TURN THE RASCALS OUT

16 TO 1

A FULL DINNER PAIL

HE KEPT US OUT OF WAR

W9-ARH-677

A NEW DEAL

A NEW AMERICA

THE NEW FRONTIER

THE GREAT SOCIETY

NIXON'S THE ONE

FRENCH-CANADIAN AMERICANS

St. Lawrence "Seaway"

3,000 miles of unfortified border

VT. 3

N.H. 4

ME. 4

First state to require literacy test

Good voting record

MUSKIELAND

Democratic shift here

Governor is likely candidate for Presidency

L. ONTARIO

N.Y. 43

FDR lived here

MASS. 14

Boston

Melting pot of Yankeeland

JFK born here

Shays' Rebellion, 1787

ERIE

New York City
The melting pot— has over 3 million voters

CONN. 8

R.I. 4

Reps.

Dems.

Stayed away from Constitutional Convention

COAL

LONG ISLAND

PA. 29

Constitutional Convention, 1787

Philadelphia
1st Presidential Convention

N.J. 17

Interstate cooperation in running Port of N.Y.

W. VA. 7
COAL POLITICS

VA. 12

Baltimore

3

Home of corporations

Birthplace of 8 presidents

DEL.

AGNEWLAND
MD. 10

N.C. 13

8

TOBACCO POLITICS

DIST. OF COL. 3

Granted vote for President by 23d Amendment

14
FLA.

Stormy Democratic politics

Miami
Home of 1968 Republican convention

THE KEY

1

Number of electoral votes

The pivotal states

Total number of electoral votes 538 for 1968 election

GOVERNMENT BY THE PEOPLE

Government

7th EDITION

The Dynamics

of American

National, State,

and Local

Government

by the People

JAMES MACGREGOR BURNS   *Williams College*

JACK WALTER PELTASON   *University of Illinois*

PRENTICE-HALL, INC., Englewood Cliffs, New Jersey

To students committed to the most difficult

and revolutionary of activities — thinking.

GOVERNMENT BY THE PEOPLE: The Dynamics of American National, State, and Local Government   SEVENTH EDITION   *Burns and Peltason*

Parts 1–6 *Copyright © 1952, 1954, 1957, 1960, 1963, 1966, 1969 by Raymond H. Young; Part 7 Copyright © 1952, 1954, 1957, 1960, 1963, 1966, 1969 by Prentice-Hall, Inc. All rights reserved.*

No part of this book may be reproduced in any form or by any means without permission in writing from the publisher.

Library of Congress Catalog Card Numbers 73-76436.

Printed in the United States of America

Design by Walter Behnke

PRENTICE-HALL INTERNATIONAL, INC., *London*

PRENTICE-HALL OF AUSTRALIA, PTY., LTD., *Sydney*

PRENTICE-HALL OF CANADA, LTD., *Toronto*

PRENTICE-HALL OF INDIA, PVT., LTD., *New Delhi*

PRENTICE-HALL OF JAPAN, INC., *Tokyo*

Current printing (last digit):

12 11 10 9 8 7 6 5 4 3 2 1

13-360651-1

PREFACE

As the 1960s give way to the 1970s, teachers of American government and textbook writers carry a double burden, for both the subject we teach and the discipline we study are rapidly changing. Political science is alive with fresh explorations, heightened disputes, new frontiers. In addition to the familiar arguments between those who believe our discipline must become more systematic, quantified, and analytic and those who argue that such systematization and quantification are either impossible or unwise, by the beginning of the seventies we find a new level of discourse about an ancient issue—the charge, especially by some of our younger members, that the discipline fails to raise fundamental issues about basic values and focuses on questions designed to preserve the *status quo*. These controversies within the discipline are, of course, reflections of the controversies within American society. Whether the changes in our society will be resolved by the American governmental system no one can say with certainty, but that the pluralistic democracy is under strain and challenge is clear.

This edition hopes to capture the excitement and the challenges of the new questioning of pluralist democracy. We have stressed social discontents and their impact on our governmental processes. We have tried to do full justice to the rise of black power, student unrest, the urban crisis, the splits within our parties, the revolt of blue-collar workers, and the "domestication" of foreign affairs, especially the Vietnam War. In addition, we have tried to incorporate the most recent scholarship in our analysis of institutions and systems.

In order to render the textbook flexible to meet the teaching needs of different types of courses, we have organized both the National and National-State-Local editions for easy adaptability to a variety of uses. For those who want a book that provides the minimum essentials of American national government, Parts Two to Five (Chapters 2 to 20) provide a self-contained core coverage. For courses also covering the basic materials of state and local government, Part Seven of the larger edition can be included. Governmental functions are described in Part Six. Part One and the Epilogue provide materials directly related to the study of American government and permit more extended coverage, either by themselves or in conjunction with any of the excellent problem or reading texts available.

In this edition, as in previous ones, the names and dates of court decisions are given in the text, but complete citations of the cases can be found in the Index.

Professors James A. Burkhart of Stephens College and Raymond L. Lee of Indiana University of Pennsylvania have produced a revised and expanded edition of their *Guide to Government by the People*, third edition, which is designed to give the student an opportunity to participate more directly in the learning process. They have also assumed the responsibility for preparing the new seventh edition of *Teaching Government with Burns' and Peltason's Government by the People* and have coordinated the supplementary materials provided for both sides of the desk in the teaching-learning process. Finally, we are pleased to announce that Professor Richard F. Heiges, Chairman of the Department of Political Science, Indiana University of Pennsylvania, has prepared a test booklet as another supplementary aid to instructors.

As with previous editions, we have asked a number of political scientists to review the current edition stringently and critically. For their host of suggestions we thank Professors Daniel J. Elazar of Temple University; Lewis A. Froman of the University of California, Irvine; Clement H. Lausberg of St. Petersburg Junior College; William C. Olson of the Rockefeller Foundation; and Martin M. Shapiro of the University of California, Irvine. A textbook covering such a vast and complex subject as the American governmental system must also rely on the work of the hundreds of scholars in the field of political science; by their books, articles, monographs, conference reports, and investigations, they have made the discipline exciting and alive. To these hundreds, and the thousands who came before, we give our thanks. Some works we cite, others are not specifically mentioned, but they have become incorporated within our work through their impact on our own intellectual development.

Professor Edward Beiser of Brown University has been of major assistance. In addition to making valuable suggestions, he directly contributed to the revision, especially in Parts Four and Five, where many of the new sections are largely in his own words. Professor Lucius J. Barker of the University of Illinois, Urbana, by his implementation of important revisions, especially in Part Three, has enabled us to profit from his specialization in the judicial process.

Professor Austin Knapp of Central Michigan University has scrutinized carefully the entire manuscript and has double-checked our statements of fact and interpretation to help us avoid error. We have also profited from the help of two young scholars, Roger Mazze and Ralph Baker of the University of Illinois. Finally, we thank Tim Peltason for his revision of the bibliography and apologize to him for the fact that consideration of book length required us to delete much of the materials he prepared. Thanks also to our good friends Warren Miller and Mrs. Maxene S. Perlmutter of the Survey Research Center at the University of Michigan and Austin Ranney of the University of Wisconsin for their efforts in making current data available to us.

Again, we wish to acknowledge the imaginative, versatile, and resourceful work of the Project Planning Department of Prentice-Hall headed by Ron Nelson and consisting of Ronni Schulbaum, our talented editor, Vera Timbanard, our cool coordinator, and Walter Behnke, our creative designer. The Product Management team at Prentice-Hall, under the leadership of Walter Welch, has given us the benefits of most useful comments from hundreds of political scientists teaching American government to all kinds of students in all kinds of institutions in all parts of the nation. We are especially grateful to those instructors who have taken the time and effort to give us the benefit of their thoughts as to how we might improve *Government by the People* as a teaching tool. We are also appreciative of the letters we have received from teachers and students, and we have tried to incorporate their suggestions in this revision. Our editor, James J. Murray III of Prentice-Hall, has provided his usual highly professional and unfailing assistance. Of our secretaries, Carolyn Higgs, Janice Parrell, and Virginia Olsen, we can say no more than we could not have done it without their help, patience, and ability. Mrs. Edward Buckley, Mrs. Ruth Greene, and Mrs. Miriam Grobois have provided valued assistance in the final preparation.

Finally, we thank Holt, Rinehart, and Winston for permission to use materials from our previously published works.

Any errors, of course, are the authors' alone — and we would greatly appreciate being notified of them.

J. M. B.   J. W. P.

CONTENTS

Contents

xvi

Contents

DEMOCRATIC GOVERNMENT IN AMERICA

PART ONE

A PROBLEM GUIDE

The American system of government is probably the most complicated on earth. It is also one of the most interesting, and—because
the United States exerts world leadership—one of the most important. Because our system is so complex, however, it is easy to get
bogged down in details and to lose perspective. The purpose of the
problem guide at the opening of each part of this book is to help
you gain an overview of the main problems that lie behind the details
of government.

The book as a whole will emphasize five sets of problems:

1 *The challenge to democratic government.* Can we answer the
claim of Communists and other antidemocrats that pluralist democracy is just a cloak for rule by a few selfish interests, that government
by the people is a luxury to be enjoyed by only a few, that for most
of mankind it is ineffective and inappropriate, and that democratic
government as we know it in America cannot compete with other
types of government throughout the world? Part One poses this
problem.

2 *The problem of constitutional government.* Should we try to
maintain a constitutional government largely shaped in 1787 in the
face of the vast and urgent demands of the 1970s? For example,
could we give our leaders enough power to do their jobs well and
still prevent them from misusing that power? How can we create
genuine teamwork within Washington and between Washington and
the state capitals and at the same time maintain a constitutional system that divides power among a host of officials? Part Two emphasizes this set of problems.

3 *The problem of individual rights.* How can pluralist democracy
maintain a balance between liberty and order, between diversity
and uniformity, between individual rights and collective needs?
The philosopher Bertrand Russell has stated this problem well:
"How can we combine that degree of individual initiative which is
necessary for progress with the degree of social cohesion that is
necessary for survival?" This set of problems is treated chiefly in
Part Three.

4 *The problem of popular representation.* How fairly do our
interest groups, opinion agencies, political parties, and elections
reflect the ideas and needs of the American people? For example,
how much influence should a popular majority (exerted perhaps
through a political party) have as compared with the major interest
groups, such as labor and business (exerted perhaps through publicity and lobbying organizations)? Does our two-party system offer
a real choice? Part Four focuses on this set of problems.

5 *The problem of responsible leadership.* How much leeway
could the people give their leaders and still keep them under broad
popular control? For example, should the President have more

1

power, at least in foreign affairs? Should we create more unity between President and Congress, or do we want them to check each other? How responsible is Congress to the people—and to what groups of people? Should we make our leaders—executive and legislative and even judicial—more responsible to the majority of the people? If so, how could this be done? Part Five is largely concerned with this set of governmental problems.

However, because American government is a "seamless web," it is impossible (and undesirable) to separate one problem sharply from another. Most of these problems are closely interrelated—for example, constitutionalism in Part Two is related to individual liberty in Part Three, representation in Part Four is related to responsible leadership in Part Five. Hence every one of the major problems is bound to spill over into every part of this book. The problem guides simply suggest the part of the book in which certain sets of problems are emphasized.

Government by the People?

1 On the eve of a new decade Americans were still trying to come to grips with the tumultuous events of the 1960s. The 1950s had been a decade of relative calm under the benign Presidency of Dwight Eisenhower. Then in the 1960s, a dynamic young man was elected President on a platform of "getting America moving again"; the long-smouldering civil rights struggle burst into flame; Americans and Communists confronted each other in Cuba, Berlin, Vietnam, and a dozen other tension points; John F. Kennedy was assassinated in Dallas; the new President, a moderate Texas Democrat, promptly took an advanced position on civil rights and social welfare measures; the Republicans nominated an all-out conservative in Barry Goldwater and were decisively beaten; and Lyndon Johnson, whose public experience and political instincts lay mainly in domestic affairs, faced rising dissatisfaction and division over the protracted war in Vietnam.

As if these events were not enough, the decade came to a climax in the presidential election year of 1968. The dramatic victories of Eugene McCarthy in the New Hampshire primary and others; the belated candidacies of Robert F. Kennedy and Nelson Rockefeller; Johnson's sudden renunciation of another term; the assassinations of Martin Luther King and Robert Kennedy — these and other tragic, turbulent events seemed both to cap and to symbolize the upheavals of the sixties.

But perhaps the most dramatic and, in the long run, significant event of the late 1960s was the revolt of the youth. Some called it the "children's crusade"; others saw it as some kind of subversive force — but none could ignore it. Students picketed and demonstrated, took over administration buildings, set up their own courses. From New Hampshire to California many campaigned for their hero, Senator McCarthy; others worked for Rockefeller; and still others, for "Bobby."

Was the ferment in the colleges a temporary eruption—just another campus fad—or would it have its influence on the politics of the 1970s? As the new decade opened it seemed likely that although the political skirmishes of 1968 might be forgotten, the fresh, challenging, stimulating ideas that lay behind much of the student revolt would have a lasting effect on American politics.

The Attack on Pluralist Democracy

The late sixties were not the first time American college men and women had protested and rebelled. Students had been part of the national ferment in the days of Theodore Roosevelt and Woodrow Wilson and earlier; they had joined radical causes in the early 1930s, and campuses became centers of isolationist and interventionist campaigns as war neared later in that decade. Young Democrats and Republicans and third-party groups have long been active on hundreds of campuses.

But there was something different about the revolt of the 1960s. Never before had American college students attacked so vehemently not only a particular party or President but the whole governmental and social and economic system under which they live. And that system, as the students freely granted, is no reactionary czardom or brutal police state. That system incorporates the values and practices of *pluralist democracy*—the Bill of Rights, constitutional diffusion of power and checks and balances, two-party government, gradual social reform, tolerance of the opposition.

The protesting students, of course, were only a small fraction of the college population of America. And they were not the only ones who attacked our form of pluralist democracy: black Americans denounced racism, poverty, and Vietnam with equal vehemence, and many other Americans who happened to be neither youthful nor black exhibited a deep disillusionment with American democracy. But the disaffection of articulate college students was the most significant development of the late 1960s. For college enrollment was due to reach seven million by 1970—almost double the enrollment of 1960—and the Census Bureau estimated that by 1970 *half* of our population would be twenty-seven years of age or under. Clearly student attitudes toward democracy American-style would affect popular views for years to come.

Their indictment of pluralist democracy listed these points:

1   *The Constitutional system of pluralist democracy grew out of, and still sustains, not "government by the people" but the rule over the many by the few.* To be sure, the critics are not always agreed as to just who the few comprise, but the typical charge is that big business and other organized interests exploit the weak, the poor, and especially the Negro.

2   *The constitutional mechanics of pluralist democracy, designed to distribute power widely among many public, semipublic, and private agencies,*

5 *actually protects the power of the few.* The best hope for reform is for the people as a whole to use their government to regulate the powerful and to protect the weak, but governmental power is so divided within the federal government; among the federal, state, and local governments; and between the formal government and "informal" governments—business, unions, churches, etc.—that the people cannot organize and unite government to advance the general interest.

3 *The essence of pluralist democracy—individual liberty, defense of minority rights, protection of dissent—allows liberty in fact to be crushed.* Big corporations treat both executives and workers as cogs in the machine; labor union leaders become separated from the real needs of the rank and file; above all—and here the critics challenge pluralist democracy most bluntly—tolerance and respect for views one hates—even for antidemocratic views—may have had a liberating role in history, but today they have become corrupted. Today tolerance protects the powerful rather than the powerless, actually blocks dissent by the oppressed and the poverty-ridden. Students like to quote philosopher Herbert Marcuse: If the way of a submerged but rising majority of the people is blocked, he has said, its reopening "may require apparently undemocratic means. They would include the withdrawal of toleration of speech and assembly from groups and movements which promote aggressive policies, armament, chauvinism, discrimination on the grounds of race and religion, or which oppose the extension of public services, social security, medical care, etc."[1]

4 *Pluralist democracy is unrepresentative.* Party politics—especially two-party politics as in America and Britain—gives little real choice to the mass of people. Both parties are controlled by conservatives and moderates who exclude the McCarthys and the Rockefellers and others with fresh ideas. Unorganized interests are underrepresented in Congress, the bureaucracy, state governments. A poor man cannot be elected President or even senator or governor.

5 *Pluralist democracy is remote, slow, unresponsive to human needs.* Daring new programs die in Congress. Some major new measures do get passed, but they seem to have little impact on people living in ghettos and rural slums. Huge welfare bureaucracies become so entangled in their own red tape that they forget the needs of the people they are supposed to serve. The poor, as always, get the crumbs. Pluralist democracy simply cannot get to the root of things.

6 *Pluralist democracy cannot cope with conflict and violence.* American society is and has been one of the most violent on earth, with one of the bloodiest civil wars in history, savage labor-management battles, assassinations of national leaders, lynchings, organized crime on a vast scale, riots. The 1970s, some critics forecast, will see the final failure of pluralist democracy to cope with tumult and upheaval in America—unless our democracy is radically transformed.

No one summed up the objects of criticism better than Richard M. Nixon. The college people, he said, were angry about:

[1]Herbert Marcuse, in Robert Paul Wolff, Barrington Moore, Jr., and Herbert Marcuse (eds.), *A Critique of Pure Tolerance* (Beacon Press, 1965), p. 100.

Drawing by Stevenson; © 1966 The New Yorker Magazine, Inc.

"I'll tell you why they keep losing. They keep losing because a lot of left-wing, bleeding-heart professors have brainwashed all the fight out of them."

A materialism that robs the individual of his sense of self.

A widening gulf between the individual and his government, as effective power moves farther and farther away.

A welfare system that breaks families apart rather than holding them together.

A disillusionment with wars that seem avoidable, in places that seem remote.

An anxiety about the future and about the place of the individual—who more and more seems alone and powerless against an overwhelming society.[2]

What do the youthful rebels want? A democracy of *participation*, in which the individual shares in all the social decisions affecting the quality and direction of his life. A politics stimulating and responding to criticism, protest, popular movements. A government that is bolder, more effective in meeting human needs, closer to the people—hence a government that is decentralized, centered in the community, the neighborhood, the ghetto itself. And if such a government is impossible through conventional political action, then the creation of parallel institutions—separate parties, unofficial community projects, student-run college courses, cooperatives, local forums and assemblies.

Such is the indictment and the program of the student revolt. But we must not draw a sharp line between the young and "those over thirty." Robert Kennedy summed up the basic identity between the generations shortly before his death:

The protest of the young both reflects and worsens their elders' own lack of self-confidence. Self-assured societies, confident of their wisdom and purpose, are not afflicted with rebellions of the young. But if the young question our involvement in Vietnam, surely this in part reflects their elders' own division and uncertainty of opinion. If the young reject a life of corporate bureaucracy and surburban sameness, surely this reflects their parents' dissatisfaction with their own lives, the realization at forty or fifty that money and status have not brought happiness or pride along with them. If the young scorn conventional politics and mock our ideals, surely this mirrors our own sense that these ideals have too often and too easily been abandoned for the sake of comfort and convenience. We have fought great wars, made great sacrifices at home and abroad, made prodigious efforts to achieve personal and national wealth. Yet we ourselves are uncertain of what we have achieved and whether we like it. Most of us can remember, after all, when

[2]Radio speech by Richard M. Nixon, June 28, 1968, New York, New York.

the aim of youth was to grow into the society of its elders. Now it seems that the young no longer want to exchange their innocence for responsibility; instead many adults seek to recapture childish things. Thus to the extent that we confront the question of our disaffecting young, we confront also our own dissatisfactions and problems, as individuals and as a society.[3]

Democracy: Ends and Means

The authors take their stand with pluralist democracy. With all its failings, this kind of democracy nourishes a tolerance for differing ideas, a respect for minority rights, and a concern for the individual that we consider essential in a decent and ordered society. But our intention in this book is not to defend pluralist democracy; our intention is to show, as objectively as we can, how it works in the United States. To debate, people must communicate; the first step must be to define what we mean by democracy both as a set of values and as a system of government. In Chapter 20 we shall look at different models of democracy and critiques of them.

Democracy—like liberty and equality and other lofty words—is hard to define precisely. The term has won such great popularity that even the Communists have tried to take it over; Communist-controlled East Germany, for example, is called the German Democratic Republic. The word itself is made up of two Greek roots—*demos*, the people, and *kratia*, authority—and was used by the Greeks to mean government by the many, as contrasted with government by the few (oligarchy) or by one (autocracy). The word came into English usage in the seventeenth century and was originally used to denote only direct democracy, the kind of government under which all

[3]Robert F. Kennedy, *To Seek a Newer World* (Doubleday, 1967), p. 10.

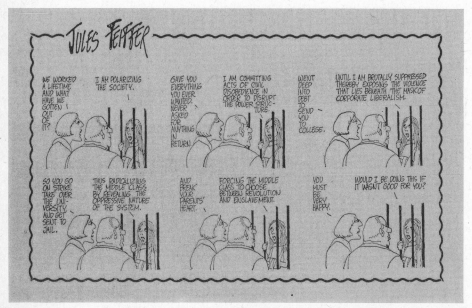

© 1968 Jules Feiffer; courtesy of Publishers-Hall Syndicate.

enfranchised citizens come together to discuss and pass laws, such as that which existed in the Greek city-states.

The term *democratic government* is also ambiguous and confusing. Some writers distinguish between democratic and republican governments, the former meaning governments in which decisions are made directly by a majority of the people—as in a New England town meeting—and the latter meaning governments in which the people's wishes are filtered through a series of representative bodies, such as Congress. But in this book we shall use the term *democratic government* to mean a representative democracy and shall use *democratic* and *republican governments* interchangeably to mean any government in which those who do the actual governing acquire their power to do so by means of a fair, free, and vigorous contest for the people's votes.

So much, then, for what we mean generally by "government by the people." What are the essential values that buttress and perpetuate democratic government?

THREE BASIC DEMOCRATIC VALUES

Democracy rests on a belief in the fundamental dignity and importance of the individual, in the essential equality of human beings, and in the individual's need for freedom. The emphasis on the supreme worth of the individual has run unbroken through democratic thought. It is woven into the writings of Thomas Jefferson, especially in the Declaration of Independence, in which he proclaimed that all men have been endowed by their Creator with certain inalienable rights and that men create governments to secure these rights. This doctrine of *individualism* (not to be confused with the doctrine of laissez faire) demands that we should, in the words of a great philosopher, Immanuel Kant, "so act as to treat humanity, whether in thine own person or in that of any other, in every case as an end withal, never as means only." Individualism makes the individual the central measure of value. The state, the union, and the corporation are valued solely in terms of their usefulness for individuals.

The doctrine of *statism,* on the other hand, makes the state the measure of value and holds that public policies and governmental forms are good if they promote the well-being of the state. Democratic political theory has refused to glorify the state or to shroud it in metaphysical abstractions. The state is nothing more than the organized political society that operates through government. The welfare of the state has no meaning except in terms of the welfare of the individuals who comprise it.

The second basic premise of democracy is the right of each individual to be treated as a unique and inviolable human being. The democrat does not insist that all men are equal in talents, virtues, or capabilities; he does insist that the claims of one individual to his life, liberty, and property must be treated as important as those of any other individual—no man should be treated as a slave or tool for the use of others.

The third basic premise of democracy is the belief that liberty is desirable, that freedom is good. *Liberty* and *freedom,* as we are using them here, mean that each individual should have the maximum opportunity to select his own purposes in life and to choose the means to accomplish those purposes. The core of liberty is self-determination. "Positive freedom consists," wrote Erich Fromm, "in the spontaneous activity of the total, integrated personality." Liberty and freedom mean more than the absence of external restraints; they connote the power to act positively toward the goals one has chosen.

The freedom to make choices and to act upon them is essential to the development of those faculties that make one a human being. It is only through the use of his freedom that an individual develops a sense of responsibility and self-restraint. It is only by acting as free and responsible individuals that men are able to exploit their full capacity for growth. From the viewpoint of society, freedom is desirable because both history and logic suggest that liberty is the key to social progress. The greater the area of freedom, the greater the probability of discovering better ways of living. Progress is stifled wherever an authoritarian group or even social custom imposes an orthodoxy that none may question. Denial of freedom, moreover, generates personal frustration, which in turn may erupt into aggressive, antisocial behavior.

There is nothing new about these basic principles of democracy. They express ancient ideals of brotherhood, compassion, justice, and the dignity of man—ideals that have deep roots in the civilization of the world.

WHAT WE MEAN BY DEMOCRATIC GOVERNMENT

Because in all but the most simple societies the day-by-day operation of government must be in the hands of a small group of people, democracy is essentially a device to determine which of several competing groups shall run the government. In a democracy the electorate chooses the major policy officials in free and relatively frequent elections. And the proportion of the adult population that must be given a voice in the political affairs of the community in order to conform to democratic ground rules must be large enough so that the electorate will represent all the interests and the interests of all.

The elections must be free. There is no meaning to sham elections in which no criticism is permitted and no opposition party allowed to bid for votes. In the Soviet Union it may well be that a large number of citizens actually support their leaders and consent to their rule. But it is a consent of ignorance, because the ruling elite secures the citizens' support by monopolizing all the sources of information. The only way the rulers in a dictatorship may be removed from office is by revolution, assassination, or internal *coup d'état.* In a democratic government the recurring choice of rulers is a matter of routine.

In order for elections to be free, citizens must enjoy the rights to have access to the facts, to criticize, to participate in political deliberations, and to organize for political purposes. The last right is of especial importance in modern societies in which the units of politics are organized groups. Individuals can become most politically effective by joining with others. Those who hold power can be checked only when the people are free to form pressure groups and political parties and to use all methods of peaceful persuasion.

A democratic government operates in accord with the decisions of majorities, which are determined by voting. He who gets the most votes wins the election. The people do not speak with a united voice; they are divided about candidates and public policies. The majority is not necessarily right, but it is right to do what the majority wishes.

Finally, a democratic government is one in which all citizens have equal voting power. This does not mean that all must or will have equal political influence. Some men, by virtue of wealth, talent, or position, have much greater political power than their fellow citizens. A newspaper publisher undoubtedly has considerably more influence in determining who gets elected to public office and what policies are enacted into law than most of those who read his paper, but when the votes are counted the publisher has no more nor less voting power than the ordinary citizen.

From our analysis of democratic government we can see that the crucial factor determining whether or not to consider a government democratic is not how much power the public officials have but how public officials secure and retain their offices. The vanquished in a political election are required by the rules of democracy to allow the victorious to govern, but the same rules require the victorious to allow today's minorities to try to become tomorrow's political majorities. You can win a tennis match by jumping over the net and hitting your opponent on the head with a racket, but then you are no longer playing tennis. You can win an election by throwing your opponents in jail, but then you are no longer operating democratically. "To see popular sovereignty, political equality, individual political rights, and majority rule . . . is to see four aspects of the same general principle. . . . More than merely compatible with one another, they are necessary to one another."[4]

CONSTITUTIONALISM—LIMITED GOVERNMENT

Constitutionalism concerns the limits set on the power of public officials. A constitutional government is one in which there are recognized and generally accepted limits to the power of those who govern. Officials have only the authority that the constitution has delegated to them, and any official who exceeds the scope of this authority surrenders his claim to obedience.

Our American government is both democratic and constitutional. There are recognized limits to what government may do, even a government that speaks for a majority, and the individual has certain basic rights that he enjoys merely because he is a human being. Not everyone agrees on the concrete content of these rights, but it is agreed that there are certain things that government may not do and other things that it may do only according to proper and fair procedure. At a minimum, the government may not deprive any person of his life, liberty, or property except by just and fair procedures of law.

Although there have been constitutional governments that were not democratic, it is unlikely that a constitutional government could be maintained in any industrialized modern nation unless it is also democratic. The prima-

[4]Thomas Landon Thorson, *The Logic of Democracy* (Holt, 1962), p. 143.

ry sanctions for ensuring that those who hold public power do not exceed the limits of their authority are the rights of unfettered criticism and the necessity for those in office to win elections periodically in order to retain their power. Constitutionalism, with its emphasis on limited government, and democracy, with its emphasis on the right of the people to decide who shall wield governmental power, are not exclusive categories but mutually supporting institutions.

So much for definitions. We must be equally particular about the intellectual tool we employ to understand democracy, its form, and its workings.

The Discipline: Political Science

Some college students are impatient to get on with the business of the world and feel that in the midst of times crying for reform their teachers and texts ask for refined distinctions that make little difference. This desire to substitute more exciting ventures for study was not unknown to earlier generations of college students. As Justice Oliver Wendell Holmes counseled some law students years ago: "Young gentlemen, you had better learn torts before you twist the Cosmos by the tail."

Other students are disappointed that they do not find a sharp break with the kind of work they did in secondary schools. This feeling of lack of intellectual freshness is in part inevitable, for the new material in college must grow out of the old. But there is one important distinction between high school and college: the mark of the more advanced scholar is his self-consciousness about his intellectual preconceptions, equipment, and deficiencies. To the unsophisticated, a fact is easy to see, and common sense is sufficient to explain it. Their assumptions about how things operate are not very complicated. Everybody has some generalized notions about the dynamics of the political system, even if not everyone is aware of these assumptions.

In college one should develop some self-consciousness about his own underlying assumptions (sometimes called frames of reference, standards of relevance, and so on), for these assumptions are not neutral—they precondition both what one looks at and what one sees when he looks. It is because of this phenomenon of selective perception that two individuals can live through the same events and each honestly see two different versions of what happened; each will select out of the environment those things that fit with his own underlying assumptions.

The intellectual discipline of political science with which you are working has certain assumptions and tools. The authors of this book are political scientists. Your teacher is a political scientist. What you are taught by this textbook and by your teacher is, then, preconditioned by the discipline of political science.

Political scientists' assumptions precondition what we look at and see and teach. Thus we teach students that some senators are Republicans and some are Democrats because our studies indicate that the fact of party membership has some relevance to how senators behave. But if our assumptions are inadequate, they may divert our attention from data of significance. And one of the primary goals in the study of American government is to become aware of our basic frames of reference and to acquire more adequate ones so that we will have standards of relevance by which we can sort out the trivial from the significant.

Political science is one of the oldest fields of knowledge—some say the oldest because it deals with the ordering of affairs among men. Plato and Aristotle were among the earliest political scientists and jointly illustrate one of the classic predicaments (or blessings) of the discipline—its linking-factual or empirical description of the political world as it is with philosophical speculation and preaching about what the political world ought to be.

PART 1
Democratic
Government
in America

© 1961 by United Feature Syndicate.

The history of political science since the Greeks is studded with great names: St. Augustine and St. Thomas Aquinas; the Italian Machiavelli; the Englishmen Hobbes and Locke; the Frenchmen Montesquieu and Rousseau; the Germans Hegel, Marx, and Engels; and many others. These men were not merely political scientists; they were philosophers who dealt with fundamental and enduring problems of politics—the nature of the state, the legitimacy of rulers, the political obligations of the ruled, the right of revolution, the nature of representation. Political science was relatively slow in becoming established in the United States. Often it was hardly distinguishable from the study of law or history or philosophy. Sometimes, political scientists were content merely to collect endless facts, describe the more obvious institutions, pile up minutiae about laws and procedures. There was little attempt to order data in a meaningful way, to speculate boldly, or to hypothesize explicitly. Political science was essentially descriptive.

Political science in the United States has come of age during the last half century. Today, in midpassage from its rather primitive beginnings to the much greater promise of the future, political science in America can be characterized as folows:

1   It continues to deal with the classic questions of politics. "How do we acquire knowledge about politics and about political life? How do we distinguish politics from other aspects of human life? In what ways are political systems similar to one another? In what ways do political systems differ from one another? What is the role of authority and power in political systems? How do men behave in politics? What are the special characteristics, if any, of *homo politicus*, political man? What kinds of conditions make for stability,

for change, or for revolution in a political system? What is required if social peace is to be maintained and violence to be avoided? What sort of political system is the best? How should we and how do we decide questions about what is 'the best' in politics?"[5]

2 It uses more sophisticated techniques in dealing with immense varieties of data. Without rejecting either classical philosophical speculation or traditional historical analysis, political science exploits techniques—polls, surveys, oral history, depth interviewing, case studies, participant-observer studies—developed within its own discipline and sister fields. It is trying to become more scientific in its use of controlled observation and even experimentation, correlations, quantification, mathematical models, probability theory. It is seeking to find patterns and regularities, to generalize more widely, to look more systematically (and less undiscriminatingly) for casual factors.

3 Political science is a profession. This is important, because a profession and professional associations provide continuing centers of communication, discussion, and controversy for their members. American political scientists are loosely organized in the American Political Science Association and in several regional and more specialized ones. They meet annually; they lecture one another and dispute one another, but they do so within an ongoing universe of discourse that provides some continuity and coherence to their debates.

4 Political scientists concentrate, not only in certain areas, such as American government or world politics or public administration or constitutional law, but even more intensively within such fields. Some are teachers; others never enter a classroom. Some move freely in and out of their neighboring disciplines of history, anthropology, sociology, psychology, economics; others prefer to stay within their field. They differ widely in temper, technique, and philosophy. They may be essentially political theologians, concerned with the enduring questions about political man and the good society; they may be political historians, reconstructing in detail the political leaders, politics, and philosophies of the past; they may be political engineers, who seek to make government more efficient or honest or representative; they may be political anecdotalists, who, as historians of the present, report on specific political activities and problems to the wider public; or they may be political behaviorists, who try to apply scientific procedures to the analysis of political data and borrow widely from the other social sciences.[6]

5 Political science is marked by internal differences as well as by solidarities. Political scientists, beginning with Plato and Aristotle, have long been divided over matters of method and substance. Today the main quarrel within political science is over the extent to which it can and should be a real science. The behaviorists, as they have come to be called, do not want to leave political science in the hands of the theologians, engineers, or anecdotalists. They believe that the discipline must develop solid generalizations about the political behavior of human beings and that the tests of "proof" are

[5]Robert A. Dahl, "What Is Political Science?" in Stephen K. Bailey (ed.), *American Politics and Government* (Basic Books, 1965), p. 4.
[6]From Nelson W. Polsby, Robert A. Dentler, and Paul A. Smith, *Politics and Social Life* (Houghton Mifflin, 1963), pp. 2–5.

those "acceptable according to the canons, conventions, and assumptions of modern empirical science."[7] A political behaviorist typically believes that in dealing with political institutions he should state his findings in "quantitative terms if he can and in qualitative terms if he must."[8] Moreover, he agrees that as a scientist he must distinguish how men act from how he thinks they ought to act. In short, the behaviorists try to emphasize the science in political science.

Critics of the behavioral school contend that political science cannot possibly emulate "real" science because of the vast complexity of political life, the fragmentary data of political science, the impossibility of conducting controlled experiments for lack of a laboratory, the crudeness of quantitative measurements (in part because of the difficulty of comparing so many unlike entities in political science), and the problem of attaining objectivity about political phenomena—politicians, laws, institutions—in which a political scientist is also involved as a citizen or as a Republican or Democrat. Above all, the critics fear that the behaviorists would drain political science of its proper moral and ethical concerns. "'Politics' should refer to power, but the term should also refer to some conception of human welfare or the public good. The achievement of Plato and Aristotle is in part a result of their starting out by asking some of the right questions; above all, what is politics *for*?"[9] Thus, it is said, the emphasis should be on the political in political science —meaning the key questions of human needs and ethical standards.

This Book: How to Use It

Thus the student—and certainly the critic—of the American form of pluralist democracy must do more than learn the facts of American government. He must understand the ends and means of democracy in general. He must test American democracy by the democratic standards it purports to satisfy. He must see the relation between democracy and limited government. And he must know something of the discipline of political science within which he works.

This book will help you with some of these tasks more than with others. It is, first of all, a description of the background, mechanics, and organization of American government. The book will occasionally note aspects of American government that are relevant to other governments, but the relation is sometimes implicit rather than explicit and for a systematic treatment you

---

[7]Robert A. Dahl, "The Behavioral Approach in Political Science: Epitaph for a Monument to a Successful Protest," *The American Political Science Review* (December 1961), p. 767.

[8]David B. Truman, *Items* (Social Science Research Council, December 1951), pp. 37–39. See also Heinz Eulau, "Recent Developments in the Behavioral Study of Politics" (Stanford Univ. Press, 1961); James C. Charlesworth (ed.), *The Limits of Behavioralism in Political Science* (American Academy of Political and Social Science, 1962); Austin Ranney (ed.), *Essays on the Behavioral Study of Politics* (Univ. of Illinois Press, 1962); David Easton, *A Framework for Political Analysis* (Prentice-Hall, 1965), pp. 6–9.

[9]Christian Bay, "Politics and Pseudopolitics: A Critical Evaluation of Some Behavioral Literature," *The American Political Science Review* (March 1965), p. 40. See also Vernon Van Dyke, *Political Science: A Philosophical Analysis* (Stanford Univ. Press, 1960), especially Chap. 15.

should take a course in comparative government. The book does not treat the economic and social context of government extensively—for this you should study economics, history, anthropology, psychology, sociology, or political science courses that borrow heavily from those fields. As for the discipline of political science, this book tries to be self-conscious about its intellectual tools, within space limitations. Above all, this book will try to confront you with key problems that require careful analysis and investigation, that raise questions both of basic values and of political analysis:

1   *The essential problem of democratic government.* Is government by the people just a pious pretension, or does it in fact exist in the United States? Is democratic government really just a cloak for rule by a small number of leaders and powerful minorities, or is there a connection between what the people want and what the government does? If so, which people?

2   *The problem of constitutional government.* Does a governmental system largely shaped in the eighteenth century provide an adequate means for the American society to govern itself in the face of the vast and urgent demands of the 1970s? Does our system of dividing authority among a host of officials in order to prevent government from becoming too powerful lead to such a diffuse structure of authority that we lack adequate means to deal with the problems of today?

3   *The problem of individual rights.* How can a democratic government be used as an instrument to promote liberties rather than to suppress them? Sometimes we use a shorthand to describe this as a problem of maintaining a balance between liberty and order, between diversity and uniformity, between individual rights and collective needs. But care should be taken in reading this shorthand to recognize that the conflicts are not between order and liberty but between *people*, that the conflicts are about which rights of which people are to be protected and promoted. This whole set of problems is treated chiefly in Part Three.

4   *The problem of representation.* What segments of the American people are represented by our interest groups, opinion agencies, and political parties? Do our electoral arrangements produce results consistent with the desires of the majority? Is the general interest best served by a free competition among organized groups or is there a general interest beyond and different from the claims of organized groups?

5   *The problem of responsible leadership.* If there is some general interest

THE GIRLS by Franklin Folger; courtesy Publishers-Hall Syndicate.

"When you say that it's all about government, do you mean it doesn't make sense?"

beyond what the people seem to want, how can we realize that general interest? How much choice should our elected leaders have? Should the President have more constitutional and political authority, especially in handling foreign affairs? Should we try to make Congress more responsive to popular majorities? Or should we try to free President and Congress from popular pressure and control and enable them to respond more to the needs of future generations and not simply to the passing needs of the present? In short, is *responsible* government something more than *representative* government? Part Five is largely concerned with this set of problems.

THE RULES AND HOW THEY GREW

PART TWO

Felix Frankfurter once observed that "talking constitutionality" was a disease that afflicted many Americans. A student may wonder why he should care about what went on in Philadelphia during the summer of 1787 or how the Constitution later developed. Our concern with constitutional history is not that of an antiquarian. We are interested in the detailed "rules of the game" and their origins and evolvement because of their *present* effect on who wins and loses in American politics and government. By identifying the values and interests that the Framers intended to advance, we set the stage for a basic question of this book: What values and interests does the American system favor today?

Forty men gathered in Philadelphia in 1787 to write the Constitution. They faced the problem of building a national government strong enough to perform its tasks but not so strong as to antagonize the people. They also faced the problem of compromising among many different ideas of government and many different interests and sections. Chapter 2 describes how the Framers met these problems.

The Constitution posed further problems, however, that have challenged Americans ever since 1787. Basically, a constitution both grants and controls power. Ideally, it gives the leaders enough power to meet the nation's needs, but it also prevents them from abusing this power. It sets up the rules that determine how leaders must win office (for example, through fair elections) and how they must exercise power once they are in office.

Now the Framers—and most other Americans in 1787—feared government, especially a *national government*, even though they knew that some government was necessary. So they designed a government that could handle the tasks facing the nation but that would not be able to seize or wield too much power. To check national power the Framers depended on two devices: (1) *free and fair elections*, so nobody could take elective office unless he was acceptable to a majority of the voters; and (2) an elaborate system of *balancing power*.

This system of balancing power is the heart of our constitutional system and rests, in turn, on two devices: (1) a *distribution of governmental power* among the several branches of the national government (for example, between President and Congress); and (2) a *system of checks and balances* that makes the branches of government responsible to different sources of popular support (for example, senators are elected by state electorates and representatives by numerous small districts based on *population*).

Although this system has stood the test of time, it created a set of difficult problems: Is a system of checks and balances that was adequate for the "horse-and-buggy age" good enough for the space age? Does it allow the people direct and strong control over their leaders? By dividing up national power among many officials, each responding to different groups of voters, does it make coordinated policies too difficult? Does it allow leaders to "pass the buck" so that the voters have trouble finding out who does what, when, and how well? Does the Constitution incorporate a systematic bias in favor of certain groups or interests at the expense of others? Chapter 3 takes up this set of problems.

Closely related to these problems is the question of how flexible and adaptable should our Constitution be. After all, it was drawn up over 180 years ago, and the demands on government are much greater now. Is the Constitution a timeless charter whose principles and methods are as sound today as ever? Or should it be possible to amend it easily to keep it attuned to new demands? Chapter 3 discusses these questions too.

Finally, there are the problems created by *federalism*—the division of power between the national and state governments. Our country has undergone vast economic, social, and military changes, and the national government has taken on heavier and heavier burdens. Relatively, the states have lost ground. Is federalism obsolete? Does it deprive the national government of the power it needs to handle its huge tasks? Or is federalism as valid as ever? In either case, who should decide what the states should do and what the national government should do? What devices have been worked out to foster cooperation among the states and between the national and state governments, despite the division of power under the Constitution? Chapters 4 and 5 deal with these and related problems.

Examining these questions will help us organize our thinking about the basic problem of Part Two. Can we and should we maintain a constitutional system largely shaped in 1787 in the face of the urgent demands of the 1970s? The answer is determined partly by what we mean by *constitutional*. Do we mean all the detailed provisions and requirements in the Constitution of 1787? Or do we mean the essential idea of constitutionalism—free elections, civil liberties, limited governmental authority, and fair procedures in government? Or do we mean the main general feature of our Constitution, namely the system of balanced powers? Part Two sets forth these problems, but they will reappear throughout the book.

The Birth of a Nation

2 On a bright Sunday afternoon in May 1787, General George Washington, escorted by three other generals and a troop of light horse, arrived in Philadelphia to the sound of chiming bells and cheering citizens. After depositing his baggage where he was to stay, Washington went to call on an old friend, Benjamin Franklin. They had many important matters to discuss and much to work out. For Washington, as a delegate from Virginia, and Franklin, as a delegate from Pennsylvania, were in the vanguard of a group of illustrious men who were to spend the hot summer of 1787 writing a new constitution for the thirteen American states.

A constitution that is to endure must reflect the hard experience and high hopes of the people for whom it is written. It cannot emerge merely from the inspiration of a few leaders. Those who framed our Constitution built with the institutions and ideas that they knew, but they did construct; their creative feat can hardly be exaggerated. They did not, of course, complete the job of constitution-making, for it is a process that began long before the Constitutional Convention met and it still continues today. Constitutions—even written ones—are growing and evolving organisms rather than documents that are merely "struck off, at a given time, by the brain and purpose of man" (as Gladstone once described our Constitution).

Toward Independence and Self-government

To trace the Constitution back to its ultimate sources would be to write an intellectual history of Western civilization. For our purposes it is enough to note that the first immigrants to this continent brought with them English political concepts and institutions. For the next 150 years these English ideas were adapted to fit the conditions of the New World. (Sometimes we forget that this nation was part of the British Empire for almost as long as it has been independent.) By July 4, 1776, the colonists had shaped basic governmental arrangements, some of which still serve us.

THIRTEEN SCHOOLS OF GOVERNMENT

It was in the colonies that Americans first learned of the difficult art of government. There were three kinds of colonial governments—*royal*, *proprietary*, and *charter*—but in practice the differences were slight. All the colonies had basic laws that established the form of government and that set forth the rights of colonists. These laws were not subject, many colonists argued, to change by ordinary law. The laws of the eight royal colonies had been granted by the King and gave the Crown considerable power of supervision. The three proprietary colonies—Maryland, Pennsylvania, and Delaware—were each governed in accordance with a charter issued by their respective proprietors, who had received a patent from the King granting them the right to establish a colony. But by the middle of the eighteenth century the Crown exerted almost the same control over proprietary colonies as it did over royal ones.

The two charter colonies—Rhode Island and Connecticut—operated under charters issued by the King confirming the governmental compacts that the colonists themselves had drawn up. These two colonies had the greatest measure of local autonomy. They were required to conform to the laws of England and to recognize the right of the Privy Council in London to review decisions of their courts, but, unlike the other colonies, their legislatures elected the colonial governor, and they did not have to send their own laws to England for review.

In all the colonies governmental authority was divided among the legislative, executive, and judicial branches. All but one (Pennsylvania) had a *bicameral* (two-house) legislature. The upper house, composed of a dozen or so landed gentlemen and wealthy merchants, advised the governor, heard appeals from colonial courts, and reviewed legislation submitted by the lower chamber. The members of the upper house were *appointed* by the Crown or the proprietor on the recommendation of the governor.

The lower house of the colonial legislature consisted of *elected* representatives. The suffrage varied from colony to colony—some colonies even had religious requirements—but in all it was limited to property-owning adult males. The lower chambers insisted that they alone had authority to raise taxes from the colonists and to appropriate funds, and because they staunchly refused to pass permanent revenue measures, the royal authorities were often forced to make concessions in order to secure the money needed to run the government. The lower houses used this control over the purse to gain further powers. Over the years, they gradually assumed power to pass general laws, subject to veto by the upper house, the governor, and imperial authorities in England.

In the royal colonies the governors were appointed by the King and served as his representatives; it was through the governors that instructions from London were transmitted. In proprietary colonies the proprietor selected the governor subject to confirmation by the Crown, and the governors were pledged to execute the laws of Parliament relating to America. Governors of the charter colonies were named by the colonial assemblies. The royal and proprietary governors were very powerful. They could exercise an absolute veto over legislation and dissolve the legislatures, and they appointed administrative subordinates, commanded the colonial militia, and presided over religious and social activities.

The judicial system grew more slowly than the other two branches, but eventually both lower and higher courts were established. The judges were appointed by the Crown, although in some colonies they depended on the legislatures for their salaries. In most cases appeals could be taken from colonial courts to the Privy Council in London, an important device of British control to ensure that colonial legislation conformed to the laws of England.

Thus it was during the colonial period that the basic pattern of American government was laid down. Relations between the colonies and England familiarized Americans with the division of powers between central and constituent governments and made federalism a natural development. The role of the Privy Council in enforcing English law as superior to colonial legislation was a forerunner of the Supreme Court's task of deciding whether state acts violate the Constitution or national law. The familiar separation of powers and the bicameral legislatures also were developed during this time.

Politically minded Americans became experts at operating or, at times, evading this governmental machinery. By the latter part of the eighteenth century, it was becoming clear that there might soon be a heightened demand for such experts.

THE KINDLING OF NATIONALISM

Despite their experience with government within the colonies, the colonists had little training in *inter*colonial problems, for under a divide-and-rule policy, London tried to keep the colonies separate and dependent on England. The colonists themselves developed little sense of unity until the events leading to the Revolutionary War stirred latent American patriotism. Until a few years before the Revolution, most colonists considered themselves Englishmen, and their national loyalty was to the British Crown. The local loyalty of each was to his colony, not to America, although there was some sectional feeling based on familiarity and identity of interests; thus New England, the South, and, to a lesser extent, the Middle Colonies became identifiable communities.

Yet even during the colonial period, the demands of war and the need for common defense forced the colonies on occasion to think of problems beyond their own boundaries. American federalism and American patriotism are rooted in this period. As early as 1643 the New England Confederation was organized to provide unified action in response to the threats of the Indians, Dutch, and French; it lasted as an effective organization until 1664. Not for almost a hundred years was there another successful proposal for intercolonial cooperation.

In 1754, the British Ministry called the seven northern colonies into conference at Albany to discuss Indian Affairs, and Benjamin Franklin seized the opportunity to propose a scheme of continental government. Franklin's proposals, known as the Albany Plan, called for the creation of a Grand Council composed of delegates elected by the colonial assemblies and a President General appointed by the King. This central government was to be given the power to regulate trade with the Indians, make war and peace, and levy taxes and collect customs duties in order to secure military and naval forces. Meeting under the threat of attack by the French and Indians, the delegates to the Albany conference avowed that some form of union was necessary to preserve the colonies. They recommended proposals for unity to the colonial assemblies, but not a single assembly approved. Those who controlled colonial affairs saw no need to subordinate their authority to an intercolonial government. Among the people themselves, there were no common American loyalties, no consciously shared experiences, no universally popular ideas. It was to take another thirty years and two wars before a strong central government would be acceptable to the colonists.

But the groundwork was being laid. During the French and Indian War, known in Europe as the Seven Years' War, American war heroes began to emerge. Gradually the colonists became aware of American, as distinct from English or purely regional, interests. "By the early 1770s, the colonists were sufficiently different from their English contemporaries that they comprised a political community—embryonic in some respects, perhaps, but nonetheless a distinct American political community."[1] Persistent trouble with the mother country intensified this sense of American identity.

Prior to the end of the French and Indian War, the imperial authorities had allowed the colonists to handle their own affairs with relatively little interference from London. But, at considerable expense, the British had driven the French from the North American continent and had made new territories available for settlement. The ministers therefore decided it would be only fair to ask the colonists to pay some of the cost of defending their own frontiers. Steps were taken to raise revenue among the Americans, to enforce trade regulations more rigorously, and generally to tighten English control over colonial affairs. But what seemed just to the English authorities was viewed differently on this side of the Atlantic. Colonial businessmen wanting to develop their own industries, merchants and shippers wishing to trade with nations other than England, planters believing they could get better prices from the Dutch and French than from the English, speculators

[1]Richard L. Meritt, *Symbols of American Community 1735–1775* (Yale Univ. Press, 1966), p. 182.

wishing to buy western land—these and others chafed under the heavier taxes and harsher restrictions.

But these restless colonists hardly thought of independence; they merely wanted Parliament to repeal the onerous laws and to leave the colonists alone as much as possible. However, to make their protests, which were couched in legal and constitutional phraseology, more effective, these essentially conservative men stirred up the feelings of other elements in the colonies. Many of the small artisans, lesser merchants, and farmers were not directly affected by the tax and trade laws, and many of them did not have the right to vote; nevertheless, the actions of the English government affronted their developing national feeling. Leadership of the protest movement began to pass from the hands of the more restrained group to those who were asking for more radical action—men like Sam and John Adams in Massachusetts and Patrick Henry and Thomas Jefferson in Virginia. These leaders gave more stress to the concepts of the natural rights of men and of government resting on the consent of the governed and less stress to constitutional and legal arguments. They started to talk about individual liberty and human rights.[2]

These arguments had a double edge. They could be used against the dominant groups within the colonies as well as against the British. Gradually some of the conservatives began to lose their enthusiasm for protest, fearing that revolution might lead not merely to changes in Empire relations but also to domestic reform. Popular feeling against England, however, became sharper. The colonists were forced, first for political and then for military purposes, to join together in defense of their common cause. Colonial leaders began to keep in closer touch with one another. The Committees of Correspondence, the Stamp Act Congress, and the First Continental Congress stimulated awareness of the common bond and gave the colonists experience in intercolonial cooperation. Finally, in 1775, the Second Continental Congress began to speak for *Americans*.

THE SURGE TOWARD INDEPENDENCE

Even after minutemen began fighting with redcoats in 1775, many Americans found the idea of independence quite unacceptable and hoped for reconciliation with England. But the fighting continued through the months, and the English government refused to make concessions to American demands. In August 1775, the King issued a proclamation declaring the colonies to be in a state of rebellion, and in December 1775, Parliament forbade all trade with the colonies. These actions played into the hands of the radicals and strengthened their cause. Then, in January 1776, Thomas Paine issued his pamphlet *Common Sense*, calling on Americans to proclaim their independence. Seldom in history has a single pamphlet had so much influence. "It rallied the undecided and the wavering, and proved a trumpet call to the radicals."[3]

[2] J. F. Jameson, *The American Revolution Considered as a Social Movement* (Princeton Univ. Press, 1926). For a detailed analysis of American political thought from 1765 to 1776, see Clinton Rossiter, *Seedtime of the Republic* (Harcourt, Brace & World, 1953).

[3] S. E. Morison and H. S. Commager, *The Growth of the American Republic*, 5th ed. (Oxford Univ. Press, 1962), p. 188.

Those clamoring for independence became stronger. In Pennsylvania the struggle was especially bitter; the radicals finally gained control, established a new government, drew up a new constitution, and instructed their delegation in Congress to work for independence. On June 7, Richard Henry Lee, following instructions from the Virginia Assembly, moved in Congress "that these United Colonies are, and of right ought to be, Free and Independent States." After bitter debate, Lee's motion was adopted on July 2. The Congress had already appointed a committee, consisting of Thomas Jefferson, John Adams, Benjamin Franklin, Roger Sherman, and Robert Livingston, to prepare a formal declaration of "the causes which impelled us to this mighty resolution." This Declaration of Independence was adopted on July 4, 1776.[4]

The Declaration is more than a justification of rebellion. It is also a statement of the American democratic creed, "designed to justify the past and chart the future,"[5] and is set forth in succinct and eloquent language:

We hold these Truths to be self-evident, that all Men are created equal, that they are endowed by their Creator with certain unalienable Rights, that among these are Life, Liberty, and the Pursuit of Happiness.—That to secure these Rights, Governments are instituted among Men, deriving their just powers from the Consent of the Governed, that whenever any Form of Government becomes destructive of these Ends, it is the Right of the People to alter or to abolish it, and to institute new Government, laying its Foundation on such Principles, and organizing its Powers in such Form, as to them shall seem most likely to effect their Safety and Happiness. . . .

Here we find the democratic beliefs in man's natural rights, in popular consent as the only just basis for political obligations, in limited government, and in the right of the people to revolt against tyrannical government.

SOME INTELLECTUAL LUGGAGE

To most American patriots in 1776, these doctrines were just plain common sense. Jefferson, who wrote the Declaration, stated in a letter to Henry Lee that he did not feel it his duty to set out "new principles . . . never before thought of," but to "place before mankind the common sense of the subject, in terms so plain and firm as to command their assent, and to justify ourselves in the independent stand we are compelled to take." These ideas had become fully synthesized in America. But in essence they were part of the intellectual luggage that the colonists had brought with them, or later imported, from the Old World.

The man most responsible for popularizing these doctrines was John Locke, whose famous *Second Treatise of Civil Government*, written a century before, had been used to justify the English Revolution of 1688. Locke's arguments were tailor-made for the defense of the American cause. He profoundly influenced the patriot leaders, and his ideas, along with some of his phraseology, found their way into the Declaration.

[4]David Hawke, *A Transaction of Free Men: The Birth and Course of the Declaration of Independence* (Scribner, 1964).
[5]Ralph Barton Perry, *Puritanism and Democracy* (Vanguard, 1944), pp. 124–125.

Prior to the establishment of organized society and government, Locke had written, man lived in a state of nature. This was not a lawless condition, however, because the natural law was known to all men through the use of reason and was binding on all. (The meaning of "natural law" has been argued by philosophers for centuries; for our purposes it is enough to think of the laws of nature as inherent, inescapable rules of proper human behavior—laws, in Cicero's words, that are in accordance with nature, apply to all men, and are unchangeable and eternal.) According to the natural law, each individual has a basic, inalienable right to his life, liberty, and that property with which he has mixed his own labor. Whoever deprives another of his natural rights violates the natural law and can justly be punished.

Most men obeyed the natural law, but living in a state of nature was inconvenient. There were always a few lawless souls; and whenever a person's natural rights were violated, he had to enforce the law himself. Furthermore, when people had differences, there was no impartial judge to whom they could turn for a decision. Therefore, men decided to end this inconvenience by contracting among themselves to form a society and to establish a government for the purpose of protecting each man's natural rights. By the terms of this social contract, each individual promised to abide by the decisions of the majority and to surrender to society his private right to enforce the law.

Government was thus limited by the purpose for which it was established. It had only the authority to enforce the natural law. *When government becomes destructive of man's inalienable rights*, it ceases to have a claim on his allegiance. The people then have the duty to revolt and to create a government better designed to promote their natural rights.

Does this sound like a radical doctrine? It must be remembered that while Locke's ideas would give power to the people, they also put checks on that power. Depending on one's interpretation of natural rights, these theories could be used either to strengthen or to weaken the right of the people to control their relations with one another through the agency of government.[6]

Early Americans were also influenced by other Old World philosophers. One of the most prominent of these was Montesquieu, who, in the time of Louis XIV and Louis XV, believed that liberty must be secured *against* government. Montesquieu's importance lies in the fact that he had a very practical scheme—the *separation of powers*—to keep government from violating man's natural right to liberty. The way to prevent the abuse of power is to check power with power, said Montesquieu, by giving some authority to the legislative branch, some to the executive, and some to the judicial. This kind of organization safeguards liberty against government.

These were the ideas that set the intellectual tone during the period when Americans were replacing English authority with their own governments.

---

[6]Willmoore Kendall, *John Locke and the Doctrine of Majority Rule* (Univ. of Illinois Press, 1941), takes the view that Locke, properly understood, advocated majoritarianism. (Kendall's reconsidered views about the problem of majority rule are presented in "The Two Majorities," *Midwest Journal of Political Science*, November 1960, pp. 317–345.) See also Peter Laslett (ed.), *Locke's Two Treatises of Government* (Cambridge Univ. Press, 1960). For a contrary view of Locke as a defender of natural rights to restrain the political majority (the view accepted by most of the Framers), see Carl L. Becker, *The Declaration of Independence; A Study in the History of Political Ideas* (Knopf, 1951).

26 Broadly speaking, our forefathers leaned more heavily on Locke in setting up government under the Articles of Confederation, more heavily on Montesquieu in framing the Constitution of 1787.

Experiment in Confederation

Alexis de Tocqueville, the perceptive nineteenth-century French visitor to the New World, asserted that "the great advantage of the Americans is that they have arrived at a state of democracy without having to endure a democratic revolution. . . ."[7] Tocqueville had not forgotten about the war of 1776. He meant that the American Revolution was primarily a rebellion of colonies against an empire. In the modern sense, it was hardly a revolution at all; there were no sharp breaks with the past and no great social, economic, or political upheavals. Contrast the colonists' demand for the "rights of Englishmen" with the Frenchmen's demand for the "rights of man" in 1789. America experienced a *conservative revolution* that sought a return to previous conditions rather than an advance to a utopian future. As a result, the American Revolution did not open class wounds. Neither a radical tradition nor a tradition of reaction developed. The political system based on such a revolution would be one of consensus rather than conflict.

And yet in significant ways the new governments were different from those existing before the Revolution. The English had tried to regulate the colonists from London; now power was to be held firmly in the hands of state governments. The imperial authorities had trampled on men's liberties; now the new state constitutions incorporated bills of rights and abolished most religious qualifications and liberalized property and tax-paying requirements for voting.[8]

The most glaring difference between the old colonial charters and the new state constitutions was the concentration of power in the legislatures. The legislative branches had enhanced their prestige as champions of popular causes. The emphasis on the consent of the governed, borrowed from Locke and others, also stressed the legislature as the repository of that consent. The governor, on the other hand, smacked of royalty and stirred unpleasant memories. In most of the states the governors were made dependent on the legislature for election, their terms of office were shortened, their veto power reduced, their power to appoint officials curbed. Judges, too, carried overtones of royalty. The new state legislatures saw no reason why they should not override judicial decisions and scold judges whose rulings were unpopular. The legislative branch, complained *Federalist No. 48* later, was "drawing all power into its impetuous vortex."

[7]Alexis de Tocqueville, *Democracy in America*, F. Bowen, ed. (Sever and Francis, 1873), vol. II, pp. 12, 123. See also Daniel J. Boorstin, *The Genius of American Politics* (Univ. of Chicago Press, 1953), p. 68; Louis Hartz, *The Liberal Tradition in America*, (Harcourt, Brace & World, 1955).

[8]Elisha P. Douglass, *Rebels and Democrats* (Univ. of North Carolina Press, 1955). See also R. R. Palmer, *The Age of the Democratic Revolution* (Princeton Univ. Press, 1959), pp. 217-135; Chilton Williamson, *American Suffrage; From Property to Democracy 1760-1860* (Princeton Univ. Press, 1960), p. 92; Robert A. Rutland, *The Birth of the Bill of Rights 1776-1791* (Univ. of North Carolina Press, 1955).

What about the central government? The Continental Congress, like the colonial legislatures, had assumed governmental powers at the outbreak of hostilities. Although the Congress appointed General Washington commander in chief of the Continental Army, carried on negotiations with foreign countries, raised and supported troops, and borrowed and printed money, its powers were based only on a revolutionary act. A more permanent constitutional arrangement was needed. Accordingly, in June 1776, the Congress created a committee to draft a constitution. A few days after the Declaration of Independence was adopted, this committee submitted a plan for a "league of friendship and perpetual Union," but not until a year later, after months of debate, did Congress submit the Articles of Confederation to the states for their approval. Within two years all the states except Maryland had ratified the Articles; however because unanimous consent was required, the Articles did not go into effect until 1781, when Maryland finally ratified.

The Articles more or less constitutionalized existing arrangements. They frankly established only a league of friendship and cooperation—not a national government. Each state retained its "sovereignty, freedom, and independence, and every power, jurisdiction, and right" that was not *expressly* delegated to "the United States, in Congress assembled." The states had jointly declared their independence of the King and had jointly fought against him, but they considered themselves free and independent sovereignties and were loath to part with any of their newly won powers. After fighting a war against centralized authority, they did not want to create another central government, even though it would be American rather than English. Most of the patriots shared the belief that republican governments could exist only in small states and feared that a strong central government would fall into the hands of those who would nullify the work of the Revolution.

There was, nevertheless, a universal recognition of the need for "the more convenient management of the general interests of the United States," and for this purpose a Congress was established in which each state was to be represented by not fewer than two nor more than seven delegates. The voting in Congress was by states, each state having one vote regardless of size or contributions to the general treasury. Delegates were chosen by the state legislatures, and their salaries were paid from their respective state treasuries. Because the delegates were state representatives rather than national legislators, they were subject to recall by their state legislatures.

Under the Articles, Congress was given the power to determine peace and war, to make treaties and alliances, to coin money, to regulate trade with the Indians, to borrow money, to issue bills of credit, to build and equip a navy, to establish a postal system, and to appoint senior officers of the United States Army (composed of state militias). In short, Congress was given substantially the same powers that the Continental Congress had already been exercising. Approval of nine of the thirteen states was required to make important decisions. Amendments required unanimous consent.

The two most important powers *denied* to Congress were the power to levy taxes and the power to regulate commerce, for it was the British government's abuse of these two powers that had precipitated the Revolutionary War. All that Congress could do was to ask the states for funds and hope that the state governments would collect taxes and turn the money over to the central treasury. And though the states promised to refrain from discriminating against one another's trade, Congress had no power to prevent such discrimination or to pass positive measures to promote national commerce. Only through treaties could Congress regulate foreign commerce, but here, too, it had no enforcement powers.

Clearly Congress under the Confederation was a feeble body. Furthermore, neither a federal executive nor a federal judiciary existed to enforce what decisions the Congress did make. There was simply the promise of each state to observe the Articles and abide by the decisions of Congress. The Articles — more like a treaty than a constitution — were ratified by the several state legislatures, not by the voters. The Articles could be amended, but — again more like a treaty than a constitution — the approval of all thirteen state legislatures was needed. In some respects the national government was like the United Nations today, although the similarity has often been exaggerated.

Nevertheless, the government created by the Articles of Confederation was what most people wanted. They believed that the goals of the Revolution could be achieved only through strong local governments and that centralized authority was dangerous. A truly national government at this time could have been established only by the sword and probably would have been destroyed by the sword. The Articles reflected public sentiment and rested on political reality. As current newspaper headlines confirm, a unified national government cannot be created by documents; it must either be based on the support of interests and individuals within the community or be held together by force.

POSTWAR PROBLEMS

The war was over and independence won. Could the new nation — a nation just becoming conscious of its own nationality — survive? The practical difficulties confronting it would have tested the strongest and best-entrenched government. Within the limits of its powers, the government of the Confederation did an excellent job: It adopted a program for governing and developing western lands; it established diplomatic relations with other nations; it laid the foundations of a central bureaucracy; and it met the financial problems growing out of the war. By the time the Constitutional Convention assembled, the postwar depression was giving way to a period of business and commercial expansion.

Yet the problems were great and the central government was unable to provide strong leadership. Newly won independence deprived Americans of some of the special trading and commercial privileges they had enjoyed as members of the British Empire. The profitable trade with the English West Indies was prohibited. Congress found it difficult to negotiate favorable trade treaties with other nations because of a general belief in Europe that the states would not comply with the treaties. The Spanish closed the mouth of the Mississippi at New Orleans to all American goods, and Barbary pirates freely looted American shipping in the Mediterranean. There was no uniform medium of exchange, because each state provided its own money, which fluctuated greatly in value. Paper money issued by Congress to finance the war was circulating at about one thousandth of its face value. Lacking confidence in the ability of Congress to redeem its pledges, creditors were reluctant to lend money to the central government except at high interest rates. Public securities sold at a fraction of their face value. The states themselves began to default in their payments to the federal treasury. Each state regulated its own commerce, some discriminating against their neighbors; and the lack of uniformity of trade regulations made it difficult to develop interstate commerce. The end of the war reduced the sense of urgency that had helped to unite the several states, and conflicts among the states were frequent.

Within the states, affairs went badly too. Delinquent debtors—primarily farmers, who faced the loss of their property and the prospect of debtors' prison—began to exert pressure on the state legislatures for relief. In several of the states they were successful, and the legislatures extended the period for the payment of mortgages, issued legal-tender paper money for the payment of debts, and scaled down the taxes. Creditors resented these interferences. Throughout the nation the conflicts grew bitter between debtor and creditor, between poor and rich, between manufacturer and shipper.

To add to the difficulties, neither the English nor the states would live up to the terms of the treaty of peace. The English refused to withdraw their troops from the western frontier until American debtors had paid their English creditors and until the states had repaid the Loyalists for confiscated property. Congress lacked the power to force either the English or the states to comply. To the English on the west and the Spanish and French in the south, the new nation, internally divided and lacking a strong central government, made a tempting prize.

MOVEMENT FOR REVISION

Was it surprising that in the face of postwar problems of demobilization, economic changes and expansion, foreign threats, and conflicts among the various sectional and economic interests, some of the democratic ardor of the revolutionary days began to wane? The radicals, who had engineered the Revolution, began to lose power. Most of the conservatives—the property owners, the creditors, the shippers, the "better" people—had never been satisfied with the Articles of Confederation, considering them too democratic and too feeble. The inability of the Confederation to provide a strong union against foreign dangers, to prevent the states from interfering with business, and to pay its creditors added to the conviction of the conservatives that the central government must be strengthened and that checks must be placed on the state governments. They undoubtedly did, for partisan purposes, "paint dark the picture of the times and blame the supposed woes of the country on the Articles of Confederation,"[9] but they were genuinely alarmed. It was,

[9]Merrill Jensen, *The Articles of Confederation* (Univ. of Wisconsin Press, 1940), p. 245.

after all, their contracts that the state legislatures were interfering with, their bonds that the central government was unable to pay, their businesses that needed uniform commercial regulations and national protective tariffs, their manufacturing for which they wanted bounties. But beyond this, they were concerned about the dangers of foreign attack, disunion, anarchy, and tyranny.

These fears were sharpened by the growth of a small but powerful group, composed chiefly of men who had never believed in government by the people. These men began to argue publicly that republican government was a failure—that a strong monarchical government was needed to protect persons and property. Washington, who, fortunately for the nation, would have nothing to do with the persistent attempts to make him a king or dictator of the United States, wrote in alarm in August 1786 to John Jay, Secretary of Foreign Affairs:

> What astonishing changes a few years are capable of producing! I am told that even respectable characters speak of a monarchical form of Government without horror. . . . But how irrevocable and tremendous! What a triumph for our enemies to verify their predictions! What a triumph for the advocates of despotism to find that we are incapable of governing ourselves, and that systems founded on the basis of equal liberty are merely ideal and fallacious! Would to God that wise measures be taken in time to avert the consequences we have but too much reason to apprehend.[10]

The politicians, creditors, and others who believed that wise measures should be taken to avert disaster felt that the situation was so critical that it would not be enough merely to amend the Articles of Confederation. They wanted to alter the basic nature of the Union and to create a strong national government with coercive powers. They wanted to place checks on the state legislatures to prevent interference with property rights.

The desire for a strong national government to control internal dissensions was not the only—perhaps not even the most important—reason why the nationalists were anxious to strengthen the central government. As William H. Riker has shown in his careful study of the origins of federalism, the pressures toward unity stemmed from fear of outside military and diplomatic threats.[11] The nationalists wanted a strong national government to provide diplomatic and military protection. They saw federalism as the only alternative to disunion because a total amalgamation of the states into a single unitary government was politically impossible short of military conquest by the more populous states.

How could closer union be achieved? Although there was growing recognition of the need to amend the Articles in order to give Congress the power to collect taxes and to regulate commerce among the states, many Americans were still suspicious of a central government with coercive powers. Many of the people did not think things were so bad, certainly not bad enough to call for any basic alterations in the governmental structure. Nevertheless, practical problems—problems of boundaries, navigation, tariffs, and so on—con-

[10]John C. Fitzpatrick (ed.), *The Writings of George Washington*, vol. XXVIII (U.S. Government Printing Office, 1938), p. 503.

[11]William H. Riker, *Federalism: Origin, Operation, Significance* (Little, Brown, 1964), pp. 19–20.

tinued to arise, and often these problems were common to most or all of the states. In the fall of 1786 the Virginia legislature, guided by James Madison, invited the states to send delegates to Annapolis to discuss uniform trade regulation. This was the ostensible purpose of the convention, but, as Madison wrote Jefferson, "Many gentlemen both within and without Congress wish to make this meeting subservient to a plenipotentiary Convention for amending the Confederation."[12] Only five states sent delegates, and many who wanted action lost hope. But Alexander Hamilton seized the opportunity to push through the Annapolis Convention a discreetly worded resolution requesting Congress to ask the states to send commissioners to Philadelphia to "devise such further provisions as shall appear to them necessary to render the Constitution of the Federal Government adequate to the exigencies of the Union." But Congress, apathetic and perhaps suspicious that Hamilton had more in mind than amending the Articles, was loath to act. Some state legislatures appointed delegates, but throughout the states not much more than polite interest was shown.

INCIDENT IN MASSACHUSETTS

In the fall and winter of 1786–1787, however, events in western Massachusetts seemed to justify the dire predictions that the country was on the verge of anarchy. Many farmers faced imprisonment through inability to meet their mortgages or their taxes and had unsuccessfully petitioned the Massachusetts legislature for relief. Finally, the angry farmers rallied around Daniel Shays, a Revolutionary War captain, and marched into Northampton, where they blocked the entrance to the courthouse and forcibly restrained the judges from foreclosing mortgages on their farms.

The militia readily put down the uprising, but the revolt sent a shudder down the spines of the more substantial citizens. The outraged General Knox, Secretary of War, wrote to Washington: "This dreadful situation has alarmed every man of principle and property in New England. . . . Our government must be braced, changed or altered to secure our lives and property. . . ."[13] As the story of this open rebellion spread through the nation, it took on lurid overtones and, in the minds of many, became a personal threat to life and fortune. Some reacted by abandoning any pretense of support for republican principles. Madison warned that the "turbulent scenes" in Massachusetts had done inexpressible injury to the republican cause and had caused a "propensity toward Monarchy" in the minds of some leaders.[14]

The more respectable leaders were not ready to plunge into either monarchy or disunion. Fortunately, an instrument was at hand that promised a better way to deal with the crisis—the proposed Philadelphia Convention. Shays's rebellion served as a catalyst, and throughout the states there was a quickening of interest in the recommendation of the Annapolis Convention. Seven states appointed delegates without waiting for Congress to act. Finally Congress jumped on the convention bandwagon with a cautiously worded request to the states to appoint delegates for the "sole and express purpose

---

[12]Quoted in Charles Warren, *The Making of the Constitution* (Little, Brown, 1937), p. 22.
[13]*Ibid.*, p. 31.
[14]Madison to Edmund Pendleton, February 28, 1787. Cited in Warren, *ibid.*, p. 45.

of revising the Articles of Confederation . . . to render the Federal Constitution adequate to the exigencies of Government, and the preservation of the Union." The careful congressmen specified that no recommendation would be effective unless approved by Congress and confirmed by all the state legislatures as provided by the Articles.

Eventually every state except Rhode Island appointed delegates. (The debtors and farmers who controlled the Rhode Island legislature suspected that the very purpose of the convention was to place limits on their power.) Many of the delegations were bound by instructions only to consider amendments to the Articles of Confederation. Delaware went so far as to forbid her representatives to consider any proposal that would deny any state equal representation in Congress.

The Philadelphia Story

The first step in the birth of the new nation had been the destruction of English governmental authority; the second step was the creation of new state governments to replace the colonial governments. The Constitutional Convention, which began in Philadelphia in the summer of 1787, was the third step. The delegates to the convention were presented with a condition, not a theory. They had to establish a national government with enough power to provide for the common defense and to prevent the nation from degenerating into anarchy or despotism.

Although seventy-four delegates were appointed by the various states, only fifty-five put in an appearance in Philadelphia, and of these, approximately forty took a real part in the work of the convention. But it was a distinguished gathering. Many of the most important men of the nation were there—successful merchants, planters, bankers, and lawyers, former and present governors and congressional representatives (thirty-nine of the delegates had served in Congress). As theorists, they had read Locke, Montesquieu, and other philosophers. As men of affairs, they were interested in the intensely practical job of constructing a national government.[15] Theory played its part, but experience was to be their main guide.

THE CAST

Although most of the Revolutionary leaders eventually supported the Constitution in the ratification debate, only eight of the fifty-six signers of the Declaration of Independence were present at the Constitutional Convention. Among the Revolutionary leaders absent were Jefferson, Paine, Henry, Richard Henry Lee, Sam and John Adams, and John Hancock. The convention was as representative as most meetings of the time. Although the delegates to the convention were mainly aristocrats, in the 1780s the common man was not expected to participate in politics; and even today small farmers and workingmen are seldom found in the ranks of Congress. Of the

[15]Stanley Elkins and Eric McKitrick, "The Founding Fathers: Young Men of the Revolution," *Political Science Quarterly* (June 1961), p. 181.

active participants at the Constitutional Convention, several men stand out as the prime movers.

Alexander Hamilton was, as already noted, one of the most impassioned proponents of a strong national government. He had been the engineer of the Annapolis Convention and as early as 1778 had been urging the necessity for invigorating the national government. Born in the West Indies, he lacked strong local attachments and was dedicated to the vision of a unified and powerful United States. Hamilton had come to the United States when only sixteen and while still a student at Kings College (now Columbia University) had won national attention by his brilliant pamphlets in defense of the colonial cause. During the war he served as General Washington's aide, and his war experiences confirmed his distaste for a Congress so weak that it could not even supply its troops with enough food or arms. The two other delegates from New York, Robert Lansing and John Yates, were ideologically opposite to Hamilton. Thus, because the voting was by states, Yates and Lansing, when present, controlled the vote of New York. But they went home early and Hamilton followed. He returned only at the end of the summer, so New York was unrepresented most of the time.

From Virginia came three of the leading delegates—*General George Washington*, *James Madison*, and *Edmund Randolph*. Even at that time Washington was "first in war, first in peace and first in the hearts of his countrymen." Although active in the movement to revise the Articles of Confederation, he had been extremely reluctant to attend the convention and accepted only when persuaded that his prestige was needed for its success. When the Virginia legislature placed his name at the top of its list of delegates, the importance of the convention was made manifest. Washington was unanimously selected to preside over the meetings. According to the records, he spoke only twice during the deliberations, but his influence was felt in the informal gatherings as well as during the sessions. The universal assumption that Washington would become the first President under the new Constitution inspired confidence in it.

James Madison, slight of build and small in voice, was only thirty-six years old at the time of the convention, but he was one of the most learned members present. Despite his youth, he had helped frame Virginia's first constitution and had served in both the Virginia Assembly and in the Congress. Realizing the importance of the Convention, Madison had spent months preparing for it by studying the history of Greek confederacies and Italian republics. During the deliberations, he sat in the front of the room and kept full notes on what was said and done. These notes are our major source of information about the convention. Madison was also a leader of the group who favored the establishment of a strong national government.

Of less importance than either Washington or Madison, but still a man of front rank, was Edmund Randolph, the thirty-four-year-old governor of Virginia and, as such, the titular head of the Virginia delegation. His political views were ambiguous and erratic, but he usually voted with Madison. He refused to sign the Constitution but later worked actively for its ratification in Virginia.

The Pennsylvania delegation rivaled that of Virginia. Its membership included *Benjamin Franklin* and *Gouverneur Morris*. Franklin, at 81, was the convention's oldest member, and, as one of his fellow delegates said, "He is well known to be the greatest philosopher of the present age." Second only to Washington in the esteem of his countrymen, Franklin enjoyed a world reputation unrivaled by that of any other American. He was one of the first to hold a vision of a strong and united America.

Gouverneur Morris, "a very handsome, bold, and—the ladies say—a very impudent man," was more eloquent than brilliant. He addressed the convention more often than any other person. His views were those of an aristocrat with disdain for both the rabble and the uncouth moneymakers. The elegance of the language of the Constitution is proof of his facility with the pen, for he was responsible for the final draft.

Luther Martin of Maryland, John Dickinson of Delaware, and William Paterson of New Jersey were not in agreement with a majority of the delegates, but they ably defended the position of those who insisted on equal representation for all states.

Clearly, the Convention was made up of the political elite of the colonies. That men of the stature of Washington, Madison, and Randolph undertook the difficult journey to Philadelphia reflects their deep concern over the state of the Union, and their expectation that major changes were in the wind.

The proceedings of the convention were kept secret, and delegates were forbidden to discuss any of the debates with outsiders in order to encourage the delegates to speak freely. It was feared that if a member publicly took a firm stand on an issue, it would be harder for him to change his mind after debate and discussion. Also, looking ahead to the ratification struggle, the members knew that if word of the inevitable disagreements got out it would provide ammunition for the many enemies of the convention. There were critics of this secrecy rule, but without it, agreement might have been impossible.

CONSENSUS

The Constitutional Convention is usually discussed in terms of the three famous compromises: the compromise between large and small states over representation in Congress, the compromise between North and South over the counting of slaves for taxation and representation, and the compromise between North and South over the regulation and taxation of foreign commerce. But this emphasis obscures the facts that there were many other important compromises and that on many of the more significant issues most of the delegates were in substantial agreement.

A few delegates personally favored a limited monarchy, but almost all were supporters of *republican* government, and this was the only form of government seriously considered at the convention. It was the only form that would be acceptable to the nation. Most important, all the delegates, including those few who favored a monarchy, were *constitutionalists*, who opposed arbitrary and unrestrained government, whether monarchical, aristocratic, or democratic.

The common philosophy accepted by most of the delegates was that of *balanced government*. They wanted to construct a national government in which no single interest would dominate the others. Because the men in Philadelphia represented groups alarmed by the tendencies of the agrarian interests to interfere with property, they were primarily concerned with balancing the government in the direction of protection for property and business. There was an almost universal concurrence in the remark of Elbridge Gerry (delegate from Massachusetts): "The evils we experience flow from the excess of democracy. The people do not want virtue, but are dupes of pretended patriots." Likewise there was substantial agreement with Gouverneur Morris's statement that property was the "principal object of government."

Benjamin Franklin favored extending the right to vote to non-property owners, but most of the delegates agreed in general with the sentiments expressed by John Dickinson, James Madison, and Gouverneur Morris. Dickinson argued that freeholders (owners of land) were the best guardians of liberty and that only they could be counted on to resist the "dangerous influence of those multitudes without property and without principle." James Madison voiced the fear that those without property would soon become the largest part of the population and, if given the right to vote, would either combine to deprive the property owners of their rights or would become the "tools of opulence and ambition." The delegates agreed in principle on restricted suffrage, but they differed over the kind and amount of property that one must own in order to vote. Moreover, as the several states were in the process of relaxing freehold qualifications for the vote, the Framers recognized that they would jeopardize approval of the Constitution if they should make the federal franchise more restricted than the franchises within the states.[16] As a result, each state was left to determine the qualifications for electing members to the House of Representatives, the only branch of the national government in which the electorate was given a direct voice.

All the delegates were bound by their instructions from Congress merely to suggest amendments to the Articles of Confederation, and some were bound by even more strict instructions from their state legislatures. But within five days of its opening, the convention, with only Connecticut dissenting, voted to approve the Fourth Virginia Resolve that "a national government ought to be established consisting of a supreme legislative, executive, and judiciary." This decision to establish a *national government resting on and exercising power over individuals* proposed to alter the nature of the central government profoundly—changing it from a league of states to a national government.

There was little dissent from proposals to give the new Congress all the powers of the old Congress plus all other powers in which the separate states were negligent or in which the harmony of the United States might be disrupted by the exercise of individual legislation. Although the original series of proposals discussed by the delegates, known as the Virginia Plan, called for legislative supremacy, the Framers agreed that a strong executive, which had been lacking under the Articles, was necessary to provide the

[16]John P. Roche, "The Founding Fathers: A Reform Caucus in Action," *The American Political Science Review* (December 1961), pp. 799–816, emphasizes the importance of such political considerations in the Framers' deliberations.

energy and direction for the general government. And an independent judiciary was also accepted without much debate. Franklin favored a single-house national legislature, but almost all the states had had two-chamber legislatures since colonial times and the delegates were used to the system. Bicameralism also conformed to their belief in the need for balanced government, the upper house representing the aristocracy and offsetting the more democratic lower house. So the delegates established two chambers in the national government too.

CONFLICT

There were serious differences among the various groups, especially between the representatives of the large states, who favored a strong national government, which they expected to be able to dominate, and the delegates from the small states, who were anxious to avoid being dominated.

The Virginia delegation took the initiative; it had caucused during the delay before the convention and, as soon as the convention was organized, was ready with fifteen resolutions. These resolutions, the Virginia Plan, called for a strong central government. The legislature was to be composed of two chambers. The members of the lower house were to be elected by the people, those of the upper house to be chosen by the lower chamber from nominees submitted by the state legislatures. Representation in both branches was to be on the basis of either wealth or numbers, thus giving the more populous and wealthy states—Virginia, Massachusetts, and Pennsylvania—a majority in the legislature.

The Congress thus created was to be given all the legislative power of its predecessor under the Articles of Confederation and the right "to legislate in all cases in which the separate States are incompetent." Furthermore, it was to have the authority to veto state legislation in conflict with the proposed constitution. The Virginia Plan also called for a national executive to be chosen by the legislature and a national judiciary with rather extensive jurisdiction. The national Supreme Court, along with the executive, was to have a qualified veto over acts of Congress.

For the first few weeks the Virginia Plan dominated the discussion at the Convention. But by June 15 additional delegates from the small states had arrived and they began to counterattack. They rallied around William Paterson of New Jersey, who presented a series of resolutions known as the New Jersey Plan. Paterson did not question the need for a greatly strengthened central government, but he was concerned about how this strength would be used. The New Jersey Plan would give Congress the right to tax and regulate commerce and to coerce recalcitrant states but would retain a single-house legislature in which all states would have the *same vote, regardless of their size.* It provided for a plural national executive and for a national Supreme Court with considerable authority. The New Jersey Plan contained the germ of what eventually came to be a key provision of our Constitution—the supremacy clause. The national Supreme Court was to hear appeals from state judges, and the supremacy clause would require all the judges—state and national—to treat laws of the national government and the treaties of the United States as part of the supreme law of each of the states.[17] (The final draft of the Constitution made an important addition to the supremacy clause by making national laws and national treaties superior to state constitutions.)

Paterson was maneuvering to force concessions from the larger states. He favored a strong central government but not one that the big states could dominate. And he raised the issue of practical politics: To adopt the Virginia Plan, which created a powerful national government dominated by Massachusetts, Virginia, and Pennsylvania and eliminated the states as important units of government, would be to court defeat for the Convention's proposals. in the ratification struggle to come.

But the large states resisted, and for a time the Convention was deadlocked. The small states argued that states should be represented equally in Congress, at least in the upper house. The large states were adamant, insisting that representation in both houses be based on population or wealth and that national legislators be elected by the electorate rather than by the state legislatures. Finally, a Committee of Eleven was elected to devise a compromise and on July 5 it presented its proposals. Because of the prominent role of the Connecticut delegation, this plan has since been known as the Connecticut Compromise. It called for a lower house in which representation would be on the basis of population and in which all. bills for raising or appropriating money would originate and an upper house in which each state would have an equal vote. This was a setback to the large states, who agreed only when the smaller states made it clear that this was their price for union. After equality of representation for the states in the Senate was accepted, most objections to the establishment of a strong national government dissolved.

The problem of representation was complicated by the existence of slavery. Southern states with large numbers of slaves wanted them to be counted in determining representation in the House of Representatives. It was finally agreed that a slave should count as three-fifths of a free person, both in determining representation in the House of Representatives and in apportionment of direct taxes. Southerners were also fearful that a Northern majority in Congress might discriminate against Southern trade. They had some basis for this concern. John Jay, Secretary of Foreign Affairs for the Confederation, had proposed a treaty with Great Britain that would have given advantages to Northern merchants at the expense of Southern exporters. To protect themselves, the Southern delegates insisted on requiring a two-thirds majority in the Senate for the ratification of treaties. This sectional check on treaties was supplemented by a provision denying to Congress the power to levy taxes on exports. Another dispute was over the slave trade. To meet the demands of South Carolina and Georgia, Congress was denied until 1808 the right to prohibit the importing of slaves.

The delegates, of course, found other issues to argue about. Should the national government have lower courts or would one federal Supreme Court be enough? This issue was resolved by postponing the decision; the Consti-

[17]Robert H. Birkby, "Politics of Accommodation: The Origin of the Supremacy Clause," *The Western Political Quarterly* (March 1966), p. 27.

tution states that there *shall* be one Supreme Court and that Congress *may* establish inferior courts. How should the President be selected? For a long time the convention accepted the idea that the President should be elected by the Congress. But it was feared that either the Congress would dominate the President or vice versa. Election by the state legislatures was rejected because of distrust of these bodies. Finally, the electoral college system was decided upon. This was perhaps the most original contribution of the delegates, although it was patterned after procedures used by Maryland to select state senators, and is one of the most criticized provisions in the Constitution (see Chapter 13).

After three months, the delegates ceased debating. On September 17, 1787, they assembled for the impressive ceremony of signing the document they were recommending to the nation. All but three of those still present signed; others, who opposed the general drift of the convention, had already left. Their work over, the delegates adjourned to the City Tavern to relax and to celebrate a job well done.

WHAT MANNER OF MEN?

Were the delegates an inspired group of men who cast aside all thoughts of self-interest? Were they motivated by the desire to save the Union or by the desire to save themselves? Was the convention the inevitable result of the weaknesses of the Articles? Was it a carefully maneuvered *coup d'état* on the part of wealthy aristocrats? Was the difference between those who favored and those who opposed the Constitution mainly economic? Or was the difference mainly regional?

Students of history and government have held various opinions concerning these, and other questions. During the early part of our history, the members of the convention were the object of uncritical adulation; the Constitution was the object of universal reverence. Early in the twentieth century, a more critical attitude was inspired by J. Allen Smith and Charles A. Beard. Smith, in his *The Spirit of American Government* (1911), painted the Constitution as the outgrowth of an antidemocratic reaction, almost a conspiracy, against the rule of majorities. Beard's thesis was that the Constitution represented the platform of the propertied groups who wanted to limit state legislatures and strengthen the national government as a means of protecting property. In his influential book *An Economic Interpretation of the Constitution* (1913), Beard described the economic holdings of the delegates and argued that their support or opposition to the Constitution could best be explained in terms of their financial interests. He explicitly denied that he was charging the Founding Fathers with writing the Constitution for their personal benefit; rather, he contended that men's political behavior reflects their broad economic interests.

Recently, historians have questioned the soundness of Beard's scholarship and challenged his interpretation of the data. Robert E. Brown points out that there was no great propertyless mass in the United States and that "practically everybody was interested in the protection of property." "We would be doing a grave injustice to the political sagacity of the Founding Fathers," Brown has written, "if we assumed that property or personal gain was their only motive."[18] Forrest McDonald, after looking into Beard's data, has concluded that the "economic interpretation of the Constitution does not work," although he concedes an "economic interpretation renders intelligible many of the forces at work in the making of the Constitution."[19] David G. Smith concludes, "The delegates . . . protected property, but especially in order to remove sources of discord, foster economic growth, and develop interest in the government. They destroyed the dependence of the government upon the states, but more in the interests of a national citizenship than fear of democracy. . . ."[20]

Probably no interpretation imputing an exclusive role to any one motivation can be satisfactory. Analysis of the votes in the convention shows that the voting patterns cannot be explained by large versus small states, the economic interests of the delegates, the class interests represented by the state delegations, or the distribution of real property in the states.[21] On the other hand, states that were geographically contiguous did tend to vote together. Beard himself recognized that men are motivated by a complex of factors, both conscious and unconscious. Self-interest, economic or otherwise, and principles are inextricably mixed in human behavior, and the Framers were not much different from contemporary political leaders. The Founding Fathers were neither minor gods for whom self-interest or economic considerations were of no importance nor men who thought only in terms of their own pocketbooks. They were concerned with the Union and they wanted to protect the nation from aggression abroad and dissension at home. Stability and strength were needed to protect their own interests —but also to secure the unity and order indispensable for the operation of a democracy.

To Adopt or Not to Adopt

The delegates had gone far. After exceeding their authority by setting aside the Articles of Confederation, they had not hesitated to contravene Congress's instructions about ratification or to ignore Article XIII of the Articles of Confederation. This article declared the Union to be perpetual and prohibited any alteration in the Articles unless agreed to by the Congress and *by every one of the state legislatures*—a provision that had made it impossible to amend the Articles. But the convention delegates boldly declared that the Constitution should go into effect when ratified by *popularly elected conventions* in *nine* states. They had substituted this method of ratification for both practical considerations and reasons of principle. Not only were the delegates aware that there was little chance of securing approval of the new Constitution in all of the state legislatures, but many felt that the Constitution should be ratified by an authority higher than

[18]Robert E. Brown, *Charles Beard and the Constitution* (Princeton Univ. Press, 1956), pp. 197–198.
[19]Forrest McDonald, *We the People: The Economic Origins of the Constitution* (Univ. of Chicago Press, 1958), pp. vii and 415.
[20]David G. Smith, *The Convention and the Constitution* (St Martin's, 1965), p. 31.
[21]S. Sidney Ulmer, "Sub-group Formation in the Constitutional Convention," *Midwest Journal of Political Science* (August 1966), p. 302.

any governmental body. A Constitution based on popular ratification would have a higher legal status; judges would be more likely to strike down any statute that contravened it, and there would be less of a possibility that any state government would decide to withdraw. The Articles of Confederation had been a compact of state governments, but the Constitution was to be a "union of people."[22]

But even this method of ratification was not going to be easy. The nation was not ready to adopt the Constitution without a thorough debate, and soon two camps sprang up. The supporters of the new government, by cleverly appropriating the name of Federalists, took some of the sting out of the charges that they were trying to destroy the states and establish an all-powerful central government. By dubbing their opponents Antifederalists, they pointed up the negative character of the arguments of those who opposed ratification.

The split was in part geographical. The seaboard and city regions tended to be Federalist strongholds. The vast back-country regions from Maine through Georgia, inhabited by farmers and other relatively poor people, were areas in which the Antifederalists were most strongly entrenched. But, as in all political contests, no single factor—geographical or economic or ideological—completely accounted for the division between Federalist and Antifederalist. For example, in Virginia the leaders of both sides came from the same general social and economic class. New York City and Philadelphia strongly supported the Constitution, but so did predominantly rural New Jersey.

From our vantage point of hindsight, many of the criticisms raised by the Antifederalists obviously were unfounded and many of their fears unjustified. It used to be the fashion among historians and political scientists to picture these opponents of our Constitution as small-minded, selfish men who could not see beyond their own local interests. With the introduction of a more critical attitude toward the Founding Fathers, there was a swing to the other extreme; the Antifederalists were then described as the true defenders of liberty and democracy, fighting the economically motivated aristocratic Federalists. Quite obviously both these generalizations are exaggerated. Each side included able and enlightened men as well as those with less admirable motives, and, judged within the context of the eighteenth century, both Federalists and Antifederalists were confirmed defenders of republican government.

The great debate was conducted with pamphlets, papers, letters to editors, and speeches. The issue was important and the interest of those concerned intense, but the argument, in the main, was carried on in a temperate manner. This great debate stands even today as an outstanding example of a free people using open discussion to determine the nature of their fundamental laws.

THE GREAT DEBATE

In general, the Antifederalist argument developed along these lines: There is much merit in the proposed Constitution, but it contains many provisions that show the aristocratic bias of its authors. It calls for the creation of a "consolidated system" that would in the end destroy republican govern-

[22]Max Farrand, *The Records of the Federal Convention* (Yale Univ. Press, 1911), vol. II, pp. 93, 476.

ment and individual liberty as well as the independence of the states.[23] It lacks adequate guarantees of the people's fundamental rights. Present conditions are not so bad as the Federalists make out; we are at peace, and there is no danger of internal dissension. We do need a correction of the Articles of Confederation but a correction that preserves, as the Constitution does not, the power of the states and the freedom of the people. We should not ratify the proposed Constitution; but after it has been fully discussed and its defects made apparent, a second convention should be called to revise the Articles in the light of these discussions.

The Antifederalists were suspicious of the intentions of the delegates to the convention; the delegates had exceeded their instructions, deliberated in secret, and presented a Constitution that established a powerful national government. Said Amos Singletary, delegate from a western town in the Massachusetts ratifying convention, member of the Massachusetts legislature, and a veteran of the Revolutionary army:

> Mr. President, if any body had proposed such a constitution as this in that day [Revolutionary period], it would have been thrown away at once. . . . These lawyers, and men of learning, and moneyed men, that talk so finely, and gloss over matters so smoothly, to make us poor illiterate people swallow down the pill, expect to get into Congress themselves; they expect to be the managers of this Constitution, and get all the power and all the money into their own hands, and then they will swallow up all of us little folks, like the great *Leviathan*, Mr. President; yes, just as the whale swallowed up *Jonah*.

The Federalists, on the other side, argued that there were just two alternatives—adoption of the Constitution or disunion. They insisted that the Confederation was hopelessly defective and, unless it was quickly altered, the Union would be lost. Arguing that union was indispensable to liberty and security, they defended the Constitution as conforming to the true principles of republican government. They admitted that it was not perfect but held that it was the best that could be obtained and that the way was open to correct such deficiencies as were uncovered through time and experience.

One of the best attacks produced by the Antifederalists was a series of articles written by Richard Henry Lee, the man who had introduced the resolution in the Second Continental Congress calling for independence. Lee's *Letters of the Federal Farmer*, published in the fall of 1787, were widely circulated throughout the nation. On the other hand, *The Federalist*, a series of essays, is without doubt the best defense of the Constitution. Charles and Mary Beard have written, "From that day to this *The Federalist* has been widely regarded as the most profound single treatise on the Constitution ever written and as among the few masterly works on political science produced in all the centuries of history."[24] These essays were written by Alex-

---

[23]John D. Lewis (ed.), *Anti-Federalists versus Federalists* (Chandler, 1967), p. 2; Robert Allen Rutland, *The Ordeal of the Constitution: The Antifederalists and the Ratification Struggle of 1787–1788* (Univ. of Oklahoma Press, 1966).

[24]Charles A. Beard and Mary R. Beard, *A Basic History of the United States* (New Home Library, 1944), p. 136. Gottfried Dietze, *The Federalist: A Classic on Federalism and Free Government* (Johns Hopkins, 1960) is one of the few monographic analyses of these important state papers. There are also two new editions of *The Federalist* available, Benjamin F. Wright (Belknap Press of Harvard Univ., 1961), which contains an excellent introductory essay, and Jacob E. Cooke (Wesleyan Univ. Press, 1961), which provides exhaustive annotations.

ander Hamilton, James Madison, and John Jay. Over the name of Publius, they were published serially in the New York papers during the winter of 1787.

Perhaps the most telling criticism of the proposed Constitution made by Lee and others was its failure to include a bill of rights.[25] The Federalists argued that a bill of rights would be superfluous. The general government had only delegated powers, and there was no need to specify that Congress could not, for example, abridge freedom of the press. It had no power to regulate the press. Moreover, the Federalists argued, to guarantee *some* rights might be dangerous because it would then be thought that rights *not* listed could be denied. Contradictorily, they pointed out that the Constitution protected some of the most important rights—trial by jury in federal criminal cases, for example. Hamilton and others also insisted that paper guarantees were weak reeds on which to depend for protection against governmental tyranny.

The Antifederalists, as well as many who were otherwise generally favorable to ratification, were unconvinced. If some rights were protected, what could be the objection to providing constitutional protection for others? Without a bill of rights, what was to prevent Congress from using one of its delegated powers in such a manner that free speech would be abridged? If bills of rights were needed in state constitutions to limit state governments, why was one not needed in the national constitution to limit the national government—a government farther from the people and with a greater tendency, it was argued, to subvert natural rights? The Federalists, forced to concede, agreed to add a bill of rights if and when the new Constitution was approved.

THE POLITICS OF RATIFICATION

Despite the great debate, many people remained apathetic. The only direct voice the electorate had in the writing and adopting of our Constitution was in choosing delegates to the state ratifying conventions. In Connecticut and in New York all adult males were allowed to vote for representatives to the ratifying conventions, and in most of the other states suffrage requirements were liberalized. From 80 to 85 percent of the adult white males[26] were eligible to vote for delegates, yet only a fraction of those qualified to vote actually did so. "The Constitution was adopted with a great show of indifference."[27]

The political strategy of the Federalists was to secure ratification in as many states as possible before the opposition had time to organize. The Antifederalists were handicapped. They lacked access to the newspapers, most of which supported ratification. Their main strength was in the rural areas, underrepresented in some state legislatures and difficult to arouse to political action. They needed time to perfect their organization and collect their

[25]Rutland, *op. cit.* See also Alpheus T. Mason, *The States Rights Debates: Antifederalism and the Constitution* (Prentice-Hall, 1964), pp. 4, 66–97.

[26]Chilton Williamson, *op. cit.*

[27]Brown, *op. cit.*, pp. 69, 197. See also A. C. McLaughlin, *A Constitutional History of the United States* (Appleton-Century-Crofts, 1935), pp. 220–221.

strength. The Federalists, composed of a more closely knit group of leaders throughout the colonies, moved in a hurry. "Unless the Federalists had been shrewd in manipulation as they were sound in theory, their arguments could not have prevailed."[28]

In most of the small states, now propitiated by equal Senate representation, ratification was gained without difficulty; Delaware was the first state to ratify. The first large state to take action was Pennsylvania. The Federalists presented the Constitution to the state legislature immediately after the Philadelphia Convention adjourned in September 1787, urging the legislators to call for the ratifying convention to adopt the new Constitution. But the legislature was about to adjourn, and the Antifederalist minority felt that this was moving with unseemly haste (Congress had not even formally transmitted the document to the legislature for its consideration!). They wanted to postpone action until after the coming state elections, when they hoped to win a legislative majority and so forestall calling a ratifying convention. When it became clear that the Federalists were going to move ahead, the Antifederalists left the legislative chamber. With three short of a quorum, business was brought to a standstill. But Philadelphia, the seat of the legislature, was a Federalist stronghold. The next morning three Antifederalists were roused from their quarters, carried into the legislative chamber, and forced to remain. With a quorum thus obtained, the resolution calling for election of delegates to a ratifying convention was adopted. Under the astute generalship of James Wilson, the Pennsylvania convention ratified by a vote of 46 to 23 in December 1787, the opposition coming from the western districts.

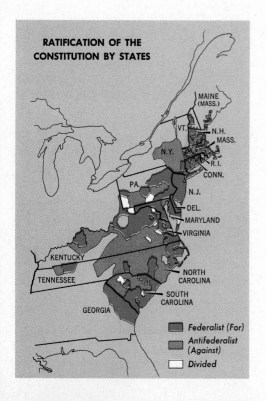

RATIFICATION OF THE CONSTITUTION BY STATES

MAINE (MASS.)
VT.
N.H.
MASS.
N.Y.
R.I.
CONN.
PA.
N.J.
DEL.
MARYLAND
VIRGINIA
KENTUCKY
TENNESSEE
NORTH CAROLINA
SOUTH CAROLINA
GEORGIA

■ Federalist (For)
■ Antifederalist (Against)
□ Divided

By early 1788 New Jersey, Connecticut, and Georgia had also ratified. The scene of battle then shifted to Massachusetts, a key state and a doubtful one. John Hancock and Samuel Adams had not declared themselves, and these gentlemen, with their great popular following, held the balance of power. The Federalists cleverly pointed out to Hancock that Washington would be the first President and that therefore the Vice President would undoubtedly be a New Englander. What citizen of New England was more distinguished than John Hancock? Whether or not this hint was the cause, Hancock eventually came out for ratification, and Adams was persuaded to vote for approval after securing a promise that a bill of rights would be forthcoming after adoption. Even so, Massachusetts ratified by the narrow margin of 187 to 168.

By June 1788, Maryland, South Carolina, and New Hampshire had ratified, so the nine states required to bring the Constitution into effect had been obtained. But neither Virginia nor

[28]Morison and Commager, *op. cit.*, p. 296.

New York had taken action, and without them the new Union would have little chance of success. Virginia was the most populous state and the home of many of the nation's outstanding leaders, and New York was important geographically.

The Virginia ratifying convention rivaled the Constitutional Convention in the caliber of its delegates. James Madison was the captain of the Federalist forces, and he had able lieutenants in Governor Randolph and young John Marshall. Patrick Henry, George Mason, and James Monroe within the convention and Richard Henry Lee outside led the opposition. Henry attacked the proposed government, point by point, with great eloquence; Madison turned back each attack quietly but cogently. At the critical juncture, Washington sent a letter to the convention urging unqualified ratification. This tipped the scale, and Virginia ratified. News was rushed to New York.

The great landowners along the Hudson, unlike their Southern planter friends, were opposed to the Constitution. They feared federal taxation of their holdings, and they did not want to abolish the profitable tax that New York had been levying on the trade and commerce of other states. When the convention assembled, the Federalists were greatly outnumbered, but they were aided by the strategy and skill of Hamilton and by word of Virginia's ratification. New York approved by a margin of three votes.

Although North Carolina and Rhode Island still remained outside the Union (the former ratified in November 1789 and the latter six months later), the new nation was created. In New York, a few members of the old Congress assembled to issue the call for elections under the new Constitution, and then Congress adjourned sine die.

The Living Constitution

3 For a time, some people remained skeptical of the new Constitution. After watching merchants and mechanics march side by side in a parade celebrating ratification, a Bostonian remarked sourly that "it may serve to please children, but freemen will not be so easily gulled out of their liberties." On the other hand, a Philadelphian said that the procession in his city had "made such an impression on the minds of our young people that 'federal' and 'union' have now become part of the household words of every family in the city." This effect on the youth was significant, for it was on the younger generation that hopes for the new government depended.

The adoption of the Constitution coincided with the return of prosperity. Markets for American goods were opening in Europe, and business was pulling out of its postwar slump. Such events seemed to justify Federalist claims that adoption of the Constitution would correct the nation's ills. Within a surprisingly short time the Constitution lost its partisan character; Antifederalists vied with Federalists in honoring it. Politicians differed less and less over whether the Constitution was good. More and more they began to argue over what it meant.

As the Constitution won the support of Americans, it began to take on the aura of natural law itself.

Here was the document into which the Founding Fathers had poured their wisdom as into a vessel; the Fathers themselves grew ever larger in stature as they receded from view; the era in which they lived and fought became a Golden Age; in that age there had been a fresh dawn for the world, and its men were giants against the sky; what they had fought for was abstracted

45

from its living context and became a set of "principles," eternally true and universally applicable."[1]

This adoration of the Constitution was important as a means of bringing unity into the diversity of the new nation. Like the Crown in Britain, the Constitution became a symbol of national loyalty, a unifying symbol that evoked both emotional and rational support from all Americans regardless of their differences. The Framers' work became part of the American creed; it stood for liberty, equality before the law, limited government—indeed, for whatever anyone wanted to build into it.

Aside from being a symbol, the Constitution is also a supreme and binding law that both *grants* and *limits* powers. "In framing a government which is to be administered by men over men," wrote Madison in *The Federalist*, "the great difficulty lies in this: you must first enable the government to control the governed; and in the next place oblige it to control itself." As an instrument, the Constitution serves a dual function. It is a *positive* instrument of government, enabling the governors to control the governed, and it is a *restraint* on government, enabling the ruled to check the rulers.

In what ways does the Constitution limit the power of the national government? In what ways does it create national power? How has it managed to serve both as a great symbol of national unity and at the same time as a somewhat adaptable and changing instrument of government?

Checking Power with Power

It is strange, perhaps, to begin by stressing the ways in which the Constitution limits national power. Yet we must keep in mind the dilemma that the Framers faced. They wanted a more effective national government but at the same time were keenly aware that the people would not accept too strong a central control. Accordingly, they allotted certain powers to the national government and reserved the rest for the states. In short, they established a system of *federalism* (the nature and problems of which will be taken up in Chapters 4 and 5). But this distribution of powers, they felt, was not enough. Other ways of limiting the national government were needed.

The most important device to make public officials observe the constitutional limits on their powers is for voters to go to the polls and throw out of office those who abuse power. But the Framers were not willing to depend solely on such *political* controls, because they did not fully trust the people's judgment. The people might be misled and vote a demagogue into office. Thomas Jefferson, a firm democrat, put it this way: "Free government is founded on jealousy, and not in confidence. . . . In questions of power, then, let no more be heard of confidence in man, but bind him down from mischief by the chains of the Constitution."[2] Even more important, the Framers feared that a majority faction might use the new central government to

[1]Max Lerner, *Ideas for the Ice Age* (Viking, 1941), pp. 241–242.
[2]Alpheus T. Mason *The Supreme Court: Palladium of Freedom* (Univ. Michigan Press, 1962), p. 10.

deprive minorities of their rights. "A dependence on the people is, no doubt, the primary control on the government," Madison admitted, "but experience has taught mankind the necessity of auxiliary precautions." Thus the Framers had inserted two different but related arrangements—separation of powers and checks and balances—that they hoped would achieve their goals of preventing public officials from abusing their power and of preventing any one group of people, even a majority, from capturing control of the government and tyrannizing the rest of the people.

DIVIDING NATIONAL POWER

The first step was the *separation of powers*, that is, dividing constitutional authority among the three branches of the national government. As we have seen, the idea of parceling out power is an old one. Locke had discussed the need for separating powers, and Montesquieu had argued that liberty could last only where powers were distributed among different departments of government. In *Federalist No. 47*, James Madison wrote, "No political truth is certainly of greater intrinsic value, or is stamped with the authority of more enlightened patrons of liberty, than that . . . the accumulation of all powers, legislative, executive, and judiciary, in the same hands . . . may justly be pronounced the very definition of tyranny."

But the force of Locke's and Montesquieu's logic alone does not account for the incorporation of the doctrine of separation of powers in our basic document. This doctrine had been, as we have seen, the operating practice in the colonies for over a hundred years. Only during the Revolutionary period was the doctrine compromised and authority concentrated in the hands of the legislature, and the experience confirmed the belief in the merits of separation of powers. Many of the Framers attributed the evils of state government and the want of energy of the central government to the lack of a strong executive who could both check legislative abuses and give energy and direction to administration.

But dividing power was not enough. For there was always the danger —from the Framers' point of view—that different officials with different powers might pool their authority and act together. In Britain today, for example, there are executive, legislative, and judicial officials, but the legislative and executive branches act together in response to directions from the Prime Minister and the Cabinet. Separation of powers by itself would not prevent government branches and officials from responding to the same pressures —for example, an overwhelming majority of the voters. If dividing power by itself was not enough, what else could be done?

CHECKS AND BALANCES—
AMBITION TO COUNTERACT AMBITION

The Framers' answer was a system of *checks and balances*, which provides that the President, legislators, and judges, although mutually dependent on one another in performing their constitutional functions, are given *political* in addition to legal independence. The Framers made these officials politically independent of one another by making them responsive to different constituencies. The President is to be chosen by a group of *electors*, so that he will have different loyalties and represent different interests from senators, chosen by *state legislators*, from representatives, directly elected by *local constituencies*, and from judges, holding office for life and appointed by the President with the consent of the Senate.

The Framers were also careful to arrange matters so that a majority could win control over only part of the government at one time. A popular majority might take control of the House of Representatives in an off-year election, but the President, representing previous popular sentiment, would still have two years to go. The majority might win the Presidency, but other forces might still control the Senate.

Moreover, each branch of the national government is given some responsibilities toward performing the functions of the others, and each is given some authority to control the operations of the others. The doctrine of separation of powers, when combined with checks and balances, is one of *interdependence* rather than independence. "The great security against a gradual concentration of the several powers in the same department," wrote Madison, "consists in giving to those who administer each department the necessary constitutional means and personal motives to resist encroachment on the others. . . . Ambition must be made to counteract ambition." Thus, Congress enacts laws, the President can veto them, and Congress can repass them over his veto. The Supreme Court can invalidate laws passed by Congress and signed by the President, but the Chief Executive appoints the judges with the Senate's concurrence. The President administers the laws, but Congress provides the money for him and his agencies. The Senate and the House of Representatives have an absolute veto on each other. The Framers created not a government of separated powers but a "government of separated institutions *sharing* powers."[3]

The Framers felt it was the legislative branch that was most likely to take over the whole government. "In republican government," Madison wrote, "the legislative authority necessarily predominates." It was in part to meet this problem that the Framers decided on two branches and made them responsible to different constituencies. Thus, said Madison, the two branches were rendered "by different modes of election and different principles of action, as little connected with each other as the nature of their common functions and their common dependence on the society will admit."

Finally, if this did not work, there were the judges. It was not until some years after the Constitution was in operation that the judges obtained the power of *judicial review*—the right to be the official interpreters of the Constitution and to refuse to enforce those laws of Congress that in the judges' opinion were unconstitutional (see Chapter 19). But from the beginning, the judges were expected to check the legislature and the groups that the congressional majority might represent. "Independent judges," wrote Alexander Hamilton in *Federalist No. 78*, would be "an essential safeguard against the effects of occasional ill humors in society. These sometimes extend no farther than to the injury of the private rights of particular classes of citizens, by unjust and partial laws."

[3]Richard E. Neustadt, *Presidential Power* (Wiley, 1960), p. 33.

Could such a system really work? What if a majority of the people should get control of all branches of government and force through radical and impulsive measures? The Framers knew that if, over a period of years, the great majority of the voters wanted to take a certain step, nothing could stop them. Nothing, that is, except despotic government, and they did not want that. The men of 1787 reasoned that all they could do—and this was quite a lot—was to stave off, temporarily, full control by the popular majority.

It may seem surprising that the people—or at least the large number of them who were suspicious of the new Constitution—did not object to these "auxiliary precautions," which often are barriers to action by a popular majority. But the Antifederalists were deeply suspicious of officeholders and were even more anxious than the Federalists to see the power of national authorities defined and restrained.[4] Early Americans did not look on government as an instrument they could seize with their votes and use for their own purposes; they viewed it as something to be handcuffed, hemmed in, and rendered harmless. The separation of powers and checks and balances were intended to make it difficult for a majority to gain control of the government and for those who govern to exceed their constitutional authority.

The Framers deliberately built inefficiency into our political system. As we shall see, these constitutional limitations on the exercise of governmental power have profound contemporary political significance. The crucial question is whether it is desirable and possible to maintain them under the vastly different conditions of the 1970s.

A STUDY IN CONTRASTS

Most Americans now take our system for granted. The separating and checking of power seem to be the very essence of constitutional government. Like Madison, we view the amassing of power in the hands of any one branch of government as the essence of tyranny. Yet it is quite possible for a government to be constitutional without such an apparatus. In the British system, the voters elect members of Parliament from districts throughout the nation (much as we elect members of the House of Representatives). The members of the House of Commons have almost complete constitutional power. The Crown appoints the leaders of the majority party to serve as executive ministers, who collectively form the Cabinet. Any time the executive officers lose support of the majority in the Commons, they must resign or call for new elections. The House of Lords once could check the Commons, but now the Lords are almost powerless. There is no High Court with power to void acts of Parliament; the Prime Minister cannot veto them (though he may ask the Crown to dissolve Parliament and call for elections for members of the House of Commons). If, tomorrow, Parliament decided to cancel elections and hold office for life, it could do so constitutionally through a majority vote. Its decisions would be carried out by the Cabinet, which constitutionally is simply the organ of Parliament, although *politically* Parliament is largely controlled by the Prime Minister and the Cabinet. And, of course, Englishmen take their system for granted, too.

[4]Cecelia M. Kenyon, "Men of Little Faith: The Anti-Federalists on the Nature of Representative Government," *William and Mary Quarterly* (January 1955), pp. 3–43.

AMERICAN SYSTEM OF SEPARATION OF POWERS

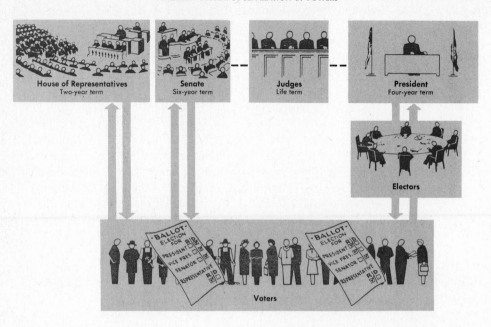

House of Representatives
Two-year term

Senate
Six-year term

Judges
Life term

President
Four-year term

Electors

Voters

BRITISH SYSTEM OF CONCENTRATION OF RESPONSIBILITY

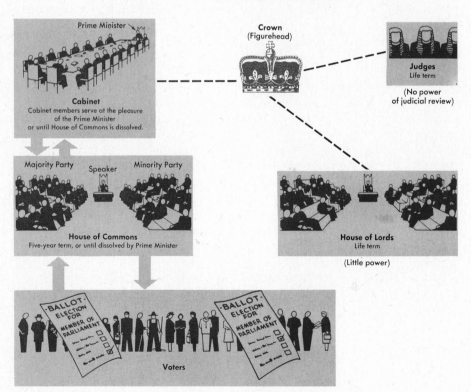

Prime Minister

Crown
(Figurehead)

Judges
Life term

(No power
of judicial review)

Cabinet
Cabinet members serve at the pleasure
of the Prime Minister
or until House of Commons is dissolved.

Majority Party   **Speaker**   **Minority Party**

House of Commons
Five-year term, or until dissolved by Prime Minister

House of Lords
Life term

(Little power)

Voters

51   The British system is based on majority rule—that is, a majority of the voters elect a majority of the legislators, who can put through (virtually without hindrance) the majority's program as long as the parliamentary majority stays together, at least until the next election rolls around. Ours usually depends for action on the agreement of many elements of the society, comprising much more than a majority. The British system *concentrates* control and responsibility in the legislature; ours *diffuses* control and responsibility among the several organs of government.

We have a written document called the Constitution; Britain does not. Yet both systems are constitutional in the sense that the rulers are subject to regular restraints. Clearly constitutionalism requires something much more basic than the existence of a document—witness the military dictatorships whose "constitutions" bear no relation to the exercise of political power. The limitations that our written Constitution and the conventions of the unwritten British constitution impose on all those who exercise governmental power rest on underlying values, attitudes, and norms that exist in both societies. One of the major concerns of political scientists today is to identify the social prerequisites of constitutional democracy. Although research in this area is far from conclusive, it seems certain that constitutional government requires more than any one particular set of formal legal rules.[5]

CHECKS AND BALANCES—RECENT MODIFICATIONS

Fragmentation of governmental power remains basic in American government, but several developments have modified the checks and balances that the Founding Fathers so carefully placed in our constitutional system.

The rise of national political parties. Political parties have served to some extent as unifying factors, drawing together the President, senators, representatives, and even judges behind a common program. But the parties, in turn, have been splintered and weakened by the workings of the system of checks and balances.

Changes in electoral methods. The Framers wanted the President to be chosen by wise, independent men free from popular passions and hero worship. Almost from the beginning, however, the presidential electors have acted as automata, pledged prior to elections to cast their electoral vote for their party's presidential candidate. And senators, who were originally elected by state legislatures, are today chosen directly by the people.

The establishment of agencies exercising all three functions—legislative, executive, and judicial. When the government began to regulate the economy, it became clear that agencies had to have some legislative and judicial as well as administrative power. It was difficult, if not impossible, to grant an agency only administrative powers when detailed rules had to be made and

[5]See Seymour Martin Lipset, *Political Man* (Doubleday, 1959), Chaps 2, 3; Seymour Martin Lipset, Martin Trow, and James Coleman, *Union Democracy* (Free Press, 1956); Harry Eckstein, *A Theory of Stable Democracy* (Princeton Univ. Center of International Studies, 1961).

judgments rendered on highly complex matters, such as policing airwaves or checking the purity of food and drugs.

The rise of the President as the dominating, unifying element in national government. Drawing on its constitutional, political, and emergency powers, the office of the Presidency has overcome some of the divisive effects of checks and balances by the growth and exercise of its power.

The Constitution as Instrument of Government

As careful as the Founding Fathers were to limit the powers they conferred on the national government, the main reason they had assembled in Philadelphia was to create a strong national government. They had learned that weak central government, incapable of governing, is a greater danger to liberty than a powerful government. They wished to establish a national government within the framework of a federal system and endow that government with enough authority to meet the exigencies of all times. They knew that to endure, the government must be capable of meeting the needs of future generations whose problems could not be anticipated. Hence they did not try to put down all the rules in black and white; they made their grants of power general, leaving the way open for succeeding generations to fill in the details and organize the structure of government in accordance with experience.

Consequently, our formal, written Constitution is only the skeleton of our system and is supplemented by a number of fundamental rules that must be considered part of our constitutional system in its larger sense. Without an understanding of the rules of the "informal" Constitution, we would have an incomplete and even misleading picture of our government, because it is primarily through changes in our informal Constitution that our constitutional system is kept up to date. These changes are to be found in certain basic statutes of Congress, decisions of the Supreme Court, actions of the President, and customs and usages of the nation.

KEEPING THE CONSTITUTION UP TO DATE

Congressional eleboration is one of the most important ways of adapting our constitutional system to new problems. Because the Framers gave Congress the authority to prescribe the structural details of the national government, it is unnecessary to amend the formal Constitution every time a change is needed. Examples of congressional elaboration appear in such fundamental legislation as the Judiciary Act of 1789, which laid the foundations of our national judicial system; in the laws establishing the organization and functions of all federal executive officials subordinate to the President; and in the rules of procedure and internal organization and practices of the Congress itself.

Presidential practices have had much to do with the development of our constitutional system. Although there has been no change in the formal Constitution in this respect, the constitutional position of the President is different today from what it was in 1789. The Presidency has become the pivotal office of our national government, and the President has become Chief Legislator as well as Chief Executive. This fundamental change in the American constitutional system has come about because of the willingness of several Presidents, especially Jackson, Lincoln, Wilson, and both Roosevelts, to respond to national crises by a vigorous use of presidential power to provide the leadership the people wanted. Other examples of how our Presidents have contributed to the building of our constitutional system are the establishment of the Cabinet, which rests on traditions going back to President Washington; the precedent established by John Tyler in 1841 (and confirmed in 1967 by the adoption of the Twenty-fifth Amendment) that the Vice President acceding to the Presidency after the death of the incumbent becomes President and not merely Acting President; and the precedent established by Wilson that the President may leave the United States and still retain the full powers of his office. The strengthened position of the Vice President and his more important role in national affairs have developed in recent years primarily through the support that Presidents Eisenhower, Kennedy, and Johnson have given to their respective Vice Presidents.

Customs and usages of the nation have rounded out our governmental system. Presidential nominating conventions and other party activities are examples of constitutional usages. Although no specific mention of these practices are in the written Constitution, they are fundamental to an understanding of our constitutional system. In fact, it has been primarily through the extraconstitutional development of national political parties and the extension of the suffrage within the states that our Constitution has become democratized. A broader electorate began to exercise control over the national government; the presidential office was made more responsive to the people; the relationship between Congress and the President was altered; and, through the growth of political parties, some of the Constitution's blocks to majority rule were overcome.

Judicial interpretation of the Constitution, especially by the Supreme Court, has played an important part in the continuous process of modernizing the constitutional system. As noted previously and discussed in fuller detail in Chapter 19, American judges have the power of judicial review, that is, the authority to refuse to enforce those laws that the judges think are in conflict with the Constitution. As a result, the Supreme Court has become the authoritative interpreter of the Constitution.

Judicial review introduces an element of rigidity into our system. Nevertheless, the words of the Constitution are broad and ambiguous enough to allow divergent interpretations. As conditions have changed and new national demands have developed, the Supreme Court's interpretation of the Constitution has changed to accommodate these new conditions and to reflect these new demands. In the words of Woodrow Wilson, "The Supreme Court is a constitutional convention in continuous session." The establishment of judicial review itself is a classic example of the importance of judicial interpretation in the development of our constitutional system. The Constitution does not specifically give the judges the power of judicial review. Rather, in the famous case of *Marbury* v. *Madison*, the Supreme Court interpreted the Constitution as requiring judges to refuse to enforce those laws that the judges believe to be in conflict with the Constitution.

Because the Constitution is so flexible and because it allows for easy adaptation to changing times, it does not require frequent formal amendment. The advantages of this flexibility may be appreciated when the national Constitution is compared with the rigid and overly specific state constitutions. Many state constitutions, more like legal codes than basic charters, are so detailed that the hands of public officials are often tied. State constitutions leave so little discretion to those who govern that in order to adapt state governments to changing conditions, the constitutions must be amended frequently or replaced every generation or so.

A RIGID OR FLEXIBLE CONSTITUTION?

This picture of a constantly changing national constitutional system disturbs many people. How, they argue, can you have a constitutional government when the Constitution is constantly being twisted by interpretation and changed by informal methods? This view fails to distinguish between two aspects of the Constitution. As an expression of basic and timeless personal liberties, the Constitution does not and should not change. For example, no government can destroy the right to free speech and remain a constitutional government. In this sense the Constitution *is* timeless and essentially unchanging.

But when we consider the Constitution as an instrument of government and a positive grant of power, we realize that if it does not grow with the nation it serves, it will soon be pushed aside. It is not disrespectful to the memory of the Framers to suggest that they could not have conceived of the problems that the government of two hundred million citizens in an industrial state would have to face in the 1970s. The general purposes of government remain the same — to establish liberty, promote justice, ensure domestic tranquility, and provide for the common defense. But the powers of government adequate to accomplish these purposes in 1787 are simply inadequate in the 1970s. No constitution can long deny to the government the right to do what its people want done.

"We the people" — the people of today and tomorrow, not just the people of 1787 — ordain and establish the Constitution. "The Constitution," wrote Jefferson, "belongs to the living and not to the dead." So firmly did he believe this that he advocated a new constitution for every generation. But new constitutions have not been necessary, because in a less formal way each generation has taken part in the never-ending process of developing the original Constitution.

Because of its remarkable adaptability, the Constitution has survived the rigors of democratic and industrial revolutions, the turmoil of civil war, the tensions of major depressions, and the dislocations of world wars. The problem is, then, to preserve the Constitution in its role as a protector of fundamental liberties, as a preserver of the essentials of justice and democracy upon which our system is based, and at the same time to permit government to operate in accordance with the wishes of the people and to adapt itself to new conditions.

Changing the Letter of the Constitution

The Framers of the Constitution knew that future experience would call for changes in the text of the Constitution itself and that some means of formal amendment was necessary. Accordingly, they set forth two ways to propose amendments to the Constitution and two ways to ratify them, and they saw to it that amendments could not be made by simple majorities.

PROPOSING AND RATIFYING

The first method of proposing amendments—the only one that has ever been used—is by a two-thirds vote of both houses of Congress. The second method is by a national convention called by Congress at the request of the legislatures of two-thirds of the states. During the first hundred years of our existence, Congress received only 10 such petitions from state legislatures, but since 1893 about 250 such petitions have been filed.

The second method is full of imponderables. Who determines whether the necessary number of state legislatures have petitioned for a convention? If Congress called a convention into being, how would delegates be chosen and how many votes would each state have? Could the convention propose amendments on a variety of subjects, perhaps even an entirely new constitution? Who determines the method of ratification, Congress or the convention? Where would the convention assemble? Because we have not had a constitutional convention since the adoption of the present Constitution, we have no precedents. But there had never appeared to be much urgency about these questions, so scholars were the only ones who had much interest in them. The general assumption was that these are political questions to be answered by Congress, either by a general law covering all such conventions or by Congress at the time it called a convention into being.

In March of 1967 these questions ceased to be academic, when the thirty-second state legislature—only two short of the required number—petitioned Congress to call a convention. The purpose was to propose an amendment that would reverse the impact of Supreme Court rulings requiring both chambers of state legislatures to be apportioned on the basis of population. Consequently, the Senate Judiciary Committee considered a proposal for a law that would have required Congress to proceed with such a convention, given each state one vote in the convention, allowed each state to determine how its delegation would be elected or appointed, imposed limitations on the convention against considering any except the amendment referred to it, and allowed Congress to determine the method of ratification.

The flurry of excitement about constitutional conventions died down when no more states petitioned Congress for a convention to consider reapportionment. And by the end of 1967 most state legislatures had been reapportioned to reflect population, so additional proposals seemed unlikely. There is, of course, no legal way to force Congress to call a convention even if the necessary two-thirds of the state legislatures petition for it, and it seems probable that in the future, as in the past, when Congress thinks an amendment necessary, it will propose the amendment itself rather than call a convention to do so. Perhaps Congress remembers the fate of its predecessor at the hands of the convention it called into being in 1787.

After an amendment has been proposed, it must be ratified by the states. Again two methods are provided—by approval of the legislatures in three-fourths of the states or by approval of specially called ratifying conventions in three-fourths of the states. Congress determines which method of ratification shall be used.

A state may ratify an amendment after it has voted against ratification, but once it approves the amendment it cannot change its mind and "unratify." Moreover, states must ratify within a "reasonable time" in order for their action to be effective. Congress determines what is a reasonable time, and the modern practice is for Congress to stipulate, either at the time it submits a proposed amendment or as part of the amendment itself, that it must be ratified within seven years. If Congress does not place a time limit on ratification when it proposes an amendment, Congress determines the effectiveness of state action at the time of ratification. For example, when Congress proposed the child labor amendment in 1924 it did not specify any time limit for ratification. To date, twenty-eight states have ratified. If ten more ratify (the three-fourths applies to the number of states presently in the Union, not the number at the time the amendment was proposed), Congress would have to determine whether the states had ratified within the "reasonable time" that is required in order to make the amendment part of the Constitution.

The procedure of submitting amendments to legislatures instead of to ratifying conventions has been criticized, because it permits the Constitution to be changed without any clear expression of the electorate's desires. State legislators who would be doing the ratifying may even have been elected before the proposed amendment was submitted to the states. In any event, state legislators are chosen because of their views on schools, taxation, bond issues, and other matters, or because of their personal popularity —they are almost never elected because of their stand on a proposed constitutional amendment.

Despite these objections to ratification by legislatures, the only amendment to be submitted to ratifying conventions was the Twenty-first (to repeal the Eighteenth or Prohibition Amendment). The "wets" rightly believed that repeal had a better chance of success with conventions than with the rural-dominated state legislatures. This strategy, rather than any desire to sub-

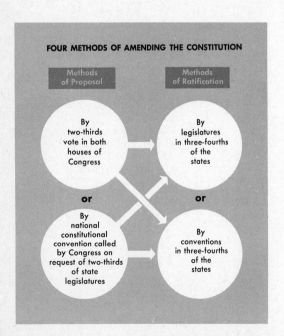

FOUR METHODS OF AMENDING THE CONSTITUTION

Methods of Proposal

Methods of Ratification

By two-thirds vote in both houses of Congress

By legislatures in three-fourths of the states

or

or

By national constitutional convention called by Congress on request of two-thirds of state legislatures

By conventions in three-fourths of the states

mit the question to the electorate, was the important factor, but many commentators mistakenly thought a new precedent had been set and that in the future Congress would choose the more democratic ratification method.[6]

The major obstacle to the adoption of constitutional amendments has not been ratification but getting Congress to propose amendments in the first place. Although dozens of resolutions proposing amendments are introduced in every session, few make any headway. But what Congress proposes is usually ratified. Of thirty amendments proposed, twenty-five have been ratified. Four of the five unratified amendments were proposed prior to the Civil War; since then, the only amendment that has failed to win the necessary state approval is the child labor amendment.

The President has no formal authority over constitutional amendments. His veto power does not extend to them, although his political influence in getting amendments through Congress is often crucial. Nor may governors veto approval of amendments by their respective legislatures, because the Constitution vests ratification in the legislatures alone.

The entire amending procedure has been criticized because neither a majority of the voters at large nor even a majority of the voters in a majority of the states can formally alter the Constitution. But when a majority of the people are serious in their desire to bring about changes in our constitutional system, their wishes are usually implemented either by formal amendment or by the more subtle methods of interpretation and adaptation.

As we have mentioned, the flexibility of our federal Constitution has reduced the need for formal amendments. If we disregard the Bill of Rights, which for all practical purposes may be considered part of the original document, the Constitution has been amended only fifteen times, and two of these amendments, the Eighteenth and Twenty-first, involving prohibition, cancel each other. The fifteen amendments adopted since the Bill of Rights are difficult to classify, but they may be grouped somewhat arbitrarily into the following categories: (1) those whose chief importance is to add to or subtract from the power of the national government; (2) those whose main effect is to limit the power of the state governments; (3) those whose chief impact has been to add to or subtract from the role of the electorate; and (4) those making structural changes in governmental machinery.

CHANGES IN NATIONAL POWER

The Eleventh Amendment. When the Constitution was adopted, it was generally assumed that no private individual could sue a state in federal courts without the consent of the state. But in 1793, when the Supreme Court ruled otherwise in the case of *Chisholm* v. *Georgia*, there was immediate alarm lest citizens flood the federal courts with suits against states defaulting on their debts. The Eleventh Amendment, which became part of the Constitution in 1798, took from federal courts any authority to hear suits commenced or prosecuted by individuals against the states, except with the consent of the state. However, in an opinion that outraged the authors of the Eleventh Amendment, Chief Justice John Marshall held that individuals

[6]Philip J. Martin, "Convention Ratification of Federal Constitutional Amendments," *Political Science Quarterly* (March 1967), p. 61.

could appeal judicial decisions to the Supreme Court, even if a state were the other party.[7] Thus a person who had been arrested could bring a state into court to defend itself against an appeal. Subsequent decisions have held that when a public official acts illegally, he is not acting in his official capacity and is not protected from suit by the Eleventh Amendment.[8] To test the validity of state legislation in the federal courts, a citizen can sue to restrain a specific official from carrying out his duties under the act. In practice, then, the Eleventh Amendment does not weaken the ability of the federal courts to prevent state governments from violating the constitutional rights of citizens and cannot be used to curb the Supreme Court; the Court, after all, has the final say as to what any amendment means.[9]

The Thirteenth Amendment. The Thirteenth Amendment abolished slavery in the United States; it is one of the two provisions of the Constitution (the other is the Twenty-first Amendment) that an individual can violate directly. In addition, it authorizes Congress to legislate against any attempt to hold a human being in slavery or involuntary servitude. In 1968, the amendment took on additional importance when the Supreme Court ruled (*Jones* v. *Mayer*) that the amendment authorizes Congress to legislate against racial discrimination whether imposed by public officials or by private individuals, for such discrimination is to impose on human beings a badge of slavery (see Chapter 7).

The Sixteenth Amendment. In 1895 the Supreme Court, overruling a long line of precedents, for all practical purposes denied to the federal government the power to levy a graduated income tax.[10] The Sixteenth Amendment, which was adopted in 1913, empowers the national government to collect such a tax.

The Eighteenth Amendment. Adopted in 1919, the Eighteenth Amendment was the culmination of a long struggle of the prohibitionists against the use of alcoholic beverages. The amendment gave Congress the power to prevent the manufacture, sale, or transportation of liquors. Although the amendment was ratified by all but two state legislatures, prohibition did not have the support of large groups of people, especially in urban areas, and during the 1920s public indifference made it impossible to enforce prohibition without adopting police-state methods. A bootlegging industry thrived, and prohibition, instead of cutting down the consumption of alcohol, served mainly to enrich criminals and to foster a callous attitude toward the law. After thirteen years of disappointment and the outbreak of the Great Depression (which made new taxes desirable), the Twenty-first Amendment was adopted in 1933, repealing the Eighteenth.

Formal amendments, it is clear, have not been very important in adding to or detracting from the power of the federal government. One amendment

[7]*Cohens* v. *Virginia* (1821).
[8]*Ex parte Young* (1908).
[9]Robert G. McCloskey, *The American Supreme Court* (Univ. of Chicago Press, 1960), p. 64.
[10]*Pollock* v. *Farmer's Loan and Trust Co.* (1895).

(the Eleventh) took away power that the national government was not thought to have had; one (the Sixteenth) added power that it was believed to have had; one grant of power (the Eighteenth) was subsequently repealed; and one (the Thirteenth) gave it power that for a hundred years was narrowed by judicial interpretation (see Chapter 7).

LIMITING STATE POWER

The Fourteenth and Fifteenth Amendments. Along with the Thirteenth, the Fourteenth and Fifteenth Amendments were adopted following and as a result of the Civil War. Whereas the major purpose of the Thirteenth was to free the slaves, the major purpose of the Fourteenth was to make them citizens and to protect their civil rights and of the Fifteenth to protect their right to vote. Although only the objectives of freedom and citizenship were immediately accomplished, the amendments had other consequences not generally anticipated, the most important being that the Supreme Court for a time used the Fourteenth Amendment to give constitutional sanction to laissez faire (see Chapter 8).

Two crucial clauses of the Fourteenth Amendment require states to guarantee *equal protection of the laws* to all persons and prohibit them from depriving any person of life, liberty, or property without *due process of law.* The equal protection and due process clauses of the Fourteenth Amendment are the Constitution's means of protecting our civil rights from infringement by state governments and have been the basis of many of the Supreme Court's decisions defending individual freedom.

These amendments substantially increased the power of the Supreme Court to review actions of the state governments and might well be placed among those that added to the power of the national government—or at least to the judicial branch of that government.

The Nineteenth Amendment. Adopted in 1920, the Nineteenth Amendment deprives the states (and the national government) of the right to deny any citizen the right to vote because of sex. Although women were voting in many states prior to its adoption, the amendment was the final step in providing the constitutional framework for universal suffrage.

The Twenty-fourth Amendment. Ever since 1939 Congress had considered action to eliminate poll taxes either by constitutional amendment or by statute. The Twenty-fourth Amendment, proposed in 1962 and adopted in 1964, forbids any state to require either the payment of a poll tax or any other action in lieu of payment of such a tax[11] as a condition for voting in any primary or election for presidential electors or for members of Congress. However, the amendment allows states to impose a poll tax as a condition of voting for state or local officials. (At the time of the amendment's adoption, four states still had poll taxes.) But in 1966 the Supreme Court held (*Harper v. Virginia Board of Electors*) that the equal protection clause of the Fourteenth Amendment precludes a state from imposing a poll tax as a require-

---

[11]*Harman* v. *Forssenius*, et al. (1965).

ment for voting in *any* election. This decision, in effect, rendered the Twenty-fourth Amendment superfluous—an intriguing example of the interplay of constitutional change.

CHANGING THE POWER OF THE VOTERS

The Seventeenth Amendment. Adopted in 1913, the Seventeenth Amendment provides that United States senators be chosen directly by the electorate instead of being selected by the state legislatures. According to the original Constitution, the House of Representatives was the only branch of the national government that the electorate chose directly. But the rise of political parties and the extension of suffrage within the states brought the presidential office under the control of the voters by the 1830s. From then on it was only a matter of time before the people would demand the right to choose their senators as well.

As the twentieth century opened, the people in many of the states were, in effect, choosing their senators, because the legislatures were simply ratifying the results of popular referendums. But in other states it was charged that great sums of money were being used to bribe state legislators into choosing as senators men of wealth and conservative outlook. The Senate came to be dubbed the Millionaires' Club, and individual senators were tagged as representatives, not of the people but of the steel trust, the sugar trust, the railroad trust, and so on. Thus the demand for constitutional change became insistent. Several times the House of Representatives approved an amendment that would require direct election, but the Senate resisted. Finally, in 1912, the Senate capitulated. The Seventeenth Amendment, passed that year, rounded out the process by which the political branches of the national government were made more directly responsive to the voters.

The Twenty-second Amendment. Adopted in 1951, the Twenty-second Amendment prevents anyone from being elected to the office of President more than twice and stipulates that a man succeeding to the Presidency and serving more than two years may be elected President in his own right only once. (Lyndon Johnson came to office after this midterm date and hence was eligible for a second full term.) The chief significance of the amendment, however, is that it limits the electorate. Prior to the third-term election of Franklin D. Roosevelt in 1940, one of the unwritten usages of the American Constitution was that a man should not run and the voters should not elect a man to this high office for more than two terms. In 1940 and again in 1944, a majority of the voters, aided by Roosevelt, "amended" this unwritten rule. But with the adoption of the Twenty-second Amendment, the restriction on the political majority was made formal.

The Twenty-third Amendment. Ratified in March 1961, the Twenty-third Amendment grants the citizens of the District of Columbia the right to vote in presidential elections for the first time since the district was founded in 1802. The amendment provides that the district shall have the number of electoral votes it would be entitled to if it were a state but in no event more than the least populous state. This means that the District of Columbia will have three votes in the electoral college, the minimum allowed to the least populous state. The ratification process took only nine months after the amendment cleared Congress. Opposition both in Congress and among the states was centered in the South, presumably because of the implications of the race issue—over half the district's population is Negro. No state of the deep South approved the proposal, and one state, Arkansas, voted against it.

CHANGING THE CONSTITUTIONAL STRUCTURE

The Twelfth Amendment. The Twelfth Amendment was adopted in 1804 to correct a deficiency in the original Constitution. The original provisions for the selection of President and Vice President were that electors should be chosen in each state according to the method prescribed by the state legislature and that each elector, without consultation with others, was to vote for the two men he deemed best qualified to serve as President. The person with the most votes, provided the number of votes represented a majority of the electors, was to be President, and the person with the next highest number of votes was to be Vice President. It was generally expected that the electors in the several states would cast their votes for the leading members of their own states and that no one would receive a majority. In such cases the House of Representatives, voting by states, was to choose the President from among the five men with the most votes. In the event that two men received the same number of votes, each representing a majority of the number of electors, the House was to choose between them.

The rise of national political parties made this system unworkable. By the time the presidential election of 1800 took place, the electors had become party functionaries pledged to vote for the candidates of their own parties. In that year the Republicans, whose candidates were Jefferson for President and Aaron Burr for Vice President, elected a majority of the electors. Each Republican elector, as pledged, cast one of his ballots for Jefferson and one for Burr, so that each man had the same number of electoral votes. As a result, the election was thrown into the House of Representatives, still controlled by the Federalists. For a while, the Federalists toyed with the idea of electing Burr to the Presidency; to some Federalist leaders this would have been the lesser of two evils. It was only with the greatest difficulty that Jefferson was finally installed in the White House. Immediately thereafter, the Twelfth Amendment was adopted. Each elector now votes separately for President and for Vice President, and the candidate with the majority of the votes in each case is elected. In the event no candidate receives a majority of the votes for President, the House, voting by states, chooses from among the three men with the most electoral votes. If no man receives a majority of the votes cast for Vice President, the Senate chooses between the two men with the most votes.

The Twentieth Amendment. Popularly known as the "lame-duck amendment," this measure was inspired largely by the late Senator George Norris of Nebraska. Before it was adopted, a President elected in November did not take office until the following March, and congressmen chosen at the same time did not legislate until thirteen months after their election. Meanwhile, congressmen who had been defeated in the elections continued to represent—or misrepresent—their constitutents in the short and ineffective December-to-March session. The Twentieth Amendment rearranged the schedule of congressional and presidential terms so that congressmen elected in November now begin their duties on January 3, and the President takes office on January 20. This also does away with the short December-to-March session of Congress, which used to specialize in filibusters.

The Twenty-fifth Amendment. Ratified in 1967, the Twenty-fifth Amendment confirms prior practice that on the death of the President, the Vice President becomes not Acting President but President. It also provides that in the event the President should resign, the Vice President would become President. But of greater significance, it provides a procedure to determine whether an incumbent President is unable to discharge the powers and duties of his office, and it establishes procedures to fill a vacancy in the vice presidency.

Sixteen times the office of Vice President has been vacant, creating (since 1947) the unsatisfactory situation of leaving the line of presidential succession open to the Speaker of the House, a man not chosen for his suitability to serve as Acting President of the United States. The Twenty-fifth Amendment provides that in the event there is a vacancy in the office of the Vice President, the President shall nominate a Vice President who shall take office upon confirmation by a majority vote of both houses of Congress. This procedure ensures the appointment of a Vice President in whom the President has confidence. If the Vice President has to take over the Presidency, he can be expected to reflect the policies of the man the people had originally elected to the office.

Five times in the past questions have been raised about the ability of the President to carry on his duties because of serious and sustained illness, but we had no agreed-upon procedure to resolve such questions. In the future, if the Vice President and a majority of the "principal officers of the executive departments"—that is, the members of the Cabinet or such body as Congress by law may provide—are of the opinion that the President is unable to discharge the powers and duties of his office, they are to so state in writing to the President pro tempore of the Senate and to the Speaker of the House. Upon such a written declaration, the Vice President is to serve immediately as Acting President and continue to do so until the President transmits in writing to the President pro tempore of the Senate and the Speaker of the House his declaration that he is prepared to resume his responsibilities. If the Vice President and a majority of the Cabinet do not think the President is ready to resume his duties, they have four days to so notify the Congress. The Congress must then assemble within forty-eight hours and come to a decision within twenty-one days. The presumption, however, favors the President. It requires a two-thirds vote of both houses to keep the President from taking over his responsibilities in the face of his declaration that he is able to do so.

The Twenty-fifth Amendment vests, for the first time, a collective responsibility in "the principal officers of the executive departments," suggesting that there may be a need for Congress to define precisely who are such principal officers, presumably only the twelve heads of the formal executive departments.

THE CHANGING CONSTITUTION—A CASE STUDY

The history of national regulation of child labor offers an interesting example of constitutional change by a combination of all the methods discussed. At the beginning of the twentieth century, people were becoming alarmed over the widespread employment in heavy and dangerous industries of children at ages when they should still have been in school. In some working places the conditions were so deplorable and the hours so long that young children of eight and ten were slowly dying of undernourishment, disease, or overwork. Wages were so low that those who exploited child labor were able to undersell their competitors. To meet the competition, other employers, in turn, were forced to hire children.

Here was an admitted evil; yet, individually, the states were unable to act. If the more progressive states outlawed child labor, they could not prevent the sale within their boundaries of cheap goods produced elsewhere by children, and they could not attract industries seeking cheap labor. Finally, in 1916, after years of agitation, Congress closed the channels of interstate commerce to goods manufactured by, or with the help of, child labor. But the Supreme Court, by a close decision and—according to some—a tortured construction of the Constitution, in *Hammer* v. *Dagenhart* (1918), struck down the law as an interference with the reserved powers of the states. Congress tried to overcome the constitutional block by placing a tax on goods produced by or with the help of children. In 1922, in *Bailey* v. *Drexel Furniture Company*, the Court ruled this law unconstitutional.

Apparently nothing could be done without a constitutional amendment. In 1924 Congress proposed an amendment that would give to the national government the power to "limit, regulate, and prohibit the labor of persons under 18 years of age." The amendment specifically stated that "the power of the several States is unimpaired by this Article except that the operations of State laws shall be suspended to the extent necessary to give effect to legislation enacted by Congress." But the opponents of the measure, behind the mask of states' rights, were able to prevent ratification by the necessary three-fourths of the states.

By 1937, although the country had experienced a major depression and a marked change in political climate, the Supreme Court was still dominated by judges who represented the views of the 1920s. Congress in 1935 had enacted a law that, if upheld, would indicate that Congress could use its power over interstate commerce to limit child labor. Would the Court approve? After much agitation by the President (see Chapter 19), including a proposal to pack the Supreme Court with justices more responsive to the political majorities of the 1930s, the Supreme Court reversed its ruling on the extent of the power of Congress over interstate commerce.[12] The following year, 1938, Congress once again enacted a law closing the channels of interstate commerce to goods produced by child labor. This time the Su-

[12]*National Labor Relations Board* v. *Jones & Laughlin Steel Corporation* (1937).

preme Court upheld the law, specifically overruling its decision of 1918.[13] It had taken twenty years, but congressional, judicial, and presidential action had at last succeeded in bringing the Constitution into line with the desires of the people. Since 1937 no state has ratified the child labor amendment, for it is no longer so vitally needed. The Constitution had been "amended" by other means.

The one principal feature of our constitutional system that remains to be examined is *federalism,* one of the most important "auxiliary precautions" against the abuse of power. The United States is not the only or even the oldest federal union, but it was the first to operate successfully a federal system on a continental scale. This has been one of America's major contributions to the science and art of government.

[13]*United States* v. *Darby* (1941).

The Dynamics
of American Federalism

4   Federalism 1787-style and federalism in the 1970s are as different as a stagecoach and a space ship. Since 1787 our federal system has been molded by a dynamic society and altered by the thoughts and actions of millions of men. This chapter will explore the nature of American federalism and its constitutional structure. But first we must define terms.

A *federal system of government* is one in which a constitution divides governmental powers between the central, or national, government and the constituent governments (called states in the United States), giving substantial functions to each. Neither the central nor the constituent government receives its powers from the other; both derive them from a common source, a constitution. This constitutional distribution of powers cannot be altered by the ordinary process of legislation—for example, by an act of the national legislature or by acts of the several constituent governments. Finally, both levels of government operate through their own agents and exercise power directly over individuals.[1] Among the countries that have a federal system of government are the United States, Canada, Switzerland, India, Mexico, Australia, and Burma.

A *unitary*, as opposed to a federal, *system of government* is one in which a constitution vests all governmental power in the central government, and constituent units exercise only the authority given to them by the central government. What the central government gives it can take away. Britain, France, Israel, and the Philippines have unitary government, and, in the

[1] Based on discussion of A. W. Macmahon (ed.), "The Problems of Federalism," *Federalism, Mature and Emergent* (Doubleday, 1955), pp. 4–5.

United States, the relation between states and their subdivisional governments, such as counties and cities, is ordinarily of this sort.

Some students distinguish a *confederation* from a federation by defining the former as a government in which the constituent governments by constitutional compact create a central government but do not give it power to regulate the conduct of individuals. The central government makes regulations for the constituent governments but it exists and operates only through their sufferance. The thirteen states operating under the Articles of Confederation fit this definition.

Unfortunately for our understanding of federalism, the founders of our Constitution used the term *federal* to describe what we now would call a confederate form of government.[2] Moreover, today *federal* is frequently used as a synonym for *national*, that is, people often refer to the government in Washington as "the federal government." In an exact sense, of course, the states *and* the national government make up our federal system.

Governments range along a continuum from highly centralized, unitary governments (in form and fact) through centralized federations to leagues of sovereign nations. And every nation is in a constant but gradual process of changing this "mix." The actual division of decision-making in any nation results not only from the constitutional division of governmental structures but also from the nature of the political party system, the ideological commitments of the electorate, the divisions within the political community, the needs of administrative efficiency, the distribution of economic resources, and other political, social, and economic factors. To determine where decisions are made and functions are performed, one must look not only at constitutional documents and political institutions but also at a nation's political behavior and practices. Constitutional forms "may or may not accurately express the social, cultural, and political realities of the society being studied."[3] The Soviet Union, for example, has a federal constitution, but because of the centralized and disciplined nature of the Communist Party, constituent unions of the U.S.S.R. have less independent authority than do the local governments under the British unitary constitution.[4]

Why Federalism?

Why do we have a federal form of government? In part, because in 1787 there was no other practical choice. After confederation had been tried and found wanting, the only choice open to those who wanted a more closely knit union was federation. A unitary system was ruled out, because the leaders knew that the overwhelming majority of the people were too deeply attached to the state governments to permit the states to be subor-

[2]Martin Diamond, "What the Framers Meant by Federalism," in Robert A. Goldwin (ed.), *A Nation of States* (Rand McNally, 1963), pp. 24–41.

[3]Charles D. Tarelton, "Symmetry and Asymmetry as Elements of Federalism: A Theoretical Speculation," *Journal of Politics* (November 1965), p. 866

[4]See Rufus Davis, "The 'Federal Principle' Reconsidered," in Aaron Wildavsky (ed.), *American Federalism in Perspective* (Little, Brown, 1967), p. 31.

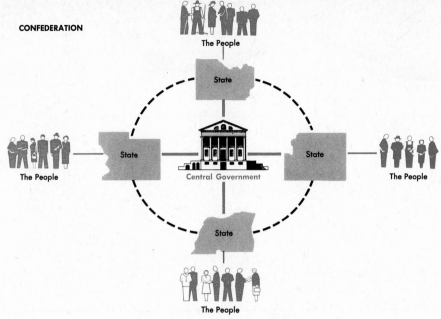

The *Confederation* was a union of *states*. The central government received power from the states and had no direct authority over the people.

—AND FEDERATION

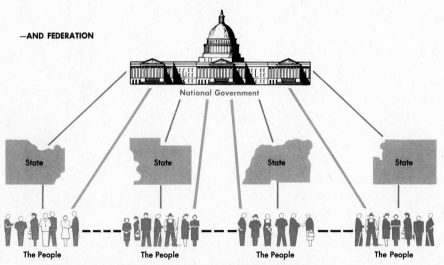

The *Federal Union* is a union of *people*. The national government and state governments receive power from the people and exercise authority directly over them.

dinated to a central government. Today, a unitary system can be operated democratically even in a large country. But in the United States of 1787 distances were too great, methods of transportation and communication too poor, and techniques of democracy too new to have made possible the operation of a large unitary state by democratic methods. In the absence of widespread cohesion and nationally shared sentiments, such a union could have been held together only by force. Federalism 1787-style went as far in the direction of union as public opinion and the technology of the time permitted.

Federalism has been the ideal system for "the great enterprise of appropriating the North American Continent to western civilization."[5] It has enabled the Union to expand from thirteen states to fifty without any disruption or revision of the governmental structure. As people moved into a new territory, they drew up a state constitution, which was then approved by the Congress and the President. Each new state became a member of the Union with the same powers and responsibilities as the original thirteen; the only changes required were the addition of new desks in the Senate and House of Representatives in Washington and new stars on the flag.

The factors that led to the creation of our federal system in 1787 and that sustain it in the 1970s should not be confused with the arguments for and against federalism. (In large measure we retain federalism because our political party structure is sufficiently decentralized to preserve the independence of the states in the face of the strong pressures that incline us to central controls.) The arguments in behalf of federalism, whatever their merits, provide an ideological tone for debate that political leaders affront at their own peril. Public debate takes place within the context of all groups' insisting that their actions will "strengthen the federal system."

UNITY WITHOUT UNIFORMITY

Even if a unitary state had been politically possible in 1787, it probably would not have been chosen, for federalism was and still is regarded as the appropriate form of government for the people of the United States. It is thought to be ideally suited to the needs of a relatively heterogeneous people who are spread over a large continent, who are suspicious of concentrated power, and who desire unity but not uniformity.

Federalism institutionalizes the American suspicion of concentrated power, for Americans tend to equate freedom and federalism. However, in the rest of the world federal forms have not been notably successful in preventing the rise of tyrannies and many unitary governments are democratic. Hence our assumption that federalism is a major factor in preserving democracy is doubtful, but federalism "lessens the risk of a monopoly of political power by providing a number of independent points where the party that is nationally in the minority at the time can maintain itself while it formulates and partly demonstrates its policies and capabilities and develops new leadership."[6] Conversely, if, as Madison pointed out in *Federalist No. 10*, "factious leaders . . . kindle a flame within their particular states," national leaders can check the spread of the "conflagration into the other states."

This diffusion of power, of course, has the defects of its virtues — it makes it difficult for a national majority to carry into effect a program of action, and it permits a majority in control of a state government to frustrate the consensus as expressed by national agencies of government. To control the three branches of the national government is sometimes not enough; power must

[5]Edward S. Corwin, "American Federalism — Past, Present, and Future," Princeton University Bicentennial Address, October 7, 1946.
[6]Macmahon, *op cit.*, p. 11.

be won at the state level too. Whether this is an advantage or a disadvantage depends on one's political outlook. To the Founding Fathers it was an advantage. As we know, they feared that the mass of people "without property or principle" would seize control of the government. Federalism, they hoped, would make such a seizure less probable, because national majorities could be checked by local majorities. Of course—and this is a point often overlooked—the size of the nation and the multiplicity of interests within it are the greatest obstacles to the formation of an arbitrary, single-interest majority. But if such a majority should be formed, the fact that it would have to work through a federal system would restrain its powers.

Under a federal system, local issues do not have to be thrust into the national arena, thereby making it easier to develop a consensus on national problems. National politicians and parties do not have to iron out every difference on every issue in every state, because issues that might prove irreconcilable in Congress are disposed of in the state legislatures. If Congress were the nation's only legislative body, it would be forced to solve all the issues that divide people along religious, racial, and social lines, but the size of the United States, with its many diverse cultures, makes it difficult to set national norms for local issues.

Suppose, for example, that Congress had to establish national policy on divorce or the content of education. The problem of securing national agreement might be infinitely complicated. Or consider the issue of controlling alcoholic beverages. Many persons living in large cities feel that the moderate use of alcohol is one of the amenities of life and that prohibition of its manufacture or sale is an infringement on personal liberty. Many people in rural areas, on the other hand, are convinced that alcohol harms health and morals, causes many social problems, and should be outlawed. Our federal system permits these battles to be fought in the state legislatures. There is no need to try to enforce an inflexible national standard on divergent areas and cultures.

THE STATES AS PROVING GROUNDS

Federalism encourages experimentation. Fifty-one governments try out new methods and enable us to compare results. By experimenting with procedures and programs, states provide a wealth of experience from which the best can be adopted. The national government often benefits from this experimentation—for example, when it adopted new budgetary methods in 1921. The Federal Rehabilitation Act of 1965 reflects the innovative practices of some of the states in the field of corrections and prisoner rehabilitation and the Federal Highway Safety Act of 1967 also builds on state experiences. New York has shown the way in its assault on water pollution; California has pioneered air-pollution control programs.[7]

The states also serve as training grounds for Presidents, congressmen, federal judges, and, to a lesser extent, federal administrators. Generally, more than half the members of Congress have had prior service in their own state legislatures, and many of our Presidents served their apprenticeship as state governors.

[7]Terry Sanford, *Storm Over the States* (McGraw-Hill, 1967), pp. 3–4.

Federalism is also defended on the grounds that it keeps governed and governors in close and continuing contact and gives the electorate a greater voice in governmental affairs. Few of us can serve the national government as President, congressman, Cabinet member, or even administrator, but many thousands can participate in the operation of state and local governments. However, analysis makes it clear that the "closeness" of state governments to the people—in such areas as provision of services, participation, control, or identification—is meaningless.[8] Voter participation in state elections is substantially below that in national elections. Survey research indicates that a solid majority of the population believes that the national government is more important than the state governments—and that it *should be*.[9] A study of the awareness among schoolchildren of the different levels of government concludes that "the state level is the last about which learning takes place."[10] Nevertheless, the belief that the states are closer to the people than is the national government remains part of the tradition of American politics.

Whatever the merits or demerits of federalism, this system is a fact of political life. Of course, the precise constitutional structure of American federalism is one of many different possible forms of federalism.

Constitutional Structure of American Federalism

The constitutional framework of federalism may be stated simply: The national government has only those powers, with one important exception, delegated to it by the Constitution; the states have all the powers not delegated to the United States except those denied to them by the Constitution; but within the scope of its operation, the national government is supreme. Furthermore, some powers are specifically denied to both national and state governments; others are specifically denied only to the states; still others are denied only to the national government. Here in outline form is the constitutional structure of our federal system.

1 *Powers of the national government.* The Constitution, chiefly in the first three Articles, delegates specific legislative, executive, and judicial powers to the national government. In addition to these *express* powers, the Constitution delegates to Congress those *implied* powers that may be reasonably inferred from the express powers. The constitutional basis for the implied powers is the "necessary and proper clause" (Article I, Section 8), which gives Congress the right "to make all Laws which shall be necessary and proper for carrying into Execution the foregoing Powers, and all other powers vested . . . in the Government of the United States. . . ." Furthermore, in the field of foreign affairs, the national government has *inherent*

---

[8]Morton Grodzins, "Centralization and Decentralization in the American Federal System," in Robert A. Goldwin (ed.), *A Nation of States* (Rand McNally, 1963), pp. 9–15.

[9]Harold Orlans, *Opinion Polls on National Leaders* (Institute for Research in Human Relations Report No. 6, 1953), pp. 2–12; cited in Fred I. Greenstein, *Children and Politics* (Yale Univ. Press, 1965), p. 61.

[10]Greenstein, *ibid.*, p. 155.

powers that do not depend on specific constitutional grants but grow out of the very existence of a nation-state.

2 *Powers of the states.* The Constitution reserves to the states (see the Tenth Amendment) all the powers not granted to the national government and not denied in the Constitution to the states. Powers that are not by express provision of the Constitution or by judicial interpretation exclusively conferred on the national government may be *concurrently* exercised by the states as long as there is no conflict with national law. The reservation of certain powers to the states, however, does not exclude the national government from regulating the subjects of that power under one of its express, implied, or inherent powers.

3 *National supremacy.* Although the national government can operate only within limited areas, within these areas it is supreme. Article VI states: "This Constitution, and the Laws of the United States which shall be made in Pursuance thereof; and all Treaties made . . . under the Authority of the United States, shall be the supreme Law of the Land; and the Judges in every state shall be bound thereby; any Thing in the Constitution or Laws of any State to the Contrary notwithstanding." Moreover, all officials, state as well as national, are bound by constitutional oath to support the Constitution. The national government may exercise its full powers over every square inch of the United States, and the states may not interfere with the constitutional activities of national officials.

4 *Constitutional limits.* The Constitution imposes certain restraints on the national or state governments or both, not only to preserve the federal system, but also to protect various individual freedoms. Most of these restraints are set forth in Article I; the Bill of Rights; and the Thirteenth, Fourteenth, and Fifteenth Amendments.

CONFLICTING INTERPRETATIONS
OF AMERICAN FEDERALISM

This outline oversimplifies and leaves unanswered some important questions. Is ours a union of states or a union of people? Should the powers of the national government be narrowly or broadly construed? Does the reservation of powers to the state determine the limits of how national power may be used? Throughout our history these questions have been constantly and heatedly debated; in 1861 they even led to war. The questions grow out of specific, controversial issues: Does the national government have the constitutional power to outlaw slavery in the territories? Do the states have the reserved power to operate racially segregated schools? Can the national government use its power to regulate interstate commerce in such a way as to determine relations between employers and employees? Although the debates are frequently couched in lofty constitutional language and appeals are made to the great principles of federalism, the real struggle is usually over very practical, immediate, and quite mundane questions of who gets what, where, when, and how, or who does what to whom.

As the issues and times have changed, so have the details of the constitutional arguments. However, it is useful to classify the approaches to our federal system into two broad schools—states' rights and nationalist.

Among those who have championed the *states' rights* interpretation, albeit with varying emphasis, are Thomas Jefferson, John C. Calhoun, the Supreme Court from the 1920s to 1937, and, today, many white Southerners. The states' righters' basic premise is that the Constitution is an intergovernmental compact among the states which thereby created the central government and gave it carefully limited authority. Because the national government is thus nothing more than the agent of the states, every one of its powers should be narrowly construed. In case of doubt whether the states gave a particular function to the general government or reserved it for themselves, the doubt should be resolved in favor of the states.

The states' righters hold that the national government should not be permitted to exercise its delegated powers in such a way as to interfere with activities reserved to the states. The Tenth Amendment, it is claimed, makes this emphatic: "The powers not delegated to the United States by the Constitution, nor prohibited by it to the States, are reserved to the States respectively, or to the people." It is contended that this amendment means, for

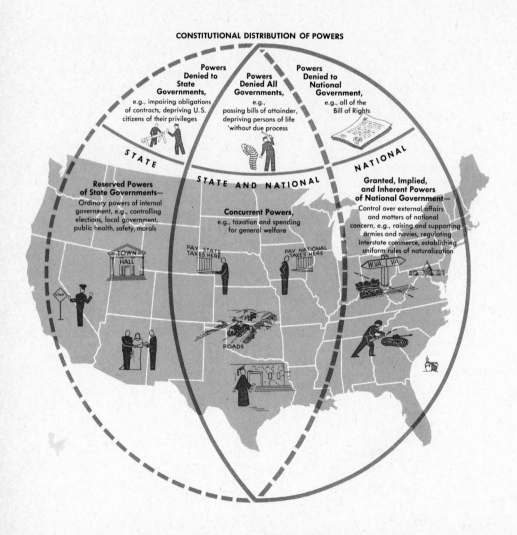

CONSTITUTIONAL DISTRIBUTION OF POWERS

Powers Denied to State Governments, e.g., impairing obligations of contracts, depriving U.S. citizens of their privileges

Powers Denied All Governments, e.g., passing bills of attainder, depriving persons of life without due process

Powers Denied to National Government, e.g., all of the Bill of Rights

STATE

STATE AND NATIONAL

NATIONAL

Reserved Powers of State Governments— Ordinary powers of internal government, e.g., controlling elections, local government, public health, safety, morals

Concurrent Powers, e.g., taxation and spending for general welfare

Granted, Implied, and Inherent Powers of National Government— Control over external affairs and matters of national concern, e.g., raising and supporting armies and navies, regulating interstate commerce, establishing uniform rules of naturalization

TOWN HALL

STOP

PAY STATE TAXES HERE

PAY NATIONAL TAXES HERE

W.VA. VA.

ROADS

example, that Congress' power to regulate commerce among the states cannot be used to regulate agriculture or to curtail child labor, because the Constitution reserves the regulation of agriculture and child labor to the states. Some of the more extreme states' righters have gone so far as to argue that the states, as sovereign entities, may exercise their reserved powers to the fullest extent even if they conflict with programs of the national government.

Underlying the states' righters' fundamental position is their insistence that the state governments are closer to the people and therefore that they more accurately reflect the people's wishes than does the national government, which they view as a distant and essentially external authority. They maintain further that the national government is inherently heavy-handed and bureaucratic and that in order to preserve our federal system and our liberties the central authority must be carefully circumscribed.

The *nationalist* position, supported, again with varying emphasis, by Chief Justice John Marshall, Abraham Lincoln, Theodore Roosevelt, Franklin Roosevelt, and, throughout most of our history, the Supreme Court, rejects the whole concept of the Constitution as an interstate compact. Rather, the Constitution is a supreme law ordained and established by the people. The national government, it is held, is an agent of the people, not of the states, for it was the people who drew up the Constitution and created the national government. The sovereign people gave the national government sufficient power to accomplish the great objectives listed in the Preamble. They intended that the central government's powers should be liberally construed and that it not be denied authority unless there is a clear conflict with express constitutional limits or a clear absence of constitutional sanction.

The nationalists contend that the national government is not a foreign entity but a government of all the people; each state speaks for only some of the people. Of course, the Tenth Amendment reserves powers to the states, but as Chief Justice Stone said, "The Tenth Amendment states but a truism that all is retained which has not been surrendered." The amendment does not deny the national government the right to exercise to the fullest extent all the powers given to it by the Constitution.[11] The supremacy of the national government does restrict the states, for a government representing part of the people cannot be allowed to interfere with a government representing all of them.

McCulloch v. *Maryland*—A NATIONALIST VICTORY

In 1819, in the famous case of *McCulloch* v. *Maryland*, the Supreme Court had the first of many chances to choose between these two interpretations of our federal system. Maryland had levied a tax against the Baltimore branch of the Bank of the United States, which had been established in accordance with a law of Congress. McCulloch, the cashier of the bank, refused to pay on the ground that a state could not tax an instrument of the national govern-

[11]Walter Berns, "The Meaning of the Tenth Amendment," in Robert A. Goldwin (ed.), *A Nation of States, op. cit.*, pp. 126–148. For an able statement of the states' rights interpretation, see James Jackson Kilpatrick, *The Sovereign States* (Regnery, 1957).

ment. Maryland's attorneys argued in the first place that the national government did not have the power to incorporate a bank, but even if it did, the state had the power to tax it.

Maryland was represented before the Court by some of the most distinguished men of the bar, including Luther Martin, a delegate to the Constitutional Convention who had left early in the deliberations when it became apparent that a strong national government was in the making. Martin, basing his argument against the constitutionality of the bank on the states' rights view of federalism, pointed out that the power to incorporate a bank is not one of the powers expressly delegated to the national government. He contended that Article I, Section 8, Clause 18, which gives Congress the right to choose whatever means are necessary and proper to carry out its delegated powers, should, like all grants of national power, be narrowly construed. So interpreted, the clause gives Congress only the power to choose those means and to pass those laws absolutely essential to the execution of its expressly granted powers. Because a bank is not absolutely necessary to the exercise of any of its delegated powers, Congress has no authority to establish it.

What about Maryland's right to tax the bank? Martin's position was simply stated: The power to tax is one of the powers reserved to the states, which they may use as they see fit.

The national government was represented by equally distinguished counsel, chief of whom was Daniel Webster. Webster conceded that the power to create a bank is not one of the express powers of the national government. But the power to pass laws necessary and proper to carry out enumerated powers is expressly delegated to Congress, and this power should be interpreted generously to mean that Congress has authority to enact any legislation convenient and useful in carrying out delegated national powers. Therefore, Congress may incorporate a bank as an appropriate, convenient, and useful means of exercising the granted powers of collecting taxes, borrowing money, and caring for the property of the United States.

As to Maryland's attempt to tax the bank, Webster contended that though the power to tax is reserved to the states, states cannot use their reserved powers to interfere with the operations of the national government. The Constitution leaves no room for doubt: In case of conflict between the national and state governments, the former is supreme.

In 1819 the Supreme Court was presided over by Chief Justice John Marshall, a nationalist and an advocate of a liberal interpretation of the central government's constitutional authority. Speaking for a unanimous Court, Marshall rejected every one of Maryland's contentions. In his usual forceful style, he wrote: "We must never forget that it is a *constitution* we are expounding. . . . [A] constitution intended to endure for ages to come, and consequently, to be adapted to the various crises of human affairs." "The government of the Union," he continued, "is emphatically and truly a government of the people. In form and substance it emanates from them, its powers are granted by them, and are to be exercised directly on them. . . . It can never be to their interest and cannot be presumed to have been their intention, to clog and embarrass its execution, by withholding the most appropriate means." Marshall summarized his views on how the powers of the national government should be broadly construed in these now-famous

words: "Let the end be legitimate, let it be within the scope of the Constitution, and all means which are appropriate, which are plainly adapted to
that end, which are not prohibited, but consist with the letter and spirit of
the Constitution, are constitutional."

Having thus established the doctrine of implied national powers, Marshall
set forth the doctrine of national supremacy. No state, he said, can use its
reserved taxing powers to tax a national instrument. "The power to tax involves the power to destroy. . . . If the right of the states to tax the means
employed by the general government be conceded, the declaration that the
Constitution, and the laws made in pursuance thereof, shall be the supreme
law of the land, is empty and unmeaning declamation."

The long-range significance of *McCulloch* v. *Maryland* in providing an
ideological support for the developing forces of nationalism can hardly be
overstated. Although many persons still support the states' rights interpretation, this case went far to establish the doctrines of liberal construction and
national supremacy. The arguments of the states' righters, if accepted, would
have strapped the national government in a constitutional straitjacket and
denied it the powers needed to handle the problems of an expanding nation.
In all probability, the Constitution would have been replaced many years
ago as succeeding generations were forced, once again, to render the central
government adequate to the needs of each new age. Marshall's vision accounts in part for the longevity of our Constitution, the oldest written constitution in the world today—and truly a living constitution.

NATIONAL POWER IN FOREIGN AFFAIRS

Even the states' rights theory of federalism recognizes that in foreign relations the national government is not restricted to powers expressly granted
or even to those that may be implied. So far as the external relations of the
United States are concerned, the national government has inherent powers
derived only indirectly from the Constitution. It has the same authority in
dealing with other nations as it would if it were a unitary government. For
example, the government of the United States may acquire territory by dis-
covery and occupation even though there is no specific constitutional basis
for such acquisition; it may also make agreements other than constitutionally
defined treaties. Even if the Constitution were silent about foreign affairs
—which it is not—the national government would have as "necessary con-
comitants of its nationality"[12] the right to declare war, make treaties, and
appoint and receive ambassadors.

Not only does the national government have inherent power over external
relations, but this power is not shared by the states; it is vested in the national
government exclusively. Of course, the fact that ours is a federal system
does have an impact on our foreign relations. National officials are sometimes cautious in making agreements with other nations that cover subjects
normally handled by the states. And although the Constitution bestows on
the national government ample and exclusive authority to conduct foreign
affairs, states have had a long-standing "unofficial" involvement in foreign

[12]*United States* v. *Curtiss-Wright Export Corporation* (1936).

relations, primarily in commerce. During the nineteenth century, states sent missions abroad to stimulate immigration, and today, many states send delegations overseas to promote commerce for their industries, and some even maintain permanent trade offices in major international markets. At times relations between the United States and other nations have been embarrassed by the failure of a state to prosecute persons who have injured foreign nationals, by state laws that discriminate against aliens, and by state policemen who stop speeding foreign diplomats.

TREATIES AND THE FEDERAL SYSTEM

The national government's power to make treaties, which is vested in the President with the advice and consent of two-thirds of the Senate, is not unlimited. The Supreme Court has "regularly and uniformly recognized the supremacy of the Constitution over a treaty."[13] The national government cannot, by treaty, abridge rights guaranteed by the Constitution. It could not, for example, deprive a person of his First Amendment rights by treaty or by a law to implement a treaty any more than it could do so by any other law. Treaties and the laws passed to implement treaties, like all other laws, must conform to the Constitution. Furthermore, Congress may, at any time, as far as its application within the United States is concerned, abrogate a treaty.

The reserved powers of the states, however, do not set bounds to the national government's treaty power. Treaties made under the authority of the United States, and laws passed by Congress to carry treaties into effect, are superior to state constitutions and state laws. A *self-executing treaty*, one that operates of itself and goes into effect without the need of any further action by Congress, is regarded by the courts on the same level as any other national law. The Framers felt that the national interest was superior to the interest of any state and that if a conflict arose between a national treaty and state policy, the state policy should give way.

In short, as long as treaties do not abridge a specific provision of the Constitution, the President and the Senate may make agreements with foreign nations regulating people, or giving Congress the power to regulate them, even though the regulations are not within the lawmaking power directly granted by the Constitution to the national government. This doctrine had been familiar for many years, but in 1920 the Supreme Court's decisions in *Missouri* v. *Holland* made its implications clear.

In 1914 Congress had passed a law dealing with the hunting of birds migrating between the United States and Canada. Two federal district courts held this law unconstitutional on the ground that Congress had no authority, express or implied, to regulate wildlife. The Supreme Court did not review these decisions. A few years later, Congress, in order to comply with a treaty between the United States and Great Britain (acting for Canada), enacted an even more stringent law governing the hunting of such birds. This time the Supreme Court did review the law and upheld its constitutionality. Justice Holmes, speaking for the Court, said that assuming Congress could not in the absence of the treaty have enacted this legislation, it did not follow that the

[13]*Reid* v. *Covert* (1957).

same law to implement a treaty would also be unconstitutional. The treaty did not contravene any prohibitory words in the Constitution. It could not be declared unconstitutional because of some "invisible radiation from the general terms of the Tenth Amendment." Since the treaty was constitutional, Congress had power to pass whatever laws were necessary and proper to implement it.

The Constitutional Position of the States

The powers of the states are also derived from the Constitution, which reserves to them all powers not granted to the national government subject only to the limitations of the Constitution. Of course, states may not use their reserved powers to frustrate national policies. (It should be recognized that local units of government are merely agents of the states exercising powers given to them by the states. What states cannot constitutionally do, local units cannot do. In our discussion of national-state relations and the constitutional structure of federalism, the local units are subsumed in all references to states.)

The Constitution, as we have noted, contains certain explicit limitations upon state power in behalf of individual liberties. In addition, the Constitution forbids the states to make treaties, impair the obligation of contracts, coin money, and pass bills of attainder or ex post facto laws (see Chapter 8). States may not, except with the consent of Congress, collect duties on exports or imports or make compacts with another state.

What if the Constitution does not vest a particular power exclusively in the national government or specifically limit state power? Does the mere vesting of a particular power in the national government by itself withdraw that power from the states? There is no general answer to this question. The Supreme Court has ruled that the very nature of some powers granted to the national government is such that they are exclusive powers—to determine the rules of naturalization, for example. On the other hand, granting to the national government the power to tax does not preclude state taxation even of the same item. Both national and state governments have concurrent powers to tax, and as long as a state tax measure does not conflict with a national law or treaty or unduly burden a function of the federal government, it may be considered constitutional.

The commerce clause granting to Congress the power to regulate interstate and foreign commerce illustrates the complexities of the situation. Some of the most difficult questions of constitutional law arise over the extent to which this clause limits the reserved powers of the state. Obviously, congressional regulation of this commerce takes precedence over any state enactments. But what if Congress has said nothing? May the states regulate interstate commerce? The answer would be simpler if the Supreme Court had adopted the position that the commerce clause totally excludes any state regulation. But the Court has ruled that the states may—when Congress has not acted—regulate those local aspects of interstate commerce that do not require uniform national treatment; they may apply their laws, designed to protect the public, to interstate commerce, if those laws do not unduly burden, obstruct, or discriminate against such commerce.

Who is to say whether a particular measure discriminates against interstate commerce or that the subject in question requires uniform national treatment? When Congress has not acted, the Supreme Court is the "arbiter of the competing demands of state and national interest." In each case, the Court must make the decision after weighing state and national considerations. State laws imposing speed limits on trains within city limits and requiring the elimination of grade crossings have been upheld, but laws requiring trains to stop at every crossing have been invalidated.[14] The Court has upheld the right of a state to refuse a permit to an interstate motor carrier because the resulting congestion on the highways would create a hazard.[15] On the other hand, it has held that a state unconstitutionally interfered with interstate commerce when it refused to grant a permit to an interstate motor carrier because of fear of excessive competition.[16]

Does all this sound complicated? It is. But complications are inevitable under federalism. For federalism means that someone — mainly legislators and judges — must apportion duties to different governments in an increasingly unified country.

OBLIGATIONS OF THE NATIONAL GOVERNMENT TO THE STATES

The Constitution obliges the national government to guarantee to each state a *republican* form of government. It does not define what is meant by a republican form — the Framers undoubtedly used the term to distinguish it from a monarchy on the one hand and a purely direct democracy on the other — and the Supreme Court has consistently held that the enforcement of this constitutional clause is a congressional obligation.[17] Congress determines whether a state has a republican form of government when it decides whether or not to permit the congressional representatives of that state to take their seats in Congress.

In addition to guaranteeing to each state a republican form of government, the national government is obliged by the Constitution to protect the states against domestic insurrection. Congress has delegated authority to the President to send troops to quell insurrections on the request of the proper state authorities. This gives the President the power to determine which of contending factions is the proper authority in a state. President Tyler's decision was binding on the courts when he threatened to send federal troops to protect the Rhode Island government against the "domestic insurrection" of a rival government contending for the right to speak for the state.[18]

---

[14]*Erb* v. *Morasch* (1900); *Erie R. Co.* v. *Board of Public Utility Commissioners* (1921); *Seaboard Air Line Ry. Co.* v. *Blackwell* (1917).

[15]*Bradley* v. *Public Utilities Commission of Ohio* (1933).

[16]*Buck* v. *Kuykendall* (1925); see also *Southern Pacific* v. *Arizona* (1945) and cases mentioned therein.

[17]*Pacific States Telephone and Telegraph Co.* v. *Oregon* (1912).

[18]*Luther* v. *Borden* (1849).

What obligations does the Constitution impose on the states in their dealings with one another? Three clauses of the Constitution, taken from the Articles of Confederation, require the states to give full faith and credit to one another's public acts, records, and judicial proceedings; to extend to one another's citizens the privileges and immunities of their own citizens; and to return persons who are fleeing from justice in sister states.

1 *Full faith and credit.* The full-faith-and-credit clause is one of the most technical provisions of the Constitution. In general, it requires each state to enforce civil judgments of other states and to accept their public records and acts as valid documents. (It does not require states to enforce the criminal laws of sister states; in fact, in most cases for one state to enforce the criminal laws of another would be unconstitutional.) The clause applies especially to noncriminal judicial proceedings. Suppose Smith obtains a $5,000 judgment against Jones from the Pennsylvania courts, but then Jones moves to California and refuses to pay up. Although California will not automatically enforce the judgment of the Pennsylvania courts, under the full-faith-and-credit clause, Smith does not have to convince a California judge or jury that he is entitled to damages from Jones. In appropriate proceedings the California courts will give full faith and credit to the Pennsylvania judgment without any inquiries into the merits of the legal dispute.[19]

Some idea of the complexity of the problems growing out of the full-faith-and-credit clause is suggested by the question: How much faith and credit must a state give to a divorce decree, a civil judgment, granted by another state? Clearly, a divorce granted by a state to two bona fide residents must be given full faith and credit by all the other states, even though they might not themselves have granted the divorce for the grounds alleged. On the other hand, what if Mrs. A., a citizen of North Carolina, goes to Reno, Nevada, in order to avoid the divorce laws of her own state, stays just the six weeks necessary to establish residence in Nevada, obtains a divorce in a proceeding in which Mr. A is not represented, and returns to North Carolina? Must North Carolina give full faith and credit to the divorce? Not necessarily, for the Supreme Court has held that under certain circumstances it is permissible for the courts of other states to rule that the divorce-granting state lacked jurisdiction over the parties; hence, there would be no validly obtained divorce decree to which full faith and credit must be given. In our example, North Carolina would not be required by the Constitution to recognize Mrs. A's divorce, though in Nevada it would, of course, be unquestioned.

2 *Interstate privileges and immunities.* States may not deny to citizens of other states the full protection of the law, the right to engage in peaceful occupations, or access to the courts. States may not tax citizens of other states

[19]Harold W. Chase, "The Lawyers Need Help with 'the Lawyer's Clause,'" in Gottfried Dietze (ed.), *Essays on the American Constitution* (Prentice-Hall, 1964), pp. 104–110.

at a discriminatory rate or otherwise arbitrarily interfere with the use of their property within the state. In short, states must extend to citizens of other states the privileges and immunities of their own citizens. However, this does not extend to political rights, such as voting and serving on juries, or admission to institutions, such as schools or hospitals, that are publicly supported.

3 Extradition.   The Constitution asserts that a state shall deliver a criminal who has fled from another state to the proper officials, when requested to do so by the governor of the state from which the criminal has fled. Congress has supplemented this provision by making the governor of the state to which the fugitive has fled responsible for returning him. However, despite the use of the word *shall*, the federal courts will not order governors to extradite (return) persons wanted in other states. A few years ago the Governor of New Jersey, horrified at the conditions under which men lived in a chain gang, refused to hand over a fugitive to Georgia officials. There was nothing that Georgia could do about it. Normally, however, extradition is handled in a routine fashion. Furthermore, Congress has partially closed this "gap" by making it a federal crime to flee from one state to another for the purpose of avoiding prosecution for a felony.

In addition to these three obligations, the Constitution also requires the states to settle their disputes with one another without the use of force. States may carry their legal arguments to the Supreme Court or may negotiate *interstate compacts*, which may also be used to establish interstate agencies and to solve joint problems (see Chapter 5). Before interstate compacts become effective, the approval of Congress is required, an approval that is sometimes given in advance. After a compact has been signed and approved by Congress, it becomes binding on all signatory states, and its terms are enforceable by the Supreme Court. Not all agreements among states, however, require congressional approval—only those, the Supreme Court held in 1893, "tending to increase the political power of the States, which may encroach upon or interfere with the just supremacy of the United States."[20]

THE SUPREME COURT
AS UMPIRE OF THE FEDERAL SYSTEM

The Supreme Court has often been called the umpire of the federal system. This role is not merely an exercise in constitutional doctrine. For, as the late Robert H. Jackson wrote before he became a Supreme Court justice:

This political role of the Court has been obscure to laymen—even to most lawyers. It speaks only through the technical forms of the lawsuit, which are not identified with politics in its popularly accepted sense. Yet these lawsuits are the chief instrument of power in our system. Struggles over power that in Europe call out regiments of troops, in America call out battalions of lawyers. When the Court decides where power will be recognized, it often thereby settles whether that power can ever effectively be exercised. A giv-

[20]*Virginia* v. *Tennessee* (1893).

en power held to reside in the states becomes at once power subdivided into forty-eight sections, each circumscribed by state boundaries—a power which can easily be defeated, evaded, or cancelled by playing one state against another. The same power held to reside in the nation is quite another matter in its effectiveness.[21]

The Court is not the only arena of conflict between those who want the national government to act and those who prefer keeping the authority in the states. Congress has much to say about the distribution of functions and the extent to which state regulations will be permitted,[22] and the President has been the major national officer to speak for national majorities. Supreme Court decisions have little significance unless they are consonant with the stand of either Congress or the President. John Marshall's great decisions in behalf of expanded national authority, for example, had little impact during his own lifetime on the actual role of the national government.[23] But the judges are not mere passive reflectors of the political currents; by their decisions they participate in the political life of the nation and in the resolution of the many battles that are fought using the language of national-state conflict.

The Supreme Court, itself a branch of the national government, has often been accused of bias. The states, it has been charged, have had to play against the umpire as well as against the national government itself. Over the years the Court's decisions have generally favored national powers. Especially in recent years, Congress has shown more of a tendency than the Supreme Court to favor local regulations. And the local majorities that control the state governments have been severe in their criticism of the Court for its decisions curtailing their authority.

Despite the frequent criticism of the Supreme Court by some outraged groups who control the machinery of state government, not many would deny the Supreme Court the power to review state actions. Support for Supreme Court review of actions of state and local governments rests upon a different basis from the argument for Supreme Court review of acts of Congress or the President. As Justice Holmes once remarked, "I do not think the United States would come to an end if we lost our power to declare an Act of Congress void. I do think the Union would be imperiled if we could not make that declaration as to the laws of the several states."[24] Or, as Justice Story wrote many years earlier, such a review is necessary to maintain "uniformity of decisions throughout the whole United States, upon all subjects within the purview of the constitution. . . . Judges of equal learning and integrity, in different states, might differently interpret a statute, or a treaty of the United States, or even the constitution itself." There must be a "revising authority to control these jarring and discordant judgments, and harmonize them into uniformity."[25]

[21]Robert H. Jackson, *The Struggle for Judicial Supremacy* (Knopf, 1941), p. xi.
[22]See Paul A. Freund, "Umpiring the Federal System," in Macmahon, *op. cit.*, p. 160.
[23]William H. Riker, *Federalism: Origin, Operation, Significance* (Little, Brown, 1964), p. 103.
[24]O. W. Holmes, *Collected Legal Papers* (Harcourt, Brace & World, 1920), pp. 295–296.
[25]*Martin* v. *Hunter's Lessee* (1816).

Growth of the National Government

The formal constitutional structure of American federalism is little changed since 1787, but the way we actually operate this system is drastically different. The words of the Constitution, wrote Justice Holmes in *Missouri* v. *Holland,* called into life a being whose development "could not have been foreseen completely by the most gifted of its begetters. It was enough for them to realize or to hope that they had created an organism; it has taken a century and has cost their successors much sweat and blood to prove that they created.a nation."[26] The Constitution established a framework in which a national government could develop, but it was some time before a viable national community to support this national government actually existed.

As we saw in the case of *McCulloch* v. *Maryland*, John Marshall argued that ours is a union of people, that the central government is both in theory and in fact a national government resting directly on the people. But there were many, foremost of whom was John C. Calhoun, who dissented and argued that the central government was only a federal, not a national, government, created by the states and receiving all its powers from the states acting in their organized sovereign capacities.

The nationalists' interpretation of government finally triumphed at Appomattox Courthouse after the Civil War, but from the beginning of our political history, events have vindicated their position. It has made no difference whether the party in power has been Federalist, Jeffersonian, Whig, Republican, or Democratic—the national government's sphere has constantly expanded. The platforms of both major parties today reflect the wishes of the major interest groups and call for programs that require greater activity by the central government. The political pressures calling for an expansion of national functions are so powerful that even President Eisenhower, who was pledged to return functions to the states, was unable to do so. It seems that the domain of the national government will continue to grow, no matter which party is in power.

CONSTITUTIONAL BASIS OF THE GROWTH

How has the expansion occurred? Not by amendment. The formal constitutional powers of the national government are essentially the same today as they were in 1789. But the Supreme Court (building on Marshall's work in *McCulloch* v. *Maryland*), the Congress, the President, and—ultimately—the people, have taken advantage of the Constitution's flexibility to permit the national government to exercise the powers needed to fight wars and depressions and to serve the needs of a modern industrial nation. The full scope of the central government's constitutional powers has been used to support

[26]*Missouri* v. *Holland* (1920).

this expansion of functions, but there are three major constitutional pillars on which the expansion has developed.

The war power. The national government is responsible for protecting the nation from external aggression and, when necessary, for waging war. In a world community that has known total war and lives under the threat of total destruction, the power needed to provide for the common defense is of a scope never dreamed of in 1789. With the possibility of attack always present, the national government cannot wait until fighting breaks out. It must keep the nation strong enough to prevent wars and if possible to win them (nonnuclear wars, for it makes no sense to talk of winning a nuclear war) if they break out. No longer does military strength depend solely on troops in the field; it also depends on the ability to mobilize the nation's industrial might and to apply its scientific knowledge to the tasks of defense. Everything from the physics courses taught in the schools to the conservation of natural resources and the maintenance of a prosperous economy affects the nation's military strength.

During times of armed conflict, the national government has the constitutional authority to organize, coordinate, and channel human and natural resources, conscript men, requisition property, control prices, encourage scientific studies, allocate resources, maintain the economy, and bolster public morale. And when the fighting ceases, the national government has authority to cope with the problems of demobilization and reconversion. It may give aid to veterans and correct war-caused maladjustments in the economy, such as housing shortages.

In brief, the national government has the power to wage war and to do what is necessary and proper to wage it successfully. In these times this almost means the power to do anything that is not in direct conflict with constitutional guarantees.

The power to regulate interstate and foreign commerce. Congressional authority extends to all commerce that affects more than one state and to all those activities, wherever they exist or whatever their nature, whose control is necessary and proper to regulate interstate and foreign commerce. The term *commerce* includes all commercial intercourse—the production, buying, selling, and transporting of goods. The power to regulate is the power to prescribe the rules by which this commerce is governed, that is, the right to foster, prohibit, promote, protect, defend all commerce that affects more states than one.

The commerce clause packs a tremendous constitutional punch. It has been construed to cover more than commercial or business transactions. In these few words the national government has been able to find constitutional justification for regulating a wide range of human activity and property. Today there are few aspects of our economy that do not affect commerce in more states than one. When farmer Filburn plants wheat in his own backyard to feed his own children and chickens, his actions affect the price of wheat in the interstate market, and therefore his activities are within the scope of congressional authority. When a large steel company fires men because they belong to a labor union, it enhances the danger of industrial strife and threatens the flow of goods in interstate commerce. Thus, national laws regulating employer-employee relations in industries that affect interstate commerce have been upheld as necessary and proper means to protect the free flow of this commerce.[27]

Some people have accused the Supreme Court of making strained and unrealistic interpretations of the commerce clause in order to find constitutional justification for national regulation. But the Court has simply recognized the obvious facts of our economic life and has refused to make its decisions in an "intellectual vacuum." Wheat planted in people's backyards does, as a matter of economic fact, affect the interstate commerce in wheat. A strike in Pittsburgh or Detroit does affect commerce in California and New York.

The power to tax and spend for the general welfare. Congress lacks constitutional authority to pass laws solely on the ground that the laws will promote the general welfare, but it may raise taxes and spend money to promote the general welfare. This distinction between legislating and appropriating frequently makes little practical difference; the distinction is primarily of legal significance. For example, Congress lacks constitutional power to regulate education or agriculture directly, but Congress has the power to appropriate money to support education or to pay farmers subsidies, and by attaching conditions to its grants of money Congress may regulate what it could not constitutionally control by legal fiat.

Congress has power to appropriate the money to the states by what are known as *grants-in-aid*. These grants are generally conditional—that is, the states must match with their own money some of the federal funds, create an agency to supervise the spending, and submit to federal inspection. Or Congress may bypass the states and give the money to individuals, local governments, or private organizations. For example, Congress has appropriated money to be used by colleges for student loans and graduate fellowships and to individual scholars for research.

Because Congress puts up the money, it has a strong voice in determining how it shall be spent. By withholding or threatening to withhold funds, the national government can influence state operations or regulate individual conduct. For example, the 1964 Civil Rights Act provides that "No person in the United States shall, on the ground of race, color, or national origin, be excluded from participation in, be denied the benefits of, or be subjected to discrimination under any program or activity receiving Federal financial assistance." Federal authorities are directed by the act to develop regulations that will ensure that federal funds, whether loans or grants, are not being used to support programs from which persons are excluded because of race or national origin.

Until recently, Congress's authority to appropriate money was almost beyond constitutional challenge. In 1923 the Supreme Court had ruled in *Frothingham* v. *Mellon* that a taxpayer's contribution to the treasury was not sufficient to give him the right to challenge before a federal court the consti-

[27]*Report of the Joint Federal-State Action Committee* (Government Printing Office, 1957).

tutionality of a federal appropriation. Then in 1968 in *Flast* v. *Cohen* the Supreme Court severely modified the Frothingham doctrine by holding that taxpayers could challenge, as a violation of the establishment of the religion and free-exercise clauses (see page 110), grants to the states under the 1965 Elementary and Secondary Education Act for the purchase of instructional materials for public and private, including church-operated, schools (see page 112). The Supreme Court did set some conditions to such taxpayer suits: A taxpayer must establish a logical link between himself and the particular spending challenged and must point to a specific constitutional limitation on the congressional power to tax and to spend; a taxpayer may not invoke the power of federal courts merely to question an appropriation because he thinks it unwise or because he deems it an interference with state functions. Nevertheless, as the result of *Flast* v. *Cohen*, there may well be an increase in the legal challenges to such measures as the 1967 amendment (the Broyhill amendment) to the Department of Health, Education, and Welfare appropriation act that forbids the use of any of the funds by any person convicted of rioting by any court.

In addition to using its appropriating authority for regulatory purposes, Congress may levy taxes that have a regulatory impact; for example, Congress has so heavily taxed white-phosphorus matches that it is no longer profitable to manufacture and sell these dangerous items. However, Congress may not use its taxing powers to deprive persons of specific rights secured by the Constitution, as it was reminded in 1968 (*Marchetti* v. *United States* and *Haynes* v. *United States*) when the Supreme Court declared unconstitutional two tax laws that forced persons to testify against themselves, contrary to the guarantee of the Fifth Amendment (see pages 186–190). One of these laws required owners of sawed-off shotguns and other such weapons to file registration papers showing possession of weapons that are illegal to possess under most state laws. The other law required professional gamblers to declare that they were engaging in activities that are illegal in forty-nine states by filing a federal tax statement and securing a federal license, both the statement and the license being available to law enforcement officials.

Congress may also use its taxing powers "to induce" states to adopt certain kinds of programs. For example, Congress has levied a tax on employers but allows them to deduct from it the state taxes they pay to support state unemployment compensation. Because the employer has to pay this money anyhow, all the states have been induced to establish unemployment compensation programs.

These three constitutional powers—the war power, the power over interstate commerce, and the power to tax and spend for the general welfare—have made possible a tremendous expansion of federal functions. If all the laws Congress has passed in pursuance of these powers were wiped off the statute books, the size of the federal government and the scope of its functions would shrink drastically.

REASONS FOR THE GROWTH

Why has this expansion of national functions occurred? Certainly not because of the superior logic of the affirmative side in the age-old debate: Resolved: that the powers of the national government should be increased. Rather, "big government" has come about because of deep-seated changes in our society and as the result of the pushing and hauling of interest groups. Since 1789 we have grown from a poor, sparsely populated, agricultural society to a rich, densely populated, industrial nation. The United States has grown from a weak, isolated debtor nation to a powerful creditor who plays a central role in the world community.

Clearly, such profound alterations in any society would have a powerful impact on the government of that society. People's attitudes toward the national government have changed, too. Whereas the government of the Confederation was viewed in the 1780s as a distant, even foreign government, today most people identify their fortunes more closely with Washington than they do with their state governments.[28] The railroad, telegraph, telephone, radio, airplane, and television have made the activities of federal officials familiar to all. Most people do not even know when their state legislature is in session, but what happens in Washington is known throughout the land in a matter of minutes. Likewise, citizens of other states are no longer considered foreign. The automobile has made us a nation on the move. Almost two hundred years of common experiences, especially the fighting of two major wars, have cemented the Union and made Washington the focus of attention. Moreover, an urban, industrial society requires much closer regulation than does an agricultural, rural one. A thousand people in the country might need only one policeman, because informal pressures can be counted on to maintain order. The same number of people living in the city, with its impersonal and diversified make-up, might require five policemen to enforce social sanctions.

The states have had to expand their functions, but because many of our problems have become national in scope, even greater responsibilities have devolved on the national government. In recent decades the national government has gradually taken over a greater role in business regulation, law enforcement, conservation, education, housing, and civil rights, among others. Much that was local in 1789, or even in 1860, is now national. A state could supervise the relations between a small merchant, who bought and sold his products within the local market, and his few employees. But only the national government can supervise the relations between a nationally organized industry that buys and sells its materials all over the world and its thousands of employees organized into national unions. With the industrialization of the United States there came about a concentration of economic power, first in the form of businesses and later in the form of labor unions. These units, which along with professional organizations, are private governments exercising political as well as economic power, necessitated the coalescing of national governmental power. If the unit of public government is not as powerful as the unit of private government it is to supervise, the regulated often regulates the regulator. The activities of a Walter Reuther or an American Telephone and Telegraph Company are too far-flung and their power too formidable to enable the states to provide the needed social

[28]See George Belknap and Ralph Smuckler, "Political Power Relations in a Mid-West City," *The Public Opinion Quarterly* (Spring 1956), p. 80. See also V. O. Key, Jr., *Public Opinion and American Democracy* (Knopf, 1961), pp. 99–120.

control. General Motors has twice the total revenue and four times as many employees as the state of California. Big business, big agriculture, big labor, all must add up to big government.

As industrialization progressed, various powerful interests began to make demands on the national government. First the business groups, who were largely responsible for building industrial America, called on the government for aid in the form of tariffs, a national banking system, a uniform and stable currency, and subsidies to railroads, airlines, and the merchant marine. Once the business groups obtained what they wanted, however, and felt strong enough to take care of themselves, they began generally to oppose governmental aid to other groups. But then the farmers learned that the national government could give them much more aid in solving their economic problems than could their states, and they too began to demand help. The farm groups used their powers to secure such laws as regulation of the railroads, antitrust legislation, paper currency, parcel post, and, finally, government support for farm prices. By the beginning of the present century, the urban groups in general, and organized labor in particular, began to press their demands. Workers found that they could not organize unions with a hostile government issuing injunctions and calling out troops. They began to work for restrictions on injunctions and for friendly administrations. Finally, with increased industrialization and urbanization, the working groups and city dwellers found that, for political reasons, they normally received more help from the national government than from the states.

INADEQUACIES OF THE STATES

Many of our states' boundaries were blocked out on the map with little reference to underlying geographic, social, or historical realities, and with the passage of time, growing discrepancies have developed between state boundaries and human problems. Many natural regions, such as river valleys, are cut in half by the surveyor's line. Many large cities have grown up along state boundaries, which means that cohesive metropolitan areas—New York City, Kansas City, and Washington, D.C., for example—are fragmented between two or three states. When the people of a river valley or a metropolitan region want their governments to act to conserve human or natural resources, they often find that no one state has jurisdiction to deal with the problems of the entire area.

Many of the problems affecting citizens most directly—housing, race relations, air pollution, economic security—require resources available only to the national government. In the 1930s, states had neither the tax resources nor a wide enough area jurisdiction to achieve recovery from the Great Depression; the national government was forced to act. In the late 1960s, faced with disorder and an urgent need to improve life for the millions of Americans living in the core of our large cities, the national government had to move on a massive scale, a scale beyond the fiscal or governmental capacity of our states.

The increased confidence of Americans in the national government has been paralleled by a diminishing sense of identity with the states, due in part, as we have noted, to the greater mobility of our population. Also, most states had no independent existence prior to becoming members of the Union. But even within the limits of their jurisdiction and their resources, many state governments have failed to retain the loyalty of large numbers of their citizens because of the states' failure to provide the programs desired by the public. Some time ago, J. Melville Broughton, a former Governor of North Carolina, wrote:

Those of us who believe in the fundamental principles of states' rights and local self-government may as well concede frankly that much of the almost terrifying expansion of federal encroachment upon the original domain of the States has come about because state governments failed to meet the challenge of the new day. Inadequate educational opportunities, archaic labor laws and regulations, unrelieved hardships and inequities suffered by the working people, low-pitched politics and unjust class and race discriminations have, all too frequently, caused the people to . . . call for relief from the Federal Government. . . .[29]

Thus far we have been speaking about federal relationships between the national government and the states as if the Union consisted of fifty identical units. Although under our constitutional system the states do have the same constitutional powers and are treated with formal-legal equality, in fact "The federal relationship, in any realistic sense, means something very much different to nearly every participant unit in the system."[30] As Professor James Fesler has warned, "generalizations about national-state relations must be read (and preferably advanced) with caution. . . . Eight of the fifty states contain about half of the national population; in four states the Federal Government owns between 64 and 94 percent of the land; the states of Alaska and Wyoming each receive Federal grants-in-aid that per capita are about six times what New Jersey or Florida receives. . . ."[31]

The primary reasons, then, for the expansion of national functions are the industrialization and urbanization of the United States, the consequent concentration of economic power, the resulting national problems that require action by a government with sufficient resources and extensive jurisdiction, external threats to our national existence, and inability of the states to solve problems that the public wants solved.

[29]"The Future of the States," *State Government* (March 1943), pp. 55–56.
[30]Charles D. Tarelton, "Symmetry and Asymmetry as Elements of Federalism: A Theoretical Speculation," *Journal of Politics* (November 1965), p. 861.
[31]James W. Fesler, "Approaches to the Understanding of Decentralization," *Journal of Politics* (August 1965), p. 537, ftn. 1.

Problems of American Federalism

5 In discussing federalism, we must be careful not to conceive of the state and national governments as hard, solid objects that collide with sharp impact. Actually these governments *mesh* with one another, for they are made up of people who govern, and are governed by, other people. To talk of states' rights is but a shorthand way of referring to the rights of people who live in states and to the authority of officials elected by them. Texans, not Texas, have rights.

National and state governments are arenas in which differing groups engage in political combat over public policies. Congressmen and state legislators often respond to the same groups and express the same ideas, and we have "national-state cooperation." At other times, congressmen and state legislators represent sharply different combinations of interest, and we have "national-state conflict." This conflict between the national and state officials is just one facet of the continuing struggle among groups that makes up our politics. "Federalism does not involve a struggle between the nation and the states, but rather a struggle among interests who have favorable access to one of the two levels of government."[1]

The Politics of Federalism

From the day the colonists first set foot on the soil of the New World, Americans have been arguing about the "proper" division of powers

[1]Harmon Zeigler, *Interest Groups in American Society* (Prentice-Hall, 1964), p. 48.

between central and local governments. From time to time various governmental commissions and private study groups have attempted to determine the proper distribution of power, but the experts discovered, as did the Founding Fathers in 1787, that there are no objective, scientific standards to distinguish the respective functions.

The questions are political in nature. Those individuals who favor national action anticipate that national officials will be most responsive to their interests, whereas those who believe that state officials will be most likely to support their goals are the champions of states' rights. At one time or another Northerners, Southerners, businessmen, farmers, workers, Federalists, Democrats, Whigs, and Republicans have thought it improper to vest a particular function in the national government. They opposed "control by Washington" in the name of maintaining the federal system. But underlying the debates were such issues as slavery, labor-management relations, government regulation of business, civil rights.

With the advent of the New Deal and the growth of organized labor's influence at the national level, most business groups became devotees of the rights of states. The national government came to be controlled by persons in whom many businessmen had little confidence and over whom they had less influence. They discovered that state legislatures and state courts are more likely than their national counterparts to make decisions favored by businessmen. As Professor Swisher has written, "It behooves us . . . to take thought before drenching our handkerchiefs when the National Association of Manufacturers and the American Bar Association bewail the prostrate position of the states before the federal colossus. These mourners are not shedding tears over the lamentable conditions of New Hampshire and North Carolina and Montana and Texas but over the enterprise caught in the grip of the federal regulatory hand. . . ."[2] On the other hand, labor leaders have found national agencies more responsive to their claims. It is not surprising that while business groups are quick to defend the states against what they call the "federal octopus," labor leaders emphasize the need for national action and charge the states with being dominated by "special interests."

In recent years those who favor segregation have rightly recognized that those who control Southern state and local governments are also likely to favor segregation. They fear that national officials, responding to different political majorities, will favor integration. Naturally, segregationists sing of the virtues of local governments "close to the people," are quick to emphasize the dangers of overcentralization, and argue at length that the regulation of civil rights is not a proper function of the national government. On the other side, those who want segregation abolished emphasize that national power should be used because they recognize that state governments controlled by segregationists will never on their own initiative move against segregation.

Of course, national-state conflicts are seldom conflicts of all the states versus the national government, for each state is different and the relations between each and the national government, as well as those among the separate states, vary. The more a state differs in its political, economic, and

[2] Carl B. Swisher, *The Growth of Constitutional Power in the United States* (Univ. of Chicago Press, 1946), p. 33.

social make-up from the rest of the nation, the more likely will that state reflect policies that will bring it into conflict with the policies being espoused by national spokesmen. For example, witness the difference in the nature of relations between Alabama and the federal government and California and the federal government.[3]

So it is that political issues are at stake in discussions of national-state relations. Nevertheless, almost all observers—however sharply they differ on particular issues—agree that a country the size of the United States needs strong and active state governments. They realize that maintaining a balance between centralized and decentralized decision-making is a major problem for our system.

The Problem of Maintaining the Balance

The awful spectacle that disturbed Hamilton—"a nation without a national government"—need frighten us no longer. The national government's activities have greatly expanded, and they will continue to do so. Today, the spectacle that frightens some people is a nation without state governments. In 1933 Luther Gulick, seeing state governments helpless before the onslaught of the Great Depression, stated, "I do not predict that the States will go, but affirm that they have gone."[4] Thirty years later Senator Dirksen intoned that before too long, "The only people interested in state boundaries will be Rand-McNally."[5] And another senator proclaimed, "State government is at a crossroad."[6] What can be done to make state governments strong instruments of public service?

MODERNIZED STATE AND LOCAL GOVERNMENTS

We hear so much about the growth of national governmental functions that we sometimes overlook the growth of state activities. An increase in the authority of one does not necessarily detract from the authority of the other. On the contrary, the entrance of the national government into new fields has in many cases strengthened the states and helped them improve their services. Despite the lamented "weakening of states" and the constant cries about national interference, today states are stronger units of government, measuring by the amount of money spent and the number of functions performed, than they were in 1787. Indeed, since the end of World War II, activities of states and their subdivisions have been increasing at a faster rate than the nondefense activities of the national government.[7] As Governor Rockefeller

---

[3]Charles B. Tarelton, "Symmetry and Asymmetry as Elements of Federalism: A Theoretical Speculation," *Journal of Politics* (November 1965), p. 871.

[4]Luther C. Gulick, "Reorganization of the State," *Civil Engineering* (August 1933), pp. 421, quoted by Terry Sanford, *Storm Over the States* (McGraw-Hill, 1967), p. 21.

[5]*The New York Times,* August 8, 1965, section IV, p. 2, quoted by Sanford, *ibid.*, p. 37.

[6]Joseph D. Tydings, "Reform is Possible," *National Civic Review* (January 1967), p. 11, quoted by Sanford, *ibid.*, p. 37.

[7]U.S. Commission on Intergovernmental Relations, *A Report to the President* (U.S. Government Printing Office, 1955), p. 36.

has pointed out, "The striking fact in our domestic political experience since World War II has not been the growth of federal government—but the far more rapid expansion of state and local government, to meet growing social needs. . . . The role of the state, within American federalism, is far from 'obsolete.' It is as dynamic and promising as is the federal idea itself." But he went on to warn, "The essential political truth is that—today more than ever—the preservation of states' rights depends upon the exercise of states' responsibilities."[8]

Clearly, then, one of the most promising approaches to maintaining a federal system is to improve, simplify, and modernize the state governments. Many reforms designed to vitalize state governments have long been advocated—reorganizing administrative machinery, streamlining legislative procedures, keeping the basis of representation in state legislatures up to date to reflect the growing urban population, shortening the ballot, and making officials responsive to wider segments of the electorate. Although recommendations for reform are often filed and forgotten, some states have made considerable progress.

FEDERALISM WITHOUT WASHINGTON—
INTERSTATE COOPERATION

States are not forced to wait for the national government to take the initiative in dealing with problems that require regional action. Several states together can deal with problems too large for any one to handle alone. And one instrument to accomplish this is the *interstate compact.*

Until the twentieth century, interstate compacts were used only to settle boundary disputes between states, but since 1900 over twenty interstate agencies have been established by compact.[9] One of the more successful of these is the Port of New York Authority, established by New Jersey and New York. This agency supervises and operates the harbor as a unit, and recently it has been given the job of coordinating the operation of airports in the area. Other promising interstate-compact agencies are those created to deal with education, abatement of water pollution, conservation of oil and gas, parole and probation, and conservation of fish.

In addition to these formal interstate agencies, state officials often get together to handle a particular problem, for example, to establish joint operations of police-radio broadcasting nets or to coordinate plans for highway safety. These efforts have on occasion given rise to formal organizations, such as the Interstate Commission on the Delaware River Basin, composed of representatives from New York, New Jersey, Pennsylvania, and Delaware. State officials have also joined together in regional conferences—e.g., the Conference of Southern Governors—and various nationwide organizations —e.g., the American Legislators' Association, the National Association of Attorneys General and of State Budget Officers. Each state now has a Commission on Interstate Cooperation. Most of the interstate agencies are co-

[8]Nelson A. Rockefeller, *The Future of Federalism* (Harvard Univ. Press, 1962), pp. 11, 14, 54.
[9]Richard H. Leach and Redding S. Sugg, Jr., *The Administration of Interstate Compacts* (Louisiana State Univ. Press, 1959), p. 6.

ordinated through the Council of State Governments, which serves as a secretariat, collects data, sponsors research, and publicizes results.

Although diversity is a virtue of federalism, it can also be a fault. Diversity of state laws on insurance, contracts, negotiable instruments, judicial procedures — in fact, on the whole scope of business transactions — increases operating costs and makes it difficult to do business on a national basis. Labeling laws designed to protect consumers against fraud, for example, are so diverse that manufacturers often have to use special labels in order to sell their products in different states. Also interstate motorists are often confused by unfamiliar traffic signs.

The application and interpretation of all these laws by the fifty-one court systems in the United States create another level of confusion. What law applies to a contract signed in California, delivered in New York, between citizens of Wisconsin and Minnesota, about property located in New Jersey? This is not a fanciful question, but an example of the actual problems confronting judges in their everyday decisions.

How can we create some measure of uniformity among state laws? Some states have adopted uniform laws dealing with, for example, stock transfers, narcotics, and criminal extradition. These attempts to bring about uniformity of the laws also have the desirable side effect of raising standards, because the best practices tend to spread throughout the states. But despite occasional successes, over sixty years' work has not significantly decreased the diversity of state laws.

How successful, then, have the states been in their efforts to cooperate? Horizontal cooperation — that is, cooperation at the state level — has perhaps made its greatest contribution "in providing central staff research and educational facilities to strengthen the competence with which the governments at a particular level do their job, so that governmental bankruptcy alone cannot justify the transference of authority to higher levels of government."[10] Horizontal federalism has brought only marginal results. What, then, about cooperation between national and state governments?

Cooperative Federalism

"There has in fact never been a time when federal, state, and local functions were separate and distinct. . . . All nostalgic references to the day of state and local independence are based upon mythical views of the past. . . . Government does more things [today] than it did in 1790 or 1861; but in terms of what government did, there was as much sharing of functions then as today."[11]

Cooperation among national and state governments takes many forms. A

[10]James W. Fesler, *Area and Administration* (Univ. of Alabama Press, 1949), p. 40.

[11]Mortin Grodzins, "Centralization and Decentralization in the American Federal System," in Robert A. Goldwin (ed.), *A Nation of States* (Rand McNally, 1963), pp. 6–7. See also Daniel J. Elazar, *The American Partnership: Intergovernmental Cooperation in the Nineteenth Century United States* (Univ. of Chicago Press, 1962).

secret service agent helped by state and local police to capture a counterfeiter is benefiting from cooperative federalism. A public health official tracking down carriers of disease uses both federal and state services. Many federal agencies, such as the U.S. Public Health Service, the U.S. Office of Education, and the Bureau of the Census, conduct surveys and gather statistics for state officials. Other agencies train local employees and help enforce state laws. This kind of cooperation avoids duplication and provides better services at less cost.

In some cases, the administration of federal programs is delegated to state governments. The TVA encouraged state and local officials to help run parts of the TVA program. The administration of the selective service system is primarily a responsibility of state and local officials. Some people favor a broad extension of state administration of national programs, arguing that the national government should lay down general policies but delegate administration to state and local governments. War on Poverty programs (discussed in Chapter 26) are in many respects joint federal-state ventures of this nature. It is doubtful, however, if this can be done except on a limited scale.

In addition, when national programs are turned over to state governments, there is the risk that they will not be administered in accordance with national policies. Philip Selznick, in his discerning study *TVA and the Grass Roots* (1949), presented evidence that TVA's policy of working with local governments often amounted to handing the TVA over to powerful local groups. And Paul H. Appleby, an experienced administrator, says, "If a program is Federal and if the responsibility is Federal, the authority should be Federal and the administering bureaucracy should almost always be Federal."[12] Conversely, there is some opposition to state administration of national policies on the grounds that it turns the states into administrative districts of the federal government.

Federalism is not merely a simple struggle between national and state officials as to who shall control a program. It also causes interactions among functional specialists and among generalists on different governmental levels. Programs that involve interactions between national and state authorities create alliances between national and state specialists—highway officials, welfare authorities, educators—who often have more in common with each other than with the general officers of their respective levels of governments. These specialists get together at professional meetings, read common journals, and jointly defend their programs against executive authorities and legislative officials whether they be national or state. As we evolve more cooperative federal-state-local programs, these alliances among specialists may become an even more significant feature of our political landscape.

GRANTS-IN-AID

More promising than turning over complete administration of federal policies to the states is the joint operation of programs through the device of the *grant-in-aid*. There are some programs for which the states have chief constitutional responsibility, but in which the entire nation has an interest. By an

[12]Paul H. Appleby, *Big Democracy* (Knopf, 1945), p. 87.

accident of geography, for example, some children may be deprived of an adequate education or people may be denied good health services, for states in which they live may lack adequate resources to provide essential services or the dominant groups within the state lack the desire to do so. These problems can no longer be considered of only local concern. Young people who have been deprived of educational opportunities or whose health has been impaired are national liabilities.

Much of our national wealth is concentrated in the industrialized areas. As a result, other areas, especially in the rural South, find it difficult to raise funds for public services.[13] The national government could, in many cases, take over the entire responsibility for the programs. But as an alternative to complete national control, Congress, through the grant-in-aid, has tried to secure a national minimum level and to encourage the states to take action on their own. Thus, the national government, with its broader tax base, taxes the wealth where it is located and turns the money over to the states for programs that Congress feels should be more adequately supported. This system of federal grants-in-aid goes back at least as far as 1802, but it got its real start in 1916 when Congress gave money to the states for the construction of rural post roads. During the Depression of the 1930s the number of federal grants greatly increased. Today the national government gives money to the states for agricultural extension work, land-grant colleges, elementary and secondary education, old-age assistance, aid to dependent children, aid to the blind, and aid to crippled children, to mention only some of the more important programs. On the average, state and local governments now receive from the national government one-fifth of the money they spend.

Most of these grants are *conditional*, that is, the states must reciprocate and match the federal funds with state funds, establish agencies to expend the funds, submit plans for advance approval, permit inspection by national officials of the completed work, and place the employees who administer the grant under a merit system. But because most grants require the states to match the federal dollars, the poor states are often unable to provide, even with federal assistance, the same services as their richer sisters. For example, a totally disabled worker in recent years might receive as much as $113 a month in California or as little as $43 in West Virginia. To help correct these inequalities, formulas for the distribution of federal funds have been proposed that take the relative needs of the several states into account. Quite naturally, the wealthy states that contribute most of the money to the federal treasury are not happy when a larger proportion goes to the less fortunate areas.

TAX SHARING AND BLOCK GRANTS

There are 21 national departments and agencies and 150 federal bureaus and divisions that administer over four hundred separate grant programs for the benefit of 50 states, 81,000 local governments, and millions of individuals. Many local governments now have specialized personnel just to keep track of the available federal grants. They need a computer to do so. Many critics

[13]Richard E. Dawson and James A. Robinson, "The Politics of Welfare," in Herbert Jacob and Kenneth N. Vines (eds.), *Politics in the American States* (Little, Brown, 1965), p. 403.

argue not only that the proliferation of detailed federal grants makes it difficult to find out what kinds of funds are available, but that such grants also deprive state and local officials of initiative. Rather than set their own priorities, these officials are tempted to use the local dollars to match federal grants. In this way, it is claimed, Congress determines what resources state and local governments should allocate to attack problems that Congress has decided need attention.

As the result of such criticisms and a growing conviction among those who support antipoverty programs that local initiative and involvement are desirable, political support has been developing for the Heller Plan, named after the former Chairman of the Council of Economic Advisors, which would have Congress return to the states some portion of federal tax revenues. Debate over tax sharing has been interrupted by the fiscal urgencies of the Vietnam crisis, but the issue is likely to reappear in the years ahead.

Others would not go so far as tax sharing but have urged Congress to make grants in terms of broad general categories—for highways, education, public assistance, public health, law enforcement. These block grants, or *subventions*, would permit states to work out local applications and uses of the funds. Congress has already moved to consolidate some grants: for example, in 1966 a dozen separate programs in the field of public health were combined into a single program by which funds are given to the states under plans prepared by each state and approved by the Surgeon General.[14] Title One of the 1968 Omnibus Crime Control and Safe Streets Act provides block grants to the states to plan and implement a law enforcement program.

Not all persons are in favor of leaving more discretion to states. They argue that if the federal government shares its taxes with the states or makes sizeable unconditional general subventions, states would "look more and more to the national government to perform the disagreeable task of extracting money from the taxpayer" and would lose their sense of financial responsibility.[15]

The debates over tax sharing and block versus detailed grants reflect a difference between those who believe that state legislatures might spend funds more wisely if they had more discretion and those who believe that Congress is more likely to determine the proper use of the money. For example, in the legislative battles over the 1968 Omnibus Crime Control Act, Southern Democrats and Republicans contended that state governments could more sensibly allocate funds to local communities than could federal bureaucrats, and they voted for block grants to be spent by a planning agency appointed by the governor in each state rather than for direct federal categorical grants to the local communities. Opponents argued that states are not equipped to handle the funds and that state governments are biased against the large cities, which thus would not get their fair share of the funds.

Because most federal grants are generated for specific goals—better highways, stronger public education, concern for public health, war against poverty, limiting racial discrimination—rather than by the abstract concern of improving the operations of state governments, fundamental changes in the

[14]Advisory Commission on Intergovernmental Relations, *Eighth Annual Report* (U.S. Government Printing Office, 1967), p. 2.

[15]U.S. Commission on Intergovernmental Relations, *op. cit.*, pp. 132–133.

nature of the federal grant-in-aid system have been slow in taking place. But with the recently developed conviction on the part of specialists concerned with solving the urgent problems of our cities that nationally programed and controlled programs may be less successful than those worked out and adapted to local conditions, there appears to be a slowly growing political support in favor of more flexible grants or some form of tax sharing.

The federal grant system is obviously here to stay. Little has happened during the last thirty years to undermine the conclusions of the late V. O. Key, Jr., who, after a careful study, reported that the federal grant system

> . . . strengthens the states and thereby strengthens but profoundly modifies the federal system. . . . The achievements of direct federal administration are not so striking as to make federal assumption an inviting alternative to the grant system. The governance of a nation of continental proportions is a matter for which no simple blueprint and specifications are available. The grant system builds on and utilizes existing institutions to cope with national problems. Under it the states are welded into a national machinery of sorts and the establishment of costly, parallel, direct federal services is made unnecessary. A virtue of no mean importance is that the administrators in actual charge of operations remain amenable to local control. In that way the supposed formality, the regularity, and the cold-blooded efficiency of a national hierarchy are avoided.[16]

INTERGOVERNMENTAL AGENCIES

In addition to a variety of intergovernmental commissions and study groups sponsored on an *ad hoc* basis, there are several significant agencies working on a continuing basis to improve the operations of our federal system. The Committees on Government Operations in both the House and the Senate have subcommittees devoted to intergovernmental relations. And in 1959 Congress created the Advisory Commission on Intergovernmental Relations, made up of representatives of federal, state, and local governments, to provide a forum for the discussion of all aspects of intergovernmental problems. This Commission has made recommendations to the Congress, the states, and local governments designed to strengthen intergovernmental cooperation. In addition, President Johnson assigned the Director of the Office of Emergency Planning to work with federal and state administrative officials to identify problems and work out solutions, and he asked the Vice President to make a special effort to work with mayors and county officers in areas where there could be more vigorous cooperative action.

A NEW PARTNER

According to the traditional concept of American federalism, the two parties to the system are the national government and the states. In a constitutional sense, all local units of government are creatures of the states. But "to refer to Chicago as but an arm of Illinois or to New York City as but an arm of New York is as unrevealing as to call the General Motors Corporation an

---

[16]V. O. Key, Jr., *The Administration of Federal Grants to States* (Public Administration Service, 1937), pp. 375, 383. See also Advisory Commission on Intergovernmental Relations, *The Role of Equalization in Federal Courts* (U.S. Government Printing Office, 1964), p. 81.

instrument of Delaware or the Southern Pacific Company an instrument of Kentucky, under whose law it is organized."[17] The federal government has dealt directly with city and county officials since the early nineteenth century, but federal-city interaction did not become significant until the Great Depression.[18] In the late 1960s, as the problems of the large cities began to be in the forefront of domestic political concern, the national government accelerated its grants and loans to the cities to build airports, provide mass transporation, get rid of slums, fight air pollution, strengthen police departments, and attack poverty. Today there are more than seventy federal programs directly supporting urban development.[19]

As might be expected, governors and state legislators do not like to see federal funds go directly to city officials. On the other hand, city officials favor such assistance—provided they have control over it. When Congress authorized federal grants to community action groups outside the structure of local governments in order to involve poor people in the administration of antipoverty programs, city officials complained about being bypassed just as loudly as had state officials. Congress responded by returning antipoverty programs to local authorities (see Chapter 25).

Many large cities—actually city-states in many respects—often have more influence within the circles of the national government than they do in their own state legislatures, which are dominated by rural and suburban representatives. President Eisenhower told the Conference of State Governors, "Today, for help in urban problems, committees of Mayors are far more likely to journey to Washington than to their own state capitals."[20] Mayor Richard Daley of Chicago told a congressional committee, "I think a city the size of Chicago should be able to go directly to its Federal Government with its programs, because we find in many instances the greater responsiveness and greater understanding."[21] And Mayor Stokes of Cleveland stated simply, "Why run to the federal government? Because that's where the money is."[22]

Reapportionment of state legislatures, which has been forced on the states as the result of the Supreme Court's decision in *Baker* v. *Carr* and its progeny, is likely to increase the voice of suburbia rather than of the central cities.[23] Nevertheless there are signs that state governments are beginning to respond to the same political forces that heretofore have had access to big-city mayors and federal authorities. By the end of 1967, twenty states had programs to help local governments construct sewage-treatment plants, eight were giving financial assistance for transportation, eleven were helping with urban renewal, and some states had even established a special state agency to deal with urban problems. Increased state—and national—action to deal

---

[17]C. B. Swisher, *Theory and Practice of American National Government* (Houghton Mifflin, 1951), p. 908.

[18]Daniel J. Elazar, *American Federalism: A View from the States* (Crowell, 1966), p. 76.

[19]Advisory Commission on Intergovernmental Relations, *Metropolitan America: Challenge to Federalism* (U.S. Government Printing Office, 1966), p. 8.

[20]Address by the President at the 1957 Governors' Conference, *Report of the Joint Federal-State Action Committee* (U.S. Government Printing Office, 1957), p. 20.

[21]*Hearings on Federal-State-Local Relations before a Subcommittee of the House Committee on Government Operations*, 85th Cong., 1st Sess., 1957, p. 391.

[22]*Chicago Tribune*, March 4, 1968.

[23]Robert S. Friedman, "The Reapportionment Myth," in Edward C. Banfield (ed.), *Urban Government* (Free Press, 1961), pp. 64–65.

with the demands of those who live in our large cities reflects the political realities of urban power and the threats to the well-being of the suburbanites and their city-based economy. There is no place to hide from the problems created by racial conflict and urban decay. State officials are beginning to respond to these realities.

The Advisory Commission on Intergovernmental Relations has warned, "The States are on the verge of losing control over the metropolitan problem; if they lose this control they lose the major responsibility for domestic government in the United States and in turn surrender a vital role in the American Federal System."[24] Yet it is doubtful that such exhortations have much impact. Cooperative federalism—or "creative federalism," as President Johnson has named it—means all things to all men. To some, it is a midway station on the road to an expansion of the responsibilities of the national government; to others, it is a way of strengthening the states. But by and large most Americans have no particular commitment to a particular level of government, as such, and are not likely to rise up in arms in defense of an abstraction such as "the states" or "the cities" or "the federal government." The concerns are with more immediate problems—clean air, equal rights, jobs, safety on the streets. They look upon the agencies of government as instruments to accomplish tasks and are willing to use whatever agencies or combinations thereof that they feel can best serve their needs. Cooperative or, as it may come to be called, creative federalism is an example of what Tocqueville noticed over a hundred years ago: "I have never been more struck by the good sense and the practical judgment of the Americans than in the manner in which they elude the numberless difficulties resulting from their Federal Constitution."[25]

Trouble Spots of Federalism

The truck driver who is stopped at the state boundary because his vehicle is six inches too long, the governor who would like to sign a new tax measure but is warned that industry may move out of the state if he does so, the woman who discovers that she is legally divorced in one state but not in another—these people, like the rest of us, face the problems of federalism. What are some of these problems and what steps have been taken to solve them?

LAW ENFORCEMENT

Not many years ago the local constabulary had little difficulty in dealing with crime. Everybody knew everybody else and detection of the guilty was relatively simple. Today, in our mobile society where anonymity makes capture difficult, criminals move swiftly across the nation by automobile or

[24]*Eighth Annual Report of the Advisory Commission on Intergovernmental Relations* (U.S. Government Printing Office, 1967), p. 9.

[25]Alexis de Tocqueville, in Phillips Bradley (ed.) *Democracy in America* (Knopf, 1944), vol. I, p. 167.

airplane, cutting across one jurisdictional boundary after another. The existence of multiple police agencies, which have overlapping responsibilities, gives criminals an advantage they are quick to exploit. On the national level, postal inspectors, T men, G men, and twenty-three other specialized federal police have limited authority to enforce specified federal laws. State police operate within the boundaries of their own states and, within the state, there are city police, county sheriffs, and township constables.

Failures of state and local police to cope with criminals have led to demands for national action. Congress has made it a federal offense to use the channels of interstate commerce to steal, kidnap, or transport women for immoral purposes; for shipment of firearms to or by convicted felons; for shipment of information or equipment used in illegal gambling; for shipment of explosives for purposes of destroying churches or public buildings. In each instance the demands for this extension of the police duties of the national government came about as a result of failure by the states to deal adequately with the problem. In recent years the failure of some state and local police authorities to protect the rights of Negroes has added fuel to the growing demand for more vigorous federal police protection.

Prior to 1968 the FBI worked with state and local law enforcement officers, but there was no comprehensive national program to combat crime. In 1967 President Johnson recommended such a program to Congress, and in 1968, he approved—reluctantly—Congress's greatly altered version of his recommendations; it is known as the Omnibus Crime Control and Safe Streets Act. Title One of the act authorizes the FBI to increase its training activities for local police and provide grants to law-enforcement students, and it creates within the Department of Justice a National Institute of Law Enforcement and Criminal Justice to encourage research in law-enforcement methods. It also authorizes substantial block grants to the states to be used to develop state plans and to recruit and train police officers. These grants are to be administered by the Law Enforcement Administration—consisting of three persons—within the Department of Justice. State agencies that receive the grants must spend at least three-fourths of the funds through local communities and local police departments.

Title One reflects the long-standing American fear that too much control over police might be concentrated in the national government. The conviction that control of crime is primarily a state and local responsibility made Congress reluctant to pass the 1968 act; it did so only because of growing public concern over crime, fear of riots, and revulsion against the assassinations, within two months, of Martin Luther King and Robert F. Kennedy. Even so, Congress built protections against federal control into the act. Title One is an example of cooperative federalism—national financing and stimulus with state and local administration.

LAW AVOIDANCE

Federalism helps people who can hardly be called criminals to evade state laws. State sales taxes on cigarettes, liquor, and gasoline, for example, can often be avoided simply by crossing the state line. "Last-chance" gasoline stations just before one enters a state with higher taxes are evidence of this everyday tax evasion. When metropolitan cities are located near state boundaries, persons who earn their living in one state and benefit from its public services can sometimes avoid paying city and state taxes by commuting to work from the adjoining low-tax state. Adoption by states of use taxes and municipal income taxes plus the enactment by Congress of laws making it difficult to use the mails in order to escape payment of state taxes have helped to close some of these loopholes.

A more spectacular form of law avoidance is carried on by those who have the money and time to go to Reno for six weeks to avoid their own state's divorce laws. Despite the efforts of the Supreme Court to protect each state's right to control the matrimonial affairs of its own citizens and at the same time to accommodate the national interest in seeing that states respect the full-faith-and-credit clause, there is greater confusion than ever about the validity of divorces. Some observers favor uniform divorce standards throughout the nation, but because all fifty state legislatures probably could never agree on standards, federal action would be required. Although Congress has no power to pass laws regulating marriage and divorce, the Supreme Court may have left the way open under the full-faith-and-credit clause for Congress to determine the grounds for divorce that would be recognized by all states.

Evasion of business laws is another problem. New Jersey in earlier years and Delaware today have been the Renos for the world of corporations. Many corporations that do most of their business and sell most of their securities in other states have responded to advertisements such as the following:

> Charters—Delaware Best, Quickest, Cheapest, Most Liberal. Nothing needs to be paid in. Do business and hold meetings anywhere. Free forms. Colonial Charter Company, Wilmington, Delaware.[26]

Corporations gaining such charters in Wilmington maintain nominal one-room—one-desk headquarters there simply to evade the stricter charter laws (designed to protect stockholders, consumers, and the public) of the states in which they do business. Periodically, proposals are made that all corporations carrying on an interstate business be required to incorporate under national law, but so far nothing has come of these proposals. Congress could also require all corporations using interstate commerce or the mails to incorporate in the state in which they maintain their real headquarters or in which they conduct the bulk of their business.

INTERSTATE COMPETITION

In their zeal to attract business, some states and cities offer free factory sites, tax exemptions, free water, and laws that make it difficult for labor to organize unions. Many states hesitate to levy taxes to pay for better schools or to increase aid to the needy for fear that the higher taxes will drive industries away to states with lower rates, even though there is no conclusive evidence that the tax rate is a cause of business migrations. Similarly, states

[26]W. Z. Ripley, *Main Street and Wall Street* (Little, Brown, 1927), p. 29, cited by G. C. S. Benson, *The New Centralization* (Holt, 1941), p. 28.

are often reluctant to enact minimum-wage laws or to extend welfare programs because the additional cost may place their industries at a competitive disadvantage to those in states without such provisions.

Competition among the states has also retarded the development of state conservation programs. Each state hesitates to require industries to follow conservation procedures—for example, preventing water pollution—for fear that the resulting expenses will cause local business firms to lose out to those operating in states with a get-rich-quick-and-never-mind-the-future philosophy. Although interstate agreements, especially in the oil and gas industry, have led to some conservation programs, such agreements have been made only when conservation coincides with more immediate economic interests—for example, controlling the supply of a commodity to prevent the depressing of prices.

MAINTAINING THE NATIONAL MARKET

One of the major goals of the Constitution was to create a free-trade area within the United States. To a large extent this goal has been achieved. Certainly one of the major reasons for the remarkable economic development of this nation has been the absence of state barriers to trade and commerce. Throughout the years, however, some state regulations have imposed restraints on the free flow of commerce. Some of these regulations are designed to protect consumers from fraud, some are in the form of health and quarantine regulations, and some are attempts to collect a fair share of taxes from those who use the roads or other tax-supported facilities. However, some laws, passed ostensibly to protect persons from disease or fraud or to protect animals and crops from infection, are actually designed to give home industries the advantage of the home market.

The interstate-commerce clause of the Constitution deprives states of any power to tax interstate commerce as such, but they may levy fees for the use of their highways and require out-of-state trucks to secure licenses, permits, and registration tickets. So long as the fee bears some reasonable relation to the use of highways, it is not unconstitutional. Although no state has yet tried to collect registration fees or permits from nonresident passenger vehicles, they all have some form of charge for out-of-state trucks. The most common forms are registration fees, mileage taxes, consumption-of-gasoline taxes, and levies on the receipts received for hauling goods. One survey reports that a trucker traveling from Alabama to South Carolina in a 5- to 6-ton truck would have to pay fees totaling several hundred dollars.

These burdens are to some extent lightened by reciprocity agreements, but only a few states grant complete freedom from fees by such agreements. States are entitled to receive some payment for the use of their highways by those who do not pay the normal state taxes. But many state highways are in part financed by federal grants drawn from federal tax funds, and the burdens placed on the free movement of goods are ultimately paid, through increased costs, by all the people of the nation.

True to the traditions of John Marshall, the Supreme Court has struck down some laws whose purpose was to discriminate against the commerce of other states. Many discriminatory practices, however, are never brought to the

Court. Moreover, the Supreme Court has a difficult task. Although it must protect interstate commerce from discriminatory treatment and must prevent the Balkanization of our national economy, it cannot permit business firms to hide behind the commerce clause in order to avoid paying their share of taxes or to escape compliance with regulations necessary to protect the public health, welfare, safety, and morals.

The Future of Federalism

As stated earlier, there are many who consider federalism as only a midway station between a confederation and a unitary state. These critics argue that modern techniques of transportation and communication have destroyed the barriers of time and distance that originally gave rise to federalism. In short, they insist that federalism has become obsolete.

Harold J. Laski, the late British political scientist, socialist writer, and critic of American federalism, argued that federalism

. . . is insufficiently positive in character; it does not provide for sufficient rapidity of action; it inhibits the emergence of necessary standards of uniformity; it relies upon compacts and compromises which take insufficient account of the urgent category of time; it leaves the backward areas a restraint, at once parasitic and poisonous, on those which seek to move forward. . . .[27]

Laski charged that our national government lacks the constitutional authority to control vested business interests and that the state governments are reluctant to regulate them lest these business interests withdraw their patronage and go elsewhere. He predicted that public pressures would force positive national action, eventually leading to the abandonment of federalism. But Laski was not so much predicting the end of our federal system as he was arguing for its abolition. Favoring more vigorous national regulation of business and more positive government management of the economy, he believed that the federal system stood in the way of achieving these goals.

William H. Riker agrees with Laski that federalism benefits economic interests, but he concludes that these benefits "pale beside the significance of the benefits to Southern segregationist whites . . . who have been given the freedom to oppress Negroes, first as slaves and later as a depressed caste. . . . The judgment to be passed on federalism in the United States is therefore a judgment on the values of segregation and racial oppression."[28]

Daniel J. Elazar, another student of the American federal system, comes to a different conclusion. He finds that all the traditional arguments in favor of federalism are demonstrated by American experience and that federalism as it operates in the United States is stronger than ever. He concludes, "In sum, the virtue of the federal system lies in its ability to develop and maintain mechanisms vital to the perpetuation of the unique combination of gov-

[27]H. J. Laski, "The Obsolescence of Federalism," *The New Republic* (May 3, 1939), pp. 367 – 369.

[28]William H. Riker, *Federalism: Origin, Operation, Significance* (Little, Brown, 1964), pp. 152 – 153.

ernmental strength, political flexibility, and individual liberty, which has been the central concern of American politics."[29]

Perhaps we attribute to federalism difficulties for which it is only partly responsible. We are a nation of continental proportions with a rich variety of sections and groups. Even if the federal form of government were abolished tomorrow, there would still be a South and a New England. Giant capitalists and trade unionists would remain strong, and white supremacists would still oppose the passage and enforcement of civil rights laws. Even without federalism there would be local units of government, and local majorities would use these units to resist national majorities. True, the ideology of states' rights and the general support for federalism permit segregationists and others who dominate state governments to work for their goals in the name of local self-government, but such appeals are not unknown in governments that operate under the unitary forms. And as far as the constitutional structure of federalism is concerned, today the national government has all the constitutional power it needs to deal with virtually every problem of national extent.

[29]Daniel J. Elazar, *op. cit.*, p. 216.

CIVIL LIBERTIES AND CITIZENSHIP

PART

THREE

How can we maintain the proper balance between liberty and order, between diversity and uniformity, between individual rights and collective needs? This is the main problem taken up in Part Three. To many Americans the safeguarding and broadening of individual freedom—of civil liberties and civil rights—is the most important task of a democratic society. These are the lofty and historic rights of the Western tradition—freedom of religion, freedom of speech, freedom of assembly, freedom of the press, equality under the law.

When we think of protecting these freedoms of the individual, we usually think of protecting them against government. We are all familiar with the struggles of oppressed peoples and individuals —Americans in 1776, Hungarians and Czechoslovakians against communist repression. But in a democracy the protection of the rights of the individual against the government is only part of the problem (though probably the major part). The other part of the problem concerns the rightful power of government over the individual. A person's freedom from governmental oppression is of little use, after all, except in a peaceful, orderly society. And government must have some power over individuals if it is to maintain peace and order.

The problem, then, is how to balance individual rights against collective needs, remembering always that individual freedom and social order are necessary to each other. Chapter 6 describes how Americans have tried to achieve this balance in several important areas—freedom of religion and of speech and of the press, for example. Which goals—individual liberties or collective needs—should receive priority if they come into conflict with each other? When and under what conditions should one or the other receive priority? Who should decide—judges, legislators, or someone else? How much individual liberty may we allow in face of our need for military security? To what extent, in a democracy, may we allow military needs to threaten individual freedom?

We have been talking about individual liberties, such as freedom of speech; there is also the matter of civil rights, such as the right to equal opportunity in education and the right to vote. Chapter 7 takes up the constitutional guarantees and political battles behind the idea that no man should suffer pains and penalties because of his race, religion, national origin, or other qualities irrelevant to his individual merit. In Chapter 8 we describe a different but equally important type of right—the right not to be arbitrarily deprived of life, liberty and property. Both sets of rights—civil rights and (mainly) procedural rights—pose the problem of the balance of individual rights against collective needs.

There is a final basic problem in Part Three—which government, state or federal, should determine the balance among and between individual rights and collective needs? What if, say, the state government should fail to protect a man's civil rights? Should the national government step in and protect those rights? Hence the problem of federalism is crucial to the problem of freedom in America. The relation of levels of governments to one another in protecting individual freedom is emphasized in Chapters 7 and 8.

Implicit in this discussion is the fact that individual freedom may be threatened directly by other individuals as well as by government. For example, a man trying to speak from a soapbox may be knocked down by a mob and arrested by a policeman. It is also possible that the policeman might protect him from the mob—a case of government guarding the liberty of one individual against other individuals. Hence it is always advisable, when considering a problem of individual freedom, to ask the question, *Whose* civil liberties are to be protected, against *what*, by *whom* (for example, what agency of government), and *how?*

Chapter 8 also deals with the status and rights of immigrants, aliens, and citizens. The Constitution does not guarantee the right of admission to the United States; aliens do not enjoy all the privileges of American citizens. But quite a few important problems of individual liberty are involved in our treatment of noncitizens.

The First Amendment
and the First Freedoms

6   "Congress shall make no law," declares the First Amendment, "respecting an establishment of religion, or prohibiting the free exercise thereof; or abridging the freedom of speech, or of the press; or the right of the people peaceably to assemble, and to petition the Government for a redress of grievances." Here in bold and imposing terms are the fundamental supports of a free society—freedom of conscience and freedom of expression.

Although the Framers drafted the Constitution, in a sense it was the people who drafted our basic charter of liberties. The Constitution drawn up at Philadelphia included no specific guarantee of the basic freedoms—an omission that aroused suspicion and distrust among the people at large. In order to win ratification, the Federalists promised to correct this oversight, and in the very first session of the new Congress they lived up to their promise. Congress proposed amendments that were ratified by the end of 1791 and became part of the Constitution. These ten amendments are known as the Bill of Rights.

Note that the Bill of Rights is addressed to the national government. As John Marshall held in *Barron* v. *Baltimore* (1833), the Bill of Rights limits the national but not the state governments. Why not the states? In the 1790s the people were confident they could control their own state officials, and most of the state constitutions already had bills of rights. It was the new and distant central government that the people feared.

But as it turned out, those popular apprehensions of 1790 were largely misplaced. The national government, responsive to tens of millions of voters from a variety of races, creeds, religions, and economic groups, has shown less tendency to curtail civil liberties than have state and local governments. It was not long after the Bill of Rights was adopted that some people began to recognize the mistake of exempting state governments from the prohibitions of the national Bill of Rights and thereby allowing state regulation of our liberties. True, each state constitution also includes a bill of rights, but for the most part state judges have not been inclined to apply these bills of rights vigorously to protect civil liberties.

With the adoption of the Fourteenth Amendment in 1868, which *does* apply to the states, litigants tried to persuade the Supreme Court to construe the due-process clause of this amendment to mean that the states are limited in the same way that the Bill of Rights limits the national government. At a minimum, they contended, freedom of speech should be brought within the confines of the Fourteenth Amendment. For decades the Supreme Court refused to interpret the Fourteenth Amendment in this way. Then in 1925, in *Gitlow* v. *New York*, the Supreme Court announced:

For present purposes we may and do assume that freedom of speech and of press—which are protected from abridgment by Congress—are among the fundamental personal rights and liberties protected by the due process clause of the Fourteenth Amendment from impairment by the states.

Gitlow v. *New York* was a decision of major, almost revolutionary, significance. Since that date the Fourteenth Amendment has placed the same restraints in behalf of free speech on states (in a constitutional sense, all subdivisional units of a state, such as cities, counties, and school districts, are part of the state) that the First Amendment places on the national government, and by 1947 the Supreme Court had brought all the other liberties of the First Amendment under the protection of the Fourteenth. Since then, most of the other provisions of the Bill of Rights have been made applicable to the states. (See pages 195–197.)

Today virtually all Americans agree that governmental power should not be used to interfere with the freedoms of speech and conscience. Yet the country seems to be almost constantly involved in quarrels about specific applications of these restraints. It is all very well to venerate our liberties in general. The trouble arises when we move from generalities to specifics. "All declare for liberty," wrote Justice Reed, "and proceed to disagree among themselves as to its true meaning."[1] In few areas are the problems more difficult to resolve and the differences more intense than in that of religious freedoms.

Each May Worship in His Own Way

The right to hold any or no religious belief is an absolute right. One's religious beliefs are inviolable, and no government in the United States has any authority whatsoever to compel the acceptance of or to censor

[1]*Breard* v. *Alexandria* (1951).

any creed. Thus a unanimous Supreme Court struck down a provision of the Maryland constitution requiring a declaration of belief in the existence of God as a prerequisite to hold public office.[2]

The right to advocate one's religion by speech or writing, like the right to use speech or writing for any other purpose, may be curbed only when there is danger of substantial injury to the rights of others. In fact, the Supreme Court has shown greater concern for religious than for political advocacy, perhaps because Congress is specifically enjoined by the First Amendment (and the states, through interpretation, by the Fourteenth) to make no law "prohibiting the free exercise" of religion.

The practice of one's religion has less protection than its advocacy. As the Supreme Court has said, "It was never intended that the First Amendment . . . could be invoked as a protection against legislation for the punishment of acts inimical to the peace, good order and morals of society."[3] Religious convictions do not exempt one from complying with otherwise valid laws designed to protect the public peace, health, safety, and morals. The Supreme Court has sustained laws forbidding the practice of polygamy, as applied to Mormons; laws requiring vaccination of schoolchildren, as applied to Christian Scientists; laws forbidding business activities on Sunday in order to promote health and rest, as applied to Orthodox Jews.[4]

Since the Civil War, the Supreme Court has consistently held that the draft laws do not violate the First Amendment, but Congress has chosen to excuse religious conscientious objectors from service. Those who oppose war on "political, sociological, or philosophical grounds" are not granted an exemption. Although the Court has interpreted the word *religious* so broadly that any deeply held humanistic opposition to all war is probably included, it has not as yet decided whether the special status given religious conscientious objectors is unconstitutional.[5]

The Court has also struck down laws under which unemployment benefits were denied to those refusing to work on Saturday, their Sabbath.[6] South Carolina argued that its statute was a general one, denying unemployment benefits to any person who refused to take a suitable job—for whatever reason. If Mrs. Sherbert did not want to work on Saturday, that was her business, but she was not entitled to special treatment just because she was a Seventh Day Adventist. The Court disagreed. If a person refuses to accept a job requiring Saturday work because he wants to go fishing, the state may deny him unemployment compensation. But if he declines the work for religious reasons, the Constitution requires the state to grant him his benefits. The Sherbert case points to a possible contradiction within the First Amendment: If the freedom-of-religion clause means that religious beliefs and practices are entitled to special consideration from the government, can the clause be reconciled with the prohibition against the establishment of religion?

[2]*Torcaso* v. *Watkins* (1961).
[3]*Reynolds* v. *United States* (1879).
[4]*McGowan* v. *Maryland* (1961).
[5]*United States* v. *Seeger* (1965).
[6]*Sherbert* v. *Verner* (1963).

What does this prohibition against the establishment of religion mean? To oversimplify, there are two general interpretations of this clause—the *no-preference* doctrine and the *wall-of-separation* doctrine. Those who accept the former hold that our Constitution forbids national and state governments to aid any particular religion, but if no preference is shown among different creeds, they may aid and encourage religious activities. The second interpretation—the one adopted by the Supreme Court—is that the Constitution creates a wall of separation between church and state and forbids governments to aid, encourage, or support any or all churches, any or all religious activities. As Justice Black said in *Everson* v. *Board of Education* (1947):

Neither a state nor the Federal Government can set up a church. Neither can pass laws that aid one religion, aid all religions, or prefer one religion over another. Neither can force nor influence a person to go or to remain away from church. . . or force him to profess a belief or a disbelief in any religion. . . . No tax in any amount, large or small, can be levied to support any religious activities or institutions, whatever they may be called, or whatever form they may adopt to teach or practice religion. Neither a state nor the Federal Government can, openly or secretly, participate in the affairs of any religions organizations or groups and vice versa. In the words of Jefferson, the clause against establishment of religion by law was intended to erect "a wall of separation between Church and State."

The Supreme Court reaffirmed the Everson doctrine when it declared unconstitutional the Champaign, Illinois, Board of Education's program of allowing privately chosen instructors to teach religion during school hours in public schoolrooms to students whose parents approved. The Supreme Court ruled: "Here not only are the State's tax-supported public school buildings used for the dissemination of religious doctrines. The State also affords sectarian groups an invaluable aid in that it helps to provide pupils for their religious classes through the use of the State's compulsory school machinery. This is not separation of Church and State."[7]

Many applauded the Supreme Court's stand in favor of the wall-of-separation doctrine, but others criticized. In the face of this criticism, the Supreme Court sustained New York City's released-time program, despite the fact that the only difference between it and the Champaign program was that it provided for the released-time classes to be held outside the public schoolbuilding in rooms made available by the various churches. Although insisting that the Court was not overruling Everson and McCollum, Justice Douglas, in his opinion (which he has since repented) for a six-man majority, appeared to be at odds with the wall-of-separation doctrine. He wrote:

The First Amendment . . . does not say that in every and all respects there shall be a separation of Church and State. . . . We are a religious people whose institutions presuppose a Supreme Being. . . . When the state

[7]*Illinois ex rel. McCollum* v. *Board of Education* (1948). For the historical background of the question, see Mark DeWolfe Howe, *The Garden and the Wilderness: Religion and Government in American Constitutional History* (Univ. of Chicago Press, 1965).

encourages religious instruction or cooperates with religious authorities by adjusting the schedule of public events to sectarian needs, it follows the best of our traditions.[8]

Since Zorach, however, the Supreme Court has specifically disavowed any intention of supporting the no-preference doctrine.[9] In 1962 (*Engel* v. *Vitale*) and in 1963 (*Abington School District* v. *Schempp*), the Court ruled that reciting nondenominational prayers or the Lord's Prayer and reading the Bible violate the Establishment Clause if made part of the program of public schools. Distinguishing ceremonial and patriotic exercises or the objective study of religion and the Bible from frankly religious ceremonies, Justice Black, in the 1962 decision, declared for the Court:

In this country it is no part of the business of government to compose official prayers for any group of the American people to recite as part of a religious program carried on by government. . . . Neither the fact that the prayer may be denominationally neutral, nor the fact that its observance on the part of the students is voluntary can serve to free it from the limitations of the Establishment Clause as it might from the Free Exercise Clause.

Justice Clark, speaking for the Court in the 1963 decision, repeated:

. . . violation of the Free Exercise Clause is predicated on coercion while the Establishment Clause violation need not be so attended. . . . To withstand the strictures of the Establishment Clause there must be a secular legislative purpose and a primary effect that neither advances nor inhibits religion.

In view of its insistence on separation of church and state, why has the Supreme Court permitted states and cities to enforce Sunday closing laws? The Court majority conceded that these laws originally had a religious purpose and effect of encouraging people to attend church, but the majority was persuaded that today they have a secular purpose and effect by providing a day of rest, recreation, and family togetherness.[10]

Only a few subjects arouse as much concern as does the question of the proper relation between governments and churches. The Supreme Court's rulings in this area have engendered many debates and comments. Some public school authorities have gone so far as to announce that, despite the Supreme Court, they would continue to include prayers and Bible readings as part of the school program. And in Congress there has been pressure for a constitutional amendment to permit religious programs in the public schools. However, those who favor the Supreme Court's construction of the Constitution have been able to block the proposed amendment. For the moment at least, the Supreme Court's construction of the Establishment Clause remains official and authoritative.[11]

To conclude that any kind of governmental aid to religion is unconstitutional does not, however, answer all the questions. What is aid to religion? May a state provide textbooks, hot lunches, and use tax money to pay the bus

[8]*Zorach* v. *Clauson* (1952).
[9]*Torcaso* v. *Watkins* (1961).
[10]*McGowan* v. *Maryland* (1961).
[11]William M. Beaney and Edward N. Beiser, "Prayer and Politics: The Impact of Engel and Schempp on the Political Process," *Journal of Public Law* (1964), vol. 13, pp. 475–503.

fare for children attending church-operated as well as public schools? In such instances the Supreme Court ruled, in *Board of Education* v. *Allen* (1968), that these practices are not aids to religion, which would be unconstitutional, but aids to education and to the welfare of children, which the Constitution does not forbid. Drawing this line was not easy; the Supreme Court was faced with a New York law that required local school boards to purchase and lend textbooks to all children residing in the district, including those enrolled in church-operated schools. (The boards made available the particular books requested by those in charge of the church-operated schools.) Justice White, speaking for a six-man majority, sustained the constitutionality of the purchases on the grounds that there is no distinction between using tax funds to provide children attending parochial schools with books or with a ride to school, which had been previously sustained in the *Everson* decision. Justice Douglas in dissent emphasized the nonideological character of a school bus as compared with a textbook that "goes to the very heart of education." The justices will soon get another opportunity to consider these complex questions. On the same day that they decided the Allen case, the Supreme Court modified *Frothingham* v. *Mellon* (see page 85) to permit taxpayers to challenge the Elementary and Secondary Education Act of 1965 in a federal district court.

For many years conflict over the wisdom and constitutionality of using federal funds to build schools, pay teachers, and purchase equipment in church as well as public schools was one of the major reasons why Congress failed to provide comprehensive federal aid for elementary and secondary schools. Some congressmen would support such a program only if federal funds were not made available to church schools; others would support such a program only if federal funds were made available to church schools.

In 1965 Congress skirted the issue: The Elementary and Secondary Education Act provides funds for almost everything except raising teachers' salaries and building classrooms. Students and teachers in private schools, including those operated by religious organizations, are eligible to participate in the federally supported public school programs and may use the books and other instructional materials that the public schools have purchased with federal funds. Whether this form of indirect aid to parochial schools will survive constitutional challenge will soon be decided. Although whatever ruling the Supreme Court makes will be sharply criticized because of the intense emotions and the difficult problems, in a world where many nations are sharply divided into religious factions, "the amicable accommodation of religious difference in America has been a significant achievement of our political experience."[12]

Free Speech and Free Men

Most democrats assume that government by the people is based on the individual's right to speak freely, to organize in groups, to question the decisions of the government, and to campaign openly against it. Only

[12]Alan P. Grimes, *Equality in America: Religion, Race, and the Urban Majority* (Oxford Univ. Press, 1964), p. 41.

through free and uncensored expression of opinion can the government be kept responsive to the electorate and can governmental power be transferred peacefully. Elections, separation of powers, and constitutional guarantees are meaningless unless each person has the right to speak frankly and to hear and judge for himself the worth of what others have to say.

Despite the fundamental importance of free speech in a democracy, some people seem to believe that speech should be free only for those who agree with themselves. Once we leave the level of abstractions and move to the level of specific questions or conflicts, there is a discouragingly low level of support for free speech among the mass public.[13] If one asks someone whether he believes in freedom of speech or the Bill of Rights, the answer will probably be "yes," but if one asks whether a Communist (or a recruiter from Dow Chemical Company) should be allowed to speak on a college campus in order to recruit persons to join the Communist party (or work for the Dow Chemical Company), the answer is often "no." One study of American opinion, for example, reported that one person in three thought that newspapers should not be permitted, even in peacetime, to criticize the government. Such people ask why evil or ignorant men should be permitted to spread falsehoods and confuse the minds of others. Why should they be allowed to utter dangerous ideas that subvert our democratic society?

THE BEST TEST OF TRUTH

Believers in democracy insist on free debate and the unlimited exchange of ideas because they feel that no group has a monopoly on truth, that no group has the right to establish in the field of politics absolute standards of what is true and what is false. A man may be convinced that he is right, that truth is on his side, but in the midst of debate he appeals, not to a philosopher-king, commissar, or oracle of wisdom, but to the power of his reason. As Justice Holmes wrote: "The best test of truth is the power of the thought to get itself accepted in the competition of the market." The insistence on free speech for others stems from the recognition that men are not infallible, that perhaps the other person is right or, at least, that "I might be wrong."

Free speech is not simply the personal right of an individual to have his say; it is also the right of the rest of us to hear him. John Stuart Mill, whose *Essay on Liberty* is an illuminating defense of free speech, put it this way: "The peculiar evil of silencing the expression of opinion, is that it is robbing the human race. . . . If the opinion is right, they are deprived of the opportunity of exchanging error for truth; if wrong, they lose, what is almost as great a benefit, the clearer perception and livelier impression of truth, produced by its collision with error."[14]

Freedom of speech is not merely freedom to express ideas that differ slightly from ours; it is, as the late Justice Jackson said, "freedom to differ on things that go to the heart of the matter." Some people profess to believe in free speech, but they draw the line at ideas they consider abhorrent or dan-

[13]Samuel Krislov, *The Supreme Court and Political Freedom* (Free Press, 1968), pp. 39ff summarizes and cites much of the relevant literature.

[14]John Stuart Mill, "Essay on Liberty," in Edwin A. Burtt (ed.), *The English Philosophers from Bacon to Mill* (Modern Library, 1939), p. 961.

gerous. But what is a dangerous idea? Who decides? The heresies of yesterday are often the orthodoxies of today. In the realm of political ideas, who can find an objective, eternally valid standard of right? The search for truth is an endless one. It involves the possibility—even the inevitability—of error. The search cannot go on unless it proceeds unfettered in the minds and speech of men. This means, in the words of Justice Holmes, not only free thought for those who agree with us, "but freedom for the thought we hate."

In short, to forbid the expression of ideas on the ground that they are dangerous is to set oneself up as an infallible judge of what speech should be permitted. Such presumptuousness stifles the fearless exchange of opinions and short-circuits the procedures of democratic government that are protected by the First Amendment. This, at least, is the assumption of democrats.

CONSTITUTIONAL GUARANTEES

Despite the fact that the First Amendment emphatically denies the national government the power to pass any law abridging freedom of speech, the amendment has never been interpreted in such sweeping terms. Liberty of expression is important, but it is not absolute. Like almost all rights, the right to freedom of speech and press is limited by the fact that its free exercise "implies the existence of an organized society maintaining public order without which liberty itself would be lost in the excess of unrestrained abuses."[15] How is the line to be drawn between permissible and unconstitutional restraint on freedom of expression?

In discussing the constitutional power of government to regulate speech, it is useful to distinguish among belief, speech, and action. At one extreme is the right to believe as one wishes, a right about as absolute as any can be for men living in organized societies. Despite occasional deviations in practice, the traditional American view is that thoughts are inviolable and that no government has the right to punish a man for his beliefs or to interfere in any way with his freedom of conscience.

At the other extreme from belief is action, which is constantly constrained. We may believe it perfectly all right to go 60 miles an hour through an intersection, but if we do so we will be punished. Because one man's action directly affects the liberty and property of others, "his right to swing his arm ends where the other fellow's nose begins."

Speech stands somewhere between belief and action; it is not an absolute (or almost absolute) right as is belief, but it is not so exposed to governmental restraint as is action. There are certain narrowly limited classes of speech that "by their very utterance inflict injury or tend to incite an immediate breach of peace"—the so-called fighting words—which government may justifiably prevent or punish. What about speech outside these categories?

THE HOLMES-BRANDEIS
CLEAR-AND-PRESENT-DANGER TEST

The first test adopted by the Supreme Court to distinguish between protected speech and that which could be regulated was announced by Justice

[15]*Cox v. New Hampshire* (1941).

115

CHAPTER 6
The
First Amendment
and the
First Freedoms

Holmes in *Schenck* v. *United States* (1919): "The question in every case is whether the words are used in circumstances and are of such a nature as to create a clear and present danger that they will bring about substantive evils that Congress has a right to prevent." Furthermore, "no danger flowing from speech can be deemed clear and present," wrote Justice Brandeis (concurring in *Whitney* v. *California*, 1927), "unless the incidence of the evil is so imminent that it may befall before there is opportunity for full discussion."

Holmes and Brandeis, although conceding that speech is not an absolute right, felt it to be so fundamental that under our Constitution no government has authority to suppress speech or punish a man for what he has said unless the connection between the speech and illegal action is so close that the speech itself takes on the character of the action. The Holmes-Brandeis clear-and-present-danger formula is primarily a rule to determine the sufficiency of the evidence. It requires that before being allowed to punish a man for what he has said or written, a government must prove clearly that his speech presents an imminent danger of a major substantive evil. Note that it is not *any* clear and present danger but only danger of a substantive evil that the government has a right to prevent—for example, rioting, destruction of property, or forceful overthrow of the government.

Let us see how the clear-and-present-danger test might be applied. Suppose, for example, a legislature has made it illegal to utter scurrilous and abusive remarks about members of another race. Under the clear-and-present-danger doctrine, a man could be punished for making such remarks only if at his trial the government has convincing evidence that his particular remarks clearly and presently might have led to a riot or some other serious substantive evil that the government rightfully may prevent.

THE DANGEROUS-TENDENCY DOCTRINE

Although the clear-and-present-danger doctrine was the first to receive formal Supreme Court support, the dangerous- or bad-tendency doctrine, stemming from the common law, is older, and it too at various times has been the official doctrine of the Court, most notably in *Gitlow* v. *New York* (1925). According to adherents of the dangerous-tendency doctrine, the Constitution, rather than requiring government to stay its hand until there is a clear and present danger flowing from a particular speech, implies that government may outlaw speech that has a tendency to lead to a substantive evil. Furthermore, those who espouse this view contend that it is primarily a legislative and not a judicial responsibility to determine what kinds of speech have a dangerous tendency. Once the legislature has made it a crime to say or write certain things that have a dangerous tendency, persons may be punished who have used the forbidden words, even if there is no immediate danger flowing from their particular speech. For the legislature has already decided that such words are dangerous.

Now let us take the example used above and apply to it the dangerous-tendency doctrine. The legislature has already determined that scurrilous and abusive remarks about members of another race are dangerous, and because it is not unreasonable to conclude that such comments have a tendency to stir up riots, all that is necessary to convict a person is to show that he in fact made such comments.

THE PREFERRED-POSITION DOCTRINE

Another test, the preferred-position doctrine, was the official view of the Supreme Court during the 1940s and is presently supported by several of the justices. This doctrine is an extension of the clear-and-present-danger formula—indeed, some of its supporters come close to the position that freedom of expression is an absolute right. Those who espouse the preferred-position interpretation believe that First Amendment freedoms hold the highest priority in our constitutional hierarchy and that courts have a special responsibility to scrutinize with extra care laws trespassing on these freedoms. Whereas legislative majorities are free to experiment and adopt various schemes regulating our economic lives, when they tamper with freedom of speech they close the channels of the political process by which error can be corrected. The majority is free via the legislature to adopt any policies it wishes, provided it leaves untouched the procedures by which new majorities may be formed. Hence, any law that on its face limits the First Amendment freedoms is presumed to be unconstitutional. Only if the government can show that limitations on speech are absolutely necessary to avoid extremely imminent and extremely serious substantive evils are such limitations to be tolerated.

If the preferred-position doctrine were applied to our example of a law against abusive racial remarks, the law would be declared unconstitutional. Restraints on such abusive speech are not absolutely necessary to prevent riots, according to this doctrine, and whatever danger may flow from such abusive remarks does not justify a restriction on free comment. Moreover, supporters of the preferred-position doctrine contend that it is not merely the application of this law to a particular speaker that is unconstitutional but that the law itself violates the Constitution.

These three doctrines are subject to a variety of interpretations and applications. And they are not the only formulas that the Supreme Court uses to measure the constitutionality of laws regulating speech. Among the other tests or doctrines or rules of thumb, perhaps the most important are the following:

Prior restraint. Of all the forms of governmental interference with speech, judges are most suspicious of those that impose prior restraint, that is, that require approval or a license before a speech can be made, a newspaper published, a motion picture shown. As Justice Brennan pointed out, "Because the censor's business is to censor, there inheres the danger that he may well be less responsive than a court . . . to the constitutionally protected interests in free expression."[16] The censor's decision may in practice be final and his views of what the public should be allowed to see or read conclusive. The Supreme Court has not gone so far as to declare all forms of prior censorship unconstitutional, but "any system of prior restraints of ex-

[16]*Freedman* v. *Maryland* (1965).

pression comes to this Court bearing a heavy presumption against its constitutional validity."[17] The judges have insisted on unusual justifications and elaborate safeguards before giving constitutional approval. For example, states or cities that wish to subject motion pictures to prior censorship must establish carefully defined standards and must provide procedures that ensure swift and easy judicial review of the censor's decision (see page 123).[18]

Vagueness. Any law is unconstitutional if it "either forbids or requires the doing of an act in terms so vague that men of common intelligence must necessarily guess at its meaning and differ as to its application. . . ."[19] Laws touching First Amendment freedoms are required to meet an even more rigid standard. These laws must not allow those who administer them so much discretion that the administrators could discriminate against those whose views they disapprove. Also the laws must not be so vague that persons are afraid to exercise protected freedoms for fear of running afoul of the law. The Supreme Court has struck down laws that condemn sacrilegious movies or publications of "criminal deeds of bloodshed or lust . . . so massed as to become vehicles for inciting violent and depraved crimes" because no one would know for sure what is or is not allowed.[20]

Overbreadth. Closely related to the vagueness doctrine and often merging with it is the requirement that a statute relating to First Amendment freedoms cannot be so broad in scope that it sweeps within its prohibitions protected as well as nonprotected activities. For example, a loyalty oath that would endanger protected forms of association as well as illegal activities would be unconstitutional. A legislature must deal more directly and precisely with the kinds of activities that it has a right to prohibit. As the Court opined in one decision, "The overly broad statute . . . creates a danger zone within protected expression may be inhibited. So long as the statute remains available to the State the threat of prosecutions of protected expression is real and substantial. Even the prospect of ultimate failure of such prosecutions by no means dispels its chilling effect on protected expression." In another, "Because First Amendment freedoms need breathing space to survive, government may regulate in the area only with narrow specificity."[21] Since the very presence on the statute books of an overbroad statute can be used to repress freedom of speech and association, such a statute, rather than just a specific application of it, may be declared unconstitutional on its face.

Least means. Related to both vagueness and overbreadth and often merged with these tests is the requirement that the legislative choice be narrowly restricted to the evil to be curbed. Outside the area of First Amendment freedoms, judges ordinarily will not invalidate a law just because the legislature might have chosen some other means to deal with a particular problem. But if the law impinges on the First Amendment, "even though the governmental purpose be legitimate and substantial, that purpose cannot be achieved by means that broadly stifle fundamental personal liberties when

[17]*Bantam Books Inc,* v. *Sullivan* (1963).
[18]*Teitel Film Corp.* v. *Cusak* (1968).
[19]*Lanzetta* v. *New Jersey* (1939).
[20]*Burstyn* v. *Wilson* (1952) and *Winters* v. *New York* (1948).
[21]Respectively, *Dombrowski* v. *Pfister* (1965) and *NAACP* v. *Button* (1963).

that end can be more narrowly achieved. The breadth of legislative abridgement must be viewed in the light of less drastic means for achieving the same basic purpose."[22] For example, a state may protect the public from the improper practice of the law, but it may not do so by a law forbidding organizations to make legal services available to their members.[23] There are other means to protect the public that do not impinge on the rights of free association.

The balancing doctrine. All judges, whatever language they use to express their opinions, weigh a variety of factors in making their decisions. But for some time the balancing doctrine took on a more restricted meaning and referred to a particular doctrine, especially as espoused by the late Justice Frankfurter and more recently by Justice Harlan. Dozens of opinions and hundreds of articles have been written supporting or condemning the balancing doctrine and explaining what it means.[24]

Essentially the Frankfurter-Harlan position is a protest by those who think the First Amendment should not be read in absolute terms, who reject the notion that First Amendment freedoms are any more sacred than any other constitutional freedoms, who believe that judges should not apply standards to measure the constitutionality of laws impinging on First Amendment freedoms that differ from those that are used to measure any other kinds of laws, and who think that judges have no mandate to protect these freedoms that is any different from their responsibilities in any other area. Laws regulating First Amendment freedoms, like all laws, must be judged by balancing the interests to be secured by the regulation against the amount of freedom that is lost or impaired. Thus Justice Harlan, using the balancing test, ruled that Congress's concern to preserve the nation against Communist subversion overbalances a witness's right before a congressional investigating committee to refuse to answer questions about his possible involvement with the Communist party.[25]

In more recent years, the Supreme Court's decisions indicate the

balancing of the Frankfurter variety has not turned out to be the dominant general formula for free speech cases that it once appeared to be becoming. [The] Court's emphasis on the need for overriding and compelling state interests before the balance will fall in its favor suggests something like a return to the old balancing cum-preferred position technique that coexisted with the clear-and-present-danger rule in the early forties. . . . For how much difference is there between saying that speech interests will be given special weight and saying that unless the state's interests are especially weighty they cannot overbalance speech.[26]

Whatever the doctrines, doctrines do not decide cases—judges do. And judges are constantly searching and seeking and explaining; hence the Su-

[22] *Shelton* v. *Tucker* (1960).

[23] *NAACP* v. *Button* (1963) and *Brotherhood of Railroad Trainmen* v. *Virginia* (1964).

[24] See, for example, Dean Alfrange, Jr., "The Balancing of Interests in Free Speech Cases: In Defense of an Abused Doctrine," *Law in Transition Quarterly* (Winter 1965), vol. II, pp. 1–29, and the many articles cited therein by Laurent Frantz, an opponent of the balancing test, and by Wallace Mendelson, an exponent of it.

[25] *Barenblatt* v. *United States* (1959).

[26] Martin Shapiro, *Freedom of Speech: The Supreme Court and Judicial Review* (Prentice-Hall, 1966), p. 83.

preme Court may undergo doctrinal changes especially when it deals with issues that lack a national consensus. Doctrines are judges' starting points, not their conclusions; each case requires them to weigh a variety of factors. *What* was said? Obscene speech, libelous statements, fighting words are not in the same category as political disputations. *Where* was it said? On the street corner, in a living room, over the radio? *How* was it said? In a flammable manner? What was the *intent* of the person who said it? To encourage people to violate the laws, to stir them to violence, or merely to cause them to think? What were the *circumstances* in which it was said? During time of war, in front of a hostile audience? *Which* government is attempting to regulate the speech? The city council that speaks for a few people or the Congress that speaks for a wide variety of people? (Only two *congressional* enactments have ever been struck down because of conflict with the First Amendment.) *How* is the government attempting to regulate the speech? By prior censorship, by punishment after the speech, by administrative procedures? *Why* is the government attempting to regulate the speech? To protect the national security, to keep the streets clean, to protect the rights of unpopular religious minorities, to prevent criticism of those in power? These and scores of other considerations are involved. And there is the further question of how much deference judges should show to the legislature's attempt to adjust these conflicting claims. In short, no test has been devised that will automatically weigh all the factors.

Freedom of the Press

"Upon what meat doth this our democracy feed?" asks Herbert Brucker, a noted newspaper editor. "It feeds upon facts brought into the minds of its citizens by the press, the radio, and the supplementary media of information."[27] So important is this system of disseminating information, says Brucker, that it constitutes the indispensable "fourth branch" of the national government. Today, information is seldom spread through street-corner meetings or public assemblies, the historic centers of debate. Rather, it is broadcast wholesale by the press, television, radio, movies, and other communication media. The Supreme Court has been zealous in guarding freedom of the press from governmental restriction. But how broad is this freedom?

Sometimes freedom of the press comes into conflict with another basic right—trial by an impartial judge and jury in a calm and judicial atmosphere. When newspapers and other mass media report in vivid detail the facts of a lurid crime and secure press releases from the prosecutor, it may be impossible to hold a trial in an atmosphere free from hysteria or to secure a jury that can decide in an impartial manner. In England the emphasis is on the side of fair trial. British courts do not hesitate to hold in contempt newspapers that comment on pending criminal proceedings. In the United States the emphasis is on the side of free comment. The Court has sustained the

[27]Herbert Brucker, *Freedom of Information* (Mamillan, 1949), p. 10.

right of the press to criticize judges, even to the point of allowing editors to threaten judges with political reprisals unless they deal with defendants in a certain fashion. As Justice Douglas put it, "Judges are supposed to be men of fortitude, able to thrive in a hardy climate" (*Craig* v. *Harney*, 1947).

Juries, on the other hand, are more susceptible to prejudicial comments and events. In 1952 a defendant was given a new trial because, after his indictment, a congressional investigating committee had conducted open hearings that, the judges believed, so inflamed public opinion that a fair trial was impossible. Similarly, the Supreme Court has reversed convictions when prejudicial newspaper publicity and prosecutors' statements to the press or the televising of the accused reading a confession have so aroused a community that a jury selected from the community could not be impartial.[28]

What about televising criminal trials? Is a defendant deprived of due process if, over his objection, the judge allows television cameras into the courtroom? Four justices of the Supreme Court were of the view that the mere fact that the trial is being televised is so likely to influence the behavior of judge, jury, witnesses, and defendants and is so inherently contrary to the idea of quiet and calm deliberation that televising trials is a violation of due process. The other justices said they would ban television from a courtroom only if there were evidence that its impact on the particular judge, jury, or witness in the trial in question interfered with a fair trial.[29]

The American Bar Association, concerned about sensational newspaper coverage, has adopted a series of rules designed, not to curb what newspapers may print, but to restrain what prosecutors, defense attorneys, judges, court employees, police, and other law enforcement officers should release. Although the ABA rules are not the law (though some judges have begun enforcing them), they do conform to the spirit of recent Supreme Court decisions instructing trial judges to use their authority to prevent the release before and during trials of prejudicial information that makes it difficult for the accused to be tried in an atmosphere that promotes calm and fair deliberations. Many newspapers have criticized the new ABA rules as infringing on free-press guarantees[30] and have been urging judges not to follow them.

Is there freedom of the press to obtain news as well as to print it? Recently, threats to the freedom of the press arising out of so-called censorship at the source have aroused the concern of newsmen. Governments have always withheld information, especially during times of war, and often public business is best done in secret. But as the cold war reached into more sectors of life, public officials classified more information as restricted or secret, so it became a crime to divulge it. Federal agencies used a 1789 "housekeeping" statute to conceal government documents from newsmen, sometimes even from congressmen. At one time the Department of Defense ordered officials not to release information unless it would "constitute a constructive contribution to the primary mission of the Department of Defense."

[28]*Delaney* v. *United States,* U.S. S.C.A. (1952); *Irvin* v. *Dowd* (1961); *Rideau* v. *Louisiana* (1963), and cases cited therein. See also Justice William O. Douglas, "The Public Trial and the Free Press," *American Bar Association Journal* (1960), vol. 46, p. 840.

[29]*Estes* v. *Texas* (1965) and *Shepperd* v. *Maxwell* (1966).

[30]For commentary and copy of ABA rules, see *American Bar Association Journal* (April 1968), pp. 343–351.

Conversely, Congress has tried to liberalize access to public records. The Freedom of Information Act, which became effective in 1967, makes public all federal records except those in certain specified categories—national security, private financial transactions, personnel records, and so on. Persons denied access to other kinds of records are given the right to sue for their production. However, in signing such congressional acts, Presidents have always emphasized that their signature is not to be interpreted as altering the President's inherent constitutional power to withhold information when the President considers its release not in the public interest.

LIBEL AND OBSCENITY

Libel prosecutions have often been a favorite weapon to suppress criticism of government officials and to prevent discussion of public issues (see page 131). But through a progressive raising of the constitutional standards, the danger of civil damages or criminal prosecution for libel no longer constitutes a serious threat to free communication. No person may be made to pay damages or be punished for any comments he makes about a *public official* unless it can be proved that the comments were made with actual malice, that is, with knowledge of their falsity or with reckless disregard of whether they were true or false. The mere fact that a statement is wrong or even defamatory of official reputation is not sufficient to sustain a charge of libel against a public official.[31] With respect to "public figures," in contrast to public officials, the Supreme Court has a somewhat less stringent rule: A person may recover damages for defamatory falsehood "substantially endangering his reputation on showing of highly unreasonable conduct constituting an extreme departure from the standards of investigation and reporting ordinarily adhered to by responsible publishers."[32]

What of obscenity? Obscene publications are not entitled to constitutional protection, but the members of the Supreme Court, like everybody else, have had great difficulty in determining what is obscene. As Justice Harlan pointed out, "The subject of obscenity has produced a variety of views among the members of the Court unmatched in any other course of constitutional adjudication."[33] In the thirteen cases since the Supreme Court entered the field in 1957 there have been a total of fifty-five separate opinions among the justices. Nonetheless, some guidelines are beginning to appear. The majority view appears to be that no material may be judged obscene until three essential constitutional criteria are met, each of which must be present. It must be established that (1) the average person, applying contemporary community standards (those of the society at large), would judge the dominant theme of the materials, taken as a whole, to be an appeal to a prurient interest in sex; (2) the material is patently offensive because it affronts contemporary standards; and (3) the material is utterly without redeeming social value.[34] The Supreme Court has also held that it cannot be made a

---

[31]*New York Times* v. *Sullivan* (1964) and *Garrison* v. *Louisiana* (1964).
[32]*Curtis Publishing Co.* v. *Butts* (1967).
[33]*Interstate Circuit, Inc.* v. *City of Dallas* (1968).
[34]*Roth* v. *United States* (1957); *Memoirs* v. *Massachusetts* (1966).

crime for a bookseller to offer an obscene book for sale; it must be shown that he *knowingly* did so.[35] Otherwise booksellers would tend to avoid placing on their shelves any book that someone might consider objectionable, and the public would be deprived of an opportunity to purchase perfectly proper books.

At the same time that the Supreme Court has insisted on a rigid definition of obscenity, it has upheld prosecutions for suggestively promoting materials, even if the materials themselves are not clearly obscene.[36] In short, as far as adults are concerned, so long as materials are discreetly promoted, governments must stay their hand against all but so-called hardcore pornography.

But what is not obscene for adults may be so for minors. The Supreme Court, recognizing the state's special interest in protecting young people, has approved regulations that prohibit the knowing sale to minors of "girly magazines" that would not be considered obscene if sold to adults.[37] But even under this "variable-obscenity" doctrine, governments are not free to move at will. For example, a Dallas ordinance was declared unconstitutional that forbade motion picture exhibitors to allow minors to see pictures that a motion picture classification board had determined were not suitable for minors. The board's standards were too vague; it classified as "not suitable for minors" films that a majority of its members thought "likely to incite or encourage crime, delinquency, or sexual promiscuity."[38]

States are primarily responsible for regulating obscene literature, but ever since Anthony Comstock started a national crusade against obscenity in the 1880s, Congress has had a concern with the subject and has made it a crime to import obscene matter or send it through the mails. Today, fears about obscenity appear to have replaced the seventeenth-century fears about heresy and the 1950s' fears about sedition. Yet there remains no conclusive evidence of a connection between the reading of obscene literature and the performance of obscene acts, although such a relationship is the primary justification for governmental regulation. Since the Supreme Court entered the field to protect reading and other materials from the too-heavy hand of the censor, Congress, responding to public concerns, has created an eighteen-member Commission on Obscenity and Pornography to study the traffic in obscene literature and the causal relationship between this matter and antisocial behavior.

In addition to federal statutes that make it a crime to distribute obscenity through the mails, Postmasters General have claimed authority to exclude obscene publications from the mails, revoke second-class mailing privileges of publications alleged to be obscene, and cut off all incoming mail to a person sending obscene matters through the mails. This claim rested on the assumption that the use of the mails is a privilege that the government may terminate at its discretion. But in 1965, the Supreme Court—on a different issue—rejected the doctrine that the use of the mails is a privilege that the government may confer or take away at its discretion. As Justice Holmes had written, ". . . the use of the mails is almost as much a part of free speech as

[35]*Smith* v. *California* (1959).
[36]*Ginzburg* v. *United States* (1966).
[37]*Ginsberg* v. *New York* (1968).
[38]*Interstate Circuit, Inc.* v. *City of Dallas* (1968).

the right to use our tongue." Congress, said the Supreme Court, cannot condition the right of an addressee to receive foreign Communist political propaganda on his returning an official notice saying that he wanted to receive it. "The regime of this Act," said the Court, "is at war with the 'uninhibited, robust, and wide-open debate' and discussion that are contemplated by the First Amendment."[39] This was the first time the Supreme Court ruled that Congress had violated the First Amendment. (For the second time, see page 136).

Until 1952 motion pictures were considered a form of entertainment and not a method of communication and therefore were not protected by the free speech and press guarantees of the Constitution. Seven states and numerous cities required all exhibitors to submit all films to censors, who determined, without any legal restraints, what could and could not be shown. Then in 1952 (*Joseph Burstyn, Inc.* v. *Wilson*), the Supreme Court brought the movies under the protection of the Constitution when it held that New York authorities lacked constitutional power to prevent the showing of a film because the authorities thought it to be "sacrilegious." Not only does *sacrilegious* lack precise meaning, the Court held, but government has no right to censor movies solely because they may offend some people's religious sensibilities. Since the Burstyn decision, the Supreme Court, in case after case, has upset attempts to ban motion pictures that various censors have alleged "tended to corrupt morals," or were "harmful," or presented "acts of sexual immorality as desirable."[40] About the only grounds on which a government may prevent the showing of a film is proof that it is obscene.

The Supreme Court has allowed films to be treated differently from books or newspapers and has refused to hold that prior censorship of films is necessarily unconstitutional under all circumstances.[41] However, laws calling for prior submission of all films to a review board are constitutional only if the review board is required promptly to grant a license or promptly to go to court for a prompt judicial hearing and determination that the film in question is obscene, and the burden is on the board to prove to the court that the film is in fact obscene.[42] Justices Black and Douglas would not even have allowed this kind of prior restraint. They argued that the public is adequately protected by the authority of the government to prosecute in a court of law those who show obscene films and that any form of censorship, no matter how speedy, is just as unconstitutional for films as it would be for newspapers.

Censorship of films and books may be imposed by a variety of means other than formal action. In some cities a local group, such as the Legion of Decency, may put pressure on the authorities, and local police have been known to threaten an exhibitor or a bookseller with criminal prosecution if he persists in showing pictures or selling books of which some local people disapprove. Such a threat is often enough to compel exhibitors to stop show-

[39]*Lamont* v. *Postmaster-General* (1965).

[40]See Paul C. Bartholomew, "Movie Censorship and the Supreme Court," *Michigan State Bar Journal* (August 1961), pp. 10–16. See also Alan F. Westin, "The Miracle Case: The Supreme Court and the Movies," in Edwin A. Bock and Alan K. Campbell (eds.), *Case Studies in American Government* (Prentice-Hall, 1962), pp. 83–131.

[41]*Times Film Company* v. *City of Chicago* (1961).

[42]*Freedman* v. *Maryland* (1965) and *Teitel Film Corp.* v. *Cusak* (1968).

ing the picture or selling the book. Of course any group is free to stay away from pictures or books that it dislikes, even to try to persuade others to stay away. What the Constitution forbids is the use of the coercive powers of government.

OTHER MEANS OF COMMUNICATION

Radio and Television. The number of frequencies that can be used for broadcasting and telecasting is limited. Chaos would result if the national government could not use its power over interstate commerce to allocate the airways and to issue licenses for broadcasting and television. The regulating agency, the Federal Communications Commission, has not tried to exercise direct power of censorship over political views or ideas presented over the airways, and doubtless it would be stopped by the courts if it did. But the First Amendment does not include "the right to use the facilities of a radio without a license" (*National Broadcasting Co.* v. *United States*, 1943). Nor does the First Amendment prevent the Federal Communications Commission from refusing or canceling a license if, in its opinion, the broadcasting station is not serving the public interest, convenience, or necessity. Federal regulation of radio and television does, however, protect these media from state regulation. When Philadelphia officials tried to censor motion pictures shown on television, a United States court of appeals ruled that the federal regulation was exclusive.

Handbills. The distribution of religious and political pamphlets, leaflets, and handbills to the public—a historic weapon in the defense of liberty—is constitutionally protected. The Supreme Court has been quick to strike down ordinances interfering with this right. Of course, cities may prosecute those who engage in fraud or libel or who deliberately litter the streets, but keeping the streets clean does not justify interference with the right to pass out political or religious literature. When Los Angeles tried to outlaw the distribution of anonymous handbills, the Supreme Court ruled that the city's interest in identifying those who might be responsible for fraud, false advertising, or libel was not substantial enough to justify a ban on all anonymous handbills.[43] When it comes to commercial handbills or advertising matter, however, there is no such sweeping constitutional protection, and such activities are exposed to much greater governmental regulation.

Picketing. Traditionally, the method used by workers to convey their messages to the public, picketing is also an economic weapon in the struggle between labor and capital. As a form of communication, it is protected by the First and Fourteenth amendments; therefore, a state law forbidding all peaceful picketing carried on for any purpose would be an unconstitutional invasion of freedom of speech.[44] However, "picketing involves elements of both speech and conduct, i.e., patrolling," and "because of this intermingling of protected and unprotected elements, picketing can be subjected to controls that would not be constitutionally permissible in the case of pure

[43]*Talley* v. *California* (1960).
[44]*Thornhill* v. *Alabama* (1940).

speech."[45] Even peaceful picketing can be restricted by a state if it is conducted for an illegal purpose.[46] But as far as trade-union picketing is concerned, federal regulations are so comprehensive and preempt so many areas from state regulation that the power of states to interfere with such picketing is much narrower than it might appear if one looks only at decisions relating to freedom of speech.[47]

Symbolic Speech. When engaged in to communicate an idea, conduct is even less protected by the First and Fourteenth amendments than is picketing, as David Paul O'Brien and his three companions discovered when they burned their draft cards in violation of a specific congressional regulation that makes it a crime to do so knowingly and deliberately. O'Brien argued that the First Amendment protects "all modes of communication of ideas by conduct." But Chief Justice Warren, speaking for eight members of the Supreme Court, stated, "We cannot accept the view that an apparently limitless variety of conduct can be labelled speech whenever the person engaging in the conduct intends thereby to express an idea."[48] Congress had chosen a necessary and proper means of implementing its power to call men to the military services.

Sound Trucks. Which is more important—the right to an undisturbed Sunday afternoon nap or the right to use a sound truck to publicize a message? In 1948, by a five-to-four decision, the Supreme Court held in *Saia* v. *New York* that the Fourteenth Amendment was violated by a city ordinance requiring an official permit from the chief of police before one could use a sound truck. Justice Douglas, speaking for the majority, said that sound trucks are "indispensable instruments of effective public speech, and . . . such abuses as they create can be controlled only by statutes narrowly drawn." The very next year, however, the authority of this ruling was thrown in doubt by another five-to-four ruling in *Kovacs* v. *Cooper*, which upheld a municipal ordinance forbidding any sound truck that emitted "loud and raucous noises." The Court majority believed that this ordinance provided a definite enough standard to guide administrators and that it was a justifiable exercise of the police power "to protect the well-being and tranquility of a community." These two cases are an excellent example of the narrow and delicate balance between civil liberties and the needs of an ordered community.

Freedom of Assembly and Petition

The right to assemble peaceably applies, not only to meetings in private homes and meeting halls, but to meetings held in public streets and parks, which, the Supreme Court has said, since ". . . time out of mind have been used for purposes of assembly . . . and discussing public

---

[45]*Amalgamated Food Employees Local 590* v. *Logan Valley Plaza, Inc.* (1968).
[46]*International Brotherhood of Teamsters* v. *Vogt* (1957).
[47]Martin Shapiro, *Law and Politics in the Supreme Court* (Free Press, 1964), pp. 75–142.
[48]*United States* v. *O'Brien* (1968).

questions" (*Hague* v. *C.I.O.*, 1939). But, under the guise of exercising freedom of peaceful assembly and petition, people are not free to incite riots, to block traffic, to take over a school, to seize and hold the office of a mayor (or a university chancellor), to hold parades, or to make speeches in the public streets during rush hours—and the government may make reasonable regulations to preserve order.

The courts will look carefully at regulations and police action that obstruct the right of public assembly, especially in circumstances that raise a suspicion that a law is not being applied evenhandedly. The Supreme Court is unwilling to approve regulations authorizing public authorities to determine, at their own discretion, which groups will be allowed to hold public meetings, or laws that are so vague that they give police broad discretion to determine whom to arrest and courts latitude to determine whom to convict. Governments may control the use of the streets, but they must do so by precisely drawn and fairly administered regulations. The Supreme Court, for example, sustained a Louisiana statute that made it an offense to picket or parade in or near a courthouse with the intent to influence a judge, juror, witness, or court order or to impede the administration of justice. On the other hand, the Court struck down another Louisiana statute that defined disturbing of the peace so broadly that it would permit arrest merely for holding a meeting on a public street or public highway.[49]

What of unpopular groups whose peaceful public meetings and nonviolent demonstrations in the public streets and parks arouse others to violence? May police arrest them and judges convict the demonstrators? If the answer were yes, then the right of unpopular minorities to hold meetings would be seriously curtailed. It is almost always easier for the police to maintain order by curbing the peaceful meetings of the unpopular minority than to move against those threatening the violence. On the other hand, if police never have the right to order a group to disperse, public order is at the mercy of those who may resort to street demonstrations just to create public tensions and provoke street battles.

The Supreme Court has refused to give a categorical answer; it depends on the circumstances. Several years ago the Court upheld the conviction of a sidewalk speaker who continued to talk after being ordered to stop by the only two policemen present. There was no evidence that the police interfered because of objection to what was being said. But in view of the hostile response of the audience, the police were fearful that a fight might ensue that they could not contain or prevent.[50] Judges have also approved of the police's breaking up demonstrations in front of public school buildings by segregationists who by taunts and threats have tried to intimidate school authorities, parents, and children attempting to carry out a court-ordered desegregation program. On the other hand, the Supreme Court has refused to approve police interference in circumstances where there is a strong suspicion that the local authorities failed to make a good-faith attempt to protect peaceful demonstrations that were not interfering with substantial rights of others.

For example, 187 Negro high school and college students were arrested

[49]*Cox* v. *Louisiana* (1965).
[50]*Feiner* v. *New York* (1951).

for holding a mass meeting in front of the South Carolina State House to protest denial of their civil rights. A crowd of about 300 onlookers watched the demonstration. The police protected the demonstrators for about forty-five minutes and then gave the students fifteen minutes in which to disperse. When they refused to do so, they were arrested and convicted for breach of the peace. The Supreme Court stressed that this was not a prosecution for violation of a precise and narrowly drawn statute limiting or prescribing specific conduct, such as interfering with traffic. All that had happened was that the opinions being expressed had been sufficiently opposed by a majority of the community to attract a crowd and necessitate police protection. "The Fourteenth Amendment," said the Court, "does not permit a State to make criminal the peaceful expression of unpopular views."[51] Justice Clark, the lone dissenter, argued that the right to express views does not include the right to do so under circumstances where law-enforcement officers conclude in good faith that a dangerous disturbance is imminent.

What of public facilities, such as libraries, courthouses, schools, and swimming pools, that are designed to serve purposes other than demonstrations? As long as persons assemble to use such facilities within the normal bounds of conduct, apparently they may not be constitutionally restrained from doing so. However, if they attempt by demonstrations such as sit-ins to interfere with programs or try to appropriate facilities for their own use, a state has the constitutional authority to punish such activities, provided the discretion accorded to those enforcing the law is properly limited and discriminatory application of the laws does not take place. In *Brown* v. *Louisiana* (1965), for example, the Supreme Court, by a five-to-four vote, ruled that five Negroes could not be punished for breach of the peace for merely remaining quietly in a library for ten to fifteen minutes in order to protest racial discrimination. There was no disorder and no intent to provoke a breach of the peace, and the protestors had a right "by silent and reproachful presence to protest the unconstitutional segregation of public facilities." But Justice Black, speaking for the four dissenting justices, wrote, "Though the First Amendment guarantees the right of assembly and the right of petition . . . , it does not guarantee to any person the right to use someone else's property, even that owned by government and dedicated to other purposes, as a stage to express dissident ideas."

A year later, a different five-to-four division of the Court, this time with Justice Black speaking for the majority, sustained a conviction for "trespass with a malicious and mischievous intent" of students from Florida A & M University. The students had marched to the jailhouse to protest the arrest and jailing of some of their fellow students the day before and, more generally, to protest against segregation within the jail. They refused to leave when ordered to do so by the sheriff. Justice Black emphasized that jails are built for security purposes and are not open to the general public and that the Constitution does not preclude a state from "even handed enforcement of its general trespass statute . . . to preserve the property under its control for the use to which it is lawfully dedicated."[52] People who wish to protest do not have a constitutional right to do so "whenever and however and wher-

[51]*Edwards* v. *South Carolina* (1963).
[52]*Adderly* v. *Florida* (1966).

ever they please." Justice Douglas, speaking for the four dissenting justices, argued that the jailhouse—just as an executive mansion, legislative chamber, or statehouse—is one of the seats of government and that when it "houses political prisoners or those whom many think are unjustly held, it is an obvious center for protest." Douglas chided the majority for treating this "petition for redress of grievances" as an ordinary trespass action.

What of private property and the right to protest? The constitutional right to assemble and to petition does not include the right to trespass on privately owned property, and governments have authority to protect property owners against those who attempt to convert such property to their own use. Nevertheless, under certain conditions, even those who own or use private property come under the restraints of the Constitution. If a company owns a town or a shopping center that it has opened to the public, its regulations cannot abridge First Amendment freedoms.[53] Furthermore, when state laws or state-enforced customs prevent proprietors from serving Negroes, the Supreme Court has been unwilling to allow governmental power to be used to punish persons for engaging in peaceful sit-ins in stores and restaurants open to the public in order to protest such state-imposed segregation. Under these circumstances, the whole procedure for denying to Negroes nonsegregated service is so infused with state support that the Constitution comes into play.

Does the right of peaceful assembly and petition include the right nonviolently but deliberately to violate a law? Again we have no unequivocal answer. The Supreme Court has sustained the right of persons to refuse peacefully to comply with segregation ordinances that are clearly unconstitutional. But speaking in general terms, "civil disobedience," even if peacefully engaged in, is not a protected right. When the late Dr. Martin Luther King and his followers refused to comply with a state court's injunction that forbade them to parade in Birmingham without first securing a permit, the Supreme Court sustained their conviction even though there was a serious doubt about the constitutionality of the injunction and the ordinance upon which it was based. Justice Stewart, speaking for the five-man majority, said, "No man can be judge in his own case, however exalted his station, however righteous his motives, and irrespective of his race, color, politics, or religion." Persons are not "constitutionally free to ignore all the procedures of the law and carry their battles to the streets."[54] The four dissenting justices emphasized that one does have a right to defy peacefully an obviously unconstitutional statute or injunction.

The many five-to-four votes of the Supreme Court in drawing a line that will preserve the rights of persons to assemble and peacefully to petition and demonstrate—but that will not deprive state and local authorities of the right to maintain order and preserve the rights of all—reflect the complexity of the problem. An explanation of the Supreme Court's attempt to distinguish between legitimate use of public authority to preserve order and the unconstitutional use of public authority to suppress the right to assemble only begins to state the problem. The Court cannot police the nation. In thou-

[53]*Marsh* v. *Alabama* (1946); *Amalgamated Food Employees Local 590* v. *Logan Valley Plaza, Inc.* (1968).
[54]*Walker* v. *Birmingham* (1967).

sands of local communities, those who really determine the extent to which people are free to exercise their constitutional right to assemble peacefully and to express unpopular views are the local law enforcement authorities, and these officials, in turn, usually reflect the views and values of the communities they serve. Despite Supreme Court opinions, local demonstrators still are arrested and demonstrations stopped. Thousands of dollars and months later, convictions may be reversed if the case is carried all the way to the Supreme Court. In the meantime the protestors are silenced. Again, we have an example of the fact that the Supreme Court can *outline* but cannot *secure* constitutional rights unless its decisions are backed by the dominant political views and values and forces of the nation.

Freedom of Association

The right to organize for the peaceful promotion of political causes is not precisely mentioned in the Constitution, but in 1958 the Supreme Court made specific what has long been implied: "It is beyond debate that freedom to engage in association for the advancement of beliefs and ideas is an inseparable aspect of the 'liberty' protected by the Constitution."[55]

Of course this right, like other rights, under certain conditions may be regulated. The Supreme Court has ruled that under certain circumstances the registration of the names of members of certain Communist organizations with the Attorney General would not by itself violate the Constitution (but see page 135).[56] Although the publicity resulting from such disclosures would impair the ability of Communists to recruit members and would subject individual Communists to social ostracism and economic reprisal, the Court majority was impressed by the evidence that Communist organizations are not ordinary political groups seeking to promote goals by peaceful means.

The Supreme Court has treated quite differently the attempts by some Southern states to prevent persons from joining the National Association for the Advancement of Colored People. This organization, which proceeds in large measure by pressing lawsuits, has aroused considerable hostility among white citizens in areas where segregationist traditions are strong. And Southern states and cities have tried by a variety of means to discourage persons from joining the NAACP, even to the extent of trying to outlaw the organization. One of the most frequently attempted anti-NAACP tactics is to force the NAACP to reveal the names of its members. In many areas, if it becomes known that a person belongs to the NAACP, he risks loss of employment, economic reprisal, even physical coercion. Under such circumstances, disclosure of membership lists would interfere with the right to join a lawful organization. Unless the state can show some compelling public purpose, it may not force the NAACP to hand over membership lists.[57]

[55] *NAACP* v. *Alabama* (1958). See also *United States* v. *Robel* (1967).
[56] *Communist Party* v. *Subversive Activities Control Board* (1961).
[57] *Bates* v. *Little Rock* (1960); *NAACP* v. *Alabama* (1958); *NAACP* v. *Button* (1963).

Along these same lines, the Supreme Court ruled that Arkansas could not demand a list of all organizations to which its teachers belong (the list ostensibly being required to determine their fitness to teach). Arkansas could get the information it was entitled to without having to impose a requirement which would discourage membership in lawful but unpopular organizations.[58]

What about the freedom *not* to associate? To oversimplify a complex problem, a majority of the justices apparently feel that under certain circumstances a legislature may constitutionally authorize compulsory membership in a union or a bar association, provided no individual is compelled to have his dues spent for political causes.[59]

Subversive Conduct and Seditious Speech

"If there is any fixed star in our constitutional constellation," Justice Jackson said, "it is that no official, high or petty, can prescribe what shall be orthodox in politics, nationalism, religion, or other matters of opinion. . . ."[60] Any group that abides by the basic rules of democracy can champion whatever position it wishes, whether vegetarianism, socialism, or even communism. But what about the American Communist party? Its leaders are unwilling to abide by democratic methods. Their organization is an instrument of a foreign power whose aggressive policies are officially held to threaten the free world.[61] Yet they claim the right under the Constitution to carry on their propaganda and other activities.

Here is a perplexing problem for American democratic government. How can the United States protect itself against Communists and other anti-democrats and at the same time preserve traditional American freedoms? The weapons in the battle against disloyalty are hazardous—there is a constant risk that they will backfire. If used clumsily, they may do more to undermine individual freedom

"Fire!"

From *The Herblock Book* (Beacon Press, 1952).

[58]*Shelton* v. *Tucker* (1960).

[59]*International Association of Machinists* v. *Street* (1961); *Lathrop* v. *Donohue* (1961).

[60]*West Virginia State Board of Education* v. *Barnette* (1943).

[61]See decision of Subversive Activities Control Board, which after fourteen months of hearings concluded that the Communist party is dominated by the Soviet Union and ordered it to register as a "communist-action organization." *Federal Register* (April 30, 1953) vol. 18, no. 83, p. 2513.

and the security of the United States than can the Communists themselves. Let us look first at the least dangerous weapons—those aimed at disloyal actions.

TRAITORS, SPIES, SABOTEURS, REVOLUTIONARIES

Laws punishing disloyal *actions* raise no constitutional questions, nor do they infringe on civil liberties, except when they are loosely drawn or indiscriminately administered. The Framers of the Constitution—themselves considered traitors by the English government—knew the dangers of loose definitions of treason. Accordingly, they carefully inserted a constitutional definition of the crime of treason by stating that it consists only of the overt acts of giving aid and comfort to the enemies of the United States or levying war against the United States. Furthermore, in order to convict a person of treason, the Constitution requires the testimony of two witnesses to the overt treasonable acts or the defendant's confession in open court.

Against what other forms of disloyal action does the national government have constitutional power to protect itself? It has the power to make it a crime to engage in espionage or sabotage, to attempt to overthrow the government by force, or to conspire to do any of these things. This power to proceed against disloyal action, however, is limited. Perhaps Congress went too far in the Internal Security Act of 1950, which outlaws any conspiratorial action, peaceful or violent, designed to contribute substantially to the establishment of a foreign-controlled dictatorship in the United States. So far, the Department of Justice has made no attempt to prosecute any person under this provision, which, unlike other antisubversive laws, is not aimed at specific acts or at the use of violence or other unlawful means but attempts to outlaw political goals.

SEDITIOUS SPEECH

It is one thing to punish men for what they *do*; it is quite another to punish them for what they *say*. The story of the development of free government is in large measure the story of making clear this distinction between speech and other kinds of activity and of restricting the power of government to define and punish seditious speech. Until recent centuries, seditious speech was so broadly defined that all criticism of those in power was considered criminal. As late as the eighteenth century in England, seditious speech was defined as covering any publication intended to incite disaffection against the King or the government or to raise discontent among the people or to promote feelings of ill will between different classes.[62] And it did not make any difference if what was said was true. On the contrary, "the greater the truth the greater the libel." For if one charged the king's ministers with being corrupt and in fact they were corrupt, such a charge would more likely cause discontent among the people than if it were false.

The adoption of the Constitution and the Bill of Rights did not result in a quick, easy victory for those who wished to establish free speech in the

---

[62]Zechariah Chafee, Jr., "The Great Liberty: Freedom of Speech and Press," in Alfred H. Kelly (ed.), *Foundations of Freedom in the American Constitution* (Harper & Row, 1958), p. 79.

United States.[63] In 1798, only seven years after the First Amendment had been ratified, Congress passed the first national sedition law. These were perilous times for the young Republic, for war with France seemed imminent. The Federalists, in control of both Congress and the Presidency, were so stung by the criticisms of the Jeffersonian Republicans that they persuaded themselves that national safety required a little suppression of speech. The Sedition Act made it a crime to utter false, scandalous, or malicious statements intended to bring the government or any of its officers into disrepute or "to incite against them the hatred of the good people of the United States."[64] The Sedition Act of 1798 marked a definite advance over the English common law, for it made truth a defense and allowed the jury to determine the seditious character of the utterances. (At about this same time in England these same procedural reforms were also being adopted.) But Federalists, like most officials wielding the power to suppress, regarded all criticism of their actions as scandalous, malicious, and false, and they used the law to punish their political opponents for criticizing the policies of the Federalist administration.

The popular reaction to the Sedition Act helped defeat the Federalists in the elections of 1800. They had failed to grasp the core of the democratic idea that a man may criticize the government of the day, he may work for its downfall, he may oppose its policies, and still be loyal to the nation. If the Sedition Act had been left on the statute books and applied in its full measure, neither a "loyal opposition" nor a free government would have been possible.

THE SEDITION ACT OF 1918

Not until World War I did such a severe measure again become the law of the land. In 1918 Congress made it a crime to print, write, or publish any "disloyal, profane, scurrilous, or abusive language about the form of government of the United States or the Constitution . . . or any language intended to bring the form of government of the United States, or the Constitution of the United States, or the military forces . . . or the flag . . . or the uniform of the Army and Navy . . . into contempt, scorn, contumely, or disrepute."

This drastic measure was not aimed at talk that might lead to specific kinds of illegal activity. Rather, it made the speech itself illegal. Like the Sedition Act of 1798, this law made it a crime not only to advocate illegal activities but even to criticize the government. Loosely drawn and poorly administered, it was applied at a time when many people, emotionally aroused by the war, were willing to restrict the liberties of their fellow citizens. As a result of the combined effort of state laws against anarchy and sedition and federal laws against interfering with drafting men for the army, it became a crime "to advocate heavier taxation instead of bond issues, to state that conscription was unconstitutional . . ., to say that the sinking of merchant vessels was legal, to urge that a referendum should have preceded our

---

[63]Leonard Levy, *Legacy of Suppression* (Harvard Univ. Press, 1960), and *Freedom of the Press from Zenger to Jefferson* (Bobbs-Merrill, 1966).

[64]See James Morton Smith, *Freedom's Fetters: The Alien and Sedition Laws and American Civil Liberties* (Cornell Univ. Press, 1956).

133

CHAPTER 6
The
First Amendment
and the
First Freedoms

declaration of war, to say that war was contrary to the teachings of Christ."[65] A twenty-one-year-old girl was sentenced to fifteen years in jail for taking part in the scattering of pamphlets attacking President Wilson and opposing American intervention in Russia.[66] During the "red scare" that followed the war, judges and juries punished hundreds of people who expressed ideas to which their neighbors objected.

THE SMITH ACT OF 1940

The next sedition law, the first to apply in peacetime since the Sedition Act of 1798, was the Smith Act of 1940. Unlike earlier sedition laws, it does not make mere criticism of the government a crime nor does it contain such loose language as "bring into contempt" or "cause discontent." The core of the offense to which this law applies is to advocate the overthrow of the government by force with the intent to bring about this overthrow. It forbids persons to advocate forceful overthrow; to distribute, with disloyal intent, matter teaching or advising the overthrow of government by violence; and to organize knowingly or to help organize any group having such purposes. According to some authorities, the act introduces into federal criminal law the concept of *guilt by association* by making it a crime for an individual to be a member of any organization that advocates forceful overthrow of the government when the individual knows that this is its purpose and joins with the intent to help the organization bring about the violent overthrow of government (even though he himself might not so advocate).

The Supreme Court construed the Smith Act and considered the constitutionality of its several provisions in a series of important cases during the 1950s. In *Dennis* v. *United States* (1951), a majority of the justices agreed that the Smith Act could be constitutionally applied to the leaders of the Communist party who had been charged with conspiring to advocate the violent overthrow of the government. Chief Justice Vinson, speaking for the majority, adopted the position of Circuit Judge Learned Hand that the probability that speech would ripen into action should not be the sole criterion, but the question was "whether the gravity of the evil, discounted by its improbability," justified such invasion of speech as was necessary to avoid the danger. The Court gave great weight to the fact that the Communist party leaders were not isolated zealots scattering a few insignificant pamphlets but members of a rigidly disciplined organization and part of a worldwide conspiracy whose purpose was to destroy democracy. Justices Douglas and Black dissented. They pointed out that there had been no evidence introduced to indicate that the Communist party leaders were teaching "methods of terror and seditious conduct," but only that they had organized people in order to teach Marxist-Leninist doctrines. Moreover, the evidence did not show that this teaching presented any clear and present danger to the government. Justice Douglas wrote,

The communists in America are miserable merchants of unwanted ideas; their wares remain unsold. The fact that their ideas are abhorrent does not

[65]Zechariah Chafee, Jr., *Free Speech in the United States* (Harvard Univ. Press, 1941), p. 51; John P. Roche, *The Quest for the Dream* (Macmillan, 1963), pp. 26–76.
[66]*Abrams* v. *United States* (1919).

make them powerful. . . . The invisible army of petitioners is the best known, the most beset, and the least thriving of any fifth column in history. . . . Unless and until extreme and necessitous circumstances are shown our aim should be to keep speech unfettered and to allow the process of law to be invoked only when the provocateurs among us move from speech to action.

THE YATES AND SCALES CASES

Following the Dennis Case, the Department of Justice and, in many states, local prosecutors proceeded to go after second-string Communist leaders, more than one hundred of whom were jailed.[67] Then the Supreme Court called a halt to the easy conviction of Communist leaders. In *Pennsylvania* v. *Nelson* (1956), the Court ruled that the Smith Act precluded state prosecutions for seditious advocacy against the national government. In *Yates* v. *United States* (1957), the Court, speaking through Justice Harlan, held that the Dennis decision had been misunderstood. The Smith Act did not outlaw the advocacy of the abstract doctrine of violent overthrow. Justice Harlan explained:

> That sort of advocacy, even though uttered with the hope that it may ultimately lead to violent revolution, is too remote from concrete action to be regarded as the kind of indoctrination preparatory to action which was condemned in Dennis. The essential distinction is that those to whom the advocacy is addressed must be urged *to do* something, now or in the future, rather than merely *to believe* in something.

The Supreme Court denied that it was reversing the Dennis case, but certainly it severely restricted the scope of that decision.

After the Yates decision, many students of constitutional law felt that the Supreme Court would not sustain the provision in the Smith Act that makes it a crime to belong knowingly to an organization that advocates the violent overthrow of the government. But in *Scales* v. *United States* (1961), the Supreme Court, by a five-to-four vote, ruled that the membership clause is constitutional. It did so, however, after narrowly construing it to apply only if there is clear evidence that the accused "specifically intended to accomplish the aims of the organization by resort to violence. A person who joins the Communist party, however active he may be, may not be prosecuted under the membership provision unless there is proof that he joined with intent to bring about the overthrow of government as speedily as circumstances would permit." So construed, the membership provision of the Smith Act is even more limited in coverage than the advocacy provision and in essence can be applied only against those who are attempting to overthrow the government by force, activity that was made criminal long before the passage of the Smith Act.

From this brief survey of laws aimed at seditious advocacy, it seems clear that seditious speech when narrowly defined to cover only the advocacy of concrete acts of violence is not constitutionally protected. Such narrowly

[67]See Robert Mollan, "Smith Act Prosecutions: The Effect of the Dennis and Yates Decisions," *Univ. Pittsburgh Law Review* (1965).

construed antisedition acts leave Communists and other totalitarians free to work for their political objectives so long as they abandon force or its advocacy.

THE INTERNAL SECURITY ACT OF 1950

With increasing tension between the United States and the Soviet world in the late 1940s, many people pressed for even more stringent restrictions on Communist political activity than the Smith Act imposed. When the cold war turned into a hot one in Korea, Congress responded with the Internal Security Act of 1950, popularly known as the McCarran act. In addition to the as yet ineffective provision previously mentioned, which outlaws conspiratorial action designed to establish a totalitarian dictatorship in the United States, the Internal Security Act strengthened laws against espionage and sedition, added to alien registration requirements, made it more difficult for Communist aliens to enter or remain in the United States, and established procedures for detaining, in the event of a national emergency, any person who could "reasonably" be expected to engage in acts of sabotage or espionage. But the most significant parts of the act were the attempts to strip the veil of secrecy from Communist political activity and to impose certain disabilities on Communists.

The act created the Subversive Activities Control Board, which determines, on the request of the Attorney General, whether a particular organization is a Communist-action, Communist-front, or Communist-infiltrated organization, as defined by the act. A Communist-action organization, for example, is defined as one that is substantially directed by the U.S.S.R. or operates primarily to advance the objectives of world communism. After the Subversive Activities Control Board issues a final order declaring an organization to be a Communist organization and this order has been sustained by the courts, various disabilities and sanctions are imposed on the organization and its members. For example, Communist-action and -front organizations must submit information about printing equipment.

Eleven years after the adoption of the Internal Security Act, the Supreme Court sustained the findings of the Subversive Activities Control Board that the Communist party is indeed a Communist-action organization as defined by the act, and the Court upheld an order requiring the party to register under the act. But this decision has had little consequence because the Supreme Court has declared unconstitutional every attempt to implement the sanctions of the act. In 1965, by an eight-to-zero decision, the Supreme Court held that individual members of the party could not be forced to register because such registration would violate the self-incrimination provision of the Fifth Amendment. The immunity conferred by Congress in the act —that the mere fact of registration should not per se constitute a violation of a federal law or be received in evidence—did not preclude the use of the registration as an investigatory lead.[68] The official spokesman for the Communist party hailed the Court's decision as "vindication," but the decision caused little stir among most Americans. With its dwindling membership and

[68]*Albertson* v. *Subversive Activities Control Board* (1965).

old-fashioned Marxist war cries, the party seemed too weak to benefit much from the decisions.

The Supreme Court also declared unconstitutional a provision that made it a criminal offense for any member of a registered Communist organization to apply for or use a passport, regardless of the extent of his involvement in the affairs of the organization or his reason for going abroad. Such a sweeping provision, said the Supreme Court, "too broadly and indiscriminately transgresses" the liberty to travel, which is part of the liberty protected by the Fifth Amendment against unreasonable governmental interference.[69] A similar fate, this time by a vote of seven to two, befell a provision of the act making it unlawful for any member of a Communist-action organization to engage in any employment in any defense facility. This statute was declared unconstitutional because it trapped within its net persons who may be inactive members of a designated organization, are unaware of the organization's unlawful aims, and are working in a nonsensitive position. Thus it contained the "fatal defect of overbreadth because it seeks to bar employment both for association which may be proscribed and for association which may not be proscribed consistently with First Amendment rights."[70]

A generation after the adoption of the Internal Security Act its constitutionality and the effectiveness of most of its provisions remain highly questionable. Members of the Subversive Activities Control Board have had so little to do that serious questions have been raised in Congress about the wisdom of continuing to pay each of them $26,000 annually. In 1967, Congress tried to salvage the act: it established a procedure by which the Board itself would register with the Attorney General the names of persons the Board had determined to be members of registered Communist organizations; it revised some of the disabilities to be imposed on members of registered organizations; it authorized the Attorney General to grant persons immunity for the purposes of enforcing the act; and it stipulated that unless the Subversive Activities Control Board held a hearing before the end of 1968 it was to be disbanded. On July 1 of that year the Attorney General petitioned the SACB to enter orders declaring that seven persons named in the petition were members of the Communist party, which action had the effect of giving the SACB a new lease on life.

THE COMMUNIST CONTROL ACT OF 1954

The purpose of the Internal Security Act of 1950 was to bring Communists out into the open. But even before this act could be applied, Congress decided to take more drastic action. Although for some time there had been agitation to outlaw the Communist party and its successors, no action was taken until 1954, partly because of doubts about the constitutionality of such a measure, partly because of doubts about its effectiveness.

In 1954 Congress declared that even the overt political activities of the Communist party serve as a front behind which the party can seduce individuals into the service of world communism and work toward the violent overthrow of the government of the United States. (Such a conspiracy,

[69]*Aptheker* v. *Secretary of State* (1964).
[70]*United States* v. *Robel* (1967).

of course, is illegal; and evidence to support this finding, if properly presented in court proceedings, would be sufficient under existing law to throw the conspirators into jail.) The party's very existence, declared Congress, renders it a "clear, present, and continuing danger to the security of the United States." Therefore, in the Communist Control Act of 1954, Congress deprived the Communist party and its successors of "any of the rights, privileges, and immunities attendant upon legal bodies created under the laws of the United States" or any of the states.

The act does not make it a crime to be a Communist (although members of the party may be subjected to the penalties that the Internal Security Act imposes on members of Communist-action organizations). The major intent of the law is to deprive the Communist party of the right to seek places on election ballots for its candidates. For the first time in our history, the national government outlawed a political party and tried to deny some citizens the opportunity to use the traditional instruments of democracy to achieve their political goals. The act presents a variety of constitutional issues, but so far they have not been raised before the courts.

Disloyalty

Spies, saboteurs, and those who advocate the forceful overthrow of the government may be tried and punished under existing laws. But what about persons who commit no crimes and yet are sympathetic to the cause of communism, or who have joined organizations that the Attorney General believes to be subversive? Should they be permitted to work for the government, serve in the armed forces, secure passports?

J. Edgar Hoover estimated that there are less than ten thousand Communists in this country and perhaps ten times that many who are sympathetic to their cause. In order to forestall this group from securing public employment, receiving government-financed fellowships, joining the merchant marine, or working in defense plants, about twenty million Americans have been subjected to some kind of federal loyalty check. In addition, Congress and at least six state legislatures have established committees to investigate un-American activities. These committees have checked into the loyalty of public employees, newspapermen, teachers, scientists, and others and have "exposed" those whom the committee members believe to be un-American.

LOYALTY-SECURITY PROGRAMS

Since 1939, Communists, Nazis, and Fascists have been disqualified from federal employment. During World War II, all applicants for government jobs were carefully investigated, and access to classified and secret information was denied to all except those who had been cleared. Then in 1947 President Truman, responding to public concern over disclosures of Communist espionage, created by executive order the first comprehensive and systematic federal loyalty-security program.

This program, as modified by acts of Congress, presidential executive orders, and Supreme Court decisions, now requires an investigation of each applicant for a position in the federal executive branch, the extent of the investigation varying with the nature of the job for which he is being considered. The applicant will be denied employment if evidence is uncovered that he would not be a good security risk because of untrustworthiness, liability to blackmail, drunkenness, and so on.

Federal employees holding sensitive positions—those directly involving national security—may, under a 1950 act of Congress, be summarily dismissed if at any time evidence is uncovered that brings their security status into question. The employee is entitled to a hearing, but the government is under no legal obligation to disclose the name of his accusers or the precise nature and source of the information against him. President Eisenhower extended these procedures to cover all federal executive employees, but the Supreme Court ruled that Congress had intended to apply such drastic dismissal regulations only to persons holding "sensitive positions."[71] The government may dismiss others of its employees, however, under civil service regulations, but these regulations provide more safeguards for the rights of the "accused."

Congress has also been concerned with the loyalty of citizens who are not federal employees. It has created a security program for employees of defense contractors. At one time, students seeking federally supported scholarships or educational loans had to sign an affidavit that they were not disloyal. Because of the opposition of leading educators and the refusal of many universities to participate in this program, in 1962 Congress repealed this requirement. It has since substituted a law that makes it a federal crime for any student who belongs to a Communist organization to apply for or to hold a scholarship or loan supported by federal funds. Every enrollee in the Job Corps must take an oath swearing allegiance to the United States and any recipient of funds under the Economic Opportunity Act of 1964 must sign an affidavit that he does not believe in, teach, or belong to any organization that advocates the overthrow of the government by illegal or unconstitutional methods.

Although few positions occupied by state and local officials directly affect our national security, many states required loyalty oaths from public employees, and some even required oaths from attorneys, students in the state university, public accountants, occupants of public housing projects, and persons applying for unemployment compensation. One state included wrestlers and fighters on the grounds, according to the executive secretary of the state athletic commission, that "we didn't want to license a professional boxer or wrestler who might become a hero in the eyes of youthful fans and then discover he was a communist."[72]

Few people object to oaths requiring one to swear or to affirm loyalty to the United States as a condition of public employment, and there has been no serious constitutional objection to such positive oaths. But loyalty oaths that reverse the normal presumption of innocence and proceed on the as-

[71]*Cole* v. *Young* (1956).
[72]See testimony before Subcommittee on Constitutional Rights of the Senate Committee on the Judiciary, Hearings, *Security and Constitutional Rights*, 84th Cong., 2d Sess., November 17, 1955, p. 350.

sumption that one is disloyal unless he swears to the contrary have run into constitutional obstacles. The Supreme Court has agreed that a state may disqualify from public employment persons who are actively attempting to overthrow the state or the United States by force or violence, but a state has no right to set as a condition of public employment the abandonment by its employees of their constitutional rights of speech and association. For a while the Supreme Court sustained oath requirements, provided the oaths were restricted to foreswearing that one did not advocate the violent overthrow of the government or knowingly belong to any organization that did so advocate. But recently even these oaths have been declared unconstitutional, for they bring within their net persons who are members of an organization but who themselves do not necessarily participate in its unlawful activities or share its unlawful purposes.[73]

The Supreme Court has not, at least as yet, reversed an earlier decision sustaining the Hatch Act, which prevents most federal employees from engaging in any active way in the affairs of political parties.[74] Presumably, a state could also neutralize its civil servants in this way, but it may not single out one kind of political activity for proscription.

Although for the most part avoiding a direct ruling on constitutional matters, the Supreme Court has also narrowly construed the federal security laws and executive orders. It has been especially suspicious of those aspects of the security regulations that attempt to extend their coverage to nongovernmental employees such as defense-plant workers (see page 136).[75] In light of recent Supreme Court decisions, it is likely that the Supreme Court, if a case were properly presented, would invalidate or narrowly construe congressional enactments that condition private citizens' participation in federal programs on the filing of loyalty affidavits, as well as provisions that make it a crime for members of Communist-action organizations to apply for federal scholarships or loans.

DISLOYALTY AND DEMOCRACY

The McCarthyism hysteria that swept through the nation in the early 1950s has died down. (Whether there will be another such wave of anti-Communist hysteria following the Vietnam war remains to be seen.) It is doubtful whether all the investigating committees and loyalty oaths prevented a single act of sabotage or espionage. Whether they suppressed the growth of communism is more difficult to assess. That thousands of innocent persons were forced to answer questions and to prove their loyalty is clear. The government was allowed to judge loyalty on the basis of hearsay evidence. Frequently, neither the accused nor the board sifting the evidence knew where the charges came from or who the informants were. Sometimes the hearings went far afield: Not untypically, in one security hearing, a witness was asked, "Do you consider Mr. V— a religious man?" and "Was he an extremist on equality?" At another hearing, one of the charges against the

---

[73]*Whitehill* v. *Elkins* (1967); *Baggett* v. *Bullitt* (1964); *Elfbrandt* v. *Russell* (1966); *Keyishian* v. *Board of Regents* (1967).
[74]*United Public Workers* v. *Mitchell* (1947).
[75]*United States* v. *Archie Brown* (1965); *United States* v. *Robel* (1967).

person under investigation was that years ago he had attended a dinner of an organization that had since been cited as a Communist front, a dinner also attended by many Washington notables.[76] Unquestionably, the morale of civil servants suffered.[77]

Are loyalty-security programs necessary? Most citizens seem to believe that the tactics of Communists and the necessities of the cold war require unusual precautions to keep Communists and "politically unstable" persons out of such sensitive areas as the Central Intelligence Agency, Atomic Energy Commission, State Department, Defense Department, and other agencies concerned directly with national security. There is far less agreement on the need for intensive investigation into the beliefs and political actions of thousands of persons in nonsensitive positions in or out of government.

Some people feel that certain of these restrictions are unjustified. Although they would use every resource to ferret out and punish anyone guilty of espionage or conspiracy to overthrow the government by force, they would not penalize persons who have combined for political action or deny antidemocrats the right to use the regular methods of democratic government. These critics of governmental restrictions are moved, not by love for Communists, but by the conviction that democracy itself is endangered when any group is punished because its ideas are abhorrent to the majority. As the late Justice Jackson stated, ". . . the right of every American to equal treatment before the law is wrapped up in the same constitutional bundle with those of the Communists."

Those who support governmental limitations on Communist activity argue that the Communists are not entitled to any rights, because they are at war with our whole democratic system. They insist that the Communists, unless carefully controlled, will take advantage of their status as a legitimate political party to camouflage their underground activities. Only by denying Communists their veil of secrecy can innocent persons be protected. Democratic government, it is contended, must curtail the freedom of those who would destroy freedom.

All recognize that we must act to protect ourselves against those who are conspiring to destroy our democratic system. On the other hand, all recognize that we must be careful not to jeopardize the rights that we have developed in order to prevent the growth of tyranny. An undemocratic but relatively insignificant minority does not justify repression. In fact, it is in times of national peril that our traditional liberties must be most steadfastly strengthened and protected.

[76]See *Vitarelli* v. *Seaton* (1959) and *Greene* v. *McElroy* (1959).
[77]U.S. Commission on Organization of the Executive Branch of the Government, Task Force on Personnel and Civil Service (U.S. Government Printing Office, 1955), p. 121.

Equality under the Law

7   The Declaration of Independence proclaims in ringing terms, "We hold these truths to be self-evident, that all men are created equal, that they are endowed by their Creator with certain inalienable rights, that among these are life, liberty, and the pursuit of happiness. That to secure these rights, governments are instituted among men. . . ." The Declaration does not talk about the equality of white, Christian, or Anglo-Saxon men, but of *all* men. This creed of individual dignity and equality is older than our Declaration of Independence; its roots go back at least as far as the teachings of Judaism and Christianity. To act by this creed, to bring practice into conformity with principles, has long been a central preoccupation of Americans.

    No doubt it might make some sense to consider the safeguarding of civil rights as a function of government, one of the areas of public policy. Yet unlike other government functions, establishing civil rights policy has the fundamental character of establishing part of the Constitution. For what we are really talking about when we talk about civil rights is the question of whether black Americans (or Mexican Americans or American Indians) are to be given the constitutional rights and the educational and social opportunities to take full part in the political system created by the American Constitution.

    Certain liberties are essential to the operation of democratic government. But these liberties are not merely means of attaining self-government; they are ends in themselves. They exist not to protect the government; the government exists to protect them. Our forefathers called them natural rights—today we speak of human rights—but the belief is still the same, the belief in the moral primacy of men over government and in the dignity and worth of each individual.

"Our inability to achieve [an] . . . accommodation of racial differences has been our most conspicuous political failure."[1] Today no problem is more compelling than that of ensuring to every American his basic civil rights—his rights to enjoy his life and liberty and to pursue his happiness—without discrimination because of his race, religion, national origin, or any other irrelevant characteristic. American democracy, despite its many triumphs, has not extended civil rights to all people, especially not to Negroes. From the time he is born until he dies, a Negro suffers handicaps that no other American has to face; he is a victim of history. This lack of racial equality is an injury that every American must live with daily.

What should we do to protect civil rights? This question has been of significance in our presidential elections; it gives rise each year to battles in Congress and to debates in state legislatures and city councils. And what we do, or fail to do, has significance beyond our national borders. Our moral stand against tyranny throughout the world loses some of its force in the light of the obvious chinks in our democratic armor. Peoples in Asia and Africa—our potential allies—follow the treatment of American Negroes with more than casual interest. And it is not only the black people who are concerned, for all who hear us talk of democracy may lose faith in a government that denies in fact the very rights that it promises in theory. As Father Hesburgh, President of the University of Notre Dame and a member of the Civil Rights Commission, has said, "Americans might well wonder how we can legitimately combat communism when we practice so widely its central folly: utter disregard for the God-given spiritual rights, freedom and dignity of every human person."[2]

Our denial of equal rights not only negates the equality that the Declaration of Independence asserts—it is also contrary to the guarantees of the Constitution. For under the Constitution each person has the right to live and work and participate in public affairs, free of discrimination because of his race, religion, or national origin. The Constitution provides two ways of protecting these civil rights: first, by seeing to it that government itself imposes no discriminatory barriers; second, by granting the national and state governments authority to act positively to protect civil rights against interference by private individuals. In this chapter we shall be concerned with both these aspects, government as a *threat* to civil rights and government as the *protector* of civil rights.

To Secure Racial Justice—An Overview

In order to put into context the court decisions, laws, and other kinds of governmental action relating to civil rights, it may be useful to review briefly the accelerating drive to make real the promises of the Declara-

[1]Alan P. Grimes, *Equality in America: Religion, Race, and the Urban Majority* (Oxford Univ. Press, 1964), p. 41. See also John P. Roche, *The Quest for the Dream* (Macmillan, 1963).

[2]United States Commission on Civil Rights, *Civil Rights, Excerpts from the 1961 Report* (U.S. Government Printing Office, 1962), p. 100.

tion of Independence and the Constitution of the United States. For the civil rights crusade is not just a series of legal decisions and statutes, as important as they may be, but an involvement of the entire social, economic, and political system of the United States. Governmental action and reaction is as much the result as the cause of the civil rights movement.

The difficulty of resolving racial tensions and providing justice is not unique to this nation, for racial conflict and discrimination are probably the most divisive internal issues faced by any nation. But Americans have had a special confrontation with the problem—before, during, and after the Civil War. Because the North won that war, the Thirteenth, Fourteenth, and Fifteenth Amendments—to abolish slavery and all badges of servitude, and grant to Negroes all rights enjoyed by every other American—became part of the Constitution. Congress enacted a series of civil rights laws to enforce these promises and established special programs, such as the Freedman's Bureau, to provide educational and social services to the recently freed slaves.

But before these programs could have much significant impact, the political community of white Americans became reunited. By 1877, Northern political leaders abandoned Negroes to their fate at the hands of their former white masters. The President no longer concerned himself with the enforcement of civil rights laws, Congress ceased to enact new ones, and the Supreme Court either declared civil rights acts unconstitutional or so narrowly construed them that they were ineffective. The Court also gave such limited construction to the Thirteenth, Fourteenth, and Fifteenth Amendments as protections against racial discrimination that there ceased to be any effective limitation on the authority of the dominant white groups to drive Negroes from the political arena.

By the end of the century, white supremacy reigned unchallenged in the South, where most Negroes lived at the time. Despite the Constitution, blacks were kept from the polls, forced to accept menial jobs, and denied educational opportunities. In 1896 the Supreme Court, by an eight-to-one vote, gave constitutional sanction to governmentally imposed racial segregation (see page 150). Even if the Court had declared segregation unconstitutional at that time, a decision so contrary to popular feeling and political realities would have had little immediate impact. Negroes were considered by many whites, North and South, to be childlike. Southern political leaders openly and unapologetically espoused white supremacy. In 1896 one Negro was lynched every fifty to sixty hours on the average, and few citizens, black or white, raised a voice in protest.

During World War I blacks began to migrate to Northern cities, and by then there were small beginnings toward educational opportunities and jobs. These trends were accelerated by the New Deal and World War II. Also, the South, through urbanization and industrialization, became more like the rest of the nation. As the migration of Negroes out of the rural South into Southern and Northern cities shifted the racial composition of cities, the votes of Negroes became important in national elections. There were more jobs, more social gains. And above all, these changes created a Negro middle class to whom segregation as a symbol of servitude and a cause of inequality became a primary target. By the middle of the twentieth century urban Negroes were no longer passive recipients of white men's favors but active and

144 politically powerful citizens. There was a growing, persistent, and insistent demand for the abolition of color barriers.

The Presidency was the first branch of the national government to become sensitized to these growing pressures from black Americans. Because of the special nature of the electoral college and the pattern of our political system (see page 320), by the 1930s no man in the White House, or hoping to live there, could afford to ignore the aspirations of Negroes. The commitment of our Presidents to the cause of equal protection under the laws became translated into the appointment of federal judges more sympathetic to a construction of the Thirteenth, Fourteenth, and Fifteenth Amendments in the manner originally intended by those who proposed them.

By the 1930s Negroes started to resort to litigation to secure their rights, especially to challenge the doctrine of segregation as a sham and a device to impose discrimination. They emphasized legal action because at the time they had no alternatives; they lacked the political power to make their demands effective before either the state legislatures or the Congress.

By the 1950s civil rights litigation began to have its impact. Under the leadership of the Supreme Court, federal judges started to construe the Fourteenth Amendment to reverse earlier decisions that rendered it and federal legislation ineffective. The Supreme Court outlawed all forms of governmentally imposed racial segregation and struck down most of the devices that had been used so long by state and local authorities to keep Negroes from voting.[3] Also, Presidents were using their executive authority to end, or to attempt to end, segregation in the armed services and federal employment and were directing more of the resources of the Department of Justice to enforce whatever civil rights laws were available.

Finally, as the 1950s came to a close, the emerging national consensus in favor of positive governmental action to protect civil rights and the growing political voice of Negroes began to have their impact on Congress. Until then, the House of Representatives had frequently adopted civil rights bills, but the intense opposition of Southern Democrats and the indifference of many conservative Republicans, combined with Senate rules that gave an advantage to a determined minority, made it impossible to secure positive Senate action. In the 1956 elections, for the first time since the New Deal there was a substantial movement of Negro voters into the Republican column, especially in the cities. Neither party could consider the Negro vote "safe"; neither could ignore the demands of those urging civil rights legislation; neither wanted to be tagged as opposed to civil rights. Southern Democrats, though still powerful enough to force concessions, were no longer able to block all civil rights legislation. They had lost their allies in the border states, and, with the addition of Hawaii and Alaska there were four more votes for civil rights legislation in the Senate. Finally, in 1957, Congress overrode a Southern filibuster in the Senate and enacted the first civil rights law since Reconstruction. Again, in 1960, 1964, and 1968 came additional and significant civil rights legislation. By the end of the 1960s all branches of the national government, reflecting a widespread and politically strong national consensus, placed their weight behind those fighting racism.

[3]For a general history of Supreme Court decisions affecting the constitutional rights of Negroes, see Loren Miller, *The Petitioners* (Meridian Books, Inc., 1967).

By the 1960s the issues and the battles were changing. During the 1950s, the conflict had been seen primarily as an attempt to use the weight of national authority to compel white Southerners to cease using state governments to segregate Negroes into inferior schools, parks, libraries, houses, and jobs. The major effort was to put down determined and sustained Southern resistance to the Supreme Court's frontal attack on segregation in the schools. Representatives of the Deep South were trying to curb the Court. "No decision of the Supreme Court," said Senator (then Governor) Herman Talmadge of Georgia, "is entitled to any greater moral weight than its content merits." Southern state legislatures, dominated by members from small towns and rural areas where segregationist sentiments are most deep-seated, reached back to pre-Civil War precedents and asserted the right to "interpose" and resist the Supreme Court's mandates; some even claimed the right to declare the Court's decisions null and void. A host of organizations sprang up to fight for segregation. The more ardent segregationists insisted not only that school boards had no duty to obey the Supreme Court but that authorities should resist judicial decrees by every possible means. Although decrying force, they urged parents to barricade and boycott schools in order to keep Negro children from attending schools previously reserved for whites. When violence flared, attempts to use police and military forces to contain it were met with cries of "federal tyranny" and "police brutality," and sociological explanations were given to explain why otherwise good citizens found it necessary to use force to keep Negro children from attending desegregated schools.

At first, Negroes had to stand up to such resistance without much help from federal authorities. Only when law and order collapsed completely or when there was open defiance of the orders of federal judges did the President intervene. By the end of the 1960s this had changed. The Department of Justice, the President, and the Congress moved to compel compliance with desegregation. Resistance to it in the South still persists and is still widespread, but now the whole nature of the struggle to secure racial justice has altered.

1963 A TURNING POINT

A decade after the Supreme Court declared public school segregation to be unconstitutional, most Negro children in the South still attended segregated schools. Furthermore, in the North, segregation in housing and education remained the established pattern in the cities. Congress had enacted laws, judges had issued injunctions, Presidents had proclaimed executive orders and appointed commissions—so most legal barriers in the path of equal rights had fallen. But black Americans still could not buy a house where they wanted, secure the job they needed, find educational opportunities for their children, or walk secure in the knowledge that they would not be subjected to insults. And what had once been thought of as a Southern problem was recognized as a national problem.

By 1963 the struggles in the courtrooms were being supplemented by a massive social, economic, and political movement. What had been largely a conflict arousing the emotions and commitments of the more highly educated and economically secure Negroes suddenly gripped the feelings of thousands of men and women, from the domestic servant to the Nobel Prize winner.

The Negro revolt of 1963 did not come unannounced, and its immediate background did not stem directly from the struggle to desegregate the public schools. In one sense it began when the first Negro slave was educated 300 years ago, but its more immediate origin was in 1955 in Montogomery, Alabama, when the Negro community engaged in a boycott of the city buses to protest segregation on them. The boycott worked. And from the Montgomery incident the civil rights movement produced its first charismatic leader — the Reverend Martin Luther King, who, through his Southern Christian Leadership Conference and his doctrine of nonviolent resistance, provided a new dimension to the struggle for civil rights. By the early 1960s, new organizational resources to support and sponsor sit-ins, freedom rides, live-ins, and mass demonstrations came into existence in almost every city.

In the summer of 1963 the forces of social discontent created a national crisis. It started with a demonstration in Birmingham, Alabama, which was countered by the use of fire hoses, police dogs, and mass arrests, and culminated in a march in Washington, D.C., where over 100,000 people heard King speak of his dream of the day when children "will live in a nation where they will not be judged by the color of their skin, but by the content of their character." By the time the summer was over there was hardly a city that had not had a demonstration, protest, or sit-in; in many, there were riots. This direct action had some effect: civil rights ordinances were enacted in many cities and existing legislation broadened; more schools were desegregated that fall than in any year since 1956; and at the national level, President Kennedy made a dramatic address to the nation and urged Congress to enact a comprehensive civil rights bill. But Congress did not act.

Late in 1963, the nation's grief over the death of John Kennedy, who had become identified with civil rights goals, added political fuel to the drive for federal action. President Johnson gave the adoption of civil rights legislation the highest priority of his program. On July 2, 1964, after months of debate and the use of cloture to end a Southern filibuster in the Senate (see page 402), President Johnson signed the Civil Rights Act of 1964 into law. The enactment of the most comprehensive and forceful civil rights law in the nation's history marked the culmination of a long drive and the beginning of a new era in the civil rights struggle.

BLACK MILITANCY, BLACK AWARENESS, AND BLACK POWER[4]

At the close of the 1960s, the legal aspects of the civil rights movement had about come to a close. Restraints previously imposed on black Americans by the instruments of government used by white Americans had been more or less removed. But as "things got better," discontents became more

[4]The growing volume of literature in this area includes Stokely Carmichael and Charles Hamilton, *Black Power* (Random House, 1967); Nathan Wright, *Black Power and Urban Unrest* (Hawthorn, 1967); Charles Fager, *White Reflections on Black Power* (Erdmans, 1967); and Floyd Barbour, *The Black Power Revolt* (Porter Sargent, 1968).

intense. Once the chains of slavery began to be withdrawn, the stings that remained hurt more. When the blacks had been completely subjugated, they had lacked resources to defend themselves. But, as is true of almost all social revolutions, as conditions began to improve, demands became more and more insistent. And the millions of impoverished black Americans, like the white Americans who came before them, have demonstrated growing impatience with the discrimination that remains—the same frustrations that are now heard by the dispossessed around the world.

Many black Americans feel that changes are not coming large enough or soon enough. But many white Americans disagree. Some, though believing in equal rights, think that changes should be made not in the streets but in legislative chambers or that until Negroes secure education and social resources, they will be unable to profit from the opportunities presently available; others view direct action (lawlessness) as confirmation of their long-held view that the Negro must be "kept in his place." Black Americans have persisted in their pursuit of equal rights, and the attitudes between and within white and black America have hardened.

It is not surprising that this highly volatile situation should give way to racial violence and disorders. By 1965, the year of the Watts riots in Los Angeles, it was all too clear that disorders were becoming a part of the American scene. In 1966 and 1967 these disorders increased in scope and intensity, with the Detroit riot in July 1967 being the worst race riot in modern American history.

On July 27, 1967, President Johnson went on nationwide television to discuss the growing urban crisis. He announced the appointment of a special Advisory Commission on Civil Disorders to investigate the origins of the disorders and to recommend measures to prevent or contain such disasters in the future. "Not even the sternest police action," said the President, "nor the most effective Federal troops can ever create lasting peace in our cities." The President concluded:

> The only genuine, long-range solution for what has happened lies in an attack—mounted at every level—upon the conditions that breed despair and violence. All of us know what those conditions are: ignorance, discrimination, slums, poverty, disease, not enough jobs. We should attack these conditions—not because we are frightened by conflict, but because we are fired by conscience. We should attack them because there is simply no other way to achieve a decent and orderly society in America.

Illinois Governor Otto Kerner was appointed chairman of the Commission; Mayor Lindsay of New York, vice chairman. The single most characteristic feature of the eleven-man Commission was that both its black and white members were drawn from the "moderate and responsible establishment." Civil rights activists were quick to attack the Commission on this score and expressed particular displeasure that moderate Negro leaders such as Senator Edward Brooke and Roy Wilkins were appointed whereas more activist leaders such as Martin Luther King, Floyd McKissick, and Stokely Carmichael were left off.

Once the Commission issued its report, however, personalities faded into relative insignificance. The urgency with which it had gone about its work was underscored by its report's being issued in March 1968, four months before the date called for by the President. In stark, clear language, a unanimous Commission said,

> What white Americans have never fully understood—but what the Negro can never forget—is that white society is deeply implicated in the ghetto. *White institutions created it, white institutions maintain it, and white society condones it.*

TWO SOCIETIES?

The basic conclusion of the Commission was that "our nation is moving toward two societies, one black, one white—separate and unequal" and that "only a commitment to national action on an unprecedented scale" could stem this trend. National action, said the Commission, should be based on these objectives:

> Opening up opportunities to those who are restricted by racial segregation and discrimination, and eliminating all barriers to their choice of jobs, education and housing.
>
> Removing the frustration of powerlessness among the disadvantaged by explicitly helping them to deal with the problems that affect their own lives and by increasing the capacity of our public and private institutions to respond to these problems.
>
> Increasing communication across racial lines to destroy stereotypes, halt polarization, end distrust and hostility, and create common ground for efforts toward public order and social justice.[5]

To fulfill these objectives, the Commission made sweeping recommendations concerning employment, education, housing, and the welfare system.[6] Without doubt, these recommendations (and the racial crisis itself) present our political leaders with their greatest legislative challenge since the Great Depression.

Where do we stand at the moment? As legal barriers have been progressively lowered by civil rights legislation, the remaining restraints appear to be primarily economic and social. Not that there is general compliance with the legislation; ways are still found to thwart, circumvent, or obstruct altogether the full force of these laws. But what now appears to stand in the way of faster and more effective advancement by Negroes are lack of modern job skills, poor education, ghetto housing, and inadequate income. In line with the Kerner Commission proposals, future legislation is more likely to be aimed at creating programs to overcome these handicaps, which are the results of decades of discrimination and poverty. Manpower training, guaranteed annual income, food-stamp programs, support for ghetto schools, housing—these probably will be the civil rights issues of the 1970s.

Still, we must expect continuing friction and cleavage among black Americans, not only over means of achieving these goals but over ends as well. Some militant black Americans see violent direct action as the only way to get the system to respond; others believe that changes can be brought about

[5]*Report of the National Advisory Commission on Civil Disorders* (U.S. Government Printing Office, 1968).
[6]*Ibid.*, Chap. 17.

through peaceful direct action. In addition, black Americans differ over where such strategy and tactics should lead. Some—usually the more moderate—see integration of the races as the end; others—such as the Black Nationalists—see complete separation of the races as the only realistic solution. Still others see separation as a necessary stage to achieve "true" integration; they believe unity of black Americans to be the only way of achieving sufficient power to bargain with white America from a position of strength. But regardless of these differences over tactics and ultimate goals, the 1960s witnessed among all black Americans a growing pride in their own race, an awareness of their culture, and a desire to reject everything from the days of slavery and oppression.

Now that we have taken an overview of the development of intensification in the struggle for racial justice, let us backtrack and look more closely at the governmental responses and initiatives in the areas of segregation, voting justice, housing, employment, and public accommodations.

The Life—and Death—of Jim Crow

Laws requiring the segregation of blacks and whites date only from the end of the nineteenth century.[7] Prior to that time it was social custom and economic status, rather than law, that kept the two races apart. But segregationists began to insist that laws were needed to maintain racial segregation, and before long, Southern states and cities had made it a crime for whites and blacks to ride in the same car on a train, attend the same theater, or go to the same school. "Jim Crow" laws, as they came to be called, soon blanketed Southern life. How could these segregation laws be adopted and enforced in the face of the Fourteenth Amendment, which declares, "No state [including any subdivision thereof] shall . . . deny to any person within its jurisdiction the equal protection of the laws"?

Before turning to the question of the constitutionality of segregation laws, let us look briefly at the more general problem of the power of government to classify people. Most laws classify, but what the Constitution forbids is *unreasonable* classification. (Although there is no equal-protection clause limiting the national government, unreasonable classification on its part is made unconstitutional by the due-process clause of the Fifth Amendment.) A classification is unreasonable when there is no relation between the classes it creates and permissible governmental goals. For example, a law prohibiting redheads from voting would be unreasonable, because there is no relation between red hair and the ability to vote. On the other hand, laws denying to persons under twenty-one the right to vote, to marry without the permission of their parents, or to drive a car are reasonable because there seems to be a relationship (to most adults, at least) between maturity and voting, marrying, and driving. Similarly, the Supreme Court has held to be reasonable classification of persons on the basis of income for tax purposes and classification of property according to its use for zoning purposes.

[7]C. Vann Woodward, *The Strange Career of Jim Crow* (Oxford Univ. Press, 1955).

Classifications based on religion, national origin, and, especially, race, have caused great controversy, however. The courts have always been particularly suspicious of these classifications, allowing them only in the most unusual cases—when the government can demonstrate some exceptional justification and show some relation between race or religion or national origin and the permissible goal. Since the end of World War II, the Supreme Court has come pretty close to the view that *all* racial classifications are inherently arbitrary and unconstitutional.[8]

IS SEGREGATION DISCRIMINATION?—*Plessy* v. *Ferguson*

With the ratification of the Fourteenth Amendment and the abolition of slavery, it became unconstitutional for governments to discriminate against Negroes or any other racial or religious groups. But in 1896 the Supreme Court, in *Plessy* v. *Ferguson*, endorsed the view that racial segregation did not constitute discrimination and that states by law could require the separation of races in public places as long as equal accommodations were provided for all. Even equal accommodations were not required except for services provided by public funds or for a limited category of public utilities, such as trains and buses. Under this *separate-but-equal* formula, several states, most of which were in the South, enforced segregation in transportation, places of pulic accommodation, and education.

Perhaps the Plessy decision was forward-looking for its time, because it did require equality as the price for a state to adopt a program of compulsory segregation. But for many years the "equal" part of the formula was meaningless. States segregated Negroes into unequal facilities and Negroes lacked a political voice to protest. The Supreme Court did not help. In 1899, for example, the Court found no denial of equal protection in the fact that a county provided a high school for white citizens but none for the sixty black children in the district.[9] The passage of time did not lessen the inequality. In 1950, in all the segregated states, there were fourteen medical schools for whites, none for blacks; sixteen law schools for whites, five for blacks; fifteen engineering schools for whites, none for blacks; five dentistry schools for whites, none for blacks.

Beginning in the late 1930s Negroes started to file lawsuits challenging the separate-but-equal doctrine as a sham. They cited facts to show that in practice separate-but-equal always resulted in discrimination against Negroes. However, the Supreme Court was not yet willing to upset the doctrine directly. Rather, it began to undermine it. The Court began to scrutinize each situation and in case after case to order facilities to be equalized.

In 1950, the Supreme Court, though refusing either to affirm or to reject the doctrine of *Plessy* v. *Ferguson*, ruled (*Sweatt* v. *Painter*) that qualified Negroes could not be denied admission to state law schools. A segregated legal education, said the Court, was not and never could be made equal to a nonsegregated one. To segregate Negroes into schools from which the state

---

[8]See *Loving* v. *Virginia* (1967), where the Supreme Court held Virginia's ban on interracial marriages to be unconstitutional.

[9]*Cumming* v. *County Board of Education* (1899). See also J. W. Peltason, *Fifty-eight Lonely Men: Southern Federal Judges and School Desegregation* (Harcourt, Brace & World, 1961), p. 248.

excluded members of the white race—which included most of the lawyers, witnesses, jurors, judges, and other officials with whom the Negroes would be dealing when they became members of the bar—in itself discriminated against Negroes.

On the same day it handed down the decision in the Sweatt case, the Supreme Court held that once a state admitted a Negro to a graduate school, it could not segregate him within the school (*McLaurin* v. *Oklahoma*). Clearly, the legal underpinnings of segregation were getting shaky. If a state could not segregate within a school, could it do so between schools? If segregated legal education is always discriminatory, why would this not be the case for *all* kinds of education? Although for a while the Court continued to avoid a specific overruling of the separate-but-equal doctrine, no one could doubt the direction of its decisions.

THE END OF SEPARATE-BUT-EQUAL: *Brown* v. *Board of Education*

Finally, in 1952, the Supreme Court agreed to consider five cases that unhesitatingly challenged the separate-but-equal doctrine; the cases involved elementary and secondary schools. For two years the Court carefully considered the issues. By May 17, 1954, the last decision day before the end of the Court's term, no decision had been forthcoming. No one except the justices themselves knew if this would be the day the decision would be announced. But by 9 A.M., a capacity crowd had already formed.

At 11 A.M. the doors to the courtroom were opened, and the Chief Justice and his eight black-robed associates took their seats. For fifty-two minutes three justices took turns reading decisions. Then at 12:52 P.M., the Chief Justice picked up a printed document and began to read in a clear voice: "Does segregation of children in public schools solely on the basis of race, even though the physical facilities and other tangible factors may be equal, deprive the children of the minority group of equal educational opportunity? *We believe it does.*" Citing psychological findings as well as legal sources, the Chief Justice continued:

In these days it is doubtful that any child may reasonably be expected to succeed in life if he is denied the opportunity of an education. . . . To separate [children] from others of similar age and qualifications solely because of their race generates a feeling of inferiority as to their status in the community that may affect their hearts and minds in a way unlikely ever to be undone.

The Supreme Court justices, knowing their decision conflicted with long-established Southern customs and recognizing the formidable problems involved, postponed any final decree for a year. Then in May 1955, after hearing suggestions from state attorneys general, the High Court issued its implementation decree. The Supreme Court directed local school authorities to proceed "with all deliberate speed" to make a prompt and reasonable start toward admitting Negroes to public schools on a racially nondiscriminatory basis. The Court stated, however, that local officials could take time to make necessary administrative adjustments and need not desegregate schools immediately. The Supreme Court did not itself formulate precise instruc-

By Baldy; © 1966 by The New York Times Company; reprinted by permission.

". . . Sure we've complied, here's our Negro!"

tions, but rather returned the cases to the federal district judges (who could best take into account the great variety of local conditions) to supervise the implementation of desegregation by local school authorities.[10]

Following its rulings in the Brown case,[11] the Supreme Court struck down law after law requiring racial segregation. The overall view was that any kind of government action at any level and in any area that denies any person access to any facility because of his race is unconstitutional. And as the result of recent Supreme Court modifications of Brown, laws and regulations imposing racial classifications may not be constitutionally enforced even briefly during a transition period.

It was one thing for the Supreme Court to declare unconstitutional racial segregation in the public schools. It has been another to abolish such segregation. In the South, some school officials have tried to circumvent desegregation orders by such tactics as assigning pupils to segregated schools for reasons other than race, closing schools to which Negroes have been assigned, using the pretext of violence as justification for delaying action. In the North, racial segregation in housing has resulted in *de facto* segregation, with the result that black children are often crowded into the worst schools with the least resources.

The Supreme Court has stood firm. Eventually federal judges have struck down all the evasive schemes. In the Little Rock, Arkansas, case (*Cooper* v. *Aaron*, 1958), in an opinion signed by all members of the Court individually —an unprecedented move to indicate their unanimity and strength of conviction—the Court stated, "The constitutional rights of children not to be discriminated against in school admission on grounds of race or color . . . can neither be nullified openly and directly by state legislators or state executives or judicial officers, nor nullified indirectly by them through evasive schemes for segregation whether attempted ingeniously or ingenuously." Community opposition, even violent protests, said the Court, could not justify and delay: "Law and order are not . . . to be preserved by depriving the Negro children of their constitutional rights." In 1963, eight years after the Brown decision, the Supreme Court pointedly stated, "Given the extended time that has elapsed, it is far from clear that the mandates of the several Brown decisions . . . would today be fully satisfied by types or plans or programs for desegregation of public educational facilities which eight years ago might have

[10]*Brown* v. *Board of Education* (1955).
[11]Also known as the school segregation case.

153 been deemed sufficient."[12] Finally in 1968, the Supreme Court stated, "The time for more mere 'deliberate speed' has run out. . . . Delays in desegregating school systems are no longer tolerable. . . . The burden on a school board today is to come forward with a plan that promises realistically to work and promises realistically to work *now*."[13]

Since 1964, Negro plaintiffs and federal judges have had assistance in trying to abolish racial segregation, for the Civil Rights Act of 1964 authorized the Attorney General to take an active role in school-desegregation suits. On signed complaints and where he is satisfied that the aggrieved individuals are unable to initiate lawsuits because of lack of funds or because they may be subject to economic injury or physical harm, the Attorney General may initiate legal proceedings in behalf of the United States. No longer do Negro parents have to bear the full burden of securing compliance with the Constitution.

Of even greater significance is the use of the congressional power of the purse. The 1964 act authorizes the Office of Eduation to give technical and financial assistance to local school systems that request such help in order to desegregate their schools. The act also stipulates that federal funds—of major importance since the adoption of the Elementary and Secondary Education Act of 1965—will be withdrawn from any school district or public institution of higher education that refuses to desegregate. School desegregation is far from being an accomplished fact. But today school segregation is not only unconstitutional, it is fiscally costly and increasingly a political liability. It has become more trouble for many school boards to try to maintain segregation than to desegregate.

Color Bar at the Polls

The Constitution leaves to the states the power to determine suffrage qualifications, but states are subject to a variety of constitutional restraints in exercising this power. The Fourteenth Amendment forbids states to deprive any person of the equal protection of the laws and thus limits their power to establish discriminatory suffrage qualifications. For example, the Supreme Court (*Carrington* v. *Rash*, 1965) held that Texas violated this amendment when it prohibited "any member of the Armed Forces of the United States who moved to Texas from voting in any election." "The uniform of our country . . . must not be the badge of disfranchisement for the man or woman who wears it," the Court declared, and "a state may not fence out from the franchise a sector of the population for fear of how it will vote." Similarly, a state law that gave whites the right to vote but denied it to Negroes otherwise qualified would also violate the equal-protection clause, because racial classifications for voting are unreasonable. In addition to restricting a state's right to discriminate against Negro voters, the Fourteenth Amendment also authorizes Congress to enact any legislation necessary and proper to enforce the prohibitions of the amendment. Federal authority can

[12]*Watson* v. *Memphis* (1963).
[13]*Green* v. *County School Board of New Kent County, Virginia* (1968).

be used to prevent any kind of governmental action designed to keep Negroes from voting because of their race.

What the Fourteenth Amendment does implicitly, the Fifteenth does explicitly: "The right of citizens of the United States to vote shall not be denied or abridged by the United States or by any State on account of race, color, or previous condition of servitude." The Fifteenth Amendment also empowers Congress to enact any law necessary and proper to enforce the prohibitions of the amendment.

For over a decade after the Civil War, the provisions of the Fourteenth and Fifteenth Amendments were backed up by federal troops. Negroes, in alliance with Northern radical Republicans (carpetbaggers) and certain white Southerners (scalawags), assumed full control of some state governments. The new regimes passed good laws as well as bad, but they were loathed by "patriotic" white Southerners. Then came the counterrevolution. Even before federal troops were withdrawn from the South in 1877, white Democrats had begun to regain power. Organizing secret societies such as the Knights of the White Camellia and the Ku Klux Klan, the aroused Southerners set out to restore Southern government to white rule. Often they resorted to threats, force, and fraud, to midnight shootings, burnings, and whippings. Many Negroes concluded that it would be healthier to stay away from the polls than to insist on their vote, and the carpetbaggers began to retreat north.

CIRCUMVENTING THE FOURTEENTH
AND FIFTEENTH AMENDMENTS "LEGALLY"

Once they had regained control of Southern state governments, Southern Democrats resolved to continue to keep the Negro from voting. At first they continued to rely only on social pressures and threats of violence. But toward the end of the nineteenth century, for the first time since the Civil War, there were two strong political parties—the Democrats and the Populists—in many parts of the South. White supremacists were fearful that the parties might compete for the Negro's vote and that the Negro might come to have a balance-of-power role. To continue to rely on extra-legal and illegal means to disfranchise the Negro had disadvantages: It undermined the moral fabric of the society, and a too flagrant use of force and fraud might cause the President and Congress to intervene.[14] So white supremacists searched for "legal" means.

Southern leaders reasoned that if they could pass laws that, while ostensibly not denying Negroes the right to vote because of their race, deprived them of it on other grounds, the Negroes would find it difficult to challenge the laws in the courts. Some whites protested, saying that such laws could be used against whites as well as Negroes. But the likelihood that the laws would keep poor whites from voting did not disturb the conservative leaders of the Democratic party who were in control of some Southern states, for they were often just as anxious to undermine white support for the Populist party as they were to disfranchise Negroes. Leaders in the states where Ne-

[14]Frederic D. Ogden, *The Poll Tax in the South* (Univ. of Alabama Press, 1958), pp. 30–31.

groes constituted a large minority and sometimes even a majority skillfully played on memories of Negro rule and Northern intervention. "The disfranchisement movement of the 'nineties,'" said V. O. Key, "gave the southern states the most impressive systems of obstacles between the voter and the ballot box known to the democratic world.[15] And "The southern states show a kind of defense in depth against the would-be Negro voter," said Dayton McKean. "If one barrier falls before courts or legislature there is another behind it."[16]

The white primary. The Fourteenth and Fifteenth Amendments forbid states to deprive Negroes of the right to vote. But in the South, for most state and local offices the decisive political contests are the primary elections within the Democratic party (see Chapter 13); in most sections, Republicans are so scarce that the Democratic nominee is an easy winner. Obviously, exclusion of the Negro from the Democratic primary would deprive him of much influence in politics. So for many years the white primary was the most important disfranchising technique. The constitutional argument was that the primary was set up by a political party, not by the state, and a political party, as a voluntary association, had as much right to exclude people from its activities as did any social group.

Then in 1944 the Supreme Court, in *Smith* v. *Allwright*, took a realistic look at the white primary. It concluded that where primaries are an essential step in the selection of public officials they comprise a basic part of governmental machinery and that discrimination by the party is as unconstitutional as discrimination by the state. Some states tried to circumvent the Smith decision. South Carolina, for example, made party primaries completely private and repealed all its laws—147 of them—controlling party nominations. But the maneuver failed. A federal district judge held that if the state turned over the control of elections to a political party, the party is no longer a private club. "It is time," he said, "for South Carolina to rejoin the Union."[17] Other devices such as primaries before the primaries were also struck down by the courts as subterfuges.

Racial gerrymandering. In 1957 the Alabama legislature redefined the city limits of Tuskegee in such a way as to remove from the city all but four or five of the four hundred Negro voters. The legislature hoped to take advantage of the fact that heretofore federal courts had been unwilling to set aside election-district boundaries. But the Supreme Court (*Gomillion* v. *Lightfoot*) ruled that this racial gerrymandering so clearly violated the Fifteenth Amendment that the lower courts were instructed to set it aside.[18]

Rural overrepresentation. Urban Negroes, along with urban whites, were underrepresented in Southern state legislatures. In Southern cities many Negroes voted, but their votes, along with those of urban whites, had less of an

[15]V. O. Key, Jr., *Southern Politics* (Knopf, 1949), p. 555.
[16]Dayton D. McKean, *Party and Pressure Politics* (Houghton Mifflin, 1949), p. 66.
[17]*Brown* v. *Baskin* (1948) and *Terry* v. *Adams* (1953).
[18]See Bernard Taper, *Gomillion v. Lightfoot: The Tuskegee Gerrymander Case* (McGraw-Hill, 1962), for a detailed account.

impact on the legislature than those of the overrepresented rural and small-town white Southerners, the group most insistent on segregation and most opposed to extending to Negroes the right to vote. Until recently, there was no legal remedy to overcome this discrimination against urban voters in the determination of election districts.

Then in 1962, in *Baker* v. *Carr*, the Supreme Court ruled that federal judges have jurisdiction to hear complaints of voters who have arbitrarily been denied fair representation in state legislatures. Two years later, in *Reynolds* v. *Sims*, the Supreme Court held that both chambers of the legislature must be apportioned on the basis of population and that the only constitutionally valid standard for determining legislative representation is population. Although these decisions were not directly aimed at discrimination against black voters, by providing more equitable representation for urban voters, they have increased the voice of white moderates and black voters in the state legislatures.

The poll tax. The best known, though perhaps the least important, disfranchising device was a tax that placed a price tag on the ballot. Although the price was not high, its payment placed an additional obstacle in the path of the voter and opened the possibility of discrimination—white voters were sometimes not asked to show their poll-tax receipt; black voters always were. By the time the Twenty-fourth Amendment, forbidding the use of poll taxes to keep persons from voting in federal elections (see page 59), had been ratified and the Supreme Court, in *Harper* v. *Virginia* (1966), had construed the Fourteenth Amendment as forbidding poll taxes as a condition of voting in any election (see page 59), the tax was of little major significance in reducing suffrage—except perhaps in Alabama and Mississippi, where it probably kept the ballot from more whites than blacks.

Discriminatory applications of registration requirements such as literacy and understanding tests. As the white primary, poll taxes, racial gerrymandering, and other laws were declared unconstitutional, those wishing to deny Negroes the right to vote placed primary reliance on registration requirements. On the surface, these requirements appear to be perfectly proper. It is the manner in which they are administered that keeps Negroes from the polls, for they are often applied by white election officers while white policemen stand guard, and white judges hear appeals—if any—from decisions of registration officials.

Registration officials often seized on the smallest error in an application blank as an excuse to disqualify a voter. In one Louisiana parish, after four white voters filed affidavits in which they challenged the legality of the registration of Negro voters on the grounds that these voters had made an "error in spilling" (*sic*) in their applications, registration officials struck 1,300 out of approximately 1,500 Negro voters from the voting rolls.[19] In other instances, Negroes were denied the right to register because when stating their ages, they did not stipulate the precise number of days.

[19]*Report of the United States Commission on Civil Rights* (U.S. Government Printing Office, 1959), pp. 103–104.

Literacy tests have also been used to deny Negroes the right to vote. Most Southern states, as well as states elsewhere, require citizens wishing to register to demonstrate that they can read or write. Literacy tests, as such, are constitutional, but it is in their application that they are abused, for the registrars have wide discretion in determining who is literate and who is not.

Some Southern states, either as an additional requirement or as a substitute for literacy tests, required an applicant to demonstrate to the satisfaction of election officials that he understood the national and state constitutions and that he was a person of good character. Even more than literacy tests, these understanding tests encouraged discrimination against Negro voters. Whites may be asked simple questions about the Constitution; Negroes could be asked questions that would baffle a Supreme Court justice. In Louisiana, where illiterates were allowed to qualify to vote if they could pass an understanding test, 49,603 illiterate white voters were able to persuade election officials they could understand the Constitution, but only two Negroes were able to do so.

Intimidation. In recent years, through intervention of the Department of Justice, the white primary, the poll tax, racial gerrymandering, and the grosser forms of discrimination in registration are no longer so readily available to those attempting to keep Negroes from voting. But in some rural areas and small towns, intimidation and threats of physical violence are still used to persuade Negroes that they should not attempt to register and vote. Even these devices, however, are ceasing to be effective. With educated leadership and more cohesive organization, Negroes can no longer be easily intimidated, and those who try to break up Negro registration drives now know that their activities are likely to be exposed to the world via television, newsreels, and the press. Moreover, there is always the danger of federal intervention.

In summary, and in the words of President Johnson:

Every device of which human ingenuity is capable has been used to deny this right. The Negro citizen may go to register only to be told that the day is wrong, or the hour is late, or the official in charge is absent. And if he persists and if he manages to present himself to the registrar, he may be disqualified because he did not spell out his middle name or because he abbreviated a word on the application. And if he manages to fill out an application, he is given a test. The registrar is the sole judge of whether he passes this test. He may be asked to recite the entire constitution, or explain the most complex provisions of state laws. And even a college degree cannot be used to prove that he can read and write. For the fact is that the only way to pass these barriers is to show a white skin.

THE NATIONAL GOVERNMENT ACTS

Although for over twenty years federal courts, under the leadership of the Supreme Court, carefully scrutinized laws and procedures in cases brought by Negroes who had been denied the right to vote, this case-by-case procedure did not open the voting booth for millions of Negroes, especially those living in rural areas of the Deep South. As the United States Civil Rights Commission reported, "Suits must proceed in a single court at a time, and they are time consuming, expensive, and difficult. After one law or procedure is enjoined, the state or county would adopt another."[20] Faced with growing and insistent economic, social, and political pressures from Negroes and a growing national consensus that the right to vote should be guaranteed by the national government, since 1957 Congress has enacted civil rights laws that have progressively expanded the national government's role in securing the right to vote for Negroes.

The Civil Rights Acts of 1957 and 1960 still left the major responsibility to the courts. The Department of Justice was empowered to seek federal injunctions, and federal judges were authorized to hold prompt hearings. Appeals were allowed directly from these courts to the Supreme Court. Federal judges were permitted to appoint registrars to register Negro voters if, on application of the Attorney General, the judges found a persistent practice of discrimination to exist. Thus each Negro did not have to file a lawsuit in order to get a chance to vote.

In the Civil Rights Act of 1964, Congress took another step. Without going outside the courtroom framework, Congress strengthened the basic federal civil rights statute that applies to voting. The 1964 act (further strengthened by the Voting Rights Act of 1965) stipulates that no person shall be denied the right to vote because of inability to read or write in English if he demonstrates that he has successfully completed the equivalent of the sixth grade in an accredited school under the American flag. In elections in which federal officials are nominated or elected, oral literacy tests are prohibited, as is the denial of the right to vote because of irrelevant and minor errors or omissions on application forms. The American flag was stipulated by the 1965 Voting Rights Act in order to protect the right to vote of Puerto Ricans who have moved to the mainland, many of whom are not able to pass literacy tests given in English.

In 1965 the Supreme Court declared unconstitutional the use of understanding tests where voting registrars are given discretion to determine who has passed. The Court also ruled that a written citizenship test could not be substituted for an understanding test unless all voters, including those previously registered, are subject to the same test.[21]

The 1964 Civil Rights Act had hardly been enacted when events in Selma, Alabama, dramatically showed the inadequacy of dependence on the courts as the major federal instrument to prevent racial barriers in polling places. The voter registration drive in that city by Martin Luther King and his associates produced police arrests, further demonstrations, marches on the state capitol, and the murdering of two civil rights workers, but there was no major dent in the color bars at the polls. The Selma protests culminated in President Johnson's making a dramatic address to the nation and to the Congress in which he called for federal action to ensure to each person that he would not be deprived of his right to vote in any election for any office be-

---

[20]*Ibid.*, and United States Commission on Civil Rights, *Civil Rights, Excerpts* (U.S. Government Printing Office, 1961), p. 18.

[21]*Louisiana* v. *United States* (1965).

cause of the color of his skin. Congress responded with an even stronger measure.

THE VOTING RIGHTS ACT OF 1965

The Voting Rights Act of 1965 is a major departure from the approach of the prior civil rights acts, which depended first on legal action and then, after the lawsuit was over, on state and local officials to carry the court order into effect. The Voting Rights Act of 1965 authorizes direct action by federal executives to register voters and to see to it that these voters are allowed to cast their ballot and that their ballots are honestly counted.[22]

By 1965, discrimination against Negro voters was concentrated in about one hundred rural counties in Alabama, Florida, Georgia, Louisiana, Mississippi, North Carolina, South Carolina, and Tennessee.[23] The Voting Rights Act of 1965 concentrates on these areas. In states or political subdivisions in which less than 50 percent of the voting-age population was registered to vote on November 1, 1964, or actually voted in the 1964 presidential elections, and which required on that date a literacy, understanding, or good-character test, the Attorney General may, *without intervening court action,* order the suspension of such tests for five years and call upon the Civil Service Commission to appoint federal examiners. Outside the covered areas, the Attorney General must secure approval for the appointment of federal examiners or the suspension of such tests by carrying his complaint of voter discrimination to a federal court.

Federal examiners (and state and local officials) are to ignore literacy and other tests that have been used to discriminate against Negroes and make their own examination to see which voters are qualified under the laws of the state or political subdivision to which they are assigned. And to keep states from constantly changing voter requirements in order to prevent Negroes from registering, in the areas covered new voting laws are not to be effective for five years unless approved by the Attorney General or a three-judge district court for the District of Columbia. Each month, up to forty-five days before any election, federal examiners transmit to the appropriate election officials a list of voters they have determined are qualified to vote.

If election officials turn away from the polls any voter that the federal examiners have determined is entitled to vote, the examiners may go into a federal district court and secure an order impounding all the ballots until persons entitled to vote are allowed to do so. In addition, the Attorney General may appoint poll watchers to enter voting places to ensure that the votes of all qualified persons are properly counted. Existing criminal provisions of civil rights laws were also strengthened by making it a federal offense, punishable by five years in prison and a $5,000 fine, for anybody, private citizen or

[22]The constitutionality of the Voting Rights Act was upheld in *South Carolina* v. *Katzenbach* (1966).

[23]United States Commission on Civil Rights, *Civil Rights, op. cit.,* p. 15. See also H. D. Price, *The Negro and Southern Politics* (New York Univ. Press, 1957), and Margaret Price, *The Negro and the Ballot in the South* (Southern Regional Council, 1959).

public official, to intimidate or otherwise interfere with any person attempting to exercise his right to vote.

States or political subdivisions subject to the Voting Rights Act of 1965 may seek exemption from it only by proving to a three-judge district court for the District of Columbia that during the last five years they have not in fact kept Negroes from voting because of their race. It is significant that Congress placed this matter outside the jurisdiction of the federal district judges sitting in the states and subdivisions subject to the act. Some of the latter judges had shown an unwillingness in past legal proceedings to scrutinize carefully state and local regulations discriminating against Negro voters or to apply civil rights statutes with vigor.

What the Voting Rights Act of 1965 means is that federal authority displaces state authority over voting in the affected counties, and the federal government may enroll and protect the right to vote of all those who are qualified to do so. States still determine the qualifications for voting, but in areas where there is a long history of the use of state and local authority to violate the Fourteenth and Fifteenth Amendments, Congress has determined that the necessary and proper way to enforce these amendments is for the national government to step in and handle voter registration directly.

THE RESULTS

Just prior to the 1968 elections, three years after the Voting Rights Act was enacted, more than 1,280,000 Negroes had registered to vote in the eleven Southern states; thus, more than half the eligible Negroes are now registered in every Southern state. Federal voting examiners were sent to fifty-eight counties and were directly responsible for registration of 150,000 Negroes. The work of the federal examiners was especially effective when combined with voter-registration projects by such organizations as the Southern Regional Council. More than 1,000 Negroes sought state, local, and party office in the South, and almost 250 were elected to public office during 1967.

Although by the spring of 1968 there were almost 3 million registered black voters in the eleven Southern states and Negroes had become a significant part of the Southern electorate, in no state was the percentage of voting-age blacks registered equal to the percentage of voting-age whites registered (there were almost 15 million white voters). And there are still 185 counties in which less than 50 percent of the voting-age blacks are registered.

As the United States Civil Rights Commission reported, restraints on black voting and registration in most areas of the South appeared, for the moment, to be more economic and social than legal. But the struggle to remove the external restraints is not over. The Commission reported that in Alabama and Mississippi state legislatures and political party committees have adopted rules to dilute the votes of the newly enfranchised blacks. In some places, persons urging blacks to register and vote and working in behalf of black candidates were subject to harassment. The Civil Rights Act of 1968 specifically makes such harassment a serious federal crime (see page 163). The Commission also urged Congress to take a close look at the situation following the 1968 elections. If voting discrimination still persists, the Commission recommended that Congress revise the provision of the Voting Rights Act of 1965 that allows a state to restore literacy tests and other devices after August 6, 1970, if it can persuade a federal court that it has not used such tests for five years for discriminatory purposes.[24]

Clearly, the Negro vote has become an important factor, especially in Southern cities. It is especially important where the political situation does not become polarized around race, that is, where voters do not find race such a salient issue that all whites vote for only white candidates and all blacks vote for only black candidates. Except in local areas where blacks outnumber whites, the black minority is most likely to have the largest political impact where its votes can provide the margin of victory. In a growing number of areas and election contests, public officials no longer find that it is always politically profitable to be identified with the more extreme white supremacists.

In the North, black voting power is beginning to assert itself in practical politics. Northern urban centers have long had large concentrations of Negro voters, and with their numbers increasing — some to majority status — they are beginning to flex their political muscles. The election of black mayors in cities such as Cleveland, Ohio, and Gary, Indiana;[25] President Johnson's appointment of a Negro Mayor for Washington, D.C.; and the increase of Negroes in elective and appointive positions at the state and local levels generally — evidence the growing influence of black Americans in the American political process.

The Struggle for Color-blind Justice

Of all the sectors of the civil rights front, perhaps the most difficult to deal with by legislation, and the one in which the role of the national government was until recently the most limited, is the administration of justice. The Constitution reserves to the states the primary responsibility for finding, prosecuting, and convicting persons who violate the laws, with the national government's functions being chiefly restricted to enforcing federal laws and supervising action by the states to secure compliance with constitutional standards.

In the 1930s the Supreme Court started to use the Fourteenth Amendment to reverse convictions by state and local courts where there was evidence that Negroes failed to receive fair treatment. The Court could free black Americans who had been jailed unfairly, but this left untouched the police and prosecutors who had deprived Negroes of their rights. Although urged to pass protective federal legislation, Congress failed to do so. Nevertheless, President Roosevelt created a Civil Rights Section in the Department of Justice to do what it could to enforce the remnants of the civil rights laws still remaining from Reconstruction days. These were primarily two statutes:

[24]United States Civil Rights Commission, *Political Participation* (May 11, 1968).
[25]Jeffrey Hadden et al., "The Making of the Negro Mayors, 1967," *Trans-action* (January-February, 1968), pp. 21–30.

the Civil Rights Act of 1866 makes it a federal crime for any person acting under the color of law willfully to deprive any person of a right secured or protected by the Constitution: and the Civil Rights Act of 1870 (Ku Klux Klan law) makes it a federal offense for two or more persons to conspire to deprive a citizen from the enjoyment of any right or privilege secured to him by the Constitution or federal laws.

At first the Civil Rights Section found it difficult to enforce these laws. The 1870 act covering conspiracies by private citizens was so narrowly construed that it was seldom used, and to secure a conviction under the 1866 act of those acting under the color of law, it was necessary to prove that the officer willfully intended to deprive a person of his constitutional rights, not just that he generally had a bad intent. Trials in some instances had to be held before juries selected in accord with state practices. The Department of Justice was unable to sustain a conviction against Sheriff Claude M. Screws of Georgia, who, along with a deputy, fatally beat for fifteen to thirty minutes a handcuffed Negro prisoner with fists and a "solid-bar blackjack about eight inches long and weighing two pounds."[26] Even when convictions were obtained, the punishment was seldom more than a year's imprisonment.

Other than these criminal statutes, about the only other federal law that offered much help to Negroes in securing their rights was the Civil Rights Act of 1871, which opened federal courts to suits for damages and injunctions against officials alleged to have deprived persons of rights secured by the Constitution. Because this act provided for civil rather than criminal remedies, damages could be won and injunctions obtained without having to prove that the officers had a specific intent to deprive a person of his federally protected rights. Negroes, working mainly through the NAACP, have had some notable successes with the act of 1871, but private litigants often find it difficult to gather evidence and to challenge state and local authorities, and it could even be dangerous for them and for the lawyers who represent them. One white lawyer, for example, told the United States Commission on Civil Rights,

> I was born in North Carolina and raised in the hills of Eastern Tennessee, and I am in favor of the Civil Rights Statutes but must live with this as silent as the grave. I see my clients beat, abused and run over all of the time and there is nothing much I can do, because when I try in Federal Court I wind up with the hell beat out of me.[27]

The failure of state and local governments to apply justice evenhandedly, the murdering within a few years of dozens of civil rights leaders, the bombing of scores of homes, and the punishment of only a few persons for these acts have caused Congress gradually to enlarge the role of the Department of Justice. The Supreme Court has more broadly construed existing legislation[28] and, most importantly, has removed any doubts about Congress's constitutional authority to do whatever is necessary and proper to

---

[26]*Screws* v. *United States* (1945).

[27]*Report of the United States Commission on Civil Rights on Justice* (U.S. Government Printing Office, 1961), p. 69. Also see generally the Commission's *Report on Law Enforcement*, 1965.

[28]*United States* v. *Price* (1966) and *United States* v. *Guest* (1966).

protect persons against racial discrimination—whether imposed by state officials, local authorities, or private individuals.

FEDERAL INTERVENTION

In 1964 Congress authorized the Attorney General to intervene, whenever he thinks the case is of public importance, in any civil suit in which there is an allegation of the denial of equal protection of the laws. Using this authority, the Department of Justice has intervened in several major suits against school districts, both in the North and the South, and in a few instances, against authorities of an entire state. Then, as part of the Civil Rights Act of 1968, Congress adopted specific federal criminal legislation to protect persons in the exercise of their civil rights against injury, intimidation, or interference either by private individuals or public officials. Under this act, it is now a crime to interfere with or attempt to interfere with or injure any person because he is voting or campaigning in any election, serving on a federal jury, working for a federal agency, or participating in any federal or federally assisted program. It is also a federal crime to interfere with or injure or intimidate any person because of his race, color, or religion, because he is attending a public school, working for any employer, serving on a state jury, or using a common carrier or public accommodation. Also protected under the law are persons who are trying to encourage or help persons secure these civil rights. Law officers are exempt from the act only during the course of their duties for actions to suppress a riot or a civil disorder. Commission of any of the acts interdicted by the federal law is also a violation of state law, so Congress limited federal prosecutions to those instances when the Attorney General certifies in writing that federal prosecution is in the public interest and necessary to secure substantial justice—thus the federal authorities will not act if the state does. Also, Congress provided for uniform provisions that should avoid any discrimination in the selection of federal juries.

The Civil Rights Act of 1968 has further strengthened the Justice Department's authority to protect constitutional rights and to act against racially motivated crimes. The Department's more active role has already had an impact; it has alerted state and local officers to the fact that they violate at their own peril the rights and privileges protected by the Constitution. But as the Civil Rights Commission has reported, "Little can be done directly to prevent police brutality itself until the police are more carefully selected, trained and controlled."[29]

THE "NEW" THIRTEENTH AMENDMENT

The Thirteenth Amendment, unlike the Fourteenth, applies to all persons and not just to those acting under the color of law . By its own force it prevents all forms of involuntary servitude. It also empowers Congress to pass whatever laws are necessary and proper to prevent slavery or involuntary servitude. For a hundred years, some people, including the first Justice

[29]*Report of the United States Commission on Civil Rights on Justice, op. cit.,* p. 9.

Harlan, have argued that the Thirteenth Amendment gave Congress the authority to legislate against all the badges of slavery, that is, against racial discrimination in all its forms, regardless of its source. But the Supreme Court construed the Thirteenth Amendment narrowly so that slavery would mean only physical compulsion or peonage (a condition of compulsory servitude based on indebtedness of the worker to the employer). Thus, it was held that Congress received no power from the Thirteenth Amendment to legislate against racial discrimination.

Then, in *Jones* v. *Mayers* (1968), Justice Stewart, speaking for a seven-man majority, adopted the view of the first Justice Harlan (his grandson, the present Justice Harlan, dissented). The immediate question before the Court was the meaning and constitutionality of an 1866 housing act. Justice Stewart, stating that the Thirteenth Amendment became part of the Constitution so that Congress could have the power to remove the "badges of slavery" from the nation, declared that discrimination against Negroes in the sale of housing, whether resulting from private or public actions, is such a badge of slavery.

Jones v. *Mayers* dealt only with discrimination in housing. It remains to be seen if the Supreme Court will stand with and expand this new meaning of the Thirteenth Amendment. Nevertheless, the ruling was highly significant and should set to rest any questions about Congress's authority to do whatever is necessary and proper to ensure that all persons within the jurisdiction of the United States secure equal justice and fair treatment in the administration of justice, and that all persons have ample protection from suffering any disabilities because of any condition of previous servitude of their father or grandfather. Doubtless there will be growing pressure on Congress to exercise its powers and to expand the federal role if state and local governments continue to fail to apply justice even-handedly or if they allow persons to go unpunished for intimidating or murdering blacks and whites trying to help Negroes secure their civil rights.

The Color Bar to Homes, Jobs, and Public Accommodations

Until recently, those who wanted to keep blacks from buying homes or eating lunch in the same stores or working in the same plants with white persons could use the power of government to enforce these discriminatory practices. Laws and regulations that interfere with equal access to homes, jobs, or public accommodations are now unconstitutional. Yet Negroes still have difficulty buying homes, getting jobs, or securing service in public places. Such discriminatory action by private individuals does not violate the Fourteenth Amendment, which only forbids discrimination by *states* including, of course, all units of the states. Unless discrimination is openly sanctioned or supported by the state, the Fourteenth Amendment offers the victim no protection or redress at all.

In recent decades, however, the Supreme Court has significantly expanded the concept of state action in support of discrimination. For example, it has ruled that though there is nothing unconstitutional about making or signing racially restrictive covenants (provisions attached to deeds restricting the sale or use of property to certain groups), court enforcement of such covenants is state action and therefore unconstitutional.[30] It has also held that trade unions whose right to engage in collective bargaining is protected by the government may not discriminate[31] and that those who lease space in public buildings to operate restaurants are subject to the Fourteenth Amendment prohibitions against state discrimination.[32] And, as we have seen, the Court has come very close to the position that the holding and conduct of elections in which public officials are nominated or elected is a governmental function and hence whoever discharges these functions is restrained by the Constitution.

Furthermore, in *Jones* v. *Mayers*, the Supreme Court hinted somewhat broadly that the whole doctrine of state action may lose its significance. If the Thirteenth Amendment, which covers private as well as state action, becomes construed by its own force to prohibit racial discrimination, there will be little need to sustain a federal lawsuit to show state involvement in the discriminatory conduct.

A more difficult constitutional issue grew out of the arrest for trespassing of Negroes who, to protest denial of service, sat in at lunch counters and other facilities that were privately owned but open to the public. Some people contended that arrest by the police and conviction by the state courts would be an unconstitutional use of state power to support discrimination. Others argued that if owners of privately owned businesses wished to refuse service to Negroes, the state could protect their right to do so. The Supreme Court had no difficulty in deciding that if state laws or actions forced the operator of a place of public accommodation to refuse nonsegregated service to Negroes, a state could not prosecute persons for peacefully attempting to secure their rights. What would happen in a community where there is no governmental pressure on the place of public accommodation to discriminate is a question that is not likely to come up, for with the passage of the Civil Rights Act of 1964 (see page 167) few businesses any longer have a legal right to discriminate against their customers because of race.

STATE CIVIL RIGHTS PROGRAMS

Although private acts of discrimination may not be unconstitutional, they may be illegal. Just as the states have the authority to protect a person's property rights against infringement by others, so they have the authority to protect his civil rights. And so does the national government (as noted below).

Should governments use their powers to make it illegal for landlords, employers, trade unions, private schools, and others to discriminate against persons because of their race or religion? No, say some people; prejudice cannot be eradicated by laws. Others respond that if laws cannot eradicate prejudice itself, they can eliminate the overt discriminatory action that de-

[30]*Shelley* v. *Kraemer* (1948) and *Barrows* v. *Jackson* (1953).
[31]*Conley* v. *Gibson* (1957).
[32]*Burton* v. *Wilmington Parking Authority* (1961).

prives people of their right to be treated as human beings and American citizens.

In the South, as we have noted, state laws require segregation, and they are still being enforced despite their unconstitutionality. But other states *outlaw* segregation and other kinds of racial or religious discrimination.[33] Discrimination by owners and operators of places of public recreation and accommodation has long been a tort (civil wrong) under the common law, and most states have special statutes making it a criminal or civil offense for places of public accommodation to refuse to serve patrons because of their race, religion, or place of national origin. In addition, many states have adopted fair-employment laws to combat discrimination in employment. Some states have made it illegal for university authorities to discriminate racially or religiously against students seeking to enter colleges or universities, except, of course, in the case of church-operated schools. Some cities forbid landlords to discriminate. Almost all states forbid discrimination in public employment.

The weakness of some of these civil rights statutes is that they make no special provision for enforcement other than by regular court action instituted by public prosecutors or through the initiation of law suits by the person being discriminated against. Frequently, the persons who are denied a job or service have neither the knowledge to bring the matter to the attention of prosecutors nor the money to undertake a civil suit. Moreover, many prosecutors have been somewhat less than eager to take action.

The ineffectiveness of criminal laws against discrimination and of dependence on damage suits brought by the aggrieved persons has led to a new development in the enforcement of civil rights.[34] In 1945 New York State created a commission charged with investigating and hearing complaints in instances of alleged discrimination, and since then eighteen additional states and numerous cities have established such special civil rights commissions with the exclusive duty of acting against discrimination.

The New York procedures are typical. The Commission for Human Rights is responsible for enforcing the state laws forbidding racial, religious, and national-origin discrimination by employers, labor unions, places of public accommodation, and governmentally aided housing projects. (Laws covering discrimination in educational institutions are enforced by the Commissioner of Education and Board of Regents.) Any person suffering such discrimination may file a complaint with the commission. If, after investigation, the commission finds the complaint is justified, it first tries to remove the cause through "conference, conciliation, and persuasion." If these efforts fail, a formal hearing takes place before at least three members of the commission. If the commission discovers evidence of violation of the law, it orders the offender to cease and desist from such practices. Violation of a Commission order is punishable by imprisonment for not more than one year or by a fine

[33]See Joseph B. Robinson and Barbara Flicker, "Summary of 1964 and 1965 State Anti-Discrimination Laws," *Law in Transition Quarterly* (Spring 1966), pp. 94–134.

[34]"Anti-Discrimination Commissions," *Race Relations Law Reporter,* (Vanderbilt Univ. School of Law, October 1958), pp. 1085–1108; *Summary of 1960 and 1961 State Discrimination Laws* (Commission on Law and Social Justice of American Jewish Congress, 1962). See generally Duane Lockard, *Toward Equal Opportunity: A Study of State and Local Antidiscrimination Laws* (Macmillan, 1968).

of not more than $500 or both. The courts may review decisions of the commission on questions of law. The Commission has seldom had to resort to its coercive powers, and through a program of education and publicity it has done much to improve human relations in this most difficult of all fields.

NATIONAL PROTECTION
AGAINST PRIVATE DISCRIMINATION

What of the national government? It was the hope of some of the congressmen who proposed the Fourteenth Amendment that its ratification would authorize federal action against nongovernmental discrimination, so in 1875 Congress made it a federal offense for any owner or operator of a public conveyance, hotel, or theater to deny accommodations to any person because of his race or color. But in the *Civil Rights Cases* (1883), the Supreme Court invalidated this law on the ground that the Fourteenth Amendment applies only to state action and does not give Congress authority to forbid discrimination by private individuals. The *Civil Rights Cases* brought to a temporary halt federal protection against nongovernmentally imposed discrimination. By 1883 Congress had ceased to have any interest in such laws, and the matter was left to the states. The trouble was that the states where most of the discrimination took place did nothing.

Since the 1940s Presidents have used their executive authority to extend civil rights. President Roosevelt ordered all contractors and subcontractors of the federal government not to discriminate against any employee or applicant for employment because of race, religion, color, or national origin. Today, the Secretary of Labor supervises a vigorous program to ensure compliance by several million government contractors. President Truman ordered the end of discrimination in federal employment and the abolition of segregation in the armed forces. President Kennedy signed an order to prevent federal funds from being used to support housing programs that are not available to Negroes. The Interstate Commerce Commission and the Civil Aeronautics Board ordered interstate carriers to cease segregating their passengers. But these actions have been swallowed in significance by the adoption of the Civil Rights Act of 1964.

PLACES OF PUBLIC ACCOMMODATION

For the first time since Reconstruction, Congress, through the Civil Rights Act of 1964, authorized the massive use of federal authority to combat privately imposed racial discrimination. Title II forbids discrimination in places of accommodation and makes it a federal offense to discriminate against any customer or patron because of his race, color, religion, or national origin. It applies to any inn, hotel, motel, or lodging establishment (except establishments with less than five rooms and occupied by the proprietor—in other words, small boarding houses); to any restaurant or gasoline station that offers to serve interstate travelers or serves food or products of which a substantial portion have moved in interstate commerce; and to any motion picture house, theater, concert hall, sports arena, or other place of entertainment that customarily presents films, performances, athletic teams, or other sources of entertainment that are moved in interstate commerce. Title II also applies to any establishment that attempts to discriminate or segregate in response to state law or order of any public official.

The Attorney General may initiate proceedings as well as intervene in cases initiated by aggrieved individuals. States with laws against discrimination in places of public accommodation are given thirty days to see if they can bring about compliance. Federal judges may refer complaints to the Community Relations Service (see page 171) in order to seek voluntary compliance. But if these procedures fail, judges are to provide prompt hearings with direct appeals to the Supreme Court whenever the Attorney General believes the case is of general public importance.

Within a few months of the enactment of Title II, the Supreme Court unanimously sustained its constitutionality (*Heart of Atlanta Motel* v. *United States*, 1964): "That Congress was legislating against moral wrongs . . . does not detract from the overwhelming evidence of the disruptive effect that racial discrimination has had on commercial intercourse." Nor does it matter that a particular motel may be considered primarily a local business. The Court had before it evidence that Negroes were unable to engage freely in interstate travel because of denial to them of facilities to eat, sleep, and purchase supplies. "If it is interstate commerce that feels the pinch, it does not matter how local the operation that applies the squeeze."

Faced with the adoption of Title II, the determination of the Department of Justice to enforce it, and an organized program of testing by Negroes to publicize lack of compliances, most larger establishments in most cities, including those in the South, have opened their doors to all customers. Smaller establishments, especially those in the rural South, still have not done so and are not likely to do so until legal, economic, and social pressures are brought to bear on them directly.

EMPLOYMENT

Title VII of the Civil Rights Act of 1964 makes it an unfair employment practice for any employer or trade union in any industry affecting interstate commerce to discriminate in any fashion or to segregate any person because of race, color, religion, sex, age, or national origin. (Religious institutions such as schools may use religious standards, and exceptions to the ban against discrimination may be made because of religion, sex, age, or national origin when there are bona fide occupational qualifications reasonably necessary to the normal operation of a particular business or enterprise. For example, it is not an unlawful employment practice for an employer to refuse to hire a woman to perform a job that requires unusual physical strength.) The law covers employers or unions with twenty-five or more employees or members.

Employers and trade unions subject to the act are required to keep records and make them available to federal authorities and to take whatever steps are necessary to bring about nondiscriminatory hirings. The Equal Employment Opportunity Commission, consisting of five members appointed by the President with the consent of the Senate, has overall responsibility for bringing about compliance. The commission is instructed to work with state authorities and to use conciliation and persuasion wherever possible. The commission may not itself order an employer or trade union to comply, but if it fails to persuade, those who have been discriminated against and the Attorney General may bring civil suits in the federal courts. If the Attorney General feels that a firm or trade union is engaged in a willful and persistent pattern of resistance, he may request a prompt hearing before a three-judge federal court from which direct appeals to the Supreme Court are possible.

The chief effect of the Civil Rights Act of 1964 has been that companies have developed more programs and policies designed to eliminate discrimination in employment; but the actual impact of the act, up to this time at least, has not been very great.[35] Many believe that until the Commission is given enforcement authority, its impact will be limited. Nevertheless, in recent years there has been a substantial gain in employment on a nondiscriminatory basis. At the moment, the chief barriers seem to be those imposed by some unions and by employers in nonindustrial areas.

DISCRIMINATION IN HOUSING: THE CIVIL RIGHTS ACT OF 1968 AND THE DISCOVERY OF THE ACT OF 1866

Discrimination in housing has remained one of the most intractable of our social problems and, in turn, has had an impact on school desegregation and the isolation of black Americans from the suburbs. Residential segregation results not from the use of governmental power to force segregated housing but from the refusal of lending agencies, brokerage agencies, and owners and operators of houses and apartments to allow Negroes to rent or buy homes for their families except within certain restricted areas.

In 1948, the Supreme Court (*Shelley* v. *Kraemer*) held that the judges of the land would no longer enforce racial restrictive covenants. And in 1962 President Kennedy ordered the Federal Housing Administration, the Veterans Administration, and other federal housing authorities to cease making federal funds or help available to any project that was operated on a segregated basis. Yet most of the nation's housing was still denied to black Americans, and they had to pay more for what was available.

President Johnson urged Congress to enact legislation to prohibit discrimination in the sale or rental of housing, and in 1968 Congress, after overcoming a filibuster in the Senate, enacted the Civil Rights Act of 1968. The act covers 80 percent of all housing for rent or sale, exempting from its coverage only private individuals owning not more than three houses who sell or rent their houses without the services of a real estate agent and who do not indicate any preference or discrimination in their advertising; dwellings that have no more than four separate living units in which the owner maintains a residence (the so-called Mrs. Murphy boarding houses); and religious organizations and private clubs housing their own members on a noncommercial basis. For all other housing, the Civil Rights Act proscribes the refusal to sell or rent to any person because of his race, color, religion, or national origin. No discriminatory advertising is to be permitted and so-called blockbusting techniques — that is, attempts to persuade persons to sell or rent a dwelling

---

[35]See Fred Luthans, "The Impact of the Civil Rights Act on Employment Policies and Programs," *Labor Law Journal* (June 1968), pp. 323–328.

by representing that Negroes, or any other racial or religious group, are about to come into the neighborhood—are outlawed. Real estate brokers and lending institutions are also prohibited from discriminatory practices.

The Civil Rights Act of 1968 depends for its enforcement primarily on the injured person; he must file a complaint with the Secretary of the Department of Housing and Urban Development. If this fails to bring action, he may file a suit in any court for injunctive relief. The Attorney General may initiate action, however, whenever he finds a pattern of discrimination of public importance. The only criminal provisions of the act cover those who interfere with any person's attempting to comply with the act or secure his rights under it.

The Civil Rights Act of 1968 had not even had time to become effective when the Supreme Court handed down a ruling concerning housing in *Jones* v. *Mayers* (1968). Mr. and Mrs. Jones had filed a complaint three years before against a housing development in St. Louis that had refused to sell them a home because Mr. Jones was a Negro. At that time few people thought they had much chance to win their case. Congress had enacted no civil rights laws to cover housing since the moribund act of 1866, and even if it did, there was some doubt about its power to make discrimination by private persons a federal offense. Even if the Joneses won, it was assumed the Supreme Court would base its decision on state involvement in the discrimination because of the financial support the state had given to the developer.

The Joneses cited the Civil Rights Act of 1866, which read, "All citizens of the United States shall have the same right, in every state and territory, as is enjoyed by white citizens thereof to inherit, purchase, lease, sell, hold, and convey real and personal property." Because of the Supreme Court's long-standing requirement of state action to bring the Fourteenth Amendment into play and its narrow construction of the Thirteenth, the 1866 act had been more or less forgotten. But the Supreme Court sustained the Joneses' petition and ruled that the Congress of 1866 meant what it had said and that the Thirteenth Amendment gave Congress ample authority to enact the law. How did the Court reconcile the fact that only a few months before, in the Civil Rights Act of 1968, Congress adopted legislation to cover discrimination in housing with more limited coverage than the act of 1866? The Supreme Court argued that the two acts reinforce each other—the 1968 act provides remedies to enforce the 1866 act.

THE FEDERAL PRESENCE AND CIVIL RIGHTS

The recently expanded involvement of the national government in the field of civil rights has produced many different agencies with responsibilities in this field. In addition to those previously mentioned, the more prominent of these federal civil rights agencies are:

United States Commission on Civil Rights. Created by the Civil Rights Act of 1957 and consisting of six national leaders, the Commission serves as a national clearing house. Its public hearings and reports to the Congress have focused national and congressional attention on the more flagrant violations of civil rights, and its recommendations have had a major impact on congressional legislation and executive actions.

Community Relations Service. Created by the Civil Rights Act of 1964, it serves as a conciliation service working with community leaders when conflict between the races has shown the lack of any local machinery to bring leaders from both races together. Federal courts also refer to the service complaints presented by lawsuits to desegregate public accommodations in order to see if voluntary compliance can be obtained.

There are dozens of other civil rights agencies. In addition, Title VI of the Civil Rights Act of 1964 directs

each federal department and agency which is empowered to extend federal financial assistance to any program or activity, by way of grant, loan, or contract to take the necessary action to insure that no person in the United States shall, on the ground of race, color, or national origin, be excluded from participation in, be denied the benefits of, or be subject to discrimination under any program or activity receiving Federal financial assistance.

Though sometimes overlooked in discussions of federal civil rights activities, the Economic Opportunity Act of 1964 may prove to be the most important federal civil rights program. This act and other antipoverty programs provide federal funds and technical assistance to states, local communities, and private agencies to support a variety of programs to motivate individuals and provide them with job skills. Negroes more than any other group have felt the impact of technological change that has made large numbers of unskilled jobs obsolete. Discriminated against, forced into urban ghettos, and suffering from the social ills of all groups that have been subjected to these conditions, many Negroes are unable to take advantage of the opportunities for employment that are progressively being made available to them. Through the programs provided under the Economic Opportunity Act, many will be given training and counseling to develop the attitudes, skills, and ambitions that will permit them to break out of the vicious cycle of discrimination and poverty.

Conclusion

It is easy to get lost in the maze of federal and state civil rights laws, to become confused by the refined distinctions made in courts of law, and to perceive the struggle to secure civil rights as one involving only constitutional and legal questions. But we are what we are, and the laws and constitutional provisions are what they are, because of a complicated interaction among social, economic, legal, and political developments.[36]

The federal presence in civil rights was a long time in coming. As we have seen, after the Civil War the federal government tried briefly to secure for the recently freed slaves some measure of protection. But Negroes were

[36]Grimes, *op. cit.*, pp. 41–85.

largely uneducated, illiterate, and completely dependent on the white community. Moreover, they were an insignificant political force. In 1877 the federal government withdrew from the field and left the blacks to their own resources. For decades, Negroes did not count politically or economically or socially, and, as a result, they were segregated and discriminated against.

At the end of World War II, the nation began a national debate over civil rights. Negro leaders and others urged Congress to adopt federal laws to protect civil rights. But white Southerners and many others contended that federal civil rights laws would upset the federal system and lead to a dangerous centralization of power. They insisted that national legislation would be ineffective and create more problems than it solved. A national program could not be enforced if it overrode local public opinion, they contended. Let the states do the job, for they can protect civil rights by laws adapted to the attitudes of the local citizenry. Anyway, they added, "you can't legislate morality."

Champions of national action argued that states had failed to protect civil rights and that, in fact, in many areas the state governments themselves were the major instruments of discrimination. Furthermore, the denial of civil rights is not merely a local matter, for it has national and international implications. The Constitution promises to every person who lives in the United States equal treatment before the law without respect to his race, religion, or national origin, and it is up to the national government to see that this promise is kept. Whatever the speculative merits of local rather than national action, as a matter of practical political fact, civil rights will be extended only by the national majority using the power of the national government. For, as one white Southerner has noted, "not one concrete step toward full rights for the southern Negro—whether in voting or education—has been achieved without the intervention of the national government."[37] By the end of the 1950s, the debate over whether the national government had a responsibility to protect civil rights was over. The question became, What should it do?

By the eve of the 1970s, discrimination had become a tougher challenge to American liberals than to conservatives. Black and white militants were challenging not just the defense of the *status quo* but the liberal pluralist value structure of individual liberty and equality. Some of them demanded recognition less of their individual rights than of their rights as a group—as blacks. Some were contending that equality was not enough—what they wanted was reverse discrimination. They wanted laws to be passed and enforced deliberately for their benefit; they wanted a social and economic "handicap" much like the handicap that favors the weaker golfer. Still others were protesting that American democratic pluralism could not do the job at all: the pluralist system was too slow, too cumbersome, too respectful of the rights of those standing in the way of progress, whereas the problem—the tangle of knotted social factors that maintain the ghetto in a city, the century-old sense of inferiority and repression in the country, and the "culture of poverty" everywhere—was simply beyond the capacity of pluralist democracy to solve.

Each year more and more Negroes have voted. Increasingly, they are

[37]James W. Prothro, "A Southerner's View of a Southerner's Book," *The Reporter* (September 20, 1956), p. 46.

comprehending more clearly the connection between voting and better schools, houses, and jobs. And with these advances, more and more Negroes are coming to insist on the abolition of segregation. The impact of the political voice of the Negro will be felt long before every Negro becomes politically self-conscious. What is happening in the United States is one facet of the worldwide "revolution of rising expectations." Colonialism is dead. White supremacy is dying. There is no stopping place between the granting of a few rights and full citizenship. Negroes are demanding the same rights as other citizens. No other Americans have asked for more than this—or settled long for less.

Rights to Citizenship, Life, Liberty, and Property

8 Public officials have great power. Under certain conditions they can seize our property, throw us into jail, and, in extreme circumstances, even take our lives. Under some conditions they can take away our citizenship. It is necessary to vest great power in those who govern—it is also dangerous. It is so dangerous that to keep officials from becoming tyrants we are unwilling to depend on the ballot box alone. For we know that political controls have little impact when a majority uses governmental power to deprive unpopular minorities of their rights.

Because public power can be dangerous, we parcel it out in small chunks and surround it with elaborate restraints. No single official can, by himself, decide to take our life, liberty, or property. And officials must proceed according to established forms. If they act outside the scope of their authority or contrary to the law, be they the President or a policeman, they have no claim to obedience.

The Constitution also protects our rights to become and to remain citizens, a right basic to the concept of self-government. True, all nations have rules that determine nationality—the condition of membership in, owing allegiance to, and being the subject of a nation-state—but in democratic theory citizenship is something more than nationality, something more than merely being a subject. Citizenship in a democracy is an office and, like other offices, carries with it certain powers and responsibilities.

The Constitution Protects Citizenship

It was not until 1868, with the adoption of the Fourteenth Amendment, that this basic right of membership in the body politic was given constitutional protection. This amendment makes "all persons *born or naturalized* in the United States and subject to the jurisdiction thereof . . . citizens of the United States and of the State wherein they reside." Thus, all persons born in the United States, with the minor exception of children born to foreign ambassadors and ministers (but not consuls), are citizens of this country regardless of the citizenship of their parents. (Congress has defined the United States to include Puerto Rico, Guam, and the Virgin Islands.) Members of Indian tribes were not made citizens of the United States by the Fourteenth Amendment, but Congress has by law conferred citizenship on persons born to members of Indian tribes.

The Fourteenth Amendment confers citizenship according to the principle of *jus soli*—by place of birth. In addition, Congress has granted, under certain conditions, citizenship at birth according to the principle of *jus sanquinis*—by blood. Thus a child born of an American parent living abroad becomes an American citizen at birth provided one of his citizen parents had been physically present in the United States or one of its possessions prior to the child's birth. In order to retain citizenship derived through only one citizen parent, a person must come to the United States before he is twenty-three and must live here for at least five years between his fourteenth and twenty-eighth birthdays.

Citizenship may also be acquired by naturalization, collective or individual. The granting of citizenship to Puerto Ricans in 1917 by an act of Congress is an example of collective naturalization. Individual naturalization requirements are determined by Congress.

Today, any nonenemy alien over eighteen years of age who has been lawfully admitted for permanent residence and who has resided in the United States for at least five years and in a state for at least six months is eligible for naturalization. The exceptions to these requirements are (1) children under sixteen who are lawful residents—they become citizens when their parents become citizens; (2) military deserters, draft dodgers, and aliens who have refused to serve in the armed forces because of allegiance to another country—they cannot become citizens; and (3) relatives of citizens and aliens in the armed services—they have lower residence requirements. An eligible alien who wished to become a citizen files a petition of naturalization, verified by two witnesses, with the clerk of a court of record, federal or state. Then an official of the Immigration and Naturalization Service examines the petitioner to ensure that he has met the residence requirements, can read, write, and speak English, and is of good moral character. The official must also determine that the petitioner understands and is attached to the fundamentals of the history, principles, and form of government of the United States; that he is well disposed toward the good order and happiness of this country; and that he does not now, nor did within the last ten years, believe in, advocate, or belong to an organization that supports opposition to organized government, overthrow of government by violence, or the doctrines of world communism or any other form of totalitarianism.

The examiner makes his report to the judge. The final step is a hearing in open court. If the judge is satisfied that the petitioner is qualified, the applicant renounces all allegiance to his former country and swears to support and defend the Constitution and laws of the United States against all enemies and to bear arms in behalf of the United States when required by law. (Those with religious beliefs against the bearing of arms are allowed to take an oath to serve in the armed forces as noncombatants or to perform work of national importance under civilian direction.) Then the court grants a certificate of naturalization.

LOSS OF CITIZENSHIP

Naturalized citizenship may be revoked by court order if the government can prove that it was procured by concealment of a material fact or by willful misrepresentation. In addition, citizenship, however acquired, may be voluntarily renounced. Under existing statutes, an American citizen living outside the United States may formally renounce his citizenship before an American diplomatic or consular official. A person living in the United States may formally renounce his citizenship only during time of war and only with the approval of the Attorney General.

Congress seems to believe that it has the power to strip a person of his citizenship as a penalty for the commission of certain kinds of crimes and that it may make an act of expatriation a certain kind of conduct that it has determined to be incompatible with undivided allegiance to the United States. The Supreme Court thinks otherwise. The justices have had difficulty in articulating their arguments and in developing a coherent and consistent majority position, but in essence the Court has ruled that what the Constitution gives, Congress may not take away. Justice Black (*Afroyim* v. *Rush,* 1967), speaking for a five-man majority, unequivocally stated, "Congress has no power under the Constitution to divest a person of his United States citizenship absent his voluntary renunciation thereof."

Of the eleven types of conduct that Congress has stipulated are to be construed as expatriating acts, five have been challenged in the courts, and all five, by a closely divided Court, have been declared unconstitutional: voting in a foreign election; conviction by a court-martial of desertion during time of war; departing from or remaining outside the United States in time of war or national emergency to avoid military service; and residence by a naturalized citizen in the country of his national origin for more than three years.[1] Among the other stipulated acts of expatriation, which have still not been challenged, the following appear to conflict with the most recent decisions of the Supreme Court, for they can hardly be considered voluntary renunciation of citizenship: conviction of treason, of attempting to overthrow the government by force, or of conspiring to advocate forceful overthrow; serving in the armed

[1]*Afroyim* v. *Rusk* (1967); *Trop* v. *Dulles* (1958); *Kennedy* v. *Mendoza-Martinez* (1963); and *Schneider* v. *Rusk* (1964). Also see John P. Roche, "The Expatriation Decisions: A Study in Constitutional Improvisation and the Uses of History," *American Political Science Review* (March 1964), pp. 72–80.

forces of another state without the approval of the Secretary of State and Secretary of Defense; and accepting a job in a foreign state that is open only to the citizens of that state. More difficult questions are presented by acts such as being naturalized in a foreign state or taking an oath of allegiance to another country, for these could be construed as voluntary renunciation of American citizenship.

RIGHTS OF AMERICAN CITIZENSHIP

American citizenship confers some very special rights. First of all, an American citizen obtains state citizenship merely by residing in a state. (*Residence*, as used in the Fourteenth Amendment, means domicile, the place one calls "home." The legal status of *domicile* should not be confused with the fact of physical presence. A person may be living in Washington, D.C., but be a citizen of California—that is, he may consider California "home." Domicile, or residence, is a question primarily of intent.) And it is from state citizenship that many of our most important rights flow. For example, states determine—subject to constitutional limitations—who shall vote, not merely for state and local officials but also for national officials. Although states could confer the right to vote on aliens, no state today does so and citizenship is an essential (but not sufficient) requirement to vote and to hold office.

Do American citizens have rights other than the right to become a citizen of the state in which they reside? The Supreme Court in the *Slaughter House Cases* (1873) carefully distinguished between privileges of United States citizens and of state citizens, holding that the only privileges attaching to national citizenship are those that "owe their existence to the Federal Government, its National Character, its Constitution, or its laws." These privileges of United States citizenship have never been completely enumerated, but they include the right to use the navigable waters of the United States; to assemble peacefully; to petition the national government for redress of grievances; to be protected by the national government on the high seas; to vote, if qualified to do so under laws, in national elections and to have one's vote counted properly; and to travel throughout the United States.

The right to travel. The right to travel, the basic freedom of persons to move from place to place, has in recent years become the subject of considerable litigation. Except for persons under legal restraint—committed to jail, subject to the draft, out on bail, and so forth—all American citizens may travel throughout the nation, and no state may impose any barriers to this freedom of movement. During World War II, however, the national government forced American citizens of Japanese ancestry to move from their homes to relocation centers. The Supreme Court reluctantly approved this denial of their liberty, accepting as reasonable the decision of military commanders that such measures were necessary to prevent sabotage and espionage. But the Supreme Court insisted that after the loyalty of these people was established, restrictions could not be placed on their freedom to travel that were not legally imposed on all other persons.[2]

---

[2]*Korematsu* v. *United States* (1944) and *Ex parte Endo* (1944).

Do American citizens have the right to travel abroad, or is that a privilege that the government may limit at its discretion? Until World War I, no passports were required, though one could be obtained as a convenience if wanted. Then, other nations began to demand passports before they would grant visas to our citizens. Under present law and presidential directives, when the United States is at war or in a state of national emergency proclaimed by the President, it is unlawful, except as otherwise provided by the President, for any citizen to depart from or enter the United States unless he bears a valid passport. Presidential proclamations have brought these provisions into effect since 1941, and, except for travel to a few nations —Mexico and Canada, for example—no citizen can lawfully leave the United States without a passport.

For many years the Secretary of State refused to give passports to citizens if he believed they were going abroad "to further the Communist cause." Before a passport application would even be considered, a noncommunist affidavit was required, and, in determining whether or not a citizen was eligible, the Department of State reserved the right to use information, the source and nature of which were not revealed to the citizen whose right to a passport was being considered. Then in 1958 (*Kent* v. *Dulles*) the Supreme Court, although holding that the right to travel is part of the liberty protected by the Fifth Amendment, avoided the underlying constitutional issues and ruled that Congress had not given the Secretary authority to withhold a passport because of a citizen's political beliefs or associations. A few years later (*Aptheker* v. *Secretary of State*, 1964), as we have seen (page 136), the Court declared unconstitutional the provision of the Internal Security Act of 1950 that made it a crime for any member of a registered Communist organization to apply for a passport.

The Supreme Court (*Zemel* v. *Rusk*, 1965) has sustained the right of the Department of State to refuse to validate passports for Cuba, China, and other iron curtain countries. The Court majority held that Congress has the authority, which it had delegated to the Secretary of State, to impose area restrictions whenever and wherever it feels that travel by American citizens is not in the best interest of the United States. However, the Supreme Court (*United States* v. *Laub*, 1967) ruled that Congress had not made it a criminal offense for a person with an otherwise valid passport to travel to a country for which his passport was invalidated. Invalidation of a passport for travel to certain countries announces to its bearer that if he goes to such a country, he cannot be assured of the protection of the United States. It does not mean that he is traveling illegally.

Because persons who travel to restricted countries may not under present law be punished, the Department of State has tried to revoke their passports. The lower federal courts ruled that the Department had no such power, so the Department has abandoned its attempt to do so, although Congress is considering legislation that would specifically authorize the Department to revoke passports of those who travel to restricted countries. The Department of State still contends that it may deny passports to persons whose travel abroad may, in the judgment of the Secretary of State, "be prejudicial to the orderly conduct of foreign relations of the United States or otherwise be prejudicial to the interests of the United States." But the Department no longer uses confidential information in passport hearings and, in recent years, has not withheld a passport for political reasons. Thus we have had no direct judicial ruling on the extent of the Department's substantive authority to deny a citizen a passport.

The right to live in the United States. Although Congress may have some limited consitutional authority to restrict the right of American citizens to travel abroad, the right of a citizen to come to the United States and to live here is not subject to any congressional limitation. In these days of war and tyranny, this is perhaps the most precious right of an American citizen. Aliens have no such right.

Congress has complete constitutional power to decide which aliens shall be admitted to the United States and under what conditions they shall remain. Despite the fact, as President Franklin D. Roosevelt reminded the Daughters of the American Revolution, that "all of us are descended from immigrants and revolutionists," Congress has made it difficult for aliens to enter the United States (though compared to many other nations, admission to the United States is relatively easy).

Beginning in 1875, Congress imposed the first of the so-called qualitative limitations, to exclude certain types of "undesirables." But the major restrictions did not come until World War I and the 1924 Immigration Act, which set a limit on the number of immigrants that could be admitted and created the national-origins quota system. Congress recodified our immigration laws in the Immigration and Nationality Act of 1952 but retained the essential features of the national-origin quota system.

The law set an overall annual limitation of around 156,000, which was divided among each nationality in proportion to the number of people of that nationality who were living in the United States in 1920. (National-origin limitations did not apply to natives of independent countries of the Western Hemisphere, to spouses and minor children of American citizens, and to a few others.) As a result, the countries of Southern and Southeastern Europe and of Asia had very small quotas. Because the largest annual allotments went to countries from which few people wanted to emigrate and the smallest to countries where there were a large number waiting, considerably fewer than the permissible 156,000 quota of immigrants came to the United States each year. In addition, Congress enacted temporary emergency measures to admit, outside the quotas, persons who had been displaced and uprooted from their homes by war and political upheavals, and each year hundreds of private bills were enacted to admit individual aliens whose special plight had attracted the attention of a congressman.

Then in 1965, after years of political pressures, Congress adopted a new immigration act that marks a major departure in our immigration policies. The quota system was phased out over a three-year period. In its place, a ceiling of 170,000 immigrants a year was established for all countries outside the Western Hemisphere, with a limitation of 20,000 from any one country in a single year. And, for the first time, a quota was imposed on immigrants from nations in the Western Hemisphere—not more than 120,000 a year for the entire hemisphere. Within these overall quotas, preferences were created for members of the arts and professions, for refugees driven from their homes by political or racial persecution, and for relatives of American citizens. Minor unmarried children, spouses, or parents of American citizens may enter without regard to quota limitations.

Once here, aliens remain in this country at the sufferance of the national government; aliens who enter illegally may be expelled without much ado. Because the Supreme Court has ruled that deportation, despite its drastic consequences, is a civil rather than a criminal proceeding, the constitutional safeguards that protect persons accused of crimes do not come into play. Thus aliens may be deported for acts that were not grounds for banishment when they were performed and for a variety of reasons, such as two convictions for crimes involving moral turpitude, joining an organization that advocates revolutionary doctrines, or engaging in activities that the Attorney General believes are "subversive to the national security." Although the Supreme Court in recent years has narrowly construed congressional statutes dealing with deportation of aliens, the basic constitutional authority of Congress to deport has not been questioned.

In summary, aliens enter and remain in the United States subject to congressional regulation, but citizens of the United States have a constitutional right to live in the United States, to move freely about within this nation, and, under most circumstances, to travel abroad. The Constitution, however, does not limit most of its protective provisions to citizens. More often it speaks of the rights of *persons*, and constitutional guarantees apply regardless of the citizenship of those whose rights are involved. For example, Congress and the states have no more right to interfere with the freedom of religion of aliens living in the United States than they do with the freedom of religion of citizens. And the Constitution protects from arbitrary governmental interference the rights to property, life, and liberty of all persons.

Courtesy The Library of Congress.

"The Last Yankee"—A cartoon attacking unrestricted immigration, 1888.

Constitutional Protection of Property

By *property rights* we mean the rights of an individual to own, use, rent, invest, or contract for property. From Aristotle, through the English philosopher Harrington, to the Founding Fathers, there has run a persistent emphasis on the close connection between liberty and private ownership of property, between property and power. This emphasis has been reflected in American political thinking and American political institutions. A major purpose of the Framers of our Constitution was to establish a government strong enough to protect each person's right to use and enjoy his property and, at the same time, a government so limited that it could not encroach upon that right. For example, the Framers were disturbed by the efforts of some state legislatures in behalf of debtors at the expense of creditors (see Chapter 2). So in the Constitution they forbade states to make anything except gold or silver legal tender for the payment of debts or to pass any law "impairing the obligation of contracts."

THE CONTRACT CLAUSE

The obligation-of-contracts clause of Article I, Section 10, was aimed at state laws extending the period during which debtors could meet their payments or otherwise relieving them of their contractual obligations. The Framers had in mind an ordinary contract between private persons. But in characteristic fashion, Chief Justice Marshall later expanded the meaning of this clause to include transactions to which the state government itself was a party. So, when the Georgia legislature annulled a grant of a large tract of land fraudulently made by an earlier legislature, the Supreme Court declared that the annulling act was an unconstitutional impairment of the obligation of contract.[3] Then in 1819 the Supreme Court ruled that charters creating corporations are contracts. Thus, whatever privileges a charter conferred on a corporation appeared to be irrevocable and untouchable by any subsequent law.[4]

In effect, the contract clause was being used to protect vested property at the expense of the power of the states to guard the public welfare. State regulations of business enterprises ran a serious risk of being declared unconstitutional. Gradually, however, the Court began to restrict the coverage of the contract clause. Finally, in the case of *Stone* v. *Mississippi* (1880), the Supreme Court ruled that all contracts are subject to the states' police power and could be regulated when necessary to protect the public health, safety, welfare, or morals. In 1934 the Supreme Court declared that even contracts between individuals—the very ones the contract clause was intended to protect—could be reasonably modified by state law in order to avert social and economic catastrophe resulting from the Depression.[5]

But in the 1880s, just as the contract clause ceased to be an important block to state regulation of property, the due process clause took over.

DUE PROCESS OF LAW

Perhaps the most difficult parts of the Constitution to understand are the clauses in the Fifth and Fourteenth Amendments that forbid national and state governments, respectively, to deny any person his life, liberty, or property without due process of law. These due process clauses have resulted

[3]*Fletcher* v. *Peck* (1810).
[4]*Dartmouth College* v. *Woodward* (1819).
[5]*Home Building and Loan Association* v. *Blaisdell* (1934).

in more Supreme Court decisions than has any other clause in the Constitution. Even so, it is impossible to give due process any exact and completely satisfactory explanation. Indeed, the Supreme Court itself has refused to give it a precise definition.

There are two types of due process: procedural and substantive. *Procedural* due process is older, for it grew out of Magna Carta and embodies the ancient notion that no man should be deprived of his life, liberty, or property unless he has violated the law and has had a fair trial. It requires, to paraphrase Daniel Webster's definition, that government render judgment against a man only after he has had a hearing in which the essentials of justice have been preserved. For the most part, procedural due process has its application in the administration of criminal justice.

Substantive due process has to do not with the procedures but with the content of law, which it requires to be reasonable and fair. Whereas procedural due process primarily restrains the executive and judicial branches, substantive due process mainly limits the lawmaking branch. Substantive due process means that even if a law has been legally passed and is being properly applied, if the law itself is unreasonable it is unconstitutional. Or to put it another way, procedural due process places limits on the manner in which governmental power may be exercised, but substantive due process withdraws certain subjects from the reach of public regulation regardless of the procedures used.

For an example of denial of substantive due process, suppose that a state legislature should adopt a law requiring employers to pay all their employees the same salary paid to the president of the firm. An employer being prosecuted for violating this law might well object that the law is unreasonable and that even though he is being given a fair trial, to make him comply with the law would be to deprive him of his property without due process. He would be raising the substantive interpretation of due process.

Substantive due process has roots in natural-law concepts and has had a long history in the American constitutional tradition. The doctrine reached its height between 1880 and 1937, when the Supreme Court was composed for the most part of conservative gentlemen who considered almost all social welfare legislation unreasonable and hence contrary to substantive due process. They used the due process clause to strike down laws regulating hours of labor, establishing minimum wages, regulating prices, and forbidding employers to discharge workers for union membership. The Supreme Court, elevating the doctrine of laissez faire into a constitutional principle, vetoed laws adversely affecting property rights unless the judges could be persuaded that such laws were necessary to protect public health or safety.

But what is "reasonable"? What is "necessary"? The trouble with the substantive interpretation of due process is that the view of the reasonableness of a law depends on a man's economic, social, and political views. In democracies, elected officials are supposed to be responsible for accommodating the clashing notions of reasonableness and for deciding what regulations of liberty and property are needed to promote the public welfare. When the Supreme Court substituted it own idea of reasonableness for the legislature's, it was acting like a superlegislature. But how competent were judges to say what the nation's economic policies should be?

183

CHAPTER 8
Rights
to Citzenship,
Life, Liberty
and Property

Under the impact of this criticism the Supreme Court since 1937 has largely abandoned substantive due process as a check on legislative regulation of the economy (but not as a check on legislative regulations of civil liberties). The Court now consists of justices who believe that determining the reasonableness of laws regulating the uses of property is a legislative and not a judicial duty. As long as it sees some connection between such a law and the promotion of the public welfare, the Supreme Court will not interfere, even if the justices personally believe the law to be unwise.

EMINENT DOMAIN

Many government regulations affect the value of the property we own, sometimes making it worth more, sometimes less. For example, a zoning law restricting a particular area to residential uses may decrease the immediate value of a particular individual's property. (Maybe he was planning to use his land for a gas station.) The government does not have to remunerate the owner for such losses, so he loses money—but the rest of the community may gain.

What if the government goes beyond reasonable regulation and takes property? Both the national and state governments have a constitutional right to do so, to exercise what is known as the power of eminent domain. But the Constitution requires that property be seized only for public purposes—for example, to build a highway or school or military installation—and that the owner must be paid a fair price. If there is any dispute about what price is fair, the final decision is made by the courts.

To sum up, where do we stand today in terms of constitutional protection of property? The obligation-of-contracts clause is no longer a major barrier to state regulation of property, and substantive due process has been abandoned as a judicially enforced limit on legislative regulation of our economy. The constitutional limits on the power of eminent domain remain as important as ever. But our right to use our property is not above regulation in the public interest. What regulations are needed is determined by the legislatures; the national courts will intervene only if the laws are outrageously arbitrary and unreasonable or are being applied without procedural due process.

Freedom from Arbitrary Arrest, Questioning, and Imprisonment

James Otis's address in 1761 protesting arbitrary searches and seizures by English customs officials was the opening salvo of the American Revolution; as John Adams later said, "American independence was then and there born." It is not surprising to find that the Fourth Amendment states:

The right of the people to be secure in their persons, houses, papers, and effects, against unreasonable searches and seizures, shall not be violated, and no Warrants shall issue, but upon probable cause, supported by Oath or affirmation, and particularly describing the place to be searched, and the persons or things to be seized.

WHAT IS AN UNREASONABLE SEARCH AND SEIZURE?

Despite television police dramas, lawmen—federal, state, or local—have no right to invade homes and break down doors; they may not search homes or people without warrants except under certain narrowly defined conditions; and they have no right to arrest except under prescribed conditions. If policemen have cause to believe that an automobile contains contraband or incriminating evidence, they may search the automobile even if they lack a search warrant—for the obvious reason that the automobile might not be there when the officers returned. Also, a police officer may stop and frisk a person when "he has reason to believe that he is dealing with an armed and dangerous individual," but the search must be confined to "an intrusion reasonably designated to discover guns, knives, clubs, or other hidden instruments for the assault of the police officer."[6] Furthermore, the police officer is not justified to stop and frisk on mere suspicion—he must have some "articulated" reason for doing so.

The police have a lawful right to arrest a person because they have either an arrest warrant or probable cause to believe that the individual is committing or has just committed a crime. In either case, during the course of the arrest the police may search the suspect and the immediate area under his control. In all other circumstances, the police need a search warrant—but not just any warrant will do. The police must furnish information and persuade a magistrate that there is probable cause for either an arrest or a search or both. The warrant the magistrate issues must describe what places are to be searched and what things are being sought. A mere blanket authorization to search indiscriminately violates the Fourth and Fourteenth Amendments.[7]

Combining the Fourth Amendment prohibition against unreasonable searches and seizures with the Fifth Amendment injunction that no person shall be compelled to be a witness against himself, the Supreme Court, in order to secure the right of privacy protected by the Fourth Amendment, has ruled that evidence unconstitutionally obtained cannot be used against persons from whom it was seized. To allow the use of this evidence would be, in effect, to force persons to testify against themselves. With such evidence excluded, police officers have every incentive to comply with the requirements of the Fourth Amendment when they make arrests and searches.

What of state courts? Until 1961 the Supreme Court held that state officers (and of course local officers) who made unreasonable searches and seizures deprived the affected person of his property without due process of law, contrary to the Fourteenth Amendment, but that it was not a denial of his liberty without due process of law for a state court to convict him on the basis of evidence unconstitutionally taken from him.[8] Then in *Mapp* v. *Ohio*, the Supreme Court reversed itself and ruled that the Constitution requires the

[6]*Terry* v. *Ohio* (1968).
[7]*Aguilar* v. *Texas* (1964).
[8]*Wolf* v. *Colorado* (1949).

states as well as the national courts to exclude from trials evidence obtained in an unconstitutional manner. Today, any conviction based on such evidence in any court violates the Constitution.

The inventions of science have confronted judges with new problems in applying the prohibition against unreasonable searches and seizures. Obviously, the framers of the Fourth Amendment had in mind physical objects such as books, papers, letters, and other kinds of documents that they felt should not be seized by police officers except on the basis of limited search warrants issued by magistrates. But what of tapping phone wires or using electronic devices to eavesdrop?[9] In *Olmstead* v. *United States*, decided in 1928, a bare majority of the Supreme Court held that there is no unconstitutional search unless there is seizure of physical objects or an actual physical entry into a premise. Justices Holmes and Brandeis wrote vigorous dissents in which they argued that the Constitution should be kept abreast of modern times and that the "dirty business" of wiretapping produced the same evil invasions of privacy that the framers had in mind when they wrote the Fourteenth Amendment.

By the middle of the 1960s, the Supreme Court was undermining the Olmstead doctrine and using the Fourth Amendment—assisted by the Fifth's due process clause and limitations on self-incrimination, and the Ninth's general reservation to the people of fundamental rights—to establish a constitutional right to privacy. For example, the Court held (*Griswold* v. *Connecticut*, 1965) that a state could not make it a crime for married couples to use birth control devices because the state had no right to intrude into the privacy of the marital estate. In 1967 the Olmstead decision was, in effect, overruled by *Berger* v. *State of New York* (see below), and in 1968 the Supreme Court declared, "The Fourth Amendment protects people—and not simply 'areas'—against unreasonable searches and seizures and the use by police officers of electronic devices to overhear a conversation inside a public telephone booth is a 'search and seizure' within the meaning of the Constitution. Wherever a man may be, he is entitled to know that he will remain free from unreasonable searches and seizures."[10]

To decide that the Fourth Amendment protects persons from unreasonable police searches of their private conversations still leaves open the question: What is an unreasonable search, an unreasonable intrusion into privacy? In the Berger case, the Supreme Court declared unconstitutional a New York State law that authorized the use by police officers of information obtained by tapping phones and overhearing conversations through the use of electronic devices when the police first secured a warrant from a magistrate. The Court felt that New York had failed to establish procedures for the granting of the warrants that would satisfy the Fourth Amendment requirement that warrants must specify what place is to be searched and what things are to be seized. The dissenting justices accused the majority of construing the Fourth Amendment in such a way as to make it impossible for wiretapping or electronic eavesdropping to satisfy the Fourth Amendment.

[9]For a study of wiretapping as it relates to the interaction of administrative, legislative, and judicial officials in the formation of public policy, see Walter F. Murphy, *Wiretapping on Trial: A Case Study in the Judicial Process* (Random House, 1965).

[10]*Katz* v. *United States* (1967).

Whether the Court will sustain the reasonableness of police wiretapping and eavesdropping through electronics is a question that is likely to be answered soon. The Crime Control Act of 1968, although making it a federal crime for any unauthorized person to tap telephone wires or to use electronic bugging devices, authorizes police and prosecutors to tap wires and engage in bugging under certain circumstances. The Attorney General may secure permission for federal police to do so by applying to a federal judge for a warrant to search for incriminating evidence for a whole range of specified federal offenses. In addition, the act authorizes the principal prosecuting attorney of any state or political subdivision to apply to a state judge for a warrant approving wiretapping or oral intercepts relating to any crime dangerous to life, limb, or property that is punishable by imprisonment for more than one year. Judges are to issue warrants if it is determined that probable cause exists that a crime was being, has been, or is about to be committed and that information relating to that crime may be obtained by the intercept. In addition to these intercepts authorized by warrants, the act permits police officers to make intercepts without a warrant for forty-eight hours in an emergency situation relating to conspiratorial activities threatening the national security or involving organized crime. The President may even authorize intercepts by nonpolice officers for national security purposes. Evidence obtained by these methods, said Congress, is to be admissible in federal courts.

President Johnson urged Congress to "immediately reconsider" the intercept procedures; he argued they could lead to "a nation of snoopers bending through the keyholes of the homes and offices of America, spying on our neighbors. No conversation in the sanctity of the bedroom . . . would be free of eavesdropping. . . ." Yet it appears unlikely that Congress will reconsider, and the issue will likely be met next in the courts of the land.

THE RIGHT TO REMAIN SILENT

During the seventeenth century, certain special courts in England forced confessions of heresy and sedition from religious dissenters. It was in response to these practices that the British privilege against self-incrimination developed, and it was because the Framers of our Bill of Rights were familiar with the history of these odious confessions that they included within the Fifth Amendment the provision that no person shall be compelled to testify against himself in criminal prosecutions. The protection against self-incrimination is designed to strengthen a fundamental principle of Anglo-American justice — that no man has an obligation to prove his innocence. Rather, the burden is on the government to prove him guilty.

Literally read, the privilege against self-incrimination applies only in criminal prosecutions, but it has always been interpreted to protect any person subject to questioning by any agency of government. Hence, a witness before a congressional committee, for example, may refuse to answer incriminating questions. But to invoke the privilege, it is not enough that the witness's answers might be embarrassing, lead to public disapproval or loss of job, or might incriminate others; there must be a reasonable fear that the answers might support a criminal prosecution or "furnish a link in the chain of evidence needed to prosecute" him for a crime.[11] A witness may refuse to answer even if his responses would not indicate guilt, for the right extends to answers that might lead to prosecution even if the witness thinks the prosecution would not lead to conviction. If defendants refuse to take the stand in their own defense, the judge must warn the jury not to draw any adverse inferences from the defendant's silence. However, if a defendant elects to take the stand, he cannot claim the privilege against self-incrimination to prevent cross-examination by the prosecution.

In 1964 (*Malloy* v. *Hogan*) the Supreme Court ruled, "The Fourteenth Amendment secures against state invasion the same privilege that the Fifth Amendment guarantees against federal infringement—the right of a person to remain silent unless he chooses to speak in the unfettered exercise of his own will, and to suffer no penalty . . . for such silence." In a subsequent decision (*Murphy* v. *Waterfront Commission*), the Court went on to rule that fear of prosecution by either national or state officials is sufficient justification to invoke the privilege against self-incrimination and refuse to answer questions put by any governmental agency.

In addition, the self-incrimination clause may not be denied to a person because he is a public employee. Governments may not dismiss police officers and other employees who invoke their right to remain silent when subject to official interrogation by grand juries and other governmental agencies (although they may be dismissed if they refuse to answer to their superiors about matters closely related to their official duties).[12]

Until the Supreme Court brought the privilege against self-incrimination within the scope of the Fourteenth Amendment and until it permitted the privilege to be invoked to prevent incrimination by either national or state governments, a person could find himself "whipsawed" between national and state authorities. He could not refuse to answer questions put to him by national authorities for fear of state prosecution, and vice versa. Thus federal and state authorities working together could use the machinery of one government to compel evidence to be used in the courts of the other government. The 1965 rulings of the Supreme Court put a stop to these practices.

Sometimes authorities would rather have answers from a witness than prosecute him. Congress has often granted immunity from subsequent prosecution in order to secure evidence. The most sweeping such law is the Immunity Act of 1954, covering national security matters and subsequently amended to include testimony about narcotics. Under this act a majority of either house of Congress, two-thirds of a congressional committee, or a United States district attorney may petition a federal district judge to grant a witness immunity against federal or state prosecution for crimes uncovered by his compelled testimony. Once given this immunity a witness must answer questions or risk punishment, because his answers can no longer lead to self-incrimination.

Under the supremacy clause in the 1954 act, Congress may confer on witnesses absolute immunity from federal or state prosecution, but a state may not completely immunize a witness from prosecution by federal authorities. However, in 1965, the Supreme Court ruled that when a state

[11]*Blau* v. *United States* (1950).
[12]*Garrity* v. *New Jersey* (1967).

grants a witness immunity, federal officials may not use the evidence uncovered by the state proceedings. Under these circumstances, then, a state
can punish witnesses who refuse to answer after being granted immunity
from state prosecution.

THE THIRD DEGREE

The questioning of suspects by the police is a key procedure for solving
crimes—and also one that can easily be abused. Policemen sometimes forget
or ignore the constitutional rights of suspects, especially of those who are
frightened and ignorant. Torture, detention incommunicado, and sustained
interrogation to wring confessions from suspects are common practices in
police states, and such tactics are not completely unknown in the United
States.

Judges, especially those on the Supreme Court, have used their power to
try to stamp out police brutality. The Supreme Court has ruled that even
though there may be sufficient evidence to support a conviction apart from a
confession, the admission into evidence of a coerced confession violates the
self-incrimination clause, deprives a person of the assistance of counsel
guaranteed by the Sixth and Fourteenth Amendments, deprives him of due
process, and vitiates the entire proceeding. Hence, any conviction by either
national or state courts on the basis of a trial in which a confession secured
by physical torture or psychological coercion has been introduced is unconstitutional.[13]

Ever since the 1930s the Supreme Court has been gradually raising the
standards to be met by all federal and state courts in the administration of
justice. Until the 1960s, it used the due process standards to reverse convictions obtained by third-degree methods—not so much because these practices amount to self-incrimination but because such brutal procedures and
the use of such unreliable evidence offend the due process clause. But what
was the good of this constitutional protection at the time of a trial, or the
guarantee of the right to assistance of counsel at the trial, or the presumption
of innocence if, long before the accused was brought before the court, he was
detained and, without the help of an attorney, forced to prove his innocence
to the police? What happened in the police station often reduced the courtroom proceedings to a mere formality.

The federal rules of criminal procedure and the laws of all our states require officers to take those whom they have arrested before a magistrate
promptly; the magistrate informs the person in custody of his constitutional
rights and allows him to get in touch with friends and to seek legal advice.
Although the police have no lawful right to hold a person for questioning prior
to his hearing before the magistrate, they are often tempted to question
first. Sometimes they lack the evidence to make an arrest stick but feel that
if they can interrogate the suspect before he knows of his constitutional
right to remain silent they can get him to confess.

At first the Supreme Court merely adopted a rule that no confession,
whether voluntary or involuntary, obtained while a person was being il-

[13]*Payne* v. *Arkansas* (1958).

legally detained by federal officers could be used in federal courts. In 1957 the Supreme Court reaffirmed this doctrine in the Mallory case, a case that made front-page headlines because it involved an especially heinous crime and because the application of the exclusion rule resulted in the release of a confessed criminal. But the Court stood fast despite criticism by many police chiefs and congressmen. In 1964, it made the Mallory decision a constitutional standard by holding, in *Massiah* v. *United States*, that incriminating statements deliberately elicited by federal agents from a suspect while he was out on bail awaiting trial deprived the suspect of his right to counsel under the Sixth Amendment; statements so elicited could not constitutionally be used against the suspect. In the Escobedo decision (*Escobedo* v. *Illinois,* 1964) the Court held that if local police question a suspect who had asked to consult with counsel and who had not been warned of his constitutional right to keep silent, the suspect is denied the assistance of counsel and no statement extracted by the police during such an interrogation could be used against him at his trial. The Supreme Court was edging close to forbidding all *in camera* interrogation of persons suspected of crime.

Then in 1966 (*Miranda* v. *Arizona*), by a five-to-four vote the Supreme Court announced that henceforth no conviction—federal or state—could stand if evidence introduced at the trial had been obtained by the police as the result of "custodial interrogation," unless the suspect had been (1) notified that he is free to remain silent, (2) warned that what he says may be used against him in court, (3) told that he has a right to have his attorney present during the questioning, (4) informed that if he cannot afford to hire his own lawyer, an attorney would be provided for him, and (5) permitted at any stage of the police interrogation to terminate it. If the suspect answers questions in the absence of his attorney, the prosecution must be prepared to demonstrate that the suspect knowingly and intelligently waived his rights to remain silent and to have his own lawyer present. Failure to comply with these requirements will lead to reversal of a conviction even if other independent evidence would be sufficient to establish guilt.

The Court still has not gone so far as to require that all interrogations be in the presence of a lawyer even when a prisoner has not asked for one or to state that a prisoner has a constitutional right to have his lawyer present at all interrogations. But the self-incrimination clause does apply to all governments; it serves to protect persons in all settings in which their freedom of action is curtailed. A government seeking to punish an individual must produce the evidence against him by its own independent labors and cannot force or coerce the suspect to contribute evidence that can be used to convict him.

As might be expected, there are many critics of the Supreme Court's decision; they argue that the Court has unnecessarily and severely limited the ability of the police to bring criminals to justice. (The importance of pretrial interrogation and investigation procedures to the administration of justice is underscored by the fact that roughly 90 percent[14] of all criminal convictions result from pleas of guilty and never reach the trial stage.) Persuaded by these critics, Congress in 1968, in Title II of the Crime Control Bill, adopted

[14]Donald J. Newman, *Conviction: The Determination of Guilt or Innocence Without Trial* (Little, Brown, 1966), p. 3.

rules for federal trials that are in direct conflict with the Court's decisions in the Mallory, Miranda, and companion cases. Congress stipulated that a confession may be admitted in a federal criminal trial if voluntarily given and that the trial judge, in determining whether a confession is voluntary, need not be bound to consider as conclusive every factor the Supreme Court ruled essential in its Miranda decision. Despite what the Supreme Court had said, Congress instructed federal courts not to rule out a confession if the defendant had not been previously informed of his constitutional rights. In addition, Congress stated that despite Mallory, a confession made by a person in the custody of law officers should not necessarily be considered inadmissible solely because of the delay in bringing the accused before a magistrate, provided the confession was given within six hours of the arrest or even longer if the trial judge found that the delay in bringing the accused before a committing officer was reasonable, considering the means of transportation and the distance to be traveled.

Congress's actions are limited to federal cases, and President Johnson instructed the Attorney General to see to it that federal prosecutors and police continue to follow the requirements stipulated by the Supreme Court. It seems likely that President Nixon's administration will rule otherwise and that in the near future the Supreme Court will either repeat its constitutional convictions or retreat in the face of Congressional interpretation.

THE WRIT OF HABEAS CORPUS

Even though the Framers did not think a Bill of Rights necessary, they considered certain rights important enough to be included in the original Constitution. Foremost is the guarantee that the writ of habeas corpus will be available unless suspended in time of rebellion or invasion. Permission to suspend the writ of habeas corpus is found in the article setting forth the powers and organization of Congress, so presumably only Congress has the right to suspend it.

There are several kinds of writs of habeas corpus and, as developed in the United States, the device has several uses. Simply stated, it is a court order to any official having a person in his custody directing the official to produce the prisoner in court and explain to the court the reasons for confining him. A person held in custody applies under oath (usually through his attorney) and states why he believes he is being held unlawfully. The judge then orders the jailer to show cause why the writ should not be issued. Testimony can be taken if there is a dispute over the facts. If the judge finds that the prisoner is being unlawfully detained, he orders the prisoner's release.

The case of Messrs. Duncan and White is a good example of one use of the writ. Duncan and White were civilians who had been convicted by military tribunals and were being held by military authorities in Hawaii during World War II. They filed petitions for writs of habeas corpus in the district court of Hawaii, citing both statutory and constitutional reasons to prove that the military had no right to keep them in prison. The court then asked the military officers to show cause why the petition should not be granted. The military replied that Hawaii had become part of an active theater of war, that the writ of habeas corpus had been suspended, that martial law had been established, and that consequently the district court had no jurisdiction to issue the writs. Moreover, the military answered, even if the writ of habeas corpus had not been suspended, it should not be issued in this case because the military trials of Duncan and White were valid. After hearing both sides, the district court, in an action eventually approved by the Supreme Court, agreed with Duncan and White and issued writs ordering their release.[15]

EX POST FACTO LAWS AND BILLS OF ATTAINDER

The Constitution forbids both the national and state governments to pass ex post facto laws or enact bills of attainder (Article I, Sections 9 and 10).

An *ex post facto law* is a retroactive criminal law that works to the detriment of an individual—for example, a law making a particular act a crime that was not a crime when committed or a law increasing the punishment for a crime after it was committed. The prohibition of ex post facto laws does not prevent the passage of retroactive civil laws—for example, increasing income tax rates as applied to income already earned—nor does it prevent the passage of retroactive penal laws that work to the benefit of an accused—for example, a law decreasing a punishment or changing the rules of evidence to make conviction more difficult.

A *bill of attainder* is a legislative act inflicting punishment on specified individuals without judicial trial. Bills of attainder have been rare in American history, but Congress has enacted two in the last two decades. In 1943 Representative Martin Dies, then chairman of the House Committee on Un-American Activities, denounced from the floor of Congress thirty-nine officials as "crackpot, radical bureaucrats." He singled out three of these men for special abuse. Shortly afterward, Congress attached a rider to an appropriation bill naming these three employees and ordering that they receive no salary from the federal government until the President had reappointed them and the Senate had confirmed their nominations. President Roosevelt, convinced that Congress had acted unconstitutionally, refused to resubmit their names. The three men kept on working and sued for their salaries in the Court of Claims, which upheld their claim. The Supreme Court, affirming that decision, ruled (in *United States* v. *Lovett*, 1946) that by accusing the men of disloyalty and denying them their pay, Congress had punished them without a trial and thus had violated the constitutional prohibition against bills of attainder.

In 1959 Congress repealed a provision of the Taft-Hartley Act that conditioned a union's access to the National Labor Relations Board on the filing of affidavits by its officers that they were not members of or affiliated with the Communist party, and then Congress enacted a law making it a crime for a member of the Communist party to serve as an officer or an employee of a labor union. Chief Justice Warren, speaking for a five-man majority, pointed out that Congress possesses power under the commerce clause to enact legislation designed to protect that commerce from political strikes. However, the 1959 enactment did not set forth a general rule, but designated by name members of a particular political group and imposed a punishment on them.

[15]*Duncan* v. *Kahanamoku* (1946).

This was a bill of attainder. The Chief Justice wrote, "Congress possesses full legislative authority, but the task of adjudication must be left to other tribunals."[16]

Rights of Persons Accused of Crime

That the innocent will go free and that the guilty will be punished; that rich and poor, educated and ignorant will secure justice under law—these are among the most ancient and honorable goals of free nations.[17] Some feel that the rights of persons accused of crime are less important than other civil liberties, but, as Justice Frankfurter observed, "The history of liberty has largely been the history of observance of procedural safeguards." These safeguards, moreover, have frequently "been forged in controversies involving not very nice people." Their purpose is not "to convenience the guilty but to protect the innocent."

THE FEDERAL COURTS

The rights of persons accused of crime by the national government can be found in the Fourth, Fifth, Sixth, and Eighth Amendments. In order to get some idea of the application of these constitutional safeguards, we shall follow the fortunes and misfortunes of John T. Crook (a fictitious name).

Crook sent circulars through the mails soliciting purchases of stock in a nonexistent gold mine, an action contrary to at least three federal laws. When postal officers uncovered these activities, they went to the district court and secured warrants to arrest Crook and to search his house for copies of the circulars. They found Crook at home, arrested him for using the mails to defraud, and seized some of the circulars. Crook was promptly brought before a federal district judge, who set bail at $1,500 and ordered him held over until the convening of the next federal grand jury in the district. After posting bond, Crook was permitted his freedom as long as he remained within the limits of the judicial district.

When the next grand jury was convened, the United States district attorney brought before the twenty-three jurors evidence to indicate that Crook had committed a federal crime. Grand jurors are concerned not with a man's guilt or innocence, but merely with whether there seems to be enough evidence to warrant bringing him to trial. No person has a right to appear before a grand jury, but he may be invited or ordered to do so. If a majority of the grand jurors agree that a trial is justified, they return what is known as a *true bill* or *indictment*. Except in cases arising in the military forces, the national government cannot force any person to stand trial for any serious crime except on grand jury indictment. In our particular case, the grand jury was in full agreement with the United States district attorney and returned a true bill against Crook.

[16]*United States* v. *Archie Brown* (1965).
[17]For a comprehensive treatment of the rights of persons accused of crime, see David Fellman, *The Defendant's Rights* (Holt, 1958).

Courtesy Charles G. Brooks and *The Birmingham News*; © 1967
by The New York Times Company; reprinted by permission.

"Quick! While I keep 'em pinned down, run and bring each of them a lawyer—and don't forget ours!"

A copy of the indictment was served on Crook and he was again ordered before a federal district judge. Crook did not know that he had a constitutional right to the assistance of counsel and that if he could not afford to pay for an attorney the national government could not bring him to trial without legal assistance. The judge saw to it that Crook was informed of his right and, after being told that the prisoner had no money, appointed a lawyer to undertake his defense. The Constitution also guarantees to the accused the right to be informed of the nature and cause of the accusation so that he can prepare his defense; consequently, the federal prosecuting officers had seen to it that the indictment clearly stated the nature of the offense, and they had given copies to Crook and his lawyer. After consulting with his lawyer, Crook entered the plea of *not guilty*.

After indictment, Crook's bail was raised to $3,000. Now the federal government was obliged to give him a speedy and public trial; the word speedy should not be taken too literally, however, because Crook had to be given time to prepare his defense. His lawyer pointed out that he had the right to a trial by an impartial jury selected from the state and district where the alleged crime was committed but that his right could be waived if he wished and the trial could be held before a judge alone. The attorney advised Crook to take his chances with a jury, though in most trials the right to jury is waived.

Crook told his lawyer that he had had dinner with George Witness on the night on which he was charged with sending the damaging circulars. But when Witness was approached, he said he was unwilling to testify at the trial. The attorney took advantage of Crook's constitutional right to obtain witnesses in his favor and had the judge subpoena Witness to appear at the trial and testify. Witness could have refused to testify on the grounds that his testimony would tend to incriminate him, but he agreed to testify. Crook himself, however, chose to use his constitutional right not to be a witness against himself and refused to take the witness stand. He knew that if he did so, the prosecution would have a right to cross-examination, and he was fearful of what might be uncovered. The federal judge conducting the trial cautioned the jury against drawing any conclusions from Crook's reluctance to testify—although nothing could prevent the jurors from being affected. All prosecution witnesses appeared in court and were available to defense cross-examination, because the Constitution insists that the accused has the right to be confronted with the witnesses against him.

At the conclusion of the trial, the jury rendered a verdict of *guilty*. The judge then raised Crook's bail to $5,000 and announced that he would hand down a sentence on the following Monday. The Eighth Amendment forbids excessive bail, the levying of excessive fines, and the inflicting of cruel and unusual punishments. Although the Bail Reform Act of 1966 gives federal judges considerable discretion to allow men freedom pending their trials or appeals, in view of Crook's past record and the nature of the offense, the bail could not be considered excessive. In addition, when the judge, in accord with the law, gave Crook the maximum punishment of $5,000 and five years in the penitentiary, the punishment could not be considered cruel and unusual.

The ban against cruel and unusual punishments forbids, for example, making drug addiction a crime because this would inflict punishment simply for being ill.[18] (The Supreme Court has refused to extend this ruling to cover alcoholism, although the vote was five to four.[19]) What of capital punishment? There are many, including some judges, who believe that for a nation that considers itself civilized any form of capital punishment should be declared cruel and unusual. Although many states have abolished it, and the Attorney General in 1968 called on Congress to do so, and the number of actual executions has drastically decreased in recent decades, so far the Supreme Court has not held capital punishment per se to violate the Eighth Amendment.

Because the Constitution forbids the federal government to place anyone twice in jeopardy for the same offense, Crook could not be tried again by federal courts for this crime. But double jeopardy does not apply to actions initiated by the defendant. Crook's lawyer appealed to the court of appeals on the ground that the judge had improperly instructed the jury. If the court of appeals had sustained the appeal, which it did not, and ordered a new trial, no double jeopardy would have been involved. Finally, the Supreme Court refused to review the case and Crook went to jail.

THE STATE COURTS
AND THE NATIONAL CONSTITUTION

After three years in the federal penitentiary, Crook was paroled. But his freedom was short-lived. The next day he was arrested by state officers, brought before a state judge, and charged with violating the state statutes against fraud. He protested that he had already been tried and punished by the federal government for using the mails for fraudulent purposes, and he pointed to the Fifth Amendment provision that no person shall "be subject for the same offense to be twice put in jeopardy of life or limb."

The judge answered that the double jeopardy provision is contained in the Fifth Amendment and the Fifth Amendment does not apply to the states. Anyway, the judge told Crook, "the Supreme Court of the United States has said that double jeopardy prevents only two trials by the *same* government for the same offense.[20] Crook, who had learned something about constitutional rights while serving in the federal penitentiary, then argued that the Fourteenth Amendment, which *does* apply to the states, forbids them to prose-

[18]*Robinson* v. *California* (1962).
[19]*Powell* v. *Texas* (1968).
[20]*United States* v. *Lanza* (1922).

cute persons for offenses for which the persons have already been tried by the federal government. But the judge pointed to a 1959 Supreme Court decision (although somewhat undermined by more recent decisions, it still has not been reversed) in which the Court had sustained a state conviction of a man for robbing a bank after he had previously been acquitted of the same offense by a federal court.[21]

What constitutional rights can Crook claim in the state courts? In the first place, every state constitution contains a bill of rights listing practically the same guarantees against state abridgement that the Bill of Rights in the national Constitution contains against national abridgement. By and large, however, state judges have been less inclined than federal judges to construe constitutional guarantees of their own state constitutions liberally in favor of those accused of crime.

To what extent does the national Constitution protect courtroom freedoms from state abridgement? The Bill of Rights does not apply to the states but the Fourteenth Amendment does, and it contains two clauses of great importance in courtroom procedures—the due process and the equal protection clauses.

The equal-protection-of-the-laws clause protects persons accused of crime against discriminatory state action. Hence, when the state provides trial by jury, it must be a fair and impartial jury. For example, a jury, either grand or petit (trial), from which Negroes have been barred because of their race would not be able constitutionally to try a Negro, for this would deny him equal protection of the laws. (Such action would also violate the civil rights of Negroes denied the opportunity to serve on juries.) Nor could a state provide different punishments for persons of different races or religions.

THE BILL OF RIGHTS, THE FOURTEENTH AMENDMENT, AND THE STATES

For some time a persistent minority of the Supreme Court justices has argued that the due process clause of the Fourteenth Amendment should be construed to impose on the states exactly the same limitations that the Bill of Rights imposes on the national government. The Supreme Court still has not gone so far as to make the due process clause of the Fourteenth Amendment a mirror image of the Bill of Rights and it still has not adopted the doctrine of "total incorporation," but it is coming closer to this position.

Until very recently the official doctrine of the Court was that only those rights "implicit in the concept of ordered liberty" that are so important that neither "liberty nor justice would exist if they were sacrificed" are, so to speak, automatically included within the Fourteenth Amendment. Outside the scope of these rights, the test in each case is whether the procedures adopted by a state are fundamentally fair—not whether the procedures are those required of the national government by the Bill of Rights.

This formula, known as the Palko test or the doctrine of selective incorporation, was formulated by Justice Cardozo.[22] Using the Palko test, the Supreme Court distinguished between such rights as the First Amendment

[21]*Bartkus* v. *Illinois* (1959).
[22]*Palko* v. *Connecticut* (1937).

freedoms, which are so fundamental that there can be no liberty or justice if they are lost, and indictment by grand jury or trials before a jury in civil cases. Replacement of these latter rights by other procedures would not necessarily be a denial of justice or liberty.

Beginning in the 1930s and accelerating after 1964, the Supreme Court has selectively incorporated provision after provision of the Bill of Rights into the requirements of the due process clause of the Fourteenth Amendment. Moreover, it has revised the Palko test. Instead of asking if a particular safeguard is necessary for a civilized society, the Court now asks if such a safeguard is fundamental to an Anglo-American regime of ordered liberty. For example, in *Duncan* v. *Louisiana* (1968) the Supreme Court brought the right to trial by jury for serious offenses into the due process clause. The justices conceded that in some societies justice might be secured without juries (in most criminal trials in England, for example, juries are not used), but "in the American States," as in the federal judicial system, "a general grant of jury trial for serious offenses is a fundamental right, essential for preventing miscarriages of justice and for assuring that fair trials are provided for all defendants."

Today, the Fourteenth Amendment imposes on the states all the requirements of the Bill of Rights except those of the Second, Third, and Tenth Amendments, which are not applicable to the states, the requirement that indictments for serious crimes must be by a grand jury, the guarantee of trial by jury in civil cases involving more than $20, and the limitation against trying a person twice for the same crime. (It seems likely that the limitation against double jeopardy will soon be brought within the scope of the Fourteenth Amendment.) The Supreme Court, however, may refrain from accepting the doctrine of total incorporation in order to allow the states to use such procedures as indictment by information.

Dissenting justices, such as John Marshall Harlan, and other critics argue that the "onward march of the . . . discredited incorporation doctrine" undermines our federal system. The Constitution, they contend, leaves each state free to adopt whatever procedures for criminal indictment that its own legislature and courts desire, provided these procedures result in fundamental fairness, and Supreme Court justices should refrain from subjecting "state legal processes to enveloping federal judicial authority."[23]

The Court majority and their defenders respond that the vague, subjective test of fundamental fairness requires the Supreme Court "to intervene in the state judicial process with considerable lack of predictability and with a consequent likelihood of considerable friction." The failure of state courts either to apply the provisions of their respective state constitutions or properly to construe Supreme Court rulings with respect to due process led to such shocking examples of injustice that the Supreme Court had to set forth clear and imperative constitutional standards. With the elaboration for state courts of the same rules that have long been followed by national courts, the state judges will know in advance how to proceed, and there should be much less need for the Supreme Court to set aside state decisions on review or for federal district judges to have to use their habeas corpus jurisdiction to

[23]*Mapp* v. *Ohio* (1961); *Malloy* v. *Hogan* (1964); *Robinson* v. *California* (1962); *Gideon* v. *Wainright* (1963); *Pointer* v. *Texas* (1965); *Washington* v. *Texas* (1967).

197

CHAPTER 8
Rights
to Citizenship,
Life, Liberty
and Property

free from state custody persons who have been denied constitutional rights by the state. "And, to deny to the states the power to impair a fundamental constitutional right is not to increase federal power, but, rather, to limit the power of both federal and state governments in favor of safeguarding the fundamental rights and liberties of the individual."[24]

Now that for practically all purposes the Bill of Rights has been incorporated into the Fourteenth Amendment, future constitutional battles are likely to develop between those who argue, like Justice Black, that "the first section of the Fourteenth Amendment not only incorporates the specifics of the first eight amendments, but it is *confined to them*,"[25] and those who believe, like Justice Douglas, that in addition to incorporating all the specific provisions of the Bill of Rights, the due process clause protects other fundamental rights too, for example, the right to privacy. Justice Douglas sees the Supreme Court as the champion of the poor and oppressed and quotes approvingly the views of the late Edmond Cahn: "Be not reasonable with inquisitions, anonymous informers, and secret files that mock American justice. . . . Exercise the full judicial power of the United States; nullify them, forbid them; and make us proud again." Justice Black, long a champion of total incorporation and vigorous enforcement of the Bill of Rights, would not allow members of the Court to impose on the country their own notions of fundamental rights except those specified in the Constitution. He quotes approvingly from Judge Learned Hand: "For myself it would be most irksome to be ruled by a bevy of Platonic Guardians, even if I knew how to choose them, which I assuredly do not."[26]

How Just Is Our System of Justice?

What are the major criticisms of the American system of justice? How have they been answered?

Too many loopholes. It is argued that in our zeal to protect the innocent and place the burden of proof on the government, we have established so many elaborate procedures that justice is delayed, disrespect for the law is encouraged, and guilty men are allowed to go unpunished. Justice should be swift and sure without being arbitrary. But under our procedures a criminal may go unpunished because (1) the police decide not to arrest him, (2) the judge decides not to hold him, (3) the prosecutor decides not to prosecute him, (4) the grand jury decides not to indict him, (5) the jury decides not to convict him, (6) the judge decides not to sentence him, (7) an appeals court decides to reverse the conviction, or (8) the executive decides to pardon, reprieve, or parole him. As a result, some complain, the public never knows whom to hold responsible when laws are not enforced. The police can blame the prosecutor, the prosecutor can blame the police, and they can all blame the grand jury.

[24]Justice Goldberg concurring in *Pointer* v. *Texas* (1965).
[25]Henry J. Abraham, *Freedom and the Court* (Oxford Univ. Press, 1967).
[26]*Griswold* v. *Connecticut* (1965).

And yet there is more to justice than simply securing convictions. We must remember that all steps in the administration of criminal laws developed out of centuries of trial and error and that each of them has been constructed to provide protection against particular abuses. History warns against entrusting the instruments of enforcing criminal law to a single functionary. For this reason responsibility is vested in many officials. And as long as these safeguards are maintained, no one need fear for his life or liberty because of the overzealous or despotic action of another.

The most debatable step in the administration of justice is the grand jury, for many people feel that this procedure is unnecessary. W. F. Willoughby summarized the criticisms of the grand jury when he stated that it

> . . . is in the nature of a fifth wheel; that real responsibility for the bringing of criminal charges is in fact exercised by the prosecuting attorney, the grand jury doing little or nothing more than follow his suggestions; that it entails delay . . . ; that it renders prosecution more difficult through important witnesses getting beyond the jurisdiction . . . or through memory of facts becoming weakened by lapse of time; that it entails unnecessary expense to the government; and that it imposes a great burden on the citizen called upon to render jury service.[27]

As a result of such criticisms, in England the grand jury has been largely replaced. And in this country twenty-eight of our states allow the prosecuting attorney to dispense with grand jury indictments for all but the most serious crimes. The prosecutor simply files an *information affidavit* that he has evidence in his possession to justify a trial.

But the grand jury has its defenders; they see it as a necessary body to protect innocent persons against arbitrary prosecutors. Although in a formal sense a man is presumed to be innocent even after he has been charged with committing a crime, in actual practice indictment injures a person's reputation and subjects him to the expense and strain of defending himself. And "the charge that the grand jury is dominated by the prosecutor is not substantiated by the available evidence."[28] Furthermore, grand juries have the power—and there are many instances when they have used it—to carry out their own independent investigations and to act when a lax prosecutor is permitting crimes to go unpunished. The grand jury is one of the few agencies with the power to limit the almost unfettered discretion of the prosecuting officers.

Too unreliable. Critics who complain that our system of justice is unreliable point to trial by jury as the chief source of trouble. Trial by jury, they argue, leads to a theatrical combat between lawyers who base their appeals on the prejudice and sentiments of the jurors. "Mr. Prejudice and Miss Sympathy are the names of witnesses whose testimony is never recorded, but must nevertheless be reckoned with in trials by jury."[29] Too often verdicts are influenced by the jurors' dislike for an attorney's personality or for a de-

---

[27]W. F. Willoughby, *Principles of Judicial Administration* (Brookings, 1929), p. 186.

[28]Robert Scigliano, "The Grand Jury, the Information, and the Judicial Inquiry," *Oregon Law Review* (June 1959), p. 303.

[29]Jerome Frank, *Courts on Trial* (Princeton Univ. Press, 1949), p. 122; Harry Kalven and Hans Zeisel, *The American Jury* (Little, Brown, 1966) reports findings of the University of Chicago's massive study of the jury system.

fendant's appearance. In addition, because of mass circulation of newspapers, untrained jurors are easily swayed by the prejudices and sentiments of the community and lack the training to distinguish between fact and fiction. No other country relies as much on trial by jury as does the United States. In short, according to this argument, the jury system is an unreliable method of sorting the guilty from the innocent.

Defenders of the system reply that trial by jury provides an invaluable check by nonprofessionals over the actions of judges and prosecutors. Justice is too important to be left to the professionals. True, juries are sometimes swayed by their feelings, but the record of judges is not substantially better. The jury system, moreover, helps to educate citizens and enables them to participate in the application of their own laws. The jury trial, said Justice Murphy, has the beneficial effect of "leavening justice with the spirit of the times." Abuses in the system call for improvement, not abolishment.

Too inflexible. The elaborate and detailed procedures of our system of justice, some critics complain, stem from the day when people wanted to limit the behavior of royal officials over whom they had no other control. But now there are better methods of preventing abuse. Modern newspapers and other media of information also reduce the danger that officials will act despotically. Then, too, hemming in the administrators of criminal laws with detailed procedures denies them the discretion that modern criminology calls for. Each criminal should be dealt with as an individual, and the findings of sociology, psychology, and criminology should be applied to protect the community and to rehabilitate the criminal. More attention should be paid to selecting better prosecutors and judges, and to ensuring them the discretion they need to administer justice.

Again, defenders of the system reply that the day of arbitrary officials has not passed. They cite cases in which prosecutors, judges, and juries have deprived individuals of justice or have failed to prosecute the guilty. So long as we have to deal with men as they are, rather than as they should be, we must limit the discretion of those who apply criminal law and trust to the Constitution itself to provide the system with the necessary flexibility.

Too discriminatory against minorities and the poor. There are two aspects to this criticism. First, it is argued that the high cost of justice gives an advantage to the man who can afford the best legal advice and who can pay for the appeals and other expenses connected with preparing his defense. The second aspect is that minority groups, especially Negroes, do not receive equal treatment before the law.

Perhaps on no problem has the Supreme Court worked harder during the last several decades than to give reality to the ideal of equal justice under the law. The Court has laid down a whole series of rules to give a poor man the same treatment before the courts as a rich man. In *Gideon* v. *Wainright* (1963), the Supreme Court ruled that just as the Sixth Amendment requires federal judges to assign counsel to all impoverished persons accused of serious federal crimes, so the Fourteenth Amendment requires state judges to be sure that all persons accused of state crimes are adequately represented by trained legal counsel. (Until Gideon, the Constitution required states to provide counsel only in cases involving capital punishment or in which peculiar circumstances—youth or ignorance of the defendant, for example—made the assignment of counsel especially necessary for a fair trial.) The Supreme Court also insisted that no appeal procedure be allowed to make it more difficult for a poor defendant to secure an appeal than a rich one. For example, if a state requires transcripts for appeals, it must see that such transcripts are made available to those who cannot afford to purchase them.[30] Congress, too, has acted. In 1964 Congress made federal funds available to pay fees and cover some of the costs of attorneys assigned by a federal court to assist indigent defendants, thereby making it more likely that the assigned counsel will be able to provide an adequate defense.

Discrimination against minorities, especially Negroes, in the administration of justice remains a major defect of our system. Police brutality is a serious problem in the United States, with Negroes feeling the brunt of it. As the United States Commission on Civil Rights reports, this brutality is largely confined to state and local police and to prison forces, but no section of the nation has a monopoly on it. The practice of Negro exclusion from juries persists "even though it has long stood indicted as a serious violation of the Fourteenth Amendment."[31] Negroes are subject to more severe punishment than whites for the same crimes, and in some regions whites who commit crimes against Negroes are not indicted by white grand juries or convicted by white jurors, who share the defendants' attitudes.

Courts and police are inevitably composed of men who reflect the prejudices and values of the society of which they are a part. When poverty and prejudice exist in the community, they will affect all institutions of the community. And yet there are few agencies that do as much as the courts to isolate prejudice and to compensate for poverty. As the Commission on Civil Rights stated, "There is much to be proud of in the American system of criminal justice. For it is administered largely without regard to the race, creed, or color of the persons involved. . . ."

In summary, some observers believe that our system of justice could be improved without sacrificing the essential safeguards. But others believe, along with the late Justice Rutledge, that "the old time-tried 'principles and institutions of the common law' perpetuated for us in the Bill of Rights" are a "basic charter of personal liberty, and there should be no experimentation with them under the guise of improving the administration of justice."[32]

The Supreme Court and Civil Liberties

In our discussion of civil liberties and civil rights, it has become clear that the judges, especially those on the Supreme Court, play a significant role in enforcing constitutional guarantees. In fact, this combination of judicial enforcement and written guarantees of enumerated liberties is one of the basic features of the American system of government. Although some of the Framers thought of the Bill of Rights as merely a statement of general principles to guide government officials, it is now regarded as a *judi-*

[30]Anthony Lewis, *Gideon's Trumpet* (Random House, 1964).
[31]*Report of the United States Commission on Civil Rights on Justice* (1962), pp. 26ff.
[32]Concurring opinion, *In re Oliver* (1948).

cially enforceable limitation on legislative and executive powers. As the late Justice Jackson wrote: "The very purpose of a Bill of Rights was to withdraw certain subjects from the vicissitudes of political controversy, to place them beyond the reach of majorities and officials and to establish them as legal principles to be applied by the courts. One's right to life, liberty, and property, to free speech, a free press, freedom of worship and assembly, and other fundamental rights may not be submitted to vote: they depend on the outcome of no elections." Or as Samuel Krislov has pointed out: "One is reminded of Godfrey Cambridge's nightmare: A telephone rings and a voice announces: 'We've had a referendum on slavery in California and you lost. Report to the auction block in four hours.'"[33]

This emphasis on constitutional limitations and judicial enforcement is an example of the "auxiliary precautions" that James Madison felt were necessary to prevent arbitrary governmental action. Other free nations rely more on elections and political checks to protect their rights, but in the United States we look to judges to hear appeals from people who feel that their freedoms are being jeopardized. All judges, not only those on the Supreme Court, have taken an oath to measure the actions of public officials against the appropriate constitutional, as well as legislative, provisions.

English judges have authority to restrain executive officials from depriving people of their legal rights, but they do not have the power to declare legislative acts unconstitutional. Moreover, Englishmen place primary reliance on an alert and aroused public opinion, operating through elected officials, to safeguard their liberty. Justice Jackson once commented: "I have been repeatedly impressed with the speed and certainty with which the slightest invasion of British individual freedom or minority rights by officials of the government is picked up in Parliament, not merely by the opposition but by the party in power, and made the subject of persistent questioning, criticism, and sometimes rebuke. There is no waiting on the theory that the judges will take care of it. . . . In Great Britain, to observe civil liberties is good politics and to transgress the rights of the individual or minority is bad politics. In the United States, I cannot say this is so."[34]

In the United States, our emphasis on judicial protection of civil liberties focuses attention on the Supreme Court. But only a small number of controversies are carried to the Court, and a Supreme Court decision is not the end of the policy-making process; compliance with its rulings "does not necessarily, universally, or automatically follow their enunciation."[35] Only now are political scientists beginning to analyze the complex process by which the policies announced by the Supreme Court justices are or are not translated into changes in the political system.[36] It is the judges of lower courts, the policemen, the superintendents of schools, and the local prosecutors who translate the doctrines enunciated by the Court and who do or do not apply them.

[33]Samuel Krislov, *The Supreme Court and Political Freedom* (Free Press, 1968), p. 35.
[34]Robert H. Jackson, *The Supreme Court in the American System of Government* (Harvard Univ. Press, 1955), pp. 81–82.
[35]See Richard M. Johnson, *The Dynamics of Compliance: Supreme Court Decision-Making from a New Perspective* (Northwestern Univ. Press, 1967), p. 3; "Interrogations in New Haven: The Impact of *Miranda*," *Yale Law Journal* (July 1967), pp. 1519–1648.
[36]Krislov, *op. cit.*, pp. 166–220.

To focus attention on the constitutionality of laws is to risk ignoring consideration of their merits. Much that is constitutional may still be unwise, and it is often more important to ask if it should be done rather than if it may constitutionally be done. Moreover, to consider civil liberties only in the context of constitutionality may cause us to ignore other factors of critical significance in determining the extent of our liberties. We cannot protect freedom merely through lawsuits and legal decisions. A society plagued by depression, hysteria, and riots offers a poor prospect for keeping freedom, no matter what is set down in the Constitution or what the judges may decide. Efforts to prevent poverty and insecurity, to preserve order and stability, may have more to do with maintaining our constitutional freedoms than the actions of our judges.

We must not, of course, underestimate the contribution of the Supreme Court in defending civil liberties. Aside from its decision-making power, its opinions are influential in clarifying the law and determining people's attitudes. And perhaps of greatest significance, the Supreme Court as an instrument of the national majority has been able to prevent local majorities in control of a state legislature or state judicial system from using their authority to deprive local minorities of constitutional rights. The Supreme Court was the first to act to end state-imposed racial segregation, to break control of rural minorities over state legislatures, and to curb local police brutality in interrogations and administration of justice.

But the Supreme Court is of little consequence unless its decisions reflect a national consensus. The judges by themselves cannot guarantee anything. Neither can the First Amendment. As the late Justice Jackson once asked: "Must we first maintain a system of free political government to assure a free judiciary, or can we rely on an aggressive, activist judiciary to guarantee free government? . . . [It] is my belief that the attitude of a society and of its organized political forces, rather than its legal machinery, is the controlling force in the character of free institutions. . . . [Any] court which undertakes by its legal processes to enforce civil liberties needs the support of an enlightened and vigorous public opinion. . . ."[37] In short, only so long as we desire liberty for ourselves and are willing to restrict our own actions in order to preserve the liberty of others can freedom be maintained.

[37]Jackson, *op. cit.*

THE PEOPLE IN POLITICS

PART
FOUR

A PROBLEM GUIDE

A central problem in realizing government by the people in a mass society is popular representation. Part Four raises the crucial question: Who really governs in democratic society? Do all people take part? Do some people have more political influence than others? Through what instruments do people express themselves politically—interest groups, mass media, political parties, demonstrations, violence? How are the people organized to take part in government by the people? And how do these different types of political organizations and forms of representation square with the ideals of democratic government?

The basic inquiry in Chapter 9 concerns the formation and expression of political attitudes. What is the nature and role of public opinion in the free society? Who are the shapers of opinion—TV news commentators, newspaper columnists, politicians? How much influence do such persons have over our political behavior? Do they really represent popular political opinion?

Chapters 10 and 11 develop the problem of popular representation in its principal forms—voting and interest-group activity. One key issue is the extent of representation. Millions of Americans do not vote because they are barred from the polls; other millions do not vote because going to the polls does not seem worth the effort. Some Americans' views are actively reflected by influential organizations. Others seem to find few, if any, organized groups promoting their interests. How serious are these problems in a democracy? How much equality of political influence do we have in America?

Chapter 12, concerning political parties, deals with this same problem of fair representation but in connection with another part of our political system. Under a two-party system, in theory at least, the party that wins a majority of the votes then proceeds to represent the interests of that popular majority in government. How effectively does the winning party speak for the majority of voters that elected it? That raises another question: Can the parties be strengthened so that they may represent their supporters more effectively? (Whether or not the parties should be strengthened is taken up in Chapter 20.) And what about the minority party—can it do the job of opposing the majority as well as it should?

A final problem of Part Four is the fairness and efficiency of the electoral system. We might think that electoral machinery would be neutral, but it is not. Some election arrangements make it difficult for people to vote. Others—for example, the electoral college—give some voters more weight than others in the election of office seekers. How fair is our system of nominating political candidates—especially the President? Chapter 13 raises such problems, which all relate to the basic question in Part Four—the question of equality of political influence for the sake of fair representation in government.

Sometimes this problem of fair representation is described in terms of special interests versus the general interest. The special interests are often pictured as small, selfish groups that "gang up" on the rest of the people, who represent the general interest. Actually, the problem is more complex. As used here, the term *special interest* means the interest (the goal or attitude) of considerably less than the whole. It is special in the sense that it immediately and directly favors and is sought by a part rather than the totality. The general interest simply means the goal or attitude of all or most of the people.

Public Opinion:
The Voices of the People

9   Government by the people is supposed to be government in accordance with the will of the people. But what is the will of the people? What does government do when people disagree? What does it do when opinions change? What does it do when most of the people are indifferent about some issues, while a minority is active and noisy? Should government itself try to influence opinion? If so, how far should it go?

Let us look at these questions from the vantage point of a senator in Washington. He wants to be the servant of the people. But he is not sure what the people want. He cannot really tell from his mail, because he is not sure that the letterwriters actually reflect opinion back home. He is suspicious of public opinion polls. He is not sure just what issues he was elected on, because he argued for and against so many propositions in his last campaign. Besides, it is five years since he was elected, and many important events have taken place in that time. He listens for the voice of the people, but the people do not speak with a single voice. No wonder he straddles the fence. From his point of view, the people are straddling the fence. But governments must act; decisions must be made. Somehow, out of the confusion, politicians must shape fairly precise and positive policies. To see the relation between political opinions and governmental actions, we must look first at the variety of people involved.

Millions of Publics

There is no one public opinion. This might seem rather obvious, but how often have you heard a politician claim that "the public wants such and such" or a columnist contend that "the people" reacted in a certain way?

A group of students takes over a college building. Think of this incident in terms of the public opinion it creates. The public is actually made up of a number of publics—the rest of the student body, the administration, the faculty, the local townspeople, parents, the taxpayers. And all react in different ways—some are sympathetic, some hostile, some neutral, many indifferent. Some people read about the incident in the newspapers, shake their heads, and forget about it; others write to the governor or their state legislator. Some suspect a Communist plot; others laugh, "boys will be boys."

In virtually all political situations, many public opinions exist because many publics exist—especially in a pluralist democracy. Translate the student episode into a national issue, and one sees the tremendous complexity of public opinion and the many publics involved. When the President makes a speech about labor legislation, his words fall differently on the ears of union members, businessmen, union leaders, farmers, Democrats, Republicans, and so on. When the Secretary of Agriculture announces a new farm program, he gets mixed reactions not only from the large nonfarming public, but also from the farm public itself—that is, from cotton farmers as against wheat farmers, from large farmers as against small farmers. When a senator calls for the end of government subsidies, many businessmen applaud because they want lower taxes, but businessmen, such as ship operators, who are receiving subsidies do not applaud. These are examples merely of different interests—but the whole process is immensely complicated by the different attitudes that people have by reason of their economic and social status, their group loyalties, their occupation, their degree of understanding or information.

What, then, are some of the important aspects of public opinions—and of the various publics that hold them?

Some kinds of political attitudes are fairly stable. People's attitudes toward certain matters may change slowly, if at all, even though the world may be changing around them. This is especially true of loyalty toward one's own group and hostility toward competitive or hostile groups. Thus, for many people political party preferences vary little over the years, as Table 9-1 suggests. In general, people remain more loyal to their groups, including their political parties, than toward issues or policies that they cannot relate to those groups.

Party preferences help stabilize other political attitudes; the political party serves as a reference point. A strong Democrat is more likely to conclude that the Democratic candidates are men of integrity and to view their policy proposals favorably than a man without any party identification or with a preference for the Republicans. In the midst of the 1956 campaign, when the Suez crisis exploded, persons who had planned to vote for Stevenson viewed the crisis as proof that Eisenhower was not doing a good job and that Stevenson was needed. But voters who had planned to support Eisenhower saw the crisis as the kind of emergency that demanded the skill and experience of a man like Eisenhower. "Most voters merely fitted the new information," points out Warren Miller, "into an old partisan frame, used the new situation further to justify their previous decision, and voted the way they had intended to vote all along."[1]

TABLE 9-1
Party Self-Identification, 1952–1966

Party Preference	1952	1954	1956	1958	1960	1962	1964	1966
Strong Democrat	22%	22%	21%	23%	21%	23%	26%	18%
Weak Democrat	25	25	23	24	25	23	25	28
Independent Democrat	10	9	6	7	8	8	9	9
Independent	5	7	9	8	8	8	8	12
Independent Republican	7	6	8	4	7	6	6	7
Weak Republican	14	14	14	16	13	16	13	15
Strong Republican	13	13	15	13	14	12	11	10
Apolitical	4	4	4	5	4	4	2	1
	100%	100%	100%	100%	100%	100%	100%	100%

SOURCE: Survey Research Center, University of Michigan.

Partisanship not only colors our response to what political leaders do; strong partisans are also likely to impute to their candidate support for ideas and issues that they favor even though the candidate himself does not. And even when a voter votes for the candidate from the opposition, he often assumes that the man he favors really supports the position the voter imputes to his own party.

Public opinion on some issues is fluid. Certain kinds of political attitudes can change dramatically, almost overnight. Isolationist feeling in 1941, for example, practically disappeared following the attack on Pearl Harbor. Changes occur less in response to the exhortations or even the acts of political leaders than to nonpolitical events—a depression, frustrations in Vietnam, the movement of people from country to city. The intensity and durability of an opinion turns largely on its *saliency*—whether it is "relatively important, at the focus of attention, crowding out other items, a pivot for organizing one's thoughts and acts."[2] What was controversial yesterday may not arouse much interest today. Following the Korean War, McCarthyism was the center of national attention, and political leaders carefully calculated

[1]Warren Miller, "The Political Behavior of the Electorate," *The American Government Annual, 1960–1961* (Holt, 1960), p. 53. V. O. Key, Jr., emphasizes in *The Responsible Electorate* (Harvard Univ. Press, 1966) that aggregate data may exaggerate party stability, because many individuals may switch parties and cancel one another out.

[2]Robert E. Lane and David O. Sears, *Public Opinion* (Prentice-Hall, 1964), p. 15.

whether to support or oppose it. By 1957 charges and countercharges about subversion ceased to attract much attention.

People vary greatly in the intensity of their beliefs. Some are mildly in favor, for example, of gun-control legislation; others are mildly opposed; still others are fanatically for or against. Such variations in intensity have important political results. Some people may have no interest in the matter at all. The attitudes of the passive can probably be easily changed. And those with strong feelings may try to organize in groups, to win votes, to campaign. (The more intense one feels about an issue, the more likely he is to do something about it; but many people satisfy their needs by talk and do nothing else.)

The public is made up of numberless subpublics. As we found in the reaction to our college incident, there are many different publics existing in our society. These subpublics vary in their interest in a given issue, their level of understanding, their basic attitudes, their religion, or race, their section or locality, their economic or social position, their education, and so on. Moreover, these thousands of subpublics cut across one another in a thousand different ways, creating millions of sub-subpublics.

The public is often indifferent to political issues. We must distinguish between the public and the "attentive public." Front-page headlines tell of a crisis in Laos, the story is featured in television specials, it makes a lead article in *Time*, and it becomes the center of conversation at the student union. Lights burn late in the White House and students organize to send telegrams. From all this activity, one might conclude that the issue has excited public attention. But careful research often reveals that the mass of the public may have a hazy notion of what is involved—but little interest. During the Suez crisis in 1956 editorial writers speculated about its impact on the electorate, but the Survey Research Center found that less than 10 percent of the voters responded in any way at all to the crisis.

Some, who discover that the general public is more concerned about sports than politics, that the New York *Daily News* has more customers than *The New York Times*, and that "The Beverly Hillbillies" draws far more television viewers than a political debate, become cynical and contemptuous of the masses or charge that behind the façade of our democratic system a "power elite" manipulates the public. Such pessimists fail to recognize that there are important links between the attentive publics and the public and that the attentive publics are not unified, monolithic entities but reflect the range of interests of the public itself.

Public opinion may be latent. Even though public attitudes on a particular issue have not crystallized, they are important, for they can be evoked and converted into action. Latent public opinion may have little direct impact on political decisions, but it has long-run political consequences; it sets rough boundaries within which the attentive publics and political leaders must operate. When leaders conclude that a public policy would give their opponents an opportunity to activate latent opinion, the issue is seldom debated. For example, leaders assume, rightly or wrongly, that the issue of United States recognition of Communist China would provoke such hostile reactions from the public that it is too hot to handle.

But latent opinion is an opportunity for political leaders as well as a danger. Especially in time of crisis, Presidents or other leaders "may capture the attention of the ordinarily inattentive public, provide cues of direction and clarification, and amass . . . support" for their policies.[3] Or, as Lasswell has summed it up, "Crisis concentrates attention; noncrisis disperses it."

Political attitudes among the most informed tend to cluster. Those who oppose federal aid to education are more likely than those who favor it also to oppose a federal social security program to provide medical care; those who feel strongly that the federal government should protect civil rights of Negroes are more likely than those who do not hold this view to oppose motion-picture censorship. Again, this generalization has to be qualified. Politicians and editorial writers sometimes assume that the public can be placed into broad categories ranging from the most conservative to the most liberal and that after identifying a citizen as a conservative, one can predict from this latent political attitude how he will respond toward various issues. But Campbell and his associates, in their studies of national samples, found that only 2 percent could be classified as persons who look at political men and events in terms of a liberal-conservative scale. "Most people," Key wrote, "[have] no latent ideological outlook along a liberal-conservative scale to be activated by the manipulation of the appropriate symbol."[4] However, political *leaders* are more likely to think and act in symbolic terms and hence their political attitudes are more likely to cluster.

Does all this mean that the "average" American has no ideology—that only his leaders have it? Much depends on what is meant by ideology. Certainly most Americans hold general notions and beliefs. The Lynds noted, in their famous study of Middletown (Muncie, Indiana) years ago, that people tended to believe such things as "America is a land of promise," "the middle way is the best way," and "if a man does not get on, it is his own fault." But even these beliefs were shot through with ambiguities and contradictions. For example, "Honesty is the best policy. *But*: Business is business, and a businessman would be a fool if he didn't cover his hand." Or, "Education is a fine thing. *But*: It is the practical man who gets things done."[5] But if by ideology we mean an integrated set of beliefs about the nature of man, the goals he should aspire to, the ways to reach those goals, and the role of the individual and the state, the average American would appear to be less ideological than the average Russian or Chinese.

Where Do Our Opinions Come From?

Living in a democracy can be confusing. Everyone seems to be trying to get our ear or catch our eye so he can press his point of view on us. Under a dictatorship life is much simpler—there is one official public

---

[3]V. O. Key, Jr., *Public Opinion and American Democracy* (Knopf, 1961), p. 285, which is also the source of the Lasswell quotation.

[4]*Ibid.*, p. 281.

[5]R. S. Lynd and H. M. Lynd, *Middletown in Transition* (Harcourt, Brace & World, 1937), pp. 402–486; R. S. Lynd, *Knowledge for What?* (Princeton Univ. Press), p. 59. For the view that Americans have a belief in liberty, equality, and fraternity—a belief rooted in Christianity and the Enlightenment—see Gunnar Myrdal, *An American Dilemma*, rev. ed. (Harper, 1962); for a differing view—that of a French Dominican priest—see R. L. Bruckberger, *Image of America* (Viking, 1959).

opinion. Some of the lesser citizenry growl and mutter under their breath, but they are in no position to take a public stand. In a democracy we sometimes complain about the babel of voices that shriek at us in the newspapers and over the airwaves, but we sense, too, that this babel is a sign of a free society and one of its basic foundations.

If we look sharply, however, we can see a pattern even in the complex workings of public opinion in a democracy. There are certain forces that shape men's ideas, and there are certain methods of persuasion and propaganda common to all opinion-molders.

POLITICAL SOCIALIZATION

In recent years social scientists have delved deep into the age-old question of where our political opinions come from. For if a political system is to function, most of its members must share certain basic attitudes and accept as legitimate certain ways to resolve conflicts. What are the major institutions, attitudes, experiences, and personality characteristics that seem to interrelate with our political opinions and behavior?

Every society has means by which it socializes the young and inculcates basic values. First of all, our opinions are molded by our culture—by the overall beliefs and behavior that characterize American society. The process is, of course, circular: beliefs and attitudes of Americans determine our culture and our culture helps determine the beliefs and attitudes of Americans. But this observation does not advance our understanding of the process of political socialization very far; for one thing, it does not explain why Americans exposed to the same political culture with shared values have diverse attitudes and views within that culture.

Probably the most important opinion-molders are parents. "Foremost among agencies of socialization into politics is the family,"[6] wrote Herbert Hyman, and his observations have been confirmed by later investigators. We begin to form our picture of the world listening to our parents talk at breakfast or to the tales our older brothers and sisters bring home from school. What we learn in the family are not so much specific political opinions, but the basic attitudes that will shape our future opinions—attitudes toward our neighbors, toward other classes or types of people, toward local rules or customs, toward society in general. "The family is bound up with all the great crises and transitions of life," says MacIver. "It is the primary agent in molding of the life habits and life attitudes of human beings."[7] Some of us may rebel against the ways of the close little group in which we live, but most of us conform. The family is a sort of link between the past and the present. It translates the world to us, but it does so on its own terms.

Schools and churches are other powerful opinion-shapers. Indeed, Hess and Torney have concluded that the "public school is the most important and effective instrument of political socialization in the United States."[8] And

[6]Herbert Hyman, *Political Socialization* (Free Press, 1959), p. 69.
[7]R. M. MacIver, *The Web of Government* (Macmillan, 1947), p. 23.
[8]Robert D. Hess and Judith V. Torney, *The Development of Basic Attitudes and Values toward Government and Citizenship during the Elementary School Years*, part I (U.S. Office of Education, 1965), p. 193.

in church, we are influenced by sermons and symbols. At an early age children begin to pick up specific political values and to acquire basic attitudes toward our system of government. Even very small schoolchildren know the name of the President and his party affiliation and have strong attitudes toward him,[9] and children as young as nine or ten begin to have a fairly precise knowledge of what a President stands for, though this perception will vary with the personality of the man. In a study of primary grade students, Roberta Sigel found that "the Kennedy image was rich, specific, and considerably more politicized than we had anticipated. He was particularly well remembered for his efforts on behalf of peace and civil rights."[10]

That parents and schools influence children's attitudes—surely this is an obvious, commonsense fact that does not require elaborate research. But political scientists are curious about the *relative* impact of these and other forces on young people, and on different types of young people—for example, working-class as against middle-class children. Investigators have also become interested in the question of whether parental and school influences tend to give young people a greater faith in existing political institutions. "The thrust of school experience is undoubtedly on the side of developing trust in the political system in general," according to one study. "Civic training in schools abounds in rituals of system support in the formal curriculum."[11] In one school that stressed the pluralist democratic creed—equality, tolerance, civic participation—there was a decided increase of support for that creed among students.[12] A recent study has indicated that even at a tender age, children begin to reflect adult feelings of mastery over their political environment.[13] These findings, if further substantiated, may have significant implications. For example, they might indicate continuity and even conservatism in the American political system and might strengthen the arguments of critics of pluralist democracy, who say that this outwardly fast-changing system conceals latent biases toward the status quo.

Still, the impact of formal institutions must not be exaggerated. We probably learn as much outside the classroom as in it, for we are reacting not merely to teachers and books but also to the behavior, manner, dress, talk, and attitudes of others. The same is true of our church—we are influenced not only by ministers, but by other members of the congregation.

COLLEGE AND OTHER INFLUENCES

College is another—and, for some, a decisive—influence on political values and attitudes. However, in college it is perhaps much less the formal instruction that is influential than the exposure to the total environment of a

[9]Fred Greenstein, *Children and Politics* (Yale Univ. Press, 1965). See also David Easton and Robert D. Hess, "The Child's Political World," *Midwest Journal of Political Science* (August 1962), pp. 229–246.

[10]Roberta S. Sigel, "Image of a President: Some Insights into the Political Views of School Children," *The American Political Science Review* (March 1968), pp. 216–226.

[11]M. Kent Jennings and Richard G. Niemi, "The Transmission of Political Values from Parent to Child," *The American Political Science Review* (March 1968), p. 178.

[12]Edgar Litt, "Civic Education, Community Norms, and Political Indoctrination," *American Sociological Review* (February 1962), pp. 69–75.

[13]David Easton and Jack Dennis, "The Child's Acquisition of Regime Norms: Political Efficacy," *The American Political Science Review* (March 1967), p. 25.

campus—when that environment is sensitive to political events outside. Of course, the currents of student activisim in politics vary—over time, from campus to campus, and within a campus from group to group. In the 1950s college students moved toward apathy, conventionality, and ambiguity. In the 1960s college students became involved in civil rights crusades and war protests, and, although such movements directly affected only a small number of students, they helped to create the climate in which other students acted and reacted.[14] A pioneering study in the late 1930s demonstrated the impact of the college experience. It found that students, most of whom came from Republican, high-income families, tended over their four years in college to move closer to the prevailing liberal, New Deal norms of the college community. A follow-up study twenty years later showed that the students had generally adhered to their changed political attitudes. Of course, students do not necessarily shift in a liberal direction; in a different institution or in a different time the movement might be in the opposite direction.[15]

During and after school other forces come to be influential. Whether it is because people tend to marry those with similar views or because after marriage they influence each other's attitudes, the fact is that husband-wife agreement on political issues is very highly correlated. "When there is disagreement between one's spouse and one's parents, there is a greater chance that the contemporary influence will win out over the historical one, rather than vice versa."[16] Husbands influence their wives more than the reverse.

Newspapers are another source of political views. Indeed, it has been estimated that only one out of every twenty families in urban areas read no daily newspaper. Perhaps a large number read only the comics, sports, headlines, and pictures, but the total circulation of American newspapers is well over sixty million copies a day. There are countless foreign-language newspapers and thousands of weeklies—ranging from mass-circulation magazines, such as *Newsweek*, *Life*, and *The Saturday Evening Post*, to more specialized journals—plus the multitude of slicks and pulps. Walter Lippmann has called the newspaper the "bible of democracy, the book out of which a people determines its conduct."

And these major opinion-forming agencies do not exhaust the list of influences that focus on us. Books, for example, play an important though often intangible role, and the many groups or persons—political parties, interest groups, governments, politicians, businessmen, bureaucrats, corporations—that seek to use the media of communication and persuasion for their own ends also have their effect. How much influence do all these forces have in molding opinion? Are they as formidable as they seem?

HOW INFLUENTIAL ARE THE MASS MEDIA?

It can be argued that newspapers do not influence opinion very much, because often the editors think one way and the people vote the opposite

---

[14]Robert E. Lane, "The Need to be Liked and the Anxious College Liberal," *The Annals* (September 1965), p. 80.

[15]Theodore M. Newcomb, *Personality and Social Change* (Holt, 1957). See also Alex S. Edelstein, "Since Bennington: Evidence of Change in Student Political Behavior," *Public Opinion Quarterly* (Winter 1962), pp. 564–577.

[16]James C. Davies, *Human Nature in Politics* (Wiley, 1963), p. 177.

way. The four elections of Franklin D. Roosevelt to the Presidency are cited to support this view; he won these elections decisively, and he swept some urban areas where he had little or no newspaper support. John F. Kennedy's victory in 1960 is another case in point. Only one-third of American daily newspapers, representing less than one-sixth of the total daily circulation, backed Kennedy, yet he won, if only barely. And city bosses have flourished for years in the face of continued denunciation by local newspapers. The vast majority of newspaper readers do not look at the editorial page.[17]

But the real question is not whether the press directly influences our choices at the polls; it is whether it gives us a conception of the world about us that indirectly influences our political behavior. Our views are shaped, in Lippmann's words, by the "pictures inside our heads." The newspaper, in its front-page makeup, its headlines, its use of pictures, its playing up of some articles and playing down of others, its distortion or suppression of important information, helps form those pictures inside our heads. Thus, although it is significant that Roosevelt won in spite of the majority of the newspapers, the central question is the extent to which he had to modify his program and actions in the face of public opinion even before he began campaigning. The press has a long-run, continuous influence on opinions that may not be obvious in a particular election. "The steady flow of the propaganda of the media between elections probably strikes people at a time when their defenses are less effectively mobilized than they are during presidential campaigns."[18]

Other media, such as radio, television, and movies, can also be effective in molding political attitudes. It is sometimes thought that radio and television, whose entertainment programs are ostensibly neutral in politics, and the movies, which disseminate no political views as such, cannot be viewed in the same light as the press, which sometimes bears an obvious party label. But on the contrary, radio, television, and movies help mold our underlying attitudes and thus our decisions at the polls, just as the daily newspaper does. Indeed, the fact that they have no obvious party ties or open intention of influencing voters may actually increase their effect. A Johnny Carson, speaking to millions, may tell a story about Washington doings that will influence the votes of many more people than the speech of a leading party politician on another network. A movie depicting American bombing or Communist brutality in dramatic terms may affect attitudes toward American foreign policy more decisively than a statement by the Secretary of State.

MASS MEDIA AND LOCAL LEADERS

It seems clear, then, that the combined weight of the mass media—the press, movies, radio, and television—in opinion-making is great. Some social scientists believe that these agencies are coming to have more influence than the family itself in shaping attitudes, but it is difficult to prove this contention, because the particular influence of the home or the press cannot be

---

[17]Charles E. Swanson, "What They Read in 130 Daily Newspapers," *Journalism Quarterly* (Fall 1955), pp. 411–421; and Percy H. Tannenbaum, "The Effect of Headlines on the Interpretation of News Stories," *Journalism Quarterly* (September 1953), pp. 189–197.
[18]Key, *Public Opinion and American Democracy, op. cit.*, p. 403.

easily isolated for study. For example, if reading a Democratic newspaper for many years influences a father and he influences his son, which is the dominant factor, home or newspaper?

We do have some evidence, however, on the relative roles of radio and television versus newspapers in national campaigns. A study of the attitudes of members of the United Automobile Workers in the 1952 elections found that more of them distrusted newspapers than television as a source of information. And in an earlier study of Erie County, Ohio, voters indicated that the radio was a more important source in helping them make up their minds than the newspapers. On the other hand, Eisenhower supporters in the 1952 election and Dewey voters in 1944 said newspapers were more important to them. Perhaps these studies show, not that television and radio are more important sources, but that the newspapers (which in 1944 favored Dewey and in 1952 favored Eisenhower) were selected by those who favored the candidates, whereas the Democrats selected the more neutral views presented on radio and television.

This much seems clear: attention is always *selective*. Out of all the speeches, articles, news stories, political pamphlets, many voters ignore much or all of them. Those who listen to the speeches on television are the ones who are also likely to read the news stories. However, we all tend to select those speeches and those stories that support our predispositions. The television debates of 1960 between Kennedy and Nixon were highly dramatic; they may also have had further effects. For the first time in modern campaigning, strong Republicans and strong Democrats were exposed to the speeches of their political *opponents*. Republicans who without the debates might have tuned in only to hear Nixon, and Democrats who otherwise might never have been exposed to the Republican candidate, were compelled by the debates to confront the candidate and arguments of the other party. True, few strong partisans changed their minds, but some with less intense feelings probably did so.[19]

But whatever the role of press, television, and the other media, we must not lose sight of the fact that, above all, it is direct, face-to-face contacts that influence people, whether in family, neighborhood, or group. Studies have shown that the more personal the means of communication, the more effective it is in changing opinions. For example, other things being equal, it seems clear that face-to-face conversation has more effect than a television speech, and a television speech is more effective than a newspaper account of it.

Does this mean that personal methods of communication have more effect on opinions than institutional methods, such as newspapers? Possibly, but the problem is not that simple. For the local opinion leaders, who influence their friends through face-to-face conversations, may have gotten their ideas from a newspaper or magazine and may pass those ideas on to other people. If a friend drops in and sells me on the need for a sales tax, and if he in turn got the idea from a popular magazine, what is the source of the influence on

[19]See Sidney Kraus (ed.), *The Great Debates: Background-Perspective-Effects* (Indiana Univ. Press, 1962); Richard S. Salant, "The Television Debates: A Revolution That Deserves a Future," *Public Opinion Quarterly* (Fall 1962), pp. 335–350; and Stanley Kelley, Jr., "Campaign Debates: Some Facts and Issues," *Public Opinion Quarterly* (Fall 1962), pp. 351–366.

me? Opinions are the product of many interrelated forces, each acting on others. It seems safe to say, however, that the mass media of communication, although they may influence local opinion leaders, will never be a substitute for them.

"How to Win Friends and . . ."

We live in what has been called the propaganda age. Propaganda is, of course, nothing new, but in the twentieth century it has truly come into its own. The mass media have become enormous enterprises: newspapers with circulations in the millions, airwaves spanning the continent, movies showing in almost every city and town in the nation. The techniques of communication have been vastly improved in a few decades, and the art of propaganda itself has been refined in our century. Harold Lasswell has said, "A new skill group has come into existence in modern civilization . . . skill in propaganda has become one of the most effective roads to power in modern states."

WHAT IS PROPAGANDA?

Is propaganda bad? Not necessarily. Indeed, it is difficult to say just where propaganda ends and education starts. Effective education may include some propaganda (in favor of, say, democratic values, the virtues of which must be taken in part on faith). And if propaganda is defined as a "method used for influencing the conduct of others on behalf of predetermined ends," then almost every person who writes or talks with a purpose becomes a propagandist. Lasswell has described propaganda as a technique of social control—"the manipulation of collective attitudes by the use of significant symbols (words, pictures, and tunes) rather than violence, bribery, or boycott." Obviously propaganda in these terms may be used for good causes as well as evil ones.

Americans are almost constantly exposed to propaganda techniques, and advertisers exploit these techniques to the full. (It has been said that Adolf Hitler borrowed some of his propaganda methods from American publicity experts.) Advertisements are cunningly designed by "practical psychologists" to appeal to our basic attitudes, especially to our desire for recognition by others (above all, by members of our own group), for prestige, and for security. Constant repetition is the hallmark of effective propaganda. Malcom M. Willey writes, "In straight advertising, for example, the morning newspaper will carry the [advertising] copy; it will appear again in the street car (or even in the flip device in the taxicab); at the office a letter or a telegram may supplement what already has been said; the menu and the matches of the restaurant will serve as another medium of transmission; the afternoon paper repeats what the morning issue has already said; billboards are employed to catch a wandering eye; the radio program has its sponsor; the motion picture has not been free of advertising influence; and more recently the neon sign takes the 'message' far into the night."[20] This bombardment of potential buyers from all directions seems to get results.

As with the advertiser, so with the politician. The latter, seeking votes instead of sales, makes use of every agency of communication—from skywriting to automobile stickers—that will influence men's attitudes and actions.

PROPAGANDA IS POLITICS

Propaganda is often denounced as dishonest and dangerous, but it is also part of the currency of a democratic politics. As Edelman has written, "If politics is concerned with who gets what, or with the authoritative allocation of values, one may be pardoned for wondering why it need involve so much talk. An individual or group can most directly get what it wants by taking it or by force and can get nothing directly by talk." But force leads to counterforce, and the employment of language "is exactly what makes politics different from other methods of allocating values. . . . Force signals weakness in politics, as rape does in sex. Talk, on the other hand, involves a competitive exchange of symbols . . . through which values are shared and assigned and coexistence attained. It is fair enough to complain that the politician is not deft in his talk, but to complain that he talks is to miss the point."[21]

In any event, propaganda is not an invincible weapon. Moreover, after a time the people—in a democracy, at least—somehow seem to get a picture of things as they are, if only through ordinary, day-to-day experience. Against the propaganda of the word is the propaganda of the deed. Facts to some extent speak for themselves. And if they are backed up by propaganda, they become doubly potent in shaping men's attitudes and behavior. In the long run, then, well-publicized truth is the most telling propaganda.

A Free Marketplace for Ideas?

Justice Holmes' classic sentence "The best test of truth is the power of the thought to get itself accepted in the competition of the market" is a doctrine that most Americans would heartily endorse. But do we have a free marketplace for ideas in the United States? Or do monopolistic practices exist in the market of opinion just as they do to some extent in the economic marketplace? Certainly we have a free market in the sense that the government does not control the main agencies of opinion. But the absence of governmental control does not in itself guarantee an open and competitive market.

THE POLITICS OF THE PRESS

Even in the case of our own justly famed free press there are at least three disturbing tendencies.

[20]M. M. Willey, "Communication Agencies and the Volume of Propaganda," *Annals of the American Academy of Political and Social Sciences*, vol. 179 (May 1935), p. 197.

[21]Murray Edelman, *The Symbolic Uses of Politics* (Univ. of Illinois Press, 1964), p. 114.

Concentration.   We live in an era of "dying dailies." Newspaper circulation keeps rising, but the number of newspapers keeps decreasing. While our population more than doubled between 1910 and 1969, the number of dailies in the country dropped by one-third. What has been the result? Many states do not have a single city with competing daily papers. Many others are without Sunday newspaper competition. A dozen companies owning big newspapers control over a quarter of our total daily circulation. Daily newspaper competition survives in only sixty of the country's six thousand cities —and in two-thirds of these the competition is only between morning and afternoon papers.

This concentration of ownership and control has led to a standardizing of news and editorial opinion. Newspapers get the bulk of their out-of-town news from great newsgathering organizations such as the Associated Press and the United Press International. The AP, for example, sells news to papers controlling over 95 percent of the total circulation in the United States. The country newspaper—once considered the citadel of rugged, independent journalism—has often become merely the local distributor of opinion canned in New York or Chicago. Over one hundred newspaper chains control almost half the total daily circulation in the country.

Some argue that absence of competition is not necessarily detrimental. If a single newspaper has a monopoly, they contend, it does not have to pander to the lowest taste of the public in order to compete for readers. The editor need not fear that if he antagonizes local advertisers or groups within the city he will lose business to his rival. Moreover, in some cities with competing newspapers the level of journalism is not as high as in some single newspaper cities. But the evidence does not "support the contention of single-ownership advocates that these papers *as a class* have been taking advantage of their more favorable economic position to improve their news, editorial, and feature content."[22]

Commercialism.   A newspaper is a business. To survive it must sell copies, for its income depends on sales and advertising. Many publishers feel, perhaps quite rightly, that they must give the public what it wants. If the readers like screaming headlines, comics, scandal, sex, crime, features, and fiction at the expense of full and balanced news stories and editorial discussion, a newspaper can hardly hold out against its customers. Such a policy, however, means that an editor may cater to the political prejudices of his readers. By giving them what they want, he may deny them the chance to break out of their bias and apathy. And he may block off the expression of controversial views for fear of alienating influential sections of his public.

Conservatism.   Newspaper publishers are businessmen. They are worried by the things that worry every businessman—labor demands, costs, sales, taxes, dividends, profits, and, as businessmen, they tend to take a conservative point of view. It is not surprising that their business attitudes are reflected in their editorial columns and sometimes in the slanting of news. Nor is it surprising that liberal candidates and proposals so often meet stout

[22]Raymond B. Nixon and Robert L. Jones, "The Content of Non-Competitive versus Competitive Newspapers," *Journalism Quarterly* (Summer 1956), p. 312, quoted by Key.

218 resistance from the press or that newspapers in 1968 supported Nixon over Humphrey by a ratio of four to one. Yet democracy demands the airing of competing views.

PART 4
The
People
in Politics

Occasionally, too, advertisers bring pressure to bear on publishers. The story of a strike in a local plant may be suppressed, or the news of the indictment of a large corporation for unfair practices may be buried in the back pages. The real problem, however, is not outright pressure or conspiracy but the community of interest that exists between the big businessman who is a publisher and the other big businessmen who advertise. An English poet satirized:

> You cannot hope to bribe or twist,
> Thank God, the British journalist;
> But seeing what the man will do
> Unbribed, there's no occasion to.

"If modern journalism tends to speak the language of corporate business instead of that of the little fellow," says Herbert Brucker, well-known editor, "it does so not because it is corrupt and venal but because it is itself a big business, a powerful institution with its interests vested in conservative economics."[23] On the other hand, many conservative publishers print the views of liberal columnists.

Certain newspapers have special political importance. *The New York Times* and the *Washington Post*, along with the *Christian Science Monitor* and the *Wall Street Journal*, although having a relatively small circulation compared to tabloids, are read by political, business, and educational leaders. They are the major instruments for supplying political leaders with open forums for political debate. They are noted for their fair and full coverage of controversial events and for their ability to confine editorial opinions to the editorial page. As V. O. Key, Jr., pointed out, these newspapers, especially the *Times*, "serve a special function in communication among the major political actors and the lesser activists."[24]

PROPOSALS FOR REFORM

Nevertheless, the problem of monopolistic tendencies—or at least of imperfect competition—in the marketplace of ideas remains a significant one. Certain solutions have been put forward. One would be to call on editors and publishers to clean their own houses, to police their own industry. It is urged that the press draw up codes of fair conduct binding on all, that newspapermen be given a greater voice in the management and editorial policy of the newspaper. The difficulty is that such codes would not be enforceable, and the worst offenders would be those least likely to conform to them.

Another proposal calls for the establishment of competing newspapers wherever possible. Unfortunately, starting a new journal becomes increasingly difficult as the years go by. Some time ago it was possible for William Allen White to establish a famous newspaper—the *Emporia* (Kansas) *Ga-*

[23]Herbert Brucker, *Freedom of Information* (Macmillan, 1949), p. 68.
[24]Key, *op. cit.*, p. 405.

zette—with a few hundred dollars and a lot of determination. To set up a newspaper today in a middle-sized or large city takes hundreds of thousands, perhaps millions, of dollars.

Finally, government intervention has been urged as a means of promoting full competition. In 1947 a Commission on Freedom of the Press, headed by then Chancellor Robert M. Hutchins of the University of Chicago, recommended that the federal government should set up, if private agencies failed to do the job, its own communications agencies—a government-owned newspaper, perhaps to tell the people of its plans and policies. To encourage criticism of the press from within and without, the commission proposed the creation of a "new and independent agency" to "appraise and report annually upon the performance of the press." Further, it urged that the antitrust laws be used to maintain competition among the larger newspapers. The commission concluded:

> The urgent and perplexing issues which confront our country, the new dangers which encompass our free society, the new fatefulness attaching to every step in foreign policy and to what the press publishes about it, mean that the preservation of democracy and perhaps of civilization may now depend upon a free and responsible press.[25]

These recommendations raise a vital question: Can government take steps to make the press more competitive and more responsible without imperiling our basic freedoms? There is no easy answer. Yet our experience with another great agency of opinion—broadcasting—may throw some light on the problem.

PROBLEMS OF RADIO AND TELEVISION

Since their infancy, radio and television have been under some kind of government regulation. When radio broadcasting first began in the early 1920s, a free-for-all occurred because broadcasters sometimes used the same wavelengths at the same time, deafening the listener with a chaos of sound. By 1927, sharp protests had brought government action. Today, by law, a broadcaster or a telecaster cannot operate without a license from the Federal Communications Commission, a federal regulatory agency (see Chapter 25). Those granted such licenses are obliged to use the public-owned airwaves and to conduct their operations in the public interest. The FCC has the power to refuse to grant or renew a license if it decides the station is not providing programs that serve the public interest.

The FCC has the ticklish task of *policing* the broadcasters without *censoring* them. On the one hand, the Communications Act of 1934 specifies that nothing therein shall be understood to give the Commission that power to interfere with the right of free speech by radio and television. And the Commission has no power to regulate the content of particular programs. On the other hand, in considering applications for the renewal of licenses, the Commission may and does take into account the content and character of the

[25]Robert D. Leigh (ed.), *A Free and Responsible Press* (Univ. of Chicago Press, 1947), pp. 105–106.

broadcaster's past programs in order to determine if he has used his license in the public interest. For instance, in 1968 the practices of a Mississippi television station, WLBT, in reporting race relations and civil rights became a factor in the renewal of its license. Network control over local programs is regulated indirectly by the limit on the number of local stations each network is permitted to own; and the FCC discourages excessive concentrated control over newspaper, television, and radio facilities in a community. In general, however, the FCC has not vigorously regulated television and radio broadcasting, and the industry operates largely under its own rules.

The FCC is also responsible for enforcing the statutory requirement that if air time is made available to one candidate for a public office it must be made available to all candidates for that office on the same terms. This section of the broadcasting act has caused difficulties, particularly in the years when national elections have been held, and Congress has occasionally suspended this rule to the extent of permitting television stations to give equal time to the presidential candidates of the two major parties without their having to give equal time to candidates of the splinter parties. In 1968 Republican Congressmen thwarted a move to suspend the provision, evidently because Nixon did not want to gamble on a debate with Humphrey.

Broadcasters also have developed ways of avoiding the requirement—for instance, by use of the news-interview format. The networks do broadcast editorials—on the grounds that their right to present a point of view labeled as such is comparable to the right a newspaper has to print editorials. Under present regulations, station owners may speak their own minds, but within reasonable limits they must also make time available to persons or parties on the opposite side.

Although the American system of radio broadcasting was determined before 1932, the television industry's came only after the end of World War II. Its system consisted, and still consists, of government allocation of channels, which are controlled privately, though regulated by a public commission, and operated for the most part on funds provided by the sale of air time. The industry considers itself responsive to the public and uses ratings and polls as justification of much prime-time programing. However, President Kennedy's FCC chairman, Newton Minow, accused broadcasters of having turned television into a "wasteland." Such criticism led to an increase in the number and quality of news and informational programs, but live dramatic shows have been steadily replaced by old movies. Technological advances abound and one in particular, the invention of video tape, which will permit the storing of programs for use by individuals at their leisure in their own homes, seems most likely to change the face of television. Cable television may eventually open a wider range of usable channels.

The British Broadcasting Corporation and the Canadian Broadcasting Corporation were established as government enterprises early, though both countries also have channels that are privately owned and commercially operated. The BBC, financed by an annual tax on radio and television sets, is rarely accused of partisanship; more often, listeners complain that its efforts to avoid taking sides have led to overcautiousness. Paradoxically, even commercial television has been accused of overcautiousness, raising the point that there seems to be no one solution to these problems.

It seems unlikely that the American system will be changed substantially, at least for the time being, even though in 1967 Congress established a Public Broadcasting Corporation—a milestone that went relatively unnoticed. The corporation was given only a paltry initial appropriation, and timidity may turn out to be its chief problem, because it was established with careful guards against political or government control.

Critics of pluralism contend (with justification) that the long-range needs of the nation continue to be blurred and undermined by a medley of narrow, commercial interests. Educational television, inadequately supported by universities and foundations and by such government agencies as the Office of Education, had provided one alternative; another, the new Public Broadcasting Corporation, was established, according to President Johnson, in order to "assist stations and producers who aim for the best in broadcasting good music, in broadcasting exciting plays, and in broadcasting reports on the whole fascinating range of human activity."

Pluralist democrats continue to believe that the best protection of the free marketplace of ideas is the variety of publics that read newspapers and watch television and the many interests engaged in the business of purveying information and opinion.[26] The 1970s seem certain to put these propositions to a hard test.

Taking the Pulse of the People

"What I want," Abraham Lincoln once said, "is to get done what the people desire to have done, and the question for me is how to find that out exactly." This perplexing question faces every politician, in office or out. Another President, Woodrow Wilson, once complained to newspapermen that they had no business to say, as they often did, that all the people out their way thought so and so: "You do not know, and the worst of it is, since the responsibility is mine, I do not know, what the people are thinking? The usual way, of course, is to look at the election yet I have got to act as if I knew. . . ."

How can the politician find out what the people are thinking? The usual way, of course, is to look at the election results. If John Brown wins over James Smith, presumably the people want what John Brown stands for. If Brown is an out-and-out prohibitionist and Smith is a 100 percent wet, evidently the majority of the people support some kind of prohibition. But we know that in practice things do not work this way. Elections are rarely fought on single issues, and candidates rarely take clear-cut stands. It is impossible, moreover, to separate issues from candidates. Did Nixon win in 1968 because of Vietnam, crime, taxes, his personality, or shifts in party support? The answer is that he won for some of these reasons and for many others. Which brings us back to the question—what do the people want?

This is where straw votes and public opinion polls come in. In this country public opinion polls are over a century old, but their main development

[26]For a vivid picture of clashing ideas and personalities within a large network, see Fred W. Friendly, *Due to Circumstances Beyond Our Control* (Random House, 1967).

has taken place in the last two or three decades. Some of the techniques were originally worked out by market research analysts hired by business-men to estimate potential sales for their products and then were adapted to measuring opinions on general issues. Today there are over one thousand polling organizations.

METHODS OF SAMPLING

Everybody conducts polls, or more precisely, most of our judgments are based on samples of evidence. The choice is not between polling (sampling) or not polling, but between biased or representative sampling. Most of us, in a majority of cases, draw conclusions from biased samples. For example: the

Courtesy David Huffine.

"Do you, or do you not, favor U.S. participation in some form of world government, under which each nation would forfeit a certain amount of its sovereignty?"

congressman who reports that he is opposed to H.R. 506 and who is sure that the voters are too because his mail has been running six to one against the bill; the reporter who writes that students are becoming more conservative, based on interviews with a dozen students on the Yale campus; the coed who predicted that Humphrey would win, based on her discussions with several of her classmates. We can have little confidence in such guesses.

If a politician or a social scientist wants to measure opinion more precisely, the first thing he must determine is the *universe*, that is, the whole group whose opinion he is interested in—every adult, all students on this campus, all students in the United States, voters in City X. If the universe consists of only thirty units—all students in a particular class—the most precise way to find out what they think on a particular issue would be to poll every one of them. But for most politically significant problems this is impossible, so pollsters *sample* the universe they are interested in. The accuracy of the results of the poll turns largely on securing a sample *representative* of the total universe. If drawn properly so that each unit in a universe has an equal chance to be included, a relatively small sample can provide accurate results. Beyond a certain point, an increase in the size of the sample reduces only slightly the *sampling error*—that is, the range between the divisions found in the sample and those of the universe.

Even a large sample can be highly inaccurate if it is unrepresentative. For example, in 1936 the *Literary Digest* sent tens of thousands of "ballots" through the mail to persons whose names were taken from telephone directories and lists of automobile owners. The results were inaccurate because the sample, large as it was, did not include persons who did not own telephones or cars or who did not bother to return the ballot. (In the 1936 election, telephone owners voted significantly differently from nontelephone owners.)

One way to develop a representative sample would be to draw the sample at random. But this type of *random sampling* is impossible for most political surveys. Instead we use *census tracts* (where these are available) which give the number of residences and their locations. By shuffling census tracts, drawing out at random the required number, and then sending interviewers to every fifth or tenth or twentieth house, one would have a random sample. A less complicated, but less reliable, sample is *quota sampling.* Here an attempt is made to secure a sample that reflects those variables among the population that might affect opinion. One polling organization, in testing opinion that is thought to be affected by income status (for example, views on the income tax), makes up a sample based on two wealthy persons, fourteen members of the upper-income class, fifty-two from the middle-income groups, and thirty-two from the poor. Interviewers are instructed to interview people in each group until they have reached the quota for that group.

An even better way to develop a sample, especially if your purpose is not so much to determine what a universe of population thinks as to study more deeply the dynamics of political behavior, is to *weight the sample.* Thus a group may be of great importance politically but may be too thinly represented in a cross-section sample for effective analysis. By weighting the sample, the analyst can include enough respondents to allow further analysis. The Survey Research Center, studying the 1964 election, wanted more than its normal 150 Negroes. So the center chose blacks at triple weight, thereby getting 450—who could be divided into subgroups for deeper analysis. There is no risk to representativeness in such a procedure provided the analyst reduces the fractional weight of each observation when he generalizes about the population as a whole.

People are often suspicious of results based on what appears to be a small sample. Is it really possible, they wonder, to generalize about the opinions of 200 million persons on the basis of a few thousand interviews? Can such a small sample be truly representative? The answer is yes. In a comparison of demographic characteristics based on census results and those based on a carefully drawn sample, the differences were very small. The census reported that 18.8 percent of the population was between the ages of 21 and 29, 23.5 percent was between 30 and 39, and 20.9 percent was between 40 and

49. The sample results were 18.4, 23.8, and 21.5, respectively.[27] Social scientists assume that if a sample chosen by modern techniques reproduces such characteristics of the population so precisely, it will replicate the attitudes and opinions of the total population equally well.

PROBLEMS OF SAMPLING

A major difficulty in securing accurate results from a survey is in phrasing the questions. If you ask a question in a certain way, you can get the answer you want. Ask a man if he favors labor unions and he may say "no." Ask him if he favors organized efforts by workers to improve their well-being, and chances are he will answer "yes." Also, trouble may arise in the alternatives that a question presents. Clearly, asking a person, "Do you favor the United States entering a world government, or do you prefer our traditional independence in determining our own affairs?" is loading the dice. Polling organizations go to great efforts to make their questions fair; some of them conduct trial runs with differently worded questions.

One way to avoid this difficulty is to ask the multiple-choice type of question. For example, a Gallup poll asked, "How far do you, yourself, think the federal government should go in requiring employers to hire people without regard to race, religion, color, or nationality?" The respondent could answer: All the way; None of the way; Depends on type of work; Should be left to state governments; or Don't know. A variation of this type—the open-end question—allows the respondent to supply his own answer. He may be asked simply, "How do you think we should deal with the problem of disloyalty in government?" (The answers to this type of question are, of course, hard to tabulate accurately.)

Interviewing itself is a delicate task. Tests show that the interviewer's appearance, clothes, language, and way of asking questions may influence the replies. Inaccurate findings may result from the bias of the interviewer or from his failure to do his job fully and carefully. And the persons interviewed may be the source of error. Respondents suspicious of the interviewer's motives may give false or confused answers. Their memories may be poor—for example, how they voted in a past election. To cover up ignorance they may give neutral answers or appear undecided. Or they may give the answers that they think the interviewer would like them to give.

Polls may give a false impression of the firmness and intensity of opinion; as we have seen, opinions may be volatile and fleeting. Moreover, polls do not differentiate among people—they give equal weight to a follower and to an opinion leader who may in the end influence other voters. Studies at the Survey Research Center at Michigan suggest that public opinion is not like an iceberg, where the movement of the top indicates the movement of the great mass under the water. The visible opinion at the top may be moving in a different direction—indeed it may even be differently located—from that of the great mass of opinion that is far less visible. In short, it is far easier to measure the surface of public opinion than its depth and intensity.

[27] Samuel A. Stouffer, *Communism, Conformity, and Civil Liberties* (Doubleday, 1955), p. 238.

Despite all these difficulties, polling is so useful a device for sounding out opinion that it is employed by a variety of organizations. During elections, parties conduct polls to discover their strong and weak points. Interest groups run polls to back up their claims that the people—or at least their own members—favor or oppose a certain bill.

INTERPRETING THE RESULTS

To the average American, preelection forecasting is the most intriguing use of surveys, for everyone likes to know in advance how an election will turn out. During the campaign, pollsters submit regular "returns" on the position of the candidates. On the whole, the record of the leading forecasters has been good, as Table 9-2 shows. The most sensational slip came in 1948, when, during the presidential battle between President Truman and Governor Dewey, the polls repeatedly indicated that Mr. Truman was running far behind. The President denounced these "sleeping polls," but the pollsters stood pat on their statistics. Early in September one of them actually announced that the race was over. Gallup gave the President 44.5 percent of the popular vote in his final forecast and Roper's prediction was 37.1 percent. Actually, Mr. Truman won 49 percent of the popular vote, and the pollsters were subjected to general ridicule. Since then the pollsters have been more cautious in making predictions from their polling data, and more careful in their methods.

TABLE 9-2
Some Recent Presidential Polls (by percentage)

Year	Actual Dem. Vote	Roper Poll	Gallup Poll	Harris Poll
1936	60.2	61.7	53.8	—
1940	54.7	55.2	55.0	—
1944	53.8	53.6	53.3	—
1948	49.4	37.1	44.5	—
1952	45.+	43.0	46.0	—
1956	42.0	40.0	40.5	—
1960	49.4	47.0	49.0	—
1964	61.4	—	61.0	—
1968	42.7	—	40.0	43.0

Election forecasters face some particularly difficult problems. Actually, all they are polling is intentions, and some respondents may change their plans at the last minute. Some may vote contrary to how they say they will vote, or they may simply fail to go to the polls. The forecasts must estimate which and how many of the people will vote, as well as how they will vote. In 1948, voting turned out to be lighter than expected, and an unusually large number of people cast ballots for state and local candidates but not for national ones. Happily for the forecasters, however, a pattern is observable in these false expectations. Almost invariably more people expect to vote than actually show up at the polls on election day. Hence, the forecasters have elaborate correction procedures to eliminate a certain proportion of the respondents who say they will vote but have characteristics that in the past have cut down their attendance at the polls. Another patterned irregularity is that more people say they will defect to the other party at the beginning of the campaign than actually do so on election day. This coming-back-home phenomenon is closely predictable — but the speed of the change is not.

Political polls have taken on increasingly more significant functions in our political system. Candidates use polls to determine where to campaign, how to campaign, and even if they should campaign. In the years and months preceding a national convention, politicians watch the polls to determine which among the hopefuls has political appeal. Kennedy used polls systematically in both his preconvention and election campaigns, as Nixon did in his 1968 campaign. Questions have been raised about this use of polls. Should candidates run for office only when it seems safe to do so? If a candidate believes in a cause, should he not defend it publicly in order to present a meaningful choice to the voters?

Surely the polls at best are no substitute for elections. Faced with his ballot, the voter must translate his opinions into concrete decisions between personalities and parties. He must decide what is important and what is unimportant. Then, out of the welter of views of all the voters, a decision emerges for some candidate who will act in terms of some program, however vague. For democracy is more than the expression of views, more than a simple mirror of public opinion. It is also the *choosing* among issues — and the governmental action that must follow. Democracy is the thoughtful participation of people in the political process; as Lasswell says, it means using heads as well as counting them. Elections, with all their failings, at least establish the link between the many voices of the people and the decisions of their leaders.

SAMPLING AS A RESEARCH TOOL

Social scientists use surveys not just to find out what people think but also to test hypotheses and to investigate the dynamics of political behavior. But all citizens must interpret and process data; and although they use less refined techniques, citizens like social scientists, must be careful in interpreting the facts. Two problems deserve brief mention.

Significance. Suppose a political scientist, after tabulating results from a well-constructed survey, discovers that 60 percent of the Democrats but only 40 percent of the Republicans favor an income tax. How does he know if this is a significant difference? How does he know that if he asked another 100 Democrats and another 100 Republicans this difference in attitude would persist? He must use statistical tests to determine if his results have any significance. As a rough rule of thumb, many statisticians consider that if the results secured could happen by chance at least once in twenty times, the results are not statistically significant.

Multivariables. Suppose a political scientist is trying to determine what factors are related to a high interest in politics. He discovers that 70 percent of the men in his sample but only 30 percent of the women have a high interest in politics. Although this difference is statistically significant, before he concludes that political interest depends on sex he decides to test another variable. It seems unlikely, he speculates, that the biological difference between men and women could account for this difference in political interest. What *is* likely, he thinks, is that in our society more women than men stay at home and perhaps this is the factor that accounts for increased political interest. So he cross-tabulates his data. This time he groups his respondents by whether they have jobs that keep them at home or jobs that take them to an office or a factory. He finds that both men and women who have jobs that keep them at home have a lower political interest than do either men or women who do not stay at home, and the difference is statistically significant. His hypothesis is verified.[28] By this type of multivariant analysis, social scientists are beginning to explore not only how people behave in politics but to understand why they so behave.

What is the relation of government to all this? Obviously, government is not an innocent bystander in the constant play and interplay of political attitudes. It has a stake in the way attitudes are formed, in the methods used to form them, such as television, and in the uses of propaganda. A democratic government is especially interested in the degree of competition in the marketplace of ideas, and in the ways that polling organizations try to meausre public opinion.

Above all, government is concerned with the makeup of public opinion itself. To stay in office, politicians must respond—or at least seem to respond—to changing opinions. They must have some sense of the scope of popular attitudes, their intensity, their stability or instability. Measuring public opinion in its many forms—perhaps by a sort of sixth sense—is the essence of the politician's job. To be successful he must have the knack of peering behind propaganda fronts and gauging the real public opinion, of spotting the areas of ignorance, the areas of apathy, the areas of understanding, the areas of action.

But politicians do not respond to public opinion in the same way. Government is made up of thousands of different people, with varying attitudes, ambitions, and loyalties. Obviously, a President responsible to the whole nation and a senator elected by a state will often react differently to public opinion. The senator will react differently from a member of the House of Representatives. And perhaps an administrative official will take still another view. Many factors lie behind the diverse attitudes of officials—their position in the government, the people by whom they are elected or appointed, the amount of security they enjoy, the date of the next election or appointment, the balance of forces in their home district or in the office of their superior, their own basic attitudes and expectations.

Nor does government merely respond to public opinion; it also creates it. Our "strong" Presidents, and even less dynamic ones such as Coolidge and Eisenhower, have known the uses of public opinion.[29] Congressional investi-

---

[28]This discussion is drawn primarily from Jane Werner Watson, *The Sciences of Mankind: Social Scientists at Work* (Golden Press, 1960), pp. 111-115.

[29]Elmer E. Cornwell, Jr., *Presidential Leadership of Public Opinion* (Indiana Univ. Press., 1965).

gation committees have learned how to make headlines with their revelations. The job of the political leader is to guide political attitudes and mediate among them as well as to follow them. This dual role enables the politician to provide the great need of modern democracies—responsible leadership. Knowing how to respond to public opinion and how to help shape it is much of the art of democratic leadership.

Politics and Public Opinion

We can sum up our discussion of public opinion with a few thumbnail conclusions:

1 Public opinion has many characteristics. In some respects it tends to be compact and stable; in others fluid and varied. One must speak not merely of public opinion but of many public opinions.

2 The public itself is many-sided in its makeup. Some people are fickle in their views; others are steady and unmoving. Actually there are many millions of publics, divided in a thousand different ways.

3 Despite its diversity, public opinion is given a certain orderliness by the fact that most Americans are subjected to common influences—family, schools, press, radio, television, and so on.

4 Much public opinion is formed by deliberate manipulation of attitudes by people with all sorts of purposes, good and bad. The development of highly efficient means of communication and persuasion has enlarged the role of the propagandist, but his influence is by no means unlimited.

5 In the offering of ideas we do not have a wholly free market. In the press and other media we find tendencies toward concentration, commercialization and conservatism. Most Americans probably want a free market, but there is no easy way to get it. The relation of government to the market is the most difficult problem of all.

6 We have fairly reliable methods for roughly measuring people's attitudes at a given time, but these methods cannot take the place of elections.

Political Behavior:
The American Voter

10   Politics is sometimes called the great American game. Thousands of politicians take part in it; millions of people follow the elections and decide who will win and who will lose. Yet the real nature of the game remains a mystery. Why does one candidate win and another lose? Why are so many Americans merely spectators? What causes some people to go to the polls and vote when others do not? How do we decide to vote the way we do? Man is a political animal, yet man knows all too little about his own political behavior—or misbehavior.

Of course, there are a lot of theories—theories that are resurrected in every election by the newspapers and by the politicians themselves. Experience often deals harshly with these theories, but they live on. For example, the old saying "As Maine goes, so goes the nation" has been disproved in election after election, but it was years before the adage died. Again, it has long been political gospel that midterm congressional elections foreshadow the results of the next presidential election, but the 1948, 1956, and 1968 results upset this theory—at least for a while.

We are still groping for some understanding of our own political behavior, and in recent years there has been a systematic effort to answer some of these basic questions of political life. Political scientists, social psychologists, cultural anthropologists, and others are making new studies that in time may throw light on the political process. Their tools—questionnaires, voting statistics, polls, interviews, intensive studies of particular campaigns, and so on—are slowly being improved. We are gaining new insights into the way relations among members of groups, between leaders and followers, and among members of families affect political activity.

Here again the keynote is change. Sometimes political change comes very quickly, as when voting returns seem to shift crazily from year to year. Far more important are underlying changes that may produce a series of voting shifts over the years. Thus we are still affected by basic forces that were unloosed in the "realigning election" of 1896.[1] In this decade we are in a period of flux in national politics. The 1964 and 1968 election campaigns were very different from most presidential election campaigns of this century. In this chapter we will deal more with the earlier elections because 1964 seemed an exceptional one and 1968 is too recent for detailed analysis. If conservative Republicans retain control of Republican presidential conventions—and Nixon easily beat Rockefeller in the Republican national convention in 1968—ideological battles between the parties may be the rule rather than the exception and one more enduring change will have registered itself in American politics.

Who Votes?

The history of suffrage in the United States has been a continuing struggle to extend the right to vote from a small group of property-owning males—perhaps one person out of every twenty or thirty—to the great bulk of the adults. In this chapter we will consider who actually votes and how and why, rather than who has the right to vote. But note that we could not even be discussing voting behavior if a lot of men and women had not fought to extend the right to vote over the last century and a half.

Three great struggles have been fought over this issue. The first was against property tests for voting. Conservatives like Chancellor Kent of New York argued that universal male suffrage would jeopardize the rights of property, that if poor people gained the right to vote they would sell their votes to the rich. The democratic, egalitarian mood of America, eastern immigration and the western frontier, and the eagerness of politicans to lower voting barriers so they could pick up votes—all these led to the end of property (and taxpaying) restrictions by the middle of the nineteenth century. The second great struggle was for women's suffrage. Husbands argued that women had no place at the polling booth, that husbands could vote for the interests of the whole family—but these arguments had a hollow ring. The aroused women conducted noisy parades, drew up petitions, organized a Washington lobby, picketed the White House, got arrested, went on hunger strikes in jail. They won the vote in some states and finally achieved a breakthrough with the passage of the Nineteenth Amendment in 1920. The third struggle—for Negro suffrage—is still going on (see Chapter 7). We will doubtless see more tumult and violence, particularly in the states of the Deep South and in Negro ghettos in large Northern cities, before this right, too, becomes guaranteed.

[1]Walter Dean Burnham, "The Changing Shape of the American Political Universe," *The American Political Science Review* (March 1965), pp. 7–28.

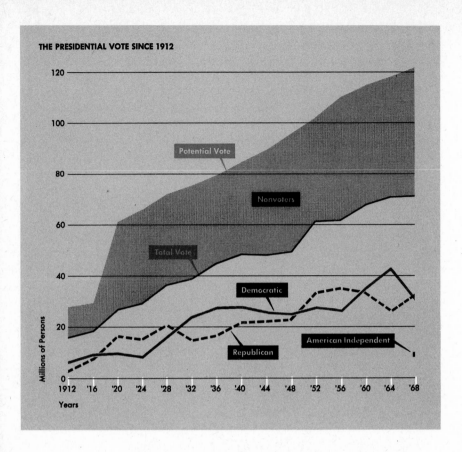

THE PRESIDENTIAL VOTE SINCE 1912

Potential Vote

Nonvoters

Total Vote

Democratic

Republican

American Independent

Millions of Persons

120

100

80

60

40

20

0

1912 '16 '20 '24 '28 '32 '36 '40 '44 '48 '52 '56 '60 '64 '68

Years

Still, the overwhelming number of Americans, including Negroes, have the right to vote. What do they do with it?

MILLIONS OF NONVOTERS

On the average, the proportion of Americans who vote is smaller than that of the British, French, Italians, West Germans, Scandinavians, or Canadians. Talk as we will about the right to vote, the fact remains that millions of Americans do not want to vote or somehow fail to get to the polls on election day. Our elections have not always been characterized by low voter participation. In 1876, 86 percent of the adult enfranchised males voted. Beginning in the early 1900s voter participation declined steadily, increasing slightly in the era of Franklin D. Roosevelt.[2] In those democracies where people have the right not to vote if they wish, there will always be some nonvoters, but the startling feature of nonvoting in America is its extent. In the 1968 presidential election about 40 percent of the potential voters did not go to the polls. About half of them will stay at home in the congressional elections of 1970. Participation in state and local elections is usually even lower.

Why do people fail to vote? Aside from outright denials of the right to

[2]*Report of the President's Commission on Registration and Voting Participation* (U.S. Government Printing Office, 1963), p. 6.

vote, "Many election laws and administrative practices are unreasonable, unfair, and outmoded. They obstruct the path to the ballot box, disfranchising millions who want to vote."[3] About eight million could not vote in 1960 because they had so recently moved from one state or county to another that they were unable to meet residence requirements. To reduce this involuntary nonvoting, a Presidential commission recommended that voter registration be made easy for citizens, for example, by authorizing registrars to canvass house by house; that state residence requirements be reduced to six months and local residence requirements to thirty days; that voting lists be kept current; that states provide absentee registration; that literacy tests be abolished; that election day be proclaimed a national holiday; that absentee voting by mail be allowed; that poll taxes be eliminated; and that states consider lowering the voting age to eighteen years.

Merriam and Gosnell, two pioneer investigators, discovered that simple lack of interest is the primary reason for nonvoting. Although about one in every eight of those interviewed said they were ill at the time and about the same number said they were away from the voting district, 10 percent simply disbelieved in voting for one reason or another—they were "disgusted with politics," or they thought that women should not vote, or something of the sort. Some found it too inconvenient to vote. A few—mostly women—did not want to disclose their ages. Some were afraid they would lose business or wages while they went to the polls. A housewife said she did her washing that day. Some nonvoters said they had intended to vote but had forgotten all about it.[4]

Most nonvoting probably results from a combination of inconvenience and low interest. That is, a young man really would vote on election day—but he forgot to register to vote two months earlier. Or an elderly woman would vote if the polls were around the corner—but the polls are actually two miles away and she lacks easy transportation. One reason that Europeans turn out in larger numbers than Americans is that they have avoided a lot of the red tape (especially registration procedures) that afflicts our system.

WHO FAILS TO VOTE?

The extent of voting varies among different types of persons, areas, and elections. Voting studies generally agree on the following patterns, which are listed here roughly in order of declining importance:

1 *The higher a person's income, the more likely he is to vote.* Our common sense might expect the opposite—that low-income people would

[3]*Ibid.*, p. 11. See also Stanley Kelley, Jr., Richard E. Ayres, and William G. Bowen, "Registration and Voting: Putting First Things First," *The American Political Science Review* (June 1967), pp. 359–377, a model of sophisticated research, which not only stresses the effect of registration procedures on voting but suggests that the adoption of demanding registration laws during the late nineteenth century was responsible to a major degree for the decline in voting turnout later.

[4]C. E. Merriam and H. F. Gosnell, *Non-Voting* (Univ. of Chicago Press, 1924); Paul F. Lazarsfeld, et al., *The People's Choice* (Duell, Sloan & Pearce, 1944), pp. 45–46. See also S. M. Lipset, *Political Man* (Doubleday, 1960); Robert E. Lane, *Political Life* (Free Press, 1959); Bernard R. Berelson, Paul F. Lazarsfeld, and William N. McPhee, *Voting* (Univ. of Chicago Press, 1954), pp. 331–347.

233

CHAPTER 10
Political
Behavior:
The American
Voter

have a strong incentive to vote because of the benefits they can gain from government. Why do low-income people vote in fewer numbers than the wealthy? They have less economic security; they feel less of a sense of control over their political environment; they feel at a disadvantage in social contacts and their social norms tend to deemphasize politics. They are subject to cross-pressures—on the one hand, their experiences and class position push them toward political action, but they are also exposed to strong upper-class and conservative influences through the press, radio, churches, and the like. Low-income-class nonvoting thus is part of a larger political and psychological environment that discourages political activity, including voting.[5]

2   *The college educated vote more than the noncollege educated.* "Practically speaking," writes Warren Miller, "almost everybody who has been to college votes,"[6] Even college-educated persons who profess little interest in or knowledge about political issues turn out to vote. People with college backgrounds exist in a climate of opinion in which voting is considered a civic duty; they tend to be more exposed to ideas, active people, newspapers, political leaders. The college education itself may have an independent effect in exposing the graduate to political ideas and personalities. In addition, persons with only a grade-school education are less likely to vote than high-school alumni.

3   *Middle-aged people tend to vote more than the younger and older.* Many young people are busy getting established, moving about, having babies, raising young children. The new husband is occupied with getting ahead; the young wife is immersed in home affairs. They find little time for politics. The more established, between thirty-five and fifty-five, are more active; then voting falls off sharply in the sixties and seventies, owing partly to the infirmities of old age. The higher incomes enjoyed by middle-aged citizens (on the average) may also spur them to greater participation.

4   *Men tend to vote more than women.*   This variation—not very great in most elections—exists in many foreign countries as well. In recent presidential elections about 61 in every 100 women have voted, about 75 in every 100 men. Women feel less social pressure to vote than men, are subject to more cross pressures concerning which way they should vote, and so tend to withdraw. Morality issues, such as prohibition, generally bring out a high women's vote, and college-educated women tend to be more active in political party work than college-educated men. There are indications that the traditional differences in the rate of voting between men and women is decreasing.

5   *Partisans tend to vote more than independents.*   "By far the most important psychological factor affecting an individual's decision to vote is his identification with a political party."[7] When the election outcome is doubtful, strong partisanship is even more likely to induce a person to vote.

[5]See Lane, *op. cit.*, pp. 50, 233–234; Angus Campbell, Philip E. Converse, Warren E. Miller, and Donal E. Stokes, *The American Voter* (Wiley, 1960); and Lipset, *op. cit.*, pp. 203–205.

[6]Warren Miller, "The Political Behavior of the Electorate," *American Government Annual, 1960–1961* (Holt, 1960), p. 50.

[7]The President's Commission, *op. cit.*, pp. 9–10.

234 A partisan is likely to have a personal interest and to be concerned about the outcome.

Summing up, if you are a young woman, with a low income, and little sense of partisanship, the chances that you will turn out even for an exciting presidential election are far less than if you are a wealthy man, in your fifties, and a strong partisan. Thus nonvoting influences are cumulative. But there also appear to be certain psychological or attitudinal differences between nonvoters and voters. Even when sex, age, education, and income are controlled, the chronic nonvoter, more characteristically than the voter, is a person with a sense of inadequacy, more inclined to accept authority, more concerned with personal and short-range issues, less sympathetic toward democratic norms, and less tolerant of those who differ from himself.[8]

EFFECT OF DIFFERENT TYPES OF ELECTIONS

Political institutions have their impact on nonvoting. So does the total political context.

1 *National elections tend to bring out more voters than state or local campaigns.* Presidential elections attract the greatest number of voters. Off-year congressional elections almost invariably draw fewer persons to the polls. City and other local elections tend to attract an even smaller number. And participation is lowest in party primaries. Even when voters are marking a ballot that offers a variety of national and local contests, some voters will check their presidential choice but not bother with others. This is one

[8]Lane, *op. cit.*, p. 342.

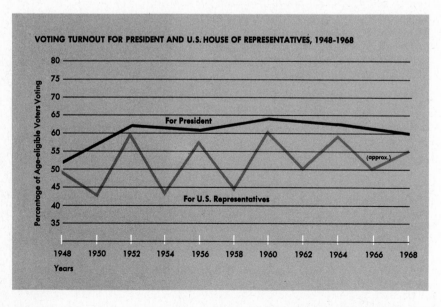

VOTING TURNOUT FOR PRESIDENT AND U.S. HOUSE OF REPRESENTATIVES, 1948-1968

SOURCES: Report of the President's Commission on Registration and Voting Participation, 1963, Appendix 3, p. 66; Hugh A. Bone and Austin Ranney, *Politics and Voters*, 2d ed. (McGraw-Hill, 1967), pp. 42–44.

reason why our governmental officials chosen by somewhat different electorates often represent different points of view. In a local election, for example, where there is little public interest, a local political organization finds it easier to control the outcome than it would in a vote for national officials.

2   *Elections for Chief Executives tend to attract more voters than elections for legislators.* Turnout for presidential elections is higher than for United States representatives; and turnout for representatives is considerably higher in years when a President is elected than in off-presidential years, as the accompanying chart indicates. A somewhat similar difference exists at the state level between gubernatorial and legislative elections. The difference in executive and legislative turnout has major implications for governmental policy; clearly the executive's constituency and the total of the legislators' constituencies differ significantly.

3   *Voting tends to be lowest in areas in which there is little two-party competition.* Thus, the lowest voting figures are likely to be found in states such as Mississippi, Georgia, and South Carolina, although undoubtedly the restraints on Negro voting are more important than lack of party competition. Recently there has been a marked upswing of voting in the South. The growth of two-party politics, the impetus of Goldwater Republicanism, and greater participation by Negroes are all having their effect.[9]

How serious is the low rate of voting? Does it indicate that our democratic system is in danger? Should we encourage—perhaps even force—everyone to vote? No, answer many authorities. F. G. Wilson suggests that it is not a low rate of voting that signals a danger for a democratic system, but a high rate.[10] A measure of nonvoting, it is argued, is a sign of widespread satisfaction, indicating that many people generally accept the status quo and have more interesting things to do than to get involved in politics.

Clearly there would be little gained from pushing into the polls people who have little knowledge about or interest in an election. And sudden upsurges in voting precipitated by a social crisis or the pull of an authoritarian leader are a danger sign, especially because large numbers of nonvoters with little sympathy for democratic values would be mobilized. All surveys and investigations suggest that persons with low levels of political sophistication tend to take a simplified view of politics, fail to show tolerance toward those with whom they disagree, and find it difficult to grasp democratic norms. And it is also clear that the level of voting as a raw statistic has little significance—compare the 99.9 percent turnout rates in the Soviet Union with those in the United States or England, for example.

What counts is the kind of participation. As long as all groups in our society are represented by the electorate, some nonvoting should not be cause for concern. But a large number of uninterested, apathetic, uninformed nonvoters provides a potential source of votes to be exploited by authoritarians and a potential factor contributing to instability in time of national crisis.

[9]Philip E. Converse, Angus Campbell, Warren E. Miller, and Donald E. Stokes, "Stability and Change in 1960: A Reinstating Election," *The American Political Science Review* (June 1961), pp. 269–280.

[10]F. G. Wilson, "The Inactive Electorate and Social Revolution," *Southwestern Social Science Quarterly*, vol. XVI (1936), pp. 73-74.

How to increase participation gradually? Moralistic preaching about the duties of citizenship fails to reach its chief target. It would be better to concentrate on political and institutional changes: Raise the level of education and economic well-being. Shorten the ballot by cutting down the number of unimportant elective positions. Simplify registration and residence requirements. Above all, make the parties more competitive in state and local as well as national elections.

So much for the nonvoter. What about the people who *do* vote?

How We Vote

Sometimes Americans are called fickle voters who switch from party to party blithely. Actually, however, the great majority of Americans stay with one party year after year, and their sons and grandsons vote for the same party long after that. Politically, these voters are "set in their ways." As a result, both parties can count on the support of an almost irreducible minimum of voters who will go Republican or Democratic almost by habit.

Of course, there are still millions of so-called independent voters. They help make our elections the unpredictable and breathless affairs that they so often are. Still, even in the variations from year to year one finds certain persistent elements. Looking closely at the complex mosaic of American politics, we can see patterns of voting habits that help us understand how we vote and a little about why we vote as we do.

PATTERNS OF VOTING

1 A pattern of *state* voting. Since the Civil War, Vermont has given its electoral votes to the Democrats only in 1964, and Maine has done so only twice since 1912. Mississippi and South Carolina, on the other hand, have given a fifth of their presidential popular votes to Republicans only twice; usually they give much less. Between these extremes some states have tended to be Republican in national elections or to be Democratic, but most states are doubtful; they cannot be considered safe by either party. Indeed, some doubtful states are consistent only in their inconsistency.

2 A pattern of *sectional* voting. The South is the most famous example. The Democratic solidarity of the states that formed the Confederacy lasted over eighty years, until it was breached in recent elections. North of the Solid South lies a band of border states that lean toward the Democrats. Republican sectionalism is not so clear-cut.

3 A pattern of *national* voting. In most states party popularity rises and falls with the national popularity of the party. National trends, in other words, are reflected in trends in most of the states. States and sections are subject to a variety of local influences, but they cannot resist the great tides that sweep the nation.

4 A pattern of voting for candidates for *different offices* in the same election. Well over half the voters usually vote a straight ticket—that is, they throw their support to every one of their party's candidates. If one candidate is an especially able vote-getter, the party's whole slate may gain. Thus it is

POLITICAL TIDES: EIGHT PRESIDENTIAL ELECTIONS, 1928-1968
(First figure, popular vote; second figure, electoral vote)

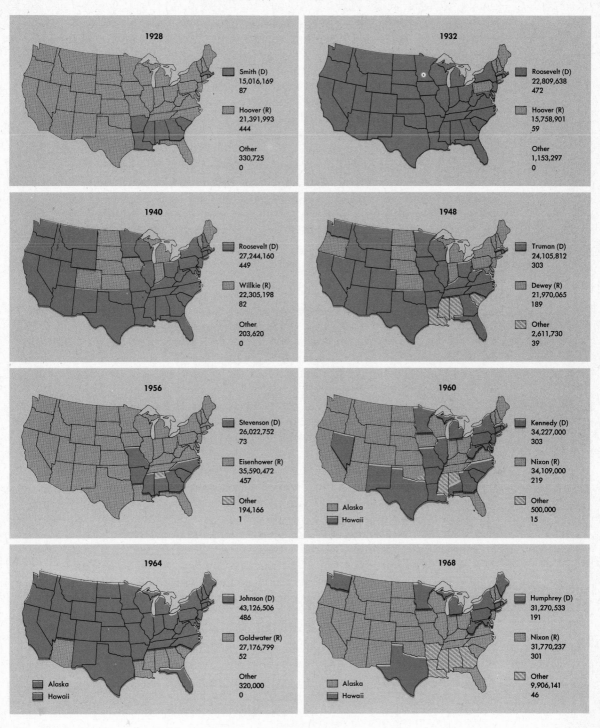

1928

Smith (D)
15,016,169
87

Hoover (R)
21,391,993
444

Other
330,725
0

1932

Roosevelt (D)
22,809,638
472

Hoover (R)
15,758,901
59

Other
1,153,297
0

1940

Roosevelt (D)
27,244,160
449

Willkie (R)
22,305,198
82

Other
203,620
0

1948

Truman (D)
24,105,812
303

Dewey (R)
21,970,065
189

Other
2,611,730
39

1956

Stevenson (D)
26,022,752
73

Eisenhower (R)
35,590,472
457

Other
194,166
1

1960

Kennedy (D)
34,227,000
303

Nixon (R)
34,109,000
219

Other
500,000
15

Alaska
Hawaii

1964

Johnson (D)
43,126,506
486

Goldwater (R)
27,176,799
52

Other
320,000
0

Alaska
Hawaii

1968

Humphrey (D)
31,270,533
191

Nixon (R)
31,770,237
301

Other
9,906,141
46

Alaska
Hawaii

said that weaker candidates ride into office on the coattails of stronger ones. The pulling power of a presidential candidate seems to help elect members of his own party to office during presidential election years. Democrats, for example, won many more seats in Congress in 1944, 1948, and 1964 than in the off-year elections in between, as did Republicans clinging to Eisenhower's coattails in 1952. It is not easy to tell, however, which candidate rides on whose coattails or just how important the relation is.[11] In 1968 Richard Nixon won the Presidency but his party failed to carry the House.

5   Finally, a pattern of voting over *time*. Great political tides seem to flow back and forth from generation to generation. A political historian, tracing the shifts in presidential and congressional elections since 1789, has found that gradual oscillations in the underlying pattern of party identifications are associated with periods of two-party equilibrium, leading to a period of realignment, followed by a period of ascendancy for one party, followed by a period of equilibrium again. This cycle seems less marked in the twentieth century than it was in the nineteenth, however, and in any case has little predictive value for any particular election.[12]

BEHIND THE TIDES

What causes the political tides to rise and fall? Business, for one thing. A drop in business activity has often preceded a loss of congressional seats by the party in power. But we cannot be sure that business cycles *cause* political cycles. Sometimes the two cycles diverge in erratic fashion. Psychological, political, traditional, sectional, international, and other forces may muddle the effect of economic forces.

If there are patterns in American politics, then, these patterns are rough and are often blurred by capricious and unexplainable variations. Indeed, the patterns may exist for many years and then disappear. For example, before the 1948 election a change in party control of Congress in an off-year election had regularly preceded a change in party fortunes in the following presidential election. But the Democrats, who lost control of Congress in 1946, won both houses of Congress and the Presidency in 1948; and despite 1954 and 1966 Democratic congressional victories, the Republicans captured the White House, though not Congress, in 1956 and 1968. So perhaps we will hear less of this "pattern" in the future.

Perhaps this murkiness in American politics is a good thing. Perhaps it shows that we are not caught in inevitable and relentless forces beyond our control. Unfathomable factors in chance and human nature still have their place. Even the opinion polls, with all their careful scientific techniques, must reckon with these factors. Men of determination in either party, campaigning skillfully and energetically, can overcome "inevitable" political trends.

[11]D. B. Truman, "Political Behavior and Voting," *The Pre-Election Polls of 1948* (Social Science Research Council, 1949), pp. 239–244. See also John W. Meyer, "A Reformulation of the 'Coattails' Problem," in William N. McPhee and William A. Glaser (eds.), *Public Opinion and Congressional Elections* (Free Press, 1962).

[12]Charles Sellers, "The Equilibrium Cycle in Two-Party Politics," *Public Opinion Quarterly* (Spring 1965), pp. 16-37, reprinted in William J. Crotty, Donald M. Freeman, and Douglas S. Gatlin (eds.), *Political Parties and Political Behavior* (Allyn and Bacon, 1966), pp. 79-102.

Why We Vote as We Do

Suppose we were able to find ten voters who represented a tiny but fairly accurate cross section of the American electorate. Suppose —shortly after an exciting and close presidential election—we asked them to tell us in a few words why they voted as they did. And suppose they gave us the *real* reason they voted as they did. What kind of answers would we get? Studies of voting indicate that the answers might go something like this:

MR. ANDERSON (*fruitgrower*): I voted Republican. I always do. I'm a businessman, you see, and the Republicans have a sound businesslike point of view. All the fruitgrowers around here voted that way.

MRS. SMITH (*housewife*): I supported the Democratic candidate. My husband said he was going to vote that way. He doesn't tell me how to vote, but I leave the politics to him. He always seem to vote Democratic anyway.

MARY BROWN (*stenographer*): Well, I didn't know what to do. I wasn't much interested, frankly, but all the girls at the office seemed to think the Democrats are doing a good job, so that's the way I decided to go.

HARRY VENUTI (*young barber*): Me? Democratic. The Venutis always vote Democratic. We go along with Tom Murphy—he's a big wheel in the party here, and he's a nice fellow too. He's done us some good turns.

DR. WHITE (*local surgeon*): I voted Republican. I don't like these medical programs the Democrats keep enacting. They'll hurt all us doctors if they go through. And I don't like their war policies.

JOHNNY BLACK (*factory worker*): I voted for the Republican candidate for President even though I'm a Democrat. All the boys in the plant were talking Democratic and one of the boys on the union committee gave us a pep talk about supporting the Democrats. But I voted Republican for President—he seemed more sincere. I didn't warm up to the Democratic candidate.

MRS. MURPHY (*housewife*): I was on the fence a long time. I read the speeches in the paper, watched on television, and finally I went Democratic. Except for Senator ———. He's been in a long time and people say he's very conscientious.

MR. SCOTT (*industrialist*): Republican, of course. We can't take these high taxes much longer. Besides the Republican candidates are obviously higher type men. They are statesmen, not politicians. I voted a straight Republican ticket.

BILL JOHNSON (*unemployed*): I didn't know what to do. My family's Republican, but the Democrats seem to want to do something to get men back to work. So I split my vote—Democratic for President, Republican for congressman.

SALLY RICE (*salesgirl*): Well, I didn't even plan to vote. I'm not much interested in politics. But I was so mad after some people booed the Republican candidate at the rally the other night that I went out and voted for him. I just voted for a couple of candidates—I didn't know all those other names.

VOTING BEHAVIOR

In what ways are these ten persons representative of Americans as a whole in the manner in which they made up their minds? First, over half of the ten supported their party almost automatically, and this voting by habit is true of most American voters, no matter what the candidates or issues. Because party identification is amazingly stable over the years,[13] each major party is sure to poll a big national vote. This traditional vote is not necessarily blind or irrational. Voting for the same party over the years may represent a person's rational view of his self-interest, as in the cases of Mr. Anderson and Harry Venuti.

But party identification is by no means the only factor. Some people, like Mr. Black, departed from their traditional party affiliation to vote for the candidate of the opposition. Most of the time even when we claim to vote for "the man and not the party," our warmness or coldness toward the candidate is related to whether or not he belongs to the party we do. But not always. An Eisenhower whose personality was so appealing to millions was able to win the vote of many Democrats.

Second, most of our ten Americans voted the same way as their families or friends or workmates were going to vote. On election day Americans mark their ballots in private, yet voting is essentially a group experience. We tend to vote as members of existing or potential groups. And the most homogeneous of all groups in molding the opinions of its members is probably the family[14] (see Chapter 9). The reasons for this uniformity are twofold. Members of the family shape one another's attitudes (often unintentionally); and members of the same family are naturally exposed to similar economic, religious, class, and geographical influences. The husband seems to be head of the house politically as well as otherwise. Most wives talk the election over with their husbands; men, on the other hand, "do not feel that they are discussing politics with their wives; they feel they are telling them."[15]

A third factor related to voting is income. Most studies of voting behavior confirm what everyday observation has already indicated: The highest proportion of persons who prefer the Republican party are in the upper-income brackets, especially with incomes over $10,000 a year. But we cannot make too much of this factor, indeed of any single factor. Eisenhower's great personal popularity seemed to blur differences in income, and the correlation between income and voting preference that developed out of the 1932 Depression tended to disappear. But the tendency of the lower socioeconomic groups to vote Democratic and of the higher to vote Republican reappeared somewhat in the 1960s.[16]

Several other factors may be noted briefly. Where one lives apparently has a relation to how one votes; Republican strength outside the South is most concentrated in the small cities. Race and religion are also related to voting, with Negroes and Catholics voting more heavily for the Democrats. Some of these factors can be seen in Table 10-1.

[13]Campbell, et al., *The Voter Decides, op. cit.*, Chap. 6.

[14]Herbert McClosky and Harold E. Dahlgren, "Primary Group Influence on Party Loyalty,"*The American Political Science Review* (September 1959), p. 775. For some interesting exceptions to this tendency, see E. E. Maccoby, R. E. Matthews, and A. S. Morton, "Youth and Political Change," *Public Opinion Quarterly* (Spring 1954), vol. 18, pp. 23-29; and Campbell, et al., *The Voter Decides, op. cit.*, pp. 109-206.

[15]Lazarsfeld, et al., *op. cit.*, p. 141. For some recent studies in this area, see articles by H. W. Riecken, C. W. Wahl, and R. D. Luce in Eugene Burdick and A. J. Brodbeck (eds.), *American Voting Behavior* (Free Press, 1959); McClosky and Dahlgren, *op. cit.*, pp. 757-776; and Lane, *op. cit.* And see generally James C. Davies, *Human Nature in Politics* (Wiley, 1963).

[16]Robert R. Alford, "The Role of Social Class in American Voting Behavior," *The Western Political Quarterly* (March 1963), pp. 180-194.

241

CHAPTER 10
Political
Behavior:
The American
Voter

TABLE 10-1

The Demography of the Vote in Recent Presidential Elections (by percentage)

Demographic Characteristic	1948 Dem.	1948 Rep.	1956 Dem.	1956 Rep.	1960 Dem.	1960 Rep.	1964 Dem.	1964 Rep.	1968 Dem.	1968 Rep.	AIP°
Religion											
Protestant	47†	53†	37	63	38	62	55	45	35	49	16
Catholic	66†	34†	51	49	78	22	76	25	59	33	8
Jewish			75	25	81	19	90	10	–	–	–
Race											
White	53†	47†	41	59	49	51	59	41	38	47	15
Negro	81†	19†	61	39	68	32	94	6	85	12	3
Union labor families	74‡	26	57	43	65	35	–	–	–	–	–
Young voters (age 21–29 yrs.)	62‡	38	43	57	54	46	64	36	47	38	15
Sex											
Women	53†	47†	39	61	49	51	62	38	45	43	12
Men	56†	44†	45	55	52	48	60	40	41	43	16

°The American Independent party, headed by George Wallace.

†Figures accompanied by an asterisk are taken from Angus Campbell et al., *The Voter Decides* (Harper & Row, 1954), pp. 70–71. Data given there were converted from a percentage of the total sample to a percentage of those voting, ignoring the "Other" column. All other data are taken from releases of the American Institute of Public Opinion (The Gallup Poll).

‡Includes Democratic, Progressive and States' Rights votes.

SOURCE: *American Government Annual* (Holt, 1965), p. 24.

But we cannot make too much of these categories. The shift of voters from Democratic to Republican between 1948 and 1956 was not peculiar to one or two groups, but in varying degrees was common to all economic classes, religions, and racial groups. In 1956, for example, the Negro vote was still primarily pro-Democratic, but Eisenhower picked up more than twice as many votes among Negroes as Dewey had won in 1948. Although Catholics still vote Democratic more than do Protestants, forty-nine percent voted for Eisenhower in 1956. Some elections, of course, tend to divide the electorate more evenly along economic lines (as in 1936) than do others (1952). Sometimes noneconomic forces are crucial. In the 1960 election, for example, religion became a highly publicized issue. Although President Kennedy won a larger ratio of the votes among Catholics than is normal for Protestant Democratic presidential candiates, he lost a much higher number of Southern white-Protestant votes than is normal for the Democratic presidential candidate. Still, even in 1960, the basic party vote was the key factor; Kennedy won mainly because he was a Democrat and the Democrats regained the majority they lost to Eisenhower during the 1950s.[17]

To indentify the political preferences of sociological groups may give a misleading picture of voting behavior, for over time these distinctions alter; and they fail to take into account the impact of national and international developments and the personality factors of the individual voter and the way he responds to candidates. "Events, communications, and attitudes—may all be more or less independent of group memberships and social classifications,"

[17]Philip E. Converse, et al., "Stability and Change in 1960: A Reinstating Election," *op. cit.* See also Andrew R. Baggaley, "Religious Influence on Wisconsin Voting, 1928-1960," *The American Political Science Review* (March 1962), p. 66ff.

242

points out Warren Miller. They all make important contributions to the individual's political behavior. But their importance is inevitably minimized in group-oriented descriptions of electoral behavior. To know someone's party affiliation does not tell us for sure how he will behave politically.

Is it a healthy sign that our political parties do not reflect too accurately basic social, economic, geographical, and religious differences? Or does this lead to a blurring of party lines, leading in turn to fuzzy programs and a failure of American government to deal with crises and problems? The fact that many Jews are Republicans, that some wealthy men are Democrats, that neither party can claim a monopoly of any group, keeps the parties from reinforcing and exaggerating differences. Lipset observes, "Where parties are cut off from gaining support among a major stratum, they lose a major reason for compromise.[18]

ALL KINDS OF INDEPENDENTS

Regularly a quarter to a third of the voters could be classed as independents. Unable to identify themselves consistently with one party or candidate, some independents cross and recross party lines from election to election. Some split their ticket and vote for some candidates from one party and other candidates from another party. Some people call themselves independents because they think it is socially more respectable, but actually they vote with the same degree of regularity for one party as do others who are not so hesitant to admit party loyalty. A study indicates that younger voters with above average incomes and college educations tend to be more independent than other groups but that the independent vote is rather evenly distributed throughout the population. On the average, about one out of every five voters calls himself independent, and twelve million independent-minded voters are a fact for any politician to reckon with.

Is the independent voter the more informed voter? There has been heated debate over this question, but much of it is fruitless because everything depends on what kind of independent we are talking about. If independents are defined as those who fail to express a preference between parties, the independent voter tends to be less well-informed than the partisan voter, for such independents include chronic nonvoters, apathetic people, and the like. But if we mean those who switch parties between elections, we find some who are highly informed and who carefully pick and choose at the polls. In

Copyright 1956, Crowell Collier Publishing Company, by Bill Mauldin.

"Me, I vote the man, not the party. Harding, Coolidge, Hoover, Landon, Dewey . . ."

[18]Lipset, *Political Man, op. cit.,* p. 31.

short, some independents are like our Mrs. Murphy, who tried to hear all sides of the argument before voting. Others resemble Sally Rice, who voted almost by whim.

Does campaigning change the votes of independents or even party regulars? From our discussion of voting behavior, we might conclude that all the speeches of vote-seekers and all the hullabaloo of their campaigns had little effect compared with the other forces at work. In part, this conclusion would be true. A campaign usually converts only a small fraction of the electorate. But it has other important effects. It reinforces the convictions of those already tending one way or another. And it activates people—that is, it arouses their interest, exposes them to particular candidates and ideas, shapes their attitudes, and stimulates them to vote on election day.

Still, events between elections and underlying attitudes, traditions, and pressures are far more important than the campaign. Does this situation discourage the vote-seeking politician? Not at all. He knows that he is dealing in margins, often in close margins. He knows that a hundred unknown intangibles will shape the final outcome. Great political forces are delicately balanced—perhaps a good push by his party and himself will tip them in the right direction.

Apathetics, Participants, Leaders

Students interviewing a cross section of a population are often surprised to find people who seem to know nothing about the questions they are asked. The newspapers may be full of headlines and discussion about a Kennedy or a Nixon or a Humphrey, but some citizens can place the names only vaguely in politics. "The first noteworthy fact about citizen participation in a democracy is that it is thin. Most citizens are little interested in playing even a small policy-making role; fully a third of American citizens neither vote, join interest groups, do party work, communicate with their representatives, nor talk politics with their friends (except occasionally in a vague and uninformed way)."[19] The completely uninvolved are dismissed as inactives, apathetics, or even as chronic know-nothings.

On the other hand some citizens are influential enough to manipulate other people's political behavior, especially how they vote. City bosses, a local newspaper editor, a national columnist sometimes have this kind of power imputed to them. The classic statement of political influence is one attributed to Boss Plunkitt, a Tammany district leader, years ago:

There's only one way to hold a district; you must study human nature and act accordin'. You can't study human nature in books. Books is a hindrance more than anything else. If you have been to college, so much the worse for you. You'll have to unlearn all you learned before you can get right down to human nature, and unlearnin' takes a lot of time. Some men can never forget what they learned at college. Such men may get to be district leaders by a fluke, but they never last.

To learn real human nature you have to go among the people, see them

[19]Charles E. Lindblom, *The Policy-Making Process* (Prentice-Hall, 1968), p. 44.

and be seen. I know every man, woman, and child in the Fifteenth District, except them that's been born this summer—and I know some of them, too. I know what they like and what they don't like, what they are strong at and what they are weak in, and I reach them by approachin' at the right side.

For instance, here's how I gather in the young men. I hear of a young feller that's proud of his voice, thinks that he can sing fine. I ask him to come around to Washington Hall and join our Glee Club. He comes and sings, and he's a follower of Plunkitt for life. Another young feller gains a reputation as a baseball player in a vacant lot. I bring him into our baseball club. That fixes him. . . . I don't trouble them with political arguments. I just study human nature and act accordin'. . . .

As to the older voters, I reach them, too. No, I don't send campaign literature. That's rot. People can get all the political stuff they want to read—and a good deal more, too—in the papers. Who reads speeches, nowadays, anyhow? It's bad enough to listen to them.[20]

THE RANGE OF ACTIVITY

In between the highly influentials—the leaders—and the apathetics are the participants who follow politics, talk about issues, and vote. But even these three groupings are oversimplified. Actually we find a range or spectrum of political participation, as Table 10-2 suggests.

TABLE 10-2

Approximate Percentage of American Citizens Participating in Various Forms of Political Activity

Holding public and party office	Less
Being a candidate for office	than
Soliciting political funds	1
Attending a caucus or a strategy meeting	
Becoming an active member of a political party	4-5
Contributing time in a political campaign	
Attending a political meeting or rally	
Making a monetary contribution to a party or candidate	10
Contacting a public official or a political leader	13
Wearing a button or putting a sticker on the car	15
Attempting to talk another into voting a certain way	25-30
Initiating a political discussion	
Voting	
Exposing oneself to political stimuli	40-70

SOURCE: Charles E. Lindblom, *The Policy-Making Process* (Prentice-Hall, 1968), p. 45.

However, the table relates only to activists and leaders. A range of activity (or inactivity) would also be found among apathetics. Some literally never vote or talk politics. Others might vote occasionally and, if not talk politics, influence the talkers by their responsiveness or indifference. Apathy and participation also vary over time. A person may ignore one national election and become intensely involved in the next; he may vote in fall elections and ignore primaries earlier in the year. And a person might be highly active in town or city elections and uninterested in state or national.

[20]W. L. Riordon, *Plunkitt of Tammany Hall* (McClure, Phillips, 1905), pp. 33-34.

245

CHAPTER 10
Political
Behavior:
The American
Voter

In general, to be sure, people active at one level of politics tend to be active at other levels. But we must be careful about generalizations concerning popular apathy, such as "the poor don't take part in politics." This may be good polemics, but as analysts we must think in terms of specific elections, types of individuals, and political situations.

WHY PEOPLE PARTICIPATE IN POLITICS

A vast amount of study has gone into the questions of how and why people get involved in politics. After an exhaustive study of the literature, Milbrath identified widely agreed-on generalizations as to the nature and causes of political participation; he sees participation as a function of the following factors:[21]

1 *Stimuli from the political environment.* Citizens contacted personally are more likely to vote and show interest in the campaign. Persons lacking education and understanding about politics tend to shut out political stimuli. Middle-class persons, men, and urban dwellers are exposed to more stimuli about politics than, respectively, working-class persons, women, and country dwellers. Children growing up in a politically involved home are more likely to maintain a high level of exposure to stimuli about politics when they become adults.

2 *Personal factors.* Those psychologically involved in politics are more likely to feel effective in political action. Persons of higher income and social status are more likely to become highly involved psychologically in politics than persons of lower status. "Perhaps the surest single predictor of political involvement," according to one study, "is number of years of formal education."[22]

3 *Political setting.* Persons contacted by party workers are more likely to vote and participate in other political activity. The relation works the other way too—persons who are more interested in politics are more likely to know party workers. Again, there is an effectiveness or efficacy factor—persons who see themselves or their group as having an impact on public policy are more likely to inform public officials of their views than are those who feel ineffective.

4 *Social position.* Persons who feel nearer the center of society are more likely to participate in politics than persons who feel near the periphery. Professional persons are the most likely to get involved in politics, especially in office-holding. Farmers are less likely to be involved in politics than businessmen. Union members are more likely to take an interest in and a stand on politics than nonunion members.

Many of these generalizations are obvious or a matter of common sense. And they do not necessarily explain the deeper causes of interest or lack of interest in political activity. But these correlations and interrelationships do help us understand how to get to the deeper causes. And they give an indi-

[21]The generalization about political participation in this section are from Lester W. Milbrath, *Political Participation* (Rand McNally, 1965); see this book also for its extensive bibliography.
[22]Angus Campbell, "The Passive Citizen," *Acta Sociologica* (1962), vol. VI, p. 20.

cation of the complexity of sources of political participation and hence help us avoid glib generalizations.

The generalizations about political activists and leaders generally parallel those about voters compared with nonvoters, noted earlier in this chapter. The extensive lack of participation in the "great game" of politics raises the same issues. Critics of pluralist democracy contend that only a few are politically involved, only a few wield power, whereas the great majority—especially poor people and "outsiders"—have neither political influence nor the incentive or means to gain it. Defenders of the system say that the range of participation makes for moderation and consensus, allows for healthy competition without extremism, and keeps open many channels of communication and wide avenues of access to governmnet for all interested people.

Voting Studies: A Research Frontier

Since at least the time of Aristotle, political scientists have been trying to understand the "what" and the "why" of politics. The "what" has been relatively easy; scholars have made detailed compilations and descriptions of election returns, political credos, the history of legislative enactments, administrative decision-making; indeed, no major area of political life has been left unexplored. The "why" has been much more difficult. Why does one man from a particular social background forge ahead relentlessly to political fame and fortune whereas another man from the same background remains apolitical all his life? Why do some people vote for the same party year after year whereas others shift back and forth? Why do millions of persons desert their old political beliefs to embrace doctrines such as Marxism or Nazism? Why do legislatures dominate some political systems and executives dominate others?

The question of why challenges historians, economists, psychologists, socialogists, anthropologists—indeed, all scholars in some way—as well as political scientists. And even the simplest event raises a host of possible answers as to why it happened. E. H. Carr, the distinguished English historian, provided an example.[23]

Jones, returning from a party at which he has consumed more than his usual ration of alcohol, in a car whose brakes turn out to have been defective, at a blind corner where visibility is notoriously poor, knocks down and kills Robinson, who was crossing the road to buy cigarettes at the shop on the corner. After the mess is cleaned up, we meet—say, at local police headquarters—to enquire into the causes of the occurrence.

Why did the accident happen? Because Jones was semi-intoxicated? Or because of the car's brakes? Or because of the blind corner? Or because Robinson smoked cigarettes? Or because Jones or Robinson, or both, were careless? Perhaps any or all of these. Then we might ask, Which are the direct and which the indirect causes? Which are purely chance and which are likely

---

[23]Edward Hallett Carr, *What Is History?* (Knopf, 1962), p. 137. Carr develops further problems of historical causation from this example.

to recur? And ultimately the political scientist might ask, Which causes could be removed (the blind corner, the defective brakes) and which could not (Jones's intoxication, Robinson's desire for cigarettes)?

The purpose of this section is to show social scientists, including political scientists, seeking to discover why Americans vote the way they do. We cannot do justice to the enormous range and variety of voting behavior studies; but to get some idea of what a professional social scientist does, let us look at some of the work that has been done in voting and opinion studies.

THE CUTTING EDGE: SOME EARLIER VOTING STUDIES

Concern with why men vote the way they do is nothing new. Scholars and journalists have speculated, have based generalizations on their own observations, have argued that it is logical to assume that men vote this way instead of that for a host of reasons that all appear to be plausible. But only recently has it been possible to find answers to these questions by looking at "hard" data and using more precise tools.

In the 1920s a young graduate student at Columbia, Stuart A. Rice, came under the intellectual influence of a sociologist who stressed quantitative research, such as the use of election statistics. Rice decided to apply quantitative methods to a study of the American farm-labor movement, in which he had been active. The resulting study of this movement led a publisher to suggest to Rice that he apply these methods to other political problems. Within three weeks Rice wove together some previously published findings with research that he had ready to be published, and his work appeared in 1928 as *Quantitative Methods in Politics*.

Rice raised many questions. What differences in political attitudes existed between urban and rural voters? How do political attitudes spread across areas? How do they change over time? To what extent are people's attitudes affected by their stereotypes—that is, by set opinions of what labor leaders, senators, Communists, and so on, are like? When William Jennings Bryan was visiting Dartmouth to denounce the theory of evolution, Rice conducted an experiment by comparing students' attitudes before and after Bryan's visit.

Rice modestly admitted that his book was only a start. Public opinion polls were still in their infancy, experimental work in social psychology was still primitive, and his data were limited. But he helped stimulate further research in voting. The 1930s saw the appearance of studies of urban-rural tensions in the election of 1896, of the extent to which labor supported Andrew Jackson in certain wards of Boston, of voting trends in particular cities or counties. The results were interesting and suggestive, but far from conclusive. There was little systematic testing of hypotheses over a long series of elections. Findings for one state might have little relation to another. The studies did not explain the reasons for individual voting choices. The "why" of voting behavior was still not clear.[24]

A psychologist then came to the fore in scholarly efforts to understand individual voting behavior. During the 1930s Paul F. Lazarsfeld had headed

[24]On these earlier voting studies see Samuel J. Eldersveld, "Theory and Method in Voting Behavior Research," *The Journal of Politics* (February 1951), vol. 13, pp. 70-87; and Peter H. Rossi, "Four Landmarks in Voting Research," in Burdick and Brodbeck (eds.), *op. cit.*, pp. 5-54.

the Office of Radio Research, which had done pioneer work on how people make up their minds about what goods they buy. Earlier, in Vienna, Lazarsfeld had studied the psychology of choice, especially the occupational choices of young people. He now proposed to survey repeatedly a sample of households to see how their choices of brands of goods could be related to their exposure to advertising. Unable to find commercial support for such a group study, he obtained funds from the Rockefeller Foundation for a panel study of the 1940 presidential campaign, as a way to test his technique of interviewing a panel over and over again. The result was *The People's Choice*, by Lazarsfeld and two associates.[25]

The place chosen for the study was Erie County, Ohio; the occasion was the election of 1940 between Roosevelt and Willkie. A carefully selected panel of 600 respondents was interviewed seven times—a Herculean task— and four matched control groups were each interviewed twice. Lazarsfeld and his colleagues emerged with many significant conclusions. Choosing candidates, it seemed, was quite different from choosing goods; voters had long-standing attachments to certain parties and had in effect decided how to vote long before the presidential campaign had begun. Many of them were apathetic; they did not even want to enter the "electoral marketplace." Other notable findings were that voting was heavily affected by family, place of work, and neighborhood influences and hence was more a *group* than an individual act; that many voters under cross-pressures became indecisive and failed to vote at all; that the candidates' campaigns tended to reach their own supporters rather than people in the opposite camp and those who were undecided; and that there was a "two-step flow of influence" in the mass media—from the media to local opinion leaders to the rank and file.

On their main question—why people voted as they did—the authors concluded that religion, socioeconomic status, and place of residence (rural or urban) were the most important factors. They constructed an Index of Political Predisposition to show these forces in their combined impact (see Table 10-3). The greater the rank number of a given cell, the greater the frequency of Democratic voting preference among the members of that cell.

TABLE 10-3

Index of Political Predisposition

Socioeconomic Status	Protestants Rural	Protestants Urban	Catholics Rural	Catholics Urban
A, B (well-to-do)	1	2	3	4
C+ (middle)	2	3	4	5
C− (lower middle)	3	4	5	6
D (lower)	4	5	6	7

The People's Choice was greeted as a major advance in understanding the "why" of voting, but both the authors and the critics agreed that there were

[25]Lazarsfeld, *The People's Choice, op. cit.*

249

CHAPTER 10
Political
Behavior:
The American
Voter

certain failings and omissions. In 1948 Lazarsfeld, Berelson, and McPhee conducted an even more elaborate study of Elmira, a small industrial city in upstate New York, in the presidential campaign of that year. They used a larger panel — 1,000 instead of 600 — but they interviewed them only four times. Field researchers also analyzed Elmira's newspapers, political party organizations, and interest groups. The result, after six years of labor, was a community and election study, entitled simply *Voting*, with far more breadth and depth than the earlier one.[26] Attention centered on the group context of voting behavior, the role of issues in the battle between Truman and Dewey, and the impact on behavior of the community and its institutions. The treatment of the two major parties and of the unions not only illuminated Elmira's politics but shed light on the role of parties and unions in the nation as a whole. Once again the authors stressed major factors such as religion and income, but they paid more attention to the structure of the community. Many scholars considered *Voting* the most useful and sophisticated community opinion and voting study that had been done.

As voting studies proliferated during the 1950s, they came under increasing criticism from antibehaviorists and others who were skeptical of the achievements and pretensions of the voting studies. In large part this criticism reflected the basic division within political science noted in Chapter 1, that is, the division over the extent to which political science could become a "real" science. But critics had some further specific questions. Voting studies, they said, were sharply limited in their applicability; if field researchers investigated Erie County in 1940, all they learned about was Erie County in 1940. They also charged that the studies came up with correlations rather than causation. If Catholics with low incomes tend to vote Democratic, this does not prove they vote Democratic *because* they are Catholics with low incomes. Finally, said some critics, the voting studies put too much emphasis on man's social milieu, because his behavior is not wholly or even mainly, determined by his environment. If a man is a Protestant or lives in the country, it does not mean that he must behave like a Protestant or like a rural dweller. Man is simply too complex and mysterious to respond predictably to external stimuli. Above all, according to this view, man is a reasoning animal — he can think rationally about his problems without being totally controlled by his environment.

INSIDE THE MIND OF THE VOTER

Of all these criticisms, those who study voting behavior have been most sensitive to the view that voters respond less directly to their social milieu than to attitudes that influence and are influenced by their group memberships. The early studies, with their emphasis on the role of groups, had been heavily influenced by political sociologists; the new emphasis would call more for psychologists (and for political scientists with some understanding of social psychology), who could discern and perhaps measure the psychological forces that operated between the individual voter and the social situation.

[26]Berelson, Lazarsfeld, and McPhee, *op. cit.*

During World War II the Program Surveys Division of the United States Department of Agriculture had conducted studies of grass-roots opinion and attitudes in connection with farm programs. After the war some of the Division's researchers moved to the University of Michigan and set up the Survey Research Center, which rapidly took leadership in public opinion research. Its work was largely sociopsychological in orientation—that is, it was "guided by the philosophy that the immediate determinants of an individual's behavior lie more clearly in *attitudes* and his *perceptual organization* of his environment than in either his social postion or other 'objective' situational factors."[27] A man might be poor and live in a city slum, for example, without seeing himself as a low-income urbanite; how he saw himself and why he behaved politically as he did would depend on his picture of reality, not on reality as someone else saw it.

Beginning in 1948 the Center conducted surveys of opinions and voting in every presidential campaign, based on a national probability sample of 2,000 respondents.[28] Because the survey was nationwide and was repeated again and again (using some of the same respondents), the studies met two of the main criticisms of the earlier efforts. Most important, they measured a number of psychological attitudes as "intervening variables linking behavior with a host of antecedent factors."[29] The major intervening variables were support for one of the political parties (party identification), concern with national governmental policy issues (issue orientation), and liking for the presidential candidates (candidate orientation). By measuring attitudes on these matters, the studies could predict with fair accuracy not only how people voted but—equally important—who would be likely to vote.

To what extent did these psychological voting studies answer the basic question of "why"? Some readers were skeptical. To be sure, they said, the studies showed that those who were Republican and "liked Ike" would vote for Eisenhower to a high degree—but did this prove very much? The political psychologists felt they had done more than explain immediate antecedent factors; they felt they had found basic influences that lay behind the immediate causes for a person voting as he did. For example, surveys may show that a woman in Virginia is still voting in reaction to the events of the Civil War or that a laborer in Massachusetts is a confirmed Democrat because of his experiences in the Depression. A psychological approach, in short, can isolate both the original motivating factor and the voter's reaction to it in a single theory of causation. This theory is shown in diagramatic form in the accompanying illustration.

A nationwide survey would obviously reveal the background of a voter only in a short and hazy manner. Is it possible to study a smaller number of persons—but far more intensively? Three psychologists in the middle 1950s selected ten "normal" men in the greater Boston area, subjected them to a battery of psychological tests, and interviewed them intensively for a total of

[27]Rossi, in Burdick and Brodbeck (eds.), *op. cit.*, p. 37 (emphasis supplied). See also Davies, *op. cit.*, Chap. 4.

[28]The most important of these studies are Angus Campbell, Gerald Gurin, and Warren E. Miller, *The Voter Decides* (Row, Peterson, 1954), and Angus Campbell, Philip E. Converse, Warren E. Miller, and Donald E. Stokes, *The American Voter* (Wiley, 1960).

[29]*The American Voter*, p. 120. The authors advance an interesting metaphor of the "funnel of causality" (pp. 31-32).

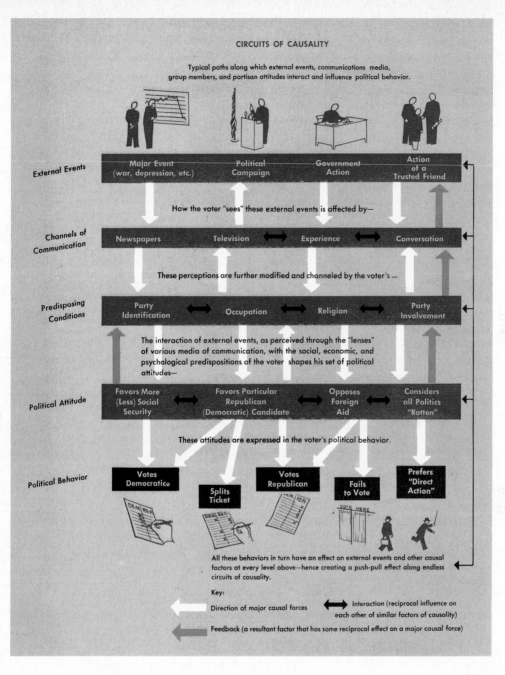

CIRCUITS OF CAUSALITY

Typical paths along which external events, communications media,
group members, and partisan attitudes interact and influence political behavior.

External Events
Major Event (war, depression, etc.) | Political Campaign | Government Action | Action of a Trusted Friend

How the voter "sees" these external events is affected by—

Channels of Communication
Newspapers | Television ⟷ Experience ⟷ Conversation

These perceptions are further modified and channeled by the voter's —

Predisposing Conditions
Party Identification ⟷ Occupation ⟷ Religion | Party Involvement

The interaction of external events, as perceived through the "lenses" of various media of communication, with the social, economic, and psychological predispositions of the voter shapes his set of political attitudes—

Political Attitude
Favors More (Less) Social Security ⟷ Favors Particular Republican (Democratic) Candidate ⟷ Opposes Foreign Aid ⟷ Considers all Politics "Rotten"

These attitudes are expressed in the voter's political behavior.

Political Behavior
Votes Democratic | Splits Ticket | Votes Republican | Fails to Vote | Prefers "Direct Action"

All these behaviors in turn have an effect on external events and other causal factors at every level above—hence creating a push-pull effect along endless circuits of causality.

Key:

⟸ Direction of major causal forces

⟷ Interaction (reciprocal influence on each other of similar factors of causality)

⟸ Feedback (a resultant factor that has some reciprocal effect on a major causal force)

Adapted from Angus Campbell, et al., *The American Voter* (Wiley, 1960).

about thirty hours each over a span of three or four months. The purpose was to collect all the available information about the subjects. The authors concluded, among many other things, that there is no rigid or easily discernible relation between a person's personality and his opinions (or voting), that opinions that develop in a person are multiple in their determinants, that the same opinions can serve several functions for their holder (for example, helping him to adjust to groups in which he participates and also helping him to cope with his own unresolved inner problems), and that the whole process of opinion formation is tremendously complex.[30] In effect, they indicated that opinion and voting studies have a long way to go before answering the real question of "why" in voting.

Evidently, then, at best we are only in midpassage in the study of voting behavior. At this point we can talk only in terms of tendencies and probabilities. Two things, though, are certain. One is that political scientists can advance in this field only in cooperation with other types of social scientists. The other is that if the problems are complex, the challenge and opportunity to the young political scientist are enormous.

[30]M. Brewster Smith, Jerome S. Bruner, and Robert W. White, *Opinions and Personality* (Wiley, 1956).

The Dynamic Role
of Interest Groups

11   The United States has been called a nation of joiners. Europeans sometimes make fun of us for setting up all sorts of organizations, and we ourselves
are often amused by the behavior of our groups—the noisy conventions of
veterans' associations, the solemn rites of great fraternal organizations, the
oratory of patriotic societies. Yet most of these groups are serious in their
aims, and they play an enormous role in politics. Moreover, joining is not an
exclusively American trait. It is a common trait of human beings—and a
biological factor as well.

How many groups are there in America? There is no way of knowing accurately. Families are groups—the most basic and important groups of all—
and there are at least forty million families in the United States. We have a
quarter of a million religious congregations, countless athletic teams, tens
of thousands of trade unions, and over two thousand trade associations. And
all these are groups in the broadest sense of the term—that is, the members
of each group share some common outlook or attitude, and interact with one
another in some way.[1]

Nor can we measure the variety of groups in America, although we know
that it is tremendous. One observer has made a list of odd organizations to
give a hint of this variety:[2]

[1]D. B. Truman, *The Governmental Process* (Knopf, 1951), Chap. 2. The basic approach of
this chapter is drawn largely from this volume and from the pioneer work, A. F. Bentley, *The
Process of Government* (Univ. of Chicago Press, 1908).

[2]From E. E. Schattschneider, *Party Government* (Holt, 1942), p. 26.

The Nonsmokers Protective League of America
Simplified Spelling Board
American Sunbathing Association
Blizzard Men of 1888 (to commemorate a famous storm)
American Hackney Horse Association
Toastmasters International

One person may belong to a great variety of groups and organizations. At home he belongs to his family, neighborhood, religious congregation, and so on. But he may also be a member of the Rotary Club, a philatelic society, the Masons, a law firm, the American Automobile Association, a taxpayers' association, the Republican party, a bowling league, the American Bar Association, the state bar association. This man is a member of all these groups but he is not *equally* a member of them. His loyalty to his family or his law firm may greatly outweigh his loyalty to all the other groups. Do the individual's allegiances to a wide variety of groups ever come into conflict with one another? Indeed yes. The AAA may demand better roads, whereas the taxpayers' association wants less governmental spending. The neighborhood this person lives in may be largely made up of Democrats whereas he is a Republican. Even without such conflicts, belonging to a variety of groups puts a great strain on his time and pocketbook.

The fact that groups are so numerous and varied raises a number of questions that go to the very heart of democratic politics in America: Why are some groups strong and organized, others weak and diffused? What happens when competing groups overlap in membership, as in the cases just mentioned? How are groups organized, led, and governed? How do they gain influence? What is their relation to the party system, to elections, to government as a whole?

Politics is concerned with the workings of all groups, but we can simplify our effort to answer these questions by limiting ourselves to a particular type, the *interest group*. This is any group whose members, as a result of sharing certain attitudes, make claims on other groups in order to realize aims arising from these attitudes. Interest groups are of many types. Some are formal associations or organizations. Others have no formal organization at all—a young people's interest group, for example. Various interest groups may even exist within a given interest group. Thus inside the American Bar Association there may be several interest groups in conflict over a particular issue. An interest group may be either broader or narrower than a particular organization. The American Federation of Labor and Congress of Industrial Organizations, for example, is opposed to a labor reform measure. But not all members of the ALF-CIO oppose the labor reform bill, and some people who are not members oppose it. The interest group working to amend or abolish this measure, then, is composed of most members of the AFL-ÇIO, but not all, along with some people outside the formal labor organization.

Politics is largely a conflict among competing groups with conflicting ideas of what is in the general interest. In political arguments we inevitably talk about special interests versus the general welfare. But in political analysis it is better to talk about this group's idea of the general welfare as compared with that group's idea. As political partisans we are all committed to particular ideas and values, but as social scientists we cannot pretend to set up a clearly defined national interest. For this is really the question at issue—What *is* the general interest?

The Crisscross of Interests

The vast majority of gainfully employed Americans are members of at least one of the big occupational associations, which have much to say about income and working conditions for employers and professional people as well as for farmers and union workers. The typical large association comprises a mosaic of local and state bodies. Usually it is the product of slow and painful growth through decades.

Probably the oldest "unions" in America are farm organizations. The earliest farm group—the South Carolina Agricultural Society—was founded even before our Constitution was written. In the late nineteenth century the National Grange, or Patrons of Husbandry, led farm rebellions against low farm prices, railroad monopolies, and grasping middlemen. The Grange, once a fighting organization with over a million members, is smaller today and more conservative than the other big farm groups. Presently, the largest farm group is the American Farm Bureau Federation, which is especially strong in the prosperous corn belt. Organized originally around government agents who helped the farmers in rural counties, the Federation today is almost a semigovernmental agency, but it retains full freedom to fight for such goals as price support and expanded farm credit facilities. The most liberal (or radical) farm organization today is the Farmers Union, founded in 1902, which represents Plains States farmers to a marked extent and works for legislation, such as government aid to family-sized farms, that will protect the small farmer. A great number of other farm organizations are based on the interests of farmers who produce specific commodities, such as the American Soybean Association or the woolgrowers' association.

Workers too have long been organized; the earliest trade union locals were founded during Washington's first administration. Throughout the nineteenth century, workers organized political parties and a host of local unions. Their most ambitious effort at national organization, the Knights of Labor, claimed 700,000 members. By the beginning of this century, the American Federation of Labor, a confederation of strong and independent-minded national unions mainly representing craftworkers, was the dominant labor organization. During the ferment of the 1930s, unions more responsive to such industrial workers as coal miners broke away from the AFL and formed a rival national organization, the Congress of Industrial Organizations. Later the AFL and CIO reunited in the big organization that exists today, but some of the industrial union leaders contend that the AFL-CIO has become too conservative and separatist tendencies remain.

Businessmen's "unions" are the most varied and numerous of all. Over two thousand national trade associations and hundreds more of local groups are as varied as the products and services they sell—automobiles, pins, cotton—the list is almost endless. The main general agency for business is the Chamber of Commerce of the United States, organized in 1912. The chamber is a federation of federations, composed of several thousand local chambers of commerce representing tens of thousands of business firms. Loosely allied with the chamber on most issues is the National Association of Manufacturers, which since its inception in the wake of the depression of 1893 has spoken for the more conservative elements of American business.

Professional people have organized some of the strongest "unions" in the nation. Some are well known, such as the American Medical Association and the American Bar Association, each of which embraces a host of state and local societies. Others are divided into many subgroups—thus, teachers are organized in the National Education Association, in the American Association of University Professors, and also in particular subject groups, such as the Modern Language Association. Many professions are closely tied in with government, especially on the state level. Lawyers, for example, are licensed by the states, which have set up, often as a result of pressure from lawyers themselves, certain standards of admission to the state bar.

Cutting across such associations based on occupation are countless other groups based on national, religious, racial, ideological, recreational, athletic, and other ties. Not many Americans are members of more than one occupational group, but they have endless nonoccupational interests and often are more emotionally and financially involved in such interests—in a veterans' organization, such as the American Legion, Veterans of Foreign Wars, or Amvets; in a nationality group, such as the multitude of Irish, German, Polish, Scandinavian, and other organzations; or in religious organizations, such as the Knights of Columbus. The variety of such memberships is remarkable; there are more than 150 nationwide organizations based on national origin alone.

It would be possible to list many other types of association. There are the women's groups, such as the League of Women Voters. There are the numerous reform groups, such as Americans for Democratic Action. There are groups concerned with particular policy areas, such as the Foreign Policy Association. A complete list would have to include the thousands of struggling groups that live for a few years, sometimes realize their objectives, then die. It would include not only existing groups but potential groups that would spring into being if certain events, such as a new depression, occurred. But our list is long enough to permit two generalizations:

First, there is a tendency for one or two large organizations to predominate in each field—for example, the AMA and the AFL-CIO in their fields, and among veterans, the Legion and the VFW. Often there are competing and even challenging organizations, but they cannot match the resources and power of the leading organizations.

Second, there is a marked continuity and stability among the major organizations. Most of them are decades old, and whatever their weaknesses, there are few signs of their being replaced. Even the AFL, which had fallen far behind the times in New Deal days, shook off the challenge of the CIO.

Both of these tendencies would seem to indicate undue continuity and even conservatism among the major organized interests. But behind the scene major changes may take place.

Interest Groups in Ferment

In many respects groups are plastic. In their internal and external relations they must respond to the deep economic and political currents that flow through the nation and the world. Successive changes in industrial organization, for example, first allowed the AFL to become dominant in labor organization and then forced it to yield ground to a rival union. Changing agricultural methods created new patterns of life on the farm, new relationships among farm groups. Recently the dynamics of group politics have been most evident in Negro organizations. The migration of thousands of Negroes from the South to Northern cities has brought changes in their economic and social opportunities, in their frustrations, and hence in their role in politics. The rise of big government has affected groups, and of course the reverse is also true — interest groups help create and shape big government. But this is more than a two-way process; it is multidirectional and multisided.

BLACK POWER

Nationality groups such as Irish-Americans or Italian-Americans may gradually lose identification with their national origins as their members become increasingly absorbed into the mainstream of American life — hence, they may lose their political leverage.[3] Racial groups may have the same experience, but the more than twenty million American Negroes will doubtless be the last to lose their separate identity. Decades of discrimination and segregation — political, economic, and social — forced Negroes to set up an almost separate life of their own. But in recent decades, as we saw in Chapter 7, black Americans have become increasingly organized and cohesive; they have begun to mass their strength behind their goal of either becoming an effective part of the American political system or branching away from it. Many politicians today consider Negroes the major shiftable block of votes in national elections.

For decades the chief Negro organization was the National Association for the Advancement of Colored People, which was established in 1910 to fight lynching and peonage and to press for the right to vote. Today, with more than five hundred chapters, the NAACP remains the single most important organization working for racial integration. It cooperates with the Urban League, another key federation of local groups — one that seeks to broaden economic opportunity. Although the leadership positions within both organizations are now filled mainly with blacks, both these "old-line" organizations are under criticism and attack from more militant Negroes, who have threatened to take over the NAACP from the so-called establishment that runs it.

[3]For contrasting views concerning how much ethnic distinctiveness and voting has declined, see Raymond E. Wolfinger, "The Development and Persistence of Ethnic Voting," *The American Political Science Review* (December 1965), pp. 896-908; and Michael Parenti, "Ethnic Politics and the Persistence of Ethnic Identification," *The American Political Science Review* (September 1967), pp. 717-726.

But most of the competition to the big Negro organizations has come from outside, from the formation of new groups. The Southern Christian Leadership Conference was organized by the late Dr. Martin Luther King and under his leadership followed the course of direct nonviolent action, such as mass demonstrations and sit-ins. The Congress of Racial Equality was started during World War II, mainly in Northern university areas, and became one of the most militant civil rights organizations of the 1950s and 1960s. It agitated to open up public accommodations, such as restaurants and skating rinks, to Negroes and picketed barbershops and chain stores that refused to serve blacks.[4] A very different Negro organization, the Black Muslims, also competes for Negro support and attacks black organizations that take part in "whitey's" politics.

For decades Negroes tended to back the Republican party—the Grand Old Party of Lincoln and emancipation—but the Depression of the 1930s and the concern of New Dealers and Fair Dealers for civil rights brought large numbers of Negroes over to the Democratic party. The anti-civil rights stand of Southern Democrats, however, has helped maintain the traditional nonpartisanship of Negro organizations.

In recent years the more militant Negro leaders have increasingly opposed the political strategy of taking part in two-party politics and the other processes of pluralist democracy. They argue in favor of building direct action groups that will take control of areas in which blacks live and work.

By the end of the 1960s most Negroes still seemed committed to achieving integration and their other goals through the methods of pluralist democracy. But critics were increasingly vocal in their claim that the American brand of democracy was loaded against the Negro and the poor; that working through pressure groups and parties was not an effective way to bring about fundamental social and political change; and that Negroes and their allies from the poor, the students, and other sectors of society must either gain control of democratic government through third parties, agitation, and other militant techniques or must "opt out" of the system and try to set up black enclaves of their own. As the 1970s got under way, one of the most urgent domestic questions was whether government by the people, American style, was able to produce major social change toward equality and freedom or whether its critics were indeed right in contending that it was controlled by a relatively few conservative or unconcerned people in both parties.

THE BASIS OF GROUP POWER

Whether a group seeks political power within or outside the framework of pluralist democracy, the main bases of its political strength are size and unity. Obviously numbers are important—an organization with three million members will overshadow one with three thousand. But numbers do not amount to much if the group is so divided that the members fail to work together in behalf of group goals. What makes a group cohesive? What causes its members to vote the same way?

By far the most important factor is the *attitude and makeup of the mem-*

[4]Marvin Rich, "The Congress of Racial Equality and Its Strategy," in H. R. Mahood (ed.), *Pressure Groups in American Politics* (Scribner, 1967), pp. 197-204.

bership. When the leaders of an organization can absolutely depend on the backing of their followers, the organization is able to put its full force into pursuing its aims, and it will have an enormous advantage in the political arena. Communist groups are said to be made up of people who devote all their time and energy to their cause; if this is true, it explains why the Communists seem to exercise influence out of proportion to their numbers. But most Americans cannot possibly give their lives over to one group—not even to their families. Most Americans are members of many groups; their loyalties are divided.

It is this fact of overlapping membership that largely determines the cohesiveness of a group. Organization leaders run up against the problem time after time. A union official, for example, asks a dozen of his members to come to a meeting. Several say they will show up. But one says he has to be with his bowling club that night. Two others have to stay home with their families. Another has a church supper. Even those who finally do show up at the union meeting are not 100 percent supporters. Perhaps they are asked to vote for a particular candidate in a coming election. Some of them will. But one may decide to vote for the other candidate because they are neighbors or because they are both Italian-Americans, both Republicans, or both Legionnaires. Or perhaps he will not know what to do and will not vote at all.

Usually a mass-membership group comprises three types of members: First, a relatively small number of formal leaders, who may hold full-time, paid postions or at least devote much of their extra time, effort, and money to the group's activities.[5] Second, a hard core of members who are highly involved in the group organizationally and psychologically; they identify themselves with the group's aims, show up at meetings, cheerfully pay their dues, do a lot of the legwork. Third, people who are members essentially in name only: they do not participate actively; they do not look on themselves as Teamsters or Rotarians or Legionnaires;[6] they cannot be depended on to vote in elections or otherwise act politically as the leadership wants. In a typical organization, for every top leader, there might be a few hundred hard-core activists and 10,000 inactive members.

A second factor in the cohesion of a group is its *organizational structure.* Some groups have no formal organization. Others consist of local organizations that have joined together in some sort of loose state or national federation. In such cases the local organizations retain a measure of separate power and independence, just as the states did when they entered the Union. Thus, there is a form of federalism in some organizations, such as the AFL-CIO and AMA, that may hinder unity.

A sort of separation of powers may be found as well. The national assembly of an organization establishes—or at least ratifies—policy. An executive committee meets more frequently. A president or director is elected to head up and speak for the group. And permanent, paid officials form the organization's bureaucracy. Power may be further divided between the organization's main headquarters and its Washington office. An organization of this sort tends to be far less cohesive than a centralized, disciplined group such as the Army or some trade unions.

[5]V. O. Key, Jr., *Public Opinion and American Democracy* (Knopf, 1961), pp. 504-507.
[6]Angus Campbell, et al., *The American Voter* (Wiley, 1960), pp. 308-309.

Closely related to this factor of cohesion is a third one—*the nature of the leadership of the group.* In a group that embraces many attitudes and interests, the leaders may either weld the various elements together or sharpen their disunity. The leader of a national business association, for example, must tread cautiously between big business and little business, between exporters and importers, between chain stores and corner grocery stores, between the makers and sellers of competing products. Yet he must not be a mere punching bag for different interests, for above all he must lead. He must show how to achieve whatever goals can be agreed on. Thus the group leader is in the same position as a President or a congressman, though his constituency is different. He must act diplomatically in his efforts to patch up differences among the subgroups. He must know when to lead his followers, when to follow them.

Finally, the power of a group is affected by the *nature of the political and governmental system in which it operates.* Because of our federal system, a group consisting of three million supporters but concentrated in a few states will have less influence than another group consisting of the same number of supporters spread out in a large number of states. (If the supporters are spread too widely, however, they might have the least impact of all.) A group whose goals are contrary to widely accepted values will have tougher going than another group that can clothe its demands in acceptable ideology. And, as we shall see in later chapters, governmental structures are significant because they allow some groups more direct access to governmental decision-makers and other groups much less.

This picture of group power suggests that the mass organizations are beset by many weaknesses and cannot act like a disciplined army. As Key said, "When the president of an organization announces to a congressional committee that he speaks for several million people, the odds are that a substantial proportion of his members can be shown to have no opinion or even to express views contrary to those voiced by their spokesmen." When the spokesmen threaten public officials with unleashing hostile votes, "they are usually pointing an unloaded gun."[7] Much of the group leader's efforts must be devoted not to influencing nonmembers of the group but to persuading his own peripheral members to support the group's line. However there is evidence that the longer a person has belonged to a group, the more likely he is to identify strongly with it.[8]

THE GROUP LEADER

Leaders of organizations use a variety of methods to hold their followers together. Directing the affairs of every group are a few insiders or old-timers who control the administrative machinery, such as admission to membership, financial affairs, correspondence, and committees. In exercising discipline and control, the leaders can withold certain services (such as lobbying assistance) from rebellious members. Sometimes they can expel members who do not follow the party line—this sanction is important if members lose their jobs when they lose their membership, as with the union shop.

[7]Key, *op. cit.*, pp. 522, 525.
[8]*Ibid.*, p. 506.

The leaders may also control the organization's propaganda. The active minority usually puts out the newspaper or magazine that goes to the members, arranges the meetings, and works up the agenda.

The leaders of a group tend to stay in control year after year. An organization that is secure in its leadership can confront its enemies and pursue its program with unity and single-mindedness. On the other hand, unchanging leadership may contribute to decay, demoralization, disunity. In order to stay in power it may resort to illegal means, or it may be enthusiastically reelected or reappointed each year by a rank and file grateful for successes achieved.

Labor unions are revealing—though by no means the only—examples of the balance of democracy and oligarchy in interest groups. On the one hand, most unions follow democratic procedures, such as regular elections, a good deal of free speech, grievance machinery, and open and much publicized conventions. On the other hand, many unions have been undemocratic in fact. Opposition has been suppressed on the convention floor, occasionally by violence. Opposition views have been barred from the union newspaper. Union presidents have been able to turn the union professional staffs into their personal political machine. Occasionally, ballots have been "lost" or miscounted.[9] Yet unions may be at least as democratic as most private associations—their failings may simply be more conspicuous because of their more open procedures and the old ideal of union democracy by which they are tested.

We must keep in mind too the question of how much labor or other group leaders should represent only the narrow interests of their groups. A union or business or veterans' leader might follow democratic procedures impeccably and speak unerringly for his group—and end up as simply a narrow-minded spokesman for some parochial interest. In fact, some leaders misrepresent their membership—not because they are dictatorial but because they have some feeling for the broader interests outside their group. Surprising gaps have been discovered between the political positions adopted by some leaders and the attitudes of their members. (Here we encounter one of the problems of representation that make up the theme of this part of the book.)

This balance of power is also upheld by external forces that operate in the whole community. One of these forces is democracy itself. Americans generally want to have a share in running their government—so naturally they want to have a say in the way their organizations are managed. Actually, most groups have the form of little democracies (although they may have their share of undemocratic practices). There are periodic elections; meetings are run in a parliamentary fashion; a member has the right to stand up in a meeting and say what he wishes. If an organization violates democratic forms year after year, it may come into bad repute. Some of its own members may turn against it, and other organizations may become hostile and refuse to work with it.

Probably the most powerful factor preventing one group from upsetting the balance of power is the existence of other groups. Organization invites

[9]For a list of nine recent studies of union government and democracy and a discriminating comment on them, see Oliver Garceau, "Book Note," *The American Political Science Review* (December 1963), pp. 982-985.

counterorganization. The increased influence of one group forces competing groups to strengthen themselves. Decades ago, for example, nationwide corporations helped stimulate nationwide labor unions, which in turn stimulated the organization of national business federations.

GROUPS IN THE POLITICAL STRUGGLE

Seen in these terms the power of organized groups does not turn only on internal factors, such as the size, unity, and leadership of groups. It also turns on external factors—the nature of the environment, the attitudes of people everywhere, the strength of other groups. Adding up all these factors, what are the main advantages and disadvantages of the major groups in the American political struggle?

Numerically, businessmen are in a minority in the United States, yet they wield great power. This power has several foundations. First, the business community is fairly cohesive. "It is almost as if the business leadership were in a continuous political caucus," says one political observer. "Conventions, committee sessions, board meetings, and corporate staff conferences, with their interlocking and overlapping memberships, build a system of face-to-face relations knitting the business community together. The airplane and the corporation expense account bring literally thousands of businessmen into conference every day, and they in turn have their relations back home with the less mobile elements of the business community."[10]

Second, business beliefs are shared by many Americans who are not businessmen. Business values have been stamped on American culture; and many people identify themselves with business.[11] Even after the Depression and the New Deal, business leaders enjoyed higher public prestige than labor leaders, according to polls. Given this situation, it becomes easier for people to accept such ideas as "What is good for business is good for you."

Third, businessmen have money and money means influence. It can be used to pay for propaganda, to support political parties, to finance lobbies, to influence public officials directly or indirectly. Fourth, business has important allies—namely, lawyers, editors, and other professional and white-collar people—who share its community of interest. Finally, businessmen have important skills, such as the ability to explain their case, experience in competition, and the like.

Business suffers certain disadvantages, too. As stated, businessmen are in a numerical minority, and in the long run in a democracy votes count most. The very concentration of business that promotes unity tends to make it a target—Americans tend to be suspicious of bigness and monopoly. Business is also a convenient scapegoat—when hard times come and jobs are scarce, it is easy to blame Wall Street.

Other groups have their own strengths and weaknesses. Industrial workers are large in numbers and have become more organizationally and politically conscious. But they are divided into organized and unorganized, white

---

[10]V. O. Key, Jr., *Politics, Parties, and Pressure Groups*, 5th ed. (Crowell, 1964), p. 90.

[11]The nature and extent of the domination of American thought and practice by business values was vividly described by Thorstein Veblen in a series of pioneering studies, especially in his *The Theory of the Leisure Class* (Funk & Wagnalls, 1967).

and black, skilled and unskilled. Moreover, many American workers refuse to identify themselves or their interests with an "inferior" class. Further-more, it is hard for labor to make alliances with farm or business groups, because the latters' views of trade unionism may be somewhat unfavorable.

The farmers' situation is almost the reverse of labor's. They are declining in numbers relative to the whole population. But their advantages are significant. The system of American federalism gives them extra political strength, for farmers are spread through all fifty states. Furthermore, farmers enjoy high esteem; in the popular mind they are frugal, hardworking, inde-pendent—the backbone of the nation. Like labor, however, the farmers are divided.

These strategic factors are not static. The external factors especially tend to change over time. Business at one time may enjoy enormous prestige, as during the prosperous 1920s when Calvin Coolidge could say the "the business of America is business." A few years later, it may be relegated to the national doghouse. Labor is usually stronger during a time of ferment and reform than during a period of prosperity.

The Weapons of Group Influence

Groups use a wide range of political techniques to reach their goals. Their capacity to use these techniques is heavily affected by the factors we have just discussed—the size of the group, its cohesion or lack of it, its organizational structure, the skills of its leaders, the external situation. Every group must exploit the particular advantages it has—for example, a small but well-organized group will probably rely on skillful lobbying rather than mass election appeals.

PERSUASION

All interest groups are propagandistic. They exploit the media described in Chapter 9—radio, press, film, leaflets, signs, and, above all, word of mouth. Business enjoys a special advantage in this arena, and businessmen have the money to hire propaganda machinery. Being advertisers on a large scale, they know how to deliver their message effectively. Most important, they generally have easy access to the means of propaganda, such as the press. The NAM puts out periodicals—one goes to educators, another to leaders of women's clubs, another to farm leaders, another to clergymen. Other fea-tures of their program of opinion-molding are a speaker-training program, motion pictures, and meetings with leaders of other groups, such as farmers and veterans. And supplementing the NAM's efforts are those of the cham-ber of commerce, trade associations, and individual corporations.

Other groups have become increasingly aware of the uses of propaganda. Organized labor is a notable example. When a business organization places full-page messages in newspapers across the nation, unions often find the funds to hire similar space for an answer. Although labor has not yet matched the propaganda skills of business, it is devoting more money and attention to this political technique. Other interest groups, such as doctors and teachers, are also making use of publicity methods. The American Medical Association spent hundreds of thousands of dollars in a decade-long campaign against the extension of social security to support hospital care for persons over sixty-five.

How effective is group propaganda? It is impossible to measure precisely the impact of propaganda campaigns, for too many other factors are involved. But we know enough to be skeptical of some of the extravagant claims made for group propaganda. For example, organized labor strongly denounced the Taft-Hartley act for years after its passage, but surveys in 1952 showed that the great majority of the public and of *union members* either wanted to keep the new law or had no opinion about it or what to do about it. Also, the more a group publicizes its position, the more it runs the risk of arousing the opposition and stimulating *its* propaganda potential. Sometimes a highly specialized interest group may improve its public image by a skillful advertising campaign, but the impact of a general propaganda campaign to affect mass attitudes on general issues may be small. The best policy for a group may be to form alliances with other groups or with a political party.[12]

ELECTIONEERING

Almost all large organizations avow that they are nonpolitical. But actually, almost all organized groups are involved in politics in one way or another. What group leaders mean when they say they are nonpolitical is that they are *nonpartisan*. A distinguishing feature of organized interest groups is that they try to work through both parties. Usually this means working for individual candidates in either party. The policy that labor has followed for years — helping friends and defeating enemies — is the policy of almost all organized interest groups.

This policy is put into action in different ways. Occasionally an organization openly endorses a candidate and actively works for his election. Thus, in 1924 many labor unions endorsed "Fighting Bob" La Follette for President; the CIO officially backed Roosevelt in 1944 and the AFL-CIO supported Humphrey in 1968. More often the organization formally stays neutral, but prominent officials take a public stand. Because of such factors as overlapping membership, an organization may set up a front organization to carry on its political activities, as in the case of the Committee on Political Education formed by the AFL-CIO.[13]

Individual labor unions, with somewhat homogeneous memberships, can sometimes afford to take a rather firm position on candidates. Other organizations are more handicapped by the diversity of their members. A local retailers' group, for example, might be composed equally of Republicans and Democrats, and many of its members might refuse to take an open position on a candidate for fear of losing business. In such cases more subtle means

[12]Samuel Halperin, *The Political World of American Zionism* (Wayne Univ. Press, 1961), Chap. 13.

[13]Harry M. Scoble, "Organized Labor in Electoral Politics: Some Questions for the Discipline," *Western Political Quarterly* (September 1963), pp. 666-685, suggests some of the difficulties in measuring the actual impact of union political activity on two-party politics.

265

CHAPTER 11
The
Dynamic Role
of Interest
Groups

may be equally effective. At meetings word is passed around that candidate X is sound from the organization's point of view. Perhaps the hat is passed around, too, and a contribution made to the cause. Members of the organization may serve as local opinion leaders in drumming up support for him.

How effective is electioneering by interest groups? No generalization is possible, because everything depends on the kinds of factors we have been discussing—the group's size, unity, objectives, political resources, leadership, and above all the political context in which it is operating. In general, though, it can be said that the power of the mass-membership organizations to mobilize their full strength in elections has been exaggerated in the press. Too many cross-pressures are operating in the pluralistic politics of America for any one group to assume a really commanding role. Some groups reach their maximum influence only by allying closely with one of the two major parties—but this means losing some of their independence and singleness of purpose.[14]

Another method of trying to win elections is to form a separate party. Third parties in the United States, however, have tended to be self-defeating (see Chapter 12). The strength of interest groups has been siphoned off into minority party politics, while the two old parties have retained control of the government.

Some groups have tried a third method—trying to infiltrate the organization and machinery of the major parties. They have placed their members on local, state, and national party committees and have helped send them to party conventions as delegates. For years, one vice president of the AFL was prominent in Republican activities and another was equally active for the Democrats.

Obviously, burrowing from within is not a new tactic; but it is being used more and more often and with increasing success. The AFL-CIO's Committee on Political Education is a good example. Technically, COPE is nonpartisan, assisting pro-labor candidates in both parties. Actually, COPE has come to concentrate most of its efforts in the Democratic party. Not only does it endorse party candidates, but in many states it has exercised electioneering functions that the parties ordinarily monopolize. COPE pays close attention to registration (see Chapter 13) in order to ensure a large vote. It takes part in primary campaigns as well as in the later election contests. It puts out posters and leaflets, holds schools on political-action techniques, provides automobiles to carry voters to the polls.

LOBBYING

Lobbying is a long-used weapon of interest groups. Generations of Americans have been stirred by exposés of the "invisible government." Some of this is based on folklore, but much of it on fact. From the time of the Yazoo land frauds 150 years ago, when a whole legislature was bribed and the Postmaster General was put on a private payroll as a lobbyist, to the latest logrolling activity in Congress, Americans have enjoyed denouncing the lobbyists.

[14]See Harmon Zeigler, *Interest Groups in American Society* (Prentice-Hall, 1964), esp. Chap. 8.

Over one thousand lobbyists are active in Washington today, but few of them are glamorous, unscrupulous, or very powerful. Most of the organizations maintaining lobbyists are highly specialized outfits such as the National Fertilizer Association, Retired Officers Association, and Institute of Shortening and Edible Oils. Lobbyists for these associations are usually hardworking attorneys, with long experience in Washington ways; their job is to watch a handful of bills and to keep in touch with a few administrative officials. Because lawmaking today is a highly technical matter, these lobbyists—or legislative counsel, as they like to be called—play a useful part in modern government. The harried congressman or administrator, threading his way through mountains of paper and seeking to appease conflicting interests, gladly turns to them for their views and information.[15]

Lobbyists for the big groups operate on a loftier scale. Their specialty is knowing just how to throw their political weight around. These lobbyists are better known throughout the country than some senators, better paid, better staffed, and more secure in their positions. The groups they represent have such broad interests that they must watch a wide variety of bills touching every phase of government. They are expert in raising such a clamor that they seem to be speaking for vast numbers of people. They exert pressure in Congress wherever they can find vulnerable points—regular committees, appropriations committees, individual legislators, even on the floor of the House and Senate (see Chapter 16). They know how to mobilize their organizations back home so that a storm of letters, telegrams, and petitions descends on Washington. They know how to draw up laws, to testify before committees, to help speed a bill through its long legislative journey, or to slow it down. They are experts in the art in influence.

Sometimes lobbyists stay in the background and make use of the legislators' own constituents. The following Hints on Lobbying sent by one organization to its members reveal this technique.

1. Interview the legislator at home if you are a constituent. If seeing him at the Capitol, impress on him that you live and vote in his district.

2. Be sure to have read the bill and to know the question with which it deals.

3. Find out main facts about legislator before interviewing him—his party, committee membership, business or profession, etc.

4. Be nonpartisan with legislator of opposite party from your own. In any case make clear our organization's nonpartisanship.

5. Don't pin legislator down to position for or against. Establish friendly relations. We will have to continue working with him in the future.

6. Use good salesmanship techniques. Our organization will be judged by the kind of interview you have.

7. Don't be "superior" even if you know far more about the question than he does. You are not there to score a point but to help get the measure passed!

8. Be patient and keep your temper.

9. Attend House and Senate galleries when bill comes up on the floor.

10. If possible, establish friendly relations with chairman and key members of at least one committee.

---

[15]On lobbying as a communication process, see Lester W. Milbrath, *The Washington Lobbyists* (Rand McNally, 1963). Also see Zeigler, *op. cit.*

When groups find the usual political channels closed to them, they may seek other ways to influence public policy.[16] The courts have increasingly become the center of such efforts. The NAACP, for example, has instituted and won numerous cases in its efforts to improve the legal protection of Negroes. The technique is not new, of course,[17] but in recent decades urban interests, feeling underrepresented in state and national legislatures, have turned increasingly to the courts.

Another technique of group activity in litigation is the device of *amici curiae*, friends of the court. The organizations present briefs supporting one side or the other in cases before the courts, thus gaining a forum for stating their organizational interests. The American Civil Liberties Union and the American Jewish Congress, for example, have often used this procedure. Another device used by interests to get their views before the courts is legal periodicals. Because judges and justices read these journals to keep abreast of legal scholarship and sometimes even cite them as authority for their rul-

[16]Lucius J. Barker, "Third Parties in Litigation: A Systemic View of the Judicial Function," *The Journal of Politics* (February 1967), vol. 29, pp. 41-69.
[17]See, for example, C. Peter Magrath, *Yazoo: Law and Politics in the New Republic* (Brown Univ. Press, 1966).

Courtesy Donald Reilly; copyright 1968 Saturday Review, Inc.

"I'm so proud of you—imagine having your hair defended by the American Civil Liberties Union!"

ings, groups may seek to have articles presenting their views published in these journals.[18]

NONVIOLENT DIRECT ACTION

Nonviolent action embraces a variety of activities ranging from passive resistance and mass demonstrations to sit-ins, strikes, and heckling of speakers. Traditionally, strikes have been used in the United States mainly by unions to win concessions from employers, but strikes and other kinds of economic pressure can also be used for political purposes. The different forms of nonviolent action have been used by many types of groups. In some places Negroes active in the civil rights movement have been denied credit or dismissed from their jobs and blacklisted, and in recent years white and black civil rights activists have counterattacked their foes by organizing boycotts of busses and stores. Negro and white college students also organized freedom rides to bring about compliance with ICC regulations on intercity buses.

Protest against the war in Vietnam in the late 1960s stimulated nonviolent direct action throughout the nation, especially on college campuses. In dozens of communities mass demonstrations and marches dramatized suppression of the right to vote, police brutality, denial of job opportunity. Using Gandhian nonviolent methods as their guide, leaders sought to restrain their followers from any form of violence, but, like the great Gandhi, they sometimes created situations in which violence easily took over.

VIOLENCE

The Whisky Rebellion of 1794 and the Civil War are sober reminders that violence is an old weapon in group struggle. For decades labor disputes have been marked by bloodshed. Only in recent years, however, has the use of violence been elevated to a kind of creed or philosophy by its practitioners.

Responding to murders, arson, and other terrors inflicted on them, some Negroes by the late 1960s were beginning to preach force as a weapon of last resort. Although most black leaders have flatly repudiated violence, force, or the threat of it, has become a central factor in the rising conflict over racial justice. Peaceful political action, it is argued, does not enable blacks and poor people to seize enough political power to influence pluralist democracy and bring about basic social reform. Violence pinpoints and dramatizes problems, attracts a good deal of attention (especially from television cameramen) and pushes far-off problems right under the noses of the apathetic middle class.

Students—who often consider themselves a politically deprived group—have recently seen their campuses turned into arenas of violence. Some student leaders contend that where undergraduates lack the opportunity to influence academic decisions because of nonrepresentation on governing councils, students must turn to nonviolent confrontation or violent action. Student leaders have discovered, however, that although violence is a ready means of attracting attention to student discontent, it has dangers and pitfalls

[18]Jack W. Peltason, *Federal Courts in the Political Process* (Doubleday, 1955), p. 52.

269

CHAPTER 11
The
Dynamic Role
of Interest
Groups

and can easily be turned against its authors. Silent or noisy nonviolent demonstrations remain the favorite student weapon.

Assassination is one of the oldest forms of political violence—and one of the newest. In the United States it has been used most significantly not as a group political weapon, but as the resort of a single fanatic or lunatic.

Whether there has been an increase in crime is still a debated question: some consider the "soaring crime rate" to be more the product of an improvement in statistical information than of a basic change in society; others see it as the product of our changing from a small-town to a large-city society. But the fact that many people believe our streets are unsafe is itself a significant political fact, as the 1968 elections suggested.

Civil disorders and violence have been the subjects of three recent presidential commissions—the Warren, Kerner, and Jenner Commissions—and of hundreds of articles and books. Some see American society as sick and find evidence that major groups are becoming alienated and are rejecting the legitimacy of pluralist democracy to resolve conflicts and maintain order.[19] Others think the evidence does not support such a pessimistic conclusion and that when viewed in the perspective of history and compared with other nations, the American system has had a remarkable ability to promote both social justice and social order.

Two problems that are often merged need to be separated—the deliberate use of force and social disorder as a reflection of social discontent. Social disorder is clearly a phenomenon of the frustration and deprivation felt by black Americans and has become an almost regular yearly event in city after city. Only recently have social scientists begun systematically to analyze civil disorders and study the conditions under which they are produced and controlled.[20] Perhaps no question is of greater urgency than how to deal with the causes of social disorder and control their consequences in a manner that will maintain confidence in the legitimacy of democracy and in the ability of our system to promote civil justice and to preserve civil order.

Interest Groups and Pluralist Democracy

Almost everyone likes to denounce pressure groups—especially somebody else's pressure group. Editorial columns are filled with protests that big business, or big labor, or the farm bloc, is taking over the country. This viewing with alarm has put organized interest groups under a cloud. Some people even look on them as a perversion of democracy—as a blot on the otherwise fair system of popular representation. Various proposals have been advanced to do away with these allegedly evil interests or at least to clip their wings.

It is easy enough to answer these critics. Obviously, organized groups are here to stay. So long as there is a modicum of freedom left in America, men

---

[19]See, for example, William H. Grier and Price M. Cobbs, *Black Rage* (Basic Books, 1968), a study by two psychiatrists of case histories of Negro men and women they have treated.

[20]William A. Gasmon, *Power and Discontent* (The Dorsey Press, 1968); Louis H. Masotti (ed.), "Urban Violence and Disorder," *American Behavioral Scientist* (March-April 1968), pp. 1–55.

will associate on some basis or other. Actually we owe a great deal to the richness and fullness of group life in America. Our progress in technological, cultural, and political areas would have been impossible without it. Yet there are three criticisms of organized interest groups in America that we must consider.

INTEREST GROUPS: ATTACK AND DEFENSE

Certain organizations, it is said, are becoming too strong. Big business was once the chief target of this criticism, but more recently farmers and unions have been pictured as the new Goliaths. Our discussion above suggests that these fears are grossly exaggerated The larger an association becomes, we noticed, the more it includes members of other groups with other allegiances. The stronger a group becomes, the more stimulus there will be for other groups to counterorganize. The real defense against group tyranny in America lies in the groups themselves.[21] So long as we have a great number and a rich diversity of groups and so long as we preserve our liberties, no single interest or combination of interests can take over America. The competition would simply be too great.

A second criticism is that interest groups tend to be oligarchical, that the group leaders misrepresent their own members. Over a half-century ago Robert Michels, after a study of European parties and groups, framed his famous "iron law of oligarchy"—that is, he who says organization says oligarchy. Organization requires leadership; and the leaders control because of their superior abilities, because the mass membership are incompetent and crave leadership, and because the leaders have the devices or organizational power—membership lists, funds, the organization's newspaper, and so on—in their own hands.

A third charge is that the sum total of groups in American politics do not represent the American people as a whole. Group leaders sometimes ignore the many people with related interests outside their own group—for example, farm associations that act only for a minority of farmers. Most important of all, it is said, many elements of the population are not represented in formal organizations at all, or at best are badly underrepresented. Not all groups receive the consideration they deserve in the clash of organized interests. Notable examples of unorganized or underorganized interests are consumers, nonunion laborers, farm workers, and certain professional and white-collar groups. Inevitably, government will tend to overrepresent the strongly organized.

But we must remember that our government is still organized on a territorial or geographical basis; we have made no attempt to build occupational representation into the structure of government. Furthermore, Americans who are underorganized can always resort to the polls, or ultimately they can organize their own associations. Admittedly this is a slow process, but it is a process that has occurred again and again in American history as less organized elements have striven to make up for their weakness by political counterorganization. In the economic sphere, for example, when business be-

[21]Truman, *op. cit.*, Chap. 16.

271

CHAPTER 11
The
Dynamic Role
of Interest
Groups

came too strong, unions and consumer groups rose to hold it in check. Or if manufacturers tried to raise prices unduly, powerful chain stores threatened to turn to other sources of supply or even to build or buy factories of their own. This doctrine of "countervailing power"[22] operates also in the political sphere; no one group can become too strong, for under a system of private checks and balances among group interests other groups will become politically active and united in opposition. The result is a system of rough justice in the representation of groups.

CONTROL OF LOBBYING: A CASE STUDY

However exaggerated, the criticisms of organized interest groups cannot be ignored. And they have not been. For years Americans have been trying to curb the excesses of "pressure groups." The attempt to control lobbying —the primary weapon of interest groups—is a revealing example of the difficulties involved in trying to regulate dynamic groups in a democracy.

Attempts to control lobbying began at least a century ago. In 1877 Georgia wrote into its constitution the simple provision that lobbying is a crime. Early in this century a number of states passed acts to regulate lobbyists, requiring that legislative counsel, or agents officially register as such and that they file statements of expenses paid or promised in connection with promoting legislation. Under the Federal Regulation of Lobbying Act of 1946, every person hired to influence or defeat bills in Congress must register and disclose the name and address of his employer, how much he is paid, and who pays him. Every three months he must file a further statement listing the names of publications that have carried his publicity and the bills he supports or opposes. Organizations whose main purpose is to influence legislation also must furnish information, which is printed regularly in the *Congressional Record*. It seems clear however, that the 1946 act has not diminished the extent of lobbying; its registration provisions, moreover, have been construed by the courts to apply only to direct pressure on Congress.

Actually, the aim of such legislation is to turn the spotlight of publicity on the expenditures and activities of lobbyists. The national lobby law has furnished a vast amount of detailed information about lobbyists—who they are, who sponsors and finances them, what bills they seek to pass or block. This information has given the public some idea of the amount of money involved; in the first four years the act was in effect, lobbyists collected about $60 million and spent approximately $30 million. About 500 persons and organizations had filed, but many hundreds of others had not, on one pretext or another.

Some hold that publicity is not enough, that what we need is actual regulation of lobbying. Most lobbyists, these critics argue, not only have no fear of publicity but, on the contrary, actually welcome it. There is much doubt, however, that Congress will try to restrict lobbyists. For one thing, such an attempt might drive the lobbyists underground, where their influence might be more insidious and just as effective, and regulation might run into serious constitutional objections based on the rights guaranteed by the First Amend-

[22]J. K. Galbraith, *American Capitalism* (Houghton Mifflin, 1952).

ment. But more important, most students of the problem feel that lobbyists serve an important and desirable function and that nothing more than publicity is needed.

These observers point out that lobbyists are a sort of "third house" of Congress. While Senate and House are set up on a geographical basis, lobbyists represent people directly in terms of their economic or other interests. Small but important groups, such as bankers, can get representation in this third house that they might not be able to get in the other two. In a nation of large and important interests, this kind of functional representation, if not abused, is highly useful as a supplement to geographical representation. The lobbyists pour vitally needed information and ideas into the legislative mill. Some European nations have gone so far as to set up legislative branches to provide functional representation; our informal third house is a welcome compromise between such extreme measures and no functional representation at all.

GROUP PLURALISM: THE NEW CRITIQUE

At the end of the 1960s the attack on the role of groups in the American pluralist democracy is taking on a new urgency and a new dimension. The problem is not so much that organized groups have too much power, though many observers are still concerned about the extent to which private groups are taking over public powers, especially in a war economy (see Chapter 18). According to the critics, the more urgent problem, in the wake of ghetto riots and burning cities, is that interest groups, big and small, perhaps have become so encrusted in the American society and economy and have such a stranglehold on the American polity that the net result is a vast conservatism, immobility, and resistance to major change in the American pluralist democracy.

The crucial question is that of quick, orderly change. The established group organizations have long been defended as little democracies in which the art of self-government could be taught (as counters to mass politics and anomic politics) and in which the little man could find some kind of psychological and political footing in "big democracy." Groups, in short, have been considered dynamic, liberalizing, transforming forces. But the critics contend that group politics, like so many other elements in pluralist democracy, have become blocks to social change rather than expediters. They have become little buttresses of the *status quo*.

Many studies have shown that large numbers of deprived Americans —Negroes, poor people, casual laborers, perhaps students—simply do not take part in the group battle on equal terms. They tend to join fewer organizations, their organizations tend to be weaker, their powers of political influence tend to be much more limited as compared to the representation that middle-class businessmen, workers, farmers, and professional people achieve at every level of government. Eventually, perhaps, the less affluent will build a network of organizations of their own—certainly Negroes have made a beginning—but in the meantime some are more likely to emphasize political techniques that bypass conventional group politics —direct action, separatism, and violence.

The Changing Parties

12

American politics is something like a deep river. The undercurrents of party attachment and voting behavior move along slowly in old and familiar channels. The subsurface currents — shifting attitudes toward candidates and issues — are somewhat more volatile and unpredictable. The 1960s have been a time of storm and commotion on the surface of American politics, but the actual effects of the dramatic elections of 1964 and 1968 will depend on the pace and direction of deep currents underneath the waters.

We can understand those deeper currents best by reviewing the long history of American parties, but first we must consider what a political party is. Much confusion arises because depicters of parties "see" different aspects. As used here a *party* comprises (1) an inner circle of office-holding and office-seeking cadres; (2) a network of party leaders — called bosses by their adversaries — who run the party machinery; (3) party activists at the grass roots who give money and time, as well as votes, to the party's candidates; (4) voters who identify with the party, almost always support its candidates, and break away from the party only as a result of major events.[1]

[1]For somewhat different definitions of party, see W. N. Chambers, "Party Development and the Mainstream," in W. N. Chambers and W. D. Burnham (eds.), *The American Party Systems* (Oxford Univ. Press, 1967), pp. 37-39; Allan P. Sindler, *Political Parties in the United States* (St Martin's Press, 1966), pp. 6-9.

The Grand Coalitions

The story of American parties is closely bound up with the economic, political, and social history of the whole nation. Looking at American parties as alliances of interest we can see three phases: first, lasting until the Civil War was the Age of the Democrats; second, stretching through the first decade of this century, was the Age of the Republicans; and third, beginning in 1930, is a period that might be called a New Age of the Democrats.

The American brand of rough-and-tumble politics did not begin in Revolutionary days. But the effect of the Revolution and the post-Revolutionary struggles was to crystallize political interests and allegiances into a more coherent and lasting form. The great service of George Washington was to give the fledgling government a sense of unity by his ability to rise above faction and party. He had hardly taken the oath of office, however, before there were signs of an emerging party split. On one side was Alexander Hamilton, who was not only Washington's Secretary of the Treasury but the leader of the Federalists. As a supporter of the Constitution, strong central government, and sound financial policies, Hamilton was spokesman for the bankers, traders, and manufacturers of the day. On the other side was Thomas Jefferson and a collection of small farmers, frontiersmen, laborers, debtors, small proprietors, slaveowners—in general, an agrarian group. Jefferson, the first national party leader, resigned as Secretary of State in Washington's second administration to devote full time to the job of welding together a party following.

The first Republican party, however, was built less by Jefferson than by Republican senators and representatives in Congress under the leadership of Jefferson's ally, James Madison. At this time the party was essentially a leadership system, lacking strong grass-roots organization. During the administration of John Adams—who was easily caricatured as a "monarchist"—Jefferson and Madison built a national party with extensive popular backing.

RISE OF THE DEMOCRATS

By the turn of the eighteenth century, Jefferson's combination had overcome the Federalists. As President, Jefferson continued to serve as party chief, using the party to put his program through Congress. The Federalists had feared that Jefferson would be a radical, demagogic leader, but as required of a multi-interest leader under a two-party system, in office he was conciliatory and moderate.[2]

Here was the first of the grand coalitions. It started out as the Democratic-Republican party, soon dropped "Democratic," later split into Republican

---

[2]William N. Chambers, *Political Parties in a New Nation* (Oxford Univ. Press, 1963), p. 177. On the final effort of the Federalists to cope with Jeffersonian supremacy, see David H. Fischer, *The Revolution of American Conservatism* (Harper & Row, 1965).

and Democratic elements, and ended up as the Democratic party. During the sixty-year period ending with Lincoln's election, the party changed in many ways. Millions of new voters were casting ballots. Americans were moving westward, and the party had to move with them. Republican leaders in office seemed to drift away from the leveling sentiments of Jefferson. The rising democratic elements, led by Andrew Jackson, gave the party a southern and westward cast. Nevertheless, the party retained two of its main features: first, it won elections, and second, it continued to play coalition politics.

How does a major party lose power? In the case of the Democrats, the party itself was split by the conflict over slavery, and the opposition hammered out a superior combination of voting groups. The 1850s were a time of party upheaval. The Democrats, sharply split between Northerners and Southerners, broke into fragments. The Whigs' coalition, composed of large sections of the propertied class, big slaveowners and planters, nativists and antislavery people, had never been stable enough or large enough to turn the tide against the Democrats, but now the conservative elements of the Whig party, especially in the South, went over to the Democrats. Other Whigs looked around for a new party.

ERA OF THE REPUBLICANS

The new winning alliance—the Republican party—was founded in 1854 (not by Abraham Lincoln, who was still a Whig). Initially the party was radical in many respects, appealing to farmers, workers, and small businessmen. To the revolutionary air of the "Marseillaise" the Republicans sang:

> Arise, arise, ye brave,
> And let your war-cry be
> Free speech, free press, free soil, free men,
> Frémont and victory.

In 1856, the Republicans lost to a Democratic coalition still strong enough to win, but four years later Lincoln led the Republicans to victory on a platform that opposed further extension of slavery and favored internal improvements, including a homestead measure for farmers and liberal wages for workingmen and mechanics. Although Lincoln received only 40 percent of the popular vote in 1860, his common appeal to North and West won him the electoral votes of all the states outside the South.

After the war, the Republican party consolidated and broadened its coalition of interests. Its liberal homestead policies helped solidify the support of farmers, especially in the Midwest, and of immigrants eager for land. Its humanitarian appeal and its high-tariff stand continued to attract many eastern workers. Its aids to business won the support of financiers, industrialists, and merchants. And as the party of Lincoln, it gained a hold on the newly freed Negroes. Veterans of the Northern armies were also part of the coalition. In short, the Republicans were the "party of the Union," with a national appeal that seemed to transcend the lines of class, group, or section.

For five decades after 1860 this coalition was to give every presidential race to the Republicans, except for Cleveland's victories in 1884 and 1892. Not all was smooth sailing for the Grand Old Party, yet it remained a grand

Courtesy *Harper's Weekly* and Thomas Nast.

Gillam in *Judge*.

1874 — The Republican elephant appears; the party symbol is introduced by Thomas Nast in *Harper's Weekly*.

1900 — Bryan is bowled over like Don Quixote by McKinley's promise to keep the workman's dinner pail full.

Tom Little in *The Nashville Tennessean*.

© 1956 Herblock in *The Washington Post*.

1940 — Willkie's new ideas rejuvenates the GOP, but a dynamic challenger succumbs to FDR's old mastery.

1956 — Eisenhower scores another great personal triumph but cannot pull his party to victory.

Scott Long in *The Minneapolis Tribune*.

1964 — Moderates are left out in the cold when Goldwater receives the Republican nomination.

Conrad in *The Los Angeles Times*.

1968 — Nixon finally wins the Presidency but only with a small popular-vote majority; moreover, he must govern with a Democratic Congress.

coalition. The secret of its success lay in its leaders, who were able to assuage conflicting elements.

THE LOYAL OPPOSITION

Discredited — in the minds of many — by the Civil War, the Democratic party survived with its hard core in the South. And acting as the loyal opposition after the war, the Democrats capitalized on the mistakes and excesses of the party in power. Along with winning the Presidency twice, and nearly winning it several times, the party occasionally took control of Congress and frequently captured state governments. Its platforms championed the principles of low tariffs, states' rights, civil service, currency reform. But the Democrats were not able to consolidate national power. Part of the trouble was their failure to win over dissident groups that spent their energies in third-party movements, but the main difficulty was that the Republicans, riding the wave of a long-term economic boom, were in accord with the main temper of the times.

For all their noisy battles during the century, both parties had remained true to the rule that under a two-party system neither side can afford to be extremist. Both parties embraced liberal and conservative elements, and both reached out for the support of members of the major interest groups, especially of the dominant business groups. Indeed, one of the main complaints of the third parties of the day was that the major parties were in a conspiracy of agreement over policy, disagreeing only over how to split up the spoils of office.[3] Both parties, however, were sensitive to shifting public sentiment. Thus from 1896 to 1912, a period of unrest and protest, the progressive wings of both parties were dominant much of the time.

In 1912 the Republican coalition split as cleanly as the Democratic coalition had in 1860. The conservative wing under President Taft kept a tight grip on the party machinery, but the progressives deserted the GOP and nominated Theodore Roosevelt on the ticket of a new Progressive party. The Democratic party, led by Woodrow Wilson, won fewer popular votes than the Republicans and Progressives combined, but it swept the electoral college. As President, Wilson used Jeffersonian precedents in putting through Congress a series of

[3] See Matthew Josephson, *The Politicos* (Harcourt, Brace & World, 1938).

notable measures including a new income tax law, a revised banking system, fair-trade and antimonopoly legislation, and lower tariffs. Wilson aimed his New Freedom program at the "common man"—laborers, farmers, small businessmen—and at the Solid South.

Wilson's coalition was not broad or firm enough, however, to stay in power for long. The Democrats barely won the Presidency in 1916 over a reunited Republican party, with Roosevelt back in the GOP fold. And the 1920s, in the wake of World War I, were years of supremacy for the Republicans as the party of prosperity. To be sure, the Republicans during this period had no specialist in group diplomacy, yet Harding, Coolidge, and Hoover triumphed easily over their Democratic opponents, perhaps because the business philosophy of the Republicans was in direct accord with the business mood of the era. The Democrats were an uneasy alliance of urban, Catholic, and "wet" groups as opposed to rural, Protestant, and "dry" elements.[4] No matter whether they presented a liberal or a conservative candidate, they could not break the GOP's hold on masses of farmers, businessmen, and even workers.

The Great Depression changed all this. The bleak years of job-hunting and breadlines created a new political temper and new political alignments. People in all classes and groups turned away from the GOP. The Democrats, under Franklin D. Roosevelt, offered a new deal to the "forgotten man," and plenty of voters felt themselves forgotten. Roosevelt not only strengthened the farmer-labor-Southern alliance that Wilson had led; he put together a grand coalition of these groups plus Negroes, unemployed, middle-class people, national and racial minorities—a coalition that in 1936 gave the Democrats the electoral votes of every state except two. Roosevelt was chief legislator as well as Chief Executive. Under his generalship Congress enacted a series of laws to provide a New Deal for American laborers, farmers, small businessmen, old people, and other groups. This grand coalition was strong enough to reelect Roosevelt three times. That it was not simply F. D. R.'s personal following was indicated when Harry Truman, who lacked some of Roosevelt's political skills, led the Democrats to an unexpected triumph in 1948.

A NEW AGE OF THE DEMOCRATS?

The election of 1952 was a sweeping victory for the Republican candidate, Dwight D. Eisenhower, and the Republicans also won control of the House and Senate. Was this the start of a new era of Republican supremacy? Some observers were doubtful. It was an *Eisenhower* victory, they said, resulting from his wartime record and his great popularity.

The 1956 election was a test of both President Eisenhower's personal popularity and the strength of the Republican party. On the first test the results were crystal clear. Running against Adlai E. Stevenson—the same man he had defeated in 1952—Eisenhower boosted both his electoral and popular-vote margins. But despite Eisenhower's victories, the Republicans

[4]David Burner, *The Politics of Provincialism: The Democratic Party in Transition, 1918-1932* (Knopf, 1968).

did not fare so well as a party. They lost control of both houses of Congress in the 1954 midterm elections and failed to regain congressional majorities in 1956 even though Eisenhower won. In 1958 the Republicans suffered a debacle reminiscent of New Deal days. The Democrats won thirteen more Senate seats, forty-seven more House seats, and five more governorships. The Grand Old Party was heartened, however, by winning the governorship of New York behind the energetic campaigning of a new figure on the political scene, Nelson Rockefeller.

Thanks to the Twenty-second Amendment, Democrats never had to fear that President Eisenhower, still very popular in the latter part of his Administration, might run for a third term. Vice President Richard M. Nixon had gained such a head start among the party faithful that he easily won the Republican party nomination. On the Democratic side, a young senator from Massachusetts, John F. Kennedy, had been campaigning for the nomination ever since the Democratic presidential defeat in 1956. And, after winning on the first ballot at the Democratic convention, Kennedy awarded the vice-presidential nomination to his chief convention opponent, Senate Majority Leader Lyndon Johnson of Texas.

The contest between Kennedy and Nixon was one of the most dramatic in American history. And the vote-counting, too, was dramatic, for the outcome was the closest in modern American history: Kennedy won 303 electoral votes (from 23 states) and 34,221,463 popular votes; Nixon won 219 electoral votes (from 26 states) and 34,108, 582 popular votes. Fifteen "independent" electors from the South voted for Senator Harry F. Byrd of Virginia. Kennedy's popular majority was only one-tenth of 1 percent.

Kennedy's election, along with the election of a strongly Democratic Congress, posed an urgent question for the Republicans. Were they doomed to be a minority indefinitely? A fundamental difference over political strategy now divided the Republican camp. Conservative members of the party, headed by Senator Barry Goldwater of Arizona, contended that the only way for the GOP to win was to stop offering the voters a watered down version of the Fair Deal and New Frontier, to stop truckling to the Eastern Establishment, to make a stronger appeal to the conservative West and South, and to take a more independent line on foreign policy than was possible under the bipartisan foreign policy approach. Liberal Republicans disagreed. They warned that the party would lose votes if it moved to the right, that a conservative appeal would antagonize Negros, immigrant, and working groups in the big cities, that the South and West did not have enough votes to carry the electoral college, that the Republicans should adhere to their progressive tradition of Lincoln and Theodore Roosevelt, and that foreign affairs in the 1960s were too critical to permit playing party politics.

By 1964 a battle royal was under way between Goldwater and the moderates. Moving early, Goldwater piled up delegate strength in state party conventions and committees and was nominated on the first ballot at the Republican convention. When the Democrats unanimously nominated President Johnson—who in his eight months in office had moved squarely into the Roosevelt-Truman-Kennedy tradition—the stage was set for a clear test of the conservative strategy. But the election outcome seemed to be a decisive repudiation of it. Not only did Johnson receive the greatest total vote, the greatest margin over an opponent, and the highest percentage of the total vote in history, but he helped pull into office the most Democratic and the most liberal Congress since 1936. Goldwater achieved a sensational breakthrough in the Deep South, but he lost all other states except his own state of Arizona.

The election had been a fascinating test of whether or not highly organized and zealous conservatives could arouse the "lost vote" that the Goldwaterites contended had not shown up in the battles between moderate Democrats and Republicans. Goldwater had in effect challenged one of the oldest rules of American politics—that to be successful a presidential candidate must be a group diplomat heading a moderate, widely based party embracing many group interests—and he had failed. The results showed that the rightists simply could not mobilize very much support in the middle of the political spectrum.[5]

In 1968 Republican presidential nominee Richard Nixon returned to the conventional strategy. He took moderate positions on domestic and foreign issues, chose as his running mate a border-state governor who also occupied a position in the center of the party spectrum, won the support both of liberal Republicans such as Nelson Rockefeller and conservative Republicans such as Barry Goldwater, and gained a narrow victory. Despite predictions that the traditional Democratic Party coalition of workers, farmers, Negroes, and ethnic groups was collapsing, Democratic presidential nominee Hubert Humphrey rallied the old battalions and came close to winning in the home stretch of the campaign. By the end of the 1960s, the political stage was set for a battle royal between a Democratic Party that was divided but still strong in grass-roots party registration and support and a Republican Party that had not achieved a durable national coalition but was led by a politically experienced President who would be able to exploit the political advantages of the White House.

Party Patterns and Functions

A striking fact emerges from a survey of party history. Our two major parties are old—both are well past their centennials. They seem to be among the more permanent and unchanging features of American politics. Only once in the past century has there been a major threat to the two-party system, and that exception—Theodore Roosevelt's desertion of the Republicans in 1912—was short-lived. George Wallace's third party in 1968 scored little electoral success—though it might be revived for an effort in 1972.

[5]On the difference in the campaign between mass opinion and the opinion of letter writers (who tended to be more ideological) in relation to the Goldwater strategy, see Philip E. Converse, Aage R. Clausen, and Warren E. Miller, "Electoral Myth and Reality: The 1964 Election," *The American Political Science Review* (June 1965), pp. 321–336. See also Chap. 11 of this book.

Why do we have a two-party system? Probably the explanation lies largely in the nature of our electoral system. Most of our election districts have a single incumbent, and the candidate with the most votes wins. Because only one candidate can win, the largest and second-largest parties monopolize the victories, and the third party, being deprived of the rewards of office, eventually gives up the fight. The system of electing the President operates in this same fashion but on a national scale. In order to win the Presidency, a party must win a majority of the electoral votes, which requires a national organization and party support in more than one region. The two major parties monopolize the Presidency; deprived of patronage and power, third parties tend to wither away. The ability of some third parties to last for two or three decades has been due largely to their hold on congressional and state offices in certain sections of the country.

PARTY PATTERNS OVER TIME

It is clear from party history that both major parties have been broad alliances of many different interests. Through parties, groups pool their interests to reach at least some of their goals. Successful party leaders must be group diplomats; they must know how to mediate among more or less hostile groups so that agreement can be reached on general principles. Hence they help build national unity, which is not simply a mystical thing, but the capacity to rise above differences (at least for a while) and pull together. Parties want to win elections. In order to win, each of them emphasizes the beliefs that unite men and plays down the issues that divide them.

A second party pattern has been moderation of party program and policy. Assuming that voters (or at least political leaders) are distributed across an ideological spectrum from left to right, each party can take its extremist supporters more or less for granted and woo the voters in the middle of the spectrum.[6] Under a multiparty system each party may range from extreme conservatism to extreme radicalism, and major parties look for support from the big groups in or close to the ideological or political mainstream. Much of the excitement of the presidential elections of 1964 and 1968 turned on calculations about the ideological spectrum.

The American pattern, as noted, has been the absence of major third, fourth, or fifth parties. This is not to minimize the role of these parties. They have drawn attention to controversial issues that the major parties either ignored or straddled. They have provided an electoral base for some able leaders such as Eugene Debs, Robert La Follette, Norman Thomas, Henry Wallace, and George Wallace. They have organized special-interest groups, such as antislavery people, prohibitionists, vegetarians, left-wing trade unionists. In some areas they may be important, as in New York City, where the Liberal Party sometimes holds the balance of power in elections. Still, it is easy to exaggerate the role of third parties, partly because some of them have had turbulent roles and charismatic leaders. The system basically operates against them.

[6]See generally Anthony Downs, *An Economic Theory of Democracy* (Harper, 1957).

Thus, the crucial functions of parties or of the two-party system are to unify the electorate and conciliate groups, sections, and ideologies by serving as "aggregators of national interest."[7] Other functions are also important:

1 To gain votes, parties simplify the alternatives. Usually they present the voters with two relatively different sets of alternatives to major problems. And almost always the two major parties limit the choice of candidates as well as issues. Hence voters can choose between a few alternatives instead of a bewildering variety of men and platforms.

2 Parties help to stimulate interest in public affairs. An election contest is exciting. Parties use all the media in order to saturate the voters with their arguments. And after a polite interval following the election, the opposition party maintains a drumfire of faultfinding against the party in power. Thousands, perhaps millions, have been mobilized to participate in public affairs through the machinery of parties.

3 Partisan activity has also been an important source of public welfare, especially in the past. Local party organizations, in their desire to win votes, gave the needy jobs, loans, free coal, picnics, and recreational facilities and helped those in trouble with such matters as pensions, unemployment benefits, taxes, and licenses. William S. Vare, leader of the Republican machine in Philadephia, used to brag that his organization was "one of the greatest welfare organizations in the United States. . . . without red tape, without class, religion, or color distinction." The creation of the welfare state has robbed parties of most of their charitable activities, but the chance to be a bridge between an impersonal government official and the ordinary voter allows big-city organizations to retain support from the poor.

4 Our parties have also served as important channels of upward mobility for integrating those on the outside into American public life. Decades ago it was the Irish-Americans who found a way to achieve status in partisan activity. Today, especially in the larger cities, parties are providing a channel of upward mobility for Negroes, although types of political action other than party activity—militant civil rights action, for example—have increasingly been attracting their attention, especially the attention of young Negroes.

5 The need of the elected official to win the most votes if he is to secure and retain power is the link between the mass public and the governing elites, and this link is essential to ensure that the decisions made by public officials do in some measure reflect the desires of the electorate. Politics has been defined as the authoritative allocation of values or as the determination of who gets what, where, when, and how. Our two-party system is one of the most important agencies in democratizing our allocation of values.

[7]Charles G. Mayo and Beryl L. Crowe (eds.), *American Political Parties: A Systemic Perspective* (Harper & Row, 1967), p. 487. See in this volume Leo D. Cagen, "Manifest Functions, Latent Functions, and the Democratic Policy" for an examination of some of the theoretical aspects of party function.

6   Parties put labels on candidates, making it easier for the voters to "reward their friends and punish their enemies." Thus parties make the "ins" and "outs" more visible and—hopefully—more accountable.

CHOOSING CANDIDATES

Certainly the function that takes most of a party's energy and interests is the recruiting and selecting of candidates for office. From the very beginning, parties have been the mechanism by which candidates for public office were selected. The earliest method was the *caucus*, a closed meeting of party leaders. It was the method used in Massachusetts only a few years after the *Mayflower* landed, and it played an important part in pre-Revolutionary politics. After the Union was established, party groups in the national or state legislatures served for several decades as the caucus. The legislators in each party simply met separately to nominate candidates. Our first presidential candidates were chosen by senators and representatives meeting as party delegates.

However, the caucus soon fell into ill repute. Its meetings smacked of secret deals and logrolling; moreover, it could not be fairly representative of the people where a party was in a minority, because only officeholders were members. Although there were efforts to make the caucus more representative, gradually a system of *party conventions* took its place. The conventions were made up of delegates, usually chosen directly by party members in towns and cities, and served several purposes. They chose the party standard-bearers. They debated and adopted a platform. And they provided a chance to whip up party spirit and perhaps to paint the town red. But the convention method in turn came in for grave criticism. It was charged—often quite rightly—that the convention was subject to control by the party bosses and their machines. At times, delegates were freely bought and sold, instructions from rank-and-file party members were ignored, meetings got completely out of control.

To democratize party selections the *direct primary* was adopted by state after state in the early years of this century. This system gives every member of the party the right to vote on party candidates in a primary election. The state usually supplies the ballots and supervises the primary election, which takes place some time before the general election in November. The direct primary was hailed by many Americans as a major cure for party corruption, but it did not cure all the existing evils, and it led to new ones.

Today the primary is the main method of picking party candidates, but the nominating convention is available in one form or another in a few of the states. The convention has also been retained nationally, of course, for picking presidential candidates. In either case, the party carries the main burden of activity, although many of its electoral activities are closely regulated by law. In the general election, too, the party has a central role. It campaigns for its candidates, mobilizes its machinery in their behalf, helps finance them, and, on election day, produces cars, advice for the voters, and workers at the polls to watch the counting of the ballots.

Party Machinery and How It Runs

On paper our parties appear to be organized like armies. They have the form of a pyramid, with millions of party members and thousands of local party officials at the base and a few national party heads at the top. They also have a hierarchy of leaders and followers, running from the national committee at the top down to town and precinct committees at the bottom. But actually, the analogy is false because the essence of an army is discipline from the top down. And discipline is precisely what our parties lack. They have been well described as "loose associations of state and local organizations, with very little national machinery and very little national cohesion."[8]

There are many reasons why our parties are decentralized and undisciplined. Perhaps the most important is the federal basis of our government. We suggested earlier that the Constitution has shaped our political system, just as the party system has affected the structure of government. Parties are an excellent example of this circular relationship. They tend to organize around elections and officeholders, and because our federal system sets up elections and offices on a national-state-local basis, our parties are organized on a similar basis. Just as state and local governments are largely independent of the national government, so the state and local parties are somewhat independent of the national party organizations. Thus, the Constitution has given us federalism in our parties as well as in our government. The nature of our party organization in turn has had a vital impact on the workings of our government, as we shall see in Part Five.

NATIONAL PARTY ORGANIZATION

The supreme authority in both major political parties is the national convention. The convention meets every four years and has four major duties: to nominate the party's candidates for President and Vice President; to write the party's national platform; to adopt the rules of the party; and to go through the formality of electing the national committee. (In Chapter 13 we shall look more closely at the convention.) But the convention is in session only briefly; most of the time party business is handled by party executives.

The Democratic and Republican National Committees are each composed of over one hundred members—one man and one woman from every state and members representing the Virgin Islands and Puerto Rico. In addition, the Republicans make each Republican state chairman a member of their National Committee if his state has cast its electoral vote for the Republican presidential candidate in the preceding election, or if a majority of his state's congressional delegation (House and Senate counted together) are Republican, or if his state has a Republican governor. In form, the committeemen of both parties are elected every four years by their respective national party

[8]"Toward a More Responsible Two-Party System," *The American Political Science Review Supplement* (September 1950), p. v.

conventions. Actually, they are chosen by state party conventions or by party committees or by party primaries.

The national committeemen are often influential in their states, but the committee itself is not very important. In fact, it rarely meets. (One of its main jobs is to choose the city where the national convention will meet, a choice usually dictated by the nature of the convention hall and facilities and by the amount of cash offered by cities for the privilege of acting as host to the convention.) The party organization is usually run by the chairman of the committee and by appointed, full-time officials.

The main job of the chairman is to manage the presidential campaign. Although in form he is elected by the national committee, actually he is chosen by the party's presidential candidate at the close of the quadrennial convention. It is through him that the presidential candidate—and perhaps later the President—runs the party nationally. By the same token, a defeated presidential candidate may have little control over the national chairman, or the national committeemen may elect a new head who responds to the balance of forces within the committee. Usually the national chairman is the chief dispenser of patronage for the President, though he does not have a great many jobs to give out. He serves at the pleasure of the President. His basic tasks have been well summarized as image maker, fund raiser, campaign manager, administrator, and hell raiser.[9]

[9]Cornelius P. Cotter and Bernard C. Hennessy, *Politics Without Power: The National Party Committees* (Atherton Press, 1964), p. 67.

FORMAL AND ACTUAL PARTY ORGANIZATION

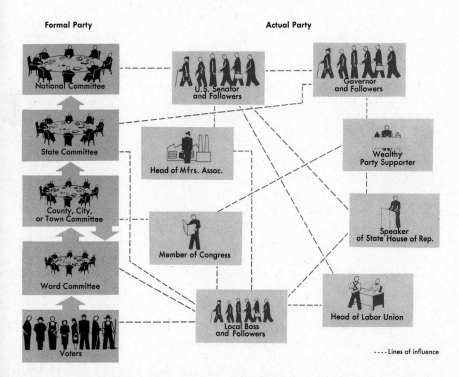

Formal Party

National Committee

State Committee

County, City, or Town Committee

Ward Committee

Voters

Actual Party

U.S. Senator and Followers

Governor and Followers

Head of Mfrs. Assoc.

Wealthy Party Supporter

Member of Congress

Speaker of State House of Rep.

Local Boss and Followers

Head of Labor Union

---- Lines of influence

It is the national chairman, backed by the President, who gives the party a measure of unity and direction when the party is in power. When the party loses a presidential race, it often has no real central leadership. The defeated nominee is called the titular leader but he usually has little power over the organization, partly because he has no jobs to hand out. As a result, the party out of power nationally may come under the control of congressional leaders.

The Congressional and Senatorial Campaign Committees aid congressmen in their campaigns for reelection. Today, both the Republican and Democratic Senatorial Campaign Committees are composed of senators chosen for two-year terms by their respective party members in the Senate. The men selected are usually from states in which there will be no senatorial election during the two years they will be committeemen. In the House of Representatives, the Congressional Campaign Committees, also composed of members chosen by each party group, are organized in somewhat similar fashion.

After candidates have been nominated, the committees send them money, provide speakers, supply campaign material, and the like. Normally they concentrate their efforts in doubtful districts and states where an expenditure of money and time can do the most good. During presidential election years, the activities of the national committee tend to overshadow the work of the Congressional and Senatorial Campaign committees. But during off-year elections, these committees often provide the only campaign that is nationally directed.

Both a cause and a result of party disorganization is the manner in which candidates are nominated. Ordinarily, politicians seeking the party nomination run on their own, while the party remains, outwardly at least, neutral toward the aspirants. Lacking organized party support, each candidate builds a personal organization; thus, because scores of candidates are usually running for a dozen or more offices, from governor to small local jobs, the party becomes a confused arena. Candidates campaign on their own, raising their own money and putting out their own publicity. In the hurly-burly of the primary campaigns there often develop sharp rivalries between Democrats or between Republicans—rivalries that may carry over into the general election, even though the party should be unified in order to put up a strong fight. Such individualistic politics is not always the case; indeed, contests within the primaries are not always the rule.[10] In cities dominated by one party, the minority party finds it difficult sometimes to persuade a politician even to run against the slates of candidates put up by the "organization."

STATE AND LOCAL PARTY ORGANIZATION

At the next lower level in the party hierarchy are the state committees, which in general resemble the national committees but are manned by committeemen chosen locally in counties or other areas. Most state commit-

[10]Austin Ranney, "Candidate Selection and Party Cohesion in Britain and the United States," paper prepared for delivery at the 1965 Annual Meeting of the American Political Science Association, September 8–11, p. 5. See also Frank J. Sorauf, *Political Parties in the American System* (Little, Brown, 1964), pp. 98–104, and *Party and Representation* (Atherton Press, 1963), Chaps. 3–5.

tees are not powerful; they are often dominated by the governor, a United States senator, or a coalition of strong local leaders, just as the President dominates his party's national committee. The state chairman is sometimes the choice of the governor or senator; occasionally, however, he is really the party's boss on the state level and is able to pick—and control—governors, senators, and other key officials. Many state parties are as undisciplined and decentralized as the national party.

Below the fifty state committees, each party hierarchy broadens out into countless district and county committees. These, too, vary tremendously in their functions and power. County chairmen are often powerful bosses such as Mayor Daley in Cook County, and many county chairmen make up the party slates for a host of offices such as county commissioner, sheriff, treasurer. Some county chairmen, however, are mere figureheads.

It is at the base of the party pyramid—at the city, town, ward, and precinct level—that we find the grass roots of the party in all its richness and profusion and variety. In some localities, party politics is a round-the-clock, round-the-year occupation. The party's sergeants and corporals—the local ward and precinct leaders—do countless favors for their constituents, from fixing parking tickets to organizing clambakes. But such strong local party organization is exceptional. Most local party committees are small, poorly financed, and inactive except during the few hectic weeks before election day. Party activities are not professional but amateurish.[11] The party committeemen are less interested in policy and program than in gaining recognition and favors from candidates and officeholders.

Our party systems are highly complex. For example, a state party organization may embrace a state committee, congressional district committees, county committees, state senatorial district committees, state judicial district committees, and precinct committees. Why such complexity? As we have seen in earlier chapters, party politics tends to be highly individualistic and personalized. It would be more nearly correct to say that we have candidate or officeholder politics rather than party politics. That is to say, political activity tends to focus on men seeking or holding political power and on the groups around them rather than on a unified, hierarchical party system. Because our constitutional arrangements provide for a multiplicity of officeholders at a number of levels of government, our parties are bound to be complicated. The diversity of our country and the absence of strong direction and control by the national party headquarters mean that party systems also vary a good deal from state to state.

This situation inevitably opens a gulf between national party headquarters and state and local parties. Deepening this gulf is the fact that most election laws are enacted and enforced by the states, not by the national government. "Political parties, as legal entities," says one authority, "are by and large state parties. . . . The national superstructure over the state party organizations, in a sense, derives its power from their consent."[12] Moreover,

---

[11]The actual effectiveness of local party work has not been systematically tested. See Phillips Cutright, "Measuring the Impact of Local Party Activity on the General Election Vote," *Public Opinion Quarterly* (Fall 1963), pp. 372–386; and Raymond E. Wolfinger, "The Influence of Precinct Work on Voting Behavior," *Ibid.*, pp. 387–398, for suggestive studies.

[12]V. O. Key, Jr., *Politics, Parties, and Pressure Groups*, 3d ed. (Crowell, 1952), p. 306.

some states hold their state and local elections in different years from national elections (partly in an effort to insulate state politics from national). New York State, for example, elects its governors for four-year terms in even-numbered years between presidential elections, and New York City elects its mayors in odd-numbered years.

The gulfs between national and state parties vary from state to state and from year to year. One factor tending to link national and local parties is mutual self-interest; each has a stake in the other's victory. Perhaps more important, most states—especially the more urban ones—are affected by political trends affecting the nation as a whole, as we saw in Chapter 10.

A DECLINE IN ONE-PARTY STATES?

In the past, most of our states have been dominated by one party, so that real party competition did not exist within the states. In the past fifty years, however, competitive two-party systems have developed within most states. Oregon and Vermont, for example, are no longer guaranteed for the Republicans, nor are Southern states assured for the Democrats, as the 1962, 1964, and 1968 elections reemphasized.

Party trends in the South are especially interesting. As a result of industrialization, urbanization, migration of Northern whites into the South and of Negroes out of it, increased Negro voting, and other economic, social, and political developments, a more competitive two-party system is slowly rising in the South.[13] One Southern student distinguishes between the "inner South," comprising the "black belt" from Georgia to Mississippi, and the "outer South," composed of the encircling states.[14] The latter, with fewer Negroes and more large cities, is fast moving toward a two-party alignment like that in the rest of the nation. This trend was reflected in the 1968 presidential election, when the outer South gave most of its electoral votes to Richard Nixon.

American Parties and Pluralist Democracy

American political parties are vital to American democracy; they do the jobs that have to be done in any healthy system of representative government. They build a bridge between people and their government. They shore up national unity by bringing conflicting interests into harmony. They soften the impact of the extremists on both sides. They stimulate and channel public discussion. They find candidates for the voters and voters for the candidates. They help run elections. Parties shoulder much of the hard, day-to-day work of democracy. Yet today our party system is under attack.

[13]Alexander Heard, *A Two Party South?* (Univ. of North Carolina Press, 1952).
[14]See Alan P. Sindler, "The Unsolid South: A Challenge to the Democratic Party," in Alan Westin (ed.), *The Uses of Power* (Harcourt, Brace & World, 1962); and Philip E. Converse, "On the Possibility of Major Political Realignment in the South," in Angus Campbell, Philip E. Converse, Warren E. Miller, and Donald E. Stokes (eds.), *Elections and the Political Order* (Wiley, 1966), pp. 212–242.

And one of the most common complaints is that the two parties do not stand for anything.

THE TWO PARTIES: TWEEDLEDUM AND TWEEDLEDEE?

The charge goes something like this: We all know that party platforms are evasive and obscure. Every four years spokesmen of interest groups appear before a bored committee on resolutions, and then a national platform is hastily pieced together. The typical platform seems to be designed to pick every stray vote rather than to speak out in a forthright manner on the vital questions of the day. The voter has almost no alternatives. Platforms are so vague and candidates' statements so ambiguous, that voters have no basis on which to choose. According to an old saying, party platforms are like train platforms — something to get in on, not to stand on.

Critics of American pluralist democracy contend that the group basis of the major parties both causes and reflects basic failings in our system. The major economic and other interests are represented in both parties, preventing them from taking clear cut stands, from mobilizing the wider electorate, and from supporting strong government. Moreover, it is said, the very weakness of the parties allows well-organized interests either to take them over or to bypass them and put pressure directly on government. In short, it is charged that compared to British and German and French parties, which take definite, definable positions on matters of policy and ideology, American parties are fuzzy, formless things. How accurate is this characterization?

In an organizational sense, party membership does not mean a great deal. In contrast to most parties abroad, the Republican and Democratic parties are not composed of regular, dues-paying members. In most states one does not join the party in any formal sense, as he must when he becomes a member of a union or a college debating group. He simply enrolls as a Democrat or Republican or requests a ballot of either party (which automatically enrolls him) at the party primaries. And if he finds the party not to his liking, he can easily drop out and become an independent or "join" the other party. Some people over the years change their party registration back and forth like a woman changing hats.

But psychologically the story is quite different. For one thing, many people see their own party or the opposition party as standing for something. "People tend to have a broad image of parties," Key reported. "They see a party as generally dedicated to the interests of a particular set of groups within society, or as committed to a broad range of policy objectives."[15] To be sure, their ideas of party philosophy and orientation may be rather crude, but they seem to make sense. For example, most business and professional people see the Republican party as the party that best serves their interests, whereas skilled and unskilled workers look on the Democrats as the party best serving them. When polled, workers offer such comments as: "The Democratic party is for the working people"; "Poor people have a better chance with the Democrats"; "The Democrats give more help to the laboring class"; "Yes, they don't be no depressions, when them Democrats is in.

[15]V. O. Key, Jr., *Public Opinion and American Democracy* (Knopf, 1961), p. 433.

They just lets that money roll on and that's what I likes." As for the Republicans, workers are quoted as saying: "The Republicans always stand for big business"; "They are all for the big man; people with money"; "It is a big business party"; "They are all right for the big shots in Wall Street."

In the second place, many people believe that there are important differences between the two parties. As we said on page 240, party identification remains stable over the years. Most people do not shift from one party to another from election to election. Furthermore, the Survey Research Center has found that about 40 percent of their national sample respond affirmatively to the question: "Do you think there are any important differences between what the Democratic and Republican parties stand for?" Another 10 percent indicates that there are differences but none of great moment. People who are strong Democrats or Republicans are likely to look at events through the eyes of their party. This phenomenon is called perceptual distortion, and the more partisan a person is, the more he may select and distort his party's positions.[16]

Critics of pluralist democracy argue that the fact that voters see differences between the major parties does not answer their charge at all. Real party differences do not exist but people are misled into thinking they do exist. Defenders of the system reply that given the nature of the American electorate, sharp differences are not likely. It is simply not possible to have two ideologically pure parties, because there is no clear-cut, bipolar cleavage in America. Moreover, it is said, the critics fail to see the true function of party in the American system. Elections are not occasions to pick complex programs; they are times to pick—and to punish—leaders and to influence the general direction of politics. The voter is a consumer making choices, and the brand name helps him.

THE ROLE OF PARTY LEADERSHIP

We have been discussing the party membership as a whole, but as we noted in our definition of party on page 273, the party is made up not just of a mass of followers but of a variety of people ranging from round-the-clock activists to mere party members. The leadership of a party, like that of any group, almost always comprises the full-time officials, a core of activists, and a larger number of fairly active members. The most important party leaders are usually the President, senators, governors, the elected state and local party chairmen, and other party officials.

Just as the Republican rank and file differs from Democratic members in socioeconomic background, so do the party leaders. A study of the occupational backgrounds of candidates for nomination for county office in three Indiana counties, for example, showed that a quarter of the Republican candidates had professional backgrounds and half had managerial, while only 12 percent had been manual workers; of the Democrats, on the other hand, over 40 percent had been manual workers, and only one-fourth managerial.[17]

[16]Angus Campbell, et al., *The American Voter* (Wiley, 1960), p. 133. See also Key, *Public Opinion and American Democracy, op. cit.*, p. 453.

[17]Frank Munger, "Two-Party Politics in the State of Indiana," unpublished master's thesis, (Harvard Univ. Press, 1955), p. 275, cited in S. M. Lipset, *Political Man* (Doubleday, 1959), p. 289.

Such contrasts, although suggestive, are not striking; it may be much more significant that most leaders in both parties come from middle-class, white-collar backgrounds.

What is the relation of party leaders and party followers? In the social scientist's language, mutually interactive or dependent. The very passivity of many followers give the leader a wide area within which to determine party policy. For example, a newly nominated presidential candidate not only may pick a new national chairman if he wishes; he can interpret the party platform almost as he wishes. But the party leader, like all group leaders, cannot go too far. He cannot antagonize big sections of his own following. And he may only manage to get his opinions superficially accepted without really changing deepseated attitudes of the rank and file.

What about leadership in the minority or opposition party? This party has very special duties: to probe, to criticize, to present alternative approaches, and to act on those alternatives if elected. But our opposition parties are not well organized to perform these functions. At the national level it has no authorized leader—except after it has named a presidential nominee. Its leadership is usually dispersed among congressional leaders, governors, former Presidents, future hopefuls. When the Democrats control one branch of the government and the Republicans another, the job of opposing is almost impossible, for each party can blame the other if things go badly. During Eisenhower's administration the Democrats established an advisory council composed of eminent Democrats such as Truman and Stevenson, and this council did a good job of proposing alternative policies to those of the Republican administration. But Democratic congressional leaders ignored the council, and it was dropped when President Kennedy took office. An all-Republican conference was established in 1962 and 1964, but Republican congressional leaders viewed it with suspicion. Following their party's presidential defeat in 1968, some Democrats pressed for the reestablishment of some kind of national forum for the loyal opposition.

A FOUR-PARTY SYSTEM?

It can be argued that, despite outward appearances, the American national party system is essentially a four-party system rather than a two-party one. According to this view, it is absurd to suppose that conservative Southern Democrats and liberal Northern Democrats make up one party, their common party label notwithstanding. Nor are conservative Middle Western and border-state Republicans members of the same party as Eastern internationalists and urbanites such as Nelson Rockefeller. Actually, it is contended, there are four parties, each with its distinctive institutional, doctrinal, sectional, and electoral makeup.

Congressional Republicans. This party is led by the committee and elected Republican leaders in the House and Senate. It is strongest in Northern rural areas, especially in the Midwest. It opposes big economic-aid programs, lower tariffs, wider presidential power in foreign affairs. Its most noted recent leaders have been Robert A. Taft, Gerald Ford, and the ranking Republican members of the major fiscal committees in the Congress, such as the Senate Finance Committee and the House Ways and Means Committee. Led by Goldwater, this party overcame the presidential Republicans in the 1964 convention and captured the presidential nomination

Presidential Republicans. This party is the party of Theodore Roosevelt at the start of the century and more recently of Wendell Willkie, Thomas Dewey, Eisenhower, and Rockefeller. It usually controls Republican national conventions, where congressional leaders have little chance of winning. Its great center of strength is the White House, just as the congressional party dominates the House and Senate. Its policies are moderately liberal and internationalist. The presidential party electorally comes into its fullest strength in presidential elections, just as the congressional parties have more weight in the more restricted voting of the off-year elections. Although Richard Nixon has been essentially a congressional Republican during most of his career, as President he is under strong pressure to lead the presidential Republicans.

Congressional Democrats. This party is as conservative as the congressional Republicans on economic matters, much more conservative on civil rights and segregation, but perhaps somewhat more internationalist on foreign economic policy. It has the same institutional strength in Congress as the congressional Republicans. Its leaders in recent years have been such men as Senator John L. McClelland, of Arkansas, Chairman of the Senate Committee on Government Operations, and Representative Wilbur Mills, also of Arkansas, Chairman of the House Ways and Means Committee. Its power in Congress rests on the mainly rural, one-party districts in the South, which enable members of Congress to accumulate seniority and hence rise to top committee positions.

Presidential Democrats. This is the party of Woodrow Wilson, Franklin D. Roosevelt, Truman, Stevenson, Johnson, Humphrey, Eugene McCarthy, and the three Kennedy brothers. It dominates the national party convention and the executive branch of the national government. In doctrine it is the most liberal and internationalist of the four parties.

Thus viewed, the two major parties are not simply divided into wings. Each of the four parties is rooted in electoral, institutional, and geographical forces—the presidential parties in the Northern, coastal, and urban areas, in presidential elections, national conventions, and the mechanics of the electoral college; the congressional parties in the off-year congressional elections, in the Southern and more inland, rural areas, and in the committee structure and parliamentary rules of Congress.[18]

To see American politics as a four-party sys-

From *The Herblock Book* (Beacon Press, 1952).

"I Have The Same Trouble!"

[18]J. M. Burns, *The Deadlock of Democracy: Four-Party Politics in America*, rev. ed., (Prentice-Hall, 1968).

tem is to see our national government not as party government, as in Britain, but as a continuously shifting coalition of four parties. The two congressional parties, for example, often coalesce in opposition to liberal social and economic policy and are denounced as an "unholy alliance of Republocrats." Perhaps the most striking example of bipartisanship is that between the two presidential parties on foreign policy: thus Johnson and Nixon broadly agreed on foreign policy; it was easy for Franklin Roosevelt to find two prominent internationalist Republicans, Stimson and Knox, to join his Cabinet during a time of international crisis in 1940; and Johnson and such Republicans as Henry Cabot Lodge collaborated closely on Vietnamese policy. This too is an alliance of Republocrats — but of a different type.

The four-party system was less conspicuous under Johnson than under his predecessors, for after the congressional Republican defeat in 1964 the President was able to unite the bulk of the two presidential parties and elements of the Congressional Democrats behind his consensus until distress over Johnson's foreign policy divided his party. Yet the basic four-party tendencies remained evident in congressional voting and in Democratic Congressional cooperation and conflict with President Nixon.

TWO BASIC PARTY WEAKNESSES

Many of the complaints against the American party system are either inaccurate or overdrawn. An example is the charge that democracy is flouted within the parties. Inside the party machinery a small group of leaders may control day-by-day events. But seen in perspective, it is apparent that these leaders must satisfy most of the voters most of the time if they wish to retain their power. Competition among parties rather than democracy within them is the safeguard.

When all is said and done, however, two major criticisms of our party system remain. One is that party machinery in virtually all the states is unwieldy and out-of-date. It is true that the informal party structure — for example, the party leadership of the President — in part makes up for the ramshackle nature of the formal organization. But powerful forces are constantly at work dividing and weakening party unity and effectiveness. The national committee, which should do the job of month-to-month governing of the party, is almost powerless. Financially, the national party usually exists from hand to mouth. It is often heavily in debt, especially in the years directly following a presidential campaign, and recovers mainly by raising funds from party "fat cats."

A situation underlying this party weakness is indeed curious: The party has no real rank-and-file membership. To be sure, individuals may join a party by voting in a primary or registering as party members. But they assume no obligations, they pay no dues, they rarely take part in party discussions of candidates or platforms. A person is usually far more active in his favorite lodge or hobby club than he is in the organization that assumes responsibility for governing the nation — the Democratic or Republican party.

The other major criticism is that of party irresponsibility — in the sense that persons elected to office on party platforms are completely free to ignore these platforms without any accounting to party leaders. Indeed, this criticism takes on all the more importance today because of the vital role that parties could play in the challenging era in which we live. Today more than ever before, governmental policies must be coordinated and coherent. One part of the government cannot pursue an inflationary policy, for example, while another is following an anti-inflationary program. Today policies must be *programmatic*—that is, they must fit into a comprehensive and consistent plan. The party—simply because it nominates and elects our chief policy-making officials—is the ideal agency to force these officials in every branch of government to pull together.

But the party does not do this job. It does not even perform the much more elementary task of making politicans live up to whatever hazy and inconsistent promises they make. This basic party weakness affects our whole government. We shall look again at the implications of this weakness (in Chapter 20) after considering how our politicians get into office and how they try to stay in office once they have won power in Washington.

Appeal to the Voters

13 The preceding four chapters have dealt with the main ingredients of American politics. We have looked at voting behavior—which people vote, how they vote, and why. We have noticed how opinions are born and shaped, the various subpublics that hold these opinions, the way opinions can be measured. We have seen something of the role of interest groups— their number and complexity, the way they cut across one another and form subgroups, their internal and external relations, their methods of gaining and wielding influence. We have considered parties as grand coalitions of interest groups, doing a variety of important jobs though not always doing them well, sometimes powerful in local activities but poorly coordinated as national agencies.

We have had to consider these factors one at a time, but they are not separate entities. Parties, groups, voting behavior, public opinion—all affect one another closely. The forming of political opinions, for example, and the way people vote are largely matters of group allegiance and activity, as we have seen. Parties are inseparable from groups, and their role and effectiveness are deeply affected by voting behavior. The close relation between public opinion and voting is obvious. We must see these political processes as a vast network of interrelationships, each process affecting others and in turn being affected by them, all part of a shifting balance of action and counteraction.

What Every Voter Should Know

Voting is a chore as well as a privilege. The manner in which elections are conducted differs widely from state to state. Their sheer number is amazing—well over a hundred thousand elections a year in all states for all offices, according to the Census Bureau. The Constitution authorizes the state legislatures to regulate the time, place, and manner of congressional elections, but Congress may alter these regulations and may also stipulate the day on which presidential electors shall be chosen and the day on which they should cast their votes. In effect, the regulation of elections for President and Congress has been left almost entirely up to the states. And, of course, each state has direct control over the election of its own and local officials.

REGISTRATION

Almost every state requires that a person must register if he wants to vote. A *registered voter* is one who has appeared before election officials during a set period and has established his right to vote. In most states an otherwise qualified voter must be over twenty-one, an American citizen, and have lived in the state for one year; in some states this residence requirement is shorter and in some states (mostly in the South) longer. The would-be voter also must have lived in the election district for a set period, often for six months. Once registered, his name appears on registration lists and it is checked off when he votes. Residence requirements are designed to give the voter a chance to inform himself about state and local conditions before voting. Some such requirements, however, have been used to deny the ballot to migratory workers or to minority groups, such as Negroes.

Registration can be *permanent* or *periodic*. Under the former system, now used by most states, the voter stays on the list as long as he remains in the election district and meets all other established requirements. In a few states a person is dropped from the list if he fails to vote in two successive elections; he must re-register in order to vote again. Permanent registration is easy on the voter but hard to administer, for election officials must see to it that those who have left the district, have died, or have been committed to public institutions are removed from the list.

Periodic registration requires voters to re-register from time to time. This system keeps the registration list up to date but is inconvenient for the voters, expensive, and a deterrent to large voter turnout. Some states allow absentee registration by persons who must be absent from the state for certain reasons.

PRIMARIES

Taking part in the selection of party candidates is often as important as voting in the election itself. As we have seen, in almost all the states candi-

dates are chosen in direct primary elections rather than in conventions. These primaries are financed by the public treasury, run by the regular election officials, and held in the same polling places as the regular election; moreover, the voters are protected by the same legal safeguards. To get on the primary ballot a candidate usually must file a petition signed by a required number of voters. In practice this means that almost anyone can get on the ballot if he does enough legwork, and the voter may find a large number of names listed on the primary ballot.

Who can vote in a party primary? In most states voters must publicly acknowledge membership in a party in order to help pick that party's nominees, but party membership in the United States is a rather ambiguous matter, and the tests are not very severe. In some states a voter may declare his party allegiance when he registers to vote; in others the voter enrolls as a party member

Courtesy Allan Kurzrok.

Panels from a pamphlet issued by The League of Women Voters to urge registration.

simply by showing up at the party primary to vote. In some states, mainly in the South, voters appearing at the primary must pledge, before receiving the ballot, that they supported the party's nominee at the last election, or will at the next, or both. In any case, a voter may change his party affiliation between elections.

This discussion refers to the *closed primary*, in which the party seeks to allow only those who are, in one way or another, party adherents to vote. But a number of states—six by latest count—have an *open primary* system, under which any qualified voter may participate in the primary of any party without having to reveal publicly his party affiliation. Except in the state of Washington, however, a voter may participate in only one party's primary. In some open systems the voter receives the ballots of all the parties and then fills out the one he prefers; in others he receives one ballot that lists the candidates of all parties for all offices.

Several states use a combination convention-primary system. Party conventions—usually called *pre-primary conventions*—or committees propose a candidate for each office. The candidate gaining the convention's endorsement then runs in the primary along with any other aspirants who may wish to compete without that endorsement. This procedure informs the voter of the official party choice but leaves him free to support any other candidate.

All primary systems allow supporters of one party to enter—or "raid"—the primary of another. The aim may be to nominate the weakest candidate in the rival party. The open primary, exposed to the depredations of one-day Republicans and next-day Democrats, makes raiding particularly easy. For this reason the open primary is deplored by party officials and advocates of strongly disciplined parties, although recent research finds no relation between the openness of primaries and subsequent support for the party, at least with respect to legislators.[1] The open primary is preferred by those who like to have a free choice on primary day as to the party contests in which they vote or who for some reason prefer not to reveal their party affiliation.

In Southern states, the Democratic nomination for state and local officers usually leads to election, because of the weakness of the Republican opposition. Sometimes so many candidates file to enter the Democratic primary that no candidate wins a majority. Then, there is a runoff primary, in which the two highest candidates run against each other in a second primary.

In the so-called *nonpartisan primary*, no party designations are permitted; candidates who qualify simply file and the two candidates who receive the most votes run against each other in the general election. *Cross-filing* also has a nonpartisan or at least a bipartisan tinge. Formerly used in California, it allows a candidate to enter the primaries of more than one party. A candidate may win both major primaries and thus in effect win the election, as former Governor Earl Warren did in California in 1946. California has since abolished cross-filing, however.

[1]Ira Ralph Telford, "Types of Primary and Party Responsibility," *American Political Science Review* (March 1965), pp. 117–118.

Nowhere are fairness and accuracy more important than in the handling of elections. In balloting, the Australian ballot system has long been accepted as a model. Under this system—used in Queensland as early as 1857—the government (rather than the parties or candidates, as had been the earlier practice) prints uniform ballots on good-quality paper, listing the names of all the candidates. Ballots are given to voters only on election day, only at the official polling place, and only by public officials. The ballots are marked secretly, folded, and deposited unopened in a ballot box. We tend to take these arrangements for granted now, but each one was adopted only after hard experience. For example, the use of good-quality paper ended the old trick of issuing tissue-paper ballots that enabled sharp-eyed party workers to see where a voter put his mark after the ballot was folded. Certain aspects of ballots and voting are worth noting:

The *office-group*, or Massachusetts-type, ballot lists together the names and party designations of all candidates for the same *office*. Candidates for the highest office usually come first and then state and local candidates. Because this type of ballot makes it impossible to vote a straight ticket with a single mark, it encourages independent and split-party voting.[2] However, it also leads to voter fatigue and to failure to vote for the offices at the bottom of the ballot.

The *party-column*, or Indiana-type, ballot groups candidates by *party* in columns. A voter can vote for all the candidates of a party simply by making his mark in a large circle or box next to the party's name and emblem. Or he may "scratch his ticket"—that is, go from column to column marking his choice for each office. The party-column ballot encourages straight party voting. Voting machines can accommodate either the office-group or party-column type.

Stickers and *write-ins* are devices for making last-minute changes in the ballot—for example, when a candidate withdraws or dies after the ballots have been printed. The voter may either paste in a gummed sticker or write in the name of the candidate of his choice. These devices are allowed in some states as a means of voting for a candidate other than the ones on the ballot, but write-in or sticker campaigns are rarely successful.

Absentee voting. Almost all the states allow certain persons, such as servicemen, to vote away from home. However, in order to prevent fraud absentee voting has been made so difficult that often only the most zealous citizen will go to the trouble of sending in an absentee ballot.

THE LONG BALLOT AND THE SHORT

A ballot has been known to be as long as 12 feet and to contain almost five hundred names. In filling out a long ballot—the form used by most states—the baffled voter must decide among a fantastic array of candidates for

[2]Angus Campbell and Warren E. Miller, "The Motivational Basis of Straight and Split Ticket Voting," *The American Political Science Review* (June 1957), pp. 293–312.

many offices. The more insignificant the office, the fewer the voters who know the qualifications of the candidates and the greater the likelihood that party organizations or interested groups can elect their favorites. And along with the candidates to be voted for, there are usually lengthy questions or propositions to be accepted or rejected.

There has long been a movement to shorten the ballot by restricting officials popularly elected to those concerned with broad policy determination, but progress has been slow. Most states have, however, adopted the *presidential short ballot*, which, instead of listing the names of all the electors of each party, carries only the names of the presidential and vice-presidential candidates to whom the electors are pledged. By casting one vote for President and Vice President, the voter in effect chooses the entire party slate of electors. But the long ballot seems certain to remain in state and local elections for a long time to come, if only because of the old fashioned—many political scientists would say misguided—view that in a democracy voters have the ability and the desire to make the most minute decisions in filling offices.

To conclude: As political scientists, we should understand that most of the voting arrangements discussed have some effect, planned or not, on voting behavior and hence on the allocation of political power. Unfortunately, research on these effects has been so limited and scattered that we still lack solid evidence and conclusions. There is indication that registration requirements and procedures are a major factor in the extent of nonvoting in the United States;[3] that party primaries tend to divide parties and their leaderships to a greater extent than do party conventions; that different types of ballots encourage or discourage straight-party voting; that even the use of voting machines instead of paper ballots has a discernible effect on voting outcomes. Further analysis of these problems, exploiting the vast amount of data available through polls and election returns, represents a major research frontier in political science.

Money and Elections

Money in politics is an important but shadowy subject. Obviously elections cost money—often a great deal of it. Estimated expenditures by the three national party organizations in the 1968 presidential campaigns totaled over $50 million. Many millions more were spent locally on state, county, and city contests and, earlier in the year, on the expensive presidential primaries in both major parties. These are the expenditures reported under the law; much—perhaps most—of the spending is never reported. In 1968 between $250 and $300 million were spent by candidates, their friends,

[3]For example, Donald R. Matthews and James W. Prothro in two articles in *American Political Science Review*, "Social and Economic Factors and Negro Registration in the South" (March 1963), pp. 24–44, and "Political Factors and Negro Voter Registration in the South" (June 1963), pp. 355–367, find that political and legal factors have a probable effect on Negro registration, but socioeconomic factors have an even greater probable effect. See also Stanley Kelley, Jr., Richard E. Ayres, and William G. Bowen, "Registration and Voting: Putting First Things First," *The American Political Science Review* (June 1967), pp. 359–377.

and other interested people for nominating and electing all public officials in the United States. A campaign for governor or senator in a large state can easily cost over a million dollars.[4]

Where does the money go? A half-hour program on a coast-to-coast television network costs (depending on the coverage) from $50,000 to $100,000. A one-minute television spot in a medium-sized city may cost $50. A full-page ad in a big-city newspaper costs $2,500. Campaign buttons cost 3 cents each, and candidates distribute tens of thousands of them. One mailing to every voter in a medium-sized state might cost $20,000.[5] Gasoline, telephone, printing, posters, rent of headquarters, salaries—all these items send expenses soaring.

One reason elections cost so much more in the United States than in other countries is the length of the campaigns. There are really two campaigns—one for nomination and one for election—and each of them lasts months. A presidential aspirant may campaign for eight or ten months before the conventions, as Kennedy did in 1960, Rockefeller and Goldwater in 1964, and McCarthy and Nixon in 1968. Candidates for governor and senator may spend far more money on their primary campaigns than on their final election campaigns—and the primary campaign expenses come out of their own pockets and from their friends, not from the party. In Great Britain, by contrast, candidates for Parliament campaign for about three weeks and depend almost wholly on their parties for money.

WHERE THE MONEY COMES FROM

Donations to party treasuries come from many sources. A little money comes from small donors, but most of the campaign chests are filled by large contributors—men who make donations of over $1,000. Only about 5 to 10 percent of the voters give any money at all to their parties or candidates. Those who have given most to the Republicans in recent presidential elections have been manufacturers, bankers, and men in the utility, insurance, mining, and oil businesses; to the Democrats, brewers, distillers, contractors, builders, professionals, merchants, and men in the entertainment and related fields. The Democrats run a series of Jackson Day dinners throughout the country, charging from $5 to $100 per plate; the Republicans have Lincoln Day dinners for the same purpose. Labor usually gives far more to the Democrats than to the Republicans.

State and local parties also receive direct gifts, but much of their money comes from candidates, especially from officeholders. Sometimes candidates give money to local parties in exchange for help. Assessing appointed officeholders is often a lucrative source of income to the parties, although this fundraising technique is usually kept under cover. It was revealed in Philadelphia, for example, that 3 to 5 percent of city workers' salaries was

---

[4]*"Financing Presidential Campaigns,"* Report of the President's Commission on Campaign Costs (U.S. Government Printing office, 1962), p. 9. See also Alexander Heard, *The Costs of Democracy* (Univ. of North Carolina Press, 1960). Estimates for 1968 are from preliminary reports of campaign spending and from estimates by the Citizens Research Foundation; see *The New York Times* (Nov. 5, 1968), p. 30.

[5]From Ivan Hinderaker, *Party Politics* (Holt, 1956), pp. 579–581.

collected by the Republican city committee, and 1 to 2 percent by the ward committees where the employees lived.

Why do people give? Mainly because they want something. City jobholders want to stay in office. Candidates want the party's good will and support. Big donors often want the party's officeholders to follow certain policies. Some big donors hope to gain prized positions, such as ambassadorships. Often what contributors want is simply an access to those in power in case the need arises.[6]

The motive for giving is not always direct self-interest, however. Thousands of contributors believe the party of their choice will govern best. Still, the number of small contributions is lamentably low. The Goldwater cause in 1964 and the Wallace campaign in 1968 attracted large numbers of small contributions, but these were exceptional.

REGULATION OF PARTY FINANCE

The national and state governments have made frequent, but not very successful, attempts to publicize party finances and to limit contributions and expenditures through corrupt practices legislation and other laws. Under certain conditions organizations receiving or spending money in two or more states to influence the election of national officials must file statements with the clerk of the House of Representatives giving the names of all persons contributing over $100, the names of all persons to whom payments of more than $10 have been made, and a total of all receipts and all expenditures. The national government and most of the states have long prohibited contributions from certain types of corporations, and in 1947 the Taft-Hartley Act barred all corporations and labor organizations from giving or spending money in connection with elections to national offices or with conventions or primaries to choose candidates for such offices. Campaign spending is supposed

© 1956 Herblock in *The Washington Post.*

"It's Terrible How The Big Money Guys Run Politics."

[6]A. Heard, *op. cit.* For excellent material on this general problem, including recommendations from political scientists and others, see "Federal Voting Assistance Act of 1955," *Hearings Before the Subcommittee on Privileges and Elections, Committee on Rules and Administration, United States Senate on S. 636, 84th Cong., 1st Sess.* (1955).

to be sharply limited. Under the 1925 Corrupt Practices Act, a candidate for representative may not spend more than $2,500, a candidate for senator not more than $10,000. As an alternative, each candidate may spend 3 cents per vote cast for all candidates for the office at the last general election—but no more than $25,000 for a senator and $5,000 for a representative. The Hatch Act of 1939, with its later amendments, limits spending by any political committee to $3 million a year and contributions by individuals to each candidate or nationally affiliated party committee to $5,000 annually. It also forbids forced contributions from government officeholders to candidates or parties and makes it "unlawful for any person employed in the executive branch of the federal government, or any agency or department thereof, to use his official authority or influence for the purpose of interfering with an election or affecting the result thereof." Such federal employees can vote, but they cannot take an active part in party affairs or political campaigns.

How effective are these regulations on campaign finance? The consensus is not very. President Johnson called the Corrupt Practice Act "more loophole than law." Full publicity is often evaded by filing reports after the election is over or by submitting inadequate or even false reports. The act does not cover primaries or expenses by committees working in a single state. Corporations make campaign contributions through personal offerings of executives and their families, labor unions through more or less voluntary offerings by their members. The limitations on expenditures are so unrealistic as to invite subterfuge.

Clearly we must change the laws relating to limitations and control over sources and permissible expenditures in political campaigns, but despite urging by the 1962 President's Commission on Campaign Costs (the Heard committee), Congress has been slow. In 1967 the Senate, by an eighty-seven-to-zero vote, approved a bill that required presidential, senatorial, and congressional candidates and all committees supporting them to file complete reports of their receipts and expenditures in both primary and general elections and repealed all restrictions on amounts that candidates and political committees could spend, but set limitations on amounts that any single person could contribute each year. A year later the House adopted a substantially similar bill, perhaps even tougher in its reporting and enforcement sections because of the proposed establishment of a Federal Election Commission. It seems clear that Congress before too long will provide more effective federal regulation and reporting of campaign spending.

A more difficult, but related question, is what, if anything, should the national government do to help parties and candidates finance campaigns. The cost of campaigning is becoming so great that to run for President or an office in a large state is difficult for any person who is not himself wealthy or does not have the backing of persons of wealth. Long ago Theodore Roosevelt urged Congress to provide funds to the two major parties from the federal treasury in order to equalize the resources available to them and to free them from dependence on private contributors. The idea still enjoys some support in Congress, but the problem of taking care of minor and new parties under such a proposal has been a major stumbling block.

In order to encourage lower- and middle-income persons to contribute to political parties, the Heard committee proposed that for an experimental

Once the candidate has entered the race he must please everyone . . .

A sore throat and temperature of 102° cannot keep him from campaigning . . .

He must be against the Taft-Hartley Law and a champion of labor . . .

A few ill-chosen words on the golf course can antagonize the church vote.

And at the same time finance his campaign with management's contributions.

And a moment of absent-mindedness will cost him the support of the vets . . .

period covering two presidential campaigns those who contribute to a national or state committee of a major political party be allowed to credit against their federal income tax half of what they contribute up to $10 a year or, alternatively, up to $1,000 a year as a regular deduction.[7] In 1966 Congress adopted (but then repealed in 1967) a plan that would allow each taxpayer to deduct a small sum from his tax bill and have it sent to either the Democratic or Republican parties.

Whatever the solution, the Heard committee concluded, there remains a major problem—the general attitude toward money in politics: "A chronic difficulty. . .has long been the lurking suspicion that contributing to political parties is somehow a shoddy business. This is unfortunate. Improvement of public understanding of campaign finance is essential."

Running for Congress

It is hard to generalize about congressional and senatorial campaigns because of the immense diversity of local factors. Much depends on the candidate—whether he is an incumbent, a novice running for the first time, an old veteran attempting a comeback. Much depends on the district —whether it is a safe district for one of the parties or highly competitive. Much depends on the time and the region, the urban, suburban, or rural makeup of the district, and local conditions.

He can lose the election by being seen in a non-union barber shop.

Is it all worth it? Only the returns on election day can tell.

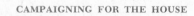

CAMPAIGNING FOR THE HOUSE

Still, there are certain patterns and rules of thumb, especially in campaigns for a seat in the House of Representatives.[8] For a person with some political experience and a moderate number of contacts throughout the district, the first question is one of timing. Does the year look good for himself and his party? Is there any kind of ground swell against the incumbents? If this is a presidential election year, will his party's ticket be headed by attractive national or state candidates, and if so, can he get a firm hold on their coattails? Would it be better to wait two or four years until he has broadened his own range of acquaintances? Or will it be too late by then?

[7] A Heard, *op. cit.*
[8] These generalizations are drawn in part from David A. Leuthold, *Electioneering in a Democracy: Campaigns for Congress* (Wiley, 1968); S. K. Bailey and H. D. Samuel, *Congress at Work* (Holt, 1952), pp. 112–135; and the illuminating studies of primary and election campaigns, "Eagleton Institute Cases in Practical Politics," sponsored by the Eagleton Foundation Advisory Board at Rutgers University (McGraw-Hill).

If he decides to "go," the candidate must first plan his primary race, unless he happens to have no opponents for his party's nomination—a piece of luck that can be expected only when his party has little chance of carrying the district. The first step in running for the nomination is to build a personal organization, because the party organization is supposed to stay neutral until the nomination is decided. A candidate can build his own organization as a holder of a lesser office, such as state representative, or simply by deliberately getting to know people, serving in civic causes, helping other candidates, and being conspicuous without being overly controversial. The next step is to enlist the support of as many interest-groups and party leaders as possible. (The latter may give their personal support even though their party committees are supposed to keep out of the contest.) A key question for the candidate is how to divide his resources—mainly money—between his primary effort and the final race. It is prudent to save most of his effort for the final race—but he always has the nagging worry that if he stints too much on the primary race he may not get to the general election at all.

Once nominated, the candidate comes into a rich inheritance—the large bloc of votes of the party faithful who will almost automatically support their party's nominee. He will also get considerable recognition from the press and from state and national leaders of his party. But the candidate for Congress usually has some woes. His party will provide him with far less financial support than he needs. Except in a few localities, such as Chicago, the party organization is either feeble or strained to the limit in trying to help all its candidates on the long ballot, and the candidate finds that he must depend on his own personal organization. But his main problem usually is one of visibility. If he campaigns in a large metropolitan area it is hard to get attention in the crowded press and on television, both of which are paying attention chiefly to the major candidates. And in rural areas the press may play down political news. He cannot afford much television, which in any event usually covers a far larger area than his district, thus wasting much of his money.

As a result congressional candidates often conclude that their best tactic is stressing personal contact—shaking hands, canvassing house to house, emphasizing local problems. One reason national representatives seem rather parochial is that their elections are usually locally instead of nationally oriented.

RUNNING FOR THE SENATE

Because states vary in population so widely, generalizing about Senate campaigns is most difficult. In a typical state, running for the Senate is big-time politics. The six-year term and the national exposure make a Senate seat a particularly glittering prize, so competition is likely to be intense. The race may easily cost several hundred thousands of dollars, whereas congressional campaigns typically cost in the tens of thousands.[9] The candidate for Senate is far more visible—he finds it more important to take positions on national problems; he cannot duck tough issues very easily; and he is likelier

[9]Leuthold, *op. cit.*, Chap. 6.

to have better access to the news media. Otherwise the problems of a senatorial candidate are much the same as those of a congressional candidate.

The advent of television has had almost as much impact on big-time Senate campaigns as on presidential. In 1948 Paul H. Douglas, long a professor of economics at the University of Chicago, ran as the Democratic nominee for Senator from Illinois. He described his campaign as follows:

> I pull up my sound-equipped jeep wagon at a factory gate during a change in shifts, or on a village street, or somewhere else near the main flow of people. I introduce myself to whatever crowd gathers, and then summarize the main themes of the campaign. Afterward I move among the clusters of people to shake hands and to distribute campaign literature which they can read at leisure. In this way I've spoken to about 225,000 people and have shaken hands with over 100,000 of them.[10]

Eighteen years later, in 1966, Charles Percy, a young Republican, took on Paul Douglas, who was completing his third term as United States Senator. A vigorous and attractive business executive, Percy emphasized television and other mass media. He made full use of independent groups working outside his party. His campaign was well financed and well organized, and he used the most modern methods of electioneering and communication. Douglas ran a strenuous campaign too, but times had changed. Percy won decisively—though doubtless he was assisted by the fact that this was an off-election year and there was a falling off of the big Democratic vote of 1964.[11]

How To Be Nominated for President

To attain the Presidency a man has to run two races and win them both. First he must be nominated at his party's national convention—and this is sometimes the harder of the two jobs. Then he must get a majority of the nation's electoral votes.

The first convention was probably held in 1808, when a few Federalist leaders met secretly in New York to nominate candidates for President and Vice President. In 1831, under Jackson's leadership, the first real national convention was held by a major party. Today the national convention is a famous and unique political institution. Every four years each party enjoys— usually for about a week—world attention; covered by batteries of cameras and microphones and by hundreds of newsmen, every incident in the great convention hall is carried to millions in this country and abroad.

The make-up of the national convention is significant. Each party has the double task of giving convention representation to the states roughly in proportion to the size of their electorates and of giving a bonus to states that have a heavier concentration of party strength. The two parties keep chang-

---

[10]Paul H. Douglas, "Running for Office Means Just That," *The New York Times Magazine* (Sept. 5, 1948), p. 5.

[11]For a full description of another high-powered campaign—that of Edward M. Kennedy for the Democratic nomination for Senator from Massachusetts in 1962—see Murray B. Levin, *Kennedy Campaigning* (Beacon Press, 1966).

ing their rules for apportioning the votes among the states in an attempt to satisfy both these requirements.

The latest Democratic allotment method, used in the 1968 convention, gives every state three convention votes for every electoral vote and awards extra convention votes to each state roughly in proportion to the extent that that state voted for the preceding Democratic presidential candidate (*i. e.*, Johnson in 1964). Tying the bonus to presidential voting alone in effect cuts down the convention strength of Southern states, who typically roll up huge majorities for Democratic candidates for governor and senator but much smaller votes for Democratic presidential candidates. Under this arrangement 2,989 delegates plus 110 national committee members cast 2,622 convention votes in the 1968 Democratic convention (some delegates have only half a vote so that more Democrats were able to take part in the convention).

Like the Democrats, the Republicans allow each state a number of delegates proportionate to its size, but they have a different method of awarding bonus votes. They allow each state extra delegates in proportion to its Republicanism. Thus, states receive extra representation roughly in proportion to how strongly they voted for the last Republican presidential candidate *or* Republican candidates for United States senator or representative. Under this arrangement, 1,333 delegates each had a single vote in the 1968 Republican convention. The key difference between this arrangement and the Democrats' is that the Republicans reward voting for both President and Congress, whereas the Democrats do so for President alone.

Each party also seats delegates from Puerto Rico and the Virgin Islands (the Democrats include the Canal Zone and Guam too), but these areas cast no electoral votes for President. And even before adoption of the Twenty-third Amendment both parties had a delegation from the District of Columbia.

CHOOSING DELEGATES

The method of selecting delegates is set by state law and varies considerably from state to state. In about two-thirds of the states, delegates are chosen by party *conventions* or committees. In about one-third, including most of the populous states, delegates are picked in state *presidential primaries*. A few states use a combination of the two methods.

The convention system tends to put selection of the delegation into the hands of a party inner circle. This may be no problem where the party leadership is representative, but that is often not the case. Most Republican party organizations in the South, for example, have tended to be controlled by a few Republican officeholders in Washington with the help of patronage. In such situations the question of who speaks for the rank and file of the party becomes very obscure. This was a main cause of the fierce fight between the Taft and Eisenhower supporters in the 1952 Republican convention, culminating in the unseating of the Taft delegations from Georgia, Louisiana, and Texas and the seating of the Eisenhower forces. Since that time the Republican party has greatly broadened its base in the South.

If state conventions are the most usual method of choosing national convention delegates, *state presidential primaries* are by far the more exciting—

and in recent years their outcome seems to have had more and more influence on the decisions of delegates from both convention and primary states. There are two main elements in state presidential primaries: presidential preference votes, as between Robert Kennedy and Eugene McCarthy in several primaries in 1968 (sometimes called popularity contests) and direct election of delegates to the national convention. The combination of these elements takes many forms, but James W. Davis has found four basic categories of primaries:

1 *Presidential preference vote with a separate election of national convention delegates by state convention.* The convention-elected delegates are legally bound to vote for the popular winner on the first ballot at the national convention. Indiana and Maryland have this kind of primary.

2 *Blended preference vote and delegate selection.* By a single X at the top of the column headed, say, "Delegates preferring Richard M. Nixon," the voter can both indicate the man he wants and vote for a delegate slate pledged to him at the national convention. California and Ohio have this kind of primary.

3 *Advisory presidential preference vote and separate delegate election on the same ballot.* The voter makes two decisions in filling out his ballot— one to indicate his preference among the presidential candidates on the ballot and one to express his choice of convention delegates from his state or district. The delegates may or may not be pledged to a candidate. Massachusetts, Illinois, New Hampshire, New Jersey, and Pennsylvania have this type of primary.

4 *Mandatory presidential preference vote and separate delegate election.* Delegates must support the popularity-poll winner on the first two convention ballots, unless that candidate releases the delegates from the pledge or receives less than 35 percent of the votes cast on a roll call. Oregon is the only state at present that has this type of primary.[12]

© 1956 Herblock in *The Washington Post.*

"Let's See—Four Oranges Plus Three Apples, Minus One Monkey Wrench, Times Two Bushels—"

The variety of methods of choosing delegates along with the variety of power patterns in state parties makes it impossible to generalize about the nature of the final delegations. Some may be under the thumb of a powerful state party leader; others may be "split wide open"; still others may operate as a unit to support

[12]Drawn from James W. Davis, *Presidential Primaries: Road to the White House* (Crowell, 1967), pp. 37–41.

a favorite son or to maximize their bargaining power. Most state delegations mirror the factions in the state party, but sometimes a strong and well-organized faction will gain control of the whole delegation.

One thing is clear. The mere adoption of a presidential primary system does not guarantee a delegation that will reflect rank-and-file wishes, any more than choosing delegates through state party conventions means that they are automatically boss-controlled. Voter turnout in most primaries tends to be low. Presidential candidates may simply ignore state primaries, as Adlai Stevenson and Hubert Humphrey did in 1952 and 1968, respectively, and still win nomination. Sometimes, on the other hand, success in presidential primaries is decisive, as in the cases of Kennedy in 1960 and Nixon in 1968.

It can be said for presidential primaries that they have stimulated interest in the early stages of presidential nominations, have opened up the party machinery to rank-and-file participation where the voters have been interested enough to use it, and have enabled the country to get a good idea of the popularity of rival candidates. Reforms have been proposed: Presidential primary ballots and procedures should be clarified and simplified. It should not be expected that candidates go through the ordeal of more than a half-dozen or so primaries. Primaries need not start so early in the presidential election year and run so late. And the system of choosing delegates through party conventions could be "made more open, better advertised and strictly regulated to insure fair procedures."[13]

Two features of the present delegating-choosing methods stand out. Increasingly, conventions seem to be ratifying popular choices. And the ordeal of winning delegations is a harsh but necessary test for the man who wants to be President. For it forces him to do two things—to show mass popularity (at least in the states with preference primaries) and to bargain effectively with a host of state leaders across the country. These are pretty good tests for the man who, in the White House, must know how to maintain some popular appeal at the same time that he must deal with rival leaders at home and abroad.

PRECONVENTION CAMPAIGNS

The preconvention campaign usually starts at least a year or two before the convention itself. The candidate—who may be a well-known governor, Cabinet member, senator, or perhaps an eminent general—is likely to assume the appearance of indecision for a time, while his scouts are busy sounding out party sentiment from Maine to Hawaii. The candidate has his choice of several preconvention strategies, depending on his political position. He can announce his candidacy months before the convention and try openly to capture state delegations. He can keep silent if he prefers not to show his hand early, especially if it is not a strong one. He can concentrate on gaining a following among the party rank and file and the voters at large through public appearances, television speeches, and the like. He can try to

[13]Gerald Pomper, *Nominating the President: The Politics of Convention Choice* (Norton, 1966), p. 276.

build his strength mainly by lining up delegates through various arrangements or deals.

John Kennedy's preconvention campaign of 1957 to 1960 may become a classic example of the activist strategy—and an example that many future presidential hopefuls will emulate.[14] Kennedy began his campaign soon after Stevenson lost to Eisenhower for the second time in 1956. After three years of intensive speaking and politicking throughout the country and amid mounting attention from the press, Kennedy announced his candidacy in January 1960. The odds seemed heavily against him. He was in his early forties and a Catholic. The old Democratic party establishment—former President Truman and the veteran Fair Deal leadership—were against him. Most Senate Democrats favored Lyndon Johnson; most House Democrats, Senator Stuart Symington. Liberal Democrats and intellectuals leaned heavily toward Stevenson. Many city bosses and most Democratic governors opposed Kennedy.

Kennedy's response was to seek every delegate vote that was possibly available, with special emphasis on the presidential primaries. He would build his party strength from the bottom up. In the early weeks of 1960 he stepped up his campaign tours and sent advance men into the key primary states. He paid special attention to Democratic governors because of their influence over state delegations and because some of them were candidates themselves or at least favorite sons.

What primaries Kennedy should enter was the candidate's main tactical problem. Clearly, he would have to invade some to show his vote-getting capacity, but other candidates' home states had to be written off—for example, Humphrey's Minnesota. Some states presented awkward problems. California's Governor Edmund "Pat" Brown had himself some hope of the presidential nomination—or at least the vice-presidential—and he wanted to keep control of his delegation for that reason—or for trading purposes. Kennedy indicated to Brown and other "neutralist" governors that he would invade their primaries unless guaranteed at least a good chunk of the delegation. Such bargaining and threatening was simple in theory, but applying these tactics to the infinitely complex politics of several large states was a hard test of Kennedy as a politician. In the end, except for Ohio and California, he entered every binding presidential primary where no legitimate favorite son was running, and he entered most of the nonbinding primaries as well.

The story of Kennedy's grand slam of the contested primaries—Wisconsin, West Virginia, Maryland, Oregon—is well known. Less known but equally important was his capture of delegations chosen in state party conventions or committees. Some sharp bargaining was necessary. In Michigan, for example, Kennedy had to make clear that its Democratic party leaders would be recognized in future party decisions, and he had to make clear his own views on forty-odd national issues. Other states presented other claims. But one thing the state politicians could not ignore—Kennedy's popularity in the

[14]This case study is drawn chiefly from Theodore C. Sorensen, *Kennedy* (Harper & Row, 1965), Chap. 5; and Theodore H. White, *The Making of the President 1960* (Atheneum, 1961), Chap 5.

primaries (and in the polls). The more primaries he won, the more state politicians realized that they had better get on the bandwagon. So in the end Kennedy's state primary campaigns and his state convention bargaining converged in a victory on the first roll call at the Democratic national convention.

CONVENTION BATTLES

In each national convention the object is simple—to win a straight majority of the votes cast on the first or any other ballot. This job is most difficult, however, for the delegates arrive in the convention city in all stages of commitment, noncommitment, or semicommitment to one candidate or another. Some delegates are pledged to a candidate only on the first ballot; others pledge themselves to one man for all ballots. Some state delegations plan to vote as a unit; others split their vote according to the position of individual delegates.

As the convention opens, the air is filled with talk of favorite sons; of stalking horses, who are used as fronts for strong candidates wishing to keep some strength in reserve; and of dark horses, who "stand restively and fully accoutered in their paddocks waiting, watching, and hoping that favorites will kill each other off, and that the convention in desperation will lead them to the starting post."[15] The big test of a candidate has been his availability, which turns on whether he has demonstrated vote-getting power, whether he seems to have presidential stature, whether or not he is closely tied to a narrow faction in the party, whether he comes from a politically strategic state or section, and —above all—whether he has alienated some vital religious, ethnic, or economic group. Governors have usually met the availability test better than senators, partly because the former can more easily dodge specific stands on national issues than the latter. But this aspect of availability may be changing, for in 1960,1964, and 1968 the voters seemed more interested in senatorial candidates who had dealt with international problems.

Both party conventions follow the same ritual. First there is a keynote speech, which lauds the party and bombards the enemy in equally flamboyant terms. Then come the election of convention officials, the reports of committees, the adoption of a platform. Some of these activities, such as the election of the permanent chairman and the seating of contested delegations, are occasions for tests of strength among leading candidates. After hearing statements from representatives of interested groups, the resolutions committee presents a proposed platform to the convention. Usually the planks are debated by the delegates, although sometimes they are accepted perfunctorily. Though drawn in generalities, negative in tone, and sometimes meaningless in detail, the platform indicates the way the wind is blowing. And on some issues, such as civil rights in the Democrats' 1948 and 1956 conventions and in the 1964 Republican convention and Vietnam in the 1968 Democratic convention, stormy debate may ensue and planks may be accepted or defeated by close votes.

By the third or fourth day the convention is ready for the main business.

[15]P. H. Odegard and E. A. Helms, *American Politics*, 2d ed. (Harper & Row, 1947), p. 532. See also Paul T. David, Ralph M. Goldman, and Richard C. Bain, *The Politics of National Party Conventions* (Brookings, 1960).

Candidates are placed in nomination in speeches depicting them as angels blessed with every virtue—above all, the ability to win elections. Pandemonium breaks forth when the name of each candidate is mentioned. Delegates march about singing and cheering in demonstrations that may last half an hour or so. Short seconding speeches come next. Then the balloting begins.

Meantime the candidates have been maneuvering for position. From their headquarters in nearby hotel rooms has emerged a stream of claims of delegate strength, counterclaims, denials, rumors, charges, and countercharges. If one candidate comes to the convention with a big lead in delegate strength, the other candidates will attempt to head him off by combining their forces, as did Nixon's and Humphrey's rivals in 1968. For if the convention can be deadlocked, a stampede may start toward even a weak candidate. Anyone controlling delegate votes must make the crucial decision of when to throw his strength to a candidate. If he throws his votes too soon, he may give them to a candidate who loses in the end. If he waits too long, some candidate may acquire enough strength elsewhere. The trick is to deliver at the right time to the winning man; the reward may be the Vice Presidency or some other prize.

Once a candidate wins a majority, some delegate who has voted against him normally moves that the nomination be made unanimous. This is done, and then another long ovation breaks out. The victorious candidate, who usually has been directing his forces from a nearby hotel suite, may appear before the convention a short while later. Smiling wife by his side, spotlighted by movie and television cameras, the happy candidate thanks the delegates for their vote of confidence and promises a winning fight.

Nominating a vice-presidential candidate usually is an anticlimax. The delegates are tired, broke, and anxious to get home. While the vice-presidential nominee is formally chosen in a roll call vote, in almost all cases the newly picked presidential nominee and his backers actually make the selection, and the convention is glad to endorse it. An effort is ordinarily made to balance the ticket by selecting for vice president a man who represents a different wing of the party, geographical area, or party faction from the presidential nominee. Sometimes the selection is partly the result of a trade by which a party faction gives its ballots to the man who wins the presidential nomination in exchange for the "consolation prize." In 1956 Stevenson tried to set a precedent by allowing the delegates to choose his running mate without any interference on his part. But in 1960 both Kennedy and Nixon reverted to the traditional practice of the new presidential nominee's choosing his own man—and they also followed tradition in selecting men who would balance them geographically and doctrinally. Johnson and Goldwater chose geographical—but not doctrinal—balance in 1964. Nixon chose a fellow "party centrist" in 1968 to gain strength in the border states and Humphrey, a fellow liberal.

SHOULD THE NATIONAL CONVENTION BE REFORMED?

One of the most-criticized party institutions is the national convention. It is charged that every party candidate is picked by party bosses in a series of unprincipled deals in smoke-filled rooms and that they usually come up with a compromise candidate who represents the dead level of party mediocrity. The manner of choosing the delegates is also under attack. Both conventions and primaries are rigged and run by state bosses, it is said, and presidential primaries are so complicated that they baffle the voter and discourage him from taking part.

The main defense of the convention system is simple—It works. During the last hundred years, it is argued, the convention system has brought before the country men of the caliber of Lincoln, Cleveland, McKinley, Wilson, Smith, Willkie, both Roosevelts, Stevenson, Eisenhower, Kennedy, and others. The genius of the convention system is that it usually produces a candidate who represents party consensus instead of merely some wing of the party. This is important, for only such a man can enjoy the united support of the party in the campaign and in the White House. Moreover, it is said, the convention increasingly manages to select the man who is the overwhelming choice of the party rank and file and who is, indeed, a national favorite rather than a dark horse. When a party convention nominates a candidate lacking consensus and moderate support at the grass roots, as the Republicans did in choosing Goldwater in 1964, the party pays a heavy price in the November election.

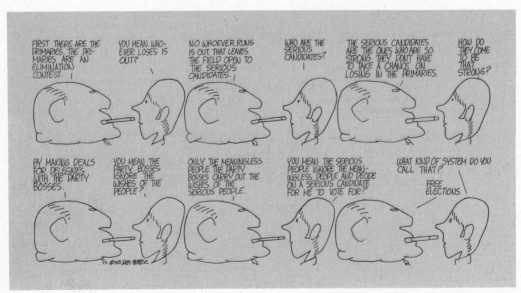

Courtesy Jules Feiffer and Publishers-Hall Syndicate.

Some favor the convention but would like to see it improved in operation. Former President Eisenhower, for example, called for cutting down the number of delegates to about a thousand; restricting demonstrations to five minutes; maintaining absolute order in the hall; and keeping all reporters and cameramen off the floor. Experienced politicians opposed such changes on the grounds that Americans liked the conventions the way they were, even with all the tumult, and that both the delegates and the public wanted reporters and cameramen on the floor—the delegates because they liked the publicity and the public because it wanted an intimate close-up of what was supposed to be going on in state delegations and smoke-filled rooms.

These questions came to a head in August 1968 at the Democratic convention in Chicago. Chosen as the convention city largely at the insistence of the powerful Democratic mayor, Richard Daley, Chicago became the setting of a furious four-day struggle as youthful protesters and hippies fought with the Chicago police. The Democrats managed to conduct a relatively orderly convention despite heavy security restrictions and even decided to banish floor demonstrations, but the general turmoil, especially in the city of Chicago, was so intense and well publicized as to bring the convention system under a cloud. Before adjourning, however, the Democrats took two important steps toward reform: they abolished the unit rule and required that all delegates be selected during the year in which the convention is held.

Some critics of the convention would abolish it completely and substitute a nationwide *direct presidential primary* system. President Woodrow Wilson in 1913 advocated legislation providing for primary elections to take place simultaneously throughout the country, in which the voters in each party would vote directly for their favorite without the intervention of nominating conventions. This system would do away with much of the confusion and inefficiencies of the present system. The proposal, which might require a constitutional amendment, has been criticized, however, by those who feel that one nationwide direct primary would disrupt party solidarity and effectiveness. We need consensus within the party, they say, so that all major elements—geographical, economic, ideological—can take part in its affairs. We need division between the major parties so that the people will have a more meaningful choice at the polls. A nationwide primary system, critics assert, would give us the reverse and would be extremely expensive for candidates.

Presidential Campaign Strategy

The convention adjourns immediately after the presidential and vice-presidential candidates deliver their acceptance speeches to the aroused and enthusiastic delegates. The presidential nominee may choose a new party chairman, who usually serves as his campaign manager. After a rest, the candidate spends the final days of the summer binding up party wounds, gearing the party for action, and planning campaign strategy. By early fall the presidential race is on.

Strategy differs from one election to another, but politicians, pollsters, and political scientists have collected enough information through experience in recent decades to agree broadly on a number of basic factors affecting it. The great bulk of the electorate votes on the basis of *party*; candidate appeal, issues, religion, etc., are important but secondary factors. Much turns on voter *turnout* as well as on habitual party disposition. Nationally the Democrats have a great advantage in party registration and support; but the Republicans have an advantage in that their partisans are more likely to turn out on election day, and they have better access to money and a somewhat more favorable press. Pledges on policy and program may not arouse the mass electorate, but they do help activate interest groups and party organizations, which in turn help get out a favorable vote. The existence of the electoral college puts a premium on votes from large two-party states.

Perhaps the clearest lesson is that in the presidential election, the major parties are quite evenly balanced—except when one of them nominates a man who can be charged with extremism, as Goldwater was in 1964. Hence much depends on the management and tactics of the campaign.[16]

CAMPAIGN TACTICS

The buildup. The personality of the candidate may be as important as the platform he runs on. If a candidate has serious personality defects, they must either be played down or transformed into virtues. The dour Calvin Coolidge had to be humanized before the presidential campaign of 1924. Franklin D. Roosevelt in 1936 had been pictured by the opposition as an arrogant dictator; his campaign tour was designed in part to show him as a warm and pleasing personality close to the people. Many in 1960 considered Kennedy too young to run for President; he had to show his maturity and judgment by his handling of bills before the Senate committees on which he served. In 1968 Nixon emphasized moderation to overcome his image as a strong partisan.

Taking the stump. By the end of September both candidates are dashing about the country by train, plane, and automobile. There was a time when candidates conducted front-porch campaigns, receiving friendly delegations at their homes. But that day seems gone forever. Today the campaign must be carried straight to the voters. Presidents Hoover, Franklin Roosevelt, and Eisenhower stayed in the White House until late in their campaigns for reelection to show their devotion to duty, but they took the stump before the end. The choice of itinerary is important. Candidates sometimes try to steer clear of areas where they might be embarrassed by a local issue or an intra-party fight.

Where to stump. The electoral college system has a strong influence on campaign strategy. Under this system, the presidential contest is not decided by the pooled votes of all those casting ballots throughout the nation, but solely by the ballots of presidential electors. *All* the electoral votes of a state go to the candidate who gains the most popular votes in that state. As a consequence, candidates concentrate their attention on big, closely divided states. This means that the Democratic candidate may write off Kansas and his Republican foe probably does the same with Massachusetts. Consequently, the candidates make most of their appearances in states such as New York, California, Pennsylvania, Illinois, and Ohio, for the election outcome may easily be decided by a large bloc of electoral votes from these states.

Building group support. The essential strategy of the campaign is to build up a winning alliance of interests—mainly sectional, economic, ideo-

[16]See Nelson W. Polsby and Aaron B. Wildavsky, *Presidential Elections: Strategies of American Electoral Politics* (Scribner, 1964), Chap. 1; Donald E. Stokes, "Some Dynamic Elements of Contests for the Presidency," *The American Political Science Review* (March 1966), pp. 19–28; and the extensive literature cited therein.

Drawing by Peter Arno; © 1946 The New Yorker Magazine, Inc.

"The big guy in front is Joseph T. Cochrane. Call him Joe. You met him in Marysville three weeks ago. Talk about hunting. He goes after deer every fall. Man on left is Leo Brown. Sixteenth District in his pocket. Don't ask about his wife. She's ditched him. Fellow with mustache is Jim Cronin. Watch your step with him. He's Cochrane's brother-in-law, and . . ."

logical, national-origin, racial, religious. Some of these interest groups are antagonistic to one another—for example, a Democratic candidate must seek to win the support of Northern Negroes without alienating too many Southern whites. Because most large organizations, such as the American Legion or the National Grange, will not commit themselves as organizations, the trick is to induce their leaders to take part in special election groups, such as Veterans for Nixon or United Farmers for Humphrey. Each party headquarters maintains active bureaus designed to mobilize support from organized groups. Campaign literature is slanted to appeal to housewives, businessmen, farmers, veterans, workers, and so on. The candidate himself must pitch his appeals so that they attract the support of divergent and overlapping groups.

Choosing issues. This is one of the basic arts of campaigning. Issues may not be more important than personalities, but actually the two are inseparable. The candidate has a wide choice of alternatives, for he is not bound by his party's platform; indeed he can openly repudiate or modify planks of the platform if he wishes, as Landon did in 1936. One basic question arises: Should the candidate take a stand on specific issues, or should he speak in generalities? Either way, he is bound both to win and to lose some votes. Traditionally, evasion of issues has been considered an effective tactic, but Truman and Kennedy took fairly definite stands. Usually the candidate tries to develop a basic theme, which is repeatedly played on with variations to suit the place and hour. But there is a good deal of improvisation as candidates and campaign managers sense last-minute changes in public feeling from their audiences and from opinion polls.

Offensive and defensive tactics. Is it better to concentrate on attacking the enemy and ignoring his charges? Or should the opposition be answered charge for charge? Is it possible to put the opposition on the defensive? How? Do Americans vote *for* candidates or *against* them? These questions plague any campaign strategist. Of course, a candidate for reelection is often on the defensive, for his public record is on display before the voters. But it is always possible to ignore the opposition's attacks and concentrate on one's own achievements. An effective tactic is to ignore the opposition's most damaging charges and to answer his weakest and wildest ones. In 1940, for example, Roosevelt said nothing about the third-term issue, but he answered at length the reckless statement of a minor Republican official that the President's only supporters were "paupers, those who earn less than $1,200 a year and aren't worth that, and the Roosevelt family."

Splitting the opposition. According to an old political maxim, a candidate should always try to separate his opponent from the party rank and file. Willkie in 1940 tried to make a distinction between New Dealers and Democrats. Humphrey in 1968 tried to sharpen the differences between Nixon and liberal Republicans. Campaigners also try to divide the groups that seem to be united behind their opponent; thus Dewey made a point of his support from organized labor, and Roosevelt made use of businessmen's organizations set up to back him. Another splitting device is to focus the attack on a minor figure in the opposition camp or on the sinister forces that are said to be in command. Republicans play up city bosses, leftists, hippies, arrogant bureaucrats; Democrats concentrate on big business, special interests, utilities, and the like. The great weakness of this device is that too much fire directed toward minor figures may leave the candidate himself unscathed.

Auxiliary organizations. While the candidate is parading himself before the voters, he must rely on his national, state, and local party organizations to carry the heavy burden of routine work. His own campaign headquarters must raise money, issue propaganda, coordinate party efforts throughout the nation, and operate special divisions to seek the vote of large groups such as Negroes, labor, and farmers. An important organizational question is whether to use auxiliary organizations independent of the party. In 1940, for example, Republicans and Independents set up thousands of Willkie Clubs, many of which had somewhat distant relations with the Republican organization. Auxiliaries can appeal more effectively to independent voters but are likely to duplicate the efforts of the party regulars and even generate serious friction. In general, a presidential candidate must rely heavily on the party machinery throughout the nation, for he does not have time to build up a nationwide personal organization. In 1968, however, Hubert Humphrey found it necessary, because of divisions in the regular party, to set up Citizens for Humphrey.

Surveys. Old-line politicians have been skeptical of the dependability of polls, partly as a result of the pollsters' debacle in 1948. But

Drawing by Robt. Day; © 1958 The New Yorker Magazine, Inc.

"How does he stand on reciprocal trade agreements? That's what I want to know."

in recent years candidates have been making increasing use of carefully conducted surveys of voters' attitudes and intentions. Kennedy employed surveys effectively both in his preconvention and election campaigns. Through the use of polls Johnson discovered in the spring of 1964 that the voters approved most of his record on economic and social issues; that they were most concerned about cold-war frustrations; that the widely feared backlash over the civil rights struggle was a potential threat but not yet an existing threat; and that no matter whom Johnson chose for his running mate, the President would win by about the same margin. When one of Johnson's close personal aides was arrested for misconduct at the height of the campaign, the President requested an immediate poll, which revealed that the incident had not had a significant impact on voters' intentions.

Timing. This is one of the most important and mysterious techniques of all. Candidates try to pace their campaigns to reach a climax just before the election. Eisenhower's promise late in October 1952 to make a personal trip to Korea if elected was perfectly timed for maximum appeal. Although it is doubtful that election climaxes can be planned with complete success, candidates usually converge on the populous areas of the East shortly before election day. The final campaign speeches usually take place on the Saturday before the Tuesday election. On election eve, the candidates usually make sober and restrained appeals to the people to do their duty at the polls next day; however, in 1968 the two major candidates held telethons that night —Nixon attempting to stem the tide of votes moving toward Humphrey, Humphrey attempting to encourage it.

An American politician can face no ordeal more exhausting or exacting than a presidential campaign. The late Adlai E. Stevenson, the unsuccessful Democratic candidate in 1952 and 1956, told how it felt to campaign.

You must emerge, bright and bubbling with wisdom and well-being, every morning at 8 o'clock, just in time for a charming and profound breakfast talk, shake hands with hundreds, often literally thousands, of people, make several inspiring, "newsworthy" speeches during the day, confer with political leaders along the way and with your staff all the time, write at every chance, think if possible, read mail and newspapers, talk on the telephone, talk to everybody, dictate, receive delegations, eat, with decorum—and discretion!—and ride through city after city on the back of an open car, smiling until your mouth is dehydrated by the wind, waving until the blood runs out of your arm, and then bounce gaily, confidently, masterfully into great howling halls, shaved and all made up for television with the right color shirt and tie—I always forgot—and a manuscript so defaced with chicken tracks and last-minute jottings that you couldn't follow it, even if the spotlights weren't blinding and even if the still photographers didn't shoot you in the eye every time you looked at them. (I've often wondered what happened to all those pictures!) Then all you have to do is make a great, imperishable speech, get out through the pressing crowds with a few score autographs, your clothes intact, your hands bruised, and back to the hotel—in time to see a few important people.

But the real work has just commenced—two or three, sometimes four hours of frenzied writing and editing of the next day's immortal mouthings so you can get something to the stenographers, so they can get something to the mineograph machines, so they can get something to the reporters, so they can get something to their papers by deadline time. (And I quickly concluded that all deadlines were yesterday!) Finally sleep, sweet sleep, steals you away, unless you worry—which I do. . . .[17]

THE ELECTORAL COLLEGE SYSTEM: MECHANICS

To win the Presidency, a candidate must put together a combination of electoral votes that will give him a majority in the electoral college. This unique institution never meets and serves only a limited electoral function. Yet it has an importance of its own. The Framers of the Constitution devised the electoral college system because they wanted the President chosen by electors exercising independent judgment, but subsequent political changes have transformed the electors into straight party representatives who simply register the electorate's decision.

The system today works as follows: In making his presidential choice on election day, the voter technically does not vote directly for a candidate but chooses between slates of *presidential electors*. Each slate is made up of men selected by the state party (in most states in party conventions) to serve this essentially honorary role. The slate that wins the most popular votes throughout the state gets to cast all the electoral votes for the state (a state has one electoral vote for every senator and representative).

The electors on the winning slate travel to their state capital the first Monday after the second Wednesday in December, go through the ceremony of casting their ballots for their party's candidates, perhaps hear some speeches, and go home. The ballots are sent from the state capitals to Washington, where early in January they are formally counted by the House and Senate and the name of the next President is announced.

Counting the electoral votes has not always been just a formality. In 1876 there was a serious and potentially explosive dispute over which slate of electoral votes from several Southern states should be counted. The election was so close that the outcome was at stake. The Senate was Republican; the House, Democratic. Finally a Commission of Fifteen was elected, composed of eight Republicans and seven Democrats. By a vote of eight to seven, the Commission ruled that the Republican electors in the disputed states had been properly elected; so Hayes became President over Tilden.

The House and Senate also must act when no candidate secures a majority of the electoral votes. This is not likely so long as there are only two serious contending parties, but it has happened twice in the case of President and once in the case of Vice President and almost happened in the very close 1968 election. The House chooses the President from among the top three candidates; each state delegation has one vote, and a majority is necessary for election. If no man receives a majority of the electoral vote in the vice-presidential contest, the Senate picks from among the top two candidates; each senator has one vote, and again a majority is required.

THE ELECTORAL COLLEGE SYSTEM: POLITICS

The operation of the electoral college, with its statewide electoral slates, sharply influences the Presidency and presidential politics. In order to win a

[17]Adlai E. Stevenson, *Major Campaign Speeches, 1952* (Random House, 1953), pp. xi–xii. Reprinted by permission of Random House, Inc. Copyright 1953 by Random House, Inc.

presidential election, a candidate must appeal successfully to urban and suburban groups in populous states such as New York, California, Pennsylvania, Illinois, and perhaps a dozen others. A Republican candidate usually enters the fray sure of the backing of rural states such as Vermont, Kansas, Oregon, and the Dakotas. Until the 1960s the Democratic candidate knew that he could depend on the support of the Solid South and some of the border states. Under the electoral college system, as we have seen, a candidate wins either *all* a state's electoral votes or *none*. Hence the presidential candidate ordinarily will not waste his time campaigning in states unless he has at least a fighting chance of carrying them; nor will he waste time in states that are assuredly on his side. Consequently, the fight usually narrows down to the big states where the balance between the parties tends to be fairly even.

Obviously the presidential candidate must win over—or at least not antagonize—masses of voters in industrial centers. He must show sensitivity to their problems—working conditions, housing, wages, social security, and relations with foreign nations, especially nations whose sons and daughters have come by the million to our shores. Moreover, the candidate's appeals must at the same time transcend local and petty matters and dramatize the great national issues. He will, of course, address himself to groups such as farmers, workers, veterans, and the like, but he will try to seize on the issues that unify these groups on a nationwide basis. The candidate, in short, strikes out for a national majority rooted in the largest states and sacrifices many narrow issues in order to exploit the broader ones. Candidates for Congress, on the other hand, often win votes by pressing local and sectional claims against those of the rest of the nation.

THE POLITICS OF ELECTORAL COLLEGE REFORM

In 1968 an elector in North Carolina chosen on the Republican ticket refused to cast his electoral vote for Nixon and gave it to George Wallace of Alabama. Although such departures from constitutional custom are rare and have never affected the outcome of an election, most people agree that it is dangerous to have a system that allows individual electors to vote for whomever they wish despite the results of the popular vote in their state. In a close election a small group of persons could frustrate the wishes of the majority of the electorate. Furthermore, in an election in which no candidate received a majority of the electoral votes, there might be a temptation for candidates to try to make deals with electors. Although under the present system fifteen states attempt by law to bind electors to vote for the presidential and vice-presidential candidates of their party, these laws would be clumsy to enforce.

The existence of the electoral college could also lead to an election being thrown into the House of Representatives. This has happened only twice in our history—both times before the establishment of our present two-party system—but if it did happen again, twenty-six state delegations could elect the President. The threat during the 1968 election that George Wallace, running essentially as a sectional candidate, might capture enough electoral votes in Southern states to deprive Nixon or Humphrey of a majority once again brought to the nation's attention the dangers of the electoral college system.

The least drastic reform was proposed by President Johnson; his plan was to abolish individual electors but retain the present winner-take-all method of counting electoral votes. This proposal received little support in the Congress, not so much because of any basic objections, but because it did not seem worth the effort to legalize the *status quo*. Others have proposed that the present winner-take-all system be retained, that electors be abolished, but that, instead of having the House of Representatives decide the election if no one candidate received a majority of the electoral votes, there should be a runoff between the candidates with the greatest number.

A much more controversial and significant proposal is to alter the winner-take-all method of counting electoral votes, which could lead to the election, as it has twice in our history, of a President who received fewer popular votes than his opponent. However, the system usually results in the exaggeration of the margin of electoral votes of the winning candidate. Thus, even when the popular vote is close, the electoral-vote margin of the winner can be substantial. In the 1960 election, for example, Kennedy's popular-vote margin was only 112,000 out of almost 69 million votes, but he received 303 electoral votes to Nixon's 209. In the absence of the electoral college unit-vote system there might have been a much greater disposition on the part of the Republicans to challenge the returns.

For decades many have urged that the electoral college system be abandoned in favor of direct election of the President. The American Bar Association formally endorsed this approach and unsuccessfully urged the Democrats and Republicans to incorporate such a plank in their 1968 platforms. Others have felt that direct election might not be accepted because the less populous states, who would not have as much voice in the election of the President as they now do with their guarantee of at least three electoral votes, would oppose it. These people propose that in order to make the electoral vote correspond more closely to the popular vote, the Constitution be amended so that each candidate would receive the same proportion of the electoral votes of a state as he won of its popular vote. For example, if a candidate secured one-third of the popular vote in a state having twelve electoral votes, he would win four of the electoral votes.

What would be the consequences of an amendment (generally known as the Lodge-Gossett proposal) distributing the electoral votes of a state in proportion to its popular vote?

Many Northern Democrats are op-

From *The Herblock Book* (Beacon Press, 1952).

"Don't Expect Me To Get This Real Accurate, Bub."

posed to this, because they believe it would strengthen the position of rural, small-town conservatives. They argue that the present system compels presidential candidates to fight especially hard to win the support of the pivotal states such as New York, Illinois, and California, because candidates can win a big batch of electoral votes in such states. As a result, presidential candidates pitch their appeals in these states to the great balance-of-power groups that tend to be composed largely of urban voters—organized labor, Catholics, nationality groups, and Negroes, who usually give majorities to Democratic candidates. The electoral college thus forces presidential candidates—and ultimately the President—to be especially responsive to the problems and interests of these groups. Since Congress overrepresents the conservative, rural areas, why should not the President overrepresent urban, liberal areas they ask. President Kennedy, when a senator, opposed electoral reform partly for this reason.

For precisely the opposite reasons some Southern Democrats and conservative Republicans favor the Lodge-Gossett proposals or some other system that would break up the unit-vote procedures—for example, having one elector chosen in each congressional district. They argue that the present system gives too much influence to the balance-of-power groups in the Northern and Western states. In 1960 and 1968, for example, a shift of 1 percent of the popular vote would have altered the electoral vote in enough states to have changed the outcome of the elections.

Who Won the Election?

The election is over. The victors and the losers exchange gracious messages. Soon the successful candidates are taking office in White House, Congress, statehouse, and city hall. These are the winners. But aside from the victorious candidates, can we say who really won the election?

NO TOTAL VICTORS

Did a party win it? Only to a limited extent, at best. No party (fortunately) ever sweeps all the national, state, and local elections, nor does any party ever elect all the members of one chamber, such as the House of Representatives. And sometimes one party captures one or both chambers of Congress while the opposition party wins or retains the Presidency, leading to divided party rule. Never in the United States does one party seize control of the legislative and executive branches of the national government to the extent that the winning party in Britain takes command in Parliament and the Cabinet. The point is that our elected candidates are not elected by or responsible to a single monolithic party, but rather to groups inside and outside the party. The party as such did not win the election.

Can we say, then, that any particular group won the election? Of course, certain groups will say that they were the ones that elected the winning candidates. But these claims are exaggerated. Few organized groups are big enough by themselves to muster enough votes for a majority. And big groups, whether economic, religious, or any other, do not vote as a bloc. The most we can say is that the election was won by a combination of segments of groups, or of subgroups.

Was the election a victory for a particular principle or set of ideas? Here again the answer must be "no." Certainly many persons will make this claim. We will hear on television or read in the paper that the election results were a victory for law and order or a repudiation of the bureaucrats. But an election is rarely, if ever, a mandate for particular policies. The party platforms are vague catchalls, and the candidates' promises are often obscure and inconsistent. An electoral majority is made up of many different elements with a variety of views. At best, the election reflects general attitudes of important segments of the voters.

Who, then, did win the election? What do the election results mean? Of course, the winners of the election may have been—at least in the long run—the whole nation, all the people. In a narrower and more immediate sense, the winners were the elected candidates and the voters supporting those candidates —*to the extent that the candidates can follow through on their followers' expectations.* The election results mean simply that the voters have made choices among candidates—choices that give only a rough idea of what the voters are thinking. Election results are not blueprints for future action, but crude guidelines to the general drift of popular feeling, and indications of popular backing for a general direction of government. "A vote," says Lippmann, "is a promise of support. It is a way of saying: I am lined up with these men, on this side."[18]

WHAT ELECTIONS ARE

To understand election results, then, we must remember what elections are and what they are not. Elections are not simply a grand rally of the people, who on their own initiative debate issues, produce candidates, and decide among them. Elections are struggles among party and group leaders who go to the voters for support. The voters are of all types, organized and unorganized, active and passive, concerned with worldwide issues and with petty ones. Elections are not the spontaneous acts of a mass of people but the periodic mobilization of voters by leaders at many levels.

Elections are only one of the ways in which the voters can have a say in their government. The people intervene in other ways between elections —by writing to their congressman and to editors, by signing petitions, by arguing and griping, by organizing in groups. This does not mean that elections are unimportant or uninspiring. Quite the contrary. William B. Munro once said:

A presidential election is merely our modern and highly refined substitute for the ancient revolution; a mobilization of opposing forces, a battle of the ins against the outs; with leaders and strategy and campaign chests and all the other paraphernalia of civil war, but without bodily violence to the warriors. This refinement of the struggle for political control, this transition

[18]Walter Lippmann, *The Phantom Public* (Harcourt, Brace & World, 1925), pp. 56–57.

Drawing by B. Tobey; © 1960 The New Yorker Magazine, Inc.

"Maybe I ought to listen. This is the year I start voting."

from bullets to ballots, is perhaps the greatest contribution of modern times to the progress of civilization.[19]

Elections are vital to democracy, not so much because through elections the citizens are able to make policy, but because through selecting those who do make policy and in a general way instructing them how to act, the citizens confer legitimacy on those who make the decisions and reinforce the idea that the decision-makers should take the citizens' wishes into account. Among the competing groups, one wins and may legitimately claim the right to make the decisions and to have those decisions obeyed. The citizens make it clear that even between elections the winners should take into account what will or will not be acceptable to the electorate. "The general rule that citizen interests should be respected in policy making is given special force by the fact of genuine elections, irrespective of whether, and how, citizens actually cast their votes."[20]

[19]William B. Munro, *The Invisible Government* (Macmillan, 1928), p. 17. For an interesting development of the view that politics is simply the manipulation of rather passive voting groups by elites vying for power, see J. A. Schumpeter, *Capitalism, Socialism, and Democracy* (Harper & Row, 1942), Chaps. 21–23.

[20]Charles L. Lindblom, *The Policy-Making Process* (Prentice-Hall, 1968), p. 45.

Elections are important to serve other functions beyond translating public wishes into governmental policies; the vote is a device to protect personal liberties, and elections create pressures on government officials to solve problems. For as Lindblom had pointed out, in the traditional despotisms a chronic problem is the inactivity of the political leadership, which fails to recognize problems or to feel any compulsion to do anything about them.

Elections set the course of government only in part. Elected officeholders share power with appointed ones, such as judges and administrative officials. All these officials, elected and appointed alike, do not exercise power freely but only within channels set by the forces discussed earlier in this book —the forces of tradition and practice, of laws and institutions, of popular wants and expectations. In the following chapters we turn to our national policy-makers and see how they share and exercise power in the never-ending ferment of ideas, interests, individuals, and institutions.

POLICY-MAKERS FOR THE PEOPLE

PART
FIVE

The main problem posed by Part Five is responsible leadership. By *leadership* we mean the readiness and ability of officials to act effectively in meeting the problems facing the country. By *responsible* we mean the ability of voters sooner or later to hold these officials accountable for their actions.

The Presidency, discussed in Chapters 14 and 15, poses these twin problems sharply. The powers of the office and the assurance of at least a four-year rule give the Chief Executive the tools of leadership, and strong Presidents have used these tools boldly. Has the Presidency gained too much power for a government by the people? This question in turn raises the problem: To whom is the President responsible? Presumably to the majority of the voters, but the Electoral College, as we saw in Chapter 13, tends to make the President especially responsive to the big urban states with their balance-of-power voting blocs.

The problem of responsible leadership also arises in the treatment of Congress in Chapters 16 and 17. How quickly and effectively can Congress take the lead in meeting problems? Except in times of crisis, it may be handicapped by the procedures described in Chapter 16, such as the committee system and the power to filibuster. To whom is Congress responsible? Mainly to the voters, of course. But to which voters? The problem here is that individual members of Congress may respond to special and local groups in their states and districts. Should Congress respond more strongly to a broader interest, such as a majority of the *national* electorate?

What about civil servants and federal judges? These officials are not directly chosen by the voters, and they are not expected to lead in the usual sense. In fact, however, bureaucrats and judges, too, must lead on occasion—for example, when an official takes some clearly desirable action although he is not specifically authorized to do so by law, or when the Supreme Court made its decision in the famous school desegregation case of 1954. To whom are these officials responsible? To the President? To Congress? To the electorate? To their own professional standards? To all these, of course. But what if officials must choose between different kinds of responsibility? These questions arise in Chapters 18 and 19.

There is one key problem running through all the chapters in this part: the problem of majority rule—that is, whether or not President and Congress should be responsible directly and primarily to the majority of voters that elected them to office. Because our political leaders win power through political parties seeking majority support, this problem raises the further question of how strongly, if at all, the winning party should control the leaders in office. Should we make our leaders, executive and legislative and even judicial, more responsible to the majority of the people? In short, do we want some kind of party government? Or do we want a looser, more decentralized political system that gives more power to shifting coalitions of minority groups working through or around our parties? This problem —and its implications for responsible leadership—is explored in Chapter 20. Chapter 20 also deals with the other four basic problems outlined in Chapter 1, including the assumptions of democratic government.

Clearly *representation*—the focal problem of Part Four—and *responsibility*—the main problem of this part—are closely intertwined. In studying representation we are looking at the problem of how the voters are organized (or disorganized or unorganized) to influence political leaders. In studying responsibility we are trying to discover which voters—in groups, in localities, in parties —the leaders are responsible to and just how they are responsible.

The Presidency:
Powers and Paradox

14

During the late 1960s the Presidency as an institution came under fire. This was nothing new—the office has been controversial during much of its existence. Conservatives in particular had long viewed the office as overly liberal, activist, and interventionist. But in the late sixties the Presidency came under fire from a new direction—the New Left—which called it the citadel of the *status quo*, the center of the industrial-military-political complex, the heart of the Establishment. Critics of pluralist democracy saw the office as compounding rather than countering the ills of the system.

The attack was as much on the President as on the Presidency—on Lyndon B. Johnson, who, it was charged, had dragged the nation into a long costly war in Vietnam with neither a formal declaration by Congress nor a mandate from the people. Implicit in this attack was a confusion of the President and the Presidency, but this was not surprising. Part of the paradox of the Presidency has been the inseparability of the person, changing every few years, from the office, continuous and growing. Lyndon Johnson once said that the office "has made every man who occupied it, no matter how small, bigger than he was; and no matter how big, not big enough for its demands." This was an arresting statement, for here was a President of the United States saying that the presidential office was much more than the man who happened to occupy it, that the Presidency had become a power—and perhaps something of a problem—in itself.

This view would have come as something of a shock to George Washington and the Framers of the Constitution. They had carefully created a presidential office with limited powers. They wanted a Chief Executive who would stay clear of parties and factions, enforce the laws passed by Congress, deal with foreign governments, and help the states put down disorders. And yet they did not want the President to be too weak either. They spent many days debating the twin questions: How strong should executive power be? And what relation should the Chief Executive have to the new Congress?

Some of the delegates, such as Alexander Hamilton and James Wilson, wanted a strong chief Executive, independent of the legislature—a Chief Executive who would lend "energy, dispatch, and responsibility" to the new government. Others, such as Roger Sherman, wished to have the Chief Executive appointed by Congress and wholly subject to the legislative will. So fearful were the delegates of a strong President that they decided several times for appointment of the Chief Executive by Congress—a move that would have made the President the instrument of Congress and probably would have given us a European type of parliamentary government. Alternative plans that would have weakened the executive consisted of setting up a plural Presidency, composed of two or three men of equal power, or allowing the President only one four-year term.

In the end the delegates compromised. On the one hand the President would be single rather than plural, eligible for reelection, and independent of the legislature. On the other, he was hemmed in by the system of checks and balances: his major appointments had to be approved by the Senate; Congress could override his veto by a two-thirds vote; he could make treaties only with the consent of two-thirds of the senators; and his power to appeal directly to the voters was muzzled by the electoral college system. Even this Presidency with its mixed set of powers worried many Americans in 1787. But those concerned about presidential power were reassured by the fact that the wise and magisterial George Washington was slated to be the first President.

Such was the origin of the office that has become the mainspring of American government. As the executive has taken on vast powers, the old questions that preoccupied the Framers have been central in the continuing debate over the shape of American government. How strong should the executive be? What should be its relation to Congress? We will return to these questions after considering how the Presidency has grown and how the President carries out his crucial roles today.

The Growth of the Presidency

The growth of the Presidency has not been steady. Washington served essentially the role that the Framers hoped, yet his administration, under the urgings of Hamilton and other activists, took strong leadership in foreign affairs and in fiscal policy. Thomas Jefferson, who had been a strict constructionist of the Constitution and had criticized it in 1787 for granting the Presidency too much power, exercised considerable leadership over Congress. Presidential power ebbed and flowed during the nineteenth century, but it has risen in a rapid and sustained fashion during the twentieth. Today it is the focus of leadership in American government; it is the center of action, "probably the single most important governmental institution in the world."[1] What are some of the basic forces behind the rise of the powerful modern Presidency?

Challenge and crisis. The President can respond to crises more quickly and forcefully than can a Congress of two houses and several hundred legislators. Almost every major domestic or foreign emergency has been seized upon by activist Presidents to make decisions; these decisions in turn set precedents that can be used by later Presidents, as illustrated by the successive intervention of three Presidents in Vietnam. Critics have denounced Presidents for ignoring or overriding Congress, but few have been able to challenge Lincoln's defense of his near-dictatorship: "Was it possible," he asked, "to lose the nation and yet preserve the Constitution? By general law, life and limb must be protected, yet often a limb must be amputated to save a life, but a life is never wisely given to save a limb."

Courtesy Tom Little; © 1965 by The New York Times Company, reprinted by permission.

Foreign affairs. The Constitution gave the President great authority in foreign affairs so that he could act swiftly and the nation could speak with a single voice. But even the perspicacious Framers could hardly have expected that the world would grow so small and the President so predominant. He can act with secrecy, speed, and force. The shrinking of the globe has produced a vast amount of multilateral diplomacy which in turn has required central coordination by the President. The sheer management of the tremendous burden of foreign affairs would go beyond the capacity of Congress today, or even of the Senate alone.

Popular need for leadership. People will turn, especially in times of distress, to the single leader rather than to obscure members and factions of a legislature. This is partly a psychological need for an authority figure, for someone who can produce miracles or at least tell people what to do. It is also partly a popular wish to give authority to a clearly identifiable person so that he can be held accountable. People fear presidential power in the abstract but often demand that specific Presidents—a Lincoln or a Roosevelt—take action even though constitutional checks and balances are disrupted. On the eve of the twentieth century a historian noted that "the greatness of the presidency is the work of the people, breaking through the constitutional form."[2] The President's ability to command radio and television and the attention lavished on his personality and family by newspapers and magazines

[1]David E. Haight and Larry D. Johnston, *The President: Roles and Powers* (Rand McNally, 1965), p. 1.
[2]Henry Jones Ford, *The Rise and Growth of American Politics* (Macmillan, 1898), p. 292.

have doubtless made the people feel more dependent than ever on the solitary figure in the White House.

Economic and social trends. The United States has become a highly urbanized and interdependent society. Such a society puts enormous pressure on government to cope with economic and social crises, to head off problems that loom on the horizon, to act quickly and decisively; and such pressures tend to focus on the President, who can act with national authority and time his moves deftly. Theodore Roosevelt directly intervened to settle a major anthracite strike in 1902, and recently the White House has often been the center of dramatic, last-minute negotiations on the eve of a strike that could paralyze a vital national industry. Franklin Roosevelt acted boldly to ward off financial collapse in 1933, and today no President would dare to sit by idly in the face of an economic recession or even a sharp slump in the stock market. Eisenhower sent troops into Little Rock, Kennedy into Mississippi, and Johnson into several cities. Recurring crises in the cities —civil rights tension, poverty, crime, urban decay—are certain to generate continuing pressures for presidential action.

Is the expansion of presidential power irreversible? From the very beginning Americans have condemned this growth as a violation of the constitutional checks and balances. Henry Clay's attacks on Jackson are part of our great political literature. During the administrations of recent strong Presidents, the criticism has become sharper and more persistent. In 1964 Barry Goldwater charged that believers in a strong Presidency held a "totalitarian philosophy that the end justifies the means." "What, then," asked the Republican presidential candidate, "is the best distribution of power for our society? Our answer to this question has traditionally been a *balance* of power among the various parts of the society. . . . I submit that this balance is being upset today by the trend toward increasing concentration of power in the Presidency. . . . *The more complete and concentrated executive power becomes, the greater will be the temptation to employ it to wipe out all opposing power.*"[3]

We will return to this controversy later. But first, to get a better idea of the size, complexity, and scope of the President's job, we must consider the Chief Executive in each of his six great roles—as chief politician, chief administrator, chief legislator, chief foreign policy maker, Commander in Chief, and chief of state. Truly, the President is many men. But although we shall explore each of these roles in turn, they must not be viewed as separate or compartmentalized. On the contrary, only in the *interweaving* of these different roles can we see the full tapestry of presidential power.

Chief Politician

First and foremost, the President is the leading politician —the most visible and potentially the most effective mobilizer of influence in the American system of power. Politician is a nasty word to many Americans,

[3]Barry Goldwater, "Powers of the Presidency," *Yale Political Review* (Fall 1964), p. 18.

and some Presidents have tried to be above politics. But a President cannot escape it. As a candidate he made promises to the people. As party leader he carries the hopes of a great political organization. To get things done he must work with many people who have somewhat differing loyalties and responsibilities. Inevitably the President is embroiled in legislative politics, judicial politics, bureaucratic politics, and of course foreign politics.

Despite his tremendous powers a President can very rarely command. He spends most of his time persuading people to do what he thinks ought to be done. Of course he has great persuasive power—it is not easy for the average politician or official to resist a President—but in the long run people think mainly of their own interests and obligations. In a government of separated institutions sharing powers,[4] some congressional leaders and even some bureaucratic leaders are beyond the political reach of the President because they have their own constituencies—a House committee, for example, or a powerful interest group. Presidents cannot simply bark out orders like a first sergeant. Before Eisenhower became President, Harry Truman said of him: "He'll sit here, and he'll say, 'Do this! Do that!' *And nothing will happen*. Poor Ike—it won't be a bit like the Army. He'll find it very frustrating."[5] *All* Presidents have found it frustrating.

The President must simply be more skillful at manipulating influence than his rivals. He must know how to marshal all the powers of his office, his own prestige, his reputation for political skill, and even his capacity to inflict political injury on his opponents in order to carry out his policies. Above all he must know how to bargain—to offer something to men who have their own political ambitions just as he does. Here again the President has the trump hand because he has so much to offer—high positions, presidential recognition, assistance to another politician on some pet project, and little courtesies and favors that can mean a great deal (an invitation to a state dinner, a special birthday note, a ride in the presidential limousine or jet). But the President's political resources are not limitless, and in a government that has so many leaders the drain on his resources is very high.

Besides the authority and trappings of his office, the President has two other special sources of political influence—his influence over public opinion and his role as party chief

THE PRESIDENT AND PUBLIC OPINION

No other politician—and few television or film stars—can achieve a closer contact with the people than does the President. Typically, he has been an active public man for years and has built up a host of followers. He has won a nomination and an election and hence has been under the public gaze for months on end. But the White House is the finest platform of all—a "bully pulpit," as Theodore Roosevelt called it. The President has his television studio, which he can use, as Lyndon Johnson did, to appeal directly to the people for understanding and support in the face of foreign crisis. He can summon the press when he wishes, accept an invitation to speak, arrange a

[4]Richard E. Neustadt, *Presidential Power* (Wiley, 1960), p. 33.
[5]Quoted in *ibid.*, p. 9.

"nonpolitical" speaking tour—and he can time all these moves for maximum advantage.

The press conference is an example of how systematically the President can employ the machinery of communication. Years ago the conferences were rather casual affairs. Franklin Roosevelt ran his conferences informally and was a master at withholding information as well as giving it. Under Truman, the conference had become

. . . an increasingly routinized, institutionalized part of the presidential communications apparatus. Preparation became elaborately formalized, as did the conduct of the meetings themselves in their new setting [a State Department auditorium]. . . . Finally, the nature of the meetings as private encounters between the Chief Executive and the newspaper representatives was rapidly changing into a semi-public performance (soon to become completely public) whose transactions were increasingly part of the public record.[6]

Kennedy authorized the first live telecast of a press conference and used it frequently for direct communication with the people. Johnson preferred non-televised meetings with reporters—sometimes while walking at a fast clip around the White House—but the big televised press conference has become a key element of presidential politics.

The President also has advantages in gauging public opinion. He sees the newspaper polls, often before they are published. He receives reports on political attitudes from local party leaders. He can get some idea of public opinion from the letters that pour into the White House, the crowds that greet him on his travels, conversations with visitors. Every President, says a former White House aide, must be a "keen judge of public opinion. He must be able to distinguish its petty whims, to estimate its endurance, to respond to its impatience, and to respect its potential power. He must know how best and how often he can appeal to the public—and when it is better left undisturbed."[7] The President must interpret public opinion not only to follow but to lead it.

Despite these advantages, the President finds difficulties in both gauging and shaping public opinion. As we have mentioned (Chapter 9), public opinion is unstable and murky and hence always somewhat baffling and unpredictable. And when the people do speak with a loud, clear voice, the President may have to ignore it. Some programs may be basically unpopular, and the President may have to move ahead in the absence of dependable support. He must know not only what to do but when to do it. Thus it is said that Kennedy's appeal for fallout shelters in the 1961 Berlin crisis overcame the existing apathy over civil defense, "but it also unleashed an emotional response which grew to near-hysterical proportions (before it receded once again to near-apathy)."[8] And the President can often mobilize opinion behind his own actions without affecting the support for other men's actions. Thus a presidential appeal for support of a civil rights measure in Congress

[6]Elmer E. Cornwell, Jr., *Presidential Leadership of Public Opinion* (Indiana Univ. Press, 1965), p. 175.

[7]Theodore C. Sorensen, *Decision-Making in the White House* (Columbia Univ. Press, 1963), p. 49.

[8]*Ibid.*, pp. 46–47.

might influence many voters—but perhaps not the constituents of key Southern Senators who might control the actual fate of the bill. In short, Presidents may not have much selective influence over public opinion.

PARTY CHIEF

A second main source of influence for the President is his political party. All Presidents since Washington have been party leaders, and generally the stronger the President, the more use he has made of party support. Men such as the two Roosevelts, Wilson, Kennedy, and Johnson fortified their executive and legislative influence by mobilizing support within their party. Yet no President has fully dominated his party, and the history of all Presidents includes party failures as well as party triumphs. How does the President direct his party? Where does his influence stop—and why?

The President is wholly master of the party organization at the national level. He has no formal position in the party structure, but his vast influence over vital national policies and over thousands of appointments commands respect from national party leaders. President and party need each other. He needs the party's backing throughout the government in order to enact his program. The party needs his direction, his prestige, and the political "gravy" that flows from the White House.

The strings of the national organization all lie in the President's hands. Formally, the national party committee picks the national party chairman; actually, the President lets the committeemen know whom he wants—and they choose him. Today the President can hire or fire national party chairmen much as he shifts department heads or even his own staff. Usually his pronouncements on national party policy are more authoritative than any party committee's, even more significant than the party platform itself. The great test of the President's influence in the party is his power to gain renomination if he wishes it, and all recent Presidents have met this test.

Yet the President's power over his party has limits, and his power often comes to an end precisely where he needs it most. He has little influence over the selection of party candidates for Congress and for state and local office. In part the reason is his limited control of state and local organizations; but even more, it is that party organizations themselves do not control their candidates in office. They do not control them because most candidates, as we have seen, win office less through the efforts of the organized party than through their own individual campaigning in both the primary and general elections. Of course the situation varies from place to place. In cities with strong Democratic party leaders, such as Chicago or Albany, a Democratic President may have great influence over the choice of candidates for Congress because (1) he has power over the machine, and (2) the machine picks faithful party men, elects them to office, and expects them to support the President. But most party organizations are not of this type.

Franklin Roosevelt's "purge" of 1938 is a dramatic example of the limits of the President's power. Despite his own sweeping victory in the 1936 election and the lopsided Democratic majorities in Congress, Roosevelt ran into heavy opposition from many Democratic senators and representatives in 1937 and 1938. Angered by this opposition within the party, Roosevelt decided to use his influence to bar the nomination of anti-New Deal candidates in the 1938 congressional primaries. He announced that not as President but as "head of the Democratic party, charged with the responsibility of carrying out the definitely liberal" 1936 Democratic party platform, he would intervene where party principles were clearly at stake. Roosevelt won a significant victory in New York City when he repudiated the anti-New Deal chairman of the House Rules Committee and helped a pro-administration Democrat win nomination. But elsewhere—mainly in the South—he was defeated.

The moral is plain. The President's control over his party has limits, no matter how strong and skillful he is. He cannot, under most circumstances, reach into local party organizations and control their nominations or the policies of their leaders. The President of course is not helpless. He can give a candidate a good deal of recognition and publicity in Washington. He can grant—or deny—campaign assistance and even (indirectly) financial assistance. If he does campaign for his candidate, he will probably encounter less criticism for "invading" the district than Roosevelt did thirty years ago. But his practical influence is sharply limited.

The upshot is that the President often must bargain and negotiate with party leaders as he does with other independent power centers. In most cases he cannot employ the kind of party discipline available to a British prime minister. Lacking full support from the whole party, the President usually falls back on his own personal organization that originally enabled him to gain the presidential nomination. The most effective political organization in the United States in 1968 was not the Republican party but the "Nixon organization" led mainly by Richard Nixon and his staff. Despite their own emphasis on their roles as party leaders, Presidents appeal to independents and even opposition party members to gain and hold power.

Thus President and party need each other—but they also conflict with each other. The President protects his own organization within the party, makes deals with the opposition party, plays down his own party when events compel him to "rise above partisan politics." The national party has its own long-term interests and traditions that may differ somewhat from White House concerns, but the party is not strong enough to elect a President by itself nor to mobilize support for the President's program from all its members on Capitol Hill. The bargaining, the cooperation, and the tension between President and party reflect some of the basic forces toward unity and diffusion in the pluralistic politics of America.

Chief Administrator

Over a century and a half ago, when Jefferson was President, the federal government employed 2,120 persons—Indian commissioners, postmasters, collectors of customs, clerks, tax collectors, marshals, lighthouse-keepers, and the like.[9] Today, by latest count, the President heads a colossal establishment of over 2.8 million federal civilian employees, who

[9]L. D. White, *The Federalists* (Macmillan, 1948), pp. 255–256.

work in more than 1,800 units of federal administration—departments, services, bureaus, commissions, boards, governmental corporations, and other agencies. They work not only in Washington but throughout the world. Their salaries and wages alone amount to well over $10 billion a year.

The Constitution charges the President to "take care that the laws be faithfully executed." But the President can be only a part-time administrator, for his other tasks demand most of his attention. Even if he could devote all his time to running the administrative establishment, it would still have to be organized for leadership and control. It is, of course, so organized. These more than 1,800 agencies are set up in great pyramids, each with its own hierarchical structure. Orders—theoretically at least—flow from President to department head to bureau chief down to the offices, services, and smaller units where they are carried out (see Chapter 18). This is the line, so-called. The President, like all top brass, is assisted by a staff, whose job it is to advise and assist him in managing the administration. This line and staff organization is inherent in any large administrative unit, whether the Army, the General Motors Corporation, or the Veterans Administration.

THE PRESIDENT AND HIS CABINET

Directly in line under the President are the executive departments: State; Treasury; Defense; Interior; Agriculture; Justice; Post Office; Commerce; Labor; Health, Education, and Welfare; Housing and Urban Development; and Transportation. The heads of these twelve departments form the President's Cabinet. Actually the Cabinet has always been a loosely designated body, and it is not always clear who belongs to it. The United States Ambassador to the United Nations, for example, in addition to his other duties, also holds Cabinet rank. Heretofore it has made little practical difference to determine precisely who belongs to the Cabinet, but since the adoption of the Twenty-fifth Amendment (see page 62) the Cabinet, defined in the amendment as "the principal officers of the executive departments," for the first time has been given a constitutional responsibility as a collective body.

It would be hard to find a more unusual or nondescript institution than the Cabinet. It has existed since early in Washington's administration; yet it is not even mentioned by name in the Constitution nor, until the Twenty-fifth Amendment was accepted, had it been referred to as a collective group. In recent years the Vice President has sat with the Cabinet, but the chiefs of great agencies such as the Veterans Administration are not members. However, Presidents often invite high officials—for example, the Budget Director or the Chairman of the Civil Service Commission—to attend Cabinet meetings. Cabinet membership carries high prestige and most Presidents have met regularly with their Cabinets; yet the discussions are often casual, perfunctory, and even listless. Presidents have turned to their Cabinets for advice on a variety of matters; yet votes are rarely taken and the President can ignore Cabinet sentiments if he wishes. (Lincoln, finding the whole Cabinet opposed to him, could say with impunity, "Seven nays, one aye—the ayes have it.") Eisenhower tried to make the Cabinet a more important agency but with little success. Kennedy rarely used his Cabinet for major decisions.

Johnson returned slightly to the Eisenhower pattern but used his Cabinet meetings less to secure advice than to make sure that all Cabinet officials understood administration policies and thus could present a unified public front in behalf of the President's programs.

Still, the Cabinet has a character and importance of its own. Membership in it continues to be the ambition of many politicians. On occasion the meetings are devoted to matters of top policy. And the discussions gain from the fact that Cabinet members usually bring lengthy political and policy-making experience to bear on the problems at hand. Most administrative problems at the White House level are really legislative and political problems.

The Cabinet may in time become a team that both sustains the President and renders him more responsible to the people. But at present the American Cabinet bears little resemblance to the Cabinet described by Harold J. Laski as a "place where the large outlines of policy can be hammered out in common, where the essential strategy is decided upon, where the President knows that he will hear, both in affirmation and in doubt, even in negation, most of what can be said about the direction he proposes to follow." What Cabinet unity there is tends to break down as soon as the members leave the Cabinet room.

In matters of prestige, partisan politics, and legislative relations alike, the Cabinet as a collectivity has only a symbolic value, a value which readily disappears when the need for action supersedes the need for a show window. In the day-to-day work of the Cabinet member, each man fends for himself without much consideration for Cabinet unity. His survival, his support, and his success do not depend on his fellow members. His performance is judged separately from theirs. This condition is but another result of the combination of the centrifugal tendencies of our political system with the low degree of institutionalization which characterizes the Cabinet.[10]

If the Cabinet's role is so limited, how does the President direct his far-flung administrative machine? He meets frequently with individual department and agency chiefs. Crucial decisions are sometimes reached in small, informal conferences between the President, the heads of two or three major departments and agencies, and staff members. Another factor in the President's control of administration is his ultimate power—subject to some limitations noted below—to hire and fire his main lieutenants as he deems fit. The Senate must ratify major appointments, but by tradition the President is allowed considerable freedom to pick his immediate subordinates—and to get rid of them.

Of a total federal civil personnel of about 2.8 million, the President, with the concurrence of the Senate, hires about 16,000. (He can appoint a limited number without Senate assent.) He chooses the department and agency heads who in turn employ thousands of civil servants. Aside from his power to hire and fire, the President directly or indirectly controls promotions, demotions, and transfers, especially at the top levels. The Supreme Court, has upheld (in *Myers* v. *United States*, 1926) the power of the President to remove executive officers at will but has ruled that he has no constitutional

[10]R. F. Fenno, Jr., *The President's Cabinet* (Harvard Univ. Pres, 1959), p. 247.

power to discharge certain officials with part judicial and part legislative functions.

THE MEN AROUND THE PRESIDENT

The single most important means of Presidential control, however, is the White House staff. Americans hear various stories about secret, invisible men who are said to control the President. The simple fact is that the President needs help. He must have advisers to help him handle the momentous questions that crowd into the White House. Much of his effectiveness turns on their loyal, disinterested, expert services.[11] So Washington commentators are right in emphasizing the importance of the men who advise the President. But they are wrong when they imply that there is anything sinister or un-American about this practice. All Presidents from Washington to Nixon have relied heavily on their own staffs.

The President's immediate staff, the White House Office, does not have fixed form; indeed, part of its value lies in its flexibility and adaptability. Most Presidents, however, have an appointments secretary, who lets the right people see the President and keeps the others away; a press secretary, who handles publicity and deals with the scores of newsmen and photographers assigned to the White House; a correspondence secretary, who watches the President's mail and often drafts important letters for his chief; a legal counsel, who advises the President on a variety of matters of broad policy (not merely on legal matters); a diplomatic aide, who acts as the President's eyes and ears on the many-sided diplomatic front in Washington; military aides; and several other key legislative, administrative, and political assistants. The President's top assistants may have far more influence than the equivalent Cabinet member; for example, the President may lean more heavily on his foreign policy assistants for an opinion on an urgent international matter than on the Secretary of State.

Just outside this inner circle of the White House Office are a complex of agencies and their heads who report directly to the President and who are roughly grouped together in what is called the Executive Office of the President. Today in addition to the White House Office, the Bureau of the Budget, Council of Economic Advisers, National Security Council, National Aeronautics and Space Council, Office of Emergency Planning, Office of Economic Opportunity, Office of the Special Representative for Trade Negotiations, National Council on Marine Resources and Engineering Development, and Office of Science and Technology are located in the Executive Office of the President (see pages 352–355). Each of these agencies and their heads report directly to the President because their responsibility is to help the President carry out his duties.

Not all the assistants in the White House Office or in the Executive Office of the President are, of course, of equal influence, and sometimes men without any formal governmental post have direct access to the President. All our Presidents have drawn around them small groups of men in whom they have confidence: Andrew Jackson had his kitchen cabinet; Abraham Lincoln his

[11]See discussion in Louis Koenig, *The Invisible Presidency* (Holt, 1960); and Francis H. Heller, *The Presidency: A Modern Perspective* (Random House, 1960), Chap. 2.

personal advisers; Woodrow Wilson his Colonel House; Franklin Roosevelt his Harry Hopkins; Dwight Eisenhower his Sherman Adams; John F. Kennedy his brother Robert, who was also Attorney General; Johnson his young aides Bill D. Moyers and Joseph Califano; and Nixon his Herbert Klein and Robert Finch, who was also a Cabinet member.

Why does the President lean so heavily on his personal staff and political advisers? Why does he not use the Cabinet or heads of vital departments for the day-to-day advice? The answer is simple. The staff can give the President the help he wants. It can do so because the President can, for the most part, juggle his staff membership and organization in a way that will be most helpful to him. He chooses the men he wants; he chooses them for their experience, for their ability to work as part of a team, and above all for their loyalty to himself. Nowhere else—not in Congress, not in his Cabinet, not in his party—can he find the loyalty, the single-mindedness, and the team spirit that he can build, if he is a leader, among his close aides. Such a staff is important to him and to the country—so important that it has come to be widely accepted that the President should have the utmost freedom in organizing his staff as he wishes.[12]

Chief Legislator

Because the national government is divided into the executive, legislative, and judicial branches, many people assume that the President has only administrative functions, the Senate and House only legislative, and the judiciary only judicial. Actually, as we have seen, the essence of the system is an intermingling of powers. The President is a prime example. The Constitution grants him certain policy-making power—that is, legislative power. And a century and a half of national growth and recurrent crises have vastly increased that power. Today he and his aides ordinarily have more influence over national policy than any single congressman or group of congressmen; truly the President is chief legislator.[13]

The Constitution ordains that the President "shall from time to time give to the Congress Information of the State of the Union, and recommend to their Consideration such Measures as he shall judge necessary and expedient." From the start, strong Presidents have exploited this power. Washington and Adams came in person to Congress to deliver information and recommendations. Jefferson and many Presidents after him sent written messages, but Wilson restored the practice of delivering a personal, and often dramatic, message. Franklin Roosevelt made personal appearances a means of drawing the attention of the whole nation to his program—with the invaluable help of radio and camera. The President can also dramatize his policies by calling either or both houses of Congress into special session, although the legislators need not act if they do not wish to.

[12]See Koenig, *op. cit.*, esp. Chap. 6.

[13]For description of the institutionalization of the President's legislative role, see Richard E. Neustadt, "Presidency and Legislation: Planning the President's Program," *The American Political Science Review* (December 1955), pp. 980–1021.

Less obvious but perhaps equally important are the frequent written messages dispatched from the White House to Capitol Hill on a vast range of public problems. Often mumbled indistinctly by a clerk, these messages may not create much stir at the moment, but they are important in defining the administration's position and giving a lead to friendly legislators. Moreover, these messages are often accompanied by detailed drafts of legislation that may be put into the hopper with hardly a change. These administration bills, the products of bill-drafting experts on the President's own staff or in the departments and agencies, may be mauled and mutilated by Congress — but many of the original provisions may survive unscathed.

THE POWER TO SAY NO

The President can *veto* a bill by returning it with his objections to the house in which it originated. Congress, by a two-thirds vote in each chamber, may then pass it over his veto. If the President does not sign or veto the bill within ten weekdays after he receives it, the bill becomes law without his signature. If Congress adjourns within the ten weekdays, however, the President, by taking no action, can kill the bill. This is known as the *pocket veto.*

The veto is sometimes a strong, sometimes a feeble, weapon. Its essential strength lies in the ordinary failure of Congress to muster a two-thirds majority of both houses in favor of a policy that the President has told the people he dislikes. Historically Congress has overridden only about 3 percent of the Presidents' vetoes.[14] Yet a Congress that can repeatedly mobilize such a majority against a President can virtually take command of the government. Such was the fate of President Andrew Johnson. Faced after 1866 with a House of Representatives almost three to one against his reconstruction policies, he was virtually helpless as bill after bill was passed stripping him of his powers; in fact, he barely escaped being ousted from office. Eisenhower, on the other hand, though faced with a Democratic-controlled Congress for six of his eight years as President, had only 2 of his 181 vetoes overturned (most of them were pocket vetoes, however).

In ordinary times, Congress can manipulate legislation to reduce the likelihood of a presidential veto. For example, it can attach irrelevant but controversial provisions, called *riders*, to vitally needed legislation; the President must either accept or reject the whole bill, for he does not have the power to strike out individual items in the bill — that is, he does not have the *item veto*. Appropriations are a special case in point. In one appropriations bill the lawmakers may combine badly needed funds for the armed forces with a host of costly pork-barrel items, but the President must take or reject the whole bill. Governors of most states do have the power of item veto, and President Eisenhower and others have urged that the President should too.

For his part, the President can use the veto power in a positive as well as a negative way. He can announce openly or let it be known quietly that a bill under consideration by Congress will be turned back at the White

[14]Carlton Jackson, *Presidential Vetoes: 1792–1945* (Univ. of Georgia Press, 1967).

House door unless certain changes have been made. He can use the threat of a veto against some bill Congress badly wants in exchange for another bill that he wants. But the veto is essentially a negative weapon, of limited use to a President who has a positive program. For it is the President who usually is pressing for action. It is Congress that has the real power to say no.

FILLING IN THE DETAILS

Most federal legislation today deals with highly complex situations. A labor law, for example, may affect a great variety of industries, a number of different unions, all kinds of labor-management relationships, and diverse attitudes and traditions in different parts of the country. Agricultural legislation may deal with certain farm problems in general, but in practice the law affects big farmers and small ones, prosperous ones and marginal ones, cotton farmers, wheat farmers, applegrowers, and so on. No matter how wise Congress might be, it could not write a law that would automatically adapt itself to such different situations. Indeed, to try to do so would be to put the administrator into a straitjacket and to make the law unworkable. Hence Congress often must content itself with prescribing general standards and delegating to the President and administrators the job of filling in the details of the laws. Such subordinate legislation is usually issued in the President's executive orders and in circulars, orders, rules, regulations, directives, and so on, issued by departments, regulatory boards, and other agencies.

Much of this delegation of legislative power allows making decisions within rather narrow limits. For example, a law may permit the President to alter tariff or minimum-wage standards to some extent, but only in terms of a standard laid down by Congress. Yet such standards vary greatly in precision. The Trade Agreement Act of 1934, its extensions, and especially the Trade Expansion Act of 1962 empowered the President to make trade agreements with foreign nations lowering existing tariff rates by as much as 50 percent and under certain conditions abolishing completely tariffs on some items. Other acts authorize him to suspend the eight-hour day for federal employees, to issue civil service rules, to prevent the export of certain raw materials.

An even wider delegation of legislative power is contained in the several Reorganization Acts. Since 1939 Congress by a series of measures has given the President authority to reduce and rearrange certain federal agencies through plans that come into effect sixty days after being sent to Congress unless disapproved by a majority of either the House or the Senate. Here is a delegation of power that amounts almost to a reversal of the usual formal relation between Congress and the Chief Executive. (Perhaps this is simply formal recognition of what in practice has come to be the relation between Congress and the President, the President initiating legislation, the Congress approving or vetoing it.)

Thus Congress, while setting objectives and standards, in practice allows the President not only to fill in the details but even to decide when action shall be taken. It is one thing to delegate the carrying out of specific provisions; it is something else to delegate the power to say when and whether a law will be invoked or applied. Why has Congress seen fit to delegate such sweeping powers? The reason is partly the willingness of the legislators to face the facts of modern life and to allow the President to do quickly and effectively what they could do, at best, haltingly and ineffectively. The reason is also that Congress is often so dominated by warring factions that it cannot find common ground on which to act. It defers to the President because he can act. The Constitution, it is true, prevents Congress from giving away its "essential" legislative powers. But as long as Congress lays down some kind of standard, the Supreme Court has been willing to approve extensive delegation of power.

THOUSANDS OF LEGISLATORS

Just as Congress must delegate legislative power to the President, so he must delegate policy-making power to hosts of administrators down the line. Obviously the Secretary of State has a decided influence on policy, as do other department heads and bureau, division, and section chiefs. In a sense, there is no level in the administrative hierarchy at which discretion ends. Even a secretary may make policy decisions by determining which matters or visitors her superior should turn to first—or at all. Routine, noncontroversial decisions are made at the lower levels, vital and difficult ones at the top echelons. But at any time the most routine matter may be called to the public's attention, perhaps by a newspaper columnist or a congressman. Then the matter will be pulled out of the lower echelon and given consideration by a bureau or department chief—perhaps even by the White House.[15]

In short, there are thousands of legislators throughout the government (and millions more, such as editors, lobbyists, and ordinary citizens, outside) who exert pressure on a democratic government. Control of legislation cannot be diagramed neatly—with Congress on top, the President in the middle, and a pyramid of department, bureau, and division heads below. Rather, it is a circular system, with President and congressmen cooperating on some matters, fighting over others, and both influencing—and being influenced by—the administrators throughout the government and political forces outside.

Moreover, history and politics have bestowed on certain agencies a degree of independence from the White House. The Federal Bureau of Investigation in the Department of Justice, the Bureau of Reclamation in the Interior Department, and the Corps of Engineers in the Department of the Army are agencies somewhat insulated from the White House because of the prestige of their chiefs or the closeness of the agencies to blocs in Congress and to interest groups outside. The independent regulatory commissions (see Chapter 18) are a special case. The President appoints the commissioners, with the consent of the Senate, but his power to discharge them is limited to that which Congress is willing to authorize. Hence they are often at liberty to make policies at variance with those of the administration. (Here is one more set of legislators on the Washington scene.)

Thus, the President shares his legislative power not only with Congress but also with administrators in the executive branch that he himself heads.

[15]Paul H. Appleby, *Policy and Adminstration* (Univ. of Alabama Press, 1949), p. 82.

The extent to which he wields legislative power turns not only on his formal constitutional position and powers but also on his political position and powers. His political powers turn on many factors. How effective is he in appealing to the public? To what extent can he dramatize official business? How magnetic is he on radio or television? How good is his timing? How active and articulate are his lieutenants—his Cabinet members and key agency heads? How close are his relations with congressional leaders? Can he mobilize public opinion on crucial issues? Does his influence reach into states and districts throughout the country?

Obviously a President's power turns to a great extent on his public prestige and standing. But in the daily task of getting things done in Washington, his effectiveness turns also on his professional reputation in a city peopled by thousands of expert politicians. These professional politicians are in Congress, the foreign embassies, the executive departments, the interest-group association headquarters, the White House itself. Because the President's power, and his employment of it, is by far the most important single influence in Washington, these professionals must watch him narrowly. Does he carry through on what he promises people? Does he reward those who help him and punish—or at least withhold favors from—those who do not? How well does he bargain with other power centers? To what extent, in short, is he on top of the struggle for power, or submerged in it, or remote from it? The President's political skill and his political power are interrelated; Washington politicians must anticipate as best they can his ability and will to make the most of the bargaining advantages he has. Out of what others think of him and his power emerge his opportunities for influence with them.[16]

Chief Foreign Policy Maker

The Framers of the Constitution foresaw a special need for speed and single-mindedness in our dealings with other nations. The Constitution makes the President the exclusive spokesman for the United States. It gives him control over relations with foreign powers. It vests in him command of the two major instruments of foreign policy—the diplomatic corps and the armed services. It gives him responsibility for negotiating with foreign powers. It permits him to make commitments in behalf of the Unites States. The Constitution specifically assigns to the President the authority to appoint, with the consent of the Senate, all United States representatives to foreign nations and to "receive ambassadors and other public ministers."

The power to appoint and receive ambassadors involves the vital power of *recognition*. The President has complete discretion to recognize or not to recognize new governments or states. In 1902 Theodore Roosevelt recognized the new state of Panama a few hours after a revolt had been staged

[16]Neustadt, *op. cit.*, p. 60.

with the help of United States forces. President Wilson withheld recognition from Mexican governments of which he disapproved, and President Hoover tried to restrain Japan by refusing to recognize its puppet Manchukuo. In 1933 President Roosevelt recognized the government of the Soviet Union, whose existence the United States had officially ignored for sixteen years. Presidents Truman, Eisenhower, Kennedy, Johnson, and Nixon withheld recognition from Red China.

EXECUTIVE AGREEMENTS

The Chief Executive shares his treaty-making power with the Senate. Presidents have found an easy way, however, to bypass the Senate under certain conditions. This is the *executive agreement*. Well over half the international agreements signed by the United States have been achieved by this procedure, which simply involves an act by the President without any participation whatsoever by Senate or House. Some executive agreements have signalized famous events, such as the Boxer Protocol of 1901 and the Atlantic Charter. In addition to executive agreements based on the President's own constitutional powers, Congress often confers authority on the Chief Executive to make agreements with other nations. The reciprocal trade program is an important example. Of course, executive agreements, like treaties, may be set aside by the legislature. But unless they are, they seem to have in the eyes of the courts much the same legal validity as treaties. To be sure, treaties possess a "constitutional and moral control over the conscience and conduct of the American people,"[17] but agreements made by Presidents with the prestige of a Franklin Roosevelt or a Dwight Eisenhower or a John Kennedy have an authority all their own.

The destroyer agreement with Britain was a striking example of the uses of executive agreements. In 1940 Britain urgently needed destroyers to protect her shores and convoys. President Roosevelt and his advisers, convinced that prompt action was vital, feared that the Senate might not act fast enough in ratifying a treaty, or might not act at all. By executive agreement the President traded fifty over-age American destroyers to the Birtish in return for long-term leases on military and naval bases in the Western Hemisphere. The move won a good deal of popular support; presented with a *fait accompli*, Congress made no attempt to repudiate the agreement.

How much power does the Chief Executive have over foreign relations? The Supreme Court has repeatedly upheld strong presidential authority in this area. In the Curtiss-Wright case in 1936 the Court referred to the "exclusive power of the President as the sole organ of the Federal Government in the field of international relations—a power which does not require as a basis for its exercise an act of Congress, but which of course, like every other governmental power, must be exercised in subordination to the applicable provisions of the Constitution." These are sweeping words. Yet Congress itself does have significant power in foreign relations. It controls the funds to back up our policies abroad. It is a forum of debate and criticism. And it can

[17]George B. Galloway, *Congress at the Crossroads* (Crowell, 1946), p. 269.

take back powers that it has delegated the President in the realm of foreign affairs.[18]

THE POWER TO ACT

The President has not only the authority but the capacity to act. For example, he has at his command unmatched sources of information. To his desk come facts channeled from the entire world. Diplomatic missions, military observers, undercover agents, personal agents, and technical experts gather tons of material which are analyzed by experts in the State Department and elsewhere. Because the President draws on the informed thinking of hundreds of specialists, his pronouncements have a tone of authority. The President and his experts are sometimes wrong and many gaps appear in their information, but his sources of information give him a clear advantage over Congress.

Diplomacy, moreover, frequently requires quick action. The President can act swiftly; Congress cannot. Diplomacy often has to be secret; as Harold Laski has said, diplomatic negotiations, like a proposal of marriage, must be made in private even if the engagement is later discussed in public. The President can act secretly; Congress cannot. For these and other reasons, Congress has granted the President wide discretion on questions affecting foreign policy and military security. Today the President has leeway in such matters as controlling foreign trade and exchange, restricting imports and exports, buying military supplies without bids, and restricting immigration—even aside from his vast constitutional powers as Commander in Chief in time of crisis (see next section). Congress thus has given up tremendous amounts of its power over foreign policy.

But the limits to presidential power should not be overlooked. Checks and balances operate in foreign policy making and cannot be ignored. For example, Congress must finance the President's policies—a power of special importance when so much of our foreign policy consists of economic and military aid to other countries.

Commander in Chief

"The President shall be Commander in Chief of the Army and Navy of the United States," reads Section 2 of Article II of the Constitution. Even though this is the first of the President's powers listed in the Constitution, the Framers intended that his military role be a limited one. As Hamilton pointed out in *The Federalist*, the President as Commander in Chief would be far less powerful than a king. The President's authority, Hamilton said, "would amount to nothing more than the supreme command and direction of the military and naval forces"; he would be a sort of first general and first admiral of the new nation. As things have turned out, how-

[18]For a penetrating analysis of presidential-congressional relations in foreign relations, see D. S. Cheever and H. F. Haviland, Jr., *American Foreign Policy and the Separation of Powers* (Harvard Univ. Press, 1952).

ever, the President has become far more powerful, as both the custodian and wielder of the nation's armed forces, than Hamilton foresaw.[19] Today the President has wide powers as Commander in Chief during peacetime, and in wartime his authority increases sharply.

IN PEACETIME

The President is supreme military commander. He appoints, with the consent of the Senate, all officers of the armed forces, from ensigns and second lieutenants to five-star generals. This is a vitally important function; it means that largely on the President's shoulders rests the job of determining who will boss our military forces and plan the overall strategy. He can also dismiss the top brass, as when President Truman relieved General MacArthur of his Far Eastern command in 1952. The President also has charge of such matters as defense plans and the disposition of forces, but these military decisions he generally leaves to the chiefs of staff and other commanders.

The President's peacetime powers are limited by the same factors that restrict him as chief administrator and chief legislator—the checks and balances within government and the strength of the opposition. Congress has the power to raise armies, to enact military regulations, and to appropriate money. In practice, Congress delegates a good deal of military rule-making to the Commander in Chief, but the legislators can revoke such grants if they wish. Congressmen also make full use of their right to investigate, to question, and to criticize, especially when the military chiefs come around requesting additional funds. Occasionally, members of Congress try to take a hand in strategic and diplomatic activities, often with unhappy results.

The Constitution delegates to Congress the authority to declare war (with the consent of the President), but in practice the Commander in Chief precipitates war. This supreme power of making war has been used by the Chief Executive time and time again. President Polk in 1846 ordered American forces to advance into disputed territory; when Mexico resisted, Polk informed Congress that war existed by act of Mexico, and a formal declaration of war was soon forthcoming. President McKinley's dispatch of a battleship to Havana, where it was blown up, helped precipitate war with Spain in 1898. In 1918, when no state of war existed between the United States and Russia, President Wilson sent American forces to Siberia to join Allied troops fighting the Bolsheviks. The United States was not formally at war with Germany until late 1941, but prior to Pearl Harbor President Roosevelt ordered the Navy to guard convoys to Great Britain and to open fire on submarines threatening the convoys. President Truman had no specific authorization from Congress in 1950 when he ordered American forces to resist aggression in Korea. Neither did President Eisenhower when he dispatched forces to Lebanon in 1958. Nor did President Kennedy when he ordered a troop buildup during the Berlin crisis of 1961, when he sent forces into Southeast Asia in the spring of 1962, or when he ordered a naval quarantine of Cuba in the fall of 1962. Nor did President Johnson when he bolstered

---

[19]E. S. Corwin, *The President: Office and Powers* (New York Univ. Press, 1957), p. 283.

American forces in Vietnam from 1965 to 1968 and sent troops into the Dominican Republic.

In the context of modern times, Congress's formal authority to declare war has become obsolete. In Korean and South Vietnamese types of hostilities, formal declarations of war are no longer made. If a total war should come, the aggressor is unlikely to make a formal declaration of war before the bombs have fallen. After they have fallen a formal declaration of war is likely to be impossible, and if possible meaningless.

THE PRESIDENT'S WAR POWERS

When the nation engages in extensive and extended military conflicts —short of a nuclear holocaust which would destroy organized society—the central need in a democracy is for unity, teamwork, discipline, in addition to the preservation of our basic liberties. The people want leadership and instinctively they turn to the President. He can tap a vast reservoir of power in planning broad strategy, raising military and industrial manpower, mobilizing the nation's economy.

In wartime the White House becomes GHQ for governmental as well as for military and industrial mobilization. Political power, which is ordinarily dispersed throughout the national government, is then largely centered in the President. He becomes a sort of constitutional dictator. For example, he makes secret diplomatic agreements with foreign powers, far surpassing in importance many treaties that in peacetime would require senatorial consent. He authorizes the allotment of billions of dollars of funds appropriated by Congress. He takes final responsibility for crucial military decisions—as in the case of Roosevelt's decision in World War II to concentrate our armed might against Hitler before finishing off Japan. Constitutional forms are not abandoned, of course. But in wartime the people become unified behind one goal—victory—and the solidarity of the people compels a unity in the government behind the President. Opposition congressmen may continue to snipe at the Commander in Chief's nonmilitary plans or policies, such as domestic economic policy or postwar peace goals, but they will not ordinarily obstruct his war program, even though they may lack confidence in it, as many senators do in the case of Vietnam.

These vast powers of the President in wartime are not a recent development. It was Lincoln, struggling to overcome the crisis of civil war, who set the vital precedents for presidential quasi-dictatorship. Congress was not in session when Lincoln was inaugurated in March 1861; despite the emergency (or perhaps because of it) the new President did not even call Congress into session for four months. Also, Congress itself has handed the President great chunks of authority during wartime. In World War II, Congress delegated vast authority to the President, who redelegated it to price, production, manpower, and transportation czars, who in turn were coordinated by super-czars. Mr. Roosevelt used Lincolnian as well as Wilsonian precedents. In 1942, when Congress refused to repeal a provision in the price-control act that protected the farmers, the President demanded that Congress act within a month—or he would. This action of Roosevelt's has been called "a claim of power on the part of the President to suspend the Constitution in a situation deemed by him to make such a step necessary."[20] In any event, Mr. Roosevelt's maneuver worked; Congress meekly repealed the provision.

Under the Constitution, a wartime President can direct military operations (taking the field himself if he wishes), establish military government in conquered lands, and end hostilities by means of an armistice. Under authority likely to be granted by Congress, he can raise armies, lend or give money or goods to other countries, take over strikebound plants, requisition property needed for defense, ration goods and set prices, shift military functions from one agency to another, censor mail, control vital imports and exports, and so on. The list is long—and a compliant Congress will delegate even more emergency powers if the President requests them.

Certain forms of the Constitution may seem to be suspended. But two basic consitutional rights remain—or a least have remained in all our wars so far. One is the ultimate control of the President by the people. In no war so far have elections been suspended. And so far, despite certain restrictions, our basic liberties of free speech and free press have survived the hard test of war.

Chief of State

As Commander in Chief the President represents the whole nation. He is not directing the war for the benefit of Republicans or Democrats; of businessmen, farmers, or workers; of Easterners, Northerners, or Southerners. He is acting for all the people. His military role, his ceremonial function, and his national responsibilities combine to make him a powerful chief of state representing the whole nation and rising above the claims of majority or minority groups.

Such was the role the Framers of the Constitution hoped the President would fulfill. Looking on him as a sort of chief magistrate, they gave him judicial duties as well. These duties stem from the "power to grant reprieves and pardons for offenses against the United States, except in cases of impeachment." This *pardoning power* leaves the President a good deal of discretion. He can withhold a pardon altogether, or simply grant a reprieve (a delay in executing sentence), or lighten the sentence (for example, by substituting life imprisonment for the death penalty), or grant a pardon subject to certain qualifications, or give a full pardon, which makes the offender, in the eyes of the law, as innocent as if he had never committed the offense. Neither Congress nor the courts can overrule a pardon. Because a President receives hundreds of applications for pardons a year, he must lean heavily on advice from the Department of Justice. The pardoning power also includes *amnesty*, a device for pardoning a specific group of persons at one stroke. In the 1860s Presidents Lincoln and Johnson granted amnesties to Southerners who had taken part in secession.

Even the Founding Fathers could hardly have foreseen the extent to which the President would become the ceremonial head of the nation. No

[20]E. S. Corwin, *Total War and the Constitution* (Knopf, 1947), p. 64; see also Nathan Grundstein, *Presidential Delegation of Authority in Wartime* (Univ. of Pittsburgh, 1961).

doubt they expected him to receive ambassadors in the manner of a king and to issue proclamations on matters of national, nonpartisan concern. But today his ritualistic role surpasses this. He pitches out the first baseball of the season, buys Christmas seals, presses buttons that start big power projects, hurries to the scene of national catastrophes, speaks on the Fourth of July and other patriotic occasions, reviews parades, and receives delegations of Boy Scouts, veterans, and the like. Often these actions may be part of a deliberate effort to humanize the man and the job, a reaching for popular support. But there is also the tendency of people to turn to him. Even in a democracy—perhaps especially in a democracy—the people need a leader. They need someone who will personalize government and authority, who will simplify politics, who will symbolize the protective role of the state, who will seem to be concerned with them. How else explain the gifts they shower on him, the tens of thousands of letters that pour into the White House, especially in time of crisis, the sense of private grief felt by masses of people when a President dies? The President is head of the political family; as a sort of father image he satisfies a deep-seated desire for a leader and protector.

The role of the national leader, then, is vital in the United States. American acceptance of leadership does not rest essentially on blind worship, as is the case with Fascists or Communists, but on an awareness that in a competitive society the exceptional leader should be allowed to emerge from the mass, take a commanding position, and receive a vote of confidence (at least at the outset). Gunnar Myrdal, a brilliant Swedish social scientist who studied American society, has remarked on the "patterns of strong and competitive personal leadership and weak followership" in the United States. He sees our type of "individual leadership as a great strength of this nation, but the passivity of the masses as a weakness."[21]

All these factors—constitutional, political, and psychological—serve to accentuate the President's role as chief of state, as leader of the nation. Yet under ordinary conditions, the President as leader of all the people keeps running headlong into the President trying to act for part of the people.

The point is that the President's functions are fundamentally inconsistent with one another. On the one hand he is a party leader, the spokesman and representative of a popular majority more or less organized in the party that he heads. As party chief he not only directs the national party organization; he also uses his powers as chief legislator to effect the party's program. On the other hand, as Commander in Chief and chief of state he must act for all the people, regardless of group or faction. As chief administrator he must faithfully administer the laws, whether these laws were passed by Democratic or Republican majorities in Congress; yet in choosing his subordinates and in applying the law, he tends to think first of the interests of his popular majority.

Sometimes the relationship between the two Presidents is uneasy. For example, the President may wish to address the nation on an important problem. As President he is entitled to free time on the radio and TV networks. But if an election is in the offing, the opposition often charges that the President is really acting in his capacity as party chief and that his party should pay for the radio or TV time. The same question comes up in connection with the

---

[21]Gunnar Myrdal, *An American Dilemma* (Harper & Row, 1962), pp. 709–719. See also Eric Hoffer, *The True Believer* (Harper & Row, 1951).

President's inspection trips, especially when he uses them as occasions for political talks and general politicking. The President is often accused, too, of executing laws in a partisan manner, of putting party regulars into administrative offices, of issuing executive orders favorable to the interests of the majority he leads.

During normal times, however, the President usually manages to combine his roles of chief of state and party leader without too much difficulty. The people expect him to hold both roles, and he moves from one to the other as conditions demand. We are accustomed to seeing the President operate as national leader in conferring with a foreign envoy, only to don partisan clothing an hour later in conferring with party leaders.

During times of emergency the problem tends to solve itself. A crisis at home or abroad demands leadership, and people in both parties instinctively turn to the White House for decision and action. The President doffs his party robes and emerges as national leader or chief of state, as Kennedy did in 1962 when he suddenly broke off campaigning in the congressional elections and returned to Washington to take charge of the threat of Russian missile bases in Cuba. Two basic changes take place. First, as we have seen, the President assumes extraordinary powers. A serious crisis invariably results in an "increase in the prestige and competence of the President."[22] The President's hold on the people is so strong, his responsibility for action is so great, that Congress almost always follows where he wishes to lead. To meet the crisis he is given wide freedom of action. The normal checks and balances in government are largely suspended.

Even more significant, the normal opposition to the President vanishes—or at least breaks into fragments. To be sure, critics remain. But most of the criticism involves relatively petty matters—problems of mechanics, of methods, of procedures. There remains little organized opposition to the President's basic strategy. This was the case with Vietnam during the early years of our involvement. If any party or group opposes the President, it may be suspected of seeking to sap the solidarity of the great majority. Such an opposition element may even be accused of lacking in Americanism. Under such conditions the opposition is likely to vanish.

All this may be inevitable. But is it healthy in a democracy? As chief of state, the President is responsible to the nation as a whole and has wide latitude in making his decisions and shaping his program. Some decisions he must make virtually alone. He lacks the guidelines that help chart the course of the party President. Being responsible to his majority is one thing. Being responsible to the whole people as chief of state is something else.

The Roles Combined: Presidential Government

We have been looking first at one function of the Presidency and then another, but we must see the Presidency as a combined operation. A President cannot conduct foreign policy or direct his political party with-

[22]C. L. Rossiter, *Constitutional Dictatorship* (Princeton Univ. Press, 1948), p. 217.

out consideration for his roles as chief administrator or chief of state. The roles may fortify each other or threaten each other. Thus the President gains influence over Congress from his role as party chief, but his obligations to his party may handicap his efforts to rise above politics and appeal to the whole electorate as chief of state.

The whole Presidency, in short, is far more than the sum of its parts. We have created a system of presidential government that may go down in history as the most striking American contribution in this century to the art of governing large democracies. Presidential government is also more than the various Presidents who come and go. It is the perpetuation and enlargement of a set of great powers; it is also the institutionalization of a vast executive establishment.

PRESIDENTIAL POWERS

The President of the United States assumes the following responsibilities:

1   Shares with Congress power over the 2.8-million-man executive establishment but has been strengthening and centralizing his own authority in recent years

2   Has a crucial initiative in policy-making and legislation and exercises a limited constitutional veto and a broader political veto over measures passed by Congress

3   Is the chief economic decision-maker through his control over the budget, the federal financial institutions, and federal spending

4   As chief politician runs his own party at the national level; establishes the ground on which the opposition party must debate and maneuver; challenges, curbs, cooperates, and bargains with major political interest groups; appeals directly to the mass public through the most powerful instruments of propaganda and persuasion

5   Can on his own decision plunge the nation into little wars, big wars, or cold wars with or without any formal participation by Congress

6   Almost wholly monopolizes power over foreign policy subject only to advice, occasional resistance over appropriations, and sporadic harassment from Capitol Hill

7   As the chief personage, symbolic leader, and spokesman of the whole nation gains continuous publicity from the press and becomes a hero to millions of his supporters throughout the nation

8   Combines all these powers in a single institution and a single person for maximum effectiveness in the mobilizing of influence at home and abroad

THE PRESIDENTIAL ESTABLISHMENT

Tourists passing by 1600 Pennsylvania Avenue often remark on the charm and simplicity of the White House. The mansion itself is small compared to those of many foreign potentates, and the administrative offices are neatly tucked away in the low west wing. Actually this west wing houses the President's main office (he also has a study on the second floor of the mansion)

The White House

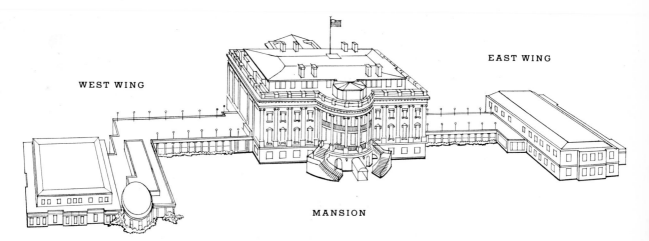

WEST WING

EAST WING

MANSION

The White House is an executive agency, a ceremonial mansion, and a home. But one man is dominant—whether instructing his aides in the West Wing, presiding over a state dinner, or talking with guests in the family living room. All the White House compartments must fit the purposes of the man in the Oval Office.

EAST WING

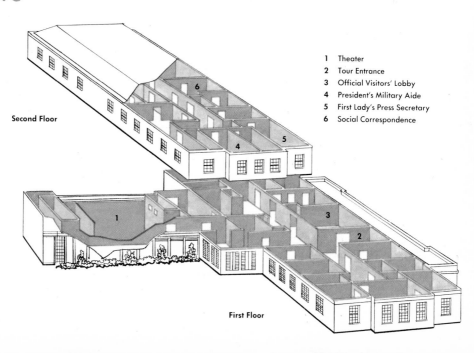

Second Floor

First Floor

1 Theater
2 Tour Entrance
3 Official Visitors' Lobby
4 President's Military Aide
5 First Lady's Press Secretary
6 Social Correspondence

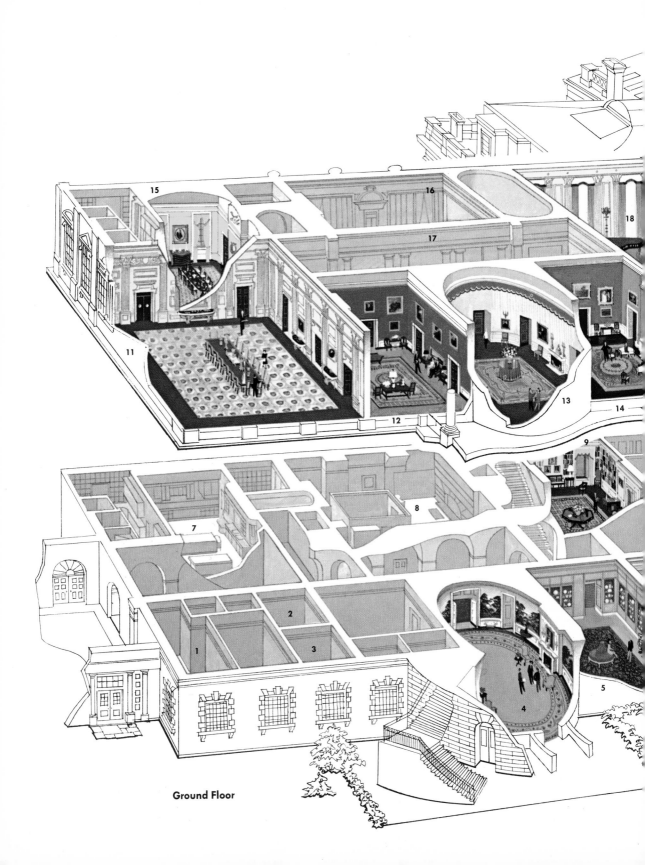

Ground Floor

Third Floor

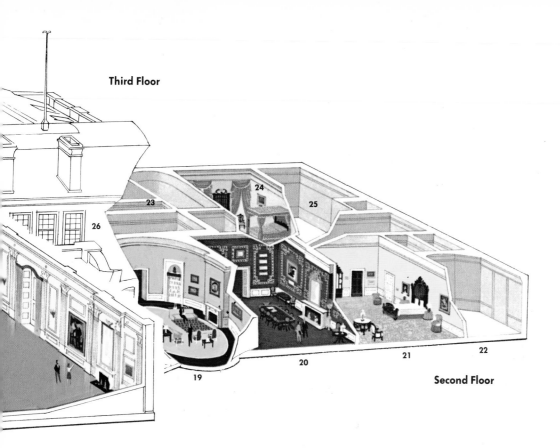

Second Floor

First Floor

MANSION

Ground Floor

1 Housekeeper
2 Secret Service
3 Doctor's Office
4 Diplomatic Reception Room
5 China Room
6 Gold Room
7 Kitchen
8 White House Curator
9 Library
10 Vaulted Arch Hallway

First Floor

11 State Dining Room
12 Red Room
13 Blue Room
14 Green Room
15 Private Dining Room
16 Entrance Hall
17 Main Hallway
18 East Room

Second Floor

19 Yellow Oval Room
20 Treaty Room (Monroe Room)
21 Lincoln Bedroom
22 Lincoln Sitting Room
23 Presidential Family Living Quarters
24 Queen's Room (Rose Room)
25 Queen's Sitting Room

Third Floor

26 Staff Living Quarters

WEST WING

1 Situation Room
2 National Security Council
3 Oval Office
4 President's Secretary
5 Cabinet Room
6 Press Lobby
7 Fish Room (conference room)
8 Press Room
9 Presidential Press Secretary
10 Swimming Pool

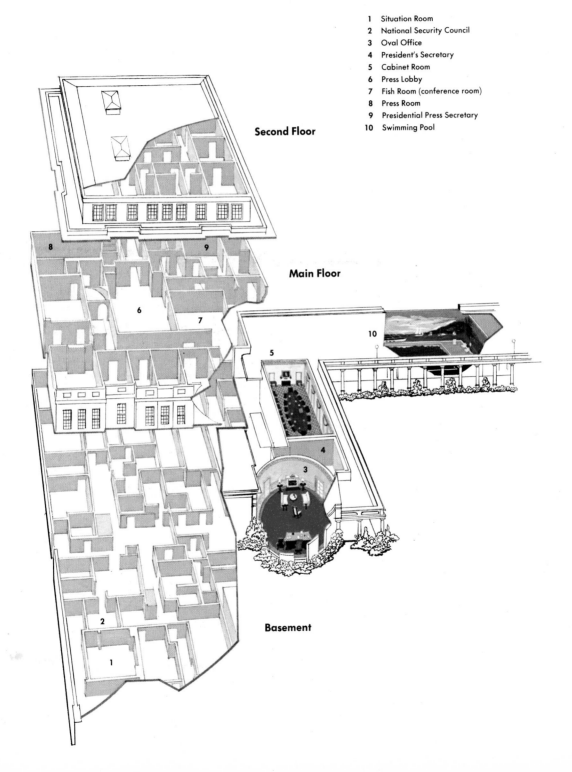

Second Floor

Main Floor

Basement

and the offices of about a dozen presidential aides who collectively, along with their Chief, are the center of initiative, action, and decision in American government. To the west of the west wing, across a small closed-off street, sits the main bureaucracy of the presidential office—the bulk of the Executive Office of the President. The rise of this office is one of the great success stories of our government.[23]

We can understand the super organization of the Presidency if we think of the Executive Office as a cluster of staff agencies that enable the President to take initiative and make decisions in crucial sectors that cut across the separate bureaus and departments. Presidential aides insist that they are simply the eyes and ears of the President, that they make few important decisions, and that they never insert themselves between the Chief Executive and the heads of departments, who are usually Cabinet members. Presidential aides and staff assistants are supposed to keep out of the limelight and to have a "passion for anonymity." In fact, as long as they have the confidence and support of the President, the men in the White House are part of the mainspring of government. Hence we can see them as occupying central command posts from which they instruct, prod, and bargain with administrators and legislators.

Administrative command post. The key agency here is certainly the Bureau of the Budget. The Director of the Bureau of the Budget advises the President in detail about the hundreds of government agencies—how much money they should be allotted in the budget and what kind of job they are doing. He and his assistants pare down the appropriations requested by the agencies to fit the President's fiscal program. They also try to improve the planning, management, and statistical work of the agencies. The Bureau makes a special effort to see that each agency conforms to presidential policies in its dealings with Congress by requiring clearance for policy recommendations to the legislature.

A budget is many things, for it deals with the purposes of men in a highly political environment. "Serving diverse purposes, a budget can be . . . a political act, a plan of work, a prediction, a source of enlightenment, a means of obfuscation, a mechanism of control, an escape from restrictions, a means to action, a brake on progress, even a prayer that the powers that be will deal gently with the best aspirations of fallible men."[24] But to the President the budget is mainly a means of control over administrators who can gang up with one another or with congressional or state politicians to thwart the presidential program and the President's control. Through the long budget-preparing process (see pages 601–604) he uses the Budget Bureau as a way to conserve and centralize his own influence. But the Bureau is more than the instrument of any single President; it is a continuing institution that has systematized its own roles, procedures, and routines, and hence it works at the heart of presidential government.

If control of money is vital to the President, control of men would seem to be more important. But the President has not enjoyed full control over hiring

---

[23]See Alex B. Lacy, Jr., "The Development of the White House Office," prepared for delivery at the 1967 annual meeting of the American Political Science Association.
[24]Aaron Wildavsky, *The Politics of the Budgetary Process* (Little, Brown, 1964), p. v.

and firing in the executive branch. The Senate, of course, has the power to confirm or reject major appointments, and during the period of congressional government after the Civil War Presidents had to struggle to keep their power to appoint and dismiss. Major control of appointments in the middle and lower ranks was vested in an independent Civil Service Commission in an effort to thwart political or patronage appointments. In recent years Presidents have gained more control of personnel, in part as the result of the warnings of organizational experts that the Chief Executive cannot really be Chief Executive unless he can hire the top men he wants and establish personnel policies down the line. The chairman of the Civil Service Commission has become the President's chief talent scout and in effect a member of the presidential staff.[25]

Economic command post. Ever since New Deal days the President has been responsible for planning against depressions and taking emergency action in the face of a sharp decline. This is not a constitutional but a political responsibility; a President knows that if he fails to act he will suffer the fate of Herbert Hoover, who was denounced for years by the Democrats for his alleged inaction during the Great Depression. The President's main staff unit in this area is the Council of Economic Advisers. The Council was established under the Employment Act of 1946, which placed responsibility on the federal government for stabilizing the economy and maintaining high levels of employment. Composed of three members appointed by the President with the consent of the Senate, the Council with the help of a small staff advises the President as to the health of the economy, analyzes existing programs, recommends new economic policies, and each year prepares for the President an economic report that enables him to review for Congress the nation's economic condition and set broad guidelines for the future. (The Budget Bureau recently has come to share some of the Council's function of formulating tax and credit policy and of working up programs for education, welfare, agriculture, and resource development.)

The Council's role has changed since its early years. Originally it was expected to be a somewhat disinterested group of experts who would give the President independent advice and might even differ with him in public. Today the Council is considered a staff arm of the President. While the members are supposed to adhere to professional standards, they are expected to support the President in testifying before Congress and to resign if they disagree with him (none has). Thus the Council is one more example of the centralization of power under the President and of the institutionalization of the Presidency.[26]

Political command post. Since every act of the President has political implications, the whole executive office is a kind of political command post. But many presidential actions are political in the narrower sense: making

[25]Laurin L. Henry, "The Presidency, Executive Staffing, and the Federal Bureaucracy," prepared for delivery at the 1967 annual meeting of the American Political Science Association, examines the background and implications of increased presidential role in personnel policy.

[26]Edward S. Flash, Jr., *Economic Advice and Presidential Leadership* (Columbia Univ. Press, 1965), stresses personal, institutional, and intellectual aspects of the Council's operations.

major appointments, planning campaigns, dealing with his party's national chairman and headquarters, mobilizing and directing presidential influence on Capitol Hill. A number of White House aides specialize in these operations. Their roles range from helping to plan the President's legislative priorities and program to deciding what state and local politicians will be allowed appointments with the President (and thus allowed to gain headlines and prestige back home). Partly because the President often does not want to seem involved in politics even when he is involved, his political staff is the least formalized and institutionalized part of the White House.[27]

Security command post. This is probably the most complex part of the President's decision-making apparatus. The President presides over the National Security Council, which is composed also of the Vice President, the Secretary of Defense, the Secretary of State, and others (described on pages 492–493). The Council has proved a useful place for discussing broad strategic matters and coordinating action but suffers from the fact that most members and participants in it represent departmental views and special agency interests. The President badly needs a single adviser who can take the same kind of presidential perspective as the Director of the Bureau of the Budget or the Chairman of the Council of Economic Advisers.

This is the job of the Special Presidential Assistant for National Security Affairs, who directs a small, highly secret command post in the basement of the White House. This office is a tiny Defense and State Department combined in one. Like other staff men, this special assistant is supposed to coordinate action rather than make decisions on his own. But as the arm of the President, he does in fact take part in decisions that in turn are carried out in the departments. This special assistant is especially useful to the President because he can coordinate actions not only in the big departments but also in a host of smaller ones that touch on national security matters. He can also work closely with other parts of the Executive Office, especially the Central Intelligence Agency, which reports formally to the National Security Council.

THE PARADOX OF THE PRESIDENCY

Presidential government is essentially the product of the interplay of traditional presidential powers, felt national needs, and strong and committed Presidents. In recent years the old interplay of personality and crisis has become much more complex to the point, indeed, of adding a whole new dimension to the Presidency. Spurred by the mass media, modern Presidents and presidential candidates not only respond to crisis, they spotlight it, dramatize it, and exploit it. The old interplay has become an intensifying spiral of (1) the fact of a national problem, such as poverty or bad health or poor education; (2) conversion of that problem by the mass media into a felt national crisis; (3) presidential exploitation of aroused public opinion about the crisis; and eventually (4) heightened popular expectations of what governments in general and Presidents in particular should do about the crisis.

Can the office meet such high expectations? The White House, as we have

[27]See Richard E. Neustadt, "Approaches to Staffing the Presidency: Notes on FDR and JFK," *The American Political Science Review* (December 1963), pp. 855–864.

noted, is a microcosm of the whole government, with the fiscal, personnel, national security, legislative, and other functions of government miniaturized in the crowded offices of the west wing and along the stately old halls of the Executive Office building. Much depends on whether this tiny organism can energize and control the vast federal bureaucracy and master the currents of social change sweeping the nation.

Critics who see the White House as the heart of the status quo contend that the White House has ossified, as have parts of the bureaucracy. Defenders of the Presidency on this score point to the fashion in which the office has kept abreast of the times in recent years by tapping the best brains in the academic community. Periodically under Kennedy and Johnson, White House aides toured campuses looking for ideas and criticism from the experts and soaking up both utopian proposals and hardheaded suggestions. Many a professor who berated the Johnson administration over Vietnam made priceless contributions in his own field. After collecting academic ideas, White House staff people set up in-house task forces to process the recommendations into policy packages, which were then routed to the Budget Bureau and other White House agencies and to the departments and bureaus.

The significance of brain trusts and academic task forces can hardly be

Courtesy John A. Ruge; copyright 1968 Saturday Review, Inc.

During the past 24 hours,—and in your rising enthusiasm for high public office, —you've promised the good people of this area clean air and rivers; safety in the streets; cheaper hunting and fishing licenses; racial peace; two dams and one hydroelectric plant; low consumer prices; higher prices for the farmer and breeder; a better image of America here and abroad; no new taxes; more police protection; a fair shake for labor; repeal of . . ."

exaggerated, it is claimed. They supply not only a constant flow of new ideas but also a constant challenge to intellectual complacency, rigidity, and dogmatism in the White House. Radical critics who are calculating that liberal political institutions will crumble like the Russian Czardom in 1917 must reckon with this built-in, self-correcting, prodding and stimulating and innovating flow of ideas.

The size and complexity of the presidential office, the President's mutually supporting and sometimes conflicting roles, the great powers and traditions of the office, the popular expectations of the office—all these lend force to former President Johnson's remark that the Presidency is much bigger than any President. They also point up a paradox of the Presidency. On the one hand, the Presidency has become so institutionalized that in effect we have a system of presidential government—a heavily organized office with an enduring structure of power and an exacting set of constitutional duties and political obligations. Presidential government will continue no matter who may occupy the oval office. On the other hand, the Presidency is vitally affected by the personality, background, temperament, loyalties, ideology, and working habits of the Chief Executive and the men around him. Hence we must look at presidential personality, tenure, and disability before we can assess the place of the President in democratic government.

The President:
Personality and Problems

15 The assassination of John F. Kennedy demonstrated the power of the personality of the man in the White House and the closeness the people feel to the President. It is estimated that the ceremonies in the capitol rotunda were witnessed in 85 percent of the American homes with television sets and that over 90 percent of American television sets—the highest total in television history—enabled over 100 million people to attend the funeral and burial services. Television and films relayed the ceremonies to many millions abroad. Kennedy's death reached even those people who usually ignore politics and political personalities. "Mourning and sadness encapsulated children" as well as adults; there was about the same proportion among grown-ups and children of headaches, loss of appetite, trouble going to sleep, and the like.[1]

The pressure on the President is a cruel test of his temperament, resilience, and sheer physical stamina. A student of the Presidency has listed the personal qualifications demanded by the job:[2]

Bounce. The President must have that "extra elasticity" that enables him to thrive on a harsh diet of work and responsibility.
Affability. "The President's heart must be not only stout but warm. . . . The Presidency is a people's office. . . ."

[1] Roberta S. Sigel, "Death of a President and School Children's Reaction To It—An Exploration Into Political Socialization" (Wayne State Univ. Press, 1965).
[2] C. L. Rossiter, *The American Presidency* (Harcourt, Brace & World, 1956), pp. 135–137. The quoted material is taken directly from this illuminating volume; the other comments are condensed or adapted from it.

Political skill. The President must be able to win popular support for his programs and deal with powerful rivals in Congress, party leaders and interest groups.

Cunning. The President must know the arts of politics — how to dodge and maneuver, when to be silent and when to speak out, when to lead the people and when to follow them.

The newspaper habit. If the President wants to maintain communication with the outside world, he must have direct lines to information and ideas beyond his immediate staff. A secretary's briefing is no substitute for reading several newspapers with different outlooks, and even glancing at the feature columns and cartoons.

A sense of history. The President must feel responsible to the generations who bequeathed us a great nation and to the generations still to come.

A sense of humor. At least two recent Presidents have said that they "could not have survived in office if they had been unable to laugh at the world and themselves."

The Presidency is the toughest job on earth; it is also the most powerful position in the Free World. And there are dangers inherent in an office on which so much depends: the hectic pace can cause physical exhaustion; there is always exposure to potential enemies. The possibility of the death or breakdown of a President makes a quick and effective transfer of power imperative.

The Vice President

The Framers of the Constitution were wise to provide for a Vice President, for four Presidents have been assassinated and four have died in office. The establishment of recognized procedures for the orderly and swift transfer of presidential power in the event of the death of the incumbent is one of the great strengths of constitutional government. And as we have seen on page 62, the ratification of the Twenty-fifth Amendment in 1967 finally established procedures to ensure that there will always be a Vice President to take over in the event of the death or disability of the President.[3]

Essential as it is to have a Vice President in the event of the President's death or disability, the nation can have only one President at a time, and one of the most troublesome problems has been to find a significant role for the Vice President when the President is healthy and hardy. Under the Constitution, the only prescribed task for the Vice President is to serve as President of the Senate, with the power to vote only if his vote is necessary to break a tie. This job is hardly sufficient to occupy the time and energy of a man of presidential ability.

It might seem that the Vice President is an ideal official to take some of the burdens off the President's shoulders and to serve as a liaison with the Congress, or a least with the Senate. Historically this has not been the case;

---

[3] For a critical view of the new procedure on the ground that it would unduly decrease the role of Congress in presidential succession, see George D. Haimbaugh, Jr., "Vice-Presidential Succession: A Criticism of the Bayh-Celler Plan," *South Carolina Law Review*, vol. 17, no. 3, (1965), pp. 1–19.

the Vice President at best was a kind of fifth wheel in administrations and at worst was a kind of joke. The Vice President was once described as "a man in a cataleptic fit. He is conscious of all that goes on but has no part in it."[4] The main reason for this weak role was that presidential candidates usually chose as running mates men who were geographically, ideologically, and in other ways likely to balance the ticket.

In recent decades, however, beginning with Roosevelt's selection of Henry Wallace as his running mate in 1940, presidential candidates have tended to choose more like-minded men for their running mates and to make full use of them when elected. Eisenhower gave Nixon a fairly prominent role in his administration, as did Kennedy to Johnson, and Johnson to Humphrey. According to one report, before offering Humphrey the vice-presidential nomination Johnson made him understand that the Vice President must have no public disputes with the President, that he must clear his speeches with the White House, and that he could disagree with the President before a decision was made but afterwards must support him.[5] Humphrey later received major assignments from his chief and remained loyal to the administration. On becoming candidate for President he was widely criticized for being a "White House puppet," especially on the issue of Vietnam; he replied that the Vice President must be a firm supporter of presidential policy.

In 1968, Nixon, Humphrey, and Wallace chose running mates close to their own political philosophy. After the election Nixon announced that he not only would give Vice President Spiro Agnew major policy-making responsibilities but would assign him an office in the White House close to the Oval Room, rather than in another building. Whatever the results of this particular experiment, it seems likely that the vice presidency has moved into the presidential orbit for good.

Kennedy, Johnson, Nixon, and the Presidency

Perhaps more than any of his predecessors, John F. Kennedy brought definite views of the nature and exercise of power to the Presidency. "I am no Whig," he said the year before his election; he believed, unlike the Whigs, that the Presidency must be the energizing and unifying force to make the divided governmental system work. And more than any other President, Kennedy campaigned for the office on the basis of how the President should exercise his power as well as what policies he would pursue. He said during the campaign:

I want to be a President who has the confidence of the people—and who takes the people into his confidence—who lets them know what he is doing and where we are going, who is for his program and who is against. I hope to set before the people our unfinished agenda—to indicate their obligations—and not simply follow their every whim and pleasure.

I want to be a President who acts as well as reacts—who originates programs as well as study groups—who masters complex problems as well as one-

[4]E. S. Corwin, *The President: Office and Powers* (New York Univ. Press, 1957), p. 73.
[5]Theodore H. White, *The Making of the President, 1964* (Atheneum, 1965), pp. 285–286.

page memorandums. I want to be a President who is the Chief Executive in every sense of the word—who responds to a problem, not by hoping his subordinates will act, but by directing them to act—a President who is willing to take the responsibility for getting things done, and take the blame if they are not done right. . . .

I am not promising action in the first 100 days alone—I am promising you 1,000 days of exacting presidential leadership.[6]

KENNEDY AS CHIEF ADMINISTRATOR

When he took office, Kennedy was aware of the two basic approaches to the role of managing the executive branch. One was best typified by Franklin D. Roosevelt. Long experienced in government and politics, Roosevelt had not been content to operate as a chairman of the board. He had administered the office in a highly personal way: he often acted through his staff assistants rather than department heads; he pounced on administrative details far down the line; he acquired information from a "myriad of private, informal, and unorthodox channels and espionage networks" rather than standard official sources; and instead of delegating power clearly and neatly, he liked to "keep grants of authority incomplete, jurisdictions uncertain, charters overlapping."[7]

The other pattern was well exemplified by President Eisenhower's methods. As perhaps befitted a military man, the General liked to follow orderly procedures, to avoid tangled lines of communication and delegation, to "go through channels." He believed in a strong staff system that would take much of the load off his own shoulders. He appointed Sherman Adams, a former governor of New Hampshire, as *the* assistant to the President—in effect a powerful chief of staff overseeing the executive department.

Kennedy greatly preferred the Roosevelt technique, not because he liked disorder or confusion, but because he wanted, whenever possible, to keep power and policy in his own hands. He had read with favor a study of presidential power by a young Columbia political scientist, Richard Neustadt, who contended that the President must not let power slip from his own hands, that he must not become too dependent on his staff, that he must check official reports against private reports, and that he must not become a prisoner of his office.[8] By building competition, diversity, and even disorder into his administration, the President would be in a better position to be the real instead of the titular head of the administration.

Observers differed in their opinions of the effectiveness of Kennedy's technique of administration. Some contended that he was taking too much on his own shoulders, that his personal intervention in administrative matters left his officials perplexed and sometimes at a loss as to what to do, that it was difficult to know sometimes whether the department or the White House was responsible for decisions. The failure of the effort to back up the invasion of Cuba in 1961 was blamed by some on tangled lines of communi-

[6]"Speeches, Remarks, Press Conferences, and Statements of Senator John F. Kennedy, Aug. 1 through Nov. 7, 1960," *Final Report of the Senate Committee on Commerce*, 87th Cong., 1st Sess., 1961, p. 904. This volume, and its counterpart on Nixon's speeches, is an invaluable source.
[7]Arthur M. Schlesinger, Jr., *The Coming of the New Deal* (Houghton-Mifflin, 1959), pp. 522–523.
[8]Richard E. Neustadt, *Presidential Power* (Wiley, 1960).

cation and decision-making between the State and Defense Departments and the White House. Others felt that the Kennedy system had proved itself. The White House was able to move speedily and simultaneously on many fronts. There was little of the genial disorder and creative disarray that characterized the Roosevelt administration, and an effective team of White House aides working closely together accomplished miracles of output. No invisible staff men or anonymous department officials were running the government behind the scenes; the President had the power and he assumed the credit or blame. There was never any real question of who was in charge. It was the President.

KENNEDY AS CHIEF LEGISLATOR

General Eisenhower had come to the White House in 1953 with a genuine regard for Congress and a respect for the tradition of governmental checks and balances. But soon disillusionment set in. Congress, though Republican-controlled, began opposing the administration in many time-honored ways — investigating it, holding up presidential appointments (in the Senate), cutting down requested appropriations, voting down White House measures. Later in his administration, when the Democrats controlled Congress, the President took somewhat stronger personal leadership, calling publicly for his legislative program and wielding his veto power freely against some measures passed by the Democrats. But he rarely threw himself into the thick of the battle on Capitol Hill, preferring to leave the infighting to friendly congressmen and agency chiefs.

Kennedy too had somewhat mixed views about the President's role as legislator. "I believe that our system of checks and balances, our whole constitutional system, can only operate under a strong President," he said in 1959. "The Constitution is a very wise document. It permits the President to assume just about as much power as he is capable of handling. If he fails, it is his fault, not the system's. I believe that the President should use whatever power is necessary to do the job unless it is expressly forbidden by the Constitution. . . ."[9]

As Kennedy faced his legislative tasks after his election, the political arithmetic of Congress seemed to him to call for presidential caution. In the 1960 congressional elections the Democrats had lost twenty-two seats in the House — most of them held by liberals and moderates. The lineup of 263 Democrats and 174 Republicans would give him a clear Democratic party majority, of course, but almost 100 of the Democrats were Southerners largely hostile to his program. The President decided on a policy of moderation and restraint. To be sure, he threw his weight into the battle to enlarge the Rules Committee (see pages 394–396), but he made it clear to the Southerners that he would not demand extensive civil rights legislation, at least for a time. And he withheld strong backing from Senate liberals in both parties who were trying to modify that great barrier to civil rights measures, the filibuster.

The President's legislative tactics in general followed this pattern: First, he made it clear, through frequent messages to Congress, addresses to the

[9] James M. Burns, *John Kennedy: A Political Profile* (Harcourt, Brace & World, 1959), p. 275.

people, comments in press conferences, and specific drafts submitted to Congress, just what he hoped Congress would do. The President's legislative aides then helped mobilize congressional support, mainly through persuasion rather than pressure. Although there were few outright deals—that is, exchanges of White House favors for specific votes—the White House aides were able to offer presidential recognition on matters close to a congressman's heart, such as funds for projects back home, patronage, defense contracts, administration help on bills especially important to the congressman, and the like. Meanwhile, the President tried to create a climate of friendly relations with Congress. Thus, his basic tactic in dealing with Congress was to use both the carrot and the stick—but much more the former than the latter.

The overall result of President Kennedy's first congressional session was mixed. On policies that aroused a bipartisan consensus over accepted types of social and economic reform—wages and hours, public housing, social security, development of depressed areas—the administration won passage of major bills. But on New Frontier efforts to "get the country moving forward" in new directions, the President made little progress. General aid to education, the financing of medical care for the aged through social security, extensive tax reform, stand-by powers for the President in coping with the threat of recession, orderly urban and transportation development, long-term financing of foreign aid, and other measures were locked in congressional committees or stalled in the labyrinthine legislative channels or defeated on the floor. Kennedy's experience with the congressional sessions of 1962 and 1963 was even more disappointing to the administration.

What verdict could be rendered on President Kennedy as Chief Legislator? Some felt that the President's tactics of caution and compromise had been wrong, that he should have aroused the country to put pressure on Capitol Hill. Others believed that the administration had done a good job considering the circumstances but that "blarney, bludgeon, and boodle," as it was called, was not enough. The one-party districts in the rural North and South, the seniority system, the filibuster, the Rules Committee, and all the other impediments in Congress were simply too strong for a President dealing with a power system beyond his power to overcome—a coalition of the congressional Republican and the congressional Democratic parties on the Hill. Some felt that such a formidable power system demanded not more manipulation and bargaining but a frontal assault by the President to clear away the institutional barriers to his program.

KENNEDY AS PARTY LEADER

Of all the presidential roles, Kennedy had probably conceived that of party leader with the least clarity and certainty. To be sure, he was fully prepared to take leadership of the national Democratic party as soon as he won the nomination. This he did by seeing that John M. Bailey of Connecticut, an early supporter, was appointed national chairman. And he stated in the campaign, "I do not intend, if successful, to ignore party leadership or party responsibility—and I do not intend to forget that I am a Democrat." But in almost the same breath he said, "I have no wish to be known as a narrowly partisan President, or as a private-interest President—I want to be President of all the people."[10] Once he took office, moreover, he faced practical difficulties in playing his part as party leader.

For one thing, Congress's Democratic majority was not a Kennedy majority. Hence it was often necessary to appeal to liberal (or presidential) Republicans to supply the necessary margin of votes. But the more Kennedy played up his role as Democratic leader, the more he might antagonize such support. In the second place, the President knew he would face many foreign crises for the handling of which he would need bipartisan support in Congress and among the electorate.

This ambivalence over party leadership was evident throughout Kennedy's three years in office. He worked closely with Democratic party leaders in Congress, attended many party rallies throughout the country, campaigned in support of Democratic candidates in the 1962 elections, and gave firm support to major pledges that the Democratic party had made in its 1960 platform. On the other hand, he did little to strengthen the party at the grass roots, he gave a good deal of recognition to friendly Republican congressmen, and in general he greatly stressed his role as national leader over that of party leader.

What kind of verdict will history render on Kennedy as chief politician? His own campaign for the Presidency may well be rated as one of the best-planned, most expertly conducted, and best-organized political operations in American political history. His legislative tactics on Capitol Hill will probably be considered less successful. Some will conclude that he was too cautious and deferential toward Congress and the congressional structure of power. On the other hand, Kennedy's critics will have to demonstrate how he could have pursued any other tactic with a Congress that was hostile to most of his bolder proposals. Doubtless it will be his capacity to inform the people, to marshal public opinion, to time his major actions, to move quickly and yet prudently in emergencies, and to conduct his office with style, humor, and zest that will secure Kennedy's reputation among the great presidential leaders.

JOHNSON: A NEW POLITICAL STYLE?

Lyndon B. Johnson's sudden elevation to the Presidency in November 1963 brought to 1600 Pennsylvania Avenue a man of considerably different political background from John F. Kennedy's. Whereas Kennedy had used the Senate mainly as a springboard to the Presidency, Johnson had carved out his political reputation in the upper chamber. He had been, above all, a "Senate man." As Democratic Majority Leader, he had shown a remarkable ability to influence Democratic senators of highly diverse points of view and some Republicans. He prided himself on being a moderate Democrat who was able to unite the liberal and conservative factions of his party.

In some respects Johnson infused the Presidency with his own personality and methods. As legislative and party leader, he relied heavily on face-to-

[10]"Speeches, Remarks, Press Conferences, and Statements of Senator John F. Kennedy, Aug. 1 through Nov. 7, 1960," *Final Report of the Senate Committee on Commerce*, 87th Cong., 1st Sess., 1961, p. 910. This volume, and its counterpart on Nixon's speeches, is an invaluable source.

face conferences with numerous politicians and on telephone calls to key people, conducted throughout the day and into the night, from his office, his limousine, and even his helicopter. He tried to use his old Senate persuasiveness on committee chairmen and other leaders of Congress. He also resisted any attempt to tie him to definite political label or philosophy. As a senator he had said in 1958: "I am a free man, an American, a United States Senator, and a Democrat, in that order. I am also a liberal, a conservative, a Texan, a taxpayer, a rancher, a businessman, a consumer, a parent, a voter, and not as young as I used to be nor as old as I expect to be—and I am all these things in no fixed order."

Still, the continuities of the Presidency as an institution seemed more significant than the change of personality in the White House. For one thing, as a Democrat, Johnson inherited Kennedy's problems and policies. He quickly made it clear that he would support the Kennedy program in Congress. He called for early passage of the tax reduction and civil rights bills and endorsed many other Kennedy proposals: expanded social welfare programs; Medicare; general federal aid to education; less discriminatory immigration barriers; youth employment legislation "to put jobless, aimless, hopeless youngsters to work on useful projects"; and stepped-up housing and urban renewal programs. President Johnson spoke out for fiscal policies that would stimulate the economy and reduce unemployment. He called vigorously for government economy, especially in the defense establishment, and for a smaller budgetary deficit, but these were policies that Presidents had preached (if not always practiced) for many years.

The President also inherited leadership of the presidential Democratic party. Although he hoped to unify the two major Democratic wings or parties, it was clear that he would follow the strategy of Franklin Roosevelt, Harry Truman, and John Kennedy in appealing to labor, consumer, and ethnic blocs in the big urban states. It was not difficult for Johnson to make this appeal, for he had started political life as a protegé of Franklin Roosevelt, and he had long reflected some of the Populist, anti-Wall Street feeling that was strong in Texas earlier in the century.

JOHNSON AS CHIEF POLITICIAN

Like Kennedy, Johnson had spent almost all his adult life in politics and knew the mazes and pitfalls of the political jungle. But the political style of the two men was quite different. Kennedy was urbane, sophisticated, and sometimes even a bit detached as he went about his political chores, whereas Johnson seemed so forceful, earthy, and transparently political that some criticized him for being little more than a wheeler-dealer and arm twister, even in the White House. But whatever the differences in style, the political aims of the two Presidents were similar—to gain support from Congress and the voters for a huge program of legislation and executive action and to win another popular mandate in the next election. Johnson inherited a host of Kennedy measures that had become stalled in Congress. In the 1964 and 1965 sessions of Congress the new President scored a series of stunning legislative victories: two major civil rights measures, school aid, Medicare, a revised immigration policy, aid to Appalachia, highway beautification, federal aid to the arts and humanities, establishment of a new Department of Housing and Urban Development.

How much of Johnson's success on Capitol Hill was due to his special political skills and experience, how much to the basic political situation? Some Washington correspondents made much of the President's "feel" for Capitol Hill, his old friendships with congressional leaders, and his uncanny knack of knowing just what combination of charm, argument, pressure, and various forms of political persuasion would win over an influential congressman or senator. Others contended that Johnson was lucky in the time that he came to power, for civil rights and other social legislation was about to achieve a breakthrough under Kennedy and that Kennedy's martyrdom accentuated public support for his major measures. But everyone agreed that the most decisive factor was the outcome of the 1964 congressional elections, for Goldwater had pulled down to defeat a number of Republican congressmen who were replaced by liberal Democrats. However in 1966 Johnson was no more successful in maintaining his party's strength in the off-year congressional elections than previous Presidents had been.

JOHNSON AS CHIEF OF STATE

Like all Presidents, Johnson somehow managed to appear to rise above politics, to be President of all the people, even when he was most partisan and political. Yet no President dedicated himself more ardently and persistently to a concept—the Great Society—that would represent a consensus of all interests. Johnson used consensus politics skillfully to win support for his program. In the 1964 election he took over the middle of the road and gained the great bulk of the independent vote as well as a large fraction of the normally Republican. He won sizable Republican backing on Capitol Hill for his legislative program. He showed a genius for discerning the formulas that united people, as in his settlement of issues that had divided railway executives and labor for decades. Although a product of the South and West, he made perhaps the strongest presidential appeal in history to the Negroes, ethnic groups, and industrial workers of the North. Abroad he maintained the bipartisan foreign policy that had long enjoyed support from both presidential parties.

Yet some were critical. Consensus politics, it was argued, was essentially a kind of brokerage politics that consisted of buying off major groups with small concessions, rather than moving boldly toward a well-defined great society. An attempt to find agreement on major policies would mean a loss of excitement and imagination and experimentation in national government. Experience suggested that in the long run consensus was impracticable as well as undesirable—in the long run people will divide over major issues and Presidents must take a stand. "The experience of past Presidents," one observer summed up, "suggests that eventually Johnson will have to make unpleasant choices that may cost him some of his broad-based support.[11]

This prediction was correct. Rising controversy over Vietnam and over law and order eroded the foundations of Johnson's broad appeal. Perhaps

[11]C. Peter Magrath, "Lyndon Johnson and the Paradox of the Presidency," *The Yale Review* (June 1965), p. 493.

the most eloquent elegy over his policy of consensus was spoken by the President himself the day after he announced that he would not be a candidate again for President:

Sometimes I have been called a seeker of "consensus"—more often in criticism than in praise. And I have never denied it. Because to heal and to build in support of something worthy is, I believe, a noble task. In the region of the country where I have spent my life, where brother was once divided against brother, this lesson has been burned deep into my memory. . . .

Yet along the way I learned somewhere that no leader can pursue public tranquility as his first and only goal.

THE NIXON PRESIDENCY

At the time of Richard Nixon's inauguration as the thirty-seventh President of the United States it was too early to know just how he would view its powers and responsibilities. Yet certain general tendencies seemed likely on the basis of earlier observations he had made of the Presidency.

According to a campaign statement, he planned, as Chief Executive, to "bring the human element into government" much more than the Democrats had. Voluntary efforts throughout the nation, he said, would not have the place they deserved "until we have leaders in Washington who are genuinely committed to the voluntary way." Volunteers at the grass roots must not be mere foot soldiers in a battle directed from Washington. It was small wonder, he added, "that more and more people, and not only the young, are in a mood of open revolt against the machinery and the men of government —against an increasingly impersonal bureaucracy, a top-heavy Washington, a statistical model of services that dehumanizes man and perpetuates a cycle of dependency."[12] Just how the new President would decentralize and "humanize" administration, and at the same time preserve drive and follow-through from the top, would be an interesting case study of pluralistic government in action.

As chief foreign policy maker, President Nixon would carry on the general bipartisan foreign policy of previous Democratic and Republican administrations. Such an approach would allow him a good deal of discretion. During international crises he could expect extensive immediate support in Congress; the test of this support would come in the long run, as the air of emergency evaporated and opposition party leaders in Congress became more critical. Nixon's problem would be compounded by the fact that he must deal with a Democratic Congress, but in this respect the bipartisan tradition would be helpful.

As Chief of State, the new President had promised, he would "rally the people, define those moral principles which are the cement of a civilized society, point the ways in which the energies of the people can be enlisted to serve the ideals of the people." Coming into office after an especially divisive year and faced with strong party opposition in Congress, Nixon after his election stressed that he would act for all the people, that he would pursue unity and consensus. These were hopeful words to a people tired of dissen-

[12]*The New York Times* (Oct. 7, 1967), pp. 1, 40.

sion and partisanship, but they raised a question—would Richard Nixon, like Lyndon Johnson, find that a consensus could crumble into fragments once the going became hard, such as in a case like Vietnam? In that event, what would the new President do—attempt to forge a new consensus, try to create and lead a new moderate Republican majority, emphasize the role of the President as one of *leading* rather than unifying, or something else?

As party leader, Richard Nixon might find himself in his natural element. Having inherited a weak Republican national party in 1960 from President Eisenhower, who had paid little attention to party politics, Nixon learned in the campaign of 1960 how crucial a well-organized party might be to the conducting of a winning presidential campaign. After the Republican debacle of 1964 he had a leading part in the rebuilding of the party. As President he was likely to see the importance of a strong national organization in order to win congressional seats in 1970 and try for reelection in 1972. Certainly President Nixon would devote time to strengthening his party—the question was how. Would he try to reestablish the party on its old presidential base, returning to the liberal Republican tradition of Lincoln and Theodore Roosevelt? Would he try to win over elements of the Democratic party, perhaps by bringing notable Democratic leaders into his administration? Or would he move closer to the old congressional party, in which he had had his political start?

Whether as a partisan or a unifier, however, President Nixon had planned to take a broad view of presidential power. "The days of a passive presidency belong to a simpler past," he stated during the campaign. "The next President must take an activist view of his office. He must articulate the nation's values, define its goals, and marshall its will."[13] Like most of his predecessors Richard Nixon would try to be both leader of the whole people and chief of his party, both an active leader in legislation and administration and a broker of interests and sections. It was by the skill with which he combined these goals that the success of his presidency would in large part be measured.

Is the Presidency Becoming Too Powerful?

Lyndon Johnson's vigorous exercise of presidential power sharpens the old question: How much power should the President have? This question is hard to answer because we cannot be certain just what powers the President does have. The Constitution, as we have seen, is somewhat vague on the matter. It seems to grant the President broad executive authority without defining it. Some scholars point out that the Constitution vests "the executive power of the United States" in the President but gives Congress only the legislative power "herein granted." They argue that in emergencies the President has wide powers to protect the public interest without specific legal authority and even at the cost of overriding existing laws. Despite considerable controversy and the Supreme Court's rebuff of President Truman's attempt to exert "inherent powers," there seem to be a kind of inherent power in the Presidency, vast but undefined, that an aggres-

[13]*Time* (Nov. 15, 1968), p. 26.

sive President could exploit in time of crisis. The President also has a good deal of undefined power as the chief forger of foreign policy—a situation that has advantages in the crisis but that makes it difficult to define presidential power.

THEORIES OF PRESIDENTIAL POWER

Presidents have had different ideas about their job, and two of them have given their views with great frankness. Theodore Roosevelt wrote in his *Autobiography* that he had insisted on

> . . . the theory that the executive power was limited only by specific restrictions and prohibitions appearing in the Constitution or imposed by the Congress under its Constitutional powers. My view was that every executive officer, and above all every executive officer in high position, was a steward of the people. . . . I declined to adopt the view that what was imperatively necessary for the Nation could not be done by the President unless he could find some specific authorization to do it. . . . Under this interpretation of executive power I did and caused to be done many things not previously done by the President and the heads of the Departments. I did not usurp power, but I did greatly broaden the use of executive power.[14]

This has been called the *stewardship* theory of presidential power, William Howard Taft, on the other hand, took a rather narrowly *constitutional* view of presidential power. He wrote in 1916:

> The true view of the Executive functions is, as I conceive it, that the President can exercise no power which cannot be fairly and reasonably traced to some specific grant of power or justly implied and included within such express grant as proper and necessary to its exercise. Such specific grant must be either in the Federal Constitution or in an act of Congress passed in pursuance thereof. There is no undefined residuum of power which he can exercise because it seems to him to be in the public interest. . . .[15]

Franklin D. Roosevelt's conception of his powers—sometimes called the *prerogative theory*—was that, in the face of emergencies, the President had the same power that John Locke once argued kings had—the power, in Locke's words, "to act according to discretion for the public good, without the prescription of the law and sometimes even against it."[16] The destroyer deal, for example, conflicted with several laws.

IS THE PRESIDENCY POWERFUL ENOUGH?

Now for the other side of the ledger. The President's power is so great that it is easy to forget all the limits on his freedom. We have seen that as chief administrator and chief legislator

[14]T. R. Roosevelt, *Theodore Roosevelt: An Autobiography* (Macmillan, 1913), pp. 388–389.
[15]W. H. Taft, *Our Chief Magistrate and His Powers* (Columbia Univ. Press, 1916), p. 139.
[16]E. S. Corwin, *The Constitution and What It Means Today*, 10th ed. (Princeton Univ. Press, 1948), p. 85.

The President must share *policy-making* power with congressmen, administrators, and others.

He must share his *treaty-making* power with the Senate.

He must share his *appointing* power with congressmen, especially senators.

His power to *dismiss* agency heads is limited.

He is powerful in his *party* but by no means all-powerful, particularly at the lower echelons.

Above all, the President is held in check by the political situation in which he operates. No matter how strong a leader he may be, he is not a free agent. Not only must he deal with key congressmen, Cabinet members, important bureaucrats, the Vice President, party chiefs, and even leaders of the opposition party, but he must also cope with the great political forces operating around the White House—public opinion in all its complexity, pressures from organized interests, demands from his own party. He must negotiate endlessly among individuals and among interests. He must act—but without stepping on too many toes. Always the fierce light of public opinion, magnified by press, radio and television, beats on the White House.

In recent years a significant curb has been put on the President's power—he has been made ineligible for a third term. Although the Framers provided for indefinite re-eligibility, Washington ran for only two terms and set a precedent that Presidents followed for a century and a half. In 1940, however, Franklin Roosevelt challenged this unwritten law and sought a third term. His victory "repealed" the tradition, but the repeal was not to last long. In 1951 the thirty-sixth state ratified the Twenty-second Amendment, which bars the President from being elected for more than two terms. It will be interesting to see if this change will survive should an immensely popular President want a third term some day. The Amendment will probably weaken Presidents during their second term, because powerful political leaders in Congress and in the administration will feel less obliged to support a man they know will be out of power on a certain date.

PROBLEM AND PROSPECTS

Have we come to the point where we are willing to accept the President as master of our fate and fortunes in time of crisis? Certainly we have rejected the concept of rigid checks on the Chief Executive, especially during crises. For example, in June 1950, a few days after North Korean troops invaded South Korea, President Truman, acting on his own, ordered American forces to resist aggression. Equally significant, the few senators who criticized him for not first going to Congress found no support except in the extreme isolationist press. President Kennedy consulted congressional leaders but not Congress as a whole when he ordered a naval quarantine of Cuba in 1962, and this time there was practically no criticism. Nor was there significant congressional opposition in 1965 when President Johnson ordered armed forces to intervene in the Dominican Republic. Today more than ever before, the President, as Woodrow Wilson once said, "is at liberty, both in law and conscience, to be as big a man as he can."

How dangerous is the tendency toward one-man rule in time of crisis? So far the danger has not been great. Perhaps we have been lucky. The great war-time leaders of the United States—Linclon, Wilson, Roosevelt—were democratic in the best sense. They did not want power for power's sake but simply as a means of overcoming national peril. Aside from one or two lapses, they maintained the basic democratic institutions of civil liberties and free elections. We may not always be so lucky. Some day we may elect a President who in time of crisis would find some pretext to postpone elections or stifle free speech. Indeed, we may elect a man who would deliberately create an emergency for the very purpose of suppressing the opposition.

The problem will grow more sinister if the twentieth century continues to be a time of endless emergencies. But one thing seems sure. We cannot eliminate the threat by trying to cut the President down to size. To do this would be to blunt the very weapon—presidential power—that has served us so well in past emergencies. Nor should we try to raise Congress into full rivalry with the President, for that would give us divided government, which might be intolerable in time of crisis. A thoughtful student of the problem, generally satisfied with the workings of the office, has advised us, "Leave Your Presidency Alone!"[17]

The problem has two edges: On the one hand we must see to it that the President is our servant not our master, that he leads us only in the direction we wish to go. On the other hand, we need to help the President. He must have enough authority to do his job.[18] He must be free of some of the obstacles that now confront him. Above all, he needs the wise counsel of men who take a broad, national point of view, who can both guide him and sustain him. He cannot always find such associates in the Cabinet, for the members, though men of his choosing, seldom have national prestige of their own. He cannot often find them in Congress, because even congressmen of the same party have their own political loyalties and responsibilities. He cannot easily find them in his own party, because our parties tend to create sectional rather than national leaders.

The need, in essence, is for *leadership*. The Presidency can be a vast reservoir of leadership, as Franklin D. Roosevelt realized:

> The Presidency is not merely an administrative office. That is the least of it. It is more than an engineering job, efficient or inefficient. It is pre-eminently a place of moral leadership. All our great Presidents were leaders of thought at times when certain historic ideas in the life of the nation had to be clarified. . . . That is what the office is—a superb opportunity for reapplying, applying in new conditions, the simple rules of human conduct to which we always go back. Without leadership alert and sensitive to change, we are all bogged up or lose our way.[19]

But what is the proper scope for such leadership? We will come to grips with this question after we have looked at our other national policy-makers.

[17]Rossiter, *op. cit.*, p. 161.
[18]Louis Brownlow, *The President and the Presidency* (Public Administration Service, 1949), pp. 114–115.
[19]*The New York Times* (Nov. 13, 1932), Sect. 8, p. 1.

Congress:

Makeup and Structure

16 Clearly, the President has come to hold the commanding position in American government. This development is just the opposite of what the Framers of the Constitution planned. They lived in a time when parliamentary assemblies were dislodging kings and royal minions, when the new legislatures embodied some of the revolutionary aspirations of the common man. The Framers expected that Congress would be the main channel of popular impulses, and the President would act as a moderating and stabilizing force. They were not quite sure how to set up the executive branch, as we have seen, but they had no major doubts about Congress. It was to be the branch that spoke for the people, and the Framers took special pride in their judicious separation of power between an upper chamber representing people by area and a lower chamber representing people by number.

What has happened to the dream of Congress as the people's branch of the government? Is its eclipse by the President simply part of a worldwide trend toward stronger executives? Certainly the past century and a half has not dealt kindly with parliaments. The German Reichstag became a mere cheering section under Hitler; the Supreme Soviet in Russia rigidly follows the party line; De Gaulle has held the French Parliament carefully in check; and the House of Commons in Britain is essentially a chamber for debating policy and rolling up an almost guaranteed majority for the Prime Minister. Congress has survived as an independent body, but hardly a year goes by without the appearance of a highly critical study of Congress, often by congressmen themselves. Still, Congress is very much a going body. Indeed it had been said: "in no other country has the legislature so much capacity for acting independently and for thwarting the will of the executive. . . ."[1]

Recruiting Congressmen

The entire membership of the House of Representatives is elected every even year. Elections for the six-year Senate terms are staggered so that one-third of the Senate is chosen at each congressional election. Hence a President, for at least half his term of office, will deal with a Congress chosen in elections in which he was not a candidate. In this way Congress tends to be insulated from the coattails effect of a popular presidential candidate.

THE SECURITY OF CONGRESSIONAL OFFICE

Although all members of the House and one-third of the senators are chosen on the same day in November, congressional elections are more local than national events, as we have seen. A candidate owes his nomination largely to political forces within his state or district, and he is almost completely dependent on local sources for such vital campaign requirements as money and workers. Of course states and districts vary greatly in this regard: In some districts the nomination is a reward for loyal service to a party organization. In others primary elections are the decisive step. And in others local ethnic groups or powerful industrial or labor organizations may play a key role.[2]

As a result of the decentralization of congressional elections, most representatives and senators have power bases independent both of the President and of the party leadership in Congress. A member of the British Parliament who opposes the national leadership of his party knows that he runs the risk of losing his party's endorsement at the next election. An American congressman knows that as long as he keeps the folks—and the interests—back home happy, he can symbolically turn his back on the White House. Conversely, the President cannot demand support from the legislators, even those of his own party, because he cannot offer them much political protection in their own constituencies.

The congressional constituencies simply do not add up to the presidential constituency. For one thing, as we have noted, off-year elections attract a much smaller electorate. Second, an overwhelming majority of senators and congressmen are assured of reelection. Well over 80 percent of the incumbents are returned, and if we consider only those seeking reelection, the percentage is even higher. The defeat of an incumbent congressman in a primary election is also rare; between 1956 and 1966 less than 2 percent of

---

[1]Lewis Froman, *The Congressional Process: Strategies, Rules and Procedures* (Little, Brown, 1967).

[2]On the relation of different forms of political organization in congressional districts with different types of congressmen, see Leo Snowiss, "Congressional Recruitment and Representation," *The American Political Science Review* (September 1966), pp. 627–639.

the House members seeking reelection lost their seats in this fashion.[3] Even more significant, at least three-quarters of the House seats are "safe" year after year. In six of the seven elections from 1950 to 1962 fewer than 100 of the 435 House seats were won by majorities of less than 55 percent.[4] Although presidential elections have been highly competitive in recent decades, the number of competitive congressional districts has decreased in the past fifty years.[5] Only one congressional seat in the entire nation changed in party control in every election from 1952 to 1960. The same pattern was evident in the 1966 and 1968 congressional elections.

As congressional districts have tended to become the exclusive preserve of one of the two major parties, statewide electorates have tended to become more competitive. This is reflected in the accompanying graph, which compares the margin of House and Senate electoral victories for the eight most populous states—the states that elect 211 of the 435 congressmen and that dominate the selection of the President through the electoral college.

The most important political consequence of the security of congressional

[3]Charles O. Jones, *Every Second Year: Congressional Behavior and the Two-Year Term* (Brookings, 1967), p. 68.

[4]H. Douglas Price, "The Electoral Arena," in David B. Truman (ed.), *The Congress and America's Future* (Prentice-Hall, 1965), p. 33.

[5]Charles O. Jones, "Inter-party Competition for Congressional Seats," *Western Political Quarterly* (September 1964), pp. 461–476.

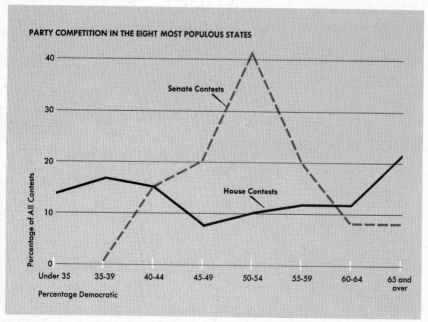

H. Douglas Price, "The Electoral Arena" in David B. Truman (ed.), *The Congress and America's Future;* © 1965 by The American Assembly, Columbia University, New York, New York; reprinted by permission of Prentice-Hall, Inc., Englewood Cliffs, New Jersey.

The graph shows the percentage Democratic for House candidates in 1962 and for all Senate candidates, 1958–1962 (includes New York, California, Pennsylvania, Illinois, Ohio, Texas, Michigan, and New Jersey).

TABLE 16-1

Percentage of Incumbents Reelected

	1950	1952	1954	1956	1958	1960	1962
House	83.4	81.6	87.1	89.5	92.1	85.6	83.9
Senate	85.4	83.3	85.4	90.6	81.3	92.0	88.0

SOURCE: Lewis Froman, *The Congressional Process: Strategies, Rules and Procedures* (Little, Brown, 1967), p. 170.

seats is that Congress is less responsive to changes in the electorate as a whole than is the President—a situation that gravely handicaps a presidential candidate who advocates substantial innovation. The electoral system guarantees that Congress will be more closely oriented to the status quo than will the President and that increasingly the House is more resistent to political change than the Senate.

Finally, popular ignorance about candidates for Congress is overwhelming. In 1958, for example, fewer than 20 percent of constituents living in districts in which a Republican and a Democrat were competing for a House seat said they had read or heard something about both candidates. "Except in rare cases, what the voter 'knew' was confined to diffuse evaluative judgments about the candidate: 'he's a good man,' 'he understands the problems,' and so forth. Of detailed information about policy stands not more than a chemical trace was found."[6] Central to the operations of a pluralist democracy is information about elected officials; yet the individual congressman, in contrast to the President, operates far from the bright lights of publicity and accountability.

THE POLITICS OF DISTRICTING

The Framers of the Constitution intended the Senate to represent areas rather than numbers, and this was to be offset by making the House of Representatives roughly reflect population. But even the lower chamber does not represent population accurately. The explanation for this is found in the way congressional districts are set up.

By act of Congress, the membership of the House is set at 435; these seats are distributed by Congress among the states according to population, with each state receiving at least one. After each ten-year census, the Bureau of the Census submits a suggested allocation of the seats, which becomes official unless Congress acts to the contrary. But Congress has left almost complete control over the drawing of congressional districts to the state legislatures.

In theory, congressional district boundaries should be as nearly equal in population as practicable and fairly compact and should not cut across unified areas such as cities. But such a theory assumes that the goal is to

[6]Warren E. Miller and Donald E. Stokes, "Constituency Influence in Congress," *The American Political Science Review* (March 1963), p. 54. See also Donald E. Stokes and Warren E. Miller, "Party Government and the Saliency of Congress," *Public Opinion Quarterly* (Winter 1962), pp. 531–546.

make the state's congressional delegation as representative as possible of the state's population and to give each voter an equal voice in the House of Representatives. In practice, the creation of congressional districts is immensely complicated by political considerations and is the product of a variety of personal, group, and party forces jockeying for advantage.

One result of this jockeying has been *gerrymandering*. The term was coined a century and a half ago when Elbridge Gerry of Massachusetts carved out a district that had the shape of a salamander; it was quickly dubbed a "gerrymander." The term is now applied to any attempt by a party or faction controlling a state legislature to draw the boundaries of districts in such a way that that party or group enjoys a close but safe margin of support in many districts, and the opposition's votes are concentrated in a few districts and thus wasted.

The accompanying map shows the congressional districts of New York City, as drawn by the Republican-controlled Legislature in 1961. District 24 in the Bronx—which may remind you of a dragon—was custom-built for former Congressman Paul Fino, Bronx County Republican leader. The area actually contains five public housing projects, whose residents tend to vote Democratic, but the Legislature was able to remove four of them from Fino's district. In addition, Staten Island did not contain sufficient population to merit its own congressman. Therefore it had to be joined to the mainland, but notice that the *fifty-one-sided* piece of central Brooklyn forming the remainder of the sixteenth district is separated from Staten Island by three other districts. *The New York Times* commented that the Legislature had drawn a line around every Republican in New York City (as a result of court action, the New York Legislature redistricted the congressional districts in 1968).

The New York sixteenth and twenty-fourth districts represent attempts to combine enough Republican voters to elect Republican congressmen. An example of the alternative tactic is provided by the twenty-eighth district in California: two chunks of Los Angeles were joined by a strip of land *three city blocks wide and five miles long.* This overwhelmingly Republican district was created by the Democratic Legislature to assure the election of Democrats in adjacent areas.

Another result of the politics of districting is sometimes called the *silent gerrymander,* a technique whereby a state legislature would make no effort to adjust its districts to population shifts within the state. Thus an urban district could double

NEW YORK CITY CONGRESSIONAL DISTRICTS

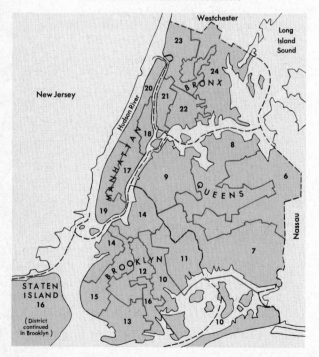

377

CHAPTER 16
Congress:
Makeup
and
Structure

in population and still have only one representative, while rural districts that declined in relative population would keep their past representation. Even if the state is awarded an additional congressman, the legislature might provide for his election "at large"—leaving the old districts intact. As the result of silent gerrymanders, Michigan's biggest congressional district in 1960 had a population of 802,994, the smallest only 177,431; and Texas districts ranged in population from 216,371 to 951,527.

The main results of the politics of districting have been to reduce the number of competitive seats in the House and to overrepresent the rural areas. Two factors lie behind the latter effect: first, because population shifts have been mainly from rural to suburban and city areas, failure to redistrict strengthened rural representation, primarily at the expense of the suburban areas; and second, most state legislatures, themselves products of gerrymandered state legislative districts that overrepresented rural areas, tended to favor their own rural supporters when drawing congressional district boundaries. City and suburban people were of course unhappy about this arrangement, but they could do little more than protest. The state legislatures were not likely to reform themselves; nor was Congress—for the same reason. The Supreme Court in *Baker v. Carr* had provided relief for voters discriminated against in the creation of state legislative districts, but this did not directly affect congressional districting.

Then in 1964, in *Wesbury* v. *Sanders*, came a dramatic challenge to gerrymandering of congressional districts. The Supreme Court, reversing an earlier decision, ruled that the Constitution required that "as nearly as is practicable one man's vote in a Congressional election is to be worth as much as another's."[7] This was a mighty boost for the ideal that one man equals one vote. Soon state legislatures were grudgingly redrawing congressional districts to conform more closely to the court's ruling that districts must be relatively equal in population.

How much difference will these actions make? Although redistricting will always lag somewhat behind the flow of population, *Wesbury* v. *Sanders* clearly has ended the egregious *population inequalities* that were previously quite common. It is much less clear that the courts will be able to prevent state legislatures from drawing the boundaries of congressional districts so as to render them *noncompetitive*. To date, the Supreme Court has not ruled that the drawing of district boundaries for partisan advantage renders them invalid.

One possible solution to the gerrymander is to take the task of redistricting away from the state legislatures and turn it over to bipartisan commissions. The use of computers might further minimize the extent of bias.[8] For it is likely that as long as the creation of congressional districts continues to be a function of the legislatures, the spirit of redistricting will be that of one Missouri Democrat: "Did the Republicans," he asked, "really expect the Democrats to draft and support a redistricting bill favorable to Republicans? If they did their political acumen hovers near the zero mark. The Republicans are entitled to the same redistricting feast at the hands of the Demo-

[7]*Wesbury* v. *Sanders* (1964).
[8]Stuart Nagel, "Simplified Bipartisan Computer Redistricting," *Stanford Law Review* vol. 17, no. 863 (1965).

crats that they would serve the Democrats if they were in power. Only that — and nothing more."[9]

Who Gets Elected?

From the "log cabin to the White House" — the idea that any boy can become President, or senator, or congressman — is one of the most pervasive myths in American politics. The legal restrictions are few indeed: members of the lower house must be at least twenty-five years old and have been citizens for seven years; senators must be age thirty and have been citizens for nine years; both must be inhabitants (but not necessarily legal residents) of the state in which they are running. Nevertheless, the recruitment process is extremely selective; members of the House and Senate do not reflect the socioeconomic composition of the nation as a whole.

THE SOCIOECONOMIC MAKEUP OF CONGRESS

The average senator or congressman is almost certain to be a white male. He will be older than the average citizen. The odds are good that he will come from a Yankee or Anglo-Saxon background and that he will belong to a Protestant church, probably a high-prestige denomination.

The typical congressman or senator's background differs from that of the average American in several important respects. Congress abounds with small-town boys. Matthews found that the birthplaces of most senators ranged in size from 2,500 to 5,000 inhabitants.[10] These small towns produced twice as many Democrats and four times as many Republicans as one might expect on the basis of chance. Matthews noted, "Places like Centerville, South Dakota; Isabel, Illinois; Ten Mile, Pennsylvania; Rising Sun, Delaware; and Honea Path, South Carolina nurtured more senators than all the cities of the United States combined."[11] If we consider the present residences of senators, the same overrepresentation of small towns and cities appears. And congressmen seem to be less mobile than the general population. A congressman is more likely than his average constituent to have been born in the state he represents.[12]

Congressmen and senators come overwhelmingly from upper and middle-class families. Table 16-2 compares the occupations of the fathers of all senators who served between 1947 and 1957 with the total labor force in 1900. The children of low-salaried workers, of industrial wage earners, and of farm laborers are significantly underrepresented in Congress.

The average congressman or senator has had considerably more formal

---

[9]Quoted in Gordon E. Baker, *The Reapportionment Revolution* (Random House, 1966), p. 88.

[10]Donald R. Matthews, *U.S. Senators and Their World* (Univ. of North Carolina Press, 1960), p. 16; William J. Keefe and Morris S. Ogul, *The American Legislative Process: Congress and the States*, 2d ed. (Prentice-Hall, 1968), Chap. 5.

[11]Matthews, *op. cit.*, p. 14.

[12]Malcolm E. Jewell and Samuel C. Patterson, *The Legislative Process* (Random House, 1966), p. 102.

379

CHAPTER 16
Congress:
Makeup
and
Structure

TABLE 16-2

Occupational Class Distribution of Senators' Fathers Compared with Labor Force in 1900

Occupational Class	Fathers of Senators	Labor Force
Professional	24%	6%
Proprietors and officials	35	7
Farmers	32	22
Low-salaried workers	2	5
Industrial wage earners	5	39
Servants	0	5
Farm laborers	0	17
Unknown	2	0
Totals	100%	100%

SOURCE: Donald R. Matthews, *U.S. Senators and Their World* (Univ. of North Carolina Press, 1960), p. 20.

education than the average citizen. He has probably gone to college and his school is more likely to be in the Ivy League than is that of the typical college graduate. Most senators and congressmen began their occupational careers in high-status positions, with law and business predominating. Indeed, the majority of the members of both houses are lawyers.

Most congressmen and senators have had political careers before entering Congress. Prior service in state legislatures or as local officials (often in law enforcement) is common for freshman congressmen. The best stepping-stones to the Senate appear to be governorships or seats in the House.[13]

It is clear, then, that most members of the House and Senate are drawn from a narrow stratum of the population. Matthews concludes that if we considered the characteristics of the typical senator to be requirements for the office, less than 5 percent of the American people would have much chance of being elected. But is this an undesirable situation? We would hardly expect to find the national percentage of high school dropouts reflected in Congress. One answer is that whereas formal education may be related to political ability, it is not clear that race, father's income, and place of birth have any such relationship. The question is whether congressmen drawn from a restricted segment of the population will be systematically biased in favor of certain points of view.

CONGRESSMEN AND EXECUTIVES: A STUDY IN CONTRASTS

Not only do members of Congress differ from the public at large, their backgrounds and career patterns differentiate them from other political elites. Thus 64 percent of the 1959 senators were raised in rural areas or in small towns and only 19 percent in metropolitan centers, whereas 52 percent of the presidents of the largest industrial corporations grew up in metropolitan centers, as did a large proportion of the political executives appointed during the Roosevelt, Truman, Eisenhower, and Kennedy administrations.[14] The difference in geographic mobility between congressmen and executives is striking. "In 1963, over one third of the top leaders of Congress (37%) but only 11 percent of administration leaders were still living in their places of birth."[15] Table 16-3 demonstrates that the career patterns of congressional leaders and administration leaders were similar in 1903 but that they had diverged considerably by 1963. Members of Congress and especially congressional leaders are likely to have worked their way up through local politics; not so members of the executive.

TABLE 16-3

Experience of National Political Leaders in State and Local Government

Offices Held	Congressional Leaders		Administration Leaders	
	1903	1963	1903	1963
Any state or local office	75%	64%	49%	17%
Elective local office	55	46	22	5
State legislature	47	30	17	3
Appointive state office	12	10	20	7
Governor	16	9	5	4

SOURCE: Samuel P. Huntington, "Congressional Responses to the Twentieth Century," in David B. Truman (ed.), *The Congress and America's Future* (Prentice-Hall, 1965), p. 14.

Huntington observes:

The differences in geographical mobility and career pattern reflect two different styles of life which cut across the usual occupational groupings. Businessmen, lawyers, and bankers are found in both Congress and the administration. But those in Congress are likely to be small businessmen, small-town lawyers, and small-town bankers. Among the sixty-six lawyers in the Senate in 1963, for instance, only two. . . had been "prominent corporation counsel" before going into politics. Administration leaders, in contrast, are far more likely to be affiliated with large national industrial corporations, with Wall Street or State Street law firms, and with New York banks.

Huntington concludes:

The absence of mobility between Congress and the executive branch and the differing backgrounds of the leaders of the two branches of government stimulate different policy attitudes. Congressmen tend to be oriented toward local needs and small-town ways of thought. The leaders of the administration and of the great private national institutions are more likely to think in national terms.[16]

Whether or not one shares Huntington's objection to the "provincialism of congressmen," it is clear that differences in recruitment patterns can contrib-

[14]Samuel P. Huntington, "Congressional Responses to the Twentieth Century," in Truman (ed.), *op. cit.*, p. 12.
[15]*Ibid.*, p. 13.
[16]*Ibid.*, pp. 14–15.

ute to different points of view in the executive and legislature and to tension between the branches.

TENURE IN OFFICE

Two consequences of the decreasing competitiveness of congressional elections (page 374) are that the number of years served by the average member is rising and that the number of new members is decreasing. Table 16-4 demonstrates the escalation in the percentage of veteran members in both houses over the past hundred years and shows that the trend in the House is more pronounced than that in the Senate. Table 16-4 records the increase in the length of the average congressional term. Huntington concludes that the "infusion of new blood has reached an all-time low."[17]

TABLE 16-4

Veteran Congressmen in Congress

Date	Representatives Elected to House More Than Once	Senators Elected to Senate More Than Once
1871	53%	32%
1887	63	45
1915	74	47
1935	77	54
1961	87	66

SOURCE: Samuel P. Huntington, "Congressional Responses to the Twentieth Century," in David B. Truman (ed.), *The Congress and America's Future* (Prentice-Hall, 1965), p. 9.

The Structure of Power

To cope with its legislative and other duties, Congress, over the decades, has developed an elaborate organization, which distributes political power in different ways to different people. The student of Congress must understand how Congress works and how its structure of power affects who gets what, when, and how.

HOW A BILL BECOMES LAW: AN OVERVIEW

The diagram on pages 382–383, indicating the formal steps a bill must go through to become law, is intended to help the student avoid getting lost in a morass of detail. Two generalizations about this process can be made at the outset. First, the complexity of the congressional system provides a tremendous built-in advantage for the *opponents* of any measure. Our diagram divides the legislative process into fifteen steps. Proponents of legislation must be victorious at every one of them; opponents need only prevail at one.

[17]*Ibid.*, p. 9.

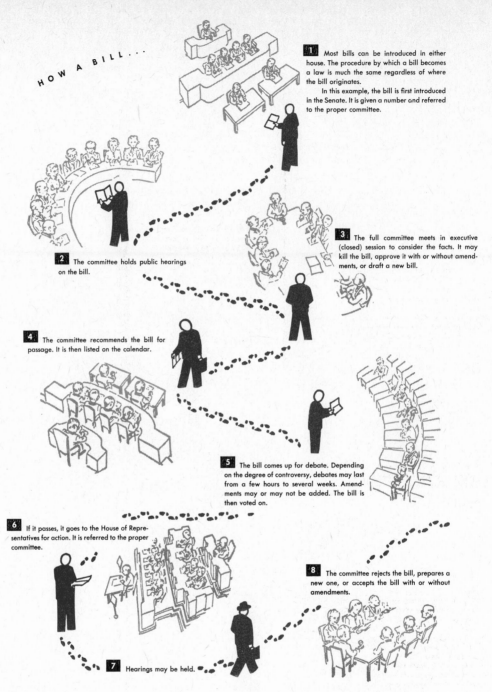

HOW A BILL...

1 Most bills can be introduced in either house. The procedure by which a bill becomes a law is much the same regardless of where the bill originates.

In this example, the bill is first introduced in the Senate. It is given a number and referred to the proper committee.

2 The committee holds public hearings on the bill.

3 The full committee meets in executive (closed) session to consider the facts. It may kill the bill, approve it with or without amendments, or draft a new bill.

4 The committee recommends the bill for passage. It is then listed on the calendar.

5 The bill comes up for debate. Depending on the degree of controversy, debates may last from a few hours to several weeks. Amendments may or may not be added. The bill is then voted on.

6 If it passes, it goes to the House of Representatives for action. It is referred to the proper committee.

7 Hearings may be held.

8 The committee rejects the bill, prepares a new one, or accepts the bill with or without amendments.

Adapted from *The Journal of the National Education Association.*

And each of these stages presents multiple opportunities for delay and defeat. Table 16-5 contains a partial list[18] of the danger points that must be

[18]Froman, *op. cit.*, p. 18.

12 If it is passed by the second body but contains differences, either house may request a conference committee. The conferees meet and try to reconcile their differences. Five conferees, representing both parties, are usually appointed from each house.

11 It goes before the entire body and is debated and voted on.

13 Generally, they reach an agreement. They report back to their respective houses. The report is accepted or rejected.

10 The Rules Committee is one of the most powerful of the committees in the House of Representatives. After a bill has been recommended for passage by the committee to which it was referred, the Rules Committee can block it or clear it for debate before the entire House.

14 If the report is accepted by both houses, the bill is signed by the Speaker of the House and the President of the Senate and is sent to the President of the United States.

9 The committee recommends the bill for passage. It is listed on the calendar and is sent to the Rules Committee.

15 The President may sign or veto the bill within ten days. If he does not sign within ten days and Congress is still in session, the bill automatically becomes law. If Congress has adjourned before the ten days have elapsed and the President has not signed the bill, it does not become law. This is known as a pocket veto. If the President returns the bill with a veto message, it may still become law if passed by a two-thirds majority in each house.

... BECOMES A LAW.

avoided—and many of these hindrances exist in both houses. To add to the complexity, many programs require dual legislative action. Thus, the supporters of a new poverty program, say, must obtain both an *authorization bill*, creating the program, and an *appropriations bill*, funding it. Opponents of the new program can ambush it at any stage of the consideration of either bill.

383

TABLE 16-5

Points at Which a Bill May Be Delayed or Defeated

Delay	Defeat
In committee:	
Referring to a subcommittee	Inaction
Prolonged hearings	Negative vote
Refusal to report	
In subcommittee:	
Prolonged hearings	Inaction
Refusal to report	Negative vote
In Rules Committee:	
Refusal to schedule hearings	Inaction
Prolonged hearings	Negative vote
Refusal to report	
Slowness in scheduling the bill	
On floor—demand for full requirements of the rules:	
Reading of the journal	Defeat of rule
Repeated quorum calls	Motion to strike enacting clause
Refusing unanimous consent to dispense with roll-call votes	Motion to recommit
	Defeat on final vote
Prolonging debate	
Various points of order	

Second, because of this complex procedure, getting a bill through Congress requires more than a simple majority of the membership. The problem of majority-building is

complicated by the existence of multiple decision-points. . . . Under normal circumstances there must be a majority in the subcommittee, a majority in the committee, a majority in the Rules Committee (if in the House), a majority to defeat amendments on the floor, often a majority against a recommittal motion, and a majority on final passage. These "majorities" involve different people in different situations at different points in time. The problems which arise in building a coalition may vary considerably at each of these decision-points.[19]

No wonder that a critic of Congress, Robert Bendiner, entitled his book *Obstacle Course on Capitol Hill.*

INTRODUCING A BILL

Although the diagram shows Senate and House acting consecutively, it is common for a bill to be introduced into each chamber and acted on simultaneously. The decision about whether to press for action in both houses or to begin in one or the other has complex political ramifications. If a bill is expected to face rough sledding in the Senate, for example, its sponsors may seek House passage, hoping that a sizable victory would spur the Senate into action. However, members of the House who would support the bill might prefer not to go on record in favor of an unpopular lost cause if they foresee a

[19]*Ibid.*, p. 19.

The Capitol

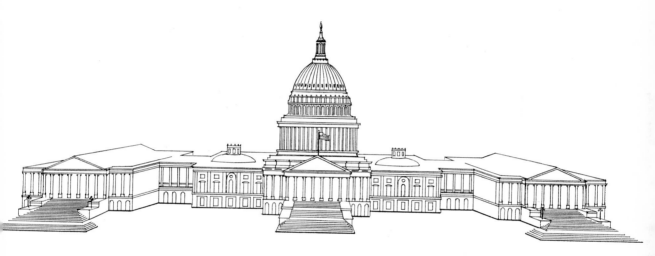

Congress is the seat of legislative authority, the center of public debate, a carry-over of folksy political traditions from earlier days—and a collection of several hundred fiercely independent politicians with separate but overlapping constituencies. The architecture of the Capitol bespeaks its ways—two chambers, endless corridors, ornate rotundas and galleries, and a rabbit warren of grand rooms, tiny offices, winding passageways. It has many entrances; it is accessible to all. There is no culminating point of authority but a multiplicity of decision centers.

HOUSE OF REPRESENTATIVES

1 Speaker's Office
2 Committee on Ways and Means
3 Parliamentarian
4 Library
5 Cloakroom
6 Members' Retiring Room
7 House Chamber
8 Committee on Appropriations
9 Minority Whip

10 House Reception Room
11 House Minority Conference Room
12 House Majority Conference Room
13 House Document Room
14 Subcommittee on Foreign Affairs
15 Representative's Office
16 Prayer Room
17 Minority Leader

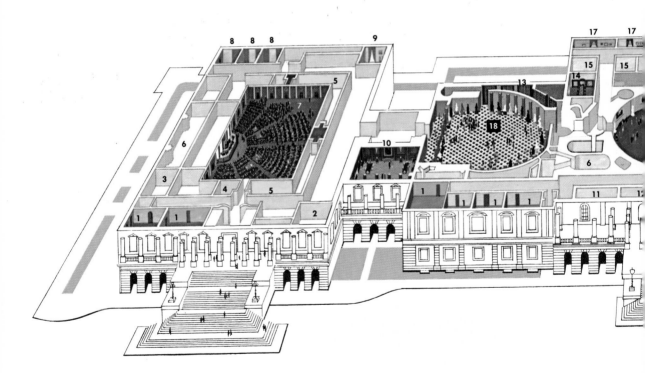

PUBLIC AREAS

18 Statuary Hall
19 Rotunda
20 Senate Rotunda
21 Old Senate Chamber
(later, Supreme Court Chamber)

SENATE

22 Senator's Office
23 Executive Clerk
24 Senate Conference Room
25 Senate Disbursing Office
26 Minority Leader
27 Majority Leader
28 Office of the Vice President
29 Senators' Reception Room

30 Cloakroom
31 Senate Chamber
32 Marble Room
33 Room of the President
34 Office of the Secretary
35 Chief Clerk
36 Bill Clerk and Journal Clerk
37 Official Reporters of Debates

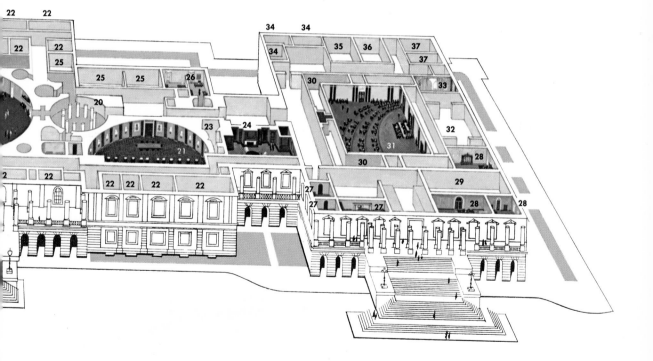

Senate filibuster against it. Here—as at all stages—the political skill and judgment of a bill's sponsors are crucial.

Although a great deal of legislation is drawn up in the executive departments (one congressman estimates that 80 percent of the bills enacted into law originate in the executive branch),[20] every bill must be introduced by a member of each house. The administration generally seeks to have its legislation introduced by the chairman of the relevant committee or by a ranking member. A bill's sponsors serve as its managers at each step, and if it is reported out of committee, they will also serve as its floor managers.

The number of bills introduced each year is tremendous. During a recent session, 20,387 bills were introduced. (This number is inflated by the House practice of many members submitting identical bills; the Senate permits joint sponsorship of a single bill.) About four or five times as many bills are introduced in the House as in the Senate.

Normally referral to a committee is automatic. Nevertheless, some political discretion may be involved. For example, the civil rights bill of 1963 was based on the commerce clause of the Constitution. In the Senate, the bill was referred to the Commerce Committee, whose chairman, Senator Warren Magnuson of Washington, was more favorably disposed to it than the chairman of the Judiciary Committee, Senator James Eastland of Mississippi. In the House, on the other hand, the bill was sent to the Judiciary Committee, chaired by Emanuel Celler of New York, rather than to the Interstate and Foreign Commerce Committee, headed by Oren Harris of Arkansas.

COMMITTEES—THE LITTLE LEGISLATURES

The main work of Congress is done in committees and subcommittees. Deluged by several thousand bills in a year, Congress could not do its job unless it delegated work to these "little legislatures." There are four types of congressional committees. *Special* or *select committees* ordinarily make specific investigations rather than introduce legislation; after submitting their report they are dissolved. When problems arise that need joint consideration, the House and Senate occasionally create *joint committees* composed of members of both chambers. *Conference committees*, a special kind of joint committee, are appointed by the presiding officers of the House and Senate when the two chambers disagree over legislation; their functions are discussed on page 405. By far the most important are the *standing committees*, which do the main work of framing legislation.

The House of Representatives has twenty standing committees with an average membership of about thirty, and these are divided into 125 subcommittees. The committees are, as Speaker Reed once said, "the eye, the ear, the hand, and very often the brain of the House." Among the most important of them are the spending and taxing committees—namely, Appropriations and Ways and Means—and the Rules Committee.

Standing committees have great power, for to them are referred all bills introduced in the House. They can defeat bills, pigeonhole them for weeks, amend them beyond recognition, or speed them on their way. In a re-

[20]Huntington, *op. cit.*, p. 23.

cent Congress, only 11 percent of the bills introduced were reported out of committee. Committee inaction will usually kill a bill. Although it can forcibly be brought to the floor of the House through a *discharge petition* signed by a majority of the House membership, congressmen are reluctant to bypass committee action. For one thing, they regard the committee members as experts in their field. A bill will be perfected in committee, whereas a bill passed without committee scrutiny may incorporate hidden pitfalls. Also there is a strong sense of reciprocity—you respect my committee's jurisdiction, and I will respect yours. It is not surprising that few discharge petitions gain the necessary number of signatures.

The Senate has sixteen standing committees, each composed of seven to twenty-seven members. Whereas a congressman generally holds only one committee assignment, each senator normally serves on three committees and often on as many as six or eight subcommittees. Among the most important Senate committees are Foreign Relations, Finance, Appropriations, and Government Operations (this committee supervises and investigates the executive agencies). Senate committees have the same powers over the framing of legislation as do those of the House, but they do not have the same degree of power to keep bills from reaching the floor, primarily because Senate rules allow unallied amendments to be attached to nonappropriation bills.

Standing committees are bipartisan. The chairman and a majority of the members are elected from the majority party, and the minority party is represented roughly in relation to the proportion of its members in the entire chamber. Getting on a politically advantageous committee is important to members of Congress. A representative from Nebraska, for example, would much rather serve on the Agriculture or Public Works Committee than on the Merchant Marine and Fisheries Committee. Members usually stay on the same committee from one Congress to the next, but freshmen, who are given minor appointments, may, when they gain seniority, move to more important committees.

How are committee members chosen? In the House of Representatives a Committee on Committees of the Republican membership allots memberships to Republican freshmen. This committee is composed of one member from each state having Republican representation in the House, and this member, chosen by his state's delegation, is almost always the senior member of the delegation. Because he has as many votes on the committee as there are Republicans in his delegation, this committee is dominated by the senior members from the large-state delegations. On the Democratic side, assignment to committees is also dominated by veterans, because the Democratic members of the House Committee on Ways and Means handle this job for the Democrats, in negotiation with senior Democrats from the respective state delegations. In both parties the procedures "are so constituted as to be virtually immune to immediate pressures brought about by electoral changes."[21] In the Senate, veterans also dominate the committee-assignment process, with each party having a small steering committee for this purpose. In both chambers it is necessary for the chamber to ratify the recommendations of party leaders, but this is done routinely.

[21]Nicholas A. Masters, "Committee Assignments in the House of Representatives," *The American Political Science Review* (June 1961), p. 350.

In making committee assignments, the party leaders are guided by a variety of considerations, but a major factor is to give each new congressman an assignment that will help him get reelected. Thus, although it might seem desirable, for example, to place an urban congressman on the Agriculture Committee to protect consumer interests, in fact, urban congressmen seldom request such an assignment and even if they do, preference will be given to congressmen from farm areas. Some committee assignments are considered more desirable than others. Appointments to key committees such as Appropriations, Foreign Affairs, or Ways and Means are rewards for members who cooperate with the leadership and show respect for the norms of the legislative way of life.

One reason Congress can cope effectively with its huge work load is that its committees and subcommittees are organized around subject-matter specialties. This allows members to develop considerable technical expertise in limited areas and to recruit skilled staffs. One consequence is that Congress is better able to criticize, challenge, and resist the experts in the executive bureaucracy. Congressmen have considerable respect for the expertise of committee members in their areas of specialization and tend to rely on their judgment. Members of interest groups and lobbyists realize the great power a specific committee has in areas of special interest to them and focus their attention on its members. Similarly, members of executive departments are careful to cultivate the chairman and members of "their" committees. One powerful Senate committee chairman reminded his constituents of the amount of federal tax money being spent in their state: "This does not happen by accident," the Senator's campaign folder says. "It takes power and influence in Congress."

Not only are committees separate little centers of power, they are discrete political systems with norms, patterns of action, and internal processes of their own. Analyzing the House Appropriations Committee, Fenno discovered that it is characterized by a remarkable agreement among its members on key issues and the role the committee should play. Leadership in the committee is stable and its members tend to remain a long time; they have worked out a way of life emphasizing conformity, give-and-take, and hard work. The subcommittee chairmen of the House Appropriations Committee become specialists on the budgets and programs of the agencies within the scope of their subcommittee's jurisdiction and often exercise more influence over administrative policy than does any other single congressman. For example, the chairman of the Appropriations Subcommittee on Foreign Aid has more influence over that program than the chairman of the House Committee on Foreign Affairs. The several appropriations subcommittees defer to one another's recommendations and back up the decisions of the parent committee.[22] The Committee has a clearly defined concept of its function —"there is no budget which cannot be cut"—and is remarkably successful in socializing new members to its norms.

Chairmen and the rule of seniority.   Crucial in protecting this separate system of power is the committee chairman, who has authority to set up sub-

[22]Richard F. Fenno, Jr., "The House Appropriations Committee as a Political System: The Problem of Integration," *The American Political Science Review* (June 1962), pp. 310–324.

committees and to appoint subcommittee chairmen. Although every member of a committee has one vote, the committee chairman is almost always the most influential member, for he holds certain formal as well as informal powers.

It is difficult to exaggerate the power of a committee chairman. Even on committees with comparatively democratic procedures, chairmen are generally able to exercise firm control, and what the committee does is seldom different from what the chairman wants it to do. Events have not served to outdate the description by Woodrow Wilson of those who command the committees: petty barons who "may at will exercise an almost despotic sway within their own shires, and may sometimes threaten to convulse even the realm itself." . . . The most awesome power of a chairman is his ability to prevent his committee from acting and thus prevent Congress from acting.[23]

Chairmen have considerable discretion regarding the scheduling of committee meetings; they also control the agendas of meetings, dominate committee procedure, and have power to recognize—or not recognize—those who wish to speak. Like the chairman, the other ranking committee members of both parties are particularly influential because they draw upon experience in committee work, legislative and parliamentary know-how, and wide contacts in Congress and outside.

Chairmanships are awarded by the rule of *seniority*. The member of the majority party who has had the longest continuous service on the committee becomes chairman. (The member of the minority party with the longest continuous service on the committee is the *ranking minority member*.) The chairman may be at odds with his fellow partisans in Congress, he may oppose his party's national program, he may even be incompetent—still, he has the right to the chairmanship under the workings of seniority.

The rule of seniority means that chairmen are not chosen by their own committees, by their party, or by the House or Senate as a whole. They are really picked by the voters in their districts and states, who give them seniority by sending them back to Congress. Thus, the key makers of national policy in Congress are locally chosen and locally responsible. The seniority rule bestows the most influence in Congress on those constituencies that are politically stable or even stagnant—where party competition is low or where a particular interest group or city or rural machine predominates. It stacks the cards against areas where the two parties are more evenly matched, interest in politics high, the number of votes large, and competition between groups keen. These are the very areas most likely to reflect quickly and typically the political tides that sweep the nation. The seniority system renders those members who are least susceptible to the displeasure of the national electorate safe from pressure within Congress and makes them its most powerful members. The *status quo* is doubly reinforced.

What groups does the seniority system benefit? When Democrats control a chamber—especially the House—committee and subcommittee chairmen

[23]Daniel M. Berman, *In Congress Assembled* (Macmillan, 1964), pp. 121, 122. See also George Goodwin, Jr., "Subcommittees: The Miniature Legislatures of Congress," *The American Political Science Review* (September 1962), pp. 596–604; and Charles O. Jones, "The Role of the Congressional Subcommittee," *Midwest Journal of Political Science* (November 1962), pp. 327–344.

tend disproportionately to be Southerners from rural and small-town areas, along with a few products of city machines. When Republicans are in control, the Middle Western rural areas tend to gain a disproportionate number of chairmanships. Whatever party controls, the chairmanships go mostly to the rural areas: In a recent Congress the 217 most urban districts produced only 26 percent of the House chairmen while the 218 least urban districts accounted for 74 percent. The imbalance is even greater if one takes into account the relative importance of the committees.

Because in both chambers the seniority system works against the urban, more liberal districts, the rule of seniority tends to make the voice of Congress a conservative one, especially in the lower chamber. It also creates conflicts between Congress and the White House. For the committee chairmanships are most likely to be in the hands of men who are least likely to support the policies sponsored by the President, whatever his party. President Eisenhower, for example, during his first two years in office, had to deal with Republican committee chairmen who had been accumulating seniority during the years of Democratic supremacy and who generally represented different groups in the Republican party from those the President represented. And President Johnson had to work with committee chairmen predominantly from the Southern or Western wing of his party, many of whom opposed key items of the President's legislative program: for example, Senator James Eastland of Mississippi was chairman of the Senate Judiciary Committee—to which all civil rights bills are referred. Senator Eastland is a vigorous opponent of the civil rights plank of the Democratic party platform, of civil rights measures favored by Democratic Presidents, and of civil rights measures favored by a majority of his own party in the Senate.

The seniority system also undermines national party cohesion. Chairmen of the committees are not accountable to their own national party for the exercise of their authority. In the words of one student, the system

. . . divides the authority of the party leaders [those elected by the party in Congress, such as the Speaker or majority leaders] and impairs their practical capacity to carry out consistently a general program of party legislation. It may even defeat the projects to which the majority of a party have been publicly pledged. . . . It makes the party system a less effective instrument than it might and should be in organizing majorities within the House for serving the manifest needs of the people of the country.[24]

Seniority may have few friends outside of Congress, but Matthews reports that "among senators, it is almost universally approved."[25] It is defended on the grounds that in elevating the most experienced members to leadership positions, it is automatic and impersonal and prevents disputes among congressmen. Basically, the argument about seniority concerns political self-interest. Rural interests naturally tend to favor the system, while it is opposed by such groups as organized labor, supporters of civil rights legislation, and

[24]A. N. Holcombe, *Our More Perfect Union* (Harvard Univ. Press, 1950), p. 185. For a scholarly treatment of the subject that warns against exaggerating the impact of the system, see George Goodwin, Jr., "The Seniority System in Congress," *The American Political Science Review* (June 1959), pp. 412–436. For a participant's defense of the system, see Emanuel Celler, "The Seniority Rule in Congress," *Western Political Quarterly* (March 1961), pp. 160–167.

[25]Matthews, *op. cit.*, p. 163.

other urban-based interests, who feel that it gives rural interests and their conservative representatives too much power in Congress. Yet liberal groups have not always been reluctant to profit from the system when it was within their power to do so. For example, the public outcry in response to the Supreme Court's school-prayer decision (page 111) was loud; a constitutional amendment to permit prayer in the public schools almost certainly would have been supported by the required two-thirds of each house, yet Chairman Emanuel Celler—much to the relief of liberals and civil libertarians—was able to kill the bill in his House Judiciary Committee.[26] If the Supreme Court's reapportionment decisions cause the rule of seniority to enhance the influence of urban-based Northern interests, it will be interesting to see if those defending and those opposing the rule of seniority switch sides.

Courtesy Tom Little, © 1965 by The New York Times Company; reprinted by permission.

The functions of congressional committees. The committee stage is the point in the congressional process at which the minute details of legislation are subjected to intensive scrutiny. A committee's staff may first conduct extensive research. When an important and controversial bill is under consideration, hearings will last for weeks; a host of administrative officials, lobbyists, technical experts, interested citizens, and members of Congress will testify. Although all committee members may not attend every hearing, they can follow the proceedings by means of verbatim transcripts. The public hearings with which we are familiar may be more interesting to visitors than House or Senate sessions, but the most important work of committees is done in *executive session,* from which visitors are barred. Committee decisions are by majority vote.

One of the most controversial activities of Congress in recent years has been committee investigations, especially the well-publicized open hearings such as those of the House Un-American Activities Committee. Why does Congress investigate? Hearings by standing committees or by their subcommittees are the most important source of information and opinion. They provide an arena in which experts can submit their views and data, statements and statistics can be entered into the record, and congressmen can quiz a wide variety of witnesses.

But committee investigations serve other functions as well. Public hearings are an important channel of communication. A committee or committee chairman may use a hearing to address his colleagues in Congress—thus, the late Senator Estes Kefauver's exposé of the drug industry was one way of impressing upon Congress the need for regulatory legislation. Committee

[26]William M. Beaney and Edward N. Beiser, "Prayer and Politics: The Impact of Engel and Schempp on the Political Process," *Journal of Public Law* (1964), pp. 475–503.

hearings may also be used to communicate with the public at large. Senator Fulbright's televised interrogation of Secretary of State Rusk was not intended to obtain new information for the Foreign Relations Committee; Fulbright was attempting to educate or at least influence the nation.

Some investigations by regular committees are related to the overseeing of administration. A committee can summon any administrative official — from Cabinet officer to stenographer — to testify in public or private hearings. Some officials greatly fear these inquiries; they dread the loaded questions of hostile congressmen and the likelihood that some adminstrative error in their agency may be uncovered and publicized.

Finally, Congress uses committee investigations to reward its friends and punish its enemies. A member of an administrative agency or a ranking military officer who supports a project being downgraded by the President but that is favored on the Hill may be called to testify. Bowing to the pressure of friendly questions, he is "forced" to agree with the distinguished senator that his agency does need more money for this vital project than the Budget Bureau has granted him. But questioning can degenerate into browbeating when the witness represents a group that is out of favor such as the Fair Play for Cuba Committee. And the problem of "witchhunting" is exacerbated when the questioning congressman is using the investigation to establish a reputation on which he hopes to build his future political career.[27]

Are there any constitutional limits to Congress's power to compel private citizens to answer questions? The Supreme Court in 1957 (*Watkins v. United States*) cautioned Congress that the First Amendment limits its power to investigate, that no committee has the power "to expose for the sake of exposure," that Congress and its committees are not courts to try and punish individuals, and that "no inquiry is an end in itself; it must be related to, and in furtherance of, a legitimate task of Congress." Nonetheless, only a minority of the Supreme Court has shown any disposition to provide a judicial check on legislative investigations in behalf of First Amendment rights.[28] The judicial checks used so far are only two: the Fifth Amendment protection against self-incrimination has been construed broadly to protect witnesses who are willing to risk public censure by invoking the amendment to refuse to answer questions; and the Supreme Court has narrowly construed the crime of contempt of Congress in order to avoid punishment of witnesses for refusing to answer questions unless these questions were *clearly pertinent* to the functions of an authorized committee.

VOTING PATTERNS IN CONGRESS

Political scientists have devoted considerable effort to identifying regular patterns of behavior in the House and Senate. They have demonstrated that on nonunanimous roll calls, the voting in Congress follows party lines more

[27]For graphic examples of the civil liberties problems involved in Congressional investigations, see Telford Taylor, *Grand Inquest: The Story of Congressional Investigations* (Simon and Schuster, 1955); and Edward Lamb, *Trial by Battle: The Case History of a Washington Witch-Hunt* (Center for the Study of Democratic Institutions, 1964).

[28]*Barenblatt* v. *United States* (1959); *Wilkinson* v. *United States* (1961); *Braden* v. *United States* (1961). For an excellent discussion of this issue, see Martin Shapiro, *Law and Politics in the Supreme Court* (Free Press, 1964), Chap. 2.

often than it is related to any other factor,[29] even though party leaders do not have the power to demand votes from members of Congress.[30] Party-line divisions, with the majority of voting Democrats arrayed against the majority of voting Republicans, have appeared on about 40 percent of the roll-call votes in recent years. In these party-line votes in the 1968 session, the average Democrat voted with the majority of his party 57 percent of the time, and the average Republican voted with his party 63 percent of the time.[31]

The accompanying illustration, based on congressional support of President Kennedy's legislative proposals in 1961, provides a good indication of the significance of the party affiliation of congressmen. It was clearly to President Kennedy's advantage to have Democratic rather than Republican legislators.

How can we explain this phenomenon? It might be that the two parties recruit or advance as candidates men with essentially different policy views. It may be that Republicans and Democrats tend to represent different kinds of constituencies. It is also possible (and there is considerable evidence to support this view) that parties function as reference groups—as important sources of voting cues.[32] Congress is organized along party lines; friendship groups tend to be intraparty more than interparty, and partisan leaders in

[29]Jewell and Patterson, *op. cit.*, pp. 416, 417.
[30]Gerald Marwell, "Party, Region and the Dimensions of Conflict in the House of Representatives, 1949–1954," *The American Political Science Review* (June 1967), pp. 380–399.
[31]*Congressional Quarterly Weekly Report* (Oct. 25, 1968), p. 2933.
[32]This discussion is based on Jewell and Patterson, *op. cit.*, p. 417.

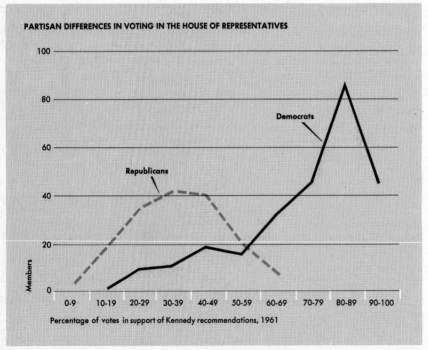

PARTISAN DIFFERENCES IN VOTING IN THE HOUSE OF REPRESENTATIVES

V.O. Key, *Politics, Parties and Pressure Groups*; copyright © 1967 by Thomas Y. Crowell Company.

both the executive and legislative branches apply rewards and sanctions primarily to members of their own party. On many issues the pressure for conformity to a party position is immediate and direct, whereas constituency pressures may be distant, vague, and contradictory. Congressmen appear to be under pressure to go along with their party, whenever possible. In the Senate "party 'discipline' may be weak, but party 'identification' is strong."[33]

One important voting pattern in Congress reflects the unofficial conservative coalition, a voting bloc of Southern Democrats and Republicans. A majority of Southern Democrats and a majority of Republicans have voted together against the majority of Northern Democrats on about 20 to 25 percent of the roll-call votes in recent years. And although the Republican debacle in 1964 weakened the coalition's strength, it reasserted itself after the 1966 elections.[34] The conservative coalition is most likely to appear on domestic issues, especially social-welfare legislation, but its overall strength in Congress cannot be measured by roll-call votes, because the many committee chairmen who are members of this group are able to prevent legislation they oppose from ever being voted on.

[33]Quoted in Jewell and Patterson, *op. cit.*, p. 417.
[34]*Congressional Quarterly Weekly Report, op. cit.*, pp. 107, 108; *Ibid.* (Nov. 1, 1968), p. 2938.

The Houses of Congress

17 The single most important fact about Congress is that each chamber has an absolute veto over the lawmaking of the other. Each house of course can run its own affairs, set its own rules, and conduct its own investigations, but the legislative role is shared. Moreover each chamber must be seen as a separate institution even though it reflects somewhat similar political forces and shares organizational patterns with the other.

The House of Representatives

A unique power institution in Congress is the House Rules Committee. Because the House handles several thousand bills a year, someone must grant priorities and control the flow of business. In an attempt to protect itself from the "tyranny" of Speaker Joseph Cannon, who presided over the House in the early years of this century, the House vested this important political power in the Rules Committee, which was expected to act as an agent of the House majority.[1] This committee is one of the regular standing committees of the lower chamber, but it has exceptional power. In the normal course of events, a bill cannot come up for action on the floor of the House without a rule from the Rules Committee. By failing to act or refusing to grant a rule, the committee can kill any bill. Furthermore, the rule granted stipulates the conditions under which the bill will be discussed, and this

394   [1]James A. Robinson, *The House Rules Committee* (Bobbs-Merrill, 1963), pp. 60–61.

may seriously affect its chance of passage. The Rules Committee may grant a rule that makes it easy for a bill to be "amended to death" on the floor. A special rule may prohibit amendments altogether or provide that only members of the committee reporting the bill may offer amendments. And the rule also sets the length of debate.

TRAFFIC COP OR ROADBLOCK?

What kind of traffic cop is this? The committee's power would seldom be questioned if the committee were fairly representative of the rank and file of the House. But it is not. It is dominated by veteran congressmen who have been reelected time and time again from "safe" districts regardless of the ebb and flow of national politics. And in recent years, a coalition of conservative Republicans and conservative Southern Democrats—the two congressional parties—has dominated the Rules Committee and created difficulties for Presidents of both parties. Liberals denounced the committee for being unrepresentative, unfair, dictatorial, and negative. Its defenders contended that the committee did just what the Framers of the Constitution wanted our system to do—prevent the House from responding too readily to new popular majorities. The committee's famous and long-time former chairman, Howard W. Smith, a conservative Democrat from Virginia, contends that the committee serves another function—it kills or delays bills that congressional sponsors do not want but feel they must openly support because of pressures from lobbyists or from their constituents.

For years House liberals attacked the committee and tried to reform it, but without much success. In 1949, the House established a twenty-one-day rule that allowed a committee chairman to call up a bill if the Rules Committee delayed it more than twenty-one days, but two years later the conservatives regained the upper hand and abolished the reform. In 1961, following John Kennedy's presidential campaign promise to "get America moving again," the reformers tried to purge from the committee a Southern Democrat who had deserted his party's national ticket and supported Richard Nixon in the campaign. This effort failed. The liberals, with the assistance of Speaker Sam Rayburn, were only able to gain an enlargement of the committee to provide a bit more representation for liberals, but in practice this new "Kennedy majority" on the committee was rather precarious.

The critics of the Rules Committee achieved something of a breakthrough when the Eighty-ninth Congress convened in January 1965. Their numbers swelled by the sweeping Democratic victories against Goldwater Republicans the preceding fall, liberal Democrats won passage of two reforms. One was a twenty-one-day rule that permitted the *Speaker*, with the approval of a majority of the House, to recognize a committee chairman so he could introduce a measure for House consideration if it had been before the Rules Committee for twenty-one days without having been granted a rule. A second change made it more difficult for the Rules Committee to delay sending a bill to a conference committee (see page 405). (Prior to 1965, a rule was required before a conference committee could be appointed; thus if the House and Senate passed different versions of a bill, the Rules Committee got two shots at it.) These changes became part of the basic House rules so that they would not have to be readopted at the beginning of each Congress. But they could be eliminated by specific House action if at a later time the members so wished. In the Ninetieth Congress the House again abolished the twenty-one-day rule but adopted other rules to curb the power of the Chairman of the Rules Committee to set meeting dates. One thing is certain: Representatives will continue to argue over House rules because these rules are part of the political process in the Congress.[2]

HOUSE PROCEDURE ON THE FLOOR

Once a bill has passed through the committee stage, how is it handled on the floor of the House of Representatives? In contrast to the Senate, the large membership of the House makes quick and orderly methods imperative.

Calendars. Bills reported out of committee to the floor of the House are assigned to one of three main calendars, or schedules. Finance measures —tax or appropriations, for example—are put on the *Union* calendar. All bills that are nonfiscal but still of a public character are placed on the *House* calendar. Private bills—bills dealing with individuals' problems, such as a veteran's pension—go on a *Private* calendar. These and other, minor calendars serve as a traffic-directing system designed to give each bill its fair turn. But there are also various means for taking up bills out of their calendar order. For example, House rules may be suspended by a two-thirds vote on certain days; or important bills may be brought up at any time by the Rules Committee; or immediate action on a measure may be won by unanimous consent.

Committee of the Whole. This committee, made up of all members of the House, is another means of expediting business. By sitting as the Committee of the Whole, members are able to operate more informally and quickly than under the regular House rules. For example, a quorum in the Committee of the Whole is 100, whereas under the House rules a majority of all the members is required. More important, there are no roll calls. Congressmen sometimes vote differently when a record is kept of their vote from the way they would otherwise. Very rarely does the whole House reject the recommendations of this committee, though it has the power to do so.

House cloture. In contrast to the smaller upper chamber, the House is too large to let everyone have his full say. Debate may be cut off simply by majority vote. This ready method of cloture (or closure) makes filibusters impossible. Most speakers are allowed only a few minutes, usually by prior agreement between party leaders on both sides.

Voting. Ordinarily, voting is conducted quickly in the House either by a viva voce (voice) vote or by a standing vote. Occasionally, though, some faction may want to make members go on record as to their stand on a controversial measure; in this case voting is conducted by the slower method of a vote by tellers (the members are checked off as they file past the Speaker's

[2]See Hugh Douglas Price, "Race, Religion, and the Rules Committee," in Alan F. Westin (ed.), *The Uses of Power* (Harcourt, Brace & World, 1962), pp. 13–20; James A. Robinson, "The Role of the Rules Committee in Regulating Debate in the U.S. House of Representatives," *Midwest Journal of Political Science* (February 1961), pp. 59–69; and James A. Robinson, "The Role of the Rules Committee in Arranging the Program of the U.S. House of Representatives," *Western Political Quarterly* (September 1959), pp. 653–669.

desk) or, upon demand of one-fifth of members present, by the still slower method of a roll call (the clerk calls each member by name).

THE SPEAKER

The Speaker's formal authority is not what it was fifty or seventy-five years ago when he could control committee assignments and wield almost complete control over House deliberations. Revolts of the rank and file in 1910 stripped the Speaker of most of his old-time authority. Still, he remains the single most important member of the House.

The Speaker's formal authority grows out of the fact that he can grant recognition to or withold it from those who wish to speak, he settles parliamentary disputes (with the help of a specialist in procedure), he appoints members of select and conference (but not standing) committees, and in general he directs the business on the floor.

Much more significant is the Speaker's political and behind-the-scenes influence. Although formally chosen by the House of Representatives, he is in fact picked by the majority party. Once in office, unlike the nonpartisan presiding officer of the British House of Commons, the Speaker is openly a party leader and is expected, subject to the rules of the game, to use his office to support the program of his party.

The late Speaker Sam Rayburn had unusual power. Because of his tremendous personal influence over his fellow Democrats, his support frequently proved decisive in key legislative battles. His decisions, like those of any Speaker, were of course subject to being overruled by the House, but as long as he kept the support of his own party, he was a man of enormous influence. When "Mr. Sam" did not want the House to do something, it seldom did it. His successor, John McCormack of Massachusetts, former Majority Leader of the House Democrats, does not enjoy the same kind of personal influence. But as Speaker he is a man of consequence.

PARTY OFFICERS AND MEETINGS

Next to the Speaker, the most important party officer in the House is the *majority floor leader*, who, like the Speaker, is chosen by the majority party caucus but, unlike the Speaker, is an officer only of his party and not of the House proper. The majority floor leader helps plan party strategy, confers with other party leaders, and tries to keep members of his party in line. The minority party elects a *minority floor leader*, who usually steps into the speakership when his party gains a majority in the House. Assisting each floor leader are the *party whips* (the term derives from the whipper-in, who in English fox hunts kept the hounds from leaving the pack). The whips serve as liaison between the House leadership of each party and the rank and file; they inform members when important bills will come up for a vote, exert mild pressure on them to support the leadership, and try to ensure maximum attendance on the floor when critical votes are imminent.

At the beginning of the session and occasionally thereafter, each party holds a *caucus* (or conference, as the Republicans call it). The caucus, composed of all the party's members in the House, meets privately to elect party

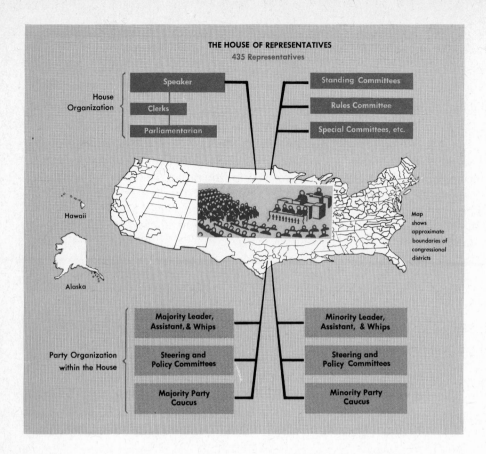

THE HOUSE OF REPRESENTATIVES
435 Representatives

House Organization

| Speaker |
| Clerks |
| Parliamentarian |

| Standing Committees |
| Rules Committee |
| Special Committees, etc. |

Hawaii

Alaska

Map shows approximate boundaries of congressional districts

Party Organization within the House

| Majority Leader, Assistant, & Whips |
| Steering and Policy Committees |
| Majority Party Caucus |

| Minority Leader, Assistant, & Whips |
| Steering and Policy Committees |
| Minority Party Caucus |

officers, approve committee assignments, discuss important legislation, and perhaps try to agree on party policy. Decisions are usually made by simple majority. In theory, the caucus is the directing party agency; in fact, this party group plays a small part in lawmaking. A decision of the Democratic caucus is binding only when approved by two-thirds of the members. When it involves a matter of constitutional interpretation (as do most measures) or when conflicting promises have been made back home (and all sorts of promises have been made), the decision is not binding at all. Republicans are not bound by any conference decision. Hardly more important than the caucus are the *steering committees*, made up of the party leadership, which do little steering but have some influence on party policy and tactics.

The House also produces a variety of groupings that come and go, some with and some without formal organization. State delegations often meet to consider business that affects the entire state. Sometimes representatives organize around common ideological concerns. For example, after the 1958 elections a group of liberal Democrats, frustrated by institutional roadblocks and by the domination of the House by the Republican-Southern Democratic coalition, formed the Democratic Study Group. The Kennedy victory and the Democratic sweep of 1964 added to the strength of the group, and it now is formally organized and has become a major instrument in securing significant alterations in rules and procedures of the House. It has bargained

398

for better representation for liberal Democrats on major House committees and has worked in behalf of legislation reflecting its liberal views.

The Senate

In many respects the Senate resembles the House. There is the same basic committee structure (but no powerful Rules Committee), the seniority system, the elected party leadership, the rather weak party committees—in short, the same dispersion of power. But the Senate is a smaller body, so its procedures can be considerably more informal.

The President of the Senate is the Vice President of the United States. But, as noted above, he does not have major influence. He is not quite a member of the "senatorial club" and can vote only in case of a tie; he will not be consulted by the leadership when many important decisions are made. The Senate also elects from among the majority party a *president pro tempore*, who is the official chairman in the absence of the Vice President. But presiding over the Senate is a thankless task and is generally carried out by the most junior members of the chamber.

Party machinery in the Senate is somewhat similar to that of the House.

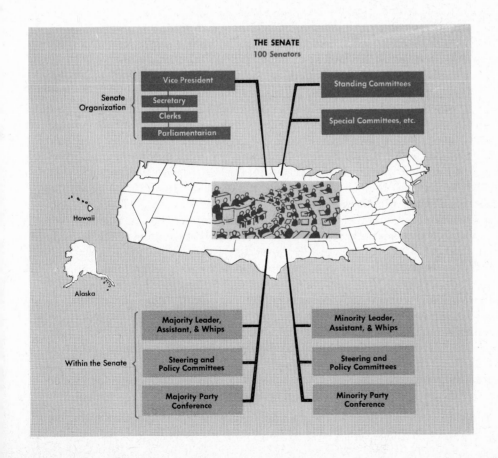

THE SENATE
100 Senators

Senate Organization
- Vice President
- Secretary
- Clerks
- Parliamentarian
- Standing Committees
- Special Committees, etc.

Hawaii

Alaska

Within the Senate
- Majority Leader, Assistant, & Whips
- Steering and Policy Committees
- Majority Party Conference
- Minority Leader, Assistant, & Whips
- Steering and Policy Committees
- Minority Party Conference

There are party conferences (in the Senate, both parties have given up the term *caucus*), majority and minority floor leaders, and party whips. In the Senate each party has a *policy committee*, composed of the leaders of the party, which is theoretically responsible for the party's overall legislative program. (In the Senate the party steering committees only handle committee assignments.) Unlike the House steering committees, the Senate's policy committees are formally provided for by law and each of them has a regular staff and a significant budget. Although the Senate policy committees have some influence on legislation, they have not asserted strong legislative leadership or managed to coordinate party policy.[3]

The majority leader, however, is usually a man of influence within the Senate and sometimes in the nation. He has the right to be the first senator to be heard on the floor and, in consultation with the minority floor leader, determines the Senate's agenda. He has much to say about committee assignments for members of his own party. But the position confers less authority than the speakership in the House, and the leader's influence depends on his political skill and the national political situation. Some majority leaders had little influence in the Senate and were relatively unknown in the nation. Others made it an important post. It was as majority floor leader that Senator Taft became "Mr. Republican."

Senator Lyndon Johnson's dramatic development of the leadership position in the Senate gave the Senate more centralized leadership than it had ever known in its history. Many hoped that Johnson's action would transform the position so that the Senate would have a means of organizing itself, identifying issues, and overcoming the divisive impact of the seniority leaders. But his successor, Senator Mike Mansfield of Montana, farmed out more of his responsibilities and displayed much less of a desire to bring Johnson's style of leadership to his position. He is quoted as saying, "I'm not the leader, really. They don't do what I tell them. I do what they tell me. . . . We've had a dispersal of responsibility. How can I know everything that's going on? The brains are in the committees."[4]

Bills are reported to the Senate floor from standing committees in much the same fashion as in the House, but there are important differences in procedure on the two floors: The Senate's Rules Committee has none of the delaying or blocking power of its counterpart in the House. The Senate uses its Committee of the Whole only for considering treaties. It has more time for debate and can carry on its business in a more informal manner. Measures in the Senate are normally debated in the order in which they are reported by committees or are taken up for discussion by unanimous consent.

THE POLITICAL ENVIRONMENT OF THE SENATE

Senators are a somewhat different breed of political animal from the average representative, and the upper chamber has a character all its own. If only

---

[3]Hugh A. Bone, "An Introduction to the Senate Policy Committees," *The American Political Science Review* (June 1956), pp. 339–359. See also Ralph K. Huitt, "Democratic Party Leadership in the Senate," *The American Political Science Review* (June 1961), pp. 333–344.

[4]Quoted by James A. Robinson, *Congress and Foreign Policy-Making* (Dorsey, 1962), pp. 215–216.

because of their six-year term, senators have more political elbow room than representatives, who, elected by smaller constituencies, may feel cramped by the necessity of devoting themselves to the needs of relatively few interest groups. In addition, senators are more likely to wield political power in their state political parties. Sometimes they virtually dominate those parties, as in the case of Huey Long of Louisiana or Robert A. Taft of Ohio. Given the relative smallness of the chamber, the average senator becomes visible and politically significant earlier in his career than the average congressman.

In a sense, the Senate is a mutual protection society. Each member tends to guard the rights and perquisites of his fellow senators—so that his own rights and perquisites will be protected in turn. Members must learn to live together. Two senators may attack each other rather sharply on the floor, only to be seen a short time later strolling together in the corridors outside.

Like any close-knit social or occupational group, the Senate has developed a set of informal but powerful folkways—standards of behavior to which new members are expected to conform.[5] New members are expected to serve an apprenticeship. "Like children," one freshman senator reported, "we are to be seen and not heard." They are to show respect to their elders and act with deference. "I attended the floor debates and voted for a year without giving a single speech," a junior senator said with pride. The new senator is encouraged to specialize—in part because of sheer necessity. Senators can be most effective in dealing with their colleagues when they restrict their speeches to areas on which they have focused. Courtesy in debate is also a cardinal rule, and debate takes place in the third person.

But by far the most important and pervasive of the folkways is reciprocity. A senator requests and receives many favors and courtesies from his fellows—always with the understanding that he will repay the kindness in some form. A senator may be out of town and request that the vote on a particular bill be delayed. A senator requests unanimous consent to suspend the rules so that he may insert material into the Congressional Record. A senator asks a committee chairman how a given bill will affect his constituents—and relies on his colleague's judgment. Reciprocity may involve seemingly trivial pleasantries—or it may involve millions of dollars in traded votes for public works appropriations. Logrolling is an institutionalized way of life.

A new senator learns the folkways by experience. If he speaks out of turn, he notices a certain coldness. Senior members subtly indicate to him that some things are simply not done. Of course, senators do deviate from the norms, but a senator who continually flouts the folkways of the Senate is likely to find that his effectiveness within the chamber is reduced.

The political import of these informal norms should not be overlooked. A senator who arrives in Washington with the conviction that basically things are well with the world can fit nicely into this pattern. He is in no hurry—especially if he is from a noncompetitive state. But a senator who arrives fired by reforming zeal is likely soon to be frustrated. Thus the folkways of the Senate buttress the *status quo* in the chamber.

[5]This discussion is based on Donald R. Matthews, *U.S. Senators and Their World* (Univ. of North Carolina Press, 1960), Chap. 5.

One major difference between the Senate and the House is that debate is sharply limited in the House and is almost unlimited in the Senate. Once a senator gains the floor, he has the right to go on talking until he relinquishes it voluntarily or through exhaustion. This right to unlimited debate may be used by a small group of senators to *filibuster*—to delay the proceedings of the Senate in order to prevent a vote.

How may a filibuster be defeated? The majority can keep the Senate in continuous session in the hope that the filibustering senator will have to give up the floor. But if three or four senators cooperate, they can keep going almost indefinitely. They merely ask one another long questions that permit their partners to take lengthy rests. So long as they keep on their feet, debate can be terminated under Senate Rule 22 only by *cloture*. Under the rule of cloture, if sixteen members sign a petition, two days later the question of curtailing debate is put to a vote. If two-thirds of the senators on the floor vote for cloture, no senator may speak for more than one hour; then the motion before the Senate must be brought to a vote.

Despite many filibusters, the Senate has acted favorably on cloture petitions only eight times since the procedure was adopted in 1917. The most spectacular filibusters of recent years have been by Southern senators determined to block civil rights legislation. During the debate on the Civil Rights Act of 1960 a group of Southern senators filibustered from February 15 to March 10. At one point in their efforts to block the legislation, the participants talked through nine days of continuous sessions. In the spring of 1962 Southern senators again organized a filibuster; it lasted thirteen days and ended with the defeat of a bill designed to eliminate discriminatory administration of literacy tests. Of the forty-three cloture votes since the rule was adopted, nineteen have been on civil rights bills. And of these, the twenty-ninth, thirty-first, and forty-second attempts (in 1964, 1965, and 1968) were the only successful ones.[6] Of course, Southern anti-civil rights senators are not the only ones who have resorted to filibustering.

The number of actual filibusters is not a proper measure of their significance. For the threat of a filibuster by an organized minority may hang over the Senate's business, and the knowledge that a bill might lead to a filibuster is often enough to force a compromise satisfactory to its opponents. Sometimes the Senate leadership, knowing that a filibuster would tie up the Senate and keep it from enacting needed legislation, does not even bother to bring a bill to the Senate floor.

Should the Senate amend Rule 22 to make it easier to end filibusters? The merits and demerits of this question are often discussed in general theoretical terms—such as, majority rule versus minority rights—but there is a policy issue behind these debates, namely, civil rights. Advocates of federal civil rights legislation know that unless they can force through a revision of Rule 22 it will be difficult to secure the kind of legislation they wish.

Significant as the filibuster is, its impact should not be exaggerated. Even

---

6"Weekly Report," *Congressional Quarterly* (March 1, 1968), p. 379.

in the area of civil rights it is gradually becoming less of a barrier. Today there are 100 senators, and those from the border states can no longer be counted on to vote against civil rights legislation. True, Southern senators can use the filibuster and the threat of it to stop civil rights bills or to force modifications, but they know that if they are too obstreperous they may force the Senate to alter Rule 22. And a really determined majority can overcome a filibuster, either by wearing the speakers down or by mobilizing the necessary votes for cloture.

"WITH THE ADVICE AND CONSENT OF THE SENATE"

The power of the Senate to confirm nominations is important constitutionally as part of our checks-and-balances system. It is even more important politically, for under the system of *senatorial courtesy* the individual senator has a virtual veto power over the major appointments in his state, provided the President belongs to his party. The arrangement is a simple one. If a senator rises and declares that a nominee to a post in his state is personally obnoxious to him, the Senate is almost certain to reject the nomination. ("Personally obnoxious" reflects not on the character of the appointee but on his politics.) In practice, therefore, the executive branch must clear nominations for such positions as postmaster or federal district judge with the senator from the relevant state. As a consequence, these positions are part of the senators' patronage power. Senatorial courtesy is a prime example of the reciprocity senators expect from one another.

The system of senatorial courtesy strengthens the senators' role both in national administration and in state politics, and it weakens national party leadership and discipline. As a curious consequence of this practice President Eisenhower was able to appoint federal district judges in the South who were much more liberal in their views on civil rights than those President Kennedy could appoint. Kennedy had to clear his appointments with the Democratic senators from the Southern states; Republican Ike had no such problem.

THE SENATE'S POWER OVER TREATIES

The Constitution provides that two-thirds of the senators present must give their consent before the President may ratify a treaty. As a result, the Secretary of State usually works closely with the Foreign Relations Committee of the Senate, and influential senators often undertake personal missions abroad and serve on delegations to the United Nations and other international bodies.

How important is the Senate's power over treaties? Secretary of State John Hay once complained that "a treaty entering the Senate is like a bull going into the arena; no one can say just how or when the final blow will fall—but one thing is certain—it will never leave the arena alive." The statistics suggest that Mr. Hay's remark was too severe. Even though a two-thirds majority is needed for treaty ratification, the Senate has unconditionally approved over 80 percent of the approximately 1,100 or more submitted to it, and many of the others were passed with amendments or reservations.

And yet it is true that some of the rejected treaties were of supreme importance; for example, Senate disapproval of the Taft-Knox arbitration treaties of
1911–1912, the Treaty of Versailles (involving United States membership in
the League of Nations), and the protocol for participating in the World Court
had a decided effect on the world role of the United States. Moreover, on
many occasions Presidents have failed to negotiate treaties, have modified
treaty provisions in advance of Senate consideration, or have even recalled
treaties already submitted in the face of opposition from various senators.

The House versus the Senate

When the Framers created a two-chamber national legisla-
ture, they anticipated that each would represent sharply different interests.
The Senate was to be a small chamber of men elected indirectly by the people and holding long, overlapping terms. The House of Representatives,
elected *in toto* every two years, was to be the direct implement of the people. The Senate did provide a conservative check on the House, especially
in the late nineteenth and early twentieth centuries when it was "a bastion
of conservatism, something of a 'rich man's club,' and highly resistant to liberal or progressive sentiment."[7] But many factors, chiefly political, have altered the character of the House and the Senate. In recent years, especially
since World War II, except for the civil rights legislation, the House has
become a conservative check on the more liberal Senate. Executive departments and agencies view the Senate as a court of appeals for their appropriations that have been "shot down" by the House.[8]

How has this come about? One reason, noted above, the large number of
relatively safe seats in the House, the impact of which is magnified by the
seniority system. And at the same time that the number of safe, noncompetitive House districts has been increasing, the number of safe, noncompetitive
Senate seats has been decreasing. Moreover, the urbanization of the nation
has left most states with large and growing metropolitan areas. Hence a senator's constituency is usually more populous than a representative's and
consists of a wider variety of interests. Compare, for example, the conservative Republican representatives from upstate New York, who have little fear
of offending those who live in New York City, with Republican Senator Jacob Javits, who must be concerned above all with the mass of voters in the
New York City area. Froman points out:

Voters with population characteristics associated with liberalism are not
randomly distributed throughout the state. For example, large numbers of Negroes are often located in only a few congressional districts within a state.
Hence most House members have few Negro constituents. Senate members,
however, have all the Negroes in the state as constituents. The same is true
for such factors as urbanism. There are more congressional districts below

[7]H. D. Price, "The Congressman and the Electoral Arena," in David B. Truman
(ed.), *The Congress and America's Future* (Prentice-Hall, 1965).
[8]Lewis A. Froman, Jr., *Congressmen and Their Constituencies* (Rand McNally, 1963), p. 142.

the state average on urbanism than above it. Since senators represent the state average, House members are by and large more conservative.[9]

TABLE 17-1 Major Differences between House and Senate	
House	*Senate*
Larger (435 members)	Smaller (100 members)
More formal	Less formal
More hierarchically organized	Less hierarchically organized
Acts more quickly	Acts more slowly
Rules more rigid	Rules more flexible
Power less evenly distributed	Power more evenly distributed
Longer apprentice period	Shorter apprentice period
More impersonal	More personal
Less prestige	More prestige
More conservative	More liberal

SOURCE: Lewis A. Froman, Jr., *Congressmen and Their Constituencies* (Rand McNally, 1963), p. 7.

Given the differences between House and Senate, it is not surprising that the version of a bill passed by one chamber may differ substantially from the version of the same bill passed by the other. Only if both houses pass an absolutely identical measure can it become law. As a general rule, one house accepts the language of the other, but about 10 percent of all bills passed must be referred to a *conference committee.*

If neither house will accept the other's bill, a special committee of members from each chamber settles the differences. Appointed to the conference committee by their presiding officers, the members are usually the first lawmakers who handled the bill in their respective chambers. The most senior senator usually serves as chairman of the conference committee, which has anywhere from three to nine members from each house. Both parties are represented, with the majority party having a larger number. The proceedings of this committee—not open to the public—are usually a shrewd and elaborate bargaining process. Concessions must be made not only to each chamber but to the more powerful groups within the chambers. Brought back to the respective chambers, the conference report can be accepted or rejected (often with further negotiations ordered), but it cannot be amended. Each set of conferees must convince its colleagues that any concessions made to the other house were on trivialities and that nothing basic in their own version of the bill was surrendered.

How much leeway does a conference committee have? Ordinarily the conferees are expected to stay somewhere between the alternatives set by the different versions, but on many matters where there is no clear middle ground, conferees are sometimes accused of exceeding their instructions and producing a new measure. Indeed, the conference committee has even been called a third house of Congress—one that arbitrarily revises Senate and House policy in secret session. Despite such criticism, however, some kind

[9]*Ibid.*, p. 14.

of conference committee is indispensable to the workings of a bicameral legislature such as ours.

The Role of the Individual Legislator

Discussions of the role of the individual legislator have centered around two contrasting (and sometimes conflicting) models—the legislator as *delegate*, accurately following the detailed wishes of his constituents, and the legislator as *trustee*, taking a "higher view" and acting in the nation's best interest. But we now know that both models bear little relationship to reality. The representative cannot follow the detailed instructions of his constituents, for, as we have seen, they do not provide such instructions.[10] But deliberation is rare too. "I have expected deliberation," one newly elected senator explained. "Instead, I . . . found haste and even a certain amount of frenzy." His colleagues agree that theirs is an impossible job. "Thousands of bills come before the Senate each Congress," said another member. "If some senator knows the fine details of more than half a dozen of them, I've never heard of him."[11] "I am appalled," said one representative, "at how much congressmen are expected to do for the nation. We have to know too much. We have to make too many decisions. . . . No matter how hardworking and conscientious a congressman is, no matter how much homework he does, he just can't master these problems. We just don't have the time to keep informed properly."[12] In addition to the tremendous flood of legislation, a congressman is expected to perform a wide variety of services for his constituents. One representative complains that he is just a glorified messenger boy, employment agency, troubleshooter, glad-hand extender, convention goer, veterans' affairs adjuster, financial wet nurse, good samaritan, and recoverer of lost baggage. In some Scandinavian countries, a special official, the ombudsman, receives and investigates complaints in behalf of the individual citizen who feels he has a grievance against a government official. The United States has 535 legislators who serve as ombudsmen.[13]

To complicate matters further, the average senator or congressman's expenses exceed his salary. A *New York Times* survey some years ago found that the additional expense averaged $3,000 a year.[14] Although many are wealthy enough to make up the deficit from investments, others must continue their connections with their law firms or businesses. Some make sizable amounts from writings and lecture tours. "I have to scrounge the countryside like the Russian Army, making speeches and lectures along the way," one senator complained. And campaigning for the next election is a never-ending process—especially for representatives, with their two-year terms.

[10]Angus Campbell, Philip E. Converse, Warren E. Miller, and Donald E. Stokes, *Elections and the Political Order* (Wiley, 1966), p. 211.

[11]Matthews, *op. cit.*, pp. 79, 95.

[12]Charles L. Clapp, *The Congressman: His Work as He Sees It* (Brookings, 1963), pp. 104–105, provides an illuminating picture of Congress as seen by members.

[13]Price, in Truman (ed.), *op. cit.* For a detailed study of ombudsmen, see Walter Gellhorn. *Ombudsmen and Others: Citizen's Protectors in Nine Countries* (Harvard Univ. Press, 1966).

[14]Matthews, *op. cit.*, p. 89.

9:00—Congressman arrives at office.

9:01—Telephone rings. Talks, signs mail.

9:58—Rushes off to committee meeting.

10 to 12—Hearing. At noon goes to floor.

1:00—Starts lunch. Call-bell rings.

3:00—Page brings note. Lady outside.

4:00—At office, sees home-state students.

4:15—Call to floor again.

7 to 12—Does homework.

6:30—Dinner with wife.

12:00—And so to bed.

How can the average congressman cope with this burden? The answer appears to be by specializing and by delegating many of his decisions to others. His legislative assistant may have considerable influence. The freshman representative or senator quickly discovers that he can master only a limited amount of the business before the Congress. He gradually identifies those areas with which he will concern himself, and he develops a communications network that will allow him to deal with the rest. He accepts cues from others—from party leaders and experts in Congress, especially ranking committee members. In reality, his vote on the many bills of no concern to him is at the disposal of one or another of these opinion leaders. Lobbyists make sure that the congressman is made aware of how a particular bill will affect his constituents.

Finally, proposals are judged on the basis of general evaluative dimensions.[15] The torrent of information from party leaders, committee chairmen, organized groups, and the executive departments interacts with the basic philosophy each congressman has built up over the years. His attitudes toward unions, business, Negroes, and so on have been molded by his life style and experience; from this stems the importance of the type of men selected to Congress.

Does this mean that the typical congressman or senator is indifferent to his constituents' attitudes? Not at all. Survey research indicates that at least on domestic issues (social welfare legislation and civil rights) there is a measurable degree of congruence between the district and the legislator.[16] "Analysis indicates that the constituencies do not influence . . . roll calls in the House. . . by selecting Congressmen whose attitudes mirror their own. Instead, Congressmen vote their constituencies' attitudes (as they perceive them) with a mind to the next election. Constituency influence is not provided by candidate recruitment but by elite cognitions."[17] Thus we are faced with a contradiction: Congressmen feel that their individual legislative actions may have considerable impact on the electorate, yet the lack of significance of a representative's voting record to his constituents implies that this is not true. To some degree this contradiction is explained by the tendency of congressmen to overestimate their visibility to the local public. It is difficult for a representative to form a correct judgment about opinion in his district. The letters he receives, the editorials he reads, the people he meets at political gatherings grossly overrepresent the degree of political information and interest in the constituency as a whole. Also, on election day, the congressman is dealing in increments and margins. Even if only a small percentage of his district is aware of his stand on a given issue, he fears that alienating this group might jeopardize his reelection. Finally, a representative reaches the public through a variety of intermediaries—the local party, the news media, economic interests, racial and nationality organizations, and so on. And these intermediaries are likely to be politically aware and sophisticated. Thus the public —or parts of it—may get a simple positive or negative impression about the

[15]Warren E. Miller and Donald E. Stokes, "Constituency Influence in Congress," *American Political Science Review* (March 1963), p. 47.

[16]*Ibid.*, p. 50.

[17]Charles F. Cnudde and Donald J. McCrone, "The Linkage between Constituency Attitudes and Congressional Voting Behavior: A Causal Model," *American Political Science Review* (March 1966), pp. 66–72. This finding is supported by Miller and Stokes, *op. cit.*

congressman from opinion leaders who were influenced by specific issues.[18] It is probably fair to conclude that the views of his constituents are only one of many pressures to which the harried congressman responds.

Congress: The Nation's Whipping Boy

In scholarly circles, in the mass media, and among many plain citizens, Congress is subject to considerable abuse. Why should this be the case? Some of the abuse stems from confusion about Congress; there is lack of agreement on what the primary functions of Congress should be. Should it hand over more of its creative lawmaking role to the President? Should it concentrate on curbing the President and the bureaucrats? "Congress is in a legislative dilemma," it has been said, "because opinion conceives of it as a legislature. . . . An assembly need not legislate to exist and to be important. . . . The primary work of legislation must be done, and increasingly is being done, by the three 'houses' of the Executive branch: the bureaucracy, the administration, and the President."[19] Some suggest that Congress should concentrate on service to constituents and administrative oversights. Others reject the notion that Congress should abandon its more traditional legislative role.

Congress is also criticized because of the way it functions. The dispersion of power among committee leaders, the Rules Committee, elected party officials, factional chieftains, and other legislators means that to get things done leaders must negotiate and bargain. The result of this "brokerage system" is that measures may be watered down or defeated or delayed, accountability for action or inaction is confused and responsibility thus eroded, and organized groups and interests are given a decided advantage. This is no accident—it is the result of our constitutional and political system that divides up authority, checks power with power, and disperses political leadership. We shall return to this problem in Chapter 20 after looking at two other parts of our system of checks and balances—the federal bureaucracy and the federal judges.

[18]The significance of voter switching in Presidential elections and its relation to public policy is discussed by V. O. Key, Jr., and Milton C. Cummings, Jr. *The Responsible Electorate: Rationality in Presidential Voting, 1936–1960* (Harvard Univ. Press, 1966).

[19]Samuel P. Huntington, "Congressional Responses to the Twentieth Century," in David B. Truman (ed.), *op. cit.* p. 29. For a severe indictment of Congress, see Drew Pearson and Jack Anderson, *The Case against Congress* (Simon and Schuster, 1968).

The Bureaucrats

18 A story making the rounds in Washington tells of a government clerk who received dozens of papers daily, which he read, initialed, and deposited in his out basket. One day a report meant for another office found its way to his desk, and he followed the usual reading, initialing, and dispatching routine. Two days later the report was returned with the following memorandum attached: "This document was not designed for you to handle. Please erase your initials and initial the erasure."[1]

What Americans call red tape is a universal complaint. However, we need to remind ourselves that all large organizations—governmental or not—are bureaucracies and are run by bureaucrats. It is quite true that some bureaucracies are inefficient, but the average work force of the 500 largest industrial corporations in the United States is over 20,000.[2] Obviously, a complex, formal system of organization providing for specialization of function and hierarchical relationships is necessary in an organization of this size. Why then is the criticism of bureaucrats in government so loud and persistent? Partly because Americans have a deep-seated fear of big government; partly because public officials work in a goldfish bowl under the sharp eyes of congressmen, columnists, radio and television commentators, and lobbyists; and partly because some pressure groups wage massive public relations campaigns to convince us that this is so.

[1]Quoted in Charles E. Jacob, *Policy and Bureaucracy* (Van Nostrand, 1966), p. 47.
[2]*Ibid.*, p. 29.

410

In this chapter, we are mainly interested in the 2.8 million people who make up the executive branch of the federal government. Certain facts about these people need to be emphasized at the outset:

1   Only a small part of the 2.8 million executive employees work in Washington. The great majority are employed in regional, field, and local offices scattered throughout the country. California alone has well over a quarter of a million federal employees.

2   More than half of these *civilian* employees work for the Army, Navy, Air Force, or other defense agencies. The continuing world crisis has put its stamp on our bureaucracy.

3   Only a small part of the bureaucrats—perhaps 10 percent—work for so-called welfare agencies, such as the Social Security Administration or the Rural Electrification Administration, and more than half of these work for the Veterans Administration. The welfare state may be a major point of controversy in our party battles, but it has a minor place in today's big government. A still smaller proportion of government employees work in regulatory agencies, such as the Interstate Commerce Commission.

4   Federal employees are not any one type. They come from all parts of the country, have a variety of religious faiths and political views, represent a great range of national origins.

5   Their work in government is equally varied. Over 15,000 different personnel skills—about two-thirds as many as are found in all private business—are represented in the federal government. Like Americans generally, most government workers are specialists in some occupation or profession. Unlike Americans as a whole, however, most federal employees are white-collar workers—stenographers, clerks, lawyers, office heads, inspectors, and the like.

How important are the bureaucrats? In a sense, of course, they are all-important. They are the core of big government. Without officials and employees, government would be a collection of politicians and lawmakers—generals without armies. So influential are the officials that sometimes the political heads seem insignificant. As Alexander Pope said over 200 years ago,

> For forms of government let fools contest,
> Whate'er is best administer'd is best.

But this sentiment goes too far. "Forms of government" help shape the political world in which the administrator lives; they influence the kind of decisions made and the way they are carried out.

Actually we cannot separate administration from politics. Our job is not to put each in a separate sphere, but to see the interrelationship between the two. How is administration carried on? What kinds of problems do administrators face? What are their powers? How are they made accountable to the electorate? In short, how can the bureaucrats do their jobs and yet remain our servants and not our masters?

The Shape of Administration

Big government is complex government. The executive branch is a cluster of twelve departments, and forty-seven independent agencies, together embracing over 1,800 bureaus, divisions, branches, offices, services, and other subunits. In size, five big agencies—the Departments of Army, Navy, and Air Force, the Post Office, and the Veterans Administration—tower over all the others. Most of the agencies are responsible to the President, but some are partly independent of him. Virtually all the agencies exist by act of Congress, and the legislators could abolish them either by passing a new law or by witholding funds. The power of Congress to set up departments and agencies is implicit in the Constitution. The Framers simply assumed—without actually specifying—that Congress might establish such functions and organizations as it saw fit.

In its first session in 1789, Congress created the Departments of Foreign Affairs (later changed to State), War, and Treasury. During the next 100 years the government grew slowly but fairly steadily. World War I brought a mushrooming of federal agencies, and many of these survived into the postwar years. World War II brought an even greater expansion, as the government mobilized armed forces of 15 million men, fought a war on many fronts, and controlled large areas of the nation's economy. The executive branch shrank after World War II (but not back to its prewar size) and increased sharply again during the Korean War. The growth of the executive establishment from 200,000 to 2.8 million people in this century is the hallmark of our bureaucratic age.[3]

FORMAL ORGANIZATION

A soldier writes to his family that he is a member of the first squad of the second platoon of Company B of the 1st Battalion of the 426th Regiment of the 95th Division of the III Corps of the Ninth Army. A friend of his works in the personnel office of the parts section of the Flint Division of the Buick Department of General Motors. A government girl in Washington tells her father that she is in the stenographic section of the administrative service of the Budget and Finance Division of the Naval Supplies System Command of the Department of the Navy in the Department of Defense.

The larger the number of people and the more complex the job, the more highly organized an agency will be. In establishing a new agency, Congress may lay down a general structural plan in legislation, the President may give further shape to it in executive orders and in private instructions, and the head of the agency and his assistants will extend the organizational skeleton of the new agency down to small units. But the executive branch as a whole, it has been said, grew up "without plan or design like the barns, shacks, silos, tool sheds, and garages of an old farm." Although different functions pro-

[3]*Ibid.*, p. 32.

duce different types of organization, in general the main agencies of government are composed of departments, corporations, independent agencies, and their subunits—bureaus, divisions, offices, and so on down the line—together with a network of regional and local offices.

The *departments* are headed by secretaries (except Post Office, which is headed by the Postmaster General, and Justice, which is headed by the Attorney General). These secretaries are also Cabinet members (except for the Secretaries of the Army, Navy, and Air Force, who report to the President through their chief, the Secretary of Defense) and thus are directly responsible to the President. Although the departments vary greatly in size, they have certain features in common: Often an undersecretary takes part of the administrative load off the secretary's shoulders, and one or more assistant secretaries direct major programs. Like the President, the secretaries have personal assistants who help them in planning, budget, personnel, legal, public relations, and other staff functions. The departments are, of course, subdivided into bureaus and smaller units, but the basis of division may differ. The most common basis is *function*; for example, the Commerce Department is divided into the Bureau of the Census, the Patent Office, the Environmental Science Services Administration, and so on. Or the basis may be *clientele* (for example, the Bureau of Indian Affairs of the Interior Department), or *work processes* (for example, the Economic Research Service of the Agriculture Department), or *geography* (for example, the Alaskan Air Command of the Department of the Air Force). The basis of organization of most departmental units—and indeed of the departments themselves—is mixed.

The score or more of *government corporations*, such as the Tennessee Valley Authority and the Federal Deposit Insurance Corporation, are a sort of cross between a business corporation and a regular government agency. Government corporations were designed to make possible a freedom of action and flexibility not always found in the regular federal agencies. For example, corporations have been free from certain regulations of the Budget Bureau and the Comptroller General. They also have had more leeway in using their own earnings as they pleased. And yet the fact that the government owns the corporations means that it retains basic control over their activities. Recently, Congress has deprived the corporations of much of their freedom, and they have taken on some of the character of regular departments—they are no longer free from the need to get annual congressional appropriations, for example. They remain, however, useful means of keeping certain government activities (especially financial) somewhat apart from the routine, congested, and centralized federal agencies and from excessive congressional and presidential control, particularly in time of emergency.

The *independent agencies* comprise many types of organization and many degrees of independence. Broadly speaking, all agencies that are not corporations and that do not fall under the executive departments (such as Treasury or Interior) are called independent agencies. Many of these agencies, however, are no more independent of the President and Congress than are the executive departments themselves. The huge Veterans Administration is not represented in the Cabinet, for example, but its chief is directly responsible to the President.

Another type of independent agency is the *independent regulatory board*

414

PART 5
Policy-makers
for the
People

or *commission*—agencies like the Securities and Exchange Commission, the National Labor Relations Board, the Interstate Commerce Commission. Congress deliberately set up these boards to keep them somewhat free from White House influence in exercising their quasi-legislative and quasi-judicial functions. Congress has protected their independence in several ways. The boards are headed by three or more commissioners with overlapping terms, they often have to be bipartisan in membership, and the President's power of removal is curbed.

Within the departments, corporations, and independent agencies are a host of subordinate units. The standard name for the largest subunit is the *bureau,* although sometimes it is called an office, administration, service, and so on. Bureaus are the working agencies of the federal government. In contrast to the big departments, which are often mere holding companies for a variety of agencies, the bureaus usually have fairly definite and clear-cut duties, for example, the Bureau of Customs and Bureau of the Mint of the Treasury Department, and the Bureau of Indian Affairs of the Interior Department. Most bureaus are overshadowed by their mother agencies, but some of them, like the Federal Bureau of Investigation and the Bureau of Reclamation, enjoy a popular prestige and political position of their own. Below the bureaus are hundreds of branches, services, sections, and other units that perform even more specialized operations.

The *field service* of the federal government embraces a vast number of regional, state, county, and local units. The local post office is part of the

FORMAL AND INFORMAL LINES OF A BUREAUCRATIC ORGANIZATION

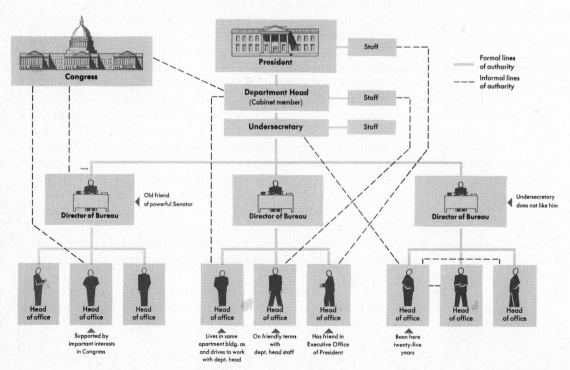

field service, as is the local recruiting center or veterans office. As the action end of government, the field service runs into many vitally important problems. Ticklish questions of coordination constantly arise. How can cooperation in the region be promoted between several federal offices with overlapping duties but responsible to different departments in Washington? How far is it possible and desirable to depart from national regulations in meeting local situations? Which decisions should be made on the spot, and which should be referred to Washington? How much collaboration should be tried with state and local governments? Washington administrators face problems, too—how far should they decentralize, what decisions should be delegated to the field, what type of field organization is best suited to their needs (there are many types), how should they combine local flexibility with national direction and responsibility.

INFORMAL ORGANIZATION

All this elaborate organization of the executive branch gives order and system to administration. It assigns certain functions to certain units, places one official (or sometimes more) at the head of each unit and makes him responsible for its performance, allows both specialization and coordination, permits ready communication, and in general makes our far-flung administration somewhat controllable and manageable. But this formal organization can be highly misleading if taken too seriously. The detailed organization chart on the office wall of some administrator may represent hope and intention rather than reality.

Why? Because people differ—in attitude, motive, ability, experience. And their very diversity leads to all sorts of complications. Relationships among officials in an agency may be based on influence rather than on formal authority. Leadership may be lodged not at the top but in a variety of places. A certain group of officials may have considerable influence, whereas another group, with the same formal status, may have much less. The loyalties of some officials may cut across the formal aims of the agency.

Consider an imaginary but typical bureau. The bureau chief is an old-line administrator who has served through four presidential administrations. He is cautious and unimaginative. He has a rival in the person of an assistant to the secretary who heads the whole department. Some officials in the bureau look to this assistant for leadership; they share his enthusiasm and support his plans, and they hope that he may take over the department some day and give them the power and position they feel they deserve. But the bureau chief has his own set of motives and attitudes; moreover, he enjoys the backing of a powerful bloc in Congress that will defend him if he is attacked. He has built a personal organization made up of two or three division chiefs, an attorney, the personnel officer, and his own staff, and this personal following is intensely loyal to him.

This, perhaps, is an extreme case, but it shows how informal organization can have a major effect on administration. A subordinate official in an agency might be especially close to his chief simply because they went to the same college or play poker together, or because the subordinate knows how to ingratiate himself with his chief. A staff official may have tremendous influence, not because of his formal authority, but because his experience, fairness, common sense, and general personality lead men to turn to him for advice. In an agency headed by a chief who is weak or unimaginative, a vacuum may develop that encourages others to try to take over. Such informal organization and communication cutting across regular channels is inevitable to some degree in any organization, public or private. Even the Army, with all its hierarchy and regimentation, abounds with these elements.

BUILDING AND MANAGING THE TEAM

The government administrator is not nearly so free in building his team as is the private businessman. Government has long followed prescribed methods of recruiting, examining, classifying, promoting, and dismissing personnel. For many years America had a notorious appointment system that was summed up in the slogan, "To the victor belong the spoils." When a new party came to power, its leaders and followers felt they had a right to take over desirable government jobs. Parties should have patronage, it was said, to encourage members to work for the party and to answer the people's demand for a new broom to sweep Washington clean. Moreover, some argued that a frequent turnover of officials would keep government democratic.

© 1968 United Feature Syndicate.

Besides, they said, the duties of public officials were so plain and simple that any intelligent person could perform them.

Later in the nineteenth century a sharp reaction set in against the spoils system. The job of government was becoming increasingly complex, and interested citizens, some of them organized in the National Civil Service Reform League, were agitating for reform. Presidents, too, were chafing under the pressures of hordes of jobseekers. Public opinion crystallized when President James A. Garfield was assassinated in 1881 by a disappointed office seeker. Two years later Congress passed the Pendleton Act, which set up the beginnings of a merit system under a three-man bipartisan board, the Civil Service Commission. The act placed certain types of employees under a new classified service, which could be entered only by passing a competitive examination. Congress put relatively few employees under the new merit system, but it gave the President power to expand the classified service. As a result of a series of executive orders over the years, about three-quarters of the federal employees today hold jobs that are covered by a merit system and protected from patronage.

Today the administrator must work closely with the Civil Service Commission in staffing his agency. With about 4,000 employees of its own, the Commission acts as a central agency for recruiting, examining, and appointing government workers. It advertises for new employees, prepares and administers oral and written examinations throughout the country, and makes up a register of names of those who pass the tests. When an agency wishes to employ a person, the Commission certifies to it three names taken from the top of the appropriate register. The administrator has some voice in the type of examination given, and he has some freedom of choice among the three job applicants, but obviously his discretion is greatly limited.

The centralization of personnel direction in the Civil Service Commission disturbs administrators eager for freedom and flexibility in their agency operations. They charge that the Commission is entangled in red tape, uses old-fashioned personnel methods, and lacks initiative and imagination. Certainly the Commission has no monopoly over basic personnel policy. The White House has taken increasing leadership, as noted above, and the departments have some autonomy. But whatever its defects, over the years the Civil Service Commission has helped to keep most federal jobs out of the spoils system.[4] Still designed to be nonpartisan, the Commission is composed of three members (no more than two of the same party) with six-year terms.

This is not to say, however, that appointment to the classified service is based on merit considerations alone. There is still a strong feeling in the United States that government jobs are a form of reward. The best example of the effects of this feeling is *veterans' preference.* Today five points are automatically added to the examination grades of all veterans, and they receive other special considerations. Disabled veterans, their wives, and their widows are given a ten-point bonus. These provisions, supported by veterans' groups in and out of Congress, have aroused much controversy. Some have charged that veterans' preference is a racket; others say that the government owes a debt to former servicemen and that it can easily find able recruits among them. At any rate, veterans' preference is probably here to stay, and it is not surprising that about half the federal employees are veterans.

Hiring is only the first step in building the administrative team. The administrator must place, train, and manage his appointees. Effective administration requires much more than knowledge of the formal legalities and power relationships. In any organization an official endowed with manipulative skills may well be able to dispense almost entirely with coercive sanctions and secure compliance by creating personal relationships and social obligations.[5]

Despite a popular notion to the contrary, government workers *can* be fired. The process, however, is hedged in by many rules to prevent arbitrary dismissals. Some inefficient employees have used cumbersome appeal pro-

[4]Wallace S. Sayre (ed.), *The Federal Government Service,* 2d ed. (Prentice-Hall, 1965) considers these and related problems.
[5]Jacob, *op. cit.,* p. 43. See also Philip M. Marcus and Dora Cafagna "Control in Modern Organizations," *Public Administration Review* (June 1965), pp. 121–127.

418 cedures to protect their jobs. In one case a stenographer appealed to four separate boards, while hanging on to her job for seventeen months, before she finally quit. But such cases are exceptional.

PART 5
Policy-makers
for the
People

Administrators as Decision-makers

A policeman stops a student who fails to bring his car to a full halt before crossing a highway. The student admits that he did not come to a full halt, but he argues that he did look both ways before entering the highway, and he did slow down enough so that he had to shift into second gear. The officer lets him off with a lecture and a warning. Why? The law requires that the student be arrested and pay a fine. But the officer knows that a full halt is not necessary at this particular corner as long as the driver is reasonably careful.

Here is a simple example of administrative discretion and decision-making. The officer is an experienced man of good sense. In this case he exercised two functions basic in the administrative process—he established his own rule and he made a judicial decision. In his own way he was participating in *administrative legislation* and *administrative adjudication*.

BIG DECISIONS

Every day in hundreds of ways federal bureaucrats make decisions that affect our jobs, our pocketbooks, our lives. We may or may not know about these decisions. The Board of Governors of the Federal Reserve System issues a ruling that affects the size of the down payment we must make on a new car. The director of the Bureau of Labor Statistics formulates a new method of computing price indexes—one that may affect the government's anti-inflation policies. Officials in charge of civil service examinations change their methods of testing. Safety officials in the Department of Transportation issue a new and more stringent set of air-safety regulations.

Wars and near-wars have vastly broadened the decision-making powers of administrative officials, especially in agencies involved in making war and peace. Obviously, the Secretary of State in dealing with foreign powers makes decisions that gravely affect the chances of peace or war. The Atomic Energy Commission and the Defense Department jointly or separately decide on crucial policies that bear on our capacity to win a war. If war comes, the fate of the nation hangs on decisions of commanders in the field. Many military decisions are secret, but some are public and even become subjects of wide discussion.

To say that bureaucrats make important decisions, however, is not to say that they have unlimited alternatives from which to choose. An administrator may have been given broad discretion by both Congress and the President and yet feel constricted by other forces. For an administrator, like a congressman or a President, works amid a complex set of political pressures. In making a key decision he must try to anticipate the attitudes of his own agency, of experts inside and outside the agency, of other agencies involved in the decision, of interest groups affected by the decision, of the press, of the attentive public as a whole,[6] of the party in power and the opposition party, of Congress and the President, perhaps even of foreign governments. He must take into account all kinds of complex organizational and psychological relationships.[7] Furthermore, he often must act in a hurry and on the basis of incomplete knowledge.

ADMINISTRATORS AS LAWMAKERS

Congress has long realized that as governmental problems become more numerous and complex, important decisions increasingly must be made by administrators. One reason for this is the increasing technical sophistication required. The granting of a license to operate a television channel by the FCC or the calculation and establishment of fair rates to be charged for electric power by the FPC are activities demanding technical training that congressmen could not readily provide.[8] Congress is composed of generalists; the delegation of rule-making authority to commissions permits legislation by specialists.

Furthermore, if Congress passed laws with very precise wording, it would get so bogged down in details that it could never complete its work. For example, assume that Congress is concerned that there be enough truck lines in operation to ensure prompt transportation services for shippers, but not so many as to lead to ruinous competition. If it attempted to specify the exact circumstances under which a new truck line should be licensed, a statute would have to read as follows:

Keokuk, Iowa, needs four truck lines unless that new superhighway that they have been talking about for ten years gets built. Then they will need five unless, of course, Uncle Charlie's Speedy Express gets rid of its Model T and gets two new tractors and vans. Then they will only need three as long as two freight trains a day also stop there.

On the other hand, Smithville, Tennessee, needs eight truck lines unless. . . .[9]

Of course, Congress does not and obviously could not write statutes like these. Instead, it declares its policy in general terms, and empowers the Interstate Commerce Commission to license new truck lines when such action would be warranted by "public convenience and necessity." The ICC then judges the situation in Keokuk and Smithville, and makes specific rules.

Well over 100 agencies have the power to issue rules and regulations affecting the public. Most of these agencies are *regulatory agencies*, like the Interstate Commerce Commission, which has power over the nation's railroads, or the Federal Communications Commission, which polices the nation's radio and television waves. The most important regulatory functions have been placed in independent boards and commissions, but on occasion

[6]G. A. Almond, *The American People and Foreign Policy* (Harcourt, Brace & World, 1950), Chap. 7; James N. Rosenau, *Public Opinion and Foreign Policy* (Random House, 1961).
[7]See H. A. Simon, *Administrative Behavior* (Macmillan, 1947); Victor A. Thompson, *Modern Organization* (Knopf, 1961).
[8]Jacob, *op. cit.*, pp. 85, 86.
[9]Martin Shapiro, *The Supreme Court and Administrative Agencies* (Free Press, 1968), p. 4.

Congress has assigned them to line agencies such as the Department of Agriculture. Congress has a special interest in the regulatory agencies, for they must interpret the laws passed by Congress and fill them out to meet specific problems. For example, Congress has recognized the right of employees to "organize and bargain collectively through representatives of their own choosing." Such a general provision leads to a hundred new questions and definitions, such as the nature of unions, the rights of employers, the definition of unfair labor practices, the rights of nonunion employees, the scope of collective bargaining, and so on. And these all-important interpretations must be made by a regulatory agency — in this case the National Labor Relations Board.

Safeguards against abuse of delegated power are of several types:

1   The agencies interpret and enforce laws of Congress; if they misinterpret a statute, Congress can always amend it to make its intent clearer. The basic legislative power of Congress compels the agencies to identify the will of Congress and to interpret and apply laws as the congressmen would wish. Congress can also exercise this control through investigations, and especially appropriations.

2   Congress has closely regulated the procedures to be followed by regulatory agencies. Under the Administrative Procedures Act of 1946, agencies must publicize their machinery and organization, must give advance information of proposed rules to interested persons, must allow such persons to present information and arguments, must allow parties appearing before the agency to be accompanied by counsel and to cross-examine witnesses.

3   Under certain conditions, final actions of regulatory agencies may be appealed to the courts.

4   Administrators in regulatory agencies, as in all agencies, are surrounded by informal political checks as well as formal ones. They must keep in mind the demands of professional ethics, the advice of experts, and the attitudes of congressmen, the President, interest groups, political parties, private persons, and so on. In the long run, these safeguards are the most important of all.

ADMINISTRATORS AS JUDGES

Among the hardest problems facing administrators are those that call for judiciousness in settling disputes or mediating among conflicting claims. The Secretary of Defense, for example, might have to reconcile the demands of two rival services, such as the Navy and Air Force. The Secretary of Agriculture might need to intervene in a conflict between two interest groups, such as growers and wholesalers of grain. A bureau chief might have to referee a jurisdictional squabble between two division heads.

The regulatory agencies bear the main burden of making judicial decisions when disputes arise between two or more private interests or between private interests and the government. Congress has delegated power to make such decisions to the regulatory agencies, a power that transforms the agencies into courts, the administrators into judges. They receive complaints, hold hearings, listen to witnesses and lawyers, study briefs, and make decisions, much like any other court.[10]

Much of this judicial business is handled informally, through the voluntary settlement of cases at lower levels in an agency. The Interstate Commerce Commission, for example, arranged voluntary settlements of all but 5 out of 3,500 complaint cases in one year. The National Labor Relations Board, even though it administers a controversial law, made formal decisions in only 4 percent of more than 12,000 cases involving unfair labor practices during the first four years of its existence.[11] Informal settlements make life a lot easier in the bureaucratic jumble of Washington. They dispose of disputes relatively quickly and inexpensively, and they take an immense burden off the courts. Moreover, they are handled by men who are experts in technical areas. And yet many persons—especially lawyers pleading cases before the regulatory agencies—have expressed concern over the extent of the judicial power vested in the agencies. They complain that the administrators violate due process of law by holding private and informal sessions, by failing to give interested parties an adequate hearing, by basing their decisions on insufficient evidence.

Partly in response to these complaints the Administrative Procedures Act of 1946 provides for broader judicial review of administrative decisions. The courts have always had the power to overturn administrative judgments on points of *law*, as in cases where an agency had exceeded its authority, or misinterpreted the law, or had simply been unfair. Under the 1946 act, however, the courts have acquired more authority to examine questions of *fact*—that is, to go over the mass of technical evidence examined by the agency. While this tendency has not gone very far, it points up the problem of maintaining the balance between judicial control and administrative efficiency and expertness. The 1946 law also provides for procedural safeguards, such as more formalized hearings and proper notice of action.

Finally, the act tackled another long-debated problem—the high concentration of both legislative and judicial power in regulatory agencies. This administrative absolutism, as some have called it, seems to run counter to the great doctrine of the separation of powers. The act provides that there should be a greater separation within regulatory agencies so that the same officials will not act as both judges and prosecutors. Officials who investigate cases and present them for action are not to have any part in deciding them.

Those who worry about the concentration of judicial power in the agencies usually express the fear that administrators will do too much prosecuting and not enough impartial judging. Yet the opposite tendency may prevail. In some cases regulatory agencies become so occupied with umpiring disputes that they pay insufficient attention to prosecuting offenders. They tend to sit back and wait for complaints to be filed instead of taking the initi-

[10]See Victor G. Rosenblum, "How to Get into TV: The Federal Communications Commission and Miami's Channel 10," in Alan F. Westin (ed.), *The Uses of Power* (Harcourt, Brace & World, 1962), pp. 173–228.

[11]*Final Report of the Attorney General's Committee on Administrative Procedure*, Senate Document 8, 77th Cong., 1st Sess., p. 35. For an admirable treatment of administrative action, see Emmette S. Redford, *Administration of National Economic Control* (Macmillan, 1952).

ative in ferreting out violations of the law. Such a course may seem to be the safe thing to do; to some extent the regular courts have forced regulatory agencies to organize themselves mainly as judicial bodies. But the result of this tendency may be inadequate protection of the very groups these agencies were set up to safeguard.

THE POLITICS OF ADMINISTRATIVE DECISION-MAKING

One of the arguments in favor of delegating policy-making to independent agencies was that railroad rates, the quality of television signals, and the elimination of stock frauds are technical questions to be settled by experts — not politicians. In fact, of course, these issues cannot be isolated from politics. Which one of six competitors should operate a TV station in Miami? Should the Springfield Armory be shut down? Should utility profits be based on the initial investment or on replacement costs? Decisions such as these, which can greatly benefit a corporation or impair the economy of a congressman's district, will inevitably lead to tremendous pressures being exerted on the decision-maker.

One of the most interesting phenomena in the field of independent regulatory agencies is the relationship that has tended to develop between the agency and the industry it is supposed to regulate. The ICC, for example, was set up to check railroad abuses and was initially opposed by the railroads. Today the ICC views itself as the protector of the railroads' interests, and they are its chief supporters.[12] Indeed, it has been said that commissions may in time be captured by the interests they regulate.[13] This is not a question of corruption — though occasionally that does occur — but of excessive interaction between the regulated and the regulator. Federal Communications Commissioners are in constant contact with members of the broadcasting industry — at conventions and conferences and in their day-to-day activities. It would be strange indeed if they were not sympathetically inclined toward the problems of the industry. Also, there is considerable personnel interchange between regulatory bodies and industry. This is not surprising. The agencies require men with technical skills; they find them in industry. Young men in government may look forward to jobs in industry. A House Armed Services Subcommittee investigation revealed that the 100 largest corporations receiving defense contracts employed more than 1,400 former officers, of which 261 were of general or flag rank. General Dynamics, which had the most government contracts when the study was made, employed 187 former officers and was headed by a former Secretary of the Army. Presumably these men still maintained close social contacts, at least, with their old comrades-in-arms.[14]

Congressmen constantly pressure bureaucrats, including members of the independent regulatory commissions. Control over agency budgets and the power to approve or deny agency requests for needed legislation give the

---

[12]Peter Woll, *American Bureaucracy* (Norton, 1963), pp. 36–40.

[13]See Bernard Schwartz, "Crisis in the Commissions," in Samuel Krislov and Lloyd D. Musolf (eds.), *The Politics of Regulation* (Houghton Mifflin, 1964), pp. 21–25.

[14]Quoted in Jacob, *op. cit.*, p. 178. See Grant McConnell, *Private Power and American Democracy* (Knopf, 1966), for a general discussion of this problem.

congressmen considerable leverage. A bureau or agency is especially careful to develop good relationships with the members of the committees handling its legislation and appropriations, as is seen from the following exchange:

OFFICIAL OF THE FISH AND WILDLIFE SERVICE: Last year at the hearings . . . you were quite interested in the aquarium there [the Senator's state], particularly in view of the centennial coming up. . . .

SENATOR MUNDT: That is right.

OFFICIAL: Rest assured we will try our best to have everything in order for the opening of that centennial.

SUBCOMMITTEE CHAIRMAN: I wrote you gentlemen . . . a polite letter about it . . . and no action was taken. . . . Now, Savannah may be unimportant to the Weather Bureau but it is important to me. . . .

WEATHER BUREAU OFFICIAL: I can almost commit ourselves to seeing to it that the Savannah weather report gets distribution in the northeastern United States. [source of tourists for the subcommittee chairman's district].[15]

The relationship between a regulatory agency, its clientele industry, and "its" congressional committee is a symbiotic one. The agency does favors for the industry and for the committee and in turn makes demands on them both. The problem with this relationship is that the decision-maker—the regulatory agency—is responsible to very limited and specialized constituencies. The broadcasters have influence with the FCC, but who speaks for the viewing public? Defense industries have highly placed friends in the Pentagon, but who represents the taxpayer? The decentralization of decision-making throughout the bureaucracy is related to the general dispersion of leadership in our political system. As we have seen, this serves to benefit some groups at the expense of others.

Administrators in Action—Two Cases

We have seen the complex of pressures and loyalties amid which a bureaucrat must work. We have seen that the good administrator must have some of the qualities of the politician, the lawmaker, the judge, the expert, the team quarterback. Day after day he must make decisions involving issues of policy, problems of organization, matters of law—and above all, people. The following two cases, based on actual administrative experience, illustrate some of the painful choices a bureaucrat may have to make, whether he is in Washington or in the field.

MR. BROWN

George Brown is chief of the Bureau of Erosion of the Department of Conservation.[16] He is still in his early forties; his appointment to the post

---

[15]Quoted in Aaron Wildavsky, *The Politics of the Budgetary Process* (Little, Brown, 1964), pp. 80, 81.

[16]The persons and agencies (except for the Budget Bureau and Post Office) in this case are fictitious, but the facts of the case are drawn from actual happenings in Washington.

was a result of both his ability and luck. When the old bureau chief retired, the President wanted to bring in a new chief from outside the agency, but influential members of Congress pressed for the selection of a former senator who had represented a farm state. As a compromise, Brown, then a division head, was promoted to bureau chief. A graduate of a Middle Western agricultural college, Brown is a career official in the federal service.

Early in March of Brown's second year in the new post, his boss, the Secretary of Conservation, summoned him and the other bureau heads to an important conference. The Secretary informed the group that he had just attended a Cabinet meeting in which the President had called for drastic economies wherever possible and had asked each department to effect at least a 10 percent cut in spending in the coming fiscal year. The President, the Secretary reported, was convinced that there was a great popular demand for retrenchment.

Brown quickly calculated what this cutback would mean for his agency. For several years, the Bureau of Erosion had been spending about $90 million a year to help farmers protect their farmland. Could it get along on about $80 million, and where could savings be made? Returning to his office, Brown called a meeting of his personnel, budget, and management officials, and his four division chiefs. After several hours of discussion it was agreed that savings could be effected only by decreasing the scope of the program—which would involve ending the jobs of about 1,200 of the Bureau's employees. He asked his subordinates to prepare a list of the 20 percent of the employees who were the least useful to the Bureau. He would decide which to drop after checking with the affected congressmen, judging whom he could and could not afford to hurt.

A few weeks later Mr. Brown presented an $80 million budget to Secretary Jones, who approved it and passed it on to the White House. The President went over the figures in a conference with the Director of the Bureau of the Budget, and a few weeks later the budget for the whole executive department, incorporating the Erosion Bureau's $80 million, was transmitted to Congress.

Meanwhile Brown was running into trouble. News of the proposed budget cut had leaked immediately to the personnel in the field. Nobody knew who would be dropped if the cut went through, and some of the abler officials were already looking around for other positions. Morale fell. Hearing of the cut, farmers' representatives in Washington notified local farm organizations throughout the country. Soon Brown began to receive letters asking that certain services be maintained. Members of the farm bloc in Congress were also becoming restless.

Shortly after the President's budget went to Congress, Representative Smith of Colorado asked Brown to see him. Smith was Chairman of the Agriculture subcommittee of the House Appropriations Committee and thus was a potent factor in congressional treatment of the budget. Brown immediately went up to the Hill. Smith began talking in an urgent tone. He said that he had consulted his fellow subcommittee members, both Democratic and Republican, and they all agreed that the Erosion Bureau's cut must not go through. The farmers needed the usual $90 million and even more. They would practically rise up in arms if the program were reduced. Members of

Congress from agricultural areas, Smith went on, were under tremendous pressure. Leaders of farm groups in Washington were mobilizing the farmers everywhere. Besides, Smith said, the President was unfair in cracking down on the farm program; he did not understand agricultural problems, and he was not cutting other expenses.

Then Smith came to the point. Brown, he said, must vigorously oppose the budget cut. Hearings on appropriations would commence in a few days and Brown as bureau chief would of course testify. At that time he must state that the cut would hurt the bureau and undermine its whole program. Brown would not have to volunteer this statement, Smith said, but just respond to leading questions put by the congressmen. Brown's testimony, he felt sure, would help clinch the argument against the cut because congressmen would respect the judgment of the administrator closest to the problem.

Smith informed Brown that other bureaucrats were fighting to save their appropriations. The Post Office Department had announced that Saturday mail deliveries would be cut immediately as part of the President's economy drive. Obviously, said Smith, they are counting on public reaction to get them an exemption from the 10 percent cutback. Smith would be foolish not to do the same.

Brown returned to his office in a state of indecision. He was in an embarrassing position. He had submitted his estimates to the Secretary of Conservation and to the President, and it was his duty to back them up. An unwritten rule demanded, moreover, that agency heads defend budget estimates submitted to Congress, whatever their personal feelings might be. The President had appointed him to his position, he reflected, and had a right to expect loyalty. On the other hand, he was on the spot with his own agency. The employees all expected their chief to look out for them. Brown had developed happy relations with "the field," and he squirmed at the thought of having to let over one thousand employees go. What would they think when they heard him defend the cut? More important, he wanted to maintain friendly relations with the farmers, the farm organizations, and the farm bloc in Congress. Finally, Brown was committed to his program. He grasped its true importance, whereas the President's budget advisers were less likely to understand it. And he knew that his pet project—to aid poverty areas in Appalachia, a program he had nurtured for several years—would be most likely to be sacrificed because it was not supported by a powerful constituency.

Brown turned for advice to an old friend in the Bureau of the Budget. This friend urged him to defend the President's budget. He appealed to Brown's professional pride as an administrator and career servant, reminding him that every student of administration agreed that the Chief Executive must have central control of the budget and that agency heads must subordinate their own interests to the executive program. As for the employees to be dropped—well, that was part of the game. A lot of them could get jobs in defense agencies; civil service would protect their status. Anyway, they would understand Brown's position. In a parting shot he mentioned that the President had Brown in mind for bigger things.

The next day Brown had lunch with the senator, wise and experienced in Washington ways, who had helped him get his start in the government. The senator was sympathetic. He understood Brown's perplexity, for many similar cases had arisen in the past. But there was no doubt about what Brown should do, the senator said. He should follow Representative Smith's plan, of course being as diplomatic as possible about it. This way he would protect his position with those who would be most important in the long run.

"After all," the senator said, "Presidents come and go, parties rise and fall, but Smith and those other congressmen will be here a long time, and so will these farm organizations. They can do a lot for you in future years. And remember one other thing—these people are elected representatives of the people. Constitutionally, Congress has the power to spend money as it sees fit. Why should you object if they want to spend an extra few million?"

Leaving the Senate Office Building, Brown realized that his dilemma was deeper than ever. The arguments on both sides were persuasive. He felt hopelessly divided in his loyalties and responsibilities. The President expected one thing of him. Congress (he was sure Smith reflected widespread feeling on Capitol Hill) expected another. As a career man and professional administrator, he sided with the President; as head of an agency, however, he wanted to protect his team. His future? Whatever decision he made, he was bound to alienate important people and interests. There was no way to compromise, because he would have to face a group of astute congressmen.

It was Brown's realization that the arguments in a sense canceled one another out that in the end helped him to make his decision. For he decided finally that the issue involved more than loyalties, ambitions, and programs. Ultimately it boiled down to two questions. First, to whom was he, Brown, legally and administratively responsible? Obviously to the Chief Executive who appointed him and who was accountable to the people for the actions of the administration. And second, which course of action did he, Brown, feel was better for the welfare of all the people? Looking at the question this way, he felt the President was right in asking for economy. As a taxpayer himself, Brown knew of the strong sentiment for retrenchment. To be sure, Congress must make the final decision. But to make the decision, Brown reflected, Congress had to know the attitude of the administration, and the administration must speak with one voice for the majority of the people or it could hardly speak at all. Despite continued pressures and mixed feelings, Brown stuck to this decision.

ASSIGNMENT IN INDONESIA

When in August 1945, shortly after the Japanese surrender, the Republic of Indonesia declared its independence from the Netherlands, a difficult political situation immediately arose.[17] The Dutch wanted to keep their rich islands; the Indonesians wanted their freedom. For several months the Dutch and Indonesian forces skirmished, especially in Batavia, the capital. The United States, deeply interested in the area for economic and strategic reasons, followed a policy of neutrality.

Representing the United States in Batavia was a sixty-year-old consul

[17]This case is drawn from an actual autobiographical account by the vice-consul involved. It was prepared for and published by the Committee on Public Administration Cases (1950) under the title *Indonesian Assignment*.

general who had served in the Indies for twelve years before the war. During this time he had enjoyed pleasant relations with Dutch officials, and he tended to feel sympathetic toward their position. As an old hand he was experienced in Indonesian affairs but was somewhat prejudiced and set in his ways. In February 1946, the consul general was joined by a vice-consul, William Jones, who was sent out by the State Department to undertake economic analysis and reporting. At this time Washington had a particular need for full and accurate information on the economic situation in Indonesia to help in developing important foreign policies.

Jones was different from his chief. A young economist, trained in American universities and in the State Department, he had studied the prewar pattern of colonialism and had developed strong sympathies for the nationalist cause. He had no established ties with the Foreign Service; indeed, his actual appointment was in the Foreign Service Reserve (see Chapter 22). Moreover, while at the State Department, Jones had learned that there was some official concern over the consul general's pro-Dutch views.

Within a few months after his arrival, the new vice-consul was busy preparing economic reports on the Indonesian islands. His relations with his chief were most cordial, but soon a difficult situation began to develop. To get complete information, Jones needed to approach Indonesian as well as Dutch officials. But the consul general wanted him to see only the Dutch. He stressed the ticklish political situation that existed and warned Jones to move slowly. Eager to maintain friendly relations with his superior, Jones followed instructions, but he had an uneasy feeling that he was not doing a full job of reporting to Washington.

Some time later a confidential airgram arrived from the State Department requesting an extensive economic report on Indonesia, adding that "if possible, and with the utmost discretion, Dutch, Indonesian, and British sources should be consulted as far as feasible." Jones was elated to have the assignment but puzzled about how he should proceed. Should he consult the Indonesian authorities?

Jones had several alternatives. He could consult the consul general, who would surely say no; this course would protect Jones's position in the Department and his friendly relations with his chief, but it would lessen the value of the report. Or he could go ahead with the report, inform the Department that he had not consulted the Indonesians and let Washington specifically request such consultation if it was still desired. This was the safest course all around, but it would mean a delayed report and perhaps a less satisfactory one. Finally, Jones could use the airgram to justify consultations with the Indonesians, at whatever risk to his relations with his chief and to Dutch-American relations.

Jones decided on the third course. Before doing so he spoke to a high Indonesian official, who assured him that he would receive useful material from the Republic and in confidence. Jones's decision proved a happy one. His talks with the Indonesians (as well as with the Dutch and British) were fruitful and he was later commended by the State Department for the report he submitted. Yet he had to pay the price. His relations with the consul general cooled markedly—not a trivial matter in a small office thousands of miles from home. Nevertheless, Jones was satisfied with his decision. He felt that he had been loyal to his profession and to the interests of his country, though at the expense of loyalty to his superior. It is clear, however, that had Jones been a veteran career man, with family responsibilities and no particular sympathy for the Indonesians, his decision might have been very different.

Can We Control the Bureaucrats?

The case histories we have just considered lead to three important generalizations:

1 Bureaucrats are people, not robots, and as people they are subject to many influences.
2 Bureaucrats do not respond merely to orders from the top but to a variety of motives stemming from their own personalities, formal and informal organization and communication, their political attitudes, their educational and professional background, and the political context in which they operate.
3 Bureaucrats are important in government. Some of them have tremendous discretion and make decisions of great significance—and the cumulative effect of all their policies and actions on our daily lives is enormous.

Put these factors together and crucial questions arise. How can we keep this powerful bureaucracy responsive to the people? How do we ensure that bureaucrats remain public servants and do not become the public's master? And underlying these questions, to which people should the bureaucrats be held accountable—the majority who elected the President, the majority reflected by the Congress, the organized interests?

CHAINS OF COMMAND

The predominant, but by no means the only, school of thought is that the President should be placed unequivocally in charge, for he is responsive to the broadest constituency. The presidential office, it is argued, must see that popular needs and expectations are converted into administrative action. If the nation votes for a conservative President who favors restricted intervention in the economy by federal agencies, that policy can be effected only if the bureaucracy responds to presidential direction. Or if the electorate chooses a President who favors a more vigorous regulation of business, the majority's wishes can be translated into action only if the bureaucrats support the presidential policies.

Yet as we have seen over and over again, under the American system of constitutional checks and political balances a single political majority winning a presidential election does not acquire control of the national government, not even the executive branch itself. For under our Constitution the President is not the undisputed master of the executive structure. Congress too has its say and wishes to keep it. Congress sets up the agencies, broadly determines their organization, provides the money, and establishes the ground rules. Congress constantly reviews the activities of the bureaucrats by appropriations hearings, special investigations, or informal inquiry. And as we have seen, the Senate helps choose the men who run the agencies.

Moreover, it is not Congress as a whole that shares the direction of the executive structure with the President. More accurately, it is the individual congressmen to whom Congress has delegated its authority. These men, primarily chairmen of committees, usually specialize in the appropriations and policies of a particular group of agencies—often the agencies serving constituents in the congressmen's own districts. But some legislators stake out a claim over more general policies; former Congressman Carl Vinson, for example, made the Navy Department his specialty. Congressmen, who see Presidents come and go, come to feel that they know more about agencies than does the President (and often they do). Thus, although Congress as an institution may prefer to have the President in charge of the executive branch so they can hold him responsible for its operation, the congressional seniority leaders often prefer to protect the agencies from presidential direction in order to maintain their own influence over public policy. Sometimes this is institutionalized—the Army Chief of Engineers, for example, is given authority by law to plan public works and report to Congress without referring to the President.

As we have seen, Congress has deliberately decided that the independent regulatory agencies should not be directly responsive to the President's control. Because these agencies make rules and decide disputes, Congress wants them to be arms of the Congress. So in addition to making these commissions multiple in membership, Congress has given their commissioners long and staggered terms. Although the President fills vacancies with the consent of the Senate, Congress has restricted his right to remove the members of these quasi-legislative, quasi-judicial agencies. The Supreme Court, in *Humphrey's Executor* v. *United States* (1935), upheld the right of Congress to do so and subsequently went further (*Wiener* v. *United States,* 1958) to rule that the President lacks any power to remove these officers unless Congress has specifically authorized him to do so.

POLITICAL CHECKS ON THE PRESIDENT

Important as these institutional breaks in the President's chain of command are, they are only part of the picture. In addition, political checks block the President. Some of the agencies have so much support among interest groups and Congress that a President would hesitate to move against them. The Federal Bureau of Investigation, for example, is politically so powerful that any President would take serious political risks if he should attempt to curtail its operations. In addition, the agencies that perform services for certain groups—the so-called clientele agencies such as the Rural Electrification Administration or the Veterans Administration—have powerful support. If a President, trying to enforce his idea of the general interest, seeks to restrict the agency, he may come into conflict with an influential group that is not without allies in the Congress.

What of the bureaucrat? Is he merely an innocent bystander in the mêlées? There are those who think he should be. They believe that bureaucrats — at least those in the lower ranks of the civil service — should be neutral in partisan politics. Not only has civil service largely overcome the patronage system, but the Hatch Acts of 1939 and 1940 extended the idea of neutrality by forbidding federal civil servants "to take any active part in political management or in political campaigns." The aim was both to prevent the building of a gigantic machine of federal officeholders and to protect the bureaucrats against having to donate money to parties or candidates in order to retain their jobs. The laws allow them to discuss politics in private and to vote but to engage in no other partisan activities. Despite some criticism that it is unwise to isolate 2.8 million people from politics and unfair to deny them the same political freedoms as anyone else, neutralization of the civil service in the political party battle seems to be a fixed feature.

Yet partisan disputes between Democrats and Republicans are not the only items of political conflict. And the Hatch Act does not mean that bureaucrats have become political nonentities. The bureaucracy is not a static force; it has political influence of its own. It seeks to maintain its own organizational system, and group loyalties to agencies and programs are forces to be reckoned with. The influence of the bureaucracy is built on the political skills of the administrator and his staff, their relations with legislative and executive officials, and the amount of support the bureau can command from interest groups and the attentive public. As we have seen, a large bureau finds public acceptance, interest-group backing, and a place in the web of government that give it a measure of political power of its own.[18]

In summary, the role of the bureaucrats in the American system of government is not to be solved merely by structural alterations. For the system of command will always end not just in the White House but in a variety of places on Capitol Hill. There are conflicting claims, including those of the bureaucrats themselves, each insisting that the administrator act "in the public interest" but each with a different definition of that interest. Defining the public interest is the crucial problem.

Organization Theory — A Research Frontier

The study of organizations or administration is a relatively young discipline and in many respects is still undefined. "Organization theory means different things to different people," report two of its most distinguished investigators.[19] The sociological orientation (also influenced by the work of political scientists) stems from the pioneering work of Max Weber, who developed analytic distinctions among various types of authority relationships — the *traditional*, the *charismatic*, and the *legal-rational*. This last

[18]For a discerning study of this problem and related questions, see H. A. Simon, D. W. Smithburg and V. A. Thompson, *Public Administration* (Knopf, 1950), especially Chaps. 18 and 19.

[19]Richard M. Cyert and James G. March, *A Behavioral Theory of the Firm* (Prentice-Hall, 1963), p. 16. See also William J. Gore, *Administrative Decision-Making: A Heuristic Model* (Wiley, 1964), pp. 30–35; and Herbert Kaufman, "Organization Theory and Political Theory," *The American Political Science Review* (March 1964), pp. 5–14.

Weberian type identifies bureaucratic structure, in which authority flows from the *office* rather than from the characteristics of the *person* who occupies the office. Today many scholars are investigating the consequences of hierarchical organization and the impact of such structures both on persons who work within them and on the larger society of which they are a part. Much attention is directed to the informal organization that exists apart from the organization chart (see p. 414); there is growing awareness that authority is a relationship that depends as much on the behavior of those to whom an order is directed as it does on the behavior of the one who issues it, that behavior is influenced not merely by instructions from the top but by many other incentives, such as prestige or power or attitudes of fellow workers.[20]

A NEW DISCIPLINE WITH OLD ROOTS

At the beginning of this century Frederick Taylor launched the scientific-management movement when he developed tools for the measurement of the efficiency of task performances. Stemming from the epic Hawthorne Experiments, the human-relations literature stresses the subjective and non-rational factors—the face-to-face interpersonal relations that take place in small groups within formal structures. Today scholars, primarily social psychologists, conduct experimental studies of such complex factors as morale and productivity.

The organization theorists whose work is of most immediate relevance to the political process are those working on administrative behavior within complex organizations. Under the banner of the Science of Public Administration, Luther Gulick and other pioneering scholars early in this century developed a formal model of administration from which they deduced certain principles: *unity of command*—every officer should have a superior to whom he reports and from whom he takes orders; *chain of command*—there should be a firm line of authority running from the top down and of formal responsibility running from the bottom up; *line and staff*—the staff advises the executive but gives no commands, whereas the line has operating duties; *span of control*—a hierarchical structure should be established so that no one person supervises more agencies directly than he can effectively handle; *decentralization*—administrators should delegate decisions and responsibilities to lower levels.

These classical principles of public administration were thought to promote efficiency and economy, to secure firm control by superiors over subordinates, and by establishing links between politically accountable policy-makers and administrative agencies, to make administration responsive to the demands of the elected officials.

HOW GOOD IS THE CLASSIC MODEL?

The classic model remains the most influential ideal for those involved in administration. However, scholars have become increasingly skeptical of the

[20]James G. March and Herbert Simon, *Organizations* (Wiley, 1958).

validity of these principles either as guides for practitioners or as models for investigators. As Herbert A. Simon wrote in his highly influential *Administrative Behavior*:

> Administrative description suffers . . . from superficiality, oversimplification, lack of realism. . . . It has refused to undertake the tiresome task of studying the actual allocations of decision-making functions. It has been satisfied to speak of "authority," "centralization," "span of control," "function," without seeking operational definitions of these terms. . . . A fatal defect of the current principles of administration is that, like proverbs, they occur in pairs. For almost every principle one can find an equally plausible and acceptable contradictory principle.[21]

Another and related challenge to the classic rational approach to decision-making is *incrementalism*. The incrementalists question the idea that men rationally approach problems with definite objectives in mind and with a clear sense of alternative ways of reaching those objectives. Men—even public administrators—simply do not know enough about the alternatives, their own goals and values are not clear enough, and the situations they face are too complex for such a broad and "rational" approach, according to this argument. Rather, they are likely to go one step at a time, to feel their way, to cling to one familiar method rather than to consider carefully all the other methods, to attack problems piecemeal, to adjust and compromise with institutions rather than overturn them and reconstruct them. Not only is this the way men *do* act, according to the incrementalists, it is the way they *should* act if they wish to go about their affairs in a sensible and effective manner.[22]

Today scholars are making intensive case studies of how decisions are made. They are developing generalizations for study and for prescription. We still lack sure knowledge to guide administrators or to speak with high confidence about the precise consequences that flow from organizational arrangements, but we have learned that the classic principles that we used to proclaim with such assurance conceal as much as they reveal.

BUREAUCRATIZATION AND INDIVIDUAL FREEDOM

It is difficult to grasp the concept that the bureaucracy is not fully subordinate to one or more of the three branches of American government. But, as we have seen, the three branches have necessarily supported the creation of a semiautonomous bureaucracy as an instrument to enable our government to meet its challenges.[23] Because it appears that bureaucracy is typical of all complex social systems, it is crucial that we understand its relationship to democracy. Surprising as it may seem, it is only in recent years that attention has been paid to this question. Two general areas are of particular importance.

Who will regulate the regulators? Who can? Who should? Is there such a thing as "the public interest" or is this simply a myth behind which special interests hide? Because it has become clear that the decisions the bureaucracy

[21]Simon, *op. cit.*, p. xiv.

[22]David Braybrooke and Charles E. Lindblom, *A Strategy of Decision* (Free Press, 1963). See also a review of this volume, Lewis A. Froman, Jr., *The American Political Science Review* (March 1964), pp. 116–117.

[23]Woll, *op. cit.*, p. 174.

makes are political decisions, the problem of keeping the bureaucracy responsible is now receiving careful attention.[24]

Most recently, scholars have begun to ask whether bureaucracy as a form of organization is itself a neutral type. Are there certain characteristics that are typical of all bureaucracies? For example, must bureaucracies be inherently conservative and resistant to change? Do bureaucracies have life cycles? Can they be rendered more flexible? Is the impersonal "multiversity" the inevitable consequence of bigness?[25] In short, does the increased bureaucratization inevitable in a modern industrial society necessarily require limitations on individual efficacy and freedom?[26] Although we are a long way from having answers to these questions, there can be no doubt that the bureaucratic phenomenon is central to an understanding of government by the people.

[24]McConnell, op. cit. See also Robert Engler, The Politics of Oil: A Study of Private Power and Democratic Directions (Macmillan, 1961).

[25]Clark Kerr, The Uses of the University (Harvard Univ. Press, 1963).

[26]Michel Crozier, The Bureaucratic Phenomenon (Univ. of Chicago Press, 1964); Anthony Downs, Inside Bureaucracy (Little, Brown, 1967); John Kenneth Galbraith, The New Industrial State (Houghton Mifflin, 1967).

The Judges

19

Foreigners are often amazed at the great power Americans give their judges, especially federal judges. In 1848, after his visit to America, the French aristocrat Alexis de Tocqueville wrote, "If I were asked where I place the American aristocracy, I should reply without hesitation . . . that it occupies the judicial bench and bar. . . . Scarcely any political question arises in the United States that it is not resolved, sooner or later, into a judicial question."[1] A century later the English laborite Harold Laski observed, "The respect in which the federal courts and, above all, the Supreme Court are held is hardly surpassed by the influence they exert on the life of the United States."[2]

Why do American federal judges have great influence and prestige? One reason is their power of judicial review—that is, their power to make the authoritative interpretation of the Constitution. Only a constitutional amendment (and the judges would interpret the amendment) or the Supreme Court itself can modify the Court's doctrine. Mr. Justice Frankfurter once put it tersely, "The Supreme Court is the Constitution."

However, even without the power to interpret the Constitution our judges would be influential decision-makers. Indeed, constitutional questions are not involved in most of the cases that come before the judges, but these cases nevertheless result in the construction of statutes and the development of

[1]Alexis de Tocqueville (Phillips Bradley, ed.), *Democracy in America* (Knopf, 1944), vol. I, pp. 278–280.
[2]Harold J. Laski, *The American Democracy* (Viking, 1948), p. 110.

434

435 rules that affect the conduct of countless numbers of people.[3] Litigation is important as a technique for resolving policy, and judicial participation is crucial in the policy-making process, but both of these are incidental results that flow from the primary function of courts—to serve as impartial tribunals for the settlement of legal disputes. Many disputes raise no major policy issues and are of little interest to any except the immediate parties to the case. But in settling peacefully the innumerable controversies that arise among individuals and between individuals and the government, judges play as notable a role as they do in deciding the more momentous cases that help shape the grand outlines of American politics.

The Law

The Constitution does not require judges to be lawyers. Yet all Supreme Court justices, as well as other federal judges, have been members of the bar. The reason for this is obvious: The business of courts is law, and law is a professional discipline, a technical subject whose mastery requires specialized training. What kind of law do federal judges apply? Where do they find it? (See Bibliography, to find out where the lay citizen can look up the law.)

TYPES OF LAW

In many instances, a judicial decision is based on *statutory law*. This is law formulated by the legislature, although it also includes treaties and executive orders; it is law that comes from authoritative and specific lawmaking sources. The legislature has no choice but to state rules in general terms, for it cannot anticipate all the questions that will arise over their meaning. Therefore, although the initial interpretation is often made by an administrator, the final interpretation is made by judges.

Intelligence alone is not enough to interpret even the simplest of laws. They must be interpreted according to the application of legal principles. In theory, judges try to discover *legislative intent*—what the legislators intended to do. When possible, this is done by studying the words of the statute, but sometimes judges must look to legislative journals, legislative debates, and committee hearings for clues to the intention of the legislators. A layman might try to consult the men who drafted, introduced, or considered the bill in committee, for they might seem to be the most informative and reliable source of legislative intent. But according to the judges' rules, which in large part they make themselves, this is not permissible.

What happens if there is no statutory law governing a case that comes before a court? What if the legislature has not formalized any rule to apply to the dispute? Then the judges must apply the *common law*. Common law is judge-made law. It has an ancient lineage reaching back through centuries of judicial decisions and originated in England in the twelfth century when

[3]Martin Shapiro, *Law and Politics in the Supreme Court* (Free Press, 1964), pp. 1–49.

royal judges began traveling around the country settling disputes in each locality according to prevailing custom. Gradually these customs became the same for the entire nation. The common law continues to develop according to the rule of *stare decisis*, which means "let the decision stand." This is the rule of precedent, which requires that once a rule has been established by a court, it shall be followed in all similar cases. (See p. 440 for a fuller discussion of this principle.)

The American common law began to branch off from the English system in the seventeenth century. Today we have forty-nine separate common-law systems, or fifty, counting the federal interpretation of state law. (In Louisiana the legal system is based on the other great Western legal tradition, the *civil law*. The civil law gives more emphasis to codes of lawgivers and less to past judicial decisions. In Louisiana the civil law has been greatly influenced by and intermingled with the common law.) There is no federal common law. Whenever federal judges have to decide disputes between citizens of two states and there is no applicable state statute, they apply the common law as interpreted by the state courts. But when there is no state interpretation, federal judges strike out for themselves. The common law governs many disputes, and even where it has been superseded by statute, the statutory law is usually a modification and codification of the old common-law rules and is normally interpreted according to the common-law tradition.

Federal judges also apply *equity*. Like common law, equity is a system of judge-made law that had its origins in England. Early in the development of the common law, it was discovered that in certain circumstances it did not ensure justice. For example, under the common law, a person whose property rights are about to be injured has no choice but to wait until the injury has taken place and then to seek money damages. But the injury may do irreparable harm for which money damages cannot provide adequate compensation. Accordingly another set of rules was worked out to be used where the law was inadequate. Under equity, a person may go to a judge, show why the common-law remedy is inadequate, and ask for equitable relief—an injunction, for example, to prevent an act that threatens irreparable harm. If the wrongdoer persists, he may be punished for contempt of court.

Sometimes judges apply *constitutional law*. Because the Constitution contains only seven thousand words and can be read in a half-hour or so, it might be assumed that any person could learn constitutional law after a little study. But the document itself sheds little light on constitutional law. Constitutional law is full of phrases like "the clear and present danger rule" and "selective absorption" that are not to be found in the written words of the Constitution. They come from the decisions of the Supreme Court. Constitutional law, in other words, consists of statements about the interpretation of the Constitution that have been given Supreme Court sanction.

Admiralty and maritime law is also applied by federal judges. This is a highly complex and technical body of rules applicable to cases arising in connection with shipping and water-borne commerce on the high seas and, by decision of the Supreme Court,[4] on the navigable waters of the United States.

[4]*The Genessee Chief* (1852).

A relatively new kind of law that has become increasingly prominent in the decisions of federal judges is *administrative law*. Within the last several decades, Congress has delegated to administrators and administrative agencies so much rule-making authority that today there is, in volume, more administrative than statutory law. Administrative law consists of the rules and regulations that are issued by administrative agencies and that deal with the operations of the government or determine private rights. An example is the Federal Trade Commission regulation that forbids interstate advertisers to use the word *free* in such a way as to mislead the reader. The rules and decisions of administrators may be reviewed by federal judges, and judges are often called on to determine whether the administrators have acted properly and within their authority.[5]

Law may also be classified as criminal or civil. *Criminal law*, which is almost entirely statutory, defines crimes against the public order and provides for punishment. Government has the primary responsibility for enforcing this type of law. The great body of criminal law is enacted by states and is enforced by state officials in the state courts, but the criminal business of federal judges is by no means negligible, and it is growing. The Constitution insists on certain minimum procedures in the trial of criminal cases (see Chapter 8), and these procedures have been supplemented by law. The Supreme Court, as supervisor of the administration of justice in the federal courts, has adopted other rules that federal judges must follow.

Civil law governs the relations between individuals and defines their legal rights. For example, Jones, who has a trademark for Atomic Pills, discovers that Smith is advertising Atomic Tablets in national magazines. If Jones wishes to protect his trademark, he may proceed against Smith before a federal judge. But the government can also be a party to a civil action. Under the Sherman Antitrust Act, for example, the federal government may initiate civil as well as criminal action to prevent violations of the law.

THE SCOPE OF JUDICIAL POWER: THE FIGHT THEORY

The American judicial process is based on the *adversary system*. A court of law is viewed as a neutral arena, in which two parties fight out their differences before an impartial arbiter. Indeed, Judge Jerome Frank suggested that the "fights" in courtrooms are civilized substitutes for primitive feuds and duels.[6] The underlying logic of the adversary system is that the best way for the court to discover the truth is for each side to strive as hard as it can to present its point of view. Macaulay said that we obtain the fairest decision "when two men argue, as unfairly as possible, on opposite sides," for then "it is certain that no important considerations will altogether escape notice."[7] Whether or not the fight theory is an adequate way of arriving at the truth—and there are those who believe it is not—the fact that it lies at the basis of our judicial system is crucial, because, first, the logic of the adversary system imposes formal restraints on the scope of judicial power and, sec-

---

[5]For a discussion of this subject, see Martin Shapiro, *The Supreme Court and Administrative Agencies* (Free Press, 1968).

[6]Jerome Frank, *Courts on Trial* (Princeton Univ. Press, 1949).

[7]*Ibid.*, p. 80.

ond, the rhetoric of the adversary system leads us to conceive of the role of the judge in a very special way.

If courts are to judge existing conflicts, then judicial power is essentially *passive*; that is, courts cannot act until combatants come to them. The judiciary is said to lack a self-starter.[8]

Not all disputes are within the scope of judicial power. Judges decide only *justiciable* disputes — those that grow out of actual cases and that are capable of settlement by legal methods. Not all governmental questions or constitutional problems are justiciable. For example, judges will not determine which government of a foreign state should be recognized by the United States. The Constitution gives this authority to the President, and judges will not question his decision. Similarly, the Supreme Court has ruled that some claims of unconstitutionality raise political and not justiciable questions. What does the Court mean by "political"? It means an issue that requires knowledge of a nonlegal character, that requires the use of techniques not suitable for a court, or that the Constitution addresses to the political branch of government. Examples of political questions are: Which of two competing state governments is the proper one? What is a republican form of state government?[9]

Theoretically, judges will not use their power unless the controversy is a real one. Two people cannot trump up a suit merely to contest the legislature. For example, in 1889 a man named Wellman tried to purchase a railway ticket the day after the Michigan legislature had fixed the rates. The ticket agent refused to sell a ticket at the new rate and Wellman brought suit. During the trial Wellman did not contest the railway company's testimony. It became clear that Wellman wanted the railway company to win; he made no attempt to present fully the facts in the case. The Supreme Court said, however, "It was never thought that, by means of a friendly suit, a party beaten in the legislature could transfer to the courts an inquiry as to the constitutionality of a legislative act."[10] (This, of course, is exactly what is done in a nonfriendly suit. In such cases, however, the two parties have an interest in getting the full facts before the Court.)

Can anybody challenge a law? Not unless he has "sustained or is immediately in danger of sustaining a direct injury. It is not sufficient that he has merely a general interest common to all members of the public."[11] Furthermore, the injury must be substantial. And the courts will not issue advisory opinions to Congress or the President.

The logic of the adversary system requires that the judge decide only what is necessary to dispose of the specific case before him. The Supreme Court has expressed its particular reluctance to go beyond the case at hand when constitutional questions are involved. As Mr. Justice Brandeis wrote,

It is not the habit of the court to decide questions of a constitutional nature unless absolutely necessary to a decision of the case. . . . The Court will not "formulate a rule of constitutional law broader than is required by the precise facts to which it is applied. . . ." The Court will not pass upon a

[8]Walter F. Murphy, Jr., *Elements of Judicial Strategy* (Univ. of Chicago Press, 1964), p. 21.
[9]*Luther* v. *Borden* (1849); *Coleman* v. *Miller* (1939).
[10]*Chicago & Grand Trunk Railway Co.* v. *Wellman* (1892).
[11]*Ex parte Levitt* (1937).

constitutional question although properly presented by the record, if there is also present some other ground upon which the case may be disposed of. . . . [It] is a cardinal principle that this Court will first ascertain whether a construction of the statute is fairly possible by which the question [of constitutionality] may be avoided.[12]

Judges do not always remain strictly within the limits set by these restrictions. At times the Supreme Court justices, despite their professed reluctance to do so, have had little hesitancy about striking down laws of Congress. Disputes have been trumped up entirely for the purpose of getting a Court decision—the Dred Scott case, for example, appears to have been a dispute of this kind. Other cases have been presented in which it was questionable whether the parties actually stood in an adverse relationship. The real significance of the technical restrictions on the Court is not that they limit judicial power, but that they give the Supreme Court considerable latitude to avoid deciding cases it does not want to confront. The first Justice Harlan (grandfather of the present Justice Harlan) made this quite clear: "The courts have rarely, if ever, felt themselves so restrained by technical rules, that they could not find some remedy, consistent with the law, for acts . . . that violated natural justice. . . ."[13]

DO JUDGES MAKE LAW?

"Do Judges make law? 'Course they do. Made some myself," remarked Jeremiah Smith, former judge of the New Hampshire Supreme Court.[14] Although such statements are now quite common, they are somehow disquieting; they do not conform to our notion of the proper judge. Why should this be? Why is it that so many still cling to the notion that judges do not make law?

The conception many people have of the role of a judge—a conception that follows quite naturally from the adversary system of adjudication—is that it is similar to that of a referee in a prizefight. What do we expect of the referee? He must be impartial; he must be disinterested; he must treat both parties as equals. Referees do not make rules; they apply the rules the boxing commission has established. Insofar as the function of a judge is analogous to that of a referee, these same expectations may be legitimately applied to him. But the analogy must not be pushed too far. The referee need do nothing more than apply the boxing commission's rules, because the boxing commission has anticipated practically every conceivable situation in the ring. But the situations with which the legislature must deal are infinitely more complex.

Herein lies the answer to the question: Do judges make law? Not only do they, but they must. Legislatures make law by adopting statutes, but judges apply the statutes to concrete situations; inevitably discretion is involved. Indeed there will be some cases to which general expressions are clearly applicable: "If anything is a vehicle, a motor-car is one."[15] But does the word

---

[12]Concurring opinion in *Ashwander* v. *T.V.A.* (1936).

[13]Quoted by Murphy, *op. cit.*, p. 30.

[14]Quoted in Paul A. Freund, *On Understanding the Supreme Court* (Little, Brown, 1949), p. 3.

[15]This discussion is based on H. L. A. Hart, *The Concept of Law* (Oxford Univ. Press, 1961), Chap. 7.

vehicle in a statute include bicycles, airplanes, and roller skates? A judge is constantly faced with situations that possess some of the features of the similar cases—but lack others. "Uncertainty at the borderline is the price to be paid for the use of general classifying terms."[16] Statutes are drawn in broad terms: Drivers shall act with "reasonable care"; No one may make "excessive noise" in the vicinity of a hospital; Employers must maintain "safe working conditions." The reason broad terms must be used is that legislators cannot have knowledge of all the possible combinations of circumstances the future may bring. Thus a statute does not settle many questions, because it could not have been anticipated that they would be raised. "In every legal system a large and important field is left open for the exercise of discretion by courts and other officials in rendering initially vague standards determinate, in resolving the uncertainties of statutes, or in developing and qualifying rules only broadly communicated by . . . precedents."[17]

These problems are further magnified when judges are asked—as American judges are—to apply the Constitution, written over 180 years ago. If Congress passed a law extending the terms of senators beyond six years, its unconstitutionality would be apparent to everyone. But if constitutional interpretation amounted only to this, judges would have no special function as interpreters of the Constitution, nor would they have much discretion. The Constitution abounds with generalizations: "due process of law," "equal protection of the laws," "unreasonable searches and seizures," "commerce among the several states." It is not likely that recourse to the intent of the Framers will help judges faced with cases involving airplanes, television, electronic wiretaps, General Motors, or birth-control pills. Because the rules by which society is governed cannot interpret themselves, judges cannot avoid making law.

STARE DECISIS

One element of the English common law that pervades our judicial system is *stare decisis*, the rule of precedent. A judge is expected to abide by all previous decisions of his own court and all rulings of superior courts. However, although the rule of precedent does impose considerable regularity on the legal system,[18] it is not nearly so restrictive as some people think.

Consider, for example, the father who, removing his hat as he enters a church, says to his son, "This is the way to behave on such occasions. Do as I do."[19] The son, like the judge trying to follow a precedent, has a wide range of possibilities open to him: How much of the performance must be imitated? Does it matter if the left hand is used, instead of the right, to remove the hat? That it is done slowly or smartly? That the hat is put under the seat? That it is not replaced on the head inside the church? The judge can *distinguish* precedents by stating that a previous case does not control the immediate one because of differences in context. In addition, in many

---

[16]*Ibid.*, p. 125.
[17]*Ibid.*, p. 132.
[18]Benjamin Cardozo, *The Nature of the Judicial Process* (Yale Univ. Press, 1921).
[19]This discussion is based on Hart, *op. cit.*, pp. 121, 122.

areas of law, there are conflicting precedents, one of which can be chosen to support a decision for either party.

The doctrine of *stare decisis* is even less controlling in the field of constitutional law. Because the Constitution, rather than any one interpretation of it, is binding, the Court can reverse a previous decision it no longer wishes to follow. Therefore Supreme Court justices are not seriously restricted by the doctrine of *stare decisis*. As the first Justice Harlan told a group of law students: "I want to say to you young gentlemen that if we don't like an act of Congress, we don't have much trouble to find grounds for declaring it unconstitutional."[20]

The Shape of Federal Justice

The Constitution provides for only one Supreme Court, leaving it up to Congress to establish inferior federal courts. (The Constitution also allows Congress to determine the size of the Supreme Court as well as of lower courts.) A Supreme Court is a necessity if the national government is to have the power to frame laws superior to those of the states. The lack of such a tribunal to maintain national supremacy, to ensure uniform interpretation of national legislation, and to resolve conflicts among the states was one of the glaring deficiencies of the central government under the Articles of Confederation.

The First Congress divided the nation into districts and created lower national courts for each district. That decision, though often supplemented, has never been seriously questioned. Today the hierarchy of the national courts of general jurisdiction consists of *district courts, courts of appeals*, and one *Supreme Court*.

THE ORGANIZATION OF FEDERAL COURTS

The workhorses of the federal judiciary are the eighty-eight district courts within the states, the district court in the District of Columbia, and the territorial district court in Puerto Rico. Each state has at least one district court; the larger states have as many as the demands of judicial business and the pressure of politics require (though no state has more than four). Each district court is composed of at least one judge, but there may be as many as twenty-four. District judges normally sit separately and hold court by themselves. There are three hundred and thirty-three district judgeships, all filled by the President with the consent of the Senate; all district judges, except those of the territorial courts, hold office for life.

District courts are trial courts of *original jurisdiction*. They are the only federal courts that regularly employ *grand* (indicting) and *petit* (trial) juries. Many of the cases tried before district judges involve citizens of different states, and the judges apply the appropriate state laws. Otherwise, district judges are concerned with federal laws. For example, they hear and decide

[20]Quoted by E. S. Corwin, *Constitutional Revolution* (Claremont and Associated Colleges, 1941), p. 38.

cases involving crimes against the United States—suits under the national revenue, postal, patent, copyright, trademark, bankruptcy, and civil rights laws. The district courts devote most of their time to civil cases, that is, to questions of property rights rather than personal rights.[21]

PART 5
Policy-makers
for the
People

District judges are assisted by clerks, bailiffs, stenographers, law clerks, court reporters, probation officers, and United States magistrates. All these persons are appointed by the judges. The magistrates, who serve eight-year terms, handle some of the preliminaries. They issue warrants for arrests and often hear the evidence to determine whether an arrested person should be held for action by the grand jury. If so, the magistrate may set the bail. A United States marshal, appointed by the President, is assigned to each district court. Although marshals no longer exercise general police jurisdiction, they maintain order in the courtroom, guard prisoners, make arrests, and carry out court orders, such as serving summonses for witnesses; at times, as in the fall

[21]Glendon A. Schubert, *Judicial Policy-Making* (Scott, Foresman, 1965), p. 62.

ORGANIZATION OF FEDERAL COURTS

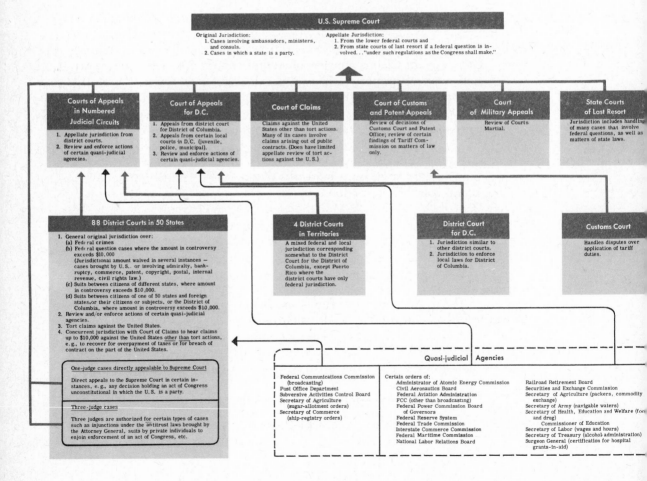

of 1962 in Oxford, Mississippi, they carry out orders of a federal court even in the face of violence.[22]

Although a few important decisions of a district court may be appealed directly to the Supreme Court, most decisions may be carried only to a United States court of appeals. (In fact, the majority of district court decisions are not appealed at all.)[23] The United States is divided into eleven judicial circuits, including the District of Columbia as a circuit, each of which has a court of appeals consisting of three to nine circuit judges, eighty-four in all. Like all judges of courts exercising the judicial power of the United States, circuit judges are appointed for life by the President with the consent of the Senate. The United States courts of appeals have only *appellate jurisdiction*—they review decisions of the district courts within their circuit and also some of the actions of certain of the independent regulatory agencies, such as the Federal Trade Commission. Each court of appeals normally utilizes panels of three judges to hear cases. One Supreme Court justice is assigned to each circuit, but today his duties as circuit justice are only nominal.

SPECIAL COURTS, LEGISLATIVE COURTS, AND ADMINISTRATIVE TRIBUNALS

In addition to the federal constitutional courts of general jurisdiction, Congress has also created constitutional courts of special jurisdiction—the Court of Claims, the Customs Court, and the Court of Customs and Patent Appeals. The Court of Claims consists of a chief and six associate judges, with jurisdiction over all property and contract damage suits against the United States. The court sits in Washington, but commissioners of the court travel throughout the United States taking evidence. The United States Customs Court, consisting of nine judges, has jurisdiction to review rulings of collectors of the customs. Its decisions in turn may be appealed to the Court of Customs and Patent Appeals, a five-member court, which also reviews decisions of the Patent Office and, on a more restricted scale, certain rulings of the United States Tariff Commission.

The United States Court of Military Appeals is the GI Supreme Court. This is a *legislative* rather than a *constitutional* court—significant mainly in that its judges need not be appointed for life. It is composed of three civilian judges appointed for fifteen years by the President with the consent of the Senate. This court applies *military law*, which is separate from the body of law that governs the rest of the federal courts. Congress develops the rules and judicial organization to protect the rights of persons in the military forces. The Constitution specifically denies to such persons the constitutional right to grand-jury indictment; and the weight of opinion, though there is considerable dissent, appears to be that the other rights of persons accused of crime that are listed in the Fifth and Sixth Amendments also do not apply to persons in the armed forces.

The Court of Military Appeals, which sits at the top of the military court

[22]Rita W. Cooley, "The Office of United States Marshal," *Western Political Quarterly* (March 1959), pp. 123–140.
[23]Schubert, *op. cit.*, p. 62.

hierarchy, must review all decisions involving a flag officer or a general, imposition of the death penalty, and questions certified to it by one of the judge advocates general and by the general counsel of the Department of Transportation acting for the Coast Guard. When petitioned by the accused, it has discretionary power to review decisions involving bad-conduct discharges or more than one year's imprisonment. The Supreme Court has not yet made clear the exact extent of civil courts' authority to review decisions of military courts, but it has indicated that their authority is exceedingly limited—probably no more than to determine whether the military courts had jurisdiction and have given fair consideration to the claims of justice.[24]

Many administrators and administrative agencies also hear and decide cases and exercise what amounts to quasi-judicial power, even though these agencies rank as neither constitutional nor legislative courts. For example, a person or company injured by the allegedly unfair competitive practices of a business engaged in interstate commerce may bring a charge to the Federal Trade Commission. Attorneys appear, present briefs, introduce evidence, and carry out regular court routine; eventually the commissioners hand down a decision—just as do judges. Appeals on questions of law and procedure in these hearings may be taken to a court of appeals and eventually to the Supreme Court.

STATE AND FEDERAL COURTS

In addition to this complex structure of federal courts, each of the fifty states maintains a complete judicial system of its own. And many of the large municipalities have independent judicial systems as complex as those of the states. This dual system of courts is not common—even among nations with federal systems. "The usual pattern in such countries is to entrust the enforcement of the federal law to the state courts. At the time of the adoption of our Constitution, however, the states and the federal government were too jealous of each other to accept a unitary judicial system."[25] The Framers gave the national courts the power to hear and decide cases in law and equity if:

1. The cases arise under the Constitution, a federal law, or a treaty.
2. The cases arise under admiralty and maritime laws.
3. The cases arise because of a dispute involving land claimed under titles granted by two or more states.
4. The United States is a party to the case.
5. A state is a party to the case (but not including suits commenced or prosecuted against a state by an individual or a foreign nation).
6. The cases are between citizens of different states.
7. The cases affect the accredited representatives of a foreign nation.

What is the relation between the federal and state courts? The common impression that all federal courts are superior to any state court is wrong. The two court systems are related, but they do not exist in a superior-inferior re-

[24]*Burns* v. *Wilson* (1953).
[25]Milton D. Green, "The Business of the Trial Courts," in Harry W. Jones (ed.), *The Courts, the Public, and the Law Explosion* (Prentice-Hall, 1965) pp. 8–9.

lationship. Over some kinds of cases only the state courts have jurisdiction; over other kinds both court systems have jurisdiction; and over others only the federal courts have jurisdiction. Moreover, except for the limited habeas corpus jurisdiction of the district courts, the Supreme Court is the only federal court that may review state-court decisions, and it may do so only under special conditions.

State courts have sole jurisdiction to try all cases not within the judicial power granted by the Constitution to the national government. As to the judicial power that is granted to the national government, Congress determines whether it shall be exclusively exercised by national courts, concurrently exercised by both national and state courts, or denied to either or both national and state courts. For example, Congress has stipulated that prosecutions for violations of federal criminal laws, suits for penalties authorized by federal laws, and cases involving foreign ambassadors are within the exclusive jurisdiction of national courts. On the other hand, legal disputes between citizens of different states involving more than $10,000 may be tried in either national or state courts. If the amount is less, the case can be tried only in state courts. (Of course, federal courts may have jurisdiction over suits between citizens of different states for some other reason, for instance if the dispute arises under national law.)

FEDERAL PROSECUTIONS

Judges decide cases; they do not prosecute persons. That job, on the federal level, falls to the Department of Justice and, more specifically, to the Attorney General, the Solicitor General, and the hundreds of United States attorneys and assistant attorneys throughout the country. A United States attorney is appointed to each district court by the President with consent of the Senate; he is appointed for a four-year term, but he may be dismissed by the President at any time. These appointments are of great interest to senators who, through senatorial courtesy (see page 403), exercise significant influence over them. Assistant attorneys are appointed by the Attorney General. Assisted by the Federal Bureau of Investigation, the district attorneys start criminal proceedings against persons who break federal laws and initiate civil actions for the government. In a criminal case, the district attorney presents to a grand jury evidence that a national law has been violated. If the jury brings an indictment, the attorney conducts the government's case against the accused

It has been said that the "prosecutor rather than the judge . . . plays the key role in the administration of criminal justice. The prosecutor must make or contribute to each of the key decisions: whether to charge an offense, which offense to charge, . . . whether to prosecute concurrently or separately if several charges are pending, and what sentence to recommend to the judge. Most of these decisions are made in the privacy of the prosecutor's office; neither newspapers nor television intrude to report the results."[26]

Although judges are the most thoroughly studied group of the federal judicial system, the role of the Department of Justice should not be underes-

[26]Herbert Jacob, *Justice in America: Courts, Lawyers, and the Judicial Process* (Little, Brown, 1965), p. 161.

timated. Attorneys from the Department of Justice and from other federal agencies participate in well over half the cases on the Supreme Court's docket.[27] Schubert suggests that one reason for increased judicial activity on behalf of Negroes in the 1960s is that "with the incumbency of the Kennedy administration, . . . the Supreme Court could count upon the support of the Department of Justice to aid and to augment the activities of the district courts in the enforcement of the Court's various . . . policies of racial integration."[28]

Within the Department of Justice special divisions—such as the criminal division, civil division, antitrust division and civil rights division—coordinate the work of the attorneys in the field, develop cases, and send out specialists to assist the attorneys. Of special importance is the Solicitor General, who appears for and represents the government before the Supreme Court. Moreover, no appeal may be taken by the United States to any appellate court without his approval.

Who Are the Judges?

THE POLITICS OF JUDICIAL SELECTION

The Constitution places the selection of federal judges in the hands of the President, acting with the advice and consent of the Senate. But political reality imposes important constraints on the President's appointment power. The selection of a federal judge is actually a complex bargaining process, in which the principal figures involved are the candidates for the judgeship, the President, United States senators, the Department of Justice, the Standing Committee on Federal Judiciary of the American Bar Association, and political party leaders.[29]

Because of the practice of senatorial courtesy (see p. 403), if the senators of the state in which the judge is to sit are of the President's party, they have an informal veto over the appointment. Until recently, the senators from the affected state often sent names to the President from which he (through his Attorney General) nominated a man for Senate consideration. "But more recent data . . . indicate that there has been at least a slight move of the pendulum toward the President."[30] The Justice Department—especially the Deputy Attorney General—now takes a more active role in selecting nominees for consideration by the Senate, but it still must find men acceptable to the senators from the state in which the judge will sit. Senatorial courtesy does not apply to appointments to the Supreme Court—the justices do not serve in any one senator's domain—so the President has considerably more discretion in making appointments to the High Court. It is not surprising

[27]Nathan Hakman, "Lobbying the Supreme Court—An Appraisal of 'Political Science Folklore,'" *Fordham Law Review* (1966).

[28]Schubert, *op. cit.*, p. 152.

[29]Harold W. Chase, "Federal Judges: The Appointing Process," *Minnesota Law Review* (1966), pp. 185–221.

[30]Joel B. Grossman, *Lawyers and Judges: The ABA and the Politics of Judicial Selection* (Wiley, 1965), p. 27. See also Chase, *op. cit.*

that judges in the lower federal courts often reflect a different consensus of values from that of the men appointed to the Supreme Court.

Candidates for judicial office may "campaign" vigorously, attempting to drum up support from men in positions to influence the decision. Alphonso Taft wrote to Chief Justice Morrison R. Waite:

"My dear Judge, I have sometimes hoped, that if Judge Swayne should retire, there might be a possibility of my being thought of for that place. I should like it. . . . If . . . you should think favorably of it, and should find oppertunity [sic] to encourage it, I should certainly be under great obligation whatever the result might be."[31]

The Chief Justice promised to "lose no opportunity" to let the President know what a fine judge Taft would make.

A candidate for judicial office wrote to the Attorney General, with whom the aspiring judge had become acquainted through his participation in the preceding presidential campaign. "Further in connection with our conversation of last week regarding the vacancy on the United States Court of Appeals for the ____ Circuit, this is to advise that both Senators . . . will support me. You will be receiving letters from them within a few days. . . ."[32] State and federal judges also often participate in the appointment procedure. Sometimes their advice is solicited by the President, but it may well come uninvited.[33] "When a recent proposed nomination to the . . . court of appeals was delayed for two years because of an intraparty dispute between the senators and the Attorney General, a number of prominent jurists, including at least two Supreme Court justices, sought to break the deadlock."[34]

Since the end of World War II, the American Bar Association—and especially its Standing Committee on Federal Judiciary—has come to play an important role in the appointment process. All federal judicial appointments are automatically sent to the committee for its evaluation. During the Eisenhower administration, the committee developed a virtual veto power over nominations,[35] and although subsequent administrations have occasionally appointed judges rated unqualified by the ABA committee, no administration is pleased to have its appointments so classified.

THE ROLE OF PARTY

When Franklin D. Roosevelt became President, over 90 percent of the federal judges were Republicans.[36] But Roosevelt's four terms in office gave him ample opportunity to redress the partisan imbalance, and as Table 19-1

---

[31]Quoted in Alpheus T. Mason, *William Howard Taft: Chief Justice* (Simon and Schuster, 1965), p. 18.

[32]Quoted in Sheldon Goldman, "Judicial Appointments to the United States Courts of Appeals," *Wisconsin Law Review* (1967), pp. 186–214. Reprinted in Thomas P. Jahnige and Sheldon Goldman (eds.), *The Federal Judicial System: Readings in Process and Behavior* (Holt, 1968), p. 16. For an excellent description of the political pressures involved in the appointment of a Supreme Court justice, see David Danelski, *A Supreme Court Justice Is Appointed* (Random House, 1964).

[33]See Walter F. Murphy, "In His Own Image," *Supreme Court Review* (1961), pp. 159–193.

[34]Grossman, *op. cit.*, p. 39

[35]*Ibid.*, p. 73.

[36]Jack W. Peltason, *Federal Courts in the Political Process* (Doubleday, 1955), p. 32.

TABLE 19-1

Federal Judgeships
as Political Patronage

President	Democrats	Republicans
Roosevelt	188	6
Truman	116	9
Eisenhower	9	165
Kennedy	111°	11
Johnson	134	8

°One New York Liberal was appointed.
SOURCE: *Congressional Quarterly Almanac* (1967), p. 1311.

indicates, he made every effort to do so.

Party considerations have always been important in the selection of judges—both state and federal. Presidents have seldom chosen a judge from the opposing party, and the use of judgeships as a form of political reward is openly acknowledged by those involved. A state party leader wrote to the Attorney General:

If ____ is not named [to the court of appeals] this would damage seriously the Kennedy forces in [this state]. ____ was openly for Kennedy before L.A. and stood strong and voted there. He is known as one of my closest friends. He is an excellent lawyer—and on the merits alone, better qualified than Judge ____.

The Senators will give you no trouble, but we have put this on the line in public, and if ____ is not appointed it will be a mortal blow.

The desired candidate was appointed.[37]

THE ROLE OF IDEOLOGY

But finding a fellow partisan is not enough. Presidents want to pick the "right" kind of Republican or "our" kind of Democrat. Especially when the appointment is to the Supreme Court, the policy orientation of the nominee is important. As President Lincoln told Congressman Boutewell when he appointed Salmon P. Chase to the Court, "We wish for a Chief Justice who will sustain what has been done in regard to emancipation and legal tender."[38] (Lincoln guessed wrong on Chase and legal tender.) Theodore Roosevelt voiced this attitude in a letter to Senator Lodge about Judge Oliver Wendell Holmes of the Massachusetts Supreme Judicial Court, whom he was considering for the Supreme Court: "Now I should like to know that Judge Holmes was in entire sympathy with our views, that is with your views and mine. . . . I should hold myself guilty of an irreparable wrong to the nation if I should [appoint] any man who was not absolutely sane and sound on the great national policies for which we stand in public life."[39]

Roosevelt was even more specific in a letter to Lodge concerning the possible appointment of Horace Lurton: "[He] is right on the negro [sic] question; he is right on the power of the Federal Government; he is right on the insular business; he is right about corporations; and he is right about labor. On every question that would come before the bench he has so far shown

[37]Goldman, *op. cit.*, p. 19.

[38]Quoted in Peltason, *op. cit.*, p. 41.

[39]Henry Cabot Lodge, *Selections from the Correspondence of Theodore Roosevelt and Henry Cabot Lodge* (Scribner, 1925), vol. I, pp. 518–519.

The Supreme Court

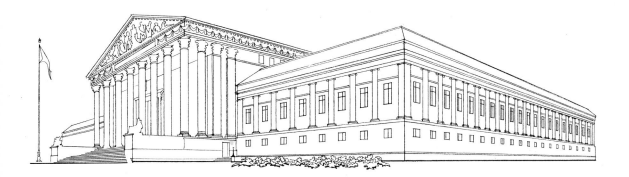

A Supreme Court must be a temple of justice in form as well as fact.
With its statuary, columns, and fountains, the Supreme Court building
produces the classic effect of serenity, detachment, wisdom. But into the
Justices' chambers stream the searing problems of a society in profound
transformation. A Chief Justice presides; nine men hear evidence and
arguments before the high bench; but decisions flow from the majority
of the moment.

THE SUPREME COURT

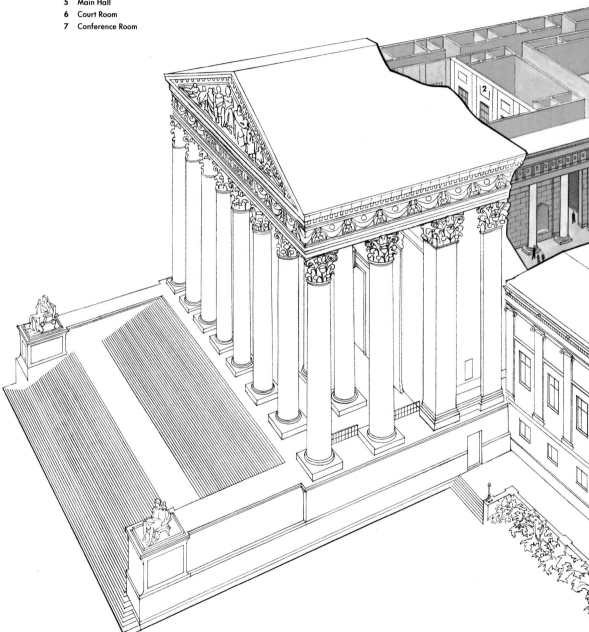

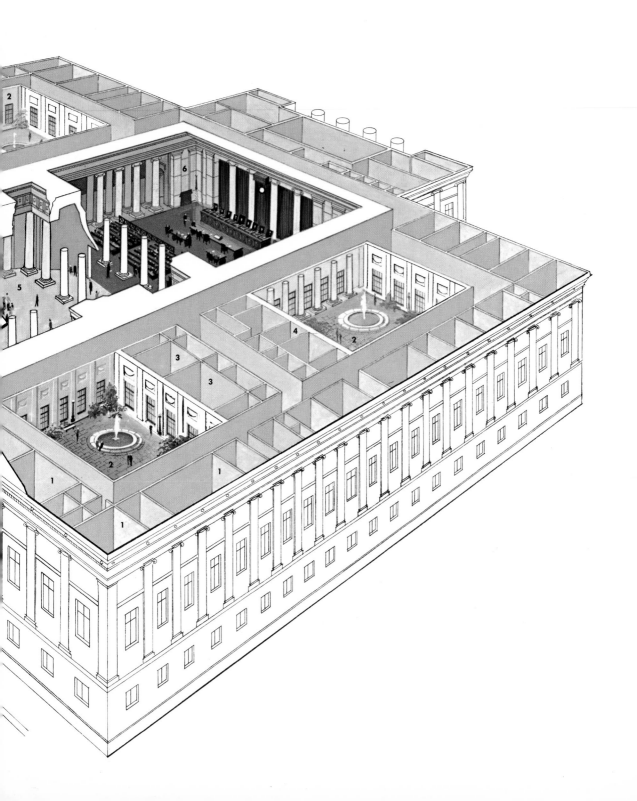

himself to be in . . . touch with the policies in which you and I believe. . . ." Senator Lodge's reply is of equal interest: "I am glad that Lurton holds all the opinions that you say he does. . . Those are the very questions on which I am just as anxious as you that judges should hold what we consider sound opinions, but I do not see why Republicans cannot be found who hold those opinions as well as Democrats."[40] The appointment went to Republican Attorney General William Moody.

Judicial ideology also plays a role in the creation of vacancies. Because federal judges serve for life, a judge can schedule his retirement so as to allow a President with whose views he is in sympathy to appoint his successor. Chief Justice Taney stayed on the bench long after he was frail to prevent Lincoln from nominating a Republican and Justice Holmes wrote to a friend that the late Chief Justice White had delayed having an operation, in part because of "determination not to give the appointment to Wilson," and that Holmes himself was pleased by Calvin Coolidge's election in 1924, which "relieves my conscience from the doubt whether I ought to resign so as to give the appointment to him."[41] In 1929 Chief Justice Taft wrote, "I am older and slower and less acute and more confused. However, as long as things continue as they are, and I am able to answer in my place, I must stay on the court in order to prevent the Bolsheviki from getting control. . . ."[42] If, as many assume, Chief Justice Warren's attempt to retire in 1968 was motivated at least in part by a desire to try to prevent Richard Nixon from selecting the next Chief Justice, he was following a well-established precedent.

CREATION AND ABOLITION OF JUDGESHIPS

Party politics is intimately involved in the creation of new judicial posts. President Eisenhower was unable to convince the Democratic-controlled Eighty-sixth Congress to create new judgeships he felt were needed—even by promising them that half the appointments would go to Democrats. With their eye on the 1960 election, the Democratic leadership in Congress decided to gamble on waiting. They won. President Kennedy was able to appoint eighty-five federal judges his first year in office. Of these, eighty-four were Democrats and one was a member of the New York Liberal Party.[43]

Congressional control over the structure and jurisdiction of the federal courts has been used successfully to influence the course of judicial decisions. Although thwarted in their attempts to impeach the judges, the Jeffersonians abolished the circuit courts that the Federalist Congress had created just prior to leaving office. In 1869 the radical Republicans in Congress used their constitutional power to alter the Supreme Court's appellate jurisdiction in order to snatch from the Court a case it was about to review involving legislation of dubious constitutionality (*Ex parte McCardle*). They also reduced the size of the Court to prevent President Johnson from filling two vacancies. After Johnson left the White House, Congress returned the Court

[40]Quoted in Glendon A. Schubert, *Constitutional Politics: The Political Behavior of Supreme Court Justices and the Constitutional Policies That They Make* (Holt, 1960), pp. 40–41.
[41]Mark De Wolfe Howe (ed.), *Holmes-Laski Letters* (Atheneum, 1963), vol. 1, pp. 264, 453.
[42]Quoted in Peltason, *op. cit.*, pp. 37, 38.
[43]Grossman, *op. cit.*, p. 34.

to its prior size to permit Grant to fill the vacancies, and the men Grant selected made it possible to reverse the Supreme Court invalidation of the Legal Tender Act. Historians are still debating whether Grant packed the Court. Certainly he was not unaware that his two appointees shared his sentiments about the desirability of reversing the earlier decision.

President Franklin D. Roosevelt's battle with the Supreme Court in 1937 is a most dramatic attempt by a political leader to influence judicial decisions by changing the size of the Court. Although Roosevelt did not succeed in packing the Court, it began to uphold New Deal legislation in the midst of the debate over his attempt to do so.[44]

PARTY AFFILIATION AND JUDICIAL BEHAVIOR

Clearly the men who select judges—especially Presidents and senators—believe it important to appoint members of their own party. But does it really matter? Is Democratic justice different from Republican justice? Political scientists have devoted much attention in recent years to this question, and several studies have concluded that *in general*, Democratic and Republican judges do behave differently. Party affiliation has been found most closely associated with judicial decision-making when the cases involved what may be called economic liberalism.[45]

Presidents have occasionally been disappointed in the men they appointed to the Supreme Court. Once on the bench, some justices have departed from the "sound policies" that the Presidents expected them to support. But by and large, through their selection of the personnel of the federal judiciary, Presidents and Senates have *eventually* been able to bring the Court into line with the general attitudes of contemporary political majorities.

Of course, "eventually" may take a long time. A judge's life tenure often keeps him in office after the political climate has changed, and he may continue to represent views of the era in which he was appointed.

WHAT MANNER OF MEN?

Who are the judges? Because all federal judges have been lawyers (though not all have been law school graduates), it is not surprising that the judges are something of an educational elite. More than a third of all the justices of the Supreme Court and more than one-quarter of the lower-federal-court judges appointed by Presidents Eisenhower and Kennedy attended Ivy League schools.[46] Federal judges and Supreme Court justices have tended to

[44]For an exciting account of the Court-packing battle, see Joseph W. Alsop and Turner Catledge, *The 168 Days* (Doubleday, 1938).
[45]Glendon A. Schubert, *Quantitative Analysis of Judicial Behavior* (Free Press, 1959), pp. 129–142; Stuart S. Nagel, "Political Party Affiliation and Judges' Decisions," *American Political Science Review* (December 1961), pp. 843–850; S. Sidney Ulmer, "The Political Party Variable in the Michigan Supreme Court," *Journal of Public Law* (1962), pp. 352–362; and Sheldon Goldman, "Voting Behavior on the United States Courts of Appeals, 1961–1964," *American Political Science Review* (June 1966), pp. 374–383.
[46]This section is based on John R. Schmidhauser, *The Supreme Court: Its Politics, Personalities, and Procedures* (Holt, 1960), and Sheldon Goldman, "Characteristics of Eisenhower and Kennedy Appointees to the Lower Federal Courts," *Western Political Quarterly* (December 1965), pp. 726–755.

come from middle- or upper-class backgrounds, and except for the appointment of Thurgood Marshall by Lyndon Johnson, Supreme Court justices have been white. Over 85 percent of Supreme Court members have been of British ethnic origin, and over 85 percent have been Protestant. But in recent years, a tradition of a Catholic seat and a Jewish seat on the Court has developed.

Federal judges at all levels are usually actively engaged in politics prior to their selection; Schmidhauser discovered that a substantial majority of the justices have been drawn from politically active families and that "every member of the Supreme Court except George Shiras held a political post of some kind prior to his appointment to the High Bench."[47] However, prior judicial experience has not been a major criterion in the selection of Supreme Court justices; only one-quarter have had really extensive judicial careers. Service on a federal district court often leads to promotion to the court of appeals, but there is no such steppingstone to the High Court. Moreover, there is little in the history of the Supreme Court to suggest that prior judicial experience produces better qualified or more objective justices. Some of the Court's most distinguished members—for example, Marshall, Taney, Miller, Hughes, Brandeis, Stone, and Frankfurter—had no judicial experience at the time of their appointments. The clamor in recent years for a requirement that only persons with judicial experience be considered for appointment to the Supreme Court is, according to one student of the Court's history, "only the most recent of the manifestations of the fact that advocacy of particular methods of judicial selection is inexorably related to desires for ideological control of the Court."[48]

How the Supreme Court Operates

The justices are in session from the first Monday in October through June. In their gleaming Corinthian building, they listen to oral arguments for two weeks and then adjourn for two weeks to consider the cases and write their opinions. Six justices must participate in each decision, and cases are decided by a majority. In the event of a tie vote, the decision of the lower court is sustained, although the case may be re-argued.

At 10 A.M. on the days when the Supreme Court sits the eight associate justices and the Chief Justice, dressed in their judicial robes, file into the Court. As they take their seats—arranged according to seniority, with the Chief Justice in the center—the clerk of the Court introduces them as the "Honorable Chief Justice and Associate Justices of the Supreme Court of the United States." Those present in the courtroom are seated, with counsel taking their places along tables in front of the bench; the attorneys for the Department of Justice, dressed in morning clothes, are at the right. The case being argued is not new to the justices—for one thing, they have already seen enough of it to determine that it was worthy of their full attention.

[47]Schmidhauser, *op. cit.*, p. 51.
[48]*Ibid.*, p. 52.

When an irate citizen vows he will take his case to the highest court of the land even if it costs him his last penny, he underestimates the difficulty of securing Supreme Court review and reveals a basic misunderstanding of the role of the High Court. The rules for appealing a case to the Supreme Court are established by act of Congress and are exceedingly complex. Certain types of cases are said to go to the Supreme Court *on appeal*; in theory, the Court is obligated to hear these cases. Other appellate cases—the great majority—come before the Court by means of a discretionary *writ of certiorari*. In addition, the Constitution stipulates that the Supreme Court has original jurisdiction in specified situations. But one basic fact lies behind all the technicalities—the Supreme Court has control of its docket and decides which cases it wants to consider. The justices closely review fewer than two hundred of the approximately three thousand cases annually presented to them.[49]

It is not enough that Jones thinks he should have won his case against Smith. There has already been at least one appellate review of the trial, either in a federal court of appeals or in a state supreme court. If the High Court had to review all cases from the courts of appeals, it would still be deciding cases today that originated in the 1920s. The Supreme Court will review Mr. Jones's case only if his claim has broad public significance. It may be that there is a conflict between the rulings of two courts of appeals on a legal point; by deciding Jones's case, the Supreme Court can guarantee that one rule is followed throughout the judicial system. It may be that Jones's case raises a constitutional issue on which a state supreme court has presented an interpretation with which the High Court justices disagree. The crucial factor in determining whether the Supreme Court will hear the case is its importance —not to Jones—but to the operation of the judicial system as a whole.

The Court accepts a case if four justices are sufficiently interested in it to request its consideration. Although the justices officially insist that their refusal to take a case does not signify that they agree with what the lower court has decided, it is probably correct to say that they tend to reject cases in which they are satisfied that a correct decision has been rendered.[50] However, the refusal to hear a case may also indicate that the justices do not wish to become involved in a political "hot potato" or that the Court is so divided on an issue that it is not yet prepared to take a stand.

THE BRIEFS

Prior to the presentation of the case in open court, the justices receive printed *briefs*, perhaps running into hundreds of pages, in which each side presents legal arguments, historical materials, and relevant precedents. Because some lawyers feel that the justices often make up their minds irrevoca-

[49]Detailed figures for the preceding term are found in each November issue of the *Harvard Law Review*.

[50]Daniel M. Berman, *It Is So Ordered: The Supreme Court Rules on School Segregation* (Norton, 1966), p. 39.

bly on the basis of the briefs alone, a considerable amount of research and effort goes into them.[51] In addition to the briefs presented by the parties to the case, the Supreme Court may receive briefs from *amici curiae*—friends of the court; these may be individuals, organizations, or government agencies who claim to have an interest in the case and information of value to the Court. This procedure guarantees that the national government is represented if a suit between two private parties calls the constitutionality of an act of Congress into question. Although sometimes a brief brought by a private party or interest group may help the court by presenting an argument or point of law that no one else had raised, it is often the case that the briefs are filed merely as a means of pressuring the Court to reach a particular decision. In the school desegregation cases, twenty-four *amicus* briefs were filed.[52]

ORAL ARGUMENT

Formal oratory before the Supreme Court, perhaps lasting for several days, is a thing of the past. As a rule, counsel for each side is now limited to a one-hour argument—in some cases even less—and the Court scrupulously enforces the time limits. (Extremely important cases will occasionally be given additional time.) Lawyers use a lectern to which two lights are attached; a white light flashes five minutes before time is up and when the red light goes on, the lawyer must stop instantly, even in the middle of a word.[53]

The entire procedure is formally informal. Sometimes, to the annoyance of the attorneys, the justices talk among themselves or consult briefs or legal volumes during the oral presentation. Justice Holmes occasionally napped during oral argument. When he found a presentation particularly bad he would frequently and ostentatiously consult his watch.[54]

The justices freely interrupt the lawyers to ask questions, and to request additional information. If a lawyer seems to be having a difficult time, they may try to help him present a better case. Occasionally the justices bounce arguments off a hapless attorney, at one another. During oral argument in the school desegregation cases, Justice Frankfurter was grilling an NAACP lawyer: "Are you saying that we can say that 'separate but equal' is not a doctrine that is relevant at the primary school level? Is that what you are saying?" he demanded. Justice Douglas tried to help the lawyer out. "I think you are saying," he ventured, "that segregation may be all right in streetcars and railroad cars and restaurants, but . . . education is different from that." The lawyer found the Douglas paraphrase to his liking. "Yes, sir," he replied. Douglas continued, "That is your argument, is it not? Isn't that your argument in this case?" Again a grateful "yes" from counsel. Frankfurter, however, was not even moderately impressed. "But how can that be your argument . . .?" he cried, and the lawyer was once again on his own.[55]

[51]*Ibid.*, p. 53.
[52]*Ibid.*, p. 56. For a good general discussion, see Samuel Krislov, "The *Amicus Curiae* Brief: From Friendship to Advocacy," *Yale Law Journal* (March 1963), pp. 694–721.
[53]Henry J. Abraham, *The Judicial Process*, 2d ed. (Oxford Univ. Press, 1968).
[54]Walter F. Murphy, *Wiretapping on Trial: A Case Study in the Judicial Process* (Random House, 1965), p. 93.
[55]Berman, *op. cit.*, p. 69.

In one case the justices interrupted counsel eighty-four times during 120 minutes of oral argument.[56] Although this may be unusually excessive, it is more unusual for counsel to complete his argument without interruption.

The participants in oral argument are by no means equal. The Solicitor General, who represents the federal government, probably enjoys a situational bias as the result of his more frequent, more intensive interaction with the justices. Similarly, though to a lesser extent, lawyers of great reputation can communicate with the Court more effectively than can a young lawyer who has been specially admitted to the Supreme Court bar to make his first appearance.[57]

THE CONFERENCE

Each Friday the justices meet in conference. During the week they have heard the oral arguments, read and studied the briefs, and examined the petitions. Before the conference, each justice receives a list of the cases that will be discussed. Each brings to the meeting a red leather book (carefully locked) in which the cases and the votes of the justices are recorded. The Friday conferences are highly secret affairs; what goes on in these meetings has to be gleaned from the infrequent comments of members of the Court.

Although the procedure varies, the conferences are marked by informality and vigorous give-and-take. The Chief Justice presides, and usually opens the discussion by briefly stating the facts, summarizing the questions of law, and making suggestions for disposing of the case. He then asks each member of the Court, in order of seniority, to give his views and conclusions. After full discussion a vote is taken, with the least senior justice voting first. The case is decided by majority vote, and one justice is designated to write the *opinion of the Court.* If the Chief Justice votes with the majority, he decides who writes the opinion. If he does not, the senior justice among the majority makes the decision. Justices who are among the minority normally select one of their number to write a *dissenting opinion*, although each dissenter is free to write his own. If a justice agrees with the majority on the decision but differs on the reasoning, he may write his own opinion; this is known as a *concurring opinion.*

OPINION WRITING: MARSHALING THE COURT

The justice selected to write the Court's opinion is faced with an exacting task. He must produce a document that will win the support of at least four —and hopefully eight—intelligent, strong-willed men, all of whom voted the same way but perhaps for very different reasons. Assisted by his law clerks, the justice tries his hand at a draft and sends it to his colleagues for their comments. If he is lucky, the majority will accept his formulation, perhaps suggesting minor changes. But it may be that his original draft is not satisfactory to the Court; then he is forced to redraft and recirculate his opinion until a majority can reach agreement.

[56]Abraham, *op. cit.*, p. 193.
[57]Schubert, *Judicial Policy-Making, op. cit.*, p. 109.

There is considerable fluidity in the judicial process at this point.[58] In fact, there are "numerous instances on record in which the justice assigned the opinion of the Court has reported back that additional study had convinced him that he and the rest of the majority had been in error."[59] Sometimes he is able to convince the Court to change its mind. Moreover, a dissenting justice can sometimes persuade the opinion writer of the merits of his protest. For example, shortly after Harlan Fiske Stone came on the Court, the justices divided seven to one in a particular case, with Stone the lone dissenter. He did not give up, however, and took to the Chief Justice (who had assigned the opinion to himself) the leading relevant articles from a dozen volumes of the Columbia and Harvard law reviews and a memorandum requesting reconsideration. Taft's draft opinion was circulated some time later, with the following note appended: "Dear Brethren: I think we made a mistake in this case and have written the opinion the other way. Hope you will agree. W. H. T." The new revised Taft opinion became the decision of a unanimous court.[60]

If the opinion writer's initial formulation is not acceptable to a majority of the Court, an elaborate bargaining process occurs. The opinion ultimately published is not necessarily the opinion the author would have liked to write—like a committee report, it represents the most common denominator. Holmes bitterly complained to Laski that he had written an opinion "in terms to suit the majority of the brethren, although they didn't suit me. Years ago I did the same thing in the interest of getting a job done. I let the brethren put in a reason that I thought bad and cut out all that I thought good and I have squirmed ever since, and swore that never again—but again I yield and now comes a petition for rehearing pointing out all the horrors that will ensue from just what I didn't want to say."[61] Holmes's files also include an opinion he had published on which he had written in his own handwriting, "This is a wholly unsatisfactory opinion," and then stated why it was unsatisfactory.[62]

The two major sanctions a justice can use against his colleagues are his vote and his willingness to write a separate opinion that will attack a doctrine the majority wishes to see adopted. A dissenting opinion is often written and circulated for the specific purpose of convincing the majority. If the opinion writer is persuaded by the logic of the dissenter, the dissenting opinion may never be published. Sometimes, however, an unpersuaded justice will be forced to give in to the demands of one of his colleagues. Especially if the Court is closely divided, one justice may be in a position to demand that a given argument be included in—or removed from—the opinion as the price of his swing vote. Sometimes this can happen even if the Court is not closely divided. An opinion writer who anticipates that his decision will elicit a critical public reaction may very much wish to have it presented as the view

---

[58]J. Woodford Howard, "On the Fluidity of Judicial Choice," *American Political Science Review* (March 1968), pp. 43–56. See also Murphy's outstanding study, *Elements of Judicial Strategy, op. cit.*

[59]*Ibid.*, p. 44.

[60]Alpheus. T. Mason, *Harlan Fiske Stone: Pillar of the Law* (Viking, 1956), p. 222. Murphy, *Elements of Judicial Strategy, op. cit.*, and Howard, *op. cit.*, contain dozens of similar examples.

[61]Howe, *op. cit.*, vol. 2, pp. 124,125.

[62]Harlan B. Phillips, *Felix Frankfurter Reminisces* (Reynal & Co., 1960), p. 298.

456 of a unanimous court and may be prepared to compromise to achieve unanimity.

OPINIONS AS MEDIA OF COMMUNICATION

As a general rule, Supreme Court decisions are accompanied by opinions that state the facts, present the issues, announce the decision, and, most importantly, attempt to justify the reasoning employed by the Court. Judicial opinions are the Court's principal method of expressing itself to the outside world, and it addresses them to various audiences. Perhaps the most important function of opinions is to instruct the lower courts and the bar how to act in future cases. Sometimes the justices go out of their way to deliver a special message. For example, in the Little Rock school desegregation case[63] the Court took the unusual step of listing the name of each justice in order to stress that it was unanimously upholding its decision in *Brown* v. *Board*. The Court was hoping to convince Southern judges, attorneys, and school boards that further resistance would be futile.

Sometimes judicial opinions are used to "drum up trade." A statement in the form "Nothing in this opinion should be taken to preclude a case in which . . ." is an invitation to attorneys and lower-court judges to act in a certain way. A dissenting or concurring opinion may be used to throw cues to the bench and bar. In one famous dissent, Justices Black, Douglas, and Murphy announced that they agreed that the present case was in accord with existing precedents, including cases they had supported in the past. But now they had changed their minds.[64] The announcement that three judicial votes would now go against a previous decision quickly led to a test case, in which the judges of a court of appeals correctly anticipated a reversal by the High Court. Judicial opinions may be directed at Congress or the President. If the Court regrets that "in the absence of action by the Congress, we have no choice but to . . ." or insists that "relief of the sort petitioner demands can only come from the political branches of government," it is clearly asking Congress to act. Sometimes the Court will interpret existing statutes so narrowly as to render them ineffective, in the hope of forcing fresh legislative action. Such a hope once prompted the following dissent from Justice Clark: "Unless the Congress changes the rule announced by the Court today, those intelligence agencies of our government engaged in law enforcement may as well close up shop. . . ." Within three months, new legislation was on the statute books.[65]

Finally, the justices use published opinions to communicate with the public. Hopefully, a well-handled opinion may increase support among specialized publics—especially lawyers and judges—and among the general population for a policy the Court is stressing. For this reason the Court delayed declaring school segregation unconstitutional until unanimity could be secured. The justices understood that any sign of dissension on the bench on this major social issue would be an invitation to ignore the Court's ruling.[66]

[63]*Cooper* v. *Aaron* (1958).
[64]*Jones* v. *Opelika* (1942).
[65]Murphy, *Elements of Judicial Strategy, op. cit.,* pp. 126, 129.
[66]Berman, *op. cit.,* p. 114; Murphy, *Elements of Judicial Strategy, op. cit.,* p. 66.

The various functions of a judical opinion are nicely illustrated by the following memorandum that Justice Frankfurter sent to Justice Murphy, discussing a dissenting opinion:

> This is a protest opinion—a protest at the Bar of the future—but also an effort to make the brethren realize what is at stake. Moreover, a powerful dissent . . . is bound to have an effect on the lower courts as well as on the officers of the law. . . . And so in order to impress our own brethren, the lower courts, and enforcement officers, it seems to me vital to make the dissent an impressive document.[67]

THE POWERS OF THE CHIEF JUSTICE

President Johnson's unsuccessful nomination in 1968 of Associate Justice Abe Fortas to the position of Chief Justice and the furor that followed led many people to ask, What special powers does the Chief Justice have? The Chief Justice has only one vote, and in terms of formal power, he is merely the first among equals.[68] However, his position gives him a unique opportunity to exercise leadership. The Chief Justice presides in open court and over the conferences, where it is he who usually presents each case to his associates—thus setting the tone of the discussion. Also, as we have seen, he assigns the writing of the opinion of the Court in all cases when he votes with the majority. This role—choosing the opinion writer—is significant because the writer determines whether an opinion is based on one ground rather than another and whether it deals narrowly or broadly with the issues. These choices may make a decision more or less acceptable to the public, may affect the decision of other justices to dissent, and may affect the value of a decision as a precedent. The Chief Justice is also the key figure in the Court's certiorari procedure; in practice, he is generally able to eliminate from the Court's docket those cases he considers trivial.

The ability of the Chief Justice to influence his Court has varied considerably. Chief Justice Hughes ran the conferences like a stern taskmaster, keeping the justices talking to the point, moving the discussion along, and doing his best to work out compromises. Frowning on dissents, he tried to achieve a unanimous vote in order to give greater weight to Court decisions. Chief Justice Stone, on the other hand, encouraged each justice to state his own point of view and let the discussion wander as it would.[69] As Danelski reminds us, "the Chief Justiceship does not guarantee leadership. It only offers its incumbent an opportunity to lead. Optimum leadership inheres in the combination of the office and an able, persuasive, personable judge."[70]

AFTER THE LAWSUIT IS OVER

Victory in the Supreme Court does not necessarily mean that a litigant will get what he wants. As a rule the High Court does not implement its own deci-

[67]Quoted in *Ibid.*, pp. 60, 61.
[68]This discussion is based on David Danelski, "The Influence of the Chief Justice in the Decisional Process of the Supreme Court," in Jahnige and Goldman (eds.), *op. cit.*, pp. 147–160.
[69]John P. Frank, *Marble Palace: The Supreme Court in American Life* (Knopf, 1958), p. 81.
[70]Danelski, in Jahnige and Goldman (eds.), *op. cit.*, p. 148.

sions. It may "remand to the lower court with instructions to act in accordance with this decision." Its ruling may require further action by administrators or local elected officials. Sometimes Supreme Court decisions are simply ignored. Despite the Supreme Court's ruling in the school-prayer case (p. 111), for example, many school boards continued their existing practices.[71] And fifteen years after *Brown* v. *Board*, the great majority of Southern schools are still not integrated.

The lower courts have considerable leeway in their interpretation of the High Court's mandates. The Constitution may be what the Supreme Court says it is, but a Supreme Court opinion means, for the moment at least, what the local judge (who is subject to local pressures) says it means.[72] A federal district judge ordered the Houston, Texas, school board to desegregate its first grade in September 1960 (six years after *Brown* v. *Board*) and to include another grade each year. Yet that same year a federal district judge in Dallas rejected the identical plan—not because the school board was moving too slowly, but because it was moving too rapidly. Eighty-two-year-old Judge Davidson, who acted only after four appeals to the court of appeals, ordered the Dallas board to submit a program of "voluntary preference" and lectured them on the dangers of racial amalgamation.

The recent history of motion-picture censorship provides another example of how lower-court judges can minimize the scope of a rule formulated by the Supreme Court. In 1952, the Supreme Court held that a state could not constitutionally refuse to license the showing of *The Miracle* because it was alleged to be sacrilegious. This standard, said the justices, was unconstitutionally vague. The following year New York judges decided that the Court's ruling did not apply to pictures alleged to be immoral, and Ohio judges sustained censorship of a film alleged to be harmful. The Supreme Court then reversed these decisions. But later, when the Illinois Supreme Court sustained a ban on *The Miracle* because it was alleged to be obscene, the Supreme Court refused (by a vote of six to three) to review the decision.[73]

As we saw in the case of the Presidency, what may appear to be a neat, hierarchical system often turns out to be a confused congeries of mutual controls and reciprocal influence, not at all like the disciplined chain of command of a military organization. So, too, are the relations of the Supreme Court with the judicial bureaucracy.[74]

The Judges—Guardians of the Constitution

Judicial review—the power of a court of law to set aside an act of the legislature that in its opinion violates the Constitution—is an American contribution to the art of government. Although only a small portion of the business of the courts involves constitutional issues, this is surely one of the most exciting and politically significant aspects of the judicial process.

[71]Robert H. Birkby, "The Supreme Court and the Bible Belt: Tennessee Reacts to the 'Schempp' Decision," *Midwest Journal of Political Science* (August 1966), pp. 304–319.

[72]Jack W. Peltason, *Fifty-Eight Lonely Men: Southern Federal Judges and School Desegregation* (Harcourt, Brace & World, 1961).

[73]This example is taken from Peltason, *Federal Courts in the Political Process, op. cit.*, p. 61.

[74]Murphy, *Elements of Judicial Strategy, op. cit.*, Chap. 4.

If an Englishman or an American is thrown into prison without cause, either can appeal to the courts of his respective country for protection. When Parliament passes a law, however, no English judge has the authority to declare it null and void because he believes it to violate the English constitution. Not the courts but Parliament is the guardian of the English constitution. But in the United States the courts, ultimately the Supreme Court, are the keepers of the constitutional conscience—not Congress and not the President. How did the judges get this tremendous responsibility?

ORIGINS OF JUDICIAL REVIEW

The Constitution itself says nothing about who should be the final arbiter of disputes that might arise over its meaning. It does not specifically grant such power to the Supreme Court. Whether the members of the Convention of 1787 intended to bestow on the courts the power of judicial review is a question that has long been debated. There is little doubt that the Framers intended the Supreme Court to have the power to declare state legislation unconstitutional, but whether they intended to give it the same power over national legislation is not clear. The late Professor Edward S. Corwin, an outstanding authority on the American Constitution, concluded that unquestionably "the framers anticipated some sort of judicial review. . . . But it is equally without question that the ideas generally current in 1787 were far from presaging the present vast role of the Court."[75] Why, then, did the Framers not specifically provide for judicial review? Probably because they believed the power rested on certain general provisions that made specific statements unnecessary.

The Federalists—the men who wrote the Constitution and controlled the national government until 1801—generally supported the courts and favored judicial review, but their opponents, the Jeffersonian Republicans, were less enthusiastic. In 1798 and 1799 Jefferson and Madison (the latter by this time had left the Federalist party) came very close in the Virginia and Kentucky Resolutions to arguing that the state legislatures and not the Supreme Court had the ultimate power to interpret the Constitution. This would seem to imply that the Supreme Court did not even have the final authority to review state legislation, something about which there had been little doubt.

When the Jeffersonians defeated the Federalists in the elections of 1800, it was still undecided whether the Supreme Court would actually exercise the power of judicial review. "The idea was in the air, the ingredients to support a doctrine of judicial review were at hand, and a few precedents could even be cited"; nevertheless, judicial review was not an established power. Then in 1803 came the case of *Marbury* v. *Madison*, a case intimately related to the political struggles between the Federalists and the Jeffersonians.

Marbury v. *Madison*

The elections of 1800 marked the rise to power of the Jeffersonian Republicans. President John Adams and his fellow Federalists did not take their

[75]Edward S. Corwin, "The Constitution as Instrument and as Symbol," *The American Political Science Review* (December 1936), p. 1078.

defeat easily; indeed, they were greatly alarmed at what they considered to be the "enthronement of the rabble." But there was nothing much they could do about it before leaving office — or was there? The Constitution gives the President, with the consent of the Senate, the power to appoint federal judges to hold office during "good behavior" — virtually for life. If the judiciary should be manned by good Federalists, reasoned Adams and his party followers, they could stave off the worst consequences of Jefferson's victory.

The Federalist lame-duck Congress created dozens of new federal judicial posts. By March 3, 1801, Adams had appointed, and the Senate had confirmed, deserving Federalists to all these new positions. Adams signed the commissions and turned them over to John Marshall, the Secretary of State, to be sealed and delivered. Marshall had just received his own commission as Chief Justice of the United States, but he was continuing to serve as Secretary of State until Adams's term expired. Working right up to nine o'clock on the evening of March 3, Marshall sealed but was unable to deliver all the commissions. The important ones were taken care of, however, and only those for the justices of the peace for the District of Columbia were left undelivered. The Chief Justice retired to his lodgings and left the commissions to be delivered by his successor.

Jefferson was highly aroused by this Federalist packing of the judiciary. When he discovered that some of the commissions had not been delivered, he told the new Secretary of State, James Madison, to hold up seventeen of those still in his possession. Jefferson could see no reason why the District needed so many justices of the peace, especially Federalist justices.

Among the commissions that were not delivered was one for William Marbury. After waiting in vain, Marbury decided to seek action from the courts. Searching through the statute books, he came across Section 13 of the Judiciary Act of 1789, which authorized the Supreme Court "to issue writs of mandamus, in cases warranted by the principles and usages of law, to . . . persons holding office, under the authority of the United States." A *writ of mandamus* is a court order directing an official to perform a nondiscretionary or ministerial act. Delivering a commission is a ministerial act; the Secretary of State is a person holding office under the authority of the United States; so why not, thought Marbury, ask the Supreme Court to issue a writ of mandamus to force Madison to deliver the commission? He and his companions went directly to the Supreme Court and, citing Section 13, they so asked.

What could Marshall do? If the Court issued the mandamus, Madison and Jefferson would probably ignore it. The Court would be powerless, and its prestige, already low, might suffer a fatal blow. On the other hand, by refusing to issue the mandamus, the judges would appear to vindicate the Republican party's claim that the Court had no authority to interfere with the executive. Would Marshall issue the mandamus? Most people thought so; angry Republicans talked of impeachment.

On February 24, 1803 the Supreme Court published its opinion. The first part of the opinion was as expected. Marbury was entitled to his commission, said Marshall, and Madison should have delivered it to him; a writ of mandamus could be issued by the proper court against even such an august officer as the Secretary of State.

Then came the surprise. Although Section 13 of the Judiciary Act purports to give the Supreme Court original jurisdiction in just such cases, this section, said Marshall, is contrary to Article III of the Constitution, which gives the Supreme Court original jurisdiction in *only* those cases in which an ambassador or other foreign minister is affected or in which a state is a party. This is a case of original jurisdiction, but Marbury is neither a state nor a foreign minister. If we follow Section 13, wrote Marshall, we have jurisdiction; if we follow the Constitution, we have no jurisdiction.

Then, in characteristic fashion, Marshall stated the question in such a way that the answer was obvious—namely, should the Supreme Court enforce an unconstitutional law? Of course not, he concluded; the Constitution is the supreme and binding law, and the courts cannot enforce any action of Congress that conflicts with it.

The real question remained unanswered. Congress and the President had also read the Constitution, and according to their interpretation (which was also reasonable), Section 13 was compatible with Article III. Where did the Supreme Court get the right to say they were wrong? Why should the Supreme Court's interpretation of the Constitution be preferred to that of Congress and the President?

Marshall, paralleling Hamilton's argument in *Federalist No. 78*, reasoned that the Constitution is law, that judges—not legislators or executives—interpret law; therefore, the judges should interpret the Constitution. "If two laws conflict with each other, the courts must decide on the operation of each," he said. Obviously the Constitution is to be preferred to any ordinary act of Congress.

Case dismissed.

Jefferson fumed. For one thing, Marshall had said that a court with the proper jurisdiction could issue a writ of mandamus even against the Secretary of State, the President's right-hand man. But there was little Jefferson could do about it, for there was not even a specific court order that he could refuse to obey. Thus, in a single stroke Marshall had given the Republicans a lecture for failing to perform their duties and had gone a long way toward acquiring for the Supreme Court the power of judicial review of acts of Congress—all in a manner that made it difficult for the Republicans to retaliate.

Marbury v. *Madison* is a masterpiece of judicial strategy. Marshall, contrary to modern canons of judicial interpretation, went out of his way to declare Section 13 unconstitutional. He could have interpreted the section to mean that the Supreme Court could issue writs of mandamus in those cases in which it did have jurisdiction. He could have interpreted Article III to mean that Congress could add to, though not subtract from, the original jurisdiction that the Constitution gives to the Supreme Court. He could have dismissed the case for want of jurisdiction without discussing Marbury's right to his commission. But none of these would have suited his purpose. Jefferson and his fellow Republicans had been threatening to use the impeachment power to remove Federalist partisans from the federal bench. Marshall was fearful for the Supreme Court's future, and he felt unless the Court spoke out it would become subordinate to the President and Congress.

Marshall's decision, important as it was, did not by itself necessarily establish for the Supreme Court the power to review and declare unconstitutional acts of Congress. *Marbury* v. *Madison* could have meant that the Supreme Court had the right to interpret the scope of *its own* powers under Article III but that Congress and the President had the authority to interpret their own powers under Articles I and II, respectively. However, Marshall's decision has not been interpreted by court or country in this way (though it was not until the Dred Scott case in 1857 that another act of Congress was declared unconstitutional). Had Marshall not spoken when he did, the Court might not have been able to assume the power of judicial review. The vital precedent had been created. Here we have a classic example of constitutional developments through judicial interpretation. There is no specific authorization in the Constitution for the Supreme Court's power to declare congressional enactments null and void; yet today it is a vital part of our constitutional system.

JOHN MARSHALL'S LEGACY

Several very important consequences followed from the fact that America has accepted John Marshall's argument that *courts* are the final arbiters of the meaning of the Constitution.[76] Because the courts refuse to give advisory opinions, Congress cannot determine whether a law will be upheld as constitutional before passing it. And an individual citizen cannot determine whether a statute is constitutional until after he violates it. Publisher Ralph Ginzburg's gamble that the Supreme Court would rule that the federal obscenity statute violated his constitutional rights won him a five-year jail sentence (*Ginzburg* v. *United States*, 1966).

In addition, because the constitutionality of a statute can only be tested by someone who is affected by it, in order to obtain a judicial ruling on a Mississippi segregation statute, for example, a Negro living in Mississippi must be willing to contest the law—and to expose himself to tremendous social and economic pressure. (See page 163 for a discussion of how recent federal civil rights acts have attempted to circumvent this problem by allowing the Attorney General to initiate suits in certain types of cases.) And litigation can be a tremendously expensive undertaking. The National Association for the Advancement of Colored People estimates that it spent "well over $200,000" in the school desegregation case *Brown* v. *Board of Education*. The average cost of Supreme Court cases testing Southern compliance with Brown has run between $50,000 and $100,000. And the steel companies spent over $1.5 million in direct legal costs and counsel fees to fight President Truman's seizure of the steel mills in 1952.[77]

Yet the most important consequence of judicial review is that even a law solemnly enacted by the Congress and approved by the President may be challenged by a single individual. Those who lack the political power to secure the support of the Congress or their own state legislature and those who wish to challenge even the authority of the President of the United

[76]Thomas P. Jahnige, "A Note on the Implications of Legal Rules and Procedures," in Jahnige and Goldman (eds.), *op. cit.,* p. 98.

[77]These examples are taken from Alan F. Westin, "Bookies and 'Bugs' in California: Judicial Control of Police Practices," in Alan F. Westin (ed.), *The Uses of Power* (Harcourt, Brace & World, 1962), pp. 161,162.

States, often through the device of a lawsuit, may secure a hearing before the courts. In the United States, litigation supplements (at times, supersedes) legislation as an instrument for the making of public policy.

Judicial Review in a Democracy

An independent judiciary is rightly considered to be one of the hallmarks of a free society. As impartial dispensers of equal justice under the law, judges should not be dependent on the pleasure of the executive, the legislature, the parties to a case, the electorate, or a mob outside the courtroom. But the very independence that is essential to protect the judge in his role as a legal technician raises basic problems when a society decides —as ours has—to allow judges to make politically significant constitutional decisions.[78]

Ours is a government of laws, not of men, we are often told, and therefore the policy views of our independent judges are (or at least should be) irrelevant. The absurdity of the assumption that law is so certain and clearly known that the human factor need not enter—that jurisprudence is a mechanical operation—is indicated by the fact that the Supreme Court of the United States divides so frequently, with each side declaring it has the appropriate interpretation of the law. In many cases, a judge has no clear mandate to decide one way or the other.

JUDICIAL ACTIVISM VERSUS JUDICIAL SELF-RESTRAINT

To recognize the facts of judicial life—that judges must choose between competing values—is not to criticize the judges. Nor is it to say that judges have unlimited discretion in deciding cases or that they give free rein to their own views. They are restricted, as we have seen, by procedural limitations. The doctrine of *stare decisis* imposes some constraints. But the total political system of which they are a part is probably the most significant restriction. If the Court is too far out of step, it is likely to get slapped down by the President or Congress.[79] It is limited by the necessity to maintain the allegiance of the judicial bureaucracy. And the never-ending task of determining what the Constitution means today and tomorrow is a process in which the voters participate—if only indirectly. By selecting Richard Nixon in preference to Hubert Humphrey in 1968 (the former made his opposition to key Supreme Court decisions one of his campaign issues), the voters decided, among other things, that the new justices appointed to the Court would be likely to be moderate-to-conservative Republicans rather than liberal-to-moderate Democrats.

In recent years, there has been considerable public debate over the proper role of the Supreme Court in our political system. Some critics, roughly characterized as judicial activists, insist that political choice is inevitable and inherent in judging and that judges should not make a false pretense of ob-

[78]Louis B. Boudin, *Government by Judiciary* (William Goodwin, Inc., 1932).
[79]See Walter F. Murphy, *Congress and the Court* (Univ. of Chicago Press, 1962).

464 jectivity. Rather, they should recognize that they are making policy, and they should consciously exercise their judicial power to achieve social justice.[80]

Judicial self-restrainers take another view. They recognize a judge's difficulties in rising above his own biases, but they insist that objectivity is the goal he should aim for. They argue that legislators and executives, as the people's political representatives, have the chief responsibility for working out the accommodation of interests that is the essence of legislation. The self-restrainers insist that judges must be very careful to avoid injecting their own wishes into the judicial process, because it is not their responsibility to determine public policy.[81]

A MIDDLE POSITION

Some take a position midway between the activists and the self-restrainers. They believe that judges should exercise restraint in using their authority to review economic and social laws affecting property rights but not hesitate to void laws that the judges believe restrict civil liberties such as free speech. Their argument for this compromise position goes like this: The political majority should not be stopped from experimenting with social and economic arrangements. If mistakes are made, new majorities will arise to correct them. But majorities should not be permitted to tamper with basic liberties. For if they go too far, the very instruments for publicizing and correcting the mistakes—such as free speech and free press—will not be able to operate

Courtesy C. B. Batchelor, in *The News*, March 5, 1967.

effectively. The Constitution does not embody any particular economic theory, and legislative majorities are free to adopt any economic policies they wish. But the Constitution is committed to the political theory of an open society, and it is the judges' special responsibility to prevent legislative tampering with the democratic process.

Before 1937, the strongest defenders of judicial review were those who supported the Supreme Court's decisions protecting the business community. These economic conservatives pointed out that the Constitution contains many limitations on precipitous majority action. Liberals denounced the Court as an enemy of majority rule. Since 1937, and especially since 1954, as a result of the Warren Court's active defense of individual liberties, liberals insist that in

[80]Arthur S. Miller and Ronald F. Howell, "The Myth of Neutrality in Constitutional Adjudication," *University of Chicago Law Review* (Summer 1960), pp. 661–695.

[81]Learned Hand, *The Bill of Rights* (Harvard Univ. Press, 1958).

protecting fundamental constitutional guarantees, the Court must be impervious to the voice of the impassioned public. In 1936–1937, political conservatives defended the Court as the bulwark of American freedom. Since 1954, political conservatives have criticized the Warren Court for "judicial legislation."

Two lessons clearly emerge from this turnabout in attitudes toward the Supreme Court. First, the Warren Court demonstrated that judicial review is by no means restricted to serving as a conservative check on liberal policies. Depending on the attitudes of the justices, the Court can take a more liberal as well as a more conservative position than either the general public or a majority in Congress.[82] Second, it is not possible to discuss the role of the Court as an abstraction, ignoring the specific political controversies at any given time.

True, the Constitution is what the judges say it is. But ultimately the Constitution is what the people want it to be.[83] The Supreme Court is able to make its decisions effective only to the extent that these decisions are supported by a considerable portion of the electorate. The main thrust of judicial policies cannot remain too far outside the main channels of American public life. The American democratic system has reached a pragmatic compromise between the desire for the independence of judges and the desire to provide political checks on their policy-making activities. Judges have no armies or police to execute their rulings. They have no authority to levy taxes. Ultimately, the power they enjoy rests on their retention of public support. No better criterion for determining the power of a government official has ever been invented.

[82]Glendon A. Schubert, *The Judicial Mind: The Attitudes and Ideologies of Supreme Court Justices, 1946–1963* (Northwestern Univ. Press, 1965), Chap. 6, for an insightful discussion of this point.
[83]Robert A. Dahl, "Decision-Making in a Democracy: The Supreme Court as a National Policy-Maker," *Journal of Public Law* (Fall 1957), p. 285.

American Pluralist Democracy: Challenge and Choice

20 Is self-government possible for Americans in the face of the emerging issues of the 1970s? Is government by the people just a pious pretension, or does it in fact exist in the United States? Is democratic government really just a cloak for rule by a small number of leaders and powerful minorities, or is there a connection between what the people want and what the government does? If so, which people?

Boiled down, these questions raise the five problems — of effective democracy, of constitutionalism, of individual rights, of representation, and of responsible leadership — summarized on the first two pages of this book and referred to often in the text. It would be easy, from the evidence in this book alone, to attack the theory and practice of government by the people. We have noted that our constitutional system hinders popular majorities from controlling government, that public opinion is often ignorant or emotional, that the individual voter is often apathetic or ill-informed, that political parties often evade issues rather than confront them, that the supposedly popular institution of Congress is mal-apportioned, that the President has vast powers and can ignore the people's wishes or respond to them.

Models of Democracy

It would be easy for students — and teachers — to debate endlessly as to whether American government meets the criteria of democracy. They would disagree over both the actual nature of American democratic gov-

466

ernment and over the norms by which it should be tested. Under such conditions polemics usually outshout analysis. As aids to analytical thinking, to more careful definitions, and to more self-consciousness about one's own values or preconceptions, political scientists use sets of assumptions, or *models*, in studying and assessing political systems. In this sense communism, anarchism, fascism, and pluralist democracy are models, though rather overgeneralized ones, for assessing political institutions and values throughout the world. It is useful to break these general models down into more sharply conceptualized ones.

THE POWER ELITE

The power-elite model is the set of assumptions about American democracy held by the New Left, as noted in Chapter 1. Mass man and mass society lack the basis and means of power. Those who make key economic decisions, have military authority, control the mass media, and have powerful social positions form a *power elite*. This elite can, within broad limits, make essentially the decisions it wants to, behind the facade of government by the people. The President, Congress, the other formal leaders have little function except to ratify decisions made elsewhere in the power structure.[1]

POPULAR RULE

The great mass of people, it is assumed under the popular-rule model, can effectively run their government provided that they are informed, interested, and basically agreed on methods and goals. The people as a whole take the initiative and the rulers follow their direction. Most people most of the time are rational, so progress is probable if not inevitable. Free and open debate with decisions made in fair, one-man, one-vote elections is the best way to get the right solutions to problems. Elected officials should be made responsive and accountable to the majority and should govern in accord with its wishes.

AMERICAN DEMOCRACY—A THIRD MODEL?

Many political scientists think in terms of a third model that is a kind of hybrid of the power-elite and popular-rule models. As they look at the evidence—community studies, voting behavior, public-opinion polls, case studies of how decisions are actually made—they see the people as far too complex to be simply categorized as informed or uninformed, rational or foolish. They see neither a simple power elite ruling an impotent mass nor the classic ideal of popular self-government based on interest, knowledge, and participation.

[1]For a spirited and informed exchange on the broader question of the relevance of elitist theories, including the problem of terminology, see Jack L. Walker, "A Critique of the Elitist Theory of Democracy," *The American Political Science Review* (June 1966), pp. 285–295, 391–392; Robert A. Dahl, "Further Reflections on 'the Elitist Theory of Democracy,'" *ibid.*, pp. 296–305.

After their pioneering classic study of Elmira, for example, Berelson and his colleagues concluded that individual voters were indeed uninvolved in politics, not well informed, parochial, and unable to think clearly and "rationally," but that the system of democracy did seem to meet certain requirements for a going political society. "The individual members may not meet all the standards but the whole nevertheless survives and grows. This suggests that where the classic theory is defective is in its concentration on the *individual citizen*. What are undervalued are certain collective properties that reside in the electorate as a whole and in the political and social system in which it functions."[2] These are the balances between involvement and indifference, stability and flexibility, progress and conservatism, consensus and cleavage, individualism and collectivism.

A comparable conclusion was reached by Almond and Verba after an intensive study of five Western nations, including the United States. Here again the investigators found a contrast between the classic ideals of civic participation and rational thinking and the reality of political passivity, narrowness, and irrationality. They agree with Schattschneider that "the problem is not how 180 million Aristotles can run a democracy, but how we can organize a community of 180 million ordinary people so that it remains sensitive to their needs. This is a problem of *leadership, organization, alternatives and systems of responsibility and confidence*."[3] They conclude that tendencies toward political apathy and intensity, toward support of the status quo and support of change, toward consensus and cleavage, and toward

[2]Bernard R. Berelson, Paul F. Lazarsfeld, and William N. McPhee, *Voting* (Univ. of Chicago Press, 1954), p. 312.
[3]E. E. Schattschneider, *The Semi-Sovereign People* (Holt, 1960), p. 138.

Courtesy Joseph Mirachi; copyright 1956 Saturday Review, Inc.

"That's the trouble with a monarchy—they can't vote you out of office."

469 other conflicting qualities are distributed widely throughout society and even within individuals and hence tend to balance one another. After all, a democracy cannot govern a citizenry every one of whom is passionately aroused politically any more than it can a people that is completely inert and ignorant.[4] Thus, according to such studies, it is in the balancing of opposite tendencies in a large public that we find the safeguards of democracy. These are the social and psychological checks and balances that parallel—and strengthen—the constitutional ones. Extremist tendencies are balanced and hence canceled.

Both these studies, and many others, prove the vital necessity of responsible leadership in a democracy. The people by themselves cannot take the initiative or carry the momentum of government. Leaders rise through the democratic process and, once in power, must have considerable leeway in exercising authority. The crucial institution is the electoral system. "An electoral system, designed to turn power over to a particular elite for a limited period of time, can achieve a balance between power and responsiveness: the elites obtain power, yet this power is limited by the periodic elections themselves, by the concern for future elections during the interelection period, and by a variety of other formal and informal checks."[5] In this sense the ideal of government *by* the people must recognize a place for government *of* the people.

Can Constitutional Government Be Efficient Government?

For centuries "strong men" have seized power from republican governments on the grounds that they were so bumbling and overloaded with constitutional checks and balances that they could not act. In the United States, especially in crisis times, voices have proclaimed that the country needed a dictator to clean up the "mess in Washington" and to get things done. More thoughtful people have criticized the vast, often slow-moving federal bureaucracy, the power of the judiciary to stall and block action, and the complex and time-consuming machinery linking the federal, state, and local governments. But the great bulk of criticism has centered on Congress, the heart of our constitutional republic.

CONGRESS UNDER ATTACK

Critics can cite many facts to demonstrate that the Congress is woefully inefficient. Procedure in both chambers—especially the Senate—is slow and cumbersome. A small group can hold up action in the House; one man can delay the majority in the Senate. The many committees, with their scores of subcommittees, operate ponderously. Congressmen spend much of their

[4]Gabriel A. Almond and Sidney Verba, *The Civic Culture* (Princeton Univ. Press, 1963), Chap. 15.
[5]*Ibid.*, p. 477.

time on time-wasting activities, such as running errands for constituents or making speeches to an almost empty chamber. Simply calling the roll in the House can take three-quarters of an hour of valuable time. One result of the inefficiency is that congressmen are constantly overworked. Above all, goes the charge, Congress does not pull with the President and hence teamwork in government is lessened.

Defenders of Congress answer these charges by pointing to the sheer volume of congressional work; Congress will consider several thousand bills in one session and enact hundreds of them. They point also to the congressional debates and to the committee hearings—much of it of a high order of excellence. But in general, students of Congress grant that its procedures are overly time consuming and even archaic. It is significant that some of the most outspoken critics of Congress are congressmen themselves.[6]

Every generation or so Congress makes an effort to modernize its procedures. In 1946 it streamlined the committee system by reducing the number by about half in each chamber and thus enabling members to concentrate on a smaller number of policy areas. Congress also strengthened the committees' professional assistance and staffs; required committees to hold regular meetings and keep better records of proceedings; and, to prevent delay and obstruction, required committee chairmen to report promptly any measures approved by their committees. But the reorganization effort of 1946 did not have the effect that some hoped. It streamlined committees, critics pointed out, but the committees simply spawned a host of subcommittees. Congress continued to go about its business in much the same way as it had in the past.

FAILURE TO MODERNIZE

Pressure for congressional improvement mounted in the early 1960s, as Congress held up or killed off many of President Kennedy's legislative proposals. A new Joint Committee on the Organization of Congress was established in 1965 consisting of six members from each chamber. Predominantly representative of the congressional establishment, the joint committee operated under restrictions that barred it from proposing any changes in the Senate or House rules and was thus precluded from considering reforms that could drastically affect the internal power structure of either chamber.

Yet as the Ninetieth Congress (1967–1968) came to a close, strong voices in both parties were speaking up for reform. The filibuster in the Senate against President Johnson's nomination of Justice Abe Fortas for Chief Justice of the Supreme Court brought more demands that the minority not be allowed to use the talkathon (as against talk) to defeat majority rule in the upper chamber. In the House, a small group of Republican liberals and moderates banded together to strengthen democratic procedures in that body. During the Ninetieth Congress, the House did adopt broad-scale re-

---

[6]See, for example (Representative) Richard Bolling, *House Out of Order* (Dutton, 1965); (Senator) Joseph S. Clark, *Congress: The Sapless Branch* (Harper & Row, 1964); and (Senator) Kenneth B. Keating, *Government of the People: The Challenge of Change* (Harcourt, Brace & World, 1964).

quirements for disclosure by members of their associations with enterprises doing business with the federal government and from which they receive income. It also acted to prevent abuses of the raising of funds through testimonial dinners and barred Congressmen from putting relatives—except for those already employed—on the congressional payroll.

Some representatives felt that these steps, useful though they were, still did not touch the crucial problems of efficiency, democracy, and leadership in the House. In 1968 Richard Bolling, a leader of the Democratic Study Group (an organization of liberal Democratic representatives) and long a lieutenant of the late Speaker Sam Rayburn, proposed sweeping reforms for his own party in the House: that the Democratic Speaker be the real operating head of the legislature; that he have power to nominate all the Democratic members of the Rules Committee and the Committee on Ways and Means and their chairmen; that the Democratic caucus have power only to accept or reject such nominations and not have the power to make nominations from the floor; and that the Speaker have extensive power over the choice of chairmen of other standing committees.[7] In one blow Bolling faced up to the main problems in the House—the dispersion of power, the weak Speaker, the seniority rule, the overly powerful committee system—in order to strengthen efficiency and central responsibility. But as the Ninety-first Congress convened there seemed to be little appetite for such basic reforms in either house of the Congress.

Is Efficient Government Free Government?

In Chapter 1 the authors urged that students of politics pause regularly to challenge their own assumptions. Here is a case in point. In the last section the authors have been blandly proceeding on the assumption that efficiency in government is a good thing. But how much value should we attach to efficiency as compared with other goals? Obviously we all want congressmen to save their time and our money—that is, we want efficiency in the narrow sense. But what about efficiency in the broader sense—what about effectiveness? Do we *want* a stronger Congress? Do we *want* more teamwork between executive and legislature? Do we *want* more partnership between national and state government?

In short, do we want a more powerful government even if it might jeopardize our highly prized civil liberties—liberties *against* government?

LIBERTY AGAINST GOVERNMENT

The answer of most of the Framers of the Constitution was, of course, no. As we have seen, they feared an overly effective government just as they did a weak government, and certainly they did not want the rulers in the nation's capital and in the states to gang up against the people and their liber-

---

[7]Richard Bolling, *Power in the House* (Dutton, 1968), pp. 266–269. Bolling would grant similar powers to the Democratic minority leader in the House.

ties. Freedom was mainly to be protected against government, not through it. The Framers were proud of their handiwork—an elaborate constitutional system that balanced the powers of government agencies against one another, which in effect meant balancing certain groups and interests against one another. The effect during most of our history has been what the Framers wanted—slow, deliberate, at times even ponderous government.

But perspectives change. The Framers tended to think of government as kings and ministers who were not politically accountable to the electorate and who were likely to suppress legislatures, arrest citizens for criticizing the authorities, search homes without warrants. Today many of us think of government as our own elected officials responsible and responsive to us. We see restraints on our liberties flowing not only from what public officials do, but from social and economic conditions of poverty and illiteracy and from the actions of other individuals—employers who might fire workers for trying to unionize, landlords who may refuse to rent homes to Negroes because of their race, vigilantes who may threaten students for working for civil rights. We have learned that, as Hobhouse said, liberty is a matter not just of the increase or decrease but of the reorganization of restraints. Indeed, we have used our political power to demand that those we elected to office employ the authority of government to extend our liberties and rights.

Yet most Americans would not overweigh the value of effective government at the expense of safe government. Elected officials, like all men, tend to view the nation's welfare from their own special and limited perspective. Some of them—revenue officials and government prosecutors, for example—have great powers when dealing with individual citizens. In our judgment, the defense of liberty against government requires not only that such officials follow due process of law and observe procedural safeguards for the individual, but that independent political bases be created for those who oppose the officials, their policies, and their methods. Perhaps the strongest inhibition on rulers is the fear that they will be driven out of power, or that their actions will be closely scrutinized, or that arbitrary methods will be checked by judges. Hence the major safeguards against oppressive governmental actions are an opposition party that strongly and continuously opposes, congressional investigations of arbitrary executive actions or practices, congressional leaders who do not depend on the President's favor for remaining in office, judges who can require enforcement officials to justify their actions, and other arrangements that were developed over the centuries to limit rulers.

CIVIL LIBERTIES—THE SUPREME VALUE?

The implication of the above, and of Part Three in general, is that individual liberty should be the supreme value in government by the people. Certainly this was the implication of the original American demand for independence from Britain. In writing the Declaration of Independence, Jefferson held that certain truths were *self-evident*—including that men were endowed by their Creator with certain unalienable rights, and that among these were life, liberty, and the pursuit of happiness. But here again we should reassess our own preconceptions.

The authors are civil libertarians in the broad sense, but even so, we would not take an absolutist position about such prized values as freedom of speech and of the press. Although the First Amendment commands Congress to make no law abridging these and certain other freedoms, there are always the competing claims of prudence, reasonableness, and common sense. Clearly, we should not allow the right of free speech to be abused by those who would use it to overthrow the government by force during wartime, even though we would allow subversives every procedural right in defending their actions. Clearly, we would not allow a freedom of the press that would permit men knowingly to sell obscene magazines to children or newspapers to publish secret military information. For the Constitution does not single out liberty as the only value; its objectives were also to establish justice, ensure domestic tranquility, and provide for the common defense, as well as to "secure the blessings of liberty." And such values often come into conflict.

Hence we must balance all individual liberties against the collective security and needs of society; we must also balance certain individual liberties against other individual liberties. The question is always which rights of which people are to be protected by what means and at what price.[8]

We must also balance traditional rights against other rights that have become increasingly important in a crowded urban society. The right of privacy as such is not mentioned in the Bill of Rights, but many city dwellers today might consider it as important as freedom of expression.

Liberty has limits. Even though the authors would place freedom of expression at the top of their hierarchy of values, there are still other competing values. And within these values there are questions concerning how conflicting specific claims can best be settled. "The practical question," John Stuart Mill said, "[is] where to place the limit—how to make the fitting adjustment between individual independence and social control." Government must represent our quest for liberty; it must also represent other goals and values of a free people.

Representation in a Pluralist Democracy

No problem of pluralist democracy is more complicated in theory and practice than that of representation. For one thing, representation is impossible in the literal sense. If you want lower taxes and better highways—as most voters do—are you being better represented if government cuts taxes or builds more highways? If every man has a host of conflicting desires, fears, and vague yearnings—as most of us do—how can government possibly represent those complex sets of desires and attitudes? Government cannot be computerized. Moreover, even if millions of people could be represented in their billions of interests, the question would remain as to *how* they were to be represented. Through direct representation, such as a New England town meeting? Through economic or vocational groups, such as

[8]Charles S. Hyneman, "Free Speech: At What Price?" *The American Political Science Review* (December 1962), p. 847.

labor guilds or Mussolini-style syndicates? Through a coalition of minority groups? Through a clear-cut majority? In a pluralist democracy a representative system can be set up by either (1) giving special representation to minority groups and allowing government to act only by consent of these groups or (2) giving strong representation to a popular majority, which can act quickly once it has gained such majority support and which guarantees the minority only the rights to agitate, put up candidates, and try to win elections. The first type of system was exemplified in the Articles of Confederation; the second type, as noted in Chapter 1, in the British government today.

In dealing with problems such as these, it may be helpful to turn to the use of models, such as those discussed at the start of this chapter.

THE BROKER-RULE MODEL

The first model, long part of American political theory, was known in its original form as the doctrine of *concurrent majority rule*. Over a century ago John C. Calhoun stated the theory in extreme form. As a Southerner representing a sectional minority he was desperately anxious to prevent the North from oppressing the planter interests in the South.

Today our system of concurrent majority rule is not so extreme as Calhoun would have wanted. Very few single interests, if any, hold a complete and final veto over the rest of the community. But the main features of the system are still with us: minority blocs in Congress strengthen their power through their control of committees, the filibuster in the Senate, and other devices for obstructing the majority; votes are traded through logrolling among the major organized interests; powerful minorities show their hand in the bureaucracy and in the Cabinet; and candidates for President are careful not to antagonize minority groups such as Negroes, Catholics, or farmers.

Today Calhoun's government by concurrent majority rule might better be called broker rule. Brokers act essentially as go-betweens; likewise, broker rule is a model of government in which leaders mediate between interest groups, tacking back and forth as political pressures rise and fall. Instead of acting for a united popular majority with a fairly set program—either liberal or conservative—the government tries to satisfy all major interests by giving them a voice in decisions and a veto over actions. In the pushing and hauling of political groups, the government does a sort of delicate balancing act. Its condition is always one of dynamic equilibrium.

BROKER RULE: PROS AND CONS

Broker rule has articulate supporters. Many thoughtful Americans believe that government by concurrent majorities is the price we pay—and not a very large price—for the maintenance of unity in a great, sprawling, diverse nation such as ours. Their arguments go something like this:

1 The system protects minorities. Broker rule does not hurt interest groups of any size because, by definition, it acts only with their support—or at least their acquiescence. At the same time, the system defends individual rights, which often find expression in minority action.

2 Broker rule safeguards our diversity. Our varied nationality, religious, racial, economic, and ideological groups are both the pride and strength of America. Our system of government should reflect the rich diversity of our group life. In short, our society is pluralistic; should our government not be pluralistic too?

3 Broker rule tames down the extremists on both sides by giving them a stake in government — and by giving them favors from government. By thus absorbing groups on the right and left, the system minimizes conflict and hardship.

4 Broker rule permits a dynamic, flexible political system just as laissez faire encourages a competitive, dynamic economy. Power is not concentrated at the top but is distributed throughout society. Everyone — not just a few key people — gets a chance to take part in the job of running the government.

5 Clearly, broker rule is the price of unity. It prevents our political parties from becoming hopelessly divided on ideological grounds, because each party embraces a diversity of interests stretching across the political spectrum. The parties serve as unifying agents. When they fail to do so, the nation is likely to become involved in civil war as it did in 1861. "A federal nation," says one historian, "is safe so long as the parties are undogmatic and contain members with many contradictory views. But when the people begin to divide according to reason, with all the voters in one party who believe one way, the federal structure is strained."[9]

Many Americans dislike certain features of broker or concurrent majority rule. They complain:

1 Broker rule is unrepresentative. True, it tends to give every big minority interest a voice in decisions. But leaders of organized interests often are not truly representative of the members of those groups. And what about the millions of Americans not organized in vocal, self-seeking groups? Does not broker rule ignore them?

2 Broker rule results in parties that do not stand for much of anything. If people think their parties will not take strong stands on important issues, they may begin to suspect that democratic government evades problems instead of solving them. If this suspicion hardens into conviction, they may turn to extremist leaders and parties, especially in time of social conflict and economic depression.

3 Broker rule may be all very well for a laissez-faire economy and a loose social organization, such as we had in the nineteenth century. But the world today is putting heavy demands on government, and these demands cannot be met by a polity of pressure groups. The shifting, unstable alliances of minority interests cannot do the job of translating nationwide policies into firm decisions and actions.

4 Broker rule does *not* protect diversity. Heterogeneity, minority interests, and individual rights thrive best in a society that is productive, stable, and secure. A depression-ridden, frightened society cannot afford — or at least does not tolerate — diversity. Only positive action can keep the na-

---

[9]Herbert Agar, *The Price of Union* (Houghton Mifflin, 1950), pp. 689–690.

tion productive and strong. If democratic government cannot act, people may turn in frustration to more drastic solutions. In short, strong—not weak—government is necessary to safeguard democracy, which in turn protects diversity.

5   Nor does broker rule lead to unity in the long run. On the contrary, by responding to pressures it sets group against group, section against section. Broker rule does not achieve genuine unity but only temporary agreements and fleeting coalitions. By responding to minority pressures so readily, it fails to achieve a basic consensus of a majority of the people, and such a consensus is the only basis of real unity.

Whatever position one takes between these two views, the implications of the problem are significant. The issue is no longer simply that of direct and faithful representation of the people. The broader question is: How much discretion should leaders have *not* to respond to what the people seem to want at a given time, provided that some day, in some election, they will have to account for their record in office?

© 1965, *Los Angeles Times*; reprinted by permission.

"Gad, when I think of the power the people have . . . it just isn't fair. . . ."

Responsibility and Leadership

The issue, then, is not so much representation as responsibility. By *responsibility* we mean two things. First, and more narrowly, we mean the final accountability of leaders to the led, presumably in some election, even though in the meantime the leaders have a great deal of freedom to act. Second, we mean a leader's concern for the general welfare of the whole nation, not just the interests of his constituents, and for the nation's long-term interests, not just its fleeting desires—that is, whether he acts responsibly from the hindsight of history. How can we provide our leaders with enough power to exercise responsibility in both senses and yet keep them accountable to the people?

Among the many answers to these questions, two are especially important for students of American government—majority rule through party government and executive (or presidential) leadership.

THE MAJORITY-RULE MODEL

Proponents of majority rule believe that leaders should be largely if not wholly accountable to the popular majority that won the last election. They value strict majority rule—the idea that when a majority of the voters elect a set of leaders to power, the new government essentially represents that majority and is responsible for enacting its wishes into law. In short, the victorious leaders have no obligation to respect the wishes of the unsuccessful popular minority—except to protect civil liberties and free elections so that the minority can try to become a majority some day.

Many Americans fear strict majority rule. They believe that the majority holds in it the seeds of tyranny. Broker rule, they suggest, minimizes conflict by absorbing forces on the right and left. Majority rule would result in violent wrenches as first one set of leaders and then a very different set of leaders came to power. The majoritarians deny this. They maintain that majority rule must be safe, because the majority, by definition, embraces a tremendous variety of attitudes and interests, even though it may not include every group across the political spectrum. Because the majority is a broad one, the leaders must act in the interests of a tremendous diversity of voters. Thus a popular majority carries built-in checks and balances.[10] Minorities —not majorities—tend to be extremist.

Majoritarians recognize that the people cannot act on their own. They can act only through political organization and leadership. The obvious political organization for a majority is the *political party.* Historically, great popular movements have turned to parties—the Jeffersonian Republicans, the Jacksonian Democrats, the rising antislavery Republicans, the New Deal Democrats—as the key political link between popular majorities and control of the government. Parties have a special advantage in that they provide a common organization for leaders in different parts of the government—especially for the Presidency and Congress—and hence can serve as a unifying force.

This is so in theory, at least. In fact, believers in majority rule and strong parties have had to recognize that, as we saw in Chapter 12, parties in the United States are loose associations of state and local groups, lacking strong national machinery or real national cohesion. National and state party organizations are virtually independent of each other. Leadership is diffused. And yet the potential of our political parties is tremendous.

MAJORITY RULE THROUGH STRONGER PARTIES

Party reformers maintain that parties should be more representative of the general public and of their own members. Parties should be less responsive to pressures from organized minority groups and local politicos and more concerned with developing positive policies reflecting a broad national consensus of party membership. The party in power must be responsible for enacting the policies on which it won election. It must be willing to discipline its members in office—especially those in Congress—if they desert the party platform. All this is true for the opposition party, too. It must act as the critic of the party in power, constantly developing and presenting alternative policies. It must serve as a strong and united opposition.

Party reformers grant that the parties must be strengthened if they are to be more responsible. These reformers would (1) build up the national party organization by improving the convention system of nominating candidates and by setting up a strong national party council that would give more direction to party program and policy; (2) make the party platform mean something, perhaps by revising it and bringing it up to date every year in a

---

[10]H. S. Commager, *Majority Rule and Minority Rights* (Oxford Univ. Press, 1943), pp. 57ff.

Courtesy Tom Little; © 1965 by The New York Times Company; reprinted by permission.

One failing of our party system is that the party out of power nationally does not have the kind of leadership that the President can provide for the party in power.

national party conference rather than only every four years in the convention; (3) strengthen the party in Congress by tightening congressional organization, focusing power in the Speaker and other party leaders, and granting the party caucus more authority; (4) develop party activity at the grass roots through better organized local committees, wider membership, and more rank-and-file activity.

Not all political scientists agree with either the diagnosis or the cure. They believe that given the conditions of American politics, as compared with British, the party-rule model is irrelevant for the United States. They fear that more discipline in parties would cut down party competition in certain areas, for the national leaders of a strong party might enforce doctrines that were unpopular in certain localities (for example, race equality in the South).[11] Not party discipline but party competition is the great need, according to this view, "Our parties are big and clumsy and loosely hung together," says Ruth C. Silva, "because our country is big and clumsy and loosely hung together."

PRESIDENTIAL LEADERSHIP AND RESPONSIBILITY

Why try the long, hard method of party reform, some critics ask, when a much better instrument is at hand to act for the popular majority, to expedite governmental action, and even to unify clashing interests? This is the Presidency. We have discussed presidential leadership in Chapters 14 and 15; let us consider it now in terms of responsibility.

Defenders of presidential power contend that, first of all, the Presidency fully meets the test of accountability. The Chief Executive must win an electoral majority to gain power. In office he is clearly responsible for his administration; he cannot pass the buck to any other leader. For four years he operates in the bright spotlight of television and is questioned by the press, attacked by the opposition, and searchingly examined by the columnists and pundits. And after four years he must face the people again. The people then can apply more general tests of accountability. Did the President observe the basic rules of the game, such as maintaining civil liberties and keeping

[11]Julius Turner, "Responsible Parties: A Dissent from the Floor," *The American Political Science Review* (March 1951), pp. 143–152.

478

the public informed? Did he abide by the Constitution? And is he willing to take responsibility for his stewardship?

But responsibility means more than accountability to a particular electorate in a particular election. It means accountability for the welfare of the nation in the long perspective of history. As we suggested above, at times it may mean *not* being immediately accountable to, or representative of, the people, because the leader sees something the people may not see. He is responsible to history, or to fundamental national values, or perhaps just to his own conscience. Lyndon Johnson described this kind of responsibility a few months after he entered the White House when he observed that the President "is not simply responsible to an immediate electorate." Johnson continued:[12]

> He knows over the long stretch of time how great can be the repercussions of all that he does or that he fails to do, and over that span of time the President always has to think of America as a continuing community.
>
> He has to try to see how his decisions will affect not only today's citizens, but their children and their children's children unto the third and fourth generation. He has to try to peer into the future, and he has to prepare for that future. . . .
>
> The President of this country, more than any other single man in the world, must grapple with the course of events and the directions of history. What he must try to do, try to do always, is to build for tomorrow in the immediacy of today. . . .

This view of presidential leadership has its critics. If the President acts according to such vague tests — the verdict of history, the welfare of our children's children — what is to stop him from acting as freely as he wishes? Why could he not become a virtual dictator on the grounds that some day he would be vindicated? Such criticism invites two comments. Whatever his broader responsibility, the President will and must be accountable to an electoral majority at the end of his term. Even if he does not run again, he will presumably want his party to win. Second, the President in a democracy needs a strong and durable opposition. This is perhaps the weakest link in the American democratic structure, as we have noted. Perhaps the most compelling task for the party reformers is not to establish party government, which can never replace our present system of presidential government, but to foster a well-organized, well-financed loyal opposition that can consistently, responsibly, and vigorously attack the President's program and offer alternatives.

Summary and Conclusions

Defenders of pluralist democracy — whether they believe in broker rule or majority rule — broadly share the following assumptions:

1 Man is a rational as well as an emotional and subjective person; he is

[12]Remarks to American Society of Newspaper Editors, The White House, April 17, 1964.

moved by objective facts and by reason as well as by symbols, prejudices, and stunted perspectives.

2   Politics is best understood as a debate not among autonomous individuals engaged in the rational pursuit of the public interest, but among individuals in a cluster of groups, each group with a different concept of the public interest.

3   Democracy is preserved not only by the convictions of the mass but also by agreement among leaders on the basic rules of the game. Competition among leaders is indispensable to democratic government.

4   Voters and interests can be organized politically in a variety of ways through a variety of representative institutions. The machinery is not neutral but often embraces and enhances values.

These assumptions have major implications for the making of public policy:

1   The most important policy issues reflect value conflicts, with differing groups and persons holding differing concepts of the public interest. It is precisely because there is no objective or scientific way to solve such conflicts that popular rule—or at least participation—is in the long run more effective than the decision-making of dictators.

2   Democratic decision-making is less a way to solve problems than to work out accommodations. Political problems are *settled* rather than solved.[13] They are settled more often by bargaining and compromise than by authority.

3   Decisions are made, even in a pluralist democracy, by a relatively small group of decision-makers, with most of the public on most issues being unconcerned and uninvolved. Yet there is a rough correspondence between what public officials do and the interests of most of the people because of competition among political decision-makers, who periodically must please most of the people most of the time in order to retain the right to make decisions. Elections may not directly determine public policies, but they legitimatize the right of one group of leaders to make these policies.

[13]Bertrand de Jouvenel, *The Pure Theory of Politics* (Yale Univ. Press, 1963), p. 207. See also Charles E. Lindblom, *The Intelligence of Democracy* (Free Press, 1965).

BIG GOVERNMENT IN ACTION

PART SIX

A PROBLEM GUIDE

In Part Six we come to what government actually *does*. In these chapters we shall explore the tremendous number and variety of federal functions, ranging from crucial foreign policy decisions to the more routine domestic tasks, such as regulating interstate commerce. As we study these functions, we shall see that they raise anew all the five major sets of problems we have explored in this book. Here we shall see how they relate to the functions of the national government.

First, *the challenge to democratic government*. Do federal functions—the tasks that are carried out by Washington officials and others—prove the Communist argument that democratic government is just a cloak for rule by a few capitalistic interests rather than the people as a whole? Do the operations of government suggest that a democratic system cannot effectively perform the big tasks of strengthening and stabilizing the economy, aiding the underprivileged, promoting peace between business and labor, coping with farm problems, and the like? Chapters 24, 25, and 26 provide the factual background necessary for considering such questions.

Second, *the problem of constitutional government*. Because of the anarchical balance-of-power relation among nations, our leaders must be able to move quickly to head off crisis or to meet it head on. They must have power to mobilize and manage our armed forces without getting the consent of the voters or even the consent of the legislators—and sometimes without announcing their plans ahead of time. Under such conditions, what happens to our traditional constitutional processes of open debate and slow, deliberative action? Foreign and military programs require unity of purpose and action. Can we afford, then, the traditional splintering of power between the executive and legislative branches, the traditional supremacy of civilian over military leaders? Such problems are raised in Chapters 21, 22, and 23.

Third, *the problem of individual rights*. This set of problems is not explored so directly in Part Six as in earlier chapters. But the increasing role of the federal government does raise the basic question of whether big government narrows or broadens individual liberty and initiative. Do the security requirements of a continuing cold war gradually impair our freedom? Are we witnessing creeping socialism that may deprive Americans of their traditional rights against government? Or can federal functions, such as aid to education, help expand liberty? Such questions are implicit in Chapters 24, 25, and 26.

Fourth, *the problem of popular representation*. For whom does the federal government perform its immense variety of tasks? Does it serve major needs of the people as a whole, or does it actually operate on behalf of hundreds of special interests? Does federal regulation of interest groups such as business or labor—regulation ostensibly undertaken for the general welfare—actually turn out to be protection of that group at the expense of the public interest? The material in Chapters 24 and 25 raises such questions. The problem of whether our fiscal machinery—raising, lending, and spending money, and so forth—is capable of serving the interests of the whole nation is taken up in Chapter 26.

Fifth, *the problem of responsible leadership.* The officials administering federal functions have great discretion and power. Do the people as a whole, acting through elected civilian officials, have adequate control over bureaucrats, technicians, military men? In matters of foreign and military policy, should federal officials be accountable to the people as a whole through bipartisan procedures, or to the party in power favoring foreign policies endorsed by a majority of the people, or to various organized minorities or interest groups? Or—the other side of the coin—does our governmental system allow our leaders enough power to act quickly and comprehensively when such action is needed? Can the system be made to work for underrepresented minorities such as Negroes and the poor?

Finally, this section will give us an opportunity to see how the various institutions, interests, ideas, and individuals that make up the American political system function in the policy-making process. Does policy result from officeholders considering all the alternatives and making the decisions they think best advance their concept of the public interest? Or does policy result from a bargaining among individuals and groups working out compromises and solutions that are acceptable to the major power sources that make up our system? Or is policy the result of changing coalitions in which groups and individuals combine with one another to give one group what it wants in return for support for what another group wants?

The first of these methods of trying to understand the policy process might be called the elite, hierarchical, or command decision-making model. The second is the political-process or bargaining model. And the third is the logrolling or coalition-formation model. Which of these models best helps us to understand how decisions are made, how policy is formulated and implemented?

Foreign Policy:
Politics and Problems

21 One momentous fact dominates foreign policy making in this country —the United States exists in a world of sovereign and independent nations. There is no world government that can guarantee to each nation its security, liberty, or property. There is little formal machinery for settling disputes. In contrast to the relatively ordered relations of people *within* the United States, the relations with other nations tremble in a state of semi-anarchy. World order rests on a precarious balance-of-power system and on some convergent patterns of self-interest from which flow a handful of international rules and customs.

Some day the present system of sovereign states may come to an end. A single nation may conquer the world and impose a "new order" directed from one super capital. Or the peoples of the world may some day join hands and establish a world government capable of making and enforcing law for everyone everywhere. But at the present time, for good or for ill, the existing system of independent states is the international framework in which the United States must strive to achieve its objectives.

What are these objectives? Have they changed significantly over the nineteen decades of our national existence? Who determines the objectives and the means of reaching them? What fundamental role is played by organized interests, political parties, public opinion? What is the role of the United Nations in our foreign policy making?

The United States in a Changing World

The chief objective of American foreign policy has been to safeguard the security of the United States. To be sure, American politicians have often preferred to speak in high moral terms about safeguarding world peace rather than to talk the blunt language of power politics. But beneath the high-flown rhetoric, the central purpose of protecting national interests has been fairly consistent.

But promoting the national interests of the United States provides no better guidelines to foreign policy makers than the standard of the public interest furnishes to those who make domestic policies. Total security is never obtainable even if it were definable. The United States lacks the resources, even if it had the will, to make the rest of the world respond to our wishes. Our policy-makers try to influence, direct, and shape events—but the rest of the world shapes and influences us. And in recent decades the world about us has been in a process of constant and rapid change.

SECURITY IN THE NINETEENTH CENTURY

At the end of the eighteenth century in his famous *Farewell Address*, George Washington said: "Europe has a set of primary interests, which to us have none, or a very remote relation. Hence she must be engaged in frequent controversies, the causes of which are essentially foreign to our concerns. Hence, therefore, it must be unwise in us to implicate ourselves, by artificial ties, in the ordinary vicissitudes of her politics, or the ordinary combinations or collisions of her friendships or enmities." Quoted over the years by thousands of politicians, these words keynoted American foreign policy making for decades.

During a good part of the nineteenth century this formula of minding our own business worked fairly well—not because American officials had some special knack of keeping out of foreign entanglements, but because Americans benefited from a world balance of power. Our ". . . Isolationism was but the shadow on the wall of a global equipoise."[1] The factors in that balance were threefold: Britannia ruled the waves, Europe was stable, and our oceans shielded us from attack.

The British navy controlled strategic sea-lanes from Gibraltar to Hong Kong, and Britain stood between our virtually undefended shores and the other major powers. Any threat by a continental nation to the United States was a threat to Britain. At the same time, the European countries could neither permit Britain to regain control over her former colonies nor allow any nation to threaten South America, because such action would upset the balance of power. That balance rested on a diffusion of military strength and on an elaborate network of treaties and understandings. Shaky though the structure was, it endured for a century.

[1]F. L. Schuman, *International Politics*, 6th ed. (McGraw-Hill, 1958), p. 590.

The United States was not insulated completely from international power politics, of course. Americans fought a war with Britain at the beginning of the nineteenth century and a war with Spain at the end of it. We had frequent brushes with other great powers. We fought a war with Mexico. President Lincoln and Secretary of State Seward had their hands full trying to prevent foreign intervention during the Civil War. There were disputes with England over fisheries and boundaries, with France over her adventures in Mexico, with Germany and England over Venezuela. And yet the essential security of the United States was not seriously threatened in the hundred years after 1815.

Then, in the chaotic years after 1914, the relatively stable world of the nineteenth century came tumbling down around us.

SECURITY IN THE SIXTIES

It is impossible to review here the past fifty years. It is important, however, to survey the strange new world with which American foreign policy makers must somehow cope.

Britain, France, Italy, and Germany are still important powers, and the 1960s saw the resurgence of Europe as an independent force in world politics. In Asia, the rise of Communist China led to a widening gulf between Peking and Moscow, bordering on actual hostility. There was a lessening of tensions between the Soviet Union and the United States, with the result that their respective allies claimed an independent role. In Eastern Europe, Communist nations tried to chart their own courses—until Soviet tanks rumbled into Prague in 1968 to suppress the independent Communist government there. And America's traditional allies, most notably France, refused to follow her lead. Nevertheless, the two super powers—the United States and the Soviet Union—were still dominating world affairs at the close of the decade.

As we move into the 1970s, the emergence of a third world power bloc is altering the international landscape and presenting new problems and challenges to our foreign policy makers. In the long run, the division between the Communist world and the West may be much less significant than the awakening of the peoples of Asia, the Middle East, and Africa. Nearly two billion people live in these lands. For centuries they have accepted squalor, hunger, and sickness as inevitable conditions of life. But in the nineteenth century, many of them were introduced to Western ideas of liberty, equality, and progress and Western technical and scientific methods. Today, that introduction is bearing fruit in national movements, reforms, and revolutions. Membership in the United Nations has almost tripled since its founding in 1945, largely as the result of the emergence of newly independent nations. This process of emergence is by no means complete. Countries in Latin America, Asia, the Middle East, and Africa are convulsed by social ferment and rebellion.

The super powers have not ignored the explosive potentialities of this "revolution of rising expectations." The main confrontation between the two powers—with Red China playing an independent role but always on the opposite side from the United States—has been in this "new" world. Korea, the Congo, the Middle East, Cuba, Santo Domingo, and Southeast Asia have been the places of crisis and confrontation. The Soviet Union and Red China have been quick to take advantage of mass unrest and social revolution, and communism sometimes has powerful appeal to people who believe that they have "nothing to lose but their chains." The Soviet Union has given economic aid and military support as it competes for influence; Red China has promoted "wars of liberation" to expand its sphere. The United States —sometimes with the support of its allies, sometimes not—has used economic aid, propaganda, and, at times, armed force to support nations and regimes whose security has been thought to be intertwined with our own. All this is a far cry from the days when American activities in Saigon, Seoul, or Cairo were restricted to the handling of trivial duties that brought Americans into contact with many members of the colonial governments but only a tiny fraction of the native population.

Finally, the world has seen immense technological changes in the past half-century. While ideologies have been tearing the world apart, technology has tended to make it one. The techniques of communication, transportation, and war have brought the continents of the world closer together than were the thirteen states of the Union in 1790. Scientific successes by both Russia and the United States in the exploration of outer space have emphasized a common interest in the unknown. Techniques of war have been revolutionized. Russian rockets located on the northern shore of Europe can lay waste the industrial areas of the United States. Polaris submarines prowl the seas, and our military bases are on constant alert, with Minuteman missiles ready to go at a moment's notice. Our geographical isolation, which, along with our powerful friends, once gave us a "cushion of time and distance," is no longer. Even the Arctic has become a strategic frontier.

NEW TIMES, NEW PROBLEMS

Such is the world that our foreign policy makers look out on—a world sharply split ideologically but closely knit technologically, a world in which tens of millions of people are demanding a larger role, a world in which the decisive events of our times are those that affect our relations with other nations. Has our thinking kept pace with these vast changes? In the nineteenth century a policy of isolationism worked, and twentieth-century America inherited a deep belief in no foreign entanglements as the best means of safeguarding our national security. Then, with shocking suddenness, national security seemed to demand that the United States play a positive and active part on the world stage. Slowly, Americans stirred themselves into action.

Recently, our foreign policies have become increasingly linked with our domestic policies. The issue of civil rights, for example, is sometimes discussed simply as a question of domestic politics. But in the perspective of world politics, the problem takes on a new dimension. The United States spends billions of dollars trying to win the friendship of the colored peoples in Africa and Asia. At the same time, every denial of civil rights to Negroes is seized upon by our enemies to create ill-feeling against the United States in these areas. Another example is "domestic" economic matters. A high level of production not only supplies Americans with goods, it helps sustain our economic and military power abroad.

This relationship between foreign and domestic issues is circular, for foreign policy has become increasingly "domesticated."[2] The makers of foreign policy must face all the facts of domestic and internal politics. In deciding what to do, they must consider the political situation in the nations throughout the world and the uncertainties and complexities of politics at home. At this time, when American power makes us the leading actor on the world scene, whether we wish the role or not, and when our mistakes may have catastrophic and irreversible consequences, foreign policy making is the most challenging and critical task facing Americans and their rulers.

Who Makes Foreign Policy?

It is the awesome responsibility of those who formulate our foreign policies to determine the basic objectives vital to our national interests and to formulate programs to achieve these objectives. American foreign policy makers are neither omnipotent nor omniscient, and they do not control the events that create problems and set limits to solutions. But to the best of their ability and resources, these men must decide how to use (or not use) the instruments available to them—bargaining or negotiation, persuasion or propaganda, economic assistance or pressures, and the threat and actual use of armed force.

Who makes our foreign policy? The Framers of our Constitution recognized that foreign policy making is inherently an executive responsibility and gave to the President control over the major instruments of foreign policy. For only the President has access to the best information; only he can act swiftly, secretly, and decisively; and only he has the legitimate claim to be the spokesman for the entire nation. We shall return later to the questions raised by presidential preeminence, but first we must look at the men within the executive departments who make up the foreign policy establishment —the men and organizations through which the President acts.

THE PRESIDENT'S RIGHT-HAND MAN

The President's chief adviser is the Secretary of State, the most important member of the Cabinet and chief of the Department of State. He is important politically too—many people who cannot identify any other member of the Cabinet know his name. The influence of the Secretary of State is suggested by the names of many famous American foreign policies or actions —the Hay Open Door Policy, the Kellogg Pact, the Stimson Doctrine, the Hull Reciprocal Trade Program, the Marshall Plan.

Officially the Secretary of State helps the President make decisions. In actual practice the Secretary formulates a great deal of foreign policy himself

[2]James N. Rosenau, "Foreign Policy as an Issue-Area," in James N. Rosenau (ed.), *Domestic Sources of Foreign Policy* (Free Press, 1967), p. 48.

He can formulate foreign policy independently—Pres. Monroe proclaimed Monroe Doctrine in 1823

He is Commander in Chief of Armed Forces—Pres. Wilson sent Marines to Haiti in 1915

He alone can recognize or not recognize a new foreign government—Pres. Coolidge and Hoover refused to recognize Soviet government

He can conclude executive agreements—FDR traded bases for destroyers in 1940

As Chief of State he represents the American people at summit meetings

He appoints U.S. ambassadors and receives representatives of other nations

Adapted from Blair Bolles, "Who Makes Our Foreign Policy?" By permission of the Foreign Policy Association, Headline Series Vol. 62.

Powers of the President as chief foreign policy maker.

and then secures the President's backing. Just how much influence the Secretary exercises depends largely on the President's personal desires. Presidents Harding, Coolidge, Hoover, and Eisenhower turned over to their Secretaries of State almost full responsibility for making important policy decisions. Other Presidents—for example, Wilson, both Roosevelts, and Kennedy—have taken a more active part themselves; indeed, at times they were their own Secretaries of State. Even so, important decisions on foreign policy are so numerous that both President and Secretary of State play important roles.

The Secretary has a large department to administer and multiple roles to fill. He receives many visits from foreign diplomats. He attends international conferences and usually heads our delegation in the General Assembly of the United Nations. He makes key statements on foreign policy, sometimes speaking directly to the people. He appears before congressional committees to explain and justify the administration's policies. He visits other nations to confer with chiefs of state and foreign ministers. He deals directly with our ambassadors and ministers in other countries.

The Secretary of State is a leading member of the President's Cabinet and may have a hand in shaping general administration policy. He serves as the President's chief agent in coordinating all those governmental actions that affect our relations with foreign nations. This role is one that, despite presidential directives, Secretaries of State have often found difficult to perform, especially when they must control the activities of the President's own inner staff or those of some powerful agency head who has close rapport with the President.

The Secretary of State is dependent on the support of the President, but he must also command some backing in the Congress. Unless he enjoys congressional confidence, the foreign policies proposed by the President may have rough going on Capitol Hill.[3] For this reason, one of the Secretary's top

[3]For an illustration of how important congressional confidence in the Secretary of State is for the President's program, see Richard F. Fenno, Jr., *The President's Cabinet* (Harvard Univ. Press, 1959), pp. 203ff.

assistants is assigned to keep congressmen in touch with the Secretary's policies and to serve as a channel of communication between the legislators and the Secretary. Broadly speaking, however, the Secretary is at the mercy of power relationships in Washington—the relations between President and Congress—all reflecting the temper of the country. In recent years, Don K. Price writes, "The Secretary of State has seemed to be the official scapegoat for a nation which resents the sacrifices of two world wars and the frustration of idealistic hopes which carried it to victory but failed to establish a firm basis for peace."[4]

THE PRESIDENT'S LEFT-HAND MEN

Decades ago, the President need call only on the Secretary of State for advice in formulating foreign policies. Today, foreign policy is intimately related to and affected by every phase of governmental activity—finance, education, agriculture, commerce, and, of course, military affairs. Suppose, for example, the President has to make a decision on a matter of international trade. The specialized knowledge and help he would need are scattered throughout the executive structure, in the Departments of Treasury, Commerce, Labor, and Agriculture, in the Federal Trade Commission, and in the United States Tariff Commission. Fifty agencies are concerned with foreign policy, and all of them are called on from time to time to furnish advice and make decisions. The Secretary of Treasury, for example, not the Secretary of State, ordinarily is responsible for discussions with other nations of matters relating to the flow of international payments and trade.

Yet next to the Secretary of State, the Secretary of Defense is likely to be the chief source of presidential advice. Because the main goal of American foreign policy is maximum security for the United States, it is not surprising that military men and defense agencies have a strong voice in the shaping of that policy. Moreover, the line between military and foreign policy is often hard to draw. In recent years, the Secretary of Defense has had more to say than the Secretary of State about our policies with respect to Cuba, Vietnam, the Dominican Republic. Also frequently called on for advice is the Chairman of the Joint Chiefs of Staff, the principal military adviser to the President and the Secretary of Defense. And generals who have been assigned to command international military forces are called upon to testify before Congress and to speak in behalf of controversial foreign policies. The influence of a MacArthur, a Marshall, or a Westmoreland on foreign policy is hard to measure but obvious to see.

THE PRESIDENT'S OWN MEN

The Secretary of State, the Secretary of Defense, the other heads of executive departments, and all their undersecretaries and assistant secretaries are in a very real sense the President's own men. He picks them, they report to

[4]Don K. Price (ed.), *The Secretary of State* (Prentice-Hall, 1960), p. 1. See also Arthur M. Schlesinger, Jr., *A Thousand Days: John F. Kennedy in the White House* (Houghton Mifflin, 1965), for a critical view of the capacity of the Secretary of State and his department to respond to presidential needs and perspectives during the Kennedy years. In the same vein see Roger Hilsman, *To Move a Nation: The Politics of Foreign Policy in the Administration of John F. Kennedy* (Doubleday, 1967).

him, and they are expected to carry out his decisions. Yet at the same time they retain a small measure of independence, and they naturally tend to reflect the views of and to defend the role of the departments and agencies they head. All our Presidents have found a need to appoint within their own office men who have no duties except to help the President make foreign policy.

These arrangements for special presidential assistants are difficult to formalize because so much depends on the nature of each President's approach to his responsibilities and his personal wishes. Wilson had his Colonel House; Roosevelt, his Harry Hopkins; Eisenhower, his Sherman Adams; Kennedy, his brother Robert and McGeorge Bundy; Johnson, his Walt Rostow. In recent administrations these arrangements have become somewhat more formal because of the establishment of the Office of the Special Assistant to the President for National Security Affairs. The Special Assistant now heads a sizable staff of experts that keeps the President apprised of happenings within the government and abroad that affect American foreign policy (see pages 492–493); he also serves the President as his own personal, and sometimes rival, Secretary of State.

INTELLIGENCE AND FOREIGN POLICY

Clearly, policy-makers must have some idea of the direction in which other nations are going to move in order to be able to counter those moves. They need, in other words, high-level foreign policy intelligence. Therefore, those who gather and analyze material are among the most important assistants to the policy-makers—they often become policy-makers themselves.

What is the significance of yesterday's election in Brazil? How many trained infantrymen are there in Czechoslovakia? What is the morale of the peasants in North Vietnam? What should we do about Communist pressures on Berlin? Before policy-makers can answer such questions, they must know a great deal about other countries—their probable reactions to a particular policy, their strengths and weaknesses, and, if possible, their strategic plans and intentions. Moreover, the makers of foreign policy must be familiar with the geographical and physical structure of the nations of the world; with the people—their number, skills, age distribution; the status of their arts, technology, engineering, and sciences; and their political and social systems.

Although most of the information comes from open sources, the term *intelligence work* conjures up visions of spies and undercover agents, and secret intelligence does often supply the crucial and coordinating data. Intelligence work involves three operations—surveillance, research, and transmission. *Surveillance* is the close and systematic observation of developments the world over; *research* is the attempt "to establish meaningful patterns out of what was observed in the past and attempts to get meaning out of what appears to be going on now"[5]; and *transmission* is getting the right information to the right people at the right time. Many agencies engage in intelligence work. There are, for example, the Bureau of Intelligence and Research (in

[5]Sherman Kent, *Strategic Intelligence for American World Policy* (Princeton Univ. Press, 1949), esp. p. 4.

the State Department), the Defense Intelligence Agency, the supersecret National Security Agency (presumably working on cryptography), and, most importantly, the Central Intelligence Agency.[6]

The CIA correlates and evaluates information gathered by other agencies, as well as collecting intelligence through its own agents located all over the world. In addition, working with other intelligence agencies, it prepares the National Intelligence Surveys, which provide encyclopedic compendia for most of the countries of the world. These surveys give our policy-makers the combined best judgments of the intelligence agencies on a whole range of topics, for example, "Chinese Communist policy in Asia in light of the Sino-Soviet split, . . . the present and likely future state of affairs in Indonesia."[7]

Located at Langley, Virginia, twenty minutes from the White House, in the second largest federal building (second only to the Pentagon), the CIA has over ten thousand employees (the precise number is a secret) and spends many more millions each year than does the Department of State. The work of this agency is so secret that even Congressmen are not sure of its appropriations, which are distributed through the federal budget; its Director can write a check for millions of dollars without explaining why he wants it (except in a general way to the President) and can hire and fire without regard to civil service regulations.

The CIA has probably well served the purpose for which it was created in 1947 — to coordinate the gathering and analysis of information that flows into the various parts of our government from all over the world. Yet organization alone cannot ensure that our policy-makers will know all they need to know. As a close student of intelligence operations has pointed out:

> In both the Pearl Harbor and Cuban crises there was plenty of information. But in both cases, regardless of what the Monday morning quarterbacks have to say, the data were ambiguous and incomplete. There was never a single, definitive signal that said, "Get ready, get set, go!" but rather a number of signals that, when put together, tended to crystallize suspicion. The true signals were always embedded in the noise or irrelevance of the false ones.[8]

Whatever the organizational arrangements, intelligence work requires men to interpret the signals, and even with the best organization and the best men, our decision-makers will often have to act on the basis of incomplete information.

A more controversial question than the way the intelligence community is organized has been the assumption by the CIA of a secret operational role. Created to gather and analyze information, the agency over the years has become an instrument to make and implement policies. It often has more men stationed in a foreign country, more money, and command of more information than does the Department of State — and the CIA operates in secrecy. Over the years it has engineered the overthrow of governments in

[6]Harry H. Ransom, *Central Intelligence and National Security* (Harvard Univ. Press, 1958).
[7]Burton M. Sapin, *The Making of United States Foreign Policy* (Brookings, 1966), p. 307.
[8]Roberta Wohlstetter, *Cuba and Pearl Harbor: Hindsight and Foresight* (The Rand Corporation, 1965), p. 36.

Iran, Laos, and Guatemala and was in charge of the ill-fated attempt to invade Castro's Cuba.[9] After the Cuban fiasco in 1961, President Kennedy tried to restore the CIA to its original intelligence function. He ordered a continuing review of its work, but an attempt in Congress to create a congressional watchdog over the agency failed.[10] Then in 1967 the CIA was again subject to public and congressional criticism when it became known that it had created "front groups" to channel funds to a variety of research and political action groups. Again Congress discussed but decided against creating special machinery to review the work of the CIA.

When the CIA was created, Congress, concerned about the dangers to a free society inherent in a secret organization not accountable in the ordinary way for what it does, stipulated that the CIA is not to engage in police work or to perform any operations within the United States. But because the ordinary procedures for ensuring that compliance with congressional (or even presidential) wishes are lacking, there is always the threat and the suspicion that the CIA has overstepped its responsibilities. Even when the CIA has done nothing, it often gets blamed because of its reputation and the secrecy surrounding its operations. As Roger Hilsman writes, "The real problem of CIA, the inherent tension in conducting secret intelligence in a free society, remains."[11] It could be added that there is an even greater problem when a secret agency designed to support the publicly accountable decision-makers itself begins to make decisions.

COORDINATING THE FOREIGN POLICY ESTABLISHMENT

With so many officials and agencies involved in some aspect of foreign policy, the problem of coordination is immense. One of the key coordinating agencies is the National Security Council, which was created by Congress in 1947 to help the President integrate foreign, military, economic, fiscal, internal security, and psychological policies that affect our national security. It consists of the Vice President, Secretary of State, Secretary of Defense, Director of the Office of Emergency Planning, and such other officers as the President shall appoint to it. The Chairman of the Joint Chiefs of Staff regularly attends meetings of the Council, as does the Director of the CIA (on organization charts, the CIA is an agency of the National Security Council). The Special Assistant to the President for National Security Affairs serves as the Executive Secretary for the Council Staff, and frequently the Director of the United States Information Agency and the Director of the Agency for International Development also sit in. Members of the Council are expected to act not merely as representatives of their departments "but as a collegiate body seeking over-all policies rather than compromises of agencies' positions."

President Eisenhower relied heavily on the National Security Council

[9]Haynes B. Johnson, *The Bay of Pigs* (Norton, 1964). See also Theodore Sorensen, *Kennedy* (Harper & Row, 1965); Schlesinger, *op. cit.*; and Hilsman, *op. cit.*

[10]Andrew Tully, *CIA, the Inside Story* (Morrow, 1962); and David Wise and Thomas B. Ross, *The Espionage Establishment* (Random House, 1967).

[11]Hilsman, *op. cit.*, p. 83.

and elaborated under it a whole series of suborganizational units. Many, including Senator Henry M. Jackson, who headed an influential Senate committee that investigated our national security machinery, were highly critical of Eisenhower's reliance on the NSC machinery. Senator Jackson charged that the NSC system was a dangerously misleading facade: "The American people, and even the Congress, get the impression that when the Council meets, fresh and unambiguous strategies are decided upon. This is not the case. . . . The NSC spends most of its time reading papers that mean all things to all men." Cabinet members who make up the bulk of the NSC membership could not devote the time necessary to develop integrated and complex policies. As Senator Jackson put it: "You know the typical week in the life of a Cabinet officer—7 formal speeches, 7 informal speeches, 7 hearings on the Hill, 7 official cocktail parties, 7 command dinner engagements. It is a schedule which leaves no time. . . . What they can do, should do, must do—and all they should be asked to do [on the National Security Council]—is to pass judgment on sharply defined policy issues."[12]

President Kennedy, in response to these criticisms and to his own desire to maintain firm control over national security policies, came to rely much less on the NSC than did President Eisenhower. Rather, Kennedy coordinated security policies through his own Special Assistant for National Security Affairs and a small personal staff but tried to avoid having his staff interpose itself between the President and the Secretary of State. His administration "deliberately rubbed out the distinction between planning and operation," because it was felt that the President's purposes could be "better served if the staff officer who keeps in daily touch with operations in a given area is also the officer who acts for the White House Staff in related planning activities."[13]

Despite his desire to avoid needless committees and specialized machinery, President Kennedy found it necessary to create a variety of special task forces—high-level, specific action-oriented groups. During the Cuban missile crisis of 1962, the President improvised an Executive Committee for the National Security Council, consisting of, in addition to himself, his Special Assistant for National Security Affairs and the Secretaries of State and Defense; this committee not only coordinated policies but kept day-by-day direction of policies in its own hands. President Johnson continued in the Kennedy tradition and even retained many of the same men in the top posts. The National Security Council remained an important channel through which broad issues of national security policy came forward for presidential decision.

Ultimately, however, the President has the final constitutional authority to coordinate national security policies. Whatever the formal arrangements, each President has the duty and discretion to determine for himself how he shall meet this crucial responsibility.

[12]"How Shall We Forge a Strategy for Survival?" Report of the Senate Subcommittee on National Security Policy Machinery, *Organizing for National Security* (U.S. Government Printing Office, 1961), vol. 2, pp. 271–272.

[13]Letter from McGeorge Bundy to Senator Jackson, quoted in full in *Ibid.*, vol. I, pp. 1335–1338.

The Politics of Foreign Policy Making

Foreign policy flows through the same institutional and constitutional structures as does domestic policy. Like domestic policy, foreign
policy is made within the context of our constitutional and political system.
Public opinion, pressure groups, political parties, elections, separation of
powers, federalism—all these are also part of the politics of foreign policy
making. But they operate somewhat differently from the way they do with
respect to internal affairs.

PUBLIC OPINION AND FOREIGN POLICY

Different foreign policy issues evoke different degrees of public involvement. In crisis situations—the Berlin airlift, the Korean invasion, the 1956
Arab-Israeli intervention, the Cuban missile crisis—decisions are made by a
small group of office-holders. "Only command post positions were involved;
the public and its institutions were far removed; the decisions made by the
elite were highly legitimate; public and semipublic responses were largely
ceremonial and affirmative. In sum, there was hardly any politics at all."[14]
Yet even in these situations the President and his advisers made their decisions with the knowledge that what they decided would ultimately have to
command support from the public and its institutions, especially Congress.
And although politics in the sense of large-scale public involvement may
have been absent, those who participated in making these crisis decisions
reported that "When decisions are made on the big questions, . . . there is
struggle and conflict. . . a push for accommodation, for compromise."[15]

In noncrisis situations the public appears to consist of three "publics."
The largest, comprising perhaps as much as 75 to 85 percent of the adult
population, is identified as the *mass public*; this group knows virtually
nothing of foreign affairs, despite the grave importance of the subject.[16] The
hard core of chronic know-nothings is even larger in respect to foreign affairs
than in respect to domestic issues. During the Berlin blockade, the Survey
Research Center found that 37 percent of the people did not even know of
any trouble in Berlin. During the Berlin crisis in 1959, a *New York Times*
survey showed that many people did not even know that Berlin was located
inside East Germany.[17] And in 1964, the Survey Research Center found that
28 percent of the people interviewed did not know that there is a Communist regime in China.

The second public is the *attentive public*. Comprising perhaps 10 percent
of the population, this group maintains an active interest in foreign policy.
The third and smallest public is the *opinion-makers*—those who transmit
information and judgments on foreign affairs and mobilize support in the
other two publics.

[14]Theodore J. Lowi, "Making Democracy Safe for the World," in Rosenau (ed.), *op. cit.*, p. 300.
[15]Hilsman, *op. cit.*, p. 541.
[16]Alfred O. Hero, *Americans in World Affairs* (World Peace Foundation, 1959), p. 10.
[17]*The New York Times* (March 22, 1959), Part IV, p. 8.

To illustrate the relationship between these three "publics," one analyst has developed this instructive analogy of a huge theater with a tense drama being played out on the stage:

> The mass public, occupying the many seats in the balcony, is so far removed from the scene of action that its members can hardly grasp the plot, much less hear all the lines or distinguish between the actors. Thus they may sit in stony silence or applaud impetuously, if not so vigorously as to shake the foundations of the theater. Usually, however, they get thoroughly bored and leave. . . . The attentive public, on the other hand, is located in the few choice orchestra seats. Its members can not only hear every line clearly, but can also see the facial expressions of the actors. Thus they become absorbed in the drama, applauding its high spots and disparaging its flaws. Indeed, their involvement is such that during the intermission they make their views known to any occupants of the balcony who may have wandered into the lobby. As for the members of the opinion-making public, they are the actors on the stage, performing their parts with gusto and intensity, not infrequently in an effort to upstage each other. Many are directing their performance at some specific portion of the orchestra audience. Others, those with especially strong vocal cords, try to make themselves heard as far as the balcony. All are keenly aware that the quality of their performance will greatly affect their bargaining power when they seek higher salaries or better parts in future productions.[18]

Over the years the plot may change, but the drama continues as the majority in the balcony remain uninvolved.

Why are so many people indifferent or uninformed? First, foreign affairs are usually more remote than domestic issues. People have more first-hand information about inflation than about Chinese communism. The worker in the factory and the boss in the front office know what labor-management relations are about, and they have strong opinions on the subject. They are likely to be less concerned about the internal struggles for power within Poland or our policy with respect to Cambodia—or to feel that they could not do much about it anyway. And the relatively fewer citizens trying to influence foreign than domestic policies is a phenomenon not unique to the United States—it is found in other democratic nations also.[19]

Lack of widespread citizen concern, knowledge, and involvement in the politics of foreign policy should not be confused with lack of intense feelings about aspects of the international scene. Since World War II, with the obviously growing importance of our foreign commitments, questions having to do with our relations with other nations have been high on the list of public concerns. And when issues such as the Vietnam conflict become domesticated—that is, when they visibly, directly, and immediately affect the people of the United States—the debate over such policies produces teach-ins, campaigns, hearings—all the trappings of the ordinary political process.[20] Foreign policy issues, then, in contrast with domestic issues have less extensity and more intensity (in the language of the social sciences). In plain

[18]James N. Rosenau (ed.), *Public Opinion and Foreign Policy* (Random House, 1961), pp. 34–35.

[19]Gabriel A. Almond and Sidney Verba, *The Civic Culture: Political Attitudes and Democracy in Five Nations* (Princeton Univ. Press, 1963).

[20]Rosenau, in Rosenau (ed.), *op. cit.*, p. 49.

English this means that until a foreign policy issue becomes critical, most Americans are unconcerned with it, but when it does become important, they become highly and intensely concerned about it.

The movement from no interest to great feeling means that the public reaction to foreign policy issues is often based on moods that have no intellectual structure or factual content.[21] The common denominator of the mass public oversimplifies the problems of foreign politics. It tends to reduce all issues to the one issue that is most urgent at the moment. It thinks of the participants in terms of heroes and villains. It favors quick and easy remedies — fire the Secretary of State, lower trade barriers, get rid of Mao and all will be well. Although the more informed members of the attentive public and the decision-makers are also subject to mood responses and oversimplification, as the level of interest and information rises, the degree of sophistication increases.

Popular indifference toward international politics means that the official policy-makers often have to dramatize the issues in order to arouse public support for their programs. On the other hand, in periods of public excitement, fear of rash public opinion causes policy-makers to be overcautious. To secure American participation in the United Nations, for example, the State Department carried on an intensive publicity campaign but, in so doing, gave many people the impression that the United Nations would ensure peace and order in the world. To arouse public support for the Truman Doctrine, people were told of the looming "crisis." But then officials had to cool down public opinion to ease demands for hasty action.

The instability of public moods makes it difficult for official policy-makers to plan ahead, to take the long view after fully considering the military, political, diplomatic, psychological, and other subtle factors involved in every major decision. The unorganized mass public does not, of course, make foreign policy. Yet public opinion determines the broad limits within which others make the decisions. Public attitudes — the political climate in general — determine the political possibilities open to the policy-makers. The President and his advisers know they must secure active public support for programs that call for large expenditures of money or for commitments that involve risk of grave danger.

Congressmen are sensitive to what they perceive to be popular feeling. The relations between the public and congressmen are direct, well known, and influential. What of the Department of State? "The Department . . . and the American public are neither old nor intimate friends," writes John Dickey.[22] Until recently, those responsible for foreign policy regarded themselves as answerable only to the President. Now the Department of State makes a systematic effort to keep the public informed, and, just as important, to keep itself informed about the state of public opinion.

On major issues of foreign policy, the President, through television addresses, messages to Congress, and public speeches, tries to educate the

[21]This material is drawn from Gabriel A. Almond, *The American People and Foreign Policy* (Harcourt, Brace & World, 1950); Rosenau, *op. cit.*; and Hero, *op. cit.* In a more recent edition of his book (Praeger, 1960), Almond has noted a "greater stabilization in foreign policy awareness and attention" in recent years.

[22]John S. Dickey, "The Secretary and the American Public," in Don K. Price (ed.), *The Secretary of State* (Prentice-Hall, 1960), p. 139.

public. The Secretary of State holds regular press conferences. The Assistant Secretary for Public Affairs heads the Bureau of Public Affairs, whose Office of Public Services operates an extensive informational program. The office sends speakers, hundreds every year, to explain American policy to private organizations; it receives and answers over 150,000 letters a year. The Office of Media Services publishes leaflets and pamphlets on many topics of general interest.[23]

The Department is just as interested in finding out what the public thinks as it is in explaining its policies to the public. The policy plans and guidance staff analyzes polls, reads resolutions and publications of organized groups, and digests daily more than ninety newspapers and sixty magazines. At one time the staff contracted for surveys so that it would be able to find out public views. But in 1957, after one poll showed general public support for foreign aid at a time when congressional mail was critical, congressmen cut off funds for these surveys. Although this incident merely demonstrated the well-known fact that congressional mail may be unrepresentative of general opinion, congressmen felt that the survey information was being used by the Department of State to discredit congressional attitudes and as propaganda in behalf of the foreign aid programs.[24]

THE ATTENTIVE PUBLIC AND FOREIGN POLICY

Group and opinion leaders sprinkled through the political society—priests and preachers, newspaper editors, radio and TV commentators, professors, and public speakers—form an attentive public whose support is actively sought by the official policy-makers and who have an influential voice in the shaping of our foreign policy. "The press is significantly more than a purveyor of information and opinion. It may not be successful much of the time in telling people what to think, but it is stunningly successful in telling its readers what to think *about*."[25] As Peter Listor has stated, "I have thought . . . that there are not one but three foreign offices in Washington—one at the *New York Times*, another at the *Washington Post*, and last, the State Department."[26]

Another important segment of the attentive public consists of the small but influential citizens' organizations devoted to increasing the public's knowledge and understanding of international politics. These organizations do not agitate for the adoption of particular policies, but they do provide information and stimulate the discussion of issues. Many of them issue their own publications, and in their meetings they bring together influential citizens and public officials. The Council on Foreign Relations and the Foreign Policy Association are examples of organizations that have assumed such lead-

[23]Robert E. Elder, *The Policy Machine: The Department of State and American Foreign Policy* (Syracuse Univ. Press, 1960), pp. 129–133.

[24]See full account in MacAlister Brown, "The Demise of State Department Public Opinion Polls: A Study in Legislative Oversight," *Midwest Journal of Political Science* (February 1961), pp. 1–17.

[25]Bernard C. Cohen, *The Press and Foreign Policy* (Princeton Univ. Press, 1963), p. 13.

[26]The Role of the Public in the Formation of American Foreign Policy," *Proceedings of the Conference Sponsored by Extension Division and Department of Political Science* (University of Illinois, 1965), p. 2.

ership responsibility. Other citizens' organizations operate in much the same manner, although they are not exclusively concerned with foreign affairs. The League of Women Voters, for example, takes stands on particular issues and carries on campaigns to raise the level of citizen understanding.

Foreign policies so affect the domestic scene that inevitably the major interest groups—agriculture, labor, and business—are closely involved. These interest groups may represent such a wide cross section of the general public, however, that they speak for broad national interests. Pacifist, patriotic, and veterans' organizations are also closely concerned with foreign policy. The patriotic and veterans' groups, for example, support large military appropriations whereas the pacifists oppose them. Farm, labor, and business interests have heavy economic stakes in foreign policy. Developments abroad affect businessmen's profits, farmers' markets, workers' jobs and wages.

Religious and national-origin publics are particularly interested in certain phases of foreign policy. These groups have intense feelings about some issues, and they are often strategically located to affect the outcome of elections. Although some scholars are skeptical about the importance of these groups, politicians are sensitive to their wishes.[27] Some Americans of Irish origin, reflecting feelings aroused by English-Irish relations, are hostile toward Anglo-American cooperation. Many Americans of German origin voted against Roosevelt in 1940 because of his strong stand against Germany.[28] The attitude of Roman Catholics has been a significant factor in shaping American policy toward Spain both during the Spanish Civil War and after World War II. American policy toward Israel has been greatly affected by the pressures of American Zionists.

It is difficult to generalize about the impact of special interest groups on American foreign policies. Their influence appears to vary by type of issue and from time to time. At moments of international crisis the President is able to mobilize so much public support for his policies that specialized groups find it difficult to exert much influence.[29] And outside the crisis areas, careful investigations into some areas of policy, such as reciprocal trade, fail to find that special groups have had a decisive role in the formulation of foreign policy.[30] Another investigation came to the same conclusion—"interest group influence on foreign policy is slight,"[31] even weaker than in the area of internal politics. Of course, what is more difficult to determine is the impact on policy stemming from the policy-makers' *anticipations* of group reactions.

[27]Louis L. Gerson, *The Hyphenate in Recent American Politics and Diplomacy* (Univ. of Kansas Press, 1964), p. 243.

[28]See also Lawrence H. Fuchs, "Minority Groups and Foreign Policy," *Political Science Quarterly* (June 1959), pp. 161–175.

[29]Nelson W. Polsby, *Congress and the Presidency* (Prentice-Hall, 1964), pp. 25–26.

[30]Raymond A. Bauer, Ithiel de Sola Pool, and Lewis Anthony Dexter, *American Business and Public Policy: The Politics of Foreign Trade* (Atherton, 1963), p. 396. See also Cohen, *op. cit.* p. 2.

[31]Lester W. Milbrath, "Interest Groups and Foreign Policy," in Rosenau (ed.), *op. cit.*, p. 251. See also analysis of group influence on foreign policy in Bernard C. Cohen, *The Influence of Non-Governmental Groups on Foreign Policy-Making* (World Peace Foundation, 1959); and Alfred O. Hero, *Voluntary Organizations in World Affairs Communication* (World Peace Foundation, 1960).

Parties, as such, do not play a major role in shaping foreign policy, for two reasons: First, many Americans would prefer to keep foreign policy out of politics. Second, parties take less clear and candid stands on foreign policy than they do on domestic policy. All the party weaknesses discussed earlier operate in full measure in foreign policy making. Party platforms often obscure the issues instead of highlighting them; many congressmen fail to follow even a very general party line; and the parties fail to discipline even the most outspoken rebels.

Should parties be concerned with foreign policy? At the end of World War II sentiment grew stronger for a bipartisan approach to foreign policy. An ambiguous term, *bipartisanship* seems to mean (1) collaboration between the executive and the congressional foreign policy leaders of both parties; (2) support of presidential foreign policies by both parties in Congress; (3) withdrawal of foreign policy issues from debate in political campaigns. In general, bipartisanship is an attempt to remove the issues of foreign policy from partisan politics. In its defense, it is argued that despite the internal differences that divide Americans, they all share a common interest with respect to other nations. During times of national danger we readily unite behind policies necessary to preserve the national well-being, and such unity is needed to support our foreign policies. American foreign policy, it is asserted, was ineffective following World War I because it became entangled in the partisan struggle between Democrats and Republicans.

Bipartisanship has appeal. In this era of chronic crisis, it seems to symbolize a people standing shoulder to shoulder as they face their enemies abroad. It provides more continuity of policy, and it ensures that a wider variety of leaders and interests are consulted in foreign policy making. Psychologically, it helps to satisfy the instinct of people to turn to one another for reassurance. Its motto—partisan politics stops at the water's edge—is comforting to the many Americans worried about disunity.

But the idea of bipartisanship has come under sharp attack. Critics charge that bipartisanship denies a basic tenet of democracy—the right of a people to choose between alternative lines of action. According to this argument, in a free society men should be allowed and even encouraged to differ. The need in a democracy is not to stifle differences, or to ignore them or to elude them. The need is to express the differences in a meaningful way, to find the will of the majority, to permit the government to act and the opposition to oppose. This is where parties come in. They present alternatives. Because they want to win as many votes as possible, parties find common denominators in the views of millions of people. Because we have a two-party system, each party distills the essence of agreement from a medley of conflicting opinions. The party that wins a majority takes office. The losing party has the equally important job of furnishing opposition.

Thus parties—and partisanship—are vital to democracy. "Why should we abandon them at the water's edge?" ask the opponents of bipartisanship. Certainly not because Americans are agreed on foreign policy—the nation abounds with differences, as recent crises have made clear. Surely not because we hope to show a united front to our enemies—we cannot deceive them with a pretense of agreement; they know our differences as well as we do. Besides, our party divisions should be something to flaunt with pride —not something to be slammed into the closet whenever foreigners seem to be looking at us.

Even more serious, the critics conclude, bipartisanship erodes responsibility. A great virtue of partisan government is that the men in office can be held to account simply because they hold authority. But when the leaders of both parties work together, responsibility fades. After things go badly, the leaders of each party maintain that it was the other party's fault. Instead of a sober consideration of alternative courses of action, there is a frantic hunt for scapegoats.

Despite these criticisms, Americans will probably continue to resort to bipartisan arrangements in foreign policy making, as in many of the decisions over Vietnam. The reason is clear. In a time of international tension and crisis, democracies must *act*. Any device that will permit action without violating constitutional forms is indispensable. The methods we use may flout ideals of responsibility and popular control, but they seem to be part of the price we must pay for living in a disorderly world of sovereign nations.

CONGRESS AND FOREIGN POLICY

It may seem strange to discuss our national legislative body as part of the attentive public rather than as part of the formal foreign policy establishment. But despite the importance of foreign policy, despite the fact that Congress can block the President's policy and undermine his decisions, Congress as an institution does not directly make much foreign policy.[32] Rather, it is the crucial link between the mass and attentive publics and those who actually make the decisions. "In foreign affairs, Congress probably serves best as discussant, critic, sharp-eyed investigator, and watchdog rather than as policy initiator and formulator."[33]

The President and his advisers do not ignore Congress. They carefully cultivate congressional leaders. Former Secretary of State Acheson estimates that he spent one-sixth of his time on the Hill explaining, justifying, and defending the policies of the President and seeking congressional support.[34] Congress has dozens of committees and subcommittees concerned about foreign policies; of these, the Senate Committee on Foreign Relations is the most important.

Because of congressmen's sensitivity to public opinion, because of their expertise, and because of their prominence, individual congressmen (in contrast to Congress) are sometimes included within the circle of those who participate in making the decisions. For example, the Chairman of the Senate Committee on Foreign Relations has been involved at times, though usually his main role is either helping to educate the public or educating the President on what will or will not run into congressional opposition. When the Chairman is out of sympathy with the policies of the President, as is Senator

[32]James A. Robinson, *Congress and Foreign Policy-Making,* (Dorsey Press, 1962).
[33]Sapin, *op. cit.,* p. 54.
[34]Dean Acheson, *A Citizen Looks at Congress* (Harper & Row, 1957), pp. 64–70.

Fulbright on Vietnam, he may use the committee to focus attention on the differences.

In summary, the politics of foreign policy making draws in the public, interest groups, political parties, elections, and the same agencies of government that are involved in the American system of government generally. There are differences of course: the President and his advisers are subject to fewer immediate political constraints, and the publics are likely to have less concern and less voice in foreign policy than in domestic policy. The political parties and the Congress—the agencies most likely to be responsive to the impact of interest groups and the mass public—have less to do with the making of foreign than domestic policies. Yet there are links between the public and the decision-makers; the publics do have effective ways to make their views felt both at election time and between elections.

Diplomats, even if misinformed about the state of public opinion, are sensitive to that opinion. That foreign policy is not divorced from the political process is well illustrated by two examples. By 1961 President Kennedy had become persuaded that sooner or later the United States must adopt a more flexible policy toward Communist China. As a small first step he considered recognition of Mongolia, an Asian Communist nation bordering on China but Soviet-oriented. The President had ample constitutional authority to recognize Mongolia, but in the face of congressional opposition, the President decided that the price he would have to pay in terms of public and congressional support—support he might need on other issues—outweighed the advantages to the national interest in recognizing Mongolia.[35] We lack the inside information to document the factors that led President Johnson to decide against running for reelection in 1968, but it seems highly plausible that criticism by influential newspapers of his policies in Vietnam and the mounting tensions within the nation over these policies had their impact on his decision. Moreover, they created a climate of restraint in which Presidents Johnson and Nixon and their advisers had to make their decisions.

Is a Democratic Foreign Policy Possible or Desirable?

Over a century ago, Tocqueville wrote that democracies were decidedly inferior to other types of governments in the conduct of their foreign relations:

Foreign politics demand scarcely any of these qualities which are peculiar to a democracy; they require, on the contrary, the perfect use of almost all those in which it is deficient. . . . [A] democracy can only with great difficulty regulate the details of an important undertaking, persevere in a fixed design, and work out its execution in spite of serious obstacles. It cannot combine its measures with secrecy or await their consequences with patience.[36]

[35]Hilsman, *op. cit.*, pp. 305–306.
[36]Alexis de Tocqueville, *Democracy in America* (Knopf, 1945), vol. 1, pp. 234–235.

More recent observers have expressed somewhat similar misgivings over the handling of foreign relations in the American democracy. Morgenthau, for example, has observed that policy-makers "either . . . must sacrifice what they consider good policy upon the altar of public opinion, or they must by devious means gain support for policies whose true nature is concealed from the public."[37] Lowi comments that our system of "separated agencies, each with constitutional or legal rights to independent identity, access, and participation, guarantee the continuity of conflict and impose a type of politics inappropriate for foreign policy." In their attempts to build coalitions, Presidents must "oversell the crisis and oversell the remedy. . . . Democracy is . . . unsafe for the world so long as democracy is not set up for consistently rational action, because the enemy can too easily miscalculate."[38] And Lippmann opines, "Mass opinion . . . has shown itself to be a dangerous master of decisions when the stakes are life and death."[39]

Tocqueville, Morgenthau, Lowi, Lippmann, and the critics they represent are concerned that our foreign policy makers are subject to too much popular control. But there is another group of critics, especially vocal in recent years, who have the opposite complaint—they are critical because the public does not have enough voice. For example, Irving Howe, representing the attitude of many critics who were frustrated by their inability to force President Johnson to abandon his Vietnam policy, wrote:

> We must conclude somewhat unhappily that on problems like Vietnam and the Dominican Republic Johnson has a relatively free hand. Confronting a Medicare bill he must calculate and measure; considering a proposal to send Marines to Latin America he can act upon what he takes to be the national interest, or what at the moment comes to little more than his, or his advisers', panic or pique.[40]

Judgments about whether we have too much or too little public involvement in our foreign policy process and whether it would be better or worse if the process of bargaining and compromise that operates to resolve internal conflicts were expanded to cover more completely the process of making foreign policy ultimately are judgments about the merits or demerits of the policies that have been adopted. If we set aside the policies of the last several years, about which emotions are so intense that judgments are difficult, and if we take an overview of American triumphs and failures in foreign policy, it is difficult to conclude that we have done any less well than those governments with less or more public involvement. Although the leaders of the Soviet Union undoubtedly have more freedom from popular control than do our leaders—it is hard to imagine that any democratic leaders could have switched overnight from a policy of nonintervention in Czechoslovakia to a flagrant invasion of that country—the Soviet Union's foreign policy has not been any more notably effective than ours. And although the British system with its disciplined parties and integrated powers should provide more inde-

---

[37]Hans Morgenthau, "The Conduct of American Foreign Policy," *Parliamentary Affairs* (Winter 1949), p. 147.

[38]Lowi, in Rosenau (ed.), *op. cit.*, p. 323.

[39]Walter Lippmann, *The Public Philosophy* (Little, Brown, 1955), p. 20.

[40]Irving Howe, "I'd Rather Be Wrong," *The New York Review of Books* (June 17, 1965), p. 3.

pendence from popular passions for the British Prime Minister and Foreign Office than our President and Department of State enjoy, one cannot say that British foreign policies have been more coherently developed and implemented than ours.[41] The American system seems to entail a pragmatic compromise that frees decision-makers from some of the restraints that would otherwise be imposed but, at the same time, makes it necessary for them to take public opinion into serious account in the making of policy.

American democracy, like other democracies, has vested primary responsibility for the making of foreign policy in its Chief Executive. The President can act swiftly and decisively. He is accountable to a national electorate and is in a position to see more readily the long-run interests of the nation above the clamor of the crowd and the tugging of special interests. He must face the people in elections—but not so often that he must follow public opinion instead of leading it. He has control of most of the instruments of foreign policy—he directs our diplomats, makes agreements with foreign nations, and is Commander in Chief of the armed forces. Yet he is no dictator and he operates subject to constant and unremitting criticism. He must persuade most of the Congress most of the time if his policies are to be effective.

Foreign policy making in a democracy does not require, nor would it be desirable, that we hold a general election before every decision is made. Everyone cannot be an expert; the people as a whole cannot actively take part in drawing up policy. "In the case of foreign affairs," it has been said, "where the given elements in a situation consist largely of the attitudes and intentions of foreign communities, to expect a very high level of information on the part of the electorate is utopian."[42] But it is equally unrealistic to conclude that the policy-makers can or should ignore the electorate. Foreign policies that commit Anerican lives and resources will have little success if Americans, through ignorance, apathy, or opposition, refuse to back them up. The electorate cannot fashion policy, but the voters can set limits on the extent of the policies they are willing to support. And when decisions can have such catastrophic consequences, there is no reason to believe from any experience of any nation that absence of some kind of popular control has made the world any safer. "Coherent policy, executed with a nice combination of caution and verve, is difficult to achieve in any political system, but no more so for democratic states than for others."[43]

---

[41]Kenneth N. Waltz, *Foreign Policy and Democratic Politics: The American and British Experience* (Little, Brown, 1967).

[42]Max Beloff, *Foreign Policy and the Democratic Process* (Johns Hopkins, 1955), p. 58.

[43]Waltz, *op. cit.*, p. 311.

Conducting Foreign Relations

22 High-level foreign policy leaders deal mainly with the key issues of state. They work at the top of an iceberg-shaped governmental structure; the organization below is wide and deep. The day-by-day administration, the handling of routine problems, and the decisions that do not immediately involve great discretion are in the hands of others. These thousands of men and women greatly influence high-level policies by gathering and evaluating data and by making the scores of little decisions out of which the big ones are often compounded. The President, Congress, the Secretary of State, and the people depend on these officials for information and advice and for the execution of policy once it has been determined. What finally emerges as a policy decision is the product of many minds.

The Role of the State Department

The State Department is the key agency in the day-by-day routine of foreign relations. This department has five traditional duties: (1) It provides the President with the information he needs to conduct international relations. Through its missions abroad, the Department collects data on political and economic events. (The *daily* volume of telegraphic traffic alone between State and the embassies is estimated at 400,000 words.) After sorting and analyzing these reports, the Department sends some to other interested departments and some to the CIA. (2) The Department assists the President

504

in forming and implementing policy. It evaluates the information and makes recommendations to the President, the National Security Council, and others, or it makes decisions in the name of the President. (3) The Department has the primary responsibility for representing the United States in our dealings with other nations and international organizations. Messages to and from other nations are routed through it. (4) The Department has the primary, but not exclusive, responsibility for carrying on negotiations with other nations and international organizations. Although only 25 percent of the United States representatives in 390 recent international meetings were from the Department of State, in most cases the heads of the delegations were State Department men. And under what is known as the Circular 175 procedure, the Department of State must approve the initiation of all negotiations with foreign governments; and all agreements, no matter how technical, must be approved by the Department. (5) The Department coordinates the activities of all the groups, agencies, and interdepartmental committees participating in the formulation and execution of foreign policy. All speeches, statements, and articles by officials of the federal government relating to foreign relations must be cleared with the Department before delivery or publication. This applies to political officials, such as the Secretary of Defense, as well as career officials.

ORGANIZATION

With the steady growth of new activities and the emergence of the United States as a major world power, the organizational structure of the Department of State has undergone constant expansion and revamping. (It has been reorganized eight times since January 1944.) Though many critics still insist that the more it changes, the more it stays the same, the Department has probably become better structured to handle the problems of the modern world. However it remains a "vast, sprawling aggregation of specialists, career men, political appointees, and bureaucrats from other agencies—so much so that it is no longer feasible to present any meaningful chart of its structure smaller than a bed sheet."[1]

The policy-making and advisory activities of the Department are centered in a group of high-ranking officers. At the top, of course, is the Secretary. Second in command is the undersecretary who serves as acting secretary during the Secretary's absence. There is another undersecretary who is sometimes designated undersecretary for political affairs, sometimes undersecretary for economic affairs; his particular designation and function depends on the interests and duties of the ranking undersecretary. Two deputy undersecretaries assist in the management and organization of the Department. Specialized assistance to the Secretary of State comes from the counselor, who is the senior policy adviser and consultant in the Department, the legal advisers, and fourteen assistant secretaries. The chairman of the Policy Planning Council, which is composed of high-level officials who are freed from operating responsibilities so they may evaluate current policy and formulate long-range programs, also advises and assists the Secretary. An executive

[1]Frederick L. Schuman, *International Politics*, 6th ed. (McGraw-Hill, 1958), p. 183.

secretariat controls the flow of papers to the Secretary and undersecretaries and follows up on decisions made by these officials. The secretariat is also responsible for the operations center, a unit set up shortly after the Bay of Pigs episode exposed the inadequacies of the Department's ability to communicate with its officials throughout the world.[2] The undersecretaries, deputy undersecretaries, assistant secretaries, and other high-ranking officials, all of whom are presidential appointees, meet with the Secretary several times a week, review developments around the world, and bring matters to the attention of the Secretary.

The actual operations of the Department of State are organized along both functional and geographic lines. Responsible for activities that cut across geographical boundaries are seven bureaus, each under the direction of an assistant secretary: International Organization Affairs, Security and Consular Affairs, Economic Affairs, International Scientific and Technological Affairs, Intelligence and Research, Public Affairs, Congressional Relations, and Educational and Cultural Affairs. Five regional bureaus, each under an assistant secretary, embrace geographic areas: Inter-American Affairs, European Affairs, East Asian and Pacific Affairs, Near Eastern and South Asian Affairs, and African Affairs. Each bureau is divided into offices, and these in turn are subdivided into what are known as *country desks*. The desk man is expected to have a thorough understanding of his country. "Almost every scrap of information which government agencies collect on an area and many policy papers from other agencies proposing action . . . cross the country desk, at a rate of 250 to 350 documents per day. . . . The Department's 114 country desk officers remain the eyes and ears, the brain and the voice, of America. . . . They keep daily watch over events in 179 political entities from Aden through Zanzibar."[3]

Inside the Department of State, but not a part of it in a real sense, are two so-called semiautonomous agencies—the Agency for International Development and the Peace Corps. The Agency for International Development (AID) operates under a director who reports directly to the Secretary of State. With a staff of over 15,000 persons, AID handles the nation's economic and technical assistance and coordinates most of the military aid programs. The agency places greater emphasis on loans than on grants and insists that each country seeking American aid first put its own house in order to ensure that the aid will lead to improved economic well-being for all the people, not just a privileged few. AID operates on the assumption that using our economic power to strengthen independent nations will improve the security of this country. The Peace Corps, first established by President Kennedy in 1961 and then confirmed by Congress, is designed to place American volunteers in the newly developing nations to help fill the critical need for skilled manpower. The Peace Corps recruits, trains, and places volunteers willing to serve for periods of from one to three years. The volunteers teach; work in agricultural extension, community development, and construction; offer medical services; and engage in a wide range of other activities (see Epilogue).

[2]Burton M. Sapin, *The Making of United States Foreign Policy* (Brookings, 1966), pp. 110–125, esp. p. 111.
[3]Robert E. Elder, *The Policy Machine* (Syracuse Univ. Press, 1959), p. 22.

The United States Arms Control and Disarmament Agency (ACDA) is not within the Department of State but its director reports to the Secretary and the President on arms control and disarmament negotiations. Established in 1961 to deal with the whole range of disarmament problems, the ACDA conducts research and sends representatives to, and prepares information for, disarmament negotiations. The 1963 test-ban treaty was based on an ACDA draft, and, also in 1963, ACDA took the lead in developing an agreement with the Soviet Union for the hot-line communications system; this system reduces the danger of an accidental war by ensuring that Moscow and Washington can always be in contact.

The United States Information Agency (USIA), which operates under the general policy guidance of the Secretary of State and the National Security Council, maintains field offices in over one hundred foreign countries. The Voice of America broadcasts are well known, but they are only a part of an elaborate program explaining American foreign policies to people abroad. It was during World War II that the United States began seriously to use propaganda as an instrument of policy. Under the Office of War Information, an independent agency, propaganda was used to soften enemy morale and gain the support of neutral countries. All kinds of propaganda—white (objective and balanced), black (slanted), and gray (mixed)—were used; today the emphasis is on making white propaganda. In addition to making radio broadcasts, the United States maintains, in foreign countries, libraries containing books and magazines about this country and its culture; we also conduct an elaborate program to help foreign students come to the United States for their education. Democracies in general, and the United States in particular, have been reluctant to establish propaganda bureaus, but the success of the Soviet Union in painting the United States as a country dominated by capitalist warmongers has forced us to engage in "campaigns of truth." The propaganda instrument is especially important in gaining the support of peoples in colonial areas, where programs must be designed in terms of local idea-systems.[4]

The creation of semiautonomous units reflects a compromise in the never-ending debate between those who believe the State Department should make policy but, except for the traditional instrument of diplomacy, leave its execution to others and those who insist that we must coordinate all facets of foreign policy in a single agency. Some believe that just as we unified the armed services into a single Defense Department, so we should unify the foreign policy agencies into a single Department of Foreign Affairs under a Secretary of Foreign Affairs. Into this new superdepartment they would place, each with its own secretary, the Department of State, a Department of Information and Cultural Affairs (consisting of the USIA and the educational and cultural bureaus now in the Department of State), and a Department of Foreign Economic Operations (consisting of the Agency for International Development).[5] Neither Congress nor recent Presidents have given any indica-

[4]Charles A. Thomson and Walter H. C. Laves, *Cultural Relations and U.S. Foreign Policy* (Indiana Univ. Press, 1963); and Wilson P. Dizard, *The Strategy of Truth: The Story of The U.S. Information Service* (Public Affairs Press, 1961).

[5]H. Field Haviland, Jr., et al., *The Formulation and Administration of United States Foreign Policy* (Brookings, 1960), pp. 3–4. A Report for the Committee on Foreign Relations of the United States Senate.

508 tion of supporting a new Department of Foreign Affairs. Whatever the scheme of organization, foreign affairs touches so many interests and activities that inevitably some of them will be handled outside the Department of State.

Americans Overseas

American diplomacy is older than the United States. Even before the Revolution, Benjamin Franklin was sent as our representative to France by the Continental Congress. Today the United States maintains 274 posts abroad, with missions in the capital cities of almost all nations with whom we carry on diplomatic relations. In addition, we maintain permanent missions at the North Atlantic Treaty Organization, the Organization of American States, European regional organizations, the United Nations, and other units such as the International Civil Aviation Organization. The heads of these missions, designated by the President with the consent of the Senate, hold the ranks of ambassador, minister, or *charge d'affaires*. Historically, ambassadors were sent to the larger and more important countries, but now we maintain embassies (each headed by an ambassador) in almost all countries. Until recently, diplomatic posts were filled primarily by political appointees, some of whom had little knowledge of foreign affairs. Today, despite the tremendous expansion in the number of nations to which we send representatives, more than 70 percent of the chiefs of missions are Foreign Service officers, many of whom are competent in the language of the nation to which they are assigned.

Diplomatic missions located in capital cities are chiefly concerned with political and economic relations between governments. Consular offices, though part of the Foreign Service, are largely concerned with the activities of individuals. Consuls are not official representatives to other governments but serve as public agents to promote the commercial interests and protect the citizens of their own country. Their powers and privileges are determined by arrangement with the countries concerned.

During our early years as a nation, the caliber of our overseas representation was high. Men like John Adams, Thomas Jefferson, and James Monroe served American interests in foreign capitals. But following the War of 1812, diplomatic posts were used mainly to reward persons for political activities. High diplomatic assignments were given to wealthy men who had contributed to the campaigns of victorious Presidents. Because the salaries of diplomats were small and their expenses large, only men of independent means could afford to take posts in the more important nations. The consular offices were in particular demand because of "the fees that went into the consul's pocket; at big ports such as Hamburg and London, the yearly plunder often exceeded the salary of the President of the United States."[6] Various minor reforms were made, but it was not until 1924 that a modern career service was established. In that year, the Rogers Act consolidated the diplomatic and consular service and provided for a Foreign Service of the United States

[6]J. Rives Childs, *American Foreign Service* (Holt, 1948), p. 6.

established on a career basis. The service was further modernized and re-organized by the Foreign Service Act of 1946.

THE AMERICAN FOREIGN SERVICE

The American Foreign Service is the eyes and ears of the United States. Although a part of the State Department, the service represents the entire government and performs jobs for many other agencies. Its main duties are to carry out foreign policy as expressed in the directives of the Secretary of State, gather data for American policy-makers, protect Americans and American interests in foreign countries, and cultivate friendly relations with foreign peoples. Although theoretically the service is only an instrument to assist policy leaders, the importance of the Foreign Service officer and his reports to policy-making are reflected in the quip, "foreign policy is made on the cables."

The Foreign Service is composed of ambassadors, ministers, officers, reserve officers, and staff.[7] At the core of the service are the Foreign Service officers, comparable to the officers of the regular army in the military services. They are a select, specially trained body of men and women who are expected to take an assignment at any place in the world on short notice. There are approximately thirty-seven hundred such officers; in most years over two hundred junior officers are appointed. They have their own training school, the Foreign Service Institute, where new officers and their wives are briefed and where experienced officers get advanced instruction. Officers have either diplomatic or consular duties and provide the general direction of our missions abroad. As a small elite group, the Foreign Service officers have a high *esprit de corps*. A Foreign Service reserve permits the Secretary of State to appoint specialists to serve for a temporary period, and a Foreign Service staff consists of technical, clerical, and custodial personnel.

The Foreign Service is one of the most prestigious and most criticized branches of the national government. During the 1950s the criticism seemed to outweigh the respect, and the service's morale suffered accordingly. In loyalty-security hearings, officers were asked to justify remarks sometimes taken out of context from confidential reports made years ago to their superiors. Critics accused the service of being infiltrated by Communist sympathizers; others charged that it was dominated by a high-society elite who were still under the impression that diplomacy was the business of gentlemen. The charges about Communist infiltration were undoubtedly overdrawn, as were claims that the service was preoccupied with refined manners. (The latter charges probably stemmed in part from the conventional stereotype of a diplomat.) Still, most of the personnel of the service did come from the same general social background—a fact that cut down on the effectiveness of their reporting, for every reporter, no matter how objective, selects and evaluates what he sees on the basis of his own attitudes and life experiences.

Prior to 1954 most stateside positions within the Department of State

[7]See Epilogue for discussion of method of appointment and preparation for entering the Foreign Service, and, for detailed background, William Barnes and John Heath Morgan, *The Foreign Service of the United States* (Department of State, 1961).

Drawing by O'Brian; © 1958 The New Yorker Magazine, Inc.

"The United States Embassy? Just follow us. We're on our way there right now."

were held by civil service employees who had no obligation to serve outside the United States, and because the Foreign Service was small, there was little opportunity to bring officers back for a tour of duty in Washington. Consequently, it was charged that Foreign Service officers had lost contact with American domestic conditions. At the same time, the civil service employees with little or no service abroad often failed to understand other nations, appreciate foreign conditions, or sympathize with the job of the men working abroad. Friction arose between the two groups: The Foreign Service officers felt that their system of selection and obligation to serve abroad made them an elite corps; the civil service employees felt that the Foreign Service officers were limited in viewpoint, lacked specialized competencies needed for modern diplomacy, and got excessively high salaries, sometimes for doing the same kind of job assigned to civil service people.

Between 1949 and 1954 five commissions or special committees studied the Foreign Service. All recommended that there should be a single service to staff both overseas and Washington positions, with all employees being obliged to serve where needed. They also recommended that the Foreign Service expand the number of specialist categories to bring within it persons with backgrounds in management, economics, and finance and training in fields other than political science, history, and international relations.[8] In 1954, as the result of the report by the Secretary of State's Public Committee on Personnel[9] (the Wriston committee), Congress authorized an expansion of the Foreign Service to bring within it State Department positions that are primarily concerned with foreign affairs or that are concerned with management of overseas operations. The Department itself put into effect many of

[8]Arthur G. Jones, *The Evolution of Personnel Systems for U.S. Foreign Affairs* (Carnegie Endowment for International Peace, 1965).
[9]"Toward A Stronger Foreign Service," *Report of the Secretary of State's Public Committee on Personnel*, U.S. Department of State Publication 5458 (U.S. Government Printing Office, 1954).

the other recommendations of the Wriston committee. Consequently, many positions formerly occupied by civil service appointees were "Wristonized," and about fifteen hundred civil servants were appointed to the Foreign Service, receiving a higher salary but with the obligation to serve abroad.

Since 1954 the Department has attempted to fill its major positions with Foreign Service officers wherever possible and has expanded its categories of specialists, but the Department has had to continue to rely on civil service employees to a substantial extent to fill positions calling for special skills and backgrounds not available with the Foreign Service. A comprehensive study of the Foreign Service, by the Carnegie Endowment's Committee on Foreign Affairs Personnel (the Herter committee), also looked at the overseas service of all the other agencies of the federal government and called for the creation of a single family of foreign affairs services. The Herter committee discovered that the Wriston reforms were working fairly well, but it also urged additional expansion of training, broader basis of selection, and further integration of civil service and Foreign Service personnel.[10] In 1964, following the Herter committee's report, the Secretary of State and the Director of the United States Information Agency announced the integration into the Foreign Service of most of the key officials of the USIA.

In order to get a better idea of the many duties of the Foreign Service, let us look at the activities of a typical American mission.

AMERICANS IN NEW DELHI

On Shantipath — Path of Peace — in New Delhi stands a handsome modern building designed by an American architect in an Eastern style. This is the American Embassy, in its diplomatic enclave in India's capital city. The entire United States mission operates from eight office buildings in this enclave and outside, spends about $3 million a year directly on its own activities, helps administer several hundred millions in loans and grants to India, and employs about sixteen hundred Americans and three thousand Indians. A dozen local units of major Washington departments and agencies — Commerce, Agriculture, and the Peace Corps, for example — are attached to the Embassy. The Ambassador — and New Delhi has received such distinguished American envoys as J. Kenneth Galbraith and Chester Bowles — is the ranking American representative in India and is responsible for coordinating all activities of the mission.

The Embassy's Division of Political-Economic Affairs, created in 1965, is unique among American Embassies; it consolidates the former Political, Economic, and Political-Military Affairs Divisions. This division is divided into an External Section, which informs the State Department of developments in India's political, military, and economic relations with other nations, and an Internal Section, which analyzes and reports on India's internal economic policies and political affairs — for example, parliamentary debates, election results, economic development, language and communal problems, Kashmir.

[10]*Personnel for the New Diplomacy* (Carnegie Endowment for International Peace, 1962). In addition, the Carnegie Endowment has published six monographs, collectively known as the Foreign Affairs Personnel Studies, prepared for use by the Herter committee.

Two key agencies are organized separately from the Embassy but operate under the Ambassador's general direction. The USAID (United States Agency for International Development) mission in India is the second largest in the world—second to the one in Vietnam—as is the economic aid program in India. USAID gives both development grants and loans for industry, agriculture, health, education, and other activities. It has made grants for malaria and smallpox eradication, craftsman training, dairy development, crop production. The United States Information Service in India is also the largest USIS post in the world—again excepting the one in Vietnam. USIS sponsors exchanges of persons and cultural programs in India; visits by American specialists; science, art, and book exhibits; and film shows. The Information Section is a huge publishing operation in itself. It puts out the *American Reporter* (circulation 450,000), a newsy fortnightly magazine filled with features and pictures about American and Indian affairs; *Span* (circulation 100,000), an attractive monthly magazine that stresses current issues in both countries and cooperation between them; *The American Review* (circulation 35,000), a cultural and intellectual quarterly; *American Labor Review* (circulation 20,000), on labor-management relations; and vast numbers of pamphlets, press releases, texts of important speeches, feature stories, and photographs for use by Indian newspapers and magazines.

And then there is the Peace Corps. India has more PCVs (Peace Corps Volunteers) than any other country—around one thousand. As in other countries, the PCVs work in the grass roots on such matters as auto mechanics, health, rural community action, and farming.

OTHER AMERICANS OVERSEAS

Of the thirty thousand Americans employed abroad, only about eight thousand are Foreign Service personnel. Prior to 1939 the Departments of Commerce, Agriculture, Treasury, and others had their own overseas staffs. In that year, however, the principle was established that there should be only one Foreign Service and that all American employees in a foreign country should be responsible to the chief of the mission. Services of the Commerce and Agriculture Departments were merged with those of the Foreign Service.

During World War II, however, many agencies set up their own offices. The diplomatic missions in many cases were overshadowed, and friction and lack of coordination resulted. The American Ambassador in London was not even kept informed of various matters affecting Anglo-American relations and was all but superseded by the American lend-lease expediter. After the war many of these agencies were abolished, and some of their duties and personnel were assigned to diplomatic and consular missions. But as postwar programs developed, the principle that the United States should have but one overseas arm was again violated, and separate overseas missions were frequently established. The Agency for International Development, the CIA, the Peace Corps, and the Foreign Agriculture Service have their own overseas career services. In many countries a Military Assistance Advisory Group reports directly to the Pentagon, and in some countries, there are operating military commands.

As a matter of official protocol, an ambassador is the President's representative and outranks all other Americans, including even the Vice President and Secretary of State when they visit the country of his mission. Recent Presidents have issued directives to clarify the ambassador's primacy and his responsibility for coordinating all American activities in the country of his mission. But in fact the primacy of the ambassador remains a polite fiction. Overseas personnel continue to deal directly with their organizational superiors in Washington, especially on important matters of budget and program. It is unlikely that coordination of our agencies overseas can proceed any faster than the coordination of programs in Washington.

The United States and International Organizations

The United States belongs to all the most important world organizations, and its representatives attend all major international conferences. These organizations and conferences are major instruments of American diplomacy. In addition to the United Nations and its related agencies, the United States is a member of more than two hundred international organizations of various types. Slowly but steadily certain functions are being transferred from the national to the international level.

THE ORGANIZATION OF AMERICAN STATES

In its own hemisphere, the United States is a member of the Organization of American States (OAS), a regional agency consisting of twenty American republics—Canada has never been a member, and Castro's Cuba was expelled in 1962. A Permanent Council of the Organization and an Economic and Social Council are continuing groups; they consist of one representative with the rank of ambassador from each member state. Decisions of the councils are not subject to a veto, but decisions on security matters are made by a second organ of the OAS—Meetings of the Ministers of Foreign Affairs —which now meets annually. Any threat of aggression is dealt with by the ministers, two-thirds of whose votes are necessary for decisions to be binding on all members, except that no state can be required to use its armed forces without its own consent. Inter-American Conferences meet about once every five years and special conferences are called occasionally. The famous Pan-American Union serves as the general secretariat for the OAS, and the Inter-American Committee on the Alliance for Progress is the secretariat for the Economic and Social Council.

THE UNITED NATIONS

The United Nations is an organization designed to bring nations together to maintain international peace and security, to develop friendly relations, to achieve international cooperation in solving world problems, to promote and encourage respect for human rights, and to harmonize the actions of nations in attaining these common goals. Although basically an association of nations, the United Nations is an international legal personality with the power to make treaties and the competence to claim reparations for injury to its agents. It maintains its own legal staff, operates its own headquarters, and has its own flag. The major United Nations organs are the Security Council, the General Assembly, the Social and Economic Council, the Trusteeship Council, the Secretariat, and the International Court of Justice.

The United States maintains a permanent diplomatic mission at the headquarters of the United Nations. This mission is headed by a chief, who has the rank of ambassador and Cabinet status, and includes three other leading diplomats, all appointed by the President with the advice and consent of the Senate. In addition, the President, again with the consent of the Senate, appoints five representatives to the General Assembly; these representatives serve for the duration of a particular session. The chief of the mission is responsible for coordinating the actions of our many delegates to other divisions of the United Nations. Within the Department of State, a separate Bureau of International Organization Affairs coordinates the policies and activities of our United Nations delegation with those of other federal agencies, helps to prepare instructions to our representatives on the delegation, serves as technical adviser to them, disseminates information to the public regarding the United Nations, and assumes general responsibility for American participation.

The United Nations' failure to solve each and every dispute among the nations of the world and its inability to resolve the conflict between the East and West have caused some Americans to become disillusioned with it. Part of their disillusionment stems from their failure to understand the nature of the organization. The United Nations is essentially the collective name of 125 nations who have organized themselves in order to facilitate cooperation. It is a diplomatic technique that simplifies the problem of multilateral consultation. The United Nations, unlike the United States of America, is not an entity separate and above its member states; its power is the power of the nations of the world. It can do only what the member nations want to do.

The United Nations is a useful organization for diplomatic consultation. It provides techniques and machinery for discussion, for working out joint plans of action, and for establishing international machinery to handle worldwide problems. As such, it has been a useful device by which the United States has been able to carry on its relations with the other nations of the world. But the United Nations, like every other agency of international politics, is affected by the fact that the world is divided into separate national sovereignties.

Conducting Foreign Relations: Three Case Studies

Foreign policy is not made according to any set formula. A great deal depends on the nature of the issue, the speed with which the problem arises, the personality of the President, the political situation, and the accidents of history. Each problem calls for new decisions; each decision creates new problems. The initiative is sometimes in the hands of our government, but unfortunately it is more often in the hands of other governments. To search for the origins of any particular policy, to isolate the critical areas, to focus on the alternatives, is not our purpose here. In the following cases we shall merely suggest the way in which the machinery works.

THE MARSHALL PLAN

In 1947 all Europe was in dire need of economic assistance. Much was already being done by the United States through the various branches of the government, but it seemed likely that unless a greater and broader program was adopted, European economies would be subject to such stresses and strains that the world situation would become highly unstable.

On March 8, 1947, Undersecretaries of State Acheson and Clayton discussed the crisis with President Truman. On May 8, in a speech at Cleveland, Mississippi, Acheson outlined the situation. This was the administration's trial balloon to sound out public and congressional opinion. The State Department, meanwhile, consulted Senator Vandenberg, the leading Senate Republican spokesman on foreign policy at the time, who warned that a carefully prepared long-range program had to be worked out. The Department's Policy Planning Staff advised that European nations should take the initiative and work out the plan. Secretary of State Marshall approved but insisted that all Europe, including Russia, be included in the program. Meanwhile, the State Department experts published a study titled *The Development of the Foreign Reconstruction Policy of the United States.*

On June 5, Secretary Marshall made a commencement address at Harvard University. Instead of an "As I look at your bright and shining faces" speech, he took advantage of the opportunity to make a major policy statement. He described the serious situation in Europe and the need for American help. But the initiative, he said, must come from Europe. The United States should aid in the drafting of a European recovery program and later support such a program.

The U.S.S.R. and her satellites refused to participate, but the other European nations seized upon the proposal. Soon, sixteen nations met in Paris and formed the Committee of European Economic Cooperation. Within the United States, groups of specialists, calling on consultants and experts outside the government, made reports covering every phase of European recovery. The State Department studied these reports and advised the President. Congress was not in session, but on November 10 Secretary Marshall appeared before a joint session of the Senate Foreign Relations Committee and the House Committee on Foreign Affairs. He outlined a program calling for an appropriation of over $6 billion for the first fifteen months of the program, which was to run for four years.

President Truman then called a special session of Congress. The legislators were presented with a proposed bill by the State Department, and administration officials made numerous appearances before committees and addresses to the public. Three special committees, composed of over 350 State Department employees, were set up in the department to work out the details of the program.

Congressmen had their own ideas. Many of them were unconvinced that such vast expenditures were needed to protect American national interests. Then, between February 23–25, 1948, the Communist coup in Czechoslovakia startled the world. Congress quickly approved the legislation—but not without amendments. The Foreign Assistance Act of 1948 was passed on April 3. The next step was to secure the appropriations. The Chairman of the House Committee on Appropriations was interested in saving money, and, despite the fact that the House had previously approved the program, he recommended and the House approved a billion-dollar reduction in the program. Senator Vandenberg used his great prestige to have the amount restored, and, except for the fact that the money was authorized for only a year instead of fifteen months, the final program was substantially as requested. The administration of the program was vested, however, not in the Department of State but in a separate Economic Cooperation Administration.

The Marshall Plan was initiated by the President and the State Department but approved by Congress—both houses of which were controlled by the opposite party to that of the Chief Executive. The leaders of the State Department and of Congress worked closely together, consulting on the details and collaborating in securing approval. Not all decisions, however, require congressional approval or permit public discussion, as the following cases indicate.

A DECISION NOT TO GO TO WAR

On March 20, 1954, General Paul Ely, the French Chief of Staff, arrived in Washington to tell the President, Secretary of State Dulles, and Chairman of the Joint Chiefs of Staff Admiral Arthur W. Radford that unless the United States intervened, Indo-China would be lost to the Communists.[11] Some time thereafter—the exact date is unknown—the National Security Council was called into special session. Admiral Radford, Vice President Nixon, and Secretary Dulles agreed that Indo-China must not be allowed to fall into Communist hands lest it set off a "falling row of dominoes" across all Southeast Asia. The Council decided that if necessary the United States should intervene, provided it could obtain the support of its allies and the French would grant Indo-China its independence. A policy paper was prepared, initialed "D. D. E." by the President to make it official.

The President had the constitutional power to put this policy into effect, but President Eisenhower usually refused, to the extent possible, to make any major foreign policy commitment without prior congressional approval. So, on April 3, 1954, eight congressmen, the foreign policy leaders of both parties, were called to a secret conference with Secretary Dulles. When they entered the State Department's fifth-floor conference room, they found that Admiral Radford and several high Defense Department officials were also present. The Secretary told the congressmen that the President wanted a joint resolution from Congress permitting the President to use air and naval power in Indo-China. (Constitutionally, the President as Commander in Chief already had this power.) Admiral Radford warned the congressmen

[11]The materials on the Indo-China decision are drawn from Chalmers M. Roberts, "The Day We Didn't Go to War," *The Reporter* (September 14, 1954), pp. 31–35.

that French forces under siege in Dienbienphu could not hold out much longer and that the fall of Indo-China would endanger all of Southeast Asia. If Congress passed the resolution, the Admiral said, the Navy and Air Force would be used for a single strike to attempt to break the siege.

The congressmen—both Republicans and Democrats—asked, "Would this mean war?" Would Communist China intervene on the other side? Radford, who long believed that a showdown with the Chinese Communists was inevitable and who felt that the sooner it came the better, minced no words: "Yes." Would land forces have to be used? No one could say for sure. As the talk continued, only Senator Knowland, Republican Senate leader, supported Dulles and Radford, and it became clear to the congressmen that the other Chiefs of Staff did not agree with Radford. Dulles, moreover, had not consulted our allies; he explained that it would take too long and that emergency action was needed if Dienbienphu was to be saved. Finally, the congressmen told Dulles that before they would try to get a joint resolution from Congress, which would in effect commit the nation to war, the Secretary should first line up the allies. Even Knowland now was cool to intervention.

Within a week Dulles had talked with the diplomatic representatives in Washington of Britain, France, Australia, New Zealand, the Philippines, Thailand, and the three associated states of Indo-China. Dulles urged these nations to be ready at the time of United States military action with a statement defending our intervention and warning the Chinese Communists against entering the war. Messages flashed back and forth. Our allies were opposed.

Dulles flew to London to talk personally with Prime Minister Churchill and Foreign Secretary Anthony Eden, but he could find little enthusiasm for American plans. Nor were the British any more ready to favor American military intervention after Dulles proposed the creation of a Southeast Asia Treaty Organization to serve as the vehicle for united action. When Dulles returned to Washington and called for a drafting meeting on April 20 to set up SEATO, London instructed the British Ambassador not to attend.

A few days later Dulles flew to Paris. The situation was more alarming than ever; when Radford arrived in Paris, he told Dulles that only a massive air attack could save Dienbienphu. On April 24 Dulles and Radford informed Eden that if the allies would agree, the President was prepared to go to Congress the next day, ask for a joint resolution, and then set the military strike for April 28. Undersecretary of State Walter Bedell Smith, who also supported intervention, gave the same proposal to the French Ambassador in Washington.

Eden balked. He said that coming on the eve of the Geneva Conference —which had been called in part to discuss means to end the seven-year Indo-China war—American military action would be disastrous. He was convinced it would lead to the use of ground troops and the spread of fighting to Communist China. Eden agreed, however, to carry the matter to the British Cabinet. But on Saturday, April 24, word came from the British Cabinet—no support. On the following Tuesday, Churchill told the House of Commons that the British government was not prepared to undertake any military action in Indo-China. Reluctantly, Dulles concluded that the United States would not intervene. Dienbienphu fell, and eventually an agreement was reached to end the Indo-China war. But that agreement brought only a temporary cessation of hostilities in what became the divided nation of Vietnam.

INTERVENTION IN SANTO DOMINGO

Late in April 1965, President Johnson summoned congressional leaders to the White House for an emergency meeting. He told them bluntly that he had ordered the landing of a detachment of marines in the Dominican Republic to protect American interests endangered by a civil war that had been raging there for over four days. He pointedly did not ask for authority to take this action but wanted Congress to know about it before the public did. Shortly thereafter the President went before the American people on TV and radio: ". . . I have ordered the Secretary of Defense to put the necessary American troops ashore in order to give protection to hundreds of Americans who are still in the Dominican Republic and to escort them safely back to this country." This first direct military intervention in Latin America by the United States since marines landed in Nicaragua in 1927 incited charges at home and abroad of "Yankee imperialism" and "gunboat diplomacy."

What lay behind this intervention? Administration officials in the 1960s had hoped that the Dominican Republic would become a showcase of democracy, for millions of Alliance for Progress dollars were channeled into the country. Political instability frustrated these dreams. The Dominicans had known only one period of calm—from 1930 until 1961—under the iron hand of Dictator Trujillo. An assassin's bullet ended his regime, but a broadly based popular rule did not develop.

From 1961 to 1965 the nation saw four coups and five changes of government. In December 1962, a valid election was won by Juan Bosch, an idealistic, well-known Latin American literary figure. A powerful military junta headed by General Wessin y Wessin sent Bosch to a Puerto Rican exile the following September; the military said they feared that Bosch's left-leaning regime was opening the door too widely for Communist participation in the nation's affairs. The military leaders installed a new civilian regime, which ruled until April 1965 when a group of junior military officers and Bosch supporters led by Colonel Francisco Caamaño Deñó seized the radio station, announced that the nation was in a state of siege, and asked the citizenry to rise up and help return the country to constitutional rule. Arms were freely distributed to the people. A military junta, led again by Wessin, regained control from the civilian government and attempted to crush the uprising. Within a week, a reported two thousand Dominicans were dead.

It was in this atmosphere that Ambassador William Tapley Bennett, Jr., requested help from Washington. The twenty-four hundred Americans and many foreign nationals needed protection and evacuation, the Ambassador pleaded by telephone, as he himself sought refuge from shattering glass under his Embassy desk. The CIA also reported to President Johnson that over fifty Communists were known to be among the rebel ranks, although the extent of their involvement was not immediately known. The President acted. Some five hundred marines from the aircraft carrier "Boxer" were sent ashore. Within two weeks a force of thirty-two thousand American fighting men were on the scene, along with a flotilla of ships and 275 aircraft.

This intervention brought most of the fighting to a halt. Rebel leader Caamaño and an estimated twelve thousand rebels were confined to a 2-square-mile sector of Santo Domingo. An American-imposed corridor prevented the junta troops from moving in on the rebels. A truce and an uneasy calm lasted for some months. The pressing need involved maintaining vital governmental services and negotiating a settlement between the warring factions. American dollars were used to meet the payrolls of civil servants and the military of both the junta and rebel factions. American troops distributed food and medicine to the citizenry.

Finding a government suitable to both factions turned out to be nearly an insoluble problem. President Johnson dispatched a personal envoy, John Bartlow Martin, who had been United States Ambassador to Santo Domingo during the Bosch regime and who was a personal friend of the deposed leader. As a result of Martin's mission, the three-man junta headed by Wessin was replaced by a more broadly based five-man junta composed of both civilians and military. Heading this group, which became known as the Government of National Reconstruction, was Brigadier General Antonia Imbert Barreras. Imbert was in some measure a national figure, because he had participated in the assassination of Trujillo, and it was hoped that he might be acceptable to the rebels. His close association with Wessin's military faction, however, precluded support from the rebels.

Thus the United States was not only interposing itself between rival military and political factions, it was going as far as helping to form a compromise government. Was this not a violation of the OAS Charter? After all, Article 15 states that no member country ". . . has the right to intervene, directly or indirectly, for any reason whatever, in the internal or external affairs of any other state." The United States' position was a difficult one to defend, especially because it was currently predicating its Vietnam policy on the principle of self-determination. To gain a measure of legitimacy for the action, President Johnson instructed Ellsworth Bunker, United States representative to the OAS, to propose the creation of a precedent-setting, inter-American peace force which would take America's place as a Dominican policeman. Under this plan, member states would send troops to serve under a unified command. As these troops became available, the United States would withdraw its forces. Many nations of Latin America had disapproved of the United States action, and acceptance of this plan was not a foregone conclusion. A great deal of United States pressure, however, resulted in approval by a fourteen-to-five vote, barely the two-thirds margin necessary for acceptance. Voting against the plan were Mexico, Peru, Chile, Ecuador, and Uruguay, with Venezuela abstaining. After the vote, Johnson sent veteran troubleshooter Averell Harriman to the various capitals to stimulate participation in the peace force. By the end of the second month of the crisis, Brazilian General Alvim had relieved the American commander, and the eighteen-thousand-man peace force had started taking on a genuine inter-American complexion.

OAS action, while relieving somewhat the onus of United States occupation, did not solve the problem of bringing political stability to the embattled nation. The United States continued its unilateral action in this regard. In May, President Johnson dispatched to Santo Domingo a top-level team of advisers—his Special Assistant for National Security Affairs McGeorge Bundy along with high officials from the Departments of State and Defense. This was more than a fact-finding mission. It was a sales effort in behalf of the new United States candidate for provisional president, Antonia Guzmán, who had been Bosch's Minister of Agriculture. A few days before, Guzmán had been flown to Washington, approved by officials, and returned to Santo Domingo. On the way south, the Bundy mission stopped off in Puerto Rico and secured Bosch's approval of Guzmán. In Santo Domingo, rebel chief Caamaño agreed to Guzmán's presidency, but Imbert disagreed on the grounds that Guzmán was merely a Bosch puppet and thus completely unacceptable to the junta. Besides, Imbert viewed *his* government as a broadly based one worthy of support, and he felt it should be allowed to wipe out the rebels. Thus the Bundy mission ended in failure.

In June a three-man OAS peace team arrived in Santo Domingo to help OAS Secretary General Jose A. Mora negotiate a settlement. This was the seventh peace-seeking mission in six weeks. This team recommended that a provisional government of nonpolitical businessmen and professors rule under a special institutional act prepared by local jurists. It also felt that the OAS should remain on the scene to keep peace and to supervise elections in six to nine months. By July both sides had agreed upon a provisional president, Héctor García Godoy, foreign minister under Bosch. Negotiations snagged, however, on other important matters, such as who would control the military. Imbert, of course, insisted that his associates would exercise military leadership in the new government. As in the past, the military in the Dominican Republic occupied a pivotal position.

The Johnson administration found that military intervention was infinitely simpler than finding a workable political arrangement. It is clear that United States action was, in the last analysis, a continuation of the policy of containment. Washington would not tolerate any more Castros or Cubas in Latin America. In his public statements, President Johnson felt the action had served its purposes:

> I think the Dominican Republic was a successful achievement. One hour after the order, troops had been landed. We brought out 5,614 people from 46 countries without a skinned ankle. . . . . But we don't have a Cuba. I told them, I told the other countries we're not going to sit here on our tail and have these people take over. We're going to have some kind of an agreement and we're going to have an election, which no Communist government would ever have allowed them to have.[12]

The imminence of a Communist take-over was not universally recognized. Juan Bosch, in whose behalf the revolt was originated, characterized this as ". . . a democratic revolution smashed by the leading democracy of the world." Should the President have consulted more closely with Congress —even asked for formal authorization? Did quick unilateral action by the United States prevent a Communist take-over in the Dominican Republic? Or did the United States actually prevent a popularly based government from returning to power? Did United States action save or permanently disable

[12]Quoted in *Newsweek* (August 2, 1965), p. 21.

the OAS as an instrument of inter-American endeavor? The crisis had raised these old questions in a new context.

As these three case studies illustrate, foreign policy making, depending in large measure on whether the issue is one that permits time for its resolution or is of a crisis character, combines both the elite decision-making model and the bargaining political model. The leaders must lead, but they cannot afford to ignore the building of political support. Foreign policy making is part of the political process, but it is a special part of it.

To Provide
for the Common Defense

23   At 8:15 on the morning of August 6, 1945, an atom bomb hurtled down toward the city of Hiroshima. At that moment there were 340,000 people living there. One minute later only 280,000 were left alive; of these, 20,000 more were to die from injuries. A total of 80,000 men, women, and children were killed by this single bomb; tens of thousands more were injured and maimed. This was a small bomb. Two days later another bomb—an "improved model" —was dropped on Nagasaki. Seven years later in the Central Pacific, a deserted island was destroyed by a fusion-type bomb—the hydrogen bomb, a device whose power far surpassed the earlier atom bomb. Spectacular improvements in nuclear-weapons technology since then have all but exhausted the supply of superlatives. Capable of delivery by intercontinental missile, the modern thermonuclear device, with its devastating blast and deadly fallout, has added a dimension of destruction to warfare that strains the imagination.

    We live in a world in which hundreds of millions of people could be killed in a single night. Although there is much dispute over precise numbers and extent of destruction, an attack on the United States could kill about 140 million people in the first sixty days. The number would continue to mount over a longer period as fallout and lack of food, shelter, and medicine took their toll.[1] Winston Churchill warned that it might no longer be possible

---

[1]Arthur T. Hadley, *The Nation's Safety and Arms Control* (Viking, 1961), pp. 34–35. See also Secretary Robert S. McNamara's testimony before the House Armed Services Committee, Feb. 18, 1964, *The New York Times* (Feb. 19, 1964), p. 10.

"for nations to fight each other and survive as nations, or even for armies to fight a battle and have at the end of it enough men on either side to fight another."[2] The age of absolute weapons has arrived.

To some, the fact that men are able to destroy their fellowmen by the millions brings the hope that they will forego such a foolish venture. To others, it means that modern civilization is doomed. But most agree that the United States must pay a high price to maintain security in a world of absolute weapons. No longer will we have a year or two to mobilize our military might while our allies hold the enemy from our shores. If an all-out thermonuclear war comes, it will be too late to start to build up our military strength. Our national policy is to have allies and arms in readiness.[3]

Friends and Neighbors

The most important of our allies are the more than 300 million people of Western Europe. They constitute an industrial and economic unit second in its productivity only to the United States and the Soviet Union and whose rate of growth in recent decades has been faster than our own or the Soviet Union's. In Western Europe are bases, plants, airports, navies, and armies, with a great military and industrial potential. True, with development of intercontinental missiles, the Soviet Union could direct an attack on this nation without occupying Western nations, and we are no longer so dependent on European bases for our own striking force, but unless Western Europe is firmly defended, its great potential could fall into the hands of the Communist world and, in the long pull of cold-war competition, its loss would vitally threaten our own security.

One of the most important links in the American defense effort is the North Atlantic Treaty Organization, composed of the United States, Canada, the United Kingdom, France, Italy, Belgium, Denmark, Iceland, Luxembourg, the Netherlands, Norway, Portugal, Greece, Turkey, and West Germany. These nations have agreed "by means of continuous and effective self-help and mutual aid" to develop their own capacities to resist armed attack. Each nation has pledged itself to regard an attack on any member of the treaty community as an attack on all.[4]

NATO has at its disposal several military commands, of which the best known are Allied Powers Europe and Allied Forces Central Europe. The United States has taken the lead in supplying troops and munitions, including nuclear weapons, to the NATO forces. We have also furnished machines, tools, and technical assistance to our allies in order to bolster their capacity to contribute to mutual defense.

Although American policy-makers envisioned a stronger NATO through an integrated military force, national differences have precluded such a thor-

[2]Paraphrase of Churchill by Roger Hilsman, *Military Policy and National Security,* William W. Kaufmann, ed. (Princeton Univ. Press, 1956), p. 44.
[3]See J. David Singer, "Stable Deterrence and Its Limits," *Western Political Quarterly* (September 1962), pp. 449–464, for a discussion of the elements of deterrence.
[4]Alvin J. Cottrell and James E. Dougherty, *The Atlantic Alliance* (Praeger, 1964).

ough combination.[5] France in particular has been a restless and even way-ward partner and has gone so far as to expel all NATO forces from her borders and to withdraw her own troops from the NATO command. The NATO council has been moved from Paris to Belgium, and other parts of the NATO structure have been dispersed to other members of the alliance. In the ever-shifting balance of European and world politics, the very nature and role of the NATO system is undergoing reconsideration.

The United States has other security commitments — we have formal defense arrangements with forty-six different nations. The OAS system, embracing Latin America, has been previously mentioned. To the north, the United States and Canada maintain a defensive alliance that predates World War II and recognizes that the two countries are a strategic entity. We have bilateral agreements of mutual defense and assistance with Nationalist China, Korea, Japan, and the Philippines and are tied to Pakistan, Iran, and Turkey through the moribund Central Treaty Organization (CTO). We are also a member of the Southeast Asia Treaty Organization (SEATO), which includes France, the United Kingdom, Australia, New Zealand, the Philippines, Pakistan, Thailand, and South Vietnam, but differences among these nations over our involvement in Vietnam have practically destroyed SEATO as an effective alliance.

Politicians, Bureaucrats, and Armed Forces

Both the President and Congress are responsible for the common defense, and both have constitutional authority to discharge that responsibility. Constitutionally, Congress appropriates the money and determines the size, structure, and organization of the fighting forces and the President is the Commander in Chief of these forces and determines where and when military power will be used. Politically, the President dominates the making of defense policy to about the same extent as he does the formulation of foreign policy.[6]

Congress declares war; the President runs it. But the declaration by Congress that a state of war exists should not be confused with the actual involvement of American armed forces in hostilities. Congress's declaration merely brings into existence a legal state that has some implications under domestic and international law. There may be fighting and no declaration of war, and there may be a declaration of war and no fighting. In fact, since World War II, Americans have fought long, costly, and bitter "wars" in Korea and South Vietnam, but Congress, although in both instances confirming and supporting the President's decisions to use military force, did not declare a formal state of war in either. In these days when an all-out use of military force by a super power could destroy the world in fifteen minutes and where limited wars engaging millions of men can be conducted without

---

[5]Wilfrid L. Kohl, "Nuclear Sharing in NATO and the Multilateral Force," *Political Science Quarterly* (March 1965), pp. 88ff.

[6]Edward A. Kolodziej, *The Uncommon Defense and Congress, 1945–1963* (Ohio State Univ. Press, 1966), pp. 484–487.

either protagonist declaring war, it may be that formal declarations by nations of a state of war are obsolete. (Since the end of World War II there has not been any declaration of war, though there have been more than 164 significant outbreaks of violence involving 82 different governments.)

The Congress, the President, the State Department, and the National Security Council make overall policy and integrate our national security programs. But the day-by-day work of developing and implementing our military programs is the job of the Department of Defense, coming to be known as DOD.

PENTAGONIA

The world's largest office building, the Pentagon, is the headquarters of the United States Defense Department, a department so big that in comparison it makes even the American Telephone and Telegraph Company look like a small-town business. The Department spends about $72 billion a year, of which $46 billion are not directly related to the Vietnam conflict. The Defense Department's expenditures equal 10 percent of the entire nation's gross national product. At work in the Pentagon are nearly 25,000 persons, including the Secretary of Defense and about 350 generals and admirals. Over 170 security officers guard the restricted areas in which the nation's military plans are made. This vast building is a communications center in constant touch with our armed forces throughout the world.

Prior to 1947 there were two separate military departments, War and Navy. But the difficulty of coordinating them during World War II led to demands for unification. In 1947 the Air Force, already an autonomous unit within the War Department, was made an independent unit, and the three military departments—Army, Navy, Air Force—were placed under the general supervision of the Secretary of Defense.[7] The Unification Act of 1947, a hesitant first step, was a bundle of compromises between the Army, which favored a tightly integrated department, and the Navy, which wanted a loosely federated structure. It also reflected compromises between congressmen who felt that disunity and interservice rivalries were undermining our defense efforts, and congressmen who, on the other hand, feared that a unified defense establishment would defy civilian control and smother dissenting views.

The 1947 act had not been long in operation before it became apparent that the Department of Defense, which was supposed to be the nation's sword, looked more like a pitchfork. All that the act had really accomplished was to bring the military services under a common organization chart. Instead of moving from two military departments to one, we had ended up with three. Despite further centralizing moves, congressional amendments in 1949, and presidential directives in 1953, each service retained considerable autonomy and the Defense Department was unable to develop an integrated military program.

In 1958, when headlines featured factional struggles among military services while the Russians were sending up sputniks, President Eisenhower

[7]For a comprehensive analysis, see Paul Y. Hammond, *Organizing for Defense: The American Military Establishment in the Twentieth Century* (Princeton Univ. Press, 1961).

came forward with Defense Department reorganization proposals. He urged Congress to appropriate all funds to the Secretary of Defense rather than to the separate military departments and to give the Secretary full control over the armed services, including the authority to transfer or abolish combatant functions and to establish direct lines of command between his office and operational forces in the field. The President also asked that the Joint Chiefs of Staff be strengthened by giving its Chairman a vote, that the staff be enlarged, and that each service chief be allowed to delegate his command duties so that he could devote most of his time to the work of the Joint Chiefs.

The President's plan to unify the Defense Department by increasing the authority of the Secretary of Defense and by centralizing the Joint Chiefs was subjected to heavy congressional fire. Many congressmen, fearful of creating a Prussian-type military establishment, argued that instead of concentrating greater authority in the Defense Secretary, what was needed was a cleaning out of the large number of assistant secretaries of defense and assistants to the assistant secretaries, positions that had been spawned in the Defense Secretary's office. They contended that with layer upon layer of civilian staffs, with so many initials to obtain on every action, and with so much red tape, nothing was getting done.

President Eisenhower felt so strongly about his proposals for Defense Department reorganization that he used the prestige and influence of his office to promote their acceptance. In the end, the Defense Department Reorganization Act of 1958 gave the President most of what he wanted. Congress, however, refused to approve the appropriation of funds to the Secretary of Defense. Furthermore, at the prompting of the Naval Air Force, Marine Corps, and National Guard (which groups, it was pointed out, live in constant fear that somebody will abolish them),[8] Congress insisted that the Secretary of Defense notify the House and Senate armed services committees if he contemplates any major change in combatant functions. If within thirty days either committee disapproves, each chamber has another forty days to stop the order from taking effect.

Congress also refused to repeal a provision, which President Eisenhower called legalized insubordination, authorizing a secretary of a military department or a member of the Joint Chiefs to make any recommendations he wishes to Congress about Defense Department matters even if his recommendations are contrary to Defense Department policy. Eisenhower's view, like that of other Presidents, was that he was the Commander in Chief, that the Secretary of Defense was his deputy, and that it was the duty of all military men to support before Congress and the country the agreed-on policies of the Defense Department regardless of their own judgment.

McNAMARA AND CREEPING UNIFICATION

Under Presidents Kennedy and Johnson there were no legislative changes in the structure of the Department of Defense, but the fact that Robert McNamara was Secretary of Defense led to greater changes in the operation of the Department of Defense than have been effected by any act of Congress.

[8]Ivan Hinderaker, "The Eisenhower Administration: The Last Years," in *American Government Annual, 1959–1960* (Holt, 1959), p. 82.

Secretary McNamara brought to the Department a small group of men, trained chiefly as economists and analysts. "Perhaps never before had so much civilian talent, sophisticated in military strategy, been assembled under a Defense Secretary himself known for exceptional intellect combined with the ability to make difficult decisions with dispatch."[9] Secretary McNamara and his "whiz kids," as they came to be called, with strong support from the White House, proceeded to coordinate the supply and intelligence activities of the services, create unified military commands, and bring more unification to the Department than Congress had been willing to sanction by legislation. Systems analysis and program budgeting were introduced as means of evaluating weapons and allocating funds among various commands and services. Secretary McNamara and his staff had their own ideas about strategic policies; unlike many past civilian leaders of the Defense Department, they raised questions about military strategy and overruled military men when they felt that the "top brass" lacked sound reasons. The Secretary, supported by Presidents Kennedy and Johnson, even redistributed military funds in order to redress what he believed had been an unbalanced reliance by the Eisenhower administration on nuclear power.[10] With the build-up of flexible, conventional military power, the United States has more options available to it in order to support its foreign policies.

Some congressmen and some military chieftains were critical of Secretary McNamara's iron-handed control of the Defense Department and of his centralization of authority in his own office and away from the civilian secretaries of each department and the military heads. After McNamara's resignation as Secretary, some doubted that the "McNamara revolution" would have a lasting impact on the Defense Department, but it had demonstrated that the power of the Secretary of Defense is more a result of his political position—chiefly of his support by the President—than it is of his legal authority or hierarchical position.[11]

KEY MILITARY AGENCIES

The Armed Forces Policy Council is the Defense Department's "little cabinet." It is composed of the Department Secretary, deputy secretary, the three civilian secretaries of the military departments, the director of defense research and engineering, the Chairman of the Joint Chiefs of Staff, and the chief of staff of each of the services. It advises the Secretary on matters of broad policy.

The Joint Chiefs of Staff serve as the principal military advisers to the President, the National Security Council, and the Secretary of Defense. They comprise the military heads of the three armed services, the commandant of the Marine Corps—whenever a matter comes up directly concerning the Marine Corps—and a chairman, all appointed by the President with the con-

---

[9]Harry Howe Ransom, *Can American Democracy Survive Cold War?* (Doubleday, 1963). See also Charles J. Hitch, *Decision-Making for Defense* (Univ. of California Press, 1966), pp. 22–58.

[10]William K. Kaufmann, *The McNamara Strategy* (Harper, 1964).

[11]John C. Ries, *The Management of Defense: Organization and Control of the U.S. Armed Services* (Johns Hopkins Press, 1964), p. 198.

sent of the Senate for a two-year term and eligible in peacetime for only one reappointment. Behind double steel doors in the Pentagon the Joint Chiefs shape strategic plans, work out joint supply programs, review major supply and personnel requirements, formulate programs for joint training, make recommendations to the Secretary of Defense on the establishment of unified commands in strategic areas, and provide American representation on the military commissions of the United Nations, NATO, and SEATO.

The Chairman of the Joint Chiefs takes precedence over all other military officers. He presides over the meetings of the Joint Chiefs, prepares the agenda, directs the staff, and informs the Secretary of Defense and the President of issues on which the Joint Chiefs have been unable to reach agreement.

At times, the Joint Chiefs are unable to develop united strategies or to agree on the allocation of resources. There is more to disputes among military services, however, than mere professional jealousies. The technological revolution in warfare has rendered obsolete existing concepts about military missions. In the past, it made sense to divide command among land, sea, and air forces, but today "technology makes a mockery of such distinctions."[12] Under the impact of ever-changing military technology and the outmoding of traditional divisions of roles and missions, each service supports a concept allowing it to claim a decisive role, each "seeks to control weapons which will enable it to carry out that role, virtually independently of operations of other services."[13]

Sometimes interservice rivalries break out in the Congress and the press. Quasi-official organizations, such as the Association of the United States Army, the Navy League, and the Air Force Association, lobby openly in behalf of their particular service. Behind the scenes the military men themselves are active. The President tries to keep interservice disputes inside the administration, but the military commander who feels that administration policy threatens the national security is in something of a quandary. He is taught to respect civilian supremacy and to obey his civilian superiors. But which civilian superiors? The President as Commander in Chief? Or should he—as he has a legal right to do—report to Congress, which is also a civilian superior? A few officers resolve the dilemma of conflicting loyalties to President, Congress, and conscience by resigning so that they will be free to

Courtesy Ed Fisher; copyright 1963 Saturday Review, Inc.

"I'll never forget his ringing words: 'Damn the Appropriations Committee—full speed ahead!'"

[12]Henry A. Kissinger, *Nuclear Weapons and Foreign Policy* (Doubleday, 1958), p. 228.

[13]William R. Kintner et al., *Forging a New Sword: A Study of the Department of Defense* (Harper, 1958), p. 172.

carry their views to the nation. More commonly, military men who wish to express dissents from official policy get their views to Congress by resorting to the Washington practice of "leaking" information to the press. Furthermore, when testifying before congressional committees it is not difficult for officers to support policies to the Defense Department only in a formal sense and to allow their real views to come across.

The continuation of interservice differences has led some to advocate the replacement of the Joint Chiefs by a single chief of staff, the complete integration of all military into a single branch, and the reassignment of forces in terms of strategic missions rather than means of locomotion. Although such a system has had the support of many high-ranking Army and some Air Force officers, it is opposed by most Navy officers and most congressmen. When McNamara was Secretary, there was considerable integration of military forces under single commands for each strategic mission but without any alterations in outward forms. Strategic policy, much like that of any other area, is the result not of a collective process of rational inquiry but of a mutual process of give and take.[14] Whether strategic policies are worked out within the Defense Department, the White House, or Congress, the decisions result from a political process in which some measure of consensus is essential; conflicts among the participants are not necesssarily evil. As one admiral put it: "How curious it is that the Congress *debates*, the Supreme Court *deliberates*, but for some reason or other the Joint Chiefs of Staff just *bicker!*"[15]

Nuclear Policy in the Space Age

During the first years of the atomic age, no basic changes in military strategy seemed to be called for. Our atomic monopoly reinforced our traditional policy of not maintaining large standing armies. Even after the Soviet Union exploded its first atom bomb, the situation was not seriously altered. We believed that our technological superiority would keep us ahead of the Soviets for many years to come and that from our overseas bases we could rain down hundreds of bombs in the event of attack. At the same time, our defense system would reduce the enemy's ability to deliver these expensive weapons to American targets. Although wars would be terribly costly, it was still possible to talk about winning such wars.

Then, on October 4, 1957 the Moscow radio announced that the Soviet Union had placed in orbit the first earth satellite. The space age was born and the military implications were terrifyingly clear. The Soviet Union had beaten us to the punch and was perfecting the intercontinental missile. Not only that, but the Soviet Union had an ample supply of nuclear weapons. A balance of terror suddenly loomed. The enemy had sufficient power to destroy us, and the fact that we could do the same to him provided little com-

[14]Samuel P. Huntington, *The Common Defense: Strategic Programs in National Politics* (Columbia Univ. Press, 1961), preface and *passim.*
[15]Quoted in *ibid.*, p. 170. See also David W. Tarr, "Military Technology and The Policy Process," *Western Political Quarterly* (March 1965), pp. 135ff.

fort to Americans. It has become clear that atomic weapons cannot be used except under extreme provocation and—we hope—the most remote circumstances.

A MILITARY STRATEGY FOR THE 1970s

The emergence of the Soviet Union as a major nuclear power and the explosion by France and Red China of their own nuclear weapons presaged the proliferation of nations capable of destroying the world. These ominous developments forced the United States to rethink its military strategy. Most people agreed that even after massing sufficient retaliatory power to destroy the enemy, it would be dangerous to relax, for he might achieve a technological breakthrough giving him a temporary advantage, such as a system to stop missiles or reduce the dangers of radiation.

Army spokesmen, however, as well as many students of foreign policy, are critical of the tendency to place so much emphasis on massive weapons at the expense of mobile tactical forces capable of being used in limited wars. They contend that the desire to balance the national government's budget by reducing the Army and relying on relatively less expensive atomic power has left us dangerously exposed to local aggressions. Neither the United States nor the Soviet Union, they argue, is likely to start a thermonuclear war of mass destruction, because such a war would lead to their own extermination. Furthermore, these critics argue, to rely only on massive retaliation and weapons of mass destruction actually increases the likelihood of all-out war. For if the Soviet Union is led to believe that these are our only weapons and that we plan to use them, the Russians might be tempted to shoot first, especially if they have a temporary missile superiority. But even more likely, leaders of the Soviet Union know that the United States will not let loose a catastrophic conflict merely to prevent aggressions such as those in Laos in 1959, Berlin in 1961, South Vietnam in 1965, or Czechoslovakia in 1968. The risk of unleashing an all-out war would be too great, and it would bring the condemnation of the entire world down on the United States. Nor, according to this view, is atomic power suitable to stop Soviet conquest of Western Europe, because its use would also destroy our allies. Hence, the Army and others argue, we must spend more on forces that can be used restrictively in order to prevent the enemy from nibbling at the edge of the free world.[16]

Air Force spokesmen and most Navy men, on the other hand, contend that to slow down the buildup of our atomic weapons would be dangerous. They argue that we have not achieved decisive superiority; and until we do, the Soviet Union will be tempted, despite the risks involved, to take advantage of any superiority it might gain. The Soviets have intercontinental missiles and a formidable air defense, so that an all-out effort is needed. We must depend on our strategic air power and atomic submarines and not divert too many resources to limited-war forces. Some spokesmen for air power—but not necessarily for the Air Force—argue that mass armies are obsolete, that air power can be used for limited conflicts, and that by concentrating on air

[16]Kissinger's book, *op. cit.*, was influential in presenting arguments for strengthening our limited-warfare forces. See also Matthew B. Ridgway, *Soldier* (Harper, 1956), pp. 295–361.

From *Straight Herblock* (Simon & Schuster, 1964).

"No Fair—I Can't Afford A Gun."

power and missiles we will be able to get more defense for less money. They believe it is foolish to commit our forces to peripheral small-scale wars and that we need only the ability to retaliate massively if the enemy starts trouble.

The election of President Kennedy and the appointment of Secretary McNamara resolved for the moment these differences over military policies, for one of President Kennedy's highest priorities was "to get the nuclear genie back into the bottle," by providing other forces as means of exerting American influence. President Johnson supported this program and during recent years, especially under the impetus of Vietnam needs, there has been a dramatic shift in emphasis toward building up conventional, flexible, and mobile military forces. Henry Kissinger, President Nixon's appointee to the post of Special Assistant for National Security Affairs, is also a proponent of limited-warfare forces. The choice of Kissinger presages the Nixon administration's support for these military strategies rather than those pursued by the Eisenhower administration.

These conflicts over appropriate military strategies clearly illustrate the interrelations between military and foreign policies. A military program that places major reliance on massive retaliation, for example, makes allies less important than does a policy of maintaining forces able to resist invasions without resorting to mass destruction. A foreign policy pledging help to nations threatened by Communist-backed guerrillas is meaningless unless we have the kind of military power to back the pledge.

SECOND LINE OF DEFENSE

In the past, our nation's practice was to rely on a small standing force that could be joined in an emergency by all able-bodied men. Today, however, our armed forces are a complex organization of trained specialists. It takes many months, even years, to train a man to serve with the modern fighting machine. The time lag between the decision to create a large military organization and its actual existence as a fighting unit can be fatal.

Today, standing behind the combat forces is a second line of defense—the Ready Reserves—consisting of the National Guard, and the Army, Navy, Air

531

Force, and Coast Guard Reserves. In a thermonuclear war, these reserves would probably be of restricted use, but in a limited war such as that in Korea and Vietnam, we have seen that these reserves can be quickly called to duty by the President. Reserve personnel take part in weekly drills and attend summer camps so that they will be ready to serve with a minimum of additional training.

Congress has long had a special interest in preserving the citizen-soldier concept, and the National Guard and other reserve components have strong political backing through the National Guard Association and the Reserve Officers Association. "Congressional primacy of interest in reserve affairs has been exceptional in comparison with the ascendancy of the executive branch in national defense policy-making."[17]

An important component of the Ready Reserves is the National Guard, composed of the organized militias of the states.[18] Except when called into federal service, the Guard is under the command of the governors of the respective states. The governors commission the officers and, through their adjutant generals, supervise the training of the militias. The national government, however, provides most of the money for training and equipment and has established minimum standards.

A state-controlled militia is an established tradition. In fact, in 1787 the states insisted on the adoption of the Second Amendment to prohibit the national government from depriving them of the right to maintain their own militias. During the War of 1812 some states would not even let their militias be used outside their own boundaries. Today, however, the national government exercises far-reaching supervision over the National Guard. Congress has the authority to call state militias into federal service, and it has given the President power to call the National Guard into immediate federal service. Once this is done, the Guard becomes an integral part of the national fighting forces, subject only to such limitations as Congress may impose.

The chief purpose of the Guard today is to provide a trained reserve for the national military forces. For this reason and because the states have not always done a good job of training, it has been suggested that the National Guard be federalized and combined with the organized reserves to provide one reserve unit as an integral part of the federal defense establishment. Every such proposal, however, has drawn little support and much opposition in Congress.

Science and Security

When the atom bomb was dropped on Hiroshima, few could doubt any longer that science had become a decisive element in defense. Wars are fought and won in large measure in a nation's scientific laboratories.

[17]William F. Levantrosser, *Congress and the Citizen-Soldier* (Ohio State Univ. Press, 1967), p. viii.

[18]See W. H. Riker, *Soldiers of the States: The Role of the National Guard in American Democracy* (Public Affairs Press, 1957). See also Martha Derthwick, *The National Guard in Politics* (Harvard Univ. Press, 1965).

The nature of war has been altered by the invention of the proximity fuse, the snorkel submarine, radar, sonar, the guided missile, and nuclear weapons. The scientists' contribution to the war effort during World War II is well known. But what is not so well known is that the scientists drew "heavily on the accumulated stockpile of fundamental scientific knowledge that was all but exhausted when fighting stopped."[19] Further advance has depended on the extension of fundamental scientific knowledge, on what is sometimes called pure science. Such science is not preoccupied with finding more powerful explosives or better devices to guide missiles, but with unlocking the mysteries of the world in which we live.

It is essential, therefore, to create the conditions under which scientific inquiry can best operate. Hitler's misunderstanding of the importance of scientific research led him to expel from Germany those who did not conform to the "new order." Our own preoccupation with applied science, and particularly with applications that have military significance, could tend to exhaust our fund of scientific knowledge without replenishing it. For this reason the government has established a National Science Foundation, which, through scholarships and other forms of assistance, helps to train scientists without regard to the immediate military value of their possible contributions.

The military departments themselves have tapped the knowledge and skill of scientists in commercial laboratories and universities.[20] In addition, the scientist has played an increasingly greater role as an adviser to the policy-maker.[21] The problem of integrating scientific and military knowledge is an essential but difficult task. Military men, like other professionals, tend to be cautious in adopting new techniques. In the past, almost every new weapon of war—gunpowder, submarines, tanks, airplanes, proximity fuses—had to be pushed on the military by civilians.

Should scientific knowledge be kept secret or disseminated as widely as possible? To stamp every new research finding "top secret" in the interests of national security would be disastrous, for scientific progress depends on the wide sharing of information. Many scientists, wishing to exchange data with their colleagues, question whether we are not losing more than we gain by our excessive concern over secrecy.

Arms Control and National Security

For many, the promise of avoiding a thermonuclear war lies not in the development of a deterrent capacity based on military weapons and elaborate civil defense, but rather in arms control and disarmament. A world in which conflicts are resolved without resort to force has been an objective of man for many centuries. Realization of such a hope in the near future indeed

[19]Vannevar Bush, *Modern Arms and Free Men* (Simon and Schuster, 1949), p. 12.
[20]Gene M. Lyons, "The Growth of National Security Research," *Journal of Politics* (August 1963), pp. 489 ff.
[21]R. Gilpin and C. Wright (eds.), *Scientists in National Policy-Making* (Columbia Univ. Press, 1964), See also Avery Leiserson, "Scientists and the Policy Process," *The American Political Science Review* (June 1965), pp. 480 ff.

seems dim as both sides in the East-West conflict continue to build massive military systems. Nevertheless, disarmament and arms control are much-debated goals and a part of policy-planning.

The policy of deterrence holds that a conflict of values is the root cause of the East-West confrontation and that military force is but a reflection of that basic conflict. Proponents of arms control and disarmament share this view to some degree, but argue that armaments themselves are also a fundamental cause of international tension. They warn of the immense risks of the deterrence system—human error, a failure in the warning network, a misguided missile, the inevitable expansion of the number of nations with nuclear weapons. But they paint an even grimmer picture of a future without arms control—one with heightened tension as the result of the development of more devastating nuclear warheads and longer-ranged, more accurate delivery vehicles; the threat of biological, chemical, and even radiological weapons; the constant surveillance of spy satellites; ever-increasing defense budgets and ever-increasing commitments of human resources to weapons technology.

Some advocates of disarmament feel this possibility can be forestalled only by general and complete renunciation of force with the elimination of virtually all military power. The Soviets purport to favor comprehensive disarmament but as yet have given no sign of willingness to move meaningfully toward that goal. A vocal minority in the West proposes that in order to save the world from nuclear destruction, the West must unilaterally take a significant first step in disarmament. A skeptical majority suspects that the Communists would not reciprocate but rather take advantage of our vulnerability.

A more feasible alternative to the arms race is limited disarmament, generally known as arms control. Beginning with nuclear weapons, gradual arms reduction by both sides has two immediate objectives: first, to reduce the likelihood of war and, if unsuccessful in this, second, to diminish the violence of armed conflict. Within this policy, mutual arms reduction would be accomplished through negotiations.[22]

The United States, Britain, and the Soviet Union began talks in 1958 to seek a treaty banning nuclear tests. Simultaneously, the three powers began a voluntary moratorium on testing. Although France, not involved in the test-ban negotiations, detonated a nuclear device in 1960, the moratorium was honored by the major powers for almost three years, until the Soviet Union resumed tests. Following the Russian tests, the United States and Britain initiated their own series. Despite testing on both sides, negotiations continued in Geneva.

On August 5, 1963, the United Kingdom, the Soviet Union, and the United States agreed on a treaty to ban all nuclear explosions in the atmosphere or in any other place if there was any danger of radioactive debris. The treaty permits nations to engage in underground testing and has an escape clause permitting nations on the basis of three months notice to withdraw from the obligations of the treaty, but its ratification by the United States and the Soviet Union and the subsequent adherence to it by more than one hundred

---

[22]For a balanced overview of arms control and disarmament see Hadley, *op. cit.*, Donald G. Brennan (ed.), *Arms Control, Disarmament and National Security* (Braziller, 1961); and Louis Henkin (ed.), *Arms Control, Issues for the Public* (Prentice-Hall, 1961).

nations is the first concrete step toward nuclear disarmament. However, there are two notable exceptions to the list of nations adhering to the test ban, France and China, both of whom have tested bombs and contaminated the atmosphere since the treaty was signed by all the other nations.

The test-ban treaty was followed in 1967 by the International Treaty on the Peaceful Uses of Outer Space, banning the use of satellites as vehicles or platforms for the launching of nuclear weapons, and in 1968 by the signing of the Nonproliferation Treaty and its presentation to the Senate for ratification. The Nonproliferation Treaty pledges the nuclear powers not to disseminate nuclear devices to nonnuclear powers for at least twenty-five years and the nonnuclear nations not to seek to acquire such devices. Again the notable absences from these treaties were Communist China and France, but the agreements marked significant steps in limiting the "nuclear club" to a relatively small number of nations and thus in avoiding the critical situation that could develop if a substantial number of nations had the capability of starting a war of total devastation. Furthermore, on the signing of the Nonproliferation Treaty, both the United States and the Soviet Union announced that they had agreed to begin talks about ways of limiting the arms race in offensive and defensive nuclear missile systems. These small signs have become the major channel through which the tensions between the East and the West have gradually started to ease. Deterrence and disarmament are both strategies of national security.

Security and Liberty—Not by Power Alone

As long as the United States exists in a world of sovereign, independent nations, it must look to its defenses. As we have seen, this means large standing military forces, adequately trained reserves, the application of scientific and other knowledge to military problems, a strong and stable economy, an alert and trained citizen body, and powerful allies. To fail to do what is necessary to provide for the common defense would be disastrous. But it would be equally disastrous to depend solely on military power to provide security. Not even the United States has sufficient resources, even if the people wished it, to control the destinies of the international community. Politics is conflict but it is also cooperation, and power should be used to help build the kind of world community in which armies and tanks will one day be archaic.

What should be the role of the military in a democratic society? A fear of the military is deeply rooted in American traditions. The Framers of the Constitution, recognizing that military domination was incompatible with free government, wove into the Constitution several precautions. The President, an elected officer, is Commander in Chief of the armed forces; with the Senate's consent, he commissions all officers. Congress makes the rules for the governance of the military services; and appropriations for the Army are limited to a two-year period. Congress has supplemented these precautions by requiring that the Secretary of Defense and the heads of the military departments be civilians and by devising elaborate procedures to prevent the military from controlling the selection of men for West Point, Annapolis, and the Air Force Academy.

In the past, professional military men were largely ignored. During time of peace, their recommendations were shrugged off or the generals were accused of wanting war. A career in the armed services was not attractive. The military mind was stereotyped as conservative, stodgy, and unimaginative. But failure to heed the words of our professional soldiers, sailors, and airmen has cost us much. At the other extreme is the danger of elevating them into positions where what they have to say is accepted uncritically. This would be disastrous both for the preservation of liberty and for the promotion of security.

War and defense today, more than ever before, are too important and too complex to leave to the generals. As we have seen, security programs require the talents of the bureaucrat, social scientist, natural scientist, labor leader, engineer, industrialist, and all other professionals. What the military expert knows must be meshed with what others know. But he may not know enough to be trusted with the running of our defense program.

Maintaining civilian supremacy over the military today is harder than ever. There is no longer a clear separation between military and civilian spheres of activity. As national security problems are brought to the fore, the generals, often reluctantly, are called upon to pass judgment on issues that in the past have not been thought to be within the scope of their competence. At the same time, their civilian superiors find it more difficult to secure the information they need to exercise control. In many cases it is the military who decide what information must remain top secret. Congressmen and the general public are at a disadvantage in exercising supremacy over the military.

The dangers to liberty arising from the *garrison state*—a nation that is constantly prepared for total war and that is organized to exert its military might—were recognized by Alexander Hamilton when he wrote:

Safety from external danger is the most powerful director of national conduct. Even the ardent love of liberty will after a time give way to its dictates. The violent destruction of life and property incident to war, the continual effort and alarm attendant on a state of continual danger, will compel nations the most attached to liberty to resort for repose and security to institutions which have a tendency to destroy their civil and political rights. To be more safe, they at length become willing to run the risk of being less free.[23]

Professor Harold D. Lasswell has summarized the impact of miltarization upon individual freedom as follows:

To militarize is to governmentalize. It is also to centralize. To centralize is to enhance the effective control of the executive over decisions, and thereby to reduce the control exercised by courts and legislatures. To centralize is to enhance the role of the military in the allocation of national resources. Continuing fear of external attack sustains an atmosphere of distrust that finds expression in spy hunts directed against fellow officials and fellow citi-

[23]*Federalist No. 8* (Modern Library, 1937), p. 42. For a recent treatment of the problem, see Samuel P. Huntington, Civilian Control and the Constitution," *The American Political Science Review* (September 1956), pp. 676–699.

zens. Outspoken criticism of official measures launched for the national defense is more and more resented as unpatriotic and subversive of the common good. The community at large, therefore, acquiesces in denials of freedom that go beyond the technical requirements of military security.[24]

The threat of militarization comes not only from the military, however. As John McCloy wrote,

> I doubt whether we need fear the men in uniform in this regard [seeking unfettered power] any more than the man or men in civil clothes to whom we have given far greater authority. Indeed, as many examples as there are of authority usurped by generals or admirals, I believe history records as many instances of usurpation on the part of civilians with at least as many disastrous results.[25]

The United States has been fortunate. It has never developed a military caste. Its generals and admirals have demonstrated respect for civilian authority. American soldiers have been imbued with democratic principles of civilian supremacy. Now that the skills required of military men are so varied, it becomes all the more necessary to educate them not only to be good soldiers but also to be good democrats. For it is by "civilianizing" the military that much can be done to prevent militarizing the civilians.[26]

In his last message to the nation as President, Dwight Eisenhower pointed out that this country is now committed to a vast armament industry and maintains "a defense establishment employing 3.5 million persons and spending huge sums." He warned:

> This conjunction of an immense military establishment and a large arms industry is new in American experience. The total influence—economic, political, even spiritual—is felt in every city, every State house, every office of the Federal government. We recognize the imperative need for this development. Yet we must not fail to comprehend its grave implications. Our toil, resources, and livelihood are involved; so is the very structure of our society.[27]

[24]Harold D. Lasswell, "Does the Garrison State Threaten Civil Rights?" *Civil Rights in America,* The *Annals* of the American Academy of Political and Social Science (May 1951), p. 111.

[25]*Task Force Report on National Security Organization,* p. 59.

[26]For a different interpretation, see Samuel P. Huntington, *The Soldier and the State* (Harvard Univ. Press, 1957), especially Chap. 17. See also Harry L. Coles (ed.), *Total War and the Cold War: Problems in the Civilian Control of the Military* (Ohio State Univ. Press, 1962).

[27]*The New York Times* (January 18, 1961), p. 22.

Government as Regulator

24　　It is impossible to draw a sharp line between the activities of the national government in waging war and peace on the one hand and its so-called domestic functions on the other. The two are inextricably intertwined. The foreign policies administered by the State Department have a direct impact on American businessmen and farmers. Fighting a war mobilizes both the nation's economy and the whole peacetime bureaucracy. Our foreign economic policies directly affect employment, wages, prices, and taxes at home. We discuss domestic activities separately from foreign affairs only for purposes of convenience.

　　Americans have always been quick to criticize their country's foreign policy, but no one has ever seriously questioned that foreign policy must be made by the national government. Even the most waspish critic of bureaucratic inefficiency has never urged that foreign affairs be turned over to businessmen, for example, or that the job of defending the country against attack be turned over to the state governments. But on domestic questions, people differ not only over what policies should be adopted, but also over whether government should act at all and, if so, which government. And if they agree that government should act, the dispute shifts to: How far should government go? What kinds of control or procedure should it use?

　　This chapter and the next two will describe some of the functions of our national government and will provide illustrations of the major techniques of governmental action, but no attempt will be made to analyze the operations of all federal agencies or all federal programs. Our concern is not so much what particular governmental bureaus do or the precise description of a particular agency's organization; it is to convey some idea of the general forms of the national government's activities and to indicate persistent problems.

In this chapter we shall explore the national government's regulatory role—regulatory in the narrow sense of trying to limit the activities of some of its citizens, to prevent bad practices, to restrict one interest from interfering with the rights of others (as defined, of course, by the men in power). This is government in a somewhat negative or restrictive sense. In the next chapter we shall turn to some of the promotional functions of government. But it is really impossible to make a sharp distinction between regulation and promotion. *Regulation* means setting restraints on individuals and groups, directly compelling them to take, or not to take, certain actions. *Promotion* means encouraging, strengthening, safeguarding, or advancing the interests of particular persons, groups, industries, or sectors of the economy. But to regulate one interest may be to promote another. Similarly, promotion can be used to regulate interests. Often either one, or a combination, can be used to carry out a public policy.

The main regulatory task of the national government is the policing of powerful interests such as business and labor. But, of course, government is not the only regulating agency. Regulatory control is also exercised by families, friends, church, and the overall social environment, as we saw in earlier chapters. In addition, the type of activity described in this chapter is only one type of regulation. Government also acts as a regulating agency in some of its newer functions, as we shall see later.

Regulating Business

Businessmen today operate in a complex web of national, state, and local laws. This was not always so. Business has never been altogether free of restrictive legislation, of course, but during much of the latter part of the nineteenth century our national policy was to leave business alone. Most of the nation's leaders, and the country at large, believed broadly in *laissez faire*—hands off. Given their head, businessmen set about developing a nation that was enormously rich in natural resources. The heroes of the 1870s and 1880s were not politicians but business magnates—the Rockefellers, Morgans, Carnegies, and Fricks. "From rags to riches" became the nation's motto.

Then, toward the end of the century, a reaction set in. Sharp depressions rocked the nation's economy and threw men out of work. Millions of people labored long hours in factory and field for little money. Muckrakers revealed that some of the most famous business leaders had indulged in shoddy practices and corrupt deals, taking a "public-be-damned" attitude. A demand for government regulation of business sprang up, and a series of national and state laws were passed to correct specific abuses. These laws followed no methodical plan or philosophy; rather, they were adopted on the pragmatic assumption that each problem could be handled as it arose.

A typical cartoon of a half-century ago against the "trusts."

We Americans have mixed feelings about big business. On one hand, we are easily impressed by bigness—the tallest skyscraper, the largest football stadium, the biggest corporation—and the efficiency and power that seem to go with bigness. On the other hand, we often assert that our economic system functions best under conditions of fair competition among small business-men. This dichotomy has been reflected in our attempts to prevent monopoly and restraint of trade.

The popular clamor for government control late in the nineteenth century culminated in attacks on monopoly. The trustbusters argued that small business was being squeezed out by huge trusts in oil, sugar, whisky, steel, and other commodities. In 1890 Congress responded to this sentiment by passing the famous Sherman Antitrust Act. Designed to foster competition and stop the growth of private monopolies, the act made clear its intention "to protect trade and commerce against unlawful restraints and monopolies." Henceforth, persons making con-tracts, combinations, or conspiracies in restraint of trade in interstate and foreign commerce could be sued for damages, required to stop their ille-gal practices, and subjected to criminal penalties.

Presidents Cleveland and McKinley showed little interest in enforcing the Sherman Act. Indeed, a Supreme Court decision in the Sugar Trust case (1895) considerably limited the scope of the act by ruling that a sugar-refining company that produced 98 percent of the sugar used in the United States was primarily engaged in manufacturing rather than interstate commerce and hence could not be regulated by the national government.[1] In 1901 Theodore Roosevelt became President, and, wielding a "big stick," he responded to the growing sentiment against monopoly. Yet even Roosevelt talked more than he acted; like most Americans he had conflicting attitudes toward big-ness. During the Taft and Wilson administrations, the trusts were prosecuted more vigorously, and court rulings gave the rather vague provisions of the act more definite meaning. Certain consolidations were not permitted if a clear intent to monopolize was proved. Voting trusts, pools, and some collu-sive practices were sharply curbed.

The Clayton Act in 1914 further clarified antitrust policy. It outlawed specific abuses affecting interstate commerce, such as charging different prices to different buyers, granting rebates, and making false statements

[1]*United States* v. *E. C. Knight Co.* (1895).

about competitors in order to take business away from them. Corporations were prohibited from acquiring stock (amended in 1950 to include assets) in competing concerns if such acquisitions substantially lessened interstate competition, and interlocking directorates in large corporations were banned. Labor had been enraged by a Supreme Court ruling that applied the Sherman Act to a union boycott against the products of a nonunion manufacturer; the Clayton Act exempted labor from the 1890 act and was greeted by unions as their Magna Carta. Later legislation exempted various business activities from the Sherman Act.

Antitrust activity languished in the 1920s. Times were prosperous; the Republican administrations were actively pro-business; and the Department of Justice, charged with enforcing the Sherman Act, paid little attention to it. Then, during the Depression popular resentment mounted against big business as abuses were revealed. At first the Roosevelt administration tried a new method—industrial self-government—under the National Industrial Recovery Act of 1933 (NIRA), which tried to promote cooperation among businessmen by allowing them to work out codes of fair competition. This was seen as a virtual suspension of government antitrust policy. The NIRA, however, was invalidated by the Supreme Court in 1935.[2]

Subsequent years saw a revival of trustbusting. In the late 1930s a well-publicized committee of congressmen and New Deal experts, the Temporary National Economic Committee, made an elaborate investigation of economic concentration and monopoly. It unanimously urged that enforcement be strengthened "to cope with the gigantic aggregations of capital which have become so dominant in our economic life." Under the leadership of Thurman Arnold, a former Yale professor, the antitrust division of the Justice Department was given a larger staff to commence trustbusting in earnest. In one year, 1940, the government instituted 345 suits; of the 280 suits that were terminated, the government won 265.

Although antitrust activity flagged during World War II, it was revived by postwar administrations, and it is evident that "vigorous antitrust enforcement has become a bipartisan policy."[3] Much of the Justice Department's attention in recent years has been focused on corporate mergers. Although mere size of a corporation is not viewed as an offense against the antitrust laws, the Department has carefully scrutinized the effect that a merger may have on the market. As the former Kennedy and Johnson antitrust chief described this policy:

The relative market size of the enterprise involved clearly is important. An acquisition or merger by a company already very large in relation to its market is far more likely to lessen competition substantially or tend to create a monopoly in violation of the antitrust laws than a similar transaction by a small company. But size alone is not controlling. . . . Competition, rather than size, is the ultimate criterion.[4]

The main burden of measuring business practices by the antitrust yardstick falls to the federal courts. In hammering out the extent of permissible

[2]*Schechter Poultry Corp.* v. *United States* (1935).
[3]Merle Fainsod, Lincoln Gordon, and J. C. Palamountain, Jr., *Government and the American Economy* (Norton, 1959), p. 616.
[4]Lee Loevinger, "Antitrust Is Pro-Business," *Fortune* (August 1962), p. 130.

corporate power consistent with antitrust laws, the judges over the years have found these factors to be relevant:

> The number of firms in the market; their effective size from the standpoint of technological development, and from the standpoint of competition with substitute materials and foreign trade; national security interests in the maintenance of strong productive facilities, and maximum scientific research and development; together with the public interest in lowered costs and uninterrupted production.[5]

In striking down mergers and sustaining antitrust prosecutions, the Supreme Court in recent years has indicated its agreement with the executive interpretation of the antitrust laws. In the DuPont case, the Supreme Court held that the big chemical company ownership of stock in General Motors gave DuPont an advantage in the market for automobile fabrics and finishes that threatened competition in that market; DuPont was ordered to divest itself of its GM stock over a ten-year period.[6] In the Brown Shoe case, the Court noted that what must be considered was a merger's ". . . probable effects upon the economic way of life sought to be preserved by Congress. . . . Congress desired to promote competition through the protection of viable, small, locally owned business. Congress appreciated that occasional higher costs and prices might result. . . . It resolved these competing considerations in favor of decentralization."[7]

Although the past decade has been one of vigorous antitrust enforcement, control over some markets by a relatively few giant corporations seems to have been unaffected by government action. It is difficult to determine precisely what is happening to the economic marketplace, because the figures are subject to varying interpretations; the interpretations are part of the argument between those who believe that bigness as such is dangerous and those who think it is not. But there is no argument about the fact that the five hundred largest corporations have well over two-thirds of all manufacturing assets and that the two thousand corporations with assets in excess of $10 million account for about 80 percent of all the resources used in manufacturing.[8] And the number of conglomerates—control by a single firm of many different noncompetitive units—continues to increase at a rapid rate. As Galbraith has written, "Many [economists] would agree that [the antitrust laws] have little real nexus with the major sources of market power. And there would be a measure of agreement that the present enforcement attacks the symbols of market power and leaves the substance."[9] For the antitrust actions of the government are aimed at monopoly, not oligopoly—that is, control over a particular market that results from the actions and reactions of a relatively few large firms.

Should bigness as such be outlawed? Yes, say some Americans; others,

[5]*United States* v. *Aluminum Co. of America* (1944).
[6]*United States* v. *E. I. du Pont de Nemours & Co.* (1957).
[7]*Brown Shoe Co., Inc.* v. *United States* (1962).
[8]"Economic Concentration: "Overall and Conglomerate Aspects." *Hearings by the Senate Subcommittee on Antitrust and Monopoly, Committee of the Judiciary*, 88th Cong., 2d. Sess. (1964), part I, p. 113.
[9]John Kenneth Galbraith, *The New Industrial State* (Houghton Mifflin, 1967), p. 188.

such as David Lilienthal, former chairman of the Atomic Energy Commission, say no. Lilienthal believes that "in Big Business we have more than an efficient way to produce and distribute basic commodities, and to strengthen the Nation's security; we have a social institution that promotes human freedom and individualism."[10] He believes that big business makes several positive contributions: it stimulates competition in ideas, products, and services; through research, it develops more and better products; it strengthens constructive labor-management relations; it produces greater stability of employment; it increases industrial output; it promotes conservation of natural resources; and it creates new opportunities for independent and small businessmen. Any danger that big business will abuse its power has been reduced to manageable proportions, argues Lilienthal, by the expanded role of government in economic affairs in recent years. Galbraith appears to agree with Lilienthal that bigness as such should not be outlawed, for it makes possible the planning needed to bring the benefits of industrialism to the people. But Galbraith is much more skeptical than is Lilienthal about the virtues of the industrial society.[11]

TRAFFIC COP FOR COMPETITION

Who controls the large corporations? In a classic study, Berle and Means showed that corporation ownership has been divorced from corporation control.[12] The ownership of stock in large corporations is widely dispersed, leaving control in the hands of a small group of managers. To whom are these managers responsible? If they are not truly responsible to the owners, should they be made more responsible to all the people through the national government? Although this problem does not directly relate to the monopoly problem, it touches on the whole role of the national government in regulating business.

Most Americans believe in vigorous but fair and open competition. In a simple economy, competition virtually enforces itself; buyers and sellers know one another and follow the old principle of *caveat emptor*—let the buyer beware. By the turn of the century, however, the American business economy was becoming so large and impersonal that a demand arose for the government to police competition; big business was especially suspect for its trade practices. The same Congress that passed the Clayton Act in 1914 also enacted the Federal Trade Commission Act.

Because our industrial life is so diverse, Congress put enforcement of the law in the hands of a five-member Federal Trade Commission (FTC), an independent regulatory board whose job is to apply the act to specific practices. As its membership slowly changed (the term of office is seven years), the FTC's conception of its job changed too. In the 1920s the Commission exercised its power rather mildly, but more recently it has taken a stricter

---

[10]David E. Lilienthal, *Big Business, A New Era* (Harper, 1953), p. ix.

[11]Galbraith, *op. cit.*

[12]A. A. Berle, Jr., and Gardiner C. Means, *The Modern Corporation and Private Property* (Macmillan, 1933). See also John Kenneth Galbraith, *American Capitalism: The Concept of Countervailing Power* (Houghton Mifflin, 1952); and A. A. Berle, Jr., *Power Without Property* (Harcourt, Brace & World, 1959).

view toward business practices and has been given new responsibilities by Congress. Today the FTC exercises a wide range of powers; it may outlaw many diverse activities.

Unfair or deceptive practices. A businessman who sells in interstate commerce must not misrepresent his products. For example, in a recent well-publicized case, the FTC enjoined a television commercial that allegedly showed sandpaper being shaved to demonstrate the "super-moisturizing power" of a shaving cream. The demonstration utilized not sandpaper but a prop consisting of sand applied to plexiglass, which of course made the job easier. The Commission's ruling that this was a deceptive trade practice was subsequently upheld by the Supreme Court.[13]

Tying contracts. The Radio Corporation of America was forbidden to require radio manufacturers to buy from RCA all vacuum tubes needed for first use in radio sets. On the other hand, when the General Motors Corporation required its Buick and Chevrolet agents to use only GM replacement parts in repair work, an FTC ban on this practice was overturned by the Supreme Court.

Price discrimination. It is unfair to sell below cost in an effort to destroy weaker competitors and thus secure a monopoly position. This practice had been a favorite one with the robber barons of old.

Monopolistic practices. There are a host of these — buying up supplies in order to stifle competition, conspiring to set uniform selling prices and conditions, harassing competitors (such as by bribing their employees or bringing vexatious lawsuits), and selling below cost in order to hinder competition. The FTC works closely with the Justice Department in trying to curb practices that improperly restrain trade among the states.

The FTC was originally designed to protect businessmen from unfair practices of competitors. Of course, the consumer was also expected to be a beneficiary of FTC regulations, but until recently this was more or less an incidental consequence. During the last several years, however, Congress has broadened FTC authority specifically for the benefit of consumers. Following are examples of such authority.

Dangerous practices. The FTC regulates the interstate marketing of apparel in order to bar the use of highly flammable materials. The Commission has also tried to protect consumers against the hazards of cigarette smoking but it ran into the opposition of the tobacco industry, which has considerable influence in Congress. When the FTC announced that it was about to require a health warning to be prominently placed on cigarette packages and in advertisements, Congress intervened and substituted an innocuous and inconspicuous warning. Three years later, the Commission reported to Congress that this warning had had no impact on reducing consumption, but Congress has been unwilling, so far, to permit the FTC to do more. However, the FTC received an assist from its fellow independent regulatory agency, the Federal Communications Commission, which ordered television and

[13]*Federal Trade Commission* v. *Colgate-Palmolive Co.* (1965).

radio stations to give equal time to those who wish to editorialize against cigarette smoking.

Truth in packaging. The FTC shares with the Department of Health, Education, and Welfare responsibility for the enforcement of the 1966 act that requires those who sell in the interstate market to adopt standards that will not mislead the consumer as to the amount or price of a product he is purchasing.

Truth in lending. The FTC shares with the Board of Governors of the Federal Reserve System the responsibility for the enforcement of the 1968 act that is designed to protect consumers from misleading advertisements about the rate of interest they will pay when they purchase homes or other products on credit or when they borrow from banks or other lending institutions.

Discriminatory advertisement of housing. The 1968 Open Housing Act empowers the FTC to prevent advertisers from offering rentals or houses for sale on a racially discriminatory basis. Prior to receiving this authority, the FTC had taken an even more vigorous step; it used its general powers to prevent false and deceptive advertising by interstate advertisers who purport to have rentals available to all persons but who refuse to rent to blacks.

POLICING THE MONEY MARKET

The American economy rests on a vast system of investment and credit. Our resources could not have been developed had people not been willing to invest money in factories and machinery, and the credit system helped make the enormous investments possible. Before World War I there were hardly half a million investors in this country, but during the war and the 1920s millions of people began to buy securities. Investment trusts and brokerage houses mushroomed.

For many years individual states had tried to cope with some of the abuses of the money markets, but it took the stock market crash of 1929 to bring vigorous national action. Investigations during the Depression revealed that abuses had been many and varied. Worthless or questionable securities had been unloaded on the public through various kinds of fraud. Insiders had used confidential information to arrange deals for themselves at the expense of thousands of small investors. Investment bankers had sponsored stock issues that created unsound corporate structures. An enormous amount of speculating on margin (buying stocks on credit), had helped precipitate the 1929 crash. Pools, rigging the market, and preferred lists were other means of manipulating the money markets.

The Federal Securities Act of 1933 and the Securities Exchange Act of 1934 were passed in response to wide bitterness and disillusionment over Wall Street practices. The 1933 act required the registration of all issues of stocks, bonds, or other securities offered in interstate commerce or by mail, along with a registration statement providing full information for potential investors. The 1934 act regulated the buying and selling of securities on exchanges throughout the country. To administer both acts, Congress established the Securities and Exchange Commission (SEC), an independent regulatory board of five men with five-year terms. All firms having listed securities must file regular reports with the SEC and with the exchanges.

The main objective of these acts is to give full publicity to stock-market transactions, but they also outlaw manipulation and other unsavory practices of the past. The SEC can investigate suspicious activities in the market and even has the power to impose new trading rules on exchanges.

The Commission has special powers over public utility holding companies —that is, corporations that control networks of operating companies. Formerly, holding companies could escape regulation by incorporating in one state to take control of operating companies in another. Many abuses developed, such as siphoning funds from operating utilities into holding companies. There was also a problem of concentration. An investigation revealed that thirteen large holding-company groups controlled three-fourths of the entire privately owned electric utility industry, and over 40 percent was concentrated in the hands of the three largest groups. To meet this problem, Congress in 1935 passed the Public Utility Holding Company Act. Not only must holding companies register full information with the SEC, but many of their transactions, such as issuing and buying securities, may be made only with the Commission's consent. Congress also required the holding companies to get rid of their extraneous operating companies and to confine themselves each to a single integrated system.

Transportation

In August 1787, the Framers of the Constitution were debating how much power they should give the new national government to regulate commerce. One day, as a relief from their labors, they junketed to the banks of the Delaware River to watch John Fitch demonstrate his sensational steamboat. "As we look back it seems that Fitch and the Founding Fathers were working at different parts of one unfolding problem." While Fitch's experiment would bring the states into closer economic relations, the Framers were granting Congress power to "regulate commerce with foreign nations, and among the several States. . . ."[14] Today Congress has virtually complete power to regulate interstate commerce, including transportation.

National power over interstate commerce is a far more powerful weapon today than the Framers could have expected. For today that power extends to hundreds of thousands of miles of railways, to water-borne commerce, to networks of pipelines, and to motor and air transportation. Congress controls not only the movement of persons, things, and words from state to state; it also has broad powers over the conduct of industries that *affect* interstate commerce.

REGULATING (AND PROTECTING) THE RAILROADS

It is hard for us today to realize how deeply railroads were involved in the politics of the late nineteenth century. At first the national government's policy was to help railroads, so in only four years, from 1862 to 1866, Congress

[14]Charles Fairman, *American Constitutional Decisions* (Holt, 1948), p. 173.

granted over 100 million acres of land to the railroad builders. But as evidence of corrupt use of these lands and of the high rates charged by the railroads came to the public's attention, demands for national regulation became insistent. To many Americans of that time, the railroads were nothing but ogres intent on ruining the little man. Farmers had especially bitter grievances; they charged that railroads extorted outrageously high rates, conspired with one another to prevent competition, discriminated against certain localities and persons, corrupted officials, evaded taxes, watered their capital, and stole money that farmers had invested in the railroads. Angry and desperate, the farmers turned to political action. The powerful Grange movement that swept the West in the 1870s and 1880s was a response to the tactics of railroads as well as to monopoly, middlemen, and the power of Eastern financiers.

The Grange movement helped to secure a number of state laws regulating railroads. But the railroads fought the new laws through appeals to the courts, and the Supreme Court of 1886 held that the commerce clause of the national Constitution deprived states of any authority to regulate transportation even within their own boundaries if it was part of commerce among the states.[15] Shippers and small businessmen joined the farmers to demand that Congress fill the void and provide national regulation. The result was the Interstate Commerce Act of 1887, which set up the Interstate Commerce Commission (ICC), the first independent regulatory commission to be created by Congress and the beginning of a new era of more positive federal regulation of business.

The 1887 act was only a modest beginning. It gave the Interstate Commerce Commission authority to prevent railroads from charging special rates, rebating, and practicing other methods of discrimination, such as charging more for a short haul than for a long haul over a line where there might be less competition. At first a hostile Supreme Court narrowly restricted the Interstate Commerce Commission's authority over rates, but, as a result of subsequent grants of jurisdiction, the Commission became a powerful agency.

. The ICC is composed of eleven commissioners, who hold seven-year overlapping terms, and a staff of over twenty-four hundred. The agency regulates railroad rates and services, mergers, corporation structures, and, in fact, most of the railroad business. In addition, the ICC has jurisdiction over motor carriers operating in interstate commerce, water carriers in domestic service (such as ships operating on canals or rivers), and certain pipelines.

Today, the ICC's major concern is no longer to prevent railroads from taking advantage of those who use their services as much as it is to help the railroads avoid financial bankruptcy in the face of increased operating costs and competition from buslines, trucklines, airlines, pipelines, shiplines, and the private automobile. By the Transportation Act of 1958, Congress authorized the ICC for a limited time to guarantee loans for railroads to maintain and improve their services and gave the Commission additional authority to permit railroads to abandon local services on which they were losing money even if a state regulatory agency opposed.

[15]*Wabash Railroad Co.* v. *Illinois* (1886).

The ICC remains the main railroad regulatory agency, but its safety functions and some promotional responsibilities have been transferred to the newly created Federal Railroad Administration, part of the Department of Transportation. The Administration dispenses federal grants to stimulate the development of high-speed railroad systems for heavily traveled corridors such as the Boston to New York to Washington run.

REGULATING THE AIRLINES

The power to regulate and promote air transportation is shared by the Civil Aeronautics Board (CAB), the Department of Transportation's National Transportation Safety Board, and the Federal Aviation Administration (FAA). The CAB is a five-member independent regulatory commission that grants licenses to airlines and regulates fares, rates, mergers, and other competitive practices. It also regulates airmail rates and, in so doing, considers the need of each air carrier for enough revenues to enable it to maintain air transportation for commerce, the postal service, and national defense.

The Federal Aviation Administration administers safety regulations and has other specialized duties but is primarily concerned with promoting and protecting air service. It is responsible for air-traffic control systems, and its agents man the control towers that direct air traffic into and out of crowded airports. The FAA works with the air-transportation industry to develop and evaluate systems for the improvement of air service and also administers the grants-in-aid that provide substantial funds to local government for the development of public airports.

The National Transportation Safety Board, a five-man agency whose members are appointed by the President with the consent of the Senate, operates as an independent unit in the Department of Transportation. The Board has taken from the CAB the responsibility for investigating accidents involving civil aircraft and for determining their cause, as well as the responsibility for hearing appeals from the rulings of the Federal Aviation Administrator that relate to air safety. The Board has somewhat similar powers over railroads and other surface transportation, as well as over national gas pipelines.

A NATIONAL TRANSPORTATION POLICY?

Congress has never declared a broad and definite transportation policy. It prefers to deal with problems as they arise and to create a separate agency to deal with each particular form of transportation. The President, who might be able to impose some kind of unified transportation program, has no direct authority over these agencies. As a result there is no single agency responsible for proposing and administering a unified transportation policy. Furthermore, each transportation industry tends to ally with the agency designed to regulate it against all other forms of transportation. The problems and prospects of the four principal modes of transportation — rail, air, highway, and water — are not identical, but many authorities believe that uncoordinated attention to specific industry problems is not adequate. A former member of the CAB stated: ". . . if we keep on trying to plan our national transportation system this way, we will wake up in a national emergency one day and find that it won't do the job."

As a hesitant first step, Congress created the Department of Transportation in 1967. However, the various segments of the transportation industry persuaded Congress to restrict the authority of the Secretary of the new Department, and the maritime industry was able to secure complete exemption from the Department for the Federal Maritime Commission, which subsidizes the building and the operation of American shipping. The new Department's principal components are the Federal Aviation Administration, formerly the Federal Aviation Agency of the Department of Commerce; a newly created Railroad Administration, which took over the functions of the Interstate Commerce Commission's Bureau of Railroad Safety and Services; a Federal Highway Administration, which absorbed the Bureau of Public Roads of the Department of Commerce; the Coast Guard, transferred from the Department of Treasury; the five-man National Transportation Safety Board, which took over the accident-investigation functions previously vested in a variety of federal agencies; and the Urban Mass Transportation Administration, which makes grants to metropolitan areas and which was transferred in 1968 from the Department of Housing and Urban Development. Left outside the Department are the principal transportation regulatory agencies—the CAB, ICC, and Maritime Commission.

The Secretary of Transportation has no authority to revise existing federal transportation policies or to change allocations of program support among the various transportation modes. At the moment his powers are limited to recommendations and to coordination. But the creation of a Cabinet-level officer with no allegiance or involvement in a single means of transportation could be a significant beginning of a more cohesive national transportation program. It was clear at the outset of the 1970s that shaping such a program would be one of the most pressing and difficult tasks of the decade.

Labor-Management Relations

As we have seen, governmental regulation of business has been essentially restrictive. Most of the laws and rules have served to curb certain business practices and steer the dynamic force of private enterprise into socially useful channels. But regulation cuts two ways. In the case of American workers, most laws in recent decades have tended not to restrict but to confer rights and opportunities on them. Actually, many labor laws do not touch labor directly; instead, they regulate its relations with employers, including the formulation of contract provisions.

Most business leaders would probably like to see government return to its old hands-off policy (though with certain exceptions, noted in the next chapter). But not labor leaders. For if governmental regulation were to be wiped out, they fear that business would impose far stricter regulations of its own —longer working hours, for example.

Labor has not always looked on government with a friendly eye. Traditionally, workers have viewed federal and state judges with particular suspicion. Early in the American experience, judges, steeped in the common law, tended to follow the *conspiracy doctrine*—the idea that men must not combine to injure others. Because organized labor's traditional weapon has been the strike, this doctrine could be used by anti-union judges to prevent workers from acting effectively. Some judges freely issued injunctions against strikes, boycotts, and other kinds of union activities. Moreover, the courts often interpreted laws in a way that hurt labor. As we saw earlier in this chapter, the Supreme Court turned the Sherman Antitrust Act against labor, even though the workers thought it had been passed to curb business combinations rather than their own unions. Finally, the courts held unconstitutional a number of acts designed to improve the worker's lot. Perhaps the most famous example was the Supreme Court's invalidation of a New York law limiting employment in bakeries to sixty hours a week and ten hours a day on the grounds that the law interfered with freedom of contract and therefore violated the due-process clause of the Fourteenth Amendment.[16]

But during the first half of this century, governmental protection and promotion were gradually extended over the whole range of labor activity and organization. This change was the result of two basic developments—labor's growing political power and the awareness of millions of Americans that a healthy and secure nation depends in large measure on a healthy and secure labor force. Both these developments were reflected in the election of pro-labor Presidents, such as Wilson and the two Roosevelts, and friendly legislators in Senate and House and the state capitols.

Labor's basic struggle was for the right to organize. For many decades trade unions had been held lawful by acts of state legislatures, but the courts had chipped away at this right by legalizing certain anti-union devices. The most notorious was the yellow-dog contract, by which anti-union employers, before they would hire a new worker, made him promise not to join a labor organization. If labor organizers later tried to unionize the worker, the employer, on the basis of yellow-dog contracts, could apply for injunctions from the courts to stop the organizers. Chafing under this restriction, labor in 1932 secured the passage of the Norris-La Guardia Act, which made yellow-dog contracts unenforceable in federal courts. Granting labor the right to organize, the act also drastically limited the issuance of labor injunctions in other respects.

By 1932 unions had won other kinds of protection from the federal government, especially over conditions of labor. Almost a century before, in 1840, the government had established the ten-hour day in its navy yards, and later Congress shortened the working day of governmental employees to eight hours and required the eight-hour day for railroad employees and for seamen. Nevertheless, progress was slow, partly because of the courts. In

[16]*Lochner* v. *New York* (1905).

1918 the Supreme Court invalidated a national law prohibiting the interstate transportation of goods produced by child labor, and a constitutional amendment to give Congress this power had not got very far. By 1932 the United States still lagged far behind several European countries in the protection afforded to labor.

A NEW DEAL FOR LABOR

In 1932, on the eve of the Roosevelt administration, the AFL was down to barely two million members—partly a result of unemployment during the Great Depression. Its political influence was small. But the new administration was sympathetic toward labor, and during the 1930s unions rose to a position of tremendous economic and political power. Under the New Deal, labor achieved both an array of protective legislation and governmental help in its campaign to organize the unorganized. The CIO split off from the AFL and unionized a number of vital industries, such as steel, automobiles, and rubber, but the AFL itself reformed its ranks and became larger and stronger than ever.

The National Industrial Recovery Act of 1933 laid the stage for the New Deal's labor policies. As mentioned above, this act was essentially a means of giving business a shot in the arm by allowing industries to work out codes of fair competition. Such codes, however, involved labor standards, such as wages, hours, and child labor, and the unions were given a part in the code-making process. Moreover, Section 7a of the act contained the famous provision that "employees shall have the right to organize and bargain collectively through representatives of their own choosing, and shall be free from the interference, restraint, or coercion of employers of labor, or their agents, in the designation of such representatives or in self-organization or in other concerted activities for the purpose of collective bargaining or other mutual aid or protection." Under the stimulus of the NIRA and the subsequent upturn in business, the unions blossomed. New members flocked into unions and violent organizational strikes occurred in many parts of the country.

The NIRA was short-lived, however, for the Supreme Court declared the act unconstitutional in 1935. But the New Deal Congress, determined to maintain national protection and encouragement of labor, passed a series of acts in the next few years that amounted to a sort of NIRA for labor.

Public contracts. The Walsh-Healey Act of 1936, as amended, requires that all national government supply contracts in excess of $10,000 must provide that no worker employed under such contracts shall be paid less than the prevailing minimum wage, as determined by the Secretary of Labor, that he must be paid overtime for all work in excess of eight hours per day or forty hours per week; that convict labor will not be used; and that child labor (boys under sixteen and girls under eighteen) will not be employed.

Wages and hours. The Fair Labor Standards Act in 1938 went much further. It set a maximum workweek of forty-four hours, to be successively reduced to forty-two and then to forty hours, for all employees engaged in interstate commerce or in the production of goods for interstate commerce (with certain exemptions). Employees could work beyond these limits only if paid at 1-1/2 times the regular rate. Minimum wages were set at 25 cents an hour but were to rise by jumps to 40 cents. Since 1938 Congress has gradually raised the minimum wage by a series of steps so that for nonfarm workers it is presently $1.60 an hour, and Congress has extended the coverage of the act so that it now includes almost forty million workers. The most notable extension came in 1966, when for the first time Congress overcame the opposition from rural districts and brought under the act certain farm workers. Congress, however, would not go all the way; it established a wage floor that provides only a $1.30 minimum for covered farm workers. The Equal Pay Act of 1963 amended the Fair Labor Standards Act to compel employers to pay equal wages to men and women doing equal work on jobs requiring equal skill, effort, and responsibility and performed under similar working conditions.

The Fair Labor Standards and Walsh-Healey Acts are administered by the Wage and Hour and Public Contracts Divisions of the Department of Labor; these two divisions are jointly administered by a head appointed by the President with the consent of the Senate. They maintain a crew of inspectors who check business firms to ensure compliance with the law, but their administrator has frequently asked Congress for more funds to permit more intensive inspection.

Child labor.   The Fair Labor Standards Act prohibited child labor (under sixteen years of age or under eighteen in hazardous occupations) in indus-

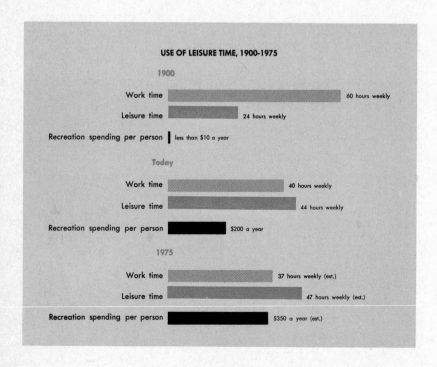

Adapted from Pictograph Corporation; © 1964 by The New York Times Company.

tries that engage in, or that produce goods for, interstate commerce. These provisions are enforced by the Wage and Hour and Public Contracts Divisions and the Bureau of Labor Standards (in the Labor Department).

Labor relations. Section 7a of the NIRA was resurrected in the National Labor Relations Act, which was passed in 1935 only two months after the Supreme Court struck down the former act. In the preamble, the Wagner Act (so called after its chief sponsor, Senator Robert Wagner of New York) declared that workers in industries affecting interstate commerce (with certain exceptions) should have the right to organize and bargain collectively and that inequality in bargaining power between employers and workers led to industrial strife and economic instability. The act made five types of action unfair for employers to practice: (1) interfering with workers in their attempt to organize unions or bargain collectively; (2) supporting company unions (unions set up and dominated by the employer); (3) discriminating against membership in unions; (4) firing or otherwise victimizing an employee for having taken action under the act; (5) refusing to bargain with union representatives. The act was intended to prevent open-shop employers from using violence, espionage, propaganda, and community pressure to resist unionization of their plants. The Wagner Act also set up machinery to decide contests over which union should represent a given group of employees. Such conflicts—which became numerous and bitter when the CIO broke away from the AFL in the mid-1930s—were to be settled by secret ballot and majority rule.

To administer the act, a board of three (now five) members, holding overlapping terms of five years each, was set up. Under the act, the National Labor Relations Board (NLRB), an independent regulatory commission, has the ticklish job of determining the appropriate bargaining unit—that is, whether the employees may organize by plant, by craft, or on some other basis. The board operates largely through regional officers, who investigate charges of unfair labor practices and may issue formal complaints, and through trial examiners, who hold hearings and submit reports to the board in Washington.

STRIKING A BALANCE

From the start the Wagner Act was a center of controversy. It strengthened the unions and helped them seize greater economic and political power. In 1936 a committee of eminent attorneys declared that the measure was unconstitutional. Taking heart from this opinion, many corporations simply ignored NLRB decisions. Unions, unwilling to wait for the slow-moving procedures of the law, organized a series of violent strikes, including the much-criticized sit-down strikes. In April 1937, during President Roosevelt's campaign to pack the Supreme Court, the Court by a five-to-four vote upheld the constitutionality of the Wagner Act.[17] The fight then shifted to Congress, where senators and representatives attacked the NLRB through denunciations, investigations, and slashes in its appropriations.

What had caused all this uproar? First, from the outset the board vigorously

---

[17]*National Labor Relations Board* v. *Jones & Laughlin Steel Corp.* (1937).

applied the pro-labor provisions of the act. For example, the act prohibited employers from interfering with employee unionization; the Board interpreted this to mean that employers could not even make public statements advising workers not to join unions. Such rulings raised a storm of protest from employers. Second, the Board got caught in the struggle between the AFL and CIO. Whichever way it decided certain representation cases, it was bound to antagonize one labor faction or the other. Third, the purpose of the act was widely misunderstood. Employers and editorial writers solemnly charged the measure and the Board with being biased in favor of labor, when the very aim of the act had been to improve the workers' bargaining power.

The controversy was sharpened by criticism of several union practices. These practices were not new, but now that labor was achieving greater power they came in for more public attention. One was *featherbedding*. Faced with labor-saving devices that cut down on the number of workers needed to do a given job, some unions demanded that the original number of workers be paid, even if they had nothing to do and merely stood around. Then there was the charge that unions were in the hands of dictators. Some union leaders stayed in office for years, even decades, and then passed control to other members of their family. To be sure, many union leaders had no more control over their unions than did many business executives over their enterprises, but unions are supposed to be run in a democratic manner. Moreover, protected by the *closed shop* — a contract under which only union members can be hired — some union heads seemed to have as much power to discipline members as had the more ruthless employers of old. And a few unions were rackets, and had connections with the underworld.

Most unions continued to be run honestly and democratically. Nevertheless, public opinion, fed by anti-union propaganda, seemed to swing against labor after World War II. Not only labor excesses but a wave of great industry-wide strikes intensified demands in Congress for a law that would equalize the obligations of labor and management. In 1946 the Republicans won majorities in both the House and Senate, paving the way for modification of the Wagner Act.

THE TAFT-HARTLEY ACT

The upshot was the Labor-Management Relations Act of 1947, commonly called the Taft-Hartley Act after its sponsors. This act, which applies with certain exceptions to industries affecting interstate commerce:

1 Outlaws the closed shop and permits the *union shop* (under which newly employed workers must join the union within a stated time period) only under certain conditions.

2 Required unions to file affidavits that their officers were not Communists, if such unions wanted to secure federal action on complaints against employers (since repealed).

3 Outlaws jurisdictional strikes (strikes arising from disputes between unions over which has the right to do a job), secondary boycotts, political expenditures by unions in connection with federal elections, excessive union dues or fees, and strikes by federal employees.

4 Makes it an unfair labor practice for unions to refuse to bargain with employers.

5 Permits employers and unions to sue each other in federal courts for violation of contracts.

6 Allows the use of the labor injunction on a limited scale, reversing the policy set by the Norris-La Guardia Act.

7 Revamped the National Labor Relations Board, increasing its membership to five and strengthening the semi-independent position of the Board's general counsel.

Organized labor greeted the new measure as a slave-labor act and vowed that it would use its political power to wipe the act from the statute books. Senator Taft saw the bill as "an extraordinary reversal along the right lines toward equalizing the power of labor unions and employers." Since 1947, organized labor has kept up its drive to repeal the Taft-Hartley Act, especially Section 14(b), which permits states to outlaw union shops. Union leaders contend that these laws undermine their organizing efforts, especially in the South, where most of the states have taken advantage of Section 14(b) to pass so-called right to work laws. But despite their opposition and the frequent support of Democratic Presidents, organized labor has never been able to muster enough votes in Congress to repeal Section 14(b).

THE LABOR REFORM ACT OF 1959

During the late 1950s public attention focused less on relations between union and management and more on the internal affairs of unions. A Senate rackets committee investigating labor activities found in some unions glaring cases of corruption, dictatorial control by a few bosses, loose financial practices, and other deplorable practices. Heavily publicized, the committee's disclosures aroused popular demand for reform. At the same time, businessmen and others, with the backing of the Eisenhower administration, wanted new restrictions on labor's use of the boycott and picketing. Union leaders hotly opposed reform on the grounds that it would harass good unions and have no effect on the bad ones. After two years of deadlock over the issue, Congress passed the Labor Reform Act of 1959 (often called the Landrum-Griffin Act), which:

1 Requires labor organizations to file comprehensive reports with the Secretary of Labor on all financial transactions and on the workings of its constitution and bylaws.

2 Under a bill-of-rights section, grants union members the unqualified right to vote in union elections by secret ballot, to speak up freely in union meetings, to get open hearings in discipline cases, and to sue in federal courts if they feel that they are not getting fair play under union rules.

3 Requires secret elections at least every three years for local union officers and at least every five years for national union officers and bars from union office Communists (since declared unconstitutional), ex-convicts, embezzlers of union funds, and any union leader with conflicting business interests.

4 Plugs loopholes in the Taft-Hartley Act's provisions against the secondary boycott. For example, the new act outlaws the "hot-cargo" weapon used by unions like the Teamsters to refuse to handle cargoes to or from firms involved in labor disputes.

5 Outlaws organizational picketing if the employer has validly recognized another union or if there has been an NLRB election within the preceding year.

KEEPING LABOR-MANAGEMENT PEACE

The Federal Mediation and Conciliation Service, with mediators located in seven regional offices, stands ready to help settle labor-management disputes in any industry affecting interstate commerce (except railroads and airlines, which are covered by the Railway Labor Act), either on request of one of the parties to the dispute or whenever the dispute threatens to cause a substantial interruption of interstate commerce. Through tact and persuasion, the troubleshooters of the Federal Mediation and Conciliation Service induce unions to call off strikes and persuade employers to make concessions. The Service has no power to dictate terms; the parties to the dispute are free 'to ignore the conciliators and their suggestions. If mediation fails, the parties may ask the service to assist in the selection of an arbitrator; under this arrangement the parties agree in advance to accept the arbitrator's decision.

The Taft-Hartley Act also set up new machinery for handling disputes affecting an entire industry or a major part of it, where a stoppage would threaten national health or safety. When such a strike breaks out, the following steps are authorized:

1 The President appoints a special board to investigate and report the facts.

2 The President may then instruct the Attorney General to seek in a federal court an eighty-day injunction against the strike.

3 The court grants this injunction if it agrees that the national health or safety is endangered.

4 If the parties have not settled the strike within the eighty days, the board informs the President of the employer's last offer of settlement.

5 The NLRB takes a secret vote among the employees to see if they will accept the employer's last offer.

6 If no settlement is reached, the injunction expires, and the President reports to Congress with such recommendations as he may wish to make.

How successful has the Taft-Hartley Act been in helping maintain labor peace? It has been invoked several times—sometimes successfully, sometimes not—against strikes in vital sectors of the economy, such as atomic energy, coal, shipping, steel, and telephone service. Often the President and the Secretary of Labor attempt to mediate strikes without resorting to the Taft-Hartley Act. The act's effectiveness is difficult to assess, because legislation is only one of the many factors affecting industrial peace and there are contrary opinions among experts whether Taft-Hartley helps or hinders the settlement of disputes.

One thing is clear, the basic issue remains unresolved—strikes are part of the price we pay for a system of free collective bargaining. But under what conditions does the price become so high that the federal government should intervene, stop the strike, and force a settlement either by setting the terms or insisting on compulsory arbitration? Congress—and the nation—will be dealing with this issue for a long time.

The policies of collective bargaining are but part of a broader set of issues. Labor is deeply concerned not only with the traditional conditions of work such as hours, wages, and pensions, but also with job security itself, now threatened by technical change and automation. Business is faced not only with rising costs but intense foreign competition, primarily from Western Europe and Japan. The public is directly affected by altered patterns of competition, quality of goods, prices, and unemployment. The impact of monopoly power of either a business or a union is felt throughout society. A healthy labor-management climate seems to require a willingness on the part of the immediate participants, the people, and their government to take a broad view of specific problems.

The Politics of Regulation

Karl Marx, the theorist of capitalist decay, maintained that the long-run interests of all capitalists were the same. He argued that the proletariat had a similar unity of interest and that eventually the exploiting class would give way to a government of the workers. Relations among the new proletarian rulers would be so harmonious that eventually the state would just wither away.

A look at the American economy today is enough to dispel the idea of a united group of businessmen facing a united group of workers. Admittedly, there is conflict between businessmen and workers. But such conflict is obscured by a vast complex of antagonistic interests operating *within* economic groups. The American political scene reflects not only the struggle of employer against worker, but also the struggles of consumer against producer, of businessmen against businessmen, of labor against labor, of section against section. And all these interests are intertwined and interlocked in such a way as to make the whole picture very complex indeed.

THE CLASH OF INTERESTS

In Chapter 11 we noted some of the characteristics and weapons of the larger economic interests. Here it might be well to look more closely at the competition among interest groups in the light of the problem of governmental regulation.

Some of the sharpest contests take place within the world of business. Early attempts to regulate the railroads, for example, reflected chiefly a struggle between the railroads and consumers. But other interests were drawn into the struggle—for example, financial control groups, railroad investors, and railroad equipment and supply industries. Later, the railroads began to meet intense competition from other forms of transportation, and railroad politics became even more intricate. Today a political battle between railroad carriers and the trucking business simmers constantly, and occasionally this battle erupts in full-page advertisements in leading newspapers. The railroads argue that the trucking business offers unfair competition. The fact that government builds and maintains the nation's highways, they protest, means that motor transportation is subsidized, whereas the railroads must provide their own facilities; the truckers reply that they contribute heavily to highway maintenance through gasoline and other taxes — and so the battle rages. The railroads also complain of the subsidies granted airlines and water shippers.[18]

The internal rivalries of labor also affect the politics of regulation. Labor, as we noted, is by no means a unified, monolithic body; it is a cluster of unions of all kinds, sizes, and interests, along with many unorganized workers. For example, the Railroad Brotherhoods and the Teamsters' Union often clash on national transportation policy simply because industrially these two groups compete with each other.

The struggle of the interests also influences regulatory procedures. Recently, for example, the Civil Aeronautics Board decided to formulate a plan for federally subsidized local air service for seven Middle Western states that were facing a transportation crisis because of contraction of railroad services. So many airlines, mayors, presidents of chambers of commerce, and others were affected by the plan that there were almost one hundred parties to the case and almost two hundred witnesses testified before one of the Board's examiners. This expert, after reading through pleadings, transcripts, exhibits, and briefs, announced his plan for air service for the area — in two volumes totaling 658 pages. More exceptions and briefs were filed by the interests affected. Then the case went before the Civil Aeronautics Board and took on more of the political atmosphere, for sixteen senators, twenty-two representatives, and three governors testified, along with spokesmen for the airlines concerned. The Board finally announced its decision — three years after the need for action became apparent.[19]

WHO REGULATES THE REGULATORS?

The influence of the independent regulatory commissions is pervasive. The late Justice Jackson observed that the rise of these commissions "probably has been the most significant legal trend of the last century and perhaps more values today are affected by their decisions than by those of all the courts. . . . They also have begun to have important consequences on personal rights."[20]

Congress has deliberately given to independent regulatory commissions the primary responsibility for restraining abuses of industrial power. As a practical matter this would not be essential. Regulatory functions can be, and

[18]Andrew Hacker, "Pressure Politics in Pennsylvania: The Truckers vs. The Railroads," in Alan F. Westin (ed.), *The Uses of Power: 7 Cases in American Politics* (Harcourt, Brace & World, 1962), pp. 323–375.

[19]Condensed from a case study in Louis J. Hector, "The New Critique of the Regulatory Agency," remarks before Section of Administrative Law, *Journal of American Bar Association* (August 25, 1959).

[20]*FTC* v. *Ruberoid Co.* (1952).

are, handled by line agencies in regular federal departments under presidential responsibility. For example, the Packers and Stockyard Administration in the Department of Agriculture regulates the packers and stockyards to protect farmers against arbitrary charges and other unfair practices. And wages and hours regulations are administered by a line agency lodged in the Labor Department. Nevertheless, Congress has generally preferred to make these special regulatory agencies relatively insulated from the President.

In creating each of the twenty regulatory commissions, Congress issued a broad policy directive but left it up to each commission, within the scope of its authority, to make the rules and issue the orders necessary to carry out the congressional mandate. Commissioners were given long, staggered terms; the President's power to remove them was limited; and he often must, in selecting commissioners, appoint men from both political parties. These arrangements have resulted in what some have called a fourth branch of government.

How independent are these independent commissions? Who regulates the regulators themselves? An answer requires consideration of three quite separate but frequently confused questions. Have the commissions operated without regard to partisan politics? Have they carried on their duties uninfluenced by improper pressures? For example, the Federal Communications Commission is supposed to decide which applicant should be licensed to use a television channel uninfluenced by personal favor, partisan preference, or the wishes even of the President of the United States. The Federal Trade Commission, in deciding if a particular company has violated the regulations concerning misleading advertising, is not supposed to be influenced by the intervention of a senator or the views of presidential assistants. By and large the independent regulatory commissions have been insulated from partisan politics and have operated in accord with standards of propriety.

A far more difficult question is: Have the commissions discharged their duties in terms of a broad concept of the public interest? Obviously the independent regulatory commissions have not and cannot be made independent of politics in the broader and more important sense of the word. No agency operating within a democracy and vested with important decision-making duties can be removed from the political system. Because independent regulatory commissions must decide big political questions calling for the adjustment of a variety of interests, their independence from the White House often makes them more dependent on the interests they regulate. For the groups most immediately affected by the decisions of a commission naturally have a more sustained interest in the regulations than does the general public. As Professor Murray Edelman has observed, "The organizational and psychological embrace of the industry around the regulatory commissioners go hand in hand. To be part of the organization in the sense of incessant exposure to its problems and decisional premises is to come to share its perspectives and values. This is not 'pressure'; it is absorption."[21]

A regulatory commission that offends a highly organized interest may discover that it is not quite as independent as its formal charter indicates. For the interests frequently work through the Congress and often can exert pres-

[21]Murray Edelman, *The Symbolic Uses of Politics* (Univ. of Illinois Press, 1964), p. 66.

sures on a commission more easily by moving through a congressional committee than by direct pressures on the commission. The Interstate Commerce Commission is often cited as one of the most judicial and independent agencies in Washington. It is rarely charged with showing favoritism of an improper sort or of being the tool for one railroad over another, but it is often accused of favoring the railroads over other forms of transportation. Whether this charge is true or not, the capture of a regulatory agency by the regulated interests is not unknown in Washington.

The independence of regulatory commissions from the President can also be exaggerated. A President may not be able and should not be allowed to influence a particular decision of a commission any more than of a court, but the general thrust of policies of an independent regulatory commission are very much a part of the President's responsibilities. A President dedicated, let us say, to a more vigorous regulation of unfair labor practices by unions or unfair methods of competition must make his influence felt. Despite their formal independence, it is difficult for commissions to withstand the impact of a powerful President who, through his influence in Congress and the nation, may bring about changes in basic statutes or alterations in appropriations. Independent regulatory commissions—even though their members are influenced by the executive, their powers derive from legislative delegation, and their decisions are subject to review in the courts—have a scope of responsibility to the American economy that may exceed that of the three regular branches of government. Aside from the many operative problems of the agencies, such as delay in processing cases, increasing judicialization of procedures, overlapping jurisdiction, and lack of interagency coordination, the key issue remains—who regulates the regulators?

Government as Promoter

25   In recent years we have heard a great deal about the welfare state. Politicians have charged that spendthrifts in Washington have been trying to buy votes through give-away programs. Supporters of federal subsidies—which we will call promotion—have denounced their opponents as heartless skinflints who would put dollars before human lives. In the heat of the argument, certain facts are sometimes ignored.

In the first place, governmental promotion is by no means a recent development in the United States. President Washington, in his first annual address to Congress, called for a tariff to protect business. Secretary of the Treasury Alexander Hamilton, in his famous *Report on the Subject of Manufactures* in 1791, proposed that government help develop business by giving bounties to new enterprises. And Henry Clay's American System, in the beginning of the nineteenth century, was a plan for federally subsidized roads and waterways, a strengthened banking system, and tariff protection. Parts of these ambitious programs were carried out during the first half of the nineteenth century, and after the Civil War the Republican party bestowed subsidies on businessmen, farmers, veterans, and other groups.

In the second place, almost all groups have at one time or another benefited directly from government aid. During much of the nation's history, business has been the main recipient of help from Washington, but farmers and veterans have been given preferred treatment as well. Governmental promotion can be used to help any group. The main questions are: Who shall be aided? In what way? And with what consequences for the general welfare?

Helping Businessmen

In the broadest sense, government assists business (as all interests) by maintaining an orderly legal and economic system. A government that protects private property and enforces contracts enables businessmen to operate in a stable situation where agreements can be enforced. A government that helps promote a prosperous economy enables businessmen to enjoy a large volume of sales and good profits. The kind of monetary system established by government—for example, tight or easy money—is of direct interest to businessmen (see Chapter 26). Aside from such obvious aids to business, the national government supplies a number of specific services and assists individual sectors of business.

THE DEPARTMENT OF COMMERCE

The Department of Commerce in Washington is the nation's "service center" for business, and the Secretary of Commerce is usually a person with a business background who is acceptable to the business community. The Department assists business in many ways; for example, the Office of Business Economics reports on business activities and prospects at home and abroad and the National Bureau of Standards makes scientific investigations and standardizes units of weight and measurement.

The Bureau of the Census has been called the greatest fact-finding and figure-counting agency in the world. The Constitution requires that a national census be taken every ten years; the results of this census, and of others in between, supply businessmen with valuable information on business and agricultural activity, incomes, occupations, employment, housing, homeownership, governmental finances, crime, and many other matters.

Another historic bureau now in the Commerce Department is the Patent Office. The first article of the Constitution authorized Congress to secure to authors and inventors for a limited period. "the exclusive right to their respective writings and discoveries." A patent, conferring the right of exclusive use of an invention for seventeen years, is a valuable property right. On receiving an application for a patent, the Patent Office must study its records to see if any prior patent might be infringed and if the invention is sufficiently original and useful to be patentable; meanwhile the applicant marks his product "patent pending." Because decisions of the Patent Office directly involve legal rights, its rulings may be appealed to a Board of Appeals in the Patent office and then to the Court of Customs and Patent Appeals or to a federal district court. Some cases even go to the Supreme Court. Although most patent problems are technical, patent policy also involves such broad problems as the stimulation of invention and the threat of monopoly and economic concentration.

The Environmental Science Services Administration, an agency created in 1965, combines two long-standing service bodies—the Weather Bureau and the Coast and Geodetic Survey. The Weather Bureau not only tries to forecast the weather but, working with private agencies, also attempts to do something about it. The Bureau makes forecasts on the basis of data funneled to it by its hundreds of field stations in this country and overseas. Its services are utilized especially by farmers, airlines, the resort business, and other industries. The use of electronic computers and such experiments as seeding clouds to induce rain suggests that the Weather Bureau may have an even greater role for both civilian and military activities in years to come.[1]

OTHER AIDS TO BUSINESS

In addition to the activities of the Department of Commerce, the government assists business through other agencies. One of these is the Small Business Administration. Created in 1953, it is an independent agency headed by an administrator appointed by the President. The Small Business Administration is designed to aid small enterprises through such services as financial counseling, research, loans to victims of natural disasters such as floods and hurricanes, loans to victims of riots, and loans for general expansion. Perhaps its major function is to ensure that a fair proportion of government purchases and contracts is placed with small business.

The government also aids business through research and experimentation carried on by a variety of agencies. Millions of dollars are spent annually for research that often directly benefits private industry. Examples include new commercial wood products resulting from work done in the laboratories of the United States Forest Service and diversified uses of bituminous coal resulting from research in the Department of the Interior. Through a wide range of promotional services, government assists the business community not only to survive but to make the necessary adjustments to a changing economy.

Facing the World Market

From one perspective the business economy seems healthy and dynamic: The gross national product is high and continues to grow; the standard of living, reflected by our purchases of consumer goods, has also been at an all-time high; and, despite some unemployment, more people have been working in American industry than ever before. Some observers are content to believe that such conditions will automatically continue if we simply tend to our business at home. But dramatic changes since World War II have made that perspective dangerously narrow.

Changed world conditions have brought three essentially new external challenges to the American economy. First, it has become clearly apparent that if we are to maintain our economic growth and high standard of living, we must sell our products abroad as well as at home. But unprecedented

[1]See Donald R. Whitnah, *A History of the United States Weather Bureau* (Univ. of Illinois Press, 1961).

economic development in the rest of the world has introduced a new kind of foreign competition. No longer are our allies simply recipients of aid to re-build war-devastated industries—they are keen competitors. In Europe, American business no longer faces a relatively weak and nationally frag-mented competitor, but an established and growing European Common Market. This entity has a potential industrial capacity equivalent to our own, and a population—and hence a market—significantly larger than ours. Japan, which has experienced tremendous industrial expansion, already effectively competes with many American manufacturers.

American business faces a second challenge in international trade from the Communist bloc. The Communists have made significant industrial ad-vances and have begun to make inroads in world trade. Undoubtedly this form of competition will be increasingly important, as the Communist lead-ers have promised an intensified "trade offensive."

The third challenge concerns the newly emerging nations. Ambitious to secure their independence through economic and social development, these nations find themselves short of necessary human and material resources. They seek economic and technical assistance and also markets for their products. Will these countries be able to sell us their goods so that they, in return, can afford to buy ours? Many of these new nations are looking for a model. Does the American business system provide a pattern that can suc-cessfully be followed by these emerging states or will they choose other economic and political systems?

The principal device used by all governments to aid their nation's business has been the *tariff*, and Congress has generally favored interests desiring high protective tariffs. Over the years, businesses jeopardized by foreign competition successfully petitioned Congress to curb competitive imports. By the beginning of this century, however, many industries protected by high tariffs had expanded to a point where sales in foreign markets were impera-tive. And Americans discovered that foreign trade is a two-way proposition —if you want people in a foreign market to buy your goods, you must be will-ing to buy theirs.

In spite of continuing protectionist pressures, in 1934 Congress began to lower tariffs. Through the Trade Agreements Act and its extensions, the President has been empowered to negotiate mutual tariff reductions with other nations. Trade barriers have been lowered, but the protectionists have managed to place restrictions on the President in the form of elaborate nego-tiating procedures, limits on the percentage of reduction allowed, and ex-emptions for industries claiming injury from the competitive imports.

In 1962 President Kennedy moved to revise substantially trade and tariff policies. He contended that continued economic growth required expanded foreign trade at a rate impossible under current policies. Tariff reductions could, through the introduction of foreign competition, help hold down our own costs and prices and increase our total productivity, which had been lagging. Lower prices and increased productivity, the President claimed, would result in a vastly improved competitive position in international trade. He asked Congress for—and received—broadened negotiating power with authority to cut existing tariffs and with discretion to deal with general categories of products rather than on an item-by-item basis. For workers losing jobs because of imports introduced by tariff cuts, he proposed a program of compensation while they were out of work, assistance for relocation to new job sites, and opportunities for retraining in new skills. For injured businesses, the President asked for loans, loan guarantees, tax benefits to encourage modernization or conversion, and technical assistance.

Armed with the authority of this Trade Expansion Act, the Kennedy—later, the Johnson—administration entered into three years of negotiations with fifty-three nations to draw up a General Agreement on Tariffs and Trade. The Kennedy Round, as these discussions came to be called, were finally concluded just under the deadline for the United States to implement the expiring Trade Expansion Act. As a result, tariffs have been eliminated (with some significant exceptions) as a major barrier to trade among industrial nations. Nontariff barriers such as quotas, minimum import prices, and restrictions on agricultural commodities still remain, although even agricultural tariffs were substantially reduced by the Kennedy Round.

By the end of the 1960s there were signs of a revival of protectionist sentiment that might lead to restrictive legislation by Congress, as American firms began to feel the impact of the flood of foreign goods being sold in the United States. But, of course, there is also a flood of American goods being sold abroad and those businessmen who profit from this trade will work to oppose the reimposition of trade barriers.

The legislative struggle for the trade-expansion program reflects some unusual interest-group alignments. Although having some reservations on specific provisions, the Chamber of Commerce, the AFL-CIO, and the Farm Bureau have supported the bills. Conversely, opposition arises from—in addition to the traditional protectionists, led by the textile industry—some groups suspicious of expanding the President's power and others wary of the long-term costs of the provisions.[2]

Perhaps the most difficult international trade issue of recent years is the unfavorable balance of payments that has caused an outflow of our gold reserves. By making dollars convertible to gold at the fixed price of $35 an ounce, the United States provides the principal medium of international exchange—the dollar. Although we still have a favorable balance of trade—we sell more abroad than we buy from foreign producers—the total balance of payments has been unfavorable because of our foreign aid and our overseas expenditures for military commitments. There has been an outflow of gold both because of these expenses and because other nations have turned in their dollars for gold. To overcome this dollar shortage, President Johnson, with a little help from Congress, tried to restrain expenditures by American tourists and businessmen abroad. This is an exceedingly difficult balancing act—we want to encourage world trade, open markets for American products, encourage foreign tourists to come and spend their money in the United States, but at the same time restrict American expenditures abroad. The problem is that we might cause foreign nations to take retaliatory action that could lead to a reversal of all the progress made under the Kennedy Round.

[2]See Raymond A. Bauer, Ithiel de Sola Pool, and Lewis Anthony Dexter, *American Business and Public Policy: The Politics of Foreign Trade* (Atherton, 1963), pp. 73–81, for the broad context in which trade policy is made.

Aiding Farmers

Nowhere is the diversity of American life more apparent than in agriculture. American farmers grow an amazing variety of crops. There are big farmers employing scores of workers on many hundreds of acres of land; there are farmers operating family-sized farms of 100 to 200 acres, with the help of one or two hired hands; there are tenant farmers working other men's farms for a share of the produce and profits; there are, finally, millions of farm laborers, many of whom move from farm to farm as the seasons change.

This wide diversity is reflected in the highly complex set of problems commonly identified simply as the farm problem. There are actually many interrelated problems, but the basic difficulty is that American agriculture is out of balance with the rest of society. Following are the general features of this imbalance.[3]

Internal imbalance. All farms are not equally successful. In most cases successful farms use more capital, more land, and less labor than the marginally prosperous ones. Yet the big farms, which have kept pace with technological developments and have made the best use of resources, constitute a minority of farms in America. And the family farms, although most numerous, supply only 15 percent of the produce.

Social imbalance. The most neglected aspect of the farm problem is the increasing imbalance between agriculture and other social institutions. Many rural communities are being bypassed by social and economic development. Some are hard pressed to provide adequate schools, fire protection, and sanitation. Moreover, the problems for the people leaving these communities may be acute. Lacking occupational skills and unprepared for urban life, thousands of families migrate each year from failing farms to find work in the city. Too often the displaced farmers remain unemployed, and their families encounter serious difficulties in adjusting to life in the city.

Economic imbalance. The American farmers' productivity often outpaces domestic demand. The adoption of improved production methods—mechanization, fertilizers, pesticides, antibiotics, and the like—has brought sharply increased total production, but these technological advances have also brought increased costs and new demands on management. Whereas costs have tended to increase or at least remain fixed, prices have been highly flexible and have tended to drop in response to increased output. As a result, the American farmer has not shared the nation's economic growth. All these facts closely affect the relation of government to agriculture.

The principal agricultural role of the federal government during the nineteenth century was clearly one of promoting production. The Homestead Act of 1862 gave settlers 160 acres of public land in exchange for a promise to occupy the land for at least five years. That same year Congress granted

[3]The following is based on Wallace Barr, "The Farm Problem Identified," in *The Farm Problem—What Are the Choices* (National Committee on Agricultural Policy, 1959), no. 1, pp. 1–4.

huge tracts of land to the states for the establishment of colleges and created the Department of Agriculture. In later years agricultural experiment stations were set up, conservation and reclamation programs undertaken, and farm cooperatives encouraged.

World War I increased governmental intervention in agriculture; the prices of food, cotton, and farmland skyrocketed, and the farmers enjoyed a boom. In 1920 the bubble burst. Prices plummeted and millions of farmers were left with surplus land, unpaid-for machinery, high taxes, and burdensome debts. Farmers turned to Washington, and Congress responded by passing measures to police the trading in contracts for future delivery of agricultural commodities, to encourage agricultural cooperatives, and to ease credit. These proved ineffectual in stemming the agricultural depression.

The Great Depression sharply intensified agricultural stagnation. Unlike industrial firms, the farmers could not retrench, lay off workers, cut down orders for materials, and decrease output. Most of the farmers' expenses continue at the same level no matter what the state of the market is. So when the price of agricultural commodities dropped, the farmers tried to grow even more—with the result that prices fell even further. And farmers were so numerous that there was no way that by themselves they could control markets.

The Roosevelt administration tried to do for farmers what businessmen were doing for themselves—restrict production in order to increase or maintain prices. It tried to create new demands and shift farm production toward commodities for which there was a better market. And since the 1930s, the federal government has developed—haltingly—a whole arsenal of devices to bring some order into agricultural markets, sustain farmers' incomes, and achieve a balance between supply and demand.

Drawing by Stevenson; © 1960 The New Yorker Magazine, Inc.

"I haven't decided which I prefer, Luke—full parity through supply-management controls, marketing quotas, and land retirement with conservation practices or . . ."

There was a temporary interruption in farm problems during World War II, but the postwar period brought their return—huge surpluses, rising production, and falling commodity prices. By the early 1960s the results were a continuing decline of the small farm, restiveness in the cities over the high cost of food, and soaring farm surpluses, costing billions of dollars each year just to handle and store. Finally, as the 1960s came to an end, the controls —or world conditions—seemed to work. For the moment, at least, the huge surpluses were disposed of and some balance began to appear between supply and demand. To maintain this balance, the government uses essentially these techniques:

Acreage allotments. Government experts estimate the probable demand for staple commodities such as cotton, wheat, and rice. Then, using an elaborate system, they break down the national acreage allotments into individual allotments for each farm.

Marketing quotas. When production becomes high and a price collapse threatens, farmers by a two-thirds vote may approve the establishment of marketing quotas. Each producer is allotted his share and pays a penalty if he markets more.

Price supports. The government, through loans, in effect takes commodities off the farmers' hands when it appears that excess production may cause prices to fall below a certain minimum. The farmers store their commodities in government warehouses and allow their loans to expire if the market falls below the loan price; the government then takes over the commodities. By discouraging farm commodities from flooding into the market after each harvest, these loans encourage orderly marketing and eliminate sharp price changes.

Conservation payments. These are grants to farmers to induce them to take certain lands from production and plant them in grass or trees or to adopt other soil-conservation practices.

Food for peace. This plan provides for long-term credit sales and sales of surplus food for foreign exchange, as well as donations of products through international relief agencies.

Food for the poor. Through the food stamp, the National School Lunch Act, and the School Milk Program, food is distributed to the needy.

Science and Government

The Founding Fathers were aware of the importance of science. Congress was given specific authority to provide for the census, to establish weights and measures, and to encourage scientific endeavors by regulating patents. But of more importance has been the broader power to appropriate money for the general welfare and for the common defense. The national government has long been involved in science: the Lewis and Clark Expedition, the Army Corps of Engineers, the National Academy of Sciences, and the Morrill Act of 1862 mark important developments. But the biggest expansion came after World War II. Today the federal government spends almost $16 billion annually on research and development ". . . of which over three-quarters is not performed by the government at all but by industry, universities, and various nonprofit institutions."[4] About 50 percent of the engineers in the United States and 25 percent of the scientists are employed by the federal government either directly or indirectly. About 65 percent of scientific research in universities and about 57 percent in private industry is financed by the federal government.[5]

The national government conducts most developmental work in its own laboratories or through contracting with private industry and universities. To support science where the concern is less with immediate solution of problems, the national government makes grants, chiefly to university scientists. These contracts and grants are sources of competition among university research centers.[6] Although Congress provides some scientific support that has no direct national security implication, especially in connection with the health sciences, the federal government's involvement in science is still heavily weighted on the side of science that has some immediate space or military benefits.

SCIENTIFIC AGENCIES

The federal government filters support for science through many agencies, the most important being the National Science Foundation, the National Institutes of Health of the Public Health Service, the Atomic Energy Commission, and the National Aeronautics and Space Administration. The Atomic Energy Commission, (AEC), established by the 1946 act, operates a vast scientific complex, but the bulk of its work is done by contract or grants. Among the many research facilities supported by AEC is the Brookhaven National Laboratory on Long Island, a facility operated by twelve universities.

Largely in response to Soviet space success, Congress passed the National Aeronautics and Space Act in 1958. The act provided for two organizations to promote research and exploration of outer space "devoted to peaceful purposes for the benefit of all mankind." The first, the National Aeronautics and Space Administration (NASA), is an independent executive agency headed by an Administrator appointed by the President with the consent of the Senate. NASA employs about thirty-five thousand persons in functions ranging from the development, construction, testing, and operation of nonmilitary aeronautical and space vehicles to the encouragement of the widest possible participation by the scientific community in space-related research. Its facilities at Edwards, California; Huntsville, Alabama; Houston, Texas; and Cape Kennedy, Florida, are known to all Americans.

The second space organization created in 1958 is the National Aeronautics and Space Council, which was placed under control of the Executive Office of the President. Headed by the Vice President, the Council is composed of the Secretaries of State and Defense, the Chairman of the Atomic Energy

---

[4]J. Stefan Dupre and Sanford A. Lakoff, *Science and the Nation* (Prentice-Hall, 1962), p. 9.

[5]Warner R. Schilling, "Scientists, Foreign Policy, and Politics," *The American Political Science Review* (June 1962), p. 288.

[6]Daniel S. Greenberg, "When Pure Science Meets Pure Politics," *The Reporter* (March 12, 1964), pp. 39 ff.

Commission, and the Administrator of the National Aeronautics and Space Administration. The Council is designed to furnish information and advise the President on matters of space exploration and related research programs.

The National Science Foundation (NSF), under the leadership of a Director appointed by the President with the consent of the Senate and the guidance of a twenty-four-man board of scientists (who spend only part time in this assignment), each year provides matching funds for research facilities, makes available graduate fellowships, and grants funds to thousands of scientists to support their investigations.

The Public Health Services' National Institutes of Health (NIH) spend millions to support the health sciences. Like the NSF, the NIH is primarily an agency to support scientific work of nongovernment scientists, but it also operates its own hospitals and other research facilities.

NSF, NIH, and AEC grants have also financed the graduate education of thousands of men and women, for a grant to a university scientist also permits him to employ graduate students as research assistants. Today a substantial percentage of the research and graduate training in the natural sciences being done in our universities is supported by the federal government. Federal aid to education at this level is no longer a debated issue; it is an accomplished fact.

What are some of the consequences of aid to science? It has not led to intensive federal control. NSF, NIH, and other agencies have exercised extreme care to ensure that only scientific standards are used in allocating funds, although at times Congress has insisted on tests of political reliability, at least to the extent of excluding from federal support scientists whose loyalty has been questioned.

University administrators, much as they welcome federal support, are alarmed by the fact that federal grants to the natural sciences could lead to an imbalance in university programs. Federal grants cover the direct cost of research but only partly cover the indirect or overhead costs. The universities must divert other funds to cover this research and thus have less to spend on the other departments. University heads also fear that the availability of federal research support for science may tend to encourage more and more young men and women into these areas, although evidence does not support these fears. There has been a drop in the proportional number of students in the humanities, but the social sciences, not the natural sciences, have gained from this decline.[7] To offset the imbalances in availability of federal research funds, the National Science Foundation has expanded its support to include the social sciences, and Congress has established a National Foundation on the Arts and Humanities to begin to do for the humanities and arts what the NSF does for the natural and social sciences.

SCIENCE, SCIENTISTS, AND PUBLIC POLICY

Scientific considerations infuse every aspect of public policy. No federal agency today considers itself properly equipped without a science adviser.

[7]Harold Orlans, *The Effects of Federal Programs on Higher Education* (Brookings, 1962), p. 43.

And few men have more influence than the Director of the Office of Science and Technology, an agency within the Executive Office of the President. Not only does the Director advise the President on scientific matters, he is also head of the President's Science Advisory Committee, a group of government and nongovernment scientists, and of the Federal Council for Science and Technology, a group representing several departments and which coordinates problems that are broader than the responsibilities of a single agency.

With scientists occupying key policy-advising positions in government and enjoying even more prestige than generals,[8] it is difficult for the non-scientists who are publicly responsible for making policy to sort out the expert, objective advice from that which reflects the primarily personal values of the scientist. Just as military domination of civilians would undermine the democratic system, so would scientific domination of politicians. And on the other hand, just as it would be dangerous for civilians to ignore military advisers, it would be even more disastrous for them to ignore their science advisers. Some scientists complain that the latter is happening today. Priorities, they say, such as in the moon program, are often based on political rather than scientific considerations. However scientists, like other mortals, often disagree with one another, even on the scientific questions involved in the larger questions of public policy.[9] This is a safeguard against the dangers to democracy that might flow from a scientific elite.

Social Welfare

There is nothing new—as the foregoing pages have shown—in the idea of governmental aid to certain sectors of the economy or to certain groups of people. For at least 160 years we have had a welfare state, to some degree. This is certainly true of social services. As far back as colonial times, parishes and counties undertook poor relief, and later on, the states set up hospitals, asylums, and other institutions. Nevertheless, until recent years American government—especially the national government—lagged far behind other countries in furnishing social services. The situation was paradoxical. On the one hand, the federal government gave huge bounties to railroads, farmers, veterans, and other groups. On the other, Washington ignored the dire need of millions of ill-clad, ill-housed, ill-nourished Americans.

One reason for this paradox is that America has traditionally been a land of opportunity. The millions of acres of free land, the enormous resources, the technical advances—all helped take care of the people who otherwise might not have made a go of it. Then, too, Americans have traditionally subscribed to a philosophy of rugged individualism and devil take the hindmost. If a man failed to get ahead, people said, it was his own fault. Rather grudgingly, the state governments—mainly during the early twentieth century—extended relief to needy groups, especially old people, blind persons,

---

[8]For detailed analysis, see Schilling, *op. cit.*, pp. 287–300. See also Daniel S. Greenberg, *The Politics of Pure Science* (New American Library, 1968).

[9]Don K. Price, *The Scientific Estate* (Harvard Univ. Press, 1965), pp. 82–119.

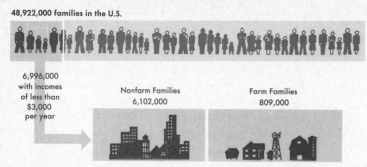

48,922,000 families in the U.S.

6,996,000
with incomes
of less than
$3,000
per year

Nonfarm Families
6,102,000

Farm Families
809,000

Of these 6,996,000 families:

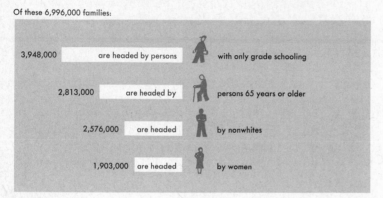

3,948,000   are headed by persons   with only grade schooling

2,813,000   are headed by   persons 65 years or older

2,576,000   are headed   by nonwhites

1,903,000   are headed   by women

Based on Bureau of Census Report, December 1967.

and orphans. But government aid was limited, and private charity was relied on to supply most social services.

Then the nation was struck by the Great Depression. Unemployment mounted to sickening heights; in the early 1930s between ten and fifteen million men were without work. Breadlines, soup kitchens, private charity, meager state and local programs—these were pitifully inadequate gestures. In 1932 the federal government began making loans to states and localities for public relief. The Roosevelt administration established a series of relief programs designed to boost the economy by increasing purchasing power. The famous WPA—Works Progress Administration—spent billions of dollars on local projects. The Public Works Administration undertook more permanent projects—dams and roads and bridges.

Before long a reaction set in to the makeshift manner in which relief was being administered. People grew critical of leaf-raking projects—popularly called "boondoggles"—and of the cost and waste of the relief program. Some wanted to go back to the dole—simple handouts of food or cash by the government. But others argued for a well-planned, long-term program that would foster both the security and self-respect of the people aided. Progress was slow. The first federal attempt at a major social security program—the Railroad Retirement Act of 1934—was declared unconstitutional by the Supreme Court.[10] Insurance companies and even certain labor groups were

[10]*Railroad Retirement Board* v. *Alton Railroad Company* (1935).

hostile to extensive social security programs. But over the last three decades the national government has built a social security program that has come to be widely accepted by the American people.

Broadly speaking, the program is based on the assumption that society must take care of old people, the unemployed, and the helpless. Such people are a cost charged against the rest of the community. Old people are a good example. In the past, when large families were common, much of the cost of social security for the aged was borne by the family itself, and the family was often large enough to bear this burden without too much difficulty. Today the typical family in an urban society will consist of mother and father and two children living in a small house. It is difficult to find space for a poor relative. Some primitive societies kill off excess and helpless people or let them starve. Some communities today put them in poorhouses at the expense of the rest of the citizens. Most modern democratic societies have governmental security systems that try to plan ahead and make provision for needy people in a fair and orderly fashion.

SOCIAL SECURITY

The foundation of the social-welfare system in the United States is the Social Security Act, passed by Congress in 1935 after elaborate study and since then frequently amended and supplemented. Today the national government's social security activities consist of several different kinds of programs.

The *unemployment insurance system* is operated jointly by the national and state governments. Until Congress acted, many states were reluctant to establish their own unemployment insurance programs for fear that the cost would place their businessmen at a competitive disadvantage with businessmen in states that had no such programs. Then, in 1935, Congress eliminated this source of reluctance by levying on all employers of eight or more persons (since amended to four or more) a payroll tax (since 1962, 3.5 percent) on the first $3,000 paid each year to each employee. If an employer contributes to a state unemployment program that meets federal standards, he may deduct from his federal payroll tax all that he pays to the state fund, provided it is no more than 90 percent of his federal tax. A state could stay out of the program, but none has done so, because the national government levies the payroll tax in any event, and the money cannot be used by the state's unemployed unless the state adopts a plan satisfactory to Washington.

The national government helps defray the administrative costs of the programs, but each state administers its own program. Programs vary in eligibility requirements, the amount paid, the period of payment, and other respects. All states levy a tax on employers; several also collect from employees. Almost half the states cover firms with fewer than four workers, and Congress has extended unemployment benefits to federal civilian employees and servicemen. These employees receive the same amounts and are governed by the same conditions as they would be if their employer were subject to state law. Payments to federal employees and ex-servicemen are made through state employment security agencies, but the federal government reimburses the states for payments made. Altogether, about fifty million

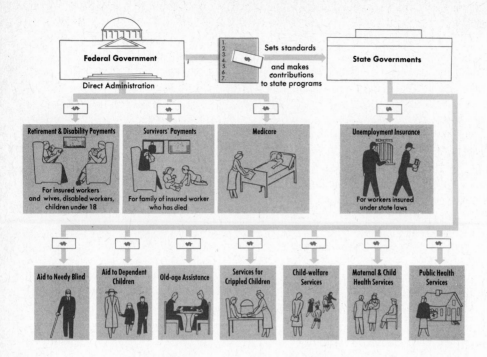

workers earn some credits toward unemployment payments. The major groups not covered by unemployment insurance are self-employed workers, agricultural employees, domestics, and—in half the states—employees of firms that have fewer than four workers. Railway workers are covered under a separate system administered by the Federal Railroad Retirement Board. During recent recessions many jobless persons exhausted their unemployment benefits, so Congress authorized emergency assistance to states in order to allow them to extend the period of payment. A number of states have taken advantage of these provisions.

The money collected by each state is deposited to that state's account in the United States Treasury. From this fund each state pays benefits to workers who report to state public employment agencies and are willing and able to work but for whom there are no jobs. Each state sets its own scale of benefits and determines who is eligible to receive them. In most states, to be eligible a person must be able to work. Indeed, if a worker is drawing benefits and becomes ill, he is no longer entitled to payments. Although states have workmen's compensation programs that pay disability benefits to some workers for industrial accidents or occupational diseases, most programs give no protection to those who are unable to work because of illness or accidents suffered off the job. Only four states—Rhode Island, California, New Jersey, and New York—pay unemployment compensation or workmen's compensation to workers who are unemployed because of nonoccupational illness or injury. Old-age insurance (see below) giving benefits to permanently disabled workers helps additional persons.

574

Federal-state cooperation meets local demand and keeps it flexible. But this combined assistance also has disadvantages. Benefits vary considerably. Recently the average weekly benefit was set at $48 in California but only $25 in Mississippi and West Virginia; the number of weeks for which benefits were paid was as low as ten and as high as twenty-six in New Jersey. Administrative services in some states have proved unduly inefficient and expensive. In some states dishonest people are able to collect payments when jobs are available—and even while holding jobs. In other states the test of unemployment is so stiff that unemployed persons find it difficult to get benefits. Because of the state-federal arrangement, administrators have sometimes had difficulty in locating jobs and steering workers to them. However, the Bureau of Employment Security in the Department of Labor, which administers the federal part of the program, does attempt to coordinate the states' efforts to place jobless workers.

Old-age, survivors', disability, and *medicare insurance,* unlike unemployment insurance, is run solely by the national government. By 1935 it was clear that the old-age problem required national action. For some time the percentage of old people in the population had been steadily increasing. Persons over sixty-five now number eighteen million; their percentage of the whole population has quadrupled in the last 100 years. This social and economic problem has affected politics, too. By 1935 the Townsend movement, clamoring for "$30 every Thursday" for the aged, had reached formidable proportions. The Social Security Act was in part a move to head off this political force.

The act of 1935 established a nationwide contributory retirement system under which payments to retired workers are made out of a fund built up from money collected equally from employers and employees through payroll taxes. Payments vary according to the earnings of the employee and the length of time his salary had been taxed. Since this is an *insurance* program, the plan pays for itself, except for the cost of administration, which the federal government assumes.

In 1939 old-age insurance was broadened to provide survivors' insurance, in 1960 disability benefits were added, and in 1965 health-care benefits were added for persons over sixty-five. Under present rates for this insurance, employers and employees each contribute 4.8 percent of the employee's income up to $7,800 a year; a self-employed person pays 6.4 percent. The rates are scheduled to increase gradually until, in 1987, they will reach 5.9 percent for employers and employees and 7.9 percent for self-employed persons.

Today the system, as recently amended, pays men and women sixty-two years of age or older monthly retirement benefits that vary from $55 to $325 in accordance with the worker's contributions and the number of persons in his family entitled to secondary benefits. (If the insured has a wife sixty years old or older or a disabled husband fifty or older, or dependent children or disabled children whatever their ages, the family receives secondary benefits.) Permanently disabled workers may retire and draw their benefits without an age minimum. Full benefits are paid between the ages of sixty-two and seventy-two only if the recipients are not earning more than $1,680 a year from jobs covered by social security. (Income from dividends, interest, rents, and annuities is not counted.) After age seventy-two a person is entitled to his retirement benefits regardless of his wages. Survivors' benefits for wives, dependent parents, and children include a lump sum of money and monthly payments. (For the health benefits, see page 577.) Benefits are subject to change by Congress, which has been liberalizing them since the system was started in 1939.

Retirement, survivors', disability, and health insurance now cover almost all workers, either on a mandatory or on a permissive basis. The only major professions not covered are public employees, who have their own special retirement systems. Approximately sixty-five million workers participate, and over twenty-three million persons are now receiving some benefits. The fact that this program has been broadened extensively under both Republican and Democratic administrations suggests that the basic system is now outside the area of party battle. Whether the system should be extended to cover other risks, for example, the costs of illness, has produced one of the most hotly debated political issues of the past two decades.

MEDICARE

After World War II Democratic Presidents proposed that the social security system be expanded to provide medical-care insurance. These proposals stirred up a hornet's nest. Leading the opposition was the prestigious American Medical Association (AMA), representing over 200,000 doctors. The AMA argued that these proposals constituted socialized medicine and that (1) tremendous strides had been made without governmental involvement; (2) the plans would bring politics into the traditionally private doctor-patient relationship; (3) standards might be lowered; (4) the programs would be expensive and wasteful; and (5) private plans such as Blue Cross and Blue Shield were covering more and more people.

Whereas the program advocated by President Truman had extremely broad coverage, the proposals advanced by Presidents Kennedy and Johnson and finally adopted centered on a limited application of the medical-insurance principle—extension of the social security system to include health-care insurance for the *aged*. Although enthusiastically supported by the Kennedy administration, efforts to establish the Medicare program failed in both the Eighty-seventh and Eighty-eighth Congresses.

Courtesy Don Hesse and McNaught Syndicate, Inc.

"Daddy's little baby must be kept warm."

Meanwhile, the political battle went on. The AMA and many insurance companies supplied doctors with anti-Medicare literature for distribution directly to patients. Doctors were urged to write, not only to their congressmen, but to local newspapers and other news media protesting the administration bills. The attack on Medicare for the aged repeated many of the objections made to earlier proposals but particularly emphasized that it was simply "a foot in the door for socialized medicine." Opponents stated further that the plan would force young people to pay for the medical expenses of older persons who had paid nothing. Finally, some critics argued that the program was not necessary at all, because existing legislation was adequate. They pointed to the Kerr-Mills Act, passed in 1960, by which the national government provides matching grants to states to help pay medical costs for the medically indigent—needy persons over 65.

Medicare supporters claimed that the Kerr-Mills programs were not adequate and were available in fewer than half of the states. The Kennedy administration contended that health insurance for the aged financed through social security was the only workable method for relieving the elderly and their children from the burden of medical expenses. Statistics were cited showing that the aged had a higher incidence of illness and thus higher medical costs than the rest of the population and that they were less capable of obtaining proper care because of their reduced incomes. It was claimed that private insurance plans provided inadequate coverage and were far too expensive for the average retired person.

Campaigning for election in 1964, President Johnson gave Medicare first priority in his proposed legislative program. The size of Johnson's electoral victory and his huge margins of support in both houses of Congress presaged the passage of Medicare in the Eighty-ninth session of Congress. After months of hearings, debate, and threats of nonparticipation by some doctors, Medicare became a reality in midsummer of 1965.

The program is administered by the social security system and applies to those sixty-five years of age or older. The cost of the benefits—which include payments for hospital and nursing-home care, but not doctors' bills, as well as certain kinds of home nursing care and outpatient service—is financed by an increase in social security taxes and from general funds. This extra tax is noted separately on workers' withholding slips so that everyone may see where his money is going. The money then goes into a separate trust fund—a concession to quell the fears of some who feel that the program might threaten the actuarial soundness of the entire social security cash-benefit system. The participation of the two million people sixty-five or older who are not covered by social security systems is financed by general revenues. Because of Republican objections, a voluntary insurance scheme was adopted to provide coverage for such things as doctors' fees, mental-hospital care, and a number of health services. To obtain this coverage costs an additional premium of $4 a month; the remainder is financed by general revenue funds.

WELFARE

When the Social Security Act was adopted, there were millions of people for whom the insurance benefits were of little help. So the national government provided substantial grants to the states to help make welfare payments to certain needy persons. That there would always be some who would need welfare — those too handicapped to work, for example — was anticipated, but it was expected that with the return of prosperity and the buildup of insurance programs over time the federal government could retire and leave to the states the burden of providing welfare to the blind, the handicapped, and orphans. This has not been so.[11]

Unemployment insurance is of little help to a person who is too unskilled to get a job or to earn enough for his family to live on. Old-age insurance is not sufficient for those who have no other resources. And a mother with small children finds it difficult when her husband dies or deserts her, especially if she lacks the basic educational skills to support her family. In good times as well as bad, one out of every nineteen Americans — nearly eight million people — receives some kind of public assistance each month. Twenty-three million meet the standards of eligibility for some kind of relief. (Not all who are entitled to assistance seek it.)

States still have the primary responsibility for welfare programs — they initiate and administer them. There are no federal minimums that the states must pay, but the federal role is important, because by various matching formulas the national government makes funds available to the states for what is called categorical assistance. As Sargent Shriver, former Director of the Office of Economic Opportunity, phrased it, "Our welfare payments . . . are a list of excuses for being poor which we middle-class Americans consider acceptable excuses and therefore reimbursable."[12] The most important of these categories for which federal funds are available are needy aged; needy and ill aged; needy blind and disabled; and families in need because of the death, desertion, or disability of a parent.

The fastest growing, most costly, and most controversial of these programs is the Aid for Families with Dependent Children (AFDC) program; it helps 4 million children, 1 million mothers, and 200,000 fathers. (Congress allows federal funds for payments to families with two unemployed parents, AFDC-UP, but only twenty-two states are in this program and it covers only 60,000 of the 200,000 fathers.) The program's aim is to keep families with children under eighteen together despite the death, disability, or desertion of the breadwinner. Many critics have charged, however, that it encourages immorality and breeds persons to whom welfare becomes a way of life. In some states attempts have been made to take away funds from families where the mother is unwed, but Congress has stopped such moves on the grounds that this punishes children rather than mothers.

An especially controversial feature of AFDC is the so-called man-in-the-house requirement. Most states, in order to encourage fathers to contribute to the support of their children, refuse to make payments if there is a man in the house. But the consequence is that a father is often given the choice of either deserting his family so that his children and wife may receive help or

[11]Gilbert Y. Steiner, *Social Insecurity: The Politics of Welfare* (Rand McNally, 1966), p. 21; Edger May, *The Wasted Americans* (Harper, 1964).
[12]R. Sargent Shriver, Jr., "New Weapons in Fighting Poverty," *Journal of the American Welfare Association* (January 1966), p. 10.

staying with them when he is unable to earn enough to support them. Further irritation is caused by the practice in some states of staging raids late at night into the homes of AFDC recipients in order to be sure that there is no man in the house.

In 1967 Congress conditioned federal assistance on a stipulation that mothers must participate in some kind of job-training program, and a certain percentage of the mother's earnings are now exempt so that she is not penalized by a loss of assistance because of the salary she earns. Congress also increased federal grants to help provide child-care centers to make it possible for mothers of small children to take jobs. Finally, Congress imposed a freeze on each state, limiting the percentage of children to be covered by AFDC to the percentage of coverage in that state in January 1968. Unless states provide more assistance, the amounts available from the federal government will be substantially reduced. Although there was general support for the 1967 amendments designed to encourage job training, there was less agreement about the desirability of forcing mothers of small children to leave the home and go to work.

Among the severest attacks on the welfare system is that of the National Advisory Commission on Civil Disorders, the Kerner Commission.

The Commission believes that our present system of public assistance contributes materially to the tensions and social disorganization that have led to civil disorders. The failures of the system alienate the taxpayers who support it, the social workers who administer it, and the poor who depend on it. As one critic told the Commission: "The welfare system is designed to save money instead of people and tragically ends up doing neither."[13]

Clearly some kind of welfare program is going to be with us for a long time, but the pressures are building for some substantial revision. What are some of the alternatives?

A WAR ON POVERTY

Suddenly—or so it seemed—poverty became a major issue of domestic politics in the 1960s. Of course, poverty was not new as a political issue; over thirty years ago Franklin Roosevelt dramatized the fact that one-third of the nation was then "ill-clad, ill-nourished, ill-housed." But in the 1960s, in the midst of national affluence, revelations about the extent and persistence of poverty came as something of a surprise. Most people believed that our expanding economy was gradually eliminating poverty and that in the meantime welfare programs were taking care of those in need. But in 1960, while traveling in West Virginia during the presidential primary race, John Kennedy saw the face of poverty and pledged that if elected he would come forward with a program to assist such areas. In 1961, President Kennedy secured the passage of the Appalachia program, which created within the Department of Commerce the Area Redevelopment Administration.

The Area Redevelopment Administration represents a new phase of co-

[13]*Report of the National Advisory Commission on Civil Disorders* (U.S. Government Printing Office, 1968), p. 252.

operative federalism under which federal authorities work with state and regional officials to provide economic stimulus to a depressed area; this stimulus is provided by the development of roads, sewers, water facilities, recreational opportunities, job training, and other measures to encourage industries and provide jobs. Despite criticism, Congress has strengthened the program in recent years and has made it possible for other areas to secure help; the aim is to determine whether the concentration of federal programs and resources in a particular area can make a substantial dent in hard-core poverty.

OTHER STRATEGIES

That the national government should do something about the persistence of poverty in the United States is not a much debated issue, but *what* it should do is. Although there is no agreement about the dimensions of the problem—how many poor exist, who are they, and why they are poor—it is clear that prosperity has passed by a substantial number of Americans, perhaps thirty million of them. These are most often the hidden poor, those who remain invisible to the majority of Americans because they exist in the dark slums of the city and in the mountains and valleys of rural America.[14]

One-third of the chronically poor are from families in which the breadwinner has been without a job for a long time. Some are headed by a father or mother whose skills are so meager that their earnings are not sufficient to support the family. A large portion of the poor live in families headed by a person over sixty-five years of age or one with little or no education. Because blacks have been subject to pervasive discrimination and denied opportunities for education, the percentage of the total black population that is poor is much greater than the percentage of the total white population that is poor. Nevertheless, three-fourths of the poor are white.

Some have argued that the best way to deal with the problem of poverty would be to do away with the existing welfare programs and to substitute some form of income maintenance, either by a negative income tax or by direct payments. They argue that it would be less expensive and more consistent with the maintenance of personal freedom to abolish the governmental agencies that presently administer welfare. Others favor some kind of income maintenance but would add it to the present welfare programs, with certain reforms in that program.

The approach pioneered by Presidents Kennedy and Johnson is different; it is built on the assumption that the causes of poverty are many and call for multiple strategies and that merely to provide cash benefits to the poor will not be sufficient. As Michael Harrington has written, "There is . . . a language of the poor, a psychology of the poor, a world view of the poor. To be impoverished is to be an internal alien, to grow up in a culture that is radically different from one that dominates the society."[15] What is

[14]Michael Harrington, *The Other America* (Penguin, 1963), pp. 23–24.
[15]*Ibid.*, pp. 23–24.

needed are programs that would help the poor to break through the cycle of poverty.

The Economic Opportunity Act of 1964, the basic antipoverty legislation, rests on the Kennedy-Johnson assumptions. This act is supplemented by a variety of other measures such as the Elementary and Secondary Education Act of 1965, the Manpower Development and Training Act, and the civil rights acts. The 1964 act created the Office of Economic Opportunity, within the Executive Office of the President, as a coordinating command post to distribute federal funds to other agencies and to operate a variety of programs through its own staff. Each program is aimed at a specific poverty-creating condition or a special clientele. Among the more important of these programs are:

Operation Headstart. Designed to get preschool children into school before the impact of a disadvantaged environment so disables them that they will be unable to profit from formal instruction when they reach the age of five or six.

Neighborhood Youth Corps. For teen-agers who have dropped out, or are in danger of dropping out, of high school. Operated by the Department of Labor, the corps provides work experiences after school hours and during the summer.

Job Corps. A high-cost, last-ditch effort to try to save as many young "dropouts from society" as possible. The Office of Economic Opportunity, through contracts with industrial firms and educational institutions, provides camps where corpsmen are given room, board, medical and dental care, and a small allowance while they learn jobs capable of providing them with an adequate income.

Community-Action Programs. The most controversial of the programs, this is an attempt to overcome what the drafters of the act thought to be the basic weaknesses of welfare programs — fragmentation and middle-class bias. To overcome these deficiencies, the federal government makes grants to local community-action groups covering most of the costs for coordinated programs "that are developed and administered with maximum feasible participation of the residents of the areas and members of the group for whose benefit the Act was passed."

In its short lifetime, the Economic Opportunity Act has been subject to intense criticism from all quarters. Some charge that the programs do not call for sufficient participation by the poor and do not make adequate funds available for a serious attack on the overwhelming problems of chronic poverty. Others charge that the act has been used to support unsavory and unsuccessful programs. Efforts have been made — with partial success — to distribute programs among previously existing agencies and to abolish the Office of Economic Opportunity. Many mayors objected to the original provisions that allowed community-action organizations to be established outside the regular governmental structure, with the result that Congress amended the act to give local authorities more control over CAPs, as they have come to be called.

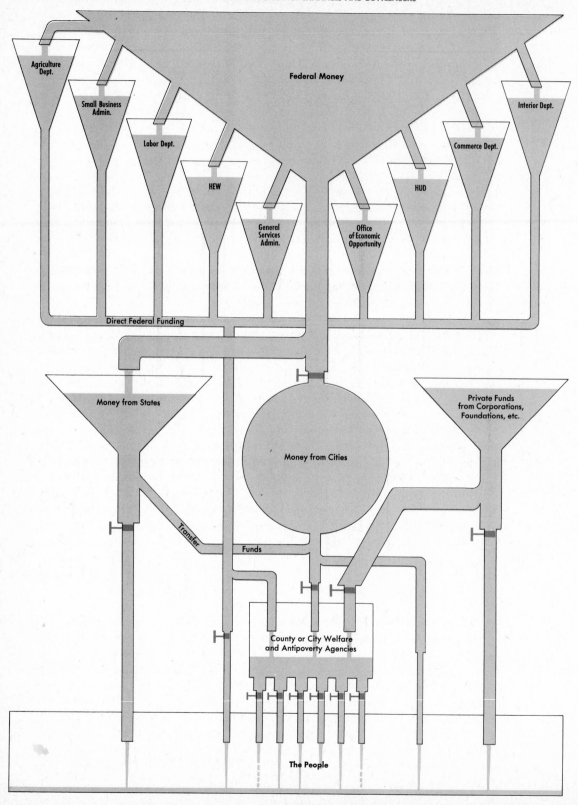

Whatever the success of the antipoverty programs, they are not likely to move quickly enough or massively enough from the perspective of the poor. The Economic Opportunity Act of 1964 was portrayed by some people as the ultimate solution to the problems of poverty; but it is only an acceleration of past efforts. For it is now clear that in the 1970s the federal government will have to confront directly the root causes of the "culture of poverty" and determine whether a pluralist democracy can overcome these root causes.

Education

Only in the 1960s did education become a major promotional activity of the federal government, for education had traditionally been viewed as essentially a function of the state and local governments. The federal government has long been indirectly involved in higher education, however. Sixty-eight land-grant colleges owe their existence largely to the Morrill Act of 1862, which granted federal public lands to the states for the establishment of agricultural and mechanical arts colleges.

For years federal educational activities have been remarkably broad and varied. At the elementary and secondary level, the federal government aids the school lunch program by providing perishable foods acquired under farm price-support operations, helps on problems of curriculum, and educates Indians and others. The federal government helps to construct and operate schools in local districts that have been flooded by new pupils from military bases or other federal installations. At the level of higher education, it provides research grants to colleges and universities, operates special educational projects (such as Howard University, the extension service of the Department of Agriculture, and the military academies), gives annual grants for agricultural and mechanical arts education at land-grant colleges, and offers special education and training for the public services. Other activities include on-farm training for students of agriculture and education in nonmilitary subjects for members of the armed services. Although these activities are administered by a variety of agencies, many of them, including vocational education and assistance to land-grant colleges, are centralized in the Office of Education in the Department of Health, Education, and Welfare.

FEDERAL AID

After World War II many Americans asked: Is the federal government doing enough for education? Casting a wary eye toward the low educational level of a sizable proportion of the population, the growing number of children pressing into our schoolrooms, and the increasing level of education required in the society, many felt that the state and local taxpayer would soon be unable or unwilling to provide the level of educational expenditures needed. The best alternative, some believed, was to turn to Washington for direct help for the schools. Proposals for federal aid to education, however, ran into heavy opposition stemming mainly from three sources: fear that the federal government might try to dictate what should be taught in public schools; a dispute over whether parochial schools should be eligible for benefits; and wide differences over whether federal money should be given to school districts that practice racial segregation.[16]

The interplay of these factors prevented comprehensive federal action in education for a number of years. But in 1957 Russia dramatized its educational and scientific achievements by launching its first Sputnik, thus stimulating many to reevaluate the state of American education and its needs. Congress responded a year later by passing the National Defense Education Act of 1958 which was primarily geared to improve the teaching of science. Attractive student loans were provided, with priority given to undergraduates preparing for careers in science, mathematics, engineering, modern foreign languages, or teacher education. The act authorized grants to high schools and private schools to help them secure better equipment for the teaching of science, mathematics, and languages and for the development of new teaching techniques, such as the use of television. Fellowships were made available from federal funds at universities undertaking new or expanded graduate programs approved by the Office of Education.

The new National Defense Education Act was widely hailed as a good start, but it did nothing, of course, to meet the shortage of classrooms. At the beginning of 1960, the public schools were short 195,000 teachers and 140,000 classrooms; there were over 1.5 million more children attending school than the schools had room for. The United States was maintaining an educational deficit estimated at between $6 and $9 billion a year. In 1961, the Kennedy administration moved to broaden and extend the National Defense Education Act. Intense opposition was again encountered in Congress along the general lines that met previous educational measures. Following a protracted conflict, the act was extended without major modification. President Kennedy signed the act "with extreme reluctance" because of its inadequacies, and he promised that he would continue to press for an enlarged program.

PINPOINTED AID

The decade of the 1960s brought revolutionary thinking about general federal aid to education. Many new departures were embodied in a task-force report presented to President-elect Kennedy in January 1961. One of these was the notion of pinpointed aid to localities badly in need of educational resources—the low-income states and densely populated, economically hardpressed areas, the urban and rural slums. Certain problems continued to persist—such as that involving aid to parochial schools—but Congress was able to pick out of the package some significant but rather noncontroversial items to consider. Shortly after John Kennedy's death, President Johnson signed into law a series of educational bills that provided for loans and grants for the construction of academic buildings for colleges, universities, and medical schools; support for improved vocational education; increased aid to college and medical students; and the broadening of the National Defense Education Act to include support for the humanities and social sciences. This

---

[16]For a case study showing the interaction of these factors, see Hugh Douglas Price, "Race, Religion and the Rules Committee: The Kennedy Aid-to-Education Bills," in Alan F. Westin (ed.), *The Uses of Power* (Harcourt, Brace & World, 1962), pp. 1ff.

flurry of congressional activity led President Johnson to laud the Eighty-eighth session as the "education Congress."

The notion of pinpointed aid, which was introduced in the 1960 task-force report, became the heart of the administration's education legislation in 1965. Recognizing that educational levels were lowest in poverty-stricken areas, President Johnson proposed, and Congress subsequently enacted, a program based primarily on the concentration of federal school aid in the depressed areas. Thus the education program was made an important pillar of the war-on-poverty program. Under the Elementary and Secondary Education Act of 1965, grants are provided for public school districts serving economically needy children. These grants are to be used as decided by local officials subject to approval by state and federal agencies. In addition to this provision, grants are authorized for text- and library-book acquisition for both public and private schoolchildren. Other funds are made available for the creation of supplementary education centers, where children from *both* pub-

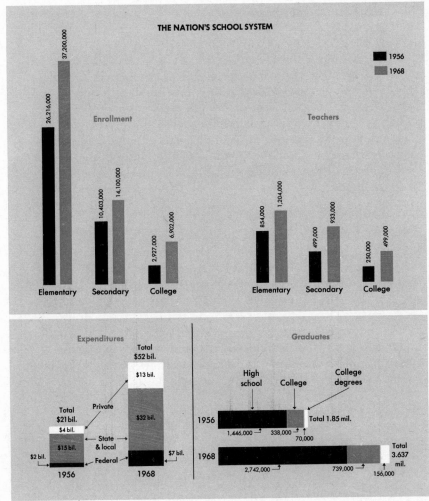

SOURCE: U.S. Department of Education.

lic and private schools can receive part of their instruction. Here special stress is placed on up-to-date and experimental methods of teaching.

These provisions were as interesting politically as they were important in substance. By tying much of the school-aid program to the war on poverty, President Johnson was able to gain congressional assent to a massive infusion of federal funds in the field of elementary and secondary education, the first time in history that federal funds were authorized for general use at these levels. Second, by providing direct aid to public schools and indirect aid to parochial schools in the form of books and materials and in the creation of the supplementary education centers, the President was able to blunt the church-state controversy that had plagued advocates of school aid for so many years. This may ease the way for later direct aid to the private schools. The special centers may prove additionally important for Northern cities as a means by which the effects of *de facto* school segregation may be overcome even while such localities may continue their tradition of the neighborhood school. Thus, by slightly altering the focus of the federal programs, interests that had previously competed for resources and through their competition had largely blocked aid at the elementary and secondary levels in particular, suddenly found themselves working in concert for a federal-aid program; success was secured.

Since the 1965 act, Congress has extended its authorizations and approved additional funds but has made no basic changes in its programs. The major conflicts in Congress have centered around attempts by some Southern representatives to restrict the Department of Health, Education, and Welfare's authority to establish guidelines for compliance with the civil rights laws and to withhold funds from states or districts that fail to comply with these guidelines. Although Congress left considerable discretion with the Department, it did stipulate that funds could not be cut off during a school year.

HEW

Presiding over and administering the major federal educational, health, and welfare programs is one of the newest and fastest growing Cabinet departments, the Department of Health, Education, and Welfare (HEW). Created in 1953, the Department in its early years was more or less a holding company for a number of separate old-line departments—the Office of Education, Social Security Administration, Welfare Administration, Food and Drug Administration, and Public Health Service. With the significant increase in federal support for education, health, and welfare programs, the Department has become increasingly prominent and has been reorganized in order to strengthen the leadership role of the Secretary.

Housing and Urban Development

Since the Depression, the federal government has helped Americans find decent housing. The FHA (Federal Housing Administration), by insuring mortgages, made it possible for persons of middle-income levels to buy homes. And the government, by guaranteeing (through the Federal Deposit Insurance Corporation) the savings accounts of depositors in savings and loan institutions, enabled these institutions to use their own money to grant mortgages. But what of the millions of Americans who are unable to purchase a home or to pay rentals for a house or an apartment? What of urban decay? What of the blacks who are trapped in ghettos?

Since 1937 the federal government has had a public-housing program, which, working with local housing authorities, has made available 500,000 units for about 1,500,000 people. Yet these programs have been criticized for providing high-rise slums for the poor without any amenities and for doing little to improve the environment for the upbringing of children. In 1949, Congress launched a more comprehensive program of urban renewal and rehabilitation by making funds available to cities for the acquisition and clearance of slum properties; the cities are then to resell the land to private builders who agree to redevelop it according to an approved plan. Congress has also made grants and loans to cities to improve municipal services.

Urban renewal, despite some success, has also failed to make central cities inhabitable, and many have criticized the program for replacing the slum homes of the poor with units that the poor cannot afford to rent or buy. And whatever was being done was not enough, for slums were being created faster than they were being replaced, and more housing units were being destroyed for highways and other civic projects than were being built.

In 1966, through the Demonstration Cities and Metropolitan Development Act, Congress tried a new technique—a select number of cities were invited to submit plans for federal support for a coordinated attack on certain target areas within the cities. The plans were to be developed with the aid of the people living in the areas concerned. This approach stemmed from past failures, in which housing, education, transportation, and recreation were each approached in a segmented and uncoordinated fashion. It was hoped that a coordinated attack on all phases of the urban environment, especially one that involves the people, would result in more progress.

In 1968, Congress adopted the Housing and Urban Development Act, which, if sufficiently funded, may mark the most significant new federal thrust in the area of housing since the Great Depression. The goal of the act is to provide six million units of new or rehabilitated housing each year for ten years and to make these units available to those with low incomes. The act is an attempt to do for the poor what the FHA had done for those with middle incomes. By a variety of devices, the federal government will subsidize mortgage or rental payments so that persons with low income can afford to live in these units. The act is designed to provide not the massive, high-rise, public-housing type of units, but those that, from the outside, are indistinguishable from other homes and apartments. The 1968 act also strengthens the Demonstration Cities programs.

Responsibility for administering housing programs is vested in the Department of Housing and Urban Development (HUD), which was established in 1965. HUD is still searching to develop its role. Its principal units are the Housing and Home Finance Agency, the Public Housing Administration, the Federal National Mortgage Association, and the Federal Housing Administration. Its responsibilities are broader than housing, but it has yet to emerge as the principal focus for the federal government's attack on the urban crisis.

The Welfare State?

A cataloguing of the federal government's promotional activities could be continued almost indefinitely, if space allowed. The government as promoter is not a new role; it is as old as the federal union itself. The intention was embodied in the preamble to the Constitution when it stated its aim to "promote the general welfare." Toward the end of the 1960s we witnessed the latest of several surges of intense governmental promotion and reawakened concern about health, education, and welfare. But even these programs, extensive as they are, do not begin to tell the story of governmental promotional activities in recent years. We have said nothing about water- and air-pollution control, development of new parks, river and recreation areas, and a variety of projects to promote the arts and protect the natural beauty of the United States.

Many disagree with these efforts by the national government to improve the quality of life, to focus resources and attention on the problems of the poor, to improve the environment in which we live. They view with distaste the bureaucracy required for these programs, and they allege that the programs are ineffective interferences with individual initiative. But although most of these programs have been initiated under Democratic Presidents, they have secured bipartisan support. Regardless of the party in power in Washington, these activities of the federal government are destined to become more significant. The pressures are for more, not less, federal involvement, and the problems are growing more gigantic and overwhelming and not less so. The welfare state seems to be a durable part of the American society.

Government as Manager

26 In the last two chapters we have been looking into two of the methods by which government influences society—regulation and promotion. Through regulation, government lays down the rules controlling what men may and may not do. Through promotion, government directly or indirectly advances the interests of certain groups. There is a third method by which government influences society—*direct management*, or control. These terms are used here in two senses. One is the direct operation or management of enterprise. The post office is a good example of this meaning. The government could allow a private company to handle the mail, and it could regulate that company in the public interest, or subsidize it, or both. Instead, the government itself took over the job long ago. The second sense in which the terms are used involves control of the economy. Government has come to intervene in the economy in so many ways and with such broad powers and effective instruments of control, that our political rulers are to a real extent our economic rulers as well.

Governmental management is no more recent a development in the United States then governmental regulation or promotion. What *is* new is the tremendous increase in governmental management during the last three decades. All over the world, in both democratic and totalitarian countries, governments have come to direct national economies and to take over operating areas hitherto reserved for private enterprise. The trend has not been so pronounced in the United States as in Britain, Sweden, or Australia, but it has clearly shown up here too.

Some call this trend socialism; others call it a drift toward the welfare state. But let us examine just what is happening. What enterprises does our federal government directly operate? With what success? To what extent does government manage the economy as a whole? What methods does it use? What political and governmental problems does this kind of management raise?

Managing Enterprises

Americans have a curiously mixed attitude toward governmental management. On the one hand, almost all of us stolidly and unquestioningly accept the fact that the federal government fights wars, runs some hospitals and public utilities, operates parks, delivers mail, manages a huge insurance system, and during emergencies takes over private enterprises such as coal mines and railroads. On the other hand, most of us oppose governmental operation of enterprises, and we can think of pretty good reasons to support our views. We dislike socialism—but we seem willing to accept it if it comes in little chunks.

Actually, most Americans approach the question of governmental ownership on a practical, matter-of-fact basis. Nobody seriously objects to the government's management of the armed forces, but few would want the government to take over retail stores. It is in the vast area between these extremes that disagreements arise. In general, we feel that most enterprises should be owned and managed privately and that the burden of proof is on those who wish to extend governmental control. Even so, the national government in recent decades has assumed direct control of important economic activities.

The types of enterprise operated by the national government range from the Forest Service to the Government Printing Office to the Hoover Dam. A survey halfway through the Eisenhower administration showed that the national government owned almost 20,000 business enterprises, with assets of more than $11 billion and employing over 250,000 people; and this report did not include the post office.[1] A review of all these activities is impossible here. Case studies of the Post Office Department, the Tennessee Valley Authority, and the Atomic Energy Commission will suggest some of the major problems involved.

WORLD'S BIGGEST BUSINESS

The United States Post Office likes to call itself the biggest single business in the world. It is the largest nonmilitary department of the national government, and its 700,000 employees account for almost one-quarter of the entire federal civil service. It handles over 76 billion pieces of mail every year, supervises about 33,000 post offices, and has annual cash transactions of $47 billion. It contracts for ship, rail, air, and truck transportation at the cost of many millions of dollars a year.

At the head of the postal service is the Postmaster General (PMG). His is a

[1] *U.S. Code Congressional and Administrative News* (June 1956), no. 9, p. i.

historic office; Benjamin Franklin served for twenty years as British Post-master General for the colonies, and for two years during the Revolution he ran the post-office system for the independent states.[2] The post office achieved Cabinet rank in 1829. For many years, however, the PMG has been more important politically than administratively, for it was long traditional for the President to appoint to the post the national chairman of his own party. The reason for putting a politician in this post is obvious—the PMG had thousands of patronage jobs to parcel out to the loyal party workers. Over the years, however, postal employees have gradually been brought under civil service. Although perhaps 20,000 jobs are still political appointments (including some top officials and first-, second-, and third-class postmasters), postal patronage is not what it used to be.[3]

The postal service, a business agency, has only its headquarters in Washington; all but a small fraction of its employees work in the field. Assisting the Postmaster General are a deputy and six assistant postmasters general, and beneath them are a host of officials supervising operations in the field. Local post offices come in all sizes. Some are enormous, like that in New York with its 100 substations. The smallest are branch offices run in retail stores by small merchants. In between are the stations run by fourth-class postmasters—almost half the total number—who are appointed by the PMG partly on a civil service, partly on a political, basis. First-, second-, and third-class postmasters are appointed by the President with Senate approval; these are prize patronage plums. But appointees now have to pass competitive examinations and, if they win permanent appointments, they may not be dismissed for political reasons.

For years the administrative structure of the post office has been called obsolete and overcentralized. Though a business-type establishment, it lacks, say its critics, the flexibility essential to good business operations; rate-making machinery is inadequate and conceals subsidies to carriers; there are still too many political appointments; and the Department has been slow to modernize and mechanize. Defenders of the post office respond that of course it loses money—because of the deliberate decision to provide services below cost. A high volume of printed matter is carried at very low rates; some airlines are subsidized at rates fixed by the CAB (see Chapter 24); and rail shipping rates are also not set by the post office but by the ICC.

In 1968 a Presidential Commission on Postal Organization, after pointing to the growing public concern over the quality of mail service, concluded that our present system is outmoded and "cannot keep pace with the demands of our society unless it is given a basic change in direction." The Commission recommended that the Post Office Department be removed from the President's Cabinet and converted to a nonprofit corporation, headed by a nine-man board of directors, which would be authorized to set postal rates after a hearing (Congress does so now); the rates would be based on actual costs of service, value to those served, and market demands; and postal employees would be transferred to a new career service. Although the Commission warned against expecting miracles and noted that the new cor-

[2] See R. L. Butler, *Doctor Franklin, Postmaster General* (Doubleday, 1928).
[3] See J. Edward Day, *My Appointed Round* (Holt, 1965), for an account by Kennedy's first Postmaster General.

poration would have to make heavy investments to secure modern equipment, the Commission estimated that the service could be improved with a 20 percent saving in cost. As to present subsidies, the Commission suggested that Congress provide these directly rather than burden the postal service with them.

What will come of these recommendations? The chairman of the House appropriations subcommittee handling postal affairs said, "Congress will think for a long time before it turns the Post Office over to a corporation."[4]

HARNESSING A RIVER: THE TVA

During World War I, in order to produce nitrogen for explosives, the federal government bought a good deal of land, a dam, a powerhouse, and other facilities at Muscle Shoals, on the Tennessee River. After the war people began to ask what the government should do with this property. Some wanted to sell it to private interests. Others, led by a man of great vision and integrity—Senator George W. Norris, a Republican from Nebraska—urged that the federal government assume responsibility for developing the whole Tennessee Valley.[5] After years of controversy, Congress in May 1933 passed a comprehensive act to improve the navigability of the Tennessee River in order to provide for flood control, reforestation, agricultural and industrial development, and the national defense. A government corporation, called the Tennessee Valley Authority (TVA) and headed by a board of three men, was set up. The TVA had a big job—to develop the physical, social, and economic resources of the whole Tennessee Valley, covering more that 40,000 square miles.

The TVA's achievements have been remarkable. Today it operates over a score of dams on the Tennessee River and its tributaries. It produces a vast quantity of electricity, much of which is used for defense activities, as in the production of atomic energy, explosives, and aluminum. It manufactures and sells fertilizers. The Tennessee is now navigable for 630 miles, and no damaging floods have swept the area since the elaborate storage system was completed. Water pollution has been reduced, malaria rendered all but extinct, hillsides reforested, fish and wildlife fostered, and recreation areas developed. But TVA's main impact has been on the people of the Valley. They benefited directly from the low electricity rates, cheap fertilizer, flood control, and construction jobs. Moreover, TVA experts have taught them how to conserve soil, use machinery, diversify their farming, and improve their education and health.

All this would suggest that the TVA experiment has turned out very well and that much of the early criticism of Valley socialism has disappeared. Nevertheless, a good many people are still asking questions. Some, for example, criticize the TVA's financial policies. Originally the agency was viewed as a yardstick against which private utilities would be measured. As

---

[4] "Weekly Report," *Congressional Quarterly* (Aug. 2, 1968), p. 2078. Morton Baratz, *Economics of the Postal Service* (Public Affairs Press, 1962), weighs alternative approaches to the mail service.

[5] See *Fighting Liberal, The Autobiography of George W. Norris* (Macmillan, 1945), esp. pp. 245–267.

things have turned out, the average kilowatt-hour price of TVA electricity is less than half the average cost for the rest of the country. But critics of TVA charge that this is not a fair yardstick, because TVA's rates do not include all the expenses that a comparable private utility would have to pay. They argue, for example, that TVA pays far less in taxation than private utilities (TVA makes some payments to local governments in lieu of taxes) and can borrow money at a lower rate of interest. Furthermore, they declare, too small a portion of the original investment was assessed to electric power, and the TVA has not returned from its sale of electricity enough funds to repay the original investment.

The truth has been shrouded in a confusion of charges, countercharges, and figure-juggling, but it does seem clear that the yardstick idea has not worked out very well. Here again we see the difficulty of judging public enterprise in terms of private-enterprise standards. On the other hand, there seems to be wide agreement on the following:

1   The Tennessee Valley Authority has been run efficiently and honestly, although management by a three-man board has raised serious problems.

2   Politics in the narrow sense of party patronage and spoils has been kept out of the agency.

3   The people in the Valley have benefited enormously from TVA's work. (Average per capita income in the Valley has grown at a faster rate than in the nation as a whole.)

4   The Tennessee Valley Authority has cost a great deal of money, much of it from the national treasury, but TVA has strengthened national defense and the whole economy. "Most of TVA's phenomenal growth in electric power production took place during World War II and the Korean War. . . ,"[6] and it has been vital to our national defense.

TVA has also made a major contribution to the science of government and has developed interesting new methods of cooperating with state and local officials. It has shown that the federal government can decentralize and still do its job. Above all, it has dramatized the enormous possibilities of unified regional development. It has proved the truth of the first Hoover Commission's judgment that

A plan for the development of a river basin cannot be devised by adding together the special studies and the separate recommendations of unifunctional agencies concerned, respectively, with navigation, flood control, irrigation, land drainage, pollution abatement, power development, domestic and industrial water supply, fishing, and recreation. These varied and sometimes conflicting purposes must be put together and integrated in a single plan of development.[7]

Will there be more TVAs? No one can say, but two obstacles may stand in the way of other unified valley authorities. One is the opposition of special

[6]Aaron Wildavsky, "TVA and Power Politics," *The American Political Science Review* (September 1961) p. 590.

[7]U.S. Commission on Organization of the Executive Branch of the Government, *Reorganization of the Department of the Interior* (U.S. Government Printing Office, 1949), p. 28.

interests in the valleys and of key officials in Washington. The other is the fear that if further regional authorities are created, the problem will arise of coordinating the different authorities. It is possible that future authorities — if any are created — might operate under the general supervision of the Department of the Interior.

ATOMIC ENERGY FOR PEACE AND WAR

Originally, the main job of the Atomic Energy Commission (AEC) was to build and stockpile atomic bombs. In its two decades of existence, the AEC has performed this task admirably — so much so that today the nation's military arsenal is brimming with nuclear weapons, and a huge surplus of fissionable material is on hand for building even more bombs. The AEC has also overseen the development of the peaceful use of the atom; at a cost of nearly $2 billion, atomic energy is beginning to compete with electricity as a power source. In fact, through its own research and development laboratories at such places as Oak Ridge, Tennessee, and the Brookhaven National Laboratory on Long Island and through contracts with universities and private research organizations, the AEC has assured the United States of leadership in nearly every phase of nuclear research. Past successes in both the military and civilian aspects of the program have in recent years permitted expenditures for atomic energy to be decreased. This great success has been achieved under terms of the Atomic Energy Act of 1946, an act that was once described as ". . . perhaps the most radical law ever enacted in the United States" — one that virtually set up "an island of socialism in the midst of a free enterprise economy."[8] How did a conservative Congress happen to pass such a measure?

In 1945 Congress found itself in the remarkable position of being able to provide in advance for the rational control of a gigantic new resource — atomic energy. Some voices were raised in favor of private control, but most congressmen decided that the opportunity was too precious to surrender. Scientists testified that the use of fissionable, fusionable, and radioactive materials would lead to further significant discoveries, which in time would create numberless and unpredictable problems. Without some kind of central control and planning, chaos would set in. So certain was Congress of the need for government development that, in the end, it socialized atomic energy with virtually no discussion at all.

Legislative battles did break out, however, over several provisions of the bill. Civilian versus military control was the most controversial issue. As first introduced, the atomic energy bill explicitly provided that members of the proposed Atomic Energy Commission might be officers of the Army or Navy. Shortly, a new type of pressure group sprang into action — atomic scientists. Many of them had chafed under military control during the war, and they feared that such control might be authoritarian, militaristic, and harmful to the spirit of free, scientific inquiry. The scientists organized citizens' committees, testified before Congress, made speeches, put out propaganda, and lobbied on Capitol Hill. Partly as a result of this skillful political action, the

[8]J. R. Newman, "America's Most Radical Law," *Harper's Magazine* (May 1947), p. 436.

bill was changed. The Commission would be entirely civilian, but it would be advised on military matters by a military liaison committee.

Although the AEC's management of atomic energy has been successful, some doubt that the commission form of control is still administratively effective. It was originally felt that diffused responsibility was a necessary check in the new and secret field and certainly preferable to the concentration of authority in a single individual. In recent years, however, as one member of the AEC put it,

> The atom has been assimilated into the affairs of the nation. . . . To an increasing extent the atomic energy enterprise has spread throughout the government and has had to be conducted by the AEC in conjunction with other agencies including the Department of Defense, State, NASA, Commerce, Interior and the Committees of Congress. Most significantly, the atomic enterprise is co-ordinated at the White House level, by the President himself, by his staff members concerned with national security affairs, and by his assistants on matters of science and technology and, as usual, or more than usual, by the Bureau of the Budget.[9]

The development of policy by the Commission has been overseen by the Joint Congressional Committee on Atomic Energy, which has taken its statutory watchdog responsibilities very seriously. The anomalous political position of the AEC, the wider dispersion of information about nuclear energy, the lessened need for dispersed authority, the great involvement of private industry ("the Atomic Energy Commission, which was hailed . . . as a triumph of socialism, supports a program in which some nine tenths of the employees work for private corporations"[10])—all these considerations led the AEC on two occasions to recommend that the commission form of management be abolished and a single administrator be placed in charge. But no action on this suggestion has as yet been taken.

Thus owing to the increased involvement with atomic energy by other departments and agencies as well as by private industry, the AEC has lost much of its previously unique status in government. Nevertheless, atomic energy is still fraught with a heavy public interest because of such problems as conflict arising from overlapping federal and state safety codes, the extent of permissible competition among private atomic enterprises, the impact of this source upon other power sources, and the effects on the economy of the location of atomic facilities. The AEC's decision to concentrate the bulk of its atomic installations in the Ohio Valley, for example, stimulated the whole economy of the region and caused a major shift in population. Hence it is safe to assume that whether the AEC continues in its present collegial form or comes to be run by a single administrator, further development of atomic energy will continue to be an enterprise principally under direct governmental management.

So much for the three cases of direct management of enterprises by the national government. Will the government continue to involve itself in this way, or does there seem to be a trend away from such arrangements? The

[9]John W. Finney, "Is the AEC Obsolete?" *The Reporter* (Nov. 19, 1964), p. 45.
[10]Don K. Price, *The Scientific Estate* (Harvard Univ. Press, 1965), p. 37.

Eisenhower administration, opposing in principle federal operation of enterprises, closed a number of federal establishments that were competing with private enterprise. But other forces—for example, technology—work in the opposite direction. The Russian success in landing a rocket on the moon in 1959 climaxed an intensive program of exploring space that compelled the United States to look at its own position in the race for space. The agency responsible for catching up with the Soviets is the National Aeronautics and Space Administration, which quickly built launching facilities capable of handling both liquid- and solid-fueled rockets; electronic tracking systems; telemetry data receiving and recording systems; range operation and control systems; and a long-range radar-tracking net. The space agency was given this vast assignment simply because no private enterprise could undertake it.

There is an important difference, however, between governmental management of space-age enterprises and their earlier counterparts discussed above. In the space-age enterprises, the greatest share of the work is not performed within the governmental establishment by civil servants but by private industry under governmental contract. For instance, nearly 80 percent of NASA's work is done by private industrial and university contractors. As many as five thousand private firms participated in the Apollo project. In the 1960s, three-quarters of the government's funds for research and development—amounting to well over $12 billion yearly—was contracted. Private concerns have been engaged for such functions as management of weapons systems, technical supervision and management of government-owned facilities, foreign technical assistance, educational activities, management analysis, and a host of additional activities. If the space-age enterprises are valid indicators of future governmental trends, then the movement is away from complete and direct governmental management of new enterprises and toward more cooperative ventures with private industry and universities.[11] But let us now turn to an even more important role of the government as manager—the indirect fiscal management of the whole economy through taxing, spending, investment, and other economic methods.

Raising the Money

Big government is expensive. By the end of the 1960s federal, state, and local governments spent over $200 billion yearly. This is between one-fourth and one-third of the income of all Americans; in short, our governments pay out about 25 cents of every dollar we earn. The national government is the biggest spender of all. In recent years Washington has disbursed more than all state and local governments combined.

Where does all this money come from? The federal government gets most of its funds from taxes and the rest from loans, commercial revenues from governmental enterprises, income from special fees and fines, and grants and gifts.

[11]See Victor K. Heyman, "Government by Contract: Boon or Boner?" *Public Administration Review* (Spring 1961), pp. 59 ff.

"In this world," Benjamin Franklin once said, "nothing is certain but death and taxes." Tax collecting is one of the oldest activities of government. Indeed, one of the few contacts that many people in earlier societies had with government was through the tax collector. He was the dread figure who symbolized the demands and authority of some far-off ruler. Putting power over taxation into the hands of the people was a landmark in the rise of self-government. "No taxation without representation" has been the war cry not only of early Americans but, in effect, the people in countries the world over.

The new Constitution in 1787 clearly provided that Congress "shall have power to lay and collect taxes, duties, imposts, and excises." But duties and excise taxes had to be levied uniformly throughout the United States; direct taxes had to be apportioned among the states according to population; and no tax could be levied on articles exported from any state. Except during the Civil War, the federal government for a century relied on the tariff for most of its revenue. This hidden tax—which many people falsely thought to be a tax on foreigners—fluctuated with the rise and fall of trade and tariff levels. Congress supplemented these taxes with excise taxes on the manufacture or sale of certain goods, and in 1894 an income tax law was enacted (such a tax had been used during the Civil War but given up shortly afterwards). The 1894 tax was not drastic—only 2 percent on all incomes over $4,000—but it seemed a portent of worse things to come. The next year, in *Pollock* v. *Farmers Loan and Trust Co.*, the Supreme Court declared the tax measure unconstitutional on the ground that it was a direct tax and therefore had to be apportioned among the states according to population. Twenty years later, in 1915, the Sixteenth Amendment was adopted authorizing Congress "to lay and collect taxes on incomes, from whatever source derived, without apportionment among the several States, and without regard to any census or enumeration."

Raising money is only one important objective of taxation; regulation and, more recently, promotion of economic growth are others. Taxation as a device to promote economic growth will be discussed later. In a broad sense, all taxation regulates human behavior; for example, a graduated income tax has a leveling influence on incomes, and a tariff act affects foreign trade. More specifically, Congress has used its taxing power to prevent or regulate certain practices. Years ago, Congress laid a 10 percent tax on the circulation of notes by state banks, immediately putting an end to such issues.

Today federal taxes are as follows:

Income taxes on individuals. Levies on the income tax of individuals account for about 40 percent of the federal government's tax revenue. Originally set at a low rate, the income tax was greatly increased during World War I and went to new heights during World War II and the Korean conflict. Over the years the income tax has grown increasingly complex as Congress has responded to claims for differing kinds of exemptions and rates, but the tax has one great advantage in its flexibility. The schedule of rates can be raised or lowered in order to stimulate or restrain economic activity. In 1964 a $12 billion tax cut proved to be a healthy stimulus to the economy. In 1968 a 10 percent surtax was added to restrain inflationary pressures.

Income taxes on corporations. These account for about 20 percent of the national government's tax dollar. As late as 1942, corporate income taxes amounted to more than individual income taxes, but returns from the latter increased more rapidly during World War II.

Excise taxes. Other than those specially earmarked, federal taxes on liquor, tobacco, automobiles, gasoline, telephones, air travel, and other so-called luxury items are scheduled to be reduced in stages until they are eliminated. However, the date for the elimination of these taxes is continually postponed by Congress, so that they still account for almost 10 percent each year.

Customs duties. Though no longer the main source of federal income, these taxes provided in recent years an annual yield of almost $500 million.

THE POLITICS AND MACHINERY OF TAXATION

When a young law assistant once commiserated with Justice Holmes on the taxes he had to pay, the old man replied, "With taxes I buy civilization." Most of us are less philsophical. We complain that our tax load is too heavy and that someone else is not carrying his fair share. People with large incomes naturally grumble about income taxes as high as 50 percent or more of their net income. Low-income people point out that even a low tax may deprive them of the necessities of life. People in the middle-income brackets feel that their plight is worst of all—their incomes are not high but their taxes are.

What is the best type of tax? Some say the *graduated income tax*, because it is relatively easy to collect, hits hardest those who are most able to pay, and hardly touches those at the bottom of the income ladder. Others argue that *excise taxes* are the fairest, because they are paid by people who are spending money for goods—especially luxury goods—and thus obviously have money to spare. Furthermore, by discouraging people from buying expensive goods, excise taxes have a desirable deflationary effect in time of rising prices. On the other hand, excise taxes are more expensive to collect than income taxes, and in some cases, such as the tax on tobacco, they may hit the poor hardest. Most controversial of all taxes is the *general sales tax*, which resembles the excise tax except that it is levied against the sales of all goods. Labor and liberal organizations

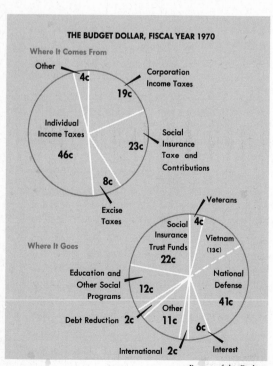

THE BUDGET DOLLAR, FISCAL YEAR 1970

Where It Comes From

Other 4c
Corporation Income Taxes 19c
Individual Income Taxes 46c
Social Insurance Taxe and Contributions 23c
Excise Taxes 8c

Where It Goes

Veterans 4c
Social Insurance Trust Funds 22c
Vietnam (13c)
Education and Other Social Programs 12c
National Defense 41c
Debt Reduction 2c
Other 11c
Interest 6c
International 2c

Bureau of the Budget.

denounce this form of tax as regressive—that is, it hurts the poor man more than the rich man, because the former uses all his earnings to buy goods, whereas the latter may devote more of his income to buying personal services or to savings. Proponents of the sales tax stress its anti-inflationary effect and point ot its successful use in a number of states.

A recent tax bill illustrated the wide impact of taxes on a variety of individuals and groups. Testifying on proposed tax changes before a congressional committee, 138 witnesses expressed their views; and scores of briefs were submitted. The printed testimony covered more than sixteen hundred pages. Business representatives opposed new taxes on corporations. Small businessmen complained that existing taxes favored big business. Spokesmen for tobacco growers, transportation interests, the wine and spirits industry, movies, the legitimate theater, candymakers, telephone companies, and bowling alley proprietors argued that the proposed tax would discriminate against them. Labor demanded a lighter burden for low-income groups and higher taxes on business. Unorganized workers and consumers, however, were not represented.

Although the Constitution provides that all revenue bills must be initiated in the House of Representatives, it is usually the President who originates tax legislation. With the help of tax experts on his staff and in the Treasury Department, he draws up a tax program not only designed to meet the government's revenue needs for the coming fiscal year but also taking into consideration the current and projected state of the economy. Often the representatives of interest groups are consulted while the bill is being formulated. Then the President submits his tax program to Congress, often along with his budget message. The powerful House Ways and Means Committee next holds hearings on the bill; administration spokesmen, headed by the Secretary of the Treasury, usually lead off the parade of witnesses, followed by representatives of interested groups, taxation experts, and others. Following committee consideration, tax measures go through Congress in much the same manner as other bills. Although the Senate cannot initiate tax legislation, it refuses to take a backseat in tax matters. It often differs with the House and forces extensive changes of bills coming from the lower chamber. Sometimes Congress refuses to follow the President's recommendations and works out a tax measure largely on its own.

The Treasury Department has the job of collecting the taxes levied by

Justus in The Minneapolis Star.

Under our form of federalism the taxpayer supports three levels of government.

Congress. One of the original departments set up in 1789 and headed by the second-highest-ranking Secretary, this Department today is a large agency employing about ninety-six thousand people. The actual tax-collecting job falls mainly to the Internal Revenue Service. Fifty-eight district directors are located throughout the country, and taxes are paid into district offices rather than directly to Washington. The Service takes in over $100 billion a year at the cost of less than 50 cents for each $100 in returns. Customs are collected by the Treasury Department's Bureau of Customs, which maintains ports of entry, inspects the discharge of cargo, assesses the value of merchandise, and, through the services of the United States Coast Guard, prevents smuggling.

UNCLE SAM, BORROWER

When a person is suddenly faced with expenses too heavy to meet out of his regular income, he may have to borrow money. The same is true of government. During military and economic crises, the federal government has gone heavily in debt. It borrowed $23 billion during World War I, about $13 billion more during the 1930s, and over $200 billion more during World War II. Between crises, the government has tried to pay off its debts, but progress has been slow. By 1970 the gross federal debt was nearing $372 billion.

Borrowing costs money. The federal government can borrow at a relatively low rate—because no security is safer than a government bond. Nevertheless, the federal debt is so huge today that the interest alone is approaching $16 billion a year. The size of the debt and of the interest payments alarms many Americans. How long can we allow the debt to grow at this staggering rate? Two considerations must be kept in mind. In the first place, the government owes most of the money to its own people rather than to foreign governments or persons; and second, the economic strength and resources of the country are more significant than the size of the public debt.

How does the government borrow money? The Constitution says that Congress may "borrow money on the credit of the United States"; it puts no limit on either the extent or method of borrowing. Under congressional authorization, the Treasury Department sells securities to banks, corporations, and individuals. Usually these securities take the form of long-term bonds or short-term treasury notes. Some bonds may be cashed in at any time, others not until their maturity. Because the United States government guarantees these bonds, they are in great demand, especially by banks and investment companies. However, the government, particularly in time of inflation, likes to induce as many individuals as possible to buy bonds, because individuals who buy bonds have less money with which to buy goods and so will not contribute to inflationary pressures.

A third source of federal funds consists of administrative and commercial revenues. The fee paid to the State Department for a passport and the fine paid by a criminal are administrative revenues that account for a portion —though a very small portion—of federal income. More important are the funds paid to the federal government in exchange for direct services—payments to the Post Office for stamps, to the Park Service for recreation, to the Government Printing Office for pamphlets.

Finally, some public-spirited people actually give money or property to the government. Mr. Justice Holmes, who did not mind taxes, left the government almost his entire estate when he died. But gifts, needless to say, are an infinitesimal source of federal revenue.

Spending the Money

All the billions of dollars the government takes in are funneled into the treasury and then rapidly move out through hundreds of channels to points throughout the nation and, indeed, throughout the world. Nothing reflects the rise of big government more clearly than the change in the amount and methods of its spending. As recently as 1933 the federal government spent only $4 billion, about $30 per capita. In 1970 the respective figures were $200 billion and over $1,000. The machinery for spending has changed, too. At one time spending was loosely administered. Records show, for example, that in an early year of the Republic one Nicholas Johnson, a Navy agent of Newburyport, Massachusetts, was handed several thousand dollars to supply "Capt. Brown for recruiting his Crew."[12] Today Mr. Johnson would have to make out detailed forms and wait for a check.

Where does the money go? Most of it, of course, is for national defense. The $198 billion unified budget estimated for the fiscal year 1970 allots about 43 percent to national security and international programs; 6 percent to interest on the national debt and 2 percent to debt reduction; 4 percent to veterans; 34 percent to social insurance, education, and other major social programs; and 11 percent to other programs, such as space and agriculture. Even in the last two decades interesting changes have taken place. In 1939 total expenditures of the federal government amounted to $9 billion. Of this, national defense took about $1 billion, interest less than $1 billion, and veterans about $600 million. It is hard to realize today that as recently as 1939 most federal expenses were for domestic relief and welfare functions. Significantly, in 1939 we spent only about 0.5 percent of the budget on international activities. The proportion has risen manyfold as we have faced up to our global responsibilities.

The sheer fact of spending $198 billion a year is most significant of all. Years ago, federal revenues and outlays were so small that national taxing and spending had little impact on the overall economy. But today the federal government cannot drain billions of dollars from certain areas of the economy and pump them back into other areas without its having a profound effect on the economy of the nation and of the world at large. This problem will be considered later in the chapter. First we must see how the federal budget is drawn up and made into law.

FORMULATING THE BUDGET

As we have seen, Congress must authorize the spending of funds, but the initiation of appropriations is a responsibility of the President. The first step

[12]L. D. White, *The Federalists* (Macmillan, 1948), p. 341.

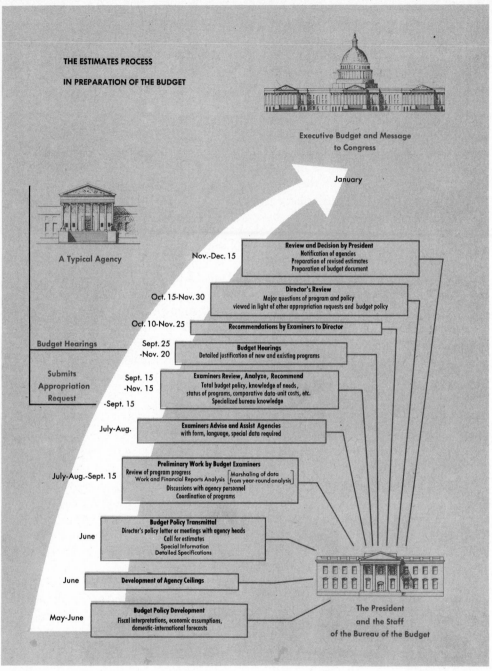

THE ESTIMATES PROCESS

IN PREPARATION OF THE BUDGET

Executive Budget and Message
to Congress

January

A Typical Agency

Nov.-Dec. 15

Review and Decision by President
Notification of agencies
Preparation of revised estimates
Preparation of budget document

Oct. 15-Nov. 30

Director's Review
Major questions of program and policy
viewed in light of other appropriation requests and budget policy

Oct. 10-Nov. 25

Recommendations by Examiners to Director

Budget Hearings

Sept. 25
-Nov. 20

Budget Hearings
Detailed justification of new and existing programs

Submits
Appropriation
Request

Sept. 15
-Nov. 15

Examiners Review, Analyze, Recommend
Total budget policy, knowledge of needs,
status of programs, comparative data-unit costs, etc.
Specialized bureau knowledge

-Sept. 15

July-Aug.

Examiners Advise and Assist Agencies
with form, language, special data required

July-Aug.-Sept. 15

Preliminary Work by Budget Examiners
Review of program progress   Marshaling of data
Work and Financial Reports Analysis from year-round analysis
Discussions with agency personnel
Coordination of programs

June

Budget Policy Transmittal
Director's policy letter or meetings with agency heads
Call for estimates
Special Information
Detailed Specifications

June

Development of Agency Ceilings

The President
and the Staff
of the Bureau of the Budget

May-June

Budget Policy Development
Fiscal interpretations, economic assumptions,
domestic-international forecasts

Bureau of the Budget.

in preparing a federal budget is for the various departments and agencies to estimate their needs.[13] This process starts early; while Congress is debating the budget for the fiscal year immediately ahead, the agencies are making

---

[13]For a discussion and graphic presentation of the budgetary cycle, see Aaron Wildavsky, *The Politics of the Budgetary Process* (Little, Brown, 1964).

budget estimates for the year following. The estimating job is handled largely by budget officers working under the direction of the agency chiefs. The agency officials must take into account not only their needs as they see them, but also the overall presidential program and the probable reactions of Congress, especially those of the House Appropriations Committee.[14] Departmental budgets are highly detailed; they include estimates on expected needs for personnel, supplies, office space, and the like.

The Bureau of the Budget handles the next phase of budget-making. A staff agency of the President, the Bureau scrutinizes each agency budget to see if it is in accord with the President's budget plans. This job is done by experienced budget examiners who usually have been long acquainted with a particular agency and can look over its requests with a sharp eye for accuracy, economy, and good program planning. Hearings are then held to give agency spokesmen a chance to clarify and defend their estimated needs. The Director of the Budget and his aides, who make the final decision, very frequently prune the agencies' requests rather severely.

For months the Budget Director has been conferring with the President and has been trying to keep the agencies below the budget ceilings set by him. Finally—it is probably December by now—the Director arrives at the White House with a single consolidated set of estimates of both revenue and expenditures, the product of perhaps a year's work. The President has reserved a day or two for a final review of the budget, and the two men check the consolidated figures. The Budget Director also helps the President prepare a budget message that will stress key aspects of the budget and tie it in with broad national plans. By January, soon after Congress convenes, the budget and the message are ready for the legislature and the people.

PRESENTING THE BUDGET

A budget as big and complex as that of the national government is not easy to understand; it is not even easy to present in a manner that makes possible comprehension of the financial picture of the national government. Until 1968 three separate budgets—the administrative budget, the consolidated cash budget, and the national income accounts budget—were presented, but the administrative budget was the one that received public attention.

The *administrative budget* shows all receipts and expenditures by the national government except for the trust funds and special accounts—for example, the account into which are paid old-age insurance taxes and from which are paid old-age insurance benefits. The *national income accounts budget* shows all transactions as they are incurred except for loans by the federal government. The *consolidated cash budget* shows all actual transactions, that is, the actual flow into and out of the federal treasury during the fiscal year, regardless of whether it consists of appropriated funds, trust accounts, loans, repayments, or whatever.

In 1968 President Johnson added a new method of presenting the budget—the unified budget—in accordance with the proposals of a bipartisan Com-

---

[14]See *ibid.*, Chap. 2; and Richard F. Fenno, Jr., "The House Appropriations Committee as a Political System," *The American Political Science Review* (June 1962), pp. 310–324.

Drawing by B. Tobey; © 1962 The New Yorker Magazine, Inc.

"Well, here's another two-hundred-million debt they're saddling our generation with."

mission on Budget Concepts. The *unified budget* includes trust-fund revenues and expenditures in addition to ordinary revenues and expenditures; it also includes as an expenditure net lending, that is, the amount the government lends for the fiscal year in excess of what it is paid. In other words, a net lending is considered for the fiscal year as if it were an expenditure for that year.

For fiscal 1970 the four different ways of presenting the federal budget are shown in Table 26-1.

TABLE 26-1
Fiscal 1970 Budget Estimates
(in billions of dollars)

Budget	Receipts	Payments	Surplus
Administrative	147.9	154.7	−6.8
National Income Accounts	202.3	199.6	2.7
Consolidated Cash	206.6	203.2	3.4
Unified	198.7	195.3	3.4

SOURCE: *Special Analyses, Budget of the United States Government, Fiscal 1970*, pages 18–19.

CHAPTER 26
Government
as
Manager

After Congress has appropriated money, it reserves the right to check up on the way the money is spent. Under the Budget and Accounting Act of 1921, the General Accounting Office (GAO) does the national government's accounting job. The GAO is headed by a Comptroller General, who is appointed by the President with the approval of the Senate. The Comptroller General enjoys some measure of independence, however, for his term of office is fifteen years, he is ineligible for reappointment, and he can be removed only for specific cause by a joint resolution of Congress.

The Comptroller General was originally intended to operate as an independent auditor serving as an arm of Congress to guard against improper and

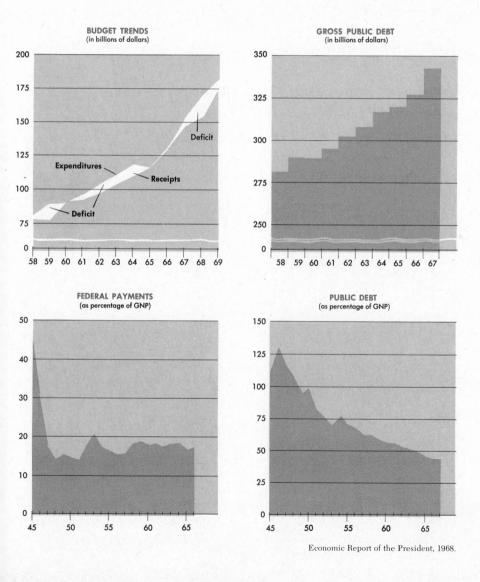

Economic Report of the President, 1968.

unauthorized expenditures. But as time went on, he was swamped by a gigantic accounting job that forced him to handle administrative matters in the executive branch even though he was not responsible to the Chief Executive. At the same time, overall management in the executive branch suffered, because daily accounting, an important instrument of administrative control, had been placed in a separate agency.

Improvements have been made in recent years. The GAO now uses spot sampling methods to check vouchers and makes its audits in the field rather than in Washington. Although the Comptroller General still has the authority to disallow expenditures, his approval is no longer needed prior to the disbursement of funds. Being relieved of personal responsibility for payments that may subsequently be disallowed, disbursing officers (provided they have acted in good faith and with reasonable diligence) have been encouraged to make their own decisions about the legality of expenditures. Moreover, in 1950 Congress gave the departments and agencies, subject to supervision of the GAO, the responsibility and authority to set up their own internal accounting operations. These procedures allow the Comptroller General to spend more time carrying out the vital legislative functions of scrutinizing administrative fiscal practices, of making sure that laws governing appropriations are correctly interpreted, of checking on the efficiency of accounting and other administrative practices—and of reporting on all these to Congress.

It might seem that accounting is a technical matter that could be settled without much argument. On the contrary, accounting is a political problem too, for it reflects two struggles in Washington—the attempt of Congress as a whole to maintain as much control as possible over the still mushrooming bureaucratic machine and the struggle of individual legislators to maintain a system that checks individual administrative payments.

Managing Money

Today's economy is essentially a money economy. Instead of using a system of barter, "civilized" peoples exchange commodities through a vast system of money and credit. We have seen the tremendous role the federal government plays in this system, simply because it gets and spends nearly $190 billion a year. But aside from its role as the biggest buyer and seller of goods and services, the federal government has a more direct impact on our money economy. It manufactures money; it regulates the value of money; and it controls the nation's credit system.

Manufacturing money is the easiest of these jobs. The Bureau of Engraving and Printing in the Treasury Department, using carefully designed plates and special types of paper, turns out millions of dollars in the form of bills, bonds, and postage stamps every week; this "folding-money" is fed into general circulation through the Treasury and the Federal Reserve banks. The Bureau of the Mint in Philadelphia, Denver, and San Francisco (also under the Treasury) manufactures various coins that together make up about one-twentieth of the country's cash.

In itself, this money is only so much paper and metal. How does the government maintain its value?

THE CURRENCY SYSTEM

The Constitution gives the federal government the right to manage the nation's monetary system. Under the Articles of Confederation, the national currency had consisted mainly of almost worthless paper money, and the individual states had maintained separate currencies. To correct this, the Constitution of 1787 vested in Congress authority to coin money and to regulate its value, carefully withholding this power from the states. Thanks partly to Secretary of the Treasury Hamilton, the early Americans scrapped the confusing British system of guineas, pounds, shillings, and pence and adopted a decimal system.

Today the United States is on the modified gold standard—the money and credit supply is backed up in part with a huge store of gold at Fort Knox, Kentucky, and the unit of monetary value is defined in terms of gold. But all the currency of the United States—Federal Reserve Notes and coins—is legal tender and cannot be freely exchanged for gold or silver. (A few United States Notes, Treasury Notes, Federal Bank Notes, National Bank Notes, or Silver Certificates are still oustanding but they are being retired.) In short, the money of the United States is freely redeemable only for other money of the United States.

Money makes up only a part of the circulating medium and is less important to our economy than credit. In the expansion and contraction of credit, the most important institutions are the nation's banks and the Federal Reserve System.

BANKS AND LENDING INSTITUTIONS

Although banking is a private business, it is subject to close governmental supervision. There are almost 14,000 banks in the United States; 4,800 are chartered by the national government, the others by the states. The national banks, however, have 50 percent of all bank deposits in their custody. The Comptroller of the Currency in the Department of the Treasury supervises their operations. Each national bank must file reports on its financial condition at least four times a year and must permit bank examiners to inspect its books at least three times every two years—at unannounced times.

Although state authorities have the primary responsibility to supervise state-chartered banks, most of these banks are also subject to federal regulation, because their deposits are insured by the Federal Deposit Insurance Corporation (FDIC). All national banks must participate in this program, and state banks that meet approved standards are also permitted to do so. All but a few hundred of the commercial bank and trust companies in the United States have their deposits insured by the FDIC, as do some of the over 500 mutual savings banks. The FDIC routinely examines banks that are not members of the Federal Reserve System (see below) and establishes rules designed to keep them solvent. When a member bank becomes insolvent, the FDIC takes over its management and pays each depositor up to $15,000.

The Federal Savings and Loan Insurance Corporation, operating under the supervision of the Federal Home Loan Bank Board, protects investors in federal savings and loan associations and those state-chartered institutions approved for participation. Like the FDIC, it guarantees savings up to $15,000 for each account.

The national government also promotes the establishment of *credit unions*, associations of persons having a common bond of occupation or residence who may secure a federal charter and receive assistance from the Bureau of Federal Credit Unions in the Department of Health, Education, and Welfare. These unions, which now number about 12,000, encourage members to deposit excess funds which may then be lent to other members at relatively low interest rates.

THE FEDERAL RESERVE SYSTEM

In many nations, a central bank owned and operated by the national government determines general monetary policies. The Constitution does not specifically authorize the national government to create such a bank—indeed, it says nothing at all about banking. But Alexander Hamilton believed that some such institution was necessary, and in 1791, on his initiative, the United States Bank was incorporated by the national government and given a twenty-year charter. This bank was partly private and partly public; the national government owned only a minority of the shares and had only a minority voice in its management. Jefferson and his supporters opposed the bank on monetary, political, and constitutional grounds; nevertheless, President Madison found it necessary to have the bank rechartered for another twenty years in 1816, after the Jeffersonians had refused to do so in 1811. In 1819 the Supreme Court in *McCulloch* v. *Maryland* (see Chapter 4) upheld the constitutionality of the bank as a necessary and proper way for the national government to establish a uniform currency and to care for the property of the United States.

After the bank closed its doors in 1836, state banks, which had previously been restrained by the second United States Bank, embarked on an orgy of issuing notes that often could not be redeemed. A military crisis forced a housecleaning. To stabilize an economy beset with war demands and to support the desires of the "dear money" groups, Congress authorized in 1863 the chartering of national banks. These are privately owned corporations not to be confused with a central bank or an institution like the United States Bank. State banks were permitted to continue in business, but a 10 percent federal tax on their notes quickly drove state bank notes out of existence.

The national bank system created during the Civil War was stable—indeed, so stable that it was inflexible. Financial crises during the late nineteenth century and in 1907 revealed an unhappy tendency of banks to restrict their loans and of national banks to contract their issuance of notes, just at the times when an *expansion* of money was needed. In order to furnish an elastic currency, and for other reasons, Congress in 1913 established the Federal Reserve System.

The act of 1913 was a compromise. Some wanted a strong central bank, but many feared that this would centralize control over currency in too few hands. So a system was established that gives us a modified central banking program with considerable decentralization. The country is divided into twelve Federal Reserve districts, in each of which there is a Federal Reserve bank (most Federal Reserve banks have branches). Each Federal Reserve bank is owned by member banks. All national banks must join the system, and state banks that meet standards are permitted to do so. Today approximately 6,100 of the 14,000 banks are members of the system; these are the largest banks and have over 85 percent of total deposits.

Each Federal Reserve bank is headed by a board of directors, of which six members are elected by the member banks and three appointed by the Board of Governors (see immediately below) in Washington. Three of the directors elected by the member banks must be bankers, and three must be active in business and industry. The three directors appointed by the Board of Governors may not have any financial interest in and may not work for any bank. The Board of Governors designates one of its appointees chairman of the board of directors, and this board in turn selects a president to serve as its chief executive officer.

A seven-man Board of Governors sitting in Washington supervises the entire system. These men are selected by the President with the consent of the Senate for fourteen-year terms, and the President designates the chairman, who has a four-year term. The Board of Governors—advised by the Federal Advisory Council, which is composed of a member from each Federal Reserve district—meets in Washington at least four times a year and determines general monetary and credit policies. It has four major devices to tighten or loosen the financial activities of the nation's banks and, in turn, of the whole economy:

1 To increase or decrease within legal limits the reserves that member banks must maintain against their deposits in the Federal Reserve bank.

2 To raise or lower the rediscount rate charged by Federal Reserve banks to member banks. The rediscount rate is the price member banks must pay to get cash from the Federal Reserve banks for acceptable commercial notes that the banks hold.

3 Through the Open Market Committee (composed of all members of the board of governors and five representatives of the Reserve banks), to sell or buy government securities and certain other bills of exchange, bank acceptances, and so on.

4 To exercise direct control over the credit that may be extended in order to purchase securities (called margin requirements). From time to time Congress has given the Board of Governors temporary authority to fix terms of consumer credit.

Through these and other devices, the Board of Governors may affect the flow of money by tightening or loosening credit. For example, if inflation is threatening, the board can depress the economy by raising member-bank reserve requirements (thus cutting down on the cash they have available for lending), by raising rediscount rates (thus forcing member banks to raise the rates for which they will lend money), by selling government securities in the open market (thus absorbing funds from the economy), and by raising margin requirements (thus reducing credit available to bid up the prices of securities). In addition, the Federal Reserve banks serve as depositories for government funds, clear checks and transfer funds among member banks, and may in case of economic emergency even lend money directly to businesses.

The Federal Reserve System is intentionally isolated from influence by the President, and, because it does not depend on annual appropriations, even Congress exercises little control over it. "Devised as a service agency for banking and commerce—to achieve a semi-automatic adjustment of the money supply—the Federal Reserve has become as well a policy-making institution with major responsibility for national economic stabilization."[15] And many observers feel that it is improper to vest this important new responsibility in an agency so divorced from public accountability. The Board of Governors, for example, often has to make a choice between fighting inflation, which may cause unemployment, and promoting employment at the expense of creating inflation. As Gardiner C. Means has said, "There is a good deal of question whether such a momentous decision should rest with the Federal Reserve Board."[16] On the other side, many, including most bankers, are anxious to preserve the system's independence. They believe that only an agency insulated from political pressures can take steps to prevent inflation that are often unpopular.

Today all agree that monetary policy must be considered as but one weapon to combat depression, control inflation, foster full employment, and encourage economic growth. Whether or not we can retain a system in which the central banking authorities "can legally . . . tell the head of [their] own Government to go fly a kite"[17] remains a moot issue.

Managing the Economy

So far we have seen how the national government directly manages certain economic activities, such as the Post Office and TVA; how it raises and spends billions of dollars a year; and how it controls currency, banking, and credit (although the banks themselves are legally under private control). We have observed the political and governmental processes that shape the way in which government operates these controls.

Does the government have the same direct control over the national economy that it has, say, over the Post Office and national forests? No. Only if we had a socialized economy administered from Washington would we have a

---

[15]See Michael D. Reagan, "The Political Structure of the Federal Reserve System," *The American Political Science Review* (March 1961), pp. 64–76, for a detailed analysis of the present structure of policy implications of the Federal Reserve System.

[16]Quoted in *ibid.*, p. 75.

[17]Elliot V. Bell, quoted in *ibid.*, p. 76.

managed economy in that sense. Actually we have an economy in which a great deal of power is left to private individuals and enterprises. And yet the government keeps a firm hand on all the gears and levers that control the general direction in which the economy will move and the rate at which it will move. These gears and levers are marked taxes, spending, credit, and the like. If these levers were operated in a haphazard, whimsical way, they might have a catastrophic effect. Operated in a carefully synchronized manner, however, they can help keep the economy on an even keel.

It is only rather recently that Americans have recognized the part that government could play in stabilizing and invigorating the economy. (There are still differences of opinion over the part that it *should* play.) The slow development of our understanding, the political struggle over the question of whether the federal government should take responsibility for full employment, the enactment of the Employment Act of 1946—these are fascinating episodes in the trend toward overall control of the economy by the federal government.

ECONOMIC GROPING

Austerity is a hard teacher. The depression of the 1930s had a tremendous impact on American thinking about the role of government in economic matters. We have had long, severe depressions before—for example, in the 1870s and 1890s. But by 1929 the United States had become a rich and powerful nation, and prosperity seemed here to stay. Then the Great Depression struck. Millions of unemployed, falling prices and income, plummeting production—all added up to mass misery. "One vivid, gruesome moment of those dark days we shall never forget," wrote one observer. "We saw a crowd of some fifty men fighting over a barrel of garbage which had been set outside the back door of a restaurant. American citizens fighting for scraps of food like animals!"[18]

Despite a wide range of initiatives on the part of the New Deal to cope with the Depression, it hung on. Faint signs of recovery could be seen in the mid-1930s, but the recession of 1937–1938 indicated that we were by no means out of the woods. Eight or nine million people were jobless in 1939. Then came the war and unemployment was cured—for a while. Millions of people had more income, more security, a higher standard of living. Lord Beveridge in England posed a question that bothered many thoughtful Americans: "Unemployment has been practically abolished twice in the lives of most of us—in the last war and in this war. Why does war solve the problem of unemployment which is so insoluble in peace?"[19] Worried that the economy might collapse after the war, thousands of people came up with plans to ensure jobs for all.

One school of thought was that the Depression persisted because the New Deal was hostile to business and intruded government too long and too extensively in the economic life of the nation. They urged the government to reduce spending, lower taxes, curb the power of labor, and generally leave business and the economy alone except for traditional regulation and aids to

[18]Quoted in F. L. Allen, *Since Yesterday* (Harper & Row, 1940), p. 64.
[19]W. H. Beveridge, *The Pillars of Security* (Macmillan, 1943), p. 51.

certain businesses. Another large group, made up of economists, labor representatives, government officials, and others, took a different tack. They said that the trouble with the New Deal was not that it had done too much but that it had done too little. The thinking of this group was deeply influenced by the work of John Maynard Keynes, the English economist. In visits to the United States during the 1930s, Keynes warned that if people did not consume enough or invest enough, national income would fall. The way to increase national income is either to spend money on consumption goods (such as clothes or food or automobiles) or on investment goods (steel mills and dock facilities) or on both. Finally, *government must do the spending and investing if private enterprise by itself would not or could not.* The Keynesian approach was related to concepts involving governmental influence on public works, wages, prices, credit, taxation, and the like. Congress, through the passage of the Employment Act of 1946, gave formal acceptance to this latter of the two basic approaches.

THE EMPLOYMENT ACT OF 1946

Congressional enactment of a measure that specifically recognized the primacy of the national government in the maintenance of full employment was bound to be difficult.[20] The bill as presented by the Truman administration embodied the viewpoint of Keynesian economists and had the support of organized labor, many senators, and members of several Senate committee staffs. Arrayed against the bill were such organizations as the NAM, chambers of commerce, the American Farm Bureau Federation, and a number of key conservatives in Congress. Although the bill fairly easily passed the Senate in close to its original form, the conservative House Rules Committee ensured that only a much weaker version would pass the lower House. Enacted in February 1946, the act declared:

> It is the continuing policy and responsibility of the Federal Government to use all practicable means consistent with its needs and obligations and other essential considerations of national policy, with the assistance and cooperation of industry, agriculture, labor, and state and local governments, to coordinate and utilize all its plans, functions, and resources for the purpose of creating and maintaining, in a manner calculated to foster and promote free competitive enterprise and the general welfare, conditions under which there will be afforded useful employment, for those able, willing, and seeking to work, and to promote maximum employment, production, and purchasing power.

If this declaration sounds like double talk, the reason may be that the bill had to be built on a series of compromises; in effect, the bill made the federal government responsible for acting in the face of rising unemployment instead of relying wholly on nongovernmental forces. Equally important, the act established machinery to carry out that responsibility.

The Council of Economic Advisers (CEA). Composed of three members appointed by the President with the consent of the Senate and located in the

---

[20]For the full history of the bill, see Stephen K. Bailey, *Congress Makes a Law* (Columbia Univ. Press, 1950).

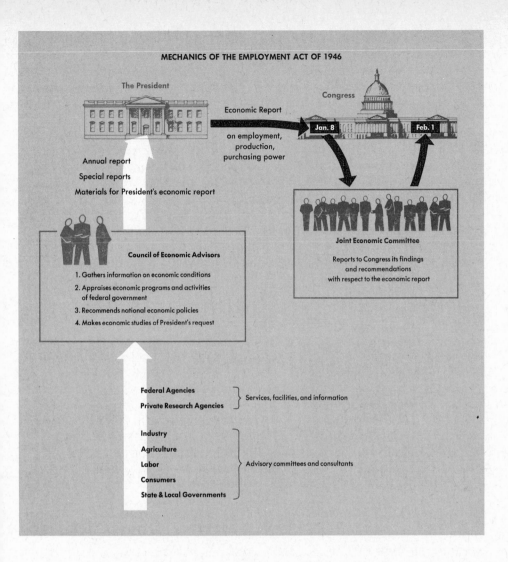

MECHANICS OF THE EMPLOYMENT ACT OF 1946

The President

Congress

Economic Report

on employment, production, purchasing power

Jan. 8   Feb. 1

Annual report

Special reports

Materials for President's economic report

Council of Economic Advisors

1. Gathers information on economic conditions

2. Appraises economic programs and activities of federal government

3. Recommends national economic policies

4. Makes economic studies of President's request

Joint Economic Committee

Reports to Congress its findings and recommendations with respect to the economic report

Federal Agencies

Private Research Agencies } Services, facilities, and information

Industry

Agriculture

Labor } Advisory committees and consultants

Consumers

State & Local Governments

Executive Office of the President, this Council with a small staff studies and forecasts economic trends, assesses the contribution of federal programs to maximum employment, and recommends to the President "national economic policies to foster and promote free competition, to avoid economic fluctuations or to diminish the effects thereof, and to maintain employment, production, and purchasing power."

The Economic Report of the President. Every January the President must submit to Congress an economic report based on the data and forecasts of the Council. The report must include a program for carrying out the policy of the act; it can also include recommendations for legislation if the President see fit.

Joint Economic Committee (JEC). This is a committee of Congress authorized by the act. Composed of seven senators and seven representatives, it must report early in each year its findings and proposals in respect to presidential recommendations. Aside from publishing various reports, such as the monthly *Economic Indicators*, the JEC is able to give Congress an overview of the economy. In this sense it is an anomaly in Congress: "a planning and theory group in a culture fiercely devoted to the short run and practical. It is committed to the panoramic view in a system that stresses jurisdictional lines. It signifies recognition that economic problems are related, in a body that deals with them piecemeal."[21]

How has the employment act worked in practice? Particularly under the Kennedy and Johnson administrations, the CEA emerged as a high-level presidential advisory body, with its chairman serving both as an adviser to the President and as a spokesman for the President before Congress and the country. The annual economic report and the budget message are major presidential statements on the role that governmental fiscal policies will play in the economy in the coming year. The JEC has played an increasingly significant role in developing information on important economic problems. For example, the effects of low income were studied in the JEC years before the Johnson war on poverty. Thus the machinery established under the act is operative and is providing both the President and Congress with the type of information and advice needed in order to shape the government's fiscal policy.[22]

The various mechanisms established by the act work, but is the information being utilized and the advice implemented? Certainly the employment act is more significant for the basic ideas it embodies than for the procedures it created. By the mid-1960s it was evident that the Keynesian economic underpinnings of the act had gained wide acceptance in Washington and elsewhere; governmental fiscal policy had been used in a straightforward fashion to stimulate the economy and cope with its fluctuations. No longer, for example, was a balanced budget viewed by Washington decision-makers as a national goal always to be pursued. It was seen that in certain instances it is better for the government to spend more than it takes in and to run a budget deficit. This is the widely recognized course of action when the economy is not operating at full capacity. When the economy is operating at full capacity, other measures may be called for—a budget surplus, for instance, may be required to check inflationary pressures under conditions of full employment. This sort of Keynesian rationale provided the basis for the $12 billion personal income tax cut in 1964 and the nearly $2 billion cut in excise taxes in 1965. Although unemployment in 1964 was moving steadily downward as the gross national product moved upward, the economy was still not at full capacity and more stimulus from the federal government was required. The increased governmental spending and the lower taxes resulting from the 1964 cut put more money in the hands of the American public, which spent more money thus creating more jobs. The economy boomed. Indeed, so successful was this action that though taxes were cut by $12 bil-

[21]Commission on Money and Credit, *Money and Credit: Their Influence on Jobs, Prices, and Growth* (Prentice-Hall, 1961), pp. 268–269.

[22]For an account of performance and politics under the Employment Act, see Harvey C. Mansfield, "The Congress and Economic Policy," in David B. Truman (ed.), *The Congress and America's Future* (Prentice-Hall, 1965), Chap. 6.

lion, $12.7 billion more was actually taken in from personal taxes in 1964. Results were so rewarding under this tax cut that the way was cleared for the excise tax cut of the following year. The same Keynesian rationale also explains the 10 percent tax surcharge and postponement in reduction of excise taxes in 1968, for by that time the economy was operating at such intensity that inflation was a serious threat; the increase in taxes was designed to slow down the overheating economy. By the end of the 1960s the United States was enjoying its longest continuous period of economic growth without a major recession and without having to suffer the travails of booms and busts.

There are still practical difficulties lying between the initiation of national economic policy and its implementation. For instance, it is necessary for Congress to pass on all revenue and expenditure proposals. This often takes time, for congressmen are called upon to deal with the very basic political problem of "who gets what." Cumbersome congressional procedures preclude the quick injection of money into the economy via a tax cut even when such a policy may be economically warranted. To remedy this it has been proposed that the President be given discretionary power to alter tax rates between certain congressionally imposed limits.[23] But Keynesian thinking has not permeated the halls of Congress to the extent of sanctioning this sort of encroachment upon its constitutional responsibilities. Also, monetary policy is a tool that may be used to affect the overall performance of the economy in that the supply of money and credit may be manipulated in ways discussed earlier. The executive, however, has no means by which it can directly influence the actions of the Federal Reserve Board of Governors, for only the latter is vested with monetary responsibilities. Consequently, it is possible for the executive and the Board to work at cross-purposes. Proposals have been made to limit the autonomy of the Board, making it more amenable to executive influence, but the chances of this kind of alteration are not bright.

The problem, in short, is not one of economic know-how. Hard experience and the work of both economists and men of affairs have taught us a lot about the workings and management of the national economy. The problem is not unwillingness to accept governmental responsibility for maintaining employment; the act of 1946 specifically recognized that responsibility. The problem is whether a governmental system such as ours can act effectively when action is needed. The true test would come if our economy took a serious turn downward after the high level of prosperity we have enjoyed for almost three decades.

The Political Economy—A Case Study

In these last three chapters we have observed that economic and political life in our society are inextricably interwoven. There are no easily discerned boundaries between private and public sectors of the econ-

[23]For example, Commission on Money and Credit, *op. cit.*, pp. 133–137.

omy. Some insist that government and the economy must be kept strictly separated, that government should not interfere in private economic affairs. Whatever its theoretical merits, this view is unrealistic. In modern American society we confront a political economy in which a decision in one area inevitably affects decisions in others. This political economy is a mixed economy—mixed in that it blends private and public enterprise, individual initiative and government promotion, personal responsibility and public regulation, federal and state governments.

We have also discovered that government regulation, promotion, and management are not really distinct approaches. Promotion may be used for regulatory purposes and regulation for promotional; government management in the broadest sense always entails both. A single case serves to demonstrate these relationships—President Kennedy's dispute with the steel industry in 1962.

For a year the Kennedy administration had been trying, mainly through exhortation, to induce both labor and employers to hold the price line. Early in April 1962 the big steel companies and the labor unions had signed a contract that the President greeted with enthusiasm as noninflationary. A few days later Roger Blough, chairman of the board of the United States Steel Corporation, went to the White House and informed the President that his corporation was raising the price of steel. The President knew that other steel companies would follow suit, the whole dike against inflation might be breached, and his policies of conciliation and persuasion would be repudiated. He knew that he must act, that he must act quickly, and that he must act across a wide front.

The events that occurred during the next three days at the White House have already been the subject of much scholarly and journalistic attention.[24] They can be summarized as follows:

First of all, the President summoned Cabinet members, economic advisers, staff assistants, statisticians, and congressional advisers to his office to plan an all-out counterattack.

Statisticians brought up to date a fact book on steel that had been put out by the Eisenhower administration two years earlier—both to be armed with the facts and to demonstrate the continuity with Eisenhower's anti-inflation policies.

The President asked congressional leaders publicly to register dismay about the steel price increase. They promptly did so.

The Justice Department announced an investigation of the steel price rise for possible violations of the antitrust laws.

The Chairman of the Federal Trade Commission told reporters that his agency had begun an informal investigation to determine whether the steel companies had violated a consent decree of 1951.

The Democratic National Committee telephoned Democratic governors to ask them to issue statements supporting the President and to ask steel producers in their own states to hold the price line. But the national com-

---

[24]A succinct account of this event is found in Grant McConnell, *Steel and the Presidency, 1962* (Norton, 1963).

mittee made no statement of its own so that this would not seem to be a party issue.

Before newsmen and television cameras at a press conference, the President denounced the price increase with controlled fury as a "wholly unjustifiable and irresponsible defiance of the public interest."

Several liberal Republicans attacked Big Steel's action. Administration leaders with connections in high places in the business world tried to induce business leaders to pressure steel against its decision.

All this was part of the administration's tactic of mobilizing public pressure on the steel companies. But its main tactic was one of divide and conquer. Much depended on how many other steel companies would follow the lead of United States Steel in raising prices. Some already had. Administration officials had networks of contacts with officials in the other companies. The government also held some economic leverage because of its huge contracts with steel companies, especially defense contracts; indeed, the Defense Department announced that it was ordering defense contractors to shift steel purchases to companies that had not raised prices. The precise nature of the negotiations between administration officials and steel company officials is not clear, but this tactic evidently turned the tide. Inland Steel and several other companies announced that they would not raise prices. Bethlehem Steel rescinded its announced increase. Soon United States Steel was left isolated, and it quickly capitulated to these market pressures. Just seventy-two hours after Blough visited the White House, he announced that his company would withdraw its price increase.

Clearly, it was a resounding immediate victory for a President pledged to hold the price line on behalf of the people as a whole. It demonstrated the power of the President—at least when a President felt that economically and politically his back was against the wall. Yet there were misgivings. Republican leaders in Congress, in a joint statement, said that a fundamental issue had been raised: "Should a President of the United States use the enormous powers of the federal government to blackjack any segment of our free society into line with his personal judgment without regard to law?" Much was made of an unfortunate action on the part of FBI agents, who routed reporters from bed to check the accuracy of certain statements of business officials; although there was no threat to the reporters themselves, for many observers the action smacked too much of the "early-morning knock on the door" in police states. A few weeks later, blame for a series of sharp dips in the stock market was laid by some to the President's action—thus linking the steel price fight to the broader question of the government's relation to economic prosperity.

Six years later, President Johnson also ordered federal agencies to refuse to buy steel from companies that had announced what the President considered to be an inflationary price increase. The steel companies again reduced their previously announced prices, although not back to the original level. But this time little was made of the President's intervention; it was now considered normal procedure.

As the case illustrates, the complex relationship between government and

618

the economy, in addition to the mutual connections between governmental techniques, makes policy evaluation indeed complicated. But we can at least begin with the knowledge that the goals of personal and national welfare are pursued in a highly political setting—a setting inevitable in a government by the people.

STATE AND LOCAL GOVERNMENT

PART SEVEN

Part Seven deals with entire systems of government at the state and local levels; hence, it raises all the problems listed at the beginning of this book. Americans in their states and localities face the same challenges as they do as a nation—the challenge of making democratic government a vital and indispensable way of ruling the people; of following basic constitutional principles, such as that of checks and balances, without letting government become stymied by internal disputes; of maintaining a balance between liberty and order; of achieving representation for all interests; of keeping state and local leaders responsible as well as responsive.

State and local governments, however, pose certain of these problems more sharply than others. Genuine political accountability is lacking in some states because of the splintering of executive power between governors and a host of independent administrative officials. The party system is often not strong enough to knit the leaders together into a team. State governments may be unable to meet the demands of modern society, and more and more functions may gradually be taken over by the federal government. This crucial question of the effectiveness of state governments is the main problem in Chapters 27, 28, 29, and 30.

What about the local governments? Here again we can recognize all of our problems, especially the focal question of the capacity of local governments to carry on their functions efficiently and responsibly. It is hard to generalize about county and municipal government because of the enormous variety of systems involved. But the questions we encountered initially in studying national government keep rising at the grass roots too. How much power does the local executive have, and to whom is he accountable? Are the various interests fairly represented in government? How well can local government mobilize the two indispensable tools of administration —able men and sufficient money—to do the job? These problems are raised in Chapters 33 and 34.

The emphasis in this book has been on the *political forces*—parties, interest groups, public opinion, and so on—that shape government. This is the emphasis in Part Seven as well. To the student of American politics the states and their subdivisions are fascinating political laboratories that allow comparison among the different systems. How strong and unified is the party system? To what extent do state and local politics mirror national political tides, to what extent are they cut off (as, for example, in some Southern states) from national politics? Does the political system foster competition between the two parties, or does one party clearly dominate? In the latter case, how much free and open competition exists between factions *within* the dominant party? In short, does the political system help the voters make intelligent choices? Do the leaders respond to the needs and wishes of the great majority of people?

619

Who Governs:
Patterns of Influence

27 We face one great advantage and one great disadvantage in taking up the study of state and local governments. The advantage is that students who have read the earlier chapters of this book and have discussed American politics in class can consider themselves as at least apprentice political scientists by now, possessing extensive information and some skill in analyzing political problems. They understand the role of constitutions; the checks and balances and division of powers in the American system; the working of interest groups, public opinion, and political parties; how the executive, legislative, and judicial branches operate; and the functions of government. They have seen, in short, the interplay of ideas, interests, institutions, and individuals in national politics, and they will find these to be familiar landmarks as they turn to state and local governments.

The disadvantage lies in the sheer variety of governments to be considered. It is one thing to study a single governmental system, vast and complex though that system may be; it is something else to study fifty separate state governments, each with its own legislature, executive, and judiciary, each with its own intricate politics and varied political traditions. Moreover, the government of each state is only part of a much larger picture. To discuss the government of Mississippi without mentioning white-black relations, the government of Massachusetts without noting the interactions between Protestants and Irish Catholics, the government of Texas without referring to cattle and oil, the government of Illinois without mentioning Chicago and Cook County politics, would be to ignore the dynamics of the political process. State governments, just like the national government, cannot be described meaningfully as structures divorced from people, as organization charts rather than as systems of politics.

Any governmental system is part of a larger social system. A government, as we have seen, is a device to resolve conflicts and to distribute those things that are valued. It is also, as we have seen, a device to achieve certain goals, to perform services desired both by those who govern and by those who are governed. As to the precise way in which a particular system of government determines who governs, how values are distributed, and what services are performed, many factors outside the governmental system itself are often more significant than the structure of the government or even the nature of its political party system. Indeed, some scholars have found that such factors as the economic system, the socioeconomic class structure, and the style of life are more important in determining the policies adopted by a particular state or municipality than the governmental structures it has adopted.[1] However, the interrelations and mutual feedbacks between the economic, social, and political systems are so complex that it is difficult to unscramble them and to decide which is cause and which is effect. Thus the interrelationship is one of reciprocal dependencies; what happens in one sector affects, and, in turn, is affected by, what happens in the other sector.

Complicated as is the picture of the state governments, it is even more complicated by the thousands of cities, counties, towns, villages, school districts, water control districts, and other governmental units that are piled one on top of another within the states. If all states or cities or towns were alike, the task might be manageable; but of course they are not. Each city, each state is unique. We need more knowledge about the political life of Ashtabula, Detroit, Washington, and California, but not merely to learn about these particular localities. The study of our state and local political systems provides a fascinating laboratory for comparative analysis, for testing our hypotheses about politics, and for developing new generalizations to be tested elsewhere. And while recognizing that our states, cities, and counties cannot be fitted into simplified categories, we must develop some patterns and search for the uniformities underlying all the "crazy mixed-up politics"; otherwise, our information is of limited utility. What we need are some tentative organizing concepts that will help us understand what is going on whether we live in rural Vermont or downtown Cleveland.

The Location of Power

How, then, can we understand the operations and problems of state and local government without becoming bogged down in endless detail? We can do so by returning to the core problems of this book—problems of democracy, constitutionalism, individual liberty, representation, and respon-

[1]Richard I. Hofferbert, "The Relation Between Public Policy and Some Structural and Environmental Variables in the American States," *American Political Science Review* (March 1966), pp. 73–82 and the literature cited therein.

sible leadership. In order to focus our attention even more, we will emphasize in these chapters a question that will throw light on all the above problems – the question of who governs. The people govern, yes – but we must probe the question further. Which people? Does political power in the states and localities tend to gravitate toward a relatively small number of people? If so, who are these "influentials"? Do they work closely together, or do they divide among themselves? Do the same influentials dominate all decision-making, or do some sets of leaders decide certain questions and leave other questions to others or to chance?

This question of who governs is, of course, an ancient one, at least two thousand years old. Not only philosophers but all people like to ask: "Who really runs things around here?" Nowhere, perhaps, has this question been asked with more fruitful results than in certain American communities during the last fifty years. In 1924, two sociologists from Columbia, a young married couple named Robert and Helen Lynd, decided that they would study a typical American city as though they were anthropologists investigating a tribe in Africa. For two years they lived in Muncie, Indiana, at that time a city of 38,000, asking lots of questions and watching how people made their living, brought up their young, used their leisure time, and joined in lodges, brotherhoods, and other groups. The Lynds reported that behind the democratic facade of Middletown, as they disguised the name of their city, a social and economic elite was actually running things.[2] Then in the middle 1940s a world-famous reporter, John Gunther, studied the United States as he had previously reported Europe and Asia – from the inside. Everywhere he went he asked people: "Who runs your state or city? What are the basic and irreversible sources of *power* – social . . ., economic . . ., political . . .?" The astonishing thing, he found, was the "luxuriant variety of answers. . . . No single person, principle, ideal, commodity, abstraction, or vested interest runs it. . . ."[3] The country was enormously conglomerate – but also interlocked.

In recent years social scientists have pressed ahead with probes of other communities and areas. Four anthropologists, analyzing a Southern city of 10,000, were struck by the tenacity of old belief systems going back a century.[4] A mining town in Montana, a Connecticut suburb, a mill city in Massachusetts, provided data on the enormous variety of communal life. One of the most ambitious studies was of an old New England seaport still living off memories of its greatness in the days of the clipper ships.[5] A score of observers, using survey data punched onto cards, found an elaborate class structure, with the old families on top even though some of them had lost their money and were poor compared to the *nouveaux-riches*.

Following their own bent, social scientists have focused on the pattern of power in communities, and they have, of course, come up with varied

---

[2]Robert S. Lynd and Helen M. Lynd, *Middletown* (Harcourt, Brace & World, 1929). See also their equally brilliant treatment of Muncie ten years later, *Middletown in Transition* (Harcourt, Brace & World, 1937).

[3]John Gunther, *Inside U.S.A.* (Harper & Row, 1947), p. xv.

[4]Allison Davis, B. B. Gardner, and M. R. Gardner, *Deep South* (Univ. of Chicago Press, 1941). The project was directed by W. Lloyd Warner.

[5]W. Lloyd Warner and P. S. Lunt, *The Social Life of a Modern Community* (Yale Univ. Press, 1941).

findings. For example, Floyd Hunter, a sociologist at the University of North Carolina, analyzing a Southern regional city (Atlanta), found a relatively small and stable group of top policy-makers drawn largely from the business class. These few operated through shifting groups of secondary leaders, who sometimes modified policy, but the power of the elite was almost always there.[6] On the other hand, Robert A. Dahl, a political scientist at Yale, studying his own university city of New Haven, concluded that while some people had a great deal of influence and others had very little, there was no solid, hard-core elite, but shifting coalitions of leaders who sometimes fell out among themselves and who always had to keep in mind what the public would bear when making their decisions.[7]

Of the two cities, Atlanta and New Haven, which is more typical of the distribution of influence in American communities? Or could it be that the differences between Hunter's and Dahl's findings stem from the questions they asked rather than from differences in the two communities? For the assumptions of the investigators and the techniques they use may produce differences in what they find.[8]

One group of investigators, chiefly sociologists such as Hunter, are mainly concerned with social stratification, for they assume that political influence is a function of the structure of the community. They try to find out who governs a community by asking a variety of citizens to identify the persons who are most influential in the community. Then these influentials, so identified, are studied to determine their social characteristics, their role in decision-making, the interrelations among influentials and between the influentials and the rest of the citizenry. Those who use this technique generally report that the upper socioeconomic groups make up the power elite, that elected political leaders are subordinate to this elite, and that the major conflicts within the community are between the upper and the lower socioeconomic classes.

Another group of investigators, primarily political scientists such as Dahl, have questioned the findings of the students of social stratification and have raised objections to their techniques. The evidence, it is contended (even that contained within the stratification studies themselves), does not support the conclusion that communities are run by a power elite. Rather, the notion of a power elite is merely a reflection of the techniques used and the assumptions of the stratification theorists. Instead of studying the activities of persons who are *thought* to have influence, one should study public policy to find out how, in fact, decisions are made. Those who make community studies in this manner usually find an open, pluralistic power structure. Some people do have more influence than others, but influence is widely shared and tends to be limited to particular issues and areas. Those who have much to say about how the public schools are run may have little influence over economic policies. And in many communities and for many issues there is no identifiable group of influentials—policy emerges not from the mani-

[6]Floyd Hunter, *Community Power Structure* (Univ. of North Carolina Press, 1953).
[7]Robert A. Dahl, *Who Governs?: Democracy and Power in an American City* (Yale Univ. Press, 1961).
[8]See Nelson W. Polsby, *Community Power and Political Theory* (Yale Univ. Press, 1963), for the perspective of a critic of social stratification theorists (and for a comprehensive bibliography of the community power studies).

pulations of a small group, but from the unanticipated and unplanned consequences of the behavior of large numbers of people. The social structure of the community is one factor—but not the determinative factor—of how goods and services and valued things are distributed within the community.[9]

Here we have an example of how the questions we ask influence the answers we find.[10] Yet the community power studies, despite differences in approach and findings, are beginning to produce enough data about enough communities so that by comparative analysis we can begin to develop generalizations about how formal governmental institutions, structure of the society, economic factors, and other variables interrelate to create a political system that determines who gets what, where, when, and how.

The Stakes of the Political Struggle

Events have given the national government enormous influence over the destiny of the American people. The advent of nuclear weapons has put into the hands of one man, the President, life-and-death control of the future of tens of millions of his fellow citizens. The assumption by the federal government of responsibility for maintaining full employment, for regulating great economic power groups such as labor and business, and for subsidizing weaker sectors of the conomy such as agriculture, has made the federal government the custodian of the nation's economic strength and security. Our economic and military aid to allies and neutrals will in the long run critically shape the nature of the late twentieth-century world.

State and local governments cannot claim anything like this momentous role. But contrary to popular impressions, the role of the states and localities is an increasingly large one on the domestic scene, not only in absolute terms but even as compared with the national government. Since World War II state and local governmental activities have increased much faster than the non-defense activities of the federal government. Presently, two-thirds of the expenditures for domestic governmental functions are carried by the states and their subdivisions.

Moreover, these governments have a far more intimate relation with the average man than does Washington, for the great neighborhood and "housekeeping" problems of Americans are closely regulated by state and local governments. The points where we come into contact with "government" most often are in school, on the highways, in a playground, at a big fire, in a hospital, in a courtroom. Some things might seem far removed from any government—for example, having a dog or a cat as a pet. But dogs are closely related to government—they need a license, a collar, to be confined, and

[9]For a critique of the pluralists, see Peter Bachrach and Morton S. Baratz, "Two Faces of Power," *American Political Science Review* (December 1962), pp. 947–952; and by the same authors, "Decisions and Non-Decisions: An Analytical Framework," *American Political Science Review* (September 1968), pp. 632–642.

[10]However, see Robert E. Agger, Daniel Goldrich, and Bert E. Swanson, *The Rulers and the Ruled* (Wiley, 1964) for a study using the decisional approach that came to conclusions similar to those based on the reputational approach.

so on—and if anyone thinks that cats are beyond the reach of the law, he should remember Adlai E. Stevenson's famous veto of the "cat bill" when he was Governor of Illinois. The bill would have imposed fines on cat-owners who let their pets run off their premises, and would have allowed cat-haters to trap them. The Governor said:

> I cannot agree, that it should be the declared public policy of Illinois that a cat visiting a neighbor's yard or crossing the highway is a public nuisance. It is in the nature of cats to do a certain amount of unescorted roaming. . . . I am afraid this bill could only create discord, recrimination, and enmity. . . . We are all interested in protecting certain varieties of birds. . . . The problem of the cat versus bird is as old as time. If we attempt to resolve it by legislation who knows but what we may be called upon to take sides as well in the age-old problem of dog versus cat, bird versus bird, or even bird versus worm. . . .[11]

So the Governor sided with cat-lovers over bird-lovers, while staying neutral between bird-lovers and worm-diggers. But the incident illustrated how the complex working of modern society draws a maze of interests into the political process.

THE MAZE OF INTERESTS

The big interest groups described in Chapter 11 are found, in varying forms, in all the states. Even industrial Rhode Island has farm organizations; even rural Mississippi has trade unions. And the big economic pressure groups operate in the states much as they do nationally—they try to build up the membership of their organizations; they lobby at the state capitol and at city hall; they propagandize the voters; they support their political friends in office and oppose their enemies. They also face the internal problems that all groups face: problems of maintaining unity within the group, of dealing with subgroups that break off in response to special needs, of maintaining both democracy and discipline within the group.

One great difference, however, is that group interests can be concentrated in states and localities, whereas their strength tends to be thinned out in the national government. Big Labor does not really run things in Washington, any more than Wall Street, or the Catholic Church, or the American Legion does. But in some states and localities certain interests are clearly dominant because of the social and economic makeup of the area. Few politicians in Wisconsin will attack dairy farmers; a candidate for office in Boston will not shout his anti-Catholicism; most white office holders in rural South Carolina are not likely to take a militant stand in favor of school desegregation.

It is the range and variety of these localized groupings that give American politics its special flavor and excitement. The auto unions and manufacturers of Michigan, the corn and hog farmers of Iowa, the French-Americans in northern New England, the gas and oil interests of Texas, the sugar growers of Colorado, the aircraft employees of southern California, copper miners in the Rockies, cotton growers in the South, the old German stock of Ohio and

[11]*Veto message*, Governor Adlai Stevenson, to members of the Senate, 66th General Assembly, Springfield, Illinois.

other Midwestern states, Pennsylvania coal miners, wool growers in Wyoming — the list of areas heavily influenced by special interests is endless.

Still, the power of these groups should not be exaggerated. None is monolithic. Studying the urban politics of St. Louis, one political scientist concluded that the labor unions were sharply divided among the teamsters, building trades, machinists, auto workers, and so on; that the business community was divided between the big industrial, banking, and commercial firms, on the one hand, and small downtown enterprises — shops, parking lot operators, and the like — on the other; and that such divisions had a direct impact on the governing of St. Louis.[12] In New England, the Irish Sons of Saint Patrick and the Italian Columbus Society have long expressed the opinions of their respective groups on various public issues, and there are also organizations to speak for the French-Canadians and the Poles. New England politicians have feared the power of such groups to influence elections, especially primaries, but after a careful look, Duane Lockard has deflated their boogeyman. He cites many examples of "Yankees" winning in heavily ethnic areas. Compared to the other considerations affecting the voter's choice, the ethnic factor may be small (although a minute precentage, of course, may still be decisive in an election). Much depends on the nature of the candidate — on the appeals he creates other than the ethnic.[13] In short, any group, no matter how strong, must cope with a variety of cross-pressures, including a general sense of the rules of the game which suggest that the voter should not vote for "one of our own" on merely that ground alone.

So much for the more general interests in certain localities; let us look further at the ones that are more specialized and that have, as noted above, a close relation to local government. Many businessmen sell to the state, or perform services for it: milk dealers, printers, contractors, parking meter manufacturers, makers of playground equipment, publishers of textbooks. Such businessmen will often formally or informally organize in order to improve and stabilize their relations with purchasing officials. Another type of group intimately concerned with public policy is the professional association. The states regulate the services of barbers, beauticians, architects, lawyers, doctors, optometrists, accountants, dentists, and many other groups. Associations representing such groups are concerned with the nature of the regulatory laws and with the makeup of the boards that do the regulating. They are especially concerned about the rules of admission to the profession — for example, architects' examinations and the required amount of education — and about the way in which professional misconduct is defined. Bar associations closely watch the appointment of judges and court officials.

The incredible profusion of groups represented in the capitol of one large state can be seen in a partial list of business activities that registered their lobbyists with the Michigan Legislature during a recent session: the Upper Peninsula Dairy Manufacturers Association, the Society of Architects, the Beauticians' Aid Association, the National Association of Margarine Manufacturers, the Funeral Directors' and Embalmers' Association, the

[12]Robert H. Salisbury, "St. Louis Politics: Relationships among Interests, Parties, and Governmental Structure," *Western Political Quarterly* (June 1960), pp. 498–507.
[13]Duane Lockard, *New England State Politics* (Princeton Univ. Press, 1959), Chap. 11.

Cash-and-carry Milk Dealers' Association, the Institute of Dry Cleaning, the Association of Private Driver-training Schools, and the Association of Civil Engineers and Land Surveyors in Private Practice.

After a survey of these and countless other lobbies in Michigan, one student concluded that there was

. . . an organization equipped to lobby for every business interest in the city, county, or state. The pattern is so complex that a particular business may be represented by an elaborate combination of groups, some with broad interests that include those of a specific calling, others dealing with a particular type of business, and the individual businessman may himself lobby before council or legislature. A supermarket chain may, for example, have its interests represented generally by the state chamber of commerce, but the company may also belong to an association of chain stores (which must parry the thrusts of the corner-grocers' lobby), to a retail-food-dealers' organization, to the package-liquor-dealers' association (if some of the stores have permits to sell same), and the company may itself register a lobbyist. In addition, if the chain is encountering labor problems, it may contribute to a "right-to-work" committee which lobbies against the union shop, and the executives of the company may choose to help support the state taxpayers' league. If the company owns its own fleet of semitrailer trucks or leases them, it may be represented by a company of additional groups dealing with the interests of this part of the business. A pluralistic society is simple in neither theory nor practice.[14]

Interest groups appear to have the most influence in the nonindustrial, nonurban states where a single party dominates political life and where party cohesion is not very strong within the state legislature.[15] In states with strong interest groups, the constitution tends to be long, frequently amended, with provision for a larger number of elected (in contrast to appointed) officials. In such states interest groups appear to be better able to isolate governmental agencies from gubernatorial and legislative influence.[16]

LOBBYISTS AT THE STATE HOUSE

There is a widespread conviction that lobbyists have a freer rein in state legislatures than they do in Congress, and, what is more, that bribery of state legislators by lobbyists is prevalent. There is no convincing evidence that corruption of legislators is so widespread, but the persistence of the belief that the lobbyists with the most money have the most influence is itself significant. In a few states a single corporation or organization has considerable influence; in others there is a "big three" or "big four" or perhaps two dominant groups or organized interests compete; but in most states there is wide-open competition among organizations, with no single group or coalition of groups standing out. In no state does any one organization or company exercise complete control of legislative policies.[17] Nonetheless, as Assem-

[14]Chares R. Adrian, *State and Local Government* (McGraw-Hill, 1960), p. 167. The list of Michigan lobbyists was drawn from the same place.

[15]Harmon Zeigler, "Interest Groups in the States," in Herbert Jacob and Kenneth N. Vines (eds.), *Politics in the American States* (Little, Brown, 1965), p. 114.

[16]Lewis A. Froman, Jr., "Some Effects of Interest Group Strength in State Politics," *American Political Science Review* (December 1966), p. 961.

[17]Zeigler, *op. cit.*, p. 128.

bly Speaker Jesse Unruh of California points out, the lobbyist, or "legislative representative," as he prefers to be called, carries the main burden of seeing through the legislature the bills in which his organization is interested. "That job is his *raison d'être*. Certainly he is concerned with other things, casually, or at times energetically, but he had better not forget for one moment the principal reason for his being there." The legislator, on the other hand, worries about not just one kind of bill but many others as well—about his party, his district, and his colleagues. The governor? "Governors come and governors go, but the lobbyists stay on forever."[18]

Some groups have a special role both because of their relations to government and because of the size and importance of the work that they are doing. Consider public school teachers, for example. They are both employees of the local government and an interest group exerting pressure on it. They must deal with many other organized groups in education: parents associated in local and state PTAs, principals and superintendents, who often have their own associations; parents of children attending private and parochial schools. Some teachers organize into unions and even use the strike as a weapon for getting better wages and working conditions; all of them try to mobilize political influence as best they can. Even local school boards often band together for better representation at the state capitol, as do teachers' colleges, state universities, and vocational schools. The educational lobby can often put up a brave front on behalf of "educational progress," but when it comes to the details they may be badly divided among themselves.

CLUSTERS OF ATTITUDES: A CASE STUDY

Analysis of the role of public opinion in the states and localities confronts us with the same problems as does the study of interest groups. On the one hand, the factors noted in Chapter 9 on the national level apply locally as well. The people speak with many voices; there are many publics and subpublics; the interested public is always changing; people holding opinions vary greatly in their intensity of belief; and public opinion may be latent as well as open and noisy. Also, most states and communities have their own sets of opinion-making agencies: schools, churches, newspapers, radio and television stations, as well as their share of the audience of national television programs, best-selling books, popular magazines, nationwide newspapers like *The New York Times*, motion pictures, and newspaper columnists. On the other hand, each locality has its own particular "mix" of these opinion-forming agencies, and powerful forces that are diluted nationally may be concentrated heavily in one area.

A good example of this latter situation is the attitude toward states' rights in the South. Almost all Americans support states' rights as a general symbol, but in the South it has a political influence far greater than that of any pressure group or party. Quoted from the lips of such Southern heroes as Jefferson and Calhoun, bolstered by the trauma of civil war, resurrected in the face of Northern civil rights programs and Supreme Court decisions on desegregation, states' rights has become a flaming symbol that can be

[18]Jesse Unruh, "A Reformed Legislature," *Journal of Public Law* (1967), vol. 16, p. 13.

evoked for a multiplicity of purposes—segregation, state control of offshore oil, local determination of welfare standards, reduction of minimum wages. It is a daring Southern politician who would defy this symbol. The combat is waged within the symbol—that is, over its meaning and relevance rather than between it and other political concepts.

Another local variation of public opinion concerns the concentration of control of local media and the resulting conformity of political attitudes. The enormous variety of opinion-shaping forces throughout the nation may dwindle sharply in its impact on a particular locality, especially one that is some distance from a big metropolitan area. Here again local conditions vary so widely that generalization is dangerous. Perhaps a case study of one community might raise suggestive questions for other localities.

The newspaper situation in New Haven, Connecticut, is typical of that in many medium-sized cities of the United States. As compared with the last century, when New Haven had three or four papers supporting different political parties, the city recently has had only two, a morning and an evening, both owned by the same family, both Republican in politics, and both heavily influenced by the family's conservative views. Almost all adults in New Haven read the evening paper, and almost all the politically active read the morning paper. Robert Dahl, analyzing the impact of the papers, concluded that their negativism and hostility to change, together with their biased news reporting, may have reduced their readers' knowledge, understanding, and concern; that they may have influenced their readers on specific policies, such as taxes; and that they probably directly influenced the attitudes of politicians who exaggerated the newspapers' influence on public opinion. The more uncertain a politician was about the stability and intensity of his own support on some measure, the more he might defer to two newspapers that seemed to speak with a single, strong voice.

But Dahl found definite limits to the power of this newspaper monopoly. For one thing, the publisher seemed more interested in immobilizing public opinion than in mobilizing it; he was less intent on initiating new policies than in balking spendthrift politicians. For another, some politicians were skeptical of the newspapers' ability to influence opinion, and they were confident of their own political strength. But the main reason why the newspapers had limited influence was the competition they received from many other sources. The more politically active the citizen was, the more likely he was to read an out-of-town newspaper such as *The New York Times*. Of the registered voters as a whole, only about four in ten said that they got more information about political affairs from newspapers than from other sources. Another four out of ten got more from radio or television, or from talking with other people. Local opinion leaders had at least as much influence as the newspapers. Dahl was prompted to conclude:

Word of mouth and personal experience are highly important sources of information that remain to a substantial extent beyond the reach of top leaders. . . . The extent to which an individual gains his information from other people than from the mass media is partly a function of his own experience. In some issue-areas, many citizens have *direct* experience; what happens there is happening to *them*, in a rather immediate way. In others, only a few citizens have any direct experience; at best the others have only derivative or vicarious experience. The more the citizens have direct experience, the more they seem to rely on talking with other people as a source of news; the more vicarious or indirect their experience, the more they seem to rely on the mass media.[19]

Direct experience, in short, could be not only a persuasive teacher, but a stubborn enemy of manipulative propaganda as well.

Ironically, the newspaper organizations themselves were not monolithic. As is the case with many big newspapers, many of the reporters on the two papers were Democrats or personally friendly with politicians opposed to the publisher. Republicans sometimes complained that their stories were buried in the back of the papers while their Democratic opponents had much of the front page. Like many a party boss or interest-group leader, the publisher found that he could not "deliver his precinct" even if he so wished.

Nevertheless, newspapers probably have greater impact on local issues and elections than on national ones. Most citizens obtain a large part of their knowledge of the local political scene from the hometown newspaper. Voters are likely to have less rigid ideas about the merits of local candidates then about national or even state candidates. A strongly partisan Republican businessman, for example, is less open to persuasion by a Democratic candidate for Congress or the Presidency than he may be by a Democratic candidate for the city council who is a friend or colleague. Attitudes toward local issues are also less likely to be rigid, or, to use the language of the social scientist, such ideas are often less structured. For their consideration of atomic testing, federal income tax revision, medical care for the aged, or the merits of Nixon over Humphrey, citizens have many sources of information, from national television to professional trade journals. But the local paper is almost the only source for weighing school-board candidacies or the desirability of a community bond issue.[20]

In such cities as Los Angeles, where political organizations are weak and authority is generally decentralized, newspapers play a more important part in the political process than in cities where political organizations are strong, e. g., Chicago.[21] The influence of the newspapers also appears to be related to the class structure. "As one ascends the social scale there is a greater sense of ease, intimacy, and personal relationship between the reader and his paper. It seems as though the better educated reader is more likely to view his hometown paper as an institution made up of people doing a job . . . . For those lower on the educational scale, the newspaper as a major institution of power appears more remote and impersonal."[22]

APATHY

To discuss pressure groups and opinion-shapers is always to run the risk of lending prominence to the activists and slighting the apathetic. But the

[19]Dahl, *op. cit.*, p. 262. This admirable work yielded the above case study.
[20]Evidence on this question is limited; but see Reo M. Christenson, "The Power of the Press—The Case of the 'Toledo Blade,' " *Midwest Journal of Political Science* (August 1959), pp. 227–240.
[21]E. C. Banfield and J. Q. Wilson, *City Politics* (Harvard Univ. Press, 1963), pp. 323–325.
[22]Leo Bogart, "Newspapers in the Age of Television," *Daedalus* (Winter 1963), p. 124.

political indifference that shows up as only a very general factor in a nation-wide survey can be seen markedly in certain regions or localities. Nonvoting, for example, is greater in the country than in the suburbs or the city. Migrant workers of the Southwest and poor whites and blacks in the South are among those who are not politically active.

It was in the little town and village that many American political thinkers, in an earlier day, saw most hope for the vitality of American democracy. Unhappily, many such communities today seem to lack an active political life. Although the little towns may be caught up in, and increasingly affected by, the social and economic trends in the urban areas, the townspeople may shrink from adopting new ways of dealing with problems. Many of these small towns are slowly declining in population; their young people are leaving for better opportunities elsewhere; their population is aging. Such political decisions as there are seem to be made by relatively few people, and usually without much discussion; there is no clear confrontation of choices; politics is highly personal and much affected by family and neighborhood relationships, petty favor-swapping, and minor deals. A town that is most in need of a searching political examination of its future, culminating in a meaningful decision, may be lacking the means for such action.[23]

But big cities, too, can provide examples of apathy. Dahl found that even in New Haven, a relatively active city politically, "political indifference surrounds a great many citizens like impenetrable armor plate and makes them difficult targets for propaganda."[24] He cites as an example a strenuous campaign to revise the city charter in 1958. City politicians debated the matter vigorously; the newspapers took an outspoken position against revision; a citizens' charter committee ran big advertisements; radio and television programs carried on the debate, fliers were even distributed from door to door. The result? Only 45 percent of those who voted in the regular election troubled to vote on the charter (and most opposed it). Boston affords an even more ominous case, for here the apathy stemmed directly from cynicism. In a hotly contested mayoralty election many voters did not even bother to vote because they were disgusted with politics, disliked both candidates or thought that neither would do a good job.[25]

Cynicism about the effectiveness of the ordinary political process is also reflected in the recent use in our big cities of the politics of confrontation—mass demonstrations, economic boycotts, even civil disorder—as ways of making demands on the governmental system. Yet at the same time, as issues become more intense and meaningful, there are signs of renewed political activity. Impoverished blacks in the ghettoes are forming into new political organizations in order to present their grievances and organize their votes more effectively. Neighborhood organizations have been formed to work for better housing and enforcement of inspection ordinances, antipoverty programs have led to the more active involvement of the poor in the

[23]Cf. A. J. Vidich and Joseph Bensman, *Small Town in Mass Society* (Princeton Univ. Press, 1958); and Laurene A. Wallace, *Carsonville: An American Village Viewed Sociologically* (Univ. of Michigan Press, 1957). See also Warner E. Mills, Jr., and Harry R. Davis, *Small City Government: Seven Cases in Decision Making* (Random House, 1962).

[24]Dahl, *op. cit.*, p. 264.

[25]Murray Levin, *The Alienated Voter* (Holt, 1960). See Levin's treatment of political alienation in Massachusetts, *The Compleat Politician* (Bobbs-Merrill, 1962).

politics of the city. In some cities officials are promoting special adult education courses. New York has begun to use both English and Spanish in all official documents as well as during voting periods in order to encourage its large population of Spanish-speaking people to become involved (since federal law now makes them potentially eligible to vote) in its political life.

State Parties: A Study in Variety

The Democratic and Republican parties almost monopolize party activity in every state, just as they do the nation's politics as a whole. But the state political parties are not miniatures of the national parties. Each has its own special features. Not only is the social and economic "mix" different for each state, as noted above, and hence the parties are different, but the states reacted differently to epochal developments in American history. The Civil War left the South heavily Democratic and portions of the North heavily Republican. The great struggle of '96 between the Democratic liberal, William Jennings Bryan, and the orthodox Republican, William McKinley, left an east-west split that has not wholly disappeared. And the traumatic experience of the Great Depression, combined with the coming of the New Deal, helped produce a surge of Democratic strength in the big cities that still influences politics sharply.

THE INTERPLAY OF NATIONAL AND STATE POLITICS

Clearly, it is impossible to separate national from state and local politics. The very structure of national party organizations, as we noted in Chapter 12, grows out of the state parties. Not only are national and state party organizations interdependent, but their fortunes and misfortunes are also interdependent; swings at the national level help produce swings at the state and local level. Whenever the Democratic party, for example, wins a presidential and congressional sweep nationally, the number of Democratic governors, state legislators, mayors, and local councilmen tends to increase. Moreover, the relationship is usually constant—the greater the national party sweep, the greater the local party victories. The famous coattails effect is at work here, but in both directions. Strong candidates at the state level help the national candidates, and strong national candidates help those running for state and local office. In 1968 strong Republican candidates helped pull Richard Nixon over the top in some states.

One effect of national politics on the state and local scene is sometimes to solidify sectional differences and strengthen one-partyism. In the one-party states of the Deep South, for example, the racial issue dominates all other problems. Here the state politicians, rallying around the symbol of states' rights, have ignored many of their other differences and stood united against the rest of the nation. On the other hand, evidence exists that industrialization and urbanization are having an impact on both the rural Republican-dominated states and the rural Democratic ones, as Republican victories in the 1966 and 1968 elections suggested. Industry brings to these regions the same issues that it brought earlier to the rest of the country—employers versus workers, large industry versus small, railroads versus truckers, and so on. These issues appear to create the same pattern of political differences that prevails in other regions and tend to move the states in the direction of two-party competition.

Sometimes state politicians try to avert national trends. Kentucky, Mississippi, New Jersey, Virginia, and Louisiana have complete electoral separation. They elect their governors and all state legislators in years when no presidential election is being held. Twenty other states elect their governors and some legislators in the off-year elections. This staggering of state elections is usually proposed as a way of concentrating the voters' attention on state issues without the distractions of a presidential campaign. But it is mainly a tactical device of party warfare, used by local politicians of one party to prevent the opposition party from benefiting by its national popularity. Of course, the tactic can backfire. Republicans in some states managed to get Republican governors elected during the Democratic 1930s and 1940s by having gubernatorial elections held when neither Roosevelt nor Truman was running; but when Eisenhower was winning in big sweeps during the 1950s these same Republicans regretted that they were not running their statewide candidates in presidential years, for they had lost the chance to get pulled in on Eisenhower's coattails.[26] Still, there is a general trend toward off-year state elections so this separation of national and state politics will probably increase in coming years.

Even when presidential and state elections are held simultaneously, the impact of national contests on state elections can be affected by the nature of the election ballot. If, for example, the Republicans have as a presidential candidate an Eisenhower type who has great electoral drawing power, it will be to their advantage if the state has a party-column or Indiana-type ballot. To reduce the impact of the presidential candidate under such circumstances, the Democrats would prefer the office-group or Massachusetts-type ballot. Still, despite all the ingenious efforts of politicians, national politics has a heavy impact on state and local government.

PARTY BALANCE AND IMBALANCE

The impact of national political forces on the particular social and economic "mix" of each state, combined with local traditions and political styles, has produced important differences among the party systems of the fifty states. The most important of these is the extent of two-party competition. State parties may be classified by three types on the basis of how the parties share state offices (often a state will vote for one party's candidate for President, or even senator or representative, but have an entirely different party preference for state officers): the *two-party* type, in which the two parties share state offices rather evenly over the years, and alternate in winning majorities; the *modified one-party* type, in which one party wins all or almost all the offices over the years, but the other party usually receives a

[26]Coleman M. Ransome, Jr., *The Office of Governor in the United States* (Univ. of Alabama Press, 1956), pp. 89–90; V. O. Key, *American State Politics* (Knopf, 1956), pp. 41–49. Austin Ranney, "Parties in State Politics," in Jacob and Vines, *op. cit.*, pp. 82–83.

large percentage of the votes, and surprises everybody—including itself—by sometimes winning; and the *one-party* type, in which one party wins all or nearly all the offices, and the second party usually receives only a small proportion of the popular vote. From the map of state party systems, based on voting patterns during the period 1956 to 1968, it can be seen that the modified one-party Democratic states are mainly the border states, but so are Virginia, North Carolina, and Florida. The six one-party Democratic states are all in the South. There are no longer any one-party Republican states, since the former rock-ribbed stalwart supporters of the Grand Old Party such as Vermont, North Dakota, and Maine in recent elections have chosen some Democrats for state office.[27]

Since the end of World War II there has been an accelerating trend toward two-party politics. In the South, Republicans have begun to make a contest of some general elections, and the old cliché that "winning the Democratic primary in the South is tantamount to election" has lost some of its validity. Although the Republican resurgence in the South has been shown mainly in voting for candidates for President and Congress, Republicans have been elected to the state legislature in Alabama, Arkansas, Florida, Georgia, and other Southern states, and Arkansas and Florida have elected Republican governors. Republicans still have to make significant gains be-

[27]This division of states is based on updated version of Austin Ranney's adaptation of the Dawson-Robinson measure in "Parties in State Politics," Jacob and Vines (eds.), *op. cit.,* p. 65.

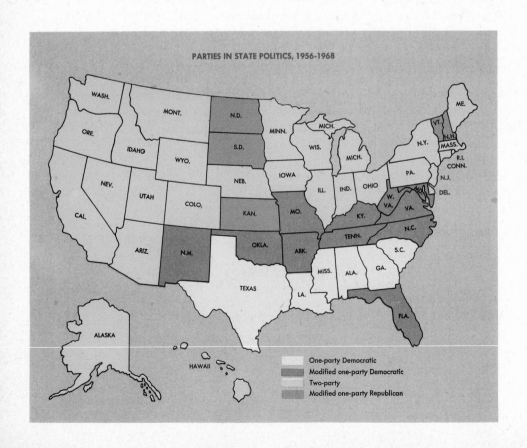

PARTIES IN STATE POLITICS, 1956-1968

One-party Democratic
Modified one-party Democratic
Two-party
Modified one-party Republican

fore we can call most Southern or border states two-party states, but the Solid South is no longer so solid, especially within the larger cities.

Outside the South there is also a gradual spread of two-partyism with the rise of Democratic strength in the formerly solid Republican states of Iowa, Kansas, Maine, New Hampshire, North Dakota, and South Dakota. "What the Democrats have lost in the South, they have regained in the rural Midwest and Northeast."[28]

What are the consequences of a fairly even party balance? When parties and their candidates compete on an even basis, each side must keep on its toes, each is more likely to be sensitive to slight changes in public opinion because even the loss of a fraction of the voters might tip the scales to the other side in the next election. Party competition tends to induce leaders within each party to work more closely together, at least as elections draw near, for any defection may throw victory into the hands of the opponents; hence, competition may produce more teamwork and efficiency in government. It is notable that states having outstanding state governments—such as Connecticut, New York, and California—are among the more competitive states; whether the party system is causally related to responsive state government is more difficult to determine.

Party imbalance may have a serious effect on the dominant party in a one-party state. Almost guaranteed a victory no matter how poor its record, the majority party may not keep itself in fighting trim. Even more important, the competition that otherwise would occur between the major parties now occurs *within* the majority party. The contests in the South, especially for control of state and local governments, often are not between Democrats and Republicans in the November election, but between Democrats—sometimes a dozen or more of them—in the Democratic primary. In these intraparty fights, issues may not be clearly drawn; personalities may dominate the campaign, with little regard for issues; voters tend not to participate to the same extent as they do where there are two-party contests. Here again one has to be careful in drawing causal connections, for lack of division within the community on major issues may cause the one-party situation as much as the other way around.

But if party imbalance disorganizes the dominant party, it utterly pulverizes the minority party. Almost without hope of ever winning at all, the minority party leaders do not put up much of a fight. They find it difficult to raise the money for campaigns or to persuade persons to become candidates for office. They have no state or local patronage jobs to give out in order to arouse hope within their ranks. Party workers and volunteers are slow to come forward. Young men wishing to succeed in politics tend to drift into the dominant party. And since the dominant party firmly controls the machinery of state and local affairs, the second party is likely only to be concerned with national politics and the patronage emanating from the White House. It may not even bother to nominate candidates for state offices or maintain local organization. For years the only Republican organization in several Deep South states was one maintained by a small group of Negroes and whites living off patronage from the Republican national committee. Indeed some

[28]*Ibid.*, p. 92.

members of these second-party organizations have a vested interest in remaining a minority. Some may fear that if their party should become a serious contender in the state, the insiders who have been running it would have to share their patronage and influence in national politics with other political leaders.[29]

We have been discussing *state* party imbalance, but imbalance can be found in even more extreme form in cities and towns. Republicans hardly ever carry Chicago, Boston, Albany, Hartford, Pittsburgh, and a host of other cities throughout the industrial North. Democrats have only a ghost of a chance in numerous towns in the rural North. Indeed, one result of this imbalance is the rapid growth, during the first half of this century, of nonpartisanship in local elections. Candidates were not able to run on major-party tickets, at least officially. The two great parties were, in effect, removed from open influence over local politics. Adopted in the name of good government, nonpartisanship had an effect on local government that will be discussed in Chapter 32; but its effect on the major parties was probably to weaken them further as organizations, for it sapped them at their foundations.

We must remind ourselves again not to overgeneralize in discussing a variety of political systems. Perhaps we can test some of these generalizations by looking at the minority party in a specific city, Elmira, in western New York. When studied by three social scientists in the early 1950s, Elmira had been Republican since 1936. What was the state of the Democratic party? Not very effective. The party did not raise much money; it did not reach many voters besides those already in the fold; it did a poor job of interpreting the national party line in a big presidential election (1948); it did not mobilize much of a vote on election day. Worst of all for the Democrats, they were not attracting new leadership from the ranks of the abler young men and women of the city. The party was run—to the extent that it was run at all—by some faithful oldtimers who could barely keep the organization from falling apart. "Thus in 1948," the study concluded, "the Democrats of Elmira had, not the vigorous spokesmen of a self-renewing opposition, but a leadership surviving from the defeats of the past—a leadership of nostalgia. . . ."[30]

PARTY WEAKNESSES

Perhaps the most striking fact about Elmira was that even Republicans, as the dominant party, were not very effective. The crucial fact about most states and localities is that *neither* party is organizationally very strong. Just as the national parties tend to break into factions revolving around individual leaders in Congress and the White House, as noted in Chapter 12, so the state and local parties tend to fragment into groups following individual candidates and officeholders. Most of the stronger leaders have their personal organizations which often crowd the regular party organizations out of the picture. Regular party committees are supposed to remain neutral during primary fights, and often do, with the result that candidates have no feeling of obliga-

[29]The classic picture of this situation at its most extreme was drawn by V. O. Key, Jr., in *Southern Politics in State and Nation* (Knopf, 1949).

[30]Bernard R. Berelson, Paul F. Lazarsfeld, and William N. McPhee, *Voting* (Univ. of Chicago Press, 1954), p. 162. These comments on Elmira are taken wholly from this brilliant analysis.

tion to the party organization once they win office. There is a tendency for every candidate in the same party to run on his own, and the devil take the hindmost. Each candidate sets up his own headquarters, puts up his own posters, sends out his own publicity, and taps his own sources of funds. Sometimes a candidate may deliberately keep clear of other candidates on the same ticket and even disassociate himself from the party label. The more offices to be voted on, the more candidates, and hence the greater the fragmentation of the party; and since most states have the "long ballot," they have fragmented parties.

What is the result of such state political systems? The late V. O. Key, Jr., of Harvard, the foremost student of state politics, expressed his concern. To paraphrase his conclusions:

1 State politics combined with constitutional arrangements, especially the nature of state legislative representation (see Chapter 29), contributes to centralization of power in the national government by incapacitating the states for action.

2 The rapid growth of state responsibilities makes it even more important to modernize the organization of political forces within the states, which at the present time is usually erratic and atomized.

3 The political system places serious obstacles in the path of popular government by making it impossible for broad popular mandates to be expressed in some situations and at some times.

4 Over the last half-century party organization has seriously deteriorated. This decay in party organization has been associated with the rise of the direct primary.[31]

In short, the problems presented by party weakness at the state level are the same as those presented at the national level—with this one difference: the national parties are roughly in balance, while state and local parties often are highly noncompetitive, where they exist at all. Many critics have suggested changes in the constitutional and administrative organization of the states, but the parties have received less attention. One reason may be that significant reforms in party structure and party balance are extremely difficult to bring about. No amount of tinkering can much alter the fact that most of the people of Kansas are Republicans and most of the people of the Deep South are Democrats. As long as strong personal factions exist within a party, preaching about the need of party cohesion will have little effect. Attitudes and political behavior change slowly and grow out of basic social, economic, and psychological conditions that reformers can do little to change.

But to recognize that political forces are relatively stable is not to say that they are impervious to change. If such institutional forces as the long ballot help to make the state and local parties what they are, institutional changes (such as the short ballot) may also affect the shape of the parties; so may changes in legislative representation or in procedures for nominating candidates.

A word about minor parties: whatever their other differences, the Demo-

[31] V. O. Key, Jr., *American State Politics: An Introduction* (Knopf, 1956), pp. 266–267.

crats and the Republicans who control the state governments agree that minor parties should be discouraged. In most states, laws relating to the formation and operation of political parties make it difficult for minor parties to become established and effective. In a few areas such as Minnesota there has been a fusion of Democrats and a minor party—e.g., the Farmer-Labor Party. In a few cities, minor parties sometimes play a balance-of-power role. In New York, for example, John Lindsay not only received the support of the Republican Party, which makes up a minority of the New York electorate, but also ran on the ticket of the Liberal Party. In short, at the level of state and local governments minor parties rarely have much influence on the outcome of elections or on the course of governmental policies.

Elections: The Struggle for Office

The Framers of the Constitution left the conduct of elections and other political matters largely in the hands of state government. This was one more safeguard, they felt, against too much national power. Today state control of elections remains a crucial fact, despite greater federal involvement to ensure compliance with the Fourteenth and Fifteenth Amendments. For one thing, it means that each state sets up its own way of managing elections, nominating candidates, regulating campaign contributions, preventing election fraud, and —most important—determining who shall be allowed to vote (always subject to limitations of the national Constitution). For another, it means that states also administer the election of national officials, presidential electors, senators, and congressmen.

NOMINATIONS IN THE STATES

Almost all party nominations in the United States—with the conspicuous exception of the nomination of the President—are made in party *primaries*. As noted in Chapter 13, primaries are of different types—the closed, the open, the run-off, and so on. The party primary is an almost uniquely American device and has had a profound influence on the nature of state and local politics. Rather than review the previous information, we might here raise some questions about the primary. Why was it adopted? What effect has it had on state and local parties and on the question of who governs? What are alternative ways of choosing party nominees?

The primaries were not always the chief means of choosing candidates. Once our parties had attained full bloom in the 1830s and 1840s, candidates for most offices were chosen in conventions. These were very much like our national conventions, but in miniature. Delegates were called to order in a local hall or hotel, candidates nominated, speeches delivered, roll call votes taken, and candidates finally chosen amid huzzahs and excitement. Not only were statewide candidates, such as the gubernatorial nominee, selected in these conclaves; local conventions were also held to select candidates for district attorney, state representative, county commissioner, and even town and city offices, such as mayor. Whatever their shortcomings, these conventions provided a vitality at the grass roots that many observers find woefully lacking today.

But conventions and caucuses had their shortcomings. In the late nineteenth century, as the rise of big cities provided lucrative contracts and franchises for politicians, local and state parties fell increasingly under the domination of bosses who used the convention as a means of control. The bosses often handpicked the delegates to conventions, refused to seat opposing delegates or ignored them if they were seated, and even used strong-arm methods. The great safeguard against such corruption was, of course, the opposition party, which could appeal to the people against bossism. But the creation of one-party states and districts as a result of the Civil War and the Bryan-McKinley fight of 1896 left most American states and localities with essentially one-party systems, especially in the South and the Northeast. So the great safeguard against bossism was gone.

The direct primary came largely as a result of this situation. During the muckraking first decade of this century, when reformers were attacking bossism, corruption, monopoly, and other conditions, the convention also came under fire. Nominations must be moved out of these boss-controlled conclaves, reformers declared, and put into the hands of the people. The means of democratizing nominations was at hand: the *direct primary*, which had first been adopted in the South. Wisconsin enacted the first state-wide primary law in 1901, and other states followed suit. Within a decade and a half —a period of progressivism dominated by Theodore Roosevelt, Robert La Follette, and Woodrow Wilson—the direct primary had been adopted for most nominations in all but a few of the states.

How has the direct primary worked out? Like most institutional reforms, it has had mixed results. On the one hand, the primary has probably diminished somewhat the power of the party leaders. It is more difficult for a boss to influence several thousand voters going to the polls than a few score of delegates going to a convention. But the difference has been only one of degree, and varies widely from place to place. Many bosses survived the coming of the primary with ease; participation in the primary was usually so light that they were able to control it by "delivering" the vote of their lieutenants, hangers-on, patronage appointees, and the friends and families of all these. Still, the primaries often encouraged insurgents to challenge the bosses.

Paradoxically, however, some people began to have second thoughts about the effect of primaries on party organization. After all, there were good party bosses as well as bad. There were party leaders who ran their organizations in a democratic fashion, tried to choose worthy candidates, and sought to live up to their other responsibilities. Good bosses were threatened, just as much as bad bosses, by factions supporting mediocre candidates and perhaps seeking to disrupt the party. The primaries had other weaknesses, some of which were noted earlier in the chapter. Primary contests were often disorganized, bewildering, and heavily influenced by local and narrow considerations. Primaries made it impossible for the parties to balance their tickets; for example, the Democratic party in Massachusetts, largely though by no means wholly made up of people of Irish descent, found it difficult to nominate a balanced ticket because the decision was made in the primaries, heavily dominated by the Boston Irish.[32] And primaries were especially hard on the minority party; up-and-coming politicians naturally gravitated to the major party primary, and the minority party nomination might go begging. In short, primaries seemed to militate against competitive, orderly, meaningful, vigorous two-party politics.

Despite these second thoughts, the trend toward the primary continues. New York and Connecticut, long the holdout states in continuing to use the convention for nomination of statewide officers, have now gone to the primary system, although they have tried to retain some of the features of the convention. In both states the candidate who secures endorsement at the convention becomes the endorsed candidate and does not have to run in a primary unless another candidate, who received 25 percent of the delegate votes (20 percent in Connecticut), wishes to challenge in a primary.[33] It is premature to suggest what will result from this combination of convention and primary, but it seems likely that there will normally be a challenge so that a primary will be held and that the results will be the same as the preprimary convention endorsements (see Chapter 13), where the real decision is in the primary. Whether the adoption of this modified primary system will undermine the strong party systems of these two states is yet to be determined. In the past, the parties were able, under the convention system, to nominate some outstanding men; indeed, the fact that New York conventions have yielded such Republicans as Theodore Roosevelt, Charles Evans Hughes, Thomas E. Dewey, and Nelson Rockefeller, and such Democrats as Alfred E. Smith, Franklin Roosevelt, Herbert Lehman, and Averell Harriman is a tribute to the convention system.

One thing is clear. The method of nominating candidates closely affects the organization of the party, and vice versa. The stronger the party—that is, the better-led, the more vigorous and competitive and unified—the more likely it can conduct its nomination fights through conventions. The weaker the party—the more disorganized and faction-ridden and decentralized—the more the voters may wish to take nominating decisions out of the hands of the parties and trust them to voters in primaries. Hence, it is quite logical that given the fact that most state and local parties are weak, primaries are the typical method of choosing nominees. By the same token, the existence of primaries may be a major cause of the structural weakness of parties. Some day there may be a trend back to the convention method, but for the moment primaries rule the day.[34]

ELECTIONS: A CASE STUDY

Perhaps the most distinctive feature of American politics is the number and variety of elections. Western Europeans, who are used to voting for one or two candidates at the national and local levels, and voting only once every

[32]Lockard, *op. cit.*, Chap. 11.

[33]Duane Lockard, *Connecticut's Challenge Primary: A Study in Legislative Politics* (Holt, 1959).

[34]The most significant work on state party systems and nominating methods has been done by V. O. Key, Jr., and his students. See his *American State Politics, op. cit.*, and his *Politics, Parties, and Pressure Groups* (Crowell, 1958), Chaps. 11,14.

two or three years, are flabbergasted by the impression they receive that Americans engage almost continuously in elections. Selection of town and local officials in the late winter may be followed by primaries to choose delegates to conventions, followed by primaries to choose party candidates, followed by general elections, all interspersed with special elections, special town or state referenda, and even in some states recall elections to throw some official out of office. Even more bewildering to many foreigners is the number of offices voted on at a particular election: from President to probate judge, from senator to sheriff, from governor to member of the library board. This is the "long ballot" in operation—whereas Europeans are more accustomed to the election of a handful of key officials, who in turn appoint career officials.

While generalizing about the nature of this enormous variety of elections would be dangerous, experienced politicians might agree on the following rules of thumb: (1) By and large, the more local the election, the less the excitement and interest aroused among the electorate, and the smaller the participation. (2) Except in areas where strong party organizations exist, candidates usually run on their own; they win through their personal organizations rather than through efforts by the party (partly because there are so many candidates running for so many offices that the party cannot give much help to any one of them). (3) Voters' familiarity with names rather than issues is of relatively greater importance in local than in state or national elections. (4) The candidate gets most of his money from his friends and from interest groups, not from his party. (5) While all kinds of propaganda are used, and often effectively, there is no substitute for personal contact between the candidate and the voters, especially in local campaigns.

The case of a recent campaign for state representative in the state of Washington exemplified some of these rules of thumb. In 1958, in the thirty-second legislative district (which includes the University of Washington), the two incumbent Republican legislators were up for reelection. Washington has the "blanket primary"—all candidates of all parties are placed on a single ballot, and the voter chooses from among them regardless of his own party affiliation. Among the Democratic candidates was a twenty-three year-old law student at the university, Wes Uhlman. With the help of leaders of the university Young Democrats, Uhlman vied with the two incumbents and with three other Democrats for nomination. He began by feeding stories to the newspapers; then, stepping up his effort, he and his helpers made up and posted hundreds of signs; sent out a carefully organized mailing to 1,300 Democrats in the district; mailed special letters on educational policy to the large number of teachers in the university area; conducted a tremendous "doorbelling" campaign; and climaxed their primary effort just before election by depositing thousands of fliers—"Be sure—Vote Uhlman"—on front porches. Money was so short during the primary campaign that Uhlman could not afford many newspaper ads, but his hard work paid off, for he placed first among the Democratic candidates. Running close behind him was another Democrat, an older man, who had done very little campaigning but who benefited from the fact that he had the same name as two well-liked politicians in the Seattle area.

With the nomination secured, Uhlman had to begin all over again for the general election. Once more he passed out literature, rang doorbells, put up signs, and put out big mailing. A massive election-eve effort to leave throwaways on front porches ran afoul of heavy winds and rain, but a small band of the faithful were still able to distribute several thousand pieces of damp literature. The Democratic party organization, which had been neutral during the primary fight, was not very active during the general election, so Uhlman had to depend on his now expanded personal organization. The Republican candidates were active too. Backed by the university Young Republicans, they countered the Democrats by publicizing the records of the incumbent representatives in extensive newspaper advertisements. But the Republicans, too, were not very effective as a party, mainly because they had to divide their efforts among campaigns for so many other offices.

When the returns were in, Uhlman, to the surprise of most observers, led the race. The next man was one of the incumbent Republicans, who thus held his seat. Uhlman's victory was credited to the hard work that he and his cohorts had done, the person-to-person contact at the polls, and his emphasis on his name rather than on his party. Political scientists might note other facts about the election battle. Organizationally, the parties did not play a major role (though the fact that most voters were either Democrats or Republicans *was* important; third parties were not involved). The candidates mainly ran on their own, emphasizing their own names. Hard work—especially "doorbelling"—was the crucial element. The whole effort was also influenced by the electoral system—the blanket primary and the fact that the district had two representatives in the legislature.

Finally, and perhaps of greatest significance, this election illustrates the openness of the American electoral system. If the Democratic nomination in the thirty-second district had been controlled by a boss, or perhaps even by a well-managed convention, Wes Uhlman, as a twenty-three-year-old newcomer to politics, probably would not have won the party nod. He was able to use the primary as a way of gaining access to the inner circles of politics.[35] Since his initial election in 1958, Uhlman has moved from the House to the Senate and has become chairman of the Senate Judiciary Committee. In a decade, an outsider became an insider.

Democracy or Oligarchy?

Who governs? We return to our central question after the quick look we have taken at the shape of politics in American states and localities. It would be easy to evade the question by saying again that the answer to the question varies according to the state or locality, as of course it does. But the nature of local and state political systems, as we have seen them briefly, does permit some generalization.

The striking fact is that American states and localities are characterized

[35]This case study is from "The Election of Wes Uhlman," in Richard T. Frost (ed.), *Cases in State and Local Government* (Prentice-Hall, 1961), pp. 79–94, which was based in turn on a case study presented by the Washington State–Northern Idaho Citizenship Clearing House.

more by *dispersion* of political influence than by concentration. The tremendous diversity of elective offices gives influence to many different officials and tends to fragmentize the political parties. The primary system of nominating candidates, used in all states, further diffuses power within the parties. A newspaper publisher, may, in effect, have a press monopoly, but he faces competition from many other media, such as television and radio, and he cannot even fully control the political influence of his own newspapers. The nominating system offers wide access to the center of influence, as in the case of Wes Uhlman.

It was not always this way. In the early days of New Haven, Robert Dahl found, the city was ruled by a small patrician-Congregationalist-Federalist elite, which exploited its high social standing, education, and wealth to achieve key positions in the church, the economy, the public life.[36] This small elite was powerful in *every* major decision-making area. But Dahl found that the situation had changed radically in the past century from what he calls "cumulative" to "dispersed inequalities." Different leaders hold different types of influence. The men who make the crucial decisions in education, for example, are not the same as those who closely influence urban redevelopment.

Roughly the same situation has been found in Chicago. Formal authority in this city, Edward Banfield discovered, was divided among thousands of governing bodies.[37] There was no small ruling elite. To be sure, the Democratic organization in Chicago was quite strong, but the mayor and the party chiefs had to bargain constantly with rebels within the organization, city officials, interest groups, and other centers of influence. Politicians and other leaders had a limited stock of power that they had to expend carefully. Everywhere there were veto groups that had to be placated, threatened, or given some kind of concession. The politics of Chicago was essentially a politics of bargaining and coalition-building. And always there was the voter who might ordinarily be uninformed and passive but who might come to the polls one day to chastize some public official who had "gone too far."

Most states and localities, in short, have pluralistic systems that are a long way from oligarchy. But this does not make them systems where every voter has roughly the same influence on political decisions. Power indeed tends to center in separate clusters of decision-makers, and large numbers of people have very little role; the fact that under the American system they could have a more active one is not an adequate reply, for ignorance, lack of education, and other factors keep many voters from wielding much influence. We can say only that along the broad range from centralization of power to dispersion of power most of our state and local governments are found nearer the latter pole.

But in the spirit of this chapter, we cannot leave the matter here. The student should look at his own state and community and ask hard questions. Who has influence and who does not? Under what conditions is influence exercised? *How* is it exercised—through authority, friendship, propaganda, deals, manipulation, coercion? What are the terms by which influence is

[36]Dahl, *op. cit.*, Chap. 1.
[37]Edward C. Banfield, *Political Influence* (The Free Press, 1961).

expended—what kind of influence does a political leader sacrifice in order to get the decision he wants?[38] In short, if most of these political systems are marked by deals, bargains, and exchanges, then who gains what, and who loses what, in the process? Does fragmented power prevent leaders from concerting efforts on behalf of the great mass of people?

[38]These questions are drawn from *ibid.*

State Constitutions:
Charters or Straightjackets?

28   "The state constitutions are the oldest things in the political history of America."[1] The early state constitutions, themselves an outgrowth of the colonial charters, were models for the national Constitution.

The people of each state, subject only to the broad limitations of the federal Constitution, are free to create whatever kind of republican government they wish. And yet all state constitutions are similar in general outline. No state has established a parliamentary system; none has deprived its judges of the power of judicial review. As people moved westward across the United States, they copied the constitutions of the older states, seemingly at times without much thought. The usual pattern of the state constitutions consists of a preamble; a bill of rights; articles providing for the separation of power, a bicameral legislature, an executive department, an independent judiciary with power of judicial review, the form and powers of local units of government; an amendment article; and miscellaneous provisions dealing with corporations, railroads, finances, and numerous other topics.

State constitutions obviously tell us much about how power is distributed within our states, and from them we learn of the essential similarity in the structure of state governments. Yet it is misleading to conclude that the similarity of formal constitutions means similarity in the actual governmental process. Much else has to be considered in determining who governs our states, as the preceding chapter suggests. The constitution is but a place to begin to learn.

[1]James Bryce, *The American Commonwealth*, vol. I (Macmillan, 1921), p. 427.

Constitutional Rigidity and Evasion

State constitutions contain more detail and are thus *longer, less adaptable*, require *more frequent formal amendment*, and remain *effective* for a *shorter period* than the federal Constitution.

California's much-amended constitution (350 amendments since 1879) goes into great detail about such matters as the taxation of fish, game, mollusks, or crustaceans, the disqualification from holding office or enjoying the right of suffrage of any person who participates in a duel, and the internal organization of several major departments. Article XX, Section 2, of Oklahoma's constitution proclaims, "Until changed by the Legislature, the flash test . . . for all kerosene oil for illuminating purposes shall be 115 degrees Fahrenheit; and the specific gravity test for all such oil shall be 40 degrees." Georgia's constitution details procedures to be followed by medical students in securing financial assistance. New Hampshire's sets the wages of its legislators in special session at a little over $3 a day. State constitutions vary in length from approximately 8,000 words in Vermont, Connecticut, and Iowa to 254,000 in Louisiana.

Although many of these detailed provisions deal with trivial subjects, others are concerned with important matters. The federal Constitution grants powers in broad and sweeping terms, letting future generations write in the details and adapt the basic charter of government to ever-changing conditions. Not so the state constitutions. They are written in restrictive terms. Whereas the federal Constitution takes only a clause to authorize Congress to spend money, state constitutions require dozens of pages to specify the purposes for which the money may be spent, how much may be spent, and in what manner.

CONSTITUTIONAL AUTOCRACY?

A written constitution, as we saw in Chapter 3, is *an instrument of government that sets forth, among other things, the terms upon which public officials are authorized to act in behalf of the sovereign voters.* The more detailed the constitution, the smaller the discretion the public officials enjoy. The earliest state constitutions had granted extensive authority to the legislatures without much restriction on how their power should be exercised; but after the legislatures gave special privileges to railroads, canal-builders, and other interests, constitutional amendments were adopted to prevent these abuses. Furthermore, reform groups, distrusting the legislatures, began to insist on having their programs incorporated into the constitution rather than settle for simple legislative adoption. In time, state constitutions became encrusted in layer after layer of detail.

What consequences does this have for democratic government? Most simply, it means that state constitutions often are less charters of self-government than straitjackets imposed on the living present by the dead past. Today's majorities find it hard to get the governmental action they wish.

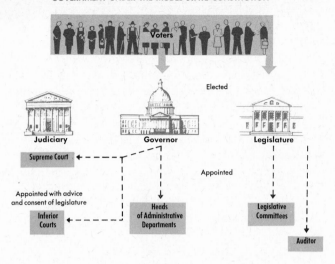

GOVERNMENT UNDER THE MODEL STATE CONSTITUTION

Voters

Elected

Judiciary — Supreme Court

Governor

Legislature

Appointed

Appointed with advice
and consent of legislature

Inferior Courts ← Heads of Administrative Departments

Legislative Committees

Auditor

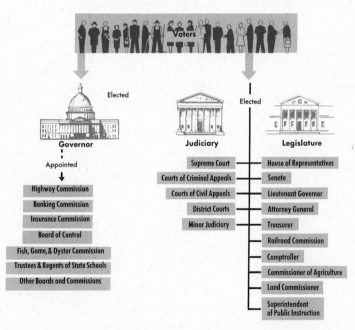

GOVERNMENT UNDER A TYPICAL STATE CONSTITUTION

Voters

Elected

Governor

Appointed

Highway Commission
Banking Commission
Insurance Commission
Board of Control
Fish, Game, & Oyster Commission
Trustees & Regents of State Schools
Other Boards and Commissions

Judiciary

Supreme Court
Courts of Criminal Appeals
Courts of Civil Appeals
District Courts
Minor Judiciary

Elected

Legislature

House of Representatives
Senate
Lieutenant Governor
Attorney General
Treasurer
Railroad Commission
Comptroller
Commissioner of Agriculture
Land Commissioner
Superintendent of Public Instruction

Adapted from charts prepared for the Committee on State Governments of the National Municipal League for the 1948 edition of the Model State Constitution, modified to reflect provisions
of the 1967 edition.

For example, construction of the Delaware Bridge, linking Philadelphia with
Camden, New Jersey, was delayed for five years because of restrictive clauses
in the Pennsylvania constitution. For many years the Oregon Legislature
could not create a state college in Portland because the constitution forbade
the founding of any new public institution outside Marion County.

The detailed enumeration of powers soon throws constitutions out of date.

Some outdated provisions are of course harmless, but more often they are roadblocks to effective government. The fixing of salaries in the constitutions, for example, makes it difficult to keep them geared to economic conditions. Prescribing a rigid administrative organization may make government incapable of accommodating changing needs. In short, details breed more details; long constitutions spawn hosts of amendments.

Under these conditions the people's representatives—the legislature—cannot act on many problems; instead, the voters are called on regularly to pass upon scores of constitutional amendments about which they know very little. In 1954, for example, the Louisiana Legislature confronted the voters with thirty-one proposed amendments. The New Orleans Bureau of Governmental Research estimated that it would take five hours just to read the texts of these proposals—and the Bureau ". . . did not guarantee that reading would make them intelligible." No wonder the Bureau termed the situation "Biennial bingo—or 31 more in '54."[2]

GETTING AROUND THE CONSTITUTION

Does all this mean that state constitutions can forever thwart the wishes of the majority? Not necessarily. The constitutional system of our states, like that of the national government, includes more than the formal written document. The unwritten rules, the practices, the basic statutes, the political parties, the interest groups, also shape the course of events. When large groups of people want their officials to act, they usually find some way to overcome formal constitutional barriers. Sometimes delicate tightrope-walking is called for, however. As a former Illinois Governor, the late Adlai E. Stevenson, explained, "For years the machinery of our state government has been kept in motion only by continued violations of plain and positive provisions in the Illinois constitution."[3] Along with the device of simply ignoring them, constitutional barriers can be overcome through judicial interpretation. Judges can interpret the meaning of words so as to remove their restrictive force. Nevertheless, rigid state constitutions create a "constitutional autocracy" by making it more difficult for new majorities to achieve their aims.

Detailed state constitutions also serve to enhance the authority of the state judiciary. The more complex the constitution, the easier it is for the judges to veto legislation. One reason for the growing length of some constitutions is that amendments are often required to reverse judicial interpretations.

Amending the Constitution

Constitutional amendments must be first *proposed* (initiated), then *ratified*. There are three ways to propose amendments: (1) by the legislature; (2) by initiative petition; and (3) by constitutional convention.

[2]Cited in and quoted by Karl A. Bosworth, "Law-making in State Governments," in *The Forty-eight States: Their Tasks as Policy Makers and Administrators* (The American Assembly, 1955), p. 90.

[3]Quoted by Richard L. Neuberger, "States in Strait Jackets," *The American Magazine* (April 1951), pp. 34–35.

CHAPTER 28
State
Constitutions:
Charters or
Straitjackets?

Proposal of constitutional amendments by initiative petition from the people is permitted in approximately one-fourth of the states. Proposal of amendments by the legislature, the most common method, is permitted in all states. Although the provisions vary among the states, the most general practice is to require the approval of two-thirds of the elected members in each chamber of the legislature in order to initiate an amendment. Some states require approval by only a simple majority, but this must be of two successive legislatures.

After an amendment has been proposed by one of these three methods, it must be ratified. In all states except Delaware (where the Legislature can ratify as well as propose amendments), ratification is by the voters. In most states, if a majority of those *voting on the amendment* approve it, the amendment becomes part of the constitution. In a few states, however, approval of a majority of *all* the voters *voting in the election* is required. Such a provision is a real obstacle, since many people who vote for candidates fail to vote at all on constitutional amendments.

Initiation of an amendment by the state legislature and ratification by a majority of voters voting on the amendment is the most common method of constitutional change. But in some states requirements are so stringent that

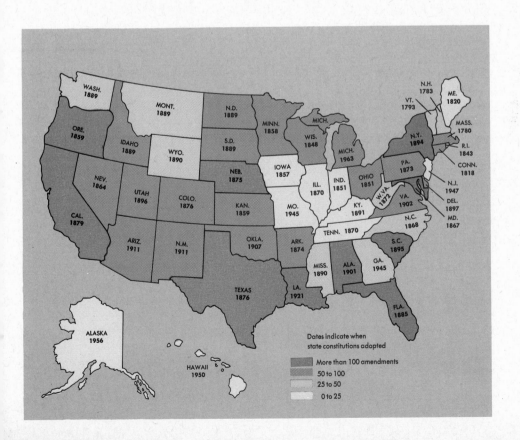

Dates indicate when
state constitutions adopted

More than 100 amendments
50 to 100
25 to 50
0 to 25

it is almost impossible to get an amendment ratified, and a relatively small minority can veto the desires of the majority. In Tennessee, for example, amending the 1870 constitution proved so difficult that not a single amendment could be pushed through until 1953. One of these amendments finally adopted in 1953 slightly liberalized the amending process. Changes in the constitutional system of Tennessee have had to come by methods other than formal amendment.

Amendments usually involve piecemeal change. Many observers, however, believe that most state constitutions are so bad that they cannot be salvaged by this kind of improvement. Rather than patching up the old model, they advocate trading it in for a new one. The officials of the National Municipal League—an organization devoted to the cause of governmental reform—have said that "most state constitutions are serious obstacles to responsible and effective state and local government." How can the people get a new constitution if they want one?

CONSTITUTIONAL CONVENTIONS

The United States is the country *par excellence* of constitutional conventions.[4] Since the nation was founded we have had over 200. Americans have always insisted on getting their constitutions down in writing, and on distinguishing clearly between fundamental and statutory law. A constitution is an expression of popular will; it is fundamental law binding on all public officials; and it can be changed only by prescribed methods. Hence, we have preferred to have our constitutions drawn up by some agency that would be more immediately expressive of popular sentiment than the legislature. The agency that we have chosen most often has been a constitutional convention.

Forty-three state constitutions authorize the legislature to submit to the voters the question of calling a convention, and in the other states the legislature is assumed to have the inherent power to do so. In ten states, the constitution requires the legislature to submit this question to the voters at fixed intervals.

If the voters approve the calling of a convention, the next step is to elect delegates. Some constitutions contain elaborate procedures governing the number of delegates, method of election, and time and place of the convention. Others leave the details to the legislature. After the delegates have been chosen for the specific job of drafting a new constitution, they assemble most frequently at the state capital.

When the convention has prepared a draft of the new constitution it is submitted to the voters, but first the delegates to the convention have to make a difficult choice. Should the voters be asked to accept or reject the new constitution as a whole? Or should they be given a chance to vote

[4]Albert L. Sturm, *Methods of State Constitutional Reform* (Univ. of Michigan Press, 1954), pp. 114–115. See also John P. Wheeler (ed.), *Salient Issues of Constitutional Revision* (National Municipal League, 1961), and John P. Wheeler, *The Constitutional Convention: A Manual on its Planning, Organization and Operation* (National Municipal League, 1961).

651

CHAPTER 28
State
Constitutions:
Charters or
Straitjackets?

on each section, as though it were an amendment to the old constitution? The advantage of the former method is that one provision of a constitution ties in with another, and in order to secure all the advantages of constitutional revision, it is desirable that the entire constitution be adopted. The disadvantage is that any group that takes issue with a particular provision may vote against the entire constitution in order to defeat the offending provision. When the convention knows that one provision is highly controversial, it may decide to submit at least that provision separately. Whichever method they choose, the proponents of constitutional change must look to their political fences in order to get their handiwork approved. The states most successful in securing new constitutions have been those that made elaborate arrangements to educate — or propagandize — the voters.

Instead of calling a constitutional convention, the legislature may appoint a small commission to make recommendations. A commission is less expensive, does not require initial voter approval, and gives the legislature final control of what is presented to the electorate. To call a convention is so difficult in some states that a commission-legislative proposal is the most effective way to secure consitutional revision: in Idaho a commission was used to frame a proposal to amend the constitution so that a convention could be called. The Legislature then had to submit this proposal to the voters.

California has been using the commission procedure to bring about significant constitutional change. The California Constitutional Revision Commission, comprising a bipartisan group of citizens and representing a wide range of interests, has been working closely with the leaders of the Legislature. In 1966 and 1968 the electorate approved revisions, originally sponsored by the Revision Commission, that made significant changes in six articles of the constitution. In some other states the revision commission has not worked so well, perhaps because it was not responsive to the political currents of the state nor representative of all the interests, thus failing to incorporate critically important compromises in its recommendations. Commissions may have the advantage of being politically disinterested, but they may propose such drastic changes that their work is rejected either by the legislature or by the voters.

The political struggle does not cease once a constitutional convention has assembled. Often, those who dominate the legislature also dominate the convention. In some cases, however, the interests that dominate conventions are different from those that run the legislature. Service in conventions usually carries greater prestige than a seat in the legislature, and many men are willing to interrupt their normal activities in order to spend some time at constitution-writing. For example, George Romney, when president of American Motors, played a vital role in the Michigan constitutional convention and went from there to the governorship and national prominence. Moreover, conventions sometimes attract greater popular attention; thus it is possible to get from conventions those changes that legislatures cannot or will not make.

Recent years have seen a renewal of interest in constitutional revision. In more than two-thirds of the states the subject is of such substantial interest that commissions have been formed or conventions called; elsewhere the question of calling a convention is presently before the legislature or the electorate. Michigan, Maryland, New York, Tennessee, New Jersey, Rhode Island, Connecticut, Hawaii, and New Hampshire, among others, have had constitutional conventions. Illinois will do so soon, and California is considering the question. Revision commissions have been at work in many states; examples are California, Idaho, Florida, Kentucky, Pennsylvania, and Wisconsin. Yet from all this activity only a few significant changes in state constitutions have resulted.

If present constitutions are so bad, why have not more states modernized them? The answer lies in the nature of the political process. Constitutions are not a neutral set of rules perched above the world of rough-and-tumble politics. On the contrary, constitutions significantly affect "who gets what" from government. The way in which a constitution is changed can help or hinder various groups in gaining what they want. Present state constitutions may be bad from the perspective of democratic theory, but they are not bad for many specific groups. Many people are indifferent to constitutional change; it is difficult to work up much excitement in a campaign for revising a state constitution. Hence, the standpatters have a built-in advantage that, when combined with the constitutional obstacles, helps to explain the lack of action.

To date, those who have a vested interest in present arrangements have been strong enough to prevent the calling of constitutional conventions or the establishment of revision commissions. Where the latter have been created, they have frequently been used as safety valves to divert demands for change into controllable hands.[5]

THE NEW YORK CONSTITUTIONAL CONVENTION:
A CASE STUDY

Although the 1894 constitution of New York provides for the automatic submission to the electorate every twenty years of a call for a constitutional convention, the call was often placed at the end of a long ballot and failed to receive the support of the electorate. In 1938 a convention was held, but its work was rejected by the voters.

By 1965, deep dissatisfaction with the workings of the state government in addition to the Legislature's inability to devise a reapportionment plan led the Legislature, by a majority vote in both houses, to resubmit the question of a constitutional convention to the voters. The call, with bipartisan support, was approved by a majority of those voting on the question. A preparatory commission, primarily composed of academics, prepared studies and alternatives for consideration by the convention. The call was the convention's last bipartisan feature. During the following year the two major parties, as well as the minor ones, named candidates for delegates to the convention. Delegates were apportioned on the same basis as the lower

[5]William C. Havard, "Notes on a Theory of State Constitutional Change: The Florida Experience," *The Journal of Politics* (February 1959), pp. 80–104.

house of the New York Legislature, with the addition of some delegates-at-large. In the November 1966 general elections the Democrats won a narrow majority of the delegates.

When the convention opened in the spring of 1967 it faced three major controversial questions: (1) how to apportion the Legislature, (2) how to select judges (by appointment, by election, or by some combination such as the Missouri Plan—see page 87), and (3) how to structure relations between churches and the state.

For the purposes of apportionment the Democrats proposed a scheme to which the Republicans objected, but since the federal Constitution requires that the legislature be apportioned by population (see pages 663–671), the partisan contention over this issue was somewhat reduced, and the Democratic apportionment proposal was adopted by the convention along with a plan to create a bipartisan commission to reapportion the Legislature after each census.

Many groups, including the League of Women Voters, hoped that the convention would reduce the number of elected judges and move to some system of appointment. But the convention adopted a plan for the election of most judges—a move that advocates of judicial reform thought was a step backward.

By far the most controversial debate centered on the so-called Blaine amendment (to the existing New York constitution) that prohibits direct or indirect aid to any religious schools. The convention substituted for the Blaine amendment language similar to that of the First Amendment to the federal Constitution, a move that was generally construed as lowering the wall between church and state. Whether this would turn out to be the case was questionable. The Blaine amendment had not kept New York courts from sustaining programs, such as the reading of prayer in the public schools, that the United States Supreme Court subsequently held to be in violation of the First Amendment. But, the fact remained that many New Yorkers thought that the proposed repeal of the Blaine amendment would open the way to closer interrelation of church and state is the significant political fact.

The convention decided to present the new constitution as a package rather than in a series of separate proposals. In the campaign for ratification, Governor Rockefeller endorsed the new constitution, the Democratic party was divided, and Republicans generally opposed it, primarily because of the belief that under the new constitution the Democrats would gain strength in the Legislature. The voters? They rejected the constitution by a vote of 3,364,630 to 1,309,897. Most of the public debate centered on the repeal of the Blaine amendment, and most observers felt that this controversy was the primary reason for the defeat of the new constitution.[6]

Other states have not had much success with constitutional conventions either. The Maryland convention consisted of delegates elected on a nonpartisan basis, the convention selected its committee chairmen without regard to party, and the convention was "one of the most carefully planned and

[6]James E. Bebout, "State Constitutions and Constitutional Revision, 1965–67," *Book of the States, 1967–1968* (Council of State Governments, 1967), pp. 6–7.

efficiently managed constitutional conventions held in recent years."[7] The proposed constitution was endorsed by most business and civic leaders, the supporters engaged in a well-financed campaign, and the voters rejected the new constitution overwhelmingly. In Rhode Island the voters also turned down a draft constitution submitted to them by their constitutional convention, "the longest one of history."[8] Michigan is one of the few states during the last decade in which the electorate approved the work of a constitutional convention, and in Michigan the new constitution is in essence a simplified version of the old one. In Tennessee, Connecticut, New Hampshire, and New Jersey the voters approved the proposals from their constitutional conventions, but these were so-called limited conventions, restricted to the consideration of only a few items, primarily that of reapportionment.

HAWAII AND ALASKA

Early in 1950, sixty-three delegates representing the several islands and various ethnic groups that made up the then Territory of Hawaii met to draft a constitution for the projected state. Five years later, fifty-five men convened in a constitutional convention in the gymnasium of the University of Alaska, and out of several weeks' effort came the constitution for what was to be the forty-ninth state of the Union.[9] The people of the two territories enthusiastically approved the labors of their conventions, and the proposed state constitutions were duly transmitted to Congress. Eventually Congress, as had its predecessors with each of the new state constitutions since 1789, found the Alaskan and Hawaiian constitutions to be republican in character and not repugnant to the Constitution of the United States or the Declaration of Independence, and resolutions admitting the new states were adopted by Congress and signed by the President. The necessary preliminaries to statehood were quickly disposed of, and Alaska and Hawaii became states in 1958 and 1959 respectively.

A hundred and seventy-odd years had passed since another group of fifty-five men met in Philadelphia to draft the national Constitution. As we have noted, these men drew heavily on the constitutions of the thirteen original states; then the new states, carved out of forest and plain as the nation moved westward, borrowed from the constitutions of their older sister states as well as from the national one. With all this experience to draw on, what kinds of constitution did Alaska and Hawaii adopt?

In general, the new constitution-writers followed tradition. The two newest state constitutions contain the usual preamble, bill of rights, provisions for separation of powers and a bicameral legislature, and articles dealing with local government. But the old patterns were not indiscriminately copied. The men who wrote these constitutions were well aware of the weaknesses and shortcomings of state constitutions depicted above and they sought to avoid many of them. For example, both constitutions are relatively short; through the avoidance of encumbering details, the legislatures have

[7]*Ibid*, p. 8.
[8]*Ibid*, p. 7.
[9]Paul C. Bartholomew, "The Constitution of the State of Alaska," *Southwestern Social Science Quarterly* (June 1959), pp. 40–53.

been left relatively free to respond to the changing needs of these two rapidly developing states.

Moreover, many specific proposals for improving state governments (some of these will be discussed in the next several chapters) have been incorporated in the constitutions of the two new states. The problem of reapportioning legislative seats as population changes—a seemingly unsolvable problem in many states—has been met by removing the responsibility from the legislature and placing it in the hands of the governor and the courts. In line with recommendations by political scientists, the number of elected executive officers has been reduced to the governor and only one other official. The organization of the judicial branch also shows the imprint of new thinking, for in both states the legislature has been left with authority to determine the organization and precise function of the lower courts. In Alaska the judges are to be selected according to the Missouri Plan (page 687), and in Hawaii by the governor with consent of the state Senate.

Alaska's and Hawaii's constitutions like those of all the other states, bear distinguishing birthmarks reflecting the peculiar demands of a given time and place. Only a few can be mentioned here. Alaska, being abundantly endowed with natural resources, devotes a sizable section of its constitution to guarantees that these resources shall be used in the public interest. Since Hawaii is the most racially mixed of all our states, several provisions of its constitution deal with race relations. Discrimination in public schools and other institutions is explicitly prohibited, as are denials of civil rights because of race, sex, or ancestry. Alaska, too, guarantees the legal and political equality of all people. Alaska also exhibits an awareness of the threat to civil liberties that arises out of efforts to deal with disloyalty. Besides containing the familiar due process clause, its constitution specifically guarantees fair and just treatment in the course of executive and legislative investigations. One final novelty—both states have departed from the mainland tradition of setting the minimum age requirement for voting at twenty-one (followed by all but Kentucky and Georgia), Alaska making it nineteen and Hawaii twenty. Hawaii continues to be a pioneer: since being admitted it has become the first state to provide for a statewide ombudsman. It also had its second constitutional convention, in 1968.

Under the Capitol Dome:
The State Legislature

29   Do you know the names of the men who represent you in your state legislature? Probably not. But in all likelihood you would if you were a member of the generation that saw war and independence come to the American colonies. Indeed, you might have counted several state legislators among your heroes. One of the significant trends in our political history has been the rise and fall of the state legislatures and of the prestige that surrounds them. During the Revolution they were the focal points of the war effort, and when peace came they occupied a powerful and prestigious position in the American community. But the guns at Yorktown had hardly fallen silent when the status of the state legislatures began to decline. In fact, the adoption of the federal Constitution was a victory for those who were disappointed with, and wished to curtail, the authority of the state legislatures. In recent times, too, state legislatures have come under heavy criticism. They have been described as unrepresentative, inefficient, badly organized, and mediocre.

   Do the legislators deserve such criticism? If so, what could be done to improve their performance? Before we turn to these problems, let us glance at the characteristic organization and procedures of our state legislatures—or assemblies, as they are often called. In all states except Nebraska, the legislature is bicameral. The lower and more numerous chamber is generally called the House of Representatives. Its size varies from a low of 35 in Delaware to a high of 400 in New Hampshire; the typical number is around 100. In most states the representatives serve for a two-year term, and the upper chamber, known in all the states as the Senate, is composed of about 40 members. State senators have a four-year term in about two-thirds of the states.

Twenty-one states hold annual legislative sessions; in others, the legislature meets in regular session once every two years (biennial sessions), usually in January of odd-numbered years. In most of the states the constitution limits the legislature to a regular session of a fixed number of days, usually sixty. A few states halt payment of legislators' salaries after a specified period; only infrequently do they stay in session after their pay stops. These restrictions reflect the old distrust of government, the feeling that "the faster we get it over with the better." The governor has the power to call the legislature into special session, a power frequently used because of the constitutional time limits on regular sessions. In some twenty-two states the legislature can discuss during the special session only those matters specified by the governor; in one-fourth of the states the legislature can call itself into special session and is not, therefore, so restricted.

The organization and procedures of the state legislature are similar to those of Congress. A speaker, chosen by the majority party, presides over the lower house. In some states the speaker has more power to control proceedings than his national counterpart; for example, in addition to all the powers of the Speaker of the national House of Representatives, he has the right to appoint committees, and thus his is a key role in determining policy. In most of the states a lieutenant governor presides over the senate; in the others, the presiding officer is chosen by the majority party in the senate. The committee system prevails, as in Congress; but in some states, notably Massachusetts, joint committees are used regularly to speed legislative action. However state "legislative standing committees are but pale shadows of their congressional counterparts"[1]; they do not have the same power over bills. Committees seldom have professional assistance; the seniority system is not as stringently followed as in Congress; and turnover is higher.

Although the formal structure and procedures of the legislatures are similar from state to state, this is not true of their actual operation. Some states, like New York, have strong political parties that take an active part in policy-making. Here and in perhaps a dozen other states the party caucus is an important part of the legislative machinery; in others, the parties assume no responsibility for the actions of their legislative members. In some states, the governor leads the legislative way; in others, he is relatively unimportant. The fairly competitive two-party system found in Congress exists in about ten states.[2] In order to describe with any accuracy the actual functioning of a particular state legislature, one must be acquainted with the entire social and political environment in which that legislature operates.[3]

WHAT THE STATE LEGISLATURES CAN—AND CANNOT—DO

What do the slightly more than 7,600 state legislators do? A former prominent state legislator replies, "We enact the laws that set speed limits on the

[1]Malcolm E. Jewell, *The State Legislature* (Random House, 1962), p. 93.
[2]Malcolm E. Jewell and Samuel C. Patterson, *The Legislative Process in the United States* (Random House, 1966), pp. 143–144.
[3]John C. Wahlke, Heinz Eulau, William Buchanan, and LeRoy C. Ferguson, *The Legislative System: Explorations in Legislative Behavior* (Wiley, 1962), is a careful and detailed analysis of the role and behavior of legislators in California, Tennessee, Ohio, and New Jersey.

highways; we specify minimum salaries for classroom teachers; we fix the content of butterfat in Grade-A milk; we draw up the rules governing the purity of drinking water; and we determine whether a citizen convicted of murder in the first degree shall be gassed, hanged, shot, electrocuted, or merely clapped behind iron bars."[4]

The state legislatures have all the governmental powers that are not given to some other agency. The Tenth Amendment to the federal Constitution makes it clear that governmental power not given to the national government or denied to the states lies with the states or with the people. The state constitutions in turn give some of this reserved power exclusively to nonlegislative agencies and specifically deny some to the legislature. What is left is inherited by the state legislatures. To be sure, some state courts have developed the doctrine of *implied limitations* on the legislatures by ruling that when the constitution authorizes the legislature to do a particular thing, by implication it denies the legislature the power to do other things.

Although subject to all these constitutional limitations, the legislature still retains a powerful voice in the determination of the crucial political questions in the state. Among other things, the legislature levies state taxes, appropriates the moneys, creates the agencies to carry out the tasks of government, allots functions among these agencies, and investigates them to make sure that they are doing what the lawmakers intended them to do. State legislators, like their national counterparts, also participate in amending constitutions, have authority to impeach and try public officials, and exercise some appointive powers.

Quite commonly, the state constitution prescribes the procedures that legislators must follow in order to legislate. In addition, the rate of taxation, the kinds of tax, the subjects that may be taxed, and the purposes of taxation are often detailed in the constitution. Special legislation — laws dealing with particular persons or localities — is usually prohibited. Many constitutions declare that special laws are to be avoided wherever possible, and in addition they list particular subjects — divorce, chartering corporations, licensing banks, affairs of local units of government — which the legislature is forbidden to deal with by special legislation. Such restrictions do not, however, prevent *classifications*, and by refined classifications (for example, a law for cities of over 14,350 and under 15,600 population when only one city in the state fits this category) legislatures can often overcome constitutional restrictions.

WHO ARE THE STATE LEGISLATORS?

In our more populous and wealthy states the trend is toward annual sessions with substantial salaries. California pays its legislators $16,000 a year; New York and Michigan, $15,000; Massachusetts, Illinois, and Wisconsin provide "living wages." But in most of the other states a legislator has only a part-time job with a commensurate salary: legislators go to the state capitol for a short time every two years and are paid so little that they are able to serve only if they are independently wealthy or have another job that can be readily combined with legislative service. In all fifty states the median *bien-*

[4]Richard L. Neuberger, "Tribulations of a State Legislator," *The Reporter* (Jan. 31, 1950), p. 31.

nial salary is not much more than $4,000 — New Hampshire provides $200 a biennium. Of course, most states provide for travel and other expenses, and this is sometimes used to overcome constitutional obstacles to providing legislators with more adequate compensation.

James Bryce argued that legislative salaries should be abolished, for they only serve, he argued, to attract men who have no interest in the job except for the money. While this attitude is still encountered, most people are persuaded that inadequate salaries discourage qualified candidates from seeking office. Few businessmen, teachers, or salaried workers, for example, can interrupt their activities to attend to legislative duties, and they cannot afford to give up their jobs and live on the salary that the state pays.

Lawyers are the largest occupational group in state assemblies, just as they are in the national Congress. Many young attorneys enter the legislature to perform a public service, secure a reputation, and build up a practice. In many states farmers are the next largest group. Since farming is more or less seasonal, it can be more readily adjusted than many professions to fit legislative schedules. However, the number of farmers serving in the legislature is decreasing as a result both of reapportionment (see pages 663–671) and of the decline in the number of farmers. Salesmen, such as insurance men and real estate dealers, are also found in significant numbers. There are a few women, and fewer Negroes, in state legislatures.[5] The women legislators — over 350 by latest count — are most often to be found in the state legislatures of the small states, especially in New England and the West, and they are predominantly Republicans.[6] Legislative service is especially attractive to those who wish to have a political career, for it is the position most often held as a preliminary to other elective offices, "the most important first rung on the ladder of political ascent."[7]

What kind of men and women are the state legislators? Bryce, writing at the end of the nineteenth century, stated that the average legislature had "fewer able and high-minded men among its members" than did the Congress. The reason, he believed, was that the state legislature "is surrounded by temptations relatively greater. It is guarded by a less watchful and less interested public opinion." All this is probably still true, although the late Senator Richard Neuberger, author and former member of the Oregon Legislature, argued that the "voters are looking right down your throat." But as Neuberger also pointed out, it is primarily the organized interest groups that are heard at the state capitols; the unorganized public probably pays even less attention to its state legislature than to Congress in faraway Washington. When Neuberger introduced a measure to limit the number of billboards on the highways, a few men, "stung on the pocket nerve," were able to make it appear that the entire state was up in arms against the bill, although the billboard-owners themselves never once appeared in testimony. The head of the Signpainters' Union called Neuberger an enemy of labor desirous of putting men out of work. The omnipresent widows and orphans came to the capi-

[5]See Crane Wilder, Jr., and Meredith W. Watts, Jr., *State Legislative Systems* (Prentice-Hall, 1968), pp. 44–48, for survey of legislative backgrounds.

[6]Emmy E. Werner, "Women in the State Legislatures," *Western Political Quarterly* (March 1968), p. 50.

[7]Lester Seligman, "Prefatory Study of Leadership Selection in Oregon," *Western Political Quarterly* (March 1959), p. 154.

tol and argued that they could not live without the rent they received from their roadside property. A delegation from the state advertising club charged that the Bill of Rights and freedom of speech were being jeopardized. The measure was stigmatized as communist in origin. Under these pressures, the bill was defeated. Without doubt, state legislators often yield to interests that comprise an extremely small segment of the population. But this weakness —if it be such—is not peculiar to the state legislators.

The state legislator enjoys far less prestige than do national congressmen, especially in states with large legislatures. Discouraged by the low salary and lack of influence, many men serve a term or two and then retire. The turnover is so large that continuity of leadership is interrupted. "Over half of the state legislators are new at each session,"[8] though the practice varies widely among the states. "Factors which appear to be relevant to turnover are the rate of compensation, responsibility sufficient to make the job attractive, electoral laws and practice which favor incumbents or discourage rotation, as well as the constitutional length of terms of office."[9]

And yet there is much to be said for the state legislator. He is usually a hardworking, public-spirited citizen. Of course, those who dislike the laws that are passed, or who like the laws that are defeated, often claim that fault lies with the intelligence of the legislators. The state legislatures probably have their share of ignorant and dishonest men, but there is little support for many of the more serious charges directed against them. And what evidence we do have indicates that there is a growing improvement in the level of legislative ethics.[10] The general level of intelligence and devotion to the public interest displayed by state legislators is probably a fairly accurate reflection of the people who elect them.

PARTIES IN THE STATE LEGISLATURES

Except in Minnesota and Nebraska, all candidates for state legislatures are nominated by political parties and elected as party members. However, the role of the parties in the management of the legislatures and in policy-making varies widely from state to state. The American Political Science Association's Committee on State Legislatures discovered strong party spirit and cohesion in seventeen state legislatures; within these states legislators in the same party tended to vote alike.[11] In eleven state legislatures the parties were found to be only moderately or occasionally strong; and in twenty, party strength was weak or nonexistent. In some states, for example, the legislature reflects a rural-versus-urban split; in others, legislators cluster in conservative or liberal coalitions; and in still others, there appear to be only shifting combinations of factions. The committee also reported a fairly even

[8]Belle Zeller (ed.), *American State Legislatures* (Crowell, 1954), p. 65. This is a report of the Committee on American Legislatures of the American Political Science Association. See also Thomas R. Dye, "State Legislative Politics," in H. Jacob and K. N. Vines (eds.), *Politics in the American States* (Little, Brown, 1965), pp. 169, 170.

[9]Wahlke, et al., *op. cit.*, p. 49. See also James D. Barber, *The Lawmakers: Recruitment and Adaptation to Legislative Life* (Yale Univ. Press, 1965), p. 8.

[10]See for example, Leonard I. Ruchelman, "A Profile of New York State Legislators," *The Western Political Quarterly* (September 1967), pp. 634–635, showing a decline in the percentage of lawmakers in New York found guilty of disreputable activity.

[11]Zeller, *op. cit.*, pp. 192ff. Wahlke, et al., *op. cit.*, supports these generalizations.

division in nineteen states between the two parties in the legislature; in nine states one of the parties dominated, but the other had a sizable number of seats in the legislature; and in eighteen states one party overwhelmingly dominated the legislature.

Party cohesion and spirit are most often to be found in the two-party legislatures. Here it is that party caucuses are most likely to function, formulating policy that party members are expected to support in the legislative sessions. Some of the two-party legislatures, however, exhibit little party cohesion, and even where party cohesion exists, the role of the party in formulating policy may be exaggerated.

In states where a single party dominates the legislature but where the minority party has a sizable number of seats, the role of the party varies widely. In some, both political parties are highly organized; in others only the majority party has cohesion, and the minority party is usually weak.[12] But the most prevalent pattern in these states is for both parties to be weak. In legislatures where a single party has overwhelming control (until recently the Democrats traditionally held every seat in both houses in five Southern states; even today there are no Republicans in the Louisiana Legislature, only one each in Alabama and Mississippi, six in Arkansas, and eight in South Carolina), parties are of little importance in conducting legislative business. Factions within the dominant party, however, are sometimes very active. Occasionally the factions in a one-party legislature organize around dominant personalities—the Long and anti-Long factions in Louisiana, for example.

In summary, parties are more likely to be strongest in the two-party legislatures, weakest in the one-party legislatures, and neither very strong nor very weak in the modified one-party legislatures. In a few state legislatures, parties seem to play a more prominent role than they do in Congress, but they are considerably weaker in most state legislatures. Party control of legislation, in short, is even weaker in most states than it is in Congress.

Improving Legislative Procedures

The weaknesses of some of our state legislatures are much like those of Congress, but they run deeper: legislative business is not conducted efficiently; committee work is not carefully planned; records are not always well kept; expert information is sometimes lacking; introducing special and private legislation is too easy; parliamentary rules impede rather than expedite action and play into the hands of minorities. Other weaknesses are peculiar to the states: the length of sessions is unnecessarily restricted;

[12]*Ibid.*, p. 206. For other studies of the parties' role in state legislatures see Thomas A. Flinn, "Party Responsibility in the States: Some Causal Factors," *The American Political Science Review* (March 1964), pp. 60–71; Jewell, *op. cit.*; Dye, in Jacob and Vines (eds.), *op. cit.*, pp. 151–206. Malcolm E. Jewell, "Party Voting in American State Legislatures," *The American Political Science Review* (September 1955), pp. 773–791. For studies of particular states, see William J. Keefe, "Parties, Partisanship, and Public Policy in the Pennsylvania Legislature," *The American Political Science Review* (June 1954), pp. 450–464; and, on a more general aspect, Leon D. Epstein, *Politics in Wisconsin* (Univ. of Wisconsin Press, 1958), pp. 33–56, and Wahlke, et al., *op. cit.*

salaries are too low; and some legislatures lack the services needed for lawmaking in a complex world.

SOME SPECIFIC RECOMMENDATIONS

Here are the recommendations made by a group of experts to improve legislative procedures in the states:

1 Constitutions should . . . leave legislatures as unhampered as possible, encouraging the development of their own self-reliance. Limitations on a legislature's power to appropriate public funds, and to address itself to public questions, should be eliminated.

2 Use of popular initiative is inconsistent with representative government, except for the call of a constitutional convention.

3 Enactment of private bills, bills affecting few persons, local and special bills should be minimized . . . .

4 As the principle of "one man, one vote" is applied, innovations in districting policies to improve patterns of representation are desirable.

5 State constitutions should provide for periodic reapportionment.

6 Adoption of a unicameral legislature may prove fruitful in some states. A small unicameral legislature may be especially appropriate in states where the cost of legislative operations is burdensome.

7 Legislatures should be of a size to make the position of legislator more important and visible.

8 To develop more responsibility in legislative performance, and more independence, legislatures should be continuing bodies meeting in annual plenary sessions, without limitation of time or subject. Legislatures should be empowered to call themselves into session.

9 Competent professional staff should be provided the legislature, including staff for the leadership, both majority and minority.

10 State legislatures should utilize a strong system of standing committees, few in number, with broad, well-defined jurisdictions.

11 To expedite consideration of legislation, devices consistent with adequate opportunity for debate and deliberation should be adopted. These include . . . electronic voting. . . .

12 Codes of ethics should be adopted, applying to career, appointed and elected officials, in all branches of state government.[13]

TWO HOUSES OR ONE?

Bicameralism became the established pattern in the United States early in our history (see Chapter 2). During colonial days, the two chambers represented distinct interests—the upper house stood for royal authority; the lower house stood for the colonial cause. The desire to balance the aristocratic

---

[13]Alexander Heard (ed.), *State Legislatures in American Politics* (Prentice-Hall, 1966). See also Robert B. Dishman and George Goodwin, Jr., *State Legislatures in New England Politics* (report of the New England Assembly on State Legislatures 1968); and Samuel C. Patterson (ed.), *Midwest Legislative Politics* (Univ. of Iowa, 1967).

against the popular interest, and the belief in a government of checks and balances, led to the retention of two-house legislatures after independence had been won. During the first decades of our history, the suffrage requirements to vote for senator and the qualifications to serve in the senate were more stringent than those for the lower house. But by the middle of the nineteenth century, the same electorate was choosing the members of both houses. Today in many states the two houses represent the same people (but usually in different districts). Why do we retain the bicameral system?

Defenders of bicameralism insist that two chambers check hasty or ill-considered legislation. But even in some states with two chambers, legislation is rushed through, especially in the closing days, with little consideration by either chamber. Sometimes the second chamber discovers unintended mistakes or errors in bills enacted by the other house and makes the necessary corrective amendments. Some bills proposed by one chamber are defeated by the other, but it is impossible to develop objective standards to determine whether the legislation so defeated was ill-considered. Critics of bicameralism are persuaded that the governor's veto, the courts, and the electorate are better checks. They believe that too many roadblocks impede legislation, with the result that minority interests find it easy to prevent legislation desired by the majority.

Another defense of bicameralism is that it balances the interests of various groups. By enabling different groups to dominate one or the other chamber, it is argued, bicameralism provides proper balance. Defenders of unicameralism answer that if this reasoning were carried to its logical conclusion, we would have a multichamber legislature with a separate chamber to represent each interest—one for the farmers, one for the businessmen, one for the workers, one for people in large cities, one for people in small towns, and so on. The interests of all groups can be fairly represented in one chamber, they insist. Moreover, bicameralism encourages buck-passing and secret legislation in conference committees, and requires elaborate committee systems.

Under the leadership of the late Senator George Norris, Nebraska created a unicameral legislature of forty-three men elected on a nonpartisan ballot. "After two and a half decades of experience, Nebraska voters appear satisfied with one house,"[14] but despite consideration by several state constitutional conventions, the single-chamber legislature has not been adopted by any other state.

Whether our legislatures are composed of one house or two, we are still faced with the perplexing problem of determining the basis on which their members shall be elected.

The Reapportionment Revolution

One of the big issues of the 1960s was the battle over representation in the state legislatures. As the decade opened, "the average value

---

[14]William Anderson, Clara Penniman, and Edward W. Weidner, *Government in the Fifty States* (Holt, 1960), p. 211. See also Roger V. Shumate, "The Nebraska Unicameral Legislature," *Western Political Quarterly* (September 1952), p. 512; and Richard D. Marvel, "The Nonpartisan Nebraska Unicameral," in Patterson, *op. cit.*, pp. 89–120.

of the vote in the big city was less than half the average value of the vote in the open country, so far as electing members of the state legislature [was] concerned.[15] Cook County, for example, had over half of Illinois's population and its residents paid more than half the state taxes, but the county elected only twenty-four of the fifty-eight members of the state Senate. Los Angeles County had more than 38 percent of California's population but elected only one out of forty senators. Dade County in Florida (Miami) contained about one-fifth of the state's population but elected only three out of ninety-five members of the lower house and only one of the thirty-eight senators. The same general picture was found in state after state.[16]

STATE LEGISLATURES V. CITY OFFICIALS

Rural Republicans running many legislatures battled city Democrats who were trying to run most of our large cities. City officials complained that the small-town and farm-dominated legislators were unsympathetic to their problems and were trying to enforce rural notions of right and wrong upon their city brethren. One student of Chicago politics noted that the office of corporation counsel of Chicago (city attorney) spent most of its time finding "ways of circumventing or changing state laws which hamper the city."[17]

George Washington Plunkitt, the Tammany Hall patriot, felt strongly about the control of the New York Legislature by rural Republicans. The hayseeds, as he called them in 1905, "think we are like the Indians to the National Government—that is, sort of wards of the state, who don't know how to look after ourselves and have to be taken care of by the Republicans of St. Lawrence, Ontario, and other backwoods counties. . . . Say, you hear a lot about the downtrodden people of Ireland . . ." continued Plunkitt. "Now, let me tell you that they have more real freedom and home rule than the people of this grand and imperial city. . . . In this state the Republican government makes no pretense at all. It says right out in the open: 'New York City is a nice big fat Goose. Come along with your carvin' knives and have a slice.' "[18]

Plunkitt accused the Republican-controlled state government of levying all the taxes on liquor, corporations, banks, and insurance companies, and then spending the money for the country people. One of his fondest dreams was to see New York City withdraw from the state. But what would happen to the people upstate? "These hayseeds," he said, "have been so used to livin' off of New York City that they would be helpless. . . . It wouldn't do to let them starve. We might make some sort of appropriation for them for a few years." Plunkitt even wanted to pass a law requiring upstate politicians to get a passport before traveling south of the Bronx. He admitted that such a law might be difficult to draw up, but as he said, "With a Tammany Constitu-

---

[15]Paul T. David and Ralph Eisenberg, *Devaluation of the Urban and Suburban Vote* (Univ. of Virginia, Bureau of Public Administration, 1961), p. 10.

[16]*Ibid.* See also Manning J. Dauer and Robert G. Kelsay, "Unrepresentative States," *National Municipal Review* (December 1955), pp. 571–575.

[17]Harold Gosnell, quoted in Thomas Page, *Legislative Apportionment in Kansas* (Univ. of Kansas, Governmental Research Series No. 8, 1952), p. 139.

[18]W. L. Riordon, *Plunkitt of Tammany Hall* (McClure, Phillips, 1905), pp. 38–39.

tion, Governor, Legislature, and Mayor, there would be no trouble in settlin' a little matter of that sort."[19]

It was not only the Plunkitts who protested against what they considered to be an injustice; at crowded meetings of the United States Conference of Mayors, the cry "Taxation without representation is tyranny!" was frequently heard. The mayors summarized their views by declaring, "Equal representation is not a mere theory or doctrine. It is a fundamental feature of democracy; and the failure of any legislative body to enforce the principle should be met with instant and vigorous protests on the part of the people affected."[20]

COUNTRY HICKS V. SUBURBANITES V. CITY SLICKERS

The battle over reapportionment was more complex than just a rural-versus-city struggle. Despite a tremendous proportional increase in the size of our population living in urban areas, large cities have not shown much gain in population. In some central cities there has even been a percentage decline. "The net result was that it was no longer cities which were the chief victims of underrepresentation but suburbia."[21] A few central cities were *over*represented: for example, Boston and Baltimore.

Many who live and do business within the central city or in the suburbs, moreover, view their political interests more like those of the farmers and small-town citizens than of their city brethren. It was not unusual to find some city dwellers seeking to maintain rural supremacy in the state legislatures. For example, many business interests were fearful that more representation in the state legislature for the city and suburban voter would result in more regulation of business. In California, "Privately owned utilities, banks, insurance companies and others . . . discovered some 'cow country' legislators more responsive to their demands and less committed to contrary points of view on key social and economic questions than were urban representatives. The urban legislator was more likely to be influenced by organized labor and by the many popular movements that ebb and flow through California politics."[22]

How did this rural domination of our state legislatures come about? It was due in part to constitutional provisions. Some state constitutions fix electoral districts with no provision for reapportionment. Some state constitutions call for equal representation in one chamber for counties or towns regardless of their population. As a result of these and other constitutional provisions, people moving from farms and small cities to the suburbs and large cities left behind depopulated "rotten boroughs" where a few people had excessive voting power.

Even where the state constitution created no inequity, and even where it was mandated that the state legislature reapportion representatives or redistrict the states every ten years, as was the case in forty states, many legisla-

[19]*Ibid.*, pp. 125–126.
[20]The United States Conference of Mayors, *Government of the People, by the People, for the People*, 1948.
[21]Robert S. Friedman, "Reapportionment Myth," *National Civic Review* (April 1960), pp. 184–188.
[22]Dean E. McHenry, "Urban vs. Rural in California," *National Municipal Review* (July 1946), p. 350.

tures simply refused to do so. Legislators from smaller towns and farmlands naturally did not wish to reapportion themselves out of a job, and their constituencies did not wish to lose their additional influence over the legislature. "Any man in this legislature who doesn't fight for his own district is a particular . . . fool," candidly observed one Illinois representative during a sharp struggle over reapportionment in that state's legislature.[23] "In perhaps no other aspect of American political life," it was said, "are constitutional . . . mandates so systematically honored in their breach . . . as they are in the matter of reapportionment."[24]

In some states where constitutional amendments may be proposed by the initiative procedure, reapportionment was forced on the legislature. Where the legislature itself must initiate constitutional amendments or summon constitutional conventions into session, reapportionment by constitutional amendment was less successful. Delegates to constitutional conventions were themselves chosen on the same basis as the legislators; hence, these delegates were no more likely to propose drastic changes in legislative representation than were the legislators.

To get around legislative opposition, some states by constitutional provision instruct the state courts to intervene if the legislature fails to do so. In other states reapportionment is assigned to some other authority—the governor or board or commission—as in Alaska, where the governor has the duty to reapportion the lower chamber and may modify senate districts after each decennial census.

How did the legislators and those who opposed reapportionment defend their failure to act? They contended that representation on the basis of population has never been consistently followed in the United States, that representation has been based on geographical areas as well as on population. The United States Senate is organized to represent states, not population clusters. If representation were based exclusively on population, they argued, city and suburban legislators would take over; that would be worse than country rule, for cities dominated by political organizations could maintain rigid control of their legislators. The "rural bias" that has existed in the United States at least since the days of Jefferson provided ideological backing for those who opposed equal voice in the state legislatures for city people. Although a majority of people in the country now live in urban areas, the belief in the superior virtues of country life and country people is still strongly held. Even among city dwellers themselves, the city is sometimes thought of as a den of iniquity and a center of un-American and radical thought.

FEDERAL COURTS TO THE RESCUE

No matter how much they protested, those underrepresented in the legislature could find no place to apply their pressures: they had no access, no leverage; the state legislatures refused to act; the judges refused to act. Even though failure of state legislatures to reapportion violated both their state constitutions and the federal Constitution, state and federal judges took

---

[23]Quoted by Gilbert Y. Steiner and Samuel K. Gove, *The Legislature Redistricts Illinois* (Univ. of Illinois Institute of Government and Public Affairs, 1956), p. 7.
[24]Page, *op. cit.*, p. 1.

the position that questions having to do with legislative districting were "political" and outside the scope of judicial authority.

In a free society formal constitutional arrangements cannot indefinitely remain far out of line with the realities of the political system. Urban Americans would not forever allow themselves to be governed by legislators from rural areas. The 1960 census showed that state legislatures were becoming more and more unrepresentative of the people. Within some of the states pressures were so strong that legislatures made slight adjustments to give somewhat greater voice to urban and suburban districts, but without making the legislatures really representative.

In 1960 the Supreme Court ruled that the Alabama Legislature had violated the Fifteenth Amendment when it redrew the boundaries of a city in order to deprive Negroes of the right to vote in city elections.[25] This ruling was not precisely pertinent to the question of legislative apportionment, but it did indicate that not all questions having to do with the drawing of election district lines were outside the scope of judicial concern. Those agitating for a more equitable representation took heart at the High Court's decision.

In Tennessee the situation was especially discouraging for city voters. The Legislature had refused to reapportion since 1901 despite population shifts; residents of some rural counties had a vote worth more than twenty-two times as much as voters in Shelby County (Memphis). Nor could the city voters secure constitutional amendments, for their state constitution could not be amended except with the consent of the rural-controlled Legislature. The state courts offered no hope, since the judges had ruled that legislative reapportionment was solely up to the state Legislature.

Having no other place to go, some urban voters challenged the constitutionality of the Tennessee apportionment practices in the federal courts. The district judges hinted that the Tennessee Legislature might be depriving urban voters of their constitutional rights, but following precedent the judges ruled that federal courts had no authority to provide relief.

When the city voters appealed to the Supreme Court, the United States Department of Justice supported their petition. In 1962, in the now famous case of *Baker* v. *Carr*, the Supreme Court held that urban voters *do* have standing to challenge legislative apportionment and that such questions may be considered by the federal courts. The Supreme Court did not itself decide that the Tennessee Legislature in fact had violated the Constitution (that had to be considered first

From *Government of the People, by the People, for the People,* published by The United States Conference of Mayors, Washington, D.C.

[25]*Gomillion* v. *Lightfoot* (1960).

by the district court) and it did not hold that legislative districts must be based on equal population. But it did say that "arbitrary and capricious" districts violate the Constitution and that federal judges may take jurisdiction over such cases.

Baker v. *Carr* started a small tidal wave. Some legislatures adopted reapportionment plans in hopes of forestalling more drastic judicial action. In almost every state in the Union underrepresented voters initiated lawsuits. The Supreme Court, however, established no standards by which a system of representation could be evaluated; it merely said in the *Baker* case that federal courts would hear cases challenging representation in state legislatures as being in violation of the equal protection of the law. Finally, in 1964, the Court enunciated the standard to be applied in a case dealing with congressional representation: ". . . *as nearly as practicable one man's vote in a congressional election is to be worth as much as another's.*"[26] Would this principle be extended to *state* representation?

The answer was yes. On the final day of the same term, in the leading case of *Reynolds* v. *Sims,* the Court held that it was ". . . clearly established that the fundamental principle of representative government in this country is one of equal representation for equal numbers of people, without regard to race, sex, economic status, or place of residence within a state." This principle was not only applicable to the lower house of the state legislature, which was usually based upon the population, but also to the *upper* house, where representation was often based upon areal factors such as counties or some other governmental unit. Defenders of this pattern had strenuously argued that so long as the lower house represented population, the upper house could represent geographical units. Look at the federal system embodied in the United States Constitution, they said. Was not representation in the United States Senate based upon area? Although many thought this to be a compelling argument, a majority of the Court did not. Chief Justice Warren explained:

Legislators represent people, not trees or acres. Legislators are elected by voters, not farms or cities or economic interests . . . the right to elect legislators in a free and unimpaired fashion is a bedrock of our political system.

The federal analogy, in short, did not hold. Political subdivisions are not and never have been sovereign entities.

ONE MAN – ONE VOTE

The constitutional requirement was simply one man – one vote. It did not even make any difference that a majority of the voters in the state had specifically approved a constitutional amendment providing for the apportionment of state senators by county while specifically rejecting one that would have established both houses on the basis of population: ". . . an individual's constitutionally protected right to cast an equally weighted vote cannot be denied even by a vote of a majority of a State's electorate, if the apportionment scheme adopted by the voters fails to measure up to the re-

[26]*Wesberry* v. *Sanders* (1964); italics added.

quirements of the Equal Protection Clause."[27] And four years later in *Avery* v. *Midland County* (1968) the Supreme Court held that the same principle must be applied to local units of government, such as county commissioners, if such units exercise legislative functions.

Critics of *Baker* v. *Carr* and *Reynolds* v. *Sims* did not accept their defeats before the Supreme Court as final. Fox Hodgon, town representative of Grany (which has a population of fifty-six and replaced its oil lamps with electricity in 1963) in the Vermont Legislature, eloquently stated the position of the rural forces: "This reapportionment will have it so we'll all be governed by these city people without the counterbalance from the country to stop runaway legislation. It will be quite a mess. . . . We'll fight and never give up."[28]

The Fox Hodgons and other opponents of the one-man–one-vote principle were almost successful. In 1964 the House of Representatives proposed to withdraw jurisdiction over legislative reapportionment from federal courts, and the Senate adopted a "sense of Congress" resolution urging judges to defer action on reapportionment in order to give the nation time to consider a constitutional amendment. In 1965 and 1966 Senator Dirksen secured a majority (but not the required two-thirds) vote in the Senate in favor of his proposed amendment that would have allowed a state to apportion one of its legislative chambers on some basis other than population. And by 1967 petitions had cumulated from almost two-thirds of the state legislatures requesting Congress to call into session a Constitutional Convention for the purpose of considering amendments allowing states greater discretion in determining how to apportion legislative seats. But 1967 was the high point of the antireapportionment campaign. By that time most of the states had completed the process of reapportioning their legislatures to conform to the dictates of the Supreme Court's decisions, and with the legislatures now in control of men elected under the new schemes, the reapportionment revolution appears to be irreversible.

UNANSWERED QUESTIONS

Even though the one-man–one-vote principle is firmly established, many other issues affecting the nature of legislative representation remain open. For example, in northern metropolitan areas the most general pattern is for the core city to be Democratic with the surrounding suburbs Republican. If the legislative district lines were drawn like spokes from the central city to the suburbs, there would be fewer Republicans elected than if the district lines were drawn in concentric circles. It is possible to have multi-member districts that are based on equal populations, but, depending on how they are drawn, they may over- or underrepresent minority groups or minor parties.[29]

Judges have insisted upon equal populations in the legislative districts, but they have not been willing to interfere beyond that unless there is demonstrable proof that race or religion has been the basis for districting. Legislatures or reapportioning commissions are still free to use single, multiple,

[27]*Lucas* v. *Forty-fourth General Assembly of Colorado* (1964).
[28]Joe Heaney, "A Vermonter Bows to Reapportionment," *Boston Globe* (June 27, 1965).
[29]Examples taken from Crane and Watts, *op. cit.*, pp. 28–31.

670 or other types of districting schemes. Thus the constitutional requirement of one man – one vote has altered but not abolished the "politics of reapportionment."

CONSEQUENCES OF REAPPORTIONMENT

In the more populous states of the North such as New Jersey, Michigan, Illinois, and New York the suburban communities have gained legislative representation as a result of the court-enforced reapportionment at the greatest cost to rural districts, but at some cost to the big cities. The traditional alliance between suburbs and rural districts against the big city appears to have been unchanged by reapportionment.

In the South, in such states as Georgia, Florida, and Tennessee (where Atlanta, Miami, and Memphis were so grossly underrepresented), reapportionment has had a more dramatic impact. In Georgia it has increased the voice of Atlanta's citizens in the state Legislature and provided opportunities for the election to that body of Negroes. In Alabama, Birmingham and Mobile have new political influence, and an alliance between these two cities could have long-range impact on the politics of that state. In Florida for the first time urban centers have the dominant voice in the Legislature.

In the West, reapportionment seems to have had little impact, although it may be a factor in creating a more competitive two-party system in the more populous states such as California.

Reapportionment has tended to benefit suburban Republicans and city Democrats at the expense of rural Republicans in the North and rural Democrats in the South, with the effect of moving toward more competitive party systems in state legislatures.

What of the policy consequences of reapportionment? Many proponents of reapportionment were especially hopeful that it would lead to legislatures more sympathetic toward big-city people, more generous in support of the welfare, transportation, educational, and financial problems of the, cities. It was also hoped that with reapportionment, state aid and shared-tax formulas would be revised toward a more favorable distribution of state funds to the cities. Opponents of reapportionment were fearful that it would lead to a decline in the quality of legislators, an increase in taxation and spending, and a reduction of state support to rural areas.

So far neither the hopes of the proponents of reapportionment nor the fears of its opponents have been realized. Specific studies of policy adopted by the several state legislatures, and the nature of their representative character in the early 1960s, failed to discover any correlation between legislative apportionment and welfare policies, distribution of state aid for public works, or support for education.[30] Metropolitan and nonmetropolitan legislators seldom oppose each other in unified voting blocs. Still, it is clear that

---

[30]Dye, in Jacob and Vines (eds.), *op. cit.*, pp. 163 – 164; Herbert Jacob, "The Consequences of Malapportionment: A Note of Caution," *Social Forces* (December 1964), pp. 256 – 261; David R. Derge, "Metropolitan and Outstate Alignments in Illinois and Missouri Legislative Delegations," *The American Political Science Review* (December 1958), pp. 1051 – 1065. See also Richard T. Frost, "On Derge's Metropolitan and Outstate Legislative Delegations," *The American Political Science Review* (September 1959), pp. 792 – 795; and Robert S. Friedman, "The Urban-Rural Conflict Revisited," *Western Political Quarterly* (June 1961), pp. 481 – 495.

the conditions of the early 1960s have been changed, and while it may be impossible precisely to correlate resulting policies with different patterns of representation, nevertheless to change the constituencies to which legislators are accountable is to make a major change in the political system. The consequences of this change are yet to be seen as we move into the 1970s.

Direct Democracy

Some of our states have given the people themselves the power to make their own laws. Around the turn of the century, one of the reformers' battle cries was to "return the government to the people" through the initiative, referendum, and recall. Give the voters the power to make or veto laws and to recall officials, they asserted, and the political machines will be destroyed and the special interests routed. Opponents vehemently replied that such measures as these would destroy representative government and open the way for crackpot and radical legislation.

During the first two decades of this century about twenty states, mostly in the West, adopted the initiative and referendum, and so did hundreds of cities, especially those with commission and city manager forms of government (see Chapter 31). A smaller number of states and cities also adopted the recall.

The details of these procedures differ, but their purpose is everywhere the same. The *initiative* allows voters to enact legislation or constitutional amendments when the legislature fails to act; the *referendum* permits a majority of the voters to veto legislation or reject constitutional amendments; the *recall* allows the electorate to eject an elected public official from his job before the end of his term.

The referendum is simply a way of letting the people vote on proposed measures; it is required in every state except Delaware for the ratification of constitutional amendments. As applied to legislation, there are two general types of referenda, *mandatory* and *optional*. The mandatory referendum calls for a waiting period, usually sixty to ninety days, before legislation goes into effect. If during this period a prescribed number of voters sign a referendum petition requesting that the act be referred to the voters, the law does not go into effect unless a majority of the voters give their approval at the next election. (The legislature may sidestep this by declaring the law to be emergency legislation to go into immediate effect.) The optional legislative referendum permits the legislature, at its discretion, to provide that a measure shall not become law until it has been approved by the voters at an election.

The *direct initiative* applies in some states to constitutional amendments and to legislation; in other states it can be used for only one or the other. In a state that permits the use of the initiative, an individual or group of voters may, on their own initiative, draft a proposed law. After the supporters have secured a certain number of signatures (often 5 to 10 percent of the total electorate), the measure is placed before the voters at the next election.

In some states, the *indirect initiative* is used, which gives the legislature an opportunity to act on the measure before it is referred to the voters. If the legislature does not approve, the proposed legislation is then placed on the ballot, although in some states additional signatures are required.

Only twelve states provide for *recall* of state officers, but many others permit the recall of local officials. Recall also requires a petition, but more signatures are usually needed than in the case of the initiative and referendum. There are various kinds of recall election. In some, the official must stand on his record; in others, candidates are permitted to file and run against him.

Governors and Judges

30 Like the national government, each state government is organized into three branches: legislative, executive, and judicial. Hence, every state is a test tube for the American experiment in government, the experiment of mingling powers among the several branches of government and of making different leaders accountable to different electorates. Each state, to a greater or less degree, makes it difficult for a simple majority of the voters to win power; each requires, to some extent, rule by concurrent majorities.

But the governmental and political systems of the states are not all alike. Formal constitutional structures may be roughly the same, but other vital aspects of government and politics—local idea-systems, interest groups, voting, parties, public attitudes, administrative arrangements—may differ widely. Indeed, the state governments dramatize the fact that constitutional *form* is only one element of government. Almost as many differences can be found between one state with a fully developed two-party system, a strong chief executive, and centralized administration, and another state with a diffused one-party system, weak governor, and decentralized administration, as can be found between our national government and that of Great Britain or France. State executives and judiciaries are a case in point.

His Excellency—the Governor

The story of the office of American governor is a progression "from detested minion of Royal power, to stepson of legislative domination, to popular figure-head, to effective executive."[1] "A strong executive is an engine of tyranny"—that was the spirit in which the office was born. Then during the period of Jacksonian Democracy, the idea spread that the people should directly elect all top officials of government, and the governor became only one of many elected officials. Nevertheless, beginning slowly and picking up speed during the last fifty years, the office of governor has grown in importance and power.

In over three-fourths of the states, the governor is elected to a four-year term; in the others, for two years. The trend is toward the longer term. In about one-fourth of the states where he has a four-year term (mostly Southern and border states) the governor is ineligible for a second consecutive term. His salary ranges from a high of $50,000 in New York to a low of $10,000 in Arkansas, with the average being about $21,000. In addition, most governors receive an expense allowance.

Because of the average governor's relatively low salary, short tenure, and limited powers, we might think that it would be difficult to get able men to run for the office. But this is not so. The governor enjoys great prestige in his state. Governors of the larger states are national figures; they often control powerful political machines. The office may be an important step toward national office—the Senate or even the Presidency.[2]

THE GOVERNOR AS CHIEF EXECUTIVE

"The executive power," says the federal Constitution, "shall be vested in the President of the United-States." Compare this flat statement with its counterpart in a typical state constitution: "The executive department shall consist of a Governor, Lieutenant Governor, Secretary of State, Auditor, Treasurer, Superintendent of Public Instruction, Attorney General," and perhaps other officials. In other words, the state governor shares the executive power with numerous other *elected* officers. Most state constitutions, nevertheless, go on to say that "the Supreme executive power shall be vested in the Governor, who shall take care that the laws be faithfully executed." And it is the governor to whom the public looks for law enforcement and the supervision of administrative agencies.

Governor Samuel W. Pennypacker, Pennsylvania's chief executive in 1903–1907, once told how he had come to office eager to ensure that the laws of the state were faithfully executed. Looking around to see what instruments he had to carry out this responsibility, he discovered that the only persons to whom he could look for help were his secretary, the janitor, and his chauffeur. The prosecutors and police, locally elected and locally controlled, were subject to little or no gubernatorial supervision. The attorney general was elected by the voters and not responsible to the governor. Of course, the governor could call out the National Guard, but that is a clumsy way to enforce the law. "So," said Governor Pennypacker, "I created the state police." Today all states have a police organization. In some states the

---

[1]William H. Young, "The Development of the Governorship," *State Government* (Summer 1958), p. 183.

[2]Duane Lockard, *The Politics of State and Local Government* (Macmillan, 1963), pp. 395–398.

governor has been given authority to supervise the activities of local prosecutors. Even so, most governors lack the means of seeing that "the laws be faithfully executed."

State governments, like their national counterpart, consist of a vast web of administrative agencies ranging from departments of finance to bureaus of rodent control. How does a governor supervise this administrative structure? During the nineteenth century, as the states took on more and more new functions, new agencies were added more or less haphazardly. Boards and commissions were established, power was parceled out among numerous officials, the long ballot (see page 299) was created with its many elective offices, and lines of authority and responsibility became hopelessly tangled. The ship of state tacked first one way, then another, and the governor had little power to control the administration.

Such was the general state of affairs until the second decade of the present century. Then in 1917 the administrative reorganization movement was born in Illinois. Following its example, state after state made some effort to unravel the tangled web that had come to characterize its administrative structure. The "executive" reorganizers hammered away at one basic formula: Reduce the number of elected officials, integrate the executive structure under the governor's direction, give the governor the executive authority he needs, and let the people hold him accountable for the effective administration of the laws. Better to make the governor the manager of the administration, they argued, than to leave the job to behind-the-scenes bosses.

The most important weapon in the governor's arsenal is his control over the *budget*. In those states in which he prepares and presents the budget to the legislature and in which he has the item veto, he can to a considerable extent control the flow of funds to the executive departments and thus shape their activities—always assuming, of course, that he has sufficient political power to sustain his budget and his veto. Purchase, fiscal, and personnel matters, moreover, are frequently centralized under the governor. When assisted by a strong staff, and backed by a strong political base in the electorate, the governor has significant control over the administration.

The trend toward integrated administration is still strong. In the urban states with a competitive party system such as New York, Illinois, New Jersey, Pennsylvania, Washington, and California, governors have considerable formal constitutional authority. But integrated administration is by no means an accomplished fact.[3] The governor is still one executive among many, with only limited authority over his subordinates. He has almost no authority over the elected officials; he neither appoints them nor can he dismiss them; if they are his political enemies, they will not accept his leadership. The governor has greater but still limited power over appointed executive officials. In most states he shares the appointive power with the senate and may remove subordinates only when they have violated the law or failed in their legal duties. There are some signs that the growing professionalism of some state administrators whose programs are supported in large measure by

[3]Joseph A. Schlesinger, "The Politics of the Executive," in H. Jacob and K. N. Vines (eds.), *Politics in the American States: A Comparative Analysis* (Little, Brown, 1965), pp. 231–232. For a general discussion of the power resources of the governor, see Lockard, *op. cit.*, pp. 367–395.

federal funds is giving them a measure of independence from the governor and greater loyalty toward, and interaction with, their functional counterparts at the national level than with other state officials. Yet with all the qualifications, the role of the governor both as political leader and as chief administrator has become more significant in the decades of this century.[4]

Governors' helpers — or enemies? In many states the other executive officials elected by the people include the lieutenant governor, secretary of state, attorney general, treasurer, and auditor. What do they do?

The *lieutenant governor* does very little. He presides over the senate and, in case of the death, disability, or absence of the governor from the state, he becomes governor or acting governor. The twelve states lacking a lieutenant governor do not seem to miss him. Since the lieutenant governor is often leader of a party faction different from that of the governor, and is sometimes even a member of the opposition party, he may become a thorn in the side of the chief executive; to try to avoid this, nine states now provide for the election of the governor and lieutenant governor as a unit. There is a tendency, though not a marked one, to enlarge the duties of the lieutenant governor.

The *secretary of state* is custodian of the state records and keeper of the state seal. He publishes the laws, supervises elections, and issues certificates of incorporation. In some states he issues automobile licenses and registers corporate securities. His office is often the dumping ground for jobs that do not seem to belong to any other office and are not important enough to justify setting up a new agency.

The *attorney general* is the state's lawyer. His office gives advice to state officials, represents the state before the courts, and supervises local prosecutors. Some attorneys general have real authority over local prosecutors and may prosecute cases on their own initiative. The attorney generalship is often a steppingstone to the governorship, and occasionally attorneys general have made political capital out of their investigations of the state administration.

The *treasurer* is custodian of state funds. Although in some states he has tax-collection duties, in most states his job is largely ministerial.

The *auditor* has two major jobs: to authorize disbursements from the treasury, and to make periodic audits of officials who handle state money. Before money can be spent, the auditor must sign a warrant indicating that he is convinced that the appropriation is authorized by law and that money is available in the treasury. This is the *pre-audit*, which many students believe should be given to a comptroller appointed by and responsible to the governor. The auditing *after* the money has been spent, however, is a job that most students believe should be vested in an officer responsible to the legislature. The auditor is the one official who, even in the opinion of some of the most extreme advocates of centralized administration, should not be responsible to the governor.

As part of the trend toward integrated administration, the duties of elected state officials have generally been limited to the functions specified in the constitution, with the more critical functions given to officials appointed by the governor. The budget directors and agency chiefs under the governor in

[4]Deil S. Wright, "Executive Leadership in State Administration," *Midwest Journal of Political Science* (February 1967), pp. 24–25.

many states have more important roles than the state treasurer or the secretary of state. Yet these elected officers with their limited but constitutionally protected duties often control patronage, attract a following, and thus develop a political base from which they can attack the governor's program and administration.

The reorganization movement and its critics.　　The wave of state reorganizations that followed World War I was repeated after World War II under the stimulus of the national Hoover Commission. Most of the states appointed their own "Little Hoover Commissions" to recommend improvements in the state governmental structure.

Attempts to reorganize state governments have not received universal praise. In many states, the commissions get together, make studies, and submit reports—which are soon filed away and forgotten.[5] Groups that profit from the existing structure—for example, those that have a pet bureau under their influence—can be counted upon to resist changes; and so can public officials who fear loss of job or prestige. Legislators who suspect that recommendations will make the governor too powerful are often reluctant to approve them. And politicians who have lived within the existing structure and know their way around in it are naturally reluctant to give up a good thing.

Another group of critics opposes not so much the idea of reorganization but the basic principle that has dominated the movement. This is the principle of *executive power* and *responsibility*. During the last several decades reorganizers have plumped for the proposition that the governor should be made the manager of the executive branch. They have developed the following canons of reorganization:

1　All agencies should be consolidated and integrated into as few departments as possible, so that similar functions will be grouped together and the governor's span of control will be manageable.

2　Lines of responsibility should be fixed and definite.

3　Single-head executives are to be preferred to boards and commissions.

4　The governor should have power to appoint and remove subordinates, including officers who are now elected, with the possible exception of the auditor.

5　The governor should have control over budgeting, accounting, reporting, purchasing, personnel, and planning, and should have the staff he needs to do these jobs.

But some critics, though they agree that centralized budgeting, purchasing, and the like, are all very well, argue that conditions differ in each state and that no "cookie cutter" pattern of administration will fit all conditions. There is little evidence, they argue, to support the proposed reforms other than the assurance of the reorganizers themselves and their citing of each other as authorities. What evidence do we have, they ask, that the people will hold the governor accountable and that the governor will devote his time and energy to administrative matters? Most governors are chiefly inter-

[5]Karl A. Bosworth, "The Politics of Management Improvement in the States," *The American Political Science Review* (March 1953), pp. 84–99.

ested in legislative problems,. not in administrative details, and are seldom judged on their executive talent. Furthermore, the critics decry the emphasis on efficiency and economy. There is a real danger, they argue, that the reorganizers are overlooking basic values in their concern with saving money. The threat of executive tyranny, they fear, is dismissed too cavalierly. As one critic put it, "Men invited to recommend a program which promises efficiency and economy for a state . . . have failed to warn their clients . . . of the enormous risk involved in creating a powerful chief executive in a state which has no responsible legislature and in many instances no effective opposition party."[6]

The reorganizers are quick to answer their critics. Of course it is ridiculous to make changes, they grant, without regard to local conditions and problems. But the basic idea—integrated authority, centralized direction, simplified structure—is sound. There would be little danger of dictatorship. In fact, it is more likely that men not responsible to the electorate will take over government when the administrative structure is cumbersome, confusing, and diffused. The legislature can more effectively supervise an administration integrated under the governor's control than one in which responsibility is diffused.[7] In states where the governor's formal authority is slight, special interests have found it easier to dominate administrative programs than in states where gubernatorial authority is strong.

Effects of reorganization.   What have been the results of a half century of reorganization? Some observers say that reorganization has not given us more efficient or democratic government. Others say it has. Still others say there is little evidence one way or another. Often the reorganizations result only in changes in organization charts but have no significant impact on actual operations. Large savings have been realized through centralized purchasing and the adoption of modern fiscal practices, but it is difficult to measure the results of the consolidation of departments and the strengthening of the governor's control over the executive branch.[8]

At the same time, the best-governed states do seem to be those in which the administrative structure has been closely integrated under the governor. Whether this integration has *caused* good government in those states is another, though closely related, question.

The basic idea of reorganization is to apply what we know to improve what we have. But to make reorganization pay the biggest dividends, it must be a continuous process of adjustment. Recently some states, notably Michigan and Alaska, have recognized this truth and adopted reorganization procedures similar to those on the national level. The governor is granted authority to submit to the state legislature reorganization proposals that if not disapproved within a certain period are automatically put into effect.

[6]C. S. Hyneman, "Administrative Reorganization: An Adventure into Science and Theology," *The Journal of Politics* (February 1939), pp. 74–75. For another presentation of this view, see Robert B. Highsaw, "The Southern Governor—Challenge to the Strong Executive Theme," *Public Administration Review* (Winter 1959), pp. 7–11.

[7]Coleman B. Ransome, Jr., *The Office of Governor in the United States* (Univ. of Alabama Press, 1956), pp. 378–386.

[8]W. H. Edwards, "Has State Reorganization Succeeded?" *State Government* (October 1938), pp. 184–185.

The reorganization of state administrative procedure is almost always justified in terms of efficiency and economy. Few would deny the importance of saving money, but it is doubtful if the costs of operating our state governments can be substantially reduced except by reducing their functions. To save money and to increase efficiency are important, but these are not the only objectives of government or the only criteria for judging its operations. The question must always be: reorganization for what? Not merely to save money but to strengthen democratic government.

THE GOVERNOR AS CHIEF LEGISLATOR

Just as the role of the President in actively determining national policy has grown over the last several decades, so has the governor become a more active participant in the making of state policy. In fact, some governors have far more influence over their legislatures than even the strongest of our presidents have had over theirs. The governor has the constitutional power to call the legislature into special session and, in some states, to specify what the legislators can discuss in such session. He is authorized to address the legislature and send messages to it. He has the responsibility in forty-three of the states to submit the budget to the legislature. Moreover, in all states except North Carolina, he has strong veto powers, usually much stronger than those of the President.

In all but nine states, the governor has, in addition to the regular qualified veto, the power to strike out—that is, veto—individual items in appropriations measures while approving the rest. In a few states, the governor can even reduce a particular appropriation. The *item veto*, like all vetoes, can be overridden by the legislature (normally a two-thirds vote in both chambers is required), but in many states most new laws are sent to the governor after the legislature has adjourned. Thus when he vetoes bills or items of appropriations, there is no chance for the legislature to override the veto. Another interesting variation is the "amendatory" or "conditional" veto of Alabama, Virginia, Massachusetts, and New Jersey that allows the governor to return a bill to the legislature with suggested changes or amendments that he wants incorporated in it. The legislature must consider the governor's recommendations before attempting to pass the bill over his veto or return it to him for reconsideration.[9]

How much legislative influence do governors have? Although their constitutional authority varies a good deal, their actual ability to influence legislative policy varies even more widely from state to state and from time to time than a reading of the constitutions might suggest. Much depends on the governor's ability, his political base, his personal popularity, and the political situation in which he operates. Some states have a long tradition of executive leadership; when the governor has the support of powerful political organizations, he can guide policy. The Governors of New York and Illinois, for example, have strong constitutional positions, and they are also likely to have strong party organizations behind them and close ties with their party

[9]Joseph E. Kallenbach, *The American Chief Executive: The Presidency and the Governorship* (Harper & Row, 1966), p. 365.

followers in the legislatures. Furthermore, Governors of these large states and others, like Ohio, Pennsylvania, and California, with active two-party systems, are potential presidential candidates. These Governors—men like Nelson Rockefeller of New York and Ronald Reagan of California—attract the national spotlight. Many of them look forward to national political careers, and each speaks with the authority of a man who might some day be President of the United States. In these states the governorship attracts able men and gives them great prestige and power. But even in states where the governor is less likely to be a national figure, he can derive power from a large popular following or a strong party organization. Also, we must be cautious in making comparative statements. The Governor of rural Mississippi has much less formal power than the Governor of New York, and on the national political scene he carries little weight. Yet within his own state his control over minor jobs, contracts, and patronage may make him a pivotal figure. The Governor of New York must operate through more formal machinery in a highly complex state containing many power sources able to compete with the Governor on his own terms.[10] Few Governors of New York have ever been able to dominate their state legislature to the same extent as some of the formally weak but politically powerful Southern governors.

Emergency powers. Emergencies enhance the authority of the executive, for they call for decisive measures. The governor is commander in chief of the state's National Guard when it is not in federal service. He is responsible for using this force when the civil authorities are inadequate—in case of riots, floods, and other catastrophes. During the riots of the 1960s many governors called up the Guard; hardly a year goes by in which the Guard of some state does not see emergency duty. In about three-fourths of the states the governor also has a state police force at his command.

The national government has the major responsibility of providing for the national defense, but the states also have vital jobs. The governor is authorized to ensure public safety in times of emergency—for example, to regulate supplies of fuel and electric power and to issue orders for air raid protection. The civil defense program places the major responsibility on the states, and in almost all cases the states have turned the job over to the governor. He is normally advised by a civil defense council which helps him supervise and coordinate the civil defense activities of local government.

A judicial function. In half the states the governor has the *pardoning power*, and in the others he shares this duty. Persons who have violated *state* law look to the governor "to temper justice with mercy." The governor may, except in cases of certain specified crimes or in cases of impeachment, pardon the offender, commute his sentence by reducing its severity, or grant a reprieve by delaying the punishment. The governor is normally assisted by pardon attorneys or pardon boards who hold hearings and sift the evidence to determine where there are extenuating circumstances. But it is the governor who is usually faced with responsibility for the decision. Many are the

[10]Schlesinger, *op. cit.*, p. 231.

stories of governors maintaining all-night vigils when men are condemned to death for their crimes. The governor as the last earthly judge has an unenviable task.

THE GOVERNOR AS PARTY CHIEF

Like the President, the governor is usually considered leader of his party in the state. But the governor faces more rivals for party leadership than the man in the White House. A United States senator may dominate the state party or a large section of it; county politics may be controlled by "courthouse rings" intent only on electing local candidates; but the most serious problems, from the governor's viewpoint, arise from the fact that the other separately elected state officials, such as the attorney general, often share power over the state party just as they share the executive power.

In theory, a state party system is supposed to help integrate all the executive officials into a functioning team. In reality, it often makes for divisions within the state administration. In one-party states, the same party wins control of all the executive officers in all or most of the elections. But it is precisely in these one-party states, where the dominant party faces the weakest opposition, that the parties have the "least capacity to tie together the work of the scattered agencies of government. . . . Whatever order and coherence develops within the administration in one-party situations must rest on some factor other than the tie of party. When one party holds both governorship and minor offices without effective challenge, the incentives for collaboration among fellow partisans are not apt to be strong."[11]

In states where parties are more evenly matched, a single party seldom carries the whole slate of executive officials. Where the Republican party tends to be stronger—as in most states outside the South and the border states—the Democrats encounter difficulty in getting a full slate elected. Although, as the lesser of the two parties, the Democrats may gather enough strength to elevate one of their men to the gubernatorial office, it takes an unusually sizable victory for them to gain control of the entire executive slate. The Republicans have the same difficulty in border and other states where the Democrats are normally the larger party.

When control of the executive departments is split between the two parties, neither party is likely to assume responsibility for overall administration. Moreover, when the governor has to work with officials from the opposite party, teamwork, difficult under the best of circumstances, is almost impossible to achieve. It is precisely in states where party competition is keenest and party control of executive offices is divided that we are most likely to find strongly disciplined parties. Thus, as Key observed, we are confronted with a dilemma: In states where a party has unchallenged control of all executive positions, the party organization is apt to be too weak to impose a unified program on the several officials. But where party bonds are tight enough to impose a cohesive program, the party is often unable to win all the executive positions.

[11]V. O. Key, Jr., *American State Politics* (Knopf, 1956), pp. 200–201.

Not too long ago governors had it fairly easy; it was considered the best platform from which to launch a presidential career. The governor made speeches in favor of civic virtue, balanced the state budget, organized campaigns against crime, took a few well-publicized trips abroad to emphasize his knowledge of foreign affairs, and watched his rivals in the Senate lose political support because their roles required them to take stands on controversial issues.

Today the life of a governor is more difficult. People want better schools, including higher education for all; uncluttered six-lane highways that do not require condemnation of any land; adequate welfare payments; aid to local school districts; civil rights; safe cities; clean air and streams; and they expect the governor to meet all these needs without proposing higher taxes. The governor has become the major political power in the state, but he has acquired the liabilities that accompany the assets. Senators, as well as governors, are now leading candidates for the presidency. Of course, the situation is not quite so simple, and sometimes men leave the Senate to run for governor because of the greater ease of "standing out from the crowd." There is only one governor of the state. But governors no longer preside; they govern.

The State Judiciary

The judges of our state courts do most of the judicial business in the United States (see Chapter 19). They preside over most of the criminal trials, settle most of the disputes between individuals, and administer most of the estates. They interpret their state constitutions and apply state laws. Of course, the federal Constitution requires of them that they follow it, and that they observe all federal laws and federal treaties, "any Thing in the Constitution or Laws of any State to the Contrary notwithstanding."

Except for the practicing members of the bar, many people know little about their judges, not even the name of the chief judge of their own supreme court. But these judges—perhaps even more than those of our federal courts—are important policy-makers. The legislature passes the law, but the judges interpret it. The state judges, in determining the reasonableness of legislative classifications, in deciding whether a state regulation of business is arbitrary, in forcing county officials to comply with the law, in ruling whether the city council has exeeded its authority, in deciding whether the governor has the power to remove a local district attorney, play as vital a role as the other branches of government in determining who gets what, and when, where, and how he gets it.

Our understanding of American government is incomplete unless we know how these judges operate, what their relation is to the legislature, the executive, and interest groups, what procedures they use, how they are chosen, and what groups have the greatest voice in selecting them. Our answers must be very tentative, however; only recently have the state courts come in for serious study.[12] In the past, they tended to be obscured by the federal court system or by the other branches of the state government. Moreover, each state has its own unique court system. There is such tremendous variety in their procedures and structural arrangements that it is difficult to generalize. But for convenience, we can classify state courts into three groups: minor courts of limited jurisdiction, general trial courts, and appellate courts.

MINOR AND TRIAL COURTS

W. D. Brogan, the celebrated English student of American politics, has written of one of his adventures in America:

I had often heard of the "Jeddart justice" doled out by rural magistrates to motorists, of the iniquities of paying magistrates on a commission basis, of the insult to the law and its majesty which these methods involved. My host, whose car was moving rapidly down the great highway to the warm sun and true spring of Central Illinois after the rain, fog, and cold of the shores of Lake Michigan, had written on the subject. He had been the pupil and the collaborator of one of the greatest of American constitutional lawyers. His opinion was worth having. A car was backed off the road and a policeman signalled us in. I innocently assumed that there had been an accident, that we were being asked to take someone to hospital. How wrong I was! We were pinched for speeding. The traffic cop's not very smart uniform bore the words "Special Police." He had cartridges on his belt; they were of different colours and may have been dummies, but he was in complete command of the situation. He demanded the license which was fortunately available. He gave instructions. "Turn round and stop at the grocery store." "Can I make a U-turn?" asked my host ironically. "Sure." We entered the grocery store, and there was American justice at the receipt of custom.

The magistrate was a bronzed jurist in a shabby shirt. He had one arm and no badge of office. This was not the Old Bailey. The representative of the "Senatus Populusque Illinoisensis" required no fasces, no mace to impress his customers. He duly pointed out that the accused could claim a jury trial, but that if he didn't, and pleaded guilty, the whole thing could be expedited.

The policeman's complaint-sheet was produced; a conviction for speeding was duly entered in it; a receipt (a flimsy piece of paper) was issued. Ten dollars fine, $4 costs (which we believed went to the jurist). In two minutes it was all over. After all, there were other customers. My friend had "a record"; for the first time in his life he had been in an American police court.

In a famous opinion Mr. Justice Frankfurter had laid it down that a court of the American system was not to be compared to the court of a Cadi sitting down under a tree. There was no tree, simply a third-rate village store. I recalled Mr. Frankfurter's dictum to my friend. He was not consoled. He thought of various points he might have made. The "esprit d'escalier" worked overtime. He recalled what he had written on this aspect of the American judicial system. I tried to console him by pointing out that he had got down from his ivory tower as the song suggested. He was not amused. He had got out of the ivory tower all right, but as another song puts it, "Baby, it's cold outside."[13]

[12] See Stuart S. Nagel, "Political Party Affiliation and Judges' Decisions," *The American Political Science Review* (December 1961), pp. 843–850; Kenneth N. Vines and Herbert Jacob (eds.), *Studies in Judicial Politics* (Tulane Studies in Political Science, 1963).

[13] W. D. Brogan, "Down from the Ivory Tower," *The Manchester Guardian Weekly* (May 31, 1956), p. 11. See also Isham G. Newton, "The Justice of the Peace—An American Judicial Dilemma," *Social Science* (April 1959).

Unfortunately, this story is too typical of the way justice is administered in our *minor courts*. These courts handle summary offenses or misdemeanors and civil suits involving relatively small amounts of money. They are minor only in the sense that they provide accessible forums for the settlement of small suits and for the trial of petty offenses. But it is in these courts that most disputes are settled. A $50 judgment is "small potatoes" as these things go; but to the parties involved, it is no small matter. Although decisions of these minor courts may be appealed and tried *de novo* — that is, tried all over again without reference to what happened in the minor court — few people bother.

Of course, there is another side to the story. The defendant in the above case was clearly guilty of speeding. A basic canon of justice — the separation of the prosecuting from the judicial functions — was observed. The fine was not out of proportion to the offense. Appeal to a jury was allowed if desired. To be sure, the whole proceeding was informal and undignified, but greater dignity and formality would have meant a more expensive court and probably higher costs for the defendant, who in this case doubtless preferred expediency to publicity.

The most common type of minor courts are justice of the peace courts. The justice of the peace, or J.P., as he is popularly known, is usually elected for a two- or four-year term by the people of each township, but his jurisdiction extends throughout the county. In addition to solemnizing marriages and notarizing papers, he is the man, especially in small towns and rural places, who fines traffic violators, decides who should go to the workhouse for thirty days, and settles disputes between neighbors about who hit whom first. He usually has power to determine who should be held over for possible indictment by the grand jury. He sets bail and handles the preliminaries in more serious criminal matters.

The J.P.s are not required to be trained in the law; few of them are. Their lack of legal training has aroused much criticism, but a more glaring weakness is that they are commonly paid out of the fees they collect. Plaintiffs have their choice of several justices of the peace, some of whom, in order to get as much business as possible, have been known to advertise quietly to plaintiffs that they should bring their cases to them to be assured that justice will be done. Several studies have concluded that J. P. in effect stands for "Judgment for the Plaintiff." Even worse, despite the fact that the Supreme Court has condemned the practice, some J.P.s get larger fees in criminal matters when the defendant is found guilty and costs are assessed against him. Even when it is not abused, the fee system leads to distrust and suspicion. The justice of the peace system is slowly losing ground; some states have replaced it with magistrates who are paid a standard salary and are required to have a knowledge of the law.

In cities, there are other minor courts, some of which have more jurisdiction than the justice of the peace and handle more serious matters. Municipal courts are frequently divided into traffic courts, police courts, and juvenile and domestic relations courts. A small-claims court with informal procedures is provided by some cities to handle cases for a small set fee.

Trial courts with complete original jurisdiction are variously called county courts, circuit courts, superior courts, district courts, and common pleas courts. They administer equity, criminal, common, and statutory law (see Chapter 19). Some states maintain separate courts, however, for criminal and civil matters. More commonly, there are special probate courts to administer estates and to handle related matters. Although decisions of the general trial courts may be reviewed by appellate courts, in practice the trial court has final say in almost all cases.

The following story as related by Harry W. Jones illustrates well the importance of trial courts in the administration of justice:

A certain Bishop of Paris, known throughout Europe for his great learning and humility, came to the conclusiong that he was unworthy of his high place in the Church and successfully petitioned the Pope for reassignment of service as a simple parish priest. . . . After less than a year of parish work, the former bishop was back in Rome with another petition, this one praying for his restoration to episcopal status, and for good and sufficient reason. "If I am unworthy to be Bishop of Paris," he said, "how much more unworthy am I to be priest of a parish. As bishop, I was remote from men and women of lowly station, my shortcomings and weaknesses concealed from them by distance and ecclesiastical dignity. But as parish priest, I move intimately each day among the members of my flock, endeavoring by comfort, counsel and admonition to make their hard lot on earth seem better than it is. I *am* the Church to them; when my faith flags or my wisdom fails or my patience wears thin, it is the Church that has failed them. *Demote* me, Your Holiness, and make me bishop again, for I have learned how much easier it is to be a saintly bishop than to be a godly priest."

The trial judge is the parish priest of our legal order. The impression that prevails in society concerning the justice or injustice of our legal institutions depends almost entirely on the propriety, efficiency, and humaneness of observed trial court functioning.[14]

APPELLATE COURTS

In most states, appeals from the trial courts are carried to the state supreme court, but fourteen states have set up intermediate appeals courts that fit into the court structure in much the same way that the United States courts of appeals fit into the federal structure.

The court of final resort is usually called the supreme court. (In New York, the Supreme Court is a trial court, and the court of last resort is called the Court of Appeals.) Unless a federal question is involved, the state supreme courts are the highest to which a case may be carried.

The appellate courts vary from three to nine in membership, with seven being the most common number. State judges have the power of judicial review and may refuse to enforce state laws on the grounds that they violate the state or national constitution. They may also declare federal laws unconstitutional, although of course such decisions are subject to review by the United States Supreme Court. All state judges take an oath to uphold the supremacy of the federal Constitution, laws, and treaties, despite anything in their own constitutions or laws.

Some states permit the supreme court to give *advisory opinions* to the legislature or the governor upon request. These advisory opinions are not

[14]Harry W. Jones (ed.), *The Courts, The Public, and the Law Explosion* (Prentice-Hall, 1965), p. 125.

binding except in Colorado; they are regarded as the opinions of the judges rather than as court decisions.

HOW ARE JUDGES CHOSEN?

Judges are chosen in several ways. Popular election is used in about three-fourths of the states. In the others—primarily Eastern states—the judges are either appointed by the governor (with the consent of the senate or executive council) or elected by the legislature. Recently, some members of the bar have grown dissatisfied with the method of choosing judges by popular election. They argue that the voters are not competent to assess legal erudition and judicial abilities. Popular election, they assert, puts a premium on personality and popularity, requires judges to enter the political arena, and discourages many able lawyers from running for the office. Furthermore, they insist, judges are often in effect appointed by party leaders despite the elective apparatus. Lower court judges may be active members of the local political organization and gain and retain their offices because of faithful party service. At the appellate level the governor often makes an interim appointment to fill vacancies created by resignation, retirement, or death of a sitting judge; and the interim appointee as the incumbent usually wins at

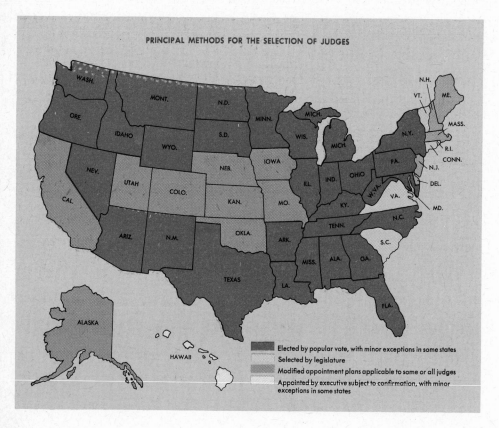

PRINCIPAL METHODS FOR THE SELECTION OF JUDGES

Elected by popular vote, with minor exceptions in some states
Selected by legislature
Modified appointment plans applicable to some or all judges
Appointed by executive subject to confirmation, with minor exceptions in some states

National Conference of Judicial Councils.

the next election. In fact, more than half of all judges sitting on elective courts of last resort first came to that court as appointees of the governor.[15]

Some states have turned to the nonpartisan primary for nominating judges or have held the election of judges on a separate day from the election of other officers, but these devices have not substantially altered the importance of party leaders. Also, those who oppose the elective system argue that the problem is not one of party but of politics. Should judges be accountable directly to the people? Should they not be indirectly responsible, so that they can better serve as a check on the popular majorities who act through the governor and the legislature? What, in short, is the role of judges in a democracy (see Chapter 19)? Those who favor the popular election of judges believe that to have them appointed by the governor would destroy popular control, divorce the judges from the electorate, give the governor too much power, and encourage judges to become the governor's pawn.

Is there any alternative method? California, Missouri, and several other states have developed ways of selecting judges that are designed to eliminate the defects of popular election but still retain popular control. In Missouri, whenever a vacancy occurs in a court to which the plan applies, a special nominating commission, composed of three lawyers elected by the bar, three laymen appointed by the governor, and the chief justice, nominates three candidates. The governor selects one who then serves as a judge for at least one year. The voters at the next general election are asked, "Shall Judge ―― be retained in office?" If a majority of the voters assent, the judge gets a full new term; if not, another person is selected by the same procedure. At the expiration of his term, the judge does not have to be renominated and reappointed; he merely certifies his wish to have his name placed on the ballot, and the voters are asked whether they want to retain him in office.[16]

The dispute over the relative merits of appointive and elective systems of judicial selection has been raging for more than 150 years. Courts in appointive states seem to have generally, but not always, a higher standing among members of the bar than those in elective states. Leaders of lawyers' groups tend to favor the appointive method. Yet there is little clear-cut evidence that the method of judicial selection makes any difference in the kinds of judicial decisions made.[17]

[15]James Herndon, "Appointment as a Means of Initial Accession to Elective Courts of Last Resort," *North Dakota Law Review* (1962), vol. 38, pp. 60–73; Emmett W. Bashful, *The Florida Supreme Court: A Study in Judicial Selection* (Florida Bureau of Governmental Research and Service, 1958); Kenneth N. Vines, "The Selection of Judges in Louisiana," in Vines and Jacob (eds.), *op. cit.*, pp. 99–119; and Bancroft Henderson and T. C. Sinclair, *The Selection of Judges in Texas, an Exploratory Study* (Univ. of Houston Public Affairs Research Center, 1965).

[16]Robert F. Karsch, *Essentials of Missouri Government*, 3d ed. (Lucas Bros., 1953), pp. 113–115. See also Harry Gershenson, "Experience in Missouri," *American Bar Association Journal* (March 1960), pp. 287ff; Richard A. Watson, Rondal G. Downing, and Frederick C. Spiegel, "Bar Politics, Judicial Selection, and the Representation of Social Interests," *American Political Science Review* (March 1967), p. 54.

[17]Herbert Jacob, *Justice in America* (Little, Brown, 1965), pp. 206–207.

Government
at the Grass Roots

31   There are over 81,000 units of local government in the United States (about 80,000 too many, some people feel). Illinois alone has over 6,400. Rhode Island, with fewer than any other state except Alaska and Hawaii, has 109. Cities, counties, school districts, townships, water control districts, park districts—all are crowded together and piled on top of one another. The average citizen lives under five or six layers of government. He pays taxes to all of them—federal, state, county, municipal, and others—and he is supposed to participate in the selection of the persons in charge of all these governments.

    Why do we have such a patchwork of governments? The basic pattern was imported from England, like so many of our governmental forms. As the years passed, new governments were created to take on new jobs when the existing units were too small or were not up to the task. Decades of compromise and struggle among conflicting groups have given us our present system. It creaks and groans. It costs a lot of money. It is not very efficient. But there it is.

    Local governments vary in structure, size, power, and relation to one another. But in a constitutional sense, they are all the same in that they all live on power "borrowed" from states. The states of our Union are basically *unitary* governments—that is, constitutionally all power is vested in the state government, with local units existing only as agents of the states and exercising power given to them by the state government.

NUMBER OF LOCAL GOVERNMENTS, BY STATES: 1967

Ill.
Pa.
Neb.
Minn.
Calif.
Kan.
S.D.
N.Y.
Texas
Ohio
Mo.
Mich.
N.D.
Ind.
Wis.
Iowa
Okla.
Wash.
Oreg.
N.J.
Ark.
Colo.
Ga.
Mont.
Ky.
Idaho
Fla.
Ala.
Tenn.
Miss.
N.C. *
La.
Maine
Vt.
Mass.
S.C.
N.H.
Wyo.
W.Va.
Utah
Conn.
Ariz.
Va. *
Md. *
N.M. *
Del.
Nev.
R.I.
Alaska
Hawaii

School districts

Governments other
than school districts

* Public school system not on school
district basis

0   2   4   6

(Number in Thousands)

U.S. Department of Commerce, Census of Governments.

"Little Federalism":
State-Local Relations

How does the *unitary* nature of state-local relations contrast with the *federal* nature of nation-state relations? The slicing up of governmental power among the various local units and the state government leads to many of the same problems that we have noted in the chapters on federalism. There is the same conflict between groups that want the state to do something and groups that fear an invasion of local rights. There is the same difficulty of constantly adjusting functions among the various units of government as economic and social conditions alter. And there are the same vexing disputes over whether a local majority or a statewide majority is to have its way.

Since local governments are created by the state legislatures and have no power in their own right, weaker pressures and fewer constitutional obstacles act against state interference in local matters than against national interference in state affairs. State officers participate in local government to a much greater extent than do federal officers in state politics. When doubt arises about the authority of local governments, the courts have generally decided against them.

But the difference between the unitary state-local and the federal nation-state relations can be exaggerated; as in so many matters of politics, the difference is one of degree rather than of kind. Moreover, during the last several decades "home rule" amendments have been added to some state constitutions. These amendments authorize certain local governments to run their own affairs and limit the power of state officials to interfere. Thus *constitutional home rule* introduces in a small way the federal principle into state constitutions.

In the beginning, the state legislatures were given almost unlimited constitutional authority over local governments and ran them pretty much as they wished. They granted, amended, and rescinded city charters, established counties, determined city and county structure, set their debt limits, and passed ordinances for them. But by the end of the nineteenth century, many state constitutions had been amended to forbid the legislature to pass laws dealing with particular local governments, and in the place of legislative enactments, constitutional provisions determined the structure—in some cases, even the process—of local governments.

The hedging in of the legislature's power did not, however, put an end to state domination of local government; while the legislature's authority was being curtailed, the power of state administrative officials was being expanded. Problems once thought to be local came to be viewed as statewide. Many local governments lacked the money to do essential jobs; they could not afford specialists, and their administrative standards were notoriously low. Moreover, the states were encouraged to enter new fields by a host of unfamiliar social and economic problems. Sometimes the states just took over a job previously handled by local people; sometimes the state offered local governments financial assistance, with certain strings attached. Gradually, state officials were given more and more authority to supervise local officials. This tendency has been especially evident in the fields of law enforcement, finance, health, highways, social security, and police (see Chapter 33).

The extent of state control over local units varies from state to state and, within each state, among the different kinds of local government. States supervise the activities of local governments through a host of devices that vary greatly in the amount of control they give to state officials. At one extreme—giving states the least amount of control—are requirements for reports by local officials to specified state officials. At the other extreme are requirements that local officials be appointed and removed by the state officers.[1]

Government by the People, County-Style

For those who live outside the city, the county and township (in New England, the town) are the most important units of local government. Although counties are not alternatives to city governments but merely additional layers, city people look to the city hall as the place where community affairs are managed. Where there is no city hall, the county courthouse stands unrivaled as the center of politics.

All states are divided into counties, though in Louisiana they are called parishes and in Alaska boroughs. With a few exceptions (such as Connecticut and Rhode Island where counties have lost their governmental function), county governments exist in all the territory of the United States. Numbering over 3,000, they vary in size and population. Some are inhabited by few men and much desert; most of them are predominantly rural.

County governments are least active in New England states where the county is essentially a judicial district; county officials do a little road-building

[1] Dale Pontius, *State Supervision of Local Government: Its Development in Massachusetts* (Public Affairs Press, 1942), pp. 1–9.

but not much else. Elsewhere the traditional functions of counties are law enforcement, highway construction and maintenance, tax collection and property assessment, recording of legal papers, and welfare. Despite assertion that the counties are dying governments, they have within recent years taken over more jobs than they have lost. Although counties in some states have given up major responsibility for relief or highway construction, they have taken on planning, zoning, licensing of businesses, airport-building and operation, ambulance service, health services, and other new functions.

COUNTY GOVERNMENT

How are counties organized to do their jobs?[2] Counties, even more than municipalities, exist to enforce state laws and to serve as administrative units of state government. In general, most counties have little legislative power, but the typical county has a group of officials who act in some fashion as the governing body. These agencies have a variety of titles—board of commissioners, supervisors of roads, county court, commissioners' court, and so on. They vary in size from one to more than fifty members. They administer state laws, levy taxes, appropriate money, issue bonds, sign contracts in behalf of the county, and handle whatever jobs the state laws and constitution assign to them.

County boards, as we shall call these agencies, are of two types. The larger boards are usually composed of township supervisors or other township officials; about 20 percent of the smaller boards are elected from the county at large. The rural county board is the one "legislative" body in the United States in which lawyers are outnumbered by farmers. Members of county boards are often key political leaders and in some states control local affairs through their power over state patronage. Consequently, they are much more important then a mere enumeration of their formal powers might suggest. Road problems and the granting of contracts to road contractors are frequently the major topics discussed at board meetings.

The county board shares its powers with a number of other officials, most commonly the sheriff, the prosecutor, the county clerk, the coroner, and the auditor. These are generally elected officials. Often, county treasurers, health officers, and surveyors are also found on the ballot. There is seldom a single administrative head or chief executive responsible for coordinating the activities of the many officials—though sometimes the officials are coordinated by a strong party organization.

WHAT DO COUNTY OFFICIALS DO?

Sheriff. Except in Rhode Island, where he is appointed by the governor, the sheriff is elected by the people of the county, usually for a two- or four-year term. He is charged with enforcing the law and keeping the county jail; in addition, he is an officer of the county's court of record. In some metropolitan counties in the North and in rural counties in the South, sheriffs are active as law-enforcement officers, but in most counties the sheriff lets the city

[2]For a comprehensive review of county and township government, see Clyde F. Snider, *Local Government in Rural America* (Appleton-Century-Crofts, 1957).

police do the job within the cities, and the state police in the rural areas; in some of the latter, however, the sheriff and his deputies are the only ones to keep law and order. If the sheriff meets serious trouble, he can summon a posse of able-bodied men to come to his assistance.

Law enforcement is a dangerous business, and it does not pay very much. Especially in counties where the sheriff is paid on a fee basis, he is likely to spend his time on the more profitable jobs of acting as court official and keeping the jail. The sheriff serves legal processes issued by the court, summons jurors, subpoenas witnesses, and sells property to satisfy judgment. In many states he receives a fixed sum for the custody and feeding of prisoners. Some sheriffs have been known to make a substantial profit from this operation.

Prosecutor. The prosecuting attorney—also known as county attorney, state's attorney, or district attorney—is commonly elected by voters of the county. He aids the grand jury in preparing indictments, and in some states he may on his own authority bring persons to trial by what is known as "information." He prosecutes state law violators and represents the state and county in civil suits. His discretion is wide, and the decision whether or not to prosecute is often made by him alone. The job is especially attractive to young law graduates, and it often serves as a steppingstone to higher political posts.

Coroner. This is another ancient office found in most counties. Generally elected for a short term, the coroner is principally responsible for holding inquests to determine the cause of accidental or suspicious deaths. In many states he selects a jury of about six men to help conduct each inquest. If the coroner and his jury believe that a crime has been committed, they turn their report over to the police and prosecutor. The coroner and his jury may actually name the person they suspect of foul play and then issue a warrant for his arrest.

The office of coroner has been severely criticized. One student of government in rural America, Lane Lancaster, has written: "The office nearly everywhere is held in something approaching contempt. . . . In many counties it goes by default; in many others it ranks simply as a wizened and wormy fruit from the political plum tree, being held by a dreary succession of down-at-the-heel party waterboys. . . . If the coroner is wide-awake . . . he may add to his income by discreet connections with local funeral directors. Indeed it is a lugubrious fact that in a good many counties the office is held by an undertaker who thus is in a strategic position to add to his business."[3] Many authorities feel that the coroner should be replaced by an appointed medical examiner, a qualified physician with training in pathology who would be paid a set salary. The legal aspects of the work, they feel, should be turned over to the prosecutor. This is the system now used in at least seven states. Some counties are too small or too poor to support a full-time trained examiner, and it has been suggested that several counties together provide for a qualified official.

County Clerk. The office of the county clerk is found in about half the states. In other states, the *clerk of the court* often performs his jobs. The

[3]Lane W. Lancaster, *Government in Rural America*, 2d ed. (Van Nostrand, 1952), p. 171.

county clerk is secretary to the county board and has such miscellaneous duties as supervision of elections, issuance of hunting, fishing, and marriage licenses, and the granting of permits for operation of amusement establishments outside city limits. In some states he is also clerk of the court of record.

County treasurer. The treasurer, also elected by the people, receives, keeps, and distributes county funds in accordance with the law. In some counties he collects taxes for the townships and those due the state, and then remits the proper shares to these governments. Some counties have abolished the office of county treasurer, transferring his functions to other officials or designating banks to assume his task.

County assessor. The assessor is responsible for locating property and determining its value for tax purposes, often with the assistance of a large staff. In most places the county assessor does the job for city, township, and state tax purposes.

The "courthouse gang." County governments are not always as headless as it might appear. "It is safe to say that, in nine-tenths of the counties in the United States, public affairs are in the hands of what the irreverent call the 'courthouse gang.' This 'gang' may be described as a more or less permanent group of elective and appointive officeholders together with private individuals whose business normally brings them into contact with public officials."[4] Here are found road contractors, printers, purveyors of supplies, lawyers in criminal and probate work, and "ex-officials who have grown old in party service and who have become masters of the lower sorts of intrigue and so habituated to playing politics as to make residence at the county seat a psychological necessity."[5] Lancaster also points out that the county is also an electoral district and that members of the state legislature "are normally graduates of the school of courthouse politics."[6]

Frequently, one member of the courthouse elite is recognized as the boss. It may be the editor of the local newspaper, the president of the local bank, the chairman of the county farm bureau, the head of the oldest family, or the leader of a local party or faction. Certain county officials are also recognized as having general, if informal, supervisory powers; sometimes it is the chairman of the governing body. In Indiana, Ohio, Minnesota, and South Dakota, it is often the county auditor; in Illinois, the chairman of the board of county commissioners or supervisors; in Missouri, the judge of the county court; in Tennessee, Kentucky, and Alabama, the county or probate judge.

COUNTY REORGANIZATION

How well do the counties do their job? Not very well. In the first place, there are too many of them. When counties were first organized, the idea was to provide a county seat within a day's journey of anyone in the county. The farmer could pile his family into the wagon and head for the courthouse. While he was attending to his business, the family could shop and pick up the local gossip. They could all get home in time to do the evening chores.

[4]*Ibid.*, p. 57.
[5]*Ibid.*, p. 58.
[6]*Ibid.*, p. 59.

Today, farmers driving high-speed cars over modern highways can travel through ten or eleven average-sized counties in a single day. The small area and population of many counties lead inevitably to inefficiency. Study after study has shown that money could be saved and services improved by *consolidating* counties. Though there is much talk about such action, few consolidations have been achieved.

County residents take pride in their county and do not like to see it lose its identity. Officeholders, their families, and their friends do not want county jobs to disappear. Businessmen at the county seat depend on officers, employees, and persons drawn to the city by county business for much of their patronage. In view of the practical obstacles to county consolidation, "Those interested in the improvement of county government would . . . seem well advised to waste little time or effort in the support of consolidation but to concentrate on more practicable means, such as internal reorganization and the consolidation of functions."[7]

Reorganization and consolidation, however, have already demonstrated their value and practicality. Counties have joined together to provide health officers, to share equipment, to purchase materials, and for numerous other purposes. There is still great opportunity for better services through greater cooperation and consolidation of functions.

What progress has been made in reorganizing county structure? Unfortunately, not enough. The headless character of county administration has long been lamented. The same arguments for integration of national and state administration have been put forth to support county reorganization. Many counties are even worse off than the states. Each state at least has a governor who in some fashion or other acts as chief executive.

A few counties have made formal attempts to provide executive leadership. This is especially true in urban or suburban counties such as Nassau and Westchester in New York, Cook County in Illinois, and Los Angeles County in California. Sixteen counties have some kind of county-manager plan. More common are counties with a chief administrative officer, as in California. In several states some counties elect their executive. Among the rural counties, however, the traditional pattern still remains dominant.

Most county governments still lack merit systems or modern fiscal and purchasing methods, and auditing practices often leave much to be desired. Even such an obvious money-saving program as centralized purchasing has not been widely adopted. But progress is being made, slow as it is.

Townships and Towns

North of the Ohio River, east of the Dakotas and Kansas, and outside of New England, the general practice is to subdivide counties into townships. The township is gradually losing many of its functions either to

[7]C. F. Snider, "American County Government: A Mid-Century Review," *The American Political Science Review* (March 1952), p. 68.

the counties or to the cities.[8] Oklahoma, after whittling township functions down to almost nothing, recently abolished them altogether. In Iowa, townships still exist formally, but they have lost so many of their functions that the Census Bureau has stopped counting them. Where they exist, townships often handle outdoor relief, build and maintain roads, and sometimes serve as districts for school purposes. In some states, all the voters of the townships are entitled to attend an annual meeting to elect officers and to levy taxes and make appropriations. These town meetings are usually poorly attended.

A board of supervisors, a justice of the peace, and a constable are the typical township officials; all are elected. The township constable is to the justice of the peace what the sheriff is to the county courts. Since constables make their fees from court work, they do little law enforcement except for catching traffic violators.

The Middle Western and Middle Atlantic townships are often confused with the New England towns. But they are essentially different types of government. The town is the principal kind of rural government in New England. It is sometimes difficult for outsiders to understand that a New England town is an area of government that includes whatever villages there may be, plus the open country. Except where a municipality has been incorporated, the town does most of the things that a county does elsewhere.

Each town holds an annual meeting open to all voters. In the United States, this town meeting is the outstanding example of a *direct democracy*, where all the voters participate directly in making the rules, passing new laws, levying taxes, and appropriating money. Before each meeting the selectmen issue a warrant designating the time and place of the meeting and setting forth the agenda. At the appointed time, a moderator is chosen to preside; the items on the agenda are then taken up, and the floor is open to any citizen who wishes to have his say. Before or during the meeting, the polls are open for the voters to choose the town officers.

The meeting may choose a board of selectmen, usually consisting of three or five members, who carry on the business of the town between meetings, have charge of town property, grant licenses, supervise other town officials, and call special town meetings. A town clerk, treasurer, assessor, overseer of the poor, constable, school board, and numerous other persons are elected by the voters or appointed by the selectmen. The town meeting often elects a finance committee to prepare the town budget.

The New England town meeting has long been a celebrated institution. The picture of sturdy and independent citizens coming together to talk over public affairs and speak their minds is a stirring one. The New England town has often been pointed to as the one place in the United States where no political bosses exist. In fact, however, a recognized group of town leaders often provides leadership. Politics is inevitable—even at a town meeting. This is not to disparage the New England town but to recognize that under conditions of freedom and diversity, groups will be formed and leaders will emerge.

[8]James W. Drury, "Townships Lose Ground," *National Municipal Review* (January 1955), pp. 10–13. Paul W. Wager, "Townships on the Way Out," *National Municipal Review* (October 1957), pp. 456–460, 475–476.

More than a hundred towns, especially the more populous ones, have created the position of *town manager*. Like the city manager (see page 700), he appoints the principal administrative officials and is responsible to the voters through the selectmen. In spite of such innovations, the traditional New England town government still flourishes. Some larger towns have adopted a limited town meeting, under which the town is divided into precincts; the voters in each precinct elect a number of delegates, and the delegates in turn form the town meeting. Any voter may speak at the town meeting, but only the delegates may vote. In some larger towns, city governments may be more appropriate, but the people cling to their traditional town government.

Our Fair Cities

What does the word "city" call to mind? Bright lights, crowded streets, museums, slums, skyscrapers, and lots of people. To some of us, the city may be Main Street, Courthouse Square, the old cannon, and farm families shopping and talking on Saturdays. For a city is not merely improved real estate. It is also people, an exciting conglomerate of men and women living and working together.

In our state statutes, this exciting thing, the city, is made to sound like a dull bit of lawyers' talk. For in law, a city is a *municipal corporation*; there are over 18,000 of them in the United States. Some have millions of people, others a few hundred. Sometimes the smaller ones are called villages, boroughs, or towns. Although not all densely populated places are governed as a municipality, the city is the major kind of local government for the urban dweller.

Each city has two major functions. One is to provide government within its boundaries in order that the citizenry may maintain law and order, keep their streets clean, educate their children, dispose of their garbage, purify their water, create parks, and in other ways make their city a good place in which to live. But the city has a second function—it is an instrumentality of the *state* to carry out *state* functions. It is distinguished from a county, a quasi-corporation, in the greater amount of discretion given to the local officials and by the greater emphasis on their local functions. A county, on the other hand, is supposed to operate primarily as an administrative unit of the state. The distinction is of course one of emphasis.

Each city has its own charter. This is not necessarily a single document; in some states one has to read the state statutes to discover the organization, powers, and functions of cities. The charter is to the city what a constitution is to the national or state government. It outlines the structure of government, sets the authority of the various officials, and provides for their selection. Where do the charters come from? Who draws them up?

In about ten states the legislature writes a *special* charter for each city and may amend the charter as it pleases, although in a few of these states the charter must be submitted to the local voters for their approval. In practice, local groups often draft the charter in consultation with their legislative representatives; other members of the legislature usually defer to the legislative delegation from the city. Since legislators need local support to stay in office, in practice the groups that dominate local politics often write their own charters, even though it is the state legislature that has the constitutional authority to do so. When the legislature is controlled by groups hostile to those in control of the city, however, a major battle may shape up.

In most states the constitution requires the legislature to classify cities and provide a charter for each class of city. If the legislature makes sufficiently refined classifications, it can, in effect, write a special charter for each city; in many states the constitution specifically permits special legislation for the largest city. Many legislatures list several kinds of charter and permit the local citizenry to choose the particular kind they wish. This is known as the *optional charter plan.*

HOME RULE

European cities can do anything that is not expressly forbidden; American cities have only those powers expressly conferred on them. State legislatures still exercise a great deal of control over city affairs. In addition to drawing up charters for the cities, the legislature allots functions to local officials and withdraws them at will. In case of conflict between a state law and a local ordinance, the state law is enforced. In some states, every time a city wants to put a stop light on the corner of Broadway and High, the city fathers have to get permission of either the legislature or certain state officials.

Some states have *legislative* home rule. The legislature delegates authority over certain subjects so that the cities do not have to ask permission to deal with these problems. However, any state law in conflict with a local ordinance supersedes the ordinance, and whatever powers the legislature gives to the local governments it may take away.

In about one-half of the states, however, the constitution, not the state legislature, delegates to citizens of certain-sized cities authority that they may exercise regardless of the wishes of the legislature. These are the *home-rule states.* Where the constitution so permits, a few states extend this power to all municipalities, and the people of the city may elect a group of citizens who draw up a charter. After the charter has been approved by local voters (in some states it must also be approved by either the legislature or the governor, or both, to ensure that it will not conflict with the constitution), it becomes the city's basic instrument of government and may be amended by local citizens. Furthermore, home-rule cities have the general power to dispose of matters of local concern without special authorization from the legislature.

Constitutional home rule thus introduces the federal principle. About two-thirds of our cities of over 200,000 population have some measure of home rule. "It would be a great mistake to think of these cities as being really independent, however."[9] Home rule cities may have some freedom in determining the general structure of their city government, but home rule has not significantly increased their substantive powers; very few items do not have some impact outside the city boundaries, and general grants to dispose of matters of local concern have been narrowly construed by the courts.

[9]Edward C. Banfield and James Q. Wilson, *City Politics* (Harvard Univ. Press, 1963), p. 67.

Since it is the courts that determine whether a given ordinance is within the scope of authority granted to the city by constitutional home rule, the major impact of constitutional home rule seems to have been to transfer some authority from the state legislature to the state courts.[10]

Is home rule worth the struggle for it? Despite the relatively small increase in local autonomy, and despite the fact that constitutional home rule introduces an element of rigidity into state-local relations and enhances the authority of judges, most reform groups favor its adoption. It frees the legislature from the necessity of dealing with local matters. More important, it gives the voters of a particular city the power to decide for themselves the general structure of their municipal government.

FORMS OF CITY CHARTERS

The formal charters are good sources of information for learning how the people in our 18,000 cities govern and are governed. But to look at just a city charter can be very misleading. The actual constitutions—in the sense of the rules by which our cities are governed in contrast to their legal charters—vary "from the narrowest oligarchy to the freest democracy," and "from the most brutal tyranny to a near philosopher-king."[11] But until we have more comparative studies and more detailed investigation, classification of city governments by the form of their charter is still the best available.

The mayor-council charter. The mayor-council charter is the oldest and the most popular charter in the smallest and largest of cities. Under this type of charter, the city council is usually a single chamber, although the bicameral form lingers on in a few cities. The size of the council varies—some have only two members, some as many as fifty. Seven members is the median in cities with over 5,000 people.

Many methods are used to select the councilmen—nonpartisan and partisan elections by small wards, by large wards, from the city at large, by proportional representation. It is artificial to isolate the method of electing councilmen from party structures, social structure, and interest groups, but the way councilmen are chosen is an important factor in determining how power is distributed in a city. Large cities that elect councilmen in partisan elections generally choose them by small districts rather than at large. This combination tends to support strong party organizations. Nonpartisan at-large elections make party organization difficult. The larger the election districts for councilmen, the more likely citywide considerations will be brought to bear in the selection of councilmen and the greater the influence of citywide institutions such as the local newspaper in the election of councilmen. The larger the election districts, the less likely racial and ethnic groups will be represented on the city council, for the voting strength of neighborhood minorities cannot be concentrated behind local councilmen. Larger districts are easier to gerrymander, but with small districts it is harder to draw lines so that a particular racial group will have no chance of winning.[12]

[10]*Ibid.*
[11]Norton E. Long, *The Polity* (Rand McNally, 1962), pp. 222–241, especially p. 230.
[12]These generalizations are based on studies of Banfield and Wilson, *op. cit.*, pp. 89–100.

Voters

Mayor

Council

Appoints with approval of the council

Department Heads

The powers of the mayor vary from charter to charter (and even more widely from city to city and mayor to mayor). The mayor is elected by the people, but in some cases the charter assigns little more than ceremonial powers to him; he welcomes visiting firemen and gives them the key to the city. In some cities his appointive power is limited, and he shares administrative authority with the other elected officials and numerous boards and commissions. This is known as the *weak mayor-council* system.

Tracing the office of mayor through various charters, one finds a general trend toward an increase in his authority. Like the Presidency and the governorship, the office of mayor over the years has grown in importance. Many cities have altered their charters in order to give the mayor power to appoint and remove heads of departments and investigate their activities, to send messages to the city council, to prepare the budget, and to veto council ordinances. In other words, he has been given a share in policy-making, and city administration has been centralized under his direction. A recent development is the creation of a chief administrative officer, appointed by the mayor to assist him in directing city administration. In New York, Chicago, and Philadelphia, for example, these city administrators manage the housekeeping functions of the city government and provide professional administration, conferring some of the advantages that are thought to come with the adoption of the council-manager form of government (see below).

Many people believe that the *strong mayor-council* is the best charter for the large cities. This charter, they argue, gives the city a strong political leader, makes efficient administration possible, and by centering authority in the hands of a few individuals makes less likely the growth of "invisible government" by men who have power but who are not publicly accountable for its use.

The commission charter. In 1900 the city of Galveston was inundated by a tidal wave. Over 6,000 people lost their lives, and property worth millions was destroyed. The mayor and aldermen seemed incapable of action. In the emergency, power began to fall into the hands of a group of businessmen who had been discussing methods of improving the harbor. They decided to act. After studying the charters of several cities, they went to the legislature with what was then almost a novel proposal for a new charter. They asked that control of the city be vested in five commissioners. The legislature approved.

About five years later, the attorney for the city of Des Moines, Iowa, took a business trip to Galveston. He was so favorably impressed with the commission government that he returned to Iowa with the proposal that the Iowa legislature permit cities to adopt commission charters.

699

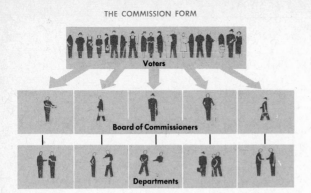

THE COMMISSION FORM

Voters

Board of Commissioners

Departments

The placing of all governmental powers in the hands of five men flew in the face of the traditional doctrine of separation of powers. Many felt that it was too dangerous to give a small group of men control over both administration and legislation. For this reason the Des Moines Plan, as it was known, included the initiative, referendum, recall, and nonpartisan ballots for primaries and elections in addition to the ideas of the Galveston businessmen. The plan became very popular, and by 1917 over 500 cities were so governed. Since that time the number has declined, although Portland, St. Paul, Memphis, and nearly 250 other cities with populations over 5,000 still have this kind of charter.

The commissioners, usually five, collectively constitute the city council; individually they are the heads of the departments of city administration. Most commissioners devote full time to their jobs and actively administer the affairs of their particular departments. One of the commissioners is designated as mayor, but he normally has little more power than the other commissioners.

The commission charter was widely heralded as an introduction of safe and sane business methods to city affairs, but after a brief wave of popularity, the new idea lost some of its glamour; the party bosses were suspicious and the city reformers disappointed. Although providing for more integrated control than the old mayor-council system, the commission charter left the city without a single responsible administrative head; in fact, a commission city has five mayors. Moreover, commissioners chosen because they represent major groups within the city often leave something to be desired as administrators of departments of public welfare, public safety, and so on. By 1917, reformers had discovered a new kind of charter which they believed had greater merit.

The council-manager charter. The council-manager, also known as city-manager or commission-manager, plan was acclaimed by James Bryce as "the latest word in municipal reform." It is one of our most significant governmental innovations. In 1908 the little city of Staunton, Virginia, appointed a general manager to direct the city's work. Little note was taken of the step, but Richard Childs, an advertising man active in the short-ballot movement, became very much interested.

Childs was enthusiastic about the commission plan (discussed above) because it applied two basic ideas, *unification of power* and a *short ballot*, to city affairs. But it did not go far enough. Add to this a chief administrative officer, he reasoned, and the results should be even better. So, as he said, he became "the minister who performed the ceremony that united" the commission plan with the idea of a general manager.

The city-manager plan was adopted by a few small cities but it did not receive much publicity. Then in 1913, Dayton, Ohio, had a flood (city

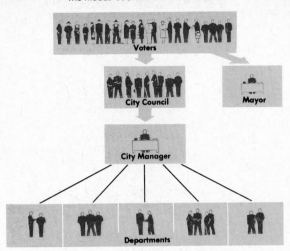

THE MODEL COUNCIL-MANAGER FORM

Voters

City Council

Mayor

City Manager

Departments

charters seem to owe much to tidal waves and floods), which came in the midst of a campaign to select members for a charter commission. The existing city officials, like their predecessors in Galveston, demonstrated their inability to meet the emergency, and the disaster added to the strength of those advocating the city-manager plan. These reformers argued that a city is a corporation and should be run like any other corporation. The voters, as "stockholders," should elect a board of directors, and these directors should select a professional administrator. This is the essence of the city-manager plan, and its adoption by Dayton attracted national attention.

Over 2,000 cities, located in almost all the states, operate under a council-manager charter, and each year new municipalities adopt the council-manager plan. Although of those cities with more than half a million people only Cincinnati, Kansas City, Dallas, and San Diego have a city manager, over half the cities of 25,000 to 100,000 people have adopted this form of city government, and over 40 million Americans live in cities governed by a council-manager system.

Under the council-manager charter, the council is usually elected in non-partisan primaries and elections, either on a citywide basis or by election districts much larger than the wards in mayor-council cities. The number of council members varies, but there are usually fewer than in cities with mayor-council charters. The council appoints a city manager, supervises his activities, and fires him when he is unsatisfactory. It makes the laws, approves the budget, and—although it is not supposed to interfere in administration—it supervises city government through the manager. A mayor is usually provided for the purpose of presiding over the council and representing the city on ceremonial occasions.

The city manager advises the council on policy and supervises the administration of city business. Since the council-manager plan envisages the selection of the best available person, most charters do not require the council to appoint a local citizen, nor do they prescribe detailed qualifications. Twenty universities now have special courses for the training of city managers. The International City Managers' Association has its own code of ethics and works to develop higher standards among its members. City managers receive substantial salaries; as more and more cities adopt this form of government, the opportunities for advancement continue to increase.

City-manager charters imply a nonpolitical city manager who merely carries into execution policies proclaimed by the council, and councilmen who refrain from interfering with the administration of city affairs. In fact, there is no such sharp distinction between policy-making and policy-applying. Most city managers operating behind the symbol of administration are the ma-

701

jor source within the city government for the initiation of policies and programs. "The city manager is a participant in the political process of the community whether he plays an active role in initiating policy, a passive role by merely drawing council attention to emerging problems, or a neutral role by refusing to commit himself publicly on a controversial question. . . . Refusal of a manager to commit himself can be interpreted by opposing groups as taking a position antagonistic to their own."[13] The unavoidable involvement of the manager in the politics of the community means that when there is a change in the control of the council, managers often are fired. The dismissal of a manager is usually explained in other than political terms—lack of sufficient management training, a personality conflict between manager and council, interference by the manager in the business of the council; or the manager may resign because of council meddling in administration. The explanations, however, are often "superficial rationalizations of the intrinsic political struggles of the community."[14]

How has the city-manager plan worked out? Cities that adopted this kind of charter have generally enjoyed an improvement in standards of public employment, a reduction in unit costs, and better services. Moreover, the city-manager cities have become institutions "with a broader and more vital function in the community."[15]

POLITICAL ETHOS AND POWER STRUCTURES

Forms of government are merely patterns for organizing the activities of people, and much depends on who the people are and the kind of government they want. "Many council-manager cities are upper-class or middle-class in character; few if any are predominantly lower-class."[16] City-manager government appeals to the concept of the public interest of these groups, a concept that stresses "good," disinterested government, efficiency and economy, business methods and procedures, and civic growth. The city-manager form of government, with its emphasis on nonpartisanship, thus tends to put into control of government persons who share these attitudes. In large cities where low-income groups have more political influence, city-manager forms are less likely to be adopted and less likely to function in the fashion contemplated by those who seek their adoption.

Political attitudes and governmental forms are related, but the relationship is complex. Regardless of form of government, our cities have political cultures, although again we must be wary of too much reliance on what must be sweeping generalizations. These political cultures have shown considerable consistency over time and are variables of some importance in understanding the political process.

A number of studies have shown that the majority partisan views in a community create an environment that itself reinforces the majority views. People who move to a city whose political atmosphere is Republican are

[13]Gladys M. Kammerer et al., *The Urban Political Community* (Houghton Mifflin, 1963), p. 5; see also by the same authors, *City Managers in Politics* (Univ. of Florida Press, 1962).
[14]*Ibid.*, p. 193.
[15]Harold A. Stone, Don K. Price, and Kathryn H. Stone, *City Manager Government in the United States* (Public Administration Service, 1940), p. 260.
[16]Banfield and Wilson, *op. cit.*, p. 169.

likely to become Republicans, even some of those who were previously Democrats. These factors of community reinforcement seem to be especially strong for those who become political activists through voluntary organizations and friendships rather than through political party activity.[17]

In addition to partisan predispositions, cities have a more general political ethos that may be classified in terms of two general political orientations[18]: the first, called the "public-regarding" view, looks upon city government as a means to perform in a disinterested fashion, as economically and efficiently as possible, service for the general good of the community. Those who hold to the public-regarding basic attitude believe that partisanship at the city level should be minimized, that decisions should be based on careful calculations of the community good, and that civic, in contrast to political, organizations and issues call for participation by all good citizens in order to make the city the "best darn place" in which people can live in peace and harmony.

The other political culture has been called "private-regarding," although the term should not be thought to suggest that it is somehow less respectable than the public-regarding concept. This basic orientation looks upon the city government as an instrument designed to provide jobs, protection, housing, and to meet the particular needs of its citizens. It views political partisanship as a legitimate device in order to secure one's share. It considers as legitimate the appointment to office of one's friends who, in return for political support, should use their office to reward those who put them there. It tends to deemphasize the possibility that all interests and groups within the community can be made equally happy and expects government to support those who support it.

These differences in attitude toward political life are correlated with class. Middle- and upper-class persons, especially those of white Protestant third- and fourth-generation backgounds, tend to believe in the public-regarding culture; while the poor, the recently arrived immigrants (Polish, Irish, Italian), and the blacks tend to operate within the private-regarding culture. These attitudes, however, do not determine the structure of city government; at least the evidence of the interrelationship has not yet been found.[19] But these differences in political culture are often more important than the form of government in determining how a city operates and how officials and party leaders do what is expected of them.

That the class structure of a community affects its governmental forms, and that these affect the class structure, is another hypothesis long held by political observers. Generally, in the communities that have strong partisan organizations where party and class coincide and where no single party dominates, decision-making tends to be in the hands of no single group. Middle-class communities—small dormitory suburbs, for example—tend to have a more closed group of decision-makers and a more public-regarding ethos. In communities where the lower-class party—usually the Democratic—has a clear majority, the business, professional, and middle-class groups

[17]Robert D. Putnam, "Political Attitudes and the Local Community," *American Political Science Review* (September 1966), p. 652.
[18]Banfield and Wilson, *op. cit.*
[19]Raymond E. Wolfinger and John Osgood Field, "Political Ethos and the Structure of City Government," *The American Political Science Review* (June 1966), pp. 324–326.

will be in favor of nonpartisan elections, the short ballot, and the city-manager form of government. And in general middle-class groups tend to promote voluntary organizations outside the party system, while lower-class groups are more likely to rely on partisan organizations.[20] But so complicated and complex and subject to changing tides and trends are the political systems of our cities, that all our generalizations must be accepted cautiously and tentatively.

[20]Based on Peter H. Rossi, "Power and Community Structure," *Midwest Journal of Political Science* (November 1960), pp. 390–401.

Metropolis: The Urban Crisis

32

"If we forget the map of America drawn to a scale of statute miles and see only the people and their distribution," writes Scott Greer, "we find a nation of mushrooming metropolitan areas, stagnant small towns, and dying open country neighborhoods. . . . The farming areas grow increasingly prairie-like as the density of human population dwindles and the size of holding increases; many small towns lose their reason for being, changing to villages and ghost towns; the small cities become 'metropolitan areas' and the great cities expand until they form vast urban regions. . . ."[1]

Today it is metropolis, not the farm or the small town so beloved in American fact and fiction, where most of us live, and most of us who do not now live in metropolis soon will. During the 1950s over 96 percent of our total population increase occurred in metropolitan areas. By 1980 over four-fifths of all Americans will be living in these areas. By the year 2000 the nation will find itself with several large metropolitan regions of solid settlement: the Eastern Seaboard, the West Coast, and an urban Middle West uniting St. Louis, Chicago, Cleveland, Detroit, Indianapolis, and Buffalo.[2]

And what is this urban environment of modern man like the world over?

[1]Scott Greer, *The Emerging City* (Free Press, 1962) pp. 29–30.
[2]Philip M. Hauser, *Population Perspectives* (Rutgers Univ. Press, 1961). The Growth of Urbanization, by States, 1870–1960. From John R. Borchert, "The Urbanization of the Upper Midwest: 1930–1960," *Upper Midwest Economic Study, Urban Report Number 2* (Feb. 1963), p. 2.

·Circle over London, Buenos Aires, Chicago, Sydney, in an airplane, or view the cities schematically by means of an urban map and block plan. What is the shape of the city and how does it define itself? The original container has completely disappeared: the sharp division between city and country no longer exists. As the eye stretches toward the hazy periphery one can pick out no definite shapes except those formed by nature; one beholds rather a continuous shapeless mass, here bulging or ridged by buildings, there broken by a patch of green or an unwinding ribbon of concrete. The shapelessness of the whole is reflected in the individual part, and the nearer the center, the less as a rule can the smaller parts be distinguished. . . .

As one moves away from the center, the urban growth becomes ever more aimless and discontinuous, more diffuse and unfocussed, except where some surviving town has left the original imprint of a more orderly life. Old neighborhoods and precincts, the social cells of the city, still maintaining some measure of the village pattern, become vestigial. No human eye can take in this metropolitan mass at a glance. No single gathering place except the totality of its streets can hold all its citizens. No human mind can comprehend more than a fragment of the complex and minutely specialized activities of its citizens. The loss of form, the loss of autonomy, the constant frustration and harassment of daily activities, to say nothing of gigantic breakdowns and stoppages—all these become normal attributes of the metropolitan regime. There is a special name for power when it is concentrated on such a scale: it is called impotence. . . ."[3]

Sprawling giantism, congestion, slums, smog, tension, rootlessness, shapelessness, loss of a sense of community, impersonal and unfriendly human relationships—all these terms have been used to describe the giant city of today. The big city has simply lost control of itself, Mumford continues. Even worse, it carries the seeds of the destruction of civilization. Historically, the city has grown from shelter to fortress to industrial center and to a mechanical way of life. *Polis*— the old Greek type of small city—gave way to metropolis and then to megalopolis and then to "tyrannopolis" and finally to necropolis—the city of death (an idea that takes on frightening prophetic possibilities in an age of the ever-present possibility of nuclear warfare).[4]

Mumford's strictures against the city are in keeping with a long-standing tradition of anti-city bias on the part of major social critics, starting with Thomas Jefferson, running through Lord Bryce, Lincoln Steffens, Theodore Dreiser, and infusing much of American social science. These critics project the image of the city as an impersonal, cold, brutal environment in which crime flourishes and man loses his dignity. The big city is contrasted with the "wholesome" small community in which men live "whole lives" of total relationships. Some of the less sophisticated critics of metropolis appear to measure the modern city against a small town inhabited by Anglo-Saxons who speak with a New England or Middle Western accent and who spend their leisure eating Mom's apple pie or sitting around the stove at the general store engaged in high-level discussions of local politics.

But metropolis and urban values have their defenders. The big city, they contend, is not just a place of smog and sprawl. It is the center of innovation, excitement, diversity, and vitality. It is where the pluralistic social base for diversity can be found, where community pressures to conform are bearable.

[3]Lewis Mumford, *The City in History* (Harcourt, Brace & World, 1961), pp. 543–544.
[4]Lewis Mumford, *The Culture of Cities* (Harcourt, Brace & World, 1938), Chap. 4.

The large community is a meeting place for talent from all over the nation and the world, and of all types: dancers, musicians, writers, actors, leaders of the world's commerce, finance, transportation. Despite all the complaints, many people *like* living in the big city. And they point out that within metropolis there are often fairly homogeneous smaller communities that retain their identity.[5] Perhaps the best known example would be Greenwich Village in lower New York City.

Metropolis: Core City versus Suburbia

The sharpest single social, political, and governmental division in the United States is fast becoming that between the central city and its suburbs. Into our large cities are moving the poor and dispossessed—both white and black, but in recent years mostly black—from the rural areas. Out to the suburbs are moving—some say they are fleeing—the economically better-off whites. Today the twelve largest cities contain over two-thirds of the Negro population outside the South, and one-third of the total Negro population of the United States. In the last few years the inflow into our central cities of blacks has accelerated the outflow of whites; as the Kerner Commission warns: "Our nation is moving toward two societies, one black, one white —separate and unequal."[6]

In charge of this metropolitan area of city and suburbs there exists no single government, but rather dozens, in some cases even hundreds, of governments. There are many Clevelanders—that is, people who work in Cleveland, shop in Cleveland, sell goods in Cleveland, hire men in Cleveland, read Cleveland newspapers—who do not *live* in Cleveland, and by and large they tend to be whiter and wealthier than those who do live in Cleveland. Only about half the St. Louisans live in St. Louis, and again, those who do live there tend to be less well-off than those who live in the suburbs. "The Pennsylvania section of the Philadelphia metropolitan area contains five counties, Philadelphia included. Less than half that region's residents now live in the central city; less than half the labor force works there."[7] And so it is with most of our metropolitan areas.

In recent years suburbs have been the fastest-growing units in the United States. Today most who can afford it leave the crowded and blighted business areas and move out into more pleasant living quarters. They go in search of cheaper land, lower taxes, more room, better air. New shopping centers rise in outlying communities. Industries also move from the central city in search of cheaper land, lower taxes, and escape from city building and health codes. "Suburbia no longer stands for the well-to-do, but rather for the scale from decent home-owning people up to the millionaires."[8]

[5]Greer, *op. cit.*, p. 133 delineates the bias pro and con running through literature with respect to urban values and life. See also Anselm Strauss, *Images of the American City* (Free Press, 1961).

[6]National Advisory Commission on Civil Disorders (U.S. Government Printing Office, 1968), p. 1.

[7]Charles E. Gilbert, *Governing the Suburbs* (Indiana Univ. Press, 1967), p. 3.

[8]Greer, *op. cit.*, p. 31. Also Kevin Lynch, "The Pattern of the Metropolis," in Lloyd Rodwin (ed.), *The Future Metropolis* (Braziller, 1961), p. 105.

Despite the fact that suburbanites often look on the politics of the central city as corrupt and something to escape from, the politics of central city are very much a part of their lives. When they read their morning papers on the way to work, they find little news about the officials of their own suburbs, but much about Mayor Yorty or Mayor Daley or Mayor Lindsay or Mayor Stokes, or of some other big-city mayor. Moreover, the major problems in which they are interested—transportation, crime, taxation of downtown businesses where they work—are more influenced by the decisions of the officials of central city than those of suburbia. And although the suburbanite has some influence in his central city through his business association or trade union, he has no direct vote in electing those whose decisions vitally affect him.

What of government and politics in the suburbs? It is dangerous to generalize. Suburbs are not all alike. Some are the exclusive residences of the rich and established, with first-rate schools, governed by an efficient cluster of specialists. Others are havens for criminals. Still others are lower-middle-class neighborhoods of blue-collar workers. And others are chosen by young executives and their wives who have little interest in their community and view their surroundings as a stepping-stone from which to move with the next promotion.

Dangerous as it is to generalize nevertheless we must. Some suburbanites tend to look at their local government as a device to protect their property, their schools, and their homes against "invasion" by minority groups, such as Negroes. Occasionally, suburban dwellers become aroused over major local problems like educational policy or taxation. In the absence of such explosive issues, suburban local politics tend to be trivial. Each suburban city is so limited in its jurisdiction that it cannot cope with the major problems of urban life. As a result, even suburbanites who are active in state and national politics seldom have much interest in what happens at their city hall. They may complain to the city officials, but since these deal with relatively minor issues, they have little interest in their work. It is often difficult to find people to run for local office.

Scott Greer, after evaluating the various studies and surveys of local suburban politics, concludes: "Whether the election in question is for school board member or mayor of the municipality, a smaller proportion of the eligibles will turn out to vote in the suburbs than will do so in the central city."[9] Of course some suburbanites are politically active, but "the small-scale community of limited liability in the suburbs does not have the 'box office' appeal that major government manifests. Staying close to home, operated by amateurs and part-time politicians . . . the suburban political community has been overlooked or rejected by a substantial proportion of its citizenry."[10]

The sheer management of suburbia often makes for frustration. Each suburban city has its own government, fire and police departments, school system, street-cleaning equipment, and building and health codes. Also, many

[9]Greer, *op. cit.*, p. 141.
[10]*Ibid.*, pp. 142–143. See also S. Greer, "The Citizen and his Local Governments: Central City and Suburban County" in J. C. Bollens (ed.), *Exploring the Metropolitan Community* (Univ. of California Press, 1961).

of the major tasks of suburban government are bound together with those of the metropolis at large. Criminals do not stop at city boundaries. The central city usually maintains an elaborate police department with detective bureaus, crime-detection laboratories, and an elaborate communications network, but its jurisdiction stops at the city line. Suburban police are fewer, and often untrained in criminology. Or consider traffic problems. Superhighways run through suburbia, with a number of access roads; these form a transportation unity, but in the midst of governmental disunity. In matters of health, too, there are often wide differences in health standards between parts of metropolis. But germs, pollution, and smog do not notice city signposts.

The Special Problems of the Central City

"He who moves from Boston to Concord or Acton, or to Weston or Needham, leaves a considerable part of his municipal burdens behind him," Cherington wrote. "He leaves tremendous problems of public health and public welfare back in the central urban core, or back in the industrial soot of Cambridge or Somerville or Chelsea. He leaves Boston to solve its own street problem while he drives to work on a state supported, federally aided highway, or he may park his car at the end of the rapid transit line and ride into State Street on the Metropolitan Transit Authority's deficit. He knows that his suburban government is cheaper and in terms of his own mythology it is 'better'. He draws a State Street salary but pays a farmer's taxes. We can scarcely find a better example of having your cake and eating it too."[11]

The fundamental problem of the core city is that while many upper-income families and high-tax-paying businesses have been moving out, low-income groups have been moving in, and the need for city services has greatly expanded. In a recent six-year period, Adrian reports, retail sales rose by 20 percent in the city of St. Louis, but by 80 percent in St. Louis County. In one year more was spent for new plants and equipment in the Illinois suburbs of St. Louis than was spent in the city and St. Louis County suburbs combined. "To heap trouble upon trouble . . . the majority of migrants will settle first in the city, probably in the decaying zone of transition. Because they are culturally marginal people — that is to say, they live in the culture of a large city but still have many of the values they earlier received from a quite different rural culture — they are likely, in their isolation, resentment, or economic desperation, to create police and juvenile problems. They are insecure and confused people. . . ."[12] In the last century they were newly arrived immigrants from Europe. In this century they are migrants from the rural areas, especially blacks and whites from the South. The center of the city tends "toward a vast ethnic ghetto, surrounding the 'white lights' and surrounded, in turn, by miles of residential streets of a shabby gentility

[11]Charles R. Cherington, "Pattern for Greater Boston," *National Municipal Review* (February 1949), p. 70.
[12]Charles R. Adrian, *State and Local Governments* (McGraw-Hill, 1960), p. 238.

whose residents consider the approach of the Puerto Ricans, the Negroes, the Mexicans, or the Okies,"[13] and live in constant fear that their own neighborhoods will become "less desirable."

Pressing problems accumulate in the core city. The large numbers of migrants from Puerto Rico mean that the schools must be specially equipped to deal with children who may not speak English. The arrival of black families from the rural South poses new problems for the public schools, which have to face tensions between blacks and whites and to provide additional services and resources to compensate for centuries of discrimination. Lower-income families in general, and especially migrants from areas where medical services have been limited, make heavy demands on the public health facilities of the city. The migration of persons lacking the job skills now needed for our increasingly automated and complicated economy puts heavy demands on welfare agencies. The crowding of persons into segregated districts accelerates the process of urban decay and slum-building. To meet stepped-up housing needs by people who cannot pay high rents, the city moves in with public housing programs, and the building of public housing projects creates tensions among those who are forced to move out of the area as well as for those who are forced to move into the public housing once it is available. People who live in congested areas always require more police protection, but police problems abound when different racial groups live closely together in slum areas with all the resulting disruption of family and community life and with forces making for juvenile delinquency. And, as if

[13]Greer, *op. cit.*, p. 31. See also Hal Bruno, "Chicago's Hillbilly Ghetto," *The Reporter* (June 4, 1964), pp. 28–31.

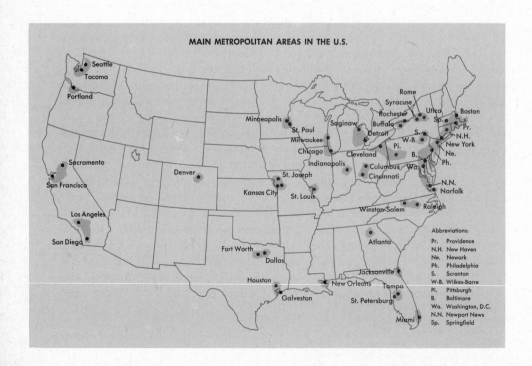

MAIN METROPOLITAN AREAS IN THE U.S.

Abbreviations:
Pr.   Providence
N.H.   New Haven
Ne.   Newark
Ph.   Philadelphia
S.   Scranton
W-B. Wilkes-Barre
Pi.   Pittsburgh
B.   Baltimore
Wa.   Washington, D.C.
N.N. Newport News
Sp.   Springfield

these were not problems enough, there is also the movement of thousands of people into the core city in the morning and out to the suburbs in the evening, the congestion of streets, and the pollution of the air. Faced with this urban crisis, the big cities need a great deal of money, and this is precisely the resource that they lack.

Two Nations — Two Cultures

City and suburb confront each other almost as two nations, each with its own subculture. The suburbs' life-style is based on children, home, neighborhood, and single-family dwelling secure on 100-foot lots. "Surburban folk tend to be of higher social rank, of white 'old American' heritage, and committed to a familistic way of life."[14] Their concept of the public interest "Derives from the middle-class ethos, favors what the municipal reform movement has always defined as 'good government' — namely efficiency, impartiality, honesty, planning, strong executives, no favoritism, model legal codes, and strict enforcement of laws against gambling and vice."[15]

As we have warned, not all suburbs are of the same pattern, and many who live in the central city have the same life-styles and concepts. But speaking generally, the central cities consisting of older dwellings, high-rise apartments, and housing projects, and made up of ethnic minorities and nonwhite enclaves, support concepts of the public interest that tend to identify with wards or neighborhoods rather than with the city as a whole, look to politicians for help and favors, regard gambling and vice as necessary evils, respond less to calls for efficiency and impartiality, and look to the city for material benefits such as protection of civil rights, maintenance of order, jobs, homes, and help in the face of economic adversity.

"Today many central cities find that their principal antagonist in the legislature is not the rural hinterland but an alliance of the hinterland and the suburbs."[16] The long-standing lines of cleavage between city and suburbs persist as a major feature of political life in the metropolis.

But we must not draw too sharp a contrast between suburb and central-city problems. In the outlying areas the suburbanites may be feeling the bite of "suburbanitis." Many of them have discovered that the lower prices for land and the lower taxes are deceptive. Fire insurance rates are often higher, they have to pay more for garbage collection, they often have to build and maintain their own septic tanks, and other costs are higher. Moreover, as suburban real estate becomes improved, and as the suburb grows in size, new waterworks and other facilities are needed. The schools become crowded, the parks are inadequate, and part-time village government is unsatisfactory. So, common needs of government services, and their heavy expense, ultimately press on people both in the core city and in suburbia. This common

[14]Scott Greer, *Governing the Metropolis* (Wiley, 1962), p. 52.
[15]Edward C. Banfield and James Q. Wilson, *City Politics* (Harvard Univ. Press, 1963), p. 46.
[16]*Ibid.*, p. 37.

problem raises the question of whether central city and suburbia can pool their resources in order to deal with it more effectively. We will return to this question after looking more closely at the politics and government of the core city.

Government of the Central City

The core city may be decaying, but it remains the most important single governmental unit within metropolis, And its politics are still the dominant concern of the citizens of metropolis, even those who live in the suburbs. How are large cities governed? Like the federal and state governments, metropolitan government is divided into the executive, legislative, and judicial branches, with a large fourth branch of more-or-less independent agencies, commissions, and authorities.

THE MEN IN CITY HALL

The most important and most publicized big-city official is the mayor. Some men were so effective, and indeed dramatic, in this role that they made names for themselves nationally; Fiorello LaGuardia of New York, Joseph W. Folk of St. Louis, Daniel W. Hoan of Milwaukee, Tom L. Johnson of Cleveland, James M. Curley of Boston are still remembered long after their regimes have ended.

Today the mayor must be the head of a huge bureaucracy as well as a politician. "The profile of today's big-city mayor—with one difference—is quite similar to that of the chief executive of a large corporation," according to a recent report. "Typically, the mayor is a college graduate, usually with a legal or business background, and is now in his late fifties. He puts in hard, grinding hours at his desk, sometimes six or seven days a week, and his wife suffers as much as his golf game. The difference is in salary: he usually makes $20,000 to $25,000. There is also a chauffeur-driven limousine and, in some cities, an expense allowance, ranging from $2,000 (Milwaukee) to $55,000 (Chicago). 'Public relations' takes a big chunk of his time. . . . Above all the mayor is a politician."[17]

The mayor of a large city thus has the same basic functions as any major executive leader. As "chief of state" he issues proclamations, receives important city visitors, appears at endless civic breakfasts, luncheons, and dinners, launches community and charity drives. As "chief executive" he appoints the heads of agencies, draws up the budget, checks up on administration, deals with sudden emergencies, mediates among warring department chiefs, tries to get rid of incompetents or misfits. As "chief of party" he usually dominates the city organization of his party; he helps recruit candidates for office, tries to shunt aside his enemies, deals with revolts and opposition within the party, represents the party in Washington or the state capital, and perhaps works through the party to win support from state and national legislators. As chief legislator the mayor draws up proposed legislation and also makes a great deal of specific policy in "filling in the details" of general leg-

[17]Editors of *Fortune* Magazine, *The Exploding Metropolis* (Doubleday, 1958), pp. 85–86.

islative enactments. Indeed, the only powers of the President that the metropolitan mayor does not hold at the city level are "commander in chief" and "chief of foreign relations" — and even in these areas the mayor has certain duties, such as civil defense, and he must often deal with foreign consulates and nationals, especially if he is head of a great port city like San Francisco, Chicago, or New Orleans.

The mayor shares his legislative power with the city council. Typically, in the giant city the mayor has extensive power to recommend legislation and to participate in the legislative process; he has a broad veto power, for example, over both policy measures and appropriations. But the balance of power widely varies from city to city. Much depends on the basis on which the councilmen are elected — for example, whether they are elected by the same party organization that supports the mayor, or by a personal organization of their own. The mayor finds that his relation with the legislative branch is essentially a *political* problem, just as the President and the governors do. Sometimes the mayor must depend on his control of the party organization to insure support in the council. For example, Chicago would seem to have a "weak" form of mayor because the city council consists of fifty members elected in small districts, but Mayor Richard Daley has been able to exercise considerable influence over the council because of his political strength in their districts.[18] Other cities may appear to have more streamlined executive-legislative relationships, but the mayor may be weak because he has little political influence over the councilmen.

Whatever the particular combination, the mayor and the council operate in terms of the separation of powers and the checks and balances that characterize other levels of American government. Hence the mayor must ever deal with the problem of splintered and fragmented power, which in turn relates to the question of whether the big city can govern itself.

THE MAYOR AS CHIEF EXECUTIVE

The main job of the mayor is administrative in the broadest sense of that term. Under him are the big "line" agencies — police, fire, public safety, traffic, health, sanitation — and a host of special agencies, such as the board of elections, the city planning agency, and commissions that regulate particular occupations and professions. The big-city mayor usually has a large staff — though usually not so large as he would like — that carries out typical overhead functions such as personnel, budgeting, and public relations. In this respect the mayor meets the same problems as all executives — problems of coordinating a variety of different activities, assigning responsibilities, checking to see whether projects have been carried out, finding the ablest available administrators to take charge, and allotting money through his control of the budget.

The mayor has a special problem that is found on both the national and the state levels of government but not in so extreme a form as in the big city. This is the *public* or *special authority*. Essentially the same as a public corporation, such as the Tennessee Valley Authority, these authorities have

[18]Martin Meyerson and Edward C. Banfield, *Politics, Planning and the Public Interest* (Free Press, 1955).

been set up to undertake important but specialized functions in the big cities; examples are the Metropolitan Water District of Southern California and the Port of New York Authority. As these suggest, the authority oversees functions lying outside as well as inside the boundaries of the metropolitan district. It has legal authority granted it by the state (or states) to raise money, hire experts, and take over some of the big-city jobs, such as transport, water, and housing. The authority has been called "the fastest-growing division of local government" in the United States.

Why public authorities? In part because state legislatures are often hostile to big-city mayors and prefer to place important functions of metropolis outside his reach and that of his political "machine"; in part because the authority has great financial flexibility (for example, it can incur debt outside the limits imposed on the city by the state); but most of all, as suggested above, because many problems, such as transportation, are simply too big, and also cover too wide a geographic area, to be properly governed by the city itself. Robert Moses of New York City, himself a member of many public authorities, summed up knowledgeably the case for this kind of device: "The nearest thing to business in government is the public authority, which is business with private capital under public auspices, established only when both private enterprise and routine government have failed to meet an urgent need, and this device is often attacked because it is too independent of daily pressures, too unreachable by the boys and therefore essentially undemocratic."[19]

Whatever the general pros and cons of the authority—and the debate runs on and on—it poses a special problem for the big-city mayor. Not only are vital functions of metropolitan government beyond his direct control, but even worse, special authorities managing big functions like transit and sanitation constantly come into contact—and conflict—with "line" agencies dealing with closely related problems, such as intercity traffic and law enforcement. It is hard enough for the mayor to coordinate and mediate among his own agencies; it is infinitely harder to deal with independent authorities. But if the authority is a problem for the mayor, it is also a temptation. By helping to sponsor these independent agencies, he can sometimes cut down on his direct load of administration. He can tap other sources of funds and hence keep his own city's tax rate lower than it otherwise would be. If things go wrong he can more easily shift the blame by saying that he did not have authority over a certain function and hence cannot be held responsible. But what might in certain instances make things easier for the mayor may not be necessarily good for the metropolitan welfare—or for the capacity of the city dwellers as a whole to govern themselves effectively.

Metropolitics: The Political Life of the Big City

The stakes and prizes of big-city politics are tremendous. Since the city government touches personal and group interests at many points, these persons and interests must continually mobilize as much

[19]Editors of *Fortune, op. cit.*, p. 99.

influence as they can. The stakes and prizes are manifold: appointments to city offices, the incidence of taxation, regulation of businesses, professions, and other activities, the question of who gets contracts from the city, the allotment of various city benefits, like education and sanitation. Beyond all this is the general interest in honest, efficient, and farseeing metropolitan government.[20]

INTEREST GROUPS IN CENTRAL CITY

Around all these stakes and prizes interest groups tend to form in varying degrees of size, solidarity, and effectiveness. The politicians of metropolis must deal with the basic group interest found anywhere in an industrial society—with organized workers and businessmen, professional associations, good government associations, doctors, ethnic groups. But all these are much closer at hand for the city fathers than they may be for a governor or a President. The mayor of a big city is constantly operating in the eye of a political hurricane.

To a greater extent than a President or governor, the mayor must deal with special types of interest groups. One of these is the "problem" group—people who share a concern over a particular city problem even though they are members of many different economic interests. Parent-teacher associations, welfare organizations such as the United Fund, and groups concerned with special problems such as beautifying the city or developing a park are examples of such problem groups. These interests, supported by the local newspapers, can mobilize a good deal of pressure on city hall, but once the problem is solved or somehow disappears, the group may disappear with it. Another special type of interest in the big city is good government and reform groups. Some of these have enjoyed such strong leadership and wide support that they have operated virtually as political parties, as in Cincinnati. But in most big cities the reform groups are simply one more pressure on city hall, and they are often divided among themselves. Their activities range all the way from trying to improve the whole metropolitan area, as in the case of the Greater Philadelphia Movement, to simply collecting facts and figures, as in the case of the Cleveland Bureau of Governmental Research and the Milwaukee Citizens' Research Bureau.

Another interest group of particular importance in the big city is the association or union of city employees. Police, firemen, street cleaners, teachers, and most other such employees are organized into unions, many of which are affiliated with the national AFL-CIO. Professional employees band together in voluntary associations of their own. While all these groups are more or less concerned about the city as a whole, they are mainly interested in specific matters such as their pay, working conditions, job security, and the like. Although in most states strikes by city employees working in vital services are prohibited by law, enforcement of the law is difficult. Teachers, welfare workers, sanitation employees, and city bus drivers have used the strike, or threat of strike, to force cities to increase wages and provide better benefits.

[20]For an excellent description of the "stakes and prizes" of one city's politics, see Wallace S. Sayre and Herbert Kaufman, *Governing New York City* (Russell Sage, 1960), Chap. 2.

Ordinarily, group interests in metropolis pursue their activities much like pressure groups anywhere; they put out propaganda, hold meetings, write letters to the mayor and council, and mount all the pressure they can. Occasionally, a local interest group provides a striking example of the effective mobilization of influence. In 1957, for example, the Esso Standard Oil Company, which employed 1,800 people in Bayonne, New Jersey, and paid a fourth of the city's taxes, threatened to leave if local officials went ahead with a planned tax increase. The oil company, in combination with other businesses, channeled its efforts through citizens' and research organizations. Contending that the city's civil service was overstaffed, the businessmen asked for budget cuts as the price of their staying in the city. The five city commissioners and the school board complied by cutting the pay of city laborers, effecting economics in textbooks and athletic programs, and reducing various city services. Esso then announced that it would continue its modernization plan.[21]

The effectiveness of metropolitan group interests turns not only on their own size, unity, and leadership, but also on the kind of government they are dealing with. The politics and government in most of our big cities, as in the states and the nation as a whole, are pluralistic, so that group interests must deal with many centers of power and decision. "Whether a city has a loose and many-centered politics or a powerful organization or political leader dominating the scene," Lockard says, "there is always bargaining between interests, bargaining between interests and leaders in government, bargaining between interests and the bureaucracy. Bargaining yes, but the patterns of bargaining vary with different kinds of political systems. In a city with focused leadership bargaining goes on in an atmosphere of deference to the power potential of the leadership. Direct negotiations with the leader or his deputies become common for all interests, and while other negotiations of course continue to be carried on, the fact that there is a central source of power conditions the manner and consequences of interest group demands. In a multi-centered pattern of politics a more free-for-all kind of bargaining is common."

The interest configuration of central city is in many ways similar to that of the national electorate now that this is an urban nation. However, within the city the electorate is biased in favor of the foreign-born, Negroes, Puerto Ricans, and blue-collar workers. In national elections these groups support the Democratic party, and these partisan affiliations hold for local politics. "Labor unions, the NAACP and the Urban League, the Sons of Garibaldi and Kosciusko, and others, including (not least) the professionals of the Democratic party," writes Greer, "are the corporate actors that contend for patronage, power, profit, and the control of the policy in the central city." But as Greer points out, to gain control of central city the politicians must also appeal to the "outer wards," populated by the middle classes with interests much like those of suburbia. Thus, politics of central city "represent most of urban America—but in a biased fashion."[22]

[21]Duane Lockard, *The Politics of State and Local Government* (Macmillan, 1963), pp. 257, 258.
[22]Greer, *The Emerging City, op. cit.*, pp. 148–149.

Who puts together these political configurations? The big city "machine."

At the turn of the century the boss was the typical ruler of many of our larger cities, and some of our smaller ones. After touring the United States, Lincoln Steffens, the famous muckraker, reported: "St. Louis exemplified boodle; Minneapolis, police graft; Pittsburgh, a political and industrial machine; and Philadelphia, general civic corruption."[23] Why were the big American cities boss-ridden? Many reasons were advanced: lack of public interest and the refusal of leading citizens to take part in public affairs; the influx of immigrants who found that the ward leaders and precinct men were their friends and that politics offered the main means of climbing the economic and social ladder; faulty structural organization of the city, leading to such weak government that some political leader had to take charge; and finally—a favorite argument of Steffens and his fellow reformers—business interests that stood behind the bosses and used them to secure favorable franchises and contracts and protection from regulation.

Few strong, citywide political machines exist today. But one that does, in Chicago, illuminates the methods of the past as well as the way that America's second largest city, until recently, at least, has conducted its political affairs. A study of the city's politics reported that in a formal sense, as noted above, Chicago was run by a city council consisting of 50 aldermen and by the mayor, who was its presiding officer. Actually it was run by the mayor and half a dozen of the most powerful Democratic aldermen. These "Big Boys," as they were called, controlled the rest of the aldermen by granting or denying them good committee assignments, appropriations for their wards, and other important political favors. One of the "Big Boys" was chairman of the Council's Finance Committee and hence was able to control appropriations, even to the extent of having city services reduced in some ward if its aldermen refused to "play ball."[24]

Behind this concentration of governmental power was a disciplined party. An alderman had to work closely with the party leader in his ward; often he himself was the leader. Not only was he the elected representative of the local party members; "in fact he was commonly the 'boss' of the ward; the party organization in the ward 'belonged' to him. He decided who would run on the party's ticket within the ward, he appointed and dismissed precinct captains at will, and he dispensed patronage." Sometimes aldermen rebelled against the city machine; often they formed factional alliances or geographical blocs. But rarely could an alderman fight the machine successfully. "The leaders of the Central (Party) Committee could bring him into line by withholding patronage or discharging public employees from his ward, by denying him financial support from the party's general coffers at election time, or by allowing an investigation of graft and corruption to take place in his

---

[23]Lincoln Steffens, *The Shame of the Cities* (Peter Smith: republished 1948; original edition 1904), p. 16.

[24]The description of the Chicago machine, including the quotations, is from Meyerson and Banfield, *op. cit.*, pp. 66–67.

ward." The central committee could even destroy a whole ward organization, but it usually preferred not to use such disruptive measures.

The key man in the organization was the precinct captain. A typical captain, who had spent nineteen years in precinct work, described this work as follows:

> I try to establish a relationship of personal obligation with my people. . . . I spend two or three evenings a week all year round visiting people, playing cards, talking, and helping them with their problems. . . . I know 90 per cent of my people by their names. Actually I consider myself a social worker for my precinct. I help my people get relief and driveway permits. I help them on unfair parking fines and property assessments. The last is most effective in my neighborhood. The only return I ask is they register and vote. . . . I never take leaflets or conduct rallies in my precinct. After all, this is a question of personal friendship between me and my neighbors.[25]

THE DECLINE OF THE BOSS?

There has been a steady decline in the number and power of citywide party bosses since the turn of the century. This decline is due in small part to a steady drumbeat of criticism and opposition by reform groups. It is due mainly to more basic causes: the shrinking of patronage as more and more city jobs came under civil service; the decrease in immigration; stricter supervision of the expenditure of funds by the state and national governments; a more affluent society, making city dwellers less dependent on the machine; and above all, the rise of the welfare state, which supplies social security, unemployment insurance, medical assistance, and relief checks, as compared to the Christmas basket, the half-ton of coal, or the outing up the river that the organization provided free in the old days. The change should not be overdrawn. Ward bosses still dispense some of the old kind of aid, and their services are especially needed to help less educated people to get around big-city regulations, such as parking restrictions. And there are some basic forces at work supporting the machines. The exodus to the suburbs is leaving the central city more and more in the hands of the less well-off: Puerto Ricans, blacks, Southern whites, who are being "restricted" to the central city and who need and can profit from the help of a political machine.[26]

If there is no political machine in a city, what takes its place? To some extent the personal organizations of mayors or other powerful city officials. Big-city politics abhors political vacuums — somebody must organize and govern. Mayors like Robert Wagner of New York built their own "machines" that could often defeat the old type of boss, as the case study of the New York mayor will suggest. But more often the machine has been succeeded by a much less centralized system. Political influence may shift to the hands of a number of powerful and perhaps competing office holders — a few councilmen or aldermen, perhaps, or the chairman of the school committee or the head of the

[25]Quoted by Fay Calkins, *The CIO and the Democratic Party* (Univ. of Chicago Press, 1952), pp. 67–68.

[26]James Q. Wilson, "Politics and Reform in American Cities," Ivan Hinderaker (ed.), *American Government Annual 1962–1963* (Holt, 1962), p. 38.

finance board or some other commission that controls the budget; or into the hands of state and federal officials from the metropolitan area, such as a United States senator, a congressman who may head an important committee in Washington, a state senator; or even into the hands of nonoffice holders such as a newspaper publisher, a union head, leaders of ethnic groups, or some combination of these and others.

While the pattern of power varies widely from city to city, the problem remains the central one that has occupied us throughout this book. Granted that bossism is an evil, how much better off is a metropolis that has no central system of power, that may be politically nothing more than a collection of warring fiefdoms or tongs. One virtue of the boss was that occasionally he *did* want to do things for the people and at least he had the power to operate through the various units of government. A divided government might be much more honest but less effective, especially in shaping and administering programs for the lower-income groups and for the long-run improvement of the city. To be sure, a strong mayor can sometimes gather the reins into his own hands, as we noted, but the difficulty with this is that his power is likely to last only as long as he holds office. LaGuardia was a strong mayor who built a personal organization in New York, as did Joseph Clark more recently, in Philadelphia, but neither man converted his personal organization into a lasting *party* organization.[27]

Party weakness is intensified by the fact that most metropolitan areas tend to favor one party, usually the Democrats. The absence of real two-party politics has somewhat the same effect on the city as it does on the South: one party is so big, and wins with such little effort, that it fails to keep in fighting trim, grows fat and sluggish, and sometimes disintegrates into factions. The minority party is too weak to have much hope of success, fails to provide a strong opposition or meaningful alternatives, and often plays a very negative type of politics. Just as the South is still responding to the politics of the Civil War, so the big cities are still dominated by the Depression, the New Deal action in the 1930s, and the sympathy and help they get from the urban-oriented Democrats. If metropolis existed by itself, as an island, its two major parties might come into balance, one governing effectively and one opposing strongly. But the one-party system discourages "party government" of this sort and raises the kind of basic questions about the nature of political organization that we discussed in Chapters 12 and 20.

A TYPOLOGY OF BIG-CITY POLITICS

Because there are so many cities and because only recently have scholars systematically studied these governmental and political units, it is difficult to generalize about city political patterns. What is true in Chicago may or may not be an accurate picture of Cleveland or Detroit or Los Angeles. One scholar, James Q. Wilson, has drawn on well-supported studies to make a tentative classification of big-city political systems.

1 *Machine politics*—Chicago and Albany, as examples. Wilson suggests that small districts or wards based on fairly homogeneous ethnic or religious

[27]James Reichley, *The Art of Government* (Fund for the Republic, 1959).

neighborhoods, a large number of elective offices, and a polyglot, lower-income population in the city as a whole tend to promote organization or machine politics.

2 *Factional alliances or coalition of groups*—Kansas City, Boston, Cleveland, St. Louis, Jersey City, and Cincinnati. In these cities, although a single party, usually the Democrats, wins the elections, officeholders are not bound together by the party and are responsive to separate and independent political constituencies. One may represent a political club, another the civil servants, another the business community, another the Negro wards, and so on.

3 *Nonpolitical elite systems* where control over public policy is in the hands of newspaper publishers, businessmen, labor leaders, lawyers, bankers, and so on—Houston, Los Angeles, Detroit. In these cities the party organizations have little to say in selecting candidates, and elective officials remain aloof from party affairs. As Wilson points out, in these "nonpartisan cities"—and here we refer to actual conduct, not to the formal charter provisions—city policies tend to favor the business community.[28]

Elements of all three types—machine, factional, nonpartisan elite—are, of course, found in all large cities. The differences are a matter of emphasis; it is also true that, in time, the political situation in cities changes. In almost all cities there are also to be found a variety of reform groups, some working outside the established dominant party, some working within.

THE RISE (AND DECLINE?) OF THE AMATEUR

Old-style machine politics based on serving the needs of the masses of newly arrived immigrants and financed by undisguised graft is on the way out. New-style politics, where political leaders must mediate among interests no longer satisfied merely with a few jobs on the city payroll, are developing. And one facet of this new politics is the emergence of a new type, the amateur politico.

Adlai Stevenson's candidacy for President brought many of these amateurs into politics. Joining the Volunteers for Stevenson, working at doorbell ringing, and fund raising, whetted the taste for politics of these enthusiastic housewives, young public relations men, lawyers, and college professors; they then organized political clubs to stay in politics. In 1968 the presidential nominating campaign of Senator Eugene McCarthy also attracted a large number of amateurs from similar backgrounds.

The amateurs consist largely of highly educated, white, middle-class groups, cosmopolitan in outlook, under forty-five years of age, uncommonly articulate, acting in the tradition of an earlier generation of New Deal liberals and Progressive reformers. Concerned about the failure of the party professionals to emphasize issues—the professionals simply want to be *elected*—and the inability of party leaders to develop programmatic platforms, the new amateurs formed their own clubs, where they discussed civil rights,

[28]Drawn from James Q. Wilson, in Hinderaker (ed.), *op. cit.*, pp. 37–55.

urban renewal, civil defense, education, nuclear policy. But these are not merely debating societies; they are also action-oriented, working at the grass roots to secure the nomination of candidates, often against the leadership of the regular Democratic organizations.

Whether the reform clubs will have any staying power and will set the style for modern city politics remains to be seen. Party professionals and some political scientists are highly skeptical. They accuse these amateurs of being more interested in talk than in action, of preferring to be right rather than effective, of intolerance toward those who do not share their own goals. The "pros" also contend that the amateurs are unrealistic in hoping to develop programmatic, cohesive, disciplined parties of liberal orientation within our large cities.

In fact, it is argued, the amateurs are making it difficult for the party professionals to secure the goals the amateurs profess. The great mass of the urban population does not share these goals, but if the amateurs force elected officers to hew to the "new party line" and fail to recognize the essential compromises necessary to gain power, they will merely throw political control of the city into the hands of those who will exploit mass sentiments for illiberal purposes. In time, endorsement of candidates by a club may become a political liability; the clubs will wither away. As James Q. Wilson, a critic of the clubs, writes: "The debate over issues becomes, in a strict sense, a spurious debate, because it is not a responsible discussion of real policy alternatives but a device for generating incentives for party activities."[29]

Others take a different view of the clubs. They view them as a means of activating citizens who otherwise find local politics of no significance. The clubs can discuss and shape party policies of much more relevance to metropolitan than to traditional "bread-and-butter" issues—preserving and enhancing attractive neighborhoods, improving city planning, increasing the city's concern for artistic and cultural activity. Moreover, even if the amateurs have a rather narrow perspective about politics and are at the moment much too rigid and unwilling to accept political realities, they will learn in time to function as a regular party unit.

Can the Mayor Lead?—A Case Study

The mayor is the most important and the most visible political figure in the big city. Like the President, he is supposed to enunciate the city's goals, play the leading role in getting them accepted by the people and adopted by the city government, and to carry them out. But, like the President, he is hemmed in on many sides. Since big cities vary widely in their politics, and mayors in their powers, we might explore the problem of mayoral leadership by taking one example—the mayor of New York. His job has been considered as second only to the President's in complexity and man-

[29]James Q. Wilson, *The Amateur Democrat: Club Politics in Three Cities—New York, Chicago, Los Angeles* (Univ. of Chicago Press, 1962), is a careful analysis of the goals, composition, and role of the clubs.

ageability, for not only is New York the nation's biggest city and one of the financial, cultural, intellectual, and trading centers of the world, but it in effect sprawls over parts of three states and hence continually faces problems of city-state-federal relationship.[30]

THE ADMINISTRATIVE CHIEF?

The mayor of New York City is supposed to be the administrative boss of the city government, and in many respects he is. For one thing, he appoints the heads of virtually all departments, such as police or fire; members of city boards and commissions, such as the parole commission; and city magistrates and justices. Unlike the President and most governors, he does not share his appointive power with legislative bodies. The mayor's authority to remove subordinates, despite numerous restrictions, is also fairly sweeping. In short, in his power to "hire and fire," the mayor of New York is truly "the chief executive officer of the city," as the city charter says.

In other respects, however, the mayor finds himself restricted as administrative chief. This is especially the case in the most crucial administrative area, budget and finance. "The Mayor is not the chief fiscal officer of the city; the Comptroller has greater financial powers than does the Mayor," according to Sayre and Kaufman. "Nor does the Mayor have budget powers comparable to those of the President or the Governor; he has the formal power to direct the preparation of 'the executive budget' step in the expense budget process, together with a minor role in the preparation of the capital budget, but the modification, and thus the larger elements of the administration of both budgets, belong to the Board of Estimate,"[31] an agency described below. The mayor's power to reorganize agencies and departments is much more limited than the President's. He has an immediate staff of about sixty, but this is hardly adequate for coordinating the huge and varied departments that actually run the city.

The mayor also exercises limited administrative power over the city's myriad independent authorities. Some of the heads of authorities have won such wide recognition that they are politically effective in their own right. Most notable of these by far was Robert Moses, who might well have been labeled "Mr. Authority." His jobs suggest the variety of special agencies as well as the versatility of this brilliant, aggressive, and often flammable man. Moses was chairman of the Triborough Bridge and Tunnel Authority, commissioner of the Park Department, a member of the City Planning Commission, chairman of the Mayor's Committee on Slum Clearance, a member of the New York City Youth Board, president of the Jones Beach State Parkway Authority, besides holding many other jobs. In all these positions he attracted friends (and enemies) within the city's administration as well as from the public. Clearly, in dealing with Moses the mayor was dealing with an independent leader who had his own "constituency" separate from the mayor's—and relations between the two were often exacerbated

[30]This case study, except where otherwise noted, is taken wholly from Sayre and Kaufman, *op. cit.*
[31]*Ibid.*, p. 670.

because Moses was a lifelong Republican, and most New York mayors are Democrats.[32]

The case of Robert Moses reminds us of a central fact of administration that we noted in Chapter 18: administrators are *people*, and they have their own interests, attitudes and loyalties that may conflict with those of the mayor. This is certainly the case in New York City. Even the great "line" departments such as police and fire, theoretically under the direct control of the mayor, are not composed simply of men drilled and marshaled and deployed from the top. The heads of the departments are experienced men who have worked their way up from the ranks, who have strong loyalties and obligations to their colleagues and subordinates, who may entertain professional and perhaps political ambitions of their own, and who enjoy direct access to newspaper editors, party leaders, interest groups, and professional associations inside and outside New York. The rank-and-file employees—the firemen, policemen, sanitation men, city hospital workers, guards at the city jails—have their unions or associations, desires for higher pay and shorter hours, all kinds of internal specializations (for example, corner cops and city detectives), jealousies, and mutual defense coalitions against excessive interference from the top.

So we must forget the notion of the mayor as a real administrative "boss." He has great administrative resources, but he must ever ride herd on a collection of many thousands of human beings with crosscutting interests and attitudes. And his powers are even more limited in his other roles.

LEGISLATIVE LEADER?

The mayor of New York, like any other mayor, finds his policy-making power splintered and fragmented from the moment he takes office, for he is working within a federal system of government that divides power among the national, state, and local governments, and among many officials at each level. Practically speaking, the mayor must often coordinate or at least clear his major policies with the President, the Governor of New York, one or two United States senators from the state, several members of Congress, a host of state legislators from the city, and numerous other officials, such as the state attorney general, members of Congress from the adjoining states of New Jersey and Connecticut, and perhaps a Cabinet member or two. Within the city government his legislative power is further fragmented.

To be sure, the mayor has formal responsibility for shaping and presenting the legislative program. Indeed, formally or informally, he presents it several times—to the council, to the Governor and the state Legislature, and to such other officials or bodies as affect his program or policies. But the formal lawmaking power is vested in the city council, consisting of twenty-five councilmen elected by the same districts that choose state senators, and the president of the council, who is elected on a citywide basis. While on

[32]For a provocative and colorful account of an independent authority *not* run by Mr. Moses, see Edward T. Chase, "How to Rescue New York from Its Port Authority," *Harper's Magazine* (June 1960), pp. 67–74, which describes the political context of the authority and the political controversy surrounding it.

paper the council would appear to be virtually a little Congress, actually it has played a rather passive role, allowing the mayor or other officials to take the leadership. The council fails to exercise the historic weapon of legislative bodies against executives—the appropriating power. It is almost monopolized by one party—the Democratic—and hence lacks vigorous internal controversy in decision-making. Weakness begets weakness; as the council has failed to exercise its power over policy, it has failed to attract strong men who might convert it into a stronger agency.

The main fiscal control of the city is exercised neither by the mayor nor by the council, but by the board of estimate. This is a rather curious institution for a city that prides itself on modernity and streamlining in so many other areas of life. Composed of eight members with varying numbers of votes (four each for the mayor, the comptroller, and the president of the council; two each for the five borough presidents), the board of estimate is not as such elected directly by the people; its members are all elected to other positions. Still, it has the dominant role in three vital areas—the enactment of local laws, the expense budget, and the capital budget. Unlike the council, it does not obligingly follow the mayor's lead; usually it prefers to fight him. Sayre and Kaufman sum up its role as follows: "It has the most generous grant of formal powers of all the city's governmental institutions; its eight members are the most influential elected officials in the city government; it has developed a mode of operation which maximizes both its formal and informal powers; the relationships of its members with the party leaders are close and usually stable; it has high prestige with the other participants (in the city's political process), particularly with those to whom it provides a public forum; and its institutional life, especially its informal processes, is surrounded by a helpful amount of mystery."[33] Like Congress on the national level, the board is the main countervailing power to the mayor.

A city councilman need not automatically be hostile to the mayor. The extent to which a mayor can induce cooperation from a councilman or a member of the board of estimate turns mainly on the extent to which the mayor can shape the political pressures working on the legislator in city hall and in the latter's district. In city hall the mayor can deal in jobs, favors, personal recognition, and the other usual currency of practical politics. But this may not be enough, just as it is often not enough in Washington, for the usual currency of political influence is limited, and rival political leaders have some of that currency too. Ultimately, the mayor's power depends on the extent to which he can mobilize support for himself and his program that can be converted to support for, or threats to, the councilman or member of the board of estimate. And this balance in turn depends on political organization.

PARTY LEADER?

The mayor of New York is the most powerful single party leader in the city. Still, he must share his party power with a host of other officials and with party leaders. There is no single citywide political party organization; thus Democrats are organized on the basis of county committees from the

[33]Sayre and Kaufman, *op. cit.*, p. 626.

five boroughs, which in turn oversee vast hierarchies of precinct, ward, and assembly district organizations. The mayor deals not with a unified party organization but with five county leaders, who may be members of the United States Congress, borough presidents (who have power in the board of estimate), or traditional party bosses who hold no major office, as was the case with Carmine De Sapio, but who exert considerable influence over their county organization through the "machine." Sometimes the mayor benefits from the absence of citywide unity, for he can follow the tactic of "dividing and conquering" the county leaders, but the party divisions may handicap him in pushing through a new program. The Republicans are somewhat more unified than the Democrats, but they lack the numbers to play competitive politics.

What a strong mayor must do is to build his own personal organization inside and outside the regular political party. This is a formidable task. He has considerable patronage, but jobs are not enough to build a political machine, for the mayor faces the classic problem, in handing out a job, of creating "nine enemies and one ingrate." Unlike the President, who can lean on the national party committee as well as his numerous personal staff, the mayor has few political aides. He must deal with party committeemen who may be much more interested in working for other candidates and officeholders than for him. Usually the mayor finds that his personal organization is not enough by itself; he must supplement it by bargaining for allies among the other office holders and heads of personal organizations.

Usually the mayor and the party leaders work hand in glove; the mayor "recognizes" the party leaders through patronage, and the party leaders help the mayor by insuring his renomination and helping his reelection. Occasionally the mayor and the machine have a falling-out. A dramatic and suggestive example of this was the struggle in 1961 between Mayor Robert F. Wagner and Carmine De Sapio, head of the regular Democrats in Manhattan, better known as Tammany. In earlier decades the mayor was often subordinated to the machine; Tammany chiefs like the nefarious William Tweed and the more genteel Charles Murphy dictated key Democratic nominations. In 1961, making full use of the personal machine that he had built up in his seven years in office, Wagner trounced De Sapio and the Tammany candidate in a bitter battle for renomination.

Wagner then announced that he would take the leadership in reorganizing and strengthening the Democratic party. Following his election he proposed new party rules under which the party would open its ranks to all interested citizens, improve its procedures for internal democracy, and play a more prominent role in drawing up and publicizing party programs. He forced some of the old party leaders out of their positions and even took on Representative Charles Buckley, long the Democratic boss of the Bronx. Yet there were many who were skeptical of any lasting improvement in the city's Democratic party.

LEADER OR HEAD BARGAINER?

The evidence is quite clear: the mayor of New York is severely restricted, no matter how great his ability. Most of the time he must piece together a coalition out of various politicians and fragments of influence. He is less the leader who draws his sword, points out the direction, and rallies his battalions, than the horse trader who talks and swaps and persuades and compromises. His governmental role tends to be more defensive than affirmative. He is continually involved in the process of building administrative, legislative, or party coalitions, and the price of such coalitions is usually weakened programs and policies. Usually he is in the middle of the political marketplace; little of importance can be done without his consent. But he finds effective action along a wide front, or even long-range planning, to be very difficult.

Whether or not one approves of this situation depends on one's views of the organization of political power. Some would contend that more progress comes of loose political arrangements like those of New York City than of a highly centralized and disciplined system. Lasting progress, they contend, comes here and there, two feet forward and one foot back, and is not dependent on direction from the top. Others hold that a city as sprawling and disorganized as New York needs a strong mayor and effective city government to lead it, and that too much bargaining and compromising will make impossible "mastery of the metropolis" by the city people as a whole.

Many New Yorkers favor moderate changes to give the mayor more leadership. They see several alternative routes. One is to change the city charter so that the mayor would have more authority and responsibility; significant charter changes in this direction have now gone through. Others believe that the mayor cannot really become a leader unless the party is reorganized; they believe in the kind of party discipline discussed in Chapter 12. Others feel that metropolitan self-government is hopeless, that the people of the giant city cannot really govern themselves, and that the job should be taken over by other governments. The election of John V. Lindsay as mayor of New York on a Republican-Liberal party ticket in 1965 offered a dramatic test of whether a reform-minded mayor could meet the challenge of metropolis. In his tenure Mayor Lindsay has already experienced some of the most critical aspects of municipal administration. He has faced strikes by city employees, rebuffs in seeking financial help in Albany and Washington, the ever-present danger of civil disorder and racial conflict, and week after week of school closures as the teachers' union clashed with leaders of independent school districts.

Can We Master Metropolis?

Most of this chapter would seem to answer with a big "yes" our theme question: Have the people of metropolis lost the power to govern themselves? The division between central city and suburbia, divided executive authority, fragmented legislative power, splintered and noncompetitive political parties, the absence of strong central government for the whole metropolitan region, the need for the mayor and other city leaders to bargain with a host of national, state, and local officials—all this would seem to suggest that the people as a whole cannot master the shapeless giants that have arisen in a score of areas across the nation.

Who governs, then? In the last century reformers were afraid of boss domination. But in modern metropolis, the mayor of the central city, as we have seen, lacks authority over all the agencies within the city alone, not counting the hundreds of other units of government. Political machines do not run central city, let alone the whole metropolis. The "interests" do not control metropolis, nor does a "business elite," nor any other kind of "they." Who, in fact, governs metropolis? Nobody? Or perhaps everybody? For the "issue is not the manipulation of the citizenry by a small elite, but rather the inability of elites to create the conditions required for making decisions."[34]

What needs to be done? Some argue that piecemeal, patchwork measures are inadequate. Metropolis is a single community, they argue; it needs a single government, a government adequate to handle the total problems of the metropolitan community. How to achieve this integration?

One suggestion is to make the county the major unit of government. Where the county covers the entire metropolitian region, real integration could be achieved. Moreover, three-fourths of all metropolitan areas are entirely within a single county.

Various kinds of city-county consolidations, or city-county separations, or transfer of all functions to the county, have been suggested for metropolitan regions, but they have not been widely adopted. In Virginia, however, all cities over 10,000 are separated from the county, and St. Louis, Baltimore, and several other cities have withdrawn from their counties. This move avoids duplication of effort within the central city, but it sometimes leaves the people in the county out in the cold. It can also further complicate relations between the central city and the suburbs. More successful in solving some metropolitan problems has been the transfer by cities of selected functions to the county. For example, Erie County in New York has taken over health, hospital, library, and welfare services formerly handled by the cities within the county. Los Angeles County has assumed many functions for the hundreds of communities in that sprawling metropolitan region. And in 1963 Davidson County, which includes Nashville, assumed responsibility for almost all local government functions, an example of a most ambitious attempt to govern a metropolis through the machinery of country government.

Another proposal to deal with problems of metropolitan regions is to permit the central city to *annex* all the surrounding units of government. Whatever the speculative merits of such a program, however, it is often politically impossible for the central city to take over after suburbs have established their own governments.

Finally, many reformers advocate a "federated metropolitan" governmental system. They would allow each local city to retain its identity and remain in charge of certain functions, but would create a central metropolitan government to deal with area-wide functions. Although several major cities in other nations—Toronto, London, Berlin—have moved to a federal-city plan, the only metropolitan region in the United States to try it is Dade County (Miami),

[34]Morris Janowitz (ed.), *Community Political Systems* (Free Press, 1961), Preface.

Florida. (New York has some aspects of a federal city, since each borough has its own president who administers such functions as street repairs and building maintenance, but the central government of all five boroughs really governs the entire city.)

THE FEDERAL-CITY PLAN: A CASE STUDY

Until 1957 the Miami metropolitan area was typical of many big cities — the population had mushroomed, but its political structure remained unchanged. Miami, the core city, was surrounded by twenty-five separate municipalities and wide expanses of unincorporated areas. Duplication of governmental services between Dade County and the several municipalities in some areas and inadequate service in others were all complicated by an inequitable tax structure. Then in 1956 the first step toward improving the situation was taken when the people of Florida approved a constitutional amendment giving Dade County constitutional home rule. The next year the voters of the entire county adopted a home-rule charter creating a countywide metropolitan government.

The new charter provides for a federated structure. The city of Miami and all the suburban cities retain their own identity and those functions not assigned to "Metro," the county government. Metro has jurisdiction over such activities as fire and police protection, slum clearance, major transportation facilities, planning, water, and sewerage systems; is governed by a board of commissioners elected on a countywide basis who in turn select a county manager.[35]

During the first year of its operation under the new charter, Metro was sued 150 times by opponents of metropolitan federation, but it has won all the decisive legal battles. In 1959 a move to amend the charter to reduce the powers of Metro and return many functions to the separate cities was soundly defeated.[36] It is too soon to make any definitive statements on the workings of this "bold experiment," but success of the federated-city program in Dade County may serve to encourage other areas to take the plunge. Some kind of federal-city system offers real advantages, especially for the twenty-two large metropolitan regions that are cut into pieces by state boundaries.[37]

THE POLITICS OF METROPOLITAN REORGANIZATION

In the last several decades, hundreds of surveys have been made of metropolitan governments, and today in almost every metropolitan area there is at least one official or semiofficial body working to rationalize governmental structure.[38] Yet, as one distinguished student of the subject has pointed out,

[35]See *The Government of Metropolitan Miami* (Public Administration Service, 1955).

[36]O. W. Campbell, "Progress Report on Metropolitan Miami," *Public Management* (April 1959), pp. 85–89. See also Reinhold Wolff, *Three Years of Progress; 1957–1960: A Report to the People, Miami Metro* (Univ. of Miami Bureau of Business & Economic Research).

[37]Daniel R. Grant, "The Government of Interstate Metropolitan Areas," *The Western Political Quarterly* (March 1955), pp. 90–107.

[38]Edward C. Banfield, "The Politics of Metropolitan Area Organization," *Midwest Journal of Political Science* (May 1957), p. 77. Most of the materials in this section are taken from this illuminating article.

"So far we have accomplished little more than a world's record for words used in proportion to cures effected."[39] Why has progress been so slow? To answer this question, we must review the politics of metropolitan reorganization.

In most metropolitan regions, to combine city and suburbs would be to shift political power to the suburbs. In most Northern centers it would give Republicans control of city affairs. In other cases it would enable Democrats to threaten the present Republican one-party systems in the suburbs. In any event, it would upset current political arrangements in a fashion difficult to predict exactly. Under these circumstances, neither Democratic rulers of the central cities nor Republicans in control of the suburbs show much enthusiasm for metropolitan government schemes.

However, "It would be a mistake to suppose that the conflict lies altogether or even mainly between the two party organizations or among the professional politicians who have a stake in them. The party differences are important . . . , but they reflect deeper and still more important differences. Metropolitan government would mean the transfer of power over the central cities from the largely lower-class Negro and Catholic elements who live in them to the largely middle-class white and Protestant elements who live in the suburbs."[40]

Apart from these political, social, racial, and economic differences which make metropolitan reorganization difficult, the fact is that most of the residents of metropolis are not sufficiently dissatisfied with the present governmental structure to favor major structural changes. Of course they want better services, but these they hope to achieve by negotiation and other special devices. There is no rebellion against the existing governmental structure.[41] Moreover, it may not be the best arrangement but it does work, after a fashion.

COOPERATION IN PRACTICE

Drastic alteration of the constitutional structure of metropolis seems unlikely, at least in the near future. Yet metropolis is not likely to disappear. "Rather than dwindle or collapse," writes Kevin Lynch, "it is more likely to become the normal human habitat."[42] And through patchwork, piecemeal, pragmatic arrangements, the services the public wants and is willing to pay for are being provided.

The special metropolitan districts, such as the Cook County Sanitary District and the Metropolitan (Park) District Commission for Boston, have been mentioned. Central cities and county governments are providing services for the satellite cities. For example, thirty-three suburban communities buy water from Chicago. Los Angeles County supplies a variety of services to the smaller cities within the county on a contractual basis.[43]

[39]T. H. Reed, "Hope for 'Suburbanitis,' " *National Municipal Review* (December 1950), p. 542.

[40]Banfield, *op. cit.*, p. 87.

[41]Robert C. Wood and V. V. Almendinger, *1400 Governments: The Political Economy of the New York Metropolitan Region* (Harvard Univ. Press, 1961), Chap. 3.

[42]Kevin Lynch, "The Pattern of the Metropolis," in Lloyd Rodwin (ed.), *The Future Metropolis* (Braziller, 1961), p. 105.

[43]Vincent Ostrom, Charles M. Tiebout, and Robert Warren, "The Organization of Government in Metropolitan Areas: A Theoretical Inquiry," *The American Political Science Review* (December 1961), p. 831.

The fiscal problems of metropolis are being met by two devices: Central cities are beginning to levy taxes on the earnings of all who work in the city no matter where they live; more important, the federal government by grants to states and cities is providing a larger portion of the funds to deal with city planning, improvement of mass transportation facilities, urban redevelopment, hospital building and operations, and welfare.

It is not a flawless or tidy system; problems are plentiful; but as Webb S. Fiser writes, "Our difficulties derive from more than fragmentation of governmental units. . . . Creating a more desirable urban environment depends upon a combination of private and governmental action."[44] A relation between government and private interests that expedites rather than suffocates action for the general welfare is a crucial need of metropolis.

A SOLUTION OUTSIDE METROPOLIS?

Many political scientists, for reasons discussed in this chapter, hold that the solution is beyond the capacity of metropolis itself. They have advanced a variety of proposals. Some favor strong controls by the federal government; and as a start they feel the setting up of the new Department of Housing and Urban Development in Washington will assist and aid megalopolis. Others believe that the job must be done by the states, which hold the fundamental constitutional power. Still others advocate bold new proposals to establish *regional* governments that would rule over huge regions embracing a host of metropolitan areas—most notably the long stretch of congested urban areas from south of Washington, D.C., to north of Boston. Big-city mayors have made it clear that in their judgment the urban crisis is acute, and that we must rearrange our priorities and allocate billions of dollars for massive aid—a Marshall Plan—to our large cities, for the cities themselves and their officials lack the resources and political jurisdiction necessary to attack the basic causes of urban pathology.

All these solutions have their opponents. Court-stimulated redistricting of congressional districts is beginning to alter the rural bias of Congress, as reflected in congressional enactment in 1965 of President Johnson's proposal for a Department of Housing and Urban Development, but Congress still does not show an overly sympathetic response to the pleas from big-city mayors. State control? Reapportionment has made some state legislatures more responsive to urban needs, but states are unable easily to deal with the problem of giant cities that stretch over state lines. New regional governments? A fascinating idea, but one that is probably beyond the reach of constitutional power and the capacity of the American people to engineer.

The issue, however, goes deeper than this—it goes back to the very heart of the question of government by the people. Can popular government best be effected through a strong executive leader of the Lindsay or Daley type —a man who wins or builds a strong position of political power and then tries to pull the divided city government together behind his program? Many scholars would answer yes; they contend that progress can come only as a result of strong, central controls at the top, even though they want the leader

[44]Webb S. Fiser, *Mastery of the Metropolis* (Prentice-Hall, 1962), p. 5.

to be willing to make concessions to particular groups and local areas. Not only can executive leadership bring about the drastic changes that may be necessary in metropolis, according to this point of view, but only through a strong mayor and a powerful organization (personal or party) can metropolitan government work for the benefit of the great majority of the people, especially low-income groups who are not fully represented in city councils or other legislative assemblies of metropolis. Just as the nation has needed Jacksons and Lincolns and Roosevelts, so the cities need popular, even charismatic, leadership.

Others disagree. Progress in the giant city, they hold, comes from piecemeal efforts, from lengthy bargaining among a multitude of leaders of all types, from community action, from exerting pressure here and there, from hammering out agreements or "treaties" among diverse groups. They grant that government by negotiation is often slow, and that makeshift arrangements sometimes result, but, given the nature of megalopolis, it is impossible to do better. Instead of grandiose schemes of regional government and city planning and disruptive urban renewal of whole blocks, they would like to see more moderate and prudent efforts. In the process they hope to hold on to some of the values of metropolis today—the unique streets, some of the older buildings, the little houses and apartment buildings that they prefer to the great hunks of concrete and glass and steel so beloved, they feel, by the city planners and reformers.

There are many positions in between these extremes. But perhaps the extremes pose once again our crucial problem of central political control versus pluralism that runs throughout this volume.

State and Local Government
in Action

33 Late in August, 1968, while the Democrats were holding their national convention and nominating Hubert Humphrey for President, Chicago erupted in violence. For a moment the nation saw a microcosm of all its problems—a nation that had been unable to end violence abroad or in its cities; a city "boss" who had been a great builder of public works but seemed to have no realization of the attitudes and needs of young militants; a city police force that was physically well prepared for the occasion but tended to overreact and demonstrate its basic incapacity; and—four miles to the south—a convention adopting a strong platform on the urban crisis even while facing, throughout the country, failures of both parties and of all levels of government to cope with questions about the quality of American life.

The roads we ride on, the schools we attend, the teachers we listen to, the electric light bills we pay, the purity of the water we drink, the safety of the elevators we ride in, when and whom we can marry—all these matters and many others are affected by what state and local officials do. Merely to list the activities of state and local officials would require a large book, and make a dull one.

And yet all these activities are part and parcel of the exciting business of politics. Listen to the debates in the state legislature, attend the meetings of the city council, watch the candidates on the stump, and you come face to face with the problems of law enforcement, education, welfare, highways. Should the city build another school? Where? Will the voters approve a bond issue to construct a new hospital? Should the state superintendent of schools be given authority to establish minimum standards for teachers? Are the gambling syndicates being protected by the police? What can be done about the traffic jam on Main Street? Everybody—mayors, legislators, judges, ward bosses, civic commissions, unions, chambers of commerce—participates in the process of determining what the officials shall do, which ones of them shall do it, and how they shall do it.

It is obviously impossible to explore each activity of our states, cities, counties, school districts, townships, and so on. But we can at least review a few of the highlights.

"The Public Safety Is a Public Trust"

THE CITY POLICE

In spite of the fact that one of the government's oldest and most accepted functions is to maintain law and order, until recently the role of the police officer has generally been ignored. "The policeman is the most important American . . . ," wrote former Attorney General Ramsey Clark. "He works in a highly flammable environment. A spark can cause an explosion. He must maintain order without provocation which will cause combustion."[1] The police officer has a vital role in preserving (or restricting) civil liberties, he determines who shall be arrested, he gives daily reality to the protections of our constitution, and, as recent events in our large cities make clear, he has much to do with preventing or causing riots. Yet this man on whom we depend for so much, the only man in our civil society whom we arm with deadly weapons, receives an annual median salary of only $5,843.

Although we have over 40,000 separate law enforcement agencies, composed of more than 368,000 men and women, our annual statistics show more than 2,780,000 felonies, 52,500 traffic deaths, and property damages estimated in the hundreds of millions of dollars, with each of these statistics rising rapidly every year.

One of the most acute problems of our domestic society is the tension between the police officer and our ethnic minorities, especially the black community congregated in the ghettos or our large cities. The President's Commission on Law Enforcement and Administration of Justice and the President's National Advisory Commission on Civil Disorders have amply documented Judge Edwards' observation, "Most Negro citizens do not believe that we have equal law enforcement in any city in this country. Whether the stated belief is well founded or not is at least partly beside the point. The existence of the belief is damaging enough."[2] Black Americans see the policeman as the enforcer of the white man's law; there are too many documented studies of prejudice on the part of white police officers and too many examples of undignified, if not brutal, police treatment of blacks to ignore.

As a result of the mutual hostility between police and the communities

[1]Foreword to George Edwards, *The Police on the Urban Frontier* (Institute of Human Relations Press, The American Jewish Committee, 1968), p. viii. See also Arthur Niederhoffer, *Behind the Shield: The Police in Urban Society* (Doubleday, 1967).
[2]Edwards, *op. cit.*, p. 28.

they are commissioned to protect, there has developed a wall of isolation that blocks understanding. Police officers tend to work together and to play together, not only in isolation from the black community but from the entire community. Too often police have been recruited from sections of the city that exhibit the strongest anti-Negro attitudes, are trained by hardened law officers who reinforce such attitudes, and are first assigned to areas of high crime rate, where Negroes are the prime suspects.

It would be as faulty of us to overgeneralize about the behavior of the police officer as it is of some police to overgeneralize about those who live within slum areas. The issue is the conditions that produce both kinds of behavior; there is too much at stake to content oneself with charges of police brutality. Consider the problems a policeman faces daily:

> A car runs out of gas in the middle of a crowded expressway. A child is impaled on a steel reinforcing rod in a building excavation. . . . A bookie is using a complex electronic device, called a "cheese box," to conceal his telephone number. . . . A motorist has to be removed from the tangled wreckage of a head-on collision. Black nationalists are holding an angry street meeting in the heat of the summer, in the city's most crowded neighborhood. . . .[3]

In performing their tasks, officers often discover that the public is indifferent, even hostile. Little wonder that they are sometimes impatient with reformers and academics who talk about the complexities of the cycle of poverty or the refinements of the law governing search and seizure, for it is the police officer and not the scholar who at 2 A.M. must go into an area of high crime rate in the middle of a hostile population to search a dark alley in response to a call about a prowler.

Finally, in the late 1960s, for a variety of reasons—fear of riots, concern about organized crime, desire to provide better and more understanding protection for the rights of persons, black and white—there was initiated a sustained drive to improve the quality of police services and to understand better the problems the police face.[4] In 1968, as we have seen, Congress through the Crime Control Act made federal funds available to help states and cities improve police standards and training. In the larger cities steps have been taken to professionalize the police, improve their training, provide them with an opportunity better to understand the complexities of social problems, and to establish community relations programs in order to open communications between the police and the communities they serve. This was a beginning, but much remains to be done.

THE STATE POLICE

The famous Texas Rangers began as a small border patrol when they were organized back in 1835. In 1865 Massachusetts appointed a few state constables to suppress commercialized vice, a job the local police had been unwilling or unable to do. But it was not until 1905, with the organization of the Pennsylvania State Constabulary, that a real state police system came

---

[3]*Ibid.*, p. 4.

[4]See *The Challenge of Crime in a Free Society*, a report by the President's Commission on Law Enforcement and Administration of Justice (U.S. Government Printing Office, 1967).

A GENERAL VIEW OF THE CRIMINAL JUSTICE SYSTEM

This chart seeks to present a simple yet comprehensive view of the movement of cases through the criminal justice system. Procedures in individual jurisdictions may vary from the pattern shown here. The differing weights of line indicate the relative volumes of cases disposed of at various points in the system, but this is only suggestive since no nationwide data of this sort exists.

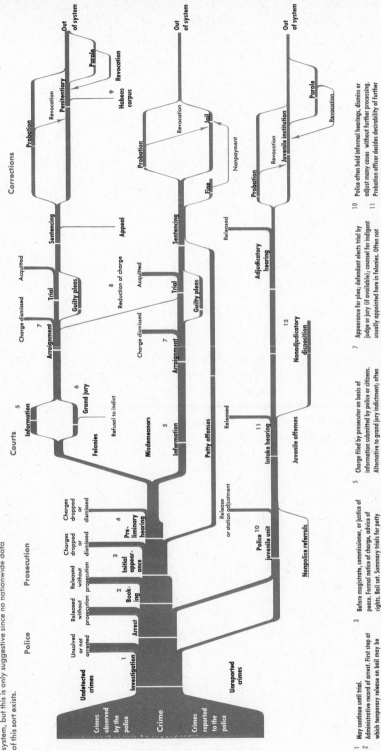

1 May continue until trial.
2 Administrative record of arrest. First step at which temporary release on bail may be available.
3 Before magistrate, commissioner, or justice of peace. Formal notice of charge, advice of rights. Bail set. Summary trials for petty offenses usually conducted here without further processing.
4 Preliminary testing of evidence against defendant. Charge may be reduced. No separate preliminary hearing for misdemeanors in some systems.

5 Charge filed by prosecutor on basis of information submitted by police or citizens. Alternative to grand jury indictment; often used in felonies, almost always in misdemeanors.
6 Reviews whether government evidence sufficient to justify trial. Some states have no grand jury system; others seldom use it.

7 Appearance for plea; defendant elects trial by judge or jury (if available); counsel for indigent usually appointed here in felonies. Often not at all in other cases.
8 Charge may be reduced at any time prior to trial in return for plea of guilty or for other reasons.
9 Challenge on constitutional grounds to legality of detention. May be sought at any point in process.

10 Police often hold informal hearings, dismiss or adjust many cases without further processing.
11 Probation officer decides desirability of further court action.
12 Welfare agency, social services, counselling, medical care, etc., for cases where adjudicatory handling not needed.

The Challenge of Crime in a Free Society, a report by the President's Commission on Law Enforcement and Administration of Justice (U.S. Government Printing Office, 1967), pp. 8–9.

into being. This system was so successful that other states followed suit. At present only a third of the state police organizations utilize full law enforcement authority; twelve states restrict their police to highway traffic regulations and to the prevention of crime committed on the highways.

State police became a part of our law enforcement system for a variety of reasons. The breakdown of rural law enforcement, the advent of the automobile (demanding greater protection on the highways and a mobile force for apprehending fleeing criminals), the need of the governor to have a police force at his disposal so that he may execute his responsibilities, and the need for a trained force to maintain order during strikes, fires, floods, and other emergencies—all this led to the creation of state police.

Not too many years ago the state police were used to break up strikes; organized labor promptly dubbed them the "American Cossacks." Although state police have not served as strikebreakers for some time, the old wariness of them among some labor leaders still lingers on. To be sure that state police will not be used for strikebreaking, many states stipulate by law that the state police cannot be moved into a strike situation until actual violence has taken place, and even then only with the specific authorization of the governor.

The establishment of the Pennsylvania State Constabulary marked a sharp break with traditional police methods. The force was a mounted and uniformed body organized on a military basis, with centralized control vested in a superintendent who, in turn, was directly responsible to the governor. This pattern has been followed by other states—New York, Michigan, and Massachusetts, to mention a few. These forces are now among the most respected police organizations in the world. They are equipped with automobiles and airplanes, modern systems of communication, and elaborate crime-detection laboratories. They maintain high standards of conduct and rigid discipline.

The military organization of these forces shields them from temptation, builds morale, and helps develop an *esprit de corps* that contrasts sharply with the cynical attitude of some urban police. Because of their mobility and professional character, the state police are less accessible to "the smaller fry of urban and rural politics." Moreover, they maintain rigorous systems of recruitment and training, and exercise close supervision over personnel.

Other state police systems have developed out of the rather modest highway patrols of a few decades ago. During the 1930s traffic control in rural regions became an acute problem, and state after state organized highway patrols, usually as subordinate units of the highway or motor vehicle department. Gradually their authority was extended from enforcing the rules of the road to exercising the usual powers of the police. Generally speaking, the state police that have grown out of highway patrols do not have such effective training programs or such high standards as those that have been modeled after the Pennsylvania force. Even when they have statewide jurisdiction, most state police may not go into cities unless ordered by the governor or requested by local officials. Local police resent such intrusion as a reflection on their own abilities—which it often is.

State police are not the only law enforcement agencies maintained by state governments. Liquor and law enforcement officials, fish and game wardens, fire wardens, independent detective bureaus, special motor-vehicle-law police, and other specialized forces abound. This dispersion of functions has been widely criticized, but each department insists that it needs its own law enforcement agency to handle its own special problems. So far, fragmentation rather than centralization of state law enforcement agencies has been the order of the day.

Government as Educator

Centuries ago, Plato and Aristotle insisted that education was the vital task of government. Indeed, to them government itself was essentially an educational institution. Thomas Jefferson was convinced that an educated citizenry was essential to democratic government. But only during the last century has the idea become generally accepted that government should provide tax-supported schools.

Many groups opposed "free" education. They argued that it would lead to social unrest, undermine the family, give government control over the minds of the young, require an extensive bureaucracy, and result in a fatal mixture of education and politics. Was it fair, they asked, to tax people who could afford to educate their own children in private schools in order to educate others?

Today, however, compulsory education through the public primary and secondary schools is an established fact (although parents may, if they choose, send their children to approved private schools). A strong movement has developed to extend public education downward to kindergarten and nursery school, upward through college and adult education, outward to cover more subjects, and deeper to cover them better. Today a third of all expenditures of state and local government is for education—more than for any other function—with the richer states spending a larger proportion of their budgets on schools than do the poorer states.[5]

THE GOVERNANCE OF EDUCATION

The city, the county, the township, or the school district has the chief responsibility for providing public elementary and secondary education. The school district, of which there are nearly 30,000, is the basic unit. In each district the voters elect a board of education. This board levies taxes, in most cases independently of the city or county. It appoints a superintendent of schools and other supervisory personnel, hires the teachers, and runs the schools from grade one through twelve.

Each state has a superintendent of public instruction or a commissioner of education. In a little over half of the states he is popularly elected, and in almost all states he shares some authority with a state board of education.

[5]Richard E. Dawson and James A. Robinson, "Inter-Party Competition, Economic Variables, and Welfare Policies in the American States," *Journal of Politics* (May 1963), pp. 286–289; Robert H. Salisbury, "State Politics and Education," in H. Jacob & K. N. Vines (eds.) *Politics in the American States* (Little, Brown, 1964), p. 353.

Although the immediate operation of the public schools is the responsibility of the local community, state officers have important supervisory powers. For one thing, they distribute financial assistance. State money is passed out according to many formulas, but the trend is toward the equalization of resources among the local communities, with the states giving more money to the poorer communities.

State officials often certify competence of teachers and set minimum salaries. They are sometimes consulted by local authorities, who wish to build new school buildings, to ensure that the buildings meet the minimum specifications set by the state. Some state officials have the authority (subject to the state constitution and laws) to prescribe the course of study and to determine what must be taught and what may not be taught. Generally in the South·and West, state authorities determine which books will be used in the schools.

Until recently most local school districts provided only for elementary and secondary education, although some of the larger cities also supported junior colleges and universities. Since the end of World War II there has been a major expansion of community colleges, as the junior colleges are now coming to be called, so that students may attend the first two years of college or, after high school, secure technical education within their own community. The trend is to create separate college districts with their own boards to operate and raise funds for the local community college, although in some areas the college is part of the regular public school system.

There is also a land-grant university in each state stemming from the 1862 Morrill Act. In addition, most states support an array of other universities and colleges. Public colleges and universities are governed by boards, in some states appointed by the governor, in some elected by the voters. Moreover, state after state has created a superboard or coordinating board with varying degrees of control over public institutions of higher education. The superboard reviews budgets and programs before they are presented to the state legislature and governor. Today, with over half of the seven million college students attending publicly supported institutions, questions of control and support of higher education are becoming increasingly significant features of the political life of our states.

Since the days of the Northwest Ordinance the national government has encouraged the states to provide educational opportunities. As briefly noted in Chapter 25, the national government's educational role has been growing rapidly in recent years: it makes substantial yearly grants for facilities, equipment, scholarships, loans, research, and for general aid. The Secretary of Health, Education, and Welfare and the Commissioner of Education who heads the Office of Education have become national leaders in the formulation of educational programs.

Despite widespread public education, private schools still flourish, especially at the college and university level (although many private universities receive significant federal assistance), but also at the primary and secondary level, where 15 percent of all students attend private, usually church-operated, schools. Several decades ago the Supreme Court made it clear that although a state may compel parents to send their children to school, parents have a right to have their children educated in private schools if they so prefer. The state, in turn, has authority to supervise private schools to ensure that they maintain certain standards. The diversity of our schools, the variety of administrative patterns, and their dependence on numerous sources of funds and support, help prevent control of our educational system by any single party, class, religion, or section.

EDUCATIONAL ISSUES

The number and popularity of books, articles, and newspaper stories bearing titles such as "Education at the Crossroads," "Our Educational Crisis," "Ghettos and Their Schools," and so on, attest to the many educational problems confronting the nation. School buildings are overcrowded, trained teachers are difficult to find, and some school districts are too small, while others are too large.

Education and educational policy have long been part of the democratic policy-making process. What shall be taught and who shall teach are hotly contested issues. Schools are favorite targets for all groups eager to have students taught the "right" things. Patriotic groups are concerned about "un-American" doctrines sneaking into textbooks or classrooms. Labor leaders are concerned that students receive the right impression about labor and its role in society. Business leaders want the children to see the free-enterprise system in the correct light. Spokesmen for minorities desire that textbooks and other materials accurately reflect the history and contributions of the groups they represent. Educators, however, try to keep the schools as isolated as possible from the demands of outside groups. They argue that censors, whether public or private, must be prevented from determining what the pupils should be taught.[6]

Some believe that the professional educators have too much authority over the schools. Others assert that only the professionals are qualified to determine teacher competence and school curriculum. Controversies also rage over the desirability and constitutionality of religious education, the virtues of progressive education, and the ways and techniques of teaching reading, spelling, and mathematics.

Today, however, the most acute problems and intense issues stem from the fact that "The vast majority of inner-city schools are rigidly segregated" and are underfinanced and undersupported to meet their overwhelming educational responsibilities.[7] As the Office of Education's report, *Equality of Educational Opportunity*," generally known as the Coleman Report, states, "Segregation has operated to reduce the quality of education provided in schools serving disadvantaged Negro neighborhoods."[8] Although in recent years state aid has increased at a rate proportionately greater for city than for suburban schools, states continue to contribute more per pupil to subur-

[6]See in general Thomas H. Eliot, "Toward an Understanding of Public School Politics," *The American Political Science Review* (December 1959), pp. 1032–1051.

[7]The National Advisory Commission on Civil Disorders, *Report* (U.S. Government Printing Office, 1968) p. 237.

[8]Department of Health, Education, and Welfare, *Equality of Educational Opportunity* (U.S. Government Printing Office, 1966), p. 20.

ban schools than to inner-city schools. Federal help, while concentrated on the inner-city schools, has not been of a scale to remove the disparity: the children who need the most and the best education are getting the least and the worst.

In many cities intense battles have occurred over the question of busing students from one neighborhood to another in order to achieve a better racial balance. Proponents of busing point to the Coleman Report findings that transferring minority pupils from homes without much educational strength to a school attended by children from families with a more advantaged background increases the achievement of the children from the depressed areas without impairing the accomplishment of others. Opponents of busing stress the desirability of maintaining neighborhood schools.

Whether or not students from ghettos are bused to schools of the more prosperous neighborhoods, most children living in the inner city will attend schools within the inner city. For such students the Kerner Commission recommends: "A comprehensive approach designed to reconstruct the ghetto child's social and intellectual environment, compensate for disadvantages already suffered and provide necessary tools for development of essential literacy skills. This approach will entail adoption of new and costly educational policies and practices beginning with early childhood and continuing through elementary and secondary schools."[9] Clearly, the question of how much should be spent and for what kinds of programs to provide the poor and depressed with the education they need to become self-sufficient will be one of the continuing and controversial issues of the 1970s.

EDUCATION AND GOVERNMENTS

Whatever the precise arrangements to govern and to operate our schools and colleges, with a few exceptions elaborate attempts have been made to isolate from the rest of government school boards, boards of trustees, boards of regents, and other agencies that govern educational institutions. This isolation is strongly supported by well-organized groups such as the Parent-Teacher Associations, the National Educational Association, the American Association of University Professors, and other university and educational groups; it is also supported by the general conviction of most citizens that education must be kept out of the hands of the politicans. The special responsibility of educational institutions to search for the truth and to teach without fear of retribution makes it undesirable to govern educational institutions by the same kind of arrangements that are appropriate for institutions that are primarly concerned with power.

Education and educational policies, however, are of such concern to so many people, and there are so many different ideas about how the schools should be run, that education cannot be completely divorced from the political system. Educational policies, like those in agriculture, law enforcement, or any other field, are determined in our government by the political processes available to a free people.

[9]Commission on Civil Disorders, *op. cit.*, p. 244.

Social Services

The poor, the blind, the sick, the handicapped, the homeless children, the old, the unskilled—what happens to these people? How are they taken care of? Prior to the Great Depression these deprived people had to rely for the most part on privately operated social agencies, charities, and haphazard systems of public relief. Today all our governments carry on extensive welfare programs. Public welfare has neither replaced private social services and charity nor lessened their importance. But it is no longer merely a depression activity; despite the prosperity of the postwar period, state public assistance payments grew from $1.1 billion in 1946 to over $5 billion in the late 1960s.

Not too many years ago poverty was considered a disgrace, mental illness a moral weakness, and public assistance a waste. The state maintained a few institutions for the poor, often run by political appointees untrained and unconcerned about those under their care. But most of the needy were taken care of at the county poorhouse, where unfortunates of all kinds were crowded together—the infirm, the handicapped, drug addicts, alcoholics, the mentally ill, and those who simply had no place to live. Each county or township supplemented this *indoor* relief by a program of outdoor relief—that is, those unable to make their own living but who did not require institutional care were given money or goods. This basic public welfare arrangement was little improvement over the Elizabethan Poor Law of 1601.

When the American economy went down the toboggan slide in the early 1930s, local communities were overwhelmed with persons in distress. Their facilities overtaxed, they sent out a call for help. State governments, in turn, were unable to handle the problem. The national government entered the field on a large-scale basis, first with emergency doles and work relief programs, then with a long-range program of federally encouraged and supported social security and insurance. During the next thirty years, these New Deal–inaugurated welfare programs were expanded, but the basic approach was unaltered. Now, as we have seen in Chapter 25, it has become clear in the past decade that despite the nation's wealth and sustained prosperity, existing programs fail to meet the needs of the large number of Americans caught within a poverty complex—people in minority groups, often with rural backgrounds, possessing skills no longer needed because of automation and technological changes, hidden from sight, segregated geographically and culturally. The existing programs fail to develop self-sustaining and economically self-reliant people.

As a result, the national government has started a war against poverty to supplement existing welfare programs. The emphasis is on education and training, with special attention to the needs of the young within the culture of poverty. The war against poverty through a variety of programs hopes to provide people with assistance in developing attitudes and skills to permit them to break away from the cycle of poverty.

Every state now has some kind of department of welfare. This agency either directly administers welfare programs or, as in most states, supervises local officials, usually of the county, who actually administer the programs. The county welfare departments, which in order to qualify for federal help must also be manned by persons selected on the basis of merit, determine which individuals are entitled to assistance (appeals can be taken to state welfare departments), and deal with clients. Within the limits of the federal program, each state is free to determine the size and details of its own welfare assistance.

General relief is almost entirely an activity of state and local government. General noninstitutionalized relief is essentially a county responsibility. Some townships do this job, but most welfare workers believe that townships are too small to support adequate welfare departments. A properly administered department requires trained caseworkers to process applications, make home visits, and help rehabilitate individuals and maintain families.

The county poorhouse is still the basic institution for general institutionalized relief. Although outdoor relief programs have slightly reduced the need for institutions, there are still many who have no home of their own, who are ill, and who require care. Today county poorhouses, often renamed county homes, are more attractive places than they used to be. The physical plant is being improved, children have special homes, and the mentally ill are being placed in state hospitals. Some counties have joined together to maintain one adequate home rather than two or more inadequate ones for the chronically ill and persons of advanced age.[10]

Most states have assumed the responsibility for insane, feebleminded, or emotionally disturbed people, and have set up reformatories for juvenile delinquents. In some states, institutions for youthful lawbreakers have been placed under the jurisdiction of welfare rather than penal authorities. Although many of these institutions are still run by incompetents, in recent years there has been encouraging progress toward trained staffs. Since distressed persons are unlikely to be politically organized, their needs are apt to be overlooked unless other citizens champion their cause.

PUBLIC HEALTH

During a summer in the 1780s, the streets of Philadelphia were deserted. All who could afford to do so had taken their families and fled to the country. Every night the mournful sounds of the death cart echoed through the empty city. Philadelphia had been stricken by a yellow-fever epidemic. Only when cool weather returned did the disease abate and the city resume normal activity. There were few families that did not lose a child, father, or mother.

Yellow fever, dysentery, malaria, and other dread scourges have periodically swept American cities. These catastrophes were one of the hazards of

[10]See Clyde F. Snider, "The Fading Almshouse," *National Municipal Review* (February 1956), pp. 60–65.

city life. As late as 1878–1879 yellow fever struck the South; Memphis was nearly depopulated. Drastic action seemed imperative. State after state, following the lead of Louisiana and Massachusetts, established a board of health. Spurred by the medical discoveries of Pasteur and other scientists, authorities inaugurated programs for the protection of public health. Open sewers were covered and other hygienic measures instituted. In fact, it was not until contagious diseases had been brought under control that the large city became a relatively safe place to live.

Today thousands of local governments—counties, cities, townships, special health districts—have some kind of public health program. Every state has an agency, usually called a department of health, that administers the state program and supervises local officials. The United States Public Health Service conducts research, assists state and local authorities, and administers federal grants to encourage them to expand their programs.

Despite the supposed virtues of country life and health hazards of city living, today it is the city people who have the best health records and the best public health protection. The bigger cities have a full-time health officer assisted by a well-staffed department. The counties have lagged behind; about 40 million Americans, most of them living in rural places, are protected either by a part-time agency or none at all. The American Public Health Association, the professional society of public health workers, recommends that counties and cities join to establish health districts with at least 50,000 people, the number they believe necessary to maintain a minimum program. Again, the trend toward larger units is apparent.

Prevention and control of communicable disease is still one of the major public health activities. Doctors are required to report cases of communicable disease; health department officials then investigate to discover the source of the infection, isolate the afflicted persons, and take whatever action seems to be called for. Most state health departments give doctors free vaccine and serum, and many local departments give free vaccinations to those who cannot afford to go to private physicians—in some cases this service is open to everyone. Since the public shows more enthusiasm for specific programs than for general disease control, some diseases have come in for special attention. The national government provides financial assistance for such activities as tuberculosis and venereal disease control. Mobile x-ray units take free x-rays of school children, teachers, and the general public. Public health officials protect water supplies and see to it that waste and sewage are safely disposed of. They protect the community's food supply by inspecting hotels, restaurants, and food markets. Many cities now require domestic servants, waiters, cooks, and other food-handlers to secure a special license and undergo a health-department medical examination. Meat and milk are of special concern. Meat products shipped in interstate and foreign commerce are inspected by federal officials, and under the Wholesome Meat Act of 1967 states must establish safeguards that meet federal standards; in those that fail to do so, federal inspectors assume this responsibility.

State and local public health officials work in a wide variety of fields. Health and educational officials make periodic inspections among school children and carry on educational programs. They keep vital statistics —recording births and deaths—and maintain laboratories for diagnosis of disease and for testing the purity of certain products. They enforce quarantine regulations. One of the most important of these persons is the public health nurse. Traveling throughout the community, she advises on prenatal and postnatal care, assists mothers in childbirth and in caring for their children, and in general provides nursing services for the sick.

In 1948 a lethal smog descended on Donora, Pennsylvania. The death of many residents dramatized the menace of air pollution. Since then the smogs of Los Angeles and other industrial areas have become notorious. Industrial waste not only infects the air we breathe but pollutes rivers and streams as well. The internal combustion engines of automobiles have been identified as a chief culprit in polluting the air; Congress, following the lead of California, has imposed standards governing the design of exhaust systems. There is growing concern over the critical levels of air and water pollution, and Congress has responded with federal programs providing funds and minimal standards to encourage state and local action, but a full-scale attack to purify our air and water has yet to be mounted.

Planning the Urban Community

Are our cities good places in which to live and work? Crowded shopping areas, dented fenders, shattered nerves, slums and blighted areas, inadequate parks, impossible traffic patterns—are all these evils and inconveniences necessary?

Many city people have asked these questions. Reorganization, city-manager charters, consolidated cities and counties, and the like—these are fine things, they argue, but the problem may lie deeper. Structural changes in the government are not enough; in addition, we need intelligent planning to avoid the kinds of problems that now confront us. Some have argued that we need a Marshall Plan to allocate billions to make of our cities environments that encourage and enrich rather than discourage and alienate.

For many decades American cities were allowed to grow in a haphazard fashion: industrialists were permitted to erect factories wherever they wished; towering buildings shut off sunlight from the streets below; traffic conditions transformed drivers into malevolent maniacs, pedestrians into traumatized wrecks. Schools were sandwiched in where the land was cheap or where the political organization could make a profit on the sale.

The most common method of assuring orderly growth is zoning— the creation of areas and the limitation on uses to which buildings may be put in each area. A community may be divided into areas for single-family dwellings, two-family dwellings multi-family dwellings, commercial purposes, and light and heavy industry. Other regulations restrict the height of buildings or their area, or require that buildings be located a certain distance apart and a certain distance from the front of the lot.

Zoning attempts to keep garbage dumps from being located next to residential areas, stabilizes property values, and enables the city or county government to coordinate services with land use. A zoning ordinance, however, is no better than its enforcement. This is usually the responsibility of a building inspector who makes sure that a projected building is consistent with building, zoning, fire, and sanitary regulations before he grants a building permit. In most cases, a zoning or planning commission or the city council can amend the zoning ordinances and make exceptions to the regulations. These officials are often under tremendous pressure to grant exceptions; but if they go too far in permitting special cases, the whole purpose of zoning is defeated.

Zoning is, however, only one phase of community planning. Until recently, planners were primarily concerned with streets and buildings. Today, many city planners are concerned with broader matters, and planning covers almost all the activities of people. The basic job of the planners is to collect all the information they can about the city and then prepare long-range plans. Which sections of the cities are growing? Where should new schools be built? Where should main highways be constructed to meet future needs? Will the water supply be adequate ten years hence? Are the parks accessible to all the people?

Obviously, planning must be built upon public support. No plan, however good it looks on paper or pleasing it may be to experts, will be effective unless it reflects the interests and values of the major groups within the community. Effective planning is a product of the political process.

Today many communities are attempting to make order out of the chaos of random growth. Most cities have some kind of planning agency, especially under the stimulus of the present federal requirement that cities applying for redevelopment assistance first develop a master plan. Further federal encouragement was provided by the so-called Model Cities Act (see page 587) in which cities may receive federal help in the rehabilitation of their inner-city areas. The participating cities must submit plans, proof of administrative structures to run the program, and most significantly of all, they must involve the residents of the target areas in the planning process.

As we also noted in Chapter 25, the federal government supports local public housing agencies and urban renewal projects, and has increased the scope of its aid to help persons of lower income find decent housing.

Although housing is only one aspect of improving the urban community, it is a vital part of it. Millions of families are presently crowded into substandard dwellings, and the cost of such slums in terms of damage to the individuals is difficult to calculate. In addition, cities have a direct financial interest in improving urban housing. The costs of education, police and fire protection, and public welfare are considerably higher in slums than in other areas. Slum areas account for 45 percent of the major crimes, 50 percent of all arrests, 55 percent of juvenile delinquency, 50 percent of all diseases, and 35 percent of all fires. In Baltimore each acre of slums produced a $2,500 yearly deficit for the city; in Atlanta it was discovered that 53 percent of all city services went to slum regions that produced only 6 percent of the real estate taxes.[11]

It is a mistake, however, to think that slums exist only in our cities, for as we

[11]Donald Robinson, "Slum Clearance Pays Off," *National Municipal Review* (October 1955), p. 461.

saw in Chapter 25, there are depressed rural regions where slums produce all the pathological types and conditions of human behavior that we sometimes regard as exclusively urban problems.

Government as Builder

State and local governments build highways, public buildings, airports, parks, and recreational facilities. But by far the major program is *building roads*. State and local governments spend more money on roads than on anything else except education and welfare.

Until the advent of the automobile, canals and railroads were the major method of long-distance travel. Local roads, such as they were, were built and repaired under the direction of city, township, and county officials. Able-bodied male citizens were required either to put in a certain number of days working on the public roads or to pay taxes for that purpose.

By the 1890s safety brakes and the pneumatic tire had been invented; and in the Gay Nineties, those who could not afford a carriage began to use the bicycle. Bicycle clubs began to urge the building of hard-surfaced roads, but it was not until the 1900s and the Age of the Automobile that road building became a major industry. It is not surprising that the function of road building gradually was transferred from the township to larger units of government—more and more to the state. But counties and townships still have important roadbuilding and maintenance problems; nearly four-fifths of the rural road mileage is under their control. The other one-fifth, which includes almost all the main highways and most of the hard-surfaced roads, is built and maintained by the state.

Ever since 1916 the national government has supported state highway construction, but with the Federal Highway Act of 1956 federal aid substantially increased. States do the planning, estimate the costs, get the construction done, but receive most of the money from the federal treasury. In order to receive federal support, however, states must submit their plans to, and have their work inspected by, the Department of Transportation's Federal Highway Administration. All federally backed highways must meet certain standards governing the engineering of the roadbed, employment conditions for construction workers, and weight and load conditions for trucks using the roads.

Under the Federal Highway Act of 1956, the states are to plan and build a National System of Interstate and Defense Highways by 1974. When completed, the Interstate will consist of 42,500 miles of superhighways linking almost all cities with a population of 50,000 or more. All but 7,000 miles will be at least four lanes, grades are to be no more than a three-foot rise per 100 feet, there will be a limited number of entry roads, and the number of signs, roadside stands, and filling stations on the right-of-way will be regulated. The federal government pays 90 percent of the costs, securing most of the money from user taxes—gasoline, tires, trucks—which are placed in a trust fund designated for that purpose. Funds are distributed among the states according to a formula that gives greater weight to population than has been given in other federal-aid highway programs. No federal money may be used for toll roads, bridges, or tunnels, although these may be part of the Interstate System. In 1959 Congress offered any state a small bonus if it would agree to restrict billboards along interstate highways in accordance with national standards. This "carrot" had little effect, so in 1965 Congress responded to President Johnson's recommendation that it use the "stick" approach. Additional federal funds were made available for landscaping, for removing billboards, and for hiding junkyards. As of 1968, states that fail to control such eyesores are faced with the loss of 10 percent of all federal highway funds. States that do not have a satisfactory program by January 1, 1971, may lose another 10 percent.

Few aspects of government are more enmeshed in patronage politics than highway building. The large sums of money spent and the army of workers needed offer many opportunities for graft and favoritism. In some states the highway department is the chief means by which a political organization maintains its power; contractors are rewarded for their support and loyal party members are given jobs.

An array of potent interest groups supports highway development. Automobile manufacturers, tire-makers, oil companies, motel and restaurant associations, automobile and tourist clubs, trucking associations, and others join hands to protect their common cause. In most states they have been strong enough to persuade legislatures to allocate gasoline taxes, automobile drivers' license fees, trucking fees, and other user-taxes for road purposes. But there is always conflict over how the money should be spent. Farmers want secondary roads developed, but truckers and tourists favor the improvement of main highways. Merchants want the roads to come their way, and their representatives try to get top priority for roads in their districts.

The 1956 highway act, though sending large sums of money to the states, also adds to state officials' troubles. Because present routes are so crowded by commercial establishments, most of these new superhighways will be in new locations. It is too costly to buy out the service stations, eating places, garages, and souvenir shops in order to get the land needed to add three or more lanes with a strip of land down the middle. Congressmen report that they are being asked by constituents to tell them where the new roads will be, so the speculators can buy land for roadside services before the prices go shooting up. State highway departments feel pressures from all sides. Farmers object to having their lands cut in two, especially since they are not able to cross the highways except at the nearest exchange or grade separation, perhaps miles away. Roadside businesses on present routes resist the loss of business. Some cities want the expressways to go through them; others do not.

Regulation at the Grass Roots

Corporations receive their charters from the state. Banks, insurance companies, securities dealers, doctors, lawyers, barbers, and various other businesses and professions are licensed, and their activities are supervised by state officials. State regulations range from stringent measures to protect the public to mere window dressing. Both farmers and workers — especially union members — are regulated as such. But of all the businesses, those that we designate as public utilities are the most closely restricted.

PUBLIC UTILITY REGULATION

It is easier to list than to define public utilities. Water-plants, electric power companies, telephone companies, railroads, and buses are among the main ones. They are distinguished from other businesses by the fact that the government gives them certain special privileges such as the power of eminent domain, the right to use public streets, and protection from competition. In return, public utilities are required to give the public adequate services at reasonable rates. Public utilities are used to render essential services in fields where normally competitive enterprise is not suitable.

In the United States, private enterprise subject to public regulation rather than public ownership has been the more general method of providing these essential services. Nevertheless, more than two-thirds of our cities own their own water works, about 100 operate their own gas utilities, and over 50 — and the number here is steadily increasing — operate their own transit systems. But other services — intercity transportation, railroads, airplanes, telephone, and telegraph — are almost everywhere provided by private enterprise subject to governmental regulation and some subsidization.

Since public utilities are not subject to the same restraints that competition brings to other businesses, the question of how they are regulated is very important. Every state has a utility commission whose responsibility it is to see that utilities operate in the interest of the public they serve. In most states utility commissioners are appointed for overlapping terms by the governor with the consent of the senate, but in some Southern and Western states they are elected by the voters and in two they are chosen by the legislature. The most common number of commissioners is three. The extent of commission regulation varies with the type of utility, but usually utility commissions have the authority to set rates, require uniform systems of accounts, approve issues of securities, pass on reorganization and merger plans, and permit abandonment of services.

Most states have only one utility commission, which combines the duties performed at the national level by the Interstate Commerce Commission, the Federal Communications Commission, the Federal Power Commission, the Civil Aeronautics Board, and (in some states) the Securities and Exchange Commission. Although the state utility commissions have broad legal powers, the general public is normally indifferent to their work and fails to give the commissions the political backing that many observers feel is necessary if they are to protect the public. On the other hand, utility managers are just as convinced that the commissions are doing a good job of regulating them — perhaps too good.

Here are some of the problems of utility regulation:

1   The requirements for a good utility commissioner are staggering; he is supposed to inspect the quality of gas and locomotives, set rates in a variety of fields, assess valuations of complex properties to protect the public interest,

and listen to company grievances. Hence, a commissioner needs the technical knowledge of the accountant, the lawyer, the engineer, the economist, and the political scientist. Not many states provide either the salary or the challenge to attract that kind of man.

2   The judges have complicated the work of the commissions. Until recently, they had a habit of setting aside commission rulings, listening to the arguments all over again, and coming to their own conclusions. In 1898 the Supreme Court decided (in *Smyth* v. *Ames*) that the Constitution required utility commissioners to set rates that would allow a "reasonable return" on "the fair value of the property being used by the utility for the convenience of the public." In the view of James Bonbright, a noted utility specialist, this formula made it impossible for commissioners to develop adequate standards of regulation. Instead, it fastened on them a formula that is fatal to administration, since the controversial task of evaluating a complex utility calls for heavy expenses and time-wasting efforts.[12] Often it took ten years or more to settle a controversy; and by that time conditions had so changed that the settlement was obsolete. Moreover, this form of regulation encourages mediocrity and invites inefficiency on the part of private management. Knowing that their rates are likely to be cut if their profits seem excessive, companies have no incentive to practice economies or to make voluntary rate reductions in the hope of increasing the demand for their services.

3   Most utility commissions are understaffed and underfinanced: in most states annual budgets are less than $400,000; commissions often have fewer than a half dozen professionals—lawyers, engineers, accountants—and, in half of the cases, fewer than fifty persons on the entire commission staff. Yet these men are expected to process the accounts, make rate-valuations, study managerial efficiency, and so on. Since they do not have time to make studies of comparative costs or to gather independent data, they often have to rely on data furnished by outside groups—including the utilities themselves. As two critics of the effectiveness of state regulation have pointed out: "Responsible for protection of the public interest in many and diverse fields, but lacking the staff and funds with which to exercise their responsibility, some commissions are able to do little more than accept and approve what is put before them by the hundreds of companies under their jurisdiction."[13]

All the states make some attempt to isolate the utility commissions from the rest of the executive structure. James Fesler has after close study concluded, however, that freeing a regulatory commission from direct control of the governor may merely drive it into the hands of groups outside the executive department. To call a utility commission independent does not free it from "this necessity of winning friends—so as to influence legislators. The method of winning these friends varies with each state and with different periods in each state's political history."[14] More often than not it includes a "reasonable" attitude toward the groups it is supposed to regulate.

[12]James C. Bonbright, *Public Utilities and the National Power Policies* (Columbia Univ. Press, 1940), pp. 16–17.
[13]Senator Lee Metcalf and Vic Reinemer, *Overcharge* (McKay, 1967), p. 29.
[14]James W. Fesler, *The Independence of State Regulatory Agencies* (Public Administration Service, 1942), p. 61.

Despite the expanded role of the national government, state and local officials still have much to say about working conditions. Here are some of the laws they enforce.

Health and safety legislation. In the opening years of this century dramatic episodes like the fire in a New York plant in which hundreds of garment workers burned to death and the revelations about sweatshop working conditions led to corrective legislation. States now require proper heating, lighting, ventilation, fire escapes, and sanitary facilities in work areas. Machinery must be equipped with safety guards, and standards have been established to cut down occupational diseases. Health, building, and labor inspectors tour industrial plants to ensure compliance with the laws.

Workmen's compensation. The common law made an employer liable for the injury or death of workers resulting from his failure to provide reasonably safe conditions of work. But it also gave him three defenses that made it almost impossible for an employee or his family to win a case. The employer was not liable if he could show that: (1) the employee contributed to the accident by his own negligence, (2) a "fellow-servant" caused the accident, (3) the employee had assumed the risk of injury that flowed from dangers ordinarily associated with the job.

Today all states have abolished these common-law defenses and have created workmen's compensation programs based on the belief that employees should not have to assume the costs of accidents. As with depreciation of machinery and other items, the costs of accidents are borne by the employer and, like other costs, are part of the price the consumer of the product must ultimately pay. No longer does the employee have to sue and prove that his employer was at fault. If he is injured or contracts a disease in the ordinary course of his employment, he is entitled to compensation set by a pre-arranged schedule.

Workmen's compensation programs vary from state to state. Most commonly, a board determines the awards. Employers either take out insurance or furnish proof that they are financially able to make payments when called upon to do so. In most states the insurance is sold by private companies, but about one-fourth of the states operate their own insurance programs. Although all states have workmen's compensation laws, their coverage varies. Agricultural, domestic, and temporary workers are not commonly covered, nor are those who work for a company employing only one or two workers. About half of the working force is presently protected.

Child labor. All states forbid child labor, but laws vary widely in their coverage and in their definition of child labor. A good many states set the minimum age at only fourteen. Higher age requirements are normal for employment in hazardous occupations and during school hours.

Hours and wages. Women and young people are protected by maximum-hours laws in most states. Men are covered only in certain dangerous occupations, or where the public safety is directly involved—operation of buses and trucks, for example. Sunday closing laws, and laws requiring that employees be allowed at least one day of rest in seven, generally apply to men as well as to women and children.

About half the states have minimum-wage laws, but in only four do they apply to men. Since the minimums have not kept up with inflation and rising wages and prices, these laws currently have little effect.

Regulation of unions and collective bargaining. National regulation of collective bargaining applies only to industries in, or affecting, *inter*state commerce. Although national law takes precedence over state enactments, states are left to impose their own regulations in many important areas of labor-management relations. Furthermore, the Labor-Management Reform Act of 1959 authorizes state labor relations boards to take jurisdiction over collective bargaining disputes in industries whose effect on interstate commerce is slight and over which the National Labor Relations Board has not taken jurisdiction.

During the 1930s state laws were patterned after national regulations and were aimed mainly at protecting the workers' right to form unions and engage in collective bargaining. Since World War II, state laws have been more restrictive of union activities. State courts have also shown a trend in postwar years to supervise picketing practices and to ban picketing whose purpose is to force conduct that is illegal or, in the opinion of the judges, contrary to public policy.

Men and Money

34   "Say, did you hear about that civil service reform association kickin' because the tax commissioners want to put their 55 deputies on the exempt list and fire the outfit left to them by Low [previous reform mayor]? That's civil service for you. Just think! Fifty-five Republicans and mugwumps holdin' $3,000 and $4,000 and $5,000 jobs in the tax department when 1,555 good Tammany men are ready and willin' to take their places! It's an outrage! What did the people mean when they voted for Tammany? What is representative government, anyhow? Is it all a fake that this is a government of the people, by the people, and for the people? If it isn't a fake, then why isn't the people's voice obeyed and Tammany men put in all the offices?"

This is our old friend Boss Plunkitt talking. Though we might disagree with the Sage of Tammany Hall, he did have a knack of cutting through to the heart of matters political. Plunkitt was a realist. He was interested in the tax department not merely because of the patronage involved. He also wanted to retain Tammany control over the agency that collected the city's tax dollars and turned them over to the city officials.

To Plunkitt, government was a matter of men and money. So it is today: men must be elected and hired, salaries must be paid and materials purchased. The cost of government depends partly on the ability of the men, and their ability depends in part on how much money they have to spend.

Where Do the Men Come From?

When we talk about the "state," the "city," or the "county," we are simply using shorthand symbols for groups of people. Although we say that the "government" builds the roads or runs the schools, what we really mean is that a group of men whom we call public officials or public employees build the roads or run the schools. About seven million people —engineers, clerks, governors, teachers—work for our state and local governments. In a sense they *are* the state and local governments. How are these people chosen?

A few of them are elected, but only a very few. It is probably a safe guess to say that well over half of the rest are chosen because they know the right person and belong to the right political faction. Many of these persons are qualified, and some are among the best public officials in the nation. Nevertheless, they were chosen for patronage or party reasons, and no systematic attempt was made to choose them on the basis of merit.

STATE AND LOCAL MERIT SYSTEMS

Thirty-four states—including most of the larger and more populous ones—use merit systems in choosing public servants. And in all the states welfare workers who administer grants under the national social security law are selected on the basis of merit, since this is a condition attached to receiving federal money.

The most general method of administering merit systems is by a civil service commission, usually composed of three members appointed by the governor with the consent of the senate, for six-year overlapping terms. The commission prepares and administers examinations, provides "eligible" registers for various jobs from which appointments may be made, establishes job classifications and prepares salary schedules, administers a system of efficiency ratings, makes and gives promotional examinations, administers regulations having to do with sick leaves, vacations, and so on, and serves as a board of appeal for persons who are discharged. Commissions are becoming increasingly active in providing for in-service training and other programs to improve the morale of public servants.

How well do the commissions do their job? Their many critics complain that they are too slow and wrapped up in red tape and cumbersome rules. Eligible lists are not kept up to date; it takes weeks to fill vacancies, they say. But a more serious charge is that civil service commissions have deprived responsible officials of authority over subordinates. There is too much emphasis, it is argued, on "keeping the rascals out" and on insulating public servants from political coercion. As a result, employees enjoy so much job security that administrators cannot get rid of incompetents. Cases have been cited where it took months and several elaborate hearings to dismiss secretaries who could not type or librarians who could not read.

It has been suggested that merit-system commissions be replaced by a director of personnel who in turn would be responsible to the governor, and that administrators be given greater discretion in choosing and disciplining their subordinates. Today some states—for example, Maryland, Connecticut, Virginia, Wisconsin, Minnesota—have what amounts to a single personnel director.

The mere passage of civil service legislation does not automatically create a merit system. Many states have put laws on the books and appointed civil service commissions, but the commissions are nothing more than window dressing; the patronage system still flourishes behind the scenes. Legislatures cripple the commissions by reducing their budgets and limiting their staffs. Payrolls are crowded with temporary or provisional employees. "Friendly" civil service commissioners are appointed. Employees with friends in the legislature get amendments to civil service laws that exempt their jobs from the regulations. In some states, incumbents have been able to get technical amendments that give them what is tantamount to life tenure.

The largest American cities have merit systems, and so do many of the smaller ones. Most cities over 10,000 choose their city employees by some form of merit system; in addition, some state laws require that certain kinds of employees, such as policemen and firemen, be chosen by merit. Relatively few counties maintain a merit system. School teachers are almost always chosen by school boards, but only after they have earned the appropriate certificates.

The salaries of civil servants vary greatly from state to state, city to city, and county to county. Most jobs, however, do not pay as much as do corresponding jobs in business and industry. Many able people are thus discouraged from entering state or local government service. Perhaps even more damaging is the lack of integration in the merit systems. Each state, if it has a merit or career system at all, has its own program, each city has its own career service, and so on. A young man entering the service of a city cannot look forward to advancement through the ranks to other cities or to the state service. If he leaves one service to enter another, he often loses retirement benefits and other privileges.

FALLACIES ABOUT PUBLIC SERVANTS

Three decades ago a Commission of Inquiry on Public Service Personnel published a famous and influential report entitled "Better Government Personnel."[1] The Commission stated: "It is apparent that the weakest link in American democracy, the point at which we fall most conspicuously behind the other self-governing peoples, is in the appointive services where the great bulk of the work of modern government is carried on." The Commission concluded that the failure of our governments to attract able men to public service was rooted in certain "fallacies." What are these fallacies?

1   "The false notion that 'to the victor belong the spoils.' . . ."
2   "The mistaken idea that duties of governmental employees are, as President Jackson said, 'so plain and simple that men of intelligence can readily qualify themselves for their performance.' . . ."

[1]*Better Government Personnel* (McGraw-Hill, 1935).

3   "The false idea that charity begins on the public payroll. Too many people are elected or appointed to office because they need a job or have suffered some misfortune. The cost is poor service and lowered morale of other employees."

4   "The erroneous assumption that 'patronage is the price of democracy,' that the parties which we need for self-government cannot exist without spoils." Perhaps the Commission had in mind George Washington Plunkitt's famous "sillygism." Said Plunkitt: "First, this great and glorious country was built up by political parties; Second, parties can't hold together if their workers don't get offices when they win; Third, if the parties go to pieces, the government they built up must go to pieces, too; Fourth, then there'll be hell to pay. Say, honest, now; can you answer that argument?" But said the Commission, "There are, it is true, large cities, certain states, and other areas where political parties . . . are *at present* sustained by patronage. But in great sections of the United States, and in other democracies of the world, democracy exists, . . . parties thrive, without the spoliation of the appointive administrative services. The truth is, as Theodore Roosevelt once observed, that patronage is the curse of politics."

5   "The idea that 'the best public servant is the worst one.' . . ." The Commission pointed out that groups who have selfish reasons for desiring bad government indulge in the vilification of public employees. "Indiscriminate vilification lessens the morale of all public officials, dissuades capable persons from entering the public service, and discredits the authority of government. . . ."

6   "The erroneous thought that 'tenure is the cure of spoils.' . . ."

7   "The superficial thought that the way to eradicate spoils and favoritism is to begin at the bottom. . . ." In many states and cities the top administrative positions are exempt from the merit system, but these are the very positions where spoilsmen can demoralize the entire service.

8   "The belief in 'home town jobs for home town boys.' . . . Residence qualifications," reports the Commission, "are a benefit only to incompetent applicants and petty politicians."

9   "The notion that 'the public service is always less capable and efficient than private enterprise.'" The Commission came to the conclusion that business and governments are about on a par, "what business gains through the profit motive and elasticity being apparently lost in many instances through hereditary management, labor difficulties, and outside control." Governments as a rule do not take over a job until private agencies have demonstrated their inability or unwillingness to do it themselves.

10   "The erroneous idea that the spoils system, the eleemosynary system and the other corrosive influences can be driven out of the public service through the prohibition of specific abuses. . . . What is clearly required is not negative laws, but the positive militant handling of the problem of personnel with the active backing of the public and the press."[2]

The slow progress that has been made in the years since the commission made its report indicates that these fallacies are still widely entertained. But

---

[2]*Ibid.*, pp. 16–22.

progress has been made. Gradually people are coming to realize that "government is only as good as the men in it." But government needs more than able men. It needs financial resources, too.

Where Does the Money Come From?

State and local governments, like the national government, get most of their money through taxation. But the state and local governments definitely play second fiddle to the national government. In response to the demands of depression, wars, and defense, national taxes have surpassed those collected by states and local communities.[3]

The duplication—or virtually quadruplication—of governments by which the American people regulate their lives complicates the tax picture. Tax policies often conflict with one another. When the national government is reducing taxes to encourage spending by the public, states may be raising taxes. When the national government increases taxes in order to reduce inflation, the states may lower taxes. Indeed, state and local governments normally spend most during periods of inflation and least during periods of deflation. Each level of government pays little attention to the tax policy of the other.

The number of taxing authorities also makes tax-gathering an expensive operation. National officials collect taxes on gasoline, state officials collect taxes on gasoline, and so do some local officials. Each maintains its own tax-gathering organization. Naturally, the taxpayer is confused. He is allowed to deduct certain business expenses from his federal income tax, but not from his state income tax. To complicate matters even more, changes in state laws often affect the amount of federal tax a man must pay. For example, the national government permits taxpayers to deduct amounts paid for state taxes from their federal income tax return; thus, if a state increases its taxes, the national government gets less money.

No matter who collects the taxes, however, all the money comes out of a single national economy. Each of the governments has a different tax base, and each of the taxes hits particular groups; but all government services, just as all our national wealth, rest on the productivity of the American people. And in turn, that productivity is increased by many of the activities of government. With their taxes the people buy police protection, school buildings, highways, and other things that they think desirable. Who pays for these services?

WHO SHALL PAY THE TAXES?

A good tax might be defined as one that the other fellow has to pay; a bad tax, one that I have to pay. Who shall bear the cost of state and local government is decided in the United States by politics. The people of any state are free to collect whatever taxes they wish from whomever (in that state) they

---

[3]H. M. Groves, *Financing Government*, 6th ed. (Holt, 1964).

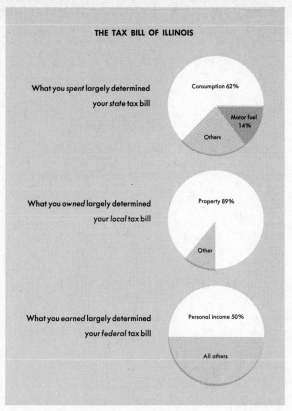

THE TAX BILL OF ILLINOIS

What you *spent* largely determined
your *state* tax bill

Consumption 62%

Motor fuel
14%

Others

What you *owned* largely determined
your *local* tax bill

Property 89%

Other

What you *earned* largely determined
your *federal* tax bill

Personal income 50%

All others

Department of Finance, State of Illinois.

wish, subject only to the restrictions imposed by the people of the United States through the federal Constitution.

The Constitution forbids states to tax exports or imports, or to levy tonnage duties without the consent of Congress; to use their taxing power to interfere with federal operation; to discriminate against interstate commerce, unduly burden it, or directly tax it; or to use their taxing power to deprive persons of equal protection of the law or to deprive them of their property without due process. Constitutional lawyers and judges spend much of their time trying to apply these generalities to concrete situations. Out of hundreds of disputes, they have decided, among other things, that states may not tax tangible property located outside the state but may tax intangible property located outside the state but owned by their own citizens, may collect sales taxes from interstate sales, may collect income taxes from persons and corporations within the state even though the income was earned from interstate business, but may not tax the privilege of engaging in interstate commerce or the unapportioned gross receipts from interstate transaction.

State constitutions also restrict state taxing power. Certain kinds of property are exempt from taxation—property used for educational, charitable, or religious purposes, for example. State constitutions frequently list the taxes that may be collected, forbidding those not mentioned. The amount of tax that may be collected from various sources is also often stipulated.

The ability of people in a city, county, or other local unit to tax themselves is even more restricted. Local governments have no inherent power of taxation. Their officials can levy only those taxes, in the amount, by the procedures, and for the purposes which the state constitution or the state legislature authorizes. What kinds of tax can they collect?

GENERAL PROPERTY TAX

Widely lambasted as "one of the worst taxes known to the civilized world," the *general property tax* is still the chief revenue source for local governments. It used to be the major state tax too, but in most states it is now of minor importance. The tax is cumbersome to administer, conducive to favoritism and inequities, and takes insufficient account of ability to pay.

A hundred years ago, wealth was primarily *real* property—land and buildings—which was relatively easy to value. Assessors could guess the value of

Courtesy *Nation's Business.*

Politically speaking, the property tax raises the loudest squawks.

the property a man owned, and this was a good test of his ability to help pay for government. Today wealth takes on many forms. People own large amounts of *personal* property—both *tangible*, such as furniture, jewels, washing machines, expensive rugs, high-priced paintings, and *intangible*, such as stocks, bonds, money in the bank. A man can concentrate a large amount of wealth, difficult to value and easy to conceal, in a small rented apartment. Real property too has changed. It no longer consists mainly of barns, houses, and land, but of large industrial plants, great retail stores, and office buildings, the value of which is hard to measure.

Furthermore, property ownership is less likely these days to correspond to ability to pay. The old couple with a large house valued at $40,000 may be living on a small allowance provided by their children. They have to pay higher local taxes than does the young couple living in a rented apartment, both of whom work and have sizable incomes. Or compare the case of a man who borrows $20,000 to buy a $25,000 house and who is paying off the mortgage out of his $12,000-a-year-job, and the case of the man who owns a $25,000 house debt-free and has a $12,000-a-year job. They both pay the same tax on their homes.

Although many communities stipulate that the general property tax be imposed on all property, the tax falls in fact on limited amounts of real property.

Over 20 percent of real property in cities is exempt. Intangible personal property is seldom taxed. Some communities place a lower rate on intangible property in order to induce owners to announce their ownership. Tangible personal property, such as watches, rings, and so on, often escapes taxation or is grossly undervalued. In most cities an unwritten understanding develops concerning the kind of property the honest taxpayer should list. The good citizen who attempts to follow the written word of the law is kindly advised by the assessor that it is not necessary.

The general property tax is also inflexible. During times of rising prices, assessed values move up much more slowly than the general price level. Thus when governments need more money, the lagging tax basis fails to provide it. Conversely, when prices fall, valuations do not drop at the same rate. When persons cannot pay taxes, much property is thrown into the market for tax delinquency. During the 1930s for example, the general property tax added to the miseries of many homeowners and to the problems of state and local officials.

The general property tax rate is difficult to compare from community to community. The rate in one city may be only $10 per thousand as compared with another city with a rate of $40 per thousand. But in the second city, valuation may be computed only at a tenth of "real" value. Claims of local politicians that they have kept down the tax rate must be scrutinized.

Despite its weaknesses, the general property tax will probably remain an important source of revenue for local government; it is especially well suited because real property rather than personal property is the chief beneficiary of many local services, such as fire protection. Alternative taxes are few, and they have their own disadvantages. Moreover, some of the bad features of the general property tax can be and are being corrected by more sensible administration, including elimination of duplicate assessments of the same property, upgrading of qualifications for the position of assessor, adoption of more systematic methods of appraising property, better record-keeping systems, and elimination of duplicate collection.

But even with improved tax administration the general property tax is not supplying local units of government with all the money they need to render the services their citizens want. Moreover, states have tended to leave the property tax to local units and thus need other sources for their funds. What other taxes do they collect?

OTHER TAXES

Sales taxes. This depression-born tax is now one of the most important sources of money for many of the states. Today forty-four states impose some kind of general sales tax, normally on retail sales. City sales taxes are less common, though more than one thousand cities collect them. City sales taxes are readily evaded; people simply do their shopping outside the city limits. Sales taxes are unpopular with local merchants, who fear that they drive trade away. Most cities and states try to prevent evasion by imposing a *use tax* payable by persons who purchase items outside the city or state for use within the city or state. Most use taxes are, however, difficult to collect.

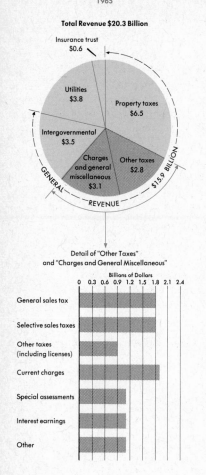

REVENUE OF MUNICIPAL GOVERNMENTS, 1965

Total Revenue $20.3 Billion

Insurance trust $0.6

Utilities $3.8

Property taxes $6.5

Intergovernmental $3.5

Charges and general miscellaneous $3.1

Other taxes $2.8

GENERAL

$15.9 BILLION

REVENUE

Detail of "Other Taxes" and "Charges and General Miscellaneous"

Billions of Dollars
0 0.3 0.6 0.9 1.2 1.5 1.8 2.1 2.4

General sales tax

Selective sales taxes

Other taxes (including licenses)

Current charges

Special assessments

Interest earnings

Other

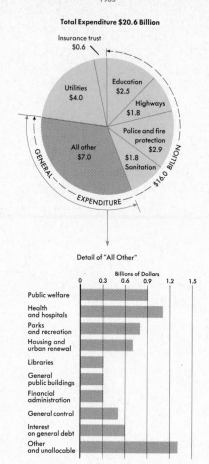

EXPENDITURE OF MUNICIPAL GOVERNMENTS, 1965

Total Expenditure $20.6 Billion

Insurance trust $0.6

Utilities $4.0

Education $2.5

Highways $1.8

Police and fire protection $2.9

All other $7.0

$1.8 Sanitation

GENERAL

$16.0 BILLION

EXPENDITURE

Detail of "All Other"

Billions of Dollars
0 0.3 0.6 0.9 1.2 1.5

Public welfare

Health and hospitals

Parks and recreation

Housing and urban renewal

Libraries

General public buildings

Financial administration

General control

Interest on general debt

Other and unallocable

Municipal Year Book, 1967.

Sales taxes, especially those levied by the state, are relatively easy to administer and produce large amounts of revenue. Despite their regressive nature (that is, their tendency to bear hardest on the lower-income groups), their popularity is increasing. They seem relatively painless, since the consumer puts out the few cents on each item rather than pay a large tax bill at one time. Labor groups and persons with small incomes are generally opposed to the sales tax and would favor wider use of the progressive income tax. They argue that persons with small incomes spend a larger part of their budget for food and clothing than do the wealthy, and sales taxes fall heaviest on those least able to pay. In some states, food has been exempted from the sales tax. In others, passage of sales taxes has been coupled with an income tax.

Income taxes. Personal income taxes are now collected in thirty-six states, but in most the income tax is a less important source of money than the sales tax. Income taxes are generally progressive or graduated—that is, the rate goes up with the size of the income. State income tax rates, however, do not rise as sharply as the federal tax and rarely go over 10 percent.

In most states exemptions are generous enough to exclude large numbers of people. Corporation incomes are frequently taxed at a flat rate. Because of the importance and burden of the federal income tax, there is a strong feeling that states should go slow.

Some cities, following the lead of Philadelphia and Toledo, now collect a payroll tax. Philadelphia imposes a relatively small flat tax on salaries of all persons and net profits of unincorporated businesses and professions. The Toledo tax applies also to corporate profits. Municipal income taxes enable hard-pressed cities to collect money from "daytime" citizens who use city facilities but reside in the suburbs. This tax is especially popular among cities in Ohio and Pennsylvania, but is also being collected by Washington, D.C., New York City, Detroit, Pittsburgh, St. Louis, and Louisville.[4]

Special excise taxes. All states tax gasoline and alcohol, and all but North Carolina tax cigarettes. Since many cities also tax these items, the local, state, and federal levies often double the cost of these "luxury" items to the consumer. Gasoline taxes are sometimes combined with the funds collected from automobile and drivers' licenses and earmarked for highway purposes. Liquor taxes often consist of licenses to manufacture or sell alcoholic beverages and levies on the sales or consumption of the beverage. Some states own their own liquor dispensaries with the profits going to the state treasury. High taxation of liquor is justified on the grounds that it re-

[4]Louis H. Masotti and Jerry E. Kugelman, "The Municipal Income Tax as an Approach to the Urban Fiscal Crisis," *Journal of Urban Law* (Fall 1967), pp. 113–128.

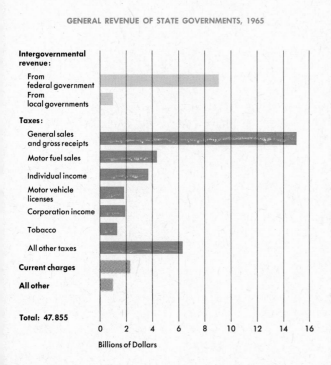

GENERAL REVENUE OF STATE GOVERNMENTS, 1965

Intergovernmental revenue:
From federal government
From local governments
Taxes:
General sales and gross receipts
Motor fuel sales
Individual income
Motor vehicle licenses
Corporation income
Tobacco
All other taxes
Current charges
All other

Total: 47.855

0   2   4   6   8   10   12   14   16
Billions of Dollars

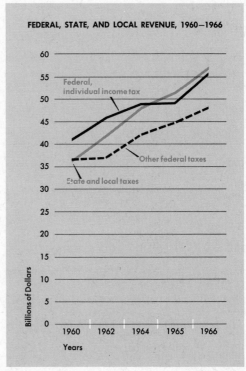

FEDERAL, STATE, AND LOCAL REVENUE, 1960–1966

Federal, individual income tax

Other federal taxes

State and local taxes

Billions of Dollars

1960   1962   1964   1965   1966
Years

Book of the States, 1967–1968.

duces the amount consumed, falls on an item that is not generally considered a necessity of life, and, through licensing, eases the task of law enforcement. If the tax is raised too high, however, liquor tends to be diverted into illegal channels, and tax revenues fall off.

This list does not begin to exhaust the kinds of tax collected by states and their subdivisional governments. Admissions taxes, stock transfer taxes, inheritance taxes, parimutuel taxes, corporate franchise taxes, license fees, and others are quite common. The tax on the privilege of "severing" natural resources such as coal, oil, and timber is important in some states; in Texas, New Mexico, Louisiana, and Oklahoma, for example, the severance tax on oil and natural gas accounts for more than 10 percent of state taxes.

NONTAX REVENUES

In addition to taxation, states derive some revenue from fees and special service charges. In fact, about 10 percent of the money collected by the states and local governments comes from these sources. Fees are charged for building inspection, recording of titles, court costs, licensing of professions, garbage disposal, and other special services. Parking meters have become an important revenue source for many cities. Special assessments against property-owners whose property is benefited by public improvements, such as streets or sewers, are a general practice.

Some cities run business enterprises from which they make money (and sometimes lose it too). Municipally owned waterworks or gas and light companies often contribute to the city treasury. In some cases, utility profits are large enough to make other city taxes unnecessary.

Grants from one level of government to another have become increasingly important during the last several decades. As we have noted, the national government through grants-in-aid allots large sums to the states. The states are giving more and more money to the local governments in the form of state grants to support particular programs or in the form of shared taxes. In the latter case, state officials return to local governments revenues collected from certain taxes, often without specifying the purposes for which the money shall be used.

When all the taxes and fees are added together, state and local governments collect large sums. But often they are still not enough to build the highways, or provide the amount of public assistance to the elderly, or perform the other functions that the voters have insisted upon. What then? Even as you and I do, our governments often have to borrow money.

Borrowing Money

During the early years of the nineteenth century, states and cities often subsidized railroad- and canal-builders. The money for this as well as for financing other public improvements came from bonds issued by the city or state. Frequently, the standards were not high, and bribery and favoritism were common. Provision for payment of debts was inadequate; at times, the people were burdened with old debts for improvements long after the improvements had lost their value. As a result, default on obligation frequently occurred, and city and state credit fell off.

Aroused by the legislatures' abuse of their powers, voters insisted on constitutional amendments reducing legislative discretion. Today most state constitutions put elaborate restrictions on the power of state and local legislatures to borrow money or pledge credit. In large measure, therefore, the power to borrow money for a long term has been transferred from the legislatures and city councils to the voters.

Fiscal planning to ensure that taxes are collected in time to cover necessary operating expenses has reduced the amount of short-term borrowing. Even so, officials sometimes need to borrow money for a short term. This "floating debt" consists of bank loans, tax-anticipation warrants, and other notes, and is paid out of current revenues.

States and cities sometimes need to borrow money for longer periods —fifteen or twenty years. During the Depression, money was needed for relief. Since the end of World War II many states have gone into debt in order to pay bonuses to veterans. Expenditures for highway construction, school buildings, slum clearance, and so on, are so large that it is not feasible to pay for them out of current revenue. Moreover, these improvements have a long life and add to the wealth of the community, so it is desirable to pay for them by spreading the cost. For this purpose, governments issue bonds. The best practice—now required by many constitutions—is to issue *serial bonds*, a portion of which come due each year and are retired out of current revenues.

State and local bonds are especially attractive to wealthy investors, since the interest received from them is exempt from federal income tax. For this reason, these governments can borrow money at a lower interest rate than can private businesses. The credit of most cities and states is good, and they readily find buyers for their bonds. Some bonds are *general obligation bonds* and are backed by the credit of the issuing governments. Other bonds, *revenue bonds*, are backed only by the income from the particular project in which the money is invested. Governments are often permitted to issue revenue bonds beyond the limitations on their general indebtedness, and this type is used whenever possible.

During World War II, with incomes high and tax collections good, many states were able to pay off much of their debt. Since the end of the war, state and municipal borrowing has increased to cover veterans' bonuses and to finance improvements that had been postponed by the emergency. Debts of state and local governments have mounted sharply in recent years, climbing from $19.3 billion in 1942 to over $110 billion in 1967, with the bulk of the increase going to education and highways.

Spending the Money

State and local governments are spending more money for more things than they did fifty years ago. Spending by state and local governments has nearly quintupled since World War II years, rising from $14.1

billion in 1946 to $83 billion in 1966. But the percentage of the national income taken by these governments has not materially increased. Their relative expenditures in terms of real and not inflated dollars are not much greater than they were twenty years ago, despite the fact that they have more duties than they ever had before. Even with their weaknesses—and there are many—state and local governments are giving better services than they did in the past without taking any appreciably larger part of the national income. And most citizens are probably getting their money's worth.

Who controls the purse strings? City councils, town meetings, school boards, the legislature—all share in deciding how much and what kinds of taxes shall be collected and how much and for what purpose the money shall be spent, subject to constitutional limitations. But the preparation of the budget and the responsibility for planning the state or city's program is becoming more and more the job of the chief executive. In at least forty states the governor prepares the budget; his staff reviews estimates from the various departments, correlates the program, and transmits it to the legislature. The mayor or manager has the same job in many municipalities. In other places, either the legislature or a group of officials prepares the budget.

The *executive budget* is preferred, because the governor or mayor who manages the administration can review programs from the point of view of the overall needs of the government. Each department head is always convinced that his department needs more money, but the chief executive has to balance the needs of all the departments. The budget is prepared in much the same way as the national budget. In fact, the practice of the national government was adapted to the needs of the states. The legislative body, normally through its committees, holds hearings and acts on the executive's recommendations. In some states and in a few cities, however, the legislature cannot increase amounts or add items to what the executive has recommended. Most governors probably have greater control over state expenditures than does the President over national. In addition to the item veto, governors often have control over the allotment of funds to departments even after appropriations have been approved by the legislature. This power over the budget makes it possible for the executive to control departmental operations, to prevent duplication and overlapping, and to require efficient management.

Epilogue:
Challenge and Opportunity

Government by the people needs thinkers and doers, leaders who heed the injunction, "Think as men of action, act as men of thought." Government by the people also requires talents, a variety of talents not monopolized by any one individual or group. How can you put your knowledge and your belief in democratic government to good use?

Needed: 100,000,000 Politicians

College men and women do not need to be told how important it is for them to take part in politics. Since grade school, they have had this sermon dinned into their ears. Nor do they agree with Boss Plunkitt that "if you have been to college, so much the worse for you" in the rough-and-tumble of American politics. They do not feel the need to "unlearn" all that they learned in college. The question is, have they learned enough?

Playing an effective part in politics depends on more than good will and interest in community affairs. It demands a good deal of political know-how. It would be pleasant to be able to say about political activity that "there's nothing to it—just learn as you go." But this would not be true. American political mechanics are a complex affair.

Many of the procedures of American politics discussed above may seem dull and difficult. So they are, until you suddenly come face to face with them in a real situation. Registration requirements, for example, seem of little import until someone publicly challenges your right to vote. Getting out the vote on election day seems a remote problem—until you find yourself in campaign headquarters at 2 A.M. waiting tensely for the last wards to report in. Limitations on campaign spending seem unimportant—until the opposition accuses your candidate of trying to buy the election.

PLUNGING IN

The first step is to find the name of the local chairman of your party; someone will know at city hall or at the courthouse. Calling on the chairman to tell him that you would like to help out in the campaign is the next step; he will doubtless give you a warm welcome.

Voting lists must be checked, letters stamped, leaflets distributed, meetings arranged, publicity sent out, posters put up. Special skills will come in handy. Anyone in the advertising business can help with radio or newspaper publicity. Amateur sign painters will have ample occasion to make use of their talents. A good money-raiser can help meet the problems of campaign expenses—usually the worst headache of all. Typists, from the hunt-and-peck variety on up, are needed (with their typewriters). Good organizers are required to direct doorbell-ringing, an art and a science in itself. Cars and drivers are wanted for the countless errands that must be run.

One of the most important jobs in a political campaign is to get people registered to vote. How does one go about getting people registered? At best,

Courtesy Ed Fisher; copyright 1968 Saturday Review, Inc.

"Before winding up the rally I've been asked to pass on a few announcements from schools in the area about homework assignments. . . ."

it is a chore. First, one must find names and addresses of those not registered. One way to do this is to check city directories or police lists against registration lists. Another, and more common, practice is to check the membership lists of organizations such as the American Legion or a labor union for names not on the voting lists. Then the unregistered person must be approached by mail, over the phone, or, best of all, in his home.

The unregistered voter is often an apathetic citizen. He may not see much point in voting. He will probably not know when the registration period comes. He may ask: Will they want to know my age? Will they make me take a reading test? Do I have to pay anything? How long do I have to live in the area? Answers to these questions—almost always they can be reassuring ones—will be expected of anyone taking part in a registration drive. In many cases, transportation and baby-sitters also must be provided.

Another highly important task in political campaigning is to get people to vote on election day. The most effective work here is usually done by party committees and candidates. Workers are stationed at every polling booth to check off the names of persons as they vote. Then "checkers" send hourly reports to people at party headquarters, who begin telephoning voters who have not shown up. Other party workers drive voters to the polls. The success of the whole operation depends on good timing, carefully checked lists, and efficient communication and transportation.

The heart of registration and voting drives lies in approaching the individual voter in person, but the approach is much more effective if it comes as part of a general drive. This is especially true of registration drives. A non-partisan, community-wide program is often the most fruitful procedure. The drive is carried on through the press, radio, television, posters, civic groups, trade unions, veterans' organizations, window displays, churches, schools, door-to-door canvassing, rallies—even skywriting! In some communities police cars have carried "get-out-the-vote" signs, "vote-mobiles" have toured the area with sample voting machines or sample ballots, and REGISTER TO VOTE has been stenciled on the sidewalks.

Much of this work would be simple drudgery under any other circumstances. In the heat of a campaign, however, it takes on an aura of the dramatic. Volunteers are part of a team engaged in a keen struggle. Party headquarters is always crowded; the phone seems always to be ringing. Crisis follows crisis. Candidates dash in to make arrangements for coming meetings, rush out to speak at the Odd Fellows' barbecue. Rumors flow thick and fast. And occasionally one of them may even be true.

Taking part in party politics is a rewarding business. Perhaps the biggest satisfaction comes on election day. The blinders have been taken off; the names on the ballot are those of flesh-and-blood persons. Politics has taken on a new dimension. At this stage you can feel that you are no longer an outsider, but an insider in party affairs. You have learned something of the rules and gimmicks of the political game.

After the election, what then? We shall be told on all sides that "politics is now adjourned." But politics is never adjourned. It is a year-round business—at least for the professionals. The only question is whether they will have the game all to themselves.

Vitally important decisions are made between elections. New members are added to local party committees, precinct captains are selected, perhaps new chairmen are elected. Members of state committees and delegates to conventions are chosen. Plans are made for registration drives, election of delegates to national conventions, future campaigns. These activities determine the shape of politics in the elections ahead. Obviously, running a party, like running a war, is too important to be left to the professionals. The period between elections is the ideal time for public-spirited citizens to make their influence felt in the party councils—an influence that will be all the greater because important party decisions are made by relatively few persons.

In most cases party workers will have no trouble gaining a foothold in the party organization. Occasionally, the old-line leaders may try to close out newcomers to keep the organization as their private preserve. They should not be allowed to succeed without a struggle. If necessary, one can often work with another part of the organization, or join or form auxiliary groups like the Young Democrats or Young Republicans.

Our mental picture of a local party leader is usually one of the ruthless boss, complete with cigar, jowls, and a taste for "honest graft." In real life the party leader usually turns out to be an amiable, honest person. Of course, unscrupulous bosses are to be found. But one should not be discouraged from taking part in politics because the local party organization seems to be controlled by a disreputable group. It is far easier to clean the organization from within than from without. Party bosses can ignore the criticism of outsiders, but they cannot resist those who outwork and outvote them within their own domain.

Let there be fair warning: Anyone going into party politics with illusions about the way the parties operate is likely to be in for a shock. On the local level, organization is often stagnant, if not moribund. Committees rarely meet and attendance is poor. Where the local organization is energetic and influential, it is usually because a leader has infused some life into it. His reward is to be called the local "boss"—whether or not he is serving private rather than public needs.

The South is spoken of slightingly as a one-party area, but in many parts of the North only one effective party organization can be found. A rival party may exist in name but not in fact. Often, especially in the cities, one party organization is the captive of the other. It exists on crumbs of patronage handed out by the dominant organization, which is willing to pay for token opposition in order to prevent real competition. True rivalry cannot be expected in a situation like this.

Most disillusioning of all is the inglorious nature of local party operations. Any hope that men have banded together for the sake of grand principles may quickly evaporate. The main reason for party activity often turns out to be the "cohesive power of public plunder." Doubtless, local politics has been purified a bit since the days of the muckrakers, but many city and county organizations are still occupied with personalities and petty business.

This is disconcerting to the citizen who has gone to party headquarters to stay. The local problems worrying him concern schools for his children, lower taxes, better roads, faster snow removal in winter, a new library building. He has only one consolation, but it is a good one: The greater the need for improving the character of local politics, the larger the opportunity for him and his fellows to pitch in and do something.

"You're the boss," Mr. Edward J. Flynn, former boss of the Bronx, told us reassuringly. But he added an important proviso. We're the boss only if we are willing to dirty our hands a bit at the grass roots of party politics.

Running for Office

For those interested in making a career of politics there are few set rules. Generalizations about the road to election-day victories are risky; the exceptions to the rules are legion. But before entering politics, the individual would be wise to reflect on his assets and liabilities. If he is sensitive to criticism, excessively shy, if he dislikes "good fellowship" and wants to lead a quiet, peaceful life, the chances are against his being successful — or at least happy — in politics. On the other hand, if he enjoys working with others, likes to speak, and can look forward to countless dinners of cold peas and roast beef, then politics offers an exciting and rewarding career.

"One who enters politics must realize that he is to live dangerously," a candidate has said. "In business, the line between the red and the black divides anxiety and comfort, but a businessman can survive a bad year; in politics .1 percent on one's biennial gross vote can mean the difference between prosperity and ruin."[1]

SOME HINTS FROM AN EXPERT

Hugh D. Scott, Jr., a Senator, former Chairman of the Republican National Committee, and an experienced politician, believes that the following traits are helpful to politically active men and women:

1. Be politically informed.
2. Integrity is the most valuable tool of the trade. Despite cynicism about politics, a dishonest politician is almost always exposed sooner or later.
3. "Patience is a prime political virtue," says Scott after observing that he had spent "twenty years or so of being stopped several times a day by people with something on their mind, of having my lapels seized firmly or my sleeve tugged by someone who wants something done that he feels I may be able to do, of long interviews with people with a grievance, a petition, a plan, an invention, or just a two-way ball-bearing tongue."
4. Courtesy — "on Ballot Boulevard there's no market at all for the sour stuff."
5. Gregariousness.
6. Hard Work. "To know your neighborhood and to help your neighbors is a 365-day-a-year job."

[1] Stimson Bullitt, *To Be a Politician* (Doubleday, 1959), p. 53.

7. A sense of humor. Freshman members of Congress are warned by their elders, "Don't violate Rule Six." And what is Rule Six? "Don't take yourself too seriously." And Rules One to Five? "Don't take yourself too seriously." A sense of proportion, a sense of humor.

8. Courage.[2]

Politics does not offer much in the way of job security. It is, therefore, helpful if the aspiring politician has some other source of income. In American politics this has often been the case. Lawyers have more of an opportunity to combine politics and business than do doctors, teachers, workers, or others. The young law school graduate is forbidden by the ethics of his profession to advertise, but he can run for office. If he wins, he will make valuable contacts. If he loses, he can return to the practice of law with a name that is better known to the public.

Insurance and farming are other professions that may be readily combined with politics. But one need not be a lawyer, insurance man, or farmer to enter politics. The avenues to public office are many, and the halls of Congress and the offices of the executive departments are filled with men and women who came into politics from every conceivable background and occupation.

DO'S AND DON'T'S

Here are some of the do's and don't's of politics that should prove useful to the neophyte.

1   Be a joiner. Try to join as great a variety of organizations as possible. By working for the Community Chest, becoming active in the union, the chamber of commerce, the service club, the lodges, and in church work, the candidate makes his name familiar, wins friends, and learns the skills of this trade.

2   Be one of the boys and avoid snobbish mannerisms, but be colorful.

3   Learn to remember names and faces, but don't be effusive.

4   Ignore unfriendly attacks. "Never get into an argument with a newspaper or a preacher; the newspaper always has the last word with its readers and the preacher always calls on Heaven as witness that he is right."[3]

5   Know your facts.

6   "Don't overestimate the people's knowledge or underestimate their intelligence."

7   Remember that a nice personality and a mastery of all the do's and don't's of politics are no substitute for intelligence, integrity, and conviction.

A Career in the Civil Service

Political work often leads to appointive as well as elective public positions. Lawyers who have come to the aid of their party are sometimes in line for judgeships, and others may be appointed to places in state or local government. But today more and more of the positions in the federal

[2]From Hugh D. Scott, Jr., *How to Go into Politics* (John Day, 1949) pp. 26ff.
[3]*Ibid.*, p. 32.

administrative structure are open to qualified nonpoliticians. These positions offer much to those who have a desire for public service — but little liking for politics — and for people who have administrative talents. The government needs all kinds of people with all kinds of skills. These positions offer reasonable compensation, considerable security, and an exciting challenge.

HOW TO GET INTO GOVERNMENT

How does one go about getting a position in one of the civilian agencies of government? There are now approximately 2.8 million civilian positions in the federal government. Only 537 of these are filled by election — namely, 435 representatives, 100 senators, the President, and the Vice President. To secure one of these positions it is necessary to go into politics. The same is generally true of an appointment to the Supreme Court or a lower federal court, district attorneyship, or appointment as a first-, second-, or third-class postmaster, or a Cabinet member. These and other such positions are filled by presidential appointment with the consent of the Senate.

But well over 90 percent of the positions in the executive branch are open to qualified citizens regardless of their politics, except that they must be loyal to the United States and not be Fascists or Communists. Most of these positions are filled through civil service examinations. Veterans receive preference on these examinations, which are held at the various regional headquarters of the Civil Service Commission. If one does not live in a city with a regional headquarters, information can be secured from the civil service secretary at the local post office.

Only about 10 percent of these positions are in Washington. The rest are scattered throughout the world. Unlike English practice, American civil service examinations are for particular kinds of jobs. Positions calling for professional training are filled through unassembled examinations. Such examinations are not examinations in the usual sense, but questionnaires that enable the Civil Service Commission and the appointing agencies to examine the competence and experience of the individual.

Civil service jobs are now graded in a general schedule of eighteen grades, with salaries ranging from $3,776 to $27,055. The work normally involves a five-day, forty-hour week with annual vacations of thirteen to twenty-six days and generous sick leave. Low-cost life insurance is available, employees are entitled to unemployment compensation, and there is an attractive retirement system. The Hatch Act protects civil servants from being obliged to contribute to political funds, but it also bars them from participating in any partisan political activity.

Several federal agencies have their own personnel systems and are not covered by regular civil service rules. The TVA, the FBI, the National Security Agency, the USIA, and the Central Intelligence Agency, for example, recruit and hire their own employees. The FBI appoints its special agents from among physically and mentally eligible lawyers (those who have graduated from an accredited law school) and accountants (with at least three years' experience). G-men receive a starting salary of $8,821 plus overtime pay and after a probationary period are given raises and permanent appointments.

In addition to opportunities in the federal service; many attractive positions are open in state and municipal public service. Since each year the states and cities improve the conditions of their public service, opportunities are becoming more attractive for able people.

Although positions with the United Nations are difficult to secure because the American quota is usually filled, the effort may be worthwhile, for service with the United Nations offers many advantages in pay and other benefits, in addition to the satisfaction of working for the community of mankind.

Entering the Foreign Service

The Foreign Service has attractions for many people. In some ways it is the glamour service of the federal government, but, as we point out in Chapter 22, much of the work is routine, and life can be dull and even unpleasant in some posts. Yet the Service has many advantages.

The Foreign Service consists of a Staff Corps and an Officer Corps. To qualify for employment in the Staff Corps one must (1) be at least twenty-one years old; (2) have been a citizen of the United States for at least five years; (3) be single and without dependents; (4) be a high school graduate; and (5) possess the necessary secretarial skills. As a secretary for the Foreign Service you may be called upon to serve anywhere in the world, including Washington, D.C., for your first twelve months.

In order to be eligible to take the Foreign Service officer examinations one must (1) be at least twenty-one and less than thirty-one years old (at least twenty if the junior year of college has been successfully completed); (2) have been a citizen of the United States for at least seven-and-a-half years; (3) not be married to an alien at the time of appointment. Examinations for these positions are written, oral, and physical. The written examination is usually held in May and December in almost 300 cities in the United States, and at any American diplomatic or consulate post that candidates residing abroad may designate. The oral examinations are held in Washington, at certain regional centers in the United States, and at certain posts abroad. Persons who wish to take the examinations may receive application forms from the Board of Examiners for the Foreign Service, Department of State, Washington, D.C. 20520; these applications should be completed at least six weeks before the date set for the examination.

FOREIGN SERVICE EXAMINATIONS

Taking a full day to complete, the written examination is composed of four parts. The first part is a general ability test (75 minutes) designed to measure the candidate's basic learning skills—ability to read, to analyze, to interpret data in a variety of quantitative forms, and to make simple mathematical deductions. The second part is an English expression test (105 minutes), intended to examine the candidate's ability to recognize and use correct, effective, and well-organized written English. Each candidate is required to write on two assigned topics during the test. The third part is a general background test (90 minutes) consisting of approximately 50 percent social sciences, 25 percent humanities, and 25 percent science questions. The final part consists of special optional tests (75 minutes). Candidates must select one of the following four optional tests: Option A—History, Government, Social Sciences, and Public Affairs; Option B—Administration; Option C—Economics; Option D—Commerce.

The oral examination is designed to test qualities such as resourcefulness and versatility, appearance, manner, diction, and personality. The Service uses the oral interview to eliminate candidates who are "shy, aggressive, boorish, unable to defend their views, who give evidence of low standards of conduct, and who show a lack of knowledge of the United States." To test this last quality, natives of one section of the country are often questioned on other sections. Factual knowledge is given less weight than "ability to form thoughtful opinions based on the facts at the candidate's disposal, to organize his views logically, and to speak clearly and understandably." While the examinations are exacting, they are less so than formerly, and the number of positions open has recently been increased.

SERVICE ABROAD

The President, with the consent of the Senate, appoints successful candidates as Foreign Service officers (since 1956, most of them at Class 8). Their salaries begin at $6,734. Officers may work up the scale until they get to the top class, where the salary is $28,750 for a career ambassador. For those serving abroad, salaries are supplemented by quarters allowances; officers receive from thirteen to twenty-six days of annual leave; and after two years abroad they are entitled to home leave in the United States with pay and travel expenses for their families. Other attractive fringe benefits are life and family health insurance, pension, and so on. Unless an officer is promoted within a maximum period in each class, except for the top two classes, he must retire.

Before foreign assignment, Foreign Service officers are trained at the Foreign Service Institute, and throughout their careers they continue special studies. There is no single method of preparation for the Foreign Service, but persons interested in taking the examination should, while in college, learn to write clear and correct English, master a foreign language, and take enough social science, humanities, and science courses to be able to pass the examinations.

PEACE CORPS: FOREIGN AND DOMESTIC

The Peace Corps recruits from a wide range of skilled Americans for overseas work. After careful screening and intensive training, volunteers are assigned to countries requesting Peace Corps services. Applicants must be citizens of the United States, eighteen years of age or older, single or married provided that applicants have no dependents under eighteen. Volunteers receive no regular salary payments but receive allowances to cover the cost of clothing, housing, food, and incidental expenses so that they live at an economic level equivalent to counterparts in the host country. Upon completion of service, Peace Corps volunteers receive a separation allotment based upon time spent overseas. The payment accumulates at the rate of $75 a month. Peace Corps questionnaires are available at most colleges, universities, and post offices, or may be obtained by writing to Peace Corps, Washington, D.C. 20520.

An important component of the War on Poverty, the Volunteers in Service to America (VISTA) is, in many respects, the domestic counterpart of the Peace Corps. Individuals volunteer for a one-year period to lend their talents to the service of communities that are striving to solve their pressing economic and social problems. After an intensive six-week training period which stresses field experience and discussions of the nature and causes of poverty in the United States, volunteers are sent to work in Job Corps camps, migrant worker communities, Indian reservations, rural and urban community action programs, hospitals, schools, and mental health facilities. In short, workers, may be sent wherever poverty exists in any of the fifty states or in territories under the American flag. VISTA volunteers are paid only subsistence expenses and a modest monthly stipend and personal allowance. The program is administered by the Office of Economic Opportunity in Washington.

A Last Word

Some of you have no interest in learning about political or administrative jobs. Your future lies elsewhere. Even so, you can and should have a political career—in the party of your choice. As we have seen, our parties badly need strengthening at every level. The country needs more party politicians to hunt out good candidates and help elect them, drive workers to the polls on election day, spread the party gospel, and remind the officeholders of their responsibilities to the people.

Every individual in a democracy contributes to its success or failure. Those who, because of ignorance or indifference, try to stay on the sidelines nevertheless influence the course of events, negative and destructive though their influence may be. If the 200 million Americans are to keep their free government, it will be mainly because of the activities of the people as a whole. Leaders dedicated to the principles of free government and leaders with vision and courage are essential; it is from private citizens that these leaders are recruited. The standards and values of the people broadly determine the type of leadership they get.

"Fourscore and seven years ago" said Abraham Lincoln in the midst of a crucial struggle, "our fathers brought forth on this continent a new nation, conceived in liberty, and dedicated to the proposition that all men are created equal." Lincoln saw that struggle as a test of whether government of the *people*, by the *people*, for the *people* could endure. Eighty years later another President, Franklin D. Roosevelt, could report in the midst of another great war that "the state of this Nation is good—the heart of this Nation is sound—the spirit of this Nation is strong—the faith of this Nation is eternal." Government by the people has met and mastered many crises. How well will it meet the tests to come?

KEEPING INFORMED: BIBLIOGRAPHY

Newspapers, radio, and television are important sources of information, but the person who depends solely on these sources will have an imperfect picture of the world around him. They give only a disconnected story of the sensational—the newsworthy—events. They tell little of the whys and wherefores. The successful negotiation of a hundred collective-bargaining contracts during a day goes unnoticed while public attention is focused on the one case in which negotiations break down.

To some extent magazines supplement the news. Some give background information; others digest the weekly events for those too busy to read daily papers. *Time* and *Newsweek*, with their clipped and dramatic reporting of the week's events, are major sources of information for many citizens. The weekly *U.S. News & World Report* presents the news in graphic form and is especially aimed toward influential members of the business community. This latter magazine is right of center, whereas *The Nation, The New Leader*, and *The New Republic* are journals of opinion that report the week's events from left to center and the *National Review* discusses events from the conservative point of view. Though these last four, compared to the others, have a relatively small circulation, their audience includes many leaders of opinion—clergymen, teachers, lawyers, public officials, and the like.

Among the monthly magazines, *Harper's Magazine, Atlantic Monthly*, and *Fortune* have relatively small audiences but great influence, because they are read by strategically placed individuals. The first two are more liberal than *Fortune*, but all three attempt to present a balanced diet. *Fortune* features materials of interest to businessmen but covers all phases of American society. By far the largest-circulation monthly is *The Reader's Digest*, read each month by millions of persons. In addition to features written by its own staff members, *The Reader's Digest* selects and abridges articles that appear in other magazines. It has conservative leanings.

Magazines of general circulation contain useful material, but they do not go deeply into particular questions. Where do you find a law? How do you look up a court decision? Where can you find information on the United Nations? How do you find out how your congressman has voted? What are some good books on the U.S.S.R.? Many aids and services have been designed to make such information readily available.

Important information-dispensing centers are the more than seventy-five hundred public libraries and the many hundreds of private libraries that are open to the public. In these libraries can be found, in addition to magazines of general interest, many specialized journals such as *The American Political Science Review*. There are also a number of periodical indexes, of which the *Public Affairs Information Service* is especially useful because it indexes books, pamphlets, and reports, as well as articles from hundreds of periodicals on topics in a broad range of current public interest. Major political science journals are included in the *International Index*. The *International Political Science Abstracts*, edited by the International Political Science Association, provides précis of articles from all major political science journals throughout the world. The *Reader's Guide to Periodical Literature* includes mainly popular magazines with mass or family circulation. The *Index to Legal Periodicals* and *Business Periodicals Index* are also useful. Most of these indexes are published monthly and indexed cumulatively at the end of the year; they can help you locate materials on most subjects. In addition to these periodical guides, Robert B. Harmon's *Political Science: A Bibliographical Guide to the Literature* (1965), Lubomyr Wynar's *Guide to Reference Materials in Political Science,* vol. I (1966), and *The ABS Guide to Recent Publications in the Social and Behavioral Sciences* (1965) are useful. The card catalog in the library will reveal the books that are available in the library. You may be able to learn something about an author's reputation and some informed opinions about a particular book in *The Book Review Digest*; this digest, though, should be used in a limited fashion because reviews are taken from a selected list of publications and therefore a full picture of the reviews of a particular book is not necessarily presented.

One of the most useful volumes is the *United States Government Organization Manual*, an annual publication. This manual, which can be obtained from the Superintendent of Documents, Government Printing Office, covers the authority, organization, and functions of all branches of the government. It has up-to-date organization charts, tells which individuals hold the higher executive positions, and gives a brief description of the work of each unit of government. The *Congressional Directory*, also published annually, has some of the materials found in the *Manual*, and it includes autobiographical sketches of members of Congress, lists of congressional committees and committee assignments, election statistics for the last several congressional elections, and maps of congressional districts. The *Directory* is the place to find out the name of your congressman, a short sketch of his life, what committees he is on, and the boundaries of the district he represents.

Of special interest to persons interested in public affairs is the *Encyclopedia of the Social Sciences*, published in 1930 under the editorship of Edwin R. A. Seligman and Alvin Johnson; it contains articles on various topics—political parties, sovereignty, representation, John Locke, for example—that are among the best short treatments to be found. The *International Encyclopedia of the Social Sciences*, which was edited by David L. Sills and published in 1968, complements its predecessor and brings the information up to date.

Although both encyclopedias contain a great deal of biography, the *Dictionary of National Biography* and the *Dictionary of American Biography* are the prime sources for this type of data. Included are some outstanding articles; one by Carl Becker on Benjamin Franklin, for example, is found in the *Dictionary of American Biography*. In *Current Biography* you can find materials and background information on men in the news, and there is a companion set, *Biography Index*, in case specific information has not been written up fully in *Current Biography* for ten years or so.

Certain important tools for quick reference to current events are available, such as *Facts on File, The New York Times Index, The Wall Street Journal Index*, and *Keesing's Contemporary Archives*.

If you want raw figures, consult the *Statistical Abstract of the United States*, another yearly publication of the Government Printing Office. The reference librarian will be able to point out other useful tools of this nature, such as the *Historical Statistics of the United States*, the *Congressional District Data Book*, and the many publications from the Bureau of the Census.

Where can you find a law? We often hear people talk about some statute without having seen it. Where can the actual text be found? The laws of the United States as passed by Congress are first printed individually and are known as slip laws. Each law has a number; in recent years public laws are numbered according to the term of Congress in which they are enacted. At the end of each year the laws are collected and published by the Government Printing Office under the title of *United States Statutes at Large*. Each year's collection is separately numbered, though there are two separate parts for each number. Part One contains *public laws*, that is, laws affecting the people generally or having to do with governmental organization. Part Two contains *private laws*, those having to do with particular groups or individuals. The laws in the *Statutes at Large* are listed chronologically, each law constituting a separate chapter. The Taft-Hartley Act, for example, is Chapter 120 of Volume 61, on page 136; it is cited as 61 Stat. 136.

The volumes of *Statutes at Large* are useful for research, but they include many laws of only specialized interest. Furthermore, many of the measures modify earlier legislation and are themselves modified by later legislation. To find *current* laws on a topic, it is best to go to the *United States Code*, which contains the public laws of the United States that are in force at the present time. The official edition of the *United States Code* is published every six years. Supplements are issued annually between editions. The laws are arranged according to fifty titles, each title is divided into sections, and each section into paragraphs that are consecutively numbered for each title. The fifty titles cover such subjects as Congress, Title 2; Army, Title 10; Bankruptcy, Title 11; Labor, Title 29; and so on. The *Code* is cited by title and paragraph. The citation of the Taft-Hartley Act, for example, is 29 U.S. C. 141ff.

The *Code*, like the *Statutes at Large*, is printed by the Government Printing Office, but there are also commercially published editions known as *United States Code Annotated* (U.S.C.A.) and the *Federal Code Annotated*

(F.C.A.). These annotated editions include notes on judicial interpretations of the law as well as the law itself. If available, they are more useful than the *Code* itself.

The series *Treaties in Force* is the best source of information about treaties and executive agreements. These volumes are published annually and are organized chronologically.

Where does one find the rules and regulations issued by the President and the executive agencies? Every day except Sunday and Monday the government publishes *The Federal Register*, which contains executive orders, regulations, and proclamations issued by the President, as well as the orders and regulations promulgated by the executive agencies (including the independent regulatory commissions). These administrative rules and regulations are collected, codified, and kept up to date in the *Code of Federal Regulations*, organized on the same plan as the *United States Code*. The *Code of Federal Regulations*, *The Federal Register*, along with the *United States Government Organization Manual* previously mentioned and a new publication, *Public Papers of the President*, are part of what is known as the Federal Register System. The *Public Papers of the President* contain public messages, speeches, and statements of the President.

The laws as they finally appear on the statute books give, however, only part of the story. Where do you find out what went on before the laws were passed or why certain laws were not passed? This information can, in part, be found in one of the most edifying and interesting items of American letters—the *Congressional Record*. The *Record* is issued every day Congress is in session and is bound and indexed at the end of each session. It contains everything that is said on the floors of the two chambers, plus a lot that is not said. Congress freely gives its consent to requests of its members "to revise and extend their remarks," which is a polite way of saying that congressmen are permitted to include in the *Record* statements they did not make before Congress. These speeches are then reprinted and distributed to the folks back home. Congressmen, with the unanimous consent of their colleagues, also place in the *Record* poems, articles, letters, editorials, and other materials they find interesting. Each day's *Record* is now accompanied by a *Daily Digest* that highlights the events on both the floor of Congress and in committees. Action on specific items can be traced by searching through the index. An easier method is to use the *Digest of Public General Bills* which gives a brief summary of all the public bills and traces their progress in the legislative assembly line.

There are several commercial services that provide convenient references to congressional activities. *The Congressional Quarterly Weekly Report* contains voting records, legislative action, reports on lobbying, and other materials about Congress in action. This is the best source for materials on lobbying activity. The materials are indexed and collected in an *Annual Almanac*. The *United States Code: Congressional and Administrative News* and the *Congressional Index* also provide ready reference to congressional acitvity.

Because most of the real work of Congress is done in committees, the reports of these committees and the printed records of hearings are important sources of information. The hearings and reports may be found in any of the 550 depository libraries in the United States. (A depository library is one that receives regularly publications issued by the Government Printing Office. Of these libraries, only 125 are full depository libraries; the rest receive publications in selected categories and subjects.)

Congress is not the only branch of the federal government that keeps a record of its work. All the other agencies have their own publications, describing their work and supplying the citizen with general and specialized information. These can be obtained from the Superintendent of Documents, Government Printing Office, Washington 25, D.C., at a nominal price. They are indexed in the *Monthly Catalog of United States Government Publications*. One of the several general guides to government publications is Laurence F. Schmeckebier's and Roy B. Eastin's *Government Publications and Their Use* (Brookings, 1961).

Where can you find the reports of the federal judiciary? Legal bibliography is a complex subject, but the law is too important to leave to lawyers. The decisions of the Supreme Court are published by the government in numbered volumes known as the *United States Reports*. Cases are cited by volume and page number, e.g., *Illinois et rel McCollum v. Board of Education*, 333 U.S. 203 (1948) means that this case can be found in the 333d volume of the *United States Reports* on page 203 and that the opinion was handed down in 1948. Decisions of the Court prior to 1875 are cited by the name of the Supreme Court reporter. Thus, *Marbury* v. *Madison*, 1 Cranch 137 (1803), can be found in the first volume of Cranch's Supreme Court reports on page 137; the opinion was announced in 1803. Two other editions of Supreme Court opinions are commercially published and each has its own form of citation. Some of the federal district court rulings are now commercially published in volumes known as the *Federal Supplement*. Those of the federal courts of appeals are now also published by the same commercial publisher in volumes known as the *Federal Reporter*. These reports are not available in many general libraries, but in many communities a special law library, usually located in the courthouse, contains the reports of the cases plus other materials needed by lawyers in their professional work.

Selected Bibliography

This bibliography makes no pretense of including all the good books pertinent to the American experiment in government by the people. Its purpose is to provide an *initial* guide to the literature. With few exceptions, the rich periodical literature is not mentioned.

PART ONE: DEMOCRATIC GOVERNMENT IN AMERICA

General Sources

R. T. Alford, *Party and Society: The Anglo-American Democracies* (1963). A comparison of political behavior in Britain, Australia, United States, and Canada.

H. R. Alker, *Mathematics and Politics* (1965). A concise study of the increasingly important role of mathematics in political science.

G. Almond and S. Verba, *The Civic Culture: Political Attitudes and Democracy in Five Nations* (1963). Presents a theory of political development and tests by sample survey methodology.

C. W. Anderson, Fred R. von der Mehden, and Crawford Young (eds.), *Issues of Political Development* (1967). The stages of evolution of political systems.

D. E. Apter (ed.), *Ideology and Discontent* (1964). Toward a definition and explanation of ideology.

A. F. Bentley, *The Process of Government* (1967). Seminal study in methodology and systematic treatment of the role of interest groups in the political process.

W. T. Bluhm, *Theories of the Political System: Classics of Political Thought and Modern Political Analysis* (1965). Relates modern political analysis to classical thought.

A. Brecht, *Political Theory: The Foundations of Twentieth Century Political Thought* (1959). Thorough analysis of "value-fact" controversy.

E. H. Buehrig (ed.), *Essays in Political Science* (1966). Readings on the state of the discipline.

J. C. Charlesworth (ed.), *Contemporary Political Analysis* (1967). Eight approaches to political study.

J. M. Claunch (ed.), *Mathematical Applications in Political Science* (1965). Four essays concerning the use of mathematics in political science.

W. E. Connolly, *Political Science and Ideology* (1967). Toward a neutral definition and application of ideology.

B. Crick, *The American Science of Politics: Its Origins and Conditions* (1959). Critical study of American political science.

R. A. Dahl, *Modern Political Analysis* (1963). Excellent short introduction to the systematic study of politics.

——— (ed.), *Political Oppositions in Western Democracies* (1966). The nature of political opposition in nine Western European nations and the United States.

J. C. Davies, *Human Nature in Politics: The Dynamics of Political Behavior* (1963). Argues that political behavior is rooted in man's organic needs.

K. W. Deutsch, *The Nerves of Government: Models of Political Communication and Control* (1963). Toward a general theory of politics through the use of communication systems metaphor.

R. S. Downie, *Government Action and Morality* (1964). Toward a morality-oriented democratic theory.

D. Easton, *A Framework for Political Analysis* (1965). Seeking a general theory of politics.

———, *A Systems Analysis of Political Life* (1965). Seeking a general theory of politics.

M. Edelman, *The Symbolic Uses of Politics* (1964). Provocative analysis of the meanings of political acts.

H. W. Ehrmann (ed.), *Democracy in a Changing Society* (1964). The need for democracy to adapt itself to a changing world.

J. Ellul, *The Political Illusion* (1967). Opinions on modern politics.

R. E. Flathman, *The Public Interest: An Essay Concerning the Normative Discourse of Politics* (1966). Relations between reason and morals in decision-making.

C. J. Friedrich, *Man and His Government: An Empirical Theory of Politics* (1963).

——— (ed.), *Nomos XII: Rational Decision* (1964). Papers on a wide range of problems dealing with the concept of rational decision-making.

F. M. Frohock, *The Nature of Political Inquiry* (1967). A study in methodology.

D. W. Gotshalk, *Human Aims in Modern Perspective* (1966). Human aims and their implications for public policy.

C. S. Hyneman, *The Study of Politics; The Present State of American Political Science* (1959). Survey of current research, problems, methods, and data.

B. de Jouvenel, *The Art of Conjecture* (1967). The methodological problems of anticipating future developments.

———, *The Pure Theory of Politics* (1963).

H. D. Lasswell, *The Future of Political Science* (1963). A blueprint for the discipline by an eminent social scientist.

G. E. Lenski, *Power and Privilege: A Theory of Social Stratification* (1966). Causes and effects of the distribution of political and economic power.

L. Lipson, *The Democratic Civilization* (1964). General study of democratic systems.

J. R. Lucas, *The Principles of Politics* (1967). Comprehensive political philosophy.

N. A. McDonald, *Politics: A Study of Control Behavior* (1965). Search for a general explanatory theory.

R. M. MacIver, *The Web of Government* (1947). Analysis of government.

E. J. Meehan, *Contemporary Political Thought* (1967).

———, *The Theory and Method of Political Analysis* (1965). A scientific approach to political phenomena.

M. F. Neufeld, *Poor Countries and Authoritarian Rule* (1965). Tendency toward authoritarian governments in poverty-stricken countries.

I. de Sola Pool (ed.), *Contemporary Political Science* (1968). Toward an empirical theory.

L. W. Pye and S. Verba (eds.), *Political Culture and Political Development: Studies in Political Development*, 5th ed. (1965). An examination of individual and group political development.

781

A. Ranney (ed.), *Political Science and Public Policy* (1968). Role of political science in policy analysis.

M. Rejai (ed.), *Democracy: The Contemporary Theories* (1967). Readings in modern democratic theory.

K. de Schweinitz, Jr., *Industrialization and Democracy* (1964). Survey of the relationship in developing and developed nations.

Y. Simon, *The Tradition of Natural Law: A Philosopher's Reflections* (1965). Basic philosophical questions of government.

A. Somit and J. Tanenhaus, *American Political Science: A Profile of a Discipline* (1964). Study of the discipline from questionnaires sent to political scientists.

H. J. Storing (ed.), *Essays on the Scientific Study of Politics* (1962). Critical essays on current trends in political science.

D. Strickland, L. Wade, and R. Johnston, *A Primer of Political Analysis* (1968). Introduction to advanced political concepts.

M. J. Swartz, V. W. Turner, and A. Tuden (eds.), *Political Anthropology* (1966). Framework for the analysis of political systems.

P. Thoenes, *The Elite in the Welfare State* (1966). Causes, operation, and effects of the political phenomenon of the welfare state.

D. B. Truman, *The Governmental Process* (1951). Builds on Bentley's work; analysis of political interests and public opinion.

V. Van Dyke, *Political Science: A Philosophical Analysis* (1960). Analysis of various approaches to the study of politics.

S. J. P. Woelfl, *Politics and Jurisprudence* (1966). Classical criticism of modern political science.

General Treatments of American Government and Society

M. Beloff, *The American Federal Government* (1959). Critical analysis by noted British scholar.

D. W. Brogan, *Politics in America* (1954). Special emphasis on party system.

J. Bryce, *The American Commonwealth*, 2 vols. (1888). Ranks with Tocqueville; more descriptive and less analytical.

S. B. Clough and T. F. Marburg, *The Economic Basis of American Civilization* (1968). The history of United States economy and its role in the shaping of American civilization as a whole.

G. Dietze, *America's Political Dilemma* (1968). Contends that America's democratic development has taken the system from bad to worse.

J. Ellul, *The Technological Society* (1967). A study in the motives for societal development and a commentary on the present state of society.

J. K. Galbraith, *The Affluent Society* (1958). Study of American economy challenging many present assumptions.

M. Harrington, *The Accidental Century* (1965). A treatise on the state of man and society in the twentieth century.

M. C. Havens, *The Challenges to Democracy: Consensus and Extremism in American Politics* (1965). A reappraisal of the moral bases of the American political system.

L. Heren, *The New American Commonwealth* (1967). Reaction of America's political system to the events of the last thirty years.

R. Hofstadter, *Anti-intellectualism in American Life* (1963).

I. Howe (ed.), *The Radical Papers* (1966). Propositions for shaping American society through politics.

R. F. Kennedy, *To Seek a Newer World* (1968). Propositions for social and political improvement.

R. Kirk, *The Intemperate Professor and Other Cultural Splenetics* (1965). Essays on the state of contemporary political science and contemporary American society.

M. Lerner, *America as a Civilization: Life and Thought in the United States Today* (1957). Wide-ranging study of American pluralism.

S. Lipset and L. Lowenthal (eds.), *Culture and Social Character* (1961). Critical examination of Riesman's thesis.

E. McCarthy, *First Things First: New Priorities for America* (1968). A suggested political course for the United States.

D. Martindale, *American Social Structure* (1960). General survey of historical antecedents and contemporary analysis of major features of American society.

J. Messner, *Social Ethics: Natural Law in the Western World* (1965).

G. Myrdal, *An American Dilemma* (1944). Monumental study of American society with special attention to the problems of Negro-white relationships.

R. Niebuhr, *Man's Nature and His Communities* (1965). A study of man in society by a leading theologian.

P. H. Odegard, *Political Power and Social Change* (1966). The concept of political power in contemporary context.

N. A. Rockefeller, *Unity, Freedom, and Peace: A Blueprint for Tommorrow* (1968). Suggestions for political and social development.

A. de Tocqueville, *Democracy in America*, 2 vols. (Phillips Bradley edition, 1964, first published in 1835). Classic study of American government.

R. M. Williams, *American Society* (1960) Sociological interpretation.

R. De Visme Williamson, *Independence and Involvement: A Christian Reorientation in Political Science* (1964). Political concepts in the light of the Christian faith and the Christian community in the present political scene.

American Political Thought

P. Bachrach, *The Theory of Democratic Elitism: A Critique* (1967). Examines contemporary theories of democracy.

C. L. Becker, *Modern Democracy* (1941). Study accenting the economic basis of democracy and the discrepancy between the ideal and the actual.

E. Berg, *Democracy and the Majority Principle: A Study in Twelve Contemporary Political Theories* (1965). Study of the majority principle and its role in achieving popular government.

F. K. Beutel, *Democracy or the Scientific Method in Law and Policy Making* (1965). An argument for the obsolescence of democracy and proposals for a new science-run political order.

T. B. Bottomore, *Elites and Society* (1964). A broader approach to elitist theory.

J. H. Bunzel, *Anti-Politics in America* (1967). The growing negative strains in American politics.

H. S. Commager, *Majority Rule and Minority Rights* (1943). Defense of majority-rule principle and attack on the limitations of judicial review.

W. F. Craven, *The Legend of the Founding Fathers* (1956). Emphasizes contributions of the Puritans.

R. A. Dahl, *A Preface to Democratic Theory* (1956). Constructs model of democracy and finds Madisonian and populistic models inadequate.

A. Downs, *An Economic Theory of Democracy* (1957). Deductive model for analysis and investigation.

H. Wentworth Eldredge, *The Second American Revolution* (1964). Case against democracy.

H. Eulau (ed.), *Political Behavior in America: New Directions* (1966). Readings.

C. Frankel, *The Democratic Prospect* (1962). An examination of democracy in an age of science and technology.

R. H. Gabriel, *The Course of American Democratic Thought*, 2d ed. (1956). Interpretation of democratic thought from 1815 to present.

E. K. Garber and John M. Crossett, Jr. (eds.), *Liberal and Conservative: Issues for College Students* (1968). Basic issues of the conflict between liberal and conservative thought.

L. Hartz, *The Liberal Tradition in America: An Interpretation of American Political Thought since the Revolution* (1955). Emphasizes uniqueness of American liberal tradition.

R. Hofstadter, *The American Political Tradition and the Men Who Made It* (1954). Study of the ideology of American statesmen, emphasizing the basic agreement underlying their political conflicts.

———, *The Paranoid Style in American Politics and Other Essays* (1965). Varied opinions on contemporary politics.

W. Kendall, *John Locke and the Doctrine of Majority-Rule* (1941). Written by an exponent of the majority-rule principle.

R. Lane, *Political Ideology: Why the American Common Man Believes What He Does* (1962). Study of political belief systems.

A. D. Lindsay, *The Modern Democratic State* (1943). Statement of the nature of democracy, its development, its essence, and defense of it, by an English scholar.

W. Lippmann, *Essays in the Public Philosophy* (1956). Antiparliamentarian, Burkean defense of democracy.

C. B. Macpherson, *The Real World of Democracy* (1966). Examines democracy in the world scene.

A. T. Mason and R. H. Leach, *In Quest of Freedom: American Political Thought and Practice* (1959).

H. B. Mayo, *An Introduction to Democratic Theory* (1960). Historical survey.

D. Meiklejohn, *Freedom and the Public; Public and Private Morality in America* (1965). Governmental obligation concerning moral awareness.

C. E. Merriam, *A History of American Political Theories* (1903; reissued, 1936). Standard classic.

J. S. Mill, *Representative Government* (1882). One of the most important books on foundations and problems of democracy.

D. W. Minar, *Ideas and Politics: The American Experience* (1964). Reexamination of the traditional concepts of American political thought.

J. S. Murphy, *Political Theory: A Conceptual Analysis* (1968). The philosophy of political concepts.

R. Niebuhr, *The Children of Light and the Children of Darkness* (1944). Short defense of democracy by one of America's leading theologians.

V. L. Parrington, *Main Currents in American Thought* (1927–1930). Interpretation of American literature, including the writings of the major political theorists and practitioners.

J. R. Pennock, *Liberal Democracy* (1950). Defense of democracy, major threats to it, and the limitations on the majority in democratic government.

R. B. Perry, *Puritanism and Democracy* (1944). Study of two American ideals; has been called a "Thesaurus of democratic thought and an arsenal of democratic defense."

D. K. Price, *The Scientific Estate* (1965). Basic questions of power and freedom and the use of knowledge in American politics.

N. Riemer, *The Revival of Democratic Theory* (1962). Call for renewed theoretical efforts based on the democratic premise.

H. U. Rhodes, *Utopias in American Political Thought* (1967). Utopian thought, especially Bellamy, Donnelly, Skinner, and George.

A. M. Rose, *The Power Structure: Political Process in American Life* (1967). Influence of economic elites in the political process.

C. L. Rossiter, *Seedtime of the Republic* (1953). Political ideas of the men who founded the Republic.

D. V. Sandifer and L. R. Scheman, *The Foundations of Freedom: The Inter-Relationship between Democracy and Human Rights* (1966). Theory and reality in the relation between human rights and democracy.

G. Sartori, *Democratic Theory* (1962). The concept of democracy as practiced by many different nations.

D. Spitz, *Patterns of Anti-democratic Thought* (1949). Refutation of the major critics of democracy from the "right."

T. L. Thorson, *The Logic of Democracy* (1962). Stimulating attempt to justify democracy logically.

H. Tingsten, *The Problem of Democracy* (1965). Concerned with problems of democracy in terms of its sociological and ideological development.

J. Tussman, *Obligation and the Body Politic* (1960). Commitments of a democrat.

Constitutionalism

C. J. Friedrich, *Constitutional Government and Democracy*, rev. ed. (1950). Analysis of relations between democracy and constitutionalism; covers all major contemporary constitutional governments.

W. B. Gwyn, *The Meaning of Separation of Powers* (1965). Analysis of the evolution of the Constitution from its origin to its adoption.

W. H. Hamilton, "Constitutionalism," *Encyclopedia of the Social Sciences*, vol. 9.

C. H. McIlwain, *Constitutionalism: Ancient and Modern*, rev. ed. (1947). Papers and essays by distinguished scholar showing the evolution of the concept of limited government.

C. P. Magrath (ed.), *Constitutionalism and Politics: Conflict and Consensus* (1968). The nature of a living constitution.

M. J. C. Vile, *Constitutionalism and the Separation of Powers* (1967). Origins and interpretation of the separation-of-powers doctrine.

F. M. Watkins, *The Political Tradition of the West* (1948). Traces development of modern liberalism.

PART TWO: THE RULES AND HOW THEY GREW

Revolution and Confederation

B. Bailyn, *Pamphlets of the American Revolution, 1750–1776*, vol. I, *1750–1765*. (1965). Colonial publications on conflicts immediately preceding the Revolution.

C. L. Becker, *The Declaration of Independence* (1942).

D. J. Boorstin, *The Americans; the Colonial Experience* (1958). Emphasis on colonial uniqueness and its influence on the development of the American character.

W. N. Chambers, *Political Parties in a New Nation: The American Experience, 1776–1809* (1963). The development and role of the party system in a new polity.

E. Dumbauld, *The Declaration of Independence and What It Means Today* (1950). A phrase-by-phrase explanation of the Declaration, placing it in the context of the days in which it was written.

J. F. Jameson, *The American Revolution Considered as a Social Movement* (1926).

M. Jensen, *The New Nation* (1950). Study of the Confederation, contains sharp criticism of the "chaos and patriots-to-the-rescue" interpretation.

A. C. McLaughlin, *The Confederation and the Constitution, 1783–1789* (1905). Standard work.

J. T. Main, *The Social Structure of Revolutionary America* (1965). Life in America at the time of the Revolution.

R. L. Merritt, *Symbols of American Community, 1735–1775* (1966). A content analysis of colonial newspapers and the growth of American community in the prerevolutionary period.

H. H. Miller, *The Case for Liberty* (1965). The colonial origins of the basic constitutional freedoms.

J. C. Miller, *Origins of the American Revolution* (1943).

J. R. Pole, *Political Representation in England and the Origins of the American Republic* (1966). An analysis of English political activity and its effect on the political development of colonial America.

Keeping
Informed:
Bibliography

The Constitutional Convention and the Ratification Campaign

C. A. Beard, *An Economic Interpretation of the Constitution of the United States* (1913). Caused a popular furor and has had a strong influence on historians and political scientists.

R. E. Brown, *Charles Beard and the Constitution: A Critical Analysis of "An Economic Interpretation of the Constitution"* (1956).

W. W. Crosskey, *Politics and the Constitution*, 2 vols. (1953). Argument that Framers intended to create a unitary system.

P. Eidelberg, *The Philosophy of the American Constitution: A Reinterpretation of the Intentions of the Founding Fathers* (1968). A philosophical interpretation of the Constitution.

J. Elliot, *The Debates in the Several Conventions on the Adoption of the Federal Constitution*, 2d ed., 5 vols. (1835–1846). Contains the debates in the state ratifying conventions.

M. Farrand, *The Records of the Federal Convention of 1787,* 4 vols., rev. ed., (1966).

J. Jay, J. Madison, and A. Hamilton, *The Federalist* (1788). Basic source material, classic exposition of Constitution.

S. J. Konefsky, *John Marshall and Alexander Hamilton* (1964). The contributions of these two men to the Constitution.

J. D. Lewis, *Anti-Federalists versus Federalists: Selected Documents* (1967).

F. McDonald, *We the People: The Economic Origins of the Constitution* (1958). Examination of Beard's thesis; concludes that economic interpretation is inadequate.

A. T. Mason, *The States Rights Debate: Antifederalism and the Constitution* (1964). Antifederalist thought as seen through debates in state ratifying conventions.

J. T. Main, *The Antifederalists: Critics of the Constitution, 1781–1788* (1961). A contemporary scholar supports Beard's thesis.

Notes of Debates in the Federal Convention of 1787, reported by J. Madison (intro. by Adrienne Koch; 1966). James Madison's record of the Constitutional Convention.

C. Rossiter, *1787: The Grand Convention* (1966). Studies of the delegates to the Constitutional Convention and what they accomplished there.

R. A. Rutland, *The Ordeal of the Constitution: The Antifederalists and the Ratification Struggle of 1787–1788* (1966). State-by-state, blow-by-blow account of the ratification campaign.

D. G. Smith, *The Convention and the Constitution: The Political Ideas of the Founding Fathers* (1965). Theories of government underlying the constitution as it was originally formed.

J. A. Smith, *The Spirit of American Government* (1911). Spirited statement of thesis that the Constitution is the platform of an antidemocratic movement.

W. U. Solberg, *The Federal Convention and the Formation of the Union of the American States* (1958). Documentary account.

C. Van Doren, *The Great Rehearsal* (1948). Popularly written account of the Constitutional Convention.

C. Warren, *The Making of the Constitution* (1937). Disputes the Beard thesis, contains day-by-day account of the activities of the delegates.

B. F. Wright, *Consensus and Continuity, 1776–1787* (1958). Another criticism of Beard, with emphasis on consensus among the Framers.

The Living Constitution

E. S. Corwin, *The Constitution and What It Means Today*, 12th ed. (1958). Phrase-by-phrase explanation.

——— and J. W. Peltason, *Understanding the Constitution* (1967). More elementary phrase-by-phrase explanation.

G. Dietze (ed.), *Essays on the American Constitution* (1965).

A. N. Holcombe, *Our More Perfect Union* (1950). Defense of American constitutional principles as expounded by Madison and other Founding Fathers.

F. McDonald, *E Pluribus Unum: The Formation of the American Republic, 1776–1790* (1965). Toward an alternative to Beard's economic interpretation of the Constitution.

L. B. Orfield, *Amending the Federal Constitution* (1942).

C. H. Pritchett, *The American Constitution* (1968). General treatment of our constitutional system.

N. J. Small (ed.), *The Constitution of the United States of America: Analysis and Interpretation* (revised and annotated, 1964), Senate Document 39, 88 Cong., 1st Sess., 1964.

J. M. Smith and P. L. Murphy (eds.), *Liberty and Justice: A Historical Record of American Constitutional Development* (1958). Collection of documents.

A. E. Sutherland, *Constitutionalism in America: Origin and Evolution of its Fundamental Ideas* (1965). A series of papers marking constitutional development from the Petition of Right in 1628 to the present.

C. B. Swisher, *The Growth of Constitutional Power in the United States* (1946). The Constitution as symbol, as limitation, and as grant of power.

Federalism

C. A. Amlund, *Federalism in the Confederacy* (1966). The author contends that the Confederacy operated from a strong central government and its states' rights were mostly on paper.

W. Anderson, *The Nation and the States, Rivals or Partners?* (1955). History and present status, by senior political scientist and member of Commission on Intergovernmental Relations.

W. V. Barton, *Interstate Compacts in the Political Process* (1967). Studies the formation of agencies or districts to help resolve interstate or state-national conflicts.

W. H. Bennett, *American Theories of Federalism* (1968).

G. F. Break, *Intergovernmental Fiscal Relations in the United States* (1967). The fiscal problems of a multijurisdictional political system.

J. P. Clark, *The Rise of a New Federalism* (1938). Pioneering discussion of the several varieties of federal-state cooperation.

Commission on Intergovernmental Relations, *A Report to the President for Transmittal to Congress* (1955). Recommendations and survey of national-state relations with emphasis on financial aspects; generally known by name of its chairman as the Kestenbaum Report.

V. Earle (ed.), *Federalism: Infinite Variety in Theory and Practice* (1968). A collection of essays.

D. J. Elazar, *American Federalism: A View From the States* (1966). Combines a general text, an essay, and a report on a research project.

J. W. Fesler, *Area and Administration* (1949). Lectures on problems arising from functional and regional administration.

C. J. Friedrich, *Trends of Federalism in Theory and Practice* (1968). A comparative survey of modern federal systems.

R. A. Goldwin (ed.), *A Nation of States: Essays on the American Federal System* (1963).

W. B. Graves, *American Intergovernmental Relations: Their Origins, Historical Development, and Current Status* (1964). Problems of twentieth-century federalism.

M. Grodzins (D. J. Elazar, ed.), *The American System* (1966). American federalism examined by a noted scholar. Edited after his death by a longtime friend.

R. M. Hutchins, *Two Faces of Federalism* (1961). A stimulating treatment of the function of federalism as an instrument in limiting government.

J. J. Kilpatrick, *The Sovereign States* (1957). Presentation of states'-rights position.

R. H. Leach and R. S. Sugg, Jr., *The Administration of Interstate Compacts* (1959). Review of administrative machinery and case studies of several compacts.

A. Maass (ed.), *Area and Power* (1959). Theoretical analysis of areal division of powers.

A. W. Macmahon (ed.), *Federalism: Mature and Emergent* (1955). Symposium dealing with federalism throughout the world.

W. H. Riker, *Federalism: Origin, Operation, Significance* (1964). A penetrating and sophisticated study.

J. R. Schmidhauser, *The Supreme Court as Final Arbiter in Federal-State Relations, 1789–1957* (1958). Study of the Supreme Court as "umpire of the federal system."

L. D. White, *The States and the Nation* (1953). Another distinguished political scientist's interpretation with somewhat different emphasis from Anderson's.

A. Wildavsky (ed.), *American Federalism in Perspective* (1967). Thirteen essays written between 1945 and 1966.

PART THREE: CIVIL LIBERTIES AND CITIZENSHIP

The Problem of Civil Liberty

H. J. Abraham, *Freedom and the Court* (1967). Civil rights, civil liberties, and Supreme Court doctrine.

American Civil Liberties Union, *Annual Reports*. The state of civil liberties in the United States.

L. J. Barker and T. W. Barker, Jr., *Freedom, Courts, Politics: Studies in Civil Liberties* (1965). Problems of civil liberties placed in their political contexts.

I. Dilliard (ed.), *The Spirit of Liberty: Papers and Addresses of Learned Hand* (1962). Distinguished jurist on the problems of liberty.

W. O. Douglas, *The Right of the People* (1958), *A Living Bill of Rights* (1961). Defense of judicial activism with regard to civil liberties by a Supreme Court justice.

T. I. Emerson, D. Haber, and N. Dorsen, *Political and Civil Rights in the United States*, 2 vols., 4th ed. (1967). Comprehensive collection of civil liberty materials.

W. Gellhorn, *Individual Freedom and Governmental Restraints* (1956). Governmental developments encroaching on freedom of the individual.

L. Hand, *The Bill of Rights* (1958). Famous judge's statement of need for judicial self-restraint in the area of civil liberties.

R. A. Horn, *Groups and the Constitution* (1956). Constitutional rights of groups; their role in constitutional development.

A. H. Kelley (ed.), *Foundations of Freedom in the American Constitution* (1958). Articles on problems of national security and constitutional liberties.

D. J. Kemper, *Decade of Fear: Senator Hennings and Civil Liberties* (1965). Political and personal biography of a leading figure in the Senate from the 1930s to the 1950s.

M. R. Konvitz, *Expanding Liberties, Freedom's Gains in Postwar America* (1966). Social challenges to civil liberty and judicial responses.

———— and C. Rossiter (eds.), *Aspects of Liberty* (1959). Essays presented to R. E. Cushman on aspects of civil liberty.

S. Krislov, *The Supreme Court and Political Freedom* (1968). Role of the Court.

L. W. Levy, *Origins of the Fifth Amendment* (1968). A historical and analytical approach.

R. P. Longaker, *The President and Individual Liberties* (1961). The role of the executive branch in the maintenance of civil liberties.

F. E. Oppenheim, *Dimensions of Freedom* (1961). Systematic analysis of the concept of freedom.

L. Pfeffer, *The Liberties of an American* (1956). General discussion of Supreme Court cases dealing with civil liberties.

R. Pound, *The Development of Constitutional Guarantees of Liberty* (1957). Noted American legal scholar analyzes the circumstances giving rise to guarantees of liberty in England and America.

R. S. Rankin and W. R. Dallmayr, *Freedom and Emergency Powers in the Cold War* (1964). Treats the problem of preservation of liberties when strong government is needed.

J. P. Rocke, *Courts and Rights* (1961). Introduction to the role of the judiciary in maintaining human rights.

————, *The Quest for the Dream: The Development of Civil Rights and Human Relations in Modern America* (1963). Emphasis on political and social history with less attention to legal development.

R. A. Rutland, *The Birth of the Bill of Rights 1776–1791* (1962). Best single-volume history of origins and early years.

R. J. Tresolini, *These Liberties: Case Studies in Civil Rights* (1968). An introductory text in civil liberties.

W. W. Turner, *Invisible Witness: The Use and Abuse of the New Technology of Crime Investigation* (1968).

Freedom of Religion

D. E. Boles, *The Bible, Religion, and the Public Schools* (1961). The problem of religion in public education.

D. Fellman, *Religion in American Public Law* (1965). Religious liberty in the United States, from public law and Supreme Court pronouncements.

M. De Wolfe Howe, *The Garden and the Wilderness* (1965). Supreme Court interpretation and misinterpretation in the field of religious liberty.

A. W. Johnson and F. H. Yost, *Separation of Church and State in the United States*, rev. ed. (1948). Theory and development of American law.

P. B. Kurland, *Religion and the Law: Of Church and State and the Supreme Court* (1962).

D. R. Manwaring, *Render unto Caesar* (1962). A study of the flag-salute controversy.

W. K. Muir, Jr., *Prayer in the Public Schools* (1968). Activities and attitudes of school officials in the aftermath of rulings on school prayer.

F. W. O'Brien, *Justice Reed and the First Amendment: The Religion Clauses* (1958).

J. M. O'Neill, *Religion and Education under the Constitution* (1949).

A. P. Stokes, *Church and State in the United States*, 3 vols. (1950). Encyclopedic source material.

U. S. Department of Health, Education, and Welfare, *The State and the Non-Public School* (1958).

Freedom of Speech

I. H. Carmen, *Movies, Censorship, and the Law* (1966). Results of Supreme Court rulings on movie censorship.

Z. Chafee, *Free Speech in the United States*, rev. ed. (1941). Most comprehensive study of restrictions on speech during and after World War I; discussion of dangers inherent in sedition laws.

M. L. Ernst and A. V. Schwartz, *Censorship: The Search for the Obscene* (1964). An argument that the dangers inherent in censorship are greater than those in pornography.

D. M. Gillmor, *Free Press and Fair Trial* (1966). A survey of several cases and the problems created by press coverage.

J. Lofton, *Justice and the Press* (1966). Suggests voluntary restraints for the press in trial coverage.

A. Meiklejohn, *Free Speech and Its Relation to Self-Government* (1948). Attack on clear-and-present-danger doctrine and defense of the absolute right of political speech.

787

J. S. Mill, *Essay on Liberty* (1859; many editions). Famous defense of free speech.

T. J. Murphy, *Censorship: Government and Obscenity*. 1963. A discussion of what is obscene and a defense of a reasonable censorship to discharge hard-core pornography.

J. C. Paul and M. Schwartz, *Federal Censorship: Obscenity in the Mail* (1960). Review and analysis of regulation of obscenity.

C. Rembar, *The End of Obscenity: The Trials of Lady Chatterley, Tropic of Cancer and Fanny Hill* (1968).

O. J. Rogge, *The First and the Fifth* (1960). Analysis of the interrelationship between these two important guarantees.

F. E. Rourke, *Secrecy and Publicity* (1961). The continuing problem of freedom of information in a free society.

M. Shapiro, *Freedom of Speech: The Supreme Court and Judicial Review* (1966). An argument for judicial activism in the defense of free speech.

J. M. Smith, *Freedom's Fetters* (1956). Study of alien and sedition laws.

S. Zagri, *Free Press, Fair Trial* (1966). The press and new media and the judicial process in the James Hoffa investigation.

The Battle against Subversive Conduct and Seditious Speech

Association of the Bar of the City of New York, Special Committee on Federal Loyalty-Security Program, *The Federal Loyalty-Security Program* (1956). Critical report by this influential body.

R. S. Brown, *Loyalty and Security; Employment Tests in the United States* (1958). Critical study of loyalty and security programs.

H. W. Chase, *Security and Liberty* (1955). Legislative and judicial handling of native Communists, 1947–1955.

Commission on Government Security, *Report* (1957). Study of the internal security program; popularly known as the Wright Report.

T. I. Cook, *Democratic Rights versus Communist Activity* (1954). Defends view that it is consistent with democratic principles and practices to make Communist political activity illegal.

M. Grodzins, *The Loyal and the Disloyal* (1956). Discussion of factors that make men loyal.

S. Hook, *Political Power and Personal Freedom: Critical Studies in Democracy, Communism, and Civil Rights* (1959).

J. E. Hoover, *Masters of Deceit: The Story of Communism in America and How to Fight It* (1958). By the Director of the FBI.

H. M. Hyman, *To Try Men's Souls: Loyalty Tests in American History* (1959). Historical background.

H. D. Lasswell, *National Security and Individual Freedom* (1950). Pressures created by cold war, with recommendations.

E. Latham, *The Communist Controversy in Washington—From the New Deal to McCarthy* (1966). Study of Communist activity in the federal government and the phenomenon of McCarthyism.

W. Schneir and M. Schneir, *Invitation to an Inquest* (1965). Examination of the trial and execution of Julius and Ethel Rosenberg for spying.

J. H. Schoar, *Loyalty in America* (1957). Analysis of the concept of loyalty.

S. H. Stouffer, *Communism, Conformity and Civil Liberties* (1955). Survey of American attitudes.

F. A. Warren III, *Liberals and Communism: The Red Decade Revisited* (1966). An analysis of Communist influence on liberal thought in the United States in the 1930s.

Equality under the Law

C. Abrams, *Forbidden Neighbors: A Study of Prejudice in Housing* (1955).

F. B. Barbour (ed.), *The Black Power Revolt* (1968).

R. H. Barrett, *Integration at Ole Miss* (1965). Liberal Southerner's account of the desegregation crisis at the University of Mississippi.

A. P. Blaustein and C. C. Ferguson, Jr., *Desegregation and the Law* (1957). Legal aspects of desegregation.

W. A. Brophy and S. Aberle, *The Indian: America's Unfinished Business* (1966). The injustices done to the American Indian, past and present.

H. Brotz (ed.), *Negro Social and Political Thought: 1850–1920* (1966). An anthology of Negro thought on the dilemma of the American Negro.

V. Countryman, *Discrimination and the Law* (1965).

H. Cruse, *The Crisis of the Negro Intellectual* (1968). The Negro intellectual in the white world.

L. W. Dunbar, *A. Republic of Equals* (1966). A liberal white Southerner's view of the racial question and the South.

R. L. Gates, *The Making of Massive Resistance: Virginia's Politics of Public School Desegregation, 1954–1956* (1963). One state's response to Supreme Court policy.

W. Gillette, *The Right to Vote: Politics and the Passage of the Fifteenth Amendment* (1965). A concise history of the passage of the Fifteenth Amendment.

E. Ginzberg and A. S. Eichner, *The Trouble-*

788

some Presence: American Democracy and the Negro (1964). The Negro and the path to true democracy.

J. Greenberg, Race Relations and American Law (1959). Comprehensive coverage of legal aspects.

W. H. Grier and P. M. Cobbs, Black Rage (1968). The effects of racism on the mind, by two black psychiatrists.

A. P. Grimes, Equality in America: Religion, Race and the Urban Majority (1964). Essays illustrating the impact of Supreme Court decisions in modern America.

_____, The Puritan Ethic and Woman Suffrage (1967). A new theory on the origins of woman suffrage.

M. Grodzins, Americans Betrayed: Politics and the Japanese Evacuation (1949). Treats what many considered a violation of civil liberties during World War II.

R. L. Hale, Freedom through Law (1952). Public control of private power.

R. Harris, The Quest for Equality (1960). Historical and constitutional study of events leading to the Brown decision.

B. Hays, A Southern Moderate Speaks (1959). Discussion of the race issue by the former congressman from the Little Rock area.

J. A. Higbee, Development and Administration of the New York State Law against Discrimination (1968). Survey of public hearings, litigation, and conciliation activities of the New York State Commission for Human Rights.

J. C. Hough, Jr., Black Power and White Protestants (1968). Christian response to current trends in black thought.

L. Ianniello (ed.), Milestones Along the March: Twelve Historic Civil Rights Documents—from World War II to Selma (1965). With introduction by John P. Roche.

J. B. James, The Framing of the Fourteenth Amendment (1965). The Fourteenth Amendment as viewed by its contemporaries.

H. Kalven, Jr., The Negro and the First Amendment (1965). The civil rights movement and interpretation of the First Amendment.

S. Katz, Negro and Jew: An Encounter in America (1968). The strange history of black-Jewish relations.

L. Killian and C. Grigg, Racial Crisis in America: Leadership in Conflict (1964). The sit-in in perspective.

D. B. King and C. W. Quick (ed.), Legal Aspects of the Civil Rights Movement (1965). Essays on the civil rights movement.

M. R. Konvitz (ed.), Law and Social Action (1951). Essays on infringement of civil rights by private groups.

S. Krislov, The Negro in Federal Employ-

ment: The Quest for Equal Opportunity (1967). An important aspect of the civil rights movement.

E. C. Ladd, Jr., Negro Political Leadership in the South (1966). A report on Negro political activity, primarily on the urban level, in the South.

J. C. Leggett, Class, Race, And Labor (1967). Class consciousness and race relations, from a case study in Detroit.

J. Lester, Look Out Whitey! Black Power's Gon' Get Your Mama! (1968).

C. M. Lightfoot, Ghetto Rebellion to Black Liberation (1968).

D. Lockard, Toward Equal Opportunity: A Study of State and Local Anti-Discrimination Laws (1968). Problems of enacting and enforcing antidiscrimination legislation.

P. McCauley and E. D. Ball (eds.), Southern Schools: Progress and Problems (1959).

G. Marx, Protest and Prejudice: A Study of Belief in the Black Community (1968). Black attitudes toward Jews.

D. R. Matthews and J. W. Prothro, Negroes and the New Southern Politics (1966). Negro political participation in a changing South.

W. Mendelson, Discrimination (1962). Based on reports of the United States Commission on Civil Rights.

L. Miller, The Petitioners: The Story of the Supreme Court of the United States and the Negro (1966). Struggle for racial justice in the courts.

National Advisory Commission on Civil Disorders, Report (1968). The Kerner Commission's probing analysis, with recommendations, of the racial disorders of 1967.

I. A. Newby, Jim Crow's Defense: Anti-Negro Thought in America, 1900–1930 (1965). A survey of scholarly and popular racism.

_____, The Segregationists: Readings in the Defense of Segregation and White Supremacy (1968). White supremacist thought since 1890.

P. H. Norgren and S. E. Hill, Toward Fair Employment (1964). A study of racial discrimination in employment and suggested programs for correcting the present situation.

J. W. Peltason, Fifty-eight Lonely Men: Southern Federal Judges and School Desegregation (1962).

J. R. Pennock and J. W. Chapman (eds.), Nomos IX: Equality (1967). Eighteen essays concerned with definition and role of equality in the context of the contemporary political scene.

W. Record, Race and Radicalism (1964 and 1966). The author finds little or no Communist influence in the civil rights movement.

P. I. Rose, *The Subject is Race* (1968). The teaching of race relations in the United States from the nineteenth century to the present.

B. Smith, *They Closed Their Schools, Prince Edward County, Virginia, 1951–1964* (1965). The desegregation battle in Virginia public schools.

Southern School News. Periodic reports on desegregation in public schools.

M. I. Sovern, *Legal Restraints on Racial Discrimination in Employment* (1966) The implementation of fair employment legislation from a lawyer's viewpoint.

D. S. Strong, *Negroes, Ballots, and Judges* (1968). Federal pronouncements on Negro voting and Southern legislative and judicial resistance.

B. E. Swanson, *The Struggle for Equality* (1966). The struggle to desegregate the New York City public schools.

K. E. Taeuber and A. F. Taeuber, *Negroes in Cities: Residential Segregation and Neighborhood Change* (1965). Comprehensive data on and interpretation of recent happenings in Negro housing and residential segregation.

J. Ten Broek, et al., *Prejudice, War, and the Constitution* (1954). Origins, politics, and legality of Japanese-American evacuations in World War II.

N. C. Thomas, *Rule 9: Politics, Administration, and Civil Rights* (1966). Fair-housing controversy in Michigan.

M. M. Tumin, et al., *Desegregation: Resistance and Readiness* (1958). Study of attitudes toward the Negro and desegregation.

United States Commission on Civil Rights, *Annual Reports.* Findings and recommendations of the commission created by the Civil Rights Act of 1957.

United States President's Committee on Civil Rights, *To Secure These Rights* (1947).

C. E. Vose, *Caucasians Only* (1959). Comprehensive discussion of Supreme Court's decisions on restrictive covenants.

C. V. Woodward, *The Strange Career of Jim Crow* (1955). Account of the growth of segregation laws.

Rights to Life, Liberty, and Property

W. M. Beaney, *Right to Counsel in American Courts* (1955). Survey of law and decisions.

E. S. Corwin, *Liberty against Government* (1948). Essays on the growth and decline of substantive due process.

D. Fellman, *The Constitutional Right of Association* (1963). A legal scholar looks at case law pertaining to the constitutional guaranty.

H. Kalven, Jr., and H. Zeisel, *The American Jury* (1966). Differences between judge and jury in determining the guilt of criminal defendants.

W. R. LaFave, *Arrest: The Decision to Take a Suspect into Custody* (1965).

J. W. Landynski, *Search and Seizure and the Supreme Court* (1966). Historical and analytical account of the Court's interpretation of the Fourth Amendment.

A. Lewis, *Gideon's Trumpet* (1964). Exciting account of the landmark right-to-counsel decision from the perspective of the appellant.

E. V. Long, *The Intruders: The Invasion of Privacy by Government and Industry* (1967). Evaluation of governmental wiretapping and related practices by a former United States Senator.

W. F. Murphy, *Wiretapping on Trial* (1965). A case study of the Osborn case and the judicial development of the right of privacy.

D. J. Newman, *Conviction: The Determination of Guilt or Innocence without Trial* (1966).

President's Commission of Law Enforcement and Administration of Justice, *The Challenge of Crime in a Free Society* (1967). A report on crime in America and what can be done about it.

A. S. Trebach, *The Rationing of Justice* (1964). Concerns the problems of the accused, employing modern social science techniques.

Immigration and Citizenship

O. Handlin, *Race and Nationality in American Life* (1957).

——, *The Uprooted* (1952). Moving history of immigration from the perspective of the immigrants.

M. A. Jones, *American Immigration* (1960).

W. Preston, Jr., *Aliens and Dissenters: Federal Suppression of Radicals, 1903–1933* (1963).

PART FOUR: THE PEOPLE IN POLITICS

Public Opinion

Of special interest is the *Public Opinion Quarterly.*

American Institute for Political Communication, *The Vietnam Issue: University Student Attitudes and the 1966 Congressional Election* (1966). Formation of student opinion on Vietnam and resulting effect on the 1966 congressional elections.

B. Berelson and M. Janowitz (eds.), *Reader*

in Public Opinion and Communication (1953). Readings on all major phases of subject.

M. Choukas, *Propaganda Comes of Age* (1965). The massive role of propaganda in our age.

R. Christenson and R. O. McWilliams, *Voice of the People*, rev. ed. (1968). Survey of current issues and research in public opinion.

J. Dewey, *The Public and Its Problems* (1927).

A. C. Dicey, *Law and Public Opinion in England* (1905).

F. I. Greenstein, *Children and Politics* (1965). An investigation of the molding of political attitudes during the period from four to eight years of age.

B. C. Hennessy, *Public Opinion* (1965). Introduction to theory and method of public opinion.

A. O. Hero, Jr., *Opinion Leaders in American Communities* (1959). Effect of primary-group communications on opinions.

————, *The Southerner and World Affairs* (1965). Analysis of the development of political thought from 1936 to 1962 in the South contrasted with the rest of the nation.

S. Kelley, Jr., *Professional Public Relations and Political Power* (1956). Role of "Madison Avenue" in American politics.

V. O. Key, Jr., *Public Opinion and American Democracy* (1961). Most recent full-scale treatment of concepts and issues.

R. E. Lane and D. O. Sears, *Public Opinion* (1964). Short but excellent examination of the dynamics of opinion formation.

L. C. Lewin (ed.), *A Treasury of American Political Humor* (1964).

°W. Lippmann, *Public Opinion* (1922).

A. L. Lowell, *Public Opinion and Popular Government* (1913).

N. R. Luttbeg (ed.), *Public Opinion and Public Policy: Models of Political Linkage* (1968). Mechanism by which public opinion is articulated to the policy-makers.

F. H. O'Neal, *Humor: The Politician's Tool* (1964).

G. Wallas, *Human Nature in Politics* (1919). Marked a reaction from earlier overrationalistic interpretations of politics and public opinion.

Public Opinion Polls

H. Cantril (ed.), *Public Opinion: Directory of Polls, 1935–1946* (1951). Comprehensive collection of poll data.

Center for the Study of Democratic Institutions, *Opinion Polls* (1962). Comments on issues and significance of polls by Elmo Roper and George Gallup.

C. Y. Glock (ed.), *Survey Research in the Social Sciences* (1967).

F. Mosteller, et al., *The Pre-Election Polls of 1948* (1949). Essays by experts who investigated the reasons for the 1948 polling fiasco.

M. B. Parten, *Surveys, Polls, and Samples* (1950). Description of polling procedures.

L. Rogers, *The Pollsters* (1949). Criticism of procedures and attack on contribution of public opinion polls.

F. F. Stephan and P. J. McCarthy, *Sampling Opinions: An Analysis of Survey Procedure* (1958).

Media of Communication

R. W. Budd, R. K. Thorp, and L. Donohew, *Content Analysis of Communication* (1967). A study of the communications process.

D. Cater, *The Fourth Branch of Government* (1959). Critical evaluation of the relations of the press with the national government.

Center for the Study of Democratic Institutions, *Television* (1962). Provocative discussion on status of and trends in television.

Z. Chafee, *Government and Mass Communications* (1947). Published under auspices of the Commission on Freedom of the Press.

R. R. Fagen, *Politics and Communication* (1966). Communications as a factor in the political process.

P. Fisher and R. L. Lowenstein (eds.), *Race and the News Media* (1967). Speeches and papers on the civil rights struggle and the role of mass media.

A. O. Hero, *Mass Media and World Affairs* (1959). Study of mass media's influence on opinions toward foreign affairs.

R. E. Hiebert, *The Press in Washington* (1966). Articles by Washington journalists.

D. Lacy, *Freedom and Communications* (1965). Lectures on communications systems in contemporary America.

P. F. Lazarsfeld, *Radio and the Printed Page* (1940). Role of radio in the communication of ideas.

W. Lippmann, *Liberty and the News* (1920). Critical essay by one of America's famous journalists.

F. L. Mott, *American Journalism* (1941). Standard history.

D. D. Nimmo, *Newsgathering in Washington: A Study in Political Communication* (1964). Interaction of government and the press.

W. L. Rivers, *The Opinionmakers* (1965). Relationship between reporters and government officials and a critical evaluation of the effect of the press on public opinion.

A. E. Rowse, *Slanted News: A Case Study of the Nixon and Stevenson Fund Stories* (1957).

B. Rubin, *Political Television* (1967). Influence of television on elections and the Presidency.

W. A. Wood, *Electronic Journalism* (1967). Accomplishments and problems of television news and public affairs programs.

G. Wyckoff, *The Image Candidates: American Politics in the Age of Television* (1968).

Interest Groups

R. Baker, *The American Legion and American Foreign Policy* (1954).

C. A. Beard, *The Economic Basis of Politics* (1922). The importance of economic interests in the political process.

D. C. Blaisdell, *Economic Power and Political Pressures* (1941). TNEC Monograph 26. Pioneering study.

P. Blau and O. D. Duncan, *The American Occupational Structure* (1967). Causes and effects of individual occupational status.

F. Calkins, *The C.I.O. and the Democratic Party* (1952). Five case studies in 1950 elections by research assistant of CIO-PAC.

J. A. Crampton, *The National Farmers Union: Ideology of a Pressure Group* (1965). The ideology of the National Farmers' Union.

J. Deakin, *The Lobbyists* (1966). The history of lobbying with brief character sketches of some lobbyists.

L. E. Ebersole, *Church Lobbying in the Nation's Capital* (1951). The religious lobbies—the causes for which they work and the methods they use.

H. W. Ehrmann, *Interest Groups on Four Continents* (1958). Discussions of interest groups in several countries, including the United States.

R. Engler, *The Politics of Oil* (1961). Review and analysis of petroleum industry's political influence.

P. O. Foss, *Politics and Grass* (1960). Interest-group behavior relating to grazing-land allocation.

J. Frank, *If Men Were Angels* (1942). Social, economic, and psychological factors in the working of administrative agencies.

J. Gaer, *The First Round: The Story of the CIO Political Action Committee* (1944). Contains facsimile examples of CIO pamphlets.

O. Garceau, *The Political Life of the American Medical Association* (1941). Pioneering study of the political activities of America's doctors.

L. L. Gerson, *The Hyphenate in Recent American Politics and Diplomacy* (1964). The influence of various ethnic groups in the United States from 1890 to 1956.

W. A. Glaser and D. L. Sills (eds.), *The Government of Associations* (1966). Articles on the subject of voluntary associations.

J. Gray and V. H. Bernstein, *The Inside Story of the Legion* (1948). Critical of the American Legion.

J. R. Gusfield, *Symbolic Crusade: Status Politics and the American Temperance Movement* (1963). An attempt to separate symbolic from instrumental politics.

S. Halperin, *The Political World of American Zionism* (1961). Interest-group analysis in a broad social context.

E. P. Herring, *Group Representation before Congress* (1929). Relations between interest groups and formal institutions of government.

——, *Public Administration and the Public Interest* (1936). Interaction between interest groups and administrative machinery.

A. Holtzman, *Interest Groups and Lobbying* (1966). Interest groups and lobbying based on previous work by noted scholars.

R. S. Jones, *A History of the American Legion* (1946). The official history.

L. C. Kesselman, *The Social Politics of FEPC* (1948). A study in reform pressure movements.

O. M. Kile, *The Farm Bureau through Three Decades* (1948). The official history.

E. Lane, *Lobbying and the Law* (1964). A survey of state regulation.

E. Latham, *The Group Basis of Politics* (1952). Interplay of group pressures in basing-point legislation.

S. M. Lipset, M. A. Trow, and J. S. Coleman, *Union Democracy: The Inside Politics of the International Typographical Union* (1956). Conditions of democratic and oligarchic control of voluntary organizations.

A. Maass, *Muddy Waters* (1951). Indictment of the Army Corps of Engineers as "the lobby that can't be licked."

G. McConnell, *Private Power and American Democracy* (1966). Influence of private power groups on public policy.

D. D. McKean, *Pressures on the Legislature of New Jersey* (1938). By a political scientist and former member of New Jersey legislature.

H. R. Mahood (ed.), *Pressure Groups in American Politics* (1967).

L. W. Milbrath, *The Washington Lobbyists* (1963). The role of the lobbyist in the formation of public policy.

R. J. Monsen, Jr., and M. W. Cannon, *The Makers of Public Policy: American Power Groups and Their Ideology* (1965). Formal and informal power groups and their influence on public policy.

P. H. Odegard, *Pressure Politics: The Study of the Anti-saloon League* (1928). Standard source.

M. Olson, Jr., *The Logic of Collective Action: Public Goods and the Theory of Groups* (1965). An explanation and investigation of the motivating forces in group action.

S. M. Peck, *The Rank-and-File Order* (1963). Class consciousness in the worker class.

C. M. Rehmus and D. B. McLaughlin (eds.), *Labor and American Politics* (1967). A history of labor's political involvement.

F. W. Riggs, *Pressures on Congress: A Study of the Repeal of Chinese Exclusion* (1950). Informing case study.

E. E. Schattschneider, *Politics, Pressures, and the Tariff* (1935). Case study based on mass of evidence from hearings on the Smoot-Hawley tariff bill.

A. M. Scott and M. A. Hunt, *Congress and Lobbies: Image and Reality* (1966). How congressmen view interest groups.

Select Committee on Lobbying Activities of the House, *Hearings*, 81st Cong., 2d Sess. (1950). Important congressional investigation; materials on some major organizations.

M. Steadman, Jr., *Religion and Politics in America* (1964). Churches in the American power structure.

P. Taft, *Organized Labor in American History* (1964). A comprehensive study.

B. R. Twiss, *Lawyers and the Constitution* (1942). How *laissez faire* came to the Supreme Court.

D. Wecter, *When Johnny Comes Marching Home* (1944). Study of return of soldiers after Revolutionary, Civil, and First World Wars.

H. Zeigler, *Interest Groups in American Society* (1964). An interpretation of the role of organized interest groups in policymaking.

_____, *The Political Life of American Teachers* (1967). A summary of ideas from the earlier work.

_____, *The Political World of the High School Teacher* (1966). A study of the political culture and behavior of American high school teachers.

Voting and Voting Behavior

H. M. Bain and D. S. Hecock, *Ballot Position and Voter's Choice* (1957). Effect of candidate's position on the ballot on voting behavior.

D. Bell (ed.), *The Radical Right* (1963). Eight famous social scientists view the ideas and activities of the current "far right."

B. R. Berelson, P. F. Lazarsfeld, and W. N. McPhee, *Voting* (1954). Voting in 1948 in a New York community, with useful summary of findings of other voting studies.

A. Boshoff and H. Zeigler, *Voting Patterns in a Local Election* (1964).

E. Burdick and A. J. Brodbeck (eds.), *American Voting Behavior* (1959). Collection of essays.

A. Campbell, P. Converse, W. Miller, and D. Stokes, *The American Voter* (1960). Analysis of 1956 election based on national sample data.

A. Campbell and H. C. Cooper, *Group Differences in Attitudes and Votes* (1956). Study of the 1954 election based on a nationwide survey.

A. Campbell, G. Gurin, and W. E. Miller, *The Voter Decides* (1954). Study of the 1952 election based on data gathered by sampling.

B. Cosman, *Five States for Goldwater: Continuity and Change in Southern Presidential Voting Patterns* (1966). Changing groupings in Southern voting behavior.

H. Eulau, *Class and Party in the Eisenhower Years* (1962). Interplay of class and voting behavior.

W. H. Flanigan, *Political Behavior of the American Electorate* (1968). Taken from four major national surveys from 1952 to 1964.

L. A. Froman, Jr., *People and Politics: An Analysis of the American Political System* (1962). Development of a theory of politics.

L. Fuchs, *The Political Behavior of American Jews* (1956).

H. F. Gosnell, *Democracy, the Threshold of Freedom* (1948). Discussion of theories of citizenship and of the premises of the right to vote.

M. K. Jennings and L. H. Zeigler (eds.), *The Electoral Process* (1966). Readings on the phenomenon of elections in a democratic society.

V. O. Key, Jr., *The Responsible Electorate* (1966). A defense of the much maligned voting public.

_____, *Southern Politics in State and Nation* (1949). The impact of the "Negro problem" on Southern politics.

A. Kornhauser, A. J. Mayer, and H. L. Sheppard, *When Labor Votes: A Study of Auto Workers* (1956). Detroit auto workers in the 1952 presidential election.

W. Kornhauser, *The Politics of Mass Society* (1959). Analysis of difference between citizen participation and spectatorship.

R. E. Lane, *Political Life: How People Get Involved in Politics* (1958).

P. F. Lazarsfeld, B. R. Berelson, and H.

Gaudet, *The People's Choice* (1948). Demonstrates the technique of panel interviewing on "How the voter makes up his mind in a presidential campaign."

G. Lenski, *The Religious Factor* (1961). Thorough analysis based on survey in Detroit area.

S. M. Lipset, *Political Man* (1960). Important series of articles on political sociology.

C. E. Merriam and H. F. Gosnell, *Nonvoting* (1924). Pioneering study.

L. W. Milbrath, *Political Participation: How and Why Do People Get Involved in Politics* (1965). Catalogue of knowledge on the subject and a few propositions.

K. H. Porter, *A History of Suffrage in the United States* (1918). Single-volume history.

E. L. Tatum, *The Changed Political Thought of the Negro, 1915–1940* (1952). Causes and consequences of changing political allegiances of Negroes.

D. Wallace, *First Tuesday: A Study of Rationality in Voting* (1964). Analysis of voting behavior and public opinion in suburban Westport, Connecticut.

R. E. Wolfinger (ed.), *Readings in American Political Behavior* (1966). Collection of empirical research and case studies.

Political Parties

H. Agar, *The Price of Union* (1950). History stressing the thesis that loosely organized and undisciplined parties are essential to the preservation of the Union.

W. E. Binkley, *American Political Parties, Their Natural History*, 3d ed. (1958). Stresses role of parties as coalitions of interest groups.

D. Burner, *The Politics of Provincialism: The Democratic Party in Transition, 1918–1932* (1967).

J. M. Burns, *The Deadlock of Democracy: Four Party Politics in America* (1962). Old and new political alignments.

W. N. Chambers and W. D. Burnham (eds.), *The American Party Systems: Stages of Political Development* (1968). History of United States competitive party politics.

Committee on Political Parties of the American Political Science Association, *Toward a More Responsible Two Party System* (1950). By committee of sixteen authorities under chairmanship of Professor Schattschneider; recommendations for strengthening the American party system.

B. Cosman and R. J. Huckshorn (eds.), *Republican Politics* (1968). The Republican party during and after the 1964 election.

E. N. Costikyan, *Behind Closed Doors: Politics in the Public Interest* (1966). Political and personal memoirs of a member of New York's Reform Democratic movement.

C. P. Cotter and B. C. Hennessey, *Politics Without Power: The National Party Committees* (1964). Emphasis on the national chairman and the committee staffs.

W. J. Crotty, *Approaches to the Study of Party Organization* (1968). Problems of internal party organization.

N. E. Cunningham, *The Jeffersonian Republicans: The Foundation of Party Organization, 1789–1801* (1957).

Eagleton Foundation, *Case Studies in Practical Politics*. Continuing series of studies of concrete political situations.

L. Eisenstein and E. Rosenberg, *A Stripe of Tammany's Tiger* (1966). An epitaph to machine politics.

S. Eldersveld, *Political Parties: A Behavioral Analysis* (1963).

M. Stanton Evans, *The Future of Conservatism: From Taft to Reagan and Beyond* (1968).

J. H. Fenton, *People and Parties in Politics* (1966). Political parties and interest groups in the political process.

G. F. Gilder and B. K. Chapman, *The Party That Lost Its Head: The Republican Collapse and Imperatives for Revival* (1966). A study of the contemporary dilemmas of the Republican party.

R. M. Goldman, *The Democratic Party in American Politics* (1966). The evolution of the party with special focus on contemporary trends.

F. Greenstein, *The American Party System and the American People* (1963). Handy synthesis of recent research.

J. Hart, *The American Dissent: A Decade of Modern Conservatism* (1966). Summary of the thought of William Buckley's conservative journal, *The National Review*, over the last ten years.

E. P. Herring, *The Politics of Democracy* (1940; reissued 1966). Interpretation and defense of present system; interpretations somewhat contrary to those of Schattschneider and the committee report mentioned below.

D. G. Herzberg and G. M. Pomper (eds.), *American Party Politics: Essays and Readings* (1966). Political parties as factors in voting behavior, elections, and the governmental process.

A. N. Holcombe, *The Political Parties of Today* (1924), *The New Party Politics* (1933), *The Middle Classes in American Politics* (1940). Interpretation of American politics as moving from sectional to urban or "class" politics with the middle class holding the balance and preserving free government.

C. O. Jones, *The Republican Party in American Politics* (1965). The implications of being the minority party.

J. LaPalombara and M. Weiner (eds.), *Political Parties and Political Development*

(1966). Political parties and party systems and their role in political development.

A. Larson, *A Republican Looks at His Party* (1956). Views of a member of the liberal wing of the Republican party.

H. D. Lasswell, *Politics: Who Gets What, When, How* (1946; reissued 1958). One of Lasswell's more popular treatments.

K. Lawson, *Political.Parties and Democracy in the United States* (1968).

A. Leiserson, *Parties and Politics, An Institutional and Behavioral Approach* (1958).

R. G. Martin, *The Bosses* (1964). Political machinery in United States history.

G. H. Mayer, *The Republican Party 1854–1966* (1968).

C. G. Mayo and B. L. Crowe (eds.), *American Political Parties: A Systematic Perspective* (1967). Articles on the structure and function of political parties.

R. Michels, *Political Parties* (reprinted in 1949). Important sociological study of the oligarchical tendencies of European democratic political parties.

H. P. Nash, Jr., *Third Parties in American Politics* (1958). Their role and history.

R. F. Nichols, *The Invention of the American Political Parties* (1967). Traces the old-world origins of the American party system, which took shape in the 1850s.

S. Neumann (ed.), *Modern Political Parties* (1956). Discussions of the party systems in several nations, including the United States.

R. D. Novak, *The Agony of the G.O.P. 1964* (1965). The four-year struggle within the Republican party that culminated in the nomination of Barry Goldwater.

M. Ostrogorski, *Democracy and the Organization of Political Parties*, 2 vols. (1908). Early, classic interpretation of development of parties in the United States and England.

K. A. Porter and D. B. Johnson, *National Party Platforms, 1840–1964* (1966).

A. Ranney and W. Kendall, *The American Party System* (1956). Examination of American parties as instruments of democratic government; defense of existing party system.

E. E. Schattschneider, *Party Government* (1942); *The Struggle for Party Government* (1948). Case for more centralized and disciplined parties by an outstanding scholar who has virtually developed a school of thought about American politics.

H. Scott, *Come to the Party* (1968). The last three decades of Republican national politics.

J. H. Silby, *The Shrine of Party: Congressional Voting Behavior, 1841–1852* (1967). Whig and Democrat interests in Congress.

F. J. Sorauf, *Party Politics in America* (1968). The parties as political structures in the political process.

M. Stedman and S. Stedman, *Discontent at the Polls* (1950). Account of legal, political, and other aspects of third parties.

F. J. Turner, *The Significance of Sections in American History* (1937). The importance of sectionalism in American politics was first projected by Turner at the beginning of the twentieth century.

M. Viorst, *Fall From Grace: The Republican Party and the Puritan Ethic* (1968).

N. L. Zucker, *The American Party Process: Readings and Comments* (1968).

Leadership

J. D. Barber (ed.), *Political Leadership in American Government* (1964). Excellent collection of materials on political leadership.

L. Bennett, Jr., *What Manner of Man* (1964). The life of Martin Luther King.

J. M. Burns, *Roosevelt: The Lion and the Fox* (1956). Problems and practices of FDR as a Democratic leader.

E. F. Goldman, *The Tragedy of Lyndon Johnson: A Historian's Personal Interpretation* (1968).

A. Gottfried, *Boss Cermak of Chicago: A Study of Political Leadership* (1962).

A. W. Gouldner (ed.), *Studies in Leadership* (1950). Essays on apathy and various kinds of leadership.

J. Jacobs and the editors of *American Heritage, RFK: His Life and Death* (1968).

H. Johnson and B. M. Gwertzman, *Fulbright: The Dissenter* (1968). One of the Senate's most outspoken members.

H. Lasswell, *Psychopathology and Politics* (1930), and *Power and Personality* (1948). *Through use of interviews, observations, and psychological techniques, Lasswell has developed a typology of political leaders and related their public careers to their psychological characteristics.*

D. Marvick (ed.), *Political Decision-Makers* (1961). Diverse approaches to the study of political leadership.

P. Salinger, *With Kennedy* (1966). The Kennedy era—especially government-press relations—by President Kennedy's press secretary.

A. M. Schlesinger, Jr., *The Age of Roosevelt: The Crisis of the Old Order*, vol. I (1958); *The Coming of the New Deal*, vol. II (1959); *The Politics of Upheaval*, vol. III (1960). Studies by leading historian.

J. A. Schlesinger, *Ambition and Politics: Political Careers in the United States* (1966). Behavior as a factor of goals and ambitions in a political career.

A. Steinberg, *Sam Johnson's Boy: A Close-*

Up of the President from Texas (1968). A biography of LBJ.

S. Verba, *Small Groups and Political Behavior: A Study of Political Leadership* (1961). Experimental findings related to notions of the political process.

W. F. Whyte, Jr., *Street Corner Society* (1943). Close study of informal leadership.

Elections

J. Abels, *The Degeneration of Our Presidential Election: A History and Analysis of an American Institution in Trouble* (1968). An argument for reform in election procedures.

H. E. Alexander, *Financing the 1964 Election* (1966). Study of party and campaign finance.

_____ (ed.), *Studies of Money in Politics, A Series of Seven Monographs* (1965). Aspects of campaign finance.

W. Buchanan and A. Bird, *Money as a Campaign Resource: Tennessee Democratic Senatorial Primaries, 1948–1964* (1966). Case studies in campaign finance.

A. Campbell, P. E. Converse, W. E. Miller, and D. E. Stokes, *Elections and the Political Order* (1966). The functions of elections in the total political system.

M. C. Cummings, Jr., *Congressmen and the Electorate: Elections for the U.S. House and the President, 1920–1964* (1964). The relationship between congressional and presidential elections.

_____ (ed.), *The National Election of 1964* (1966). Seven essays discussing various aspects of the phenomenon of an election.

P. T. David, R. M. Goldman, and R. C. Bain, *The Politics of National Party Conventions* (1960). Analysis of the nominating process.

P. T. David, et al., *Presidential Nominating Politics in 1952* (1954). Five-volume report undertaken by over 150 political scientists.

J. W. Davis, *Presidential Primaries: Road to the White House* (1967). The evolution of the primary system and a study of some past primary strategies.

_____, *Springboard to the White House: Presidential Primaries: How They Are Fought and Won* (1967). A study of the increasingly important presidential primaries.

B. F. Donahoe, *Private Plans and Public Dangers: The Story of FDR's Third Nomination* (1966). A study of the struggle for the 1940 Democratic presidential nomination.

H. Faber (ed.), *The Road to the White House* (1965). The 1964 presidential primaries

and campaign, by *The New York Times* staff.

B. L. Felknor, *Dirty Politics* (1966). A study of campaign techniques and the state of contemporary campaigning, with emphasis on the growing political role of public relations.

D. Frost, *The Presidential Debate, 1968* (1968). Interviews with nine leading contenders for the Presidency.

H. G. Greenhill, *Labor Money in Wisconsin Politics, 1964* (1966). Organized labor in the 1964 Wisconsin elections; financial and political aid.

S. Harris, *The Economics of the Political Parties* (1962). Major parties' fiscal positions.

A. Heard, *The Costs of Democracy* (1960). Authoritative study of campaign finance.

_____ (ed.) and J. W. Haydon, D. F. Daley, and C. E. Schutz, *Bipartisan Political Fund Raising: Two Experiments in 1964* (1967). A study in campaign finance.

J. B. Johnson, *Registration for Voting in the United States*, rev. ed. (1946). Survey of methods used.

S. Kelley, *Political Campaigning* (1960). A study in strategy and technique.

S. Kraus (ed.), *The Great Debates* (1962). Analysis of Kennedy-Nixon debates.

K. Lamb and P. Smith, *Campaign Decision-Making* (1968).

M. B. Levin, *Kennedy Campaigning: The System and the Style as Practiced by Senator Edward Kennedy* (1966). Documents the 1962 campaign for the Democratic senatorial nomination in Massachusetts.

R. G. Martin, *Ballots and Bandwagons* (1964). Complete analysis of the nominating convention.

M. Moos, *Politics, Presidents, and Coattails* (1953). Study of congressional elections, emphasizing interaction of presidential and congressional elections.

National Municipal League, *Presidential Nominating Procedures in 1964: A State-by-State Report* (1965). An analysis and questionnaire study.

F. D. Ogden, *The Poll Tax in the South* (1968). A complete study of the poll tax and its effect on the democratic process.

J. R. Owens, *Money and Politics in California: Democratic Senatorial Primary* (1964). Case study in campaign finance.

N. R. Pierce, *The People's President: The Electoral College in American History and Direct-Vote Alternative* (1968). A critique of the present electoral process.

N. W. Polsby and A. B. Wildavsky, *Presidential Elections*, 2d ed. (1968). The context within which presidential elections are fought and the strategies employed.

G. M. Pomper, *Elections in America: Control and Influence in Democratic Politics* (1968). Elections, their effect on public policy, and the true efficacy of the American ballot.

———, *Nominating the President: The Politics of Convention Choice* (1963). Analysis and appraisal of the nominating-convention system.

I. deS. Pool, R. P. Abelson, and S. Popkin, *Candidates, Issues, and Strategies* (1965). Campaign technique and public response.

President's Commission on Campaign Costs, *Financing Presidential Campaigns* (1962). Recommendations on improved financing of national election campaigns.

D. W. Rae, *The Political Consequences of Electoral Laws* (1967). Relationship of electoral laws to legislative representation of political parties.

E. H. Roseboom, *A History of Presidential Elections* (1964). A United States history with special focus on presidential politics.

R. H. Rovere, *The Goldwater Caper* (1965).

A journalist's reflections on Goldwater and his presidential candidacy.

R. M. Scammon, *America Votes*. Collection of recent election statistics, additional volumes every two years.

S. C. Shadegg, *How to Win an Election: The Art of Political Victory* (1964). Campaign techniques for the political aspirant.

J. B. Shannon, *Money and Politics* (1959).

Subcommittee of the Senate Committee on the Judiciary, *Hearings, Nomination and Election of President and Vice-President* 84th Cong., 1st Sess. Testimony on several proposals to alter electoral college.

M. R. Weisbord, *Campaigning for President* (1964). Presidential campaigns from 1860 to 1964.

T. H. White, *The Making of the President, 1960* (1961). Pulitzer Prize account of the 1960 national campaign.

———, *The Making of the President, 1964* (1965). Similar treatment of 1964 campaign.

L. Wilmerding, *The Electoral College* (1958). Critical analysis of its operation and of proposals for change.

PART FIVE: POLICY-MAKERS FOR THE PEOPLE

The Legislative Process

J. Bibby and R. Davidson, *On Capitol Hill; Studies in the Legislative Process* (1967). Case studies illustrating the legislative process in Congress.

J. L. Freeman, *The Political Process: Executive Bureau—Legislative Committee Relations* (1965). The interaction of bureaucrats, congressmen, and lobbyists in policy-making.

H. F. Gosnell, *Democracy, the Threshold of Freedom* (1948). Contains discussion of the functions of representatives and representative assemblies.

A. de Grazia, *Public and Republic* (1951). History of who represents what and how.

C. E. Lindblom, *The Intelligence of Democracy: Decision Making through Mutual Adjustment* (1965). The role of many interacting individuals and groups in the formulation of policy in a democracy.

E. V. Schneier, *Policy Making in American Government* (1968). Essays on the formulation of public policy.

T. V. Smith, *The Legislative Way of Life* (1940). Defense of the legislature by an ex-congressman, ex-state legislator, philosopher, and political scientist.

J. C. Wahlke and H. Eulau (eds.), *Legislative Behavior: A Reader in Theory and Research* (1959). Studies of several aspects of legislative behavior.

Congress

T. B. Alexander, *Sectional Stress and Party Strength: A Computer Analysis of Roll-Call Voting Patterns in the United States House of Representatives, 1836–1860* (1967). Party cohesion and sectionalism from the Twenty-fourth to the Thirty-sixth Congress.

S. K. Bailey, *Congress Makes a Law* (1950). Detailed account of the enactment of the Employment Act of 1946.

S. K. Bailey, *The New Congress* (1966). An encouraging assessment of Congress.

D. M. Berman, *A Bill Becomes a Law* (1962). Legislative case study of the Civil Rights Act of 1960.

R. Bolling, *House Out of Order* (1965). Personal account of the workings of the House by a liberal congressional reformer.

J. Boyd, *Above the Law* (1967). An account of the congressional investigation of Senator Thomas J. Dodd.

F. L. Burdette, *Filibustering in the Senate* (1940). Standard source.

J. Burnham, *Congress and the American Tradition* (1959). Congress viewed as losing its rightful authority.

C. H. Cherryholmes and M. J. Shapiro, *Representatives and Roll Calls: A Computer Simulation of Voting in the Eighty-Eighth Congress* (1968).

C. L. Clapp, *The Congressman: His Work as*

He Sees It (1963). The House as observed by a number of its members.

J. S. Clark, *Congress, The Sapless Branch* (1964). A Senator's look at congressional reform and party leadership in Congress.

―――― (ed.), *Congressional Reform: Problems and Prospects* (1965). Essays on congressional reform.

J. C. Cleveland, *We Propose: A Modern Congress* (1966). Proposals for congressional reform from leading members of the House Republican Task Force.

R. A. Dahl, *Congress and Foreign Policy* (1950). Evaluation of Congress's role in the making of foreign policy; suggestions for improving its functioning.

R. J. Dangerfield, *In Defense of the Senate: A Study in Treaty-Making* (1933). Evidence that Senate's obstruction is less serious than usually thought.

R. H. Davidson, D. M. Kovenock, and M. K. O'Leary, *Congress in Crisis: Politics and Congressional Reform* (1966). The organization of the Congress and proposals for reform.

R. G. Dixon, Jr., *Democratic Representation: Reapportionment in Law and Politics* (1968). An analysis of reapportionment rulings in courts and legislatures.

R. F. Fenno, Jr., *The Power of the Purse: Appropriations Politics in Congress* (1966). A complete study of the appropriations procedure and its political characteristics and implications.

L. A. Froman, Jr., *The Congressional Process: Strategies, Rules, and Procedures* (1967). Studies the relation between formal and informal rule structures and policy outputs of the Congress.

―――― , *Congressmen and Their Constituencies* (1963). Focuses on congressional elections and constituency influences on congressional decision-making.

G. B. Galloway, *History of the House of Representatives* (1962).

―――― , *The Legislative Process in Congress* (1953). Organization, procedures, and problems by political scientist who played leading role in reorganization of Congress in 1946.

A. de Grazia, *Republic in Crisis: Congress against the Executive Force* (1965). A study of the distribution of power at the Federal level.

―――― et al., *Congress: the First Branch of Government* (1966). Twelve studies of the organization and workings of Congress.

B. M. Gross, *The Legislative Struggle* (1953). Probing analysis of Congress as the battleground of interest struggles.

A. Hacker, *Congressional Districting: The Issue of Equal Representation* (1963).

J. P. Harris, *The Advice and Consent of the Senate* (1953). A study of the confirmation of appointments by the United States Senate.

S. Horn, *The Cabinet and Congress* (1960). Historical background, discussion of proposals to improve cabinet-congressional relations.

C. E. Jacobs and J. F. Gallagher, *The Selective Service Act: A Case Study of the Governmental Process* (1967). The interplay of forces and interests that produces a law.

Joint Committee on Organization of the Congress, *Organization of Congress*, Senate Report 1011, 79th Cong., 2d Sess., 1946. Favorable report on reorganization act.

C. O. Jones and R. B. Ripley, *The Role of Political Parties in Congress: A Bibliography and Research Guide* (1966). A comprehensive listing of books and articles on the role of parties in Congress.

K. Kofmehl, *Professional Staffs of Congress* (1962).

T. J. Lowi, *Legislative Politics, U.S.A.* (1962). Selected readings on Congress and the forces that shape it.

D. R. Matthews, *U.S. Senators and Their World* (1960). Study of the Senate as an institution and the behavior of its members.

D. R. Mayhew, *Party Loyalty among Congressmen* (1966). Congressional behavior as affected by party status.

D. G. Morgan, *Congress and the Constitution* (1966). A challenge to Congress in the legislative-judicial division of power.

J. T. Patterson, *Congressional Conservatism and the New Deal* (1967). Origins of the Republican–conservative Democrat coalition in Congress.

R. L. Peabody and N. W. Polsby (eds.), *New Perspectives on the House of Representatives* (1963). Essays on the House as a political institution.

N. W. Polsby, *Congress and the Presidency* (1964). A study of the Congress and the division of powers.

J. L. Pressman, *House vs. Senate: Conflict in the Appropriations Process* (1966).

F. M. Riddick, *The United States Congress* (1949). Authoritative discussion of organizational and procedural aspects.

M. E. Ridgeway, *The Missouri Basin's Pick-Sloan Plan* (1955). A case study in congressional policy determination.

J. A. Robinson, *Congress and Foreign Policy-Making*, rev. ed. (1967). Probing analysis of Congress in the foreign policy process.

D. J. Rothman, *Politics and Power: The United States Senate, 1869–1901* (1966). A study of the development of specific patterns of behavior within the legislature.

H. M. Scoble, *Ideology and Electoral Action*

(1967). Study of the National Committee for an effective Congress.

D. C. Tompkins (compiled), *Changes in Congress: Proposal to Change Congress, Term of Members of the House; A Bibliography* (1966). Literature of the last twenty years on congressional reform.

D. B. Truman (ed.), *The Congress and America's Future* (1965). Papers for an American Assembly on Congress.

———, *The Congressional Party: A Case Study* (1959). The party system in Congress, analyzed through studies of roll calls.

J. Turner, *Party and Constituency* (1952). Measurement of relative impact of parties and constituencies on congressional voting behavior.

W. S. White, *Citadel: The Story of the United States Senate* (1956). Readable account of the Senate with emphasis on the unwritten rules.

———, *The Story of the U.S. House of Representatives* (1965). The journalist's attention turns to the House.

W. Wilson, *Congressional Government* (1885). Classic interpretation.

Committees

A. Barth, *Government by Investigation* (1955).

C. Beck, *Contempt of Congress* (1959). Discussion of a serious problem flowing from congressional investigations.

W. F. Buckley, Jr., et al., *The Committee and Its Critics* (1962). Defense of the House Committee on Un-American Activities.

R. K. Carr, *The House Un-American Activities Committee* (1952). Balanced discussion of congressional investigations.

H. N. Carroll, *The House of Representatives and Foreign Affairs* (1958).

D. N. Farnsworth, *The Senate Committee on Foreign Relations* (1961).

W. Goodman, *The Committee: The Extraordinary Career of the House Committee on Un-American Activities* (1968). A vivid history and critique of the controversial committee.

C. O. Jones, *Party and Policy Making: The House Republican Policy Committee* (1964). Power of a party policy committee in Congress.

D. H. Riddle, *The Truman Committee: A Study in Congressional Responsibility* (1964). An important wartime investigating committee is examined.

T. Taylor, *Grand Inquest* (1955). Critical study of congressional investigations.

The President

T. A. Bailey, *Presidential Greatness; The Image and the Man from George Washington to the Present* (1966). Proposed and applied criteria for evaluating presidential greatness.

B. J. Bernstein and A. J. Matusow, *The Truman Administration: A Documentary History* (1966). A selection of materials instrumental in policy-making of the Truman administration.

W. Binkley, *The Man in the White House* (1959). Growth of the Presidency and the many facets of the office.

S. G. Brown, *The American Presidency: Leadership, Partisanship, and Popularity* (1966). A survey of presidential action and popularity with relation to domestic and foreign issues.

J. MacG. Burns (ed.), *To Heal and Build: The Programs of Lyndon B. Johnson* (1968).

M. W. Childs, *Eisenhower—Captive Hero: A Critical Study of the General and the President* (1958). Readable biographical account of the man and his administration.

F. J. Cook, *What So Proudly We Hailed* (1968). An angry evaluation of the Johnson administration.

E. E. Cornwell, Jr., *Presidential Leadership of Public Opinion* (1962)., Presidential mobilization of public and congressional support.

E. S. Corwin, *The President: Office and Powers*, rev. ed. (1957). Comprehensive discussion of the historical and constitutional development.

——— and L. W. Koenig, *The Presidency Today* (1956).

C. P. Cotter and J. M. Smith, *Powers of the President During National Crises* (1961).

J. Deakin, *Lyndon Johnson's Credibility Gap* (1968).

R. J. Donovan, *The Inside Story* (1956). Taken from notes on the Eisenhower Cabinet meetings; gives picture of this and other aspects of the Eisenhower administration.

D. D. Eisenhower, *The White House Years, Waging Peace. 1956–1961* (1965). White House affairs from the viewpoint of the President and his staff.

J. D. Feerick, *From Failing Hands, The Story of Presidential Succession* (1965). Presidential disability and succession by a contributor to the Bayh amendment.

H. Finer, *The Presidency: Crisis and Regeneration* (1960). Analysis with provocative recommendations.

B. M. Gross (ed.), *A Great Society?* (1968). Aims and achievements of the Johnson presidency.

E. C. Hargrove, *Presidential Leadership* (1966). The link between personality and policy in six American Presidents.

L. C. Hatch, *A History of the Vice-Presidency of the United States* (1934). Standard source.

R. S. Hirschfield (ed.), *The Power of the Presidency* (1968),

E. J. Hughes, *The Ordeal of Power: A Political Memoir of the Eisenhower Years* (1963). A view from the inside.

S. Hyman, *The American President* (1954). Interpretative study.

C. Jackson, *Presidential Vetoes: 1792–1945* (1967). The historical utility of presidential veto power.

J. E. Kallenbach, *The American Chief Executive: The Presidency and the Governorship* (1966). Treats both background and present-day status of the Presidency and the governorship.

L. W. Koenig, *The Chief Executive* (1964). Up-to-date general analysis of the President performing many roles.

H. J. Laski, *The American Presidency* (1940). Dynamics of the Presidency by famous British political scientist.

H. L. Laurin, *Presidential Transitions (1960). Experience and problems in the transition from election to inauguration.*

W. E. Leuchtenberg, *Franklin D. Roosevelt and the New Deal, 1932–1940* (1963). A thorough chronicle of the New Deal era.

E. R. May (ed.), *The Ultimate Decision: The President as Commander in Chief* (1961). Analysis of presidential behavior during national emergencies.

G. McConnell, *The Modern Presidency* (1967). Brief study of the changing office.

_____, *Steel and the Presidency* (1963). Story of the exciting confrontation between President Kennedy and "big steel."

R. Neustadt, *Presidential Power* (1960). Influential work on the politics of the Presidency.

C. Phillips, *The Truman Presidency: The History of a Triumphant Succession* (1966). A journalistic account of the Truman era.

C. Rossiter, *The American Presidency* (1956). Analysis of the growth and uses of the Presidency.

A. M. Schlesinger, Jr., *A Thousand Days* (1965). The Kennedy administration treated in historical depth by the "resident intellectual" in the White House.

G. A. Schubert, Jr., *The Presidency in the Courts* (1957). Study of the Supreme Court's interpretation of the office and powers.

R. C. Silva, *Presidential Succession* (1951). Study of "history, interpretation, statutory development, and practical application of the provisions . . . for presidential succession."

T. C. Sorenson, *Decision-Making in the White House: The Olive Branch or the Arrows* (1963). With a foreword by John F. Kennedy.

_____, *Kennedy* (1965). The late President as seen by an intimate advisor.

I. Stone, *They Also Ran: The Story of the Men Who Were Defeated for the Presidency* (1966). A study of the men who almost became President and a historical evaluation of the electorate's competence in picking the best man.

W. H. Taft, *Our Chief Magistrate and His Powers* (1916). Presents a much more limited concept of the Presidency.

R. G. Tugwell, *FDR: Architect of an Era* (1967). A popular biography of a now historical figure.

_____, *How They Became President: Thirty-Five Ways to the White House* (1964). Brief analyses of the way in which each of our Presidents was elected and the way in which each served.

L. D. White, *The Federalists* (1948), *The Jeffersonians* (1951), *The Jacksonians* (1955), and *The Republican Era, 1869–1901* (1958). Cover the early years and emphasize the administrative organization of the executive.

T. Wicker, *JFK and LBJ: The Influence of Personality on Politics* (1968). An evaluation of two administrations.

I. G. Williams, *The Rise of the Vice-Presidency* (1956). History and role.

W. Wilson, *Constitutional Government in the United States* (reprinted 1921). Written before he became President; indicates Wilson's concept of the role and responsibility of the office.

E. W. Wough, *Second Consul: The Vice-Presidency—Our Greatest Political Problem* (1956). History and analysis of the office.

President as Administrator

E. R. Canterbery, *The President's Council of Economic Advisers* (1962). Study of its functions and influence on the Chief Executive's decisions.

R. F. Fenno, Jr., *The President's Cabinet* (1959). Analysis of Cabinets from Wilson to Eisenhower.

C. E. Jacob, *Leadership in the New Deal: The Administrative Challenge* (1967). A study of FDR, the administrator.

L. W. Koenig, *The Invisible Presidency* (1960). A study of the President's personal advisers.

President's Committee on Administrative Management, *Reports . . . with Studies of Administrative Management in the Federal Government* (1937). Influential studies; primary source for understanding the problems of high-level governmental administration.

L. G. Seligman and E. E. Cornwell, Jr. (eds.), *New Deal Mosaic: Roosevelt Confers with His National Emergency Council* (1965). Verbatim report of the proceedings of the National Emergency Council.

C. Silverman, *The President's Economic Advisors* (1959). A case study.

Public Administration

P. H. Appleby, *Policy and Administration* (1949). Interpretations of the dynamic aspect of administration; the interrelations between policy and administration.

P. M. Blau, *The Dynamics of Bureaucracy* (1955). Interpersonal relationships of civil servants.

C. H. Dillon, *The Area Redevelopment Administration: New Patterns in Developmental Administration* (1964). Complete analysis of the Area Redevelopment Administration.

A. Etzioni, *Modern Organizations* (1964). A broad survey of administrative theory.

R. T. Golembiewski, (ed.), *Perspectives on Public Management: Cases and Learning Designs* (1968). Case studies in managerial behavior and method.

F. J. Goodnow, *Politics and Administration* (1900). Another pioneering volume; attempt to isolate administration from politics as separate branch of study.

W. J. Gore and J. W. Dyson (eds.), *The Making of Decisions: A Reader in Administrative Behavior* (1964). Articles on the significant aspects of decision-making.

B. M. Gross, *The Managing of Organizations* (1964). A complete work on administration and its many forms.

K. M. Henderson, *Emerging Synthesis in American Public Administration* (1966). Current status of the discipline and practice of public administration in the United States.

C. S. Hyneman, *Bureaucracy in a Democracy* (1950). Study of the control and role of the bureaucracy with special attention to the question of legislative and executive responsibilities.

J. M. Landis, *The Administrative Process* (1966). The administrative process within agencies.

J. G. March (ed.), *Handbook of Organizations* (1965). Twenty-eight papers covering all aspects of organizations and organization theory.

_____ and H. A. Simon, *Organizations* (1958). Study of the theory of organizations.

R. C. Martin (ed.), *Public Administration and Democracy: Essays Honoring Paul H. Appleby* (1965). Essays on public administration and "big democracy" since the 1920s.

R. K. Merton, et al., *Reader in Bureaucracy* (1951). Collection of articles by authorities in sociology and political science.

J. Messner, *The Executive: His Key Position in Contemporary Society* (1965). A study in social organization.

J. D. Millett, *Government and Public Administration: The Quest for Responsible Performance* (1959). The control of bureaucracy.

_____, *Organization for the Public Service* (1966). Public administration and public service.

F. C. Mosher, *Democracy and the Public Service* (1968). The appointive public service and the democratic process.

C. N. Parkinson, *Parkinson's Law* (1957). The "laws" of bureaucratic expansion.

R. Presthus, *Behavioral Approaches to Public Administration* (1965). Relevance of behavioral studies to public administration.

P. Selznick, *Leadership in Administration: A Sociological Interpretation* (1957). Study of leadership in administrative organizations.

H. Sherman, *It All Depends* (1966). Discussion of organization and management.

H. A. Simon, *Administrative Behavior* (1950). A study of decision-making processes in administrative organization.

J. D. Thompson, *Approaches to Organizational Design* (1966). The design, functions, and interworking of organizations.

_____, *Organizations in Action* (1967). A theoretical essay on the sociology of complex organizations.

V. Thompson, *Modern Organizations* (1961). Perceptive analysis suggestive of political applications.

G. Tullock, *The Politics of Bureaucracy* (1965). The political relationships in an administrative structure.

V. H. Vroom (ed.), *Methods of Organizational Research* (1967). Four essays on structure and behavior of the complex organization.

D. Waldo, *The Administrative State* (1948). The theory of American public administration; survey of the various schools of thought.

_____, *Perspectives on Administration* (1968). Central issues in administrative theory and research.

H. L. Wilensky, *Organizational Intelligence* (1967). The use and abuse of intelligence information in modern agencies.

W. Wilson, "The Study of Administration," *Political Science Quarterly* (June 1887). Classic essay marking the beginning of the modern study of administration.

P. Woll, *American Bureaucracy* (1963). A study of administrative responsibility in the federal government.

Federal Administrative Structure

A. A. Altshuler, *The Politics of the Federal Bureaucracy* (1968). The role of the bureaucracy in the political process.

S. H. Aronson, *Status and Kinship in the Higher Civil Service* (1964). A historical study of presidential appointment.

W. Gellhorn, *When Americans Complain* (1966). Existing governmental procedures in handling grievances.

General Services Administration, *United States Government Organization Manual*, published annually. Contains descriptions of legislative, judicial, and executive branches—their organization and functions, organization charts of the major agencies, select lists of government publications, and other information.

C. E. Jacob, *Policy and Bureaucracy* (1966). Study of administration and policy formulation.

O. Kraines, *Congress and the Challenge of Big Government* (1958). History of the first congressional investigation into administrative structure and organization.

D. E. Mann, *The Assistant Secretaries: Problems and Processes of Appointment* (1965). A study of the complexities of administrative transitions.

L. Merriam and L. K. Schmeckebier, *Reorganization of the National Government* (1939). Critical discussion of the reports of the President's Committee on Administrative Management.

R. Polenberg, *Reorganizing Roosevelt's Government, 1936–1939: The Controversy over Executive Reorganization* (1966). An account of the revamping of the federal administrative structure.

D. T. Stanley, *Changing Administrations* (1965). A study of the working of the bureaucratic structure in changing administrations.

———, *The Higher Civil Service: An Evaluation of Federal Personnel Practices* (1964). A study of a group of civil servants whose decisions have a great effect on American life.

———, D. E. Mann, and J. W. Doig, *Men Who Govern: A Biographical Profile of Federal Political Executives* (1967). A study of executive appointments covering the last five administrations.

W. S. Sayre (ed.), *The Federal Government Service: Its Character, Prestige, and Problems*, 2d ed. (1965). An American Assembly Symposium.

S. C. Wallace, *Federal Departmentalization* (1941). Critical analysis of the theories of federal departmentalization.

Regulatory Administration

H. A. Bennet, *The Commission and the Common Law* (1964). Critique of Interstate Commerce Commission activity.

M. H. Bernstein, *Regulating Business by Independent Commissions* (1955). Critical study of politics of regulation.

W. L. Cary, *Politics and the Regulatory Agencies* (1967). The political relationships of six prominent independent agencies.

R. E. Cushman, *The Independent Regulatory Commissions* (1941). General discussion of the independent regulatory commissions.

H. J. Friendy, *The Federal Administrative Agencies: The Need for Better Definition of Standards* (1962). Advocates improvement in commission personnel and standards.

J. M. Landis, *The Administrative Process* (1938). Perceptive analysis.

E. Latham, *The Politics of Railroad Coordination, 1933–1936* (1959). Politics of railroad regulation during the first years of the New Deal.

S. A. Lawrence, *United States Merchant Shipping Policies and Politics* (1966). Analysis of Merchant Marine policy and the politics of its regulation.

D. H. Nelson, *Administrative Agencies of the U.S.A.: Their Decisions and Authority* (1964). An analysis of the adjudicatory power of federal administrative agencies.

B. Schwartz, *The Professor and the Commissions* (1959). Story of congressional investigation of regulatory commissions and trials and tribulations of a former committee counsel.

Public Personnel Management

M. H. Bernstein, *The Job of the Federal Executive* (1958). Description of the work of top career and political executives; problems of keeping able men in government.

J. J. Corson and R. S. Paul, *Men Near the Top: Filling Key Posts in the Federal Service* (1966). A study based on questionnaires and interviews of federal employees.

P. T. David and R. Pollock, *Executives in Government: Central Issues of Federal Personnel Administration* (1957). Problems of recruiting and keeping high-level personnel.

F. P. Kilpatrick, et al., *The Image of the Federal Service* and *Source Book of a Study of Occupational Values and the Image of the Federal Service* (1964). Companion volumes.

S. B. Sweeney (ed.), *Education for Administrative Careers in Government Service* (1958). Problems of training public administrators.

P. Van Riper, *History of the United States Civil Service* (1959). History of public employment in the United States; emphasis on the period since the beginning of civil service reform.

W. B. Vosloo, *Collective Bargaining in the*

United States Civil Service (1966). Study and critique of the Kennedy program of management-employee cooperation in the federal service.

K. O. Warner (ed.), *Collective Bargaining in the Public Service; Theory and Practice* (1967). Essays on public personnel management in Canada and the United States.

———— (ed.), *Developments in Public Employee Relations: Legislative, Judicial, Administrative* (1965). Management-employee relations in government.

———— and M. L. Hennessy, *Public Management at the Bargaining Table* (1967). Collective bargaining in the public services of Canada and the United States.

W. L. Warner, et al., *The Federal Executive* (1963). Social and personal characteristics of American civil and military leaders.

The Judges

See also the titles listed under "The Living Constitution," p. 784.

T. L. Becker, *Political Behavioralism and Modern Jurisprudence* (1964).

D. M. Berman, *It Is So Ordered* (1966). The federal judicial process illustrated by the path of the school desegregation case in reaching the Supreme Court.

B. N. Cardozo, *The Nature of the Judicial Process* (1921). One of the American classics in legal theory.

J. Frank, *Law and the Modern Mind* (1930). Discussion of the various factors, especially psychological, that affect men, including judges.

F. Frankfurter, *Law and Politics* (1939). Articles, book reviews, occasional papers written before the author became a justice.

R. L. Goldfarb, *The Contempt Power* (1963).

H. Jacob, *Justice in America* (1965).

H. James, *Crisis in the Courts* (1968).

H. W. Jones (ed.), *The Courts, the Public, and the Law Explosion* (1965). Discrepancy between theory and practice in the judicial process.

W. F. Murphy, *Elements of Judicial Strategy* (1964). Judicial behavior analyzed from perspective of stratagems to maximize policy preferences.

J. W. Peltason, *Federal Courts in the Political Process* (1955).

V. G. Rosenbaum, *Law as a Political Instrument* (1955). The legal system as part of the political process.

G. A. Schubert (ed.), *Judicial Behavior: A Reader in Theory and Research* (1964).

———— (ed.), *Judicial Decision-Making* (1963).

———— and D. J. Danelski, *Comparative Judicial Behavior: Cross Cultural Studies in Political Decision-Making in the East and West* (1969).

J. A. Sigler, *An Introduction to the Legal System* (1968). The role of the legal subsystem in the political system.

The Supreme Court

H. J. Abraham, *The Judicial Process* (1962). Comparative study of United States, English, and French systems.

L. Baker, *Back to Back: The Duel between FDR and the Supreme Court* (1967). An account of the Roosevelt court-packing fight.

M. G. Baxter, *Daniel Webster and the Supreme Court* (1966). Daniel Webster and the Court's doctrinal development in the first half of the nineteenth century.

T. L. Becker (ed.), *The Supreme Court Decision: Readings on Causes and Effects* (1968).

A. S. Bedi, *Freedom of Expression and Security: A Comparative Study of the Function of the Supreme Courts of the United States of America and India* (1966). American influences on the Indian legal system.

A. M. Bickel, *The Least Dangerous Branch: The Supreme Court at the Bar of Politics* (1962). Discussion of the "proper" role of the Court in the American system.

————, *Politics and the Warren Court* (1965). Essays on the activities of the Warren Court, covering civil rights, reapportionment, and religion.

A. Cox, *The Warren Court: Constitutional Decision as an Instrument of Reform* (1968).

C. P. Curtis, *Lions under the Throne* (1947). Interpretation of role of courts in the American system.

D. Danelski, *The Appointment of a Supreme Court Justice* (1965). The story behind the appointment of Pierce Butler.

J. P. Frank, *Marble Palace: The Supreme Court in American Life* (1958). Organization and work of the Court.

M. Freedman, W. M. Beaney, and E. V. Rostow, *Perspectives on the Court* (1967). Lectures on the Supreme Court from the perspectives of journalism, political science, and law.

P. A. Freund, *On Understanding the Supreme Court* (1950). Analytical lectures with comments on the Supreme Court and Supreme Court commentators.

J. B. Grossman, *Lawyers and Judges, The ABA and the Politics of Judicial Selection* (1965).

G. G. Haines, *The Role of the Supreme Court in American Government and Politics, 1789–1835* (1944). Detailed history of the formative years.

R. S. Hirshfield, *The Constitution and the Court* (1962). Briefs from decisions and comments.

S. Krislov, *The Supreme Court and Political Freedom* (1968).

P. B. Kurland (ed.), *The Supreme Court Review.* Annual collection, since 1959, of commentary articles on Supreme Court activity.

C. M. Lytle, *The Warren Court and Its Critics* (1968). The Warren Court's major decisions and public reaction.

R. McCloskey, *The American Supreme Court 1789–1960* (1960). Analytical history.

C. P. Magrath, *Yazoo: Law and Politics in the New Republic, The Case of Fletcher vs. Peck* (1966). The background and eventual consequences of a famous 1810 decision on property rights.

A. T. Mason, *The Supreme Court from Taft to Warren* (1958). Interpretive history.

W. Mendelson (ed.), *The Supreme Court: Law and Discretion* (1967). Supreme Court cases and the conflict between judicial activism and judicial restraint.

A. S. Miller, *The Supreme Court and American Capitalism* (1968).

G. T. Mitau, *Decade of Decision: The Supreme Court and the Constitutional Revolution* (1968).

W. F. Murphy, *Congress and the Court* (1962). Along with the Pritchett volume, useful for comprehensive coverage of a recent Supreme Court controversy.

———— and C. H. Pritchett (eds.), *Courts, Judges, and Politics* (1961). An introduction to the organization and function of the American judiciary.

C. H. Pritchett, *Civil Liberties and the Vinson Court* (1954). Continuation of earlier volume during period 1946–1953.

————, *Congress versus the Supreme Court* (1961).

————, *The Political Offender and the Warren Court* (1959). Analysis of Warren Court reaction to anti-Communist legislation.

————, *The Roosevelt Court* (1948). Survey of the Court from 1937 to 1947 with statistical charts on each justice's "batting average" on particular issues.

———— and A. F. Westin (eds.), *The Third Branch of Government* (1963). Eight cases that place Supreme Court decisions in their contexts.

J. R. Schmidhauser, *The Supreme Court: Its Politics, Personalities and Procedures* (1960). Internal politics of the Court.

G. R. Schubert, *The Judicial Mind: Attitudes and Ideologies of Supreme Court Justices, 1946–1963* (1965). A study of eighteen Supreme Court justices and the causes and results of their actions.

————, *Quantitative Analysis of Judicial Behavior* (1959). Diverse approaches to judicial behavior.

Senate Committee on the Judiciary, *Hearings of Subcommittee to Investigate the Administration of the Internal Security Act and Other Internal Security Laws,* 85th Cong., 1st and 2d Sess. (1957 and 1958). Hearings on the Jenner Bill, which would have curbed the power of the Supreme Court in security cases; rich source of data on public reactions to the Court's decisions.

Senate Committee on the Judiciary, *Hearings, Reorganization of the Federal Judiciary,* 79th Cong., 2d Sess. (1937). Verbatim testimony of the many people who appeared for and against President Roosevelt's Court Plan.

M. Shapiro, *Law and Politics in the Supreme Court* (1964).

————, *The Supreme Court and Administrative Agencies* (1968).

———— (ed.), *The Supreme Court and Public Policy* (1968). The Supreme Court's internal organization and external effect on the political process.

C. B. Swisher, *The Supreme Court in Its Modern Role* (1958).

A. L. Todd, *Justice on Trial: The Case of Louis D. Brandeis* (1964). The Political struggle in the appointment of Brandeis to the Supreme Court.

A. F. Westin (ed.), *An Autobiography of the Supreme Court: Off-the-Bench Commentary by the Justices* (1963). The judicial process as seen by the justices themselves.

Judicial Review

C. L. Black, *The People and the Court* (1960). An interpretation of modern judicial review.

F. V. Cahill, Jr., *Judicial Legislation* (1952). Analytic survey of modern American jurisprudence, stressing the problem of right of the judiciary to review acts of other levels of government.

E. S. Corwin, *Court over Constitution, A Study of Judicial Review as an Instrument of Government,* 2d ed. (1942).

————, *The Doctrine of Judicial Review* (1914). Essays including famous article on *Marbury* v. *Madison.*

H. E. Dean, *Judicial Review and Democracy* (1966). Case for judicial review as an integral part of the democratic process.

C. G. Haines, *The American Doctrine of Judicial Supremacy,* 2d ed. (1932). Balanced investigation of the role of the Supreme Court and its use of judicial review.

C. S. Hyneman, *The Supreme Court on Trial*

(1963). Ramifications of the segregation rulings for the political system.

R. H. Jackson, *The Struggle for Judicial Supremacy* (1941). Critical discussion of Supreme Court, especially its activities during the New Deal period.

E. V. Rostow, *The Sovereign Prerogative: The Supreme Court and the Quest for Law* (1962). A liberal's evaluation of contemporary Supreme Court policy.

G. Sawer, *Law in Society* (1965). Sociology of law.

J. N. Shklar, *Legalism* (1964). Study of selected ideas about law and legalism.

J. Stone, *Law and the Social Sciences* (1966). The social sciences and the judicial process.

S. E. Stumpff, *Morality and the Law* (1966). The moral connotations of the law.

R. J. Tresolini, *American Constitutional Law* (1965). Political impact of judicial decisions.

C. Warren, *The Supreme Court in United States History*, rev. ed., 2 vols. (1932). Standard history, sympathetic to the Court's use of judicial review.

H. Wechsler, *Principles, Politics and Fundamental Law* (1961). A controversial interpretation of judicial review.

A. F. Westin, *The Anatomy of a Constitutional Law Case* (1958). Case study of *Youngstown Sheet and Tube Co.* v. *Sawyer*, "the steel seizure decision."

Judicial Biography

A. J. Beveridge, *The Life of John Marshall*, 4 vols. (1916–1919). History; has become the prototype of judicial biography.

V. Countryman, *Douglas and the Supreme Court: A Selection of His Opinions* (1959). Contains a biographical sketch of Douglas.

C. Fairman, *Mr. Justice Miller and the Supreme Court* (1939). Contains account of the Court's work and Reconstruction politics during the critical years 1860–1890.

J. P. Frank, *Mr. Justice Black* (1949). By leading legal thinker.

H. J. Friendly, *Benchmarks* (1967). Reflections on judges, judging, and some past judicial action.

E. C. Gerhart, *America's Advocate: Robert H. Jackson* (1958).

G. S. Hellman, *Benjamin N. Cardozo* (1940).

L. B. Hellor, *Do You Solemnly Swear?* (1968). Reminiscences and commentary by a New York State Supreme Court judge.

S. Hendel, *Charles Evans Hughes and the Supreme Court* (1951).

M. D. Howe, *Justice Oliver Wendell Holmes: The Shaping Years, 1841–1870* (1957).

L. Katcher, *Earl Warren: A Political Biography* (1967). The origins of Chief Justice Warren's political and judicial attitudes.

W. L. King, *Melville Weston Fuller, Chief Justice of the United States* (1950). Study of a moderately able justice and oustanding Chief Justice; informative on the internal working of the Court.

S. J. Konefsky, *The Constitutional World of Mr. Justice Frankfurter* (1949). Collection of opinions with introductory notes by editor.

_____, *The Legacy of Holmes and Brandeis* (1957). Study of the constitutional philosophy of two outstanding justices.

M. Lerner (ed.), *The Mind and Faith of Justice Holmes* (1943). Collection of Justice Holmes's speeches, essays, letters, and judicial opinions, with introduction and notes by the editor.

A. T. Mason, *Brandeis: A Free Man's Life* (1946).

_____, *Harlan Fiske Stone* (1956).

_____, *William Howard Taft, Chief Justice* (1965).

W. Mendelson, *Justices Black and Frankfurter* (1961). Conception of the Court's role in terms of the careers of these two jurists.

D. G. Morgan, *Justice William Johnson: The First Dissenter* (1954).

H. F. Pringle, *The Life and Times of William Howard Taft*, 2 vols. (1939). Biography of former President and Chief Justice.

M. J. Pusey, *Charles Evans Hughes*, 2 vols. (1951). Biography.

H. Shanks (ed.), *The Art and Craft of Judging: The Decisions of Judge Learned Hand* (1968).

C. P. Smith, *James Wilson, Founding Father* (1956).

C. B. Swisher, *Roger B. Taney* (1935).

_____, *Stephen J. Field, Craftsman of the Law* (1930). Biography of a justice who had much to do with the development of substantive due process.

C. Williams, *Hugo L. Black* (1950).

PART SIX: BIG GOVERNMENT IN ACTION

International Politics

R. Aron, *The Great Debate: Theories of Nu-* *clear Strategy* (1965). The implications of the thermonuclear age for defense policies of all nations.

J. W. Burton, *International Relations: A*

General Theory (1965). An appraisal of and suggestions for contemporary theories of international relations.

R. W. Cottam, *Competitive Interference and Twentieth Century Diplomacy* (1967). The effects of interference as a tactic in foreign policy.

A. Etzioni, *Winning without War* (1964). Optimistic alternative to most theories of foreign relations.

E. B. Haas, *Beyond the Nation-State: Functionalism and International Organization* (1964). The process of international integration.

E. E. Harris, *Annihilation and Utopia: The Principles of International Politics* (1966). A philosophy-oriented approach to international relations and national security.

A. Herzog, *The War-Peace Establishment* (1965). Present strategies and future prospects for war and peace.

S. Hoffmann, *Contemporary Theories in International Relations* (1960).

_____, *The State of War* (1965). Historical-sociological perspective on international politics.

F. C. Iklé, *How Nations Negotiate* (1964). A systematic analysis of one of the principal techniques of diplomacy.

M. A. Kaplan, *System and Process in International Politics* (1957). Systematic theoretical analysis of international politics.

C. O. Lerche, Jr., *The Cold War—and After* (1965). A study of the changing character of the cold war.

H. J. Mackinder, *Democratic Ideals and Reality* (1919; republished, 1942). Seminal study of what is too narrowly called geopolitics.

C. B. Marshall, *The Exercise of Sovereignty: Papers on Foreign Policy* (1965). A collection of essays on the persistence of sovereignty as a problem of international relations.

E. S. Mason, *Foreign Aid and Foreign Policy* (1964). Foreign aid as a tool of foreign policy.

M. C. McGuire, *Secrecy and the Arms Race: A Theory of the Accumulation of Strategic Weapons and How Secrecy Affects It* (1965). An examination of the production and handling of the strategic weapons of the world powers.

J. D. Montgomery, *Foreign Aid in International Politics* (1967). Motives and methods of United States foreign aid.

N. J. Padelford and G. A. Lincoln, *The Dynamics of International Politics* (1962). Overview and analysis.

J. N. Rosenau, *International Aspects of Civil Strife* (1964). Internal war as an international event.

T. C. Schelling, *Arms and Influence* (1966). An analysis of international strategies.

C. P. Schleicher, *International Relations:* *Cooperation and Conflict* (1962). A general view.

A. M. Scott, *The Revolution in Statecraft: Informal Penetration* (1965). Informal foreign relations—the government of one nation reaches the people of another.

R. C. Synder, et al. (eds.), *Foreign Policy Decision-Making: An Approach to the Study of International Politics* (1962).

H. Sprout and M. Sprout, *The Ecological Perspective on Human Affairs with Special References to International Politics* (1965). An investigation into the environmental effects on human behavior as they relate to international politics.

B. Ward, *The Lopsided World* (1968). Contends that international economic inequities are endangering the world's political and economic stability.

The Worldmark Encyclopedia of Nations (1960). A general guide to important features of all nations, their international relationships, and the UN system.

American Foreign Policy

T. A. Bailey, *A Diplomatic History of the American People,* 5th ed. (1955). Lively account emphasizing the role of public opinion and interest groups.

D. A. Baldwin, *Economic Development and American Foreign Policy 1943–1962* (1966). Domestic goals of foreign-aid recipients; possible conflicts between recipient and donor.

_____, *Foreign Aid and American Foreign Policy: A Documentary Analysis* (1966). Documents for study of the role of foreign aid in foreign policy.

G. W. Ball, *The Discipline of Power: The Essentials of a Modern World Structure* (1968). Urges longer perspective.

R. Bartlett, *Policy and Power: Two Centuries of American Foreign Relations* (1965). A history of the major policy decisions in American foreign policy for the last 200 years.

S. F. Bemis, *American Secretaries of State and Their Diplomacy* (1957).

_____, *A Diplomatic History of the United States* (1950).

_____, *A Short History of American Foreign Policy and Diplomacy* (1959).

D. Brandon, *American Foreign Policy beyond Utopianism and Realism* (1966). The intellectual and political sources of American foreign policy from the postrevolutionary period to the present.

D. W. Brogan, *Worlds in Conflict* (1967). A broad commentary on American foreign policy by a leading British political scientist.

H. Cleveland, *The Obligations of Power: American Diplomacy in the Search for Peace* (1966). The unique task of American foreign policy, past attempts to meet this task, and future proposals.

B. C. Cohen, *Foreign Policy in American Government* (1963). A reader focusing on various dimensions of foreign policy making.

———, *The Press and Foreign Policy* (1963). The organization and conduct of reporting on foreign affairs.

W. S. Cole, *An Interpretive History of American Foreign Relations* (1968). A basic diplomatic history.

P. H. Coombs, *The Fourth Dimension of Foreign Policy: Educational and Cultural Affairs* (1964). A plea for a human oriented approach to foreign policy.

J. Davids (ed.), *Documents on American Foreign Relations*, (1965). Council on Foreign Relations' annual summary of American foreign policy.

——— (ed.), *The United States in World Affairs: 1964* (1965).

A. A. Ekirch, Jr., *Ideas, Ideals and American Diplomacy* (1966). The major trends and forces in American foreign policy from the beginning of the republic to the present.

L. Farago, *The Broken Seal: The Story of Operation "Magic" and the Pearl Harbor Disaster* (1967). Intrigue in international strategies.

H. Feis, *Foreign Aid and Foreign Policy* (1964). A discussion of the relationship between assistance and diplomacy.

W. T. R. Fox and A. B. Fox, *NATO and the Range of American Choice* (1967). NATO and restrictions on United States action.

C. Frankel, *The Neglected Aspect of Foreign Affairs: American Educational and Cultural Policy Abroad* (1965). United States cultural and educational foreign policy.

E. S. Furniss, Jr. (ed.), *The Western Alliance: Its Status and Prospects* (1965). Examines a crumbling NATO and prospects for the future.

W. P. Gerberding, *United States Foreign Policy: Perspectives and Analysis* (1966). Introductory survey of United States foreign affairs.

D. B. Gobel, *A Documentary Chronicle of American Foreign Policy: 1776–1960* (1961).

H. K. Jacobson and E. Stein, *Diplomats, Scientists, and Politicians* (1966). A complete study of the nuclear test ban negotiations.

H. G. Johnson, *Economic Policies toward Less Developed Countries* (1967). Present and proposed policies.

W. Johnson and F. J. Colligan, *The Fullbright Program: A History* (1965). A history and analysis of the Fullbright program for international educational exchange.

L. S. Kaplan (ed.), *Recent American Foreign Policy: Conflicting Interpretation* (1968). Selected issues of recent American foreign policy.

G. F. Kennan, *From Prague after Munich: Diplomatic Papers, 1938–1940* (1968). Documents from United States embassies in Germany and Czechoslovakia immediately preceding the war.

———, *Realities of American Foreign Policy* (1966). New edition of a 1954 work.

———, *Russia, the Atom and the West* (1958). Kennan's argument for disengagement in Central Europe.

H. S. Kissinger, *Nuclear Weapons and Foreign Policy* (1957). Influential discussion of the strategic impact of nuclear technology and defense of policy of limited nuclear war.

———, *Problems of National Strategy: A Book of Readings* (1966). Readings on varied aspects of foreign policy.

———, *The Troubled Partnership: A Reappraisal of the Atlantic Alliance* (1965). The difficulties besetting the Atlantic Alliance.

C. O. Lerche, Jr., *Last Chance in Europe: Bases for a New American Policy* (1967). Suggestions for a renovation of America's European policy in light of a weakened NATO.

G. Liska, *Imperial America: The International Politics of Primacy* (1967). America as the dominant power in international relations.

J. B. Martin, *Overtaken by Events: The Dominican Crisis from the Fall of Trujillo to the Civil War* (1966). The United States embassy in the Dominican crisis.

R. F. Mikesell, *The Economics of Foreign Aid* (1968).

H. J. Morgenthau, *A New Foreign Policy for the United States* (1968). An evaluation of past policy and future recommendations.

M. C. Needler, *Understanding Foreign Policy* (1966). The basic trends and working processes of American foreign policy.

J. M. Nelson, *Aid, Influence, and Foreign Policy* (1968). Foreign aid as an instrument of foreign policy.

D. Perkins, *The American Approach to Foreign Policy*, rev. ed. (1962). Topical historical analysis of American foreign policy.

J. W. Pratt, *A History of United States Foreign Policy*, 2d ed. (1965).

W. A. Reitzel, M. A. Kaplan, and C. G. Coblentz, *United States Foreign Policy, 1945–1955* (1956). A historical and topical analysis of American policy.

E. B. Skolnikoff, *Science, Technology, and American Foreign Policy* (1967). New opportunities and challenges in foreign policy.

J. Slater, *The OAS and United States Foreign Policy* (1967). The past and future of United States–Latin American policy.

N. J. Spykman, *America's Strategy in World Politics* (1942). Geopolitical analysis of American policy.

R. P. Stebbins (ed.), *Documents on American Foreign Relations, 1963* (1964).

—— (ed.), *The United States in World Affairs, 1963* (1964). A crisis year in United States foreign affairs. Studies by the Council on Foreign Relations.

E. Stillman and W. Pfaff, *Power and Impotence: The Failure of America's Foreign Policy* (1966). A criticism of the prevailing trends of American foreign policy for the last decade.

R. B. Textor (ed.), *Cultural Frontiers of the Peace Corps* (1966). A survey and analysis of Peace Corps activities.

P. A. Toma, *The Politics of Food for Peace* (1967). Origins and activities of a United States foreign aid program.

K. N. Waltz, *Foreign Policy and Democratic Politics: The American and British Experience* (1967). A comparison of American and British foreign policy formulation.

A. F. Westwood, *Foreign Aid in a Foreign Policy Framework* (1966). An analysis of United States aid policies from the Marshall Plan to the Alliance for Progress.

C. E. Wilson, *Diplomatic Privileges and Immunities* (1967). Theory, practice, and scope of diplomatic privileges.

D. Wise and T. B. Ross, *The Invisible Government* (1964). Espionage and intelligence agencies in the United States system.

—— and ——, *The Espionage Establishment* (1967). Espionage on the international scene.

T. P. Wright, Jr., *American Support for Free Elections Abroad* (1964). The anticipated and actual results of American support of free elections.

American Foreign Policy: Vietnam

V. Bator, *Vietnam, A Diplomatic Tragedy: The Origins of the United States Involvement* (1965). The 1953 beginnings of United States involvement in Vietnam.

J. Buttinger, *Vietnam: A Political History* (1968). Vietnamese history.

W. R. Corson, *The Betrayal* (1968). A critique of the United States in Vietnam by a Marine colonel.

T. Draper, *Abuse of Power* 1966. Analysis and critique of American policy in Vietnam since 1945.

D. J. Duncanson, *Government and Revolution in Vietnam* (1967).

R. A. Falk (ed.), *The Vietnam War and International Law* (1968).

B. B. Fall, *Hell in a Very Small Place* (1967). The story of the siege of Dien Bien Phu.

——, *Last Reflections on a War* (1967). Articles on the history and present status of United States involvement in Vietnam.

W. R. Fishel (ed.), *Vietnam: Anatomy of a Conflict* (1968). History and analysis of United States activity in Vietnam.

V. Hartke, *The American Crisis in Vietnam* (1968).

H. Kahn, et al., *Can We Win in Vietnam?* (1968).

W. J. Lederer, *Our Own Worst Enemy* (1968). Alleged corruption and waste in Vietnam.

C. E. Lemay (with D. O. Smith), *America Is in Danger* (1968).

M. Ray, *The Two Shores of Hell* (1968). Account of French photographer held prisoner for three weeks by the Vietcong.

D. Schoenbrun, *Vietnam: How We Got In, How to Get Out* (1968).

D. Wit, *Thailand: Another Vietnam* (1968). Communist insurgency in Thailand.

How Foreign Policy Is Made

G. A. Almond, The *American People and Foreign Policy* (1950). Analysis of the effect of the public, interest groups, and opinion leaders in shaping foreign policy.

W. Barnes and J. H. Morgan, *The Foreign Service of the United States* (1961). Origins, development, and functions of the diplomatic corps.

V. M. Barnett, Jr. (ed.), *The Representation of the U.S. Abroad* (1956). Study papers for a meeting of The American Assembly.

R. A. Bauer, I. Pool, and L. A. Dexter, *American Business and Public Policy: The Politics of Foreign Trade* (1963). The political process is viewed from the perspective of foreign-trade policy.

P. W. Buck and M. Travis, Jr. (eds.), *Control of Foreign Relations in Modern Nations* (1957). Study of the machinery and methods of making and executing policy in several nations, including the United States.

H. N. Carroll, *The House of Representatives and Foreign Affairs* (1958).

D. S. Cheever and H. F. Haviland, Jr., *American Foreign Policy and the Separation of Powers* (1952). Survey of constitutional arrangements, case studies, and recommendations for improving machinery of government.

H. Cleveland, G. Mangone, and J. C. Adams, *The Overseas Americans* (1960). Analysis and recommendations relating to Americans on overseas assignments.

B. C. Cohen, *The Influence of Non-Governmental Groups on Foreign Policy-Making* (1959). Survey of interest-group patterns in the foreign-policy process.

Commission on the Organization of the Government, *Task Force Report on the Organization of the Government for the Con-*

duct of Foreign Affairs (1949). Prepared under direction of H. H. Bundy and J. G. Rogers; generally considered one of the better Task Force Reports.

C. V. Crabb, Jr., *Bipartisan Foreign Policy: Myth or Reality* (1957). The virtues and hazards of bipartisanship.

W. P. Dizard, *The Strategy of Truth* (1961). Description of United States Information Service.

R. E. Elder, *The Information Machine: The United States Information Agency and American Foreign Policy* (1968).

———, *Overseas Representation and Services for Federal Domestic Agencies* (1965). A discussion of problems involved when domestic agencies must reorient some segments of their institutions for foreign service.

———, *The Policy Machine* (1960). Description of policy-making process in the State Department and related agencies.

H. Feis, *The Atomic Bomb and the End of World War II* (1966). Causes and effects of the decision to drop the atomic bomb.

F. Fielder and G. Harris, *The Quest for Foreign Affairs Officers — Their Recruitment and Selection* (1965).

V. L. Galbraith, *World Trade in Transition* (1965).

B. Glad, *Charles Evans Hughes and Illusions of Innocence* (1966). A critique of the policies of Hughes in the 1920s.

J. E. Harr, *The Anatomy of the Foreign Service — A Statistical Profile* (1965).

———, *The Development of Careers in the Foreign Service* (1965). A study of the difficulties in career development in the foreign service.

R. Hilsman, *Strategic Intelligence and National Decisions* (1956). Discussion of the place of strategic intelligence in decision-making.

S. Huddleston, *Popular Diplomacy and War* (1954). Critical comments about the impact of mass opinion on diplomacy.

A. G. Jones, *The Evolution of Personnel Systems for U.S. Foreign Affairs* (1965). A history of the Foreign Service from its inception to the present.

C. O. Lerch, *Foreign Policy of the American People,* 3d ed. (1967). Trends in formulation and execution of foreign policy.

———, *The Uncertain South: Its Changing Pattern of Politics in Foreign Policy* (1964). Another side of changing southern politics.

J. J. McCloy, *The Challenge to American Foreign Policy* (1953). Brief discussion of problems of making and executing foreign policy, with special attention to problem of civil-military relations, by former United States High Commissioner for Germany.

M. K. O'Leary, *The Politics of American*

Foreign Aid (1967). Domestic sources of foreign-aid policy.

D. K. Price (ed.), *The Secretary of State* (1961). Examination of the office.

H. B. Price, *The Marshall Plan and Its Meaning* (1955). Evaluation and history.

H. H. Ransom, *Central Intelligence and National Security* (1958). Study of the organization and procedures of American intelligence agencies.

L. N. Rieselbach, *The Roots of Isolationism: Congressional Voting and Presidential Leadership in Foreign Policy* (1966). An analysis of congressional action on foreign policy over the last twenty years.

J. A. Robinson, *Congress and Foreign Policy-Making: A Study in Legislative Influence and Initiative* (1967). Congress in the foreign-policy process.

J. N. Rosenau (ed.), *Domestic Sources of Foreign Policy* (1967). A study of domestic policy as an ingredient in foreign-policy formulation.

———, *Public Opinion and Foreign Policy* (1961). Treatment of public's role in decision-making.

B. M. Sapin, *The Making of United States Foreign Policy* (1965). The structure and function of contemporary foreign-policy machinery.

Secretary of State's Public Committee on Personnel, *Toward a Stronger Foreign Service* (1954). The important Wriston Report, which resulted in major organizational changes in foreign service.

G. H. Stuart, *The Department of State* (1949). Comprehensive history.

A. Tully, *CIA* (1962). Popular account of the intelligence agency and the formation of policy.

A. Vagts, *Defense and Diplomacy: The Soldier and the Conduct of Foreign Relations* (1956). Role of the military in American foreign policy from a historical perspective.

R. Walther, *Orientations and Behavioral Styles of Foreign Service Officers* (1965).

H. B. Westerfield, *Foreign Policy and Party Politics* (1955). Role of the parties and bipartisanship in Congress.

H. M. Wriston, *Diplomacy in a Democracy* (1956). Discussion of the problems of foreign policy in a democracy.

The United Nations and World Organization

A. Beichman, *The "Other" State Department* (1968). A study of United States representation and activity in the UN.

A. L. Burns and N. Heathcote, *Peace-Keeping by U.N. Forces from Suez to the Congo.* A study of UN intervention concentrating especially on actions taken in the Congo from July 1960 to December 1962.

I. L. Claude, Jr., *Swords into Ploughshares* (1956). Analysis of the problems of international organizations.

C. M. Eichelberger, *U.N.: The First Twenty Years* (1965). A historical analysis of the United Nations from its beginnings to the present.

T. R. Fehrenbach, *This Kind of Peace* (1966). The origins of the UN; the intentions and hopes of its founders.

F. B. Gross (ed.), *The United States and the United Nations* (1964). The role of the UN in the East-West conflict.

P. C. Jessup and H. J. Taubenfeld, *Controls for Outer Space and the Antarctic Analogy* (1959). Examination of the problems and possibilities of international control of outer space.

J. Larus (ed.), *From Collective Security to Preventive Diplomacy* (1965). Eight international security crises from 1920 to 1960 and their handling by international bodies.

W. H. C. Laves and C. A. Thomson, *UNESCO: Purposes, Progress, Prospects* (1957). Account of the organization's first ten years.

C. Manly, *The UN Record* (1955). By severe critic who believes UN to be a failure and an instrument of subversion.

F. S. C. Northrup, *The Taming of the Nations* (1953). A study of the cultural basis of international policy.

C. C. O'Brien and F. Topolski, *The United Nations: Sacred Drama* (1968).

R. E. Riggs, *Politics in the United Nations: A Study of United States Influence in the General Assembly* (1958). Study of the extent of American influence and the techniques used.

A. Ross, *The United Nations: Peace and Progress* (1966). The UN as a political phenomenon.

R. B. Russell, *The United Nations and United States Security Policy* (1968).

W. A. Scott and S. B. Withey, *The United States and the United Nations: The Public View, 1945–1955* (1958). American attitudes toward the organization as revealed in opinion polls.

War and National Defense

A. Beaufre, *Deterrence and Strategy* (1966). Implications of the nuclear age and possibilities for international nuclear deterrence.

D. B. Bobrow (ed.), *Components of a Defense Policy* (1965). Articles analyzing defense policy.

C. W. Borklund, *The Department of Defense* (1968).

———, *Men of the Pentagon: From Forrestal to McNamara* (1966). The evolution of the Department of Defense.

B. Brodie, *Escalation and the Nuclear Option* (1966). Political and military considerations of the thermonuclear age.

———, *Strategy in the Missile Age* (1959). Effects of technical advances on military planning.

D. Caraley, *The Politics of Military Unification: A Study of Conflict and the Policy Process* (1966). Conflict over military unification from 1943 to 1947 and the resolution of the conflict as part of the policy process.

W. J. Coats, *Armed Force as a Power: The Theory of War Reconsidered* (1966). The relevant political and philosophical considerations in the use of military force.

A. H. Dean, *Test Ban and Disarmament: The Path of Negotiation* (1966). The complexities of U.S.-U.S.S.R. disarmament negotiations.

J. M. Gavin, *War and Peace in the Space Age* (1958). Critical evaluation of American military policy by a former Army chief of research and development.

P. Hammond, *Organizing for Defense* (1961). Comprehensive analysis of the American military organization.

C. J. Hitch, *Decision-Making for Defense* (1965). The pentagon management of the largest part of our budget.

S. P. Huntington, *The Common Defense: Strategic Programs in National Politics* (1961). Essays analyzing the dynamics of postwar defense policy-making.

H. Kahn, *On Escalation: Metaphors and Scenarios* (1965). Modern military strategy.

W. R. Kintner, et al., *Forging a New Sword* (1958). Study of Defense Department and recommendations for improving its operations.

K. Knorr, *On the Uses of Military Power in the Nuclear Age* (1966). The impact of nuclear weapons on political and military strategies.

J. H. McBride, *The Test Ban Treaty: Military, Techological, and Political Implication* (1967). The hawk case for nuclear power.

W. Millis, *Arms and Men* (1956). History of American military institutions.

———, H. C. Mansfield, and H. Stein, *Arms and the State: Civil-military Elements in National Policy* (1958). Relations of military and civilian factors in the making of recent American policy.

R. G. O'Connor (ed.), *American Defense Policy in Perspective from Colonial Times to the Present* (1965). Historical survey of American military policy.

D. K. Palit, *War in the Deterrent Age* (1968).

P. W. Powers, *A Guide to National Defense: The Organization and Operations of the U.S. Military Establishment* (1964). Purposes and operations of the American defense establishment.

J. D. Singer, *Deterrence, Arms Control and Disarmament: Toward a Synthesis in National Security Policy* (1962).

G. H. Snyder, *Stockpiling Strategic Materials: Politics and National Defense* (1966). The storage of weapons and supplies and the many conflicts that it presents.

J. J. Stone, *Containing the Arms Race, Some Specific Proposals* (1966). Analysis and proposals on questions of national strategy.

———, *Strategic Persuasion: Arms Limitation through Dialogue* (1968).

Science and National Security

R. J. Barber, *The Politics of Research* (1966). Government and scientific research.

M. Berkowitz and P. G. Bock (eds.), *American National Security: A Reader in Theory and Policy* (1965). Readings by prominent men on a pressing problem.

Bulletin of Atomic Scientist, published monthly. Articles on science and international security.

D. W. Cox, *America's New Policy Makers: The Scientists' Rise to Power* (1964). Science-government relations from 1790 to the present.

J. S. Dupre and S. A. Lakoff, *Science and the Nation: Policy and Politics* (1962). Appraisal of the ever-widening influence of government in science and technology.

W. Gellhorn, *Security, Loyalty, and Science* (1950). Presents the view that national security and scientific development are being jeopardized by overzealous concern for security and secrecy.

R. Gilpin, *American Scientists and Nuclear Weapons Policy* (1962). An analysis of participation in policy-making by an important new elite.

——— and Christopher Wright (eds.), *Scientists and National Policy Making* (1964). Essays by nine authors on the changing role of science in government.

P. Green, *Deadly Logic: The Theory of Nuclear Deterrence* (1966). A scientific approach.

Y. Harkabi, *Nuclear War and Nuclear Peace* (1966). Probable and possible implications of a new kind of warfare.

A. A. Jordan, Jr. (ed.), *Issues of National Security in the 1970's* (1967). Fourteen articles from the military viewpoint.

L. B. Kirkpatrick, Jr., *The Real CIA* (1967). Defense by the CIA's former executive director.

R. E. Lapp, *The New Priesthood: The Scientific Elite and the Uses of Power* (1965). A somewhat pessimistic view of the scientific establishment's handling of its societal obligations.

G. M. Lyons and O. Morton, *Schools for Strategy: Education and Research in National Security Affairs* (1965). Study of training in national security affairs.

W. L. Laurence, *The Hell Bomb* (1951). The hydrogen bomb—its implications and recommendations for American policy toward its use. By *The New York Times* science editor.

H. L. Nieburg, *Nuclear Secrecy and Foreign Policy* (1964). The effect of nuclear power on foreign policy.

H. Orlans, *Contracting for Atoms* (1967). Government role in nuclear research.

A. K. Smith, *A Peril and a Hope: The Scientists' Movement in America 1945–47* (1965). A chronicle of the entry of many scientists into the political realm.

B. L. R. Smith, *The RAND Corporation: Case Study of a Nonprofit Advisory Corporation* (1966). History, structure, operations, and future of the RAND Corporation.

D. Van Tassel and M. G. Hall (eds.), *Science and Society in the United States* (1966). Scientific development and its part in the shaping of American history.

A. Weinberg, *Reflections on Big Science* (1967). Essays on science and social science in the governmental structure.

J. B. Wiesner, *Where Science and Politics Meet* (1965). By John Kennedy's science adviser.

A. Wolfers, et al., *The United States in a Disarmed World* (1966). A somewhat pessimistic appraisal of United States disarmament proposals.

Military and Civilian

H. L. Coles, *Total War and the Cold War* (1961). Problems of civilian control of the military.

V. Davis, *Postwar Defense Policy and U.S. Navy, 1943–1946* (1966). The Navy's fight for survival in the immediate post-war period.

M. Derthick, *The National Guard in Politics* (1965). A study of a very successful pressure group.

A. A. Ekirch, Jr., *The Civilian and the Military* (1956). Survey of American tradition and discussion of contemporary application.

S. P. Huntington, *The Soldier and the State* (1957). Study of civil-military relations in the United States.

M. Janowitz (ed.), *The New Military: Changing Patterns of Organization* (1964). A collection of eight studies of the internal and external evolution of the military.

E. A. Kolodziej, *The Uncommon Defense and Congress, 1945–1963* (1966). The role of Congress in formulation of military policy.

H. D. Lasswell, *National Security and Individual Freedom* (1950). Recommenda-

811

tions as to how to avoid the "garrison state."

W. F. Levantrosser, *Congress and the Citizen-Soldier* (1967). Congressional participation in formulation of policy on the Federal Armed Forces Reserve.

J. C. Miller, III (ed.), *Why The Draft?* (1968). A comparative study of the ways to raise an army.

C. R. Mollenhoff, *The Pentagon* (1967). An analysis and criticism of the concentration and use of power.

The Peace Education Division of the American Friends Service Committee, *The Draft?* (1968). A moral case against the draft.

Senate Committee on Armed Services and Committee on Foreign Relations, *Hearings, Military Situation in Far East*, 82d Cong., 1st Sess. (1951). MacArthur hearings contain materials on how decisions are made and the relations among the President, his military advisers, and his civilian advisers.

L. Smith, *American Democracy and Military Power* (1951). Survey of democratic theory, constitutional law, and administrative practices and evaluation of their adequacy to preserve civilian control of the armed forces.

J. W. Spanier, *The Truman-MacArthur Controversy and the Korean War*, 2d ed (1965). Study of wartime civil-military relationships.

H. Stein (ed.), *American Civil-Military Decisions* (1968). Comprehensive study of civil-military relationship through eleven case studies.

Government and the Economy

J. E. Anderson, *Politics and the Economy* (1967). Trends and policy patterns in national economic policy.

A. A. Berle, *Economic Power and the Free Society* (1957). Essay on the prevailing currents in economic life and their impact on individual freedom.

A. F. Burns, *The Management of Prosperity* (1966). A report on national economic development and the Employment Act of 1946.

T. C. Cochran, *The American Business System* (1957). Interpretative history since 1900.

R. A. Dahl and C. E. Lindblom, *Politics, Economics and Welfare* (1953). Patterns of economic and political power; suggests new theoretical approaches.

M. E. Dimock, *The New American Political Economy* (1962). Challenging suggestion for reform in the American political-economic system.

D. W. Ewing, *The Practice of Planning* (1968).

E. S. Flash, *Economic Advice and Presidential Leadership: The Council of Economic Advisers* (1965). History of the Council of Economic Advisers.

J. K. Galbraith, *American Capitalism* (1952). Role of government, business, and labor in modern American competitive economy, "the concept of countervailing power.

———, *The New Industrial State* (1967). Controversial view of modern economic life.

H. K. Girvetz, *From Wealth to Welfare* (1950). Interpretation of the forces that have led to the welfare state.

L. M. Hacker, *American Capitalism* (1957). Role of capitalism in American society.

E. W. Hawley, *The New Deal and the Problem of Monopoly: A Study in Economic Ambivalence* (1966). The domestic economic program of FDR's New Deal.

W. W. Heller, *New Dimensions of Political Economy* (1966). Modern economics as a means to social good.

C. B. Hoover, *The Economy, Liberty and the State* (1959). Study of the relation of the state to the economy in several nations, including the United States.

L. A. Lecht, *Goals, Priorities, and Dollars: The Next Decade* (1966). The cost of achieving national objectives for the next decade.

H. Schoeck and J. W. Wiggins (eds.), *Central Planning and Neomercantilism* (1964). The centralization of governments and a defense of laissez faire.

A. Shonfield, *Modern Capitalism: The Changing Balance of Public and Private Power* (1965). The change in capitalism since World War II.

G. Soule, *Planning U.S.A.* (1967). History and analysis of United States economic planning.

Government and Business

W. Adams and H. M. Gray, *Monopoly in America* (1956). Evidence to support argument that government policy in recent years tends to promote monopoly.

T. W. Arnold, *The Folklore of Capitalism* (1937). Mythology of business and trust-busting, with emphasis on its futility, by a man who subsequently became an active trustbuster.

R. A. Bauer, I. de S. Pool, and L. A. Dexter, *American Business and Public Policy* (1963). A major study of public opinion and congressional activity on business politics.

A. A. Berle and G. C. Means, *The Modern Corporation and Private Property* (1933). Analysis of the growth of large industry, the separation between ownership and control, and problems of social control.

H. Brayman, *Corporate Management in a World of Politics: The Public, Political, and Governmental Problems of Business* (1967). Corporate management and communication.

S. Buchanan, *The Corporation and the Republic* (1958). The emergent role of the corporation in society.

J. W. Burns, *A Study of Anti-trust Laws* (1958). Emphasis on legal aspects.

J. M. Edelman, *The Licensing of Radio Services in the U.S., 1927 to 1947* (1950). Study in administrative formulation of policy.

C. D. Edwards, *Maintaining Competition* (1949). Recommendations for a governmental policy.

M. G. Glaeser, *Public Utilities in American Capitalism* (1957). Study of problems and policies of regulation.

J. Landis, *Report on Regulatory Agencies to the President-Elect* (1960). Policy recommendation to President Kennedy.

R. E. Lane, *The Regulation of Businessmen* (1954). Responses of businessmen to regulation.

W. Letwin, *Law and Economic Policy in America: The Evolution of the Sherman Anti-Trust Act* (1965).

D. E. Lilienthal, *Big Business: A New Era* (1952). Argument for an affirmative program to help develop big business and discussion of its contributions.

R. E. Low (ed.), *The Economics of Antitrust* (1968).

E. S. Redford, *Administration of National Economic Controls* (1952). Analysis of process by which policy is made and instruments through which it is executed.

J. Scoville and N. Sargent, *Fact and Fancy in the T. N. E. C. Monographs* (1942). Critical review of TNEC reports prepared under auspices of NAM.

I. L. Sharfman, *The Interstate Commerce Commission*, 4 vols. (1931–1937). Comprehensive study of the oldest federal regulatory agency.

G. M. Smerk, *Urban Transportation: The Federal Role* (1965). The problem to date and recommendations for the future.

S. N. Whitney, *Anti-trust Policies: American Experience in Twenty Industries*, 2 vols. (1958). Analysis of the effectiveness of antitrust action.

Government and Agriculture

M. R. Benedict, *Farm Policies of the United States, 1790–1950* (1953). Origins and development of governmental policy.

H. F. Breimyer, *Individual Freedom and the Economic Organization of Agriculture* (1965). A discourse on agricultural policy and the maintenance of freedom.

D. E. Conrad, *The Forgotten Farmers: The Story of Sharecroppers in the New Deal* (1965). Roosevelt's Department of Agriculture and the small farmer.

D. F. Hadwiger and R. B. Talbot, *Pressures and Protests: The Kennedy Farm Program and the Wheat Referendum of 1963* (1965). Agricultural accomplishments of the Kennedy administration.

R. S. Kirkendall, *Social Scientists and Farm Politics in the Age of Roosevelt* (1966). Agricultural policy in the New Deal.

J. L. Shover, *Cornbelt Rebellion: The Farmers' Holiday Association* (1965). The protests of United States farmers during the Depression and the New Deal.

Conservation

M. Clawson and B. Held, *The Federal Lands: Their Use and Management* (1957).

———, ———, and C. H. Stoddard, *Land for the Future* (1960).

R. A. Cooley, *Politics and Conservation: The Decline of the Alaska Salmon* (1963). A study of pressure politics.

H. Jarrett (ed.), *Perspectives on Conservation: Essays on America's Natural Resources* (1958).

J. V. Krutilla and O. Eckstein, *Multiple Purpose River Development* (1958). General treatment of water resources.

C. McKinley, *Uncle Sam in the Pacific Northwest* (1952). Detailed study of federal government's program for management of natural resources in the area.

R. J. Morgan, *Governing Soil Conservation: Thirty Years of the New Decentralization* (1966). The agricultural and administrative problems of soil conservation.

G. Pinchot, *Breaking New Ground* (1947). Autobiography of a crusader for conservation.

President's Materials Policy Commission, *Resources for Freedom* (1952). With five supporting volumes, one of the most significant studies of resources and public policy in recent years.

E. F. Renshow, *Toward Responsible Government: An Economic Appraisal of Federal Investment in the Water Resources Program* (1957). Critical of the program.

R. M. Robbins, *Our Landed Heritage* (1942). History of public-land policies.

M. W. Straus, *Why Not Survive?* (1955).

N. I. Wengert, *Natural Resources and the Political Struggle* (1955). History and politics of conservation.

The Labor Movement

L. E. H. Chamberlin, et al., *Labor Unions and Public Policy* (1958). Critical of the power that unions now have.

J. R. Commons, et al., *History of Labor in*

the United States, 4 vols. (1935). One of the best labor histories covering period before the New Deal.

M. M. Kampelman, *The Communist Party vs. the CIO: A Study of Power Politics* (1957). Study of attempted Communist infiltration and union counteraction.

M. Karson, *American Labor and Politics, 1900–1918* (1958).

R. A. Lester, *As Unions Mature: An Analysis of the Evolution of American Unionism* (1958). Background and current problems.

C. E. Lindblom, *Unions and Capitalism* (1949). Questions the compatibility of unions and capitalism.

H. A. Millis and R. Montgomery, *Organized Labor* (1945). Outstanding labor history.

C. W. Mills, *The New Men of Power* (1948). Study of the leaders of organized labor by a sociologist.

J. G. Rayback, *A History of American Labor* (1959).

F. Tannenbaum, *A Philosophy of Labor* (1951). Interpretation of unions as a conservative force in modern capitalistic society.

G. Tyler, *A New Philosophy for Labor* (1959). Interpretation of labor's situation and prospects.

Government Labor Policy

H. A. Millis and E. C. Brown, *From the Wagner Act to Taft-Hartley* (1950). Labor policy from the New Deal to Taft-Hartley.

S. Petro, *Power Unlimited: The Corruption of Union Leadership* (1959). Interpretation and summary of the McClellan committee disclosures.

P. Sultan, *Right to Work Laws: A Study of Conflict* (1958). Balanced discussion of the background and arguments on both sides.

U.S. Department of Labor, *Federal Labor Laws and Agencies* (1957, supp. 1960). Periodically revised. Provides quick reference to laws and regulations.

Social Security

A. J. Altmeyer, *The Formative Years of Social Security* (1966). A history of the program.

I. Deutscher and E. J. Thompson (eds.), *Among the People: Encounters with the Poor* (1968). An intensive study of poverty.

J. C. Donovan, *The Politics of Poverty* (1967). The formation and operation of the Economic Opportunities Act of 1964.

J. D. Hagan and F. A. J. Ianni, *American Social Legislation* (1957). Appraisal of problems and alternatives; sociological emphasis.

M. Herman and M. Munk, *Decision Making In Poverty Programs* (1968). Twenty case studies from youth-work agencies.

J. Larner and I. Howe (eds.), *Poverty: Views from the Left* (1968).

O. Lewis, *La Vida: A Puerto Rican Family in the Culture of Poverty—San Juan and New York* (1966). The migrant life of a composite family.

P. Marris and M. Rein, *Dilemmas of Social Reform: Poverty and Community Action in the United States* (1968). Contemporary problems and future prospects of programs for social reform.

National Association of Social Workers, *The Social Welfare Yearbook.* Annual collection of articles.

L. Rainwater and W. L. Yancey, *The Moynihan Report and the Politics of Controversy* (1967). A thorough study of this controversial government report, public and private response, and the effect on the policy process.

A. U. Romasco, *The Poverty of Abundance* (1965). Herbert Hoover's response to the Great Depression.

S. Scheibla, *Poverty Is Where the Money Is* (1968).

B. B. Seligman, *Permanent Poverty: An American Syndrome* (1968).

———, *Poverty as a Public Issue* (1965). Searching studies of the war on poverty.

T. D. Sherwood (ed.), *Social Welfare and Urban Problems* (1967). Papers from the 1967 National Conference on Social Welfare.

G. Y. Steiner, *Social Insecurity: The Politics of Welfare* (1966). A wide view of United States welfare programs and policies.

J. G. Turnhill, et al., *Economic and Social Security: Public and Private Measures against Economic Insecurity* (1957). General treatment of problems and policies.

United States Social Security Administration, *Social Security Bulletin.*

J. C. Vadakin, *Children, Poverty, and Family Allowances* (1968). An economic approach to social stability and social justice.

E. E. Witte, *The Development of the Social Security Act* (1962).

Health Insurance

G. Rosen, *A History of Public Health* (1958). General review of programs through several centuries.

H. M. Somers and A. R. Somers, *Doctors, Patients, and Health Insurance* (1961). Comprehensive, balanced examination.

U. S. Department of Health, Education, and Welfare, *Annual Report.* Useful information on current problems.

Education

S. K. Bailey, et al., *The Economics and Politics of Public Education* (1962–1963). An eight-volume inquiry that places education in a political context.

J. S. Coleman (ed.), *Education and Political Development, Studies in Political Development* (1965). A series of essays about the relationship between education and political development and the degree to which educators and political scientists have neglected each other.

Committee on Economic Development, *Paying for Better Schools* (1960). Recommendations on educational finance.

K. Goldhammer, J. E. Suttle, W. D. Aldridge, and G. L. Becker, *Issues and Problems in Contemporary Educational Administration* (1967). Finds that many public school superintendents are inadequately prepared for their rapidly changing vocation.

B. R. Keenan (ed.), *Science and the University* (1966). Government policy toward university science.

A. Kerber and W. Smith (eds.), *Educational Issues in a Changing Society* (1962). Discussion of current problems.

D. M. Knight, *The Federal Government and Higher Education* (1961). Analysis of growing relationships.

M. Mayer, *The Schools* (1961). Provocative general treatment of American public education.

P. Meranto, *The Politics of Federal Aid to Education in 1965: A Study in Political Innovation* (1967). Factors in the 1965 passage of the federal aid to education program.

Rockefeller Brothers Fund, *The Pursuit of Excellence: Education and the Future of America* (1958). Study of needs, problems, and philosophy.

Housing

M. Anderson, *The Federal Bulldozer* (1964). A critical look at federal urban renewal programs from 1949 to 1962.

R. M. Fisher, *Twenty Years of Public Housing: Economic Aspects of the Federal Program* (1959). History of federal policy and activities.

Housing and Home Finance Agency, *Annual Report*. Valuable factual data.

Joint (Congressional) Committee on Housing, *Final Majority Report*, Housing Study and Investigation, House Report 1564, 80th Cong., 2d Sess. (1949).

Federal Policemen

M. Lowenthal, *The Federal Bureau of Investigation* (1950). Criticism of the FBI.

D. Whitehead, *The F.B.I. Story* (1956). Readable, sympathetic, and wide-ranging account.

Government as Manager

A. Griffith, *The National Aeronautics and Space Act* (1962). The birth of NASA.

I. L. Horowitz (ed.), *The Rise and Fall of Project Camelot* (1967). The relationship between social science and practical politics in the Project Camelot experience.

S. A. Lakoff (ed.), *Knowledge and Power: Essays on Science and Government* (1966). Essays covering varied aspect of science-government relations.

D. E. Lilienthal, *TVA: Democracy on the March*, rev. ed. (1953). Defense by former director of TVA as major instrument of grass-roots democracy.

C. McKinley, *The Management of Land and Related Water Resources in Oregon: A Case Study in Administrative Federalism* (1965).

L. Metcalf and V. Reinemer, *Overcharge* (1967). A study of the inflated prices of the electric power industry.

H. L. Nieburg, *In the Name of Science* (1966). Examines the "contract state," a system of ties between private interests and public programs.

J. L. Penick, Jr., C. W. Pursell, Jr., M. B. Sherwood, and D. C. Swain (eds.), *The Politics of American Science: 1939 to the Present* (1965). Policy and administration in the scientific community.

D. K. Price, *Government and Science* (1954). Shows major role of government in scientific activity.

C. H. Pritchett, *The Tennessee Valley Authority: A Study in Public Administration* (1943). Standard study of TVA administration.

P. Selznick, *TVA and the Grass Roots* (1949). Sociological interpretation.

M. Thomas and R. M. Northrop, *Atomic Energy and Congress* (1956).

V. Van Dyke, *Pride and Power: The Rationale of the Space Program* (1964). Analysis of America's program for man in space.

Fiscal and Monetary Policy

The several reports resulting from the Employment Act of 1946 are primary sources for the whole problem of governmental fiscal and monetary policy. These include the President's Economic Report to the Congress, Report of the Council of Economic Advisers, and Reports and Hearings of the Joint Congressional Committee on Economic Report. These are issued regularly.

J. M. Buchanan, *Public Finance in Democratic Process, Fiscal Institutions and*

Individual Choice (1967). A discussion of individual decision-making in public goods and expenditures and in future taxation policies.

Bureau of the Budget, *The Federal Budget in Brief*. Published annually, summary of budget; many illustrations.

J. Burkhead, *Government Budgeting* (1956). Description of the budgetary process.

G. Colm and P. Wagner, *Federal Budget Projections* (1966). Studies and supports programs for long-range budget forecast in Washington.

M. S. Comiez, *A Capital Budget Statement for the U.S. Government* (1966). A restatement of federal expenditures, denoting which were capital and which operational, and a discussion of political consequences.

R. T. Golembiewski (ed.), *Public Budgeting and Finance: Readings in Theory and Practice* (1968). Readings in budgeting technique and theory.

J. M. Keynes, *The General Theory of Employment, Interest, and Money* (1936). One of the most influential books of modern times; interpretation of economics that calls for governmental fiscal and monetary policy and public works to offset unemployment.

L. H. Kimmel, *Federal Budget and Fiscal Policy, 1789–1958* (1959). General survey of policies and procedures.

D. Novick (ed.), *Program Budgeting—Program Analysis and the Federal Budget* (1965). A series of essays that discusses the role of budgeting in governmental decision-making and the general concept of program budgeting.

D. J. Ott and A. F. Ott, *Federal Budget Policy* (1965). A nontechnical study of the budget and its relationship to the economy.

J. A. Pechman, *Federal Tax Policy* (1966). The formation and implementation of tax policy.

M. D. Reagan, *The Managed Economy* (1963). The evolution of free-enterprise economy.

Senate Committee on Banking and Currency, *Federal Reserve Policy and Economic Stability, 1951–1957*, study prepared by A. Achinstein, Senate Report No. 2500, 85th Cong., 2d Sess. (1958).

R. A. Wallace, *Congressional Control of Federal Spending* (1962). Study of congressional role in fiscal policy.

A. B. Wildavsky, *The Politics of the Budgetary Process* (1964). The strategies and calculations of participants in the budget-making process.

PART SEVEN: STATE AND LOCAL GOVERNMENTS

Many of the books mentioned in the other sections of this bibliography, especially in connection with federalism, also pertain to government of the states and their subdivisions. Except in a few cases, they will not be listed again here; nor will the standard texts be noted. Furthermore, the wealth of materials—some produced by individual scholars and some by the many research organizations connected with universities, cities, state organizations, and various associations of officials—dealing with the government of a particular state, city, county, region, or area are not mentioned, but only the more general works.

Annuals, Manuals, and Periodicals

American City Magazine Corporation, *The American City* (published monthly). A trade journal of city officials.

American Judicature Society, *Journal of the American Judicature Society* (published monthly). Devoted to the cause of judicial reform and improvement in the administration of justice.

Council of State Governments, *The Book of the States* (published biennially with semiannual supplements. A basic source; contains bibliography of state government, short articles on current developments, charts and lists of personnel.

———, *State Government* (published monthly). Articles by state officials and scholars and reports on programs of state governments.

B. J. Halevy (comp.), *A Select Bibliography on State Constitutional Revision* (1963).

J. Herndon, C. Press, and O. P. Williams (comps. and eds.), *A Selected Bibliography of Materials in State Government and Politics* (1963).

International City Managers' Association, *The Municipal Yearbook* (published yearly). Contains up-to-date information on every aspect of municipal activity.

Library of Congress, *Monthly Checklist of State Publications*. A state-by-state list of publications.

National Association of County Officials, *The County Officer* (published monthly). Trade journal of county officials.

National Municipal League, *National Civic Review* (published monthly). The trade journal of city officials; articles dealing with problems of those who run our cities.

C. Press, O. Williams, *State Manuals, Blue Books and Election Results* (1962).

State Manuals (published by most states yearly). Usually contain directories of public officials, election statistics, descriptions of activities of various government agencies, and so on.

United States Conference of Mayors, *The U. S. Municipal News* (published biweekly). Newsletter of current events; suggests political pressures operating on mayors.

Patterns of State and Local Politics

R. A. Agger, D. Goldrich, and B. E. Swanson, *The Rulers and the Ruled: Political Power and Importance in American Communities* (1964). Research report of decision-making in four communities.

E. C. Banfield, *Political Influence* (1961). Political patterns in Chicago.

———— and J. Q. Wilson, *City Politics* (1963). City government is viewed in the context of the total urban setting.

E. A. Bock (ed.), *State and Local Government* (1968). Twenty-five case studies illustrating major problems of state and local government.

W. E. Brigman and E. C. Buell (eds.), *The Grass Roots: Readings in State and Local Government* (1968). The interrelationship of government and politics in regional governmental structures.

J. C. Buechner, *State Government in the Twentieth Century* (1967).

T. D. Clark and A. D. Kirkman, *The South since Appomattox: A Century of Regional Change* (1967). An account of social, economic, and political development.

A. L. Clem, *Prairie State Politics: Popular Democracy in South Dakota* (1967). A historical-structural study of South Dakota politics over the last century.

R. A. Dahl, *Who Governs? Democracy and Power in an American City* (1961). Important study of city politics.

T. R. Dye, *Politics, Economics, and the Public Policy Outcomes in the American States* (1966). The effect of economic development on public-policy outcome.

J. H. Fenton, *Midwest Politics* (1966). Historical development of party politics in each of six Middle Western states.

J. H. Fenton, *Politics of the Border States* (1957). Politics of Maryland, West Virginia, Kentucky, and Missouri.

J. D. Fleer, *North Carolina Politics* (1968).

D. W. Grantham, *The Democratic South* (1963). Southern politics exclusive of the race issue—public opinion and political groupings.

L. S. Greene, M. E. Jewell, and D. R. Grant, *The States and the Metropolis* (1968). Present problems and future prospects for government in states and metropolises.

L. C. Hardy, *California Government,* 2d ed. (1967). An examination of state and local politics in California and their relation to national government.

R. B. Highsaw (ed.), *The Deep South in Transformation* (1968). Essays on the social, political, and economic development of the South over the last ten years.

G. Hill, *Dancing Bear: An Inside Look at California Politics* (1968). A political history and analysis.

J. E. Holmes, *Politics in New Mexico* (1967). A history and analysis that is of general interest in the study of state politics.

H. Jacob and K. N. Vines (eds.), *Politics in the American States: A Comparative Analysis* (1965). Systematic comparative analysis of problems of state politics.

F. H. Jonas (ed.), *Western Politics* (1961). Survey of politics in the burgeoning West.

V. O. Key, Jr., *American State Politics* (1956). Comparative study with important insights for understanding national politics.

———— and A. Heard, *Southern Politics* (1949). Brilliant studies of regional politics.

M. M. Leiman, *Jacob N. Cardozo: Economic Thought in the Ante-Bellum South* (1966). A study of pre-Civil War economic thought in the South from the work of Jacob Cardozo, a Charleston editor.

E. Litt, *The Political Cultures of Massachusetts* (1965). The process of political change in Massachusetts.

D. Lockard, *New England. State Politics* (1959). Politics of Vermont, New Hampshire, Maine, Massachusetts, Rhode Island, and Connecticut.

R. L. Morlan (ed.), *Capital, Courthouse, and City Hall: Readings in American State and Local Government* (1966).

F. Munger (ed.), *American State Politics: Readings for Comparative Analysis* (1966). A regional approach to basic issues of state governments.

R. B. Nye, *Midwestern Progressive Politics* (1951). Historical interpretation.

G. Ostrander, *Nevada: The Great Rotten Borough, 1859–1964* (1966). Alleges that Nevada has used its equal representation in the Senate to further local, rather than national, interests.

R. Presthus, *Men at the Top: A Study in Community Power* (1964). A study of two small New York communities.

T. Sanford, *Storm over the States* (1967). An analysis of the present problems and future prospects of state governments by a former North Carolina governor.

A. H. Syed, *The Political Theory of American Local Government* (1966). Basic concepts and suggestions for reorientation of local government.

G. B. Tindall, *The Emergence of the New South 1913–1945,* vol. 10, *A History of the South* (1967).

O. P. Williams and C. R. Adrian, *Four Cities: A Study in Comparative Policy-Making*

(1963). Who governs in four middle-sized cities.

State Constitutions

J. W. Fesler (ed.), *The Forty-eight States: Their Tasks as Policy Makers and Administrators* (1955). Symposium prepared for American Assembly conference evaluating how well the states are doing their jobs.

W. B. Graves (ed.), *American Commonwealth Series*, a current series of volumes on the government and administration of the states; to date, about twelve states have been covered.

_____, *Major Problems in State Constitutional Revision* (1960). General treatment.

The National Municipal League, *Bill of Rights* (1960).

_____, *The Constitutional Convention: A Manual* (1961).

_____, *The Governor* (1960).

_____, *The Model State Constitution*, 6th ed. (1963).

_____, *Reapportionment* (1960).

_____, *Salient Issues of Constitutional Revision* (1961).

_____, *The Shape of the Document* (1960).

_____, *The Structure of Administration (1961).*

New York State Constitutional Convention Committee, *Constitutions of the States and the United States*, vol. III (1938). Most comprehensive and recent collection.

V. A. O'Rourke and D. W. Campbell, *Constitution-Making in a Democracy* (1943). Case study of a New York constitutional convention.

A. L. Sturm, *Methods of State Constitutional Reform* (1954). Monograph covering background and methods for change.

C. B. Swisher, *Motivations and Political Techniques in the California Constitutional Convention, 1878–1879* (1930). Study of the constitutional convention as part of the process of government.

Under the Capitol Dome

L. F. Anderson, M. W. Watts, Jr., and A. R. Wilcox, *Legislative Roll-Call Analysis* (1966). Primarily a manual in research technique.

T. J. Anton, *The Politics of State Expenditure in Illinois* (1966). Major steps of the state budgetary process.

C. W. Bain, *Annexation in Virginia: The Use of the Judicial Process for Readjusting County-City Boundaries* (1966). Virginia's unique system of annexation through judicial processes.

G. E. Baker, *Rural Versus Urban Political Power* (1955). Problems and consequences.

J. D. Barber, *The Lawmakers: Recruitment and Adaptation to Legislative Life* (1965). Theory of political recruitment and adaptation emerges from intensive interviews.

G. S. Blair and H. I. Flournoy, *Legislative Bodies in California* (1967). State and local legislative processes in California.

A. C. Breckenridge, *One House for Two: A Study of Nebraska's Unicameral Legislature* (1957). Review of its operations.

Congressional Quarterly Service, *Representation and Apportionment* (1966). Report on reapportionment activities of the Congress and the courts and their political effects.

L. W. Eley, *The Executive Reorganization Plan: A Survey of State Experience* (1967). Attempts at executive reorganization in the states.

H. Eulau and J. D. Sprague, *Lawyers in Politics: A Study in Professional Convergence* (1964). Examination of role perceptions of lawyer-legislators.

R. Hanson, *The Political Thicket* (1966). The democratic case for reapportionment.

A. Heard (ed.), *State Legislatures in American Politics* (1966). Review of current thought on American state legislatures.

M. E. Jewell (ed.), *The Politics of Reapportionment* (1962). Case studies of struggles for legislative reapportionment and congressional redistricting.

G. Schubert, *Reapportionment* (1965). Reapportionment in both Congress and the state legislatures.

F. J. Sorauf, *Party and Representation: Legislative Politics in Pennsylvania* (1963). Sophisticated view of recruitment processes.

J. C. Wahlke, H. Eulau, W. Buchanan, L. C. Ferguson, *The Legislative System* (1962). Comparative analysis in four states.

B. Zeller (ed.), *American State Legislatures* (1954). Report of the American Political Science Association's Committee on American Legislatures.

Governors and Judges

J. R. Bell and T. J. Ashley, *Executives in California Government* (1967). Roles and functions of California state and local executives.

J. C. Bollens, *Administrative Reorganization in the States since 1939* (1947). Updates Buck's work.

G. E. Brooks, *When Governors Convene* (1961). Study of the annual national governors' conference.

A. E. Buck, *Reorganization of State Governments in the United States* (1938). Comprehensive discussion of 1917 to 1938 reorganization movement; state-by-state survey.

F. Gantt, Jr., *The Chief Executive in Texas: A Study in Gubernatorial Leadership* (1964). A history and current study of the Texas governorship.

C. S. Hyneman, "Administrative Reorganization: An Adventure into Science and Theology," *Journal of Politics*, vol. I (1939). One of the better-known "broadsides" against reorganization principles.

L. Lipson, *American Governor: From Figure-head to Leader* (1939). Basic source of the development of the governor's office; special attention to the reorganization period and experiences of Virginia, Massachusetts, New York, and Illinois.

R. D. Morey, *Politics and Legislation: The Office of Governor in Arizona* (1965). Executive-legislative relationships.

B. Nispel, *Reform of the Office of Lieutenant Governor (1958).*

C. B. Ransone, Jr., *The Office of Governor in the United States* (1956). Its historical development, present status, and problems.

W. H. Riker, *Soldiers of the State: The Role of the National Guard in American Democracy* (1957).

J. A. Schlesinger, *How They Became Governor: A Study of Comparative State Politics, 1870–1950* (1957).

The State Judiciary

B. B. Cook, *The Judicial Process in California* (1967). Formal and informal judicial procedure in California.

Council of State Governments, *The Courts of Last Resort of the Forty-Eight States* (1950). Comparative study of major aspects of organization and operation of the highest state courts.

————, *Trial Courts of General Jurisdiction in the Forty-Eight States* (1951). Companion report.

E. Haynes, *The Selection and Tenure of Judges* (1944). The standard history; a basic source.

J. W. Peltason, *Missouri Plan for Selection of Judges* (1945). Description of the Missouri system and the activities of a judicial reform interest group.

R. Pound, *Organization of the Courts* (1940). By leader in judicial reform movement and famous legal scholar.

K. N. Vines and H. Jacob, *Studies in Judicial Politics* (1962). The role of the judiciary in state and local politics.

Government at the Grass Roots

W. Anderson and E. W. Weidner (eds.), *Research in Intergovernmental Relations* (1950–1952). Series of ten monographs on various phases of state-local relations.

C. W. Bain, *A Body Incorporate: City-County Separation in Virginia* (1967). Development and operation of the practice of city-county separation.

J. D. Barber, *Power in Committees: An Experiment in the Governmental Process* (1966). The dynamics of committee activity, from a study of twelve local government committees.

J. C. Bollens, *Special District Governments in the United States* (1956). Number, kinds, and jobs done.

Bureau of the Census, *Governments in the United States*. Number and kinds.

T. N. Clark, *Community Structure, Power, and Decision-Making* (1968). A comparative analysis of community decision-making.

H. J. Gans, *The Levittowners* (1967). A study of social and political life in a lower-middle-class suburb.

R. B. Highsaw and J. A. Dyer, *Conflict and Change in Local Government* (1965). Rural governmental cooperation; four case studies from Alabama.

R. C. Martin, *Grass Roots* (1968). A critical look at small-town government.

W. E. Mills, Jr., and H. R. Davis, *Small City Government* (1962). Seven instructive case studies.

National Municipal League, *Model County Charter* (1956).

C. F. Snider, *Local Government in Rural America* (1957). Study of all forms of rural government.

A. J. Vidich and J. Bensman, *Small Town in Mass Society: Class, Power, and Religion in a Rural Community* (1960). Sociological study.

P. W. Wager (ed.), *County Government across the Nation* (1950). Case studies of county and township government in the states.

E. W. Weidner, *The American County, Patchwork of Boards* (1946). Comments on trends and suggestions for improvement.

Metropolis

E. C. Banfield, *Big City Politics* (1965). A collection of studies of the political systems of nine big cities.

J. C. Bollens (ed.), *Exploring the Metropolitan Community* (1961). Survey of social-political problems.

———— and H. J. Schmandt, *The Metropolis: Its People, Politics, and Economic Life* (1965). A primer in the functions of metropolitan government and politics.

A. Boskoff, *The Sociology of Urban Regions* (1962). Sociological discussion of major facets or urban life.

M. B. Clinard, *Slums and Community Development: Experiments in Self Help*

(1966). Study of slums and the possibilities of urban reform.

Committee for Economic Development, *Modernizing Local Government* (1966). Recommendations for urban governmental reorganization.

M. N. Danielson, *Federal-Metropolitan Politics and the Commuter Crisis* (1965). A thorough study of the urban transportation problem and the conflict between federal, state, and local governments involved.

J. C. Davies III, *Neighborhood Groups and Urban Renewal* (1966). A study of the role of the informal group in the urban political process.

W. M. Dobringer (ed.), *The Suburban Community* (1958). Essays in the sociology of suburbia.

J. W. Doig, *Metropolitan Transportation Politics and the New York Region* (1966). A case study of the New York–New Jersey metropolitan area and the political considerations of transportation reform.

T. R. Dye and B. W. Hawkins (eds.), *Politics in the Metropolis: A Reader in Conflict Cooperation* (1967). Readings toward a theory of conflict resolution in metropolitan conflict.

Editors of Fortune, *The Exploding Metropolis* (1958). Essays on various aspects of metropolitan problems.

E. K. Faltmyer, *Redoing America: A Nationwide Report on How to Make Our Cities and Suburbs Livable* (1968).

W. S. Fiser, *Mastery of the Metropolis* (1962). Approaches to the multiple problems of the metropolitan complex.

B. J. Frieden, *Metropolitan America: Challenge to Federalism* (1966). The deficiencies of our present governmental systems in handling the urban crisis.

E. Ginzberg (ed.), *Manpower Strategy for the Metropolis* (1968).

C. N. Glaab, *The American City: A Documentary History* (1963).

S. Greer, *The Emerging City* (1962). Sociological view of the modern urban setting.

———, *Metropolitics: A Study of Political Culture* (1963).

———, *Urban Renewal and American Cities* (1965). History and analysis of urban renewal.

L. H. Gulick, *The Metropolitan Problem and American Ideas* (1962). Cites failures of current approaches to "metropolitanism" and recommends solutions.

J. K. Hadden, L. Masotti, C. J. Larson (eds.), *Metropolis in Crisis* (1967). Readings on the political process in today's urban clusters.

B. W. Hawkins, *Nashville Metro: The Politics of City-County Consolidation* (1966). Prospects for consolidated metropolitan governments.

V. M. Jones, *Metropolitan Government* (1942). Standard source; discussion of basic problems.

J. R. Lowe, *Cities in a Race with Time: Progress and Poverty in America's Renewing Cities* (1967). Urban renewal and public housing in five large cities over the last twenty years.

B. McKelvey, *The Emergence of Metropolitan America, 1915–1966* (1968). The urban migration and the challenge to city governments.

S. J. Makielski, *The Politics of Zoning: The New York Experience* (1966). A history and analysis of the politics of zoning.

J. R. Meyer, J. F. Kain, and M. Wohl, *The Urban Transportation Problem* (1965). Examines basic issues of the urban transportation problem.

M. Meyerson and E. Banfield, *Boston: The Job Ahead* (1966). The good and bad about today's Boston and what must be done in the future.

L. Mumford, *The City in History* (1961). Interpretative account of the emergence of the urban community.

L. Mumford, *The Urban Prospect* (1968).

W. Owen, *The Metropolitan Transportation Problem*, rev. ed. (1966). The classic work on the subject. Suggests a demand-oriented treatment of the problem.

O. R. Pilat, *Lindsay's Campaign: A Behind-the-Scenes Diary* (1968).

A. R. Pred, *The Spatial Dynamics of U. S. Urban-Industrial Growth, 1800–1914: Interpretive and Theoretical Essays* (1966). The early evolution of the cities.

H. J. Schmandt (with W. H. Standing), *The Milwaukee Metropolitan Study Commission* (1965). Intensive case study of Milwaukee Metropolitan work.

S. Scott (ed.), *The San Francisco Bay Area: Its Problems and Future*, vols. I and II (1966). A comprehensive study of the political, economic, and social aspects of the San Francisco Bay area.

T. D. Sherrard (ed.), *Social Welfare and Urban Problems* (1968).

G. M. Smerk (ed.), *Readings in Urban Transportation* (1968).

R. Starr, *The Living End: The City and Its Critics* (1966). Proposals for altering the metropolitan political structure.

S. B. Warner, Jr., *The Private City: Philadelphia in Three States of Its Growth* (1968).

R. O. Warren, *Government in Metropolitan Regions: A Reappraisal of Fractionated Political Organization* (1966). The Los Angeles metropolitan area and the efforts of local units to meet changing urban needs.

R. C. Weaver, *Dilemmas of Urban America* (1965). Proposals for successful urban renewal.

Y. Willbern, *The Withering Away of the City*

(1964). The current challenges to metropolitan areas.

R. C. Wood, *Suburbia: Its People and Their Politics* (1959). Sociological and political analysis of the movement to the suburbs.

Urban Government

Advisory Commission on Intergovernmental Relations, *Metropolitan Social and Economic Disparities: Implications for Intergovernmental Relations in Central Cities and Suburbs* (1965). A report on the state of urban areas in the United States. Several conclusions, in terms of policy, are reached.

A. A. Altshuler, *The City Planning Process: Political Analysis* (1966). An analysis of planning concepts drawn from data on the Minneapolis-St. Paul area.

E. C. Banfield (ed.), *Urban Government* (1961). Selected readings.

A. T. Brown, *The Politics of Reform—Kansas City's Municipal Government, 1925–1950* (1958).

R. S. Childs, *The First Fifty Years of the Council-Manager Plan of Municipal Government* (1965). An assessment, by the originator, of a system designed to divorce partisan politics from urban government.

J. D. Crumlish, *A City Finds Itself: The Philadelphia Home Rule Charter Movement* (1959). Case study in the politics of municipal reform.

W. V. D'Antonio and W. H. Form, *Influentials in Two Border Cities: A Study in Community Decision Making* (1965). A study that contrasts and compares patterns of influence in city governments of El Paso, Texas, and Ciudad Juarez, Mexico.

J. P. East, *Council-Manager Government: The Political Thought of its Founder, Richard S. Childs* (1965). A study of Childs, the man, and the council-manager form of government—his attempt to separate local government from partisan politics.

C. E. Gilbert, *Governing the Suburbs* (1967). Comparative analysis of community politics.

N. Glazer and D. P. Moynihan, *Beyond the Melting Pot: The Negroes, Puerto Ricans, Jews, Italians and Irish of New York City* (1963). The political consequences of ethnicity.

L. E. Goodall (ed.), *Urban Politics in the Southwest* (1967). Profiles of eleven Southwestern urban governments.

P. M. Hauser and L. F. Schnore (eds.), *The Study of Urbanization* (1965). The causes and effects of the massive urban movement.

W. C. Havard and F. L. Corty, *Rural-Urban Consolidation: The Merger of Governments in the Baton Rouge Area* (1964). Problems in adapting local governments to changing urban needs.

G. M. Kammerer, et al., *City Managers in Politics: An Analysis of Manager Tenure and Termination* (1962).

E. O. Laumann, *Prestige and Association in an Urban Community: An Analysis of an Urban Stratification System* (1966). The urban social structure and political and economic attitudes.

T. J. Lowi, *At the Pleasure of the Mayor: Patronage and Power in New York City, 1898–1958* (1964).

R. P. Lowry, *Who's Running this Town? Community Leadership and Social Change* (1965). A study of the effects of rapid change on the American suburb.

R. C. Martin, *The Cities and the Federal System* (1965). An appraisal of present-day relations between federal and urban governments.

R. L. Mott, *Home Rule for American Cities* (1949). How home rule works and why it is desirable; published by the American Municipal Association.

National Municipal League, *Model City Charter* (1948).

N. W. Polsby, *Community Power and Political Theory* (1963). Patterns of influence in community decision-making.

W. S. Sayre and H. Kaufman, *Governing New York City* (1960).

L. F. Schnore and H. Fagin (eds.), *Urban Research and Policy Planning* (1967). Major developments since World War II.

F. M. Stewart, *A Half Century of Municipal Reform* (1950). The history of the National Municipal League.

R. A. Straetz, *PR Politics in Cincinnati: Thirty Years of City Government Through Proportional Representation* (1958).

O. P. Williams and C. Press (ed.), *Democracy in Urban America* (1961). Various approaches to the study of municipal government and politics.

J. Q. Wilson (ed.), *City Politics and Public Policy* (1968). Public policy differences among American cities.

W. O. Winter, *The Urban Polity* (1968). Toward a general theory of urban politics.

The International City Managers' Association publishes several specialized training manuals on municipal finance, police, fire, public works, personnel administration, municipal recreation, local planning, and municipal administration.

Public Safety

D. J. Bordua (ed.), *The Police* (1967). Six essays on sociological aspects of police work.

R. M. Cipes, *The Crime War: The Manufactured Crusade* (1968). A calm look at the current hysterical reports of a massive increase in crime.

A. C. Germann, F. D. Day, R. R. J. Gallati, *Introduction to Law Enforcement and Justice* (1968). A comprehensive study of evaluation of all aspects of law enforcement.

S. L. Halleck, *Psychiatry and the Dilemmas of Crime* (1968). The nature of the criminal and problems of today's methods of crime control.

E. H. Johnson, *Crime, Correction, and Society* (1968). The principles of social science applied to the study of criminology.

H. T. Klein, *The Police: Damned if They Do, Demned if They Don't* (1968).

C. Leiden and K. M. Schmidt (eds.), *The Politics of Violence* (1968).

A. Neiderhoffer, *Behind the Shield: The Police in Urban Society* (1967). Police response to social change.

G. Radano, *Walking the Beat* (1968). By a New York City police officer.

Report of the National Advisory Commission on Civil Disorders (1968). By the President's commission.

W. W. Turner, *The Police Establishment* (1968).

Government as Educator

J. S. Brubacher and W. Rudy, *Higher Education in Transition: An American History, 1636–1956* (1958). Comprehensive single-volume history.

Committee on Government and Higher Education, *The Efficiency of Freedom* (1959). The relation of the states to higher education.

N. Edwards and H. G. Richey, *The School in the American Social Order* (1947). History of education and discussion of relation between educational policy and social change.

R. B. Kimbrough, *Political Power and Education Decision Making* (1964). The power structure of a local school board.

L. H. Masotti, *Education and Politics in Suburbia: The New Trier Experience* (1967). A case study in the politics of education.

N. A. Masters, R. H. Salisbury, and T. H. Eliot, *State Politics and the Public Schools* (1964).

V. Miller and W. B. Spalding, *The Public Administration of American Schools*, 2d ed. (1958).

A. Nevins, *The State Universities and Democracy* (1962). Historical evaluation.

F. Rudolph, *The American College and University: A History* (1962). Wide-ranging study.

Services

E. C. Banfield and M. Grodzins, *Government and Housing in Metropolitan Areas* (1958).

B. Y. Landis, *Rural Welfare Services* (1949).

H. M. Leyendecker, *Problems and Policy in Public Assistance* (1955). General treatment.

H. E. Martz, *Citizen Participation in Government* (1948). A study of county welfare boards.

M. Meyerson and E. C. Banfield, *Politics, Planning and the Public Interest* (1955). Case study of public housing in Chicago that emphasizes the policy-making process.

H. M. Somers and A. R. Somers, *Workmen's Compensation* (1954). Covers all aspects of oldest social-insurance program.

Regulation at the Grass Roots

Council of State Governments, *Occupational Licensing Legislation in the States* (1952). State-by-state data.

J. W. Fesler, *The Independence of State Regulatory Agencies* (1942). Discussion of existing practices, problems, weaknesses, and solutions.

D. V. Harper, *Economic Regulation of the Motor Trucking Industry by the States* (1959).

Money and Men

A. K. Campbell and S. Sacks, *Metropolitan America: Fiscal Patterns and Governmental Systems* (1967). Fiscal patterns of local political systems.

Civil Service Assembly of the United States and Canada, *A Digest of State Civil Service Laws*.

———, *Public Personnel Review*, (published quarterly). Articles and reports on developments.

O. Eckstein, *Trends in Public Expenditure in the Next Decade* (1959).

H. M. Groves, *Financing Government*, 6th ed. (1964). Standard text.

A. H. Hansen and H. S. Perloff, *State and Local Finance in the National Economy* (1944). Problems of integrated national fiscal policy as complicated by federal system.

International City Managers' Association, *Municipal Personnel Administration* (1950). Day-to-day problems of city administrators.

J. A. Maxwell, *Financing State and Local Governments* (1965). A survey of revenue sources and local governments.

Municipal Finance Officers' Association, *Municipal Finance* (published quarterly). Report on current developments.

822

National Civil Service League, Civil Service Assembly, and National Municipal League, *A Model State Civil Service Law* (1946). Each section is accompanied by explanatory comments.

D. Netzer, *Economics of the Property Tax* (1966). A study of the operation and effects of the property tax.

C. Penniman and W. Heller, *State Income Tax Administration* (1960). Overview and analysis.

Tax Foundation, Tax Institute, and Tax Policy League, among other organizations, publish numerous monographs dealing with problems of state and local taxation, expenditure, and debt.

U. S. Bureau of Census. Numerous reports dealing with state and local finances.

EPILOGUE: CHALLENGE AND OPPORTUNITY

Politics and You

S. Bullitt, *To Be a Politician* (1959). An intellectual reflects on his experience in the world of "practical politics."

J. M. Cannon (ed.), *Politics U.S.A.: A Practical Guide to the Winning of Public Office* (1960). Insiders' advice on campaign politics.

J. E. McLean, *Politics Is What You Make It* (1952). Pamphlet on how to be an effective citizen-politician.

R. E. Merriam and R. M. Goetz, *Going Into Politics* (1957). A guide for citizens.

S. A. Mitchell, *Elm St. Politics* (1959). Former chairman of Democratic National Committee discusses the role of "amateurs" in politics and outlines how a citizen can become active in politics.

National Municipal League, *The Citizen Association: How to Organize and Run It* (1953).

———, *The Citizen Association: How to Win Civic Campaigns* (1953).

E. E. Schattaschneider, V. Jones, and S. Bailey, *A Guide to the Study of Public Affairs* (1952). Practical guides to gathering political information.

H. D. Scott, Jr., *How to Go into Politics* (1949). By former chairman of Republican National Committee, now a senator.

H. Scott, *How to Run for Public Office, and Win!* (1968).

P. Tillett (ed.), *The Political Vocation* (1965). Readings from ancient Greece to the present.

A. Zeitlin, *To the Peace Corps with Love* (1965). An account of personal experiences.

POLITICAL NOVELS

Books of fiction often provide useful insights into political life. Many novelists have developed specifically political themes whereas others have presented political implications for the broader human drama. Three general studies — Irving Howe, *Politics and the Novel* (1957); Joseph Blotner, *The Modern American Political Novel: 1900–1960* (1966); and Gordon Milne, *The American Political Novel:* (1966) — discuss aspects of the interrelationship between politics and the novelists' art. Following is a brief listing of a few leading American political novels.

H. Adams, *Democracy* (1880). Classic in American political fiction.

E. Burdick, *The Ninth Wave* (1956). A powerful account of applied political psychology.

———, and H. Wheeler, *Fail-Safe* (1962). Policy-making and accidental war.

J. Dos Passos, *Number One* (1943). A study in the pathology of political corruption.

A. Drury, *Advise and Consent* (1960). A fictional version of the Senate's confirmation of a controversial presidential appointment.

P. Frank, *Affair of State* (1948). Dilemmas in the life of a foreign-service officer.

W. J. Lederer and E. Burdick, *The Ugly American* (1959). Vignettes of several types of Americans on overseas assignments.

S. Lewis, *It Can't Happen Here* (1936). America under a fascist dictatorship.

E. O'Connor, *The Last Hurrah* (1955). A delightful portrait of a big-city boss and his machine.

J. G. Schneider, *The Golden Kazoo* (1956). Public relations men transform a presidential campaign.

R. P. Warren, *All the King's Men* (1946). The rise and fall of a southern demagogue in the mold of Huey Long.

THE CONSTITUTION OF THE UNITED STATES

We the People of the United States, in Order to form a more perfect Union, establish Justice, insure domestic Tranquility, provide for the common defence, promote the general Welfare, and secure the Blessings of Liberty to ourselves and our Posterity, do ordain and establish this Constitution for the United States of America.

ARTICLE I

Section 1. All legislative Powers herein granted shall be vested in a Congress of the United States, which shall consist of a Senate and House of Representatives.

Section 2. The House of Representatives shall be composed of Members chosen every second Year by the People of the several States, and the Electors in each State shall have the Qualifications requisite for Electors of the most numerous Branch of the State Legislature.

No Person shall be a Representative who shall not have attained to the Age of twenty five Years, and been seven Years a Citizen of the United States, and who shall not, when elected, be an Inhabitant of that State in which he shall be chosen.

Representatives and direct Taxes shall be apportioned among the several States which may be included within this Union, according to their respective Numbers, which shall be determined by adding to the whole Number of free Persons, including those bound to Service for a Term of Years, and excluding Indians not taxed, three fifths of all other Persons. The actual Enumeration shall be made within three Years after the first Meeting of the Congress of the United States, and within every subsequent Term of ten Years, in such Manner as they shall by Law direct. The Number of Representatives shall not exceed one for every thirty Thousand, but each State shall have at Least one Representative; and until such enumeration shall be made, the State of New Hampshire shall be entitled to chuse three, Massachusetts eight, Rhode-Island and Providence Plantations one, Connecticut five, New-York six, New Jersey four, Pennsylvania eight, Delaware one, Maryland six, Virginia ten, North Carolina five, South Carolina five, and Georgia three.

When vacancies happen in the Representation from any State, the Executive Authority thereof shall issue Writs of Election to fill such Vacancies.

The House of Representatives shall chuse their speaker and other Officers; and shall have the sole Power of Impeachment.

Section 3. The Senate of the United States shall be composed of two Senators from each State, chosen by the Legislature thereof, for six Years; and each Senator shall have one Vote.

Immediately after they shall be assembled in Consequence of the first Election, they shall be divided as equally as may be into three Classes. The Seats of the Senators of the first Class shall be vacated at the Expiration of the second Year, of the second Class at the Expiration of the fourth Year, and of the third Class at the Expiration of the sixth Year, so that one third may be chosen every second Year; and if Vacancies happen by Resignation, or otherwise, during the Recess of the Legislature of any State, the Executive thereof may make temporary Appointments until the next Meeting of the Legislature, which shall then fill such Vacancies.

No Person shall be a Senator who shall not have attained to the Age of thirty Years, and been nine Years a Citizen of the United States, and who shall not, when elected, be an Inhabitant of that State for which he shall be chosen.

The Vice President of the United States shall be President of the Senate, but shall have no Vote, unless they be equally divided.

The Senate shall chuse their other Officers, and also a President pro tempore, in the Absence of the Vice President, or when he shall exercise the Office of President of the United States.

The Senate shall have the sole Power to try all Impeachments. When sitting for that Purpose, they shall be on Oath or Affirmation. When the President of the United States is tried, the Chief Justice shall preside: And no Person shall be convicted without the Concurrence of two thirds of the Members present.

Judgment in Cases of Impeachment shall not extend further than to removal from Office, and disqualification to hold and enjoy any Office of honor, Trust or Profit under the United States: but the Party convicted shall nevertheless be liable and subject to Indictment, Trial, Judgment and Punishment, according to law.

Section 4. The Times, Places and Manner of holding Elections for Senators and Representatives, shall be prescribed in each State by the Legislature thereof; but the Congress may at any time by Law make or alter such Regulations, except as to the Places of chusing Senators.

The Congress shall assemble at least once in every Year, and such Meeting shall be on the first Monday in December, unless they shall by Law appoint a different Day.

Section 5. Each House shall be the Judge of the Elections, Returns and Qualifications of its own Members, and a Majority of each shall constitute a Quorum to do Business; but a smaller Number may adjourn from day to day, and may be authorized to compel the Attendance of absent Members, in such Manner, and under such Penalties as each House may provide.

Each House may determine the Rules of its Proceedings, punish its Members for disorderly Behaviour, and, with the Concurrence of two thirds, expel a Member.

Each House shall keep a Journal of its Proceedings, and from time to time publish the same, excepting such Parts as may in their Judgment require Secrecy; and the Yeas and Nays of the Members of either House on any question shall, at the Desire of one fifth of those Present, be entered on the Journal.

Neither House, during the Session of Congress, shall, without the Consent of the other, adjourn for more than three days, nor to any other Place than that in which the two Houses shall be sitting.

Section 6. The Senators and Representatives shall receive a Compensation for their Services, to be ascertained by Law, and paid out of the Treasury of the United States. They shall in all Cases, except Treason, Felony and Breach of the Peace, be privileged from Arrest during their Attendance at the Session of their respective Houses, and in going to and returning from the same; and for any Speech or Debate in either House, they shall not be questioned in any other Place.

No Senator or Representative shall, during the Time for which he was elected, be appointed to any civil Office under the Authority of the United States, which shall have been created, or the Emoluments whereof shall have been encreased during such time; and no Person holding any Office under the United States, shall be a Member of either House during his Continuance in Office.

Section 7. All Bills for raising Revenue shall originate in the House of Representatives; but the Senate may propose or concur with Amendments as on other Bills.

Every Bill which shall have passed the House of Representatives and the Senate, shall, before it become a Law, be presented to the President of the United States; If he approve he shall sign it, but if not he shall return it, with his Objections to that House in which it shall have originated, who shall enter the Objections at large on their Journal, and proceed to reconsider it. If after such Reconsideration two thirds of that House shall agree to pass the Bill, it shall be sent, together with the Objections, to the other House, by which it shall likewise be reconsidered, and if approved by two thirds of that House, it shall become a Law. But in all such Cases the Votes of both Houses shall be determined by Yeas and Nays, and the Names of the Persons voting for and against the Bill shall be entered on the Journal of each House respectively. If any Bill shall not be returned by the President within ten Days (Sundays excepted) after it shall have been presented to him, the Same shall be a Law, in like Manner as if he had signed it, unless the Congress by their Adjournment prevent its Return, in which Case it shall not be a Law.

Every Order, Resolution, or Vote to which the Concurrence of the Senate and House of Representatives may be necessary (except on a question of Adjournment) shall be presented to the President of the United States; and before the Same shall take Effect, shall be approved by him, or being disapproved by him, shall be repassed by two thirds of the Senate and House of Representatives, according to the Rules and Limitations prescribed in the Case of a Bill.

Section 8. The Congress shall have Power To lay and collect Taxes, Duties, Imposts and Excises, to pay the Debts and provide for the common Defence and general Welfare of the United States; but all Duties, Imposts and Excises shall be uniform throughout the United States;

To borrow Money on the Credit of the United States;

To regulate Commerce with foreign Nations, and among the several States, and with the Indian Tribes;

To establish an uniform Rule of Naturalization, and uniform Laws on the subject of Bankruptcies throughout the United States;

To coin Money, regulate the Value thereof, and of foreign Coin, and fix the Standard of Weights and Measures;

To provide for the Punishment of counterfeiting the Securities and current Coin of the United States;

To establish Post Offices and post Roads;

To promote the Progress of Science and useful Arts, by securing for limited Times to Authors and Inventors the exclusive Right to their respective Writings and Discoveries;

To constitute Tribunals inferior to the supreme Court;

To define and punish Piracies and Felonies committed on the high Seas, and Offences against the Law of Nations;

To declare War, grant Letters of Marque and Reprisal, and make Rules concerning Captures on Land and Water;

To raise and support Armies, but no Appropriation of Money to that Use shall be for a longer Term than two Years;

To provide and maintain a Navy;

To make Rules for the Government and Regulation of the land and naval Forces;

To provide for calling forth the Militia to execute the Laws of the Union, suppress Insurrections and repel Invasions;

To provide for organizing, arming, and disciplining, the Militia, and for governing such Part of them as may be employed in the Service of the United States, reserving to the States respectively, the Appointment of the Officers, and the Authority of training the Militia according to the discipline prescribed by Congress;

To exercise exclusive Legislation in all Cases whatsoever, over such District (not exceeding ten Miles square) as may, by Cession of particular States, and the Acceptance of Congress, become the Seat of the Government of the United States, and to exercise like Authority over all Places purchased by the Consent of the Legislature of the State in which the Same shall be for the Erection of Forts, Magazines, Arsenals, dock-Yards, and other needful Buildings;—And

To make all Laws which shall be necessary and proper for carrying into Execution the foregoing Powers, and all other Powers vested by this Constitution in the Government of the United States, or in any Department or Officer thereof.

Section 9. The Migration or Importation of such Persons as any of the States now existing shall think proper to admit, shall not be prohibited by the Congress prior to the Year one thousand eight hundred and eight, but a Tax or duty may be imposed on such Importation, not exceeding ten dollars for each Person.

The Privilege of the Writ of Habeas Corpus shall not be suspended, unless when in Cases of Rebellion or Invasion the public Safety may require it.

No Bill of Attainder or ex post facto Law shall be passed.

No Capitation, or other direct, Tax shall be laid, unless in Proportion to the Census or Enumeration herein before directed to be taken.

No Tax or Duty shall be laid on Articles exported from any State.

No Preference shall be given by any Regulation of Commerce or Revenue to the Ports of one State over those of another: nor shall Vessels bound to, or from, one State, be obliged to enter, clear, or pay Duties in another.

No Money shall be drawn from the Treasury, but in Consequence of Appropriations made by Law; and a regular Statement and Account of the Receipts and Expenditures of all public Money shall be published from time to time.

No Title of Nobility shall be granted by the United States: And no Person holding any Office of Profit or Trust under them, shall, without the Consent of the Congress, accept of any present, Emolument, Office, or Title, of any kind whatever, from any King, Prince, or foreign State.

Section 10. No State shall enter into any Treaty, Alliance, or Confederation; grant Letters of Marque and Reprisal; coin Money; emit Bills of Credit; make any Thing but gold and silver Coin a Tender in Payment of Debts; pass any Bill of Attainder, ex post facto Law, or Law impairing the Obligation of Contracts, or grant any Title of Nobility.

No State shall, without the Consent of the Congress, lay any Imposts or Duties on Imports or Exports, except what may be absolutely necessary for executing its inspection Laws: and the net Produce of all Duties and Imposts, laid by any State on Imports or Exports, shall be for the Use of the Treasury of the United States; and all such Laws shall be subject to the Revision and Controul of the Congress.

No State shall, without the Consent of Congress, lay any Duty of Tonnage, keep Troops, or Ships of War in time of Peace, enter into any Agreement or Compact with another State, or with a foreign Power, or engage in War, unless actually invaded, or in such imminent Danger as will not admit of delay.

ARTICLE II

Section 1. The executive Power shall be vested in a President of the United States of America. He shall hold his Office during the Term of four Years, and, together with the Vice President, chosen for the same term, be elected, as follows

Each State shall appoint, in such Manner as the Legislature thereof may direct, a Number of Electors, equal to the whole Number of Senators and Representatives to which the State may be entitled in the Congress: but no Senator or Representative, or Person holding an Office of Trust or Profit under the United States, shall be appointed an Elector.

The Electors shall meet in their respective States, and vote by Ballot for two Persons, of whom one at least shall not be an Inhabitant of the same State with themselves. And they shall make a List of all the Persons voted for, and of the Number of Votes for each; which List they shall sign and certify, and transmit sealed to the Seat of the Government of the United States, directed to the President of the Senate. The President of the Senate shall, in the Presence of the Senate and House of Representatives, open all the Certificates, and the Votes shall then be counted. The Person having the greatest Number of Votes shall be the President, if such Number be a Majority of the whole Number of Electors appointed; and if there be more than one who have such Majority, and have an equal Number of Votes, then the House of Representatives shall immediately chuse by Ballot one of them for President: and if no Person have a Majority, then from the five highest on the List the said House shall in like Manner chuse the President. But in chusing the President, the Votes shall be taken by States, the Representation from each State having one Vote; A quorum for this Purpose shall consist of a Member or Members from two thirds of the States, and a Majority of all the States shall be necessary to a Choice. In every Case, after the Choice of the President, the Person having the greatest Number of Votes of the Electors shall be the Vice President. But if there should remain two or more who have equal Votes, the Senate shall

chuse from them by Ballot the Vice President.

The Congress may determine the Time of chusing the Electors, and the Day on which they shall give their Votes; which Day shall be the same throughout the United States.

No Person except a natural born Citizen, or a Citizen of the United States, at the time of the Adoption of this Constitution, shall be eligible to the Office of President; neither shall any Person be eligible to that Office who shall not have attained to the Age of thirty five Years, and been fourteen Years a Resident within the United States.

In Case of the Removal of the President from Office, or of his Death, Resignation, or Inability to discharge the Powers and Duties of the said Office, the Same shall devolve on the Vice President, and the Congress may by Law provide for the Case of Removal, Death, Resignation or Inability, both of the President and Vice President, declaring what Officer shall then act as President, and such Officer shall act accordingly, until the Disability be removed, or a President shall be elected.

The President shall, at stated Times, receive for his Services a Compensation, which shall neither be encreased nor diminished during the Period for which he shall have been elected, and he shall not receive within that Period any other Emolument from the United States, or any of them.

Before he enter on the Execution of his Office, he shall take the following Oath or Affirmation: — "I do solemnly swear (or affirm) that I will faithfully execute the Office of President of the United States, and will to the best of my Ability, preserve, protect and defend the Constitution of the United States."

Section 2. The President shall be Commander in Chief of the Army and Navy of the United States, and of the Militia of the several States, when called into the actual Service of the United States; he may require the Opinion, in writing, of the principal Officer in each of the executive Departments, upon any Subject relating to the Duties of their respective Offices, and he shall have Power to grant Reprieves and Pardons for Offences against the United States, except in Cases of Impeachment.

He shall have Power, by and with the Advice and Consent of the Senate, to make Treaties, provided two thirds of the Senators present concur; and he shall nominate, and by and with the Advice and Consent of the Senate, shall appoint Ambassadors, other public Ministers and Consuls, Judges of the supreme Court, and all other Officers of the United States, whose Appointments are not herein otherwise provided for, and which shall be established by Law; but the Congress may by Law vest the Appointment of such inferior Officers, as they think proper, in the President alone, in the Courts of Law, or in the Heads of Departments.

The President shall have Power to fill up all Vacancies that may happen during the Recess of the Senate, by granting Commissions which shall expire at the End of their next Session.

Section 3. He shall from time to time give to the Congress Information of the State of the Union, and recommend to their Consideration such Measures as he shall judge necessary and expedient; he may, on extraordinary Occasions, convene both Houses, or either of them, and in Case of Disagreement between them, with Respect to the Time of Adjournment, he may adjourn them to such Time as he shall think proper; he shall receive Ambassadors and other public Ministers; he shall take Care that the Laws be faithfully executed, and shall Commission all the Officers of the United States.

Section 4. The President, Vice President and all civil Officers of the United States, shall be removed from Office on Impeachment for, and Conviction of, Treason, Bribery, or other High Crimes and Misdemeanors.

ARTICLE III

Section 1. The judicial Power of the United States, shall be vested in one supreme Court, and in such inferior Courts as the Congress may from time to time ordain and establish. The Judges, both of the supreme and inferior Courts, shall hold their Offices during good Behaviour, and shall, at stated Times, receive for their Services, a Compensation, which shall not be diminished during their Continuance in Office.

Section 2. The judicial Power shall extend to all Cases, in Law and Equity, arising under this Constitution, the Laws of the United States, and Treaties made, or which shall be made, under their Authority;—to all Cases affecting Ambassadors, other public Ministers and Consuls;—to all Cases of admiralty and maritime Jurisdiction;—to Controversies to which the United States shall be a Party;—to Controversies between two or more States; between a State and Citizens of another State;—between Citizens of different States;—between Citizens of the same State claiming Lands under Grants of different States, and between a State, or the Citizens thereof, and foreign States, Citizens or Subjects.

In all Cases affecting Ambassadors, other public Ministers and Consuls, and those in which a State shall be Party, the supreme Court shall have original Jurisdiction. In all the other Cases before mentioned, the supreme Court shall have appellate Jurisdiction, both as to Law and Fact, with such Exceptions, and under such Regulations as the Congress shall make.

The Trial of all Crimes, except in Cases of Impeachment, shall be by Jury; and such Trial shall be held in the State where the said Crimes shall have been committed; but when not committed within any State, the Trial shall be at such Place or Places as the Congress may be Law have directed.

Section 3. Treason against the United States, shall consist only in levying War against them, or in adhering to their Enemies, giving them Aid and Comfort. No Person shall be convicted of Treason unless on the Testimony of two Witnesses to the same overt Act, or on Confession in open Court.

The Congress shall have Power to declare the Punishment of Treason, but no Attainder of Treason shall work Corruption of Blood, or Forfeiture except during the Life of the Person attainted.

ARTICLE IV

Section 1. Full Faith and Credit shall be given in each State to the public Acts, Records, and judicial Proceedings of every other State. And the Congress may by general Laws prescribe the Manner in which such Acts, Records and Proceedings shall be proved, and the Effect thereof.

Section 2. The Citizens of each State shall be entitled to all Privileges and Immunities of Citizens in the several States.

A Person charged in any State with Treason, Felony, or other Crime, who shall flee from Justice, and be found in another State, shall on Demand of the executive Authority of the State from which he fled, be delivered up, to be removed to the State having Jurisdiction of the Crime.

No Person held to Service or Labour in one State, under the Laws thereof, escaping into another, shall, in Consequence of any Law or Regulation therein, be discharged from such Service or Labour, but shall be delivered up on Claim of the Party to whom such Service or Labour may be due.

Section 3. New States may be admitted by the Congress into this Union; but no new State shall be formed or erected within the Jurisdiction of any other State; nor any State be formed by the Junction of two or more States, or Parts of States, without the Consent of the Legislatures of the States concerned as well as of the Congress.

The Congress shall have Power to dispose of and make all needful Rules and Regulations respecting the Territory or other

Property belonging to the United States; and nothing in this Constitution shall be so construed as to Prejudice any Claims of the United States, or of any particular State.

Section 4. The United States shall guarantee to every State in this Union a Republican Form of Government, and shall protect each of them against Invasion; and on Application of the Legislature, or of the Executive (when the Legislature cannot be convened) against domestic Violence.

ARTICLE V

The Congress, whenever two thirds of both Houses shall deem it necessary, shall propose Amendments to this Constitution, or, on the Application of the Legislatures of two thirds of the several States, shall call a Convention for proposing Amendments, which, in either Case, shall be valid to all Intents and Purposes, as Part of this Constitution, when ratified by the Legislatures of three fourths of the several States, or by Conventions in three fourths thereof, as the one or the other Mode of Ratification may be proposed by the Congress; Provided that no Amendment which may be made prior to the Year One thousand eight hundred and eight shall in any Manner affect the first and fourth Clauses in the Ninth Section of the first Article; and that no State, without its Consent, shall be deprived of its equal Suffrage in the Senate.

ARTICLE VI

All Debts contracted and Engagements entered into, before the Adoption of this Constitution, shall be as valid against the United States under this Constitution, as under the Confederation.

This Constitution, and the Laws of the United States which shall be made in Pursuance thereof; and all Treaties made, or which shall be made, under the Authority of the United States, shall be the supreme Law of the Land; and the Judges in every State shall be bound thereby, any Thing in the Constitution or Laws of any State to the Contrary notwithstanding.

The Senators and Representatives before mentioned, and the Members of the several State Legislatures, and all executive and judicial Officers, both of the United States and of the several States, shall be bound by Oath or Affirmation, to support this Constitution; but no religious Test shall ever be required as a Qualification to any Office or public Trust under the United States.

ARTICLE VII

The Ratification of the Conventions of nine States, shall be sufficient for the Establishment of this Constitution between the States so ratifying the Same.

Done in Convention by the Unanimous Consent of the States present the Seventeenth Day of September in the Year of our Lord one thousand seven hundred and eighty seven and of the Independence of the United States of America the twelfth. In witness whereof We have hereunto subscribed our Names.

(The first 10 Amendments were ratified December 15, 1791, and form what is known as the "Bill of Rights.")

AMENDMENT 1

Congress shall make no law respecting an establishment of religion, or prohibiting the free exercise thereof; or abridging the freedom of speech, or of the press; or the right of the people peaceably to assemble, and to petition the Government for a redress of grievances.

AMENDMENT 2

A well regulated Militia, being necessary to the security of a free State, the right of the people to keep and bear Arms, shall not be infringed.

AMENDMENT 3

No Soldier shall, in time of peace be quartered in any house, without the consent of the Owner, nor in time of war, but in a manner to be prescribed by law.

AMENDMENT 4

The right of the people to be secure in their persons, houses, papers, and effects, against unreasonable searches and seizures, shall not be violated, and no Warrants shall issue, but upon probable cause, supported by Oath or affirmation, and particularly describing the place to be searched, and the persons or things to be seized.

AMENDMENT 5

No person shall be held to answer for a capital, or otherwise infamous crime, unless on a presentment or indictment of a Grand Jury, except in cases arising in the land or naval forces, or in the Militia, when in actual service in time of War or public danger; nor shall any person be subject for the same offence to be twice put in jeopardy of life or limb; nor shall be compelled in any criminal case to be a witness against himself, nor be deprived of life, liberty, or property, without due process of law; nor shall private property be taken for public use, without just compensation.

AMENDMENT 6

.In all criminal prosecutions, the accused shall enjoy the right to a speedy and public trial, by an impartial jury of the State and district wherein the crime shall have been committed, which district shall have been previously ascertained by law, and to be informed of the nature and cause of the accusation; to be confronted with the witnesses against him; to have compulsory process for obtaining witnesses in his favor, and to have the Assistance of Counsel for his defence.

AMENDMENT 7

In Suits at common law, where the value in controversy shall exceed twenty dollars, the right of trial by jury shall be preserved, and no fact tried by a jury, shall be otherwise re-examined in any Court of the United States, than according to the rules of the common law.

AMENDMENT 8

Excessive bail shall not be required, nor excessive fines imposed, nor cruel and unusual punishments inflicted.

AMENDMENT 9

The enumeration in the Constitution, of certain rights, shall not be construed to deny or disparage others retained by the people.

AMENDMENT 10

The powers not delegated to the United States by the Constitution, nor prohibited by it to the States, are reserved to the States respectively, or to the people.

AMENDMENT 11

[Ratified February 7, 1795]

The Judicial power of the United States shall not be construed to extend to any suit in law or equity, commenced or prosecuted against one of the United States by Citizens of another State, or by Citizens or Subjects of any Foreign State.

AMENDMENT 12

[Ratified July 27, 1804]

The Electors shall meet in their respective states and vote by ballot for President and Vice-President, one of whom, at least,

shall not be an inhabitant of the same state with themselves; they shall name in their ballots the person voted for as President, and in distinct ballots the person voted for as Vice-President, and they shall make distinct lists of all persons voted for as President, and of all persons voted for as Vice-President, and of the number of votes for each, which lists they shall sign and certify, and transmit sealed to the seat of the government of the United States, directed to the President of the Senate;—The President of the Senate shall, in the presence of the Senate and House of Representatives, open all the certificates and the votes shall then be counted;—The person having the greatest number of votes for President, shall be the President, if such number be a majority of the whole number of Electors appointed; and if no person have such majority, then from the persons having the highest numbers not exceeding three on the list of those voted for as President, the House of Representatives shall choose immediately, by ballot, the President. But in choosing the President, the votes shall be taken by states, the representation from each state having one vote; a quorum for this purpose shall consist of a member or members from two-thirds of the states, and a majority of all the states shall be necessary to a choice. And if the House of Representatives shall not choose a President whenever the right of choice shall devolve upon them, before the fourth day of March next following, then the Vice-President shall act as President, as in the case of the death or other constitutional disability of the President.—The person having the greatest number of votes as Vice-President, shall be the Vice-President, if such number be a majority of the whole number of Electors appointed, and if no person have a majority, then from the two highest numbers on the list, the Senate shall choose the Vice-President; a quorum for the purpose shall consist of two-thirds of the whole number of Senators, and a majority of the whole number shall be necessary to a choice. But no person constitutionally ineligible to the office of President shall be eligible to that of Vice-President of the United States.

AMENDMENT 13

[Ratified December 6, 1865]

Section 1. Neither slavery nor involuntary servitude, except as a punishment for crime whereof the party shall have ben duly convicted, shall exist within the United States, or any place subject to their jurisdiction.

Section 2. Congress shall have power to enforce this article by appropriate legislation.

[Ratified July 9, 1868]

Section 1. All persons born or naturalized in the United States, and subject to the jurisdiction thereof, are citizens of the United States and of the State wherein they reside. No State shall make or enforce any law which shall abridge the privileges or immunities of citizens of the United States; nor shall any State deprive any person of life, liberty, or property, without due process of law; nor deny to any person within its jurisdiction the equal protection of the laws.

Section 2. Representatives shall be apportioned among the several States according to their respective numbers, counting the whole number of persons in each State, excluding Indians not taxed. But when the right to vote at any election for the choice of electors for President and Vice President of the United States, Representatives in Congress, the Executive and Judicial officers of a State, or the members of the Legislature thereof, is denied to any of the male inhabitants of such State, being twenty-one years of age, and citizens of the United States, or in any way abridged, except for participation in rebellion, or other crime, the basis of representation therein shall be reduced in the proportion which the number of such male citizens shall bear to the whole number of male citizens twenty-one years of age in such State.

Section 3. No person shall be a Senator or Representative in Congress, or elector of President and Vice President, or hold any office, civil or military, under the United States, or under any State, who, having previously taken an oath, as a member of Congress, or as an officer of the United States, or as a member of any State legislature, or as an executive or judicial officer of any State, to support the Constitution of the United States, shall have engaged in insurrection or rebellion against the same, or given aid or comfort to the enemies thereof. But Congress may by a vote of two-thirds of each House, remove such disability.

Section 4. The validity of the public debt of the United States, authorized by law, including debts incurred for payment of pensions and bounties for services in suppressing insurrection or rebellion, shall not be questioned. But neither the United States nor any State shall assume or pay any debt or obligation incurred in aid of insurrection or rebellion against the United States, or any claim for the loss or emancipation of any slave; but all such debts, obligations and claims shall be held illegal and void.

Section 5. The Congress shall have power to enforce, by appropriate legislation, the provisions of this article.

[Ratified February 3, 1870]

Section 1. The right of citizens of the United States to vote shall not be denied or abridged by the United States or by any State on account of race, color, or previous condition of servitude.

Section 2. The Congress shall have power to enforce this article by appropriate legislation.

AMENDMENT 16

[Ratified February 3, 1913]

The Congress shall have power to lay and collect taxes on incomes, from whatever source derived, without apportionment among the several States, and without regard to any census or enumeration.

AMENDMENT 17

[Ratified April 8, 1913]

The Senate of the United States shall be composed of two Senators from each State, elected by the people thereof for six years; and each Senator shall have one vote. The electors in each State shall have the qualifications requisite for electors of the most numerous branch of the State legislatures.

When vacancies happen in the representation of any State in the Senate, the executive authority of such State shall issue writs of election to fill such vacancies: *Provided,* That the legislature of any State may empower the executive therof to make temporary appointments until the people fill the vacancies by election as the legislature may direct.

This amendment shall not be so construed as to affect the election or term of any Senator chosen before it becomes valid as part of the Constitution.

AMENDMENT 18

[Ratified January 16, 1919]

Section 1. After one year from the ratification of this article the manufacture, sale, or transportation of intoxicating liquors within, the importation thereof into, or the exportation thereof from the United States and all territory subject to the jurisdiction thereof for beverage purposes is hereby prohibited.

Section 2. The Congress and the several States shall have concurrent power to enforce this article by appropriate legislation.

Section 3. This article shall be inoperative unless it shall have been ratified as an amendment to the Constitution by the legislatures of the several States, as provided in the Constitution, within seven years from the date of the submission hereof to the States by the Congress.

AMENDMENT 19

[Ratified August 18, 1920]

The right of citizens of the United States to vote shall not be denied or abridged by the United States or by any State on account of sex.

Congress shall have power to enforce this article by appropriate legislation.

AMENDMENT 20

[Ratified January 23, 1933]

Section 1. The terms of the President and Vice President shall end at noon on the 20th day of January, and the terms of Senators and Representatives at noon on the 3d day of January, of the years in which such terms would have ended if this article had not been ratified; and the terms of their successors shall then begin.

Section 2. The Congress shall assemble at least once in every year, and such meeting shall begin at noon on the 3d day of January, unless they shall by law appoint a different day.

Section 3. If, at the time fixed for the beginning of the term of the President, the President elect shall have died, the Vice President elect shall become President. If a President shall not have been chosen before the time fixed for the beginning of his term, or if the President elect shall have failed to qualify, then the Vice President elect shall act as President until a President shall have qualified; and the Congress may by law provide for the case wherein neither a President elect nor a Vice President elect shall have qualified, declaring who shall then act as President, or the manner in which one who is to act shall be selected, and such person shall act accordingly until a President or Vice President shall have qualified.

Section 4. The Congress may by law provide for the case of the death of any of the persons from whom the House of Representatives may choose a President whenever the right of choice shall have devolved upon them, and for the case of the death of any of the persons from whom the Senate may choose a Vice President whenever the right of choice shall have devolved upon them.

Section 5. Sections 1 and 2 shall take effect on the 15th day of October following the ratification of this article.

Section 6. This article shall be inoperative unless it shall have been ratified as an amendment to the Constitution by the legislatures of three-fourths of the several States within seven years from the date of its submission.

AMENDMENT 21

[Ratified December 5, 1933]

Section 1. The eighteenth article of amendment to the Constitution of the United States is hereby repealed.

Section 2. The transportation or importation into any State, Territory, or possession of the United States for delivery or use therein of intoxicating liquors, in violation of the laws thereof, is hereby prohibited.

Section 3. This article shall be inoperative unless it shall have been ratified as an amendment to the Constitution by conventions in the several States, as provided in the Constitution, within seven years from the date of the submission hereof to the States by the Congress.

AMENDMENT 22

[Ratified February 27, 1951]

Section 1. No person shall be elected to the office of the President more than twice, and no person who has held the office of President, or acted as President, for more than two years of a term to which some other person was elected President shall be elected to the office of the President more than once. But this Article shall not apply to any person holding the office of President when this Article was proposed by the Congress, and shall not prevent any person who may be holding the office of President, or acting as President, during the term within which this Article becomes operative from holding the office of President or acting as President during the remainder of such term.

Section 2. This article shall be inoperative unless it shall have been ratified as an amendment to the Constitution by the legislatures of three-fourths of the several States within seven years from the date of its submission to the States by the Congress.

AMENDMENT 23

[Ratified March 29, 1961]

Section 1. The District constituting the seat of Government of the United States shall appoint in such manner as the Congress may direct:

A number of electors of President and Vice President equal to the whole number of Senators and Representatives in Congress to which the District would be entitled if it were a State, but in no event more than the least populous State; they shall be in addition to those appointed by the States, but they shall be considered, for the purposes of the election of President and Vice President, to be electors appointed by a State; and they shall meet in the District and perform such duties as provided by the twelfth article of amendment.

Section 2. The Congress shall have power to enforce this article by appropriate legislation.

AMENDMENT 24

[Ratified January 23, 1964]

Section 1. The right of citizens of the United States to vote in any primary or other election for President or Vice President, for electors for President or Vice President, or for Senator or Representative in Congress, shall not be denied or abridged by the United States or any State by reason of failure to pay any poll tax or other tax.

Section 2. The Congress shall have power to enforce this article by appropriate legislation.

AMENDMENT 25

[Ratified February 10, 1967]

Section 1. In case of the removal of the President from office or of his death or resignation, the Vice President shall become President.

Section 2. Whenever there is a vacancy in the office of the Vice President, the President shall nominate a Vice President who shall take office upon confirmation by a majority vote of both Houses of Congress.

Section 3. Whenever the President transmits to the President pro tempore of the Senate and the Speaker of the House of Representatives his written declaration that he is unable to discharge the powers and duties of his office, and until he transmits to them a written declaration to the contrary, such powers and duties shall be discharged by the Vice President as Acting President.

Section 4. Whenever the Vice President and a majority of either the principal officers of the executive departments or of such other body as Congress may by law provide, transmit to the President pro tempore of the Senate and the Speaker of the House of Representatives their written declaration that the President is unable to discharge the powers and duties of his office, the Vice President shall immediately assume the powers and duties of the office as Acting President.

Thereafter, when the President transmits to the President pro tempore of the Senate and the Speaker of the House of Representatives his written declaration that no inability exists, he shall resume the powers and duties of his office unless the Vice President and a majority of either the principal officers of the executive department or of such other body as Congress may by law provide, transmit within four days to the President pro tempore of the Senate and the Speaker of the House of Representatives their written declaration that the President is unable to discharge the powers and duties of his office. Thereupon Congress shall decide the issue, assembling within forty-eight hours for that purpose if not in session. If the Congress, within twenty-one days after receipt of the latter written declaration, or, if Congress is not in session, within twenty-one days after Congress is required to assemble, determines by two-thirds vote of both Houses that the President is unable to discharge the powers and duties of his office, the Vice President shall continue to discharge the same as Acting President; otherwise, the President shall resume the powers and duties of his office.

INDEX

INDEX

WASHINGTON

Centers of Decision

*Cross sections of the White House, Capitol, and Supreme Court
are shown in color inserts in the text*

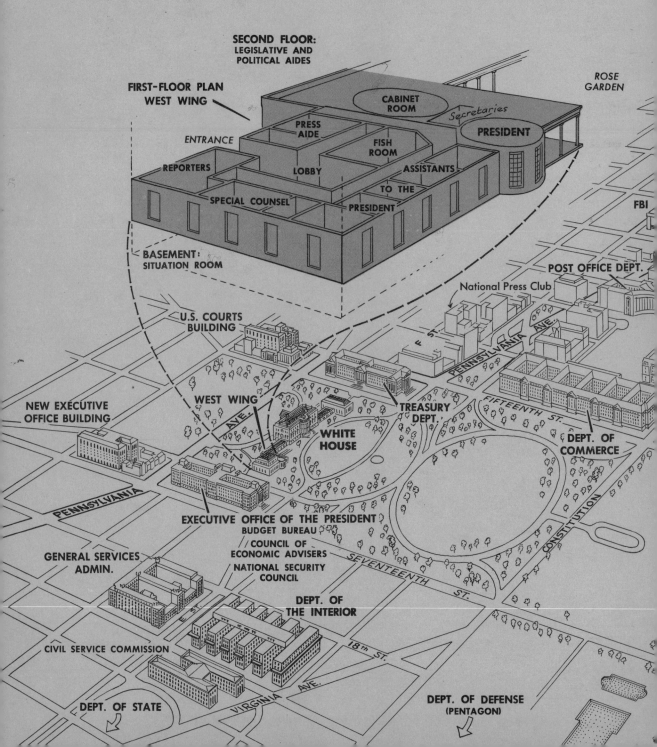

SECOND FLOOR:
LEGISLATIVE AND
POLITICAL AIDES

ROSE
GARDEN

FIRST-FLOOR PLAN
WEST WING

CABINET
ROOM

Secretaries

PRESIDENT

ENTRANCE

PRESS
AIDE

FISH
ROOM

REPORTERS

LOBBY

ASSISTANTS

FBI

SPECIAL COUNSEL

TO THE

PRESIDENT

BASEMENT:
SITUATION ROOM

POST OFFICE DEPT.

National Press Club

U.S. COURTS
BUILDING

NEW EXECUTIVE
OFFICE BUILDING

WEST WING

TREASURY
DEPT.

WHITE
HOUSE

PENNSYLVANIA AVE.

FIFTEENTH ST.

DEPT. OF
COMMERCE

PENNSYLVANIA

EXECUTIVE OFFICE OF THE PRESIDENT
BUDGET BUREAU

COUNCIL OF
ECONOMIC ADVISERS

GENERAL SERVICES
ADMIN.

NATIONAL SECURITY
COUNCIL

SEVENTEENTH ST.

CONSTITUTION

DEPT. OF
THE INTERIOR

CIVIL SERVICE COMMISSION

18th ST.

DEPT. OF STATE

VIRGINIA AVE.

DEPT. OF DEFENSE
(PENTAGON)